Mathematical Methods

Units 1 & 2

Michael Evans
Douglas Wallace
Kay Lipson
David Greenwood

Cambridge Senior Mathematics
Australian Curriculum/VCE

CAMBRIDGE UNIVERSITY PRESS

INCLUDES INTERACTIVE TEXTBOOK POWERED BY CAMBRIDGE HOTMATHS

CAMBRIDGE
UNIVERSITY PRESS

University Printing House, Cambridge CB2 8BS, United Kingdom

One Liberty Plaza, 20th Floor, New York, NY 10006, USA

477 Williamstown Road, Port Melbourne, VIC 3207, Australia

314–321, 3rd Floor, Plot 3, Splendor Forum, Jasola District Centre, New Delhi – 110025, India

79 Anson Road, #06–04/06, Singapore 079906

Cambridge University Press is part of the University of Cambridge.

It furthers the University's mission by disseminating knowledge in the pursuit of education, learning and research at the highest international levels of excellence.

www.cambridge.org
Information on this title: www.cambridge.org/9781107520134

© Michael Evans, Douglas Wallace, Kay Lipson, David Greenwood 2015

This publication is in copyright. Subject to statutory exception and to the provisions of relevant collective licensing agreements, no reproduction of any part may take place without the written permission of Cambridge University Press.

First published 2015
20 19 18 17 16 15 14 13 12 11 10 9

Cover designed by Loupe Design
Typeset by Jane Pitkethly and diacriTech
Printed in China by C & C Offset Printing Co. Ltd.

A catalogue record for this book is available from the National Library of Australia at www.nla.gov.au

ISBN 978-1-107-52013-4 Paperback

Additional resources for this publication at www.cambridge.edu.au/seniormaths

Reproduction and communication for educational purposes
The Australian *Copyright Act 1968* (the Act) allows a maximum of one chapter or 10% of the pages of this publication, whichever is the greater, to be reproduced and/or communicated by any educational institution for its educational purposes provided that the educational institution (or the body that administers it) has given a remuneration notice to Copyright Agency Limited (CAL) under the Act.

For details of the CAL licence for educational institutions contact:

Copyright Agency Limited
Level 11, 66 Goulburn St,
Sydney NSW 2000
Telephone: (02) 9394 7600
Facsimile: (02) 9394 7601
Email: memberservices@copyright.com.au

Reproduction and communication for other purposes
Except as permitted under the Act (for example a fair dealing for the purposes of study, research, criticism or review) no part of this publication may be reproduced, stored in a retrieval system, communicated or transmitted in any form or by any means without prior written permission All inquiries should be made to the publisher at the address above.

Cambridge University Press has no responsibility for the persistence or accuracy of URLS for external or third-party internet websites referred to in this publication, and does not guarantee that any content on such websites is, or will remain, accurate or appropriate. Information regarding prices, travel timetables and other factual information given in this work is correct at the time of first printing but Cambridge University Press does not guarantee the accuracy of such information thereafter.

Contents

Introduction ... ix

Acknowledgements ... xi

An overview of the Cambridge complete teacher and learning resource ... xii

1 Reviewing linear equations ... 1

    1A Linear equations ... 2
    1B Constructing linear equations ... 8
    1C Simultaneous equations ... 11
    1D Constructing simultaneous linear equations ... 17
    1E Solving linear inequalities ... 20
    1F Using and transposing formulas ... 23
    Review of Chapter 1 ... 28

2 Coordinate geometry and linear relations ... 33

    2A Distance and midpoints ... 34
    2B The gradient of a straight line ... 37
    2C The equation of a straight line ... 43
    2D Graphing straight lines ... 51
    2E Parallel and perpendicular lines ... 55
    2F Families of straight lines ... 59
    2G Linear models ... 62
    2H Simultaneous linear equations ... 65
    Review of Chapter 2 ... 72

3 Quadratics ... 81

    3A Expanding and collecting like terms ... 82
    3B Factorising ... 87

3C	Quadratic equations	92
3D	Graphing quadratics	96
3E	Completing the square and turning points	101
3F	Graphing quadratics in polynomial form	106
3G	Solving quadratic inequalities	110
3H	The general quadratic formula	112
3I	The discriminant	116
3J	Solving simultaneous linear and quadratic equations	120
3K	Families of quadratic polynomial functions	123
3L	Quadratic models	132
	Review of Chapter 3	136

4 A gallery of graphs — 145

4A	Rectangular hyperbolas	146
4B	The truncus	150
4C	The graph of $y = \sqrt{x}$	151
4D	Circles	154
4E	Determining rules	160
	Review of Chapter 4	164

5 Functions and relations — 169

5A	Set notation and sets of numbers	170
5B	Relations, domain and range	174
5C	Functions	180
5D	One-to-one functions and implied domains	188
5E	Piecewise-defined functions	192
5F	Applying function notation	194
5G	Inverse functions	196
5H	Functions and modelling exercises	199
	Review of Chapter 5	202

6 Polynomials — 209

6A	The language of polynomials	210
6B	Division of polynomials	215
6C	Factorisation of polynomials	220
6D	Solving cubic equations	229
6E	Cubic functions of the form $f(x) = a(x - h)^3 + k$	232
6F	Graphs of factorised cubic functions	236
6G	Solving cubic inequalities	242
6H	Families of cubic polynomial functions	243
6I	Quartic and other polynomial functions	247
6J	Applications of polynomial functions	252

	6K	The bisection method	257
		Review of Chapter 6	259

7 Transformations — 267

	7A	Translations of functions	268
	7B	Dilations and reflections	272
	7C	Combinations of transformations	276
	7D	Determining transformations	278
	7E	Matrices	280
	7F	Identities, inverses and determinants for 2×2 matrices	287
	7G	Using matrices with transformations	290
	7H	Transformations of graphs of functions with matrices	296
		Review of Chapter 7	298

8 Revision of Chapters 2–7 — 302

	8A	Technology-free questions	302
	8B	Multiple-choice questions	304
	8C	Extended-response questions	308

9 Probability — 313

	9A	Sample spaces and probability	314
	9B	Estimating probabilities	322
	9C	Multi-stage experiments	327
	9D	Combining events	332
	9E	Probability tables	337
	9F	Conditional probability	341
	9G	Independent events	350
	9H	Solving probability problems using simulation	356
		Review of Chapter 9	360

10 Counting methods — 367

	10A	Addition and multiplication principles	368
	10B	Arrangements	371
	10C	Selections	377
	10D	Applications to probability	382
	10E	Pascal's triangle and the binomial theorem	384
		Review of Chapter 10	388

11 Discrete probability distributions — 392

	11A	Discrete random variables	393
	11B	Sampling without replacement	399
	11C	Sampling with replacement: the binomial distribution	402
		Review of Chapter 11	413

12 Revision of Chapters 9–11 — 419

- 12A Technology-free questions ... 419
- 12B Multiple-choice questions ... 421
- 12C Extended-response questions ... 424

13 Exponential functions and logarithms — 429

- 13A The index laws ... 430
- 13B Rational indices ... 437
- 13C Graphs of exponential functions ... 440
- 13D Solving exponential equations and inequalities ... 446
- 13E Logarithms ... 450
- 13F Using logarithms to solve exponential equations and inequalities ... 454
- 13G Graphs of logarithm functions ... 457
- 13H Exponential models and applications ... 462
- 13I Logarithmic scales ... 471
- Review of Chapter 13 ... 477

14 Circular functions — 483

- 14A Measuring angles in degrees and radians ... 484
- 14B Defining circular functions: sine and cosine ... 487
- 14C Another circular function: tangent ... 489
- 14D Reviewing trigonometric ratios ... 490
- 14E Symmetry properties of circular functions ... 491
- 14F Exact values of circular functions ... 494
- 14G Graphs of sine and cosine ... 496
- 14H Solution of trigonometric equations ... 503
- 14I Sketch graphs of $y = a \sin n(t \pm \varepsilon)$ and $y = a \cos n(t \pm \varepsilon)$ ... 508
- 14J Sketch graphs of $y = a \sin n(t \pm \varepsilon) \pm b$ and $y = a \cos n(t \pm \varepsilon) \pm b$ ... 510
- 14K Further symmetry properties and the Pythagorean identity ... 512
- 14L The tangent function ... 515
- 14M Numerical methods with a CAS calculator ... 518
- 14N General solution of trigonometric equations ... 521
- 14O Applications of circular functions ... 524
- Review of Chapter 14 ... 527

15 Revision of Chapters 13–14 — 533

- 15A Technology-free questions ... 533
- 15B Multiple-choice questions ... 535
- 15C Extended-response questions ... 537

16 Rates of change — 541

- **16A** Recognising relationships — 542
- **16B** Constant rate of change — 546
- **16C** Average rate of change — 550
- **16D** Instantaneous rate of change — 555
- **16E** Position and average velocity — 561
- Review of Chapter 16 — 568

17 Differentiation and antidifferentiation of polynomials — 574

- **17A** The derivative — 576
- **17B** Rules for differentiation — 583
- **17C** Differentiating x^n where n is a negative integer — 591
- **17D** Graphs of the derivative function — 594
- **17E** Antidifferentiation of polynomial functions — 602
- **17F** Limits and continuity — 608
- **17G** When is a function differentiable? — 614
- Review of Chapter 17 — 618

18 Applications of differentiation and antidifferentiation of polynomials — 623

- **18A** Tangents and normals — 624
- **18B** Rates of change — 627
- **18C** Stationary points — 632
- **18D** Types of stationary points — 635
- **18E** Applications to maximum and minimum problems — 640
- **18F** Applications of differentiation to kinematics — 647
- **18G** Applications of antidifferentiation to kinematics — 655
- **18H** Families of functions and transformations — 658
- **18I** Newton's method for finding solutions to equations — 661
- Review of Chapter 18 — 665

19 Revision of Chapters 16–18 — 674

- **19A** Technology-free questions — 674
- **19B** Multiple-choice questions — 675
- **19C** Extended-response questions — 680

20 Further differentiation and antidifferentiation — 685

- **20A** The chain rule — 686
- **20B** Differentiating rational powers — 691
- **20C** Antidifferentiating rational powers — 694
- **20D** The second derivative — 697
- **20E** Sketch graphs — 698
- Review of Chapter 20 — 703

21 Integration — 707

- **21A** Estimating the area under a graph … 708
- **21B** Finding the exact area: the definite integral … 713
- **21C** Signed area … 718
- Review of Chapter 21 … 724

22 Revision of Chapters 20–21 — 731

- **22A** Technology-free questions … 731
- **22B** Multiple-choice questions … 732

23 Revision of Chapters 1–22 — 734

- **23A** Technology-free questions … 734
- **23B** Multiple-choice questions … 737
- **23C** Extended-response questions … 741

A Appendix A: Further polynomials and systems of linear equations — 745

- **A1** Synthetic substitution and division … 745
- **A2** The rational-root theorem … 748
- **A3** Systems of equations … 750

Glossary — 755

Answers — 763

Included in the Interactive and PDF Textbook only

Appendix B: Guide to the TI-Nspire CAS Calculator (OS4) in VCE Mathematics

Appendix C: Guide to the Casio ClassPad II CAS Calculator in VCE Mathematics

Appendix D: Chapter 12 from Specialist Mathematics 1&2

Sampling and sampling distributions

- 12A Populations and samples
- 12B The distribution of the sample proportion
- 12C Investigating the distribution of the sample proportion using simulation
- 12D Investigating the distribution of the sample mean using simulation

Chapter summary

Introduction

Cambridge Mathematical Methods Australian Curriculum/VCE Units 1&2 provides a complete teaching and learning resource for the VCE Study Design to be implemented in 2016. It has been written with understanding as its chief aim and with ample practice offered through the worked examples and exercises. All the work has been trialled in the classroom, and the approaches offered are based on classroom experience and the responses of teachers to earlier versions of this book.

Mathematical Methods Units 1 and 2 provide an introductory study of simple elementary functions, algebra, calculus, probability and statistics and their applications in a variety of practical and theoretical contexts. The course is designed as preparation for Mathematical Methods Units 3 and 4 and contains assumed knowledge and skills for these units. The changes in this course reflect the requirements of the Australian Curriculum subject Mathematical Methods.

The book has been carefully prepared to reflect the prescribed course. New material such as the bisection method, Newton's method for solving equations and the rational root theorem has been included and the probability has been written to reflect the introduction of statistical inference in Mathematical Methods Units 3 and 4.

The book contains six revision chapters. These provide technology free, multiple-choice questions and extended-response questions.

The TI-Nspire calculator examples and instructions have been completed by Russell Brown and those for the Casio ClassPad have been completed by Maria Schaffner.

The integration of the features of the textbook and the new digital components of the package, powered by Cambridge HOTmaths, are illustrated on pages xii to xiii.

Introduction

About Cambridge HOTmaths

Cambridge HOTmaths is a comprehensive, award-winning mathematics learning system - an interactive online maths learning, teaching and assessment resource for students and teachers, for individuals or whole classes, for school and at home. Its digital engine or platform is used to host and power the interactive textbook and the Online Teaching Suite, and selected topics from HOTmaths' own Years 9 and 10 courses area are available for revision of prior knowledge. All this is included in the price of the textbook.

Acknowledgements

The author and publisher wish to thank the following sources for permission to reproduce material:

Cover: Used under license 2015 from Shutterstock.com / John M Anderson

Images: Shutterstock.com / ILeysen, **p.1**, 313 / Joanna Dorota, **p.22** / 1000 Words, **p.24** / Mauro Fabbro, **p.33** / My Good Images, **p.71** / LizaLutik, **p.81**, 419 / Flashon Studio, **p.109** / wavebreakmedia, **p.135** / Melamory **p.145**, 392 / Curly Pat, **p.169**, 302 / Redcollegiya, **p.209** / kentoh, **p.267** / Bardocz Peter, **p.321** / RTimages, **p.349** / bellenxie, **p.367** / bikeriderlondon, **p.401** / Micha Klootwijk, **p.412** / Phil Date, **p.414** / Monkey Business Images, **p.426** / fotosav, **p.427** / vanillamilk, **p.429**, 83 / tristan tan, **p.466** / Yenyu Shih, **p.476** / Lester / Max Krasnov, **p.533** / MRTfotografie, **p.540** / Attitude, **p.541** / Hakki Arslan, **p.574** / Iterum, **p.623** / metrue, **p.674** / Kittikorn Phongok, **p.685** / Apostrophe, **p.707** / oksanka007, **p.731** / Excellent backgrounds, **p.734**

Every effort has been made to trace and acknowledge copyright. The publisher apologises for any accidental infringement and welcomes information that would redress this situation.

An overview of the Cambridge complete teacher and learning resource

For more detail, see the guide in the online Interactive Textbook

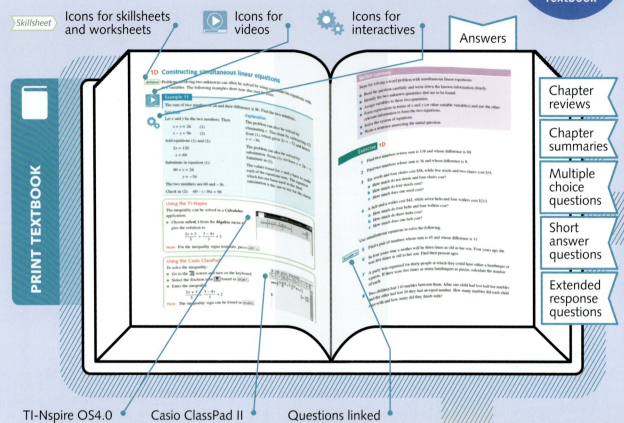

- Icons for skillsheets and worksheets
- Icons for videos
- Icons for interactives
- Answers
- Chapter reviews
- Chapter summaries
- Multiple choice questions
- Short answer questions
- Extended response questions

PRINT TEXTBOOK

- TI-Nspire OS4.0 examples
- Casio ClassPad II examples
- Questions linked to examples

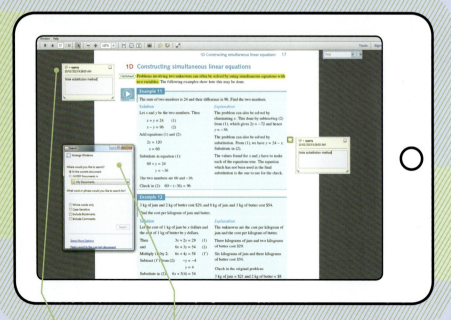

PDF TEXTBOOK

Downloadable

Included with print textbook and interactive textbook

- Note-taking
- Search functions

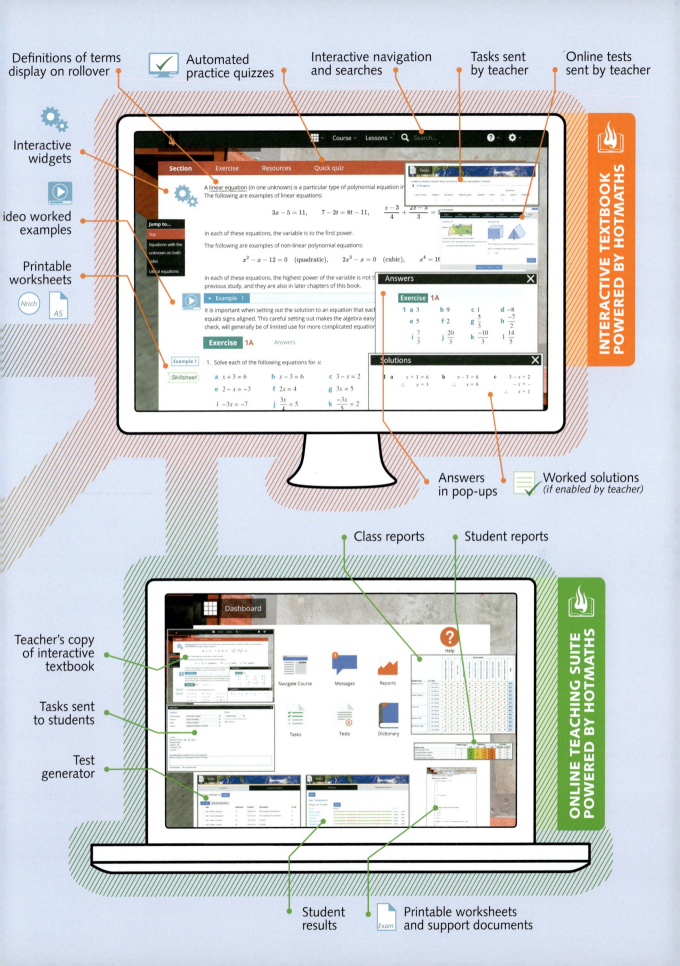

Chapter 1

Reviewing linear equations

Objectives

▶ To solve **linear equations** in one unknown.
▶ To construct linear equations.
▶ To use linear equations to **solve problems**.
▶ To solve **simultaneous linear equations** by substitution and elimination methods.
▶ To solve **linear inequalities**.
▶ To use and **transpose** formulas.

Many problems may be solved by first translating them into mathematical equations and then solving the equations using algebraic techniques. An equation is solved by finding the value or values of the variables that would make the statement true.

Consider the equation $2x + 11 = 3 - 2x$. If $x = -2$, then

$$\text{LHS} = 2(-2) + 11 = 7 \quad \text{and} \quad \text{RHS} = 3 - 2(-2) = 7$$

The statement is true when $x = -2$. The solution to the equation is therefore $x = -2$. In this case there is no other value of x that would give a true statement.

The equations that we deal with in this chapter are called linear equations since they are related to the equation of a straight line.

Linear equations have either one solution (as shown in the example above), no solutions or infinitely many solutions. The equation $2x + 3 = 2x + 4$ has no solutions, since no value of x makes the statement true. The equation $2(x + 3) = 2x + 6$ has infinitely many solutions, since it is true for all values of x.

We note that the equation $x^2 = 16$ has exactly two solutions, $x = 4$ or $x = -4$, but this equation is not linear.

1A Linear equations

A **linear equation** (in one unknown) is a particular type of polynomial equation in which the variable is to the first power. The following are examples of linear equations:

$$3x - 5 = 11, \qquad 7 - 2t = 8t - 11, \qquad \frac{z-3}{4} + \frac{2z-5}{3} = 11$$

In each of these equations, the variable is to the first power.

The following are examples of non-linear polynomial equations:

$$x^2 - x - 12 = 0 \quad \text{(quadratic)}, \qquad 2x^3 - x = 0 \quad \text{(cubic)}, \qquad x^4 = 16 \quad \text{(quartic)}$$

In each of these equations, the highest power of the variable is not the first power. You have met some of these in your previous study, and they are also in later chapters of this book.

▶ Solving linear equations

It is important when setting out the solution to an equation that each step is written under the previous one with the equals signs aligned. This careful setting out makes the algebra easy to check. Unsystematic methods, such as guess and check, will generally be of limited use for more complicated equations.

It is often helpful to look at how the equation has been constructed so that the steps necessary to 'undo' the equation can be identified. It is most important that the steps taken to solve the equation are done in the correct order.

Linear equations of the form $ax + b = c$

Many linear equations that arise in applications are of the form $ax + b = c$.

> **Example 1**
>
> Solve the equation $3x + 4 = 16$ for x.
>
> | Solution | Explanation |
> |---|---|
> | $3x + 4 = 16$ | |
> | $3x = 12$ | Subtract 4 from both sides. |
> | $x = 4$ | Divide both sides by 3. |
> | Check: | Once a solution has been found it may be checked by substituting the value back into both sides of the original equation to ensure that the left-hand side (LHS) equals the right-hand side (RHS). |
> | LHS $= 3(4) + 4 = 16$ | |
> | RHS $= 16$ | |
> | $\therefore$ the solution is correct. | |

The first three equations in the above example are equivalent equations. Obtaining the second two equations enables us to solve the first equation.

1A Linear equations

Given an equation, an equivalent equation can be formed by:
- adding or subtracting the same number on both sides of the equation
- multiplying or dividing both sides of the equation by the same non-zero number.

Importantly, two equivalent equations have the same solution. By forming suitable equivalent equations, we solve linear equations.

Equations with the unknown on both sides

Group all the terms containing the variable on one side of the equation and the remaining terms on the other side.

Example 2

Solve $4x + 3 = 3x - 5$.

Solution

$$4x + 3 = 3x - 5$$
$$x + 3 = -5$$
$$x = -8$$

Check:
$$\text{LHS} = 4(-8) + 3 = -29$$
$$\text{RHS} = 3(-8) - 5 = -29$$

∴ the solution is correct.

Explanation

Subtract $3x$ from both sides and then subtract 3 from both sides.

The solution can be checked as previously shown.

Equations containing brackets

A frequently used first step is to remove brackets and then to follow the procedure for solving an equation without brackets.

Example 3

Solve $3(2x + 5) = 27$.

Solution

$$3(2x + 5) = 27$$
$$6x + 15 = 27$$
$$6x = 12$$
$$x = 2$$

Check:
$$\text{LHS} = 3(2 \times 2 + 5) = 27$$
$$\text{RHS} = 27$$

∴ the solution is correct.

Explanation

We note that since 27 is divisible by 3, the following method is also possible:

$$3(2x + 5) = 27$$
$$2x + 5 = 9$$
$$2x = 4$$
$$x = 2$$

Equations containing fractions

A frequently used first step is to multiply both sides of the equation by the lowest common multiple of the denominators of the fractions.

Example 4

Solve $\dfrac{x}{5} - 2 = \dfrac{x}{3}$.

Solution

$$\dfrac{x}{5} - 2 = \dfrac{x}{3}$$

$$\dfrac{x}{5} \times 15 - 2 \times 15 = \dfrac{x}{3} \times 15$$

$$3x - 30 = 5x$$

$$-2x = 30$$

$$x = -15$$

Check: LHS $= \dfrac{-15}{5} - 2 = -3 - 2 = -5$

RHS $= \dfrac{-15}{3} = -5$

∴ the solution is correct.

Explanation

The denominators of the fractions are 3 and 5. The lowest common multiple of 3 and 5 is 15.

Multiply both sides of the equation by 15. This means that each term of the LHS and the RHS of the equation is multiplied by 15.

Example 5

Solve $\dfrac{x-3}{2} - \dfrac{2x-4}{3} = 5$.

Solution

$$\dfrac{x-3}{2} \times 6 - \dfrac{2x-4}{3} \times 6 = 5 \times 6$$

$$3(x - 3) - 2(2x - 4) = 30$$

$$3x - 9 - 4x + 8 = 30$$

$$-x = 31$$

$$x = -31$$

Check:

LHS $= \dfrac{-31 - 3}{2} - \dfrac{2 \times (-31) - 4}{3}$

$= \dfrac{-34}{2} - \dfrac{-66}{3} = -17 + 22 = 5$

RHS $= 5$

∴ the solution is correct.

Explanation

Remember that the line separating the numerator and the denominator (the vinculum) acts as brackets.

Multiply both sides of the equation by 6, the lowest common multiple of 2 and 3.

1A Linear equations

Using the TI-Nspire

- To find the solution to the linear equation, use a **Calculator** application.
- Select menu > **Algebra** > **Solve**.
- Enter the equation
$$\frac{x-3}{2} - \frac{2x-4}{3} = 5$$
- Press enter to obtain the solution.

Note: A template for fractions may be obtained by pressing ctrl ÷.
For more details on the use of the calculator refer to the TI-Nspire appendix in the Interactive Textbook.

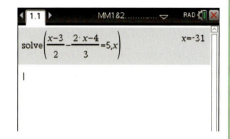

Using the Casio ClassPad

- Go to the $\sqrt{\alpha}$ **Main** screen and turn on the keyboard.
- Select the fraction icon found in the Math1 keyboard.
- Enter the equation
$$\frac{x-3}{2} - \frac{2x-4}{3} = 5$$
- Highlight the equation using the stylus and select **Interactive** > **Equation/Inequality** > **solve**.
- Tap on OK to obtain the solution. (Note that the default variable is x.)

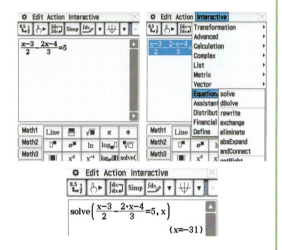

Note: For more details on the use of the calculator refer to the Casio ClassPad appendix in the Interactive Textbook.

Literal equations

An equation for the variable x in which all the coefficients of x, including the constants, are pronumerals is known as a **literal equation**.

Example 6

Solve $ax + b = cx + d$ for x.

Solution	Explanation
$ax + b = cx + d$ $ax - cx = d - b$	Collect terms in x on the left-hand side and constants on the right-hand side.
$(a - c)x = d - b$	Factorise the left-hand side.
$x = \dfrac{d - b}{a - c}$	

Using the TI-Nspire

- To solve the literal equation $ax + b = cx + d$, use a **Calculator** application.
- Select menu > **Algebra** > **Solve**.
- Enter $ax + b = cx + d$ as shown.
- Press enter to obtain the solution.

Note: Ensure a multiplication sign is placed between the letters of the expression, otherwise the calculator will read them as a single variable rather than a product. That is, enter $a \times x$ and not ax.

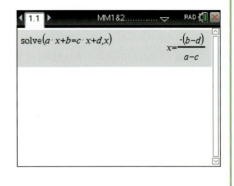

Using the Casio ClassPad

- To solve the literal equation $ax + b = cx + d$, first go to the $\sqrt{\alpha}$ Main screen and turn on the keyboard.
- Select the Var keyboard. This will bring up the variables.
- Enter the equation $ax + b = cx + d$ and highlight it.
- Select **Interactive** > **Equation/Inequality** > **solve** and ensure that the variable selected is x.
- Tap on OK to obtain the solution.
- If necessary, the answer may be simplified further by copying the answer into the next line and then selecting **Interactive** > **Transformation** > **simplify**.

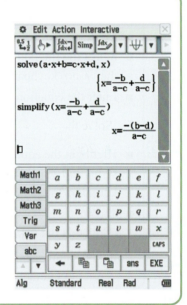

Section summary

- An equation is solved by finding the value or values of the variables that would make the statement true.
- A linear equation is one in which the variable is to the first power.
- There are often several different ways to solve a linear equation. The following steps provide some suggestions:
  1. Expand brackets and, if the equation involves fractions, multiply through by the lowest common denominator of the terms.
  2. Group all of the terms containing a variable on one side of the equation and the terms without the variable on the other side.

Exercise 1A

1 Solve each of the following equations for x:
- **a** $x + 3 = 6$
- **b** $x - 3 = 6$
- **c** $3 - x = 2$
- **d** $x + 6 = -2$
- **e** $2 - x = -3$
- **f** $2x = 4$
- **g** $3x = 5$
- **h** $-2x = 7$
- **i** $-3x = -7$
- **j** $\dfrac{3x}{4} = 5$
- **k** $\dfrac{-3x}{5} = 2$
- **l** $\dfrac{-5x}{7} = -2$

2 Solve each of the following literal equations for x:
- **a** $x - b = a$
- **b** $x + b = a$
- **c** $ax = b$
- **d** $\dfrac{x}{a} = b$
- **e** $\dfrac{ax}{b} = c$

Example 1 **3** Solve the following linear equations:
- **a** $2y - 4 = 6$
- **b** $3t + 2 = 17$
- **c** $2y + 5 = 2$
- **d** $7x - 9 = 5$
- **e** $2a - 4 = 7$
- **f** $3a + 6 = 14$
- **g** $\dfrac{y}{8} - 11 = 6$
- **h** $\dfrac{t}{3} + \dfrac{1}{6} = \dfrac{1}{2}$
- **i** $\dfrac{x}{3} + 5 = 9$
- **j** $3 - 5y = 12$
- **k** $-3x - 7 = 14$
- **l** $14 - 3y = 8$

Example 2 **4** Solve the following linear equations:
- **a** $6x - 4 = 3x$
- **b** $x - 5 = 4x + 10$
- **c** $3x - 2 = 8 - 2x$

5 Solve the following linear equations:

Example 3
- **a** $2(y + 6) = 10$
- **b** $2y + 6 = 3(y - 4)$
- **c** $2(x + 4) = 7x + 2$
- **d** $5(y - 3) = 2(2y + 4)$
- **e** $x - 6 = 2(x - 3)$
- **f** $\dfrac{y + 2}{3} = 4$

Example 4
- **g** $\dfrac{x}{2} + \dfrac{x}{3} = 10$
- **h** $x + 4 = \dfrac{3}{2}x$
- **i** $\dfrac{7x + 3}{2} = \dfrac{9x - 8}{4}$

Example 5
- **j** $\dfrac{2(1 - 2x)}{3} - 2x = -\dfrac{2}{5} + \dfrac{4(2 - 3x)}{3}$
- **k** $\dfrac{4y - 5}{2} - \dfrac{2y - 1}{6} = y$

Example 6 **6** Solve the following literal equations for x:
- **a** $ax + b = 0$
- **b** $cx + d = e$
- **c** $a(x + b) = c$
- **d** $ax + b = cx$
- **e** $\dfrac{x}{a} + \dfrac{x}{b} = 1$
- **f** $\dfrac{a}{x} + \dfrac{b}{x} = 1$
- **g** $ax - b = cx - d$
- **h** $\dfrac{ax + c}{b} = d$

7 Solve each of the following for x:
- **a** $0.2x + 6 = 2.4$
- **b** $0.6(2.8 - x) = 48.6$
- **c** $\dfrac{2x + 12}{7} = 6.5$
- **d** $0.5x - 4 = 10$
- **e** $\dfrac{1}{4}(x - 10) = 6$
- **f** $6.4x + 2 = 3.2 - 4x$

8 Solve $\dfrac{b - cx}{a} + \dfrac{a - cx}{b} + 2 = 0$ for x.

9 Solve $\dfrac{a}{x + a} + \dfrac{b}{x - b} = \dfrac{a + b}{x + c}$ for x.

1B Constructing linear equations

As stated earlier, many problems can be solved by translating them into mathematical language and using an appropriate mathematical technique to find the solution. By representing the unknown quantity in a problem with a symbol and constructing an equation from the information, the value of the unknown can be found by solving the equation.

Before constructing the equation, each symbol and what it stands for (including the units) should be stated. It is essential to remember that all the elements of the equation must be in units of the same system.

Example 7

A chef uses the following rule for cooking a turkey:
'Allow 30 minutes for each kilogram weight of turkey and then add an extra 15 minutes.'

If the chef forgot to weigh a turkey before cooking it, but knew that it had taken 3 hours to cook, calculate how much it weighed.

Solution

Let the weight of the turkey be x kilograms.
Then the time taken is $(30x + 15)$ minutes.

$$\therefore \quad 30x + 15 = 180$$
$$30x = 165$$
$$x = 5.5$$

The turkey weighed 5.5 kilograms.

Explanation

Assign a variable to the quantity that is to be found. In this example, the weight of the turkey is x kilograms.

Find, in terms of x, the time to cook the turkey. Then form the equation. Note that 3 hours is 180 minutes.

State the solution to the problem in words.

Example 8

Find the area of a rectangle whose perimeter is 1.08 m, if it is 8 cm longer than it is wide.

Solution

Let length = ℓ cm.
Then width = $(\ell - 8)$ cm.

$$\begin{aligned} \text{Perimeter} &= 2 \times \text{length} + 2 \times \text{width} \\ &= 2\ell + 2(\ell - 8) \\ &= 4\ell - 16 \text{ cm} \end{aligned}$$

Perimeter = 108 cm

$$\therefore \quad 4\ell - 16 = 108$$
$$4\ell = 124$$
$$\ell = 31 \text{ cm}$$

The length is 31 cm and the width is 23 cm.

Therefore the area is $31 \times 23 = 713 \text{ cm}^2$.

Explanation

We know that

$$\text{Perimeter} = 2 \times \text{length} + 2 \times \text{width}$$

and that the width is 8 cm less than the length. Let ℓ cm be the length. Then the width is $(\ell - 8)$ cm.

Find the perimeter in terms of ℓ. Find the length and width, and hence find the area.

Example 9

Adam normally takes 5 hours to travel between Higett and Logett. One day he increases his speed by 4 km/h and finds the journey from Higett to Logett takes half an hour less than the normal time. Find his normal speed.

Solution

Let x km/h be his normal speed.

The distance from Higett to Logett is $x \times 5 = 5x$ kilometres.

Adam's new speed is $(x + 4)$ km/h.

Hence
$$(x + 4) \times \frac{9}{2} = 5x$$
$$9(x + 4) = 10x$$
$$9x + 36 = 10x$$
$$36 = x$$

His normal speed is 36 km/h.

Explanation

In problems such as this, the speed is the average speed.

We note that
$$\text{distance} = \text{speed} \times \text{time}$$

Section summary

Steps for solving a word problem with a linear equation:

- Read the question carefully and write down the known information clearly.
- Identify the unknown quantity that is to be found.
- Assign a variable to this quantity.
- Form an expression in terms of x (or the variable being used) and use the other relevant information to form the equation.
- Solve the equation.
- Write a sentence answering the initial question.

Exercise 1B

1 For each of the following, write an equation using the variable x, then solve the equation for x:

  a A number plus two is equal to six.

  b A number multiplied by three is equal to ten.

  c Six is added to a number multiplied by three and the result is twenty-two.

  d Five is subtracted from a number multiplied by three and the result is fifteen.

  e Three is added to a number. If the result of this is multiplied by six, then fifty-six is obtained.

  f Five is added to a number and the result divided by four gives twenty-three.

2 $48 is divided among three students, A, B and C. If B receives three times as much as A, and C receives twice as much as A, how much does each receive?

3 The sum of two numbers is 42, and one number is twice the other. Find the two numbers.

Example 7 **4** A chef uses the following rule for cooking food on a spit: 'Allow 20 minutes for each kilogram weight and then add an extra 20 minutes.' If the chef forgot to weigh the food before cooking it but knew that it had taken 3 hours to cook, calculate how much it weighed.

Example 8 **5** Find the area of a rectangle whose perimeter is 4.8 m, if it is 0.5 m longer than it is wide.

6 Find three consecutive whole numbers with a sum of 150.

7 Find four consecutive odd numbers with a sum of 80.

8 Two tanks contain equal amounts of water. They are connected by a pipe and 3000 litres of water is pumped from one tank to the other. One tank then contains 6 times as much water as the other. How many litres of water did each tank contain originally?

9 A 120-page book has p lines to a page. If the number of lines were reduced by three on each page, the number of pages would need to be increased by 20 to give the same amount of writing space. How many lines were there on each page originally?

Example 9 **10** A rower travels upstream at 6 km/h and back to the starting place at 10 km/h. The total journey takes 48 minutes. How far upstream did the rower go?

11 A shopkeeper buys a crate of eggs at $1.50 per dozen. He buys another crate, containing 3 dozen more than the first crate, at $2.00 per dozen. He sells them all for $2.50 a dozen and makes $15 profit. How many dozens were there in each of the crates?

Example 9 **12** Jess walked for 45 minutes at 3 km/h and then ran for half an hour at x km/h. At the end of that time she was 6 km from the starting point. Find the value of x.

13 A man travels from A to B at 4 km/h and from B to A at 6 km/h. The total journey takes 45 minutes. Find the distance travelled.

14 A boy is 24 years younger than his father. In two years time the sum of their ages will be 40. Find the present ages of father and son.

1C Simultaneous equations

A linear equation that contains two unknowns, e.g. $2y + 3x = 10$, does not have a single solution. Such an equation actually expresses a relationship between pairs of numbers, x and y, that satisfy the equation. If all possible pairs of numbers (x, y) that satisfy the equation are represented graphically, the result is a straight line; hence the name **linear relation**.

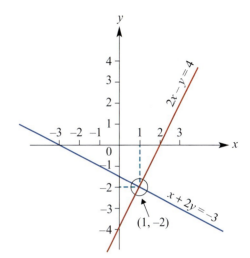

If the graphs of two such equations are drawn on the same set of axes, and they are non-parallel, the lines will intersect at one point only. Hence there is one pair of numbers that will satisfy both equations simultaneously.

The intersection point of two straight lines can be found graphically; however, the accuracy of the solution will depend on the accuracy of the graphs.

Alternatively, the intersection point may be found algebraically by solving the pair of simultaneous equations. We shall consider two techniques for solving simultaneous equations.

Example 10

Solve the equations $2x - y = 4$ and $x + 2y = -3$.

Solution	Explanation
Method 1: Substitution	
$2x - y = 4$ (1) $\quad$ $x + 2y = -3$ (2)	Using one of the two equations, express one variable in terms of the other variable.
From equation (2), we get $x = -3 - 2y$.	
Substitute in equation (1): $2(-3 - 2y) - y = 4$ $-6 - 4y - y = 4$ $-5y = 10$ $y = -2$	Then substitute this expression into the other equation (reducing it to an equation in one variable, y). Solve the equation for y.
Substitute the value of y into (2): $x + 2(-2) = -3$ $x = 1$	Substitute this value for y in one of the equations to find the other variable, x.
Check in (1): LHS $= 2(1) - (-2) = 4$ RHS $= 4$	A check can be carried out with the other equation.

Method 2: Elimination

$$2x - y = 4 \quad (1)$$
$$x + 2y = -3 \quad (2)$$

To eliminate x, multiply equation (2) by 2 and subtract the result from equation (1).

When we multiply equation (2) by 2, the pair of equations becomes:

$$2x - y = 4 \quad (1)$$
$$2x + 4y = -6 \quad (2')$$

Subtract (2′) from (1):

$$-5y = 10$$
$$y = -2$$

Now substitute for y in equation (2) to find x, and check as in the substitution method.

If one of the variables has the same coefficient in the two equations, we can eliminate that variable by subtracting one equation from the other.

It may be necessary to multiply one of the equations by a constant to make the coefficients of x or y the same in the two equations.

Note: This example shows that the point (1, −2) is the point of intersection of the graphs of the two linear relations.

Using the TI-Nspire
Calculator application

Simultaneous equations can be solved in a **Calculator** application.

- Use menu > **Algebra** > **Solve System of Equations** > **Solve System of Equations**.
- Complete the pop-up screen.

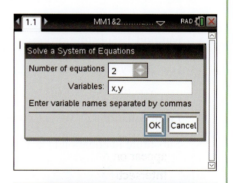

- Enter the equations as shown to give the solution to the simultaneous equations $2x - y = 4$ and $x + 2y = -3$.

Note: The solution can also be found with solve($2x - y = 4$ and $x + 2y = -3, x, y$).

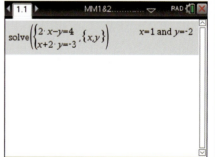

Graphs application

The simultaneous equations can also be solved graphically in a **Graphs** application.

Entering the equations:

- The equations can be entered directly in the form $a \cdot x + b \cdot y = c$ using menu > **Graph Entry/Edit > Equation > Line > a·x + b·y = c**.
- Enter the equations as shown.

Hint: Use ▼ to enter the second equation.

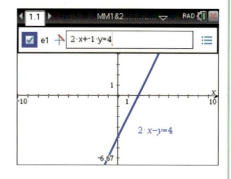

Alternatively:

- The equations can be rearranged to make y the subject. The equations in this form are $f1(x) = 2x - 4$ and $f2(x) = \dfrac{-3 - x}{2}$.
- Enter these in the default function entry line.

Note: If the entry line is not visible, press tab or double click in an open area. Pressing enter will hide the entry line.

Finding the intersection point:

- Use menu > **Geometry > Points & Lines > Intersection Point(s)**.
- Use the touchpad to move the cursor to select each of the two graphs.

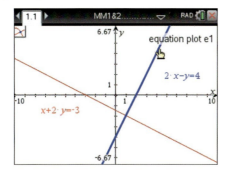 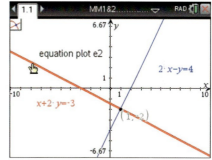

- The intersection point's coordinates will appear on the screen. Press esc to exit the **Intersection Point(s)** tool.

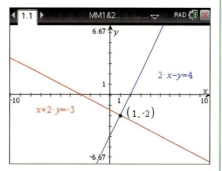

Note: You can also find the intersection point using menu > **Analyze Graph > Intersection**.

Using the Casio ClassPad

To solve the simultaneous equations algebraically:

- Go to the $\sqrt{\alpha}$ Main screen and turn on the keyboard.
- Open the Math1 keyboard and select the simultaneous equations icon.
- Enter the two equations

  $2x - y = 4$

  $x + 2y = -3$

  into the two lines.
- Type x, y in the bottom-right square to indicate the variables.
- Select EXE.

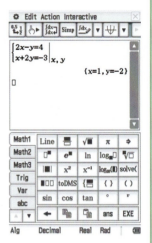

The simultaneous equations can also be solved graphically:

- Tap on the graph icon to display the graph screen.
- Using your stylus, highlight the first equation $2x - y = 4$ and drag it down into the graph screen. Lift the stylus off the screen for the graph to appear.
- Repeat by highlighting the second equation $x + 2y = -3$ and dragging it down into the graph screen. Lift the stylus off the screen for the second graph to appear.

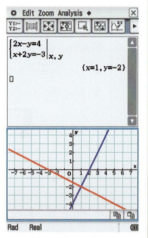

- To find the solution, tap into the graph screen to select it, and then select **Analysis** > **G-Solve** > **Intersection**.

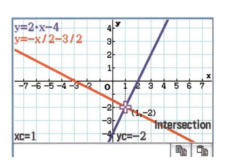

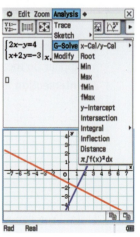

▶ The geometry of simultaneous equations

Two distinct straight lines are either parallel or meet at a point.

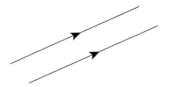 

There are three cases for a system of two linear equations with two variables.

	Example	Solutions	Geometry
Case 1	$2x + y = 5$ $x - y = 4$	Unique solution: $x = 3, \ y = -1$	Two lines meeting at a point
Case 2	$2x + y = 5$ $2x + y = 7$	No solutions	Distinct parallel lines
Case 3	$2x + y = 5$ $4x + 2y = 10$	Infinitely many solutions	Two copies of the same line

This is further discussed in Chapter 2.

Section summary

We have two methods for solving simultaneous linear equations in two variables by hand.

1 Substitution

Make one of the variables the subject in one of the equations and substitute for that variable in the other equation.

For example, for the equations:

$$3x + y = 6 \quad (1)$$
$$5x + 3y = -2 \quad (2)$$

- From (1), we have $y = 6 - 3x$.
- Substitute this into (2), and solve the resulting equation $5x + 3(6 - 3x) = -2$ for x.
- Substitute this value for x back into one of the original equations to find the value of the other variable, y.
- Check that your solution satisfies the original equations.

2 Elimination

In this method, one of the variables is eliminated. For example, with the same equations considered above:

$$3x + y = 6 \quad (1)$$
$$5x + 3y = -2 \quad (2)$$

- Decide which variable to eliminate. We will eliminate y.
- If necessary, multiply both sides of one or both equations by a number to obtain the same or opposite coefficient for the variable to be eliminated. With this example, multiply (1) by 3:

$$9x + 3y = 18 \quad (1')$$

- Add or subtract the equations to eliminate the chosen variable. In this example, subtract (2) from (1').
- Solve the resulting equation, and then proceed as with the substitution method.

Exercise 1C

1 Solve each of the following pairs of simultaneous equations by the substitution method:

- **a** $y = 2x + 1$
  $y = 3x + 2$
- **b** $y = 5x - 4$
  $y = 3x + 6$
- **c** $y = 2 - 3x$
  $y = 5x + 10$
- **d** $y - 4 = 3x$
  $y - 5x + 6 = 0$
- **e** $y - 4x = 3$
  $2y - 5x + 6 = 0$
- **f** $y - 4x = 6$
  $2y - 3x = 4$

2 Solve each of the following pairs of simultaneous equations by the elimination method:

- **a** $x + y = 6$
  $x - y = 10$
- **b** $y - x = 5$
  $x + y = 3$
- **c** $x - 2y = 6$
  $x + 6y = 10$

Example 10

3 Solve each of the following pairs of simultaneous linear equations by either the substitution or the elimination method:

- **a** $2x - 3y = 7$
  $y = 5 - 3x$
- **b** $2x - 5y = 10$
  $4x + 3y = 7$
- **c** $2m - 1 = n$
  $2n + m = 8$
- **d** $7x - 6y = 20$
  $3x + 4y = 2$
- **e** $3s - 1 = t$
  $5s + 2t = 20$
- **f** $4x - 3y = 1$
  $4y - 5x = 2$
- **g** $15x - 4y = 6$
  $9x - 2y = 5$
- **h** $2p + 5q = -3$
  $7p - 2q = 9$
- **i** $2x - 4y = -12$
  $2y + 3x - 2 = 0$

4 For each of the following pairs of simultaneous linear equations, state whether there is one, none or infinitely many solutions:

- **a** $3x + y = 6$
  $6x + 2y = 7$
- **b** $3x + y = 6$
  $6x + 2y = 12$
- **c** $3x + y = 6$
  $6x - 2y = 7$
- **d** $3x - y = 6$
  $6x + 2y = 7$

1D Constructing simultaneous linear equations

Skillsheet Problems involving two unknowns can often be solved by using simultaneous equations with two variables. The following examples show how this may be done.

Example 11

The sum of two numbers is 24 and their difference is 96. Find the two numbers.

Solution

Let x and y be the two numbers. Then

$$x + y = 24 \quad (1)$$
$$x - y = 96 \quad (2)$$

Add equations (1) and (2):

$$2x = 120$$
$$x = 60$$

Substitute in equation (1):

$$60 + y = 24$$
$$y = -36$$

The two numbers are 60 and -36.

Check in (2): $60 - (-36) = 96$

Explanation

The problem can also be solved by eliminating x. Subtracting (2) from (1) gives $2y = -72$ and hence $y = -36$.

The problem can also be solved by substitution. From (1), we have $y = 24 - x$. Substitute in (2).

The values found for x and y have to make each of the equations true. The equation which has not been used in the final substitution is the one to use for the check.

Example 12

3 kg of jam and 2 kg of butter cost $29, and 6 kg of jam and 3 kg of butter cost $54. Find the cost per kilogram of jam and butter.

Solution

Let the cost of 1 kg of jam be x dollars and the cost of 1 kg of butter be y dollars.

Then $\quad 3x + 2y = 29 \quad (1)$
and $\quad 6x + 3y = 54 \quad (2)$

Multiply (1) by 2: $\quad 6x + 4y = 58 \quad (1')$
Subtract (1') from (2): $\quad -y = -4$
$\quad y = 4$

Substitute in (2): $\quad 6x + 3(4) = 54$
$\quad 6x = 42$
$\quad x = 7$

Jam costs $7 per kg and butter $4 per kg.

Explanation

The unknowns are the cost per kilogram of jam and the cost per kilogram of butter.

Three kilograms of jam and two kilograms of butter cost $29.

Six kilograms of jam and three kilograms of butter cost $54.

Check in the original problem:

3 kg of jam = $21 and 2 kg of butter = $8
Total = $29

6 kg of jam = $42 and 3 kg of butter = $12
Total = $54

Section summary

Steps for solving a word problem with simultaneous linear equations:

- Read the question carefully and write down the known information clearly.
- Identify the two unknown quantities that are to be found.
- Assign variables to these two quantities.
- Form expressions in terms of x and y (or other suitable variables) and use the other relevant information to form the two equations.
- Solve the system of equations.
- Write a sentence answering the initial question.

Exercise 1D

1. Find two numbers whose sum is 138 and whose difference is 88.

2. Find two numbers whose sum is 36 and whose difference is 9.

3. Six stools and four chairs cost $58, while five stools and two chairs cost $35.
    a. How much do ten stools and four chairs cost?
    b. How much do four stools cost?
    c. How much does one stool cost?

4. A belt and a wallet cost $42, while seven belts and four wallets cost $213.
    a. How much do four belts and four wallets cost?
    b. How much do three belts cost?
    c. How much does one belt cost?

Use simultaneous equations to solve the following.

5. [Example 11] Find a pair of numbers whose sum is 45 and whose difference is 11.

6. In four years time a mother will be three times as old as her son. Four years ago she was five times as old as her son. Find their present ages.

7. A party was organised for thirty people at which they could have either a hamburger or a pizza. If there were five times as many hamburgers as pizzas, calculate the number of each.

8. Two children had 110 marbles between them. After one child had lost half her marbles and the other had lost 20 they had an equal number. How many marbles did each child start with and how many did they finish with?

9 One hundred and fifty tickets were sold for a basketball match and $560 was the total amount collected. Adult tickets were sold at $4.00 each and child tickets were sold at $1.50 each. How many adult tickets and how many child tickets were sold?

10 The sum of the numerator and denominator of a fraction expressed in simplest form is 17. If 3 is added to the numerator, the value of the fraction will be 1. What is the fraction?

11 Linda thinks of a two-digit number. The sum of the digits is 8. If she reverses the digits, the new number is 36 greater than her original number. What was Linda's original number?

12 Tickets to a musical cost $30 for adults and $12 for children. At one particular performance 960 people attended and $19 080 was collected in ticket sales. Find the number of adults and the number of children who attended the performance.

13 An investor received $1400 interest per annum from a sum of money, with part of it invested at 10% and the remainder at 7% simple interest. This investor found that if she interchanged the amounts she had invested she could increase her return by $90 per annum. Calculate the total amount invested.

Example 12 **14** A shopkeeper sold his entire stock of shirts and ties in a sale for $10 000. The shirts were priced at 3 for $100 and the ties $20 each. If he had sold only half the shirts and two-thirds of the ties he would have received $6000. How many of each did he sell in the sale?

15 A tent manufacturer produces two models, the Outback and the Bush Walker. From earlier sales records it is known that 20 per cent more of the Outback model is sold than the Bush Walker. A profit of $200 is made on each Outback sold, but $350 is made on each Bush Walker. If during the next year a profit of $177 000 is planned, how many of each model must be sold?

16 Oz Jeans has factories in Mydney and Selbourne. At the Mydney factory, fixed costs are $28 000 per month and the cost of producing each pair of jeans is $30. At the Selbourne factory, fixed costs are $35 200 per month and the cost of producing each pair of jeans is $24. During the next month Oz Jeans must manufacture 6000 pairs of jeans. Calculate the production order for each factory, if the total manufacturing costs for each factory are to be the same.

17 A tea wholesaler blends together three types of tea that normally sell for $10, $11 and $12 per kilogram so as to obtain 100 kilograms of tea worth $11.20 per kilogram. If the same amounts of the two higher priced teas are used, calculate how much of each type must be used in the blend.

1E Solving linear inequalities

Skillsheet An **inequality** is a mathematical statement that contains an inequality symbol rather than an equals sign: for example, $2x + 1 < 4$. When you solve the inequality $2x + 1 < 4$, you answer the question:

'Which numbers x satisfy the property that $2x + 1$ is less than 4?'

You will find that your answers can be described using a number line. This is a good way to represent the solution, as there are infinitely many numbers that satisfy an inequality such as $2x + 1 < 4$. For example:

$$2(1) + 1 = 3 < 4, \quad 2(0) + 1 = 1 < 4, \quad 2\left(\frac{1}{2}\right) + 1 = 2 < 4, \quad 2(-1) + 1 = -1 < 4$$

To solve linear inequalities, proceed exactly as for equations with the following exception:

- When multiplying or dividing both sides by a negative number, the 'direction' of the inequality symbol is reversed.

Example 13

Solve the inequality $2x + 1 < 4$.

Solution	Explanation
$2x + 1 < 4$	
$2x < 3$	Subtract 1 from both sides.
$x < \dfrac{3}{2}$	Divide both sides by 2.
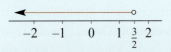	The solution can be represented on a real number line.

Note: In a number-line diagram, the 'endpoint' of an interval is indicated with a closed circle if the point is included and with an open circle if it is not.

Example 14

Solve the inequality $3 - 2x \leq 4$.

Solution	Explanation
$3 - 2x \leq 4$	
$-2x \leq 1$	Subtract 3 from both sides.
$x \geq -\dfrac{1}{2}$	Divide both sides by -2. Note that the inequality symbol is reversed.

Example 15

Solve the inequality $\dfrac{2x+3}{5} > \dfrac{3-4x}{3} + 2$.

Solution

$$\dfrac{2x+3}{5} > \dfrac{3-4x}{3} + 2$$

$$3(2x+3) > 5(3-4x) + 30$$

$$3(2x+3) - 5(3-4x) > 30$$

$$6x + 9 - 15 + 20x > 30$$

$$26x - 6 > 30$$

$$x > \dfrac{36}{26}$$

$$\therefore \quad x > \dfrac{18}{13}$$

Explanation

Multiply both sides by 15, the lowest common denominator of 5 and 3.

Collect the terms containing x on the left-hand side of the inequality.

Using the TI-Nspire

The inequality can be solved in a **Calculator** application.

- Choose **solve( )** from the **Algebra** menu to give the solution to

$$\dfrac{2x+3}{5} > \dfrac{3-4x}{3} + 2$$

Note: For the inequality signs template, press `ctrl` `=`.

Using the Casio ClassPad

To solve the inequality:

- Go to the $\sqrt{\alpha}$ Main screen and turn on the keyboard.
- Select the fraction icon found in Math1.
- Enter the inequality

$$\dfrac{2x+3}{5} > \dfrac{3-4x}{3} + 2$$

Note: The inequality sign can be found in Math3.

- Highlight the inequality using the stylus.
- Select **Interactive** > **Equation/Inequality** > **solve** and ensure that the variable selected is x.
- Tap on OK to obtain the solution.

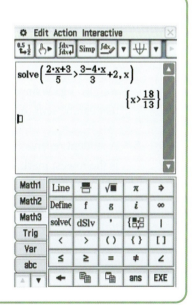

Section summary

- We can add or subtract the same number on both sides of an inequality, and the resulting inequality is equivalent to the original.
- We can multiply or divide both sides of an inequality by a positive number, and the resulting inequality is equivalent to the original.
- If we multiply or divide both sides of an inequality by a negative number, then we must reverse the inequality sign so that the resulting inequality is equivalent.

Exercise 1E

Example 13, 14

1 Solve each of the following inequalities for x:

   a $x + 3 < 4$
   b $x - 5 > 8$
   c $2x \geq 6$

   d $\dfrac{x}{3} \leq 4$
   e $-x \geq 6$
   f $-2x < -6$

   g $6 - 2x > 10$
   h $\dfrac{-3x}{4} \leq 6$
   i $4x - 4 \leq 2$

Example 14, 15

2 Solve for x in each of the following and show the solutions on a real number line:

   a $4x + 3 < 11$
   b $3x + 5 < x + 3$
   c $\dfrac{1}{2}(x + 1) - x > 1$

   d $\dfrac{1}{6}(x + 3) \geq 1$
   e $\dfrac{2}{3}(2x - 5) < 2$
   f $\dfrac{3x - 1}{4} - \dfrac{2x + 3}{2} < -2$

   g $\dfrac{4x - 3}{2} - \dfrac{3x - 3}{3} < 3$
   h $\dfrac{1 - 7x}{-2} \geq 10$
   i $\dfrac{5x - 2}{3} - \dfrac{2 - x}{3} > -1$

3 a For which real numbers x is $2x + 1$ a positive number?
   b For which real numbers x is $100 - 50x$ a positive number?
   c For which real numbers x is $100 + 20x$ a positive number?

4 In a certain country it costs \$1 to send a letter weighing less than 20 g. A sheet of paper weighs 3 g. Write a suitable inequality and hence state the maximum number of pages that can be sent for \$1. (Ignore the weight of the envelope in this question.)

5 A student receives marks of 66 and 72 on two tests. What is the lowest mark she can obtain on a third test to have an average for the three tests greater than or equal to 75?

1F Using and transposing formulas

Skillsheet An equation containing symbols that states a relationship between two or more quantities is called a **formula**. An example of a formula is $A = \ell w$ (area = length × width). The value of A, called the subject of the formula, can be found by substituting in given values of ℓ and w.

Example 16

Find the area of a rectangle with length (ℓ) 10 cm and width (w) 4 cm.

Solution	Explanation
$A = \ell w$	
$A = 10 \times 4$	Substitute $\ell = 10$ and $w = 4$.
$A = 40$ cm^2	

Sometimes we wish to rewrite a formula to make a different symbol the subject of the formula. This process is called **transposing** the formula. The techniques for transposing formulas include those used for solving linear equations detailed in Section 1A.

Example 17

Transpose the formula $v = u + at$ to make a the subject.

Solution	Explanation
$v = u + at$	
$v - u = at$	Subtract u from both sides.
$\dfrac{v - u}{t} = a$	Divide both sides by t.

If we wish to evaluate an unknown that is not the subject of the formula, we can either substitute the given values for the other variables and then solve the resulting equation, or we can first transpose the formula and then substitute the given values.

Example 18

Evaluate p if $2(p + q) - r = z$, and $q = 2$, $r = -3$ and $z = 11$.

Solution
Method 1: Substituting then solving

	Explanation
$2(p + 2) - (-3) = 11$	First substitute $q = 2$, $r = -3$ and $z = 11$.
$2p + 4 + 3 = 11$	Then solve for p.
$2p = 4$	
$p = 2$	

Method 2: Transposing then substituting

$$2(p+q) - r = z$$
$$2(p+q) = z + r$$
$$p + q = \frac{z+r}{2}$$
$$p = \frac{z+r}{2} - q$$
$$\therefore \; p = \frac{11 + (-3)}{2} - 2$$
$$p = 2$$

First solve for p.

Substitute $q = 2$, $r = -3$ and $z = 11$.

Example 19

A path x metres wide surrounds a rectangular lawn. The lawn is ℓ metres long and b metres wide. The total area of the path is A m².

a Find A in terms of ℓ, b and x.

b Find b in terms of ℓ, A and x.

Solution

a

$b + 2x$ m

b m

ℓ m

$\ell + 2x$ m

The area of the path is

$$A = (b + 2x)(\ell + 2x) - b\ell$$
$$= b\ell + 2x\ell + 2xb + 4x^2 - b\ell$$
$$\therefore \; A = 2x\ell + 2xb + 4x^2$$

b $A - (2x\ell + 4x^2) = 2xb$

Therefore

$$b = \frac{A - (2x\ell + 4x^2)}{2x}$$

Example 20

For each of the following, make c the subject of the formula:

a $e = \sqrt{3c - 7a}$

b $\dfrac{1}{a} - \dfrac{1}{b} = \dfrac{1}{c - 2}$

Solution

a $e = \sqrt{3c - 7a}$

Square both sides of the equation:

$$e^2 = 3c - 7a$$

Therefore

$$3c = e^2 + 7a$$

$$c = \dfrac{e^2 + 7a}{3}$$

b $\dfrac{1}{a} - \dfrac{1}{b} = \dfrac{1}{c - 2}$

Establish common denominator on the left-hand side of the equation:

$$\dfrac{b - a}{ab} = \dfrac{1}{c - 2}$$

Take the reciprocal of both sides:

$$\dfrac{ab}{b - a} = c - 2$$

Therefore $c = \dfrac{ab}{b - a} + 2$

Using the TI-Nspire

Literal equations can be solved for a given variable in a **Calculator** application.

- Use **solve( )** from the **Algebra** menu to make c the subject of the formula

$$\dfrac{1}{a} - \dfrac{1}{b} = \dfrac{1}{c - 2}$$

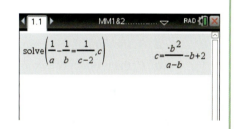

Using the Casio ClassPad

To solve a literal equation for a given variable:

- Go to the $\sqrt{\alpha}$ (Main) screen and turn on the keyboard.
- Select the fraction icon found in Math1.
- Select the Var keyboard.
- Enter and highlight the equation

$$\dfrac{1}{a} - \dfrac{1}{b} = \dfrac{1}{c - 2}$$

- Select **Interactive > Equation/Inequality > solve** and ensure that you change the selected variable to c.
- Tap on OK to obtain the solution.
- If necessary, copy the solution and use **Interactive > Transformation > expand** to produce a neater answer.

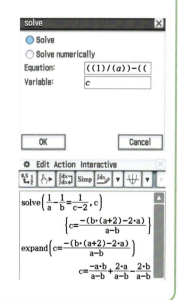

Section summary

- A formula relates different quantities: for example, the formula $A = \pi r^2$ relates the radius r with the area A of the circle.
- The variable on the left is called the subject of the formula: for example, in the formula $A = \pi r^2$, the subject is A.
- To calculate the value of a variable which is not the subject of a formula:

    Method 1 Substitute the values for the known variables, then solve the resulting equation for the unknown variable.

    Method 2 Rearrange to make the required variable the subject, then substitute values.

Exercise 1F

1 For each of the following, find the value of the letter in parentheses:

a $c = ab$, $a = 6$, $b = 3$ (c)

b $r = p + q$, $p = 12$, $q = -3$ (r)

c $c = ab$, $a = 6$, $c = 18$ (b)

d $r = p + q$, $p = 15$, $r = -3$ (q)

e $c = \sqrt{a}$, $a = 9$ (c)

f $c = \sqrt{a}$, $c = 9$ (a)

g $p = \dfrac{u}{v}$, $u = 10$, $v = 2$ (p)

h $p = \dfrac{u}{v}$, $p = 10$, $v = 2$ (u)

2 For each of the following, construct a formula using the given symbols:

a S, the sum of three numbers a, b and c

b P, the product of two numbers x and y

c the cost, $\$C$, of five CDs which each cost $\$p$

d the total cost, $\$T$, of d chairs which cost $\$p$ each and c tables which cost $\$q$ each

e the time, T, in minutes, of a train journey that takes a hours and b minutes

Example 16

3 Find the values of the following:

a $E = IR$, when $I = 5$ and $R = 3$

b $C = pd$, when $p = 3.14$ and $d = 10$

c $P = \dfrac{RT}{V}$, when $R = 60$, $T = 150$ and $V = 9$

d $I = \dfrac{E}{R}$, when $E = 240$ and $R = 20$

e $A = \pi r \ell$, when $\pi = 3.14$, $r = 5$ and $\ell = 20$

f $S = 90(2n - 4)$, when $n = 6$

Example 17

4 For each of the following, make the symbol indicated the subject of the formula:

a $PV = c$; V

b $F = ma$; a

c $I = Prt$; P

d $w = H + Cr$; r

e $S = P(1 + rt)$; t

f $V = \dfrac{2R}{R - r}$; r

Example 18

5 Find the value of the unknown symbol in each of the following:

a $D = \dfrac{T + 2}{P}$, when $D = 10$, $P = 5$

b $A = \tfrac{1}{2}bh$, when $A = 40$, $h = 10$

c $V = \tfrac{1}{3}\pi r^2 h$, when $\pi = 3.14$, $V = 100$, $r = 5$

d $A = \tfrac{1}{2}h(a + b)$, when $A = 50$, $h = 5$, $a = 10$

6 The diagram represents the brick wall of a dwelling with three windows. Each of the windows is h m high and w m wide. Other dimensions are as shown.

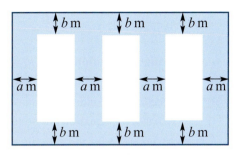

a Find the length of the wall.
b Find the height of the wall.
c Find the total area of the three windows.
d Find the total area of brickwork.

7 A lampshade has a metal frame consisting of two circular hoops of radii p cm and q cm joined by four straight struts of length h cm. The total length of metal is T cm.

a i Find an expression for T in terms of p, q and h.
   ii Find T when $p = 20$, $q = 24$ and $h = 28$.
b The area of the material covering the frame is A cm^2, where $A = \pi h(p + q)$. Find an expression for p in terms of A, h, q and π.

8 Find the value of the unknown symbol in each of the following:

a $P = \dfrac{T - M}{D}$, $P = 6$, $T = 8$, $M = 4$
b $H = \dfrac{a}{3} + \dfrac{a}{b}$, $H = 5$ and $a = 6$

c $a = \dfrac{90(2n - 4)}{n}$, $a = 6$
d $R = \dfrac{r}{a} + \dfrac{r}{3}$, $a = 2$ and $R = 4$

Example 19

9 Right-angled triangles XYZ and ABC are similar.
$$\dfrac{XY}{AB} = \dfrac{YZ}{BC} = \dfrac{ZX}{CA} = k$$

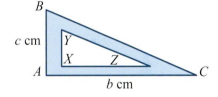

If $AB = c$ cm and $AC = b$ cm, find:

a the area, D cm^2, of the shaded region in terms of c, b and k
b k in terms of D, b and c
c the value of k if $D = 2$, $b = 3$ and $c = 4$.

10 Two rectangles each with dimensions c cm × b cm are used to form a cross as shown. The arms of the cross are all of equal length.

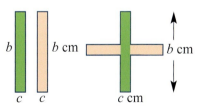

a Find the perimeter, P cm, of the cross in terms of b and c.
b Find the area, A cm^2, of the cross in terms of b and c.
c Find b in terms of A and c.

Example 20

11 For each of the following, make the symbol in brackets the subject of the formula:

a $a = \sqrt{a + 2b}$ (b)
b $\dfrac{a + x}{a - x} = \dfrac{b - y}{b + y}$ (x)

c $px = \sqrt{3q - r^2}$ (r)
d $\dfrac{x}{y} = \sqrt{1 - \dfrac{v^2}{u^2}}$ (v)

Chapter 1: Reviewing linear equations

Chapter summary

- A **linear equation** is one in which the variable is to the first power.
- It is often helpful to look at how the equation has been constructed so that the steps necessary to 'undo' the equation can be identified. It is most important that the steps taken to solve the equation are done in the correct order.
- An equation for the variable x in which all the coefficients of x, including the constants, are pronumerals is known as a **literal equation**: for example, $ax + b = c$.
- The two methods for solving simultaneous linear equations are **substitution** and **elimination**.
- An **inequality** is a mathematical statement that contains an inequality symbol rather than an equals sign: for example, $2x + 1 < 4$.
- To solve linear inequalities, proceed exactly as for equations except that, when multiplying or dividing both sides by a negative number, the 'direction' of the inequality symbol is reversed.
- An equation containing symbols that states a relationship between two or more quantities is called a **formula**. An example of a formula is $A = \ell w$ (area = length × width). The subject of this formula is A.
- If we wish to evaluate an unknown that is not the subject of the formula, we can either substitute the given values for the other variables and then solve the resulting equation, or we can first transpose the formula and then substitute the given values.

Technology-free questions

1 Solve each of the following equations for x:

   a $2x + 6 = 8$ **b** $3 - 2x = 6$ **c** $2x + 5 = 3 - x$

   d $\dfrac{3 - x}{5} = 6$ **e** $\dfrac{x}{3} = 4$ **f** $\dfrac{13x}{4} - 1 = 10$

   g $3(2x + 1) = 5(1 - 2x)$ **h** $\dfrac{3x + 2}{5} + \dfrac{3 - x}{2} = 5$

2 Solve each of the following for t:

   a $a - t = b$ **b** $\dfrac{at + b}{c} = d$ **c** $a(t - c) = d$

   d $\dfrac{a - t}{b - t} = c$ **e** $\dfrac{at + b}{ct - b} = 1$ **f** $\dfrac{1}{at + c} = d$

3 Solve each of the following inequalities for x:

   a $2 - 3x > 0$ **b** $\dfrac{3 - 2x}{5} \geq 60$

   c $3(58x - 24) + 10 < 70$ **d** $\dfrac{3 - 2x}{5} - \dfrac{x - 7}{6} \leq 2$

4 Make x the subject of the formula $z = \tfrac{1}{2}x - 3t$. Find x when $z = 4$ and $t = -3$.

5 A number d is equal to the square of a number e plus twice a number f.
  a Find a formula for d in terms of e and f.
  b Make f the subject of the formula.
  c Find f when $d = 10$ and $e = 3$.

6 The surface area of a sphere of radius r is given by the formula $A = 4\pi r^2$. Calculate the surface area of a sphere of radius 10 cm. Give your answer in terms of π.

7 The volume of metal in a tube is given by the formula $V = \pi \ell [r^2 - (r - t)^2]$, where ℓ is the length of the tube, r is the radius of the outside surface and t is the thickness of the material. Find V when:
  a $\ell = 100$, $r = 5$ and $t = 0.2$
  b $\ell = 50$, $r = 10$ and $t = 0.5$

8 For each of the following, make the variable in brackets the subject of the formula:
  a $A = \pi rs$ (r)
  b $T = P(1 + rw)$ (w)
  c $v = \sqrt{\dfrac{n - p}{r}}$ (r)
  d $ac = b^2 + bx$ (x)

9 Let $s = \left(\dfrac{u + v}{2}\right)t$.
  a Find the value of s if $u = 10$, $v = 20$ and $t = 5$.
  b Find the value of t if $u = 10$, $v = 20$ and $s = 120$.

10 The volume, V cm^3, of a cylinder is given by $V = \pi r^2 h$, where r cm is the radius and h cm is the height. Find the radius of the cylinder if the volume of the cylinder is 500π cm^3 and the height is 10 cm.

11 A rope of length 205 m is cut into 10 pieces of one length and 5 pieces of another length. The total length of three of the first 10 lengths exceeds that of two the second length by 2 m. Find the lengths of the pieces.

12 If I add one to the numerator of a fraction $\dfrac{m}{n}$ it simplifies to $\dfrac{1}{5}$. If I subtract one from the denominator it simplifies to $\dfrac{1}{7}$. Find the fraction $\dfrac{m}{n}$.

13 Mr Adonis earns $7200 more than Mr Apollo, and Ms Aphrodite earns $4000 less than Mr Apollo. If the total of the three incomes is $303 200, find the income of each person.

14 Solve each of the following pairs of simultaneous equations for a and b:
  a $4a - b = 11$
      $3a + 2b = 6$
  b $a = 2b + 11$
      $4a - 3b = 11$

15 A motorist travelled a total distance of 424 km, and had an average speed of 80 km/h on highways and 24 km/h while passing through towns. If the journey took six hours, find how long the motorist spent travelling on highways.

Multiple-choice questions

1. The solution of the linear equation $3x - 7 = 11$ is
   A $\frac{4}{3}$ B $\frac{11}{3}$ C $\frac{-3}{4}$ D 6 E -6

2. If $\frac{x}{3} + \frac{1}{3} = 2$ then $x =$
   A $\frac{1}{3}$ B $\frac{2}{3}$ C $\frac{7}{3}$ D 5 E 7

3. The solution of the equation $x - 8 = 3x - 16$ is
   A $x = \frac{-8}{3}$ B $x = \frac{11}{3}$ C $x = 4$ D $x = 2$ E $x = -2$

4. The statement that 7 is 11 times the result of subtracting 2 from x can be written as
   A $7 = 11(x - 2)$ B $11x - 2 = 7$ C $7 = 11(x + 2)$
   D $\frac{11}{x - 2} = 7$ E $\frac{7}{11} - 2 = x$

5. The solution of the simultaneous equations $2x - y = 10$ and $x + 2y = 0$ is
   A $x = -2$ and $y = 3$ B $x = 2$ and $y = -3$ C $x = 4$ and $y = -2$
   D $x = 6$ and $y = 2$ E $x = 1$ and $y = -8$

6. I bought x CDs for $\$a$ and y DVDs for $\$b$. The average price paid, in dollars, is
   A $\frac{x + y}{a + b}$ B $\frac{a + b}{y + x}$ C $\frac{xa + yb}{y + x}$ D $\frac{y + x}{xa + yb}$ E $\frac{a}{x} + \frac{b}{y}$

7. The solution of the equation $\frac{x + 1}{4} - \frac{2x - 1}{6} = x$ is
   A $x = \frac{8}{5}$ B $x = \frac{5}{13}$ C $x = 1$ D $x = -\frac{1}{5}$ E $x = -1$

8. The values of z that satisfy the inequality $\frac{72 + 15z}{3} > 4$ are
   A $z > 4$ B $z > -4$ C $z = -4$ D $z < 4$ E $z < -4$

9. If $A = \frac{hw + k}{w}$ then
   A $w = \frac{k}{A - h}$ B $w = \frac{ht + k}{A}$ C $w = \frac{A - 2k}{2h}$
   D $w = \frac{3Ah}{2} - k$ E $w = \frac{2}{3}h(A + k)$

10. Bronwyn walks one lap of an oval at 2.5 km/h and then jogs another eight laps of the oval at 5 km/h. If it takes her 30 minutes in total, how long in metres is each lap?
    A 200 m   B 250 m   C 300 m   D 350 m   E 400 m

11 Which of the following equations has no solutions?

  A $3x + 6 = 2x + 4$ **B** $2(x + 3) = 2x + 6$ **C** $3x - 4 = 5 - x$
  D $3x + 6 = 2x + 6$ **E** $2x + 4 = 2x + 6$

12 Which of the following equations is true for all values of x?

  A $4x - 6 = 2x + 4$ **B** $5(x + 3) = 5x + 15$ **C** $3x - 4 = 10 - x$
  D $7x + 6 = -2x + 6$ **E** $2x + 4 = 2x + 6$

Extended-response questions

1 The formula for converting degrees Celsius, C, to degrees Fahrenheit, F, is $F = \dfrac{9}{5}C + 32$.

  a Convert 30°F to Celsius.
  b Convert 30°C to Fahrenheit.
  c If $x°C = x°F$ find x.
  d If $(x + 10)°C = x°F$ find x.
  e If $2x°C = x°F$ find the value of x.
  f If $k°F = (-3k)°C$ find k.

2 For a spherical mirror of radius r cm, $\dfrac{1}{v} + \dfrac{1}{u} = \dfrac{2}{r}$, where u cm is the distance from the mirror to the object and v cm is the distance from the mirror to the image. The magnification is given by $m = \dfrac{v - r}{r - u}$.

  a Find r in terms of v and u from the first formula.
  b Find m in terms of v and u only.

3 The diagram shows a section of wire mesh w metres in width and ℓ metres in length.

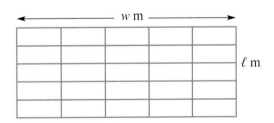

  a Find an expression in terms of w and ℓ for the total length of wire required for the mesh.

  b **i** If $w = 3\ell$, find an expression in terms of w for the total length of wire required.
      ii If the length of wire used is 100 m, find the value of w and the value of ℓ.

  c The total length of wire, L m, required for another type of rectangular mesh of dimensions x m by y m, is given by the formula $L = 6x + 8y$.
      i Find y in terms of x and L.
      ii Find y if $L = 200$ and $x = 4$.

  d A third type of mesh can also be used to cover a rectangular region of dimensions x m by y m. In this case, the type of mesh introduced in part c requires 100 m of wire and so $6x + 8y = 100$. This third type of mesh requires 80 m and this gives the equation $3x + 2y = 40$. Find the values of x and y.

4 Tom leaves town A and travels towards town B at a constant speed of u km/h. At the same time, Julie leaves town B and travels towards town A at a constant speed of v km/h. Town B is d km from town A.
  a How far has each travelled after t hours?
  b By considering that the sum of their distances travelled must be d km when they meet, find:
    i the time it takes for them to meet
    ii their distance from town A when they meet.
  c If $u = 30$, $v = 50$ and $d = 100$, find the time it takes for them to meet and their distance from town A.

5 Xiu travels from town A to town B at u km/h and then returns at v km/h. Town A is d km from town B.
  a Find the average speed at which Xiu travels for the complete journey, in terms of u and v. Remember that
  $$\text{average speed} = \frac{\text{total distance travelled}}{\text{total time taken}}$$
  b If it takes T hours to travel from A to B, find the time taken:
    i for the return trip from B to A, in terms of T, u and v
    ii for the entire trip, in terms of T, u and v.

6 A man on a bicycle rides one-third of the way from town A to town B at a speed a km/h and the remainder of the way at $2b$ km/h.
  a If the distance between the two towns is 9 km, find the time taken to ride from A to B.
  If the man had travelled at a uniform rate of $3c$ km/h, he could have ridden from A to B and back again in the same time.
  b Show that $\dfrac{2}{c} = \dfrac{1}{a} + \dfrac{1}{b}$.
  c i Make c the subject of this formula.
    ii Find c, when $a = 10$ and $b = 20$.

7 A man walks 70 km. He walks x km at 8 km/h and y km at 10 km/h.
  a Find the length of time he was walking at 8 km/h in terms of x, and the length of time he was walking at 10 km/h in terms of y.
  b Find his average speed in terms of x and y.
  c If the man walks at 10 km/h for the time he was walking at 8 km/h and at 8 km/h for the time he was walking at 10 km/h, he walks 72 km. Find x and y.

8 Prove that the lines with equations $2y - x = 2$, $y + x = 7$ and $y - 2x = -5$ meet at the one point.

Coordinate geometry and linear relations

Objectives

▶ To find the **midpoint** of a line segment.
▶ To find the **distance** between two points.
▶ To calculate the **gradient** of a straight line.
▶ To calculate the **angle of slope** of a straight line given the gradient.
▶ To interpret and use different forms of an equation of a straight line.
▶ To establish and use necessary and sufficient conditions for two lines to be **perpendicular** or **parallel**.
▶ To use a parameter to describe families of straight lines.
▶ To apply knowledge of linear relations to solving problems.
▶ To solve and apply **simultaneous linear equations**.

The number plane (Cartesian plane) is divided into four quadrants by two perpendicular axes. These axes intersect at a point called the origin. The position of any point in the plane can be represented by an **ordered pair** of numbers (x, y), called the **coordinates** of the point. Given the coordinates of two points, we can find the equation of the straight line through the two points, the distance between the two points and the midpoint of the line segment joining the points. These are the beginning ideas of coordinate geometry. The topic of calculus, which is introduced later in this book, builds on these ideas.

A **relation** is defined as a set of ordered pairs in the form (x, y). Sometimes we can give a rule relating the x-value to the y-value of each ordered pair, such as $y = 2x + 1$, and this is a more convenient way of describing the relation. A relation may also be represented graphically on a set of axes. If the resulting graph is a straight line, then the relation is called a **linear relation**.

2A Distance and midpoints

Skillsheet In this first section we look at the method to find the coordinates of the midpoint of a line segment and we apply Pythagoras' theorem to find the distance between two points.

▶ Midpoint of a line segment

Finding the midpoint of a line segment parallel to an axis is a simple special case, and it is useful in obtaining the more general result.

A line segment parallel to an axis

The midpoint of the line segment AB with endpoints $A(2, 3)$ and $B(2, -4)$ is the point P with coordinates $(2, -\frac{1}{2})$.

Note that $-\frac{1}{2}$ is the average of 3 and -4. The line through A and B is parallel to the y-axis.

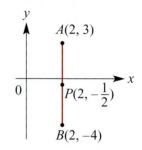

Similarly for the line segment CD with endpoints $C(-1, 2)$ and $D(3, 2)$, the midpoint is the point P with coordinates $(1, 2)$.

Note that 1 is the average of -1 and 3. The line through C and D is parallel to the x-axis.

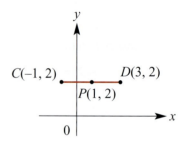

A line segment not parallel to one of the axes

Let $P(x, y)$ be the midpoint of the line segment joining $A(x_1, y_1)$ and $B(x_2, y_2)$, where the line through A and B is not parallel to either axis.

Let points C and D be chosen so that AC and PD are parallel to the x-axis, and PC and BD are parallel to the y-axis.

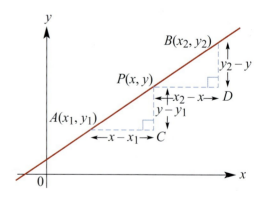

The triangles APC and PBD are congruent (AAS). Hence

$$AC = PD \quad \text{and} \quad PC = BD$$
$$\therefore \quad x - x_1 = x_2 - x \qquad y - y_1 = y_2 - y$$
$$2x = x_1 + x_2 \qquad 2y = y_1 + y_2$$
$$x = \frac{x_1 + x_2}{2} \qquad y = \frac{y_1 + y_2}{2}$$

We have proved the following result.

The coordinates of the midpoint P of the line segment AB joining $A(x_1, y_1)$ and $B(x_2, y_2)$ are

$$\left(\frac{x_1 + x_2}{2}, \frac{y_1 + y_2}{2}\right)$$

That is, we take the average of the x-coordinates and the average of the y-coordinates.

Example 1

Find the midpoint of the line segment joining $A(2, 6)$ with $B(-3, -4)$.

Solution

The midpoint of line segment AB has coordinates

$$\left(\frac{2 + (-3)}{2}, \frac{6 + (-4)}{2}\right) = \left(-\frac{1}{2}, 1\right)$$

Explanation

The coordinates of the midpoint of the line segment joining $A(x_1, y_1)$ and $B(x_2, y_2)$ are

$$\left(\frac{x_1 + x_2}{2}, \frac{y_1 + y_2}{2}\right)$$

▶ The distance between two points

The distance between given points $A(x_1, y_1)$ and $B(x_2, y_2)$ can be found by applying Pythagoras' theorem to the triangle ABC:

$$AB^2 = AC^2 + BC^2$$
$$= (x_2 - x_1)^2 + (y_2 - y_1)^2$$

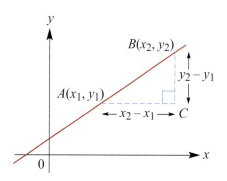

Therefore, the distance between the two points $A(x_1, y_1)$ and $B(x_2, y_2)$ is

$$AB = \sqrt{(x_2 - x_1)^2 + (y_2 - y_1)^2}$$

Example 2

Calculate the distance EF if E is $(-3, 2)$ and F is $(4, -2)$.

Solution

$$EF = \sqrt{(x_2 - x_1)^2 + (y_2 - y_1)^2}$$
$$= \sqrt{(4 - (-3))^2 + (-2 - 2)^2}$$
$$= \sqrt{7^2 + (-4)^2}$$
$$= \sqrt{65}$$
$$= 8.06 \quad \text{(to two decimal places)}$$

Explanation

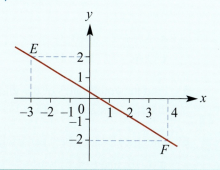

Section summary

- The coordinates of the midpoint of the line segment joining $A(x_1, y_1)$ and $B(x_2, y_2)$ are
$$\left(\frac{x_1 + x_2}{2}, \frac{y_1 + y_2}{2}\right)$$
- The distance between points $A(x_1, y_1)$ and $B(x_2, y_2)$ is
$$\sqrt{(x_2 - x_1)^2 + (y_2 - y_1)^2}$$

Exercise 2A

Example 1

1 Find the coordinates of M, the midpoint of AB, where A and B have the following coordinates:

   a $A(2, 12)$, $B(8, 4)$
   b $A(-3, 5)$, $B(4, -4)$
   c $A(-1.6, 3.4)$, $B(4.8, -2)$
   d $A(3.6, -2.8)$, $B(-5, 4.5)$

2 Find the midpoints of each of the sides of a triangle ABC, where A is $(1, 1)$, B is $(5, 5)$ and C is $(11, 2)$.

3 The secretary of a motorcross club wants to organise two meetings on the same weekend. One is a hill climb starting from point $A(3.1, 7.1)$ and the other is a circuit event with the start at $B(8.9, 10.5)$, as shown on the map. Only one ambulance can be provided. The ambulance can be called up by radio, so it is decided to keep it at C, halfway between A and B.
What are the coordinates of C?

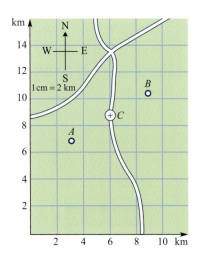

4 If M is the midpoint of XY, find the coordinates of Y when X and M have the following coordinates:

   a $X(-4, 2)$, $M(0, 3)$
   b $X(-1, -3)$, $M(0.5, -1.6)$
   c $X(6, -3)$, $M(2, 1)$
   d $X(4, -3)$, $M(0, -3)$

5 Find the coordinates of the midpoint of the line segment joining $(1, 4)$ and (a, b), in terms of a and b. If $(5, -1)$ is the midpoint, find the values of a and b.

Example 2

6 Find the distance between each of the following (correct to two decimal places):

   a $(3, 6)$ and $(-4, 5)$
   b $(4, 1)$ and $(5, -3)$
   c $(-2, -3)$ and $(-5, -8)$
   d $(6, 4)$ and $(-7, 4)$

7 Calculate the perimeter of a triangle with vertices (−3, −4), (1, 5) and (7, −2).

8 The diagram shows the four points A(6, 6), B(10, 2), C(−1, 5) and D(−7, 1). If the midpoint of AB is P and the midpoint of CD is M, calculate the distance PM.

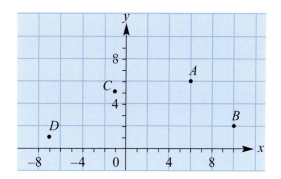

9 There is an off-shore oil drilling platform in Bass Strait situated at D(0, 6), where 1 unit = 5 km. Pipes for this oil drill come ashore at M(−6, 1) and N(3, −1). Assuming the pipelines are straight, which is the shorter DM or DN?

2B The gradient of a straight line

Through any two points it is only possible to draw a single straight line. Therefore a straight line is defined by any two points on the line.

In coordinate geometry the standard way to define the **gradient of a line segment** AB is $\dfrac{\text{rise}}{\text{run}}$ where:

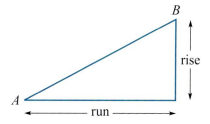

- rise is the change in the y-values as you move from A to B
- run is the change in the x-values as you move from A to B.

The **gradient of a line** is defined to be the gradient of any segment within the line. This definition depends on the fact that any two segments of a line have the same gradient. Hence given any two points on the line, $A(x_1, y_1)$ and $B(x_2, y_2)$, the gradient of the line can be found. The symbol used for gradient is m.

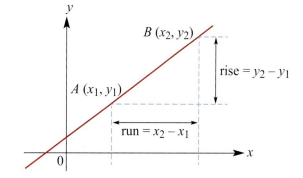

$$\text{Gradient } m = \frac{\text{rise}}{\text{run}} = \frac{y_2 - y_1}{x_2 - x_1}$$

Note that since

$$\frac{y_2 - y_1}{x_2 - x_1} = \frac{y_1 - y_2}{x_1 - x_2}$$

it does not matter which point we take as the first and which point we take as the second.

Example 3

Find the gradient of each line:

a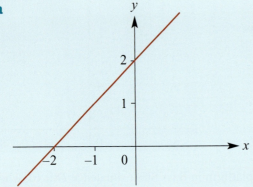

b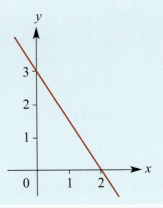

Solution

a Gradient $m = \dfrac{2-0}{0-(-2)}$

$= \dfrac{2}{2}$

$= 1$

b Gradient $m = \dfrac{0-3}{2-0}$

$= -\dfrac{3}{2}$

Explanation

Let $(x_1, y_1) = (-2, 0)$ and $(x_2, y_2) = (0, 2)$.

Gradient $m = \dfrac{y_2 - y_1}{x_2 - x_1}$

Let $(x_1, y_1) = (0, 3)$ and $(x_2, y_2) = (2, 0)$.

Gradient $m = \dfrac{y_2 - y_1}{x_2 - x_1}$

Notes:
- The gradient of a line that slopes upwards from left to right is **positive**, as illustrated in Example 3a.
- The gradient of a line that slopes downwards from left to right is **negative**, as illustrated in Example 3b.
- The gradient of a **horizontal line** (parallel to the x-axis) is zero, since $y_2 - y_1 = 0$.
- The gradient of a **vertical line** (parallel to the y-axis) is undefined, since $x_2 - x_1 = 0$.

Example 4

Find the gradient of the line that passes through the points $(1, 6)$ and $(-3, 7)$.

Solution

$m = \dfrac{y_2 - y_1}{x_2 - x_1}$

$= \dfrac{7 - 6}{-3 - 1}$

$= -\dfrac{1}{4}$

Explanation

The gradient can also be found using

$m = \dfrac{y_1 - y_2}{x_1 - x_2}$

$= \dfrac{6 - 7}{1 - (-3)} = -\dfrac{1}{4}$

The tangent of the angle of slope

We will look first at the case when the gradient is positive and then when the gradient is negative.

Positive gradient

From Year 10 you will be familiar with the trigonometric ratio

$$\tan \theta = \frac{\text{opposite}}{\text{adjacent}}$$

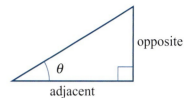

Consider a straight line with positive gradient. The line forms an acute angle, θ, with the positive direction of the x-axis.

The gradient, m, of the line is given by

$$m = \frac{y_2 - y_1}{x_2 - x_1} \quad (x_1 \neq x_2)$$

From the diagram, it follows that

$$m = \tan \theta$$

where θ is the angle that the line makes with the positive direction of the x-axis.

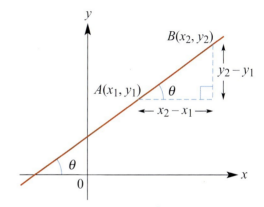

Example 5

Determine the gradient of the line passing through the points $(3, 2)$ and $(5, 7)$ and the angle θ that the line makes with the positive direction of the x-axis.

Solution

$$m = \frac{7 - 2}{5 - 3}$$

$$= \frac{5}{2}$$

$$\tan \theta = \frac{5}{2}$$

$$\therefore \quad \theta = 68.1986\ldots°$$

$$= 68.20°$$

correct to two decimal places.

Explanation

The gradient is given by

$$m = \frac{y_2 - y_1}{x_2 - x_1}$$

The gradient is positive and so the angle θ is acute.

The angle can be found with a calculator using inverse tan.

Negative gradient

Now consider a line with negative gradient. The line forms an acute angle α with the negative direction of the x-axis, and an obtuse angle θ with the positive direction of the x-axis. We have $\theta = 180° - \alpha$.

From the diagram, we see that the gradient satisfies

$$m = \frac{y_2 - y_1}{x_2 - x_1} = \frac{-(y_1 - y_2)}{x_2 - x_1} = -\tan \alpha$$

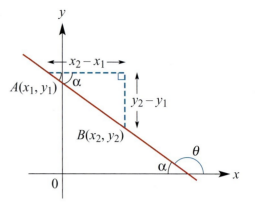

From your work on circular functions in Year 10 you may recall that

$$\tan \theta = \tan(180° - \alpha) = -\tan \alpha$$

Thus the gradient satisfies

$$m = -\tan \alpha = \tan \theta$$

Example 6

Determine the gradient of the line passing through the points $(5, -3)$ and $(-1, 5)$ and the angle θ that the line makes with the positive direction of the x-axis.

Solution

$$m = \frac{5 - (-3)}{-1 - 5}$$
$$= -\frac{4}{3}$$
$$\tan \theta = -\frac{4}{3}$$
$$\therefore \quad \theta = 180° - (53.130\ldots°)$$
$$= 126.87°$$

correct to two decimal places.

Explanation

The gradient is negative and so the angle θ between the line and the positive direction of the x-axis is obtuse.

You first use your calculator to find the adjacent supplementary angle α, which is acute. You do this by finding the inverse tangent of $\frac{4}{3}$. The magnitude of this angle is $53.130\ldots°$.

You subtract this from $180°$ to obtain θ.

Section summary

- The gradient of a line segment AB joining two points $A(x_1, y_1)$ and $B(x_2, y_2)$ is
  $$\frac{y_2 - y_1}{x_2 - x_1} \quad \text{provided } x_1 \neq x_2$$
- The gradient of a line is defined as the gradient of any line segment of that line.
- A horizontal line has gradient zero.
- A vertical line does not have a gradient.

- Let θ be the angle that a line makes with the positive direction of the *x*-axis.
  - The gradient *m* is positive if and only if θ is acute.
  - The gradient *m* is negative if and only if θ is obtuse.
  - If θ is acute or obtuse, then $m = \tan \theta$.
  - If $\theta = 0°$, then $m = \tan 0° = 0$.
  - If $\theta = 90°$, then the gradient is not defined.

Exercise 2B

Example 3

1 Calculate the gradient of each of the following lines:

a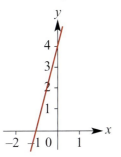

b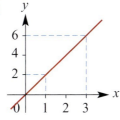

c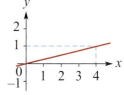

d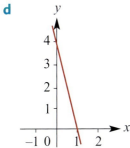

e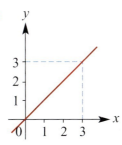

f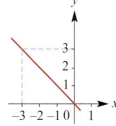

g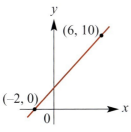

h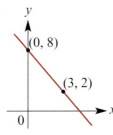

i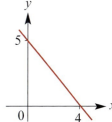

j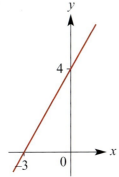

k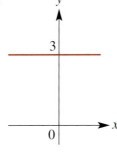

2 Sketch a graph of a line with gradient 1.

3 Sketch a graph of a line with gradient 0 which passes through the point $(1, 6)$.

Example 4

4 For each of the following, find the gradient of the line that passes through the two points with the given coordinates:

- **a** $(6, 3)$, $(2, 4)$
- **b** $(-3, 4)$, $(1, -6)$
- **c** $(6, 7)$, $(11, -3)$
- **d** $(5, 8)$, $(6, 0)$
- **e** $(6, 0)$, $(-6, 0)$
- **f** $(0, -6)$, $(-6, 0)$
- **g** $(3, 9)$, $(4, 16)$
- **h** $(5, 25)$, $(6, 36)$
- **i** $(-5, 25)$, $(-8, 64)$
- **j** $(1, 1)$, $(10, 100)$
- **k** $(1, 1)$, $(10, 1000)$
- **l** $(5, 125)$, $(4, 64)$

5
- **a** Find the gradient of the straight line that passes through the points with coordinates $(5a, 2a)$ and $(3a, 6a)$.
- **b** Find the gradient of the straight line that passes through the points with coordinates $(5a, 2a)$ and $(5b, 2b)$.

6
- **a** A line has gradient 6 and passes through the points with coordinates $(-1, 6)$ and $(7, a)$. Find the value of a.
- **b** A line has gradient -6 and passes through the points with coordinates $(1, 6)$ and $(b, 7)$. Find the value of b.

7 Find the angle, correct to two decimal places, that the lines joining the given points make with the positive direction of the x-axis:

- **a** $(0, 3)$, $(-3, 0)$
- **b** $(0, -4)$, $(4, 0)$
- **c** $(0, 2)$, $(-4, 0)$
- **d** $(0, -5)$, $(-5, 0)$

Example 5, 6

8 Find the angle, correct to two decimal places, that the lines joining the given points make with the positive direction of the x-axis:

- **a** $(-4, -2)$, $(6, 8)$
- **b** $(2, 6)$, $(-2, 4)$
- **c** $(-3, 4)$, $(6, 1)$
- **d** $(-4, -3)$, $(2, 4)$
- **e** $(3b, a)$, $(3a, b)$
- **f** (c, b), (b, c)

9 Find the gradient of a straight line which is:
- **a** inclined at an angle of $45°$ to the positive direction of the x-axis
- **b** inclined at an angle of $135°$ to the positive direction of the x-axis
- **c** inclined at an angle of $60°$ to the positive direction of the x-axis
- **d** inclined at an angle of $120°$ to the positive direction of the x-axis.

2C The equation of a straight line

Skillsheet In this section we discuss different ways of determining the equation of a straight line. In general two 'independent pieces of information' are required. The following given information is considered:

- gradient and y-axis intercept
- gradient and a point
- two points.

Sketching straight lines given the equation is discussed in Section 2D.

▶ Gradient–intercept form of the equation of a straight line

We first consider an example before stating the general result. The argument in the general case is exactly the same.

The line $y = 2x + 4$

Consider the line with gradient 2 and y-axis intercept 4. This line passes through the point $A(0, 4)$. Let $B(x, y)$ be any other point on the line.

Gradient of line segment $AB = \dfrac{y - 4}{x - 0} = \dfrac{y - 4}{x}$

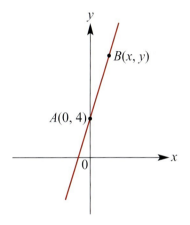

We know that the gradient of the line is 2. Therefore

$$\dfrac{y - 4}{x} = 2$$
$$y - 4 = 2x$$
$$y = 2x + 4$$

So the coordinates (x, y) satisfy the equation $y = 2x + 4$.

Conversely, if a point $B(x, y)$ in the plane satisfies $y = 2x + 4$, then

$$\dfrac{y - 4}{x} = 2$$

Thus we know that the gradient of the line segment joining point B to the point $A(0, 4)$ is 2. Therefore the line through $A(0, 4)$ and $B(x, y)$ has gradient 2 and y-axis intercept 4.

The line $y = mx + c$

In the same way as for the line $y = 2x + 4$, we can show that:

- The line with gradient m and y-axis intercept c has equation $y = mx + c$.
- Conversely, the line with equation $y = mx + c$ has gradient m and y-axis intercept c.

This is called the **gradient–intercept form**.

Example 7

Find the gradient and y-axis intercept of the line $y = 3x - 4$.

Solution

The gradient is 3 and the y-axis intercept is −4.

Explanation

$m = 3$ and $c = -4$

Example 8

Find the equation of the line with gradient −3 and y-axis intercept 5.

Solution

$y = -3x + 5$

Explanation

$y = mx + c$

Example 9

State the gradient and y-axis intercept of the line $3y + 6x = 9$.

Solution

$$3y + 6x = 9$$
$$3y = 9 - 6x$$
$$y = \frac{9 - 6x}{3}$$
$$y = 3 - 2x$$
i.e. $y = -2x + 3$

Therefore $m = -2$ and $c = 3$.

Explanation

Rearrange the equation $3y + 6x = 9$ into gradient–intercept form.

Now the gradient and y-axis intercept can be read directly from the equation.

▶ ## Point–gradient form of the equation of a straight line

If $A(x_1, y_1)$ is a point on a line with gradient m and $P(x, y)$ is any other point on the line, then

$$\frac{y - y_1}{x - x_1} = m$$

and so we have

$$y - y_1 = m(x - x_1)$$

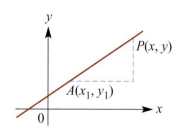

The **point–gradient form** of the equation of a straight line is

$$y - y_1 = m(x - x_1)$$

where (x_1, y_1) is a point on the line and m is the gradient.

Example 10

Find the equation of the line which passes through the point $(-1, 3)$ and has gradient 4.

Solution

Method 1

$(x_1, y_1) = (-1, 3)$ and $m = 4$.

The equation is

$$y - 3 = 4(x - (-1))$$
$$y = 4(x + 1) + 3$$
$$= 4x + 4 + 3$$
$$= 4x + 7$$

Method 2

Since $m = 4$, the equation is of the form $y = 4x + c$.

When $x = -1$, $y = 3$.

Therefore

$$3 = 4 \times (-1) + c$$
$$7 = c$$

The equation is $y = 4x + 7$.

Explanation

We use the equation $y - y_1 = m(x - x_1)$. (It is not necessary to work from first principles every time.)

Rearrange to make y the subject and write the equation in the form $y = mx + c$.

We can also use the equation $y = mx + c$ and find the value of c. The gradient is 4.

The point $(-1, 3)$ lies on the line.

Solve for c.

Example 11

Find the equation of the line that passes through the point $(3, 2)$ and has a gradient of -2.

Solution

$$y - 2 = -2(x - 3)$$
$$y - 2 = -2x + 6$$
$$y = -2x + 8$$

The equation is

$$y = -2x + 8$$

which could also be expressed as

$$2x + y - 8 = 0$$

Explanation

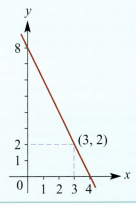

▶ A line through two points

To find the equation of the line through two given points (x_1, y_1) and (x_2, y_2), first find the gradient

$$m = \frac{y_2 - y_1}{x_2 - x_1}$$

and then use the point–gradient form

$$y - y_1 = m(x - x_1)$$

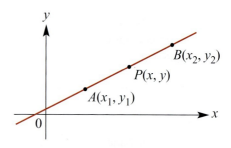

We can also find the equation directly by taking the point $P(x, y)$ and noting that

$$\frac{y - y_1}{x - x_1} = m$$

Example 12

Find the equation of the straight line passing through the points $(1, -2)$ and $(3, 2)$.

Solution

$$m = \frac{y_2 - y_1}{x_2 - x_1}$$
$$= \frac{2 - (-2)}{3 - 1}$$
$$= \frac{4}{2}$$
$$= 2$$

$$\therefore \quad 2 = \frac{y - (-2)}{x - 1}$$

$$2x - 2 = y + 2$$

$$\therefore \quad y = 2x - 4$$

Explanation

First find the gradient m and then use

$$\frac{y - y_1}{x - x_1} = m$$

Choose $(x_1, y_1) = (1, -2)$.

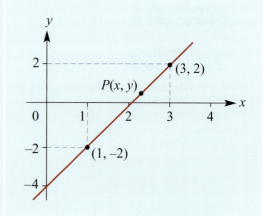

Example 13

Find the equation of the straight line with y-axis intercept -3 which passes through the point with coordinates $(1, 10)$.

Solution

The gradient is

$$m = \frac{10 - (-3)}{1 - 0} = 13$$

Therefore the equation is $y = 13x - 3$.

Explanation

Find the gradient using $(x_1, y_1) = (0, -3)$ and $(x_2, y_2) = (1, 10)$.

The general equation of a line with y-axis intercept -3 is $y = mx - 3$.

Two intercepts

A special case of finding the equation of a line given the coordinates of two points is when the intercept with each axis is known, that is, finding the line through $(a, 0)$ and $(0, b)$, where $a, b \neq 0$.

In this case, the gradient is
$$m = \frac{b - 0}{0 - a} = -\frac{b}{a}$$

Thus the equation of the line is
$$y - 0 = -\frac{b}{a}(x - a)$$

Multiplying both sides of the equation by a gives
$$ay + bx = ab$$

Dividing both sides of the equation by ab gives the following:

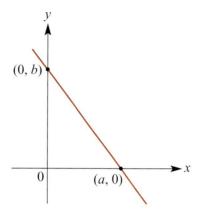

> The **intercept form** of the equation of a straight line is
> $$\frac{x}{a} + \frac{y}{b} = 1$$
> where a and b are the x-axis intercept and y-axis intercept respectively.

Example 14

Find the equation of the line shown in the graph.

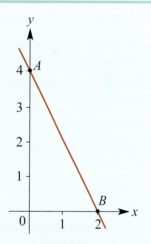

Solution

The intercept form of the equation is
$$\frac{x}{2} + \frac{y}{4} = 1$$

Multiply both sides by 4:
$$2x + y = 4$$

The equation of the line is $y = -2x + 4$.

Explanation

The coordinates of A and B are $(0, 4)$ and $(2, 0)$.

Vertical and horizontal lines

If a line is **horizontal**, then its gradient $m = 0$ and its equation is simply $y = c$, where c is the y-axis intercept.

If a line is **vertical**, then its gradient is undefined and its equation is $x = a$, where a is the x-axis intercept.

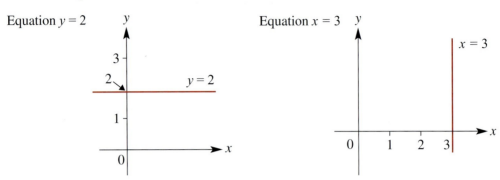

Note that the equation of a vertical line is not of the form $y = mx + c$.

General form of the equation of a straight line

We have seen that all points on the line through two given points satisfy an equation of the form $mx + ny + p = 0$, with m and n not both 0. Conversely, any 'linear equation' $mx + ny + p = 0$ is the equation of a (straight) line. This is called the **general form** of the equation of a line.

Section summary

- **Gradient–intercept form:** The line with gradient m and y-axis intercept c has equation $y = mx + c$. Conversely, the line with equation $y = mx + c$ has gradient m and y-axis intercept c.

- **Point–gradient form:** If (x_1, y_1) is a point on a line with gradient m and (x, y) is any other point on the line, then

$$\frac{y - y_1}{x - x_1} = m$$

which can be written as

$$y - y_1 = m(x - x_1)$$

- **Two points:** To find the equation of the line through two given points (x_1, y_1) and (x_2, y_2), first find the gradient

$$m = \frac{y_2 - y_1}{x_2 - x_1}$$

and then use the point–gradient form

$$y - y_1 = m(x - x_1)$$

- **Intercept form:** If a line has x-axis intercept a and y-axis intercept b, the equation of the line is
$$\frac{x}{a} + \frac{y}{b} = 1$$
- **Horizontal line:** A line parallel to the x-axis through the point (a, c) has equation $y = c$.
- **Vertical line:** A line parallel to the y-axis through the point (a, c) has equation $x = a$.
- **General form:** Every straight line satisfies an equation of the form $mx + ny + p = 0$, with m and n not both 0. Conversely, any 'linear equation' $mx + ny + p = 0$ is the equation of a straight line.

Exercise 2C

Example 7 **1** State the gradient and y-axis intercept of the graph of each equation:
  a $y = 3x + 6$ **b** $y = -6x + 7$ **c** $y = 3x - 6$ **d** $y = -x - 4$

Example 8 **2** **a** Find the equation of the straight line with gradient 3 and y-axis intercept 5.
  b Find the equation of the straight line with gradient -4 and y-axis intercept 6.
  c Find the equation of the straight line with gradient 3 and y-axis intercept -4.

Example 9 **3** State the gradient and y-axis intercept of the graph of each equation:
  a $3x - y = 6$ **b** $4x - 2y = 8$ **c** $5x - 10y = 20$ **d** $2x - 6y = 10$

4 Express in gradient–intercept form and hence state the gradient and y-axis intercept of each of the following linear relations:
  a $2x - y = 9$ **b** $3x + 4y = 10$ **c** $-x - 3y = 6$ **d** $5x - 2y = 4$

Example 10 **5** **a** Find the equation of the straight line that has gradient 3 and passes through the point with coordinates $(6, 7)$.

Example 11 **b** Find the equation of the straight line that has gradient -2 and passes through the point with coordinates $(1, 7)$.

Example 12 **6** Find the equations of the straight lines passing through the following pairs of points. (Express your answer in gradient–intercept form.)
  a $(-1, 4), (2, 3)$ **b** $(0, 4), (5, -3)$ **c** $(3, -2), (4, -4)$ **d** $(5, -2), (8, 9)$

Example 13 **7** For the straight line that has y-axis intercept 6 and passes through the point with coordinates $(1, 8)$, find:
  a the gradient   **b** the equation

8 Find the equation of the straight line that passes through the point $(1, 6)$ and has gradient:
  a 2   **b** -2

9 Write, in the form $y = mx + c$, the equations of the lines which have the given gradient and pass through the given point:
  a $m = 2$; $(-1, 4)$
  b $m = -2$; $(0, 4)$
  c $m = -5$; $(3, 0)$

Example 14
10 Find equations defining the lines which pass through the following pairs of points:
  a $(0, 4)$, $(6, 0)$
  b $(-3, 0)$, $(0, -6)$
  c $(0, 4)$, $(4, 0)$
  d $(2, 0)$, $(0, 3)$

11 Find the equations, in the form $y = mx + c$, of the lines which pass through the following pairs of points:
  a $(0, 4)$, $(3, 6)$
  b $(1, 0)$, $(4, 2)$
  c $(-3, 0)$, $(3, 3)$
  d $(-2, 3)$, $(4, 0)$
  e $(-1.5, 2)$, $(4.5, 8)$
  f $(-3, 1.75)$, $(4.5, -2)$

12 Find the equation of each of the following lines:

a
b
c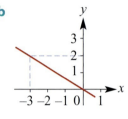

d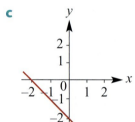
e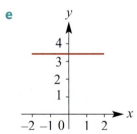
f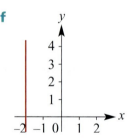

13 Do the points $P(1, -3)$, $Q(2, 1)$ and $R(2\frac{1}{2}, 3)$ lie on the same straight line?

14 For which of the following does the line pass through the origin?
  a $y + x = 1$
  b $y + 2x = 2(x + 1)$
  c $x + y = 0$
  d $x - y = 1$

15 a Find the equation of the line that is parallel to the y-axis and passes through the point with coordinates $(4, 7)$.
  b Find the equation of the line that is parallel to the x-axis and passes through the point with coordinates $(-4, 11)$.
  c Find the equation of the line that is parallel to the y-axis and passes through the point with coordinates $(11, -7)$.
  d Find the equation of the line that is parallel to the x-axis and passes through the point with coordinates $(5, -1)$.

2D Graphing straight lines

In the previous section we discussed methods of finding the equation of a straight line given suitable information. In this section we look at sketching a straight line from an equation. To sketch the graph we need to derive the coordinates of two points on the line. A convenient way to sketch graphs of straight lines is to plot the two axis intercepts.

Example 15

Sketch the graph of $2x + 4y = 10$.

Solution

x-axis intercept ($y = 0$): $2x + 4(0) = 10$
$x = 5$

y-axis intercept ($x = 0$): $2(0) + 4y = 10$
$y = 2.5$

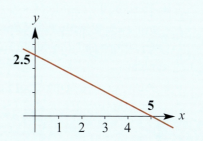

Example 16

Sketch the graph of $y = 2x - 6$ by first finding the intercepts.

Solution

x-axis intercept ($y = 0$): $0 = 2x - 6$
$x = 3$

y-axis intercept ($x = 0$): $y = 2(0) - 6$
$y = -6$

Note: You can also obtain the y-axis intercept directly from the equation.

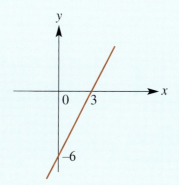

Using the TI-Nspire

To sketch the graph of $6x + 3y = 9$:

- Open a **Graphs** application: press (on) and select the **Graphs** icon, or use (ctrl)(I) and select **Add Graphs**.
- Equations of the form $ax + by = c$ can be entered directly using (menu) > **Graph Entry/Edit** > **Equation** > **Line**. Enter as $6x + 3y = 9$.

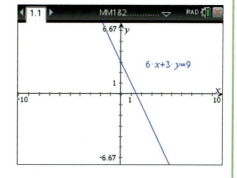

Note: The window settings (menu >
Window/Zoom > Window Settings)
will have to be changed if the axis
intercepts do not appear on the screen.

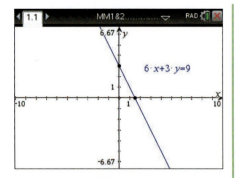

- The axis intercepts can be found using menu
  > **Geometry** > **Points & Lines** > **Intersection Point(s)**. Select the x-axis and the graph to display the x-axis intercept. Select the y-axis and the graph to display the y-axis intercept.
- To show the coordinates of these points, use menu > **Actions** > **Coordinates and Equations** and double click on each of the points.
- Press esc to exit the **Coordinates and Equations** tool.

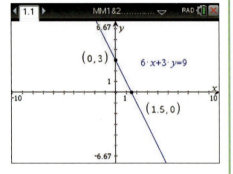

Using the Casio ClassPad

- Type the equation $3y + 6x = 9$ in the main screen $\sqrt[Main]{\alpha}$. Tap on the graph icon to display the graph screen.
- Using your stylus, highlight the equation and drag it down into the graph screen. Lift the stylus off the screen for the graph to appear.

- The graph window setting can be adjusted using the window setting icon.
- Ensure the graph window is selected and the intercepts are visible on the graph.

- To find the intercepts, go to **Analysis** > **G-Solve**. Select **y-Intercept** for the *y*-axis intercept and select **Root** for the *x*-axis intercept.

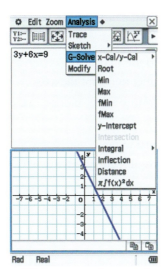
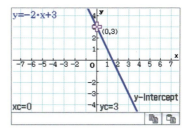
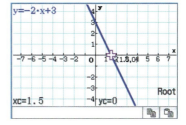

Note: The equation is displayed in gradient–intercept form in the top-left corner of the graph screen.

From Section 2B we know that the gradient of a line is the tangent of the angle of slope (that is, the angle formed by the line with the positive direction of the *x*-axis).

Example 17

For each of the following lines, find the magnitude of the angle θ (correct to two decimal places) that the line makes with the positive direction of the *x*-axis:

a $y = 2x + 3$
b $3y = 3x - 6$
c $y = -0.3x + 1.5$

Solution

a
$y = 2x + 3$
Gradient = 2
Hence $\tan \theta = 2$
Therefore $\theta = 63.43°$
correct to two decimal places

b
$3y = 3x - 6$
$y = x - 2$
Gradient = 1
Hence $\tan \theta = 1$
Therefore $\theta = 45°$

c
$y = -0.3x + 1.5$
Gradient = -0.3
Hence $\tan \theta = -0.3$
Therefore $\theta = (180 - 16.699\ldots)°$
$= 163.30°$ correct to two decimal places

Section summary

- The most practical way to sketch a straight line is to plot two points known to be on the required line and draw the line through them.
  - Two important points are the intercept with the x-axis and the intercept with the y-axis. These are the best two points to use in order to sketch a line that does not pass through the origin and is not parallel to one of the axes.
  - To sketch a line with equation of the form $y = mx$, plot one other point on the line besides the origin.
- The gradient m of a line $y = mx + c$ is equal to $\tan \theta$, where θ is the angle of slope measured between the line and the positive direction of the x-axis.

Exercise 2D

1 For each of the following, give the coordinates of the axis intercepts:
  a $x + y = 4$
  b $x - y = 4$
  c $-x - y = 6$
  d $y - x = 8$

Example 15 **2** Sketch the graphs of each of the following linear relations:
  a $2x - 3y = 12$
  b $x - 4y = 8$
  c $-3x + 4y = 24$
  d $-5x + 2y = 20$
  e $4x - 3y = 15$
  f $7x - 2y = 15$

Example 16 **3** For each of the following, sketch the graph by first finding the axis intercepts:
  a $y = x - 1$
  b $y = x + 2$
  c $y = 2x - 4$

4 Sketch the graphs of each of the following by first determining the axis intercepts:
  a $y = 2x - 10$
  b $y = 3x - 9$
  c $y = 5x + 10$
  d $y = -2x + 10$

5 Sketch the graphs of each of the following:
  a $y = x + 2$
  b $y = -x + 2$
  c $y = 2x + 1$
  d $y = -2x + 1$

6 Sketch the graphs of each of the following:
  a $x + y = 1$
  b $x - y = 1$
  c $y - x = 1$
  d $-x - y = 1$

7 Sketch the graphs of each of the following:
  a $y = x + 3$
  b $y = 3x + 1$
  c $y = 4 - \frac{1}{2}x$
  d $y = 3x - 2$
  e $4y + 2x = 12$
  f $3x + 6y = 12$
  g $4y - 6x = 24$
  h $8x - 3y = 24$

8 Sketch the graphs of each of the following:
  a $y = 3$
  b $x = -2$
  c $y = -2$
  d $x = 5$

2E Parallel and perpendicular lines

9 Find the magnitude of the angle, correct to two decimal places, made by each of the following with the positive direction of the x-axis:

  a $y = x$
  b $y = -x$
  c $y = x + 1$
  d $x + y = 1$
  e $y = 2x$
  f $y = -2x$

10 Find the magnitude of the angle, correct to two decimal places, made by each of the following with the positive direction of the x-axis:

  a $y = 3x + 2$
  b $2y = -2x + 1$
  c $2y - 2x = 6$
  d $3y + x = 7$

11 A straight line has equation $y = 3x - 4$. The points with coordinates $(0, a)$, $(b, 0)$, $(1, d)$ and $(e, 10)$ lie on the line. Find the values of a, b, d and e.

2E Parallel and perpendicular lines

▶ Parallel lines

> ■ Two non-vertical lines are **parallel** if they have the same gradient.
> ■ Conversely, if two non-vertical lines are parallel, then they have the same gradient.

This is easily proved through considering the angles of inclination of such lines to the positive direction of the x-axis and using the following two results:

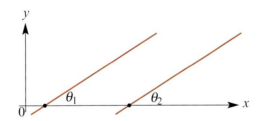

1 Two non-vertical lines are parallel if and only if the corresponding angles θ_1 and θ_2 formed by the lines and the positive direction of the x-axis are equal.

2 If θ_1 and θ_2 are two angles which are acute, obtuse or zero, then $\tan \theta_1 = \tan \theta_2$ implies $\theta_1 = \theta_2$.

For example, consider the lines

$y = 2x + 3$

$y = 2x - 4$

Both lines have gradient 2, and so they are parallel.

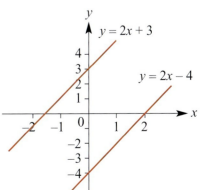

▶ Perpendicular lines

We prove that two lines are **perpendicular** if and only if the product of their gradients is -1 (or if one is horizontal and the other vertical).

> Two lines with gradients m_1 and m_2 (both non-zero) are perpendicular if and only if $m_1 m_2 = -1$.

Proof Initially we consider the case where the two lines intersect at the origin.

Step 1 Draw two lines passing through the origin with one of the lines having positive gradient, m_1, and the other negative gradient, m_2. Form right-angled triangles OPQ and OAB with $OQ = OB$.

Gradient $m_1 = \dfrac{AB}{BO}$

Gradient $m_2 = -\dfrac{OQ}{PQ}$

Product $m_1 m_2 = -\dfrac{OQ}{PQ} \times \dfrac{AB}{BO}$

$= -\dfrac{OQ}{PQ} \times \dfrac{AB}{OQ}$

$= -\dfrac{AB}{PQ}$

Step 2 We now prove: *If two lines passing through the origin are perpendicular, then the product of their gradients is -1.*

If the lines are perpendicular, then $\angle POQ = \angle AOB$. Therefore triangles OPQ and OAB are congruent. So $PQ = AB$ and therefore the product of the gradients is

$$m_1 m_2 = -\dfrac{AB}{PQ} = -\dfrac{AB}{AB} = -1$$

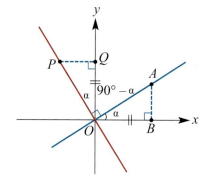

Step 3 We next prove the converse: *If for two lines passing through the origin the product of their gradients is -1, then the lines are perpendicular.*

If the product $m_1 m_2 = -1$, then $AB = PQ$, which implies that the triangles OAB and OPQ are congruent. Therefore $\angle POQ = \angle AOB$ and so $\angle AOP = 90°$.

Step 4 If we are given two lines anywhere in the plane, we can draw lines through the origin parallel to the original two lines. The slopes of the new lines are the same. So the result holds for lines that do not necessarily pass through the origin.

Example 18

Find the equation of the straight line which passes through $(1, 2)$ and is:

a parallel to the line with equation $2x - y = 4$

b perpendicular to the line with equation $2x - y = 4$.

Solution

The equation $2x - y = 4$ is equivalent to $y = 2x - 4$. The line $y = 2x - 4$ has gradient 2.

a The required line passes through $(1, 2)$ and has gradient 2. Hence
$$y - 2 = 2(x - 1)$$
Therefore the line has equation $y = 2x$.

b The required line passes through $(1, 2)$ and has gradient $-\frac{1}{2}$. Hence
$$y - 2 = -\frac{1}{2}(x - 1)$$
Therefore $2y - 4 = -x + 1$ and equivalently $2y + x = 5$.

The line has equation $2y + x = 5$.

Explanation

A line parallel to $y = 2x - 4$ has gradient 2.

We use $y - y_1 = m(x - x_1)$ where $(x_1, y_1) = (1, 2)$ and $m = 2$.

A line perpendicular to a line with gradient m has gradient $-\frac{1}{m}$ (provided $m \neq 0$).

We use $y - y_1 = m(x - x_1)$ where $(x_1, y_1) = (1, 2)$ and $m = -\frac{1}{2}$.

Example 19

The coordinates of the vertices of a triangle ABC are $A(0, -1)$, $B(2, 3)$ and $C(3, -2\frac{1}{2})$. Show that the side AB is perpendicular to the side AC.

Solution

Let m_1 be the gradient of the line AB and let m_2 be the gradient of the line AC.

$$m_1 = \frac{3 - (-1)}{2 - 0}$$
$$= 2$$

$$m_2 = \frac{-2\frac{1}{2} - (-1)}{3 - 0}$$
$$= \frac{-1\frac{1}{2}}{3}$$
$$= -\frac{1}{2}$$

Since $m_1 \times m_2 = 2 \times (-\frac{1}{2}) = -1$, the lines AB and AC are perpendicular to each other.

Explanation

We use the fact that two lines with gradients m_1 and m_2 (both non-zero) are perpendicular if and only if $m_1 m_2 = -1$.

We show the product of the gradients is -1. Hence the lines are perpendicular.

Section summary

- Two non-vertical lines are **parallel** if they have the same gradient. Conversely, if two non-vertical lines are parallel, then they have the same gradient.
- Two lines are **perpendicular** if the product of their gradients is -1 (or if one is horizontal and the other vertical). Conversely, if two lines are perpendicular, then the product of their gradients is -1 (or one is horizontal and the other vertical).

Exercise 2E

1 Find the equation of the straight line which passes through $(4, -2)$ and is:
  a parallel to the line with equation $y = 2x + 1$
  b perpendicular to the line with equation $y = 2x + 1$
  c parallel to the line with equation $y = -2x + 1$
  d perpendicular to the line with equation $y = -2x + 1$
  e parallel to the line with equation $2x - 3y = 4$
  f perpendicular to the line with equation $2x - 3y = 4$
  g parallel to the line with equation $x + 3y = 5$
  h perpendicular to the line with equation $x + 3y = -4$.

2 For which of the following pairs of equations are the corresponding lines parallel to each other? Sketch graphs to show the pairs of non-parallel lines.
  a $2y = 6x + 4$; $y = 3x + 4$
  b $x = 4 - y$; $2x + 2y = 6$
  c $3y - 2x = 12$; $y + \frac{1}{3} = \frac{2}{3}x$
  d $4y - 3x = 4$; $3y = 4x - 3$

3 Find the equation of the line:
  a perpendicular to the line $x = 3$ and which passes through the point $(3, 4)$
  b perpendicular to the line $y = 3$ and which passes through the point $(2, 3)$
  c perpendicular to the line $x = -2$ and which passes through the point $(-2, 4)$
  d perpendicular to the line $y = -4$ and which passes through the point $(3, -4)$.

4 Find the equation of the straight line which passes through the point $(1, 4)$ and is perpendicular to the line with equation $y = -\frac{1}{2}x + 6$.

5 Points A and B have coordinates $(1, 5)$ and $(-3, 7)$ respectively. Find the coordinates of the midpoint M of the line segment AB and find the equation of the line which passes through the point M and is perpendicular to the line AB.

6 If the points A, B and C have the coordinates $A(5, 2)$, $B(2, -3)$ and $C(-8, 3)$, show that the triangle ABC is a right-angled triangle.

7 Given the points $A(3, 7)$, $B(6, 1)$ and $C(20, 8)$, prove that AB is perpendicular to BC.

8 Show that $RSTU$ is a rectangle if the coordinates of the vertices are respectively $R(2, 6)$, $S(6, 4)$, $T(2, -4)$ and $U(-2, -2)$.

9 Given that the lines $4x - 3y = 10$ and $4x - \ell y = m$ are perpendicular and intersect at the point $(4, 2)$, find the values of ℓ and m.

10 The line $y = 2x + 3$ intersects the y-axis at A. The points B and C on this line are such that $AB = BC$. The line through B perpendicular to AC passes through the point $D(-1, 6)$. Find:
   a the equation of BD
   b the coordinates of B
   c the coordinates of C.

2F Families of straight lines

  Here are three families of straight lines:

- $y = mx$, where the gradient m of the lines varies – the graphs are the straight lines through the origin.
- $y = 3x + c$, where the y-axis intercept c of the lines varies – the graphs are the straight lines with gradient 3.
- $y = mx + 2$, where the gradient m of the lines varies – the graphs are the straight lines with y-axis intercept 2. Some graphs in this family are illustrated below.

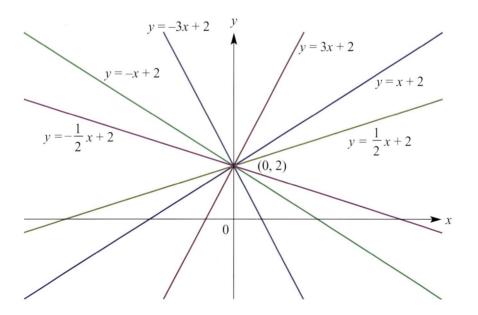

The variable m is called a **parameter**. We will consider other families of graphs in later chapters of this book.

Example 20

Find the value of m if the line $y = mx + 2$ passes through the point $(3, 11)$.

Solution

We can write

$$11 = 3m + 2$$

Therefore $3m = 9$ and hence $m = 3$. It is the line $y = 3x + 2$.

Example 21

A family of lines have equations of the form $y = mx + 2$, where m is a negative number.

a Find the x-axis intercept of a line in this family in terms of m.
b For which values of m is the x-axis intercept greater than 3?
c Find the equation of the line perpendicular to the line $y = mx + 2$ at the point $(0, 2)$.

Solution	Explanation
a When $y = 0$: $\quad mx + 2 = 0$ $\quad\quad\quad\quad mx = -2$ $\quad\quad\quad\quad\quad x = -\dfrac{2}{m}$ The x-axis intercept is $-\dfrac{2}{m}$.	To find the x-axis intercept put $y = 0$.
b $-\dfrac{2}{m} > 3$ $-2 < 3m$ $-\dfrac{2}{3} < m$ Therefore the x-axis intercept is greater than 3 for $-\dfrac{2}{3} < m < 0$.	Multiply both sides of the inequality by m. Since m is negative, the inequality sign is reversed. Then divide both sides by 3.
c The equation is $y - 2 = -\dfrac{1}{m}x$ and the gradient–intercept form is $y = -\dfrac{1}{m}x + 2$.	The perpendicular line has gradient $-\dfrac{1}{m}$ and passes through $(0, 2)$.

Section summary

Families of straight lines can be described through the use of a parameter. For example:

- All the non-vertical lines passing through $(0, 2)$ have equation of the form $y = mx + 2$, where m is a real number. (If $m = 0$, the line is horizontal.)
- All the lines with gradient 3 have equation of the form $y = 3x + c$, where c is a real number.
- All the lines with x-axis intercept 4 have equation of the form $\dfrac{x}{4} + \dfrac{y}{b} = 1$, where b is a non-zero real number.

Exercise 2F

Example 20

1 The line with equation $y = mx - 3$, where m is a positive number, passes through the point $(2, 7)$. Find the value of m.

2 The line with equation $y = 2x + c$, where c is a number, passes through the point $(3, 11)$. Find the value of c.

3 A line has equation $y = mx + 3$, where $m \neq 0$. A second line is perpendicular to this line and passes through the point $(0, 3)$.
  a Find the equation of the second line in terms of m.
  b Find the value of m if the second line passes through the point $(1, -4)$.

4 The line with equation $y = mx + 2$, where m is a positive number, passes through the point $(3, 8)$. Find the value of m.

Example 21

5 A family of lines have equations of the form $y = mx - 3$, where m is a positive number.
  a Find the x-axis intercept of a line in this family in terms of m.
  b Find the value of m if the line passes through the point $(5, 6)$.
  c For which values of m is the x-axis intercept less than or equal to 1?
  d Find the equation of the line perpendicular to the line $y = mx - 3$ at the point $(0, -3)$.

6 A family of lines have equations of the form $y = 2x + c$, where c is a number.
  a Find the x-axis intercept of a line in this family in terms of c.
  b Find the value of c if the line passes through the point $(5, 6)$.
  c For which values of c is the x-axis intercept less than or equal to 1?
  d Find the equation of the line perpendicular to the line $y = 2x + c$ at the point $(0, c)$.

7 A family of lines have equations of the form $\dfrac{x}{a} - \dfrac{y}{12} = 4$, where a is a non-zero number.
  a Find the x-axis intercept of a line in this family in terms of a.
  b Find the gradient of the line in terms of a.
  c Find the value of a if the gradient is
    i 2
    ii -2

8 A family of lines have equations of the form $y = -2x + c$, where c is a positive number.
  a Find the x-axis intercept of a line in this family in terms of c.
  b Find the value of c if the line passes through the point $(1, 7)$.
  c For which values of c is the x-axis intercept less than or equal to 1?
  d Find the equation of the line perpendicular to $y = -2x + c$ at the point $(0, c)$.
  e Let O denote the origin, and let A and B be the x-axis and y-axis intercepts of $y = -2x + c$.
    i If the midpoint M of the line segment AB is $(3, 6)$, find the value of c.
    ii If the triangle AOB has area 4, find the value of c.
    iii If the midpoint M of AB is such that $OM = 2\sqrt{5}$, find the value of c.

9 A family of lines have equations of the form $3x + by = 12$, where b is a non-zero number.

  a Find the y-axis intercept of a line in this family in terms of b.
  b Find the gradient of the line in terms of b.
  c Find the value of b if the gradient is
    i 1
    ii -2
  d Find the equation of the line perpendicular to the line $3x + by = 12$ at the point $(4, 0)$.

2G Linear models

There are many practical situations where a linear relation can be used.

Example 22

Austcom's rates for local calls from private telephones consist of a quarterly rental fee of $50 plus 25c for every call. Construct a cost function that describes the quarterly telephone bill and sketch the linear graph for this.

Solution

Let

C = cost ($) of quarterly telephone bill

n = number of calls

Then

$C = 0.25n + 50$

The number of calls is counted in whole numbers including zero.

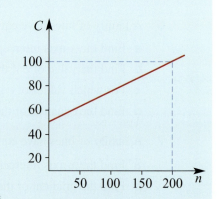

Draw the graph of the function $C = 0.25n + 50$ where n is a whole number including zero.

Note: The graph should be a series of discrete points rather than a continuous line, because n is a whole number. With the scale used it is not practical to show it correctly.

An important linear relation is the relation between distance travelled and time taken when an object is travelling with constant speed. If a car travels at 40 km/h, the relationship between distance travelled (s kilometres) and time taken (t hours) is

$s = 40t$ (for $t \geq 0$)

The graph of s against t is a straight-line graph through the origin. The gradient of this graph is 40.

Example 23

A car starts from point A on a highway 10 kilometres past the Wangaratta post office. The car travels at a constant speed of 90 km/h towards picnic stop B, which is 120 kilometres further on from A. Let t hours be the time after the car leaves point A.

a Find an expression for the distance d_1 of the car from the post office at time t hours.
b Find an expression for the distance d_2 of the car from point B at time t hours.
c On separate sets of axes sketch the graphs of d_1 against t and d_2 against t and state the gradient of each graph.

Solution

a At time t the distance of the car from the post office is $10 + 90t$ kilometres.
b At time t the distance of the car from B is $120 - 90t$ kilometres.
c

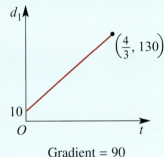

Gradient = 90

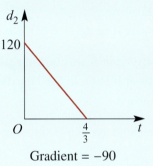

Gradient = −90

Exercise 2G

Example 22

1 The weekly wage, $w, of a vacuum cleaner salesperson consists of a fixed sum of $350 plus $20 for each cleaner sold. If n cleaners are sold per week, construct a rule that describes the weekly wage of the salesperson.

Example 23

2 a A train moves at 50 km/h in a straight line away from a town. Give a rule for the distance, d_1 km, from the town at time t hours after leaving the town.
  b A train has stopped at a siding 80 km from the town and then moves at 40 km/h in a straight line away from the siding towards the town. Give a rule for the distance, d_2 km, from the town at time t hours after leaving the siding.
  c On separate sets of axes sketch the graphs of d_1 against t ($0 \leq t \leq 4$) and d_2 against t and state the gradient of each graph.

3 a An initially empty container is being filled with water at a rate of 5 litres per minute. Give a rule for the volume, V litres, of water in the container at time t minutes after the filling of the container starts.
  b A container contains 10 litres of water. Water is then poured in at a rate of 5 litres per minute. Give a rule for the volume, V litres, of water in the container at time t minutes after the pouring starts.

4 The reservoir feeding an intravenous drip contains 500 mL of a saline solution. The drip releases the solution into a patient at the rate of 2.5 mL/minute.
  a Construct a rule which relates the amount of solution left in the reservoir, v mL, to time, t minutes.
  b State the possible values of t and v.
  c Sketch the graph of the relation.

5 The cost ($C) of hiring a taxi consists of two elements, a fixed flagfall and an amount that varies with the number (n) of kilometres travelled. If the flagfall is $2.60 and the cost per kilometre is $1.50, determine a rule which gives C in terms of n.

6 A car rental company charges $85, plus an additional amount of 24c per kilometre.
  a Write a rule to determine the total charge $C for hiring a car and travelling x kilometres.
  b What would be the cost to travel 250 kilometres?

7 Two towns A and B are 200 km apart. A man leaves town A and walks at a speed of 5 km/h towards town B. Find the distance of the man from town B at time t hours after leaving town A.

8 The following table shows the extension of a spring when weights are attached to it.

x, extension (cm)	0	1	2	3	4	5	6
w, weight (g)	50	50.2	50.4	50.6	50.8	51.0	51.2

  a Sketch a graph to show the relationship between x and w.
  b Write a rule that describes the graph.
  c What will be the extension if $w = 52.5$ g?

9 A printing firm charges $35 for printing 600 sheets of headed notepaper and $47 for printing 800 sheets.
  a Find a formula, assuming the relationship is linear, for the charge, $C, in terms of number of sheets printed, n.
  b How much would they charge for printing 1000 sheets?

10 An electronic bank teller registered $775 after it had counted 120 notes and $975 after it had counted 160 notes.
  a Find a formula for the sum registered ($C) in terms of the number of notes (n) counted.
  b Was there a sum already on the register when counting began?
  c If so, how much?

2H Simultaneous linear equations

> Skillsheet

In this section we revisit the geometry of simultaneous equations, first introduced in Section 1C, and also make use of parameters to explore these properties. Finally we consider some of the many applications of simultaneous equations.

▶ The geometry of simultaneous equations

There are three possible outcomes when considering a system of two simultaneous linear equations in two unknowns:

- There is a unique solution. (Lines intersect at a point.)
- There are infinitely many solutions. (Lines coincide.)
- There is no solution. (Lines are parallel.)

Example 24

Explain why the simultaneous equations $2x + 3y = 6$ and $4x + 6y = 24$ have no solution.

Solution

First write the equations in the form $y = mx + c$. They become

$$y = -\frac{2}{3}x + 2 \quad \text{and} \quad y = -\frac{2}{3}x + 4$$

Each of the lines has gradient $-\frac{2}{3}$. The y-axis intercepts are 2 and 4 respectively. The equations have no solution as they correspond to parallel lines and they are different lines.

Example 25

The simultaneous equations $2x + 3y = 6$ and $4x + 6y = 12$ have infinitely many solutions. Describe these solutions through the use of a parameter.

Solution

The two lines coincide, and so the solutions are all points on this line. We make use of a third variable λ as the parameter. If $y = \lambda$, then $x = \dfrac{6 - 3\lambda}{2}$. The points on the line are all points of the form $\left(\dfrac{6 - 3\lambda}{2}, \lambda\right)$.

Using the TI-Nspire

Simultaneous equations can be solved in a **Calculator** application.

- Use menu > **Algebra** > **Solve System of Equations** > **Solve System of Equations**.
- Complete the pop-up screen.

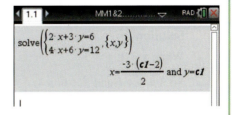

The solution to this system of equations is given by the calculator as shown. The variable $c1$ takes the place of λ.

Using the Casio ClassPad

To solve the simultaneous equations $2x + 3y = 6$ and $4x + 6y = 12$:

- Open the Math1 keyboard.
- Select the simultaneous equations icon.
- Enter the two equations into the two lines and type x, y in the bottom-right square to indicate the variables.
- Select EXE.

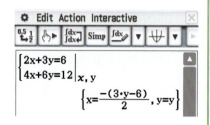

Choose $y = \lambda$ to obtain the solution $x = \dfrac{6 - 3\lambda}{2}$, $y = \lambda$ where λ is any real number.

Example 26

The family of lines $y = mx + 2$ with varying gradient m all pass through the point $(0, 2)$.

a For what values of m does the line $y = mx + 2$ not intersect the line $y = 5x - 3$?

b For what values of m does the line $y = mx + 2$ intersect the line $y = 5x - 3$?

c If the line $y = mx + 2$ intersects the line $y = 5x - 3$ at the point $(5, 22)$, find the value of m.

Solution

a The y-axis intercept of $y = mx + 2$ is 2 and the y-axis intercept of $y = 5x - 3$ is -3. The lines will not intersect if they are parallel, that is, if they have the same gradient. So $m = 5$.

b The lines intersect when $m \neq 5$.

c If $(5, 22)$ lies on the line $y = mx + 2$, then

$$22 = 5m + 2$$
$$20 = 5m$$
$$m = 4$$

Thus the lines intersect at $(5, 22)$ when $m = 4$.

Example 27

The lines $y = x + k$ and $y = mx + 4$ intersect at $(1, 3)$. Find the values of m and k.

Solution

When $x = 1$, $y = 3$.

So $3 = 1 + k$ and $3 = m + 4$.

Hence $k = 2$ and $m = -1$.

Example 28

The lines $(m-2)x + y = 2$ and $mx + 2y = k$ intersect at $(2, 8)$. Find the values of m and k.

Solution

$$(m-2)x + y = 2 \quad (1)$$
$$mx + 2y = k \quad (2)$$

When $x = 2$, $y = 8$. Substituting these values into equations (1) and (2), we have the equations

$$2(m-2) + 8 = 2 \quad (3)$$
$$2m + 16 = k \quad (4)$$

From (3), we have $2m - 4 + 8 = 2$. Therefore $m = -1$.

From (4), we have $2(-1) + 16 = k$. Therefore $k = 14$.

Example 29

Consider the simultaneous linear equations $(m-2)x + y = 2$ and $mx + 2y = k$. Find the values of m and k such that the system of equations has:

a no solution **b** infinitely many solutions **c** a unique solution.

Solution

$$(m-2)x + y = 2 \quad (1)$$
$$mx + 2y = k \quad (2)$$

We know that for *no solution* or *infinitely many solutions*, the corresponding lines are parallel or coincide. If the corresponding lines are parallel or coincide, the gradients are the same.

Gradient of line (1) $= 2 - m$

Gradient of line (2) $= -\dfrac{m}{2}$

Hence $\quad 2 - m = -\dfrac{m}{2}$

$\quad\quad\quad 4 - 2m = -m$

$\quad\quad\quad\quad\quad m = 4$

Substitute $m = 4$ in equations (1) and (2). We have

$$2x + y = 2$$
$$4x + 2y = k$$

a There is no solution if $m = 4$ and $k \neq 4$.
b If $m = 4$ and $k = 4$, there are infinitely many solutions as the equations are equivalent.
c The solution is unique if $m \neq 4$ and k is any real number.

Applications of simultaneous equations

Example 30

There are two possible methods for paying gas bills:

Method A   A fixed charge of $25 per quarter + 50c per unit of gas used
Method B   A fixed charge of $50 per quarter + 25c per unit of gas used

Determine the number of units which must be used before method B becomes cheaper than method A.

Solution

Let C_1 = charge ($) using method A
    C_2 = charge ($) using method B
    x = number of units of gas used

Then $C_1 = 25 + 0.5x$
    $C_2 = 50 + 0.25x$

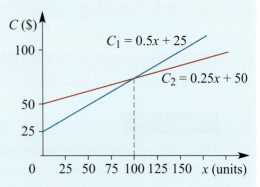

From the graph we see that method B is cheaper if the number of units exceeds 100.

The solution can be obtained by solving simultaneous linear equations:

$$C_1 = C_2$$
$$25 + 0.5x = 50 + 0.25x$$
$$0.25x = 25$$
$$x = 100$$

Example 31

Robyn and Cheryl race over 100 metres. Robyn runs so that it takes a seconds to run 1 metre, and Cheryl runs so that it takes b seconds to run 1 metre. Cheryl wins the race by 1 second. The next day they again race over 100 metres but Cheryl gives Robyn a 5-metre start so that Robyn runs 95 metres. Cheryl wins this race by 0.4 seconds. Find the values of a and b and the speed at which Robyn runs.

Solution

For the first race: Time for Robyn − time for Cheryl = 1 s.

$$100a - 100b = 1 \quad (1)$$

For the second race: Time for Robyn − time for Cheryl = 0.4 s.

$$95a - 100b = 0.4 \quad (2)$$

Subtract (2) from (1). This gives $5a = 0.6$ and therefore $a = 0.12$.

Substitute in (1) to find $b = 0.11$.

Robyn's speed = $\dfrac{1}{0.12} = \dfrac{25}{3}$ m/s.

Section summary

- There are three cases for a system of two linear equations with two variables:
  - unique solution (lines intersect at a point), e.g. $y = 2x + 3$ and $y = 3x + 3$
  - infinitely many solutions (lines coincide), e.g. $y = 2x + 3$ and $2y = 4x + 6$
  - no solution (lines are parallel), e.g. $y = 2x + 3$ and $y = 2x + 4$.
- There are many applications of simultaneous linear equations with two variables. The problems often arise by working with two quantities both changing at a constant but often different rate.

Exercise 2H

Example 24   **1**   Explain why the simultaneous equations $x + y = 6$ and $2x + 2y = 13$ have no solution.

Example 25   **2**   The simultaneous equations $x + y = 6$ and $2x + 2y = 12$ have infinitely many solutions. Describe these solutions through the use of a parameter.

Example 26   **3**   The family of lines $y = mx + 6$ with varying gradient m all pass through the point $(0, 6)$.
  a   For what values of m does the line $y = mx + 6$ not intersect the line $y = 4x - 5$?
  b   For what values of m does the line $y = mx + 6$ intersect the line $y = 4x - 5$?
  c   If the line $y = mx + 6$ intersects the line $y = 4x - 5$ at the point $(5, 15)$, find the value of m.

Example 27   **4**   The lines $y = 2x + k$ and $y = mx - 4$ intersect at $(2, 6)$. Find the values of m and k.

Example 28   **5**   The lines $(m - 2)x + y = 4$ and $mx + 3y = k$ intersect at $(2, 8)$. Find the values of m and k.

Example 29   **6**   Find the value of m for which the simultaneous equations $mx - y = 5$ and $3x + y = 6$ have no solution.

7   Find the value of m for which the pair of simultaneous equations $3x + my = 5$ and $(m + 2)x + 5y = m$ have:
  a   infinitely many solutions
  b   no solutions.

Example 30   **8**   Two bicycle hire companies have different charges. Company A charges $\$C$, according to the rule $C = 10t + 20$, where t is the time in hours for which a bicycle is hired. Company B charges $\$C$, according to the rule $C = 8t + 30$.
  a   Sketch each of the graphs on the same set of axes.
  b   Find the time, t, for which the charge of both companies is the same.

9 John and Michael race over 50 metres. John runs so that it takes at a seconds to run 1 metre and Michael runs so that it takes b seconds to run 1 metre. Michael wins the race by 1 second. The next day they again race over 50 metres but Michael gives John a 3-metre start so that John runs 47 metres. Michael wins this race by 0.1 seconds. Find the values of a and b and the speed at which Michael runs.

10 The distances, d_A km and d_B km, of cyclists A and B travelling along a straight road from a town hall step are given respectively by $d_A = 10t + 15$ and $d_B = 20t + 5$, where t is the time in hours after 1 p.m.
  a Sketch each of the graphs on the one set of axes.
  b Find the time in hours at which the two cyclists are at the same distance from the town hall step.

11 A helicopter can be hired for $210 per day plus a distance charge of $1.60 per km or, alternatively, at a fixed charge of $330 per day for an unlimited distance.
  a For each of the methods of hiring, find an expression for cost, $C, in terms of the distance travelled, x km.
  b On one set of axes, draw the graph of cost versus distance travelled for each of the methods.
  c Determine for what distances the fixed-charge method is cheaper.

12 Three power boats in a 500 km handicap race leave at 5 hourly intervals. Boat A leaves first and has a speed for the race of 20 km/h. Boat B leaves 5 hours later and travels at an average speed of 25 km/h. Boat C leaves last, 5 hours after B, and completes the race at a speed of 40 km/h.
  a Draw a graph of each boat's journey on the same set of axes.
  b Use your graphs to find the winner of the race.
  c Check your answer algebraically.
  d Write a short description of what happened to each boat in the race.

13 If the line OT has the equation $y = -\frac{3}{4}x$ and the line HT has the equation $y = \frac{3}{2}x - 12$, determine the point over which both craft would pass.

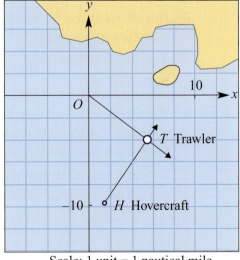

Scale: 1 unit = 1 nautical mile

14 A school wishes to take some of its students on an excursion. If they travel by tram it will cost the school $2.80 per student. Alternatively, the school can hire a bus at a cost of $54 for the day plus a charge of $1 per student.
  a For each mode of transport, write an expression for the cost (C) of transport in terms of the number of students (x).
  b On one set of axes, draw the graph of cost, C, versus number of students, x, for each mode of transport.
  c Determine for how many students it will be more economical to hire the bus.

15 Anne and Maureen live in towns that are 57 km apart. Anne sets out at 9 a.m. one day to ride her bike to Maureen's town at a constant speed of 20 km/h. At the same time Maureen sets out to ride to Anne's town at a constant speed of 18 km/h.
  a Write down a rule for the distance, d km, that each of them is from Anne's place at a time t minutes after 9 a.m.
  b On the same set of axes, draw graphs of the distance, d km, versus time, t minutes after 9 a.m., for each cyclist.
  c Find the time at which they will meet.
  d How far has each of them travelled when they meet?

Chapter summary

- The **midpoint** of the line segment joining (x_1, y_1) and (x_2, y_2) is the point with coordinates
$$\left(\frac{x_1 + x_2}{2}, \frac{y_1 + y_2}{2}\right)$$

- The **distance** between two points $A(x_1, y_1)$ and $B(x_2, y_2)$ is
$$AB = \sqrt{(x_2 - x_1)^2 + (y_2 - y_1)^2}$$

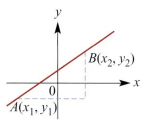

- The **gradient** of a straight line joining two points:
$$\text{Gradient } m = \frac{y_2 - y_1}{x_2 - x_1}$$

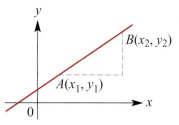

- For a line with gradient m, the **angle of slope** (θ) can be found using
$$m = \tan \theta$$
where θ is the angle the line makes with the positive direction of the x-axis.

- The gradient–intercept form of the equation of a straight line is
$$y = mx + c$$
where m is the gradient and c is the y-axis intercept.

- The equation of a line passing through a given point (x_1, y_1) and having gradient m is
$$y - y_1 = m(x - x_1)$$

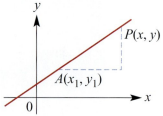

- The equation of a line passing through two given points (x_1, y_1) and (x_2, y_2) is
$$y - y_1 = m(x - x_1) \quad \text{where} \quad m = \frac{y_2 - y_1}{x_2 - x_1}$$

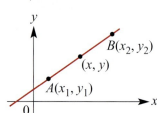

- Two straight lines are **perpendicular** to each other if and only if the product of their gradients is -1 (or if one is horizontal and the other vertical):
$$m_1 m_2 = -1$$

Chapter 2 review

Technology-free questions

1 Find the length and the coordinates of the midpoint of the line segment joining each of the following pairs of points:

  a $A(1, 2)$ and $B(5, 2)$ **b** $A(-4, -2)$ and $B(3, -7)$ **c** $A(3, 4)$ and $B(7, 1)$

2 Find the gradients of the lines joining each of the following pairs of points:

  a $(4, 3)$ and $(8, 12)$ **b** $(-3, 4)$ and $(8, -6)$ **c** $(2, 1)$ and $(2, 9)$
  d $(0, a)$ and $(a, 0)$ **e** $(0, 0)$ and (a, b) **f** $(0, b)$ and $(a, 0)$

3 Find the equation of the straight line of gradient 4 which passes through the point with coordinates:

  a $(0, 0)$ **b** $(0, 5)$ **c** $(1, 6)$ **d** $(3, 7)$

4 **a** The point $(1, a)$ lies on the line with equation $y = 3x - 5$. Find the value of a.
  b The point $(b, 15)$ lies on the line with equation $y = 3x - 5$. Find the value of b.

5 Find the equation of the straight line joining the points $(-5, 2)$ and $(3, -4)$.

6 Find the equation of the straight line of gradient $-\frac{2}{3}$ which passes through $(-4, 1)$.

7 Write down the equation of the straight line that:

  a passes through $(5, 11)$ and is parallel to the x-axis
  b passes through $(0, -10)$ and is parallel to the line with equation $y = 6x + 3$
  c passes through the point $(0, -1)$ and is perpendicular to the line with equation $3x - 2y + 5 = 0$.

8 Find the equation of the straight line which passes through the point $(2, 3)$ and is inclined at $30°$ to the positive direction of the x-axis.

9 Find the equation of the straight line which passes through the point $(-2, 3)$ and makes an angle of $135°$ with the positive direction of the x-axis.

10 Find the equation of the straight line passing through the point $(4, 8)$ and which is perpendicular to the line with equation $y = -3x + 2$.

11 A straight line has equation $y = 2x + 1$. The points with coordinates $(0, a)$, $(b, 0)$, $(2, d)$ and $(e, 7)$ lie on this line. Find the values of a, b, d and e.

12 Sketch the graph of each of the following by first determining axis intercepts. Clearly label each axis intercept.

  a $y = 2x - 8$ **b** $3x + y = 6$ **c** $3x + y + 6 = 0$
  d $y - 2x - 8 = 0$ **e** $y = -6x + 6$ **f** $2x + 5y + 10 = 0$

13 **a** Find the equation of the line parallel to the x-axis passing through the point $(8, -9)$. Sketch the graph.
  b Find the equation of the line parallel to the y-axis passing through the point $(8, -9)$. Sketch the graph.
  c Find the equation of the straight line that passes through the origin and has gradient:
    i 3   **ii** -3
  Sketch the graphs of each of these.

14 A car travels at a constant 60 km/h.
  a Write down the formula for the distance d km travelled by the car in t hours.
  b What is the gradient of the graph of d against t?

15 The weekly wage $\$S$ of a car salesperson consists of a fixed sum of $\$800$ plus $\$500$ for each car sold. If n cars are sold in a week, construct a formula that describes the weekly wage of the salesperson in terms of n.

16 A family of straight lines satisfy the rule $y = ax + 2$.
  a Find the equation of the straight line in this family for which $y = 6$ when $x = 2$.
  b **i** Find the x-axis intercept of the line with equation $y = ax + 2$.
    ii If $a < 0$, find the values of a for which the x-axis intercept is greater than 1.
  c Find the coordinates of the point of intersection of the line with equation $y = x + 3$ and the line with equation $y = ax + 2$, given that $a \neq 1$.

Multiple-choice questions

1 The coordinates of the midpoint of AB, where A has coordinates $(4, 12)$ and B has coordinates $(6, 2)$, are
  A $(4, 8)$ **B** $(4.5, 8)$ **C** $(5, 8)$ **D** $(5, 7)$ **E** $(1, 5)$

2 If $(6, 3)$ is the midpoint of the line segment joining the points $(-4, y)$ and $(x, -6)$, then the value of $x + y$ is
  A 0   **B** 16   **C** 20   **D** -10 **E** 28

3 The gradient of the line passing through the points $(5, -8)$ and $(6, -10)$ is
  A -2 **B** $-\dfrac{1}{2}$ **C** $\dfrac{1}{2}$ **D** $-\dfrac{1}{18}$ **E** $\dfrac{3}{2}$

4 The gradient of the line passing through points $(4a, 2a)$ and $(9a, -3a)$ is
  A a **B** $-5a$ **C** 1   **D** -5 **E** -1

5 The equation of the straight line with gradient 3 that passes through the point $(1, 9)$ is
  A $y = x + 9$ **B** $y = 3x + 9$ **C** $y = 3x + 6$
  D $y = -\frac{1}{3}x + 1$ **E** $y = -\frac{1}{3}x + 6$

6 A straight line passes through the points (2, −6) and (−2, −14). The equation of the line is

  A $y = x - 8$ **B** $y = \frac{1}{2}x - 7$ **C** $y = \frac{1}{2}x - 10$
  D $y = 2x - 10$ **E** $y = -\frac{1}{2}x - 8$

7 The line with equation $y = 2x - 6$ passes through the point $(a, 2)$. The value of a is

  A 2   **B** 4   **C** 5   **D** −4   **E** −2

8 The relation with graph as shown has rule

  A $y = -3x - 3$ **B** $y = -\frac{1}{3}x - 3$ **C** $y = \frac{1}{3}x - 3$
  D $y = 3x + 3$ **E** $y = 3x - 3$

9 If two lines $5x - y + 7 = 0$ and $ax + 2y - 11 = 0$ are parallel, then a equals

  A −5   **B** 5   **C** −10   **D** 10   **E** $-\frac{1}{2}$

10 The cost ($C) of hiring a car is given by the formula $C = 2.5x + 65$, where x is the number of kilometres travelled. A person is charged $750 for the hire of the car. The number of kilometres travelled was

  A 65   **B** 145   **C** 160   **D** 200   **E** 274

11 The solution of the two simultaneous equations $2ax + 2by = 3$ and $3ax - 2by = 7$ for x and y is

  A $x = 2a, \ y = \dfrac{3 - 4a^2}{2b}$ **B** $x = 2, \ y = \dfrac{3 - 4a}{2b}$

  C $x = \dfrac{2}{a}, \ y = -\dfrac{1}{2b}$ **D** $x = 0, \ y = 0$

  E $x = 3a, \ y = 7b$

Extended-response questions

1 The cost of hiring a motor cruiser consists of a down payment of $500 and a running charge of $100 per day, or part of a day. The cost of fuel is $27.50 per day. There is also a charge of $50 for filling the freshwater tanks and charging the batteries. Food for a cruise of n days costs $62.50 per day.

  a Give a formula for C, the total cost in dollars of hiring the cruiser for n days (all costs to be included).

  b For how many days can a cruiser be hired if the cost of a cruise is to be no more than $3000?

  c A rival company has a fixed rate of $300 per day. For how many days would it be cheaper to hire from this company?

2 The cost of fitting a new plug and cable for an electric drill is $C, when the length of the cable is x metres and $C = 4.5 + 1.8x$.

    a What meaning could be given for the constant term 4.5?
    b What could be the meaning of the coefficient 1.8?
    c What would be the gradient of the graph of C against x?
    d What length of cable would give a total cost of $24.50?

3 The profit made on a single journey of an Easyride bus tour is $P, when there are x empty seats and $P = 1020 - 24x$.

    a What do you think is the meaning of the constant term 1020?
    b What is the least number of empty seats which would result in a loss on a single journey?
    c Suggest a meaning for the coefficient 24.

4 A quarterly electricity bill shows the following charges:

- For the first 50 kWh (kilowatt hours): 9.10c per kWh
- For the next 150 kWh: 5.80c per kWh
- Thereafter: 3.56c per kWh

    a Write down a formula relating cost, $C, to n, the number of kWh of electricity used:

        i for the first 50 kWh
        ii for the next 150 kWh
        iii for more than 200 kWh.

    b Draw a graph of C against n. Use the graph, or otherwise, to determine the charges for:

        i 30 kWh
        ii 90 kWh
        iii 300 kWh

    c How much electricity could be used for a cost of $20?

5 O is the position of the air traffic control tower at an airport. An aircraft travelling in a straight line is identified at $A(2, 10)$ and again at $B(8, -4)$.

    a What is the equation that describes the flight path of the aircraft?
    b How far south of O is the aircraft when $x = 15$ km?

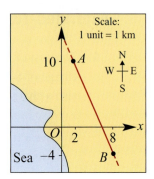

6 A construction company estimates that for every 1% of air left in concrete as it is being laid the strength of the hardened concrete decreases by 7%. Let x represent the percentage of air in the concrete (by volume), and the strength of the concrete be s units, where $s = 100$ when $x = 0$.

  a Write a formula for s in terms of x.
  b Sketch a graph of s against x.
  c Calculate how much air can be allowed to remain in the concrete for a strength of at least 95%.
  d Estimate how much air the concrete will contain at 0% strength.
  e Is the model sensible at 0% strength?
  f State the possible values of x.

7 The diagram shows a plan view of a paddock over which a Cartesian framework has been superimposed. From an observation point O, a rabbit has been spotted first at $A(0, 2)$ and then at $B(4, 6)$. A fox is seen at $C(3, 0)$ and later at $D(5, 4)$.

  a Find the equations of the lines AB and CD.
  b Assuming that both the rabbit and the fox were running along straight lines, calculate whether the fox's path would cross the rabbit's track before the irrigation channel.

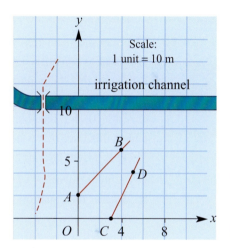

8 The diagram shows the side view of a rough, uncut diamond fixed in position on a computer-controlled cutting machine. The diamond is held at the points $A(-4.5, 2)$, $B(0.25, 7)$, $C(5, 1.5)$ and $D(1.5, 0)$.

  a If a straight cut is made joining A and B, find the y-coordinate of the point V at which the cut will cross the vertical axis.
  b Find the equation of the line joining V and C.
  c Would the cuts AB and VC be equally inclined to the vertical axis? Explain your answer.

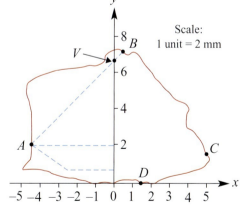

9 A new light beacon is proposed at $P(4, -75)$ for air traffic flying into an airport located at $O(0, 0)$. It is intended that the aircraft should follow a course over beacons at P and $Q(36, -4)$, turning at Q towards the runway at O.

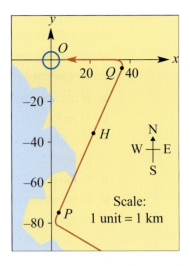

  a Would a direct line from P to Q pass directly over a hospital located at $H(20, -36)$?
  b If not, state how far east or west of H the aircraft would be when the y-coordinate of an aircraft's flight path is -36.

10 The map shows an area where it is proposed to construct a new airport. It is thought that the main runway of the airport will have one end of its centre line at $A(48, 10)$, but the position of the other end of this line, B, has not been decided. There is a light aircraft airport at $E(68, 35)$ and a radio beacon at $C(88, -10)$.

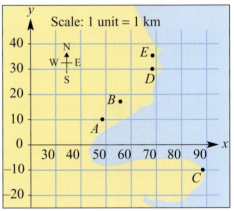

  a What is the equation that will define the new runway if aircraft coming in to land from the east must be on the extended central line of the new runway when they are 5 km due south of E?
  b If B is to be 8 km to the east of A, what will be its coordinates?
  c A marker beacon is to be built at $D(68, 30)$ and it is proposed that several auxiliary beacons should be placed on the line CD. What is the equation of the line CD?
  d If one of the auxiliary beacons is to be placed due east of A, what are the coordinates of its position?

11 The diagram shows a quadrilateral. Angle BAD is a right angle and C lies on the perpendicular bisector of AB. The equation of the line through points B and C is $3y = 4x - 14$. Find:

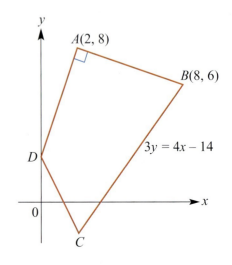

  a the equation of the line AD
  b the coordinates of D
  c the equation of the perpendicular bisector of AB
  d the coordinates of C
  e the area of triangle ADC
  f the area of the quadrilateral $ABCD$.

12 Wheelrite, a small company that manufactures garden wheelbarrows, has overhead expenses of $30 000 per year. In addition, it costs $40 to manufacture each wheelbarrow.

  a Write a rule which determines the total cost, C, of manufacturing x wheelbarrows per year.

  b If the annual production is 6000 wheelbarrows, what is the overall cost per wheelbarrow?

  c How many wheelbarrows must be made so that the overall cost is $46 per wheelbarrow?

  d Wheelrite sells wheelbarrows to retailers for $80 each. Write a rule which determines the revenue, R, from the sale of x wheelbarrows to retailers.

  e Sketch the graphs for C and R against x on the same axes.

  f What is the minimum number of wheelbarrows that must be produced for Wheelrite to make a profit each year?

  g Write a rule which determines the profit, P, from the manufacture and sale of x number of wheelbarrows.

13 An electricity supply authority is offering customers a choice of two methods of paying electricity bills. Method 1 involves payment annually and method 2 involves payment each quarter (that is, every three months). The charges for each method are as follows:

Method 1 – per year
Fixed charge $100
Price per unit $0.08125

Method 2 – per quarter
Fixed charge $27.50
Price per unit $0.075

  a Suppose a customer used 1560 units of electricity in a year. Calculate which is the cheaper method of payment.

  b Copy and then complete the following table:

	Number of units of electricity			
	0	1000	2000	3000
Cost ($) calculated by method 1				
Cost ($) calculated by method 2				

  c Use these values to plot graphs of the costs for each method of paying for electricity. Clearly indicate the approximate number of units of electricity for which the cost is the same for both methods of payment.

  d If C_1 is the cost by method 1, C_2 is the cost by method 2, and x is the number of units of electricity used in a year, write down the two formulas which show the cost of x units calculated by each method. Use these formulas to calculate the exact number of units for which the cost is the same for both methods.

14 In a metal fabricating yard which has been flooded by overflow from a local river, a large steel frame has been partly submerged. The ends A, B, C and D are the only parts visible above the level of the flood water. The coordinates of the ends relative to an overhead crane are $A(10, 16)$, $B(16, 20)$, $C(24, 8)$ and $D(18, 4)$. The overhead crane moves east–west along its rail, and the distance east from a point $O(0, 0)$ is denoted by x. The crane's hook moves north–south across the frame and the distance to the north of the south rail is denoted by y. Units are in metres. The steel frame is to be raised out of the water by lifting it at the midpoint, M, of its middle section.

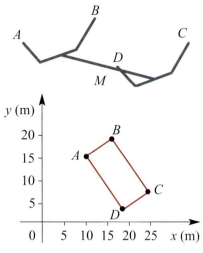

a Find the coordinates, x and y, of the point to which the hook must be moved so that it will be directly above the midpoint, M, of the steel frame.

b In order to minimise the risk of the hook slipping, the hook will be moved slowly along a line parallel to AB. Find the equation of the line along which the hook will be moved.

15 The diagram below shows part of a micro-electronics circuit, as seen through a magnifying glass; the circuit has been etched onto a chip of plated silica.
The four points A, B, C and D stand away from the chip itself. A is $(100, 60)$, B is $(200, 100)$, C is $(160, 200)$ and D is $(60, 160)$. Units are in $\frac{1}{25}$ mm.
The unit S is a moveable micro-soldering unit, its tip being at $P(0, 120)$. It is desired to program the tip of the soldering iron, P, to solder wires to the points A, B, C and D, moving along the dashed lines as shown in the graph.

a Find equations for the lines defining each section of the path along which P must be programmed to move.

b Will any of the turns be through right angles? Explain.

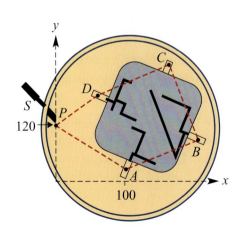
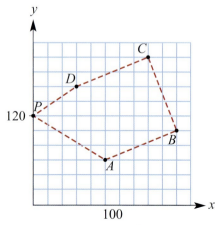

Scale: 1 unit = $\frac{1}{25}$ mm

Chapter 3
Quadratics

Objectives

- To recognise and sketch the graphs of **quadratic polynomials**.
- To find the key features of the graph of a quadratic polynomial: axis intercepts, turning point and axis of symmetry.
- To determine the **maximum** or **minimum** value of a quadratic function.
- To **solve quadratic equations** by factorising, completing the square and using the general formula.
- To apply the **discriminant** to determine the nature and number of solutions of a quadratic equation.
- To apply quadratic functions to solving problems.

A **polynomial function** has a rule of the type

$$y = a_n x^n + a_{n-1} x^{n-1} + \cdots + a_1 x + a_0$$

where n is a natural number or zero, and $a_0, a_1, \ldots, a_n$ are numbers called **coefficients**.

The **degree** of a polynomial is given by the value of n, the highest power of x with a non-zero coefficient. For example:

- $y = 2x + 3$ is a polynomial function of degree 1
- $y = 2x^2 + 3x - 2$ is a polynomial function of degree 2.

This chapter deals with polynomials of degree 2. These are called **quadratic polynomials**.

The graph of a linear polynomial function, $y = mx + c$, is a straight line and the graph of a quadratic polynomial function, $y = ax^2 + bx + c$, $a \neq 0$, is a **parabola**. Polynomials of higher degree will be studied in Chapter 6.

3A Expanding and collecting like terms

In order to sketch graphs of quadratics, we need to find the x-axis intercepts (if they exist), and to do this we need to solve quadratic equations. As an introduction to the methods of solving quadratic equations, the first two sections of this chapter review the basic algebraic processes of expansion and factorisation.

An algebraic expression is the sum of its **terms**. For example:

- The terms of the linear expression $3x - 1$ are $3x$ and -1.
- The terms of the quadratic expression $-2x^2 + 3x - 4$ are $-2x^2$, $3x$ and -4.

Example 1

Simplify $2(x - 5) - 3(x + 5)$ by first expanding.

Solution

$$2(x - 5) - 3(x + 5) = 2x - 10 - 3x - 15$$
$$= 2x - 3x - 10 - 15$$
$$= -x - 25$$

Explanation

Expand each bracket.

Collect like terms.

Example 2

Expand $2x(3x - 2) + 3x(x - 2)$.

Solution

$$2x(3x - 2) + 3x(x - 2) = 6x^2 - 4x + 3x^2 - 6x$$
$$= 9x^2 - 10x$$

For expansions of the type $(a + b)(c + d)$, proceed as follows:

$$(a + b)(c + d) = a(c + d) + b(c + d)$$
$$= ac + ad + bc + bd$$

Example 3

Expand the following:

a $(x + 3)(2x - 3)$ **b** $(x - 3)(2x - 2\sqrt{2})$

Solution

a $(x + 3)(2x - 3)$
$$= x(2x - 3) + 3(2x - 3)$$
$$= 2x^2 - 3x + 6x - 9$$
$$= 2x^2 + 3x - 9$$

Explanation

Each term in the second pair of brackets is multiplied by each term in the first.

b $(x-3)(2x-2\sqrt{2})$

$= x(2x - 2\sqrt{2}) - 3(2x - 2\sqrt{2})$

$= 2x^2 - 2\sqrt{2}x - 6x + 6\sqrt{2}$

$= 2x^2 - (2\sqrt{2} + 6)x + 6\sqrt{2}$

Be careful with negative signs.

You can also complete binomial expansions with a table; this emphasises the terms.

	x	-3
$2x$	$2x^2$	$-6x$
$-2\sqrt{2}$	$-2\sqrt{2}x$	$6\sqrt{2}$

You add the terms to complete the expansion.

Example 4

Expand $(2x - 1)(3x^2 + 2x + 4)$.

Solution

$(2x - 1)(3x^2 + 2x + 4) = 2x(3x^2 + 2x + 4) - 1(3x^2 + 2x + 4)$

$\qquad = 6x^3 + 4x^2 + 8x - 3x^2 - 2x - 4$

$\qquad = 6x^3 + x^2 + 6x - 4$

Using the TI-Nspire

To expand the expression

$(2x - 1)(3x^2 + 2x + 4)$

use menu > **Algebra** > **Expand**.

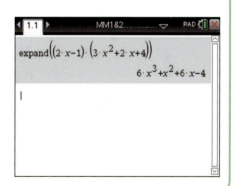

Using the Casio ClassPad

Enter the expression

$(2x - 1)(3x^2 + 2x + 4)$

into $\sqrt{\alpha}$. Highlight the expression and select **Interactive** > **Transformation** > **expand**.

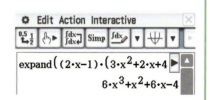

▶ Perfect squares

Consider the expansion of a perfect square, $(a+b)^2$:

$$(a+b)^2 = (a+b)(a+b)$$
$$= a(a+b) + b(a+b)$$
$$= a^2 + ab + ab + b^2$$
$$= a^2 + 2ab + b^2$$

Thus the general result can be stated as:

$$(a+b)^2 = a^2 + 2ab + b^2$$

That is, to expand $(a+b)^2$ take the sum of the squares of the terms and add twice the product of the terms.

Example 5

Expand $(3x - 2)^2$.

Solution

$$(3x-2)^2 = (3x)^2 + 2(3x)(-2) + (-2)^2$$
$$= 9x^2 - 12x + 4$$

Explanation

Use the expansion $(a+b)^2 = a^2 + 2ab + b^2$.
Here $a = 3x$ and $b = -2$.

▶ Difference of two squares

Consider the expansion of $(a+b)(a-b)$:

$$(a+b)(a-b) = a(a-b) + b(a-b)$$
$$= a^2 - ab + ab - b^2$$
$$= a^2 - b^2$$

Thus the expansion of the difference of two squares has been obtained:

$$(a+b)(a-b) = a^2 - b^2$$

Example 6

Expand:
a $(2x-4)(2x+4)$
b $(x - 2\sqrt{7})(x + 2\sqrt{7})$

Solution

a $(2x-4)(2x+4) = (2x)^2 - (4)^2$
$$= 4x^2 - 16$$

b $(x - 2\sqrt{7})(x + 2\sqrt{7}) = x^2 - (2\sqrt{7})^2$
$$= x^2 - 28$$

Example 7

Expand $(2a - b + c)(2a - b - c)$.

Solution

$$(2a - b + c)(2a - b - c) = ((2a - b) + c)((2a - b) - c)$$
$$= (2a - b)^2 - c^2$$
$$= 4a^2 - 4ab + b^2 - c^2$$

Section summary

- A **polynomial function** has a rule of the type
  $$y = a_n x^n + a_{n-1} x^{n-1} + \cdots + a_1 x + a_0$$
  where n is a natural number or zero, and $a_0, a_1, \ldots, a_n$ are numbers called **coefficients**.
- The **degree** of a polynomial is given by the value of n, the highest power of x with a non-zero coefficient.
- A polynomial function of degree 2 is called a **quadratic function**. The general rule is of the form $y = ax^2 + bx + c$, where $a \neq 0$. The graph of a quadratic function is called a **parabola**.
- General binomial expansion:
  $$(a + b)(c + d) = a(c + d) + b(c + d)$$
  $$= ac + ad + bc + bd$$
- Perfect square expansion:
  $$(a + b)^2 = a^2 + 2ab + b^2$$
- Difference of two squares expansion:
  $$(a + b)(a - b) = a^2 - b^2$$

Exercise 3A

1 Expand each of the following:
  - **a** $2(x - 4)$
  - **b** $-2(x - 4)$
  - **c** $3(2x - 4)$
  - **d** $-3(4 - 2x)$
  - **e** $x(x - 1)$
  - **f** $2x(x - 5)$

2 Collect like terms in each of the following:
  - **a** $2x + 4x + 1$
  - **b** $2x - 6 + x$
  - **c** $3x + 1 - 2x$
  - **d** $-x + 2x - 3 + 4x$

Example 1

3 Simplify each of the following by expanding and collecting like terms:
  - **a** $8(2x - 3) - 2(x + 4)$
  - **b** $2x(x - 4) - 3x$
  - **c** $4(2 - 3x) + 4(6 - x)$
  - **d** $4 - 3(5 - 2x)$

4 Simplify each of the following by expanding and collecting like terms:
  a $2x(x-4) - 3x$
  b $2x(x-5) + x(x-5)$
  c $2x(-10 - 3x)$
  d $3x(2 - 3x + 2x^2)$
  e $3x - 2x(2-x)$
  f $3(4x - 2) - 6x$

5 Simplify each of the following by expanding and collecting like terms:
  a $(3x-7)(2x+4)$
  b $(x-10)(x-12)$
  c $(3x-1)(12x+4)$
  d $(4x-5)(2x-3)$
  e $(x-\sqrt{3})(x-2)$
  f $(2x-\sqrt{5})(x+\sqrt{5})$
  g $(3x-2\sqrt{7})(x+\sqrt{7})$
  h $(5x-3)(x+2\sqrt{2})$
  i $(\sqrt{5}x-3)(\sqrt{5}x-32\sqrt{2})$

6 Simplify each of the following by expanding and collecting like terms:
  a $(2x-3)(3x^2+2x-4)$
  b $(x-1)(x^2+x+1)$
  c $(6-2x-3x^2)(4-2x)$
  d $(5x-3)(x+2) - (2x-3)(x+3)$
  e $(2x+3)(3x-2) - (4x+2)(4x-2)$

7 Simplify each of the following by expanding and collecting like terms:
  a $(x-4)^2$
  b $(2x-3)^2$
  c $(6-2x)^2$
  d $\left(x-\dfrac{1}{2}\right)^2$
  e $(x-\sqrt{5})^2$
  f $(x-2\sqrt{3})^2$

8 Simplify each of the following by expanding and collecting like terms:
  a $(x-3)(x+3)$
  b $(2x-4)(2x+4)$
  c $(9x-11)(9x+11)$
  d $(2x-3)(2x+3)$
  e $(2x+5)(2x-5)$
  f $(x-\sqrt{5})(x+\sqrt{5})$
  g $(2x+3\sqrt{3})(2x-3\sqrt{3})$
  h $(\sqrt{3}x-\sqrt{7})(\sqrt{3}x+\sqrt{7})$

9 Simplify each of the following by expanding and collecting like terms:
  a $(x-y+z)(x-y-z)$
  b $(2a-b+c)(2a-b-c)$
  c $(3w-4z+u)(3w+4z-u)$
  d $(2a-\sqrt{5}b+c)(2a+\sqrt{5}b+c)$

10 Find the area of each of the following by:
  i adding the areas of the four 'non-overlapping' rectangles (two of which are squares)
  ii multiplying length by width of the undivided square (boundary in blue).

a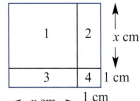

b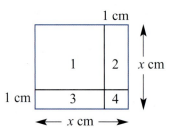

3B Factorising

Four different types of factorisation will be considered.

▶ Factorisation using common factors

If each term in an algebraic expression to be factorised contains a **common factor**, then this common factor is a factor of the entire expression. To find the other factor, divide each term by the common factor. The common factor is placed outside the brackets. This process is known as 'taking the common factor outside the brackets'.

Example 8

a Factorise $9x^2 + 81x$.
b Factorise $2a^2 - 8ax^2$.

Solution

a $9x^2 + 81x = 9x \times x + 9x \times 9$
$\qquad = 9x(x + 9)$

b $2a^2 - 8ax^2 = 2a \times a - 2a \times 4x^2$
$\qquad = 2a(a - 4x^2)$

Note: The answers can be checked by expanding.

Explanation

The common factor $9x$ is 'taken out' of the brackets.

The common factor $2a$ is 'taken out' of the brackets.

In general, take out as many common factors as possible.

Example 9

Factorise $7x^2y - 35xy^2$.

Solution

$7x^2y - 35xy^2 = 7xy(x - 5y)$

Explanation

The common factor $7xy$ is 'taken out' of the brackets.

▶ Grouping of terms

This method can be used for expressions containing four terms.

Example 10

Factorise $x^3 + 4x^2 - 3x - 12$.

Solution

$x^3 + 4x^2 - 3x - 12 = (x^3 + 4x^2) - (3x + 12)$
$\qquad = x^2(x + 4) - 3(x + 4)$
$\qquad = (x^2 - 3)(x + 4)$

Explanation

The terms in this expression can be grouped as shown.

The common factor $(x + 4)$ is 'taken out' of the brackets.

▶ Difference of two squares

You will recall the following identity from the previous section:

$$(a + b)(a - b) = a^2 - b^2$$

We can now use the result the other way in order to factorise:

$$a^2 - b^2 = (a + b)(a - b)$$

Example 11

a Factorise $3x^2 - 75$.
b Factorise $9x^2 - 36$.

Solution	Explanation
a $3x^2 - 75 = 3(x^2 - 25)$ $ = 3(x + 5)(x - 5)$	First 'take out' the common factor 3. Use the difference of squares identity.
b $9x^2 - 36 = 9(x^2 - 4)$ $ = 9(x - 2)(x + 2)$	First 'take out' the common factor 9. Use the difference of squares identity.

Example 12

Factorise $(x - y)^2 - 16y^2$.

Solution	Explanation
$(x - y)^2 - 16y^2 = (x - y)^2 - (4y)^2$ $ = (x - y + 4y)(x - y - 4y)$ $ = (x + 3y)(x - 5y)$	Use the difference of squares identity $a^2 - b^2 = (a + b)(a - b)$ with $a = (x - y)$ and $b = 4y$.

▶ Factorising quadratic polynomials

A quadratic polynomial is an expression of the form $ax^2 + bx + c$ with $a \neq 0$. We have seen in the previous section that we can expand a product of two binomial factors to obtain a quadratic expression. For example:

$$(x + 2)(x - 4) = x(x - 4) + 2(x - 4)$$
$$= x^2 - 4x + 2x - 8$$
$$= x^2 - 2x - 8$$

We want to be able to reverse this process. That is, we want to start from the expanded expression and obtain the factorised form. We have already done this for expressions that are differences of squares. We now turn our attention to the general case.

Example 13

Factorise $x^2 - 2x - 8$.

Solution

Using the method described in the explanation opposite, we can factorise without any further setting out:

$$x^2 - 2x - 8 = (x - 4)(x + 2)$$

Alternatively, we can reverse the process we used for expanding:

$$\begin{aligned} x^2 - 2x - 8 &= x^2 - 4x + 2x - 8 \\ &= x(x - 4) + 2(x - 4) \\ &= (x - 4)(x + 2) \end{aligned}$$

Explanation

We want

$$\begin{aligned} x^2 - 2x - 8 &= (x + a)(x + b) \\ &= x^2 + (a + b)x + ab \end{aligned}$$

The values of a and b are such that $ab = -8$ and $a + b = -2$.

Values of a and b which satisfy these two conditions are $a = -4$ and $b = 2$.

A quadratic polynomial is called a **monic quadratic polynomial** if the coefficient of x^2 is 1. The quadratic polynomial $x^2 - 2x - 8$ factorised in the previous example is monic.

Factorising non-monic quadratic polynomials involves a slightly different approach. We need to consider all possible combinations of factors of the x^2 term and the constant term. The next example and the following discussion give two methods.

Example 14

Factorise $6x^2 - 13x - 15$.

Solution

There are several combinations of factors of $6x^2$ and -15 to consider. Only one combination is correct.

$$6x^2 - 13x - 15 = (6x + 5)(x - 3)$$

Factors of $6x^2$	Factors of -15	'Cross-products' add to give $-13x$
$6x$	$+5$	$+5x$
x	-3	$-18x$
		$-13x$

Here is a second method for factorising $6x^2 - 13x - 15$ which still requires some trial and error but is more systematic. It is the reverse process of expanding $(x - 3)(6x + 5)$.

We let

$$ax^2 + bx + c = (\alpha x + \gamma)(\beta x + \delta)$$

Expanding the right-hand side gives

$$ax^2 + bx + c = \alpha\beta x^2 + (\gamma\beta + \alpha\delta)x + \gamma\delta$$

Note that $ac = \alpha\beta\gamma\delta$ and $b = \gamma\beta + \alpha\delta$.

We now apply this to factorising $6x^2 - 13x - 15$.

First we look for two numbers that multiply together to give ac and add to give b. That is, we look for two numbers whose product is $6 \times (-15) = -90$ and whose sum is -13.

The two numbers are -18 and 5. We write:

$$6x^2 - 13x - 15 = 6x^2 - 18x + 5x - 15$$
$$= 6x(x - 3) + 5(x - 3)$$
$$= (x - 3)(6x + 5)$$

Example 15

Factorise $8x^2 + 2x - 15$.

Solution

$8x^2 + 2x - 15 = 8x^2 + 12x - 10x - 15$
$ = 4x(2x + 3) - 5(2x + 3)$
$ = (4x - 5)(2x + 3)$

Explanation

$ac = 8 \times (-15) = -120$ and $b = 2$.

The two numbers are 12 and -10. So we write $2x = 12x - 10x$.

It is sometimes possible to take out a common factor first to simplify the factorisation.

Example 16

Factorise $2x^2 + 6x - 20$.

Solution

$2x^2 + 6x - 20 = 2(x^2 + 3x - 10)$
$ = 2(x + 5)(x - 2)$

Explanation

The common factor 2 is 'taken out' first.

Example 17

Factorise $(x + 1)^2 - 2(x + 1) - 3$.

Solution

$(x + 1)^2 - 2(x + 1) - 3 = a^2 - 2a - 3$
$ = (a - 3)(a + 1)$
$ = (x + 1 - 3)(x + 1 + 1)$
$ = (x - 2)(x + 2)$

Explanation

The substitution $a = x + 1$ makes it easier to recognise the required factorisation.

Using the TI-Nspire

To factorise the expression $6x^2 - 13x - 15$, use menu > **Algebra** > **Factor**.

Using the Casio ClassPad

Enter the expression

$$6x^2 - 13x - 15$$

into Main $\sqrt{\alpha}$. Highlight the expression and select **Interactive > Transformation > factor**.

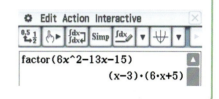

Section summary

- Difference of two squares identity: $a^2 - b^2 = (a + b)(a - b)$.
- Factorisation of monic quadratics: To factorise a quadratic of the form $x^2 + bx + c$, find two numbers whose sum is the coefficient of x and whose product is the constant term.
- Factorisation of general quadratics: To factorise a quadratic of the form $ax^2 + bx + c$, find two numbers e and f whose product is ac and whose sum is b. Split the middle term bx as $ex + fx$ and then factorise by grouping.

Exercise 3B

1 Factorise each of the following:
- **a** $2x + 4$
- **b** $4a - 8$
- **c** $6 - 3x$
- **d** $2x - 10$
- **e** $18x + 12$
- **f** $24 - 16x$

Example 8

2 Factorise:
- **a** $4x^2 - 2xy$
- **b** $8ax + 32xy$
- **c** $6ab - 12b$
- **d** $6xy + 14x^2y$
- **e** $x^2 + 2x$
- **f** $5x^2 - 15x$
- **g** $-4x^2 - 16x$
- **h** $7x + 49x^2$
- **i** $2x - x^2$

Example 9

3 Factorise:
- **a** $6x^3y^2 + 12y^2x^2$
- **b** $7x^2y - 6y^2x$
- **c** $8x^2y^2 + 6y^2x$

Example 10

4 Factorise:
- **a** $x^3 + 5x^2 + x + 5$
- **b** $xy + 2x + 3y + 6$
- **c** $x^2y^2 - x^2 - y^2 + 1$
- **d** $ax + ay + bx + by$
- **e** $a^3 - 3a^2 + a - 3$
- **f** $2ab - 12a - 5b + 30$
- **g** $2x^2 - 2x + 5x - 5$
- **h** $x^3 - 4x + 2x^2 - 8$
- **i** $x^3 - bx^2 - a^2x + a^2b$

Example 11

5 Factorise:
- **a** $x^2 - 36$
- **b** $x^2 - 81$
- **c** $x^2 - a^2$
- **d** $4x^2 - 81$
- **e** $9x^2 - 16$
- **f** $25x^2 - y^2$
- **g** $3x^2 - 48$
- **h** $2x^2 - 98$
- **i** $3ax^2 - 27a$
- **j** $a^2 - 7$
- **k** $2a^2 - 5$
- **l** $x^2 - 12$

Chapter 3: Quadratics

Example 12 **6** Factorise:
- **a** $(x-2)^2 - 16$
- **b** $25 - (2+x)^2$
- **c** $3(x+1)^2 - 12$
- **d** $(x-2)^2 - (x+3)^2$
- **e** $(2x-3)^2 - (2x+3)^2$
- **f** $(2x-1)^2 - (3x+6)^2$

Example 13 **7** Factorise:
- **a** $x^2 - 7x - 18$
- **b** $y^2 - 19y + 48$
- **c** $a^2 - 14a + 24$
- **d** $a^2 + 18a + 81$
- **e** $x^2 - 5x - 24$
- **f** $x^2 - 2x - 120$

Example 14, 15 **8** Factorise:
- **a** $3x^2 - 7x + 2$
- **b** $6x^2 + 7x + 2$
- **c** $5x^2 + 23x + 12$
- **d** $2x^2 + 9x + 4$
- **e** $6x^2 - 19x + 10$
- **f** $6x^2 - 7x - 3$
- **g** $12x^2 - 17x + 6$
- **h** $5x^2 - 4x - 12$
- **i** $5x^3 - 16x^2 + 12x$

Example 16 **9** Factorise:
- **a** $3y^2 - 12y - 36$
- **b** $2x^2 - 18x + 28$
- **c** $4x^2 - 36x + 72$
- **d** $3x^2 + 15x + 18$
- **e** $ax^2 + 7ax + 12a$
- **f** $48x - 24x^2 + 3x^3$

Example 17 **10** Factorise:
- **a** $(x-1)^2 + 4(x-1) + 3$
- **b** $2(x-1)^2 + 5(x-1) - 3$
- **c** $(2x+1)^2 + 7(2x+1) + 12$

3C Quadratic equations

Skillsheet This section looks at the solution of quadratic equations by simple factorisation. There are three steps to solving a quadratic equation by factorisation:

Step 1 Write the equation in the form $ax^2 + bx + c = 0$.

Step 2 Factorise the quadratic expression.

Step 3 Use the result that $mn = 0$ implies $m = 0$ or $n = 0$ (or both); this is known as the **null factor theorem**.

For example, to solve the equation $x^2 - x = 12$:

$$x^2 - x = 12$$
$$x^2 - x - 12 = 0 \qquad \text{(Step 1)}$$
$$(x-4)(x+3) = 0 \qquad \text{(Step 2)}$$
$$\therefore \quad x - 4 = 0 \quad \text{or} \quad x + 3 = 0 \qquad \text{(Step 3)}$$
$$x = 4 \quad \text{or} \quad x = -3$$

In the simplest cases, the first two steps may have been done already.

Example 18

Solve $x^2 + 11x + 24 = 0$.

Solution

x^2	+24	+11x
x	+3	+3x
x	+8	+8x
		+11x

Factorising gives

$$x^2 + 11x + 24 = 0$$
$$(x + 3)(x + 8) = 0$$
$$\therefore \quad x + 3 = 0 \quad \text{or} \quad x + 8 = 0$$
$$x = -3 \quad \text{or} \quad x = -8$$

Explanation

The quadratic can also be factorised in the following way:

$$x^2 + 11x + 24 = x^2 + 8x + 3x + 24$$
$$= x(x + 8) + 3(x + 8)$$
$$= (x + 8)(x + 3)$$

Note: We can check the answer for this example by substituting into the equation:

$$(-3)^2 + 11(-3) + 24 = 0$$
$$(-8)^2 + 11(-8) + 24 = 0$$

Example 19

Solve $2x^2 + 5x - 12 = 0$.

Solution

$2x^2$	−12	+5x
$2x$	−3	−3x
x	+4	+8x
		+5x

Factorising gives

$$2x^2 + 5x - 12 = 0$$
$$(2x - 3)(x + 4) = 0$$
$$\therefore \quad 2x - 3 = 0 \quad \text{or} \quad x + 4 = 0$$
$$x = \frac{3}{2} \quad \text{or} \quad x = -4$$

Explanation

The quadratic can also be factorised in the following way:

$$2x^2 + 5x - 12 = 2x^2 + 8x - 3x - 12$$
$$= 2x(x + 4) - 3(x + 4)$$
$$= (2x - 3)(x + 4)$$

Applications of quadratic equations

Problems involving the solution of quadratic equations arise in many situations. We will meet more such problems in Section 3L.

Example 20

The perimeter of a rectangle is 20 cm and its area is 24 cm². Calculate the length and width of the rectangle.

Solution

Let x cm be the length of the rectangle and y cm the width.

Then $2(x + y) = 20$ and thus $y = 10 - x$.

The area is 24 cm² and therefore $xy = x(10 - x) = 24$.

i.e. $\quad 10x - x^2 = 24$

$x^2 - 10x + 24 = 0$

$(x - 6)(x - 4) = 0$

Thus the length is 6 cm or 4 cm. The width is 4 cm or 6 cm.

Section summary

To solve a quadratic equation by factorisation:

Step 1 Write the equation in the form $ax^2 + bx + c = 0$.

Step 2 Factorise the quadratic polynomial.

Step 3 Use the result that $mn = 0$ implies $m = 0$ or $n = 0$ (or both).

Exercise 3C

1 Solve each of the following for x:
  a $(x - 2)(x - 3) = 0$
  b $x(2x - 4) = 0$
  c $(x - 4)(2x - 6) = 0$
  d $(3 - x)(x - 4) = 0$
  e $(2x - 6)(x + 4) = 0$
  f $2x(x - 1) = 0$
  g $(5 - 2x)(6 - x) = 0$
  h $x^2 = 16$

2 Use a CAS calculator to solve each of the following equations. Give your answer correct to two decimal places.
  a $x^2 - 4x - 3 = 0$
  b $2x^2 - 4x - 3 = 0$
  c $-2x^2 - 4x + 3 = 0$

Example 18 **3** Solve for x in each of the following:
  a $x^2 - x - 72 = 0$
  b $x^2 - 6x + 8 = 0$
  c $x^2 - 8x - 33 = 0$
  d $x(x + 12) = 64$
  e $x^2 + 5x - 14 = 0$
  f $x^2 = 5x + 24$

Example 19

4 Solve for x in each of the following:
   a $2x^2 + 5x + 3 = 0$
   b $4x^2 - 8x + 3 = 0$
   c $6x^2 + 13x + 6 = 0$
   d $2x^2 - x = 6$
   e $6x^2 + 15 = 23x$
   f $2x^2 - 3x - 9 = 0$
   g $10x^2 - 11x + 3 = 0$
   h $12x^2 + x = 6$
   i $4x^2 + 1 = 4x$
   j $x(x + 4) = 5$
   k $\frac{1}{7}x^2 = \frac{3}{7}x$
   l $x^2 + 8x = -15$
   m $5x^2 = 11x - 2$

5 Calculate the value of x.

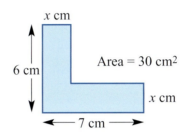

6 The bending moment, M, of a simple beam used in bridge construction is given by the formula
$$M = \frac{w\ell}{2}x - \frac{w}{2}x^2$$
If $\ell = 13$ m, $w = 16$ kg/m and $M = 288$ kg m, calculate the value of x.

7 The height, h metres, reached by a projectile after t seconds travelling vertically upwards is given by the formula $h = 70t - 16t^2$. Calculate t if h is 76 metres.

8 A polygon with n sides has $\frac{n(n-3)}{2}$ diagonals. How many sides has a polygon with 65 diagonals?

9 For a particular electric train, the tractive 'resistance' R at speed v km/h is given by $R = 1.6 + 0.03v + 0.003v^2$. Find v when the tractive resistance is 10.6.

Example 20

10 The perimeter of a rectangle is 16 cm and its area is 12 cm². Calculate the length and width of the rectangle.

11 The altitude of a triangle is 1 cm shorter than the base. If the area of the triangle is 15 cm², calculate the altitude.

12 Tickets for a concert are available at two prices. The more expensive ticket is $30 more than the cheaper one. Find the cost of each type of ticket if a group can buy 10 more of the cheaper tickets than the expensive ones for $1800.

13 The members of a club hire a bus for $2100. Seven members withdraw from the club and the remaining members have to pay $10 more each to cover the cost. How many members originally agreed to go on the bus?

3D Graphing quadratics

A quadratic polynomial function is defined by the general rule

$$y = ax^2 + bx + c$$

where a, b and c are constants and $a \neq 0$. This is called **polynomial form**.

▶ The parabola $y = x^2$

The simplest quadratic function is $y = x^2$. If a table of values is constructed for $y = x^2$ for $-3 \leq x \leq 3$, these points can be plotted and then connected to produce a continuous curve.

x	-3	-2	-1	0	1	2	3
y	9	4	1	0	1	4	9

Features of the graph of $y = x^2$:

- The graph is called a **parabola**.
- The possible y-values are all positive real numbers and 0. (This is called the **range** of the quadratic and is discussed in a more general context in Chapter 5.)
- The graph is symmetrical about the y-axis. The line about which the graph is symmetrical is called the **axis of symmetry**.
- The graph has a **vertex** or **turning point** at the origin $(0, 0)$.
- The minimum value of y is 0 and it occurs at the turning point.

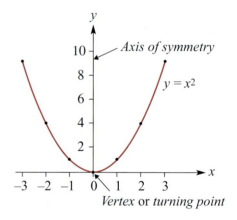

▶ Transformations of $y = x^2$

By a process called **completing the square** (to be discussed in Section 3E), all quadratics in polynomial form $y = ax^2 + bx + c$ may be transposed into what will be called the **turning point form**:

$$y = a(x - h)^2 + k$$

We first consider the effect of changing the value of a for our basic graph of $y = x^2$.

We then consider the effect of changing h and k for graphs of the form $y = ax^2$. Graphs of the form $y = a(x - h)^2 + k$ are formed by **translating** the graph of $y = ax^2$. The graph of $y = a(x - h)^2 + k$ is exactly the same shape as $y = ax^2$. All of these graphs are indeed congruent to $y = ax^2$ and each other.

Graphs of $y = ax^2$

We first consider graphs of the form $y = ax^2$. In this case both $h = 0$ and $k = 0$. In the basic graph of $y = x^2$, the value of a is 1.

The following graphs are shown on the same set of axes:

$y = x^2$
$y = 2x^2$ $(a = 2)$
$y = \frac{1}{2}x^2$ $(a = \frac{1}{2})$
$y = -2x^2$ $(a = -2)$

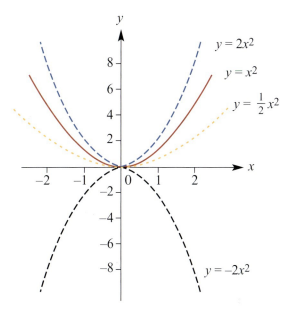

If $a > 1$, the graph is 'narrower'. If $0 < a < 1$, the graph is 'broader'. The transformation which produces the graph of $y = 2x^2$ from the graph of $y = x^2$ is called a **dilation of factor 2 from the x-axis**.

When a is negative, the graph is reflected in the x-axis. The transformation which produces the graph of $y = -x^2$ from the graph of $y = x^2$ is called a **reflection in the x-axis**.

Graphs of $y = x^2 + k$

On this set of axes are the graphs of

$y = x^2$
$y = x^2 - 2$ $(k = -2)$
$y = x^2 + 1$ $(k = 1)$

As can be seen, changing k moves the basic graph of $y = x^2$ in a vertical direction.

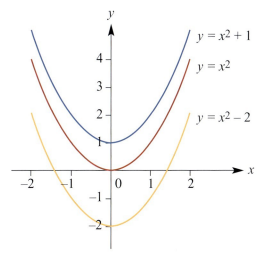

- When $k = -2$ the graph is **translated** 2 units in the negative direction of the y-axis. The vertex is now $(0, -2)$ and the range is now all real numbers greater than or equal to -2.
- When $k = 1$ the graph is **translated** 1 unit in the positive direction of the y-axis. The vertex is now $(0, 1)$ and the range is now all real numbers greater than or equal to 1.

All other features of the graph are unchanged. The axis of symmetry is still the y-axis.

Graphs of $y = (x - h)^2$

On this set of axes are the graphs of

$y = x^2$
$y = (x - 2)^2$ $(h = 2)$
$y = (x + 3)^2$ $(h = -3)$

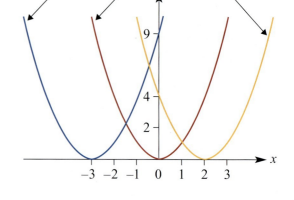

As can be seen, changing h moves the graph in a horizontal direction.

- When $h = 2$ the graph is **translated** 2 units in the positive direction of the x-axis. The vertex is now $(2, 0)$ and the axis of symmetry is now the line $x = 2$.

- When $h = -3$ the graph is **translated** 3 units in the negative direction of the x-axis. The vertex is now $(-3, 0)$ and the axis of symmetry is now the line $x = -3$.

In both cases, the range is unchanged and is still all non-negative real numbers.

Examples of transformations

By combining dilations, reflections and translations, we can sketch the graph of any quadratic expressed in the form $y = a(x - h)^2 + k$:

- The vertex is the point (h, k).
- The axis of symmetry is $x = h$.
- If h and k are positive, then the graph of $y = a(x - h)^2 + k$ is obtained from the graph of $y = ax^2$ by translating h units in the positive direction of the x-axis and k units in the positive direction of the y-axis.
- Similar results hold for different combinations of h and k positive and negative.

Example 21

Sketch the graph of $y = x^2 - 3$.

Solution

The graph of $y = x^2 - 3$ is obtained from the graph of $y = x^2$ by translating 3 units in the negative direction of the y-axis.

The vertex is now at $(0, -3)$. The axis of symmetry is the line with equation $x = 0$.

To find the x-axis intercepts, let $y = 0$:

$0 = x^2 - 3$
$x^2 = 3$
$\therefore \quad x = \pm\sqrt{3}$

Hence the x-axis intercepts are $\pm\sqrt{3}$.

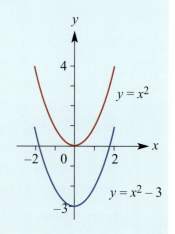

Example 22

Sketch the graph of $y = -(x + 1)^2$.

Solution

The graph of $y = -(x + 1)^2$ is obtained from the graph of $y = x^2$ by a reflection in the x-axis followed by a translation of 1 unit in the negative direction of the x-axis.

The vertex is now at $(-1, 0)$.

The axis of symmetry is the line with equation $x = -1$.

The x-axis intercept is -1.

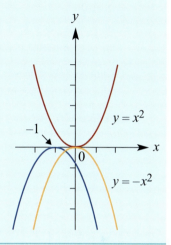

Example 23

Sketch the graph of $y = 2(x - 1)^2 + 3$.

Solution

The graph of $y = 2x^2$ is translated 1 unit in the positive direction of the x-axis and 3 units in the positive direction of the y-axis.

The vertex has coordinates $(1, 3)$.

The axis of symmetry is the line $x = 1$.

The graph will be narrower than $y = x^2$.

The range will be $y \geq 3$.

To add further detail to our graph, we can find the axis intercepts:

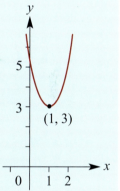

y-axis intercept
When $x = 0$, $y = 2(0 - 1)^2 + 3 = 5$.

x-axis intercepts
In this example, the minimum value of y is 3, and so y cannot be 0. Therefore this graph has no x-axis intercepts.

Note: Another way to see this is to let $y = 0$ and try to solve for x:

$$0 = 2(x-1)^2 + 3$$
$$-3 = 2(x-1)^2$$
$$-\tfrac{3}{2} = (x-1)^2$$

As the square root of a negative number is not a real number, this equation has no real solutions.

Example 24

Sketch the graph of $y = -(x+1)^2 + 4$.

Solution

The vertex has coordinates $(-1, 4)$ and so the axis of symmetry is the line $x = -1$.

When $x = 0$, $y = -(0+1)^2 + 4 = 3$.
∴ the y-axis intercept is 3.

When $y = 0$, $-(x+1)^2 + 4 = 0$
$$(x+1)^2 = 4$$
$$x + 1 = \pm 2$$
$$x = \pm 2 - 1$$

∴ the x-axis intercepts are 1 and -3.

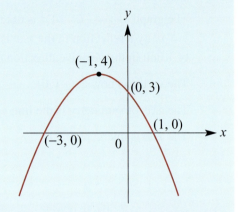

Section summary

- The graph of $y = x^2$ is called a parabola. The vertex (or turning point) is the point $(0, 0)$ and the axis of symmetry is the y-axis.
- The graph of $y = -x^2$ is the reflection of the graph of $y = x^2$ in the x-axis.
- For $y = ax^2$ and $a > 1$, the graph is 'narrower' than the graph of $y = x^2$.
- For $y = ax^2$ and $0 < a < 1$, the graph is 'broader' than the graph of $y = x^2$.
- All quadratic functions in polynomial form $y = ax^2 + bx + c$ may be transposed into the turning point form $y = a(x - h)^2 + k$.
- The graph of $y = a(x - h)^2 + k$ is a parabola congruent to the graph of $y = ax^2$.
  - The vertex (or turning point) is the point (h, k).
  - The axis of symmetry is $x = h$.
  - If h and k are positive numbers, then the graph of $y = a(x - h)^2 + k$ is obtained from the graph of $y = ax^2$ by translating h units in the positive direction of the x-axis and k units in the positive direction of the y-axis.
  - Similar results hold for different combinations of h and k positive and negative.

Exercise 3D

For each of the following, find

　i　the coordinates of the turning point
　ii　the axis of symmetry
　iii　the x-axis intercepts (if any)

and use this information to help sketch the graph.

Example 21   **1**   **a** $y = x^2 - 4$ **b** $y = x^2 + 2$ **c** $y = -x^2 + 3$
             d $y = -2x^2 + 5$ **e** $y = -x^2 + 4$ **f** $y = 3x^2 - 9$

Example 22   **2**   **a** $y = (x-2)^2$ **b** $y = (x+3)^2$ **c** $y = -(x+1)^2$ **d** $y = -\frac{1}{2}(x-4)^2$

Example 23, 24   **3**   **a** $y = (x-2)^2 + 1$ **b** $y = (x-2)^2 - 1$ **c** $y = (x-1)^2 + 2$
                  d $y = (x+1)^2 - 1$ **e** $y = -(x-3)^2 + 1$ **f** $y = (x+2)^2 - 4$
                  g $y = 2(x+2)^2 - 18$ **h** $y = -3(x-4)^2 + 3$ **i** $y = -\frac{1}{2}(x+5)^2 - 2$
                  j $y = 3(x+2)^2 - 12$ **k** $y = -4(x-2)^2 + 8$ **l** $y = \frac{1}{3}(x-1)^2 - 3$

3E Completing the square and turning points

In order to use the techniques from the previous section for sketching quadratics, it is necessary for the quadratic to be expressed in **turning point form**. This can be done by two different but related methods: by completing the square and by using the equation of the axis of symmetry.

▶ Completing the square

To transpose a quadratic in polynomial form we can **complete the square**.

Consider the expansion of a perfect square:

$$(x + a)^2 = x^2 + 2ax + a^2$$

The last term of the expansion is the square of half the coefficient of the middle term.

Now consider the quadratic polynomial

$$x^2 + 2x - 3$$

This is not a perfect square. However, by adding and subtracting a new term, we can form a perfect square as part of a new expression for the same polynomial.

We have that

$$x^2 + 2x + 1 = (x + 1)^2$$

which is a perfect square. In order to keep our original quadratic 'intact', we both add and subtract the 'correct' new term. For example:

$$x^2 + 2x - 3 = (x^2 + 2x + 1) - 1 - 3$$

This can now be simplified to

$$(x + 1)^2 - 4$$

Hence the quadratic $y = x^2 + 2x - 3$ is expressed in turning point form as $y = (x + 1)^2 - 4$, and so the **vertex** (turning point) of its graph is the point with coordinates $(-1, -4)$.

In the above example, the coefficient of x^2 was 1. If the coefficient is not 1, this coefficient must first be 'factored out' before proceeding to complete the square.

A geometric representation of completing the square

Completing the square for $x^2 + 2x$ is represented in the following diagrams. The diagram on the left shows $x^2 + 2x$. The small rectangle to the right is moved to the 'base' of the x by x square. The red square of area 1 unit is added. Thus $x^2 + 2x + 1 = (x + 1)^2$.

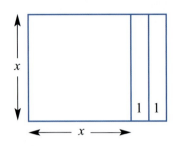
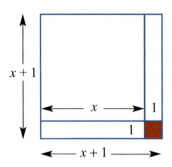

Using the TI-Nspire

Use menu > **Algebra** > **Complete the Square** to rearrange the expression $x^2 - 5x + 2$.

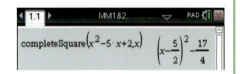

Solving equations by completing the square

The process of completing the square can also be used for the solution of equations.

Example 25

Solve each of the following equations for x by first completing the square:

a $x^2 - 3x + 1 = 0$ **b** $2x^2 - 3x - 1 = 0$

Solution

a Completing the square:

$$x^2 - 3x + 1 = 0$$

$$x^2 - 3x + \left(\frac{3}{2}\right)^2 - \left(\frac{3}{2}\right)^2 + 1 = 0$$

$$\left(x - \frac{3}{2}\right)^2 - \frac{5}{4} = 0$$

$$\left(x - \frac{3}{2}\right)^2 = \frac{5}{4}$$

Therefore $x - \frac{3}{2} = \pm\frac{\sqrt{5}}{2}$

and so $x = \frac{3}{2} \pm \frac{\sqrt{5}}{2} = \frac{3 \pm \sqrt{5}}{2}$

Explanation

$\frac{1}{2} \times (-3) = -\frac{3}{2}$

We add and subtract $\left(-\frac{3}{2}\right)^2 = \frac{9}{4}$ on the left-hand side of the equation.

This gives an equivalent expression to the expression of the left-hand side.

Solve the equation as shown.

b Completing the square:

$$2x^2 - 3x - 1 = 0$$

$$2\left(x^2 - \frac{3}{2}x - \frac{1}{2}\right) = 0$$

$$x^2 - \frac{3}{2}x + \left(\frac{3}{4}\right)^2 - \left(\frac{3}{4}\right)^2 - \frac{1}{2} = 0$$

$$\left(x - \frac{3}{4}\right)^2 = \frac{17}{16}$$

Therefore $x - \frac{3}{4} = \pm\frac{\sqrt{17}}{4}$

and so $x = \frac{3}{4} \pm \frac{\sqrt{17}}{4} = \frac{3 \pm \sqrt{17}}{4}$

Divide both sides by 2 before completing the square.

$$\frac{1}{2} \times \left(-\frac{3}{2}\right) = -\frac{3}{4}$$

We add and subtract $\left(-\frac{3}{4}\right)^2 = \frac{9}{16}$ on the left-hand side of the equation.

Sketching the graph of a quadratic polynomial after completing the square

Completing the square enables the quadratic rule to be written in turning point form. We have seen that this can be used to sketch the graphs of quadratic polynomials.

Example 26

Find the coordinates of the vertex by completing the square and hence sketch the graph of $y = -2x^2 + 6x - 8$.

Solution

Take out -2 as a common factor and then complete the square:

$$y = -2x^2 + 6x - 8$$
$$= -2(x^2 - 3x + 4)$$
$$= -2\left(x^2 - 3x + \left(\frac{3}{2}\right)^2 - \left(\frac{3}{2}\right)^2 + 4\right)$$
$$= -2\left(\left(x - \frac{3}{2}\right)^2 - \frac{9}{4} + 4\right)$$
$$= -2\left(\left(x - \frac{3}{2}\right)^2 + \frac{7}{4}\right)$$
$$\therefore \; y = -2\left(x - \frac{3}{2}\right)^2 - \frac{7}{2}$$

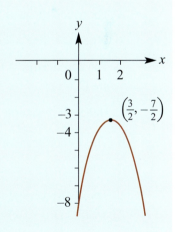

Therefore the vertex is $\left(\frac{3}{2}, -\frac{7}{2}\right)$ and the axis of symmetry is $x = \frac{3}{2}$.

The y-axis intercept is -8.

The graph has maximum value of $-\frac{7}{2}$, and so there are no x-axis intercepts.

▶ The equation for the axis of symmetry of a parabola

We first complete the square for $y = ax^2 + bx + c$:

$$y = ax^2 + bx + c$$

$$= a\left(x^2 + \frac{b}{a}x + \frac{c}{a}\right)$$

$$= a\left(x^2 + \frac{b}{a}x + \frac{b^2}{4a^2} - \frac{b^2}{4a^2} + \frac{c}{a}\right) \quad \text{completing the square}$$

$$= a\left(x + \frac{b}{2a}\right)^2 - \frac{b^2}{4a} + c$$

> For a quadratic function written in polynomial form $y = ax^2 + bx + c$, the axis of symmetry of its graph has the equation $x = -\dfrac{b}{2a}$.

Therefore the x-coordinate of the turning point is $-\dfrac{b}{2a}$. Substitute this value into the quadratic polynomial to find the y-coordinate of the turning point.

Example 27

Use the axis of symmetry to find the turning point of the graph and hence express in turning point form:

a $y = x^2 - 4x + 3$ **b** $y = -2x^2 + 12x - 7$

Solution

a The x-coordinate of the turning point is 2.

When $x = 2$, $y = 4 - 8 + 3 = -1$.

The coordinates of the turning point are $(2, -1)$.

Hence the equation is $y = (x - 2)^2 - 1$.

b The x-coordinate of the turning point is 3.

When $x = 3$, $y = -2 \times (3)^2 + 12 \times 3 - 7 = 11$.

The coordinates of the turning point are $(3, 11)$.

Hence the equation is $y = -2(x - 3)^2 + 11$.

Explanation

Here $a = 1$ and $b = -4$, so the axis of symmetry is $x = -\left(\dfrac{-4}{2}\right) = 2$.

For the turning point form $y = a(x - h)^2 + k$, we have found that $a = 1$, $h = 2$ and $k = -1$.

Here $a = -2$ and $b = 12$, so the axis of symmetry is $x = -\left(\dfrac{12}{-4}\right) = 3$.

For the turning point form $y = a(x - h)^2 + k$, we have found that $a = -2$, $h = 3$ and $k = 11$.

Section summary

- Quadratic equations can be solved by completing the square. The method of completing the square allows us to deal with all quadratic equations, even though there may be no solution for some quadratic equations.

- To complete the square of $x^2 + bx + c$:
  - Take half the coefficient of x (that is, $\frac{b}{2}$) and add and subtract its square $\frac{b^2}{4}$.
- To complete the square of $ax^2 + bx + c$:
  - First take out a as a factor and then complete the square inside the bracket.
- The axis of symmetry of the graph of the quadratic function $y = ax^2 + bx + c$ is $x = -\frac{b}{2a}$.
- To convert the quadratic function $y = ax^2 + bx + c$ into turning point form using the axis of symmetry:
  1. The x-coordinate h of the vertex of the parabola is $-\frac{b}{2a}$.
  2. Find the y-coordinate k of the vertex by substituting in $y = ax^2 + bx + c$.
  3. Substitute these values for h and k in $y = a(x - h)^2 + k$.

Exercise 3E

1 Expand each of the following:
 a $(x - 1)^2$ **b** $(x + 2)^2$ **c** $(x - 3)^2$ **d** $(-x + 3)^2$
 e $(-x - 2)^2$ **f** $(x - 5)^2$ **g** $\left(x - \frac{1}{2}\right)^2$ **h** $\left(x - \frac{3}{2}\right)^2$

2 Factorise each of the following:
 a $x^2 - 4x + 4$ **b** $x^2 - 12x + 36$ **c** $-x^2 + 4x - 4$ **d** $2x^2 - 8x + 8$
 e $-2x^2 + 12x - 18$ **f** $x^2 - x + \frac{1}{4}$ **g** $x^2 - 3x + \frac{9}{4}$ **h** $x^2 + 5x + \frac{25}{4}$

Example 25 **3** Solve each of the following equations for x by first completing the square:
 a $x^2 - 2x - 1 = 0$ **b** $x^2 - 4x - 2 = 0$ **c** $x^2 - 6x + 2 = 0$
 d $x^2 - 5x + 2 = 0$ **e** $2x^2 - 4x + 1 = 0$ **f** $3x^2 - 5x - 2 = 0$
 g $x^2 + 2x + k = 0$ **h** $kx^2 + 2x + k = 0$ **i** $x^2 - 3kx + 1 = 0$

Example 26 **4** Express each of the following in the form $y = a(x - h)^2 + k$ by completing the square. Hence state the coordinates of the turning point and sketch the graph in each case.
 a $y = x^2 - 2x + 3$ **b** $y = x^2 + 4x + 1$ **c** $y = x^2 - 3x + 1$

5 Express each of the following in the form $y = a(x - h)^2 + k$ by completing the square. Hence state the coordinates of the turning point and sketch the graph in each case.
 a $y = 2x^2 - 2x - 5$ **b** $y = 4x^2 + 8x + 8$ **c** $y = 3x^2 - 6x - 4$

Example 27 **6** Express each of the following in the form $y = a(x - h)^2 + k$ using the axis of symmetry. Hence state the coordinates of the turning point and sketch the graph in each case.
 a $y = x^2 - 8x + 12$ **b** $y = x^2 - x - 2$ **c** $y = 2x^2 + 4x - 2$
 d $y = -x^2 + 4x + 1$ **e** $y = -2x^2 - 12x - 12$ **f** $y = 3x^2 - 6x + 12$

3F Graphing quadratics in polynomial form

It is not always essential to convert a quadratic to turning point form in order to sketch its graph. We can sometimes find the *x*- and *y*-axis intercepts and the axis of symmetry from polynomial form by other methods and use these details to sketch the graph.

Step 1 **Find the *y*-axis intercept**

Let $x = 0$. For the general quadratic $y = ax^2 + bx + c$, this gives
$$y = a(0)^2 + b(0) + c$$
$$y = c$$

Hence the *y*-axis intercept is always equal to c.

Step 2 **Find the *x*-axis intercepts**

Let $y = 0$. In general, this gives
$$0 = ax^2 + bx + c$$

In order to solve such an equation it is necessary to factorise the right-hand side and then use the **null factor theorem**.

Step 3 **Find the equation of the axis of symmetry**

Once the *x*-axis intercepts have been found, the equation of the axis of symmetry can be found by using the symmetry properties of the parabola. The axis of symmetry is the perpendicular bisector of the line segment joining the *x*-axis intercepts.

Step 4 **Find the coordinates of the turning point**

The axis of symmetry gives the *x*-coordinate of the turning point. Substitute this into the quadratic polynomial to obtain the *y*-coordinate.

Example 28

Find the *x*- and *y*-axis intercepts and the turning point, and hence sketch the graph of $y = x^2 - 4x$.

Solution

Step 1 $c = 0$. Therefore the *y*-axis intercept is 0.

Step 2 Let $y = 0$. Then
$$0 = x^2 - 4x$$
$$0 = x(x - 4)$$
$$\therefore \quad x = 0 \text{ or } x = 4$$

The *x*-axis intercepts are 0 and 4.

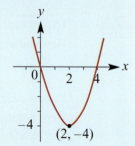

Step 3 The axis of symmetry is the line with equation $x = \dfrac{0 + 4}{2}$, that is, $x = 2$.

Step 4 When $x = 2$, $y = (2)^2 - 4(2) = -4$. The turning point has coordinates $(2, -4)$.

3F Graphing quadratics in polynomial form 107

Example 29

Find the x- and y-axis intercepts and the turning point, and hence sketch the graph of $y = x^2 - 9$.

Solution

Step 1 $c = -9$. Therefore the y-axis intercept is -9.

Step 2 Let $y = 0$. Then
$$0 = x^2 - 9$$
$$0 = (x + 3)(x - 3)$$
$$\therefore \quad x = -3 \text{ or } x = 3$$

The x-axis intercepts are -3 and 3.

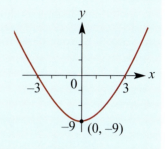

Step 3 The axis of symmetry is the line with equation
$x = \dfrac{-3 + 3}{2}$, that is, $x = 0$.

Step 4 When $x = 0$, $y = (0)^2 - 9$
$\qquad\qquad\qquad\quad = -9$

The turning point has coordinates $(0, -9)$.

Example 30

Find the x- and y-axis intercepts and the turning point, and hence sketch the graph of $y = x^2 + x - 12$.

Solution

Step 1 $c = -12$. Therefore the y-axis intercept is -12.

Step 2 Let $y = 0$. Then
$$0 = x^2 + x - 12$$
$$0 = (x + 4)(x - 3)$$
$$\therefore \quad x = -4 \text{ or } x = 3$$

The x-axis intercepts are -4 and 3.

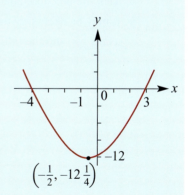

Step 3 The axis of symmetry is the line with equation
$x = \dfrac{-4 + 3}{2} = -\dfrac{1}{2}$

Step 4 When $x = -\dfrac{1}{2}$, $y = (-\dfrac{1}{2})^2 + (-\dfrac{1}{2}) - 12$
$\qquad\qquad\qquad\qquad = -12\dfrac{1}{4}$

The turning point has coordinates $(-\dfrac{1}{2}, -12\dfrac{1}{4})$.

Using the TI-Nspire

To graph the quadratic function with rule $y = x^2 + x - 12$:

- Enter the rule in the entry line of a **Graphs** application as shown, and press (enter).

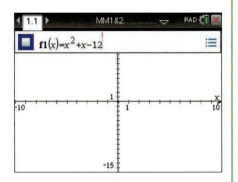

- Using (menu) > **Window/Zoom** > **Window Settings**, select the window settings $-10 \leq x \leq 10$ and $-15 \leq y \leq 15$ to obtain the graph shown.

Note: You can also double click on the end values to change the window settings.

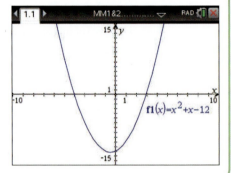

Using the Casio ClassPad

- Open the menu ; select **Graph & Table** .
- Type the expression $x^2 + x - 12$ in y1.
- Tick the box and tap the graph icon .
- It may be necessary to change the view window by using and the settings shown below.

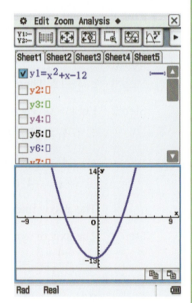

Section summary

Steps for sketching the graph of a quadratic function given in polynomial form:

Step 1 Find the y-axis intercept.
Step 2 Find the x-axis intercepts.
Step 3 Find the equation of the axis of symmetry.
Step 4 Find the coordinates of the turning point.

Exercise 3F

1 **a** A parabola has x-axis intercepts 4 and 10. State the x-coordinate of the vertex.
  b A parabola has x-axis intercepts 6 and 8. State the x-coordinate of the vertex.
  c A parabola has x-axis intercepts -6 and 8. State the x-coordinate of the vertex.

2 **a** A parabola has vertex $(2, -6)$ and one of the x-axis intercepts is at 6. Find the other x-axis intercept.
  b A parabola has vertex $(2, -6)$ and one of the x-axis intercepts is at -4. Find the other x-axis intercept.
  c A parabola has vertex $(2, -6)$ and one of the x-axis intercepts is at the origin. Find the other x-axis intercept.

Example 28, 29 **3** Sketch each of the following parabolas, clearly showing the axis intercepts and the turning point:

  a $y = x^2 - 1$
  b $y = x^2 + 6x$
  c $y = 25 - x^2$
  d $y = x^2 - 4$
  e $y = 2x^2 + 3x$
  f $y = 2x^2 - 4x$
  g $y = -2x^2 - 3x$
  h $y = x^2 + 1$

Example 30 **4** Sketch each of the following parabolas, clearly showing the axis intercepts and the turning point:

  a $y = x^2 + 3x - 10$
  b $y = x^2 - 5x + 4$
  c $y = x^2 + 2x - 3$
  d $y = x^2 + 4x + 3$
  e $y = 2x^2 - x - 1$
  f $y = 6 - x - x^2$
  g $y = -x^2 - 5x - 6$
  h $y = x^2 - 5x - 24$

3G Solving quadratic inequalities

Skillsheet In Chapter 1 we looked at solving linear inequalities. The situation is a little more complex for quadratic inequalities. We suggest one possible approach.

To solve a quadratic inequality (for example, $x^2 + x - 12 > 0$):

Step 1 Solve the corresponding equation (for example, $x^2 + x - 12 = 0$).

Step 2 Sketch the graph of the quadratic polynomial (for example, $y = x^2 + x - 12$).

Step 3 Use the graph to determine the set of x-values which satisfy the inequality.

Example 31

Solve $x^2 + x - 12 > 0$.

Solution

Step 1 Solve the equation
$$x^2 + x - 12 = 0$$
$$(x + 4)(x - 3) = 0$$
$$\therefore \quad x = -4 \text{ or } x = 3$$

Step 2 Sketch the graph of the quadratic
$y = x^2 + x - 12$.

Step 3 From the graph it can be seen that
$x^2 + x - 12 > 0$ when $x < -4$ or $x > 3$.

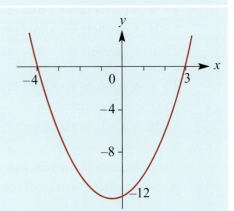

Using the TI-Nspire

The calculator may be used to solve quadratic inequalities.

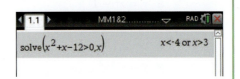

Using the Casio ClassPad

To solve the inequality $x^2 + x - 12 > 0$:

- Enter the inequality in the main screen $\sqrt{\alpha}$.
  (The inequality symbol can be found in the [Math3] keyboard.)
- Highlight the inequality using the stylus.
- Select **Interactive** > **Equation/Inequality** > **solve** and ensure the variable is x.
- Tap on OK to obtain the solution.

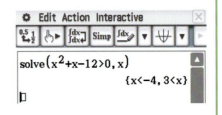

3G Solving quadratic inequalities

Section summary

When solving quadratic inequalities of the form $ax^2 + bx + c \leq 0$ (or with $\geq$, $>$ or $<$), it is best to sketch the graph of $y = ax^2 + bx + c$.

Exercise 3G

Example 31

1 a Solve the equation $x^2 - 2x - 8 = 0$.
   b Sketch the graph of $y = x^2 - 2x - 8$.
   c Solve the inequality $x^2 - 2x - 8 \leq 0$.
   d Solve the inequality $x^2 - 2x - 8 > 0$.

2 Solve each of the following inequalities:
   a $(x - 3)(x + 2) \geq 0$
   b $(x + 4)(x + 3) < 0$
   c $(2x - 1)(x + 4) \leq 0$
   d $(x - 6)(2x - 4) > 0$
   e $(2x - 6)(2x - 4) < 0$
   f $(7 - 2x)(2x - 3) \geq 0$
   g $(2x + 7)(2x - 4) < 0$
   h $(3x + 6)(2x - 5) \leq 0$
   i $(5 - 2x)(5 + x) < 0$
   j $(7 - 2x)(x + 2) \geq 0$
   k $(7 - 2x)(5x - 2) < 0$
   l $(11 - 2x)(5 - 2x) \geq 0$

3 Solve each of the following inequalities:
   a $(5 - x)(5 + x) < 0$
   b $4 - 9y^2 \geq 0$
   c $16 - y^2 < 0$
   d $36 - 25x^2 \geq 0$
   e $1 - 16y^2 \leq 0$
   f $25 - 36y^2 < 0$

4 Solve each of the following inequalities:
   a $x^2 + 2x - 8 \geq 0$
   b $x^2 - 5x - 24 < 0$
   c $x^2 - 4x - 12 \leq 0$
   d $2x^2 - 3x - 9 > 0$
   e $6x^2 + 13x < -6$
   f $-x^2 - 5x - 6 \geq 0$
   g $12x^2 + x > 6$
   h $10x^2 - 11x \leq -3$
   i $x(x - 1) \leq 20$
   j $4 + 5p - p^2 \geq 0$
   k $3 + 2y - y^2 < 0$
   l $x^2 + 3x \geq -2$

5 Solve each of the following inequalities:
   a $x^2 + 3x - 5 \geq 0$
   b $x^2 - 5x + 2 < 0$
   c $2x^2 - 3x - 1 \leq 0$
   d $8 - 3x - x^2 > 0$
   e $2x^2 + 7x + 1 < 0$
   f $2x^2 - 8x + 5 \geq 0$

6 Explain why $(x - 3)^2 \geq 0$ for all x.

7 Explain why $-(x - 1)^2 \leq 0$ for all x.

8 Complete the square for $x^2 + 2x + 7$ and hence show that $x^2 + 2x + 7 \geq 6$ for all x.

9 Complete the square for $-x^2 - 2x - 7$ and hence show that $-x^2 - 2x - 7 \leq -6$ for all x.

3H The general quadratic formula

Not all quadratics can be factorised by inspection, and it is often difficult to find the x-axis intercepts this way. There is a general formula for finding the solutions of a quadratic equation in polynomial form. This formula comes from 'completing the square' for the general quadratic.

In Section 3E we showed that

$$y = ax^2 + bx + c$$
$$= a\left(x + \frac{b}{2a}\right)^2 - \frac{b^2}{4a} + c$$

We can use this to solve the general quadratic equation:

$$ax^2 + bx + c = 0$$
$$a\left(x + \frac{b}{2a}\right)^2 - \frac{b^2}{4a} + c = 0$$
$$a\left(x + \frac{b}{2a}\right)^2 = \frac{b^2}{4a} - c$$

Now divide both sides by a:

$$\left(x + \frac{b}{2a}\right)^2 = \frac{b^2}{4a^2} - \frac{c}{a} = \frac{b^2 - 4ac}{4a^2}$$

$$x + \frac{b}{2a} = \pm\sqrt{\frac{b^2 - 4ac}{4a^2}}$$

$$\therefore \quad x = -\frac{b}{2a} \pm \sqrt{\frac{b^2 - 4ac}{4a^2}} = \frac{-b \pm \sqrt{b^2 - 4ac}}{2a}$$

> The solutions of the quadratic equation $ax^2 + bx + c = 0$, where $a \neq 0$, are given by the **quadratic formula**
>
> $$x = \frac{-b \pm \sqrt{b^2 - 4ac}}{2a}$$

Note: The quadratic formula provides an alternative method for solving quadratic equations to 'completing the square', but it is probably not as useful for curve sketching as 'completing the square', which gives the turning point coordinates directly.

It should be noted that the equation of the axis of symmetry can be derived from this general formula: the axis of symmetry is the line with equation

$$x = -\frac{b}{2a}$$

Also, from the formula it can be seen that:

- If $b^2 - 4ac > 0$, there are two solutions.
- If $b^2 - 4ac = 0$, there is one solution.
- If $b^2 - 4ac < 0$, there are no real solutions.

This will be further explored in the next section.

A CAS calculator gives the result shown opposite.

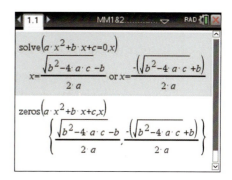

Example 32

Solve each of the following equations for x by using the quadratic formula:

a $x^2 - x - 1 = 0$ **b** $x^2 - 2kx - 3 = 0$

Solution

a $x^2 - x - 1 = 0$

Here $a = 1$, $b = -1$ and $c = -1$.
The formula gives

$$x = \frac{-(-1) \pm \sqrt{(-1)^2 - 4 \times 1 \times (-1)}}{2 \times 1}$$

$$= \frac{1 \pm \sqrt{5}}{2}$$

b $x^2 - 2kx - 3 = 0$

Here $a = 1$, $b = -2k$ and $c = -3$.
The formula gives

$$x = \frac{-(-2k) \pm \sqrt{(-2k)^2 - 4 \times 1 \times (-3)}}{2 \times 1}$$

$$= \frac{2k \pm \sqrt{4k^2 + 12}}{2}$$

$$= k \pm \sqrt{k^2 + 3}$$

Explanation

$$x = \frac{-b \pm \sqrt{b^2 - 4ac}}{2a}$$

Note that $k^2 + 3 \geq 0$ for all values of k, since $k^2 \geq 0$.

Using the TI-Nspire

- Use menu > **Algebra** > **Solve** to solve the equation $x^2 - 2kx - 3 = 0$ for x.
- Alternatively, use menu > **Algebra** > **Zeros**.

Note: You must use a multiplication sign between the k and x.

Using the Casio ClassPad

To solve the equation $x^2 - 2kx - 3 = 0$ for x:

- Enter and highlight the equation. (Use the Var keyboard to enter the variables.)
- Select **Interactive** > **Equation/Inequality** > **solve** and set the variable to x.

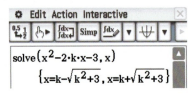
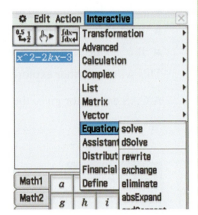

Example 33

Sketch the graph of $y = -3x^2 - 12x - 7$. Use the quadratic formula to calculate the x-axis intercepts.

Solution

Since $c = -7$, the y-axis intercept is -7.

Axis of symmetry $\quad x = -\dfrac{b}{2a}$

$$= -\left(\dfrac{-12}{2 \times (-3)}\right)$$

$$= -2$$

Turning point

When $x = -2$, $y = -3(-2)^2 - 12(-2) - 7 = 5$. The turning point coordinates are $(-2, 5)$.

x-axis intercepts

$-3x^2 - 12x - 7 = 0$

$x = \dfrac{-b \pm \sqrt{b^2 - 4ac}}{2a}$

$= \dfrac{-(-12) \pm \sqrt{(-12)^2 - 4(-3)(-7)}}{2(-3)}$

$= \dfrac{12 \pm \sqrt{60}}{-6}$

$= \dfrac{12 \pm 2\sqrt{15}}{-6}$

$= -2 \mp \tfrac{1}{3}\sqrt{15}$

≈ -3.29 or -0.71 (to two decimal places)

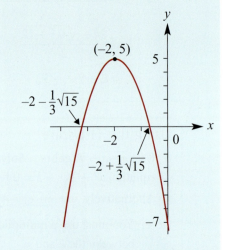

Section summary

The solutions of the quadratic equation $ax^2 + bx + c = 0$, where $a \neq 0$, are given by the **quadratic formula**

$$x = \frac{-b \pm \sqrt{b^2 - 4ac}}{2a}$$

From the formula it can be seen that:
- If $b^2 - 4ac > 0$, there are two solutions.
- If $b^2 - 4ac = 0$, there is one solution.
- If $b^2 - 4ac < 0$, there are no real solutions.

Exercise 3H

1 For each of the following, the coefficients a, b and c of a quadratic $y = ax^2 + bx + c$ are given. Find:

  i $b^2 - 4ac$ **ii** $\sqrt{b^2 - 4ac}$ in simplest surd form

  a $a = 2$, $b = 4$ and $c = -3$
  b $a = 1$, $b = 10$ and $c = 18$
  c $a = 1$, $b = 10$ and $c = -18$
  d $a = -1$, $b = 6$ and $c = 15$
  e $a = 1$, $b = 9$ and $c = -27$

2 Simplify each of the following:

  a $\dfrac{2 + 2\sqrt{5}}{2}$
  b $\dfrac{9 - 3\sqrt{5}}{6}$
  c $\dfrac{5 + 5\sqrt{5}}{10}$
  d $\dfrac{6 + 12\sqrt{2}}{6}$

Example 32   **3** Solve each of the following for x. Give exact answers.

  a $x^2 + 6x = 4$
  b $x^2 - 7x - 3 = 0$
  c $2x^2 - 5x + 2 = 0$
  d $2x^2 + 4x - 7 = 0$
  e $2x^2 + 8x = 1$
  f $5x^2 - 10x = 1$
  g $-2x^2 + 4x - 1 = 0$
  h $2x^2 + x = 3$
  i $2.5x^2 + 3x + 0.3 = 0$
  j $-0.6x^2 - 1.3x = 0.1$
  k $2kx^2 - 4x + k = 0$
  l $2(1 - k)x^2 - 4kx + k = 0$

Example 33   **4** Sketch the graphs of the following parabolas. Use the quadratic formula to find the x-axis intercepts (if they exist) and the axis of symmetry and, hence, the turning point.

  a $y = x^2 + 5x - 1$
  b $y = 2x^2 - 3x - 1$
  c $y = -x^2 - 3x + 1$
  d $y + 4 = x^2 + 2x$
  e $y = 4x^2 + 5x + 1$
  f $y = -3x^2 + 4x - 2$
  g $y = -x^2 + 5x + 6$
  h $y = 4x^2 - 3x + 2$
  i $y = 3x^2 - x - 4$

3I The discriminant

Skillsheet In the previous section we found that the solutions to the quadratic equation $ax^2 + bx + c = 0$ are given by

$$x = \frac{-b \pm \sqrt{b^2 - 4ac}}{2a}$$

The expression under the square root sign is called the **discriminant**. We write

$$\Delta = b^2 - 4ac$$

▶ The number of x-axis intercepts

There are three different possibilities for the number of x-axis intercepts of a parabola:

- zero – the graph is either all above or all below the x-axis
- one – the graph touches the x-axis and the turning point is the x-axis intercept
- two – the graph crosses the x-axis.

For a parabola $y = ax^2 + bx + c$, we can use the discriminant $\Delta = b^2 - 4ac$ to determine when each of these three situations occur.

- If the discriminant $b^2 - 4ac < 0$, then the equation $ax^2 + bx + c = 0$ has no solutions and the corresponding parabola will have no x-axis intercepts.

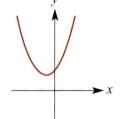

- If the discriminant $b^2 - 4ac = 0$, then the equation $ax^2 + bx + c = 0$ has one solution and the corresponding parabola will have one x-axis intercept. (We sometimes say the equation has two coincident solutions.)

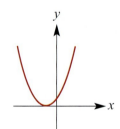

- If the discriminant $b^2 - 4ac > 0$, then the equation $ax^2 + bx + c = 0$ has two solutions and the corresponding parabola will have two x-axis intercepts.

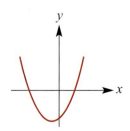

Example 34

Find the discriminant of each of the following quadratics and state whether the graph of each crosses the x-axis, touches the x-axis or does not intersect the x-axis.

a $y = x^2 - 6x + 8$ **b** $y = x^2 - 8x + 16$ **c** $y = 2x^2 - 3x + 4$

Solution

a Discriminant $\Delta = b^2 - 4ac$
$= (-6)^2 - (4 \times 1 \times 8)$
$= 4$

As $\Delta > 0$, the graph intersects the x-axis at two distinct points, i.e. there are two distinct solutions of the equation $x^2 - 6x + 8 = 0$.

b $\Delta = b^2 - 4ac$
$= (-8)^2 - (4 \times 1 \times 16)$
$= 0$

As $\Delta = 0$, the graph touches the x-axis, i.e. there is one solution of the equation $x^2 - 8x + 16 = 0$.

c $\Delta = b^2 - 4ac$
$= (-3)^2 - (4 \times 2 \times 4)$
$= -23$

As $\Delta < 0$, the graph does not intersect the x-axis, i.e. there are no real solutions for the equation $2x^2 - 3x + 4 = 0$.

Example 35

Find the values of m for which the equation $3x^2 - 2mx + 3 = 0$ has:

a one solution **b** no solution **c** two distinct solutions.

Solution

For the quadratic $3x^2 - 2mx + 3$, the discriminant is $\Delta = 4m^2 - 36$.

a For one solution:
$\Delta = 0$
i.e. $4m^2 - 36 = 0$
$m^2 = 9$
$\therefore \quad m = \pm 3$

b For no solution:
$\Delta < 0$
i.e. $4m^2 - 36 < 0$

From the graph, this is equivalent to
$-3 < m < 3$

c For two distinct solutions:
$\Delta > 0$
i.e. $4m^2 - 36 > 0$

From the graph it can be seen that
$m > 3$ or $m < -3$

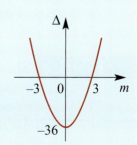

▶ The nature of the solutions of a quadratic equation

The discriminant can be used to assist in the identification of the particular type of solution for a quadratic equation $ax^2 + bx + c = 0$.

For a, b and c rational numbers:

- If $\Delta = b^2 - 4ac$ is a perfect square and $\Delta \neq 0$, then the quadratic equation has two rational solutions.
- If $\Delta = b^2 - 4ac = 0$, then the quadratic equation has one rational solution.
- If $\Delta = b^2 - 4ac$ is not a perfect square and $\Delta > 0$, then the quadratic equation has two irrational solutions.

Example 36

Show that the solutions of the equation $3x^2 + (m - 3)x - m = 0$ are rational for all rational values of m.

Solution

$$\begin{aligned}\Delta &= (m - 3)^2 - 4 \times 3 \times (-m) \\ &= m^2 - 6m + 9 + 12m \\ &= m^2 + 6m + 9 \\ &= (m + 3)^2 \geq 0 \quad \text{for all } m\end{aligned}$$

Furthermore, Δ is a perfect square for all m.

Section summary

The **discriminant** Δ of a quadratic polynomial $ax^2 + bx + c$ is

$$\Delta = b^2 - 4ac$$

For the equation $ax^2 + bx + c = 0$:

- If $\Delta > 0$, there are two solutions.
- If $\Delta = 0$, there is one solution.
- If $\Delta < 0$, there are no real solutions.

For the equation $ax^2 + bx + c = 0$ where a, b and c are rational numbers:

- If Δ is a perfect square and $\Delta \neq 0$, then the equation has two rational solutions.
- If $\Delta = 0$, then the equation has one rational solution.
- If Δ is not a perfect square and $\Delta > 0$, then the equation has two irrational solutions.

Exercise 3I

1 Determine the discriminant of each of the following quadratics:

   a $x^2 + 2x - 4$ **b** $x^2 + 2x + 4$ **c** $x^2 + 3x - 4$

   d $2x^2 + 3x - 4$ **e** $-2x^2 + 3x + 4$

Example 34 2 Without sketching the graphs of the following quadratics, determine whether they cross or touch the x-axis:
   a $y = x^2 - 5x + 2$
   b $y = -4x^2 + 2x - 1$
   c $y = x^2 - 6x + 9$
   d $y = 8 - 3x - 2x^2$
   e $y = 3x^2 + 2x + 5$
   f $y = -x^2 - x - 1$

3 By examining the discriminant, find the number of distinct solutions of:
   a $x^2 + 8x + 7 = 0$
   b $3x^2 + 8x + 7 = 0$
   c $10x^2 - x - 3 = 0$
   d $2x^2 + 8x - 7 = 0$
   e $3x^2 - 8x - 7 = 0$
   f $10x^2 - x + 3 = 0$

4 By examining the discriminant, state the nature and number of distinct solutions for each of the following:
   a $9x^2 - 24x + 16 = 0$
   b $-x^2 - 5x - 6 = 0$
   c $x^2 - x - 4 = 0$
   d $25x^2 - 20x + 4 = 0$
   e $6x^2 - 3x - 2 = 0$
   f $x^2 + 3x + 2 = 0$

Example 35 5 Find the values of m for which each of the following equations:
   i has no solutions   ii has one solution   iii has two distinct solutions.
   a $x^2 - 4mx + 20 = 0$
   b $mx^2 - 3mx + 3 = 0$
   c $5x^2 - 5mx - m = 0$
   d $x^2 + 4mx - 4(m - 2) = 0$

Example 36 6 For m and n rational numbers show that $mx^2 + (2m + n)x + 2n = 0$ has rational solutions.

7 Find the values of p for which the equation $px^2 + 2(p + 2)x + p + 7 = 0$ has no real solution.

8 Find the values of p for which the equation $(1 - 2p)x^2 + 8px - (2 + 8p) = 0$ has one solution.

9 Find the value(s) of p for which:
   a $px^2 - 6x + p = 0$ has one solution
   b $2x^2 - 4x + 3 = p$ has two solutions
   c $3x^2 = 2x + p - 1$ has two solutions
   d $x^2 - 2x + 2 = p$ has two solutions.

10 Find the values of p for which the graph of $y = px^2 + 8x + p - 6$ crosses the x-axis.

11 Show that the equation $(p^2 + 1)x^2 + 2pqx + q^2 = 0$ has no real solution for any values of p and q ($q \neq 0$).

12 a Find the discriminant of $x^2 + 4mx + 24m - 44$.
   b Show the equation $x^2 + 4mx + 24m - 44 = 0$ has a solution for all values of m.

13 a Find the discriminant of $4mx^2 + 4(m - 1)x + m - 2$.
   b Show the equation $4mx^2 + 4(m - 1)x + m - 2 = 0$ has a solution for all values of m.

14 Find the discriminant of the equation $4x^2 + (m - 4)x - m = 0$, where m is a rational number, and hence show that the equation has rational solution(s).

15 Find the discriminant of the equation $x^2 - (m + 2n)x + 2mn = 0$, where m and n are rational numbers, and hence show that the equation has rational solution(s).

16 If both a and c are positive, what can be said about the graph of $y = ax^2 + bx - c$?

17 If a is negative and c is positive, what can be said about the graph of $y = ax^2 + bx + c$?

3J Solving simultaneous linear and quadratic equations

As discussed in Section 2H, when solving simultaneous linear equations we are actually finding the point of intersection of the two corresponding linear graphs.

If we wish to find the point or points of intersection between a straight line and a parabola, we can solve the equations simultaneously.

It should be noted that depending on whether the straight line intersects, touches or does not intersect the parabola we may get two, one or zero points of intersection.

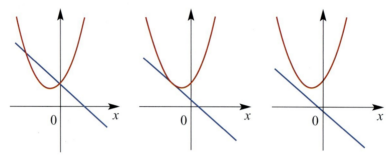

Two points of intersection   One point of intersection   No point of intersection

If there is one point of intersection between the parabola and the straight line, then the line is a **tangent** to the parabola.

As we usually have the quadratic equation written with y as the subject, it is necessary to have the linear equation written with y as the subject. Then the linear expression for y can be substituted into the quadratic equation.

Example 37

Find the points of intersection of the line with equation $y = -2x + 4$ and the parabola with equation $y = x^2 - 8x + 12$.

Solution

At the point of intersection:

$$x^2 - 8x + 12 = -2x + 4$$
$$x^2 - 6x + 8 = 0$$
$$(x - 2)(x - 4) = 0$$

Hence $x = 2$ or $x = 4$.

When $x = 2$, $y = -2(2) + 4 = 0$.

When $x = 4$, $y = -2(4) + 4 = -4$.

Therefore the points of intersection are $(2, 0)$ and $(4, -4)$.

The result can be shown graphically.

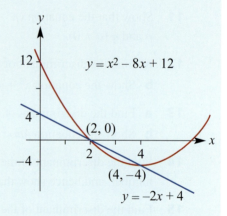

3J Solving simultaneous linear and quadratic equations

Using the TI-Nspire

To solve the simultaneous equations
$y = -2x + 4$ and $y = x^2 - 8x + 12$:

- Use menu > **Algebra** > **Solve System of Equations** > **Solve System of Equations**.
- Press enter to accept the default settings of two equations with variables x and y, and then complete the template as shown.

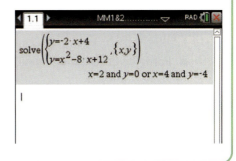

Using the Casio ClassPad

- In the $\sqrt{\alpha}$ Main screen, turn on the keyboard and select the simultaneous equations icon from Math1.
- Enter the simultaneous equations

$$y = -2x + 4$$
$$y = x^2 - 8x + 12$$

into the two lines, and enter x, y as the variables.
- Tap EXE.

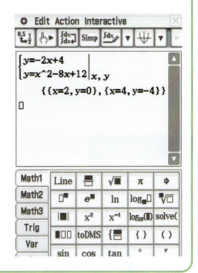

Example 38

Prove that the straight line with the equation $y = 1 - x$ meets the parabola with the equation $y = x^2 - 3x + 2$ once only.

Solution

At the point of intersection:

$$x^2 - 3x + 2 = 1 - x$$
$$x^2 - 2x + 1 = 0$$
$$(x - 1)^2 = 0$$

Therefore $x = 1$ and $y = 1 - 1 = 0$.

The straight line just touches the parabola at $(1, 0)$.

This can be illustrated graphically.

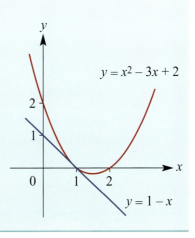

Section summary

To find the points of intersection of a straight line $y = mx + c_2$ and a parabola $y = ax^2 + bx + c_1$:

- Form the quadratic equation
$$ax^2 + bx + c_1 = mx + c_2$$
- Rearrange the equation so that the right-hand side is zero:
$$ax^2 + (b - m)x + (c_1 - c_2) = 0$$
- Solve the equation for x and substitute these x-values into the equation of the line to find the corresponding y-values.

The discriminant applied to the second equation, $ax^2 + (b - m)x + (c_1 - c_2) = 0$, can be used to determine the number of intersection points:

- If $\Delta > 0$, there are two intersection points.
- If $\Delta = 0$, there is one intersection point.
- If $\Delta < 0$, there are no intersection points.

Exercise 3J

1 *Example 37*

   a Find the points of intersection of the line with equation $y = x - 2$ and the parabola with equation $y = x^2 - x - 6$.

   b Find the points of intersection of the line with equation $x + y = 6$ and the parabola with equation $y = x^2$.

   c Find the points of intersection of the line with equation $5x + 4y = 21$ and the parabola with equation $y = x^2$.

   d Find the points of intersection of the line with equation $y = 2x + 1$ and the parabola with equation $y = x^2 - x + 3$.

2 Solve each of the following pairs of equations:

   a $y = x^2 + 2x - 8$
   $y = 2 - x$

   b $y = x^2 - x - 3$
   $y = 4x - 7$

   c $y = x^2 + x - 5$
   $y = -x - 2$

   d $y = x^2 + 6x + 6$
   $y = 2x + 3$

   e $y = 6 - x - x^2$
   $y = -2x - 2$

   f $y = x^2 + x + 6$
   $y = 6x + 8$

3 *Example 38* Prove that, for each of the following pairs of equations, the straight line meets the parabola only once:

   a $y = x^2 - 6x + 8$
   $y = -2x + 4$

   b $y = x^2 - 2x + 6$
   $y = 4x - 3$

   c $y = 2x^2 + 11x + 10$
   $y = 3x + 2$

   d $y = x^2 + 7x + 4$
   $y = -x - 12$

4 Solve each of the following pairs of equations:
  a $y = x^2 - 6x$
     $y = 8 + x$
  b $y = 3x^2 + 9x$
     $y = 32 - x$
  c $y = 5x^2 + 9x$
     $y = 12 - 2x$
  d $y = -3x^2 + 32x$
     $y = 32 - 3x$
  e $y = 2x^2 - 12$
     $y = 3(x - 4)$
  f $y = 11x^2$
     $y = 21 - 6x$

5 a Find the value of c such that $y = x + c$ is a tangent to the parabola $y = x^2 - x - 12$.
      Hint: Consider the discriminant of the resulting quadratic.
   b i Sketch the parabola with equation $y = -2x^2 - 6x + 2$.
      ii Find the values of m for which the straight line $y = mx + 6$ is tangent to the parabola. Hint: Use the discriminant of the resulting quadratic.

6 a Find the value of c such that the line with equation $y = 2x + c$ is tangent to the parabola with equation $y = x^2 + 3x$.
   b Find the possible values of c such that the line with equation $y = 2x + c$ twice intersects the parabola with equation $y = x^2 + 3x$.

7 Find the value(s) of a such that the line with equation $y = x$ is tangent to the parabola with equation $y = x^2 + ax + 1$.

8 Find the value of b such that the line with equation $y = -x$ is tangent to the parabola with equation $y = x^2 + x + b$.

9 Find the equation of the straight line(s) which pass through the point $(1, -2)$ and is (are) tangent to the parabola with equation $y = x^2$.

3K Families of quadratic polynomial functions

Skillsheet In Chapter 2 we considered the information that is necessary to determine the equation of a straight line and we also studied families of straight lines. In this section these two ideas are extended for our study of quadratic polynomials.

▶ Families of quadratics

Here are some examples of families of quadratic polynomial functions:

$y = ax^2$, $a \neq 0$	The parabolas with their vertices at the origin.
$y = a(x - 2)^2 + 3$, $a \neq 0$	The parabolas with turning point at $(2, 3)$.
$y = a(x - 2)(x + 5)$, $a \neq 0$	The parabolas with x-axis intercepts 2 and -5.
$y = a(x - h)(x - 2)$, $a \neq 0$	The parabolas with x-axis intercept 2.
$y = ax^2 + bx$, $a \neq 0$ and $b \neq 0$	The parabolas with two x-axis intercepts, one of which is the origin.

We recall from Chapter 2 that the letters *a*, *b* and *h* are called parameters. Varying the parameter produces different parabolas. For example, for $y = ax^2 + bx$ some possible curves are shown below.

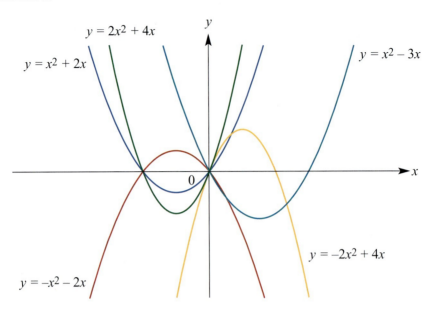

Example 39

A family of parabolas have rules of the form $y = ax^2 + c$. For the parabola in this family that passes through the points $(1, 7)$ and $(2, 10)$, find the values of a and c.

Solution

When $x = 1$, $y = 7$ and when $x = 2$, $y = 10$.

$7 = a + c$ (1)

$10 = 4a + c$ (2)

Subtract (1) from (2):

$3 = 3a$ and hence $a = 1$.

Substitute in (1):

$7 = 1 + c$ and therefore $c = 6$.

The equation is $y = x^2 + 6$.

Explanation

Substitute $x = 1$, $y = 7$ in the equation $y = ax^2 + c$ to obtain (1).

Substitute $x = 2$, $y = 10$ in the equation $y = ax^2 + c$ to obtain (2).

Example 40

A family of parabolas have rules of the form $y = ax^2 + bx + 2$, where $a \neq 0$.

a For a parabola in this family with its turning point on the *x*-axis, find *a* in terms of *b*.

b If the turning point is at $(4, 0)$, find the values of *a* and *b*.

Solution

a The discriminant $\Delta = b^2 - 8a$.

We have $\Delta = 0$ and therefore $a = \dfrac{b^2}{8}$.

b We have $-\dfrac{b}{2a} = 4$, which implies $b = -8a$.

From part a, we have $a = \dfrac{b^2}{8}$.

Hence $a = \dfrac{64a^2}{8} = 8a^2$.

Thus $a(1 - 8a) = 0$ and, since $a \neq 0$, $a = \tfrac{1}{8}$.

Substituting for a in $b = -8a$ gives $b = -1$.

Explanation

The discriminant of $ax^2 + bx + c$ is $\Delta = b^2 - 4ac$. In this case $c = 2$.

The discriminant $\Delta = 0$ since the parabola touches the x-axis at its turning point.

The axis of symmetry has equation $x = -\dfrac{b}{2a}$.

▶ **Determining quadratic rules**

At the beginning of this section we looked at different families of quadratic polynomial functions. We now consider three important such families which can be used as a basis for finding a quadratic rule from given information. These are certainly not the only useful forms. You will see others in the worked examples.

1 $y = a(x - e)(x - f)$ This can be used if two x-axis intercepts and the coordinates of one other point are known.

2 $y = a(x - h)^2 + k$ This can be used if the coordinates of the turning point and one other point are known.

3 $y = ax^2 + bx + c$ This can be used if the coordinates of three points on the parabola are known.

Example 41

A parabola has x-axis intercepts -3 and 4 and it passes through the point $(1, 24)$. Find the rule for this parabola.

Solution

$y = a(x + 3)(x - 4)$

When $x = 1$, $y = 24$.

Therefore $24 = a(1 + 3)(1 - 4)$

$24 = -12a$

$a = -2$

The rule is $y = -2(x + 3)(x - 4)$.

Explanation

Two x-axis intercepts are given. Therefore use the form $y = a(x - e)(x - f)$.

Example 42

The coordinates of the turning point of a parabola are $(2, 6)$ and the parabola passes through the point $(3, 3)$. Find the rule for this parabola.

Solution

$y = a(x - 2)^2 + 6$

When $x = 3$, $y = 3$.

Therefore

$3 = a(3 - 2)^2 + 6$

$3 = a + 6$

$a = -3$

The rule is $y = -3(x - 2)^2 + 6$.

Explanation

The coordinates of the turning point and one other point on the parabola are given. Therefore use $y = a(x - h)^2 + k$.

Example 43

A parabola passes through the points $(1, 4)$, $(0, 5)$ and $(-1, 10)$. Find the rule for this parabola.

Solution

$y = ax^2 + bx + c$

When $x = 1$, $y = 4$.
When $x = 0$, $y = 5$.
When $x = -1$, $y = 10$.

$4 = a + b + c$ (1)

$5 = c$ (2)

$10 = a - b + c$ (3)

Substitute from equation (2) into equations (1) and (3):

$-1 = a + b$ (1′)

$5 = a - b$ (3′)

Add (1′) and (3′):

$4 = 2a$

$a = 2$

Using equation (1′), we obtain $b = -3$.

The rule is $y = 2x^2 - 3x + 5$.

Explanation

The coordinates of three points on the parabola are given. Therefore substitute values into the polynomial form $y = ax^2 + bx + c$ to obtain three equations in three unknowns.

Example 44

Determine the quadratic rule for each of the following parabolas:

a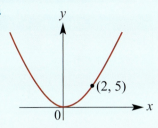

b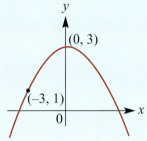

c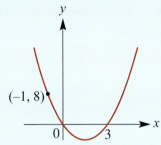

d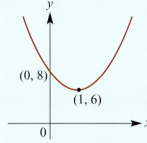

Solution

a This is of the form $y = ax^2$

For $(2, 5)$: $\quad 5 = 4a$

$\quad \therefore a = \dfrac{5}{4}$

Hence the rule is $\quad y = \dfrac{5}{4}x^2$

b This is of the form $y = ax^2 + c$

For $(0, 3)$: $\quad 3 = a(0) + c$

$\quad \therefore c = 3$

For $(-3, 1)$: $\quad 1 = a(-3)^2 + 3$

$\quad 1 = 9a + 3$

$\quad \therefore a = -\dfrac{2}{9}$

Hence the rule is $\quad y = -\dfrac{2}{9}x^2 + 3$

c This is of the form $y = ax(x - 3)$

For $(-1, 8)$: $\quad 8 = -a(-1 - 3)$

$\quad 8 = 4a$

$\quad \therefore a = 2$

Hence the rule is $\quad y = 2x(x - 3)$

$\quad y = 2x^2 - 6x$

d This is of the form $y = a(x - 1)^2 + 6$

For $(0, 8)$: $\quad 8 = a + 6$

$\quad \therefore a = 2$

Hence the rule is $\quad y = 2(x - 1)^2 + 6$

$\quad y = 2(x^2 - 2x + 1) + 6$

$\quad y = 2x^2 - 4x + 8$

Using the TI-Nspire

The equation $y = ax^2 + bx + 2$ and the two points $(-1, 0)$ and $(1, 2)$ are used to generate equations in a and b. These equations are then solved simultaneously to find a and b.

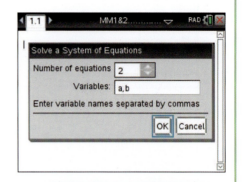

You can either substitute the values for x, y prior to entering or substitute in the command line as shown.

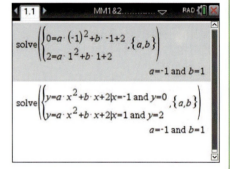

Using the Casio ClassPad

Substituting the points $(-1, 0)$ and $(1, 2)$ in the equation $y = ax^2 + bx + 2$ generates two equations in a and b.

These equations are then solved simultaneously to find a and b.

Note: To substitute $x = -1$ into $ax^2 + bx + 2 = 0$, use the symbol | found in Math2. Remember to use Var to enter the variables a and b.

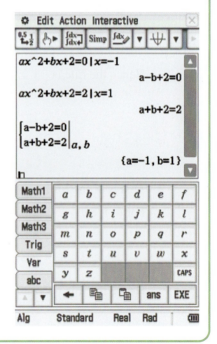

Section summary

To find a quadratic rule to fit given points, first choose the best form of quadratic expression to work with. Then substitute in the coordinates of the known points to determine the unknown parameters. Some possible forms are given here:

i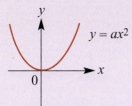

One point is needed to determine a.

ii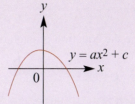

Two points are needed to determine a and c.

iii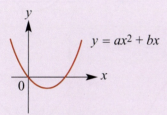

Two points are needed to determine a and b.

iv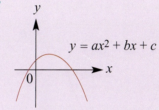

Three points are needed to determine a, b and c.

Exercise 3K

Example 39   **1**   A family of parabolas have rules of the form $y = ax^2 + c$. For the parabola in this family that passes through the points $(-1, 2)$ and $(0, 6)$, find the values of a and c.

Example 40   **2**   A family of parabolas have rules of the form $y = ax^2 + bx + 4$, where $a \neq 0$.
     a Find the discriminant of the quadratic polynomial $ax^2 + bx + 4$.
     b For a parabola in this family with its turning point on the x-axis, find a in terms of b.
     c If the turning point is at $(-4, 0)$, find the values of a and b.

Example 41   **3**   **a** A parabola has x-axis intercepts -2 and 6 and it passes through the point $(1, -30)$. Find the rule for this parabola.

Example 42   **b** The coordinates of the turning point of a parabola are $(-2, 4)$ and the parabola passes through the point $(3, -46)$. Find the rule for this parabola.

Example 43   **c** A parabola passes through the points $(1, -2)$, $(0, -3)$ and $(-1, -6)$. Find the rule for this parabola.

4   A quadratic rule for a particular parabola is of the form $y = ax^2$. The parabola passes through the point with coordinates $(2, 8)$. Find the value of a.

5 A quadratic rule for a particular parabola is of the form $y = ax^2 + bx$. The parabola passes through the point with coordinates $(-1, 4)$ and one of its x-axis intercepts is 6. Find the values of a and b.

6 A quadratic rule for a particular parabola is of the form $y = a(x - b)^2 + c$. The parabola has vertex $(1, 6)$ and passes through the point with coordinates $(2, 4)$. Find the values of a, b and c.

Example 44

7 Determine the equation of each of the following parabolas:

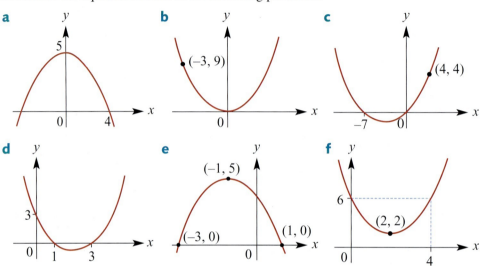

8 A parabola has vertex with coordinates $(-1, 3)$ and passes through the point with coordinates $(3, 8)$. Find the equation for the parabola.

9 A parabola has x-axis intercepts 6 and -3 and passes through the point $(1, 10)$. Find the equation of the parabola.

10 A parabola has vertex with coordinates $(-1, 3)$ and y-axis intercept 4. Find the equation for the parabola.

11 Assuming that the suspension cable shown in the diagram forms a parabola, find the rule which describes its shape. The minimum height of the cable above the roadway is 30 m.

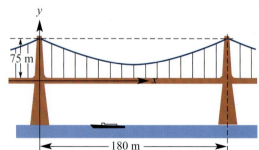

12 A parabola has the same shape as $y = 2x^2$, but its turning point is $(1, -2)$. Write its equation.

13 A parabola has its vertex at $(1, -2)$ and passes through the point $(3, 2)$. Write its equation.

14 Which of the curves could be most nearly defined by each of the following?

 a $y = \frac{1}{3}(x+4)(8-x)$
 b $y = x^2 - x + 2$
 c $y = -10 + 2(x-1)^2$
 d $y = \frac{1}{2}(9 - x^2)$

A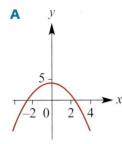
B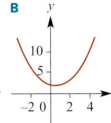
C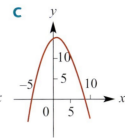
D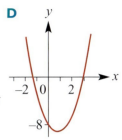

15 A family of parabolas satisfies the rule $y = ax^2 + 2x + a$.

 a Express $ax^2 + 2x + a$ in the form $a(x+b)^2 + c$ for real numbers b and c.
 b Give the coordinates of the turning point of the graph of $y = ax^2 + 2x + a$ in terms of a.
 c For which values of a is $ax^2 + 2x + a$ a perfect square?
 d For which values of a does the graph of $y = ax^2 + 2x + a$ have two x-axis intercepts?

16 A parabola has its vertex at $(2, 2)$ and passes through $(4, -6)$. Write its equation.

17 Write down four quadratic rules that have graphs similar to those in the diagram.

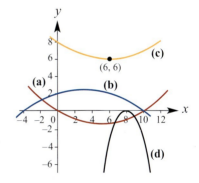

18 Find quadratic expressions which could represent the two curves in this diagram, given that the coefficient of x is 1 in each case. The labelled points are $A(2, 3)$, $B(2, 1)$, $C(0, -5)$ and $D(0, 2)$.

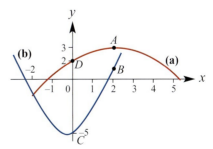

19 The rate of rainfall during a storm t hours after it began was 3 mm per hour when $t = 5$, 6 mm per hour when $t = 9$ and 5 mm per hour when $t = 13$. Assuming that a quadratic model applies, find an expression for the rate of rainfall, r mm per hour, in terms of t.

20 **a** Which of the graphs shown below could represent the equation $y = (x-4)^2 - 3$?
b Which graph could represent $y = 3 - (x-4)^2$?

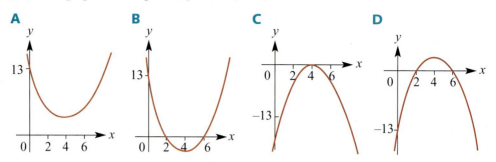

21 Find the equation of the quadratic which passes through the points with coordinates:

a $(-2, -1)$, $(1, 2)$, $(3, -16)$ **b** $(-1, -2)$, $(1, -4)$, $(3, 10)$
c $(-3, 5)$, $(3, 20)$, $(5, 57)$

3L Quadratic models

Skillsheet — In this section it is shown how quadratics can be used to solve worded problems, including problems which involve finding the maximum or minimum value of a quadratic polynomial that has been used to model a 'practical' situation.

Example 45

Jenny wishes to fence off a rectangular vegetable garden in her backyard. She has 20 m of fencing wire which she will use to fence three sides of the garden, with the existing timber fence forming the fourth side. Calculate the maximum area she can enclose.

Solution

Let A = area of the rectangular garden
x = length of the garden

Then width = $\dfrac{20 - x}{2} = 10 - \dfrac{x}{2}$

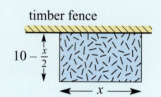

Therefore

$A = x\left(10 - \dfrac{x}{2}\right)$

$= 10x - \dfrac{x^2}{2}$

$= -\dfrac{1}{2}(x^2 - 20x + 100 - 100)$

(completing the square)

$= -\dfrac{1}{2}(x^2 - 20x + 100) + 50$

$= -\dfrac{1}{2}(x - 10)^2 + 50$

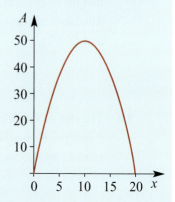

Hence the maximum area is 50 m² when $x = 10$.

Example 46

A cricket ball is thrown by a fielder. It leaves his hand at a height of 2 metres above the ground and the wicketkeeper takes the ball 60 metres away again at a height of 2 metres. It is known that after the ball has gone 25 metres it is 15 metres above the ground. The path of the cricket ball is a parabola with equation $y = ax^2 + bx + c$.

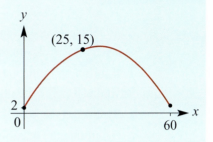

a Find the values of a, b and c.
b Find the maximum height of the ball above the ground.
c Find the height of the ball when it is 5 metres horizontally before it hits the wicket-keeper's gloves.

Solution

a The data can be used to obtain three equations:

$$2 = c \quad (1)$$
$$15 = (25)^2 a + 25b + c \quad (2)$$
$$2 = (60)^2 a + 60b + c \quad (3)$$

Substitute equation (1) in equations (2) and (3):

$$13 = 625a + 25b \quad (2')$$
$$0 = 3600a + 60b \quad (3')$$

Simplify (3') by dividing both sides by 60:

$$0 = 60a + b \quad (3')$$

Multiply this by 25 and subtract from equation (2'):

$$13 = -875a$$

$$\therefore a = -\frac{13}{875} \quad \text{and} \quad b = \frac{156}{175}$$

The path of the ball has equation

$$y = -\frac{13}{875}x^2 + \frac{156}{175}x + 2$$

b The maximum height occurs when $x = 30$ and $y = \frac{538}{35}$.

$\therefore$ maximum height is $\frac{538}{35}$ m.

c When $x = 55$, $y = \frac{213}{35}$.

$\therefore$ height of the ball is $\frac{213}{35}$ m.

Exercise 3L

1 A farmer has 60 m of fencing with which to construct three sides of a rectangular yard connected to an existing fence.

    a If the width of the yard is x m and the area inside the yard is A m², write down the rule connecting A and x.
    b Sketch the graph of A against x.
    c Determine the maximum area that can be formed for the yard.

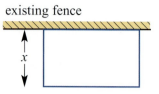

2 A rectangle has a perimeter of 20 m. Let x m be the length of one side. Find a formula for the area A of the rectangle in terms of x. Hence find the maximum area A.

3 The efficiency rating, E, of a particular spark plug when the gap is set at x mm is said to be $400(x - x^2)$.

    a Sketch the graph of E against x for $0 \leq x \leq 1$.
    b What values of x give a zero efficiency rating?
    c What value of x gives the maximum efficiency rating?
    d Use the graph, or otherwise, to determine the values of x between which the efficiency rating is 70 or more.

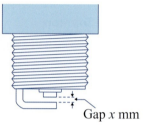

4 A piece of wire 68 cm in length is bent into the shape of a rectangle.

    a If x cm is the length of the rectangle and A cm² is the area enclosed by the rectangular shape, write down a formula which connects A and x.
    b Sketch the graph of A against x for suitable x-values.
    c Use your graph to determine the maximum area formed.

5 A piece of wire 80 cm long is to be cut into two pieces. One piece is to be bent into a square and the other into a rectangle four times as long as it is wide.

    a Let x cm be the length of a side of the square and y cm be the width of the rectangle. Write a formula connecting y and x.
    b Let A cm² be the sum of the areas of the square and the rectangle.
        i Find a formula for A in terms of x.
        ii Find the length of both pieces of wire if A is to be a minimum.

6 A construction firm has won a contract to build cable-car pylons at various positions on the side of a mountain. Because of difficulties associated with construction in alpine areas, the construction firm will be paid an extra amount $\$C$ for each pylon, given by the formula $C = 240h + 100h^2$, where h is the height in km above sea level.

    a Sketch the graph of C as a function of h. Comment on the possible values of h.
    b Does C have a maximum value?
    c What is the value of C for a pylon built at an altitude of 2500 m?

7 A tug-o-war team produces a tension in a rope described by the rule
   $T = 290(8t - 0.5t^2 - 1.4)$ units, where t is the number of seconds after commencing the pull.
   a Sketch a graph of T against t, stating the practical domain.
   b What is the greatest tension produced during a 'heave'?

Example 46

8 A cricketer struck a cricket ball such that its height, d metres, after it had travelled x metres horizontally was given by the rule $d = 1 + \frac{3}{5}x - \frac{1}{50}x^2$, $x \geq 0$.
   a Use a CAS calculator to graph d against x for values of x ranging from 0 to 30.
   b i   What was the maximum height reached by the ball?
      ii If a fielder caught the ball when it was 2 m above the ground, how far was the ball from where it was hit?
      iii At what height was the ball when it was struck?

9 An arch on the top of a door is parabolic in shape. The point A is 3.1 m above the bottom of the door. The equation $y = ax^2 + bx + c$ can be used to describe the arch. Find the values of a, b and c.

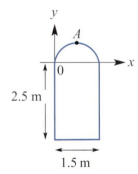

10 It is known that the daily spending of a government department follows a quadratic model. Let t be the number of days after 1 January and s be the spending in hundreds of thousands of dollars on a particular day, where $s = at^2 + bt + c$.

t	30	150	300
s	7.2	12.5	6

   a Find the values of a, b and c.
   b Sketch the graph for $0 \leq t \leq 360$. (Use a CAS calculator.)
   c Find an estimate for the spending when:
      i $t = 180$
      ii $t = 350$

Chapter summary

- The general expression for a quadratic function is $y = ax^2 + bx + c$.
- Methods for **factorising**:
  - Taking out a common factor
    e.g. $9x^3 + 27x^2 = 9x^2(x + 3)$
  - Grouping of terms
    e.g. $x^3 + 4x^2 - 3x - 12 = (x^3 + 4x^2) - (3x + 12)$
    $= x^2(x + 4) - 3(x + 4)$
    $= (x^2 - 3)(x + 4)$
  - Difference of two squares: $x^2 - a^2 = (x + a)(x - a)$
    e.g. $16x^2 - 49 = (4x - 7)(4x + 7)$
  - Factorising quadratic expressions
    e.g. $x^2 + 2x - 8 = (x + 4)(x - 2)$
    $6x^2 - 13x - 15 = (6x + 5)(x - 3)$
- The graph of a quadratic may be sketched by first expressing the rule in **turning point** form, $y = a(x - h)^2 + k$. The graph can then be obtained from the graph of $y = ax^2$ by translating h units in the positive direction of the x-axis and k units in the positive direction of the y-axis (for h, k positive).

  e.g. for $y = 2(x - 1)^2 + 3$

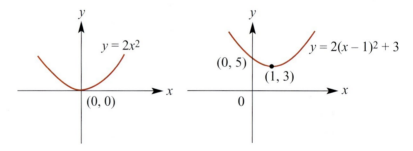

- A quadratic equation $ax^2 + bx + c = 0$ may be solved by:
  - Factorising
  - Completing the square
  - Using the general **quadratic formula** $x = \dfrac{-b \pm \sqrt{b^2 - 4ac}}{2a}$
- The following steps can be used to sketch the graph of a quadratic function in **polynomial** form, $y = ax^2 + bx + c$:
  - If $a > 0$, the function has a minimum value.
  - If $a < 0$, the function has a maximum value.
  - The value of c gives the y-axis intercept.
  - The equation of the axis of symmetry is $x = -\dfrac{b}{2a}$.
  - The x-axis intercepts are determined by solving the equation $ax^2 + bx + c = 0$.

- The number of solutions of a quadratic equation $ax^2 + bx + c = 0$ can be found from the **discriminant** $\Delta = b^2 - 4ac$:
  - If $\Delta > 0$, the quadratic equation has two distinct solutions.
  - If $\Delta = 0$, the quadratic equation has one solution.
  - If $\Delta < 0$, the quadratic equation has no real solutions.
- To find a quadratic rule to fit given points, choose an appropriate form. For example:

  $y = a(x - e)(x - f)$ This can be used if two x-axis intercepts and the coordinates of one other point are known.

  $y = a(x - h)^2 + k$ This can be used if the coordinates of the turning point and one other point are known.

  $y = ax^2 + bx + c$ This can be used if the coordinates of three points on the parabola are known.

Technology-free questions

1 Express each of the following in the form $(ax + b)^2$:

  a $x^2 + 9x + \dfrac{81}{4}$
  b $x^2 + 18x + 81$
  c $x^2 - \dfrac{4}{5}x + \dfrac{4}{25}$
  d $x^2 + 2bx + b^2$
  e $9x^2 - 6x + 1$
  f $25x^2 + 20x + 4$

2 Expand each of the following products:

  a $-3(x - 2)$
  b $-a(x - a)$
  c $(7a - b)(7a + b)$
  d $(x + 3)(x - 4)$
  e $(2x + 3)(x - 4)$
  f $(x + y)(x - y)$
  g $(a - b)(a^2 + ab + b^2)$
  h $(2x + 2y)(3x + y)$
  i $(3a + 1)(a - 2)$
  j $(x + y)^2 - (x - y)^2$
  k $u(v + 2) + 2v(1 - u)$
  l $(3x + 2)(x - 4) + (4 - x)(6x - 1)$

3 Express each of the following as a product of factors:

  a $4x - 8$
  b $3x^2 + 8x$
  c $24ax - 3x$
  d $4 - x^2$
  e $au + 2av + 3aw$
  f $4a^2b^2 - 9a^4$
  g $1 - 36x^2a^2$
  h $x^2 + x - 12$
  i $x^2 + x - 2$
  j $2x^2 + 3x - 2$
  k $6x^2 + 7x + 2$
  l $3x^2 - 8x - 3$
  m $3x^2 + x - 2$
  n $6a^2 - a - 2$
  o $6x^2 - 7x + 2$

4 Solve each of the following equations for x by first factorising:

  a $x^2 - 2x - 15 = 0$
  b $x^2 - 9x = 0$
  c $2x^2 - 10x + 12 = 0$
  d $x^2 - 24x - 25 = 0$
  e $3x^2 + 15x + 18 = 0$
  f $x^2 - 12x + 36 = 0$
  g $2x^2 - 5x - 3 = 0$
  h $12x^2 - 8x - 15 = 0$
  i $5x^2 + 7x - 12 = 0$

5 Sketch the graphs of each of the following:
  a $y = 2x^2 + 3$
  b $y = -2x^2 + 3$
  c $y = 2(x - 2)^2 + 3$
  d $y = 2(x + 2)^2 + 3$
  e $y = 2(x - 4)^2 - 3$
  f $y = 9 - 4x^2$
  g $y = 3(x - 2)^2$
  h $y = 2(2 - x)^2 + 3$

6 Express in the form $y = a(x - h)^2 + k$ and hence sketch the graphs of the following:
  a $y = x^2 - 4x - 5$
  b $y = x^2 - 6x$
  c $y = x^2 - 8x + 4$
  d $y = 2x^2 + 8x - 4$
  e $y = -3x^2 - 12x + 9$
  f $y = -x^2 + 4x + 5$

7 For each of the following, find
  i the axis intercepts
  ii the axis of symmetry
  iii the turning point
  and hence sketch the graph:
  a $y = x^2 - 7x + 6$
  b $y = -x^2 - x + 12$
  c $y = -x^2 + 5x + 14$
  d $y = x^2 - 10x + 16$
  e $y = 2x^2 + x - 15$
  f $y = 6x^2 - 13x - 5$
  g $y = 9x^2 - 16$
  h $y = 4x^2 - 25$

8 Find the value(s) of p that will make the quadratic $(5p - 1)x^2 - 4x + (2p - 1)$ a perfect square.

9 Solve the following quadratic inequalities:
  a $x^2 > x$
  b $(x + 2)^2 \leq 34$
  c $3x^2 + 5x - 2 \leq 0$
  d $-2x^2 + 13x \geq 15$

10 Use the quadratic formula to solve each of the following:
  a $x^2 + 6x + 3 = 0$
  b $x^2 + 9x + 12 = 0$
  c $x^2 - 4x + 2 = 0$
  d $2x^2 + 7x + 2 = 0$
  e $2x^2 + 7x + 4 = 0$
  f $3x^2 + 9x - 1 = 0$

11 Find the equation of the quadratic, the graph of which is shown.

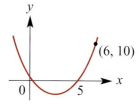

12 A parabola has the same shape as $y = 3x^2$ but its vertex is at $(5, 2)$. Find the equation corresponding to this parabola.

13 Find the values of m if $(2m - 3)x^2 + (5m - 1)x + (3m - 2) = 0$ has two solutions.

14 Two numbers have a sum of 30. Find the maximum value of the product of such numbers.

15 Find the rule of the quadratic function which describes the graph.

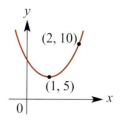

16 Find the coordinates of the points of intersection of the graphs with equations:
  a $y = 2x + 3$ and $y = x^2$
  b $y = 8x + 11$ and $y = 2x^2$
  c $y = 3x^2 + 7x$ and $y = 2$
  d $y = 2x^2$ and $y = 2 - 3x$

17 a A parabola has x-axis intercepts -4 and 1 and it passes through the point $(-1, -12)$. Find the rule for this parabola.
  b The coordinates of the turning point of a parabola are $(-1, 3)$ and the parabola passes through the point $(1, -5)$. Find the rule for this parabola.
  c A parabola passes through the points $(1, -3)$, $(0, -3)$ and $(-1, 1)$. Find the rule for this parabola.

18 The surface area, S, of a cylindrical tank with a hemispherical top is given by the formula $S = ar^2 + brh$, where $a = 9.42$ and $b = 6.28$. What is the radius of a tank of height 6 m which has a surface area of 125.6 m^2?

19 a For what value(s) of m does the equation $2x^2 + mx + 1 = 0$ have exactly one solution?
  b For what values of m does the equation $x^2 - 4mx + 20 = 0$ have real solutions?

20 Consider the family of quadratics with rules of the form $y = x^2 + bx$, where b is a non-zero real number.
  a Find the x-axis intercepts.
  b Find the coordinates of the vertex of the parabola.
  c **i** Find the coordinates of the points of intersection of the graph of $y = x^2 + bx$ with the line $y = x$, in terms of b.
    ii For what value(s) of b is there one point of intersection?
    iii For what value(s) of b are there two points of intersection?

Multiple-choice questions

1. The linear factors of $12x^2 + 7x - 12$ are
   - **A** $4x - 3$ and $3x + 4$
   - **B** $3x - 4$ and $4x + 3$
   - **C** $3x - 2$ and $4x + 6$
   - **D** $3x + 2$ and $4x - 6$
   - **E** $6x + 4$ and $2x - 3$

2. The solutions of the equation $x^2 - 5x - 14 = 0$ are
   - **A** $x = -7$ only
   - **B** $x = -7$, $x = 2$
   - **C** $x = -2$, $x = 7$
   - **D** $x = -2$, $x = -7$
   - **E** $x = -2$ only

3. For $y = 8 + 2x - x^2$, the maximum value of y is
   - **A** $-3\frac{1}{4}$
   - **B** $5\frac{1}{4}$
   - **C** 9
   - **D** $9\frac{1}{2}$
   - **E** 10

4. If the graph of $y = 2x^2 - kx + 3$ touches the x-axis, then the possible values of k are
   - **A** $k = 2$ or $k = -3$
   - **B** $k = 1$
   - **C** $k = -3$ or $k = -\frac{1}{2}$
   - **D** $k = 1$ or $k = 3$
   - **E** $k = 2\sqrt{6}$ or $k = -2\sqrt{6}$

5. The solutions of the equation $x^2 - 56 = x$ are
   - **A** $x = -8$ or 7
   - **B** $x = -7$ or 8
   - **C** $x = 7$ or 8
   - **D** $x = -9$ or 6
   - **E** $x = 9$ or -6

6. The value of the discriminant of $x^2 + 3x - 10$ is
   - **A** 5
   - **B** -5
   - **C** 49
   - **D** 7
   - **E** -2

7. The coordinates of the turning point of the graph with equation $y = 3x^2 + 6x - 1$ are
   - **A** $(\frac{1}{3}, -2)$
   - **B** $(-\frac{1}{3}, 2)$
   - **C** $(-\frac{1}{3}, -4)$
   - **D** $(1, -4)$
   - **E** $(-1, -4)$

8. The quadratic $5x^2 - 10x - 2$ in turning point form $a(x - h)^2 + k$, by completing the square, is
   - **A** $(5x + 1)^2 + 5$
   - **B** $(5x - 1)^2 - 5$
   - **C** $5(x - 1)^2 - 5$
   - **D** $5(x + 1)^2 - 2$
   - **E** $5(x - 1)^2 - 7$

9. The value(s) of m that will give the equation $mx^2 + 6x - 3 = 0$ two solutions is (are)
   - **A** $m = -3$
   - **B** $m = 3$
   - **C** $m = 0$
   - **D** $m > -3$
   - **E** $m < -3$

10. $6x^2 - 8xy - 8y^2$ is equal to
    - **A** $(3x + 2y)(2x - 4y)$
    - **B** $(3x - 2y)(6x + 4y)$
    - **C** $(6x - 4y)(x + 2y)$
    - **D** $(3x - 2y)(2x + 4y)$
    - **E** $(6x + y)(x - 8y)$

11. The turning point of a quadratic with rule $y = x^2 - ax$ has coordinates
    - **A** $(0, a)$
    - **B** $\left(\frac{a}{2}, \frac{-a^2}{4}\right)$
    - **C** $(a, 0)$
    - **D** $\left(a, \frac{-a^2}{2}\right)$
    - **E** $\left(\frac{-a}{2}, \frac{-a^2}{4}\right)$

12 The solution of the inequality $x^2 > b^2$, where $b < 0$, is

  A $x > b$ or $x < -b$ **B** $x > b$ **C** $b < x < -b$
  D $-b < x < b$ **E** $x < b$ or $x > -b$

13 The quadratic equation $x^2 - 2ax + b = 0$, where a and b are positive constants, has one solution when

  A $b = a$ and $a \neq 1$ **B** $b = \sqrt{a}$ and $b = -\sqrt{a}$ **C** $b = 1$ and $a \neq 1$
  D $a = \sqrt{b}$ or $a = -\sqrt{b}$ **E** $b = a = 2$

Extended-response questions

1 The diagram shows a masonry arch bridge of span 50 m. The shape of the curve, ABC, is a parabola. The line AC is the water level and B is the highest point of the bridge.

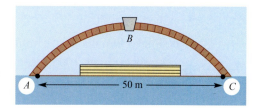

  a Taking A as the origin and the maximum height of the arch above the water level as 4.5 m, write down a formula for the curve of the arch where y is the height of the arch above AC and x is the horizontal distance from A.
  b Calculate a table of values and accurately plot the graph of the curve.
  c At what horizontal distance from A is the height of the arch above the water level equal to 3 m?
  d What is the height of the arch at a horizontal distance from A of 12 m?
  e A floating platform 20 m wide is towed under the bridge. What is the greatest height of the deck above water level if the platform is to be towed under the bridge with at least 30 cm horizontal clearance on either side?

2 A piece of wire 12 cm long is cut into two pieces. One piece is used to form a square shape and the other a rectangular shape in which the length is twice its width.

  a If x cm is the side length of the square, write down the dimensions of the rectangle in terms of x.
  b Formulate a rule for A, the combined area of the square and rectangle in cm^2, in terms of x.
  c Determine the lengths of the two pieces if the sum of the areas is to be a minimum.

3 Water is pumped into an empty metal tank at a steady rate of 0.2 litres/min. After 1 hour the depth of water in the tank is 5 cm; after 5 hours the depth is 10 cm.

  a If the volume of water in the tank is V litres when the depth is x cm and there is a quadratic relationship between V and x, write down a rule which connects V and x.
  b It is known that the maximum possible depth of water in the tank is 20 cm. For how long, from the beginning, can water be pumped into the tank at the same rate without overflowing?

4 The figure shows a section view of a freeway embankment to be built across a flood-prone river flat. The height of the embankment is x m and the width at the top is 90 m.

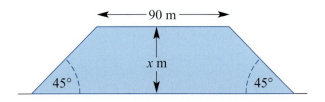

a Find a formula, in terms of x, for V, the volume of earth in m³ required to build a 120 m length of freeway embankment.

This figure shows another section of the freeway which is to be constructed by cutting through a hillside. The depth of the cutting is x m and the width of the cutting at the base is 50 m.

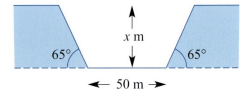

b Find a formula for the volume of earth, in m³, which would have to be excavated to form a straight 100 m section of the cutting.

c If $x = 4$ m, what length of embankment could be constructed from earth taken from the cutting?

5 100 m of angle steel is used to make a rectangular frame with three crossbars as shown in the figure.

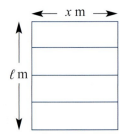

a If the width of the frame is x m, determine an expression for ℓ, the length of the frame in metres, in terms of x.

b The frame is to be covered by light aluminium sheeting. If the area of this sheeting is A m², formulate a rule connecting A and x.

c Sketch a graph of A against x, stating the axis intercepts and the turning point.

d What is the maximum area and the value of x which gives this area?

6 A shape which has been of interest to architects and artists over the centuries is the 'golden rectangle'. Many have thought that it has the perfect proportions for buildings. The rectangle is such that, if a square is drawn on one of the longer sides, then the new rectangle is similar to the original. Let the length of $AP = 1$ unit; then $AB = 1 - x$ units and $\dfrac{AP}{AD} = \dfrac{AD}{AB}$.

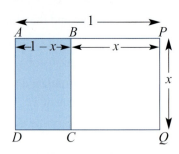

Find the value of x. (This value is the reciprocal of the 'golden ratio'.)

7 The point P is x m from B along the line BC.
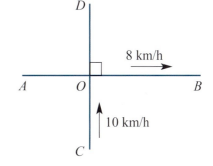
  a Find distance PA in terms of x.
  b **i** Find distance PC in terms of x.
  ii Find distance PD in terms of x.
  c Find x if $PA = PD$.
  d Find x if $PA = 2PD$. (Answer correct to three decimal places.)
  e Find x if $PA = 3PD$. (Answer correct to three decimal places.)

8 AB and CD are crossroads. A jogger runs along road AB at a speed of 8 km/h and passes O at 1 p.m. Another runner is moving along road CD. The second runner is moving at 10 km/h and passes O at 1:30 p.m.
  a Let y km be their distance apart t hours after 1 p.m.
    i Find an expression for y in terms of t.
    ii Plot the graph of y against t on a CAS calculator.
    iii Find the time(s) when the runners are 4 km apart. (Use a CAS calculator.)
    iv Find the time at which the runners are closest and their distance apart at this time.
  b Find the exact value(s) of t for which:
    i $y = 5$ **ii** $y = 6$

9 A rectangle of perimeter b cm is inscribed in a circle of radius a cm. The rectangle has width x cm and length y cm.
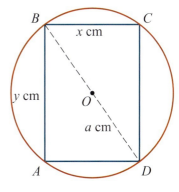
  a Apply Pythagoras' theorem in triangle BCD to show that $x^2 + y^2 = 4a^2$.
  b Form a second equation involving x, y and b.
  c Eliminate y from these equations to form a quadratic equation in terms of x, a and b.
  d As x, y and $2a$ are the sides of a triangle, $x + y > 2a$. Use this result and apply the discriminant to the quadratic equation formed in part c to show that the rectangle can be inscribed in the circle only if $4a < b \leq 4\sqrt{2}a$.
  e **i** If $a = 5$ and $b = 24$, find the values of x and y.
    ii If $b = 4\sqrt{2}a$, find the values of x and y in terms of a.
  f If $\dfrac{b}{a} = 5$, find the values of x and y in terms of a.
  g Write a program to solve the quadratic equation found in part c for suitable choices of a and b and state the values of x and y. (Answers correct to two decimal places.)

10 The equation of curve B is $y = -6 + 4x - x^2$.

  a $(h, 3)$ is the vertex of a parabola A, with equation $y = x^2 + bx + c$. Find the values of b, c and h for $h > 0$.

  b Let P be a point on curve A, and P′ be a point on curve B such that PP′ is perpendicular to the x-axis.

   i The coordinates of P are $(x, x^2 + bx + c)$. State the coordinates of P′ in terms of x.

   ii Find the coordinates of M, the midpoint of PP′, in terms of x.

   iii Find the coordinates of M for $x = 0, 1, 2, 3, 4$.

   iv Give the equation of the straight line on which all of these points lie. (This is called the locus of the midpoints.)

  c Let d be the distance PP′.

   i Express d in terms of x.

   ii Sketch the graph of d against x.

   iii Find the minimum value of d and the value of x for which this occurs.

11 A path cuts across a park. Its centreline can be described by the equation $y = \dfrac{x}{2}$, where the origin is at a point O in the park. The path starts at a point $C(-30, -15)$ and finishes at a point $D(60, 30)$.

  a How long is the path?

  One boundary of the pond in the park is parabolic in shape. The boundary passes through the points $A(-20, 45)$, $B(40, 40)$ and $E(30, 35)$. The equation of the parabola is of the form $y = ax^2 + bx + c$.

  b **i** Find the equation of the parabola.

   ii Find the coordinates of the vertex of the parabola.

  c On the one set of axes sketch the graphs of $y = \dfrac{x}{2}$ and the parabola. (Use a CAS calculator to help.)

  d Consider the rule $y = (ax^2 + bx + c) - \frac{1}{2}x$, where a, b and c have been determined in part b i.

   i What does this expression determine?

   ii Find the minimum value of this expression and the value of x for which this occurs.

Chapter 4

A gallery of graphs

Objectives

▶ To recognise the rules of a number of common algebraic relations:
  ▷ $y = x^{-1}$ (rectangular hyperbola)
  ▷ $y = x^{-2}$
  ▷ $y = \sqrt{x}$
  ▷ $x^2 + y^2 = 1$ (circle).
▶ To be able to sketch the graphs of these relations.
▶ To be able to sketch the graphs of simple transformations of these relations.
▶ To find the key features of the graphs of these relations.
▶ To determine the rules of relations of these types given sufficient information.

In Chapter 2, we looked at linear graphs, sketching them and determining their rules given sufficient information. All linear graphs can be considered as transformations of $y = x$. The features we concentrated on for linear graphs were the x-axis intercept, the y-axis intercept and the gradient.

In Chapter 3, we considered quadratics written in 'turning point form' and sketched their graphs by using transformations of the graph of the basic quadratic $y = x^2$. The features we concentrated on for graphs of quadratic polynomials were the x-axis intercepts, the y-axis intercept and the coordinates of the turning point (vertex).

In this chapter, we study some other common algebraic relations, and develop methods similar to those used in Chapter 3 to sketch the graphs of these relations. The relations in this chapter have different types of key features. For example, we introduce asymptotes for graphs of rectangular hyperbolas and graphs of the form $y = x^{-2}$, and the coordinates of the centre and the length of the radius are key features in the study of circles.

4A Rectangular hyperbolas

Consider the rule

$$y = \frac{1}{x} = x^{-1} \quad \text{for } x \neq 0$$

We can construct a table of values for $y = \dfrac{1}{x}$ for values of x between -4 and 4 as follows:

x	-4	-3	-2	-1	$-\frac{1}{2}$	$\frac{1}{2}$	1	2	3	4
y	$-\frac{1}{4}$	$-\frac{1}{3}$	$-\frac{1}{2}$	-1	-2	2	1	$\frac{1}{2}$	$\frac{1}{3}$	$\frac{1}{4}$

We can plot these points and then connect the dots to produce a continuous curve. A graph of this type is an example of a **rectangular hyperbola**.

Note that y is undefined when $x = 0$, and that there is no x-value that will produce the value $y = 0$.

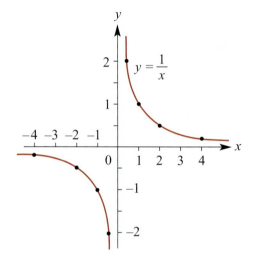

▶ Asymptotes

There are two lines associated with this graph that help to describe its shape.

Horizontal asymptote

From the graph we see that, as x approaches infinity in either direction, the value of y approaches zero. The following notation will be used to state this:

- As $x \to \infty$, $y \to 0^+$. This is read: 'As x approaches infinity, y approaches 0 from the positive side.'
- As $x \to -\infty$, $y \to 0^-$. This is read: 'As x approaches negative infinity, y approaches 0 from the negative side.'

The graph approaches the x-axis (the line $y = 0$) but does not cross this line. The line $y = 0$ is a **horizontal asymptote**.

Vertical asymptote

As x approaches zero from either direction, the magnitude of y becomes very large. The following notation will be used to state this:

- As $x \to 0^+$, $y \to \infty$. This is read: 'As x approaches zero from the positive side, y approaches infinity.'
- As $x \to 0^-$, $y \to -\infty$. This is read: 'As x approaches zero from the negative side, y approaches negative infinity.'

The graph approaches the y-axis (the line $x = 0$) but does not cross this line. The line $x = 0$ is a **vertical asymptote**.

▶ Dilations from an axis

The diagram on the right shows the graphs of

$$y = \frac{1}{x}, \quad y = \frac{2}{x} \quad \text{and} \quad y = \frac{1}{3x}$$

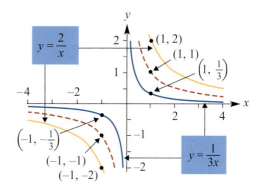

The asymptotes are the x-axis and the y-axis, and they have equations $y = 0$ and $x = 0$ respectively.

As can be seen from the diagram, the graphs of $y = \frac{2}{x}$ and $y = \frac{1}{3x}$ have the same 'shape' and asymptotes as the graph of $y = \frac{1}{x}$, but they have been 'stretched'.

The transformation that takes the graph of $y = \frac{1}{x}$ to the graph of $y = \frac{2}{x}$ is called the **dilation** of factor 2 from the x-axis. For example, the point $(1, 1)$ on the graph of $y = \frac{1}{x}$ is taken to the point $(1, 2)$ on the graph of $y = \frac{2}{x}$. Dilations will be considered formally in Chapter 7.

▶ Reflection in the x-axis

When the graph of $y = \frac{1}{x}$ is reflected in the x-axis, the result is the graph of $y = -\frac{1}{x}$.

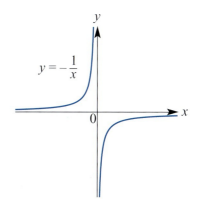

The asymptotes are still the two axes, that is, the lines $x = 0$ and $y = 0$.

Similarly, $y = -\frac{2}{x}$ is the reflection of $y = \frac{2}{x}$ in the x-axis.

Reflecting in the y-axis gives the same result for these two graphs.

▶ Translations

Now let us consider the graph of $y = \frac{1}{x - 1} + 3$.

The basic graph of $y = \frac{1}{x}$ has been translated 1 unit to the right and 3 units up.

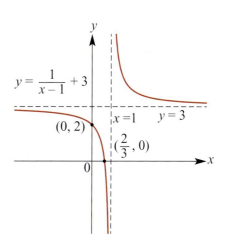

Asymptotes The equation of the vertical asymptote is now $x = 1$, and the equation of the horizontal asymptote is now $y = 3$.

Intercepts with the axes The graph now has x-axis and y-axis intercepts. These can be calculated in the usual way to add further detail to the graph.

Sketching rectangular hyperbolas

Using dilations, reflections and translations, we are now able to sketch the graphs of all rectangular hyperbolas of the form $y = \dfrac{a}{x-h} + k$.

Example 1

Sketch the graph of $y = \dfrac{2}{x+1} - 3$.

Solution

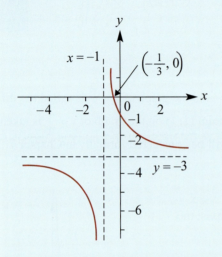

Explanation

The graph of $y = \dfrac{2}{x}$ has been translated 1 unit to the left and 3 units down. The asymptotes have equations $x = -1$ and $y = -3$.

When $x = 0$, $y = \dfrac{2}{0+1} - 3 = -1$.

∴ the y-axis intercept is -1.

When $y = 0$,

$$0 = \dfrac{2}{x+1} - 3$$

$$3 = \dfrac{2}{x+1}$$

$$3(x+1) = 2$$

$$x = -\dfrac{1}{3}$$

∴ the x-axis intercept is $-\dfrac{1}{3}$.

Example 2

Sketch the graph of $y = \dfrac{-2}{x-1}$.

Solution

The graph of $y = -\dfrac{2}{x}$ is obtained from the graph of $y = \dfrac{2}{x}$ by reflection in the x-axis.

This graph is then translated 1 unit to the right to obtain the graph of $y = \dfrac{-2}{x-1}$.

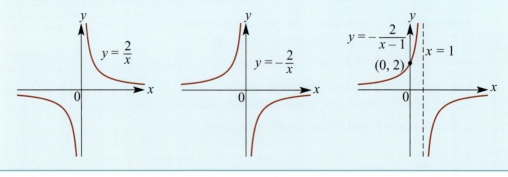

4A Rectangular hyperbolas

Section summary

- For $a > 0$, a dilation of factor a from the x-axis transforms the graph of $y = \dfrac{1}{x}$ to the graph of $y = \dfrac{a}{x}$.
- A reflection in the x-axis transforms the graph of $y = \dfrac{a}{x}$ to the graph of $y = -\dfrac{a}{x}$.
- For $h, k \geq 0$, a translation of h to the right and k upwards transforms the graph of $y = \dfrac{a}{x}$ to the graph of $y = \dfrac{a}{x - h} + k$.
- A rectangular hyperbola with rule of the form $y = \dfrac{a}{x - h} + k$ has:
  - vertical asymptote $x = h$
  - horizontal asymptote $y = k$.

Exercise 4A

Example 1, 2

1 Sketch the graphs of the following, showing all important features of the graphs:

a $y = \dfrac{1}{x}$
b $y = \dfrac{2}{x}$
c $y = \dfrac{1}{2x}$
d $y = \dfrac{-3}{x}$

e $y = \dfrac{1}{x} + 2$
f $y = \dfrac{1}{x} - 3$
g $y = \dfrac{2}{x} - 4$
h $y = \dfrac{-1}{2x} + 5$

i $y = \dfrac{1}{x - 1}$
j $y = \dfrac{-1}{x + 2}$
k $y = \dfrac{1}{x + 1} + 3$
l $y = \dfrac{-2}{x - 3} - 4$

2 Write down the equations of the asymptotes for each of the graphs in Question 1.

3 a We can write $y = \dfrac{1}{3x + 6}$ as $y = \dfrac{1}{3(x + 2)}$.

Sketch the graph of $y = \dfrac{1}{3x}$ and hence the graph of $y = \dfrac{1}{3x + 6}$.

b We can write $y = \dfrac{3}{2x + 4}$ as $y = \dfrac{3}{2(x + 2)}$.

Sketch the graph of $y = \dfrac{3}{2x}$ and hence the graph of $y = \dfrac{3}{2x + 4}$.

c We can write $y = \dfrac{-1}{2x + 4}$ as $y = -\dfrac{1}{2(x + 2)}$.

Sketch the graph of $y = -\dfrac{1}{2x}$ and hence the graph of $y = \dfrac{-1}{2x + 4}$.

d We can write $y = \dfrac{1}{2x + 1}$ as $y = \dfrac{1}{2(x + \frac{1}{2})}$.

Sketch the graph of $y = \dfrac{1}{2x}$ and hence the graph of $y = \dfrac{1}{2x + 1}$.

4 Sketch the graphs of the following, showing all important features of the graphs:

a $y = \dfrac{1}{3x + 1}$
b $y = \dfrac{1}{3x + 1} - 1$
c $y = \dfrac{-1}{3x + 1} - 1$
d $y = \dfrac{-2}{3x + 1}$

e $y = \dfrac{-2}{3x + 1} - 4$
f $y = \dfrac{-2}{3x + 1} + 3$
g $y = \dfrac{2}{3x + 2} - 1$
h $y = \dfrac{3}{3x + 4} - 1$

5 Show that $\dfrac{x+3}{x-1} = \dfrac{4}{x-1} + 1$ and hence sketch the graph of $y = \dfrac{x+3}{x-1}$.

6 Show that $\dfrac{2x+3}{x+1} = \dfrac{1}{x+1} + 2$ and hence sketch the graph of $y = \dfrac{2x+3}{x+1}$.

7 Show that $\dfrac{3-2x}{x-2} = -\dfrac{1}{x-2} - 2$ and hence sketch the graph of $y = \dfrac{3-2x}{x-2}$.

4B The truncus

Now consider the rule

$$y = \dfrac{1}{x^2} = x^{-2} \quad \text{for } x \neq 0$$

We can construct a table of values for x between -4 and 4 as follows:

x	-4	-3	-2	-1	$-\tfrac{1}{2}$	$\tfrac{1}{2}$	1	2	3	4
y	$\tfrac{1}{16}$	$\tfrac{1}{9}$	$\tfrac{1}{4}$	1	4	4	1	$\tfrac{1}{4}$	$\tfrac{1}{9}$	$\tfrac{1}{16}$

We can plot these points and then connect the dots to produce a continuous curve. A graph of this shape is sometimes called a **truncus**.

Note that y is undefined when $x = 0$, and that there is no x-value that will produce a negative value of y.

Note: As $x \to \infty$, $y \to 0^+$. As $x \to -\infty$, $y \to 0^+$.
As $x \to 0^+$, $y \to \infty$. As $x \to 0^-$, $y \to \infty$.

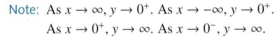

The graph of $y = \dfrac{1}{x^2}$ has asymptotes $y = 0$ and $x = 0$.

The transformations considered in the previous section can be applied to the graph of $y = \dfrac{1}{x^2}$. All graphs of the form

$$y = \dfrac{a}{(x-h)^2} + k$$

will have the same basic 'truncus' shape. The **asymptotes** will be the lines $y = k$ and $x = h$.

Example 3

Sketch the graph of $y = \dfrac{-1}{2(x+3)^2} - 4$.

Solution

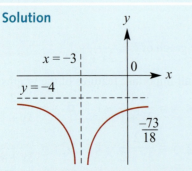

Explanation

The graph of $y = \dfrac{-1}{2x^2}$ is translated 3 units to the left and 4 units down.

The y-axis intercept is found by putting $x = 0$; it is $\dfrac{-73}{18}$.

Exercise 4B

 1 Sketch the graphs of the following, showing all important features:

a $y = \dfrac{1}{(x+3)^2}$ **b** $y = \dfrac{1}{x^2} - 4$

c $y = \dfrac{-1}{(x-2)^2}$ **d** $y = \dfrac{1}{(x-1)^2} + 3$

e $y = \dfrac{1}{2(x+3)^2} - 4$ **f** $y = \dfrac{-2}{(x-2)^2} + 1$

g $y = \dfrac{3}{(x+3)^2} - 6$ **h** $y = \dfrac{-1}{(x-4)^2} + 2$

2 Write down the equations of the asymptotes for each of the graphs in Question 1.

3 a We can write $y = \dfrac{1}{(3x+6)^2}$ as $y = \dfrac{1}{9(x+2)^2}$.

Sketch the graph of $y = \dfrac{1}{9x^2}$ and hence the graph of $y = \dfrac{1}{(3x+6)^2}$.

b We can write $y = \dfrac{3}{(2x+4)^2}$ as $y = \dfrac{3}{4(x+2)^2}$.

Sketch the graph of $y = \dfrac{3}{4x^2}$ and hence the graph of $y = \dfrac{3}{(2x+4)^2}$.

c We can write $y = \dfrac{-1}{(2x+4)^2}$ as $y = -\dfrac{1}{4(x+2)^2}$.

Sketch the graph of $y = -\dfrac{1}{4x^2}$ and hence the graph of $y = \dfrac{-1}{(2x+4)^2}$.

4C The graph of $y = \sqrt{x}$

The rule
$$y = \sqrt{x} = x^{\frac{1}{2}} \quad \text{for } x \geq 0$$

corresponds to the upper part of the graph shown opposite.
It is one arm of the parabola $x = y^2$.

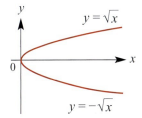

Coordinates of points on the graph of $y = \sqrt{x}$ include $(0, 0), (1, 1), (4, 2)$ and $(9, 3)$.

All graphs of the form
$$y = a\sqrt{x - h} + k$$

will have the same basic shape as the graph of $y = \sqrt{x}$.

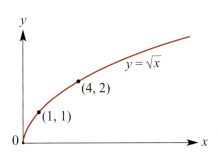

Example 4

Sketch the graph of $y = 3\sqrt{x+1} - 6$.

Solution

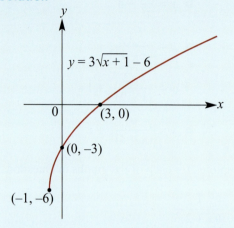

When $x = 0$, $y = -3$

When $y = 0$, $3\sqrt{x+1} - 6 = 0$

$$3\sqrt{x+1} = 6$$
$$\sqrt{x+1} = 2$$
$$x+1 = 4$$
$$x = 3$$

Explanation

The graph is formed by dilating the graph of $y = \sqrt{x}$ from the x-axis by factor 3 and then translating 1 unit to the left and 6 units down.

The rule is defined for $x \geq -1$.

The set of values the rule can take (the range) is all numbers greater than or equal to -6, i.e. $y \geq -6$.

Example 5

Sketch the graph of $y = -2\sqrt{x-1} + 3$.

Solution

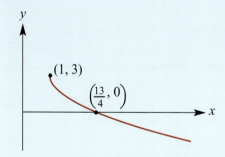

When $y = 0$: $\quad -2\sqrt{x-1} + 3 = 0$

$$2\sqrt{x-1} = 3$$

Square both sides: $\quad 4(x-1) = 9$

Therefore $x = \dfrac{9}{4} + 1 = \dfrac{13}{4}$

Explanation

The graph is formed by dilating the graph of $y = \sqrt{x}$ from the x-axis by factor 2, reflecting this in the x-axis and then translating it 1 unit to the right and 3 units up.

The rule is defined for $x \geq 1$.

The set of values the rule can take (the range) is all numbers less than or equal to 3, i.e. $y \leq 3$.

▶ The graph of $y = \sqrt{-x}$

The rule
$$y = \sqrt{-x} \quad \text{for } x \leq 0$$
yields a graph which is the reflection of the graph of $y = \sqrt{x}$ in the y-axis.

All graphs of the form
$$y = a\sqrt{-(x-h)} + k$$
will have the same basic shape as the graph of $y = \sqrt{-x}$.

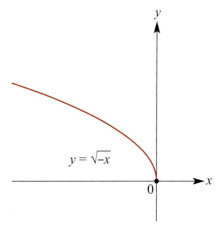

Example 6

Sketch the graph of $y = \sqrt{2-x} + 3$.

Note: $\sqrt{2-x} = \sqrt{-(x-2)}$

Solution

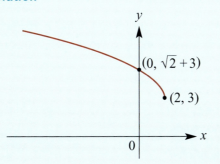

When $x = 0$, $y = \sqrt{2} + 3$.

Explanation

We can write the rule as
$$y = \sqrt{-(x-2)} + 3$$

The rule is defined for $x \leq 2$. The set of values the rule can take (the range) is all numbers greater than or equal to 3, i.e. $y \geq 3$.

Section summary

- All graphs of the form $y = a\sqrt{x-h} + k$ will have the same basic shape as the graph of $y = \sqrt{x}$. The graph will have endpoint (h, k).
- The graph of $y = \sqrt{-x}$ is the reflection in the y-axis of the graph of $y = \sqrt{x}$.

Exercise 4C

Example 4

1 For each of the following rules, sketch the corresponding graph, giving the axis intercepts when they exist, the set of x-values for which the rule is defined and the set of y-values which the rule takes:

a $y = 2\sqrt{x} + 3$
b $y = \sqrt{x-2} + 3$
c $y = \sqrt{x-2} - 3$
d $y = \sqrt{x+2} + 1$
e $y = -\sqrt{x+2} + 3$
f $y = 2\sqrt{x+2} - 3$

154 Chapter 4: A gallery of graphs

Example 5, 6

2 For each of the following rules, sketch the corresponding graph, giving the axis intercepts when they exist, the set of x-values for which the rule is defined and the set of y-values which the rule takes:

a $y = -\sqrt{x-2} + 3$

b $y = \sqrt{-(x-4)} - 2$

c $y = -2\sqrt{-(x+4)} - 1$

d $y = 2\sqrt{3-x}$

e $y = -2\sqrt{3-x}$

f $y = 4\sqrt{3-x} - 4$

3 For each of the following rules, sketch the corresponding graph, giving the axis intercepts when they exist, the set of x-values for which the rule is defined and the set of y-values which the rule takes:

a $y = \sqrt{3x}$

b $y = \sqrt{3(x-1)}$

c $y = -\sqrt{2x}$

d $y = \sqrt{2(3-x)}$

e $y = -2\sqrt{4(2-x)}$

f $y = 4\sqrt{2(3-x)} - 4$

4D Circles

Consider a circle in the coordinate plane with centre the origin and radius r. If $P(x, y)$ is a point on the circle, its distance from the origin is r and so by Pythagoras' theorem $x^2 + y^2 = r^2$.

Skillsheet

Conversely, if a point $P(x, y)$ in the plane satisfies the equation $x^2 + y^2 = r^2$, its distance from the origin is r, so it lies on a circle with centre the origin and radius r.

To the right is the graph of the circle with equation $x^2 + y^2 = 1$.

All circles can be considered as being transformations of this basic graph.

As has been seen with other graphs, the basic graph may be translated horizontally and vertically.

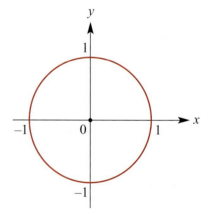

> The equation for a circle is
> $$(x-h)^2 + (y-k)^2 = r^2$$
> where the **centre** of the circle is the point (h, k) and the **radius** is r.

If the radius and the coordinates of the centre of the circle are given, the equation of the circle can be determined.

Example 7

Write down the equation of the circle with centre $(-3, 5)$ and radius 2.

Solution

If the radius is 2 and the centre is the point $(-3, 5)$, then the equation will be

$$(x - (-3))^2 + (y - 5)^2 = 4$$
$$(x + 3)^2 + (y - 5)^2 = 4$$

If the equation of the circle is given, the radius and the centre of the circle can be determined and the graph sketched.

Example 8

Find the centre and radius of the circle $(x - 1)^2 + (y - 2)^2 = 4$.

Solution

The equation
$(x - 1)^2 + (y - 2)^2 = 4$
defines a circle of radius 2 with centre at $(1, 2)$.

Explanation

We can sketch the circle with a little extra work.

When $x = 0$,

$$1 + (y - 2)^2 = 4$$
$$(y - 2)^2 = 3$$

Hence $y = 2 \pm \sqrt{3}$

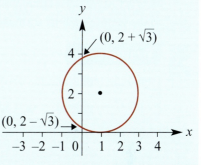

Example 9

Sketch the graph of the circle $(x + 1)^2 + (y + 4)^2 = 9$.

Solution

When $x = 0$,

$$1 + (y + 4)^2 = 9$$
$$(y + 4)^2 = 8$$

Hence $y = -4 \pm \sqrt{8}$
$ = -4 \pm 2\sqrt{2}$

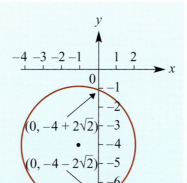

Explanation

The circle has radius 3 and centre $(-1, -4)$.

The y-axis intercepts can be found in the usual way.

The equation of a circle may not always be written in the form $(x - h)^2 + (y - k)^2 = r^2$.

Expanding the general equation of a circle gives
$$(x - h)^2 + (y - k)^2 = r^2$$
$$x^2 - 2hx + h^2 + y^2 - 2ky + k^2 = r^2$$
$$x^2 + y^2 - 2hx - 2ky + h^2 + k^2 - r^2 = 0$$

Let $c = h^2 + k^2 - r^2$. Then we obtain an alternative form for the equation of a circle:

> The **general form** for the equation of a circle is
> $$x^2 + y^2 - 2hx - 2ky + c = 0$$

You will note that there is some similarity with the general form of a straight line, $ax + by + c = 0$.

Notice that in the general form of the circle equation, the coefficients of x^2 and y^2 are both 1 and there is no xy term.

In order to sketch a circle with equation expressed in this form, the equation can be converted to the 'centre–radius' form by completing the square for both x and y.

Example 10

Find the radius and the coordinates of the centre of the circle with equation
$$x^2 + y^2 - 6x + 4y - 12 = 0$$
and hence sketch the graph.

Solution

By completing the square for both x and y we have
$$x^2 + y^2 - 6x + 4y - 12 = 0$$
$$(x^2 - 6x + 9) - 9 + (y^2 + 4y + 4) - 4 - 12 = 0$$
$$(x^2 - 6x + 9) + (y^2 + 4y + 4) = 25$$
$$(x - 3)^2 + (y + 2)^2 = 5^2$$

The radius is 5 and the centre is at $(3, -2)$.

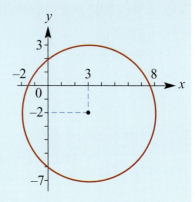

▶ Semicircles

Transposing the general equation of the circle $x^2 + y^2 = r^2$ to make y the subject, we have

$$y^2 = r^2 - x^2$$
$$y = \pm\sqrt{r^2 - x^2}$$

We can now consider two separate rules

$$y = +\sqrt{r^2 - x^2} \quad \text{and} \quad y = -\sqrt{r^2 - x^2}$$

which correspond to the top half and bottom half of the circle respectively.

Similarly, solving for x will give you the semicircles to the left and right of the y-axis:

$$x = \pm\sqrt{r^2 - y^2}$$

Example 11

Sketch the graphs of:

a $y = +\sqrt{4 - x^2}$ **b** $y = -\sqrt{4 - x^2}$
c $x = -\sqrt{4 - y^2}$ **d** $x = +\sqrt{4 - y^2}$

Solution

a $y = +\sqrt{4 - x^2}$

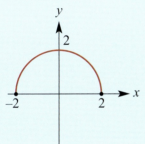

b $y = -\sqrt{4 - x^2}$

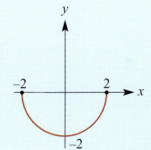

c $x = -\sqrt{4 - y^2}$

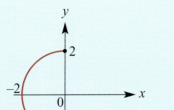

d $x = +\sqrt{4 - y^2}$

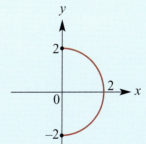

158　Chapter 4: A gallery of graphs

Example 12

Sketch the graph of $y = -2 + \sqrt{49 - (x-2)^2}$.

Solution

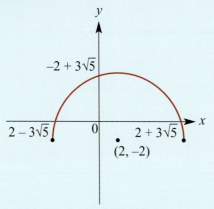

Explanation

It is a semicircle of the circle

$$(x - 2)^2 + (y + 2)^2 = 49$$

The centre is at the point $(2, -2)$.

It is the semicircle $y = \sqrt{49 - x^2}$ translated 2 units the right and 2 units down.

In the usual way, we find the x-axis intercepts and the y-axis intercept.

When $x = 0$,

$$y = -2 + \sqrt{45}$$
$$= -2 + 3\sqrt{5}$$

When $y = 0$,

$$-2 + \sqrt{49 - (x-2)^2} = 0$$
$$\sqrt{49 - (x-2)^2} = 2$$
$$49 - (x-2)^2 = 4$$
$$(x-2)^2 = 45$$
$$x = 2 \pm 3\sqrt{5}$$

Section summary

- The equation of a circle with centre (h, k) and radius r is
  $$(x - h)^2 + (y - k)^2 = r^2$$

- The **general form** for the equation of a circle is
  $$x^2 + y^2 - 2hx - 2ky + c = 0$$

- The two separate rules for semicircles with their base on the x-axis are
  $$y = +\sqrt{r^2 - x^2} \quad \text{and} \quad y = -\sqrt{r^2 - x^2}$$
  They correspond to the top half and bottom half of the circle respectively.

- The two separate rules for semicircles with their base on the y-axis are
  $$x = +\sqrt{r^2 - y^2} \quad \text{and} \quad x = -\sqrt{r^2 - y^2}$$
  They correspond to the right half and left half of the circle respectively.

Exercise 4D

1 Write down the equation of each of the following circles, with centre at $C(h, k)$ and radius r:

a $C(0,0)$, $r = 3$
b $C(0,0)$, $r = 4$
c $C(1,3)$, $r = 5$
d $C(2,-4)$, $r = 3$
e $C(-3,4)$, $r = \frac{5}{2}$
f $C(-5,-6)$, $r = 4.6$

2 Find the centre, C, and the radius, r, of the following circles:

a $(x-1)^2 + (y-3)^2 = 4$
b $(x-2)^2 + (y+4)^2 = 5$
c $(x+3)^2 + (y-2)^2 = 9$
d $(x+5)^2 + (y-4)^2 = 8$

3 Sketch the graphs of each of the following:

a $x^2 + y^2 = 64$
b $x^2 + (y-4)^2 = 9$
c $(x+2)^2 + y^2 = 25$
d $(x+1)^2 + (y-4)^2 - 169 = 0$
e $(2x-3)^2 + (2y-5)^2 = 36$
f $(x+5)^2 + (y-5)^2 = 36$

4 Find the centre, C, and the radius, r, of the following circles:

a $x^2 + y^2 - 6y - 16 = 0$
b $x^2 + y^2 - 8x + 12y + 10 = 0$
c $x^2 + y^2 - 6x + 4y + 9 = 0$
d $x^2 + y^2 + 4x - 6y - 12 = 0$
e $x^2 + y^2 - 8x + 4y + 1 = 0$
f $x^2 + y^2 - x + 4y + 2 = 0$

5 Sketch the graphs of each of the following:

a $x^2 + y^2 - 6y - 16 = 0$
b $x^2 + y^2 + 4x - 6y - 3 = 0$
c $x^2 + y^2 - 8x + 22y + 27 = 0$

6 Sketch the graphs of each of the following:

a $y = +\sqrt{9 - x^2}$
b $x = +\sqrt{9 - y^2}$
c $y = -\sqrt{16 - x^2}$
d $y = -\sqrt{25 - x^2}$
e $x = -\sqrt{49 - y^2}$
f $x = \sqrt{\frac{25}{4} - y^2}$

7 Sketch the graphs of each of the following:

a $y = \sqrt{36 - (x-2)^2}$
b $y - 2 = \sqrt{4 - (x+2)^2}$

8 The graph of $x^2 + y^2 \leq 9$ is as shown. Note that $(1, 1)$ satisfies $1^2 + 1^2 \leq 9$. The coordinates of every point in the shaded region satisfy the inequality.

Sketch the graphs of each of the following. Use a dotted line to indicate that the boundary is not included.

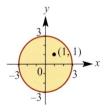

a $x^2 + y^2 \leq 4$
b $x^2 + y^2 > 1$
c $x^2 + y^2 \leq 5$
d $x^2 + y^2 > 9$
e $x^2 + y^2 \geq 6$
f $x^2 + y^2 < 8$

4E Determining rules

Skillsheet In Chapters 2 and 3 we looked at some sufficient conditions for determining the rules for straight lines and parabolas. For straight lines these included:

- the coordinates of two points
- the gradient and a point.

For parabolas these included:

- the coordinates of three points
- the coordinates of the vertex and the coordinates of one other point.

In this section we are looking at some sufficient conditions for determining the rules for the graphs of this chapter.

Example 13

a The rectangular hyperbola $y = \dfrac{a}{x} + 8$ passes through the point $(-2, 6)$. Find the value of a.

b The rectangular hyperbola $y = \dfrac{a}{x} + k$ passes through the points $(2, 7)$ and $(-1, 1)$. Find the values of a and k.

Solution

a When $x = -2$, $y = 6$. Hence

$$6 = \dfrac{a}{-2} + 8$$

$$-2 = \dfrac{a}{-2}$$

$$a = 4$$

The equation is $y = \dfrac{4}{x} + 8$.

b When $x = 2$, $y = 7$. When $x = -1$, $y = 1$.
So we have the equations

$$7 = \dfrac{a}{2} + k \qquad (1)$$

$$1 = -a + k \qquad (2)$$

Subtract (2) from (1):

$$6 = \dfrac{a}{2} + a \qquad (3)$$

Multiply both sides of equation (3) by 2:

$$12 = a + 2a$$

$$a = 4$$

From equation (2): $k = 5$.

The equation is $y = \dfrac{4}{x} + 5$.

Explanation

The general technique is to substitute the given values into the general equation

$$y = \dfrac{a}{x - h} + k$$

In this case $h = 0$ and $k = 8$.

The general technique is to substitute the given values into the general equation

$$y = \dfrac{a}{x - h} + k$$

In this case $h = 0$ and the values of a and k are unknown.

Simultaneous equations need to be formed and then solved.

4E Determining rules

Example 14

A graph which has rule $y = a\sqrt{x - h}$ passes through the points $(4, 2)$ and $(7, 4)$. Find the values of a and h.

Solution

When $x = 4$, $y = 2$. When $x = 7$, $y = 4$.
We have the equations

$$2 = a\sqrt{4 - h} \quad (1)$$
$$4 = a\sqrt{7 - h} \quad (2)$$

Divide (2) by (1):

$$2 = \frac{\sqrt{7 - h}}{\sqrt{4 - h}} \quad (3)$$

Multiply both sides of equation (3) by $\sqrt{4 - h}$:

$$2\sqrt{4 - h} = \sqrt{7 - h}$$

Square both sides of the equation:

$$4(4 - h) = 7 - h$$
$$16 - 4h = 7 - h$$
$$3h = 9$$
$$h = 3$$

Substitute in (1) to find $a = 2$.

The required equation is $y = 2\sqrt{x - 3}$.

Explanation

The general technique is to substitute the given values into the general equation

$$y = a\sqrt{x - h} + k$$

In this case $k = 0$ and the values of a and h are unknown.

Simultaneous equations need to be formed and then solved. Note that $h \neq 4$ from equation (1).

Example 15

Find the equation of the circle whose centre is at the point $(1, -1)$ and which passes through the point $(4, 3)$.

Solution

Let r be the length of the radius. Then

$$r = \sqrt{(4 - 1)^2 + (3 - (-1))^2}$$
$$= \sqrt{3^2 + 4^2}$$
$$= 5$$

Hence the equation of the circle is

$$(x - 1)^2 + (y + 1)^2 = 25$$

Explanation

We use the centre–radius form for the equation of a circle:

$$(x - h)^2 + (y - k)^2 = r^2$$

The centre is $(1, -1)$. We need to find the radius.

Exercise 4E

Example 13a 1. The rectangular hyperbola $y = \dfrac{a}{x} + 3$ passes through the point $(1, 8)$. Find the value of a.

2. A rectangular hyperbola with rule of the form
$$y = \dfrac{a}{x - h} + k$$
has vertical asymptote $x = 3$, horizontal asymptote $y = 4$ and passes through the point $(0, 6)$. Find the values of a, h and k.

Example 13b 3. The rectangular hyperbola $y = \dfrac{a}{x} + k$ passes through the points $(1, 8)$ and $(-1, 7)$. Find the values of a and k.

4. A rectangular hyperbola with rule of the form
$$y = \dfrac{a}{x - h} + k$$
has vertical asymptote $x = 2$, horizontal asymptote $y = -4$ and passes through the point $(0, 4)$. Find the values of a, h and k.

5. A graph which has rule $y = a\sqrt{x}$ passes through the point $(2, 8)$. Find the value of a.

Example 14 6. A graph which has rule $y = a\sqrt{x - h}$ passes through the points $(1, 2)$ and $(10, 4)$. Find the values of a and h.

Example 15 7. Find the equation of the circle whose centre is at the point $(2, 1)$ and which passes through the point $(4, -3)$.

8. Find the equation of the circle whose centre is at the point $(-2, 3)$ and which passes through the point $(-3, 3)$.

9. Find the equation of the circle whose centre is at the point $(-2, 3)$ and which passes through the point $(2, 3)$.

10. Find the equation of the circle with centre $(2, -3)$ which touches the x-axis.

11. Find the equation of the circle whose centre lies on the line $y = 4$ and which passes through the points $(2, 0)$ and $(6, 0)$.

12. Find the equations of the circles which touch the x-axis, have radius 5 and pass through the point $(0, 8)$.

13. Find the equation of a circle which passes through the points $A(0, 2)$, $B(2, 0)$ and $C(-4, 0)$.

14 Find the rule for each of the following graphs. The general form of the rule is given for each graph.

a $(x - h)^2 + (y - k)^2 = r^2$

b $y = a\sqrt{x - h} + k$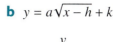

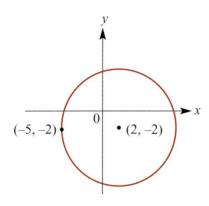

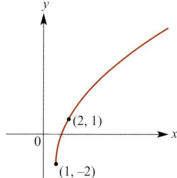

Centre at $(2, -2)$

c $y = \dfrac{a}{x - h} + k$

d $y = \dfrac{a}{x - h} + k$

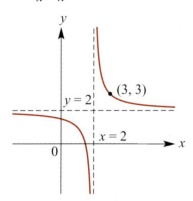

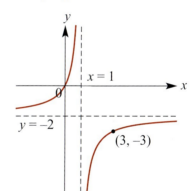

e $y = a\sqrt{h - x} + k$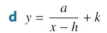

f $y = \dfrac{a}{(x - h)^2} + k$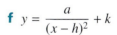

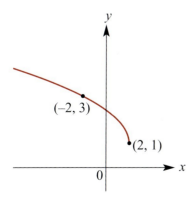

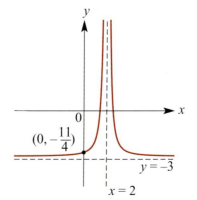

Chapter summary

- The standard graphs:

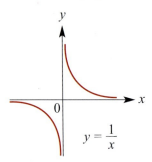

Rectangular hyperbola

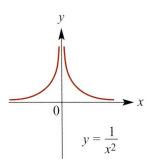

Truncus

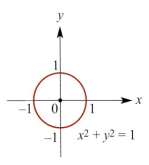

Circle

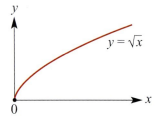

- Dilations of these graphs:

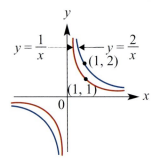

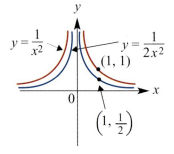

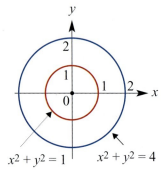

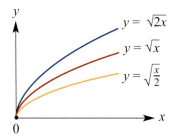

- Reflections in the axes:

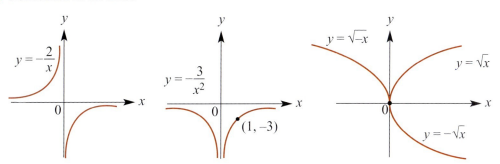

- Translations of graphs:

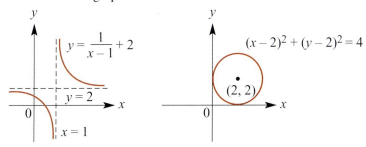

- Equation for a circle with centre at (h, k) and radius r:

$$(x - h)^2 + (y - k)^2 = r^2$$

Alternative form:

$$x^2 + y^2 - 2hx - 2ky + c = 0$$

where $c = h^2 + k^2 - r^2$.

Technology-free questions

1 Sketch the graphs of each of the following:

a $y = \dfrac{-3}{x}$ **b** $y = \dfrac{2}{x^2}$ **c** $y = \dfrac{1}{x - 1}$ **d** $y = \dfrac{2}{x + 1} + 1$

e $y = \dfrac{-2}{x^2}$ **f** $y = \dfrac{-1}{x - 1}$ **g** $y = \dfrac{4}{2 - x} + 3$ **h** $y = \dfrac{-3}{x^2} + 1$

i $y = 2\sqrt{x} + 2$ **j** $y = 2\sqrt{x - 3} + 2$ **k** $y = -2\sqrt{x + 2} + 2$

2 By completing the square, write each of the following equations in the form $(x - a)^2 + (y - b)^2 = r^2$:

a $x^2 + y^2 - 6x + 4y - 12 = 0$ **b** $x^2 + y^2 - 3x + 5y - 4 = 0$

c $2x^2 + 2y^2 - x + y - 4 = 0$ **d** $x^2 + y^2 + 4x - 6y = 0$

e $x^2 + y^2 = 6(x + y)$ **f** $x^2 + y^2 = 4x - 6y$

3 For the circle $x^2 + y^2 - 4x + 6y = 14$, find the equation of the diameter which passes through the origin.

4 For the circle $x^2 + y^2 - 3x + 2y = 26$, find the equation of the diameter which cuts the x-axis at an angle of $45°$.

5 Find the equation of the circle with centre C and radius r for each of the following and sketch the graph:
  a $C(3, 4)$, $r = 5$
  b $C(-1, 0)$, $r = 1$
  c $C(4, 4)$, $r = 2$
  d $C(\frac{1}{2}, -\frac{1}{3})$, $r = \frac{1}{6}$

6 The equation of a circle is $x^2 + y^2 + 4x - 6y = 23$. Find the centre and radius.

7 Find the length cut off on the x-axis and y-axis by the circle $x^2 + y^2 - 2x - 4y = 20$.

8 Sketch the graphs of the following semicircles:
  a $y = \sqrt{9 - x^2}$
  b $y = -\sqrt{16 - (x + 1)^2}$
  c $y - 2 = -\sqrt{1 - x^2}$
  d $y + 3 = \sqrt{4 - (x + 2)^2}$

Multiple-choice questions

1 The circle with equation $(x - a)^2 + (y - b)^2 = 36$ has its centre on the x-axis and passes through the point with coordinates $(6, 6)$. The values of a and b are
  A $a = 0$ and $b = 6$
  B $a = 0$ and $b = 0$
  C $a = 2$ and $b = 0$
  D $a = -6$ and $b = 0$
  E $a = 6$ and $b = 0$

2 The equations of the asymptotes of the graph of $y = 5 - \dfrac{1}{3x - 5}$ are
  A $x = 5$, $y = \dfrac{3}{5}$
  B $y = 5$, $x = \dfrac{5}{3}$
  C $x = 5$, $y = \dfrac{5}{3}$
  D $y = 5$, $x = \dfrac{3}{5}$
  E $x = 5$, $y = -\dfrac{5}{3}$

3 For the rule $y = \dfrac{5}{x^2} + 3$, when $x = \dfrac{a}{2}$, $y =$
  A $\dfrac{5}{4a^2} + 3$
  B $\dfrac{12a^2 + 5}{4a^2}$
  C $\dfrac{20a^2 + 3}{4a^2}$
  D $\dfrac{12a^2 + 5}{a^2}$
  E $\dfrac{20}{a^2} + 3$

4 If the y-axis is an axis of symmetry and the circle passes through the origin and $(0, 4)$, the equation of the circle shown is
  A $x^2 + (y - 2)^2 = 4$
  B $(x - 2)^2 + y^2 = 2$
  C $(x + 2)^2 + y^2 = 4$
  D $x^2 + (y + 2)^2 = 4$
  E $x^2 + y^2 - 2 = 4$

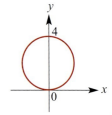

5 The equations of the asymptotes of the graph of $y = 5 + \dfrac{1}{(x-2)^2}$ are

  A $x = 2,\ y = 5$ **B** $x = -2,\ y = 5$ **C** $x = 5,\ y = 4$
  D $x = 5,\ y = 2$ **E** $x = 4,\ y = 5$

6 For the circle with equation $(x - 5)^2 + (y + 2)^2 = 9$, the coordinates of the centre and the radius are

  A $(-5, 2)$ and 3   **B** $(-5, 2)$ and 9   **C** $(5, -2)$ and 9
  D $(5, -2)$ and 3   **E** $(-2, 5)$ and 3

7 For the rule $y = -2\sqrt{x} + 3$, where $x \geq 0$, the range of possible y-values is

  A $y \geq 3$ **B** $y > -3$ **C** $y \geq -3$ **D** $y \leq 3$ **E** $y > 3$

8 The equation of the circle which has a diameter with endpoints at $(-2, 8)$ and $(6, 8)$ is

  A $(x + 2)^2 + (y - 8)^2 = 16$ **B** $(x + 2)^2 + (y + 8)^2 = 64$
  C $(x - 2)^2 + (y - 8)^2 = 16$ **D** $(x - 2)^2 + (y + 8)^2 = 4$
  E $(x - 2)^2 + (y + 8)^2 = 16$

9 Which of the following is the equation for the graph of a circle?

  A $y = 16 - x^2$ **B** $y^2 = 16 + x^2$ **C** $x + y^2 = 16$
  D $x^2 - y^2 = 16$ **E** $y^2 = 16 - x^2$

10 The equation of the semicircle shown is

  A $x^2 + (y - 3)^2 = 9$
  B $y = \sqrt{9 - x^2} + 3$
  C $y = \sqrt{9 + x^2} - 3$
  D $y = -\sqrt{9 - x^2} - 3$
  E $y = -\sqrt{9 - x^2} + 3$

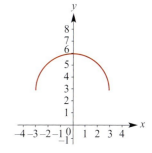

Extended-response questions

The following questions also involve techniques developed in Chapters 2 and 3.

1 The line with equation $y = mx$ is tangent to the circle with centre $(10, 0)$ and radius 5 at the point $P(x, y)$.

  a Find the equation of the circle.
  b Show that the x-coordinate of the point P satisfies the equation
   $(1 + m^2)x^2 - 20x + 75 = 0$.
  c Use the discriminant for this equation to find the exact value of m.
  d Find the coordinates of P. (There are two such points.)
  e Find the distance of P from the origin.

2 A circle has its centre at the origin and radius 4.

   a Find the equation of this circle.

   b Two lines which pass through the point $(8, 0)$ are tangents to this circle.

      i Show that the equations of these tangents are of the form $y = mx - 8m$.

      ii Use techniques similar to those used in Question 1 to find the value of m and, hence, the equations of the tangents.

3 A circle has centre at the origin and radius 5. The point $P(3, 4)$ lies on the circle.

   a Find the gradient of the line segment OP, where O is the origin.

   b Find the gradient of the tangent to the circle at P.

   c Find the equation of the tangent at P.

   d If the tangent crosses the x-axis at A and the y-axis at B, find the length of line segment AB.

4 Let $P(x_1, y_1)$ be a point on the circle with equation $x^2 + y^2 = a^2$.

   a **i** Give the gradient of the line segment OP, where O is the origin.

      ii Give the gradient of the tangent to the circle at P.

   b Show that the equation of the tangent at $P(x_1, y_1)$ is $x_1 x + y_1 y = a^2$.

   c If $x_1 = y_1$ and $a = 4$, find the equations of the possible tangents.

5 An equilateral triangle ABC circumscribes the circle with equation $x^2 + y^2 = a^2$. The side BC of the triangle has equation $x = -a$.

   a Find the equations of AB and AC.

   b Find the equation of the circle circumscribing triangle ABC.

6 Consider the curve with equation $y = \sqrt{x - b} + c$.

   a Show that if the curve meets the line with equation $y = x$ at the point (a, a), then a satisfies the equation $a^2 - (2c + 1)a + c^2 + b = 0$.

   b **i** If the line with equation $y = x$ is a tangent to the curve, show that $c = \dfrac{4b - 1}{4}$.

      ii Sketch the graph of $y = \sqrt{x} - \frac{1}{4}$ and find the coordinates of the point on the graph at which the line with equation $y = x$ is a tangent.

   c Find the values of k for which the line with equation $y = x + k$:

      i meets the curve with equation $y = \sqrt{x} - \frac{1}{4}$ twice

      ii meets the curve with equation $y = \sqrt{x} - \frac{1}{4}$ once

      iii does not meet the curve with equation $y = \sqrt{x} - \frac{1}{4}$.

7 For the curve with equation $y = \sqrt{x - 1}$ and the straight line with equation $y = kx$, find the values of k such that:

   a the line meets the curve twice

   b the line meets the curve once.

Chapter 5
Functions and relations

Objectives

▶ To understand and use the **notation of sets**, including the symbols $\in$, $\subseteq$, $\cap$, $\cup$, $\varnothing$ and $\setminus$.
▶ To use the notation for **sets of numbers**.
▶ To understand the concepts of **relation** and **function**.
▶ To find the **domain** and **range** of a given relation.
▶ To decide whether or not a given function is **one-to-one**.
▶ To find the **implied (maximal) domain** of a function.
▶ To work with **restrictions of a function** and **piecewise-defined functions**.
▶ To find the **inverse** of a one-to-one function.
▶ To apply a knowledge of functions to solving problems.

In this chapter we introduce the notation that will be used throughout the rest of the book. You will have met much of it before and this will serve as revision. The language introduced in this chapter helps to express important mathematical ideas precisely. Initially they may seem unnecessarily abstract, but later in the book you will find them used more and more in practical situations.

In Chapters 2 and 3 we looked at linear polynomials and quadratic polynomials, and in Chapter 4 we studied rectangular hyperbolas, square-root graphs, circles and semicircles. These are all examples of relations. You will meet them all again in this chapter, but using a new notation which will be carried through into the following chapters of this book.

5A Set notation and sets of numbers

Set notation

Set notation is used widely in mathematics and in this book where appropriate. This section summarises all of the set notation you will need.

- A **set** is a collection of objects.
- The objects that are in the set are known as **elements** or members of the set.
- If x is an element of a set A, we write $x \in A$. This can also be read as 'x is a member of the set A' or 'x belongs to A' or 'x is in A'. For example: $2 \in$ set of even numbers.
- If x is **not an element** of A, we write $x \notin A$. For example: $2 \notin$ set of odd numbers.
- Set B is called a **subset** of set A if every element of B is also an element of A. We write $B \subseteq A$. This expression can also be read as 'B is contained in A' or 'A contains B'.

For example, let $B = \{0, 1, 2\}$ and $A = \{0, 1, 2, 3, 4\}$. Then B is a subset of A, as illustrated in the diagram opposite.

This diagram is called a **Venn diagram**. Venn diagrams are revisited in Chapter 9.

- The set of elements common to two sets A and B is called the **intersection** of A and B, and is denoted by $A \cap B$. Thus $x \in A \cap B$ if and only if $x \in A$ and $x \in B$.
- If the sets A and B have no elements in common, we say A and B are **disjoint**, and write $A \cap B = \emptyset$. The set $\emptyset$ is called the **empty set**.
- The set of elements that are in A or in B (or in both) is called the **union** of sets A and B, and is denoted by $A \cup B$.

For example, let $A = \{1, 3, 5, 7, 9\}$ and $B = \{1, 2, 3, 4, 5\}$. The intersection and union are illustrated by the Venn diagram shown opposite:

$A \cap B = \{1, 3, 5\}$

$A \cup B = \{1, 2, 3, 4, 5, 7, 9\}$

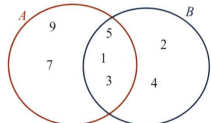

Example 1

For $A = \{1, 2, 3, 7\}$ and $B = \{3, 4, 5, 6, 7\}$, find:

a $A \cap B$ **b** $A \cup B$

Solution	Explanation
a $A \cap B = \{3, 7\}$	The elements 3 and 7 are common to sets A and B.
b $A \cup B = \{1, 2, 3, 4, 5, 6, 7\}$	The set $A \cup B$ contains all elements that belong to A or B (or both).

Note: In Example 1, we have $3 \in A$ and $5 \notin A$ and $\{2, 3\} \subseteq A$.

Set difference

Finally we introduce the **set difference** of two sets A and B:

$$A \setminus B = \{ x : x \in A,\ x \notin B \}$$

The set $A \setminus B$ contains the elements of A that are not elements of B.

> **Example 2**
>
> For $A = \{1, 2, 3, 7\}$ and $B = \{3, 4, 5, 6, 7\}$, find:
>
> **a** $A \setminus B$ **b** $B \setminus A$
>
> *Solution*
>
> **a** $A \setminus B = \{1, 2, 3, 7\} \setminus \{3, 4, 5, 6, 7\}$
> $= \{1, 2\}$
>
> **b** $B \setminus A = \{3, 4, 5, 6, 7\} \setminus \{1, 2, 3, 7\}$
> $= \{4, 5, 6\}$
>
> *Explanation*
>
> The elements 1 and 2 are in A but not in B.
>
> The elements 4, 5 and 6 are in B but not in A.

▶ Sets of numbers

We begin by recalling that the elements of $\{1, 2, 3, 4, \dots\}$ are called the **natural numbers**, and the elements of $\{\dots, -2, -1, 0, 1, 2, \dots\}$ are called **integers**.

The numbers of the form $\dfrac{p}{q}$, with p and q integers, $q \neq 0$, are called **rational numbers**. The real numbers which are not rational are called **irrational** (e.g. π and $\sqrt{2}$).

The rationals may be characterised as being those real numbers that can be written as a terminating or recurring decimal.

- The set of real numbers will be denoted by $\mathbb{R}$.
- The set of rational numbers will be denoted by $\mathbb{Q}$.
- The set of integers will be denoted by $\mathbb{Z}$.
- The set of natural numbers will be denoted by $\mathbb{N}$.

It is clear that $\mathbb{N} \subseteq \mathbb{Z} \subseteq \mathbb{Q} \subseteq \mathbb{R}$, and this may be represented by the diagram on the right.

Describing a set

It is not always possible to list the elements of a set. There is an alternative way of describing sets that is especially useful for infinite sets.

The set of all x such that ___ is denoted by $\{ x : \underline{} \}$. Thus, for example:

- $\{ x : 0 < x < 1 \}$ is the set of all real numbers strictly between 0 and 1
- $\{ x : x \geq 3 \}$ is the set of all real numbers greater than or equal to 3
- $\{ x : x > 0,\ x \text{ rational} \} = \{ x : x > 0,\ x \in \mathbb{Q} \}$ is the set of all positive rational numbers
- $\{ 2n : n = 0, 1, 2, \dots \}$ is the set of all non-negative even numbers
- $\{ 2n + 1 : n = 0, 1, 2, \dots \}$ is the set of all non-negative odd numbers.

Interval notation

Among the most important subsets of $\mathbb{R}$ are the **intervals**. The following is an exhaustive list of the various types of intervals and the standard notation for them. We suppose that a and b are real numbers with $a < b$.

$$(a, b) = \{ x : a < x < b \} \qquad [a, b] = \{ x : a \leq x \leq b \}$$
$$(a, b] = \{ x : a < x \leq b \} \qquad [a, b) = \{ x : a \leq x < b \}$$
$$(a, \infty) = \{ x : a < x \} \qquad [a, \infty) = \{ x : a \leq x \}$$
$$(-\infty, b) = \{ x : x < b \} \qquad (-\infty, b] = \{ x : x \leq b \}$$

Intervals may be represented by diagrams as shown in Example 3.

Example 3

Illustrate each of the following intervals of real numbers:

a $[-2, 3]$ **b** $(-3, 4]$ **c** $(-\infty, 5]$ **d** $(-2, 4)$ **e** $(-3, \infty)$

Solution

a $[-2, 3]$

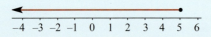

b $(-3, 4]$

c $(-\infty, 5]$

d $(-2, 4)$

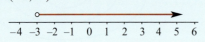

e $(-3, \infty)$

Explanation

The square brackets indicate that the endpoints are included; this is shown with closed circles.

The round bracket indicates that the left endpoint is not included; this is shown with an open circle. The right endpoint is included.

The symbol $-\infty$ indicates that the interval continues indefinitely (i.e. forever) to the left; it is read as 'negative infinity'. The right endpoint is included.

Both brackets are round; the endpoints are not included.

The symbol ∞ indicates that the interval continues indefinitely (i.e. forever) to the right; it is read as 'infinity'. The left endpoint is not included.

Notes:
- The 'closed' circle (•) indicates that the number is included.
- The 'open' circle (◦) indicates that the number is not included.

The following are subsets of the real numbers for which we have special notation:
- Positive real numbers: $\mathbb{R}^+ = \{ x : x > 0 \}$
- Negative real numbers: $\mathbb{R}^- = \{ x : x < 0 \}$
- Real numbers excluding zero: $\mathbb{R} \setminus \{0\}$

Section summary

- If x is an element of a set A, we write $x \in A$.
- If x is not an element of a set A, we write $x \notin A$.
- If every element of B is an element of A, we say B is a **subset** of A and write $B \subseteq A$.
- The set $A \cap B$ is the **intersection** of A and B, where $x \in A \cap B$ if and only if $x \in A$ and $x \in B$.
- The set $A \cup B$ is the **union** of A and B, where $x \in A \cup B$ if and only if $x \in A$ or $x \in B$.
- The set $A \setminus B$ is the **set difference** of A and B, where $A \setminus B = \{x : x \in A, \ x \notin B\}$.
- If the sets A and B have no elements in common, we say A and B are **disjoint** and write $A \cap B = \emptyset$. The set $\emptyset$ is called the **empty set**.
- Sets of numbers:
  - Real numbers: $\mathbb{R}$
  - Integers: $\mathbb{Z}$
  - Rational numbers: $\mathbb{Q}$
  - Natural numbers: $\mathbb{N}$
- For real numbers a and b with $a < b$, we can consider the following **intervals**:

  $(a, b) = \{x : a < x < b\}$ \quad $[a, b] = \{x : a \leq x \leq b\}$

  $(a, b] = \{x : a < x \leq b\}$ \quad $[a, b) = \{x : a \leq x < b\}$

  $(a, \infty) = \{x : a < x\}$ \quad $[a, \infty) = \{x : a \leq x\}$

  $(-\infty, b) = \{x : x < b\}$ \quad $(-\infty, b] = \{x : x \leq b\}$

Exercise 5A

Example 1   **1**   For $A = \{1, 2, 3, 5, 7, 11, 15\}$, $B = \{7, 11, 25, 30, 32\}$ and $C = \{1, 7, 11, 25, 30\}$, find:

     a $A \cap B$ **b** $A \cap B \cap C$ **c** $A \cup C$

     d $A \cup B$ **e** $A \cup B \cup C$ **f** $(A \cap B) \cup C$

Example 2   **2**   For $A = \{1, 2, 3, 5, 7, 11, 15\}$, $B = \{7, 11, 25, 30, 32\}$ and $C = \{1, 7, 11, 25, 30\}$, find:

     a $A \setminus B$ **b** $B \setminus A$ **c** $A \setminus C$ **d** $C \setminus A$

Example 3   **3**   Illustrate each of the following intervals on a number line:

     a $[-3, 4)$ **b** $(-\infty, 3]$ **c** $[-2, -1]$

     d $(-2, \infty)$ **e** $(-2, 3)$ **f** $(-2, 4]$

4   Describe each of the following subsets of the real number line using the interval notation $[a, b)$, (a, b), etc.

a

b
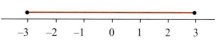

c
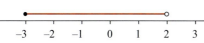

d
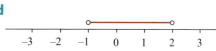

5 Use the appropriate interval notation (i.e. $[a, b]$, (a, b), etc.) to describe each of the following sets:

  a $\{x : -1 \leq x \leq 2\}$
  b $\{x : -4 < x \leq 2\}$
  c $\{y : 0 < y < \sqrt{2}\}$
  d $\left\{y : -\dfrac{\sqrt{3}}{2} < y \leq \dfrac{1}{\sqrt{2}}\right\}$
  e $\{x : x > -1\}$
  f $\{x : x \leq -2\}$
  g $\mathbb{R}$
  h $\mathbb{R}^+ \cup \{0\}$
  i $\mathbb{R}^- \cup \{0\}$

6 For $B = \{7, 11, 25, 30, 32\}$, find:

  a $(-2, 10] \cap B$
  b $(3, \infty) \cap B$
  c $(2, \infty) \cup B$
  d $(25, \infty) \cap B$

7 For each of the following, use one number line on which to represent the sets:

  a $[-2, 5]$, $[3, 4]$, $[-2, 5] \cap [3, 4]$
  b $[-2, 5]$, $\mathbb{R} \setminus [-2, 5]$
  c $[3, \infty)$, $(-\infty, 7]$, $[3, \infty) \cap (-\infty, 7]$
  d $[-2, 3]$, $\mathbb{R} \setminus [-2, 3]$

8 Write each of the following sets as a union of two intervals:

  a $\mathbb{R} \setminus \{-2\}$
  b $\mathbb{R} \setminus \{3\}$
  c $\mathbb{R} \setminus \{4\}$

9 Illustrate each of these sets on a number line:

  a $[-3, 2] \cup [4, 8]$
  b $(-\infty, 2] \cup [4, \infty)$
  c $(-\infty, -3) \cup (0, \infty)$
  d $(-5, -2] \cup (2, 6]$
  e $(-\infty, 2) \cup (2, \infty)$
  f $(-\infty, -3) \cup (-3, \infty)$

10 Describe each of the following intersections of intervals as simply as possible:

  a $(-\infty, -3) \cap (-6, \infty)$
  b $(-\infty, 1) \cap (4, \infty)$
  c $(-\infty, 0] \cap [-6, \infty)$
  d $[-3, 2] \cap [-1, 8]$
  e $[-3, 1] \cap [1, 8]$
  f $(-\infty, -1] \cap (-10, \infty)$

5B Relations, domain and range

Skillsheet In previous chapters we have looked at how to sketch the graphs of various mathematical relations. We will now look at this aspect of representing relations in a more formal way.

- An **ordered pair**, denoted (x, y), is a pair of elements x and y in which x is considered to be the first coordinate and y the second coordinate.
- A **relation** is a set of ordered pairs. The following are examples of relations:
  a $S = \{(1, 1), (1, 2), (3, 4), (5, 6)\}$
  b $T = \{(-3, 5), (4, 12), (5, 12), (7, -6)\}$
- Every relation determines two sets:
  - The set of all the first coordinates of the ordered pairs is called the **domain**.
  - The set of all the second coordinates of the ordered pairs is called the **range**.

For the above examples:

a domain of $S = \{1, 3, 5\}$, range of $S = \{1, 2, 4, 6\}$
b domain of $T = \{-3, 4, 5, 7\}$, range of $T = \{5, 12, -6\}$

Some relations may be defined by a **rule** relating the elements in the domain to their corresponding elements in the range. In order to define the relation fully, we need to specify both the rule and the domain. For example, the set

$$\{(x, y) : y = x + 1,\ x \in \{1, 2, 3, 4\}\}$$

is the relation

$$\{(1, 2), (2, 3), (3, 4), (4, 5)\}$$

The **domain** is the set $X = \{1, 2, 3, 4\}$ and the **range** is the set $Y = \{2, 3, 4, 5\}$.

▶ Representing relations

Graphing relations

We can represent a relation as a graph on a set of Cartesian axes.

On the right is the graph of the relation

$$\{(x, y) : y = x + 1,\ x \in \{1, 2, 3, 4\}\}$$

Note that we only graph the individual points of this relation.

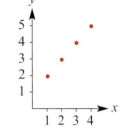

If the domain of the relation is the set of real numbers, $\mathbb{R}$, then there are infinitely many points. For example, the graph of

$$\{(x, y) : y = x + 1,\ x \in \mathbb{R}\}$$

is a continuous straight line.

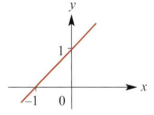

Arrow diagrams

A relation may also be represented by an arrow diagram.

This diagram represents the relation $\{(3, 6), (3, 5), (2, 5), (2, 4), (1, 2)\}$:

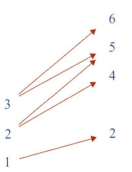

This diagram represents the relation $\{(5, 4), (4, 3), (3, 2), (2, 1)\}$:

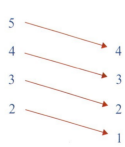

■ A relation may be written as:
 • a listed set of ordered pairs (not always convenient or possible)
 • a rule with a specified or implied domain.

■ A relation may be represented by a graph or an arrow diagram.

Example 4

Sketch a graph of each of the following relations and state its domain and range:
a $\{(-2, -1), (-1, -1), (-1, 1), (0, 1), (1, -1)\}$
b $\{(x, y) : x^2 + y^2 = 1, \ x \in [-1, 1]\}$
c $\{(x, y) : 2x + 3y = 6, \ x \geq 0\}$
d $\{(x, y) : y = 2x - 1, \ x \in [-1, 2]\}$

Solution

a
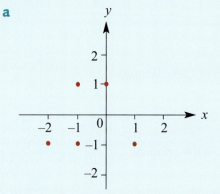

Domain = $\{-2, -1, 0, 1\}$
Range = $\{-1, 1\}$

b
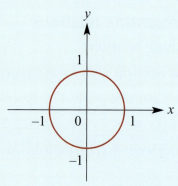

Domain = $\{x : -1 \leq x \leq 1\}$
Range = $\{y : -1 \leq y \leq 1\}$

c
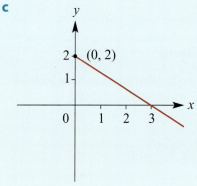

Domain = $\mathbb{R}^+ \cup \{0\}$
Range = $(-\infty, 2]$

d
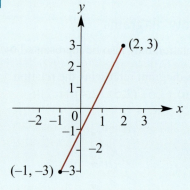

Domain = $[-1, 2]$
Range = $[-3, 3]$

Often set notation is not used in the specification of a relation. For example:

- $\{(x, y) : y = x^2\}$ is written as $y = x^2$
- $\{(x, y) : y = x + 1\}$ is written as $y = x + 1$.

This has been the case in your previous considerations of relations.

Note: In order to determine the range of a relation it is necessary to consider the graph. This strategy is used in the following examples.

Example 5

For each of the following, complete the square, sketch the graph and state the range. The domain is $\mathbb{R}$.

a $y = x^2 - 4x + 5$
b $y = -x^2 + 4x - 5$

Solution

a $y = x^2 - 4x + 5$
$= (x - 2)^2 + 1$

The range is $[1, \infty)$.

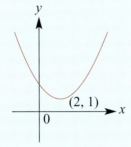

Explanation

Complete the square:
$x^2 - 4x + 5 = x^2 - 4x + 4 - 4 + 5$
$= (x - 2)^2 + 1$

The vertex is at $(2, 1)$. The minimum value of $y = x^2 - 4x + 5$ is 1.

b $y = -x^2 + 4x - 5$
$= -(x - 2)^2 - 1$

The range is $(-\infty, -1]$.

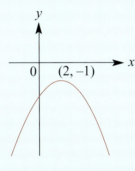

Complete the square:
$-x^2 + 4x - 5 = -(x^2 - 4x + 5)$
$= -[x^2 - 4x + 4 + 1]$
$= -[(x - 2)^2 + 1]$
$= -(x - 2)^2 - 1$

The vertex is at $(2, -1)$. The maximum value is -1.

Example 6

Sketch the graph of the relation $y = x^2 + 2$ for $x \in [-2, 1]$ and state the range.

Solution

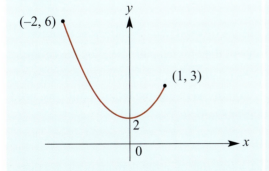

The range is $[2, 6]$.

Explanation

Note that the range is not determined by considering the endpoints alone. The minimum value is 2, not 3.

Implied (maximal) domain

When the rule for a relation is written and no domain is stipulated, then it is understood that the domain taken is the largest for which the rule has meaning. This domain is called the **maximal** or **implied domain**.

For example, the implied domain of $y = x^2$ is $\mathbb{R}$, and the implied domain of $x^2 + y^2 = 1$ is $[-1, 1]$. This concept is considered again in Section 5D.

Example 7

For each of the following relations, state the implied domain and the range:

a $(x-1)^2 + y^2 = 9$ **b** $y = \sqrt{9 - x^2} + 1$

Solution

a This relation is a circle with centre $(1, 0)$ and radius 3. The implied domain is $[-2, 4]$ and the range is $[-3, 3]$.

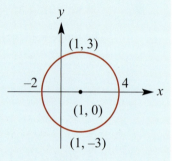

b This relation is a semicircle with centre $(0, 1)$ and radius 3. The implied domain is $[-3, 3]$ and the range is $[1, 4]$.

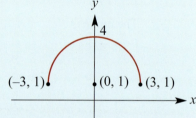

Section summary

- An **ordered pair**, denoted (x, y), is a pair of elements x and y in which x is considered to be the first coordinate and y the second coordinate.
- A **relation** is a set of ordered pairs.
  - The set of all the first coordinates of the ordered pairs is called the **domain**.
  - The set of all the second coordinates of the ordered pairs is called the **range**.
- Some relations may be defined by a rule relating the elements in the domain to their corresponding elements in the range. In order to define the relation fully, we need to specify both the rule and the domain. For example:

  $\{(x, y) : y = x + 1,\ x \in \mathbb{R}^+ \cup \{0\}\}$

- For a relation described by a rule with y in terms of x, the domain is the x-values and the range is the y-values.
- The **maximal** or **implied domain** is the largest domain for which the rule of the relation has meaning.

Exercise 5B

1 Sketch a graph of each of the following relations and state its domain and range:
  a $\{(-3, -4), (-1, -1), (-6, 7), (1, 5)\}$
  b $\{(-4, 1), (-4, -1), (-6, 7), (-6, 8)\}$
  c $\{(x, y) : x^2 + y^2 = 4, \ x \in [-2, 2]\}$
  d $\{(x, y) : 3x + 2y = 12, \ x \geq 0\}$
  e $\{(x, y) : x - y = 4, \ x \in [-1, 2]\}$
  f $\{(x, y) : y = 2x + 3, \ x \in [-4, 1]\}$

2 State the domain and range for the relations represented by each of the following graphs:

a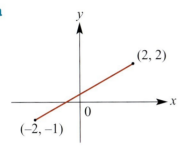

b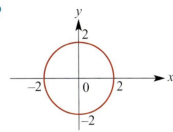

c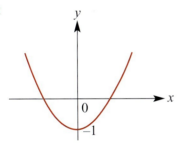

d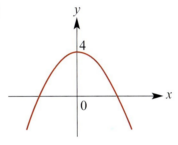

3 For each of the following, complete the square, sketch the graph and state the range:
  a $y = x^2 + 6x + 10$
  b $y = -x^2 - 4x - 6$
  c $y = 2x^2 - 4x + 6$

4 Sketch the graphs of each of the following and state the range of each:
  a $y = x + 1, \ x \in [2, \infty)$
  b $y = -x + 1, \ x \in [2, \infty)$
  c $y = 2x + 1, \ x \in [-4, \infty)$
  d $y = 3x + 2, \ x \in (-\infty, 3)$
  e $y = x + 1, \ x \in (-\infty, 3]$
  f $y = -3x - 1, \ x \in [-2, 6]$
  g $y = -3x - 1, \ x \in [-5, -1]$
  h $y = 5x - 1, \ x \in (-2, 4)$

5 Sketch the graphs of each of the following and state the range of each:
  a $y = x^2 + 3, \ x \in [-1, 1]$
  b $y = x^2 + 4, \ x \in [-2, 1]$
  c $y = x^2 - 4, \ x \in [-1, 2]$
  d $y = 2x^2 + 1, \ x \in [-2, 3]$

6 Sketch the graphs of each of the following relations, stating the range of each:
  a $\{(x, y) : y = x^2 + 1\}$
  b $\{(x, y) : y = x^2 + 2x + 1\}$
  c $\{(x, y) : y = 4 - x^2, \ x \in [-2, 2]\}$
  d $\{(x, y) : y = x^2 + 2x + 3\}$
  e $\{(x, y) : y = -x^2 + 2x + 3\}$
  f $\{(x, y) : y = x^2 - 2, \ x \in [-1, 2]\}$
  g $\{(x, y) : y = 2x^2 - 3x + 6\}$
  h $\{(x, y) : y = 6 - 3x + x^2\}$

180 Chapter 5: Functions and relations

Example 7 7 Sketch the graphs of each of the following relations, stating the implied domain and range of each:
  a $\{(x, y) : x^2 + y^2 = 9\}$
  b $(x - 2)^2 + (y - 3)^2 = 16$
  c $(2x - 1)^2 + (2y - 4)^2 = 1$
  d $y = \sqrt{25 - x^2}$
  e $y = -\sqrt{25 - x^2}$
  f $\{(x, y) : y = -\sqrt{25 - (x - 2)^2}\}$

8 Sketch the graphs of each of the following relations, stating the maximal domain and range of each:
  a $y = \dfrac{2}{2x - 5} + 3$
  b $y = \sqrt{2x - 5}$
  c $y = \sqrt{5 - 2x}$
  d $y = \sqrt{4 - (x - 5)^2}$
  e $y = \dfrac{2}{(2x - 5)^2}$
  f $y = (4 - 2x)^{\frac{1}{2}}$

9 Sketch the graphs of each of the following relations, stating the maximal domain and range of each:
  a $x = y^2$
  b $x = y^2 + 1$
  c $x = y^2 - 1$
  d $x = (y - 3)^2 + 1$

5C Functions

Skillsheet A **function** is a relation such that for each x-value there is only one corresponding y-value. This means that, if (a, b) and (a, c) are ordered pairs of a function, then $b = c$. In other words, a function cannot contain two different ordered pairs with the same first coordinate.

Example 8

Which of the following sets of ordered pairs defines a function?
a $\{(-3, -4), (-1, -1), (-6, 7), (1, 5)\}$
b $\{(-4, 1), (-4, -1), (-6, 7), (-6, 8)\}$

Solution

a $\{(-3, -4), (-1, -1), (-6, 7), (1, 5)\}$ is a function, because for each x-value there is only one y-value.

b $\{(-4, 1), (-4, -1), (-6, 7), (-6, 8)\}$ is *not* a function, because there is an x-value with two different y-values. The relation contains two ordered pairs, $(-4, 1)$ and $(-4, -1)$, with the same first coordinate.

One way to identify whether a relation is a function is to draw a graph of the relation and then apply the following test.

Vertical-line test

If a vertical line can be drawn anywhere on the graph and it only ever intersects the graph a maximum of once, then the relation is a **function**.

Example 9

a Is $y = x^2$ a function? State the maximal domain and range of $y = x^2$.

b Is $x^2 + y^2 = 4$ a function? State the maximal domain and range of $x^2 + y^2 = 4$.

Solution

a

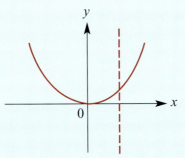

The vertical-line test shows that $y = x^2$ is a function. The maximal domain is $\mathbb{R}$ and the range is $\mathbb{R}^+ \cup \{0\}$.

b

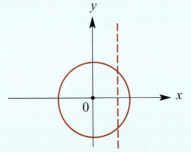

The vertical-line test shows that $x^2 + y^2 = 4$ is *not* a function. The maximal domain is $[-2, 2]$ and the range is $[-2, 2]$.

Explanation

For each x-value there is only one y-value.

The ordered pairs of the relation are all of the form (a, a^2).

Note that $(\sqrt{2}, \sqrt{2})$ and $(\sqrt{2}, -\sqrt{2})$ are ordered pairs of the relation.

There is an x-value with more than one y-value.

▶ Function notation

Functions are usually denoted with lowercase letters such as f, g, h.

If f is a function, then for each x in the domain of f there is a unique element y in the range such that $(x, y) \in f$. The element y is called 'the **image** of x under f' or 'the **value** of f at x', and the element x is called 'a **pre-image** of y'.

Since the y-value obtained is a *function* of the x-value, we use the notation $f(x)$, read as 'f of x', in place of y.

For example, instead of $y = 2x + 1$ we can write $f(x) = 2x + 1$. Then $f(2)$ means the y-value obtained when $x = 2$.

e.g. $f(2) = 2(2) + 1 = 5$

$f(-4) = 2(-4) + 1 = -7$

$f(a) = 2a + 1$

By incorporating this notation, we have an alternative way of writing functions:

- For the function $\{(x, y) : y = x^2\}$ with domain $\mathbb{R}$, we write $f: \mathbb{R} \to \mathbb{R}$, $f(x) = x^2$.
- For the function $\{(x, y) : y = 2x - 1,\ x \in [0, 4]\}$, we write $f: [0, 4] \to \mathbb{R}$, $f(x) = 2x - 1$.
- For the function $\left\{(x, y) : y = \dfrac{1}{x}\right\}$ with domain $\mathbb{R} \setminus \{0\}$, we write $f: \mathbb{R} \setminus \{0\} \to \mathbb{R}$, $f(x) = \dfrac{1}{x}$.

If the domain is $\mathbb{R}$, we often just write the rule. For example: $f(x) = x^2$.

Note that in using the notation $f: X \to Y$, the set X is the domain but Y is not necessarily the range. It is a set that contains the range and is called the **codomain**. With this notation for functions, we write the domain of f as **dom f** and the range of f as **ran f**.

A function $f: \mathbb{R} \to \mathbb{R}$, $f(x) = a$ is called a **constant function**. For such a function f, we have dom $f = \mathbb{R}$ and ran $f = \{a\}$. For example, let $f(x) = 7$. Then dom $f = \mathbb{R}$ and ran $f = \{7\}$.

A function $f: \mathbb{R} \to \mathbb{R}$, $f(x) = mx + c$ is called a **linear function**. For example, let $f(x) = 3x + 1$. Then dom $f = \mathbb{R}$ and ran $f = \mathbb{R}$. Note that if the domain of a linear function is $\mathbb{R}$ and $m \neq 0$, then the range is $\mathbb{R}$.

Example 10

Rewrite each of the following using the $f: X \to Y$ notation:

a $\{(x, y) : y = -3x + 2\}$

b $\{(x, y) : y = -2x + 5,\ x \geq 0\}$

c $y = 5x^2 + 6,\ -1 \leq x \leq 2$

d $y = \dfrac{1}{(x - 2)^2},\ x \neq 2$

Solution

a $f: \mathbb{R} \to \mathbb{R}$, $f(x) = -3x + 2$

b $f: \mathbb{R}^+ \cup \{0\} \to \mathbb{R}$, $f(x) = -2x + 5$
or $f: [0, \infty) \to \mathbb{R}$, $f(x) = -2x + 5$

c $f: [-1, 2] \to \mathbb{R}$, $f(x) = 5x^2 + 6$

d $f: \mathbb{R} \setminus \{2\} \to \mathbb{R}$, $f(x) = \dfrac{1}{(x - 2)^2}$

Example 11

If $f(x) = 2x^2 + x$, find:

a $f(3)$ **b** $f(-2)$ **c** $f(x - 1)$ **d** $f\left(\dfrac{1}{a}\right),\ a \neq 0$

Solution

a $f(3) = 2(3)^2 + 3 = 21$

b $f(-2) = 2(-2)^2 - 2 = 6$

c $f(x - 1) = 2(x - 1)^2 + x - 1$
$= 2(x^2 - 2x + 1) + x - 1$
$= 2x^2 - 3x + 1$

d $f\left(\dfrac{1}{a}\right) = 2\left(\dfrac{1}{a}\right)^2 + \dfrac{1}{a}$
$= \dfrac{2}{a^2} + \dfrac{1}{a}$
$= \dfrac{2 + a}{a^2}$

Example 12

Consider the function defined by $f(x) = 2x - 4$ for all $x \in \mathbb{R}$.

a Find the value of $f(2)$ and $f(t)$.
b Find the value of x for which $f(x) = 6$.
c Find the value of x for which $f(x) = 0$.
d For what values of t is $f(t) = t$?
e For what values of x is $f(x) \geq x$?
f For what values of x is $f(x) \leq 3x$?

Solution

a $f(2) = 2(2) - 4 = 0$
$f(t) = 2t - 4$

b $f(x) = 6$
$2x - 4 = 6$
$2x = 10$
$\therefore \ x = 5$

c $f(x) = 0$
$2x - 4 = 0$
$2x = 4$
$\therefore \ x = 2$

d $f(t) = t$
$2t - 4 = t$
$t - 4 = 0$
$\therefore \ t = 4$

e $f(x) \geq x$
$2x - 4 \geq x$
$x - 4 \geq 0$
$\therefore \ x \geq 4$

f $f(x) \leq 3x$
$2x - 4 \leq 3x$
$-4 \leq x$
$\therefore \ x \geq -4$

Using the TI-Nspire

- Use **menu** > **Actions** > **Define** to define the function $f(x) = 2x - 4$. Find $f(2)$ and $f(t)$.
- Use **menu** > **Algebra** > **Solve** to solve the equation $f(t) = t$ and the inequality $f(x) \geq x$.

Note: The symbol $\geq$ can be accessed from the symbols palette **ctrl** **menu** or by using **ctrl** **=** and selecting $\geq$.

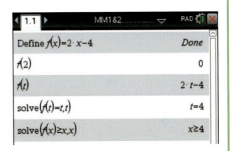

Using the Casio ClassPad

- In the main screen $\sqrt{\alpha}$, type $2x - 4$.
- Highlight the expression and go to **Interactive > Define**. Tap OK.
- Type $f(2)$ by using the **abc** keyboard. Alternatively, copy $f(x)$ and replace x with 2. Tap **EXE** for the answer.
- Type $f(t)$ and tap **EXE**.
- Type $f(t) = t$, highlight it and go to **Interactive > Equation/Inequality > solve**. Remember to change the variable to t.
- The inequality $f(x) \geq x$ can be solved similarly.

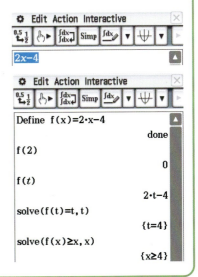

▶ Restriction of a function

Consider the following functions:

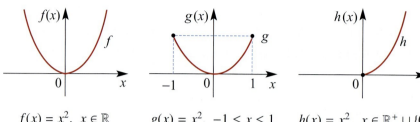

$f(x) = x^2, \ x \in \mathbb{R}$ $g(x) = x^2, \ -1 \leq x \leq 1$ $h(x) = x^2, \ x \in \mathbb{R}^+ \cup \{0\}$

The different letters, f, g and h, used to name the functions emphasise the fact that there are three different functions, even though they all have the same rule. They are different because they are defined for different domains. We say that g and h are **restrictions** of f, since their domains are subsets of the domain of f.

Example 13

Sketch the graph of each of the following functions and state its range:

a $f: [-1, 2] \to \mathbb{R}, \ f(x) = x$

b $f: [-1, 1] \to \mathbb{R}, \ f(x) = x^2 + x$

c $f: (0, 2] \to \mathbb{R}, \ f(x) = \dfrac{1}{x}$

d $f: \mathbb{R} \to \mathbb{R}, \ f(x) = x^2 - 2x + 8$

Solution

a
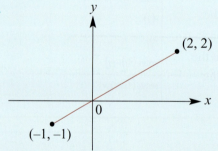

Range is $[-1, 2]$

b
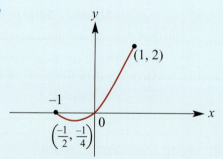

Range is $[-\frac{1}{4}, 2]$

c
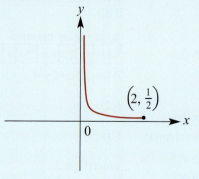

Range is $[\frac{1}{2}, \infty)$

d
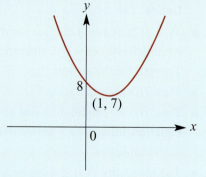

$f(x) = x^2 - 2x + 8 = (x-1)^2 + 7$
Range is $[7, \infty)$

Using the TI-Nspire

- In a **Calculator** application, use menu > **Actions** > **Define** to define the function $f : [-1, 1] \to \mathbb{R}, f(x) = x^2 + x$.

Note: The 'with' symbol | and the inequality signs can be accessed using ctrl =.

- Use menu > **Calculus** > **Function Minimum** and menu > **Calculus** > **Function Maximum** to help determine the range of this restricted function. The range is $[-\frac{1}{4}, 2]$.
- The graph of $y = f(x)$ is plotted by entering $f_1(x) = f(x)$ in a **Graphs** application.
- Use menu > **Analyze Graph** > **Minimum or Maximum** to show the key points.

Note: You can also enter the restricted function directly in the function entry line in the **Graphs** application if preferred.

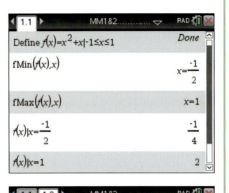

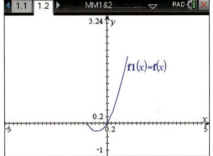

Using the Casio ClassPad

- In the Main $\sqrt{\alpha}$ screen, type $x^2 + x \mid -1 \leq x \leq 1$. (The symbol | is found in Math2.)
- Highlight the expression together with the restricted domain and go to **Interactive** > **Define**. Tap OK.
- Graphing in the main screen:
Select the graph icon. Highlight the definition of $f(x)$ and drag into the graph window.
- Alternatively, go to the menu and select **Graph & Table**. Either enter $f(x)$ in $y1$ or enter $x^2 + x \mid -1 \leq x \leq 1$ directly.

Note: The window can be adjusted using the icon. Alternatively, use Zoom Box to manually select an appropriate window.

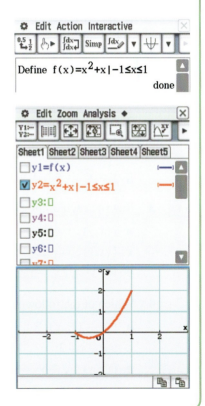

Section summary

- A **function** is a relation such that for each x-value there is only one corresponding y-value.
- **Vertical-line test**: If a vertical line can be drawn anywhere on the graph and it only ever intersects the graph a maximum of once, then the relation is a function.
- Functions are usually denoted with lowercase letters such as f, g, h.
- For an ordered pair (x, y) of a function f, we say that y is the **image** of x under f or that y is the value of f at x, and we say that x is a **pre-image** of y.
- Since the y-value obtained is a function of the x-value, we use the notation $f(x)$, read as 'f of x', in place of y.
- Notation for defining functions: For example, we write $f: [0, 4] \to \mathbb{R}$, $f(x) = 2x - 1$ to define a function f with domain $[0, 4]$ and rule $f(x) = 2x - 1$.
- A **restriction** of a function has the same rule but a 'smaller' domain.

Exercise 5C

Example 8 **1** Which of the following relations are functions? State the domain and range for each:
  a $\{(0, 1), (0, 2), (1, 2), (2, 3), (3, 4)\}$
  b $\{(-2, -1), (-1, -2), (0, 2), (1, 4), (2, -5)\}$
  c $\{(0, 1), (0, 2), (-1, 2), (3, 4), (5, 6)\}$
  d $\{(1, 3), (2, 3), (4, 3), (5, 3), (6, 3)\}$

Example 9 **2** Sketch the graph of each of the following relations, then state the range of each and specify whether the relation is a function or not:
  a $y = x^2$, $x \in [0, 4]$
  b $\{(x, y) : x^2 + y^2 = 4, \; x \in [0, 2]\}$
  c $\{(x, y) : 2x + 8y = 16, \; x \in [0, \infty)\}$
  d $y = \sqrt{x}$, $x \in \mathbb{R}^+$
  e $\left\{(x, y) : y = \dfrac{1}{x^2}, \; x \in \mathbb{R} \setminus \{0\}\right\}$
  f $\left\{(x, y) : y = \dfrac{1}{x}, \; x \in \mathbb{R}^+\right\}$
  g $y = x^2$, $x \in [-1, 4]$
  h $\{(x, y) : x = y^2, \; x \in \mathbb{R}^+ \cup \{0\}\}$

Example 10 **3** Rewrite each of the following using the $f : X \to Y$ notation:
  a $\{(x, y) : y = 3x + 2\}$
  b $\{(x, y) : 2y + 3x = 12\}$
  c $\{(x, y) : y = 2x + 3, \; x \geq 0\}$
  d $y = 5x + 6$, $-1 \leq x \leq 2$
  e $y + x^2 = 25$, $-5 \leq x \leq 5$
  f $y = 5x - 7$, $0 \leq x \leq 1$

4 Which of the following relations are functions? State the domain and range for each:
  a $\{(x, -2) : x \in \mathbb{R}\}$
  b $\{(3, y) : y \in \mathbb{Z}\}$
  c $y = -x + 3$
  d $y = x^2 + 5$
  e $\{(x, y) : x^2 + y^2 = 9\}$

5C

Example 11 5
a Given that $f(x) = 2x - 3$, find:
  i $f(0)$ ii $f(4)$ iii $f(-1)$ iv $f(6)$ v $f(x-1)$ vi $f\left(\dfrac{1}{a}\right)$

b Given that $g(x) = \dfrac{4}{x}$, find:
  i $g(1)$ ii $g(-1)$ iii $g(3)$ iv $g(2)$

c Given that $g(x) = (x-2)^2$, find:
  i $g(4)$ ii $g(-4)$ iii $g(8)$ iv $g(a)$

d Given that $f(x) = 1 - \dfrac{1}{x}$, find:
  i $f(1)$ ii $f(1+a)$ iii $f(1-a)$ iv $f\left(\dfrac{1}{a}\right)$

Example 12 6 Consider the function defined by $f(x) = 2x + 1$ for all $x \in \mathbb{R}$.
  a Find the value of $f(2)$ and $f(t)$.
  b Find the value of x for which $f(x) = 6$.
  c Find the value of x for which $f(x) = 0$.
  d For what values of t is $f(t) = t$?
  e For what values of x is $f(x) \geq x$?
  f For what values of x is $f(x) \leq 3x$?

7 Find the value(s) of x for which the function has the given value:
  a $f(x) = 5x - 2$, $f(x) = 3$
  b $f(x) = \dfrac{1}{x}$, $f(x) = 6$
  c $f(x) = x^2$, $f(x) = 9$
  d $f(x) = (x+1)(x-4)$, $f(x) = 0$
  e $f(x) = x^2 - 2x$, $f(x) = 3$
  f $f(x) = x^2 - x - 6$, $f(x) = 0$

8 Let $g(x) = x^2 + 2x$ and $h(x) = 2x^3 - x^2 + 6$.
  a Evaluate $g(-1)$, $g(2)$ and $g(-2)$.
  b Evaluate $h(-1)$, $h(2)$ and $h(-2)$.
  c Express the following in terms of x:
    i $g(-3x)$ ii $g(x-5)$ iii $h(-2x)$ iv $g(x+2)$ v $h(x^2)$

9 Consider the function $f(x) = 2x^2 - 3$. Find:
  a $f(2), f(-4)$
  b the range of f

10 Consider the function $f(x) = 3x + 1$. Find:
  a the image of 2
  b the pre-image of 7
  c $\{x : f(x) = 2x\}$

11 Consider the function $f(x) = 3x^2 + 2$. Find:
  a the image of 0
  b the pre-image(s) of 5
  c $\{x : f(x) = 11\}$

12 Consider the functions $f(x) = 7x + 6$ and $g(x) = 2x + 1$. Find:
  a $\{x : f(x) = g(x)\}$
  b $\{x : f(x) > g(x)\}$
  c $\{x : f(x) = 0\}$

Example 13 13 Sketch the graphs of each of the following functions and state the range of each:
  a $f: [-1, 2] \to \mathbb{R}$, $f(x) = x^2$
  b $f: [-2, 2] \to \mathbb{R}$, $f(x) = x^2 + 2x$
  c $f: (0, 3] \to \mathbb{R}$, $f(x) = \dfrac{1}{x}$
  d $f: \mathbb{R} \to \mathbb{R}$, $f(x) = x^2 - 2x + 3$
  e $f: (1, 6] \to \mathbb{R}$, $f(x) = x^2 - 4x + 6$
  f $f: [-3, 6] \to \mathbb{R}$, $f(x) = x^2 - 2x + 1$

5D One-to-one functions and implied domains

▶ One-to-one functions

We have seen that a function is a special type of relation such that each x-value maps to only one y-value.

A function is said to be **one-to-one** if different x-values map to different y-values. That is, a function f is one-to-one if $a \neq b$ implies $f(a) \neq f(b)$, for all $a, b \in \text{dom } f$. Another way to say this is that a one-to-one function cannot contain two different ordered pairs with the same second coordinate.

Example 14

Which of the following functions is one-to-one?

a $\{(1,4),(2,2),(3,4),(4,6)\}$ **b** $\{(1,4),(2,3),(3,2),(4,1)\}$

Solution

a $\{(1,4),(2,2),(3,4),(4,6)\}$ is *not* one-to-one, as both 1 and 3 map to 4.

b $\{(1,4),(2,3),(3,2),(4,1)\}$ is one-to-one, as different x-values map to different y-values.

The vertical-line test can be used to determine whether a relation is a function or not. Similarly, there is a geometric test that determines whether a function is one-to-one or not.

Horizontal-line test

If a horizontal line can be drawn anywhere on the graph of a function and it only ever intersects the graph a maximum of once, then the function is **one-to-one**.

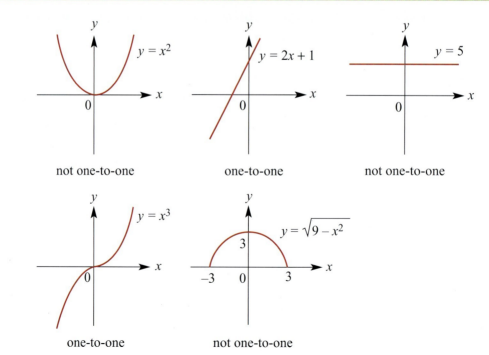

▶ Implied (maximal) domains

We considered implied domains for relations in Section 5B. We recall our definition but this time we do so for functions in particular. The **implied (maximal) domain** of a function is the set of all real numbers for which the rule of the function has meaning.

For example: $f(x) = 3x^2 - 2x$ has implied domain $\mathbb{R}$

$g(x) = \sqrt{x}$ has implied domain $[0, \infty)$

Example 15

State the implied domain, sketch the graph and find the corresponding range of each of the following:

a $f(x) = \sqrt{2x - 5}$ **b** $g(x) = \dfrac{1}{2x - 5}$

Solution

a For $f(x)$ to be defined, we need $2x - 5 \geq 0$, that is, $x \geq \frac{5}{2}$.

Hence the implied domain is $[\frac{5}{2}, \infty)$.

The range of the function is $\mathbb{R}^+ \cup \{0\} = [0, \infty)$.

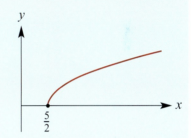

b For $g(x)$ to be defined, we need $2x - 5 \neq 0$, that is, $x \neq \frac{5}{2}$.

Hence the implied domain is $\mathbb{R} \setminus \{\frac{5}{2}\}$.

The range is $\mathbb{R} \setminus \{0\}$.

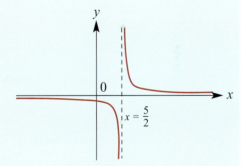

Section summary

- A function f is **one-to-one** if different x-values map to different y-values, that is, if $a \neq b$ implies $f(a) \neq f(b)$, for all $a, b \in \text{dom } f$.
- **Horizontal-line test**: If a horizontal line can be drawn anywhere on the graph of a function and it only ever intersects the graph a maximum of once, then the function is one-to-one.
- When the domain of a function is not explicitly stated, it is assumed to consist of all real numbers for which the rule has meaning. We refer to the **implied (maximal) domain** of a function, because the domain is implied by the rule.

Exercise 5D

1 State which of the following functions are one-to-one:

Example 14

- **a** $\{(1, 3), (2, 4), (4, 4), (3, 6)\}$
- **b** $\{(1, 3), (2, 4), (3, 6), (7, 9)\}$
- **c** $\{(x, y) : y = x^2\}$
- **d** $\{(x, y) : y = 3x + 1\}$
- **e** $f(x) = x^3 + 1$
- **f** $f(x) = 1 - x^2$
- **g** $y = x^2,\ x \geq 0$

2 Each of the following is the graph of a relation:
   i State which are the graph of a function.
   ii State which are the graph of a one-to-one function.

a 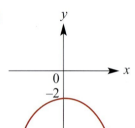   **b** 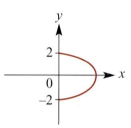   **c**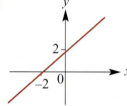

d 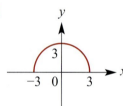   **e** 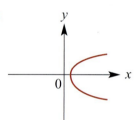   **f**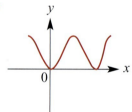

g 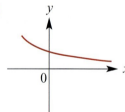   **h**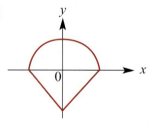

Example 15

3 For each of the following, find the implied domain and the corresponding range for the function defined by the rule:

- **a** $y = 7 - x$
- **b** $y = 2\sqrt{x}$
- **c** $y = x^2 + 1$
- **d** $y = -\sqrt{9 - x^2}$
- **e** $y = \dfrac{1}{\sqrt{x}}$
- **f** $y = 3 - 2x^2$
- **g** $y = \sqrt{x - 2}$
- **h** $y = \sqrt{2x - 1}$
- **i** $y = \sqrt{3 - 2x}$
- **j** $y = \dfrac{1}{2x - 1}$
- **k** $y = \dfrac{1}{(2x - 1)^2} - 3$
- **l** $y = \dfrac{1}{2x - 1} + 2$

4 For each of the following, state the implied domain and range:
  a $f(x) = \sqrt{x - 4}$
  b $f(x) = \sqrt{4 - x}$
  c $f(x) = 2\sqrt{x - 2} + 3$
  d $f(x) = \dfrac{1}{x - 4}$
  e $f(x) = \dfrac{1}{x - 4} + 3$
  f $f(x) = \dfrac{3}{x + 2} - 3$

5 Each of the following is the rule of a function. In each case write down the maximal domain and the range:
  a $f(x) = 3x + 4$
  b $g(x) = x^2 + 2$
  c $y = -\sqrt{16 - x^2}$
  d $y = \dfrac{1}{x + 2}$

6 The graph shown is of the relation
$$\{(x, y) : y^2 = -x + 2,\ x \leq 2\}$$
From this relation, form two functions with domain $(-\infty, 2]$ and specify the range of each.

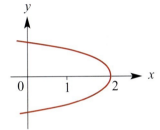

7 a Draw the graph of $f : \mathbb{R} \to \mathbb{R}$, $f(x) = x^2 - 2$.
  b By restricting the domain of f, form two one-to-one functions that have the same rule as f.

8 a Draw the graph of $f : \mathbb{R} \to \mathbb{R}$, $f(x) = x^2 - 2x + 4$.
  b By restricting the domain of f, form two one-to-one functions that have the same rule as f.

9 a Draw the graph of $f : \mathbb{R} \setminus \{2\} \to \mathbb{R}$, $f(x) = \dfrac{1}{(x - 2)^2}$.
  b By restricting the domain of f, form two one-to-one functions that have the same rule as f.

10 a Draw the graph of $x^2 + y^2 = 4$ and state the domain.
   b From this relation form two one-to-one functions that have domain $[0, 2]$.
   c From this relation form two one-to-one functions that have domain $[-2, 0]$.

5E Piecewise-defined functions

Functions which have different rules for different subsets of their domain are called **piecewise-defined functions**. They are also known as **hybrid functions**.

Example 16

a Sketch the graph of the function f given by:
$$f(x) = \begin{cases} -x - 1 & \text{for } x < 0 \\ 2x - 1 & \text{for } 0 \leq x \leq 1 \\ \frac{1}{2}x + \frac{1}{2} & \text{for } x > 1 \end{cases}$$

b State the range of f.

Solution

a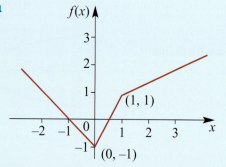

b The range is $[-1, \infty)$.

Explanation

- The graph of $y = -x - 1$ is sketched for $x < 0$. Note that when $x = 0$, $y = -1$ for this rule.
- The graph of $y = 2x - 1$ is sketched for $0 \leq x \leq 1$. Note that when $x = 0$, $y = -1$ and when $x = 1$, $y = 1$ for this rule.
- The graph of $y = \frac{1}{2}x + \frac{1}{2}$ is sketched for $x > 1$. Note that when $x = 1$, $y = 1$ for this rule.

Notes:
- For this function, the sections of the graph 'join up'. This is not always the case.
- A CAS calculator can be used to sketch this graph; see the calculator appendices in the Interactive Textbook.

Exercise 5E

Example 16

1 Sketch the graph of each of the following functions and state its range:

a $h(x) = \begin{cases} x, & x \geq 0 \\ -x, & x < 0 \end{cases}$

b $h(x) = \begin{cases} x - 1, & x \geq 1 \\ 1 - x, & x < 1 \end{cases}$

c $h(x) = \begin{cases} -x, & x \geq 0 \\ x, & x < 0 \end{cases}$

d $h(x) = \begin{cases} 1 + x, & x \geq 0 \\ 1 - x, & x < 0 \end{cases}$

e $h(x) = \begin{cases} x, & x \geq 1 \\ 2 - x, & x < 1 \end{cases}$

2 a Sketch the graph of the function:

$$f(x) = \begin{cases} \frac{2}{3}x + 3, & x < 0 \\ x + 3, & 0 \leq x \leq 1 \\ -2x + 6, & x > 1 \end{cases}$$

b What is the range of f?

3 Sketch the graph of the function:

$$g(x) = \begin{cases} -x - 3, & x < 1 \\ x - 5, & 1 \leq x \leq 5 \\ 3x - 15, & x > 5 \end{cases}$$

4 a Sketch the graph of the function:

$$h(x) = \begin{cases} x^2 + 1, & x \geq 0 \\ 1 - x, & x < 0 \end{cases}$$

b State the range of h.

5 a Sketch the graph of the function:

$$f(x) = \begin{cases} x + 3, & x < -3 \\ x^2 - 9, & -3 \leq x \leq 3 \\ x - 3, & x > 3 \end{cases}$$

b State the range of f.

6 Sketch the graph of each of the following and state the range:

a $f(x) = \begin{cases} x + 3, & x < -3 \\ x, & x > 2 \end{cases}$

b $f(x) = \begin{cases} \dfrac{1}{x+3}, & x < -3 \\ x^2, & x > 0 \end{cases}$

c $f(x) = \begin{cases} 2x + 3, & x \leq 1 \\ x, & 1 < x < 3 \\ -x, & x \geq 4 \end{cases}$

d $f(x) = \begin{cases} \dfrac{1}{x+3}, & x < -3 \\ (x + 2)^2, & x > -1 \end{cases}$

7 a Sketch the graph of the function:

$$f(x) = \begin{cases} \dfrac{1}{x}, & x > 1 \\ x, & x \leq 1 \end{cases}$$

b State the range of f.

8 Specify the function represented by this graph:

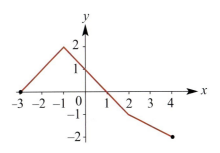

5F Applying function notation

Skillsheet The first four chapters of this book involve functions without using function notation. This section presents further questions which arise from the first four chapters of this book but where function notation can now be used.

Example 17

The volume of a sphere of radius r is determined by the function with rule $V(r) = \dfrac{4}{3}\pi r^3$. State the practical domain of the function V and find $V(10)$.

Solution

The practical domain is $(0, \infty)$.

$$V(10) = \dfrac{4}{3} \times \pi \times 10^3 = \dfrac{4000\pi}{3}$$

(The volume of a sphere of radius 10 is $\dfrac{4000\pi}{3}$ cubic units.)

Example 18

If $f: \mathbb{R} \to \mathbb{R}$, $f(x) = ax + b$ such that $f(1) = 7$ and $f(5) = 19$, find a and b and sketch the graph of $y = f(x)$.

Solution

Since $f(1) = 7$ and $f(5) = 19$,

$\qquad 7 = a + b \qquad (1)$

and $\quad 19 = 5a + b \qquad (2)$

Subtract (1) from (2):

$\qquad 12 = 4a$

Thus $a = 3$ and substituting in (1) gives $b = 4$.

Hence $f(x) = 3x + 4$.

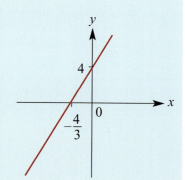

Example 19

Find the quadratic function f such that $f(4) = f(-2) = 0$ and $f(0) = 16$.

Solution

Since 4 and -2 are solutions to the quadratic equation $f(x) = 0$, we have

$\qquad f(x) = k(x - 4)(x + 2)$

Since $f(0) = 16$, we obtain

$\qquad 16 = k(-4)(2)$

$\qquad \therefore \ k = -2$

Hence $f(x) = -2(x - 4)(x + 2)$
$= -2(x^2 - 2x - 8)$
$= -2x^2 + 4x + 16$

Exercise 5F

Example 17   **1**   A metal bar is L cm long when its temperature is $T°C$. The quantities L and T are approximately related by the formula $L = 0.002T + 25$.

    a L is a function of T and the rule can be written $L(T) = 0.002T + 25$. State a possible practical domain for the function.

    b   Find:

        i $L(30)$ **ii** $L(16)$ **iii** $L(100)$ **iv** $L(500)$

Example 18   **2**   If $f(x) = a + bx$ with $f(4) = -1$ and $f(8) = 1$:

    a   find a and b

    b   solve the equation $f(x) = 0$.

3   Find a linear function f such that $f(0) = 7$ and whose graph is parallel to that of the function with rule $g(x) = 2 - 5x$.

4 f is a linear function such that $f(-5) = -12$ and $f(7) = 6$.

    a   Find:

        i $f(0)$ **ii** $f(1)$

    b   Solve the equation $f(x) = 0$.

Example 19   **5**   Find the quadratic function f such that $f(2) = f(4) = 0$ and 7 is the greatest value of $f(x)$.

6   Write $f(x) = x^2 - 6x + 16$ in the form $f(x) = (x - 3)^2 + p$ and hence state the range of f.

7 $f : \mathbb{R} \to \mathbb{R}$, $f(x) = ax^2 + bx + c$. Find a, b and c if $f(0) = 2$, $f(4) = 0$ and $f(5) = 0$.

8   Find two quadratic functions f and g such that $f(1) = 0$, $g(1) = 0$ and $f(0) = 10$, $g(0) = 10$ and both have a maximum value of 18.

9   **a**   Find the set of values of k for which $f(x) = 3x^2 - 5x - k$ is greater than 1 for all real x.

    b   Show that, for all k, the minimum value of $f(x)$ occurs when $x = \dfrac{5}{6}$. Find k if this minimum value is zero.

5G Inverse functions

Skillsheet

If f is a one-to-one function, then for each number y in the range of f there is exactly one number x in the domain of f such that $f(x) = y$.

Thus if f is a one-to-one function, a new function f^{-1}, called the **inverse** of f, may be defined by:

$$f^{-1}(x) = y \text{ if } f(y) = x, \quad \text{for } x \in \text{ran } f \text{ and } y \in \text{dom } f$$

Example 20

The set of ordered pairs $\{(1, 2), (3, 4), (5, -1), (6, -7), (0, 6)\}$ is a function f.

Describe the inverse function f^{-1} of this function as a set of ordered pairs. Give the domain and range of both f and f^{-1}.

Solution

The inverse function f^{-1} is the set of ordered pairs:
$\{(2, 1), (4, 3), (-1, 5), (-7, 6), (6, 0)\}$

The domain of f is $\{1, 3, 5, 6, 0\}$.
The range of f is $\{2, 4, -1, -7, 6\}$.

The domain of f^{-1} is $\{2, 4, -1, -7, 6\}$.
The range of f^{-1} is $\{1, 3, 5, 6, 0\}$.

Explanation

Using function notation we can define the function f as:

$$f(1) = 2, \quad f(3) = 4, \quad f(5) = -1,$$
$$f(6) = -7, \quad f(0) = 6$$

The inverse function is defined by:

$$f^{-1}(2) = 1, \quad f^{-1}(4) = 3, \quad f^{-1}(-1) = 5$$
$$f^{-1}(-7) = 6, \quad f^{-1}(6) = 0$$

It is not difficult to see what the relation between f and f^{-1} means geometrically. The point (x, y) is on the graph of f^{-1} if the point (y, x) is on the graph of f. Therefore to get the graph of f^{-1} from the graph of f, the graph of f is to be reflected in the line $y = x$.

From this the following is evident:

$$\text{dom } f^{-1} = \text{ran } f$$
$$\text{ran } f^{-1} = \text{dom } f$$

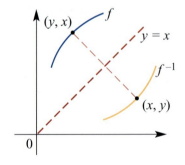

A function has an inverse function if and only if it is one-to-one.

Example 21

a Find the inverse function f^{-1} of the function $f(x) = 2x - 3$ and sketch the graph of $y = f(x)$ and $y = f^{-1}(x)$ on the one set of axes.

b Find the inverse function g^{-1} of the function $g : [2, 6] \to \mathbb{R}$, $g(x) = 2x - 3$ and state the domain and range of g^{-1}.

Solution

a The graph of f has equation $y = 2x - 3$ and so the graph of f^{-1} has equation $x = 2y - 3$, i.e. x and y are interchanged.

Solve for y:

$$x = 2y - 3$$
$$2y = x + 3$$
$$y = \tfrac{1}{2}(x + 3)$$

Hence $f^{-1}(x) = \tfrac{1}{2}(x + 3)$

with $\operatorname{dom} f^{-1} = \operatorname{ran} f = \mathbb{R}$

and $\operatorname{ran} f^{-1} = \operatorname{dom} f = \mathbb{R}$

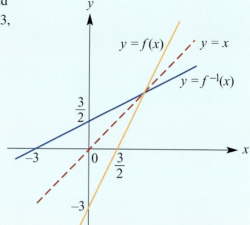

b Now consider $g : [2, 6] \to \mathbb{R}$, $g(x) = 2x - 3$.

The domain of g is $[2, 6]$. We find $g(2) = 1$ and $g(6) = 9$. The gradient of the graph of $y = g(x)$ is positive. Therefore the maximum value of the function is 9 and the minimum value is 1. The range of g is $[1, 9]$.

From part a, the rule for the inverse function is $g^{-1}(x) = \tfrac{1}{2}(x + 3)$.

Also $\operatorname{dom} g^{-1} = \operatorname{ran} g = [1, 9]$

and $\operatorname{ran} g^{-1} = \operatorname{dom} g = [2, 6]$

Using the TI-Nspire

To find the inverse of the function with rule $f(x) = 2x - 3$, use menu > **Algebra** > **Solve**. Two methods are shown.

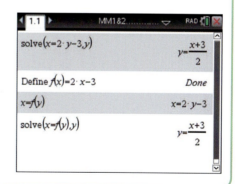

Using the Casio ClassPad

To find the inverse of the function with rule $f(x) = 2x - 3$:

- Enter and highlight the equation $y = 2x - 3$.
- Then use **Interactive** > **Equation/Inequality** > **solve**.

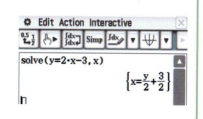

Example 22

Let $f: [3, 6] \to \mathbb{R}$, $f(x) = \left(\dfrac{x}{3}\right)^2$. Find f^{-1} and state its domain and range.

Solution

Let $y = \left(\dfrac{x}{3}\right)^2$. The inverse function has rule

$$x = \left(\dfrac{y}{3}\right)^2$$

$$\pm\sqrt{x} = \dfrac{y}{3}$$

$$\therefore\ y = \pm 3\sqrt{x}$$

But ran f^{-1} = dom f = $[3, 6]$, and so

$$f^{-1}(x) = 3\sqrt{x}$$

with dom f^{-1} = ran f = $[1, 4]$

i.e. $f^{-1}: [1, 4] \to \mathbb{R}$, $f^{-1}(x) = 3\sqrt{x}$

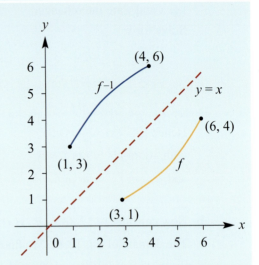

Example 23

Find the inverse of the function $f: [1, \infty) \to \mathbb{R}$, $f(x) = (x - 1)^2 + 4$.

Solution

The inverse has rule

$$x = (y - 1)^2 + 4$$
$$(y - 1)^2 = x - 4$$
$$y - 1 = \pm\sqrt{x - 4}$$
$$\therefore\ y = 1 \pm \sqrt{x - 4}$$

But ran f^{-1} = dom f = $[1, \infty)$, and so

$$f^{-1}(x) = 1 + \sqrt{x - 4}$$

with dom f^{-1} = ran f = $[4, \infty)$

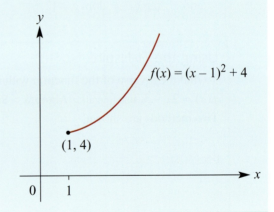

Exercise 5G

Example 20

1 For each of the following, find the inverse function and state its domain and range:
  a $\{(1, 3), (-2, 6), (4, 5), (7, 1)\}$
  b $\{(2, 3), (-1, 6), (4, -5), (1, 7), (6, -4)\}$
  c $\{(3, 3), (-2, -4), (-1, -1), (-8, 1)\}$
  d $\{(1, 3), (-10, -7), (-7, -6), (2, 8), (11, 4)\}$

Example 21

2 For each of the following, find the inverse function and state its domain and range:
  a $f: \mathbb{R} \to \mathbb{R}$, $f(x) = 6 - 2x$
  b $f: [1, 5] \to \mathbb{R}$, $f(x) = 3 - x$
  c $f: \mathbb{R}^+ \to \mathbb{R}$, $f(x) = x + 4$
  d $f: (-\infty, 4] \to \mathbb{R}$, $f(x) = x + 4$
  e $f: [-1, 7] \to \mathbb{R}$, $f(x) = 16 - 2x$

Example 22, 23

3 Find the inverse function of each of the following. State the domain and range of f^{-1}.
   a $f: [0, \infty) \to \mathbb{R}, f(x) = x^2$
   b $f: [2, \infty) \to \mathbb{R}, f(x) = (x - 2)^2 + 3$
   c $f: (-\infty, 4] \to \mathbb{R}, f(x) = (x - 4)^2 + 6$
   d $f: [0, 1] \to \mathbb{R}, f(x) = \sqrt{1 - x}$
   e $f: [0, 4] \to \mathbb{R}, f(x) = \sqrt{16 - x^2}$
   f $f: [0, \infty) \to \mathbb{R}, f(x) = (x + 4)^2 + 6$

4 a On the one set of axes sketch the graphs of $y = f(x)$ and $y = f^{-1}(x)$, where $f(x) = 2x - 6$.
   b Find the coordinates of the point for which $f(x) = f^{-1}(x)$.

5 a On the one set of axes sketch the graphs of $y = f(x)$ and $y = f^{-1}(x)$, where $f: [0, \infty) \to \mathbb{R}, f(x) = x^2$.
   b Find the coordinates of the point(s) for which $f(x) = f^{-1}(x)$.

6 $f: \mathbb{R} \to \mathbb{R}, f(x) = ax + b$, where a and b are non-zero constants, and $f(1) = 2$ and $f^{-1}(1) = 3$. Find the values of a and b.

7 $f: (-\infty, a] \to \mathbb{R}, f(x) = \sqrt{a - x}$.
   a Find $f^{-1}(x)$.
   b If the graphs of $y = f(x)$ and $y = f^{-1}(x)$ intersect at $x = 1$, find the possible values for a.

5H Functions and modelling exercises

In the following examples we see how function notation can be used when applying mathematics in 'real' situations.

Example 24

A book club has a membership fee of $60.00 and each book purchased is $10.00. Construct a cost function that can be used to determine the cost of different numbers of books, then sketch its graph.

Solution

Let $C(n)$ denote the cost (in dollars) when n books are purchased. Then

$$C(n) = 60 + 10n$$

The domain of this function is $\mathbb{N} \cup \{0\}$, the set of non-negative integers, and its graph will be as shown.

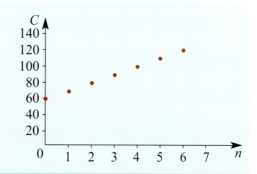

The range of this function is $\{10x : x \in \mathbb{N} \text{ and } x \geq 6\}$. Sometimes to simplify the situation we represent such functions by a continuous line. Strictly, this is not mathematically correct, but it may aid our understanding of the situation.

Example 25

The following table shows the Younanistan Post rates for sending letters.

Mass, m (g)	Cost, C ($)
Up to 50 g	$0.70
Over 50 g up to 100 g	$1.15
Over 100 g up to 250 g	$1.70
Over 250 g up to 500 g	$3.00

Sketch a graph of the cost function, C, giving its domain and range and the rules that define it.

Solution

$$C(m) = \begin{cases} 0.70 & \text{for } 0 < m \le 50 \\ 1.15 & \text{for } 50 < m \le 100 \\ 1.70 & \text{for } 100 < m \le 250 \\ 3.00 & \text{for } 250 < m \le 500 \end{cases}$$

Domain = $(0, 500]$
Range = $\{0.70, 1.15, 1.70, 3.00\}$

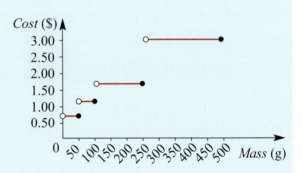

Example 26

A householder has six laying hens and wishes to construct a rectangular enclosure to provide a maximum area for the hens, using a 12 m length of fencing wire. Construct a function that will give the area of the enclosure, A, in terms of its length, ℓ. By sketching a graph, find the maximum area that can be fenced.

Solution

Let ℓ = length of the enclosure

Then width = $\dfrac{12 - 2\ell}{2} = 6 - \ell$

The area is

$$A(\ell) = \ell(6 - \ell)$$
$$= 6\ell - \ell^2$$

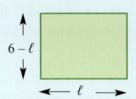

The domain of A is the interval $[0, 6]$.

The maximum area is 9 m² and occurs when $\ell = 3$ m, i.e. when the enclosure is a square.

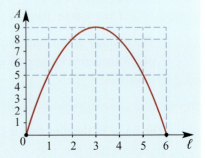

Exercise 5H

1 Vicom's rates for local calls from private telephones consist of a quarterly rental fee of $45 plus 15c for every call. Construct a cost function that describes the quarterly telephone bill.

2 Suppose that Younanistan Post charges the following rates for airmail letters to Africa: $1.20 up to 20 g; $2.00 over 20 g and up to 50 g; $3.00 over 50 g and up to 150 g.
  a Write a cost function, C ($), in terms of the mass, m (g), for letters up to 150 g.
  b Sketch the graph of the function, stating the domain and range.

3 Self-Travel, a car rental firm, has two methods of charging for car rental:
  Method 1 $64 per day + 25 cents per kilometre
  Method 2 $89 per day with unlimited travel
  a Write a rule for each method if C_1 is the cost, in dollars, using method 1 for x kilometres travelled, and C_2 is the cost using method 2.
  b Draw a graph of each rule on the same axes.
  c Determine, from the graph, the distance which must be travelled per day if method 2 is cheaper than method 1.

4 A piece of wire 100 cm long is bent to form a rectangle. Let x cm be the width of the rectangle.
  a Find the length of the rectangle in terms of x.
  b Find the rule $A(x)$ for the function A that gives the area of the rectangle in cm^2.
  c Find the allowable values for x.
  d Find the maximum possible area of the rectangle and the value of x for which this maximum occurs.

5 Assume that angles that look like right angles are right angles.
  a **i** Find an expression for the area A in terms of x and y.
     ii Find an expression for the perimeter P in terms of x and y.
  b **i** If $P = 64$ cm, find A in terms of x.
     ii Find the allowable values for x.
     iii Sketch the graph of A against x for these values.
     iv What is the maximum area?

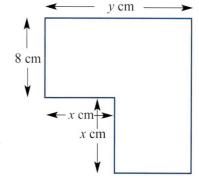

Chapter summary

- **Set notation**

  $x \in A$ x is an element of A

  $x \notin A$ x is not an element of A

  $A \subseteq B$ A is a subset of B

  $A \cap B$ $x \in A \cap B$ if and only if $x \in A$ and $x \in B$

  $A \cup B$ $x \in A \cup B$ if and only if $x \in A$ or $x \in B$

  $A \setminus B$ $\{ x : x \in A,\ x \notin B \}$

- **Sets of numbers**

  $\mathbb{N}$ Natural numbers $\mathbb{Z}$ Integers

  $\mathbb{Q}$ Rational numbers $\mathbb{R}$ Real numbers

- **Interval notation**

  $(a, b) = \{ x : a < x < b \}$ $[a, b] = \{ x : a \leq x \leq b \}$

  $(a, b] = \{ x : a < x \leq b \}$ $[a, b) = \{ x : a \leq x < b \}$

  $(a, \infty) = \{ x : a < x \}$ $[a, \infty) = \{ x : a \leq x \}$

  $(-\infty, b) = \{ x : x < b \}$ $(-\infty, b] = \{ x : x \leq b \}$

- **Relations**

  - A **relation** is a set of ordered pairs.
  - The **domain** is the set of all the first coordinates of the ordered pairs in the relation.
  - The **range** is the set of all the second coordinates of the ordered pairs in the relation.

- **Functions**

  - For a function f and an element x of the domain of f, there is a unique element y in the range such that $(x, y) \in f$. The element y is called the **image** of x under f, and the element x is called a **pre-image** of y.
  - A function f is said to be **one-to-one** if $a \neq b$ implies $f(a) \neq f(b)$, for all $a, b \in \text{dom}\, f$. In other words, f is one-to-one if every image under f has a unique pre-image.
  - The **implied domain** (or **maximal domain**) of a function is the largest subset of $\mathbb{R}$ for which the rule is defined.
  - For a function f with domain D, a new function g may be defined with domain $A \subseteq D$ and rule given by $g(x) = f(x)$ for all $x \in A$. The function g is called a **restriction** of f.

- **Inverse functions**

  If f is a one-to-one function, then for each element y in the range of f there is exactly one element x in the domain of f such that $f(x) = y$.

  Thus if f is a one-to-one function, a new function f^{-1}, called the **inverse** of f, may be defined by:

  $$f^{-1}(x) = y \ \text{ if } \ f(y) = x, \quad \text{for } x \in \text{ran}\, f,\ y \in \text{dom}\, f$$

Chapter 5 review   203

The point (x, y) is on the graph of f^{-1} if the point (y, x) is on the graph of f.

Therefore to get the graph of f^{-1} from the graph of f, the graph of f is to be reflected in the line $y = x$.

From this the following is evident:

$$\text{dom } f^{-1} = \text{ran } f$$
$$\text{ran } f^{-1} = \text{dom } f$$

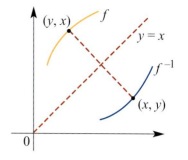

Technology-free questions

1 Describe each of the following using interval notation:

a

b

c

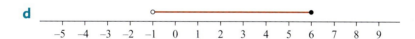

d

e

f

g

2 If f is the function with rule $f(x) = 2 - 6x$, find:

   a $f(3)$
   b $f(-4)$
   c the value of x for which f maps x to 6.

3 For $f: [-1, 6] \to \mathbb{R},\ f(x) = 6 - x$:

   a sketch the graph of f
   b state the range of f.

4 Sketch the graphs of each of the following, stating the range of each:
   a $\{(x,y) : 3x + y = 6\}$
   b $\{(x,y) : y = 3x - 2, \ x \in [-1, 2]\}$
   c $\{(x,y) : y = x^2, \ x \in [-2, 2]\}$
   d $\{(x,y) : y = 9 - x^2\}$
   e $\{(x,y) : y = x^2 + 4x + 6\}$
   f $\{(1, 2), (3, 4), (2, -6)\}$
   g $f : \mathbb{R} \to \mathbb{R}, \ f(x) = (x - 2)^2$
   h $f : \mathbb{R} \setminus \{0\} \to \mathbb{R}, \ f(x) = \dfrac{1}{x} + 2$
   i $(x - \tfrac{1}{2})^2 + (y + 2)^2 = 9$
   j $f : [-1, 3] \to \mathbb{R}, \ f(x) = x$

5 The function f has rule $f(x) = \dfrac{a}{x} + b$ such that $f(1) = \dfrac{3}{2}$ and $f(2) = 9$.
   a Find the values of a and b.
   b State the implied domain of f.

6 Given that $f : [0, 2] \to \mathbb{R}, \ f(x) = 2x - x^2$:
   a sketch the graph
   b state the range.

7 Given that $f(x) = ax + b$, $f(5) = 10$ and $f(1) = -2$, find the values of a and b.

8 Given that $f(x) = ax^2 + bx + c$, $f(0) = 0$, $f(4) = 0$ and $f(-2) = -6$, find the values of a, b and c.

9 State the implied (maximal) domain for each of the following:
   a $y = \dfrac{1}{x - 2}$
   b $f(x) = \sqrt{x - 2}$
   c $y = \sqrt{25 - x^2}$
   d $f(x) = \dfrac{1}{2x - 1}$
   e $g(x) = \sqrt{100 - x^2}$
   f $h(x) = \sqrt{4 - x}$

10 State which of the following functions are one-to-one:
   a $y = x^2 + 2x + 3$
   b $f : [2, \infty) \to \mathbb{R}, \ f(x) = (x - 2)^2$
   c $f(x) = 3x + 2$
   d $f(x) = \sqrt{x - 2}$
   e $f(x) = \dfrac{1}{x - 2}$
   f $f : [-1, \infty) \to \mathbb{R}, \ f(x) = (x + 2)^2$
   g $f : [-3, 5] \to \mathbb{R}, \ f(x) = 3x - 2$
   h $f(x) = 7 - x^2$
   i $f(x) = \dfrac{1}{(x - 2)^2}$
   j $h(x) = \dfrac{1}{x - 2} + 4$

11 Sketch the graphs of each of the following:
   a $f(x) = \begin{cases} 3x - 1, & x \in [0, \infty) \\ x^2, & x \in [-3, 0) \\ 9, & x \in (-\infty, -3) \end{cases}$
   b $h(x) = \begin{cases} 1 - 2x, & x \in [0, \infty) \\ x^2, & x \in [-3, 0) \\ -x^2, & x \in (-\infty, -3) \end{cases}$

12 Sketch the graph of each of the following and state the range:
  a $f: [0, 3] \to \mathbb{R}, f(x) = (x - 1)^2$
  b $f: [-4, 1] \to \mathbb{R}, f(x) = (x + 2)^2 + 1$
  c $f: [1, 5] \to \mathbb{R}, f(x) = \dfrac{1}{(2x - 1)^2}$
  d $f: [-2, 3] \to \mathbb{R}, f(x) = -x^2 + 3$

13 State the maximal domain and range of each of the following:
  a $f(x) = \sqrt{x - 1}$ **b** $f(x) = \sqrt{1 - x}$ **c** $f(x) = 1 - \sqrt{x}$

14 State the maximal domain and range of each of the following:
  a $f(x) = \dfrac{2}{x - 1}$ **b** $f(x) = \dfrac{2}{x + 1}$ **c** $f(x) = \dfrac{2}{x - 1} + 3$

15 State the maximal domain and range of each of the following:
  a $f(x) = \sqrt{1 - x^2}$ **b** $f(x) = \sqrt{9 - x^2}$ **c** $f(x) = \sqrt{1 - x^2} + 3$

16 For each of the following, find the inverse function, stating its rule and domain:
  a $f: [-1, 5] \to \mathbb{R}, f(x) = 3x - 2$
  b $f: [-2, \infty) \to \mathbb{R}, f(x) = \sqrt{x + 2} + 2$
  c $f: [-1, \infty) \to \mathbb{R}, f(x) = 3(x + 1)^2$
  d $f: (-\infty, 1) \to \mathbb{R}, f(x) = (x - 1)^2$

17 If $f(x) = 2x + 5$, find:
  a $f(p)$ **b** $f(p + h)$ **c** $f(p + h) - f(p)$ **d** $f(p + 1) - f(p)$

18 If $f(x) = 3 - 2x$, find $f(p + 1) - f(p)$.

19 State the range of each of the following:
  a $f(x) = -2x^2 + x - 2$ **b** $f(x) = 2x^2 - x + 4$
  c $f(x) = -x^2 + 6x + 11$ **d** $g(x) = -2x^2 + 8x - 5$

20 $f: [-1, 6] \to \mathbb{R}, f(x) = 5 - 3x$
  a Sketch the graph of f. **b** State the range of f.

21 $f: [-1, 8] \to \mathbb{R}, f(x) = (x - 2)^2$
  a Sketch the graph of f. **b** State the range of f.

22 State the implied domain and range of each of the following relations:
  a $x^2 + y^2 = 9$ **b** $(x - 2)^2 + y^2 = 1$
  c $(2x - 1)^2 + (2y - 1)^2 = 1$ **d** $(x - 4)^2 + y^2 = 25$
  e $(y - 2)^2 + x^2 = 16$

23 The domain of the function f is $\{1, 2, 3, 4\}$. Find the range of f if:
  a $f(x) = 2x$ **b** $f(x) = 5 - x$ **c** $f(x) = x^2 - 4$ **d** $f(x) = \sqrt{x}$

Multiple-choice questions

1. For $f(x) = 10x^2 + 2$, $f(2a)$ equals
    A $20a^2 + 2$ B $40a^2 + 2$ C $2a^2 + 2a$ D $100a^2 + 2$ E $10a^2 + 2a$

2. The maximal domain of the function f with rule $f(x) = \sqrt{3x + 5}$ is
    A $(0, \infty)$ B $\left(-\frac{5}{3}, \infty\right)$ C $(5, \infty)$ D $[-5, \infty)$ E $\left[-\frac{5}{3}, \infty\right)$

3. The maximal domain of the function f with rule $f(x) = \sqrt{6 - 2x}$ is
    A $(0, \infty)$ B $[3, \infty)$ C $(-\infty, 2)$ D $(-\infty, 3]$ E $[6, \infty)$

4. The range of the relation $x^2 + y^2 > 9$ when $x, y \in \mathbb{R}$ is
    A $[0, \infty)$ B $\mathbb{R}$ C $(-\infty, 0]$
    D $(3, \infty) \cup (-\infty, -3)$ E $(-\infty, 0)$

5. The range of the function $f: (-1, 2] \to \mathbb{R}$ with rule $f(x) = x^2 + 1$ is
    A $(2, \infty)$ B $(2, 5]$ C $(1, 5]$ D $[0, 5]$ E $[1, 5]$

6. For $f(x) = 7x - 6$, $f^{-1}(x)$ equals
    A $7x + 4$ B $\frac{1}{7}x + 6$ C $\frac{1}{7}x + \frac{6}{7}$ D $\frac{1}{7x - 6}$ E $\frac{1}{7}x - 6$

7. For $f: (a, b] \to \mathbb{R}$, $f(x) = 3 - x$, the range is
    A $(3 - a, 3 - b)$ B $(3 - a, 3 - b]$ C $(3 - b, 3 - a)$
    D $(3 - b, 3 - a]$ E $[3 - b, 3 - a)$

8. Which of the following functions is not one-to-one?
    A $f(x) = 9 - x^2, \, x \geq 0$ B $f(x) = \sqrt{9 - x^2}$ C $f(x) = 1 - 9x$
    D $f(x) = \sqrt{x}$ E $f(x) = \frac{9}{x}$

9. The graph of $y = \frac{2}{x} + 3$ is reflected in the x-axis and then in the y-axis. The equation of the final image is
    A $y = -\frac{2}{x} + 3$ B $y = -\frac{2}{x} - 3$ C $y = \frac{2}{x} + 3$
    D $y = \frac{2}{x} - 3$ E $y = 2x - 3$

10. For $f: [-1, 5) \to \mathbb{R}$, $f(x) = x^2$, the range is
    A $\mathbb{R}$ B $[0, \infty)$ C $[0, 25)$ D $[1, 25]$ E $[0, 5]$

11. Which of the following rules does **not** describe a function?
    A $y = x^2 - x$ B $y = \sqrt{4 - x^2}$ C $y = 3, \, x > 0$
    D $x = 3$ E $y = 3x$

Extended-response questions

1. An Easyride coach leaves town X and maintains a constant speed of 80 km/h for 4 hours, stops at town Y for $\frac{3}{4}$ hours before travelling for a further $2\frac{1}{2}$ hours at 80 km/h to its destination at town Z. A second coach leaves town Z at the same time and runs express to town X, completing its journey in $5\frac{1}{2}$ hours.
   a Construct functions that describe the distance, d km, from X of each coach at time t, stating the domain, range and rule for each.
   b Calculate the distance, from X, at which the two coaches pass each other.

2. A parking meter is designed to accept 200 twenty-cent coins.
   a Write a rule which gives the number of hours parking, P, in terms of the number n of twenty-cent coins inserted, when the cost of parking is 20c for each half hour.
   b Sketch the function, stating the domain and range.

3. The Exhibition Centre hires a graphics company to produce a poster for an exhibit. The graphics company charges $1000 and an additional $5 for each poster produced.
   a i Write the rule for a function, $C(n)$, which describes the cost to the Exhibition Centre of obtaining n posters.
      ii Sketch the graph of C against n (use a continuous model).
   b The Exhibition Centre is going to sell the posters for $15 each.
      i Write down the rule for the function $P(n)$ which gives the profit when the Exhibition Centre sells n posters.
      ii Sketch the graph of this function (use a continuous model).

4. An article depreciates by 5% of its original cost each year. If the original cost was $8000, find an expression for the value, V, of the item n years after purchase.

5. The organisers of a sporting event know that, on average, 50 000 people will visit the venue each day. They are presently charging $15.00 for an admission ticket. Each time in the past when they have raised the admission price, an average of 2500 fewer people have come to the venue for each $1.00 increase in ticket price. Let x represent the number of $1.00 increases.
   a Write the rule for a function which gives the revenue, R, in terms of x.
   b Sketch the graph of R against x.
   c Find the price which will maximise the revenue.

6. A thin wire of length a cm is bent to form the perimeter of a pentagon $ABCDE$ in which $BCDE$ is a rectangle and ABE is an equilateral triangle. Let x cm be the length of CD and let $A(x)$ be the area of the pentagon.
   a Find $A(x)$ in terms of x.
   b State the allowable values for x.
   c Show that the maximum area is $\dfrac{a^2}{4(6-\sqrt{3})}$ cm^2.

7 Let P be a point between B and C on the line BC.

Let $d(x)$ be the distance $(PA + PD)$ m, where x is the distance of P from B.

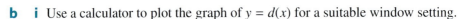

   a   **i** Find an expression for $d(x)$.

   ii Find the allowable values of x.

   b   **i** Use a calculator to plot the graph of $y = d(x)$ for a suitable window setting.

   ii Find the value of x if $d(x) = 20$ (correct to two decimal places).

   iii Find the values of x for which $d(x) = 19$ (correct to two decimal places).

   c   **i** Find the minimum value of $d(x)$ and the value of x for which this occurs.

   ii State the range of the function.

8   **a** Find the coordinates of $A(x_1, y_1)$ and $B(x_2, y_2)$.

   b Let $d(x)$ be the 'vertical' distance between the graphs for $x \in [x_2, x_1]$.

   i Find $d(x)$ in terms of x.

   ii Plot the graph of $d(x)$ against x for $x \in [x_2, x_1]$ and on the same screen the graphs of $y = 2x$ and $y = (x+1)(6-x)$.

   c   **i** State the maximum value of the function defined by $d(x)$ for $x \in [x_2, x_1]$.

   ii State the range of this function.

   d Repeat with the graphs $y = 5x$ and $y = (x+1)(6-x)$.

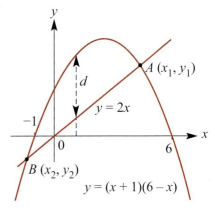

Chapter 6

Polynomials

Objectives

- To add, subtract and multiply polynomials.
- To **divide polynomials**.
- To use the **remainder theorem**, **factor theorem** and **rational-root theorem** to identify the linear factors of cubic and quartic polynomials.
- To solve **equations** and **inequalities** involving cubic and quartic polynomials.
- To recognise and sketch the graphs of **cubic and quartic functions**.
- To find the rules for given cubic graphs.
- To apply cubic functions to solving problems.
- To use the **bisection method** to solve polynomial equations numerically.

In Chapter 3 we looked at polynomial functions of degree 2, or quadratics.

A polynomial function of degree 3 is called a **cubic function**. The general rule for such a function is

$$f(x) = ax^3 + bx^2 + cx + d, \quad a \neq 0$$

A polynomial function of degree 4 is called a **quartic function**. The general rule for such a function is

$$f(x) = ax^4 + bx^3 + cx^2 + dx + e, \quad a \neq 0$$

In Chapter 3 it was shown that all quadratic functions can be written in 'turning point form' and that the graph of a quadratic has one basic form, the parabola.

This is not true of cubic or quartic functions. There is a range of different graph 'shapes' for cubic and quartic functions, depending on the values of the coefficients (a, b, c, d and e).

6A The language of polynomials

Skillsheet

- A **polynomial function** is a function that can be written in the form

$$P(x) = a_n x^n + a_{n-1} x^{n-1} + \cdots + a_1 x + a_0$$

where n is a natural number or zero, and the coefficients $a_0, \ldots, a_n$ are real numbers with $a_n \neq 0$.

- The number 0 is called the **zero polynomial**.
- The **leading term**, $a_n x^n$, of a polynomial is the term of highest index among those terms with a non-zero coefficient.
- The **degree of a polynomial** is the index n of the leading term.
- A **monic polynomial** is a polynomial whose leading term has coefficient 1.
- The **constant term** is the term of index 0. (This is the term not involving x.)

Example 1

Let $P(x) = x^4 - 3x^3 - 2$. Find:

a $P(1)$ **b** $P(-1)$ **c** $P(2)$ **d** $P(-2)$

Solution

a $P(1) = 1^4 - 3 \times 1^3 - 2$
$= 1 - 3 - 2$
$= -4$

b $P(-1) = (-1)^4 - 3 \times (-1)^3 - 2$
$= 1 + 3 - 2$
$= 2$

c $P(2) = 2^4 - 3 \times 2^3 - 2$
$= 16 - 24 - 2$
$= -10$

d $P(-2) = (-2)^4 - 3 \times (-2)^3 - 2$
$= 16 + 24 - 2$
$= 38$

Example 2

a Let $P(x) = 2x^4 - x^3 + 2cx + 6$. If $P(1) = 21$, find the value of c.

b Let $Q(x) = 2x^6 - x^3 + ax^2 + bx + 20$. If $Q(-1) = Q(2) = 0$, find the values of a and b.

Solution

a $P(x) = 2x^4 - x^3 + 2cx + 6$ and $P(1) = 21$.

$P(1) = 2(1)^4 - (1)^3 + 2c + 6$
$= 2 - 1 + 2c + 6$
$= 7 + 2c$

Since $P(1) = 21$,
$7 + 2c = 21$
$c = 7$

Explanation

We will substitute $x = 1$ into $P(x)$ to form an equation and solve.

b $Q(x) = 2x^6 - x^3 + ax^2 + bx + 20$ and $Q(-1) = Q(2) = 0$.

$$Q(-1) = 2(-1)^6 - (-1)^3 + a(-1)^2 - b + 20$$
$$= 2 + 1 + a - b + 20$$
$$= 23 + a - b$$

$$Q(2) = 2(2)^6 - (2)^3 + a(2)^2 + 2b + 20$$
$$= 128 - 8 + 4a + 2b + 20$$
$$= 140 + 4a + 2b$$

Since $Q(-1) = Q(2) = 0$, this gives

$$23 + a - b = 0 \quad (1)$$
$$140 + 4a + 2b = 0 \quad (2)$$

Divide (2) by 2:

$$70 + 2a + b = 0 \quad (3)$$

Add (1) and (3):

$$93 + 3a = 0$$
$$a = -31$$

Substitute in (1):

$$b = -8$$

Hence $a = -31$ and $b = -8$.

First find $Q(-1)$ and $Q(2)$ in terms of a and b.

Form simultaneous equations in a and b by putting $Q(-1) = 0$ and $Q(2) = 0$.

▶ The arithmetic of polynomials

The operations of addition, subtraction and multiplication for polynomials are naturally defined, as shown in the following examples.

Let $P(x) = x^3 + 3x^2 + 2$ and $Q(x) = 2x^2 + 4$. Then

$$P(x) + Q(x) = (x^3 + 3x^2 + 2) + (2x^2 + 4)$$
$$= x^3 + 5x^2 + 6$$

$$P(x) - Q(x) = (x^3 + 3x^2 + 2) - (2x^2 + 4)$$
$$= x^3 + x^2 - 2$$

$$P(x)Q(x) = (x^3 + 3x^2 + 2)(2x^2 + 4)$$
$$= (x^3 + 3x^2 + 2) \times 2x^2 + (x^3 + 3x^2 + 2) \times 4$$
$$= 2x^5 + 6x^4 + 4x^2 + 4x^3 + 12x^2 + 8$$
$$= 2x^5 + 6x^4 + 4x^3 + 16x^2 + 8$$

The sum, difference and product of two polynomials is a polynomial.

Example 3

Let $P(x) = x^3 - 6x + 3$ and $Q(x) = x^2 - 3x + 1$. Find:

a $P(x) + Q(x)$ **b** $P(x) - Q(x)$ **c** $P(x)Q(x)$

Solution

a $P(x) + Q(x)$
$= x^3 - 6x + 3 + x^2 - 3x + 1$
$= x^3 + x^2 - 6x - 3x + 3 + 1$
$= x^3 + x^2 - 9x + 4$

b $P(x) - Q(x)$
$= x^3 - 6x + 3 - (x^2 - 3x + 1)$
$= x^3 - 6x + 3 - x^2 + 3x - 1$
$= x^3 - x^2 - 6x + 3x + 3 - 1$
$= x^3 - x^2 - 3x + 2$

c $P(x)Q(x) = (x^3 - 6x + 3)(x^2 - 3x + 1)$
$= x^3(x^2 - 3x + 1) - 6x(x^2 - 3x + 1) + 3(x^2 - 3x + 1)$
$= x^5 - 3x^4 + x^3 - 6x^3 + 18x^2 - 6x + 3x^2 - 9x + 3$
$= x^5 - 3x^4 + (x^3 - 6x^3) + (18x^2 + 3x^2) - (6x + 9x) + 3$
$= x^5 - 3x^4 - 5x^3 + 21x^2 - 15x + 3$

We use the notation $\deg(f)$ to denote the degree of a polynomial f. For $f, g \neq 0$, we have

$\deg(f + g) \leq \max\{\deg(f), \deg(g)\}$

$\deg(f \times g) = \deg(f) + \deg(g)$

▶ ## Equating coefficients

Two polynomials P and Q are equal only if their corresponding coefficients are equal. For two cubic polynomials, $P(x) = a_3x^3 + a_2x^2 + a_1x + a_0$ and $Q(x) = b_3x^3 + b_2x^2 + b_1x + b_0$, they are equal if and only if $a_3 = b_3$, $a_2 = b_2$, $a_1 = b_1$ and $a_0 = b_0$.

For example, if

$P(x) = 4x^3 + 5x^2 - x + 3$ and $Q(x) = b_3x^3 + b_2x^2 + b_1x + b_0$

then $P(x) = Q(x)$ if and only if $b_3 = 4$, $b_2 = 5$, $b_1 = -1$ and $b_0 = 3$.

Example 4

The polynomial $P(x) = x^3 + 3x^2 + 2x + 1$ can be written in the form $(x - 2)(x^2 + bx + c) + r$ where b, c and r are real numbers. Find the values of b, c and r.

Solution

$(x - 2)(x^2 + bx + c) + r$
$= x(x^2 + bx + c) - 2(x^2 + bx + c) + r$
$= x^3 + bx^2 + cx - 2x^2 - 2bx - 2c + r$
$= x^3 + (b - 2)x^2 + (c - 2b)x - 2c + r$

Explanation

We first expand the brackets of

$(x - 2)(x^2 + bx + c) + r$

If $x^3 + 3x^2 + 2x + 1 = (x - 2)(x^2 + bx + c) + r$ for all real numbers x, then from the above

$$b - 2 = 3 \quad \therefore b = 5$$
$$c - 2b = 2 \quad \therefore c = 2b + 2 = 12$$
$$-2c + r = 1 \quad \therefore r = 2c + 1 = 25$$

Hence $b = 5$, $c = 12$ and $r = 25$.

This means $P(x) = (x - 2)(x^2 + 5x + 12) + 25$.

We then equate coefficients: first the coefficients of x^2, then the coefficients of x, and finally the constants.

▶ The expansion of $(a + b)^n$

We know that

$$(a + b)^2 = a^2 + 2ab + b^2$$

This is called an **identity**; it is true for all a and b. If we multiply both sides of this identity by $(a + b)$, then we obtain

$$(a + b)^3 = (a + b)(a + b)^2 = (a + b)(a^2 + 2ab + b^2)$$
$$= a(a^2 + 2ab + b^2) + b(a^2 + 2ab + b^2)$$
$$= a^3 + 2a^2b + ab^2 + ba^2 + 2ab^2 + b^3$$
$$= a^3 + 3a^2b + 3ab^2 + b^3$$

So we have a new identity:

$$(a + b)^3 = a^3 + 3a^2b + 3ab^2 + b^3$$

We can continue to build identities in this way:

$$(a + b)^4 = a^4 + 4a^3b + 6a^2b^2 + 4ab^3 + b^4$$

We will give the general expansion of $(a + b)^n$ in Chapter 10.

Section summary

- A **polynomial function** is a function that can be written in the form

  $$P(x) = a_n x^n + a_{n-1} x^{n-1} + \cdots + a_1 x + a_0$$

  where n is a natural number or zero, and the coefficients $a_0, \ldots, a_n$ are real numbers with $a_n \neq 0$. The **leading term** is $a_n x^n$ (the term of highest index) and the **constant term** is a_0 (the term not involving x).
- The **degree of a polynomial** is the index n of the leading term.
- The sum, difference and product of two polynomials is a polynomial. Division does not always lead to another polynomial.
- Two polynomials P and Q are equal only if their corresponding coefficients are equal. Two cubic polynomials, $P(x) = a_3 x^3 + a_2 x^2 + a_1 x + a_0$ and $Q(x) = b_3 x^3 + b_2 x^2 + b_1 x + b_0$, are equal if and only if $a_3 = b_3$, $a_2 = b_2$, $a_1 = b_1$ and $a_0 = b_0$.

Exercise 6A

Example 1

1. Let $P(x) = x^3 - 3x^2 - 2x + 1$. Find:
   a $P(1)$
   b $P(-1)$
   c $P(2)$
   d $P(-2)$

2. Let $P(x) = 8x^3 - 4x^2 - 2x + 1$. Find:
   a $P\left(\dfrac{1}{2}\right)$
   b $P\left(-\dfrac{1}{2}\right)$

3. Let $P(x) = x^3 + 4x^2 - 2x + 6$. Find:
   a $P(0)$
   b $P(1)$
   c $P(2)$
   d $P(-1)$
   e $P(a)$
   f $P(2a)$

Example 2

4. a Let $P(x) = x^3 + 5x^2 - ax - 20$. If $P(2) = 0$, find the value of a.
   b Let $P(x) = 2x^3 + ax^2 - 5x - 7$. If $P(3) = 68$, find the value of a.
   c Let $P(x) = x^4 + x^3 - 2x + c$. If $P(1) = 6$, find the value of c.
   d Let $P(x) = 3x^6 - 5x^3 + ax^2 + bx + 10$. If $P(-1) = P(2) = 0$, find the values of a and b.
   e Let $P(x) = x^5 - 3x^4 + ax^3 + bx^2 + 24x - 36$. If $P(3) = P(1) = 0$, find the values of a and b.

Example 3

5. Let $f(x) = x^3 - 2x^2 + x$, $g(x) = 2 - 3x$ and $h(x) = x^2 + x$. Simplify each of the following:
   a $f(x) + g(x)$
   b $f(x) + h(x)$
   c $f(x) - g(x)$
   d $3f(x)$
   e $f(x)g(x)$
   f $g(x)h(x)$
   g $f(x) + g(x) + h(x)$
   h $f(x)h(x)$

6. Expand each of the following products and collect like terms:
   a $(x - 2)(x^2 - 2x + 3)$
   b $(x - 4)(x^2 - 2x + 3)$
   c $(x - 1)(2x^2 - 3x - 4)$
   d $(x - 2)(x^2 + bx + c)$
   e $(2x + 1)(x^2 - 4x - 3)$

Example 4

7. It is known that $x^3 - 7x^2 + 4x + 12 = (x + 1)(x^2 + bx + c)$ for all values of x, for suitable values of b and c.
   a Expand $(x + 1)(x^2 + bx + c)$ and collect like terms.
   b Find b and c by equating coefficients.
   c Hence write $x^3 - 7x^2 + 4x + 12$ as a product of three linear factors.

8. Let $x^2 + 6x - 2 = (x - b)^2 + c$. Find the values of b and c so that this is true for all x.

9. a Expand $(a + b)^5$.
   b Expand $(a + b)^6$.

10. Use the identity $(a + b)^4 = a^4 + 4a^3b + 6a^2b^2 + 4ab^3 + b^4$ to expand:
    a $(x - y)^4$ (Let $a = x$ and $b = -y$.)
    b $(2x + y)^4$ (Let $a = 2x$ and $b = y$.)

6B Division of polynomials

In order to sketch the graphs of many cubic and quartic functions (as well as higher degree polynomials) it is often necessary to find the x-axis intercepts. As with quadratics, finding x-axis intercepts can be done by factorising and then solving the resulting equation using the null factor theorem.

All cubics will have at least one x-axis intercept. Some will have two and others three.

We shall first look at the techniques for dividing one polynomial by another. One process for division of polynomials is exactly the same as the long division process for numbers.

▶ Long division with positive integers

We show the process for $274 \div 13$.

$$
\begin{array}{r}
21 \\
13\overline{)274} \\
\underline{26} \\
14 \\
\underline{13} \\
1
\end{array}
$$

We have

$$274 = 13 \times 21 + 1$$

Here 274 is the **dividend**, 13 the **divisor**, 21 the **quotient** and 1 the **remainder**.

> When we divide the number p by d we obtain two integers, q the quotient and r the remainder, such that
>
> $p = dq + r$ and $0 \leq r < d$
>
> For example,
>
> $27 = 4 \times 6 + 3$
>
> If $r = 0$, then d is a **factor** of p. For example, $24 = 4 \times 6$.

▶ Long division with polynomials

The process for dividing a polynomial by a linear polynomial follows very similar steps. For example, $(x^2 + 7x + 11) \div (x - 2)$ gives

$$
\begin{array}{r}
x + 9 \\
x - 2\overline{)x^2 + 7x + 11} \\
\underline{x^2 - 2x} \\
9x + 11 \\
\underline{9x - 18} \\
29
\end{array}
$$

Divide x^2 by x. This gives x.
Multiply $x - 2$ by x and subtract from $x^2 + 7x + 11$.
This leaves $9x + 11$. Now x into $9x$ goes 9 times.
Multiply $x - 2$ by 9 and subtract from $9x + 11$.
This leaves 29 remainder.

Thus $(x^2 + 7x + 11) \div (x - 2) = x + 9$ with remainder 29. We write

$$x^2 + 7x + 11 = (x - 2)(x + 9) + 29$$

We can see in this example that $x - 2$ is *not* a factor of $x^2 + 7x + 11$. We can also write the result as

$$\frac{x^2 + 7x + 11}{x - 2} = x + 9 + \frac{29}{x - 2}$$

In this example:

- $x^2 + 7x + 11$ is the dividend
- $x - 2$ is the divisor
- 29 is the remainder.

> When we divide the polynomial $P(x)$ by the polynomial $D(x)$ we obtain two polynomials, $Q(x)$ the **quotient** and $R(x)$ the **remainder**, such that
>
> $$P(x) = D(x)Q(x) + R(x)$$
>
> and either $R(x) = 0$ or $R(x)$ has degree less than $D(x)$.
>
> Here $P(x)$ is the **dividend** and $D(x)$ is the **divisor**.

Note: If $R(x) = 0$, then $D(x)$ is a **factor** of $P(x)$. For example, let $P(x) = x^2 + 6x + 8$ and $D(x) = x + 2$. Then $P(x) = (x + 2)(x + 4) = D(x)(x + 4) + 0$.

Example 5

Divide $x^3 + x^2 - 14x - 24$ by $x + 2$.

Solution

$$\begin{array}{r}
x^2 - x - 12 \\
x + 2 \overline{\smash{)}\, x^3 + x^2 - 14x - 24} \\
\underline{x^3 + 2x^2 } \\
-x^2 - 14x - 24 \\
\underline{-x^2 - 2x } \\
-12x - 24 \\
\underline{-12x - 24} \\
0
\end{array}$$

Explanation

- Divide x, from $x + 2$, into the leading term x^3 to get x^2.
- Multiply x^2 by $x + 2$ to give $x^3 + 2x^2$.
- Subtract from $x^3 + x^2 - 14x - 24$, leaving $-x^2 - 14x - 24$.
- Now divide x, from $x + 2$, into $-x^2$ to get $-x$.
- Multiply $-x$ by $x + 2$ to give $-x^2 - 2x$.
- Subtract from $-x^2 - 14x - 24$, leaving $-12x - 24$.
- Divide x into $-12x$ to get -12.
- Multiply -12 by $x + 2$ to give $-12x - 24$.
- Subtract from $-12x - 24$, leaving remainder of 0.

In this example we see that $x + 2$ is a factor of $x^3 + x^2 - 14x - 24$, as the remainder is zero. Thus $(x^3 + x^2 - 14x - 24) \div (x + 2) = x^2 - x - 12$ with zero remainder.

$$\therefore \quad \frac{x^3 + x^2 - 14x - 24}{x + 2} = x^2 - x - 12$$

Example 6

Divide $3x^3 + x - 3$ by $x - 2$.

Solution

$$
\begin{array}{r}
3x^2 + 6x + 13 \\
x - 2 \overline{\smash{)}\, 3x^3 + 0x^2 + x - 3} \\
\underline{3x^3 - 6x^2 } \\
6x^2 + x - 3 \\
\underline{6x^2 - 12x } \\
13x - 3 \\
\underline{13x - 26} \\
23
\end{array}
$$

Explanation

Here there is no term in x^2, however we can rewrite the polynomial as $3x^3 + 0x^2 + x - 3$.

- Divide x, from $x - 2$, into $3x^3$ to get $3x^2$.
- Multiply $3x^2$ by $x - 2$ to give $3x^3 - 6x^2$.
- Subtract from $3x^3 + 0x^2 + x - 3$, leaving $6x^2 + x - 3$.
- Now divide x, from $x - 2$, into $6x^2$ to get $6x$.
- Multiply $6x$ by $x - 2$ to give $6x^2 - 12x$.
- Subtract from $6x^2 + x - 3$, leaving $13x - 3$.
- Divide x into $13x$ to get 13.
- Multiply 13 by $x - 2$ to give $13x - 26$.
- Subtract from $13x - 3$, leaving remainder of 23.

From this example, we have

$$3x^3 + x - 3 = (x - 2)(3x^2 + 6x + 13) + 23$$

Alternatively, we can write

$$\frac{3x^3 + x - 3}{x - 2} = 3x^2 + 6x + 13 + \frac{23}{x - 2}$$

▶ Equating coefficients to divide

We will briefly outline how to carry out divisions by equating coefficients as shown in the first section of this chapter.

To divide $x^3 - 7x^2 + 5x - 4$ by $x - 3$, first write the identity

$$x^3 - 7x^2 + 5x - 4 = (x - 3)(x^2 + bx + c) + r$$

We first find b, then c and finally r by equating coefficients of the left-hand side and right-hand side of this identity.

x^2 term   Left-hand side: $-7x^2$. Right-hand side: $-3x^2 + bx^2 = (-3 + b)x^2$.
                 Therefore $-3 + b = -7$. Hence $b = -4$.

x term   Left-hand side: $5x$. Right-hand side: $12x + cx = (12 + c)x$.
                 Therefore $12 + c = 5$. Hence $c = -7$.

constant term   Left-hand side: -4. Right-hand side: $21 + r$.
                 Therefore $21 + r = -4$. Hence $r = -25$.

So we can write $x^3 - 7x^2 + 5x - 4 = (x - 3)(x^2 - 4x - 7) - 25$.

We do the following example using this method. You can see how the long division has the same arithmetic steps.

Note: There is a discussion of a different method (synthetic division) in Appendix A.

Example 7

Divide $3x^3 + 2x^2 - x - 2$ by $2x + 1$.

Solution

$$\begin{array}{r} \frac{3}{2}x^2 + \frac{1}{4}x - \frac{5}{8} \\ 2x+1 \overline{) 3x^3 + 2x^2 - x - 2} \\ 3x^3 + \frac{3}{2}x^2 \\ \hline \frac{1}{2}x^2 - x - 2 \\ \frac{1}{2}x^2 + \frac{1}{4}x \\ \hline -\frac{5}{4}x - 2 \\ -\frac{5}{4}x - \frac{5}{8} \\ \hline -1\frac{3}{8} \end{array}$$

Explanation

We show the alternative method here.

First write the identity
$$3x^3 + 2x^2 - x - 2 = (2x+1)(ax^2 + bx + c) + r$$

Equate coefficients of x^3:
$3 = 2a$. Therefore $a = \frac{3}{2}$.

Equate coefficients of x^2:
$2 = a + 2b$. Therefore $b = \frac{1}{2}(2 - \frac{3}{2}) = \frac{1}{4}$.

Equate coefficients of x:
$-1 = 2c + b$. Therefore $c = \frac{1}{2}(-1 - \frac{1}{4}) = -\frac{5}{8}$.

Equate constant terms:
$-2 = c + r$. Therefore $r = -2 + \frac{5}{8} = -\frac{11}{8}$.

Using the TI-Nspire

Use **propFrac( )** from menu > **Algebra** > **Fraction Tools** > **Proper Fraction** as shown.

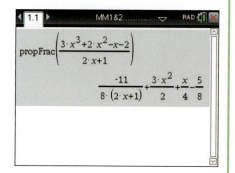

Using the Casio ClassPad

- In √☐, select ☐ from the Math1 keyboard.
- Enter the expression $\dfrac{3x^3 + 2x^2 - x - 2}{2x+1}$.
- Highlight the expression and go to **Interactive** > **Transformation** > **Fraction** > **propFrac**.

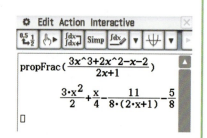

Dividing by a non-linear polynomial

We give one example of dividing by a non-linear polynomial. The technique is exactly the same as when dividing by a linear polynomial.

Example 8

Divide $3x^3 - 2x^2 + 3x - 4$ by $x^2 - 1$.

Solution

$$
\begin{array}{r}
3x - 2 \\
x^2 + 0x - 1 \overline{\smash{)}\, 3x^3 - 2x^2 + 3x - 4} \\
\underline{3x^3 + 0x^2 - 3x } \\
-2x^2 + 6x - 4 \\
\underline{-2x^2 + 0x + 2} \\
6x - 6
\end{array}
$$

$\therefore 3x^3 - 2x^2 + 3x - 4 = (x^2 - 1)(3x - 2) + 6x - 6$

Explanation

We write $x^2 - 1$ as $x^2 + 0x - 1$.

Section summary

- When we divide the polynomial $P(x)$ by the polynomial $D(x)$ we obtain two polynomials, $Q(x)$ the **quotient** and $R(x)$ the **remainder**, such that

    $$P(x) = D(x)Q(x) + R(x)$$

    and either $R(x) = 0$ or $R(x)$ has degree less than $D(x)$. The polynomial $P(x)$ is the **dividend**.
- Two methods for dividing polynomials are long division and equating coefficients. A third method is presented in Appendix A.

Exercise 6B

Example 5 **1** For each of the following, divide the polynomial by the accompanying linear expression:
  a $x^3 + x^2 - 2x + 3$, $x - 1$
  b $2x^3 + x^2 - 4x + 3$, $x + 1$
  c $3x^3 - 4x^2 + 2x + 1$, $x + 2$
  d $2x^3 - 3x^2 + x - 2$, $x - 3$

Example 6 **2** For each of the following, divide the polynomial by the accompanying linear expression:
  a $x^3 + 3x - 4$, $x + 1$
  b $2x^3 + 17x + 15$, $x + 4$
  c $x^3 + 4x^2 + 2$, $x + 3$
  d $x^3 - 3x^2 + 6x$, $x - 2$

3 For each of the following, divide the polynomial by the accompanying linear expression and hence show that the linear expression is a factor of the polynomial:
  a $x^3 - x^2 + 3x + 5$, $x + 1$
  b $2x^3 + 6x^2 - 14x - 24$, $x + 4$
  c $x^3 - 5x^2 + 18$, $x - 3$
  d $3x^3 - 7x^2 - 4x + 12$, $x - 2$

4 Find the quotient and remainder when the first polynomial is divided by the second:
  a $x^3 + 2x^2 - 3x + 1$, $x + 2$
  b $x^3 - 3x^2 + 5x - 4$, $x - 5$
  c $2x^3 - x^2 - 3x - 7$, $x + 1$
  d $5x^3 - 3x + 7$, $x - 4$

Example 7 5 For each of the following, divide the polynomial by the accompanying linear expression:
  a $x^3 + 6x^2 + 8x + 11$, $2x + 5$
  b $2x^3 + 5x^2 - 4x - 5$, $2x + 1$
  c $2x^3 + 3x^2 - 32x + 15$, $2x - 1$
  d $x^3 - 3x^2 + 1$, $3x - 1$

6 a Write $\dfrac{x^3 + 2x^2 + 5x + 1}{x - 1}$ in the form $P(x) + \dfrac{a}{x - 1}$, where $P(x)$ is a quadratic expression and a is a real number.

  b Write $\dfrac{2x^3 - 2x^2 + 5x + 3}{2x - 1}$ in the form $P(x) + \dfrac{a}{2x - 1}$, where $P(x)$ is a quadratic expression and a is a real number.

Example 8 7 For each of the following, divide the polynomial $P(x)$ by the polynomial $D(x)$:
  a $P(x) = 2x^3 - 6x^2 - 4x + 12$, $D(x) = x^2 - 2$
  b $P(x) = x^3 - 6x^2 + x - 8$, $D(x) = x^2 + 1$
  c $P(x) = 2x^3 - 6x^2 - 4x + 54$, $D(x) = x^2 - 2$
  d $P(x) = x^4 - 2x^3 - 7x^2 + 7x + 5$, $D(x) = x^2 + 2x - 1$
  e $P(x) = x^4 - x^3 + 7x + 2$, $D(x) = x^2 + 2x - 1$
  f $P(x) = 2x^4 + x^3 + 13x + 10$, $D(x) = 2x^2 - x + 4$

6C Factorisation of polynomials

▶ Remainder theorem

Since the aim of factorising a cubic is usually to solve an equation or to find the x-axis intercepts of a graph, the first step is to establish whether a particular linear expression is a factor of the given cubic or not. It is possible to do this without actually doing the division process.

Let $P(x) = x^3 + 3x^2 + 2x + 1$.

Divide $P(x)$ by $x - 2$:

$$
\begin{array}{r}
x^2 + 5x + 12 \\
x - 2 \overline{\smash{\big)}\, x^3 + 3x^2 + 2x + 1} \\
\underline{x^3 - 2x^2 } \\
5x^2 + 2x + 1 \\
\underline{5x^2 - 10x } \\
12x + 1 \\
\underline{12x - 24} \\
25
\end{array}
$$

The remainder is 25.

Now $P(2) = (2)^3 + 3(2)^2 + 2(2) + 1$
$= 8 + 12 + 4 + 1$
$= 25$

The example suggests that, when $P(x)$ is divided by $x - \alpha$, the remainder is equal to $P(\alpha)$. This is in fact true, and the result is called the **remainder theorem**.

It is proved as follows. Suppose that, when the polynomial $P(x)$ is divided by $x - \alpha$, the quotient is $Q(x)$ and the remainder is R. Then

$$P(x) = (x - \alpha)Q(x) + R$$

Now, as the two expressions are equal for all values of x, they are equal for $x = \alpha$.

$$\therefore \quad P(\alpha) = (\alpha - \alpha)Q(\alpha) + R \quad \therefore \quad R = P(\alpha)$$

i.e. the remainder when $P(x)$ is divided by $x - \alpha$ is equal to $P(\alpha)$. We therefore have

$$P(x) = (x - \alpha)Q(x) + P(\alpha)$$

More generally:

> **Remainder theorem**
>
> When $P(x)$ is divided by $\beta x + \alpha$, the remainder is $P\left(-\dfrac{\alpha}{\beta}\right)$.

Example 9

Use the remainder theorem to find the value of the remainder when:
a $P(x) = x^3 - 3x^2 + 2x + 6$ is divided by $x - 2$
b $P(x) = x^3 - 2x + 4$ is divided by $2x + 1$.

Solution	Explanation
a $P(2) = (2)^3 - 3(2)^2 + 2(2) + 6$ $= 8 - 12 + 4 + 6$ $= 6$ The remainder is 6.	We apply the remainder theorem by evaluating $P(2)$.
b $P\left(-\dfrac{1}{2}\right) = \left(-\dfrac{1}{2}\right)^3 - 2\left(-\dfrac{1}{2}\right) + 4$ $= -\dfrac{1}{8} + 1 + 4$ $= \dfrac{39}{8}$ The remainder is $\dfrac{39}{8}$.	We apply the remainder theorem by evaluating $P(-\tfrac{1}{2})$.

Note: It is not necessary to perform polynomial division to find the remainder.

Example 10

When $P(x) = x^3 + 2x + a$ is divided by $x - 2$, the remainder is 4. Find the value of a.

Solution

$P(2) = 8 + 4 + a = 4$
Therefore $a = -8$.

Explanation

We apply the remainder theorem to form a linear equation in a.

▶ Factor theorem

Now, in order for $x - \alpha$ to be a factor of the polynomial $P(x)$, the remainder must be zero. We state this result as the **factor theorem**.

Factor theorem

For a polynomial $P(x)$:
- If $P(\alpha) = 0$, then $x - \alpha$ is a factor of $P(x)$.
- Conversely, if $x - \alpha$ is a factor of $P(x)$, then $P(\alpha) = 0$.

More generally:
- If $\beta x + \alpha$ is a factor of $P(x)$, then $P\left(-\dfrac{\alpha}{\beta}\right) = 0$.
- Conversely, if $P\left(-\dfrac{\alpha}{\beta}\right) = 0$, then $\beta x + \alpha$ is a factor of $P(x)$.

Example 11

Show that $x + 1$ is a factor of $x^3 - 4x^2 + x + 6$ and hence find the other linear factors.

Solution

Let $P(x) = x^3 - 4x^2 + x + 6$
Then $P(-1) = (-1)^3 - 4(-1)^2 + (-1) + 6$
$= 0$

Thus $x + 1$ is a factor (by the factor theorem).

Divide by $x + 1$ to find the other factor:

$$\begin{array}{r} x^2 - 5x + 6 \\ x+1 \overline{\smash{\big)} x^3 - 4x^2 + x + 6} \\ \underline{x^3 + x^2} \\ -5x^2 + x + 6 \\ \underline{-5x^2 - 5x} \\ 6x + 6 \\ \underline{6x + 6} \\ 0 \end{array}$$

Explanation

We can use the factor theorem to find one factor, and then divide to find the other two linear factors.

Here is an alternative method:

Once we have found that $x + 1$ is a factor, we know that we can write

$$x^3 - 4x^2 + x + 6 = (x + 1)(x^2 + bx + c)$$

By equating constant terms, we have $6 = 1 \times c$. Hence $c = 6$.

By equating coefficients of x^2, we have $-4 = 1 + b$. Hence $b = -5$.

$\therefore \quad x^3 - 4x^2 + x + 6 = (x + 1)(x^2 - 5x + 6)$

$$\therefore x^3 - 4x^2 + x + 6 = (x + 1)(x^2 - 5x + 6)$$
$$= (x + 1)(x - 3)(x - 2)$$

The linear factors of $x^3 - 4x^2 + x + 6$ are $(x + 1)$, $(x - 3)$ and $(x - 2)$.

Thinking about the numbers involved in the process of factorisation gives us a way of searching for factors. For example, consider the polynomial $x^3 - 2x^2 - 5x + 6$. Assume this polynomial has a linear factor $x - \alpha$, where α is an integer.

Then we can write

$$x^3 - 2x^2 - 5x + 6 = (x - \alpha)(x^2 + bx + c)$$
$$= x^3 - (\alpha - b)x^2 - (\alpha b - c)x - \alpha c$$

By considering the constant term, it can be seen that $\alpha c = -6$. Therefore α divides 6. (Since α is an integer, it follows that b and c are too.)

Thus only the factors of 6 need be considered (i.e. ±1, ±2, ±3, ±6).

Try these in turn until a value for α makes $P(\alpha) = 0$. This process is completed in the following example.

Example 12

Factorise $x^3 - 2x^2 - 5x + 6$.

Solution

$P(1) = 1 - 2 - 5 + 6 = 0$

$\therefore x - 1$ is a factor.

Now divide to find the other factors:

$$\begin{array}{r}
x^2 - x - 6 \\
x - 1 \overline{) x^3 - 2x^2 - 5x + 6} \\
\underline{x^3 - x^2} \\
-x^2 - 5x + 6 \\
\underline{-x^2 + x} \\
-6x + 6 \\
\underline{-6x + 6} \\
0
\end{array}$$

$$\therefore x^3 - 2x^2 - 5x + 6 = (x - 1)(x^2 - x - 6)$$
$$= (x - 1)(x - 3)(x + 2)$$

Explanation

The factors of 6 are ±1, ±2, ±3, ±6.

We evaluate the first option, $P(1)$, which in fact equals 0. If $P(1)$ did not equal 0, we would try the other factors of 6 in turn until a zero result is found.

Note that, for some cubics, the quadratic factor may not be able to be factorised. For such cubics there will only be one linear factor. The implications of this will be discussed later in the chapter when considering the graphs of cubic functions.

Using the TI-Nspire

Use **factor( )** from menu > **Algebra** > **Factor** to factorise the expression $x^3 - 2x^2 - 5x + 6$.

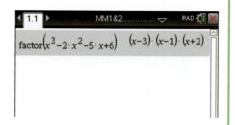

Using the Casio ClassPad

- In $\sqrt{\alpha}$ (Main), enter the expression $x^3 - 2x^2 - 5x + 6$.
- Highlight the expression and go to **Interactive** > **Transformation** > **factor**.

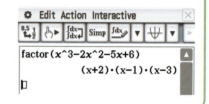

▶ Rational-root theorem

Consider the cubic polynomial

$$P(x) = 2x^3 - x^2 - x - 3$$

We can easily show that $P(1) \neq 0$, $P(-1) \neq 0$, $P(3) \neq 0$ and $P(-3) \neq 0$. Hence the equation $P(x) = 0$ has no solution that is an integer.

Does it have a rational solution, that is, a fraction for a solution?

The **rational-root theorem** helps us with this. It says that if α and β have highest common factor 1 (i.e. α and β are relatively prime) and $\beta x + \alpha$ is a factor of $2x^3 - x^2 - x - 3$, then β divides 2 and α divides -3.

Therefore, if $-\dfrac{\alpha}{\beta}$ is a solution of the equation $P(x) = 0$ (where α and β are relatively prime), then β must divide 2 and α must divide -3. So the only value of β that needs to be considered is 2, and $\alpha = \pm 3$ or $\alpha = \pm 1$.

We can test these through the factor theorem. That is, check $P\left(\pm\dfrac{1}{2}\right)$ and $P\left(\pm\dfrac{3}{2}\right)$. We find

$$P\left(\dfrac{3}{2}\right) = 2\left(\dfrac{3}{2}\right)^3 - \left(\dfrac{3}{2}\right)^2 - \left(\dfrac{3}{2}\right) - 3$$

$$= 2 \times \dfrac{27}{8} - \dfrac{9}{4} - \dfrac{3}{2} - 3$$

$$= 0$$

We have found that $2x - 3$ is a factor.

Dividing through we find that

$$2x^3 - x^2 - x - 3 = (2x - 3)(x^2 + x + 1)$$

We can show that $x^2 + x + 1$ has no linear factors by showing that the discriminant of this quadratic is negative.

Example 13

Factorise $P(x) = 3x^3 + 8x^2 + 2x - 5$.

Solution

$P(1) = 8 \neq 0,$ $P(-1) = -2 \neq 0,$
$P(5) = 580 \neq 0,$ $P(-5) = -190 \neq 0,$
$P\left(-\dfrac{5}{3}\right) = 0$

Therefore $3x + 5$ is a factor.

Dividing gives

$$3x^3 + 8x^2 + 2x - 5 = (3x + 5)(x^2 + x - 1)$$

We complete the square for $x^2 + x - 1$ to factorise:

$$x^2 + x - 1 = x^2 + x + \dfrac{1}{4} - \dfrac{1}{4} - 1$$

$$= \left(x + \dfrac{1}{2}\right)^2 - \dfrac{5}{4}$$

$$= \left(x + \dfrac{1}{2} + \dfrac{\sqrt{5}}{2}\right)\left(x + \dfrac{1}{2} - \dfrac{\sqrt{5}}{2}\right)$$

Hence

$$P(x) = (3x + 5)\left(x + \dfrac{1}{2} + \dfrac{\sqrt{5}}{2}\right)\left(x + \dfrac{1}{2} - \dfrac{\sqrt{5}}{2}\right)$$

Explanation

The only possible integer solutions are ±5 or ±1. So there are no integer solutions. We now use the rational-root theorem.

If $-\dfrac{\alpha}{\beta}$ is a solution, the only value of β that needs to be considered is 3 and $\alpha = \pm 5$ or $\alpha = \pm 1$.

Here is the complete statement of the theorem:

Rational-root theorem

Let $P(x) = a_n x^n + a_{n-1} x^{n-1} + \cdots + a_1 x + a_0$ be a polynomial of degree n with all the coefficients a_i integers. Let α and β be integers such that the highest common factor of α and β is 1 (i.e. α and β are relatively prime).

If $\beta x + \alpha$ is a factor of $P(x)$, then β divides a_n and α divides a_0.

A proof of the rational-root theorem is given in Appendix A.

▶ Special cases: sums and differences of cubes

Example 14

Factorise $x^3 - 27$.

Solution

Let $P(x) = x^3 - 27$

Then $P(3) = 27 - 27 = 0$

$\therefore x - 3$ is a factor.

Divide to find the other factor:

$$\begin{array}{r} x^2 + 3x + 9 \\ x-3 \overline{\smash{\big)}\, x^3 + 0x^2 + 0x - 27} \\ \underline{x^3 - 3x^2} \\ 3x^2 + 0x - 27 \\ \underline{3x^2 - 9x} \\ 9x - 27 \\ \underline{9x - 27} \\ 0 \end{array}$$

$\therefore x^3 - 27 = (x-3)(x^2 + 3x + 9)$

Explanation

The division can also be performed using the method of equating coefficients:

Let $x^3 - 27 = (x-3)(x^2 + bx + c)$.

Equating constant terms gives $c = 9$.

Equating coefficients of x^2 gives $-3 + b = 0$, and so $b = 3$.

In general, if $P(x) = x^3 - a^3$, then $x - a$ is a factor and so by division:

$$x^3 - a^3 = (x-a)(x^2 + ax + a^2)$$

If a is replaced by $-a$, then

$$x^3 - (-a)^3 = (x-(-a))(x^2 + (-a)x + (-a)^2)$$

This gives:

$$x^3 + a^3 = (x+a)(x^2 - ax + a^2)$$

Example 15

Factorise $8x^3 + 64$.

Solution

$8x^3 + 64 = (2x)^3 + (4)^3$

$ = (2x + 4)(4x^2 - 8x + 16)$

Section summary

- **Remainder theorem** When $P(x)$ is divided by $\beta x + \alpha$, the remainder is $P\left(-\dfrac{\alpha}{\beta}\right)$.
- **Factor theorem**
  - If $\beta x + \alpha$ is a factor of $P(x)$, then $P\left(-\dfrac{\alpha}{\beta}\right) = 0$.
  - Conversely, if $P\left(-\dfrac{\alpha}{\beta}\right) = 0$, then $\beta x + \alpha$ is a factor of $P(x)$.
- A cubic function can be factorised using the factor theorem to find the first linear factor and then using polynomial division or the method of equating coefficients to complete the process.
- **Rational-root theorem** Let $P(x) = a_n x^n + a_{n-1} x^{n-1} + \cdots + a_1 x + a_0$ be a polynomial of degree n with all the coefficients a_i integers. Let α and β be integers such that the highest common factor of α and β is 1 (i.e. α and β are relatively prime). If $\beta x + \alpha$ is a factor of $P(x)$, then β divides a_n and α divides a_0.
- Difference of two cubes: $x^3 - a^3 = (x - a)(x^2 + ax + a^2)$
- Sum of two cubes: $x^3 + a^3 = (x + a)(x^2 - ax + a^2)$

Exercise 6C

Example 9 **1** Without dividing, find the remainder when the first polynomial is divided by the second:

   a $x^3 - x^2 - 3x + 1,\ x - 1$ **b** $x^3 - 3x^2 + 4x - 1,\ x + 2$
   c $2x^3 - 2x^2 + 3x + 1,\ x - 2$ **d** $x^3 - 2x + 3,\ x + 1$
   e $x^3 + 2x - 5,\ x - 2$ **f** $2x^3 + 3x^2 + 3x - 2,\ x + 2$
   g $6 - 5x + 9x^2 + 10x^3,\ 2x + 3$ **h** $10x^3 - 3x^2 + 4x - 1,\ 2x + 1$
   i $108x^3 - 27x^2 - 1,\ 3x + 1$

Example 10 **2** Find the value of a for each of the following:

   a $x^3 + ax^2 + 3x - 5$ has remainder -3 when divided by $x - 2$
   b $x^3 + x^2 - 2ax + a^2$ has remainder 8 when divided by $x - 2$
   c $x^3 - 3x^2 + ax + 5$ has remainder 17 when divided by $x - 3$
   d $x^3 + x^2 + ax + 8$ has remainder 0 when divided by $x - 1$

Example 11 **3** Without dividing, show that the first polynomial is exactly divisible by the second polynomial:

   a $x^3 - x^2 + x - 1,\ x - 1$ **b** $x^3 + 3x^2 - x - 3,\ x - 1$
   c $2x^3 - 3x^2 - 11x + 6,\ x + 2$ **d** $2x^3 - 13x^2 + 27x - 18,\ 2x - 3$

4 Find the value of m if the first polynomial is exactly divisible by the second:

   a $x^3 - 4x^2 + x + m,\ x - 3$ **b** $2x^3 - 3x^2 - (m + 1)x - 30,\ x - 5$
   c $x^3 - (m + 1)x^2 - x + 30,\ x + 3$

5 Factorise each of the following:
   a $2x^3 + x^2 - 2x - 1$
   b $x^3 + 3x^2 + 3x + 1$
   c $6x^3 - 13x^2 + 13x - 6$
   d $x^3 - 21x + 20$
   e $2x^3 + 3x^2 - 1$
   f $x^3 - x^2 - x + 1$
   g $4x^3 + 3x - 38$
   h $4x^3 + 4x^2 - 11x - 6$

6 Find the remainder when $(1 + x)^4$ is divided by $x + 2$.

7 Use the rational-root theorem to help factorise each of the following cubic polynomials:
   a $2x^3 - 7x^2 + 16x - 15$
   b $2x^3 - 3x^2 + 8x + 5$
   c $2x^3 - 3x^2 - 12x - 5$
   d $2x^3 - x^2 - 8x - 3$

8 Factorise each of the following:
   a $x^3 - 1$
   b $x^3 + 64$
   c $27x^3 - 1$
   d $64x^3 - 125$
   e $1 - 125x^3$
   f $8 + 27x^3$
   g $64m^3 - 27n^3$
   h $27b^3 + 8a^3$

9 Factorise each of the following:
   a $x^3 + x^2 - x + 2$
   b $3x^3 - 7x^2 + 4$
   c $x^3 - 4x^2 + x + 6$
   d $6x^3 + 17x^2 - 4x - 3$

10 Find the values of a and b and factorise the polynomial $P(x) = x^3 + ax^2 - x + b$, given that $P(x)$ is divisible by $x - 1$ and $x + 3$.

11 a Show that, for any constant a and any natural number n, $x - a$ is a factor of $x^n - a^n$.
   b Find conditions (if any) on n that are required in order that:
      i $x + a$ is a factor of $x^n + a^n$
      ii $x + a$ is a factor of $x^n - a^n$.

12 The polynomial $P(x)$ has a remainder of 2 when divided by $x - 1$ and a remainder of 3 when divided by $x - 2$. The remainder when $P(x)$ is divided by $(x - 1)(x - 2)$ is $ax + b$, i.e. $P(x)$ can be written as $P(x) = (x - 1)(x - 2)Q(x) + ax + b$.
   a Find the values of a and b.
   b i Given that $P(x)$ is a cubic polynomial with coefficient of x^3 being 1, and -1 is a solution of the equation $P(x) = 0$, find $P(x)$.
      ii Show that the equation $P(x) = 0$ has no other real solutions.

6D Solving cubic equations

In order to solve a cubic equation, the first step is often to factorise. We start with an example of a cubic already written in factorised form.

Example 16

Solve $(x - 2)(x + 1)(x + 3) = 0$.

Solution

Using the null factor theorem,
$(x - 2)(x + 1)(x + 3) = 0$ implies

$x - 2 = 0$ or $x + 1 = 0$ or $x + 3 = 0$

Thus the solutions are $x = 2, -1$ and -3.

Explanation

In this example, the cubic has already been factorised.

In the following example, a common factor of x is first taken out.

Example 17

Solve each of the following equations for x:

a $2x^3 - x^2 - x = 0$

b $x^3 + 2x^2 - 10x = 0$

Solution

a
$$2x^3 - x^2 - x = 0$$
$$x(2x^2 - x - 1) = 0$$
$$x(2x + 1)(x - 1) = 0$$
$$\therefore \ x = 0 \text{ or } x = -\tfrac{1}{2} \text{ or } x = 1$$

b
$$x^3 + 2x^2 - 10x = 0$$
$$x(x^2 + 2x - 10) = 0$$
$$x(x^2 + 2x + 1 - 11) = 0$$
$$x(x + 1 - \sqrt{11})(x + 1 + \sqrt{11}) = 0$$
$$\therefore \ x = 0 \text{ or } x = -1 + \sqrt{11} \text{ or } x = -1 - \sqrt{11}$$

In the following example, grouping is used to factorise.

Example 18

Solve each of the following equations for x:

a $x^3 - 4x^2 - 11x + 44 = 0$

b $x^3 - ax^2 - 11x + 11a = 0$

Solution

a $x^3 - 4x^2 - 11x + 44 = 0$
$x^2(x - 4) - 11(x - 4) = 0$
Therefore $(x - 4)(x^2 - 11) = 0$
Hence $x = 4$ or $x = \pm\sqrt{11}$

b $x^3 - ax^2 - 11x + 11a = 0$
$x^2(x - a) - 11(x - a) = 0$
Therefore $(x - a)(x^2 - 11) = 0$
Hence $x = a$ or $x = \pm\sqrt{11}$

In the following two examples, the factor theorem is used to find a linear factor.

Example 19

Solve $x^3 - 4x^2 - 11x + 30 = 0$.

Solution

Let $P(x) = x^3 - 4x^2 - 11x + 30$

Then $P(1) = 1 - 4 - 11 + 30 \neq 0$

$P(-1) = -1 - 4 + 11 + 30 \neq 0$

$P(2) = 8 - 16 - 22 + 30 = 0$

$\therefore x - 2$ is a factor.

By division or inspection,

$x^3 - 4x^2 - 11x + 30 = (x - 2)(x^2 - 2x - 15)$
$= (x - 2)(x - 5)(x + 3)$

$\therefore (x - 2)(x - 5)(x + 3) = 0$

$\therefore x - 2 = 0$ or $x - 5 = 0$ or $x + 3 = 0$

$\therefore x = 2, 5$ or -3

Explanation

In this example we first identify a linear factor using the factor theorem.

The factorisation is completed using one of the methods given in the previous section.

Example 20

Solve $2x^3 - 5x^2 + 5x - 2 = 0$.

Solution

Let $P(x) = 2x^3 - 5x^2 + 5x - 2$

Then $P(1) = 2 - 5 + 5 - 2 = 0$

$\therefore x - 1$ is a factor.

By division or inspection,

$2x^3 - 5x^2 + 5x - 2 = (x - 1)(2x^2 - 3x + 2)$

$\therefore (x - 1)(2x^2 - 3x + 2) = 0$

$\therefore x = 1$

Explanation

First find a linear factor using the factor theorem. Then find the quadratic factor by division.

The discriminant of this quadratic is a negative number, so this quadratic cannot be factorised further. Hence there is only one linear factor and therefore only one solution.

Using the TI-Nspire

Use **solve( )** from menu > **Algebra** > **Solve** to solve the equation $2x^3 - 5x^2 + x + 2 = 0$.

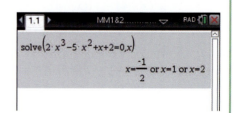

Using the Casio ClassPad

- Go to the main screen $\sqrt{\alpha}$ (Main).
- Select **solve(** from the Math1 keyboard.
- Enter the equation $2x^3 - 5x^2 + x + 2 = 0$.
- Close the bracket and tap EXE.

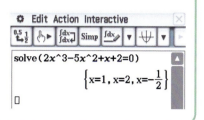

Section summary

Cubic polynomial equations can be solved by first using an appropriate factorisation technique. Factorisation may involve:

- extracting a simple common factor
- using the factor theorem
- polynomial division or equating coefficients
- sum or difference of two cubes
- using the quadratic formula to complete the factorisation.

Exercise 6D

Example 16

1 Solve each of the following:
   a $(x-1)(x+2)(x-4) = 0$
   b $(x-4)^2(x-6) = 0$
   c $(2x-1)(x-3)(3x+2) = 0$
   d $x(x+3)(2x-5) = 0$

Example 17

2 Solve each of the following:
   a $x^3 - 2x^2 - 8x = 0$
   b $x^3 + 2x^2 - 11x = 0$
   c $x^3 - 3x^2 - 40x = 0$
   d $x^3 + 2x^2 - 16x = 0$

Example 18

3 Use grouping to solve each of the following:
   a $x^3 - x^2 + x - 1 = 0$
   b $x^3 + x^2 + x + 1 = 0$
   c $x^3 - 5x^2 - 10x + 50 = 0$
   d $x^3 - ax^2 - 16x + 16a = 0$

Example 19

4 Solve each of the following:
   a $x^3 - 19x + 30 = 0$
   b $3x^3 - 4x^2 - 13x - 6 = 0$
   c $x^3 - x^2 - 2x + 2 = 0$
   d $5x^3 + 12x^2 - 36x - 16 = 0$
   e $6x^3 - 5x^2 - 2x + 1 = 0$
   f $2x^3 - 3x^2 - 29x - 30 = 0$

Example 20

5 Solve each of the following for x:
   a $x^3 + x^2 - 24x + 36 = 0$
   b $6x^3 + 13x^2 - 4 = 0$
   c $x^3 - x^2 - 2x - 12 = 0$
   d $2x^3 + 3x^2 + 7x + 6 = 0$
   e $x^3 - x^2 - 5x - 3 = 0$
   f $x^3 + x^2 - 11x - 3 = 0$

6 Solve each of the following equations for x:
  a $2x^3 = 16x$
  b $2(x-1)^3 = 32$
  c $x^3 + 8 = 0$
  d $2x^3 + 250 = 0$
  e $1000 = \dfrac{1}{x^3}$

7 Factorise each of the following cubic expressions, using a calculator to help find at least one linear factor:
  a $2x^3 - 22x^2 - 250x + 2574$
  b $2x^3 + 27x^2 + 52x - 33$
  c $2x^3 - 9x^2 - 242x + 1089$
  d $2x^3 + 51x^2 + 304x - 165$

6E Cubic functions of the form $f(x) = a(x-h)^3 + k$

In Chapter 3 we saw that all quadratic functions can be written in 'turning point form' and that the graphs of all quadratics have one basic form, the parabola. This is not true of cubic functions. Let us first consider those cubics that are of the form

$$f(x) = a(x-h)^3 + k$$

The graphs of these functions can be formed by simple transformations of the graph of $f(x) = x^3$.

For example, the graph of $f(x) = (x-1)^3 + 3$ is obtained from the graph of $f(x) = x^3$ by a translation of 1 unit in the positive direction of the x-axis and 3 units in the positive direction of the y-axis.

▶ **Transformations of the graph of $f(x) = x^3$**

Dilations from an axis and reflections in an axis

As with other graphs it has been seen that changing the value of a simply narrows or broadens the graph without changing its fundamental shape. Again, if $a < 0$, the graph is reflected in an axis. Note that reflecting in the x-axis and reflecting in the y-axis result in the same graph. This is because $(-x)^3 = -x^3$.

For example:

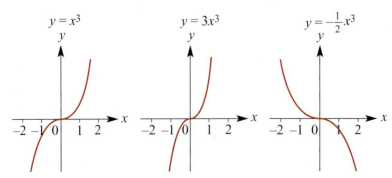

It should be noted that the implied **domain** of all cubics is $\mathbb{R}$ and the **range** is also $\mathbb{R}$.

Point of inflection

The significant feature of the graph of a cubic of this form is the **point of inflection** (a point of zero gradient). This will be discussed fully in Chapter 18, but for the moment we note that it is the 'flat point' of the graph.

The point of inflection of $y = x^3$ is at the origin $(0, 0)$.

Vertical translations

By adding or subtracting a constant term to $y = x^3$, the graph moves either 'up' or 'down'.

The graph of $y = x^3 + k$ is the basic graph moved k units up (for $k > 0$). The point of inflection becomes $(0, k)$. In this case, the graph of $y = x^3$ is translated k units in the positive direction of the y-axis.

Horizontal translations

The graph of $y = (x - h)^3$ is simply the basic graph moved h units to the 'right' (for $h > 0$). The point of inflection is at $(h, 0)$. In this case, the graph of $y = x^3$ is translated h units in the positive direction of the x-axis.

General form

> For the graph of a cubic function of the form
> $$y = a(x - h)^3 + k$$
> the point of inflection is at (h, k).

When sketching cubic graphs of the form $y = a(x - h)^3 + k$, first identify the point of inflection. To add further detail to the graph, find the x-axis and y-axis intercepts.

Example 21

Sketch the graph of the function $y = (x - 2)^3 + 4$.

Solution

The graph of $y = x^3$ is translated 2 units to the right and 4 units up.

Point of inflection is $(2, 4)$.

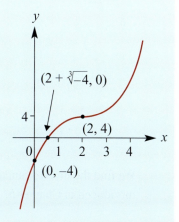

x-axis intercept:

Let $y = 0$

$0 = (x - 2)^3 + 4$

$-4 = (x - 2)^3$

$\sqrt[3]{-4} = x - 2$

$x = 2 + \sqrt[3]{-4}$

≈ 0.413

y-axis intercept:

Let $x = 0$

$y = (0 - 2)^3 + 4$

$y = -8 + 4$

$y = -4$

▶ The function $f: \mathbb{R} \to \mathbb{R}$, $f(x) = x^{\frac{1}{3}}$

The functions with rules of the form $f(x) = a(x - h)^3 + k$ are one-to-one functions. Hence each of these functions has an inverse function.

The inverse function of $f(x) = x^3$ is $f^{-1}(x) = x^{\frac{1}{3}}$.

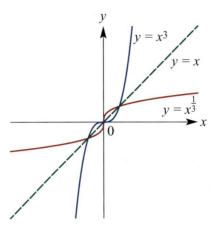

The graphs of $y = x^3$ and $y = x^{\frac{1}{3}}$ are shown above.

The graph of $y = x^{\frac{1}{3}}$ is instantaneously vertical at $x = 0$. The graphs of $y = x^3$ and $y = x^{\frac{1}{3}}$ intersect at $(1, 1)$ and $(-1, -1)$.

Example 22

Sketch the graph of $y = (x - 1)^{\frac{1}{3}} - 2$.

Solution

When $x = 0$,

$y = (-1)^{\frac{1}{3}} - 2$

$= -1 - 2$

$= -3$

When $y = 0$,

$(x - 1)^{\frac{1}{3}} - 2 = 0$

$(x - 1)^{\frac{1}{3}} = 2$

$x - 1 = 2^3$

$x = 9$

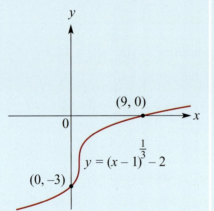

Explanation

Find the axis intercepts.

The graph of

$y = (x - 1)^{\frac{1}{3}} - 2$

is the graph of $y = x^{\frac{1}{3}}$ translated 1 unit to the right and 2 units down.

We find the inverse function of a cubic of the form $y = a(x - h)^3 + k$ by using the technique introduced in Chapter 5.

Example 23

Find the inverse function f^{-1} of $f: \mathbb{R} \to \mathbb{R}$, $f(x) = 2(x-4)^3 + 3$.

Solution

Interchange x and y:

$$x = 2(y-4)^3 + 3$$

Solve for y:

$$x - 3 = 2(y-4)^3$$
$$\frac{x-3}{2} = (y-4)^3$$
$$y - 4 = \left(\frac{x-3}{2}\right)^{\frac{1}{3}}$$
$$y = \left(\frac{x-3}{2}\right)^{\frac{1}{3}} + 4$$

Therefore $f^{-1}: \mathbb{R} \to \mathbb{R}$, $f^{-1}(x) = \left(\frac{x-3}{2}\right)^{\frac{1}{3}} + 4$

Explanation

Remember that $(x, y) \in f$ if and only if $(y, x) \in f^{-1}$.

The opposite operation to cubing is taking the cube root. That is, $\sqrt[3]{x} = x^{\frac{1}{3}}$

Section summary

- The graph of $y = a(x-h)^3 + k$ has the same shape as $y = ax^3$ but is translated h units in the positive x-axis direction and k units in the positive y-axis direction (where h and k are positive constants).
- The implied domain of all cubic functions is $\mathbb{R}$.
- The functions $f(x) = x^3$ and $f^{-1}(x) = x^{\frac{1}{3}}$ are inverse functions of each other.

Exercise 6E

Example 21

1 Using the method of horizontal and vertical translations, sketch the graph of each of the following:

- **a** $y = (x+2)^3 - 1$
- **b** $y = (x-1)^3 - 1$
- **c** $y = (x+3)^3 + 2$
- **d** $y = (x-2)^3 + 5$
- **e** $y = (x+2)^3 - 5$

2 Sketch the graphs of the following functions:

- **a** $y = 2x^3 + 3$
- **b** $y = 2(x-3)^3 + 2$
- **c** $3y = x^3 - 5$
- **d** $y = 3 - x^3$
- **e** $y = (3-x)^3$
- **f** $y = -2(x+1)^3 + 1$
- **g** $y = \frac{1}{2}(x-3)^3 + 2$

Example 22

3 Sketch the graph of each of the following:

- **a** $y = (x-1)^{\frac{1}{3}} - 2$
- **b** $y = 2x^{\frac{1}{3}}$
- **c** $y = 2(x-3)^{\frac{1}{3}} + 1$
- **d** $y = 3(x+2)^{\frac{1}{3}} - 2$
- **e** $y = -2(x-3)^{\frac{1}{3}} + 2$
- **f** $y = -2(x+3)^{\frac{1}{3}} - 2$

236 Chapter 6: Polynomials

Example 23

4 Find the inverse function of each of the following functions:

    a $f(x) = 2x^3 + 3$
    b $f(x) = 3x^{\frac{1}{3}}$
    c $f(x) = 2(x + 1)^3 + 1$

    d $f(x) = 2(x + 3)^{\frac{1}{3}} - 2$
    e $f(x) = -2(x - 1)^{\frac{1}{3}} + 4$
    f $f(x) = -2(x + 2)^{\frac{1}{3}} - 1$

6F Graphs of factorised cubic functions

The general cubic function written in **polynomial form** is

$$y = ax^3 + bx^2 + cx + d$$

There is a variety of graph shapes for cubic functions, depending on the values of the coefficients. The graph of a cubic function is not necessarily a simple transformation (dilations, translations, reflections) of the graph of $y = x^3$.

All cubics have at least one x-axis intercept. We have seen that cubic functions of the form $f(x) = a(x - h)^3 + k$ have only one x-axis intercept, but these are not the only cubic functions with one x-axis intercept. Some cubic functions have two and others have three.

The y-axis intercept is easily found by letting $x = 0$, and it is the point $(0, d)$.

When sketching the graphs of cubics which are not of the form $f(x) = a(x - h)^3 + k$, begin by finding the x-axis intercepts.

In the example below, the cubic is in factored form already.

Example 24

Sketch the graph of $y = (x - 1)(x + 2)(x + 1)$. Do not give coordinates of turning points.

Solution

To find the x-axis intercepts, let $y = 0$.

Then $0 = (x - 1)(x + 2)(x + 1)$
$\therefore x - 1 = 0$ or $x + 2 = 0$ or $x + 1 = 0$
$\therefore x$-axis intercepts are $1, -1$ and -2.

To find the y-axis intercept, let $x = 0$.
Then $y = (0 - 1)(0 + 2)(0 + 1) = -2$.
$\therefore y$-axis intercept is -2.

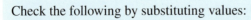

Check the following by substituting values:

- When $x > 1$, $y > 0$.
- When $-2 < x < -1$, $y > 0$.
- When $-1 < x < 1$, $y < 0$.
- When $x < -2$, $y < 0$.

(Notice how the sign of the y-value changes from one side of an x-axis intercept to the other.) Finally, consider what happens to the graph 'beyond' the x-axis intercepts:

- For $x > 1$, $y > 0$ and as x increases y increases.
- For $x < -2$, $y < 0$ and as x decreases y decreases.

6F Graphs of factorised cubic functions

The polynomial form of the cubic in this example is $y = x^3 + 2x^2 - x - 2$. The coefficient of x^3 is positive. We now see what happens when the coefficient of x^3 is negative.

The graph of the cubic function

$$y = -x^3 - 2x^2 + x + 2$$

is the reflection in the x-axis of the graph of the cubic function considered in Example 24.

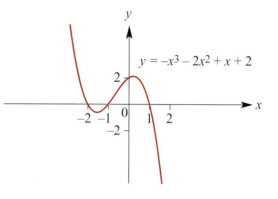

- When $x > 1$, $y < 0$.
- When $-1 < x < 1$, $y > 0$.
- When $-2 < x < -1$, $y < 0$.
- When $x < -2$, $y > 0$.

- For $x > 1$, $y < 0$ and as x increases y decreases.
- For $x < -2$, $y > 0$ and as x decreases y increases.

At this stage the location of the turning points is unspecified. However, it is important to note that, unlike quadratic graphs, the turning points are not symmetrically located between x-axis intercepts. How to determine the exact values of the coordinates of the turning points will be shown later in this book.

▶ Sign diagrams

A sign diagram is a number-line diagram which shows when an expression is positive or negative.

The following is a sign diagram for a cubic function, the graph of which is also shown.

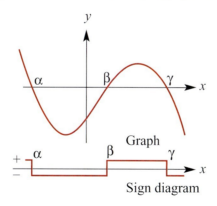

Using a sign diagram requires that the factors, and the x-axis intercepts, be found. The y-axis intercept and sign diagram can then be used to complete the graph.

This procedure is shown in Example 25.

Example 25

Sketch the graph of $y = x^3 + 2x^2 - 5x - 6$.

Solution

Let $P(x) = x^3 + 2x^2 - 5x - 6$

Then $P(1) = 1 + 2 - 5 - 6 \neq 0$

$P(-1) = -1 + 2 + 5 - 6 = 0$

$\therefore x + 1$ is a factor.

By division, $y = (x + 1)(x - 2)(x + 3)$.

$\therefore$ x-axis intercepts are -1, 2 and -3.

When $x < -3$, y is negative.

When $-3 < x < -1$, y is positive.

When $-1 < x < 2$, y is negative.

When $x > 2$, y is positive.

This gives the sign diagram.

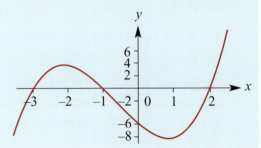

Using the TI-Nspire

In order to provide more detail, the coordinates of the turning points can be found with a CAS calculator.

- Enter $f_1(x) = x^3 + 2x^2 - 5x - 6$ in a **Graphs** application.
- Choose a suitable window (`menu` > **Window/Zoom** > **Window Settings**).

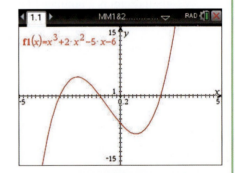

- Use `menu` > **Analyze Graph** > **Maximum**.
- Move the cursor to the left of point (lower bound), click, move to the right of point (upper bound) and click to display the coordinates.
- Repeat for other points of interest.

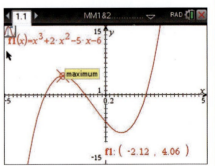

Note: Alternatively, use `menu` > **Trace** > **Graph Trace** to find the coordinates of the two turning points. A label will appear near a turning point to indicate that the calculator has found a local maximum or a local minimum.

Using the Casio ClassPad

In order to provide more detail, the coordinates of the turning points can be found with a CAS calculator.

- Go to the menu, select **Graph & Table** and tap the cursor next to $y1$.
- Enter $x^3 + 2x^2 - 5x - 6$.
- Tick the box and select to produce the graph.
- Choose a suitable window using or a combination of **Zoom Out** and **Zoom Box**.
- Tap in the graph screen to select it, then use **Analysis > G-Solve > Max** to find the local maximum and **Min** to find the local minimum.

Note: The maximum and minimum points must be visible on the screen before carrying out the analysis step.

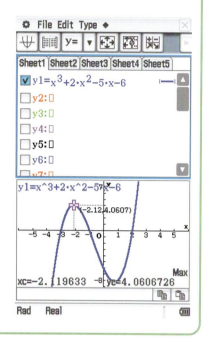

▶ Repeated factors

The polynomial function $f(x) = (x - 1)^2(x + 3)$ has a **repeated factor**. In this case $(x - 1)$ is repeated. Since the repeated factor is squared, it is easy to see that the sign of the y-value is the same on either side of the corresponding x-axis intercept. (Of course we mean 'close in' to the x-axis intercept.)

If the factorised cubic has a repeated factor and another linear factor, there are only two x-axis intercepts and the repeated factor corresponds to one of the turning points.

Example 26

Sketch the graph of $y = x^2(x - 1)$.

Solution

To find the x-axis intercepts, let $y = 0$.

Then $x^2(x - 1) = 0$.

Thus the x-axis intercepts are at $x = 0$ and $x = 1$.
Because the repeated factor is x^2, there is also a turning point at $x = 0$.

The y-axis intercept (letting $x = 0$) is at $y = 0$.

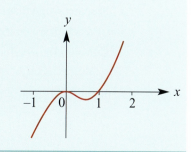

Cubics with one x-axis intercept

Cubics of the form $y = (x - a)^3$ have only one x-axis intercept. Some other cubics also have only one x-axis intercept because, when they are factorised, they are found to have only one linear factor, with the remaining quadratic factor unable to be factorised further.

Example 27

Sketch the graph of $y = -(x - 1)(x^2 + 4x + 5)$.

Solution

To find the x-axis intercept, let $y = 0$.

First, we note that the factor $x^2 + 4x + 5$ cannot be factorised further:

$$\Delta = b^2 - 4ac$$
$$= 4^2 - 4(1)(5)$$
$$= -4$$

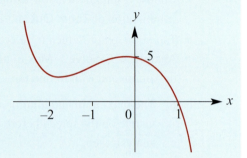

∴ there are no further linear factors.

Hence, when solving the equation $-(x - 1)(x^2 + 4x + 5) = 0$, there is only one solution.

∴ x-axis intercept is $x = 1$.

To find the y-axis intercept, let $x = 0$. Then $y = -(0 - 1)(0^2 + 4(0) + 5) = 5$.

On a CAS calculator it is found that the turning points are at $(0, 5)$ and $(-1.82, 2.91)$, where the values for the coordinates of the second point are given to two decimal places.

Section summary

- The graph of a cubic function can have one, two or three x-axis intercepts.
- If a cubic can be written as the product of three linear factors, $y = a(x - \alpha)(x - \beta)(x - \gamma)$, then its graph can be sketched by following these steps:
  - Find the y-axis intercept.
  - Find the x-axis intercepts.
  - Prepare a sign diagram.
  - Consider the y-values as x increases to the right of all x-axis intercepts.
  - Consider the y-values as x decreases to the left of all x-axis intercepts.
- If there is a repeated factor to the power 2, the y-values have the same sign immediately to the left and right of the corresponding x-axis intercept.

Exercise 6F

1 Sketch the graph for each of the following and draw a sign diagram. Label your sketch graph showing the points of intersection with the axes. (Do not determine coordinates of turning points.)

  a $y = x(x-1)(x-3)$
  b $y = (x-1)(x+1)(x+2)$
  c $y = (2x-1)(x-2)(x+3)$
  d $y = (x-1)(x-2)(x-3)$

2 Sketch the graph for each of the following and draw a sign diagram. Label your sketch graph showing the points of intersection with the axes. (Do not determine coordinates of turning points.)

  a $y = x^3 - 9x$
  b $y = x^3 - 4x^2 - 3x + 18$
  c $y = -x^3 + x^2 + 3x - 3$
  d $y = 3x^3 - 4x^2 - 13x - 6$
  e $y = 6x^3 - 5x^2 - 2x + 1$
  f $y = 2x^3 - 9x^2 + 7x + 6$

3 Sketch the graph for each of the following and draw a sign diagram. Label your sketch graph showing the points of intersection with the axes. (Do not determine coordinates of turning points.)

  a $y = (x-1)(x-2)^2$
  b $y = x^2(x-4)$
  c $y = 2(x+1)^2(x-3)$
  d $y = x^3 + x^2$
  e $y = 4x^3 - 8x^2 + 5x - 1$
  f $y = x^3 - 5x^2 + 7x - 3$

4 Sketch the graph for each of the following and draw a sign diagram. Label your sketch graph showing the points of intersection with the axes. (Do not determine coordinates of turning points.) Use your calculator to help sketch each of them.

  a $y = (x-1)(x^2+1)$ (Note: There is no turning point or 'flat point' of this cubic.)
  b $y = (x^2+2)(x-4)$ (Note: There are two turning points.)

5 Sketch the graph for each of the following, using a CAS calculator to find the coordinates of axis intercepts and local maximum and local minimum values:

  a $y = -4x^3 - 12x^2 + 37x - 15$
  b $y = -4x^3 + 19x - 15$
  c $y = -4x^3 + 0.8x^2 + 19.8x - 18$
  d $y = 2x^3 + 11x^2 + 15x$
  e $y = 2x^3 + 6x^2$
  f $y = 2x^3 + 6x^2 + 6$

6 Show that the graph of f, where $f(x) = x^3 - x^2 - 5x - 3$, cuts the x-axis at one point and touches it at another. Find the values of x at these points.

6G Solving cubic inequalities

Skillsheet As was done for quadratic inequalities, we can solve cubic inequalities by considering the graph of the corresponding polynomial.

Example 28

Find $\{x : x^3 + x^2 - 5x + 3 \leq 0\}$.

Solution

$P(x) = x^3 + x^2 - 5x + 3$

$P(1) = 1 + 1 - 5 + 3 = 0$

$\therefore x - 1$ is a factor. By division, $y = (x - 1)^2(x + 3)$.

There are only two x-axis intercepts, 1 and -3. The y-axis intercept is 3.

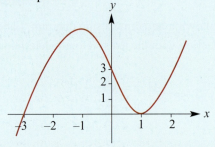

From the graph we can see that $y \leq 0$ when $x \leq -3$ or when $x = 1$.

$\therefore \{x : x^3 + x^2 - 5x + 3 \leq 0\} = (-\infty, -3] \cup \{1\}$

Explanation

- Use the factor theorem to find initial linear factor.
- Complete the factorisation.
- Find the axis intercepts.
- Sketch the graph.
  (Note that this cubic has a repeated factor, and so $(1, 0)$ is a turning point as well an intercept.)
- Solve the inequality by inspecting the graph.
- Express the solution in formal set notation.

Section summary

Cubic inequalities can be solved by sketching the graph of the corresponding cubic function and analysing the graph.

Exercise 6G

Example 28

1 Solve the following cubic inequalities:

 a $(x - 1)(x + 2)(x - 3) \leq 0$
 b $(x + 1)(x + 2)(x - 4) \geq 0$
 c $(x - 1)(x - 2)^2 < 0$
 d $x(x + 2)(x - 3) > 0$
 e $(x - 1)^3 + 8 \leq 0$
 f $x^3 - 1 \geq 0$
 g $x^2(x - 4) > 0$
 h $(x + 3)(x^2 + 2x + 5) \leq 0$

2 Solve the following cubic inequalities. Begin by getting all of the terms on one side.

 a $x^3 > 4x$
 b $x^3 < 5x^2$
 c $x^3 + 4x \leq 4x^2$
 d $x^3 > 9x$
 e $x^3 - 6x^2 + x \geq 6$
 f $2x^3 - 6x^2 - 4x < -12$

6H Families of cubic polynomial functions

 In Chapter 2 we considered the information that is necessary to determine the equation of a straight line. In Chapter 3 this was considered for quadratic functions, and in Chapter 4 for rectangular hyperbolas, circles and other types of functions.

Here are some examples of families of cubic polynomial functions:

$y = ax^3$, $a > 0$ The cubic graphs that are dilations from the x-axis of $y = x^3$.

$y = a(x - h)^3 + k$, $a \neq 0$ The cubic graphs that are translations of $y = ax^3$.

$y = a(x - 2)(x + 5)(x - 4)$, $a \neq 0$ The cubic graphs with x-axis intercepts 2, −5 and 4.

$y = ax^3 + bx^2 + cx$, $a \neq 0$ The cubic graphs that pass through the origin.

Recall that in this context we call a, b, c, h and k parameters.

▶ Finding rules for cubic polynomial functions

The method used for finding the equation from the graph of a cubic will depend on what information is given in the graph.

If the cubic function has rule of the form $f(x) = a(x - h)^3 + k$ and the point of inflection (h, k) is given, then only one other point needs to be known in order to find the value of a.

For those that are not of this form, the information given may be some or all of the x-axis intercepts as well as the coordinates of other points including possibly the y-axis intercept.

Example 29

a A cubic function has rule of the form $y = a(x - 2)^3 + 2$. The point $(3, 10)$ is on the graph of the function. Find the value of a.

b A cubic function has rule of the form $y = a(x - 1)(x + 2)(x - 4)$. The point $(5, 16)$ is on the graph of the function. Find the value of a.

Solution

a $y = a(x - 2)^3 + 2$

When $x = 3$, $y = 10$. Solve for a:

$10 = a(3 - 2)^3 + 2$

$8 = a \times 1^3$

$a = 8$

b $y = a(x - 1)(x + 2)(x - 4)$

When $x = 5$, $y = 16$.

$16 = a(5 - 1)(5 + 2)(5 - 4)$

$16 = 28a$

$a = \dfrac{4}{7}$

Explanation

In each of these problems we substitute in the given values to find the unknown.

The coordinates of the point of inflection of a graph which is a translation of $y = ax^3$ are known and the coordinates of one further point are known.

Three x-axis intercepts are known and the coordinates of a fourth point are known.

Example 30

A cubic function has rule of the form $f(x) = ax^3 + bx$. The points $(1, 16)$ and $(2, 30)$ are on the graph of the function. Find the values of a and b.

Solution

Since $f(1) = 16$ and $f(2) = 30$, we obtain the simultaneous equations

$$16 = a + b \qquad (1)$$
$$30 = a(2)^3 + 2b \qquad (2)$$

Multiply (1) by 2 and subtract from (2). This gives $-2 = 6a$ and hence $a = -\dfrac{1}{3}$.

Substitute in (1) to find $b = \dfrac{49}{3}$.

Example 31

Determine the rule for the cubic function shown in each of the following graphs:

a
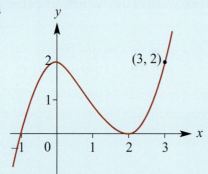

b
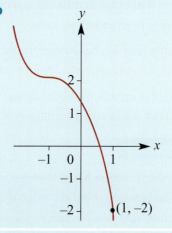

Solution

a $y = a(x + 1)(x - 2)^2$

Put $(3, 2)$ in the equation:

$$2 = a(4)(1)$$
$$\tfrac{1}{2} = a$$

The rule is $y = \tfrac{1}{2}(x + 1)(x - 2)^2$.

b $y - 2 = a(x + 1)^3$

To determine a, put the known point $(1, -2)$ into the equation:

$$-2 - 2 = a(2)^3$$
$$-4 = 8a$$
$$-\tfrac{1}{2} = a$$

The rule is $y - 2 = -\tfrac{1}{2}(x + 1)^3$.

Explanation

The x-axis intercepts are -1 and 2, and the graph touches the x-axis at 2. So the cubic has a repeated factor $(x - 2)$.

Therefore the form of the rule appears to be $y = a(x + 1)(x - 2)^2$.

This graph appears to be of the form $y = a(x - h)^3 + k$. As can be seen from the graph, $k = 2$ and $h = -1$.

6H Families of cubic polynomial functions

Example 32

A cubic function f has rule $f(x) = ax^3 + bx^2 + cx + d$. If

$$f(1) = 0, \quad f(2) = -7, \quad f(4) = 27, \quad f(5) = 80$$

find the values of a, b, c and d.

Using the TI-Nspire

- Define the function $f(x) = ax^3 + bx^2 + cx + d$.
- Use menu > **Algebra** > **Solve System of Equations** > **Solve System of Equations**. Complete the pop-up screen and enter the equations as shown to give the solution to the simultaneous equations.
- An alternative method is also shown.

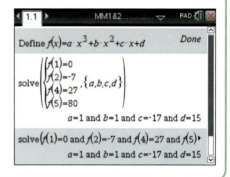

Using the Casio ClassPad

- In Main, enter $f(x) = ax^3 + bx^2 + cx + d$. (Remember to use Var when entering the variables a, b, c, d and abc when entering the function name f.)
- Highlight the expression and go to **Interactive** > **Define**. Use the default function name f and variable x.
- In Math1, select the simultaneous equations icon. Tap it twice more to expand for four simultaneous equations.
- Enter the known values $f(1) = 0, f(2) = -7, f(4) = 27$ and $f(5) = 80$ into the four lines and enter the variables a, b, c, d in the bottom right separated by commas.

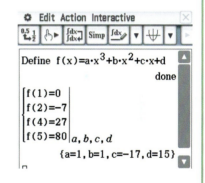

Section summary

The rule of a cubic function can be determined if:

- the coordinates of four points on the graph are known
- the form of the function is known to be $f(x) = a(x - \alpha)^2(x - \beta)$, and α and β and the coordinates of one other point are known
- the form of the function is known to be $f(x) = a(x - h)^3 + k$, and the coordinates of the inflection point (h, k) and one other point are known.

There are other sets of information which can be used to determine the rule of a cubic function and more of these will be given in Chapter 18.

Exercise 6H

1 a A cubic function has rule of the form $y = a(x - 3)^3 + 1$. The point $(4, 12)$ is on the graph of the function. Find the value of a.

b A cubic function has rule of the form $y = a(x - 2)(x + 3)(x - 1)$. The point $(3, 24)$ is on the graph of the function. Find the value of a.

c A cubic function has rule of the form $y = ax^3 + bx$. The points $(1, 16)$ and $(2, 40)$ are on the graph of the function. Find the values of a and b.

2 The graphs shown are similar to the basic curve $y = -x^3$. Find possible cubic functions which define each of the curves.

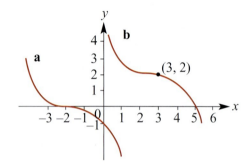

3 Find the equation of the cubic function for which the graph is shown.

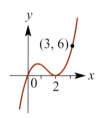

4 Find a cubic function whose graph touches the x-axis at $x = -4$, cuts it at the origin, and has a value 6 when $x = -3$.

5 The graph of a cubic function has x-axis intercepts 1, 3 and -1 and y-axis intercept -6. Find the rule for this cubic function.

6 A cubic function f has rule $f(x) = (x - 3)(x^2 + a)$ and $f(6) = 216$. Find the value of a.

7 The graphs below have equations of the form shown. In each case, determine the equation.

a $y = a(x - h)^3 + k$ **b** $y = ax^3 + bx^2$ **c** $y = ax^3$

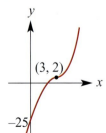 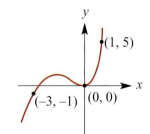 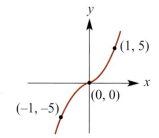

8 Find the expressions which define the following cubic curves:

a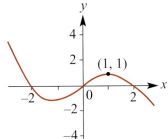

b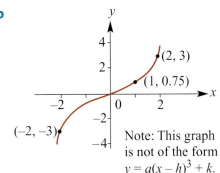

Note: This graph is not of the form $y = a(x - h)^3 + k$.

9 For each of the following, use a CAS calculator to find the values of a, b, c, d in the cubic equation $y = ax^3 + bx^2 + cx + d$, given that the following points lie on its graph:

a $(0, 270), (1, 312), (2, 230), (3, 0)$
b $(-2, -406), (0, 26), (1, 50), (2, -22)$
c $(-2, -32), (2, 8), (3, 23), (8, 428)$
d $(1, -1), (2, 10), (3, 45), (4, 116)$
e $(-3, -74), (-2, -23), (-1, -2), (1, -2)$
f $(-3, -47), (-2, -15), (1, -3), (2, -7)$
g $(-4, 25), (-3, 7), (-2, 1), (1, -5)$

6I Quartic and other polynomial functions

In this section we look at polynomial functions of degree 4 and greater.

▶ Quartic functions of the form $f(x) = a(x - h)^4 + k$

The graph of $f(x) = (x - 1)^4 + 3$ is obtained from the graph of $y = x^4$ by a translation of 1 unit in the positive direction of the x-axis and 3 units in the positive direction of the y-axis.

As with other graphs it has been seen that changing the value of a simply narrows or broadens the graph without changing its fundamental shape. Again, if $a < 0$, the graph is inverted.

The significant feature of the graph of a quartic of this form is the **turning point** (a point of zero gradient). The turning point of $y = x^4$ is at the origin $(0, 0)$.

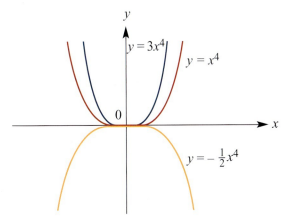

For the graph of a quartic function of the form

$$y = a(x - h)^4 + k$$

the turning point is at (h, k).

When sketching quartic graphs of the form $y = a(x - h)^4 + k$, first identify the turning point. To add further detail to the graph, find the x-axis and y-axis intercepts.

Example 33

Sketch the graph of the function $y = (x-2)^4 - 1$.

Solution

Turning point is $(2, -1)$.

x-axis intercepts:
Let $y = 0$
$$0 = (x-2)^4 - 1$$
$$1 = (x-2)^4$$
$$\pm\sqrt[4]{1} = x - 2$$
$$x = 2 + 1 \text{ or } x = 2 - 1$$
$$x = 3 \text{ or } x = 1$$

y-axis intercept:
Let $x = 0$
$$y = (0-2)^4 - 1$$
$$= 16 - 1$$
$$= 15$$

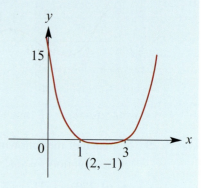

The implied **domain** of all quartics is $\mathbb{R}$, but unlike cubics the range is not $\mathbb{R}$.

▶ Other quartic functions

The techniques for graphing quartic functions in general are very similar to those employed for cubic functions. A CAS calculator is to be used in the graphing of these functions. Great care needs to be taken in this process as it is easy to miss key points on the graph using these techniques.

The graph of $y = 2x^4 - 8x^2$ is shown.

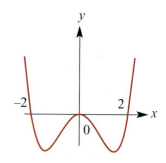

Example 34

Solve each of the following equations for x:

a $x^4 - 8x = 0$ **b** $2x^4 - 8x^2 = 0$ **c** $x^4 - 2x^3 - 24x^2 = 0$

Solution

a $x^4 - 8x = 0$

Factorise to obtain
$$x(x^3 - 8) = 0$$
$$\therefore x = 0 \text{ or } x^3 - 8 = 0$$
Thus $x = 0$ or $x = 2$.

b $2x^4 - 8x^2 = 0$

Factorise to obtain
$$2x^2(x^2 - 4) = 0$$
$$\therefore 2x^2 = 0 \text{ or } x^2 - 4 = 0$$
Thus $x = 0$ or $x = 2$ or $x = -2$.

c $x^4 - 2x^3 - 24x^2 = 0$

Factorise to obtain $x^2(x^2 - 2x - 24) = 0$
$$\therefore x^2 = 0 \text{ or } x^2 - 2x - 24 = 0$$
i.e. $x = 0$ or $(x-6)(x+4) = 0$
Thus $x = 0$ or $x = 6$ or $x = -4$.

Odd and even polynomials

In this subsection we look briefly at odd and even polynomial functions. Knowing that a function is even or that it is odd is very helpful when sketching its graph.

- A function f is **even** if $f(-x) = f(x)$. This means that the graph is symmetric about the y-axis. That is, the graph appears the same after reflection in the y-axis.
- A function f is **odd** if $f(-x) = -f(x)$. The graph of an odd function has rotational symmetry with respect to the origin: the graph remains unchanged after rotation of $180°$ about the origin.

A **power function** is a function f with rule $f(x) = x^r$ where r is a non-zero real number. In this book we focus on the cases where r is a positive integer or $r \in \{-2, -1, \frac{1}{2}, \frac{1}{3}\}$.

Even-degree power functions

The functions with rules $f(x) = x^2$ and $f(x) = x^4$ are examples of even-degree power functions.

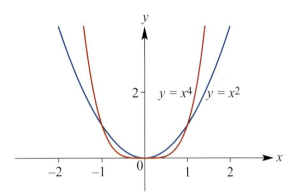

The following are properties of all even-degree power functions:

- $f(-x) = (x)$ for all x
- $f(0) = 0$
- As $x \to \pm\infty$, $y \to \infty$.

Note that, if m and n are positive even integers with $m > n$, then:

- $x^m > x^n$ for $x > 1$ or $x < -1$
- $x^m < x^n$ for $-1 < x < 1$ with $x \neq 0$
- $x^m = x^n$ for $x = 1$ or $x = -1$ or $x = 0$.

Odd-degree power functions

The functions with rules $f(x) = x^3$ and $f(x) = x^5$ are examples of odd-degree power functions.

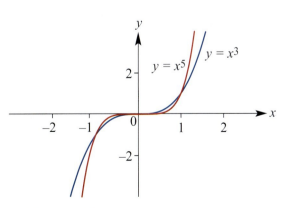

The following are properties of all odd-degree power functions:

- $f(-x) = -f(x)$ for all x
- $f(0) = 0$
- As $x \to \infty$, $y \to \infty$ and as $x \to -\infty$, $y \to -\infty$.

Note that, if m and n are positive odd integers with $m > n$, then:

- $x^m > x^n$ for $x > 1$ or $-1 < x < 0$
- $x^m < x^n$ for $x < -1$ or $0 < x < 1$
- $x^m = x^n$ for $x = 1$ or $x = -1$ or $x = 0$.

Example 35

State whether each of the following polynomials is even or odd:

a $f(x) = 6x^4 - 3x^2$ **b** $g(x) = 3x^5 - x^3 + x$

c $h(x) = x^6 - 3x^2 + 2$ **d** $m(x) = x^7 - 4x$

Solution

a $f(-x) = 6(-x)^4 - 3(-x)^2$
$= 6x^4 - 3x^2$
$= f(x)$

The function is even.

b $g(-x) = 3(-x)^5 - (-x)^3 + (-x)$
$= -3x^5 + x^3 - x$
$= -g(x)$

The function is odd.

c $h(-x) = (-x)^6 - 3(-x)^2 + 2$
$= x^6 - 3x^2 + 2$
$= h(x)$

The function is even.

d $m(-x) = (-x)^7 - 4(-x)$
$= -x^7 + 4x$
$= -m(x)$

The function is odd.

The results of the example are not surprising since:

- The sum of two even functions is even, and any constant multiple of an even function is even.
- The sum of two odd functions is odd, and any constant multiple of an odd function is odd.

Not every polynomial is even or odd. For example, the polynomial $f(x) = x^2 + x$ is neither.

Example 36

a On the one set of axes sketch the graphs of $f(x) = x^4$ and $g(x) = 2x^3$.

b Solve the equation $f(x) = g(x)$.

c Solve the inequality $f(x) \leq g(x)$.

Solution

a

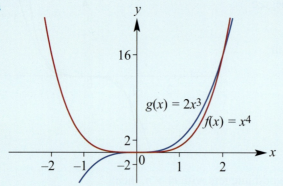

b $f(x) = g(x)$
$x^4 = 2x^3$
$x^4 - 2x^3 = 0$
$x^3(x - 2) = 0$
$x = 0$ or $x = 2$

c $f(x) \leq g(x)$
$x^4 \leq 2x^3$

From the graphs and part b, $f(x) \leq g(x)$ for $x \in [0, 2]$.

Section summary

- The graph of $y = a(x-h)^4 + k$ has the same shape as $y = ax^4$ but is translated h units in the positive x-axis direction and k units in the positive y-axis direction (for h and k positive constants).
- The implied domain of all quartic functions is $\mathbb{R}$.
- A function f is **even** if $f(-x) = f(x)$. This means that the graph is symmetric about the y-axis.
- A function f is **odd** if $f(-x) = -f(x)$. The graph of an odd function has rotational symmetry with respect to the origin.
- A **power function** is a function f with rule $f(x) = x^r$ where r is a non-zero real number.

Exercise 6I

Example 33

1 Using the method of horizontal and vertical translations, sketch the graph of each of the following:

    a $y = (x+2)^4 - 1$ **b** $y = (x-1)^4 - 1$ **c** $y = (x+3)^4 + 2$

    d $y = (x-2)^4 + 5$ **e** $y = (x+2)^4 - 5$

2 Sketch the graphs of the following functions:

    a $y = 2x^4 + 3$ **b** $y = 2(x-3)^4 + 2$ **c** $y = x^4 - 16$

    d $y = 16 - x^4$ **e** $y = (3-x)^4$ **f** $y = -2(x+1)^4 + 1$

Example 34

3 Solve each of the following equations for x:

    a $x^4 - 27x = 0$ **b** $(x^2 - x - 2)(x^2 - 2x - 15) = 0$

    c $x^4 + 8x = 0$ **d** $x^4 - 6x^3 = 0$

    e $x^4 - 9x^2 = 0$ **f** $81 - x^4 = 0$

    g $x^4 - 16x^2 = 0$ **h** $x^4 - 7x^3 + 12x^2 = 0$

    i $x^4 - 9x^3 + 20x^2 = 0$ **j** $(x^2 - 4)(x^2 - 9) = 0$

    k $(x-4)(x^2 + 2x + 8) = 0$ **l** $(x+4)(x^2 + 2x - 8) = 0$

4 Use a CAS calculator to help draw the graph of each of the following. Give x-axis intercepts and coordinates of turning points. (Values of coordinates of turning points to be given correct to two decimal places.)

    a $y = x^4 - 125x$ **b** $y = (x^2 - x - 20)(x^2 - 2x - 24)$

    c $y = x^4 + 27x$ **d** $y = x^4 - 4x^3$

    e $y = x^4 - 25x^2$ **f** $y = 16 - x^4$

    g $y = x^4 - 81x^2$ **h** $y = x^4 - 7x^3 + 12x^2$

    i $y = x^4 - 9x^3 + 20x^2$ **j** $y = (x^2 - 16)(x^2 - 25)$

    k $y = (x-2)(x^2 + 2x + 10)$ **l** $y = (x+4)(x^2 + 2x - 35)$

252 Chapter 6: Polynomials

Example 35

5 State whether each of the following polynomials is even or odd:
   a $f(x) = 5x^6 - 3x^2$
   b $g(x) = 7x^{11} - x^3 + 2x$
   c $h(x) = x^4 - 3x^2 + 2$
   d $m(x) = x^5 - 4x^3$

Example 36

6 a On the one set of axes sketch the graphs of $f(x) = x^3$ and $g(x) = 2x^2$.
   b Solve the equation $f(x) = g(x)$.
   c Solve the inequality $f(x) \leq g(x)$.

7 a On the one set of axes sketch the graphs of $f(x) = x^4$ and $g(x) = 9x^2$.
   b Solve the equation $f(x) = g(x)$.
   c Solve the inequality $f(x) \leq g(x)$.

8 a On the one set of axes sketch the graphs of $f(x) = x^3$ and $g(x) = 4x$.
   b Solve the equation $f(x) = g(x)$.
   c Solve the inequality $f(x) \leq g(x)$.

6J Applications of polynomial functions

Example 37

A square sheet of tin measures 12 cm × 12 cm.

Four equal squares of edge x cm are cut out of the corners and the sides are turned up to form an open rectangular box. Find:

a the values of x for which the volume is 100 cm³
b the maximum volume.

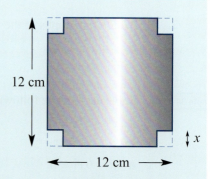

Solution

The figure shows how it is possible to form many open rectangular boxes with dimensions $12 - 2x$, $12 - 2x$ and x.

The volume of the box is

$$V = x(12 - 2x)^2, \quad 0 \leq x \leq 6$$

which is a cubic model.

We complete the solution using a CAS calculator as follows.

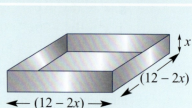

Using the TI-Nspire

Plot the graph of $V = x(12 - 2x)^2$.

a To find the values of x for which $V = 100$, plot the graph of $V = 100$ on the same screen and find the intersection points using (menu) > **Geometry** > **Points & Lines** > **Intersection Point(s)**.

b To find the maximum volume, use (menu) > **Trace** > **Graph Trace** or (menu) > **Analyze Graph** > **Maximum**.

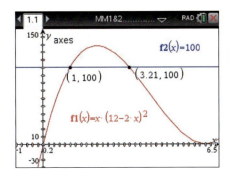
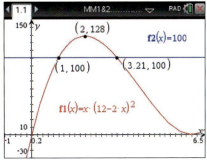

Using the Casio ClassPad

Plot the graph of $V = x(12 - 2x)^2$.

a To find the values of x for which $V = 100$:
- Plot the graph of $V = 100$ on the same screen.
- To adjust your window screen use ⬚. Set $x_{min} = 0$ and $x_{max} = 6$. Then go to **Zoom Auto**. This will automatically adjust the window to the given domain. The grid appears when the scale is adjusted to 20 units.
- Select the graph window ⬚ and go to **Analysis** > **G-Solve** > **Intersection**.
- Press the right arrow on the hard keyboard to find the other point of intersection.

b The maximum volume of the box may be found using **Analysis** > **G-Solve** > **Max**. (You must first remove the tick for y2 and redraw the graph.)

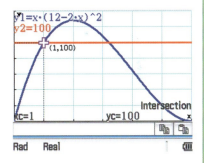
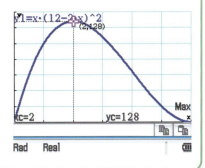

Example 38

It is found that 250 metres of the path of a stream can be modelled by a cubic function. The cubic passes through the points $(0, 0)$, $(100, 22)$, $(150, -10)$, $(200, -20)$.

a Find the equation of the cubic function.
b Find the maximum deviation of the graph from the x-axis for $x \in [0, 250]$.

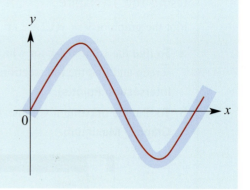

Using the TI-Nspire

- **Define** $f(x) = ax^3 + bx^2 + cx$.
- **Solve** using the **Solve System of Equations** command. Enter using the following function notation:

  $f(100) = 22, \quad f(150) = -10,$
  $f(200) = -20$

  Proceed as shown in the first screen.

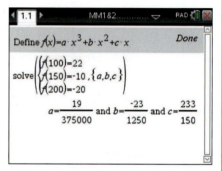

- **Store** these values as a, b and c respectively.
- Use **fMax( )** from menu > **Calculus** > **Function Maximum** to find where f obtains its maximum value.
- Use **fMin( )** from menu > **Calculus** > **Function Minimum** to find where f obtains its minimum value.

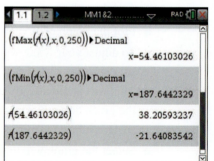

The maximum deviation is 38.21 metres.

Using the Casio ClassPad

- **Define** $f(x) = ax^3 + bx^2 + cx + d$.
- Enter the four equations shown as simultaneous equations with variables set as a, b, c, d.

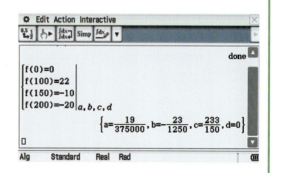

- Store the values found for a, b, c, d as shown below. (**Edit > Copy** and **Edit > Paste** are useful here. The symbol $\Rightarrow$ is found in Math1.)
- The maximum value can be found in the main screen. Type $f(x)$, highlight it and go to **Interactive > Calculation > fMin/fMax**.
- Alternatively, find the maximum value in Graph&Table. Enter and graph $y1 = f(x)$ and then use **Analysis > G-Solve > Max**.

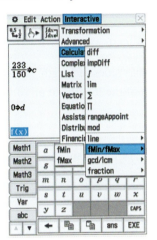 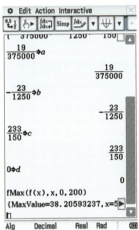 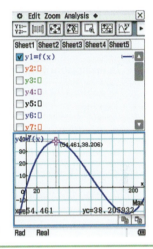

Exercise 6J

Example 37

1 A square sheet of cardboard has edges of length 20 cm. Four equal squares of edge length x cm are cut out of the corners and the sides are turned up to form an open rectangular box.

   a Find the length of each edge of the base of the box in terms of x.

   b Find the volume, V cm^3, of the box in terms of x.

   c Find the volume of the box when $x = 5$.

   d Find the values of x for which the volume is 500 cm^3.

2 A rectangular sheet of metal measuring 10 cm × 12 cm is to be used to construct an open rectangular tray. The tray will be constructed by cutting out four equal squares from each corner of the sheet as shown in the diagram.

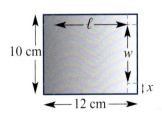

   a If the edge of each cut-out square is x cm, express ℓ and w in terms of x.

   b Write down a rule for the volume, V cm^3, of the open tray in terms of x.

   c Use a CAS calculator to help draw the graph of V against x for suitable values of x.

   d Find the value of V when $x = 1$.

   e Find the values of x for which $V = 50$.

   f Find the maximum volume of the box and the value of x for which this occurs.

3 The outside surface area of an open box is 75 cm². The base is a square with each edge x cm. Let h cm be the height of the box.
   a Find the surface area of the box in terms of x and h.
   b Hence, find h in terms of x.
   c Find V in terms of x if V cm³ is the volume of the box.
   d Find V when:
      i $x = 2$ ii $x = 5$ iii $x = 8$
   e Given that $V = 59$ when $x = 4$, find the other value of x for which $V = 59$.

4 In an upright triangular prism, the triangular base has sides of length $5x$ cm, $12x$ cm and $13x$ cm. The height of the prism is h cm. The sum of the lengths of all of its edges is 180 cm.
   a Find h in terms of x.
   b Find V in terms of x where V cm³ is the volume of the prism.
   c Find V when $x = 3$.
   d Find the values of x for which $V = 1200$.

5 The diagram shows a conical heap of gravel. The slant height of the heap is 8 m, the radius of the base x m, and the height h m.
   a Express x in terms of h.
   b Construct a function which expresses V, the volume of the heap in m³, in terms of h.
   c Use a CAS calculator to help draw the graph of V against h.
   d State the domain for the function.
   e Find the value of V when $h = 4$.
   f Find the values of h for which $V = 150$.
   g Find the maximum volume of the cone and the corresponding value of h.

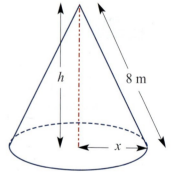

6 The figure shows a rectangular prism with a square cross-section.
   a If the sum of the dimensions, length plus width plus height, is 160 cm, express the height, h, in terms of x.
   b Write down an expression for the volume, V cm³, of the prism in terms of x.
   c State the domain.
   d Use a CAS calculator to help draw the graph of V against x.
   e Find the value(s) of x for which $V = 50\,000$.
   f Find the maximum volume of the prism.

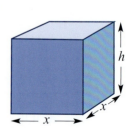

6K The bisection method

Spreadsheet

The **bisection method** is a method for finding approximate solutions of equations. Here we restrict our attention to equations involving polynomial functions.

With higher degree polynomials, the problem of finding exact solutions is more demanding, and it can be shown that beyond degree 4 there is no nice general formula to find all the solutions of a polynomial equation.

For the cubic function $f(x) = x^3 + 3x + 6$, the equation $f(x) = 0$ has only one real solution. The exact solution is

$$x = \frac{-1}{(-3 + \sqrt{10})^{1/3}} + (-3 + \sqrt{10})^{1/3}$$

Finding this by hand is beyond the requirements of this course, but we can find a numerical approximation to this solution using the bisection method.

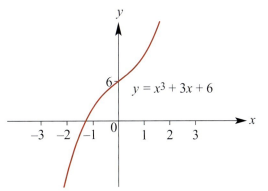

We note that $f(-2) < 0$ and $f(-1) > 0$. This observation is central to using the bisection method.

> In general, consider an equation $f(x) = 0$ that has one solution α in the interval $[a_1, b_1]$.
>
> - The sign of $f(a_1)$ is the opposite of the sign of $f(b_1)$, because $f(\alpha) = 0$ and so the function must change from being positive to being negative or vice versa.
> - Calculate $c_1 = \dfrac{a_1 + b_1}{2}$ and $f(c_1)$.
> - Choose the interval $[a_1, c_1]$ if $f(a_1) \times f(c_1) < 0$, and the interval $[c_1, b_1]$ otherwise.
> - The process is then repeated with the new interval, and then repeatedly until the required accuracy is reached.

▶ Using a spreadsheet with the bisection method

We now return to the function $f(x) = x^3 + 3x + 6$ and finding the solution of the equation $x^3 + 3x + 6 = 0$.

Step 1   We start with the interval $[-2, -1]$, since we know the solution lies in this interval.
$f(-2) = -8 < 0$ and $f(-1) = 2 > 0$.
Let $c_1 = \dfrac{-2 + (-1)}{2} = -1.5$.
Since $f(-1.5) = -1.875 < 0$, we now know the solution is between -1.5 and -1.

Step 2   Choose -1.5 as the new left endpoint. Therefore the second interval is $[-1.5, -1]$.
Now $c_2 = \dfrac{-1.5 + (-1)}{2} = -1.25$ and $f(-1.25) = 0.296875 > 0$.

Step 3 Choose -1.25 as the new right endpoint. Thus the third interval is $[-1.5, -1.25]$.

Now $c_3 = \dfrac{-1.5 + (-1.25)}{2} = -1.375$ and $f(-1.375) = -0.724609 < 0$.

Step 4 Choose -1.375 as the new left endpoint. Thus the fourth interval is $[-1.375, -1.25]$.

At this point we know that the solution is in the interval $[-1.375, -1.25]$.

We continue with the spreadsheet as shown. This spreadsheet can be modified for other functions.

	Left endpoint	Right endpoint	Midpoint c_i	$f(c_i)$
Step 1	-2	-1	-1.5	-1.87500000
Step 2	-1.5	-1	-1.25	0.29687500
Step 3	-1.5	-1.25	-1.375	-0.72460938
Step 4	-1.375	-1.25	-1.3125	-0.19848633
Step 5	-1.3125	-1.25	-1.28125	0.05294800
Step 6	-1.3125	-1.28125	-1.296875	-0.07181931
Step 7	-1.296875	-1.28125	-1.2890625	-0.00919962
Step 8	-1.2890625	-1.28125	-1.28515625	0.02193302
Step 9	-1.2890625	-1.28515625	-1.28710938	0.00638143
Step 10	-1.2890625	-1.28710938	-1.28808594	-0.00140541
Step 11	-1.28808594	-1.28710938	-1.28759766	0.00248893

We conclude that the solution is -1.29 correct to two decimal places.

Whatever equation we are working with, if the starting interval is 1 unit, then the 'error' is at most $\frac{1}{2}$ after the next step and at most $(\frac{1}{2})^{n-1}$ after n steps.

Exercise 6K

1 Find approximate solutions for each of the following. The initial interval is given and the desired accuracy is stated.

  a $x^3 - x - 1 = 0$ $[1, 2]$ 2 decimal places
  b $x^4 + x - 3 = 0$ $[1, 3]$ 3 decimal places
  c $x^3 - 5x + 4.2 = 0$ $[1, 2]$ 3 decimal places
  d $x^3 - 2x^2 + 2x - 5 = 0$ $[2, 3]$ 3 decimal places
  e $2x^4 - 3x^2 + 2x - 6 = 0$ $[-2, -1]$ 2 decimal places

Chapter 6 review 259

Chapter summary

- The sum, difference and product of two polynomials is a polynomial.
- Division of one polynomial by another does not always result in a polynomial.
- **Remainder theorem** When $P(x)$ is divided by $x - \alpha$, the remainder is equal to $P(\alpha)$.
  e.g. When $P(x) = x^3 + 3x^2 + 2x + 1$ is divided by $x - 2$, the remainder is
  $$P(2) = (2)^3 + 3(2)^2 + 2(2) + 1 = 25$$
- **Factor theorem** For a polynomial $P(x)$, if $P(\alpha) = 0$, then $x - \alpha$ is a factor. Conversely, if $x - \alpha$ is a factor of $P(x)$, then $P(\alpha) = 0$.
  e.g. For $P(x) = x^3 - 4x^2 + x + 6$,
  $$P(-1) = (-1)^3 - 4(-1)^2 + (-1) + 6 = 0$$
  and so $x + 1$ is a factor of $P(x)$.
- Sums and differences of cubes:
  $$x^3 - a^3 = (x - a)(x^2 + ax + a^2)$$
  e.g. $\quad x^3 - 27 = (x - 3)(x^2 + 3x + 9)$
  $$x^3 + a^3 = (x + a)(x^2 - ax + a^2)$$
  e.g. $\quad 8x^3 + 64 = (2x)^3 + 4^3$
  $$= (2x + 4)(4x^2 - 8x + 16)$$
- **Rational-root theorem** Let $P(x) = a_n x^n + a_{n-1} x^{n-1} + \cdots + a_1 x + a_0$ be a polynomial of degree n with all the coefficients a_i integers. Let α and β be integers such that the highest common factor of α and β is 1 (i.e. α and β are relatively prime). If $\beta x + \alpha$ is a factor of $P(x)$, then β divides a_n and α divides a_0.
- The following are the steps in the process of solving cubic equations:
  i Determine factors by using the factor theorem and dividing.
  ii Use the null factor theorem to determine solutions.
  e.g. Solve $x^3 - 4x^2 - 11x + 30 = 0$.
  Since $P(2) = 8 - 16 - 22 + 30 = 0$, we know that $x - 2$ is a factor.
  Dividing $x - 2$ into $x^3 - 4x^2 - 11x + 30$ gives
  $$x^3 - 4x^2 - 11x + 30 = (x - 2)(x^2 - 2x - 15)$$
  $$= (x - 2)(x - 5)(x + 3)$$
  $\therefore \quad (x - 2)(x - 5)(x + 3) = 0$
  $\therefore \quad x = 2, 5$ or -3
- The basic shape of the curve defined by $y = x^3$ is shown in the graph.

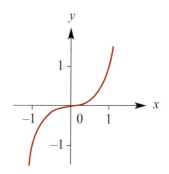

- The implied domain of all polynomial functions is $\mathbb{R}$.
- The functions $f(x) = x^3$ and $f^{-1}(x) = x^{\frac{1}{3}}$ are inverse functions of each other.
- The graph of $y = a(x - h)^3 + k$ has the same shape as $y = ax^3$ but is translated h units in the positive x-axis direction and k units in the positive y-axis direction (where h and k are positive constants).
- The basic shape of the curve defined by $y = x^4$ is shown in the graph.

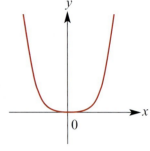

- The graph of $y = a(x - h)^4 + k$ has the same shape as $y = ax^4$ but is translated h units in the positive x-axis direction and k units in the positive y-axis direction (where h and k are positive constants). The turning point is at (h, k).
- Sign diagrams assist in sketching graphs of cubic functions.

  e.g. $y = x^3 + 2x^2 - 5x - 6$
  $= (x + 1)(x - 2)(x + 3)$

  When $x < -3$, y is negative.
  When $-3 < x < -1$, y is positive.
  When $-1 < x < 2$, y is negative.
  When $x > 2$, y is positive.

  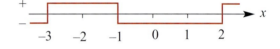

- To sketch the graph of a cubic function $y = ax^3 + bx^2 + cx + d$, the steps are:
  i Use the factor theorem and division to determine the x-axis intercepts.
  ii The y-axis intercept is d.
  iii Draw a sign diagram.

- Finding equations for given cubic graphs. The following may assist:

  i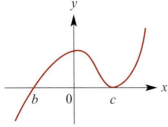

  ii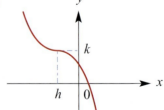

  Form: $y = a(x - b)(x - c)^2$
  Assume b and c are known, substitute another known point to calculate a.

  Form: $y = a(x - h)^3 + k$
  Substitute known values to determine a.

  Alternatively, use the general form $y = ax^3 + bx^2 + cx + d$ and the known points to determine a, b, c and d.

Chapter 6 review

- A function f is **even** if $f(-x) = f(x)$. This means that the graph is symmetric about the y-axis.
- A function f is **odd** if $f(-x) = -f(x)$. The graph of an odd function has rotational symmetry with respect to the origin.
- A **power function** is a function f with rule $f(x) = x^r$ where r is a non-zero real number.

Technology-free questions

1 Sketch the graph of each of the following:
  a $y = (x - 1)^3 - 2$
  b $y = (2x - 1)^3 + 1$
  c $y = 3(x - 1)^3 - 1$
  d $y = -3x^3$
  e $y = -3x^3 + 1$
  f $y = -3(x - 2)^3 + 1$
  g $y = 4(x + 2)^3 - 3$
  h $y = 1 - 3(x + 2)^3$

2 Sketch the graph of each of the following:
  a $y = (x - 1)^4$
  b $y = (2x - 1)^4 + 1$
  c $y = (x - 1)^4 - 1$
  d $y = -2x^4$
  e $y = -3x^4 + 1$
  f $y = -(x - 2)^4 + 1$
  g $y = 2(x + 1)^4 - 3$
  h $y = 1 - 2(x + 2)^4$

3 Solve each of the following equations for x:
  a $2x^3 + 3x^2 = 11x + 6$
  b $x^2(5 - 2x) = 4$
  c $x^3 + 4x + 12 = 7x^2$

4 a Use the factor theorem to show that $2x - 3$ and $x + 2$ are factors of $6x^3 + 5x^2 - 17x - 6$. Find the other factor.
  b Solve the equation $2x^3 - 3x^2 - 11x + 6 = 0$.
  c Solve the equation $x^3 + x^2 - 11x - 3 = 8$.
  d i Show that $3x - 1$ is a factor of $3x^3 + 2x^2 - 19x + 6$.
    ii Find the factors of $3x^3 + 2x^2 - 19x + 6$.

5 Let $f(x) = x^3 - kx^2 + 2kx - k - 1$.
  a Show that $f(x)$ is divisible by $x - 1$.
  b Factorise $f(x)$.

6 Find the values of a and b for which $x^3 + ax^2 - 10x + b$ is divisible by $x^2 + x - 12$.

7 Draw a sign diagram for each of the following and hence sketch the graph:
  a $y = (x + 2)(3 - x)(x + 4)$
  b $y = (x - 2)(x + 3)(x - 4)$
  c $y = 6x^3 + 13x^2 - 4$
  d $y = x^3 + x^2 - 24x + 36$

8 Without actually dividing, find the remainder when the first polynomial is divided by the second:
  a $x^3 + 4x^2 - 5x + 1$, $x + 6$
  b $2x^3 - 3x^2 + 2x + 4$, $x - 2$
  c $3x^3 + 2x + 4$, $3x - 1$

9 Find the rule of the cubic for which the graph is shown.

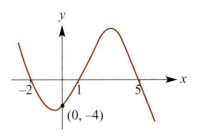

10 Find a cubic function whose graph touches the x-axis at $x = -4$, passes through the origin and has a value of 10 when $x = 5$.

11 Let $f(x) = 2x^3 + ax^2 - bx + 3$. When $f(x)$ is divided by $x - 2$ the remainder is 15 and $f(1) = 0$.
  a Calculate the values of a and b.
  b Find the other two factors of $f(x)$.

12 Solve each of the following inequalities for x:
  a $(x - 3)^2(x + 4) \leq 0$
  b $-(x + 3)(x + 4)(x - 2) \geq 0$
  c $x^3 - 4x^2 + x < -6$

13 For each of the following, find a sequence of transformations that takes the graph of $y = x^3$ to the graph of:
  a $y = 2(x - 1)^3 + 3$
  b $y = -(x + 1)^3 + 2$
  c $y = (2x + 1)^3 - 2$

Multiple-choice questions

1 If $P(x) = x^3 + 3x^2 + x - 3$, then $P(-2)$ equals
  A 1 **B** -1 **C** -25 **D** 3 **E** -5

2 If $a > b > c$ and $P(x) = (x - a)^2(x - b)(x - c)$, then $P(x) < 0$ for $x \in$
  A $(-\infty, a)$ **B** $(-\infty, b)$ **C** $(-\infty, c)$ **D** (c, b) **E** (b, a)

3 The image of the graph of $y = x^3$ under a dilation of factor 2 from the y-axis followed by a reflection in the y-axis and then a translation of 4 units in the negative direction of the y-axis is
  A $y = -\dfrac{x^3}{8} - 4$
  B $y = -\dfrac{x^3}{2} - 4$
  C $y = -8x^3 - 4$
  D $y = -\dfrac{x^3}{2} + 4$
  E $y = \dfrac{x^3}{8} + 4$

4 The equation $x^3 + 5x - 10 = 0$ has only one solution. This solution lies between
  A -2 and -1 **B** -1 and 0 **C** 0 and 1 **D** 1 and 2 **E** 2 and 8

5 Let $P(x) = x^4 + ax^2 - 4$. If $P(\sqrt{2}) = 0$ and $P(-\sqrt{2}) = 0$, the value of a is
  A 0 **B** 2 **C** -2 **D** -3 **E** 3

6 Let $P(x) = x^3 + ax^2 + bx - 9$. If $P(1) = 0$ and $P(-3) = 0$, the values of a and b are
  A $a = 1$, $b = -3$
  B $a = -1$, $b = 3$
  C $a = 5$, $b = 3$
  D $a = -5$, $b = -3$
  E $a = 0$, $b = 0$

7 If $ax^3 + 2x^2 + 5$ is exactly divisible by $x + 1$, the value of a is
  A 1 **B** 7 **C** −1 **D** 3 **E** −7

8 When the polynomial $P(x) = x^3 + 2x^2 - 5x + d$ is divided by $x - 2$, the remainder is 10. The value of d is
  A 10 **B** 4 **C** −10 **D** −4 **E** 3

9 The diagram shows part of the graph of a polynomial function.

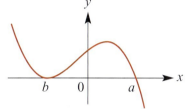

A possible equation for the rule of the function is
  A $y = (x - b)^2(x - a)$
  B $y = (x - a)^2(x - b)$
  C $y = -(x + b)^2(x - a)$
  D $y = (x - b)^2(a - x)$
  E $y = (x + b)^2(a - x)$

10 The graph of $y = f(x)$ is shown on the right. Which one of the following could be the graph of $y = 1 - f(x)$?

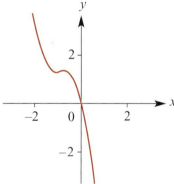

A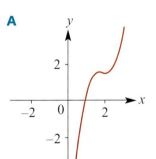
B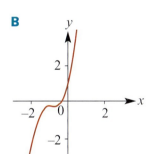

C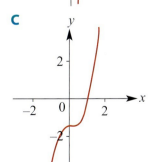
D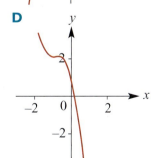
E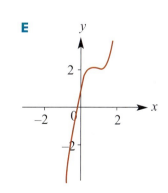

Extended-response questions

1. The volume of a cylinder is given by $V = \pi r^2 h$. It is given that $h + r = 6$.
   a. Write $V(r)$ in terms of r.
   b. State the values that r can have.
   c. Find $V(3)$.
   d. Find the values of r for which $V(r) = 27\pi$.
   e. Use your CAS calculator to find the maximum possible volume of the cylinder.

2. There is a proposal to provide a quicker, more efficient and more environmentally friendly system of inner-city public transport by using electric taxis. The proposal necessitates the installation of power sources at various locations as the taxis can only be driven for a limited time before requiring recharging.
   The graph shows the speed v m/s that the taxi will maintain if it is driven at constant speed in such a way that it uses all its energy up in t seconds. The curve is a section of a parabola which touches the t-axis at $t = 900$. When $t = 0$, $v = 25$.

   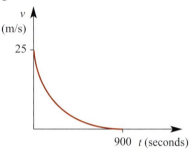

   a. Construct a rule for v in terms of t.
   b. If s metres is the distance that a taxi can travel before running out of electrical energy, write down a rule connecting s and t.
   c. Use a CAS calculator to help draw the graph of s against t.
   d. Originally the power sources were to be located at 2 km intervals. However there is a further proposal to place them at 3.5 km intervals. Is this new distance feasible?
   e. With the power sources at 2 km intervals, use your graph to determine approximately both the maximum and minimum speeds recommended for drivers. Explain your answer.

3. The figure shows part of a cubic graph that represents the relationship between the engine speed, R rpm, and the throttle setting, x mm from the closed position, for a new engine.
   It can be seen from the graph that the engine has a 'flat spot' where an increase in x has very little effect on R.

   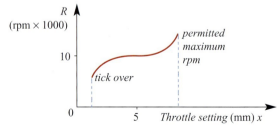

   a. Develop a cubic expression for R in terms of x of the form $R = a(x - h)^3 + k$.

b Find a if when the graph is extended it passes through the origin.

c In a proposed modification to the design, the 'flat spot' will occur when $x = 7$ mm. The speed of the engine in this case will be 12 000 rpm when $x = 7$ mm. Assuming that a cubic model still applies and that $R = 0$ when $x = 0$, write down an expression for R as a function of x.

4 A net for making a cardboard box with overlapping flaps is shown in the figure. The dotted lines represent cuts and the solid lines represent lines along which the cardboard is folded.

	Top	Top	Top	Top
	Left	Back	Right	Front
	Bottom	Bottom	Bottom	Bottom

(with vertical dimensions $\frac{w}{2}$, h, $\frac{w}{2}$ and horizontal dimensions ℓ, w, ℓ, w)

a If $\ell = 35$ cm, $w = 20$ cm and $h = 23$ cm, calculate the area of the net.

b If the area of the net is to remain constant at the value calculated in part **a** and $\ell = h$, write down an expression for V, the volume of the box in cm^3, as a function of ℓ. (The maximum volume of the box will occur when $\ell = h$).

c Use a CAS calculator to help draw the graph of V against ℓ.

d Find the value of ℓ when the volume of the box is:

  i 14 000 cm^3 **ii** 10 litres = 10 000 cm^3

e Find the maximum volume of the box and the value of ℓ for which this occurs.

5 It is found that the shape of a branch of a eucalyptus tree can be modelled by a cubic function. The coordinates of several points on the branch are (0, 15.8), (10, 14.5), (15, 15.6), (20, 15).

a The rule for the function is of the form $y = ax^3 + bx^2 + cx + d$. Find the values of a, b, c and d.

b Find the coordinates of the point on the branch that is:

  i closest to the ground
  ii furthest from the ground.

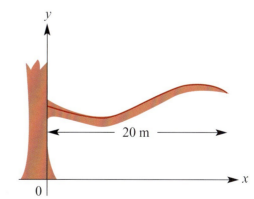

6 A reinforced box is made by cutting congruent squares of side length x cm from the four corners of a rectangular piece of cardboard that measures 48 cm by 96 cm. The flaps are folded up.

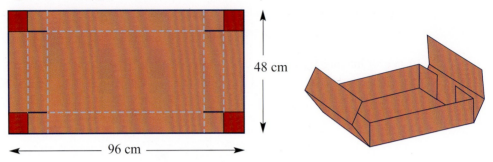

a Find an expression for V, the volume of the box formed.
b Plot a graph of V against x on your CAS calculator.
   i What is the domain of the function V?
   ii Using your CAS calculator, find the maximum volume of the box and the value of x for which this occurs (approximate values required).
c Find the volume of the box when $x = 10$.
d It is decided that $0 \leq x \leq 5$. Find the maximum volume possible.
e If $5 \leq x \leq 15$, what is the minimum volume of the box?

Chapter 7
Transformations

Objectives

▶ To introduce a notation for considering **transformations** of the plane, including translations, reflections in an axis and dilations from an axis.
▶ To use **matrices** to define transformations.
▶ To be able to use **matrix equations** in determining the image of a curve under a linear transformation.

We have studied transformations in the earlier chapters of this book without any systematic consideration of transformations of the points of the plane in general. In this chapter we offer the opportunity to develop techniques for both applying and identifying transformations.

We state the following result as an example of the relationship between the transformation of points and the graph-sketching techniques we have used earlier in this book. Similar results hold for reflections in an axis and dilations from an axis.

For the graph of $y = f(x)$, the following two processes yield the same result:

- Applying the translation $(x, y) \rightarrow (x + h, y + k)$ to the graph of $y = f(x)$.
- Replacing x with $x - h$ and y with $y - k$ in the equation to obtain $y - k = f(x - h)$ and graphing the result.

Sections 7E and 7F give a very brief introduction to matrices and their arithmetic. A more comprehensive treatment is available in the Interactive Textbook. Sections 7G and 7H discuss the application of matrices to describing these simple transformations.

It is possible to complete the rest of this book without reference to the first four sections of this chapter, but we note that many students may find this a helpful tool in their work with transformations.

7A Translations of functions*

The **Cartesian plane** is represented by the set $\mathbb{R}^2$ of all ordered pairs of real numbers. That is, $\mathbb{R}^2 = \{(x, y) : x, y \in \mathbb{R}\}$. The transformations considered in this book associate each ordered pair of $\mathbb{R}^2$ with a unique ordered pair. We can refer to them as examples of **transformations of the plane**.

For example, the translation 3 units in the positive direction of the x-axis (to the right) associates with each ordered pair (x, y) a new ordered pair $(x + 3, y)$. This translation is a transformation of the plane. Each point in the plane is mapped to a unique second point. Furthermore, every point in the plane is an image of another point under this translation.

▶ Notation

The translation 3 units to the right can be written $(x, y) \to (x + 3, y)$. This reads as '(x, y) maps to $(x + 3, y)$'.

For example, $(-1, -2) \to (-1 + 3, -2)$.

In applying this translation, it is useful to think of every point (x, y) in the plane as being mapped to a new point (x', y'). This point (x, y) is the only point which maps to (x', y'). The following can be written for this translation:

$$x' = x + 3 \quad \text{and} \quad y' = y$$

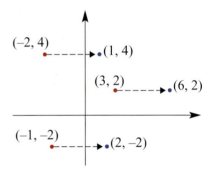

As another example, consider the translation 2 units in the positive direction of the x-axis (to the right) and 4 units in the positive direction of the y-axis (up). This can be described by the rule $(x, y) \to (x + 2, y + 4)$.

For example, $(3, 2) \to (3 + 2, 2 + 4)$.

The following can be written for this translation:

$$x' = x + 2 \quad \text{and} \quad y' = y + 4$$

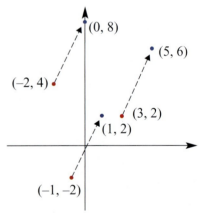

A translation of h units in the positive direction of the x-axis and k units in the positive direction of the y-axis is described by the rule

$$(x, y) \to (x + h, y + k)$$

or $\quad x' = x + h \quad \text{and} \quad y' = y + k$

where h and k are positive numbers.

---

* The first four sections could be omitted but they form a sound foundation for further study.

A translation of h units in the negative direction of the x-axis and k units in the negative direction of the y-axis is described by the rule

$$(x, y) \to (x - h, y - k)$$

or $\quad x' = x - h \quad$ and $\quad y' = y - k$

where h and k are positive numbers.

Notes:
- Under a translation, if $(a', b') = (c', d')$, then $(a, b) = (c, d)$.
- For a particular translation $(x, y) \to (x + h, y + k)$, for each point $(a, b) \in \mathbb{R}^2$ there is a point (p, q) such that $(p, q) \to (a, b)$. (It is clear that $(a - h, b - k) \to (a, b)$ under this translation.)

▶ Applying translations to sketch graphs

We look at a particular example.

Translate the set of points defined by the function

$$\{(x, y) : y = x^2\}$$

by the translation defined by the rule

$$(x, y) \to (x + 2, y + 4)$$
$$x' = x + 2 \quad \text{and} \quad y' = y + 4$$

For each point (x, y) there is a unique point (x', y') and vice versa.

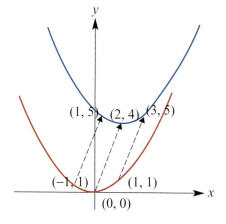

We have $x = x' - 2$ and $y = y' - 4$.

This means the points on the curve with equation $y = x^2$ are mapped to the curve with equation $y' - 4 = (x' - 2)^2$.

Hence $\{(x, y) : y = x^2\}$ maps to $\{(x', y') : y' - 4 = (x' - 2)^2\}$.

For the graph of $y = f(x)$, the following two processes yield the same result:
- Applying the translation $(x, y) \to (x + h, y + k)$ to the graph of $y = f(x)$.
- Replacing x with $x - h$ and y with $y - k$ in the equation to obtain $y - k = f(x - h)$ and graphing the result.

Proof A point (a, b) is on the graph of $y = f(x)$

$\Leftrightarrow f(a) = b$
$\Leftrightarrow f(a + h - h) = b$
$\Leftrightarrow f(a + h - h) = b + k - k$
$\Leftrightarrow (a + h, b + k)$ is a point on the graph of $y - k = f(x - h)$

Note: The double arrows indicate that the steps are reversible.

Example 1

Find the equation for the image of the curve with equation $y = f(x)$, where $f(x) = \dfrac{1}{x}$, under a translation 3 units in the positive direction of the x-axis and 2 units in the negative direction of the y-axis.

Solution

Let (x', y') be the image of the point (x, y), where (x, y) is a point on the graph of $y = f(x)$.

Then $x' = x + 3$ and $y' = y - 2$.

Hence $x = x' - 3$ and $y = y' + 2$.

The graph of $y = f(x)$ is mapped to the graph of
$y' + 2 = f(x' - 3)$

i.e. $y = \dfrac{1}{x}$ is mapped to

$$y' + 2 = \dfrac{1}{x' - 3}$$

Explanation

The rule is $(x, y) \to (x + 3, y - 2)$.

Substitute $x = x' - 3$ and $y = y' + 2$ into $y = f(x)$.

Recognising that a transformation has been applied makes it easy to sketch many graphs.

For example, in order to sketch the graph of

$$y = \dfrac{1}{x - 2}$$

note that it is of the form $y = f(x - 2)$ where $f(x) = \dfrac{1}{x}$. That is, the graph of $y = \dfrac{1}{x}$ is translated 2 units in the positive direction of the x-axis.

Examples of two other functions to which this translation is applied are:

$f(x) = x^2 \qquad f(x - 2) = (x - 2)^2$

$f(x) = \sqrt{x} \qquad f(x - 2) = \sqrt{x - 2}$

Section summary

For the graph of $y = f(x)$, the following two processes yield the same result:

- Applying the translation $(x, y) \to (x + h, y + k)$ to the graph of $y = f(x)$.
- Replacing x with $x - h$ and y with $y - k$ in the equation to obtain $y - k = f(x - h)$ and graphing the result.

Exercise 7A

1 Find the image of the point $(-3, 4)$ after a mapping of a translation:
  a of 2 units in the positive direction of the x-axis and 3 units in the negative direction of the y-axis
  b of 2 units in the negative direction of the x-axis and 4 units in the positive direction of the y-axis
  c of 3 units in the negative direction of the x-axis and 2 units in the negative direction of the y-axis
  d defined by the rule $(x, y) \to (x - 4, y + 5)$
  e defined by the rule $(x, y) \to (x - 2, y - 1)$.

2 In each of the following, find the rule for the image of the graph of $y = f(x)$ under the given translation:
  a $f(x) = \dfrac{1}{x}$ under a translation 2 units in the positive direction of the x-axis and 1 unit in the negative direction of the y-axis
  b $f(x) = \dfrac{1}{x^2}$ under a translation 4 units in the positive direction of the x-axis and 3 units in the positive direction of the y-axis
  c $f(x) = x^2$ under a translation 2 units in the negative direction of the x-axis and 3 units in the negative direction of the y-axis
  d $f(x) = x^3$ under a translation 4 units in the positive direction of the x-axis and 2 units in the negative direction of the y-axis
  e $f(x) = \sqrt{x}$ under a translation 2 units in the positive direction of the x-axis and 1 unit in the negative direction of the y-axis.

3 For $y = f(x) = \dfrac{1}{x}$, sketch the graph of each of the following, labelling asymptotes and axis intercepts:
  a $y = f(x - 1)$
  b $y = f(x) + 1$
  c $y = f(x + 3)$
  d $y = f(x) - 3$
  e $y = f(x + 1)$
  f $y = f(x) - 1$

4 For $y = f(x) = x^2$, sketch the graph of each of the following, labelling axis intercepts:
  a $y = f(x - 1)$
  b $y = f(x) + 1$
  c $y = f(x + 3)$
  d $y = f(x) - 3$
  e $y = f(x + 1)$
  f $y = f(x) - 1$

5 For $y = f(x) = x^2$, sketch the graph of each of the following, labelling axis intercepts:
  a $y = f(x - 1) + 2$
  b $y = f(x - 3) + 1$
  c $y = f(x + 3) - 5$
  d $y = f(x + 1) - 3$
  e $y + 2 = f(x + 1)$
  f $y = f(x - 5) - 1$

7B Dilations and reflections

The same techniques can be applied to dilations from an axis and reflections.

▶ Dilation from the x-axis

A dilation of factor 2 from the x-axis can be defined by the rule $(x, y) \to (x, 2y)$.

Hence the point with coordinates $(1, 1) \to (1, 2)$.

Consider the curve with equation $y = \sqrt{x}$ and the dilation of factor 2 from the x-axis.

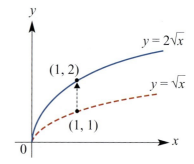

- Let (x', y') be the image of the point with coordinates (x, y) on the curve.
- Hence $x' = x$ and $y' = 2y$, and thus $x = x'$ and $y = \dfrac{y'}{2}$.
- Substituting for x and y, we see that the curve with equation $y = \sqrt{x}$ maps to the curve with equation $\dfrac{y'}{2} = \sqrt{x'}$, i.e. the curve with equation $y = 2\sqrt{x}$.

> For b a positive constant, a dilation of factor b from the x-axis is described by the rule
>
> $\quad (x, y) \to (x, by)$
>
> or $\quad x' = x$ and $y' = by$
>
> For the graph of $y = f(x)$, the following two processes yield the same result:
> - Applying the dilation from the x-axis $(x, y) \to (x, by)$ to the graph of $y = f(x)$.
> - Replacing y with $\dfrac{y}{b}$ in the equation to obtain $y = bf(x)$ and graphing the result.

▶ Dilation from the y-axis

A dilation of factor 2 from the y-axis can be defined by the rule $(x, y) \to (2x, y)$. Hence the point with coordinates $(1, 1) \to (2, 1)$.

Again, consider the curve with equation $y = \sqrt{x}$.

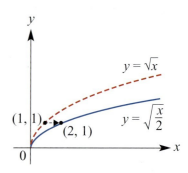

- Let (x', y') be the image of the point with coordinates (x, y) on the curve.
- Hence $x' = 2x$ and $y' = y$, and thus $x = \dfrac{x'}{2}$ and $y = y'$.
- The curve with equation $y = \sqrt{x}$ maps to the curve with equation $y' = \sqrt{\dfrac{x'}{2}}$.

For a a positive constant, a dilation of factor a from the y-axis is described by the rule

$$(x, y) \to (ax, y)$$

or $\quad x' = ax$ and $y' = y$

For the graph of $y = f(x)$, the following two processes yield the same result:
- Applying the dilation from the y-axis $(x, y) \to (ax, y)$ to the graph of $y = f(x)$.
- Replacing x with $\dfrac{x}{a}$ in the equation to obtain $y = f\left(\dfrac{x}{a}\right)$ and graphing the result.

▶ Reflection in the x-axis

A reflection in the x-axis can be defined by the rule $(x, y) \to (x, -y)$. Hence the point with coordinates $(1, 1) \to (1, -1)$.

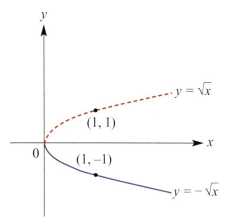

- Let (x', y') be the image of the point (x, y).
- Hence $x' = x$ and $y' = -y$, which gives $x = x'$ and $y = -y'$.
- The curve with equation $y = \sqrt{x}$ maps to the curve with equation $-y' = \sqrt{x'}$, i.e. the curve with equation $y = -\sqrt{x}$.

A reflection in the x-axis is described by the rule

$$(x, y) \to (x, -y)$$

or $\quad x' = x$ and $y' = -y$

For the graph of $y = f(x)$, the following two processes yield the same result:
- Applying the reflection in the x-axis $(x, y) \to (x, -y)$ to the graph of $y = f(x)$.
- Replacing y with $-y$ in the equation to obtain $y = -f(x)$ and graphing the result.

▶ Reflection in the y-axis

A reflection in the y-axis can be defined by the rule $(x, y) \to (-x, y)$. Hence the point with coordinates $(1, 1) \to (-1, 1)$.

- Let (x', y') be the image of the point (x, y).
- Hence $x' = -x$ and $y' = y$, which gives $x = -x'$ and $y = y'$.
- The curve with equation $y = \sqrt{x}$ maps to the curve with equation $y' = \sqrt{-x'}$, i.e. the curve with equation $y = \sqrt{-x}$.

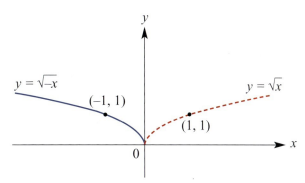

A reflection in the *y*-axis is described by the rule

$(x, y) \to (-x, y)$

or $\quad x' = -x \quad$ and $\quad y' = y$

For the graph of $y = f(x)$, the following two processes yield the same result:

- Applying the reflection in the *y*-axis $(x, y) \to (-x, y)$ to the graph of $y = f(x)$.
- Replacing x with $-x$ in the equation to obtain $y = f(-x)$ and graphing the result.

Example 2

Determine the rule of the image when the graph of $y = \dfrac{1}{x^2}$ is dilated by a factor of 4:

a from the *y*-axis **b** from the *x*-axis.

Solution

a $(x, y) \to (4x, y)$

Let (x', y') be the coordinates of the image of (x, y), so $x' = 4x, \; y' = y$.

Rearranging gives $x = \dfrac{x'}{4}, \; y = y'$.

Therefore $y = \dfrac{1}{x^2}$ becomes $y' = \dfrac{1}{\left(\frac{x'}{4}\right)^2}$.

The rule of the transformed function is $y = \dfrac{16}{x^2}$.

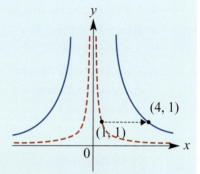

b $(x, y) \to (x, 4y)$

Let (x', y') be the coordinates of the image of (x, y), so $x' = x, \; y' = 4y$.

Rearranging gives $x = x', \; y = \dfrac{y'}{4}$.

Therefore $y = \dfrac{1}{x^2}$ becomes $\dfrac{y'}{4} = \dfrac{1}{(x')^2}$.

The rule of the transformed function is $y = \dfrac{4}{x^2}$.

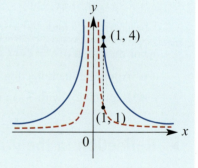

▶ Applying dilations and reflections to sketch graphs

In order to sketch the graph of $y = \sqrt{\dfrac{x}{2}}$, note that it is of the form $y = f\left(\dfrac{x}{2}\right)$ where $f(x) = \sqrt{x}$. This is the graph of $y = \sqrt{x}$ dilated by factor 2 from the *y*-axis.

Examples of other functions under this dilation are:

$f(x) = x^2 \qquad f\left(\dfrac{x}{2}\right) = \left(\dfrac{x}{2}\right)^2 = \dfrac{x^2}{4}$

$f(x) = \dfrac{1}{x} \qquad f\left(\dfrac{x}{2}\right) = \dfrac{1}{\frac{x}{2}} = \dfrac{2}{x}$

It should be noted that each of these functions formed by a dilation of factor 2 from the y-axis can also be formed by a dilation from the x-axis. This result is not true in general, as will be seen when new functions are introduced in Chapters 13 and 14.

- For the graph of $y = \sqrt{\dfrac{x}{2}}$, we can write $y = \dfrac{1}{\sqrt{2}}\sqrt{x} = \dfrac{1}{\sqrt{2}}f(x)$, where $f(x) = \sqrt{x}$. That is, it is formed by a dilation of factor $\dfrac{1}{\sqrt{2}}$ from the x-axis.

- For the graph of $y = \dfrac{x^2}{4}$, we can write $y = \tfrac{1}{4}x^2 = \tfrac{1}{4}f(x)$, where $f(x) = x^2$. That is, it is formed by a dilation of factor $\tfrac{1}{4}$ from the x-axis.

- For the graph of $y = \dfrac{2}{x}$, we can write $y = 2f(x)$, where $f(x) = \dfrac{1}{x}$. That is, it is formed by a dilation of factor 2 from the x-axis.

Section summary

For the graph of $y = f(x)$, we have the following four pairs of equivalent processes:

1.
   - Applying the **dilation from the x-axis** $(x, y) \to (x, by)$ to the graph of $y = f(x)$.
   - Replacing y with $\dfrac{y}{b}$ in the equation to obtain $y = bf(x)$ and graphing the result.

2.
   - Applying the **dilation from the y-axis** $(x, y) \to (ax, y)$ to the graph of $y = f(x)$.
   - Replacing x with $\dfrac{x}{a}$ in the equation to obtain $y = f\left(\dfrac{x}{a}\right)$ and graphing the result.

3.
   - Applying the **reflection in the x-axis** $(x, y) \to (x, -y)$ to the graph of $y = f(x)$.
   - Replacing y with $-y$ in the equation to obtain $y = -f(x)$ and graphing the result.

4.
   - Applying the **reflection in the y-axis** $(x, y) \to (-x, y)$ to the graph of $y = f(x)$.
   - Replacing x with $-x$ in the equation to obtain $y = f(-x)$ and graphing the result.

Exercise 7B

1 Find the image of the point $(-2, -3)$ after:

  a a reflection in the x-axis   **b** a reflection in the y-axis

  c a dilation of factor 4 from the x-axis   **d** a dilation of factor 4 from the y-axis.

Example 2

2 Write down the equation of the image obtained when the graph of each of the functions below is transformed by:

    i a dilation of factor $\tfrac{1}{2}$ from the y-axis   **ii** a dilation of factor 5 from the y-axis

    iii a dilation of factor $\tfrac{2}{3}$ from the x-axis   **iv** a dilation of factor 4 from the x-axis

    v a reflection in the x-axis   **vi** a reflection in the y-axis.

  a $y = x^2$ **b** $y = \dfrac{1}{x^2}$ **c** $y = \dfrac{1}{x}$ **d** $y = \sqrt{x}$

3 Sketch the graph of each of the following:

  a $y = 3\sqrt{x}$ **b** $y = -\dfrac{1}{x}$ **c** $y = \dfrac{3}{x}$ **d** $y = \dfrac{1}{2x}$ **e** $y = \sqrt{3x}$ **f** $y = \dfrac{3}{2x}$

7C Combinations of transformations

In this section, we look at sequences of transformations. For example, first consider:

- a dilation of factor 2 from the x-axis
- followed by a reflection in the x-axis.

The rule becomes
$$(x, y) \to (x, 2y) \to (x, -2y)$$

First the dilation is applied and then the reflection. For example, $(1, 1) \to (1, 2) \to (1, -2)$.

Another example is:

- a dilation of factor 2 from the x-axis
- followed by a translation of 2 units in the positive direction of the x-axis and 3 units in the negative direction of the y-axis.

The rule becomes
$$(x, y) \to (x, 2y) \to (x + 2, 2y - 3)$$

First the dilation is applied and then the translation. For example, $(1, 1) \to (1, 2) \to (3, -1)$.

Example 3

Find the equation of the image of $y = \sqrt{x}$ under:

a a dilation of factor 2 from the x-axis followed by a reflection in the x-axis

b a dilation of factor 2 from the x-axis followed by a translation of 2 units in the positive direction of the x-axis and 3 units in the negative direction of the y-axis.

Solution

a From the discussion above, the rule is $(x, y) \to (x, 2y) \to (x, -2y)$.

If (x, y) maps to (x', y'), then $x' = x$ and $y' = -2y$. Thus $x = x'$ and $y = \dfrac{y'}{-2}$.

The image has equation $\dfrac{y'}{-2} = \sqrt{x'}$ and hence $y' = -2\sqrt{x'}$.

b From the discussion above, the rule is $(x, y) \to (x, 2y) \to (x + 2, 2y - 3)$.

If (x, y) maps to (x', y'), then $x' = x + 2$ and $y' = 2y - 3$. Thus $x = x' - 2$ and $y = \dfrac{y' + 3}{2}$.

The image has equation $\dfrac{y' + 3}{2} = \sqrt{x' - 2}$ and hence $y' = 2\sqrt{x' - 2} - 3$.

Using the TI-Nspire

Use menu > **Actions** > **Define** to define the function $f(x) = \sqrt{x}$. Complete as shown.

> **Using the Casio ClassPad**
>
> Use **Interactive** > **Define** to define the function $f(x) = \sqrt{x}$, and then complete as shown.
>
> Note: The symbol $\sqrt{}$ is found in Math1.

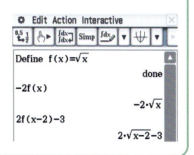

Section summary

A sequence of transformations can be applied, and the rule for transforming points of the plane can be described. For example, the sequence

- a dilation of factor 3 from the x-axis
- followed by a translation of 2 units in the positive direction of the x-axis and 3 units in the negative direction of the y-axis
- followed by a reflection in the x-axis

can be described by the rule $(x, y) \to (x, 3y) \to (x + 2, 3y - 3) \to (x + 2, 3 - 3y)$.

Let $x' = x + 2$ and $y' = 3 - 3y$. Then $x = x' - 2$ and $y = \dfrac{3 - y'}{3}$.

The graph of $y = f(x)$ maps to $\dfrac{3 - y'}{3} = f(x' - 2)$. That is, the graph of $y = f(x)$ maps to the graph of $y = 3 - 3f(x - 2)$.

Exercise 7C

Example 3

1 Find the equation of the image of the graph $y = \sqrt{x}$ when each of the following sequences of transformations have been applied:

   a a translation of 2 units in the positive direction of the x-axis followed by a dilation of factor 3 from the x-axis

   b a translation of 3 units in the negative direction of the x-axis followed by a reflection in the x-axis

   c a reflection in the x-axis followed by a dilation of factor 3 from the x-axis

   d a reflection in the x-axis followed by a dilation of factor 2 from the y-axis

   e a dilation of factor 2 from the x-axis followed by a translation of 2 units in the positive direction of the x-axis and 3 units in the negative direction of the y-axis

   f a dilation of factor 2 from the y-axis followed by a translation of 2 units in the negative direction of the x-axis and 3 units in the negative direction of the y-axis.

2 Repeat Question 1 for $y = \dfrac{1}{x}$.

3 Repeat Question 1 for $y = x^{\frac{1}{3}}$.

7D Determining transformations

Skillsheet The method that has been used to find the effect of transformations can be reversed to determine the sequence of transformations used to take a graph to its image.

For example, in order to find the sequence of transformations which maps $y = \sqrt{x}$ to $y' = -2\sqrt{x'}$, work backwards through the steps in the solution of Example 3a:

- $y = \sqrt{x}$ maps to $\dfrac{y'}{-2} = \sqrt{x'}$.
- Hence $x = x'$ and $y = \dfrac{y'}{-2}$, and therefore $x' = x$ and $y' = -2y$.
- The transformation is a dilation of factor 2 from the x-axis followed by a reflection in the x-axis.

This can also be done by inspection, of course, if you recognise the form of the image. For the combinations of transformations in this course, it is often simpler to do this.

Example 4

a Find a sequence of transformations which takes the graph of $y = x^2$ to the graph of $y = 2(x-2)^2 + 3$.

b Find a sequence of transformations which takes the graph of $y = \sqrt{x}$ to the graph of $y = \sqrt{5x - 2}$.

Solution

a By inspection

By inspection, it is a dilation of factor 2 from the x-axis followed by a translation of 2 units in the positive direction of the x-axis and 3 units in the positive direction of the y-axis.

By the method

$y = x^2$ maps to $y' = 2(x' - 2)^2 + 3$. Rearranging this equation gives

$$\dfrac{y' - 3}{2} = (x' - 2)^2$$

We choose to write $y = \dfrac{y' - 3}{2}$ and $x = x' - 2$.

Solving for x' and y' gives

$$x' = x + 2 \quad \text{and} \quad y' = 2y + 3$$

The transformation is a dilation of factor 2 from the x-axis followed by a translation of 2 units in the positive direction of the x-axis and 3 units in the positive direction of the y-axis.

b We have $y' = \sqrt{5x' - 2}$ and $y = \sqrt{x}$. We choose to write $y = y'$ and $x = 5x' - 2$. Hence

$$x' = \dfrac{x + 2}{5} = \dfrac{x}{5} + \dfrac{2}{5} \quad \text{and} \quad y' = y$$

The transformation is a dilation of factor $\frac{1}{5}$ from the y-axis followed by a translation of $\frac{2}{5}$ units in the positive direction of the x-axis.

Example 5

a Find a sequence of transformations which takes the graph of $y = \dfrac{3}{(x-1)^2} + 6$ to the graph of $y = \dfrac{1}{x^2}$.

b Find a sequence of transformations which takes the graph of $y = (5x-1)^2 + 6$ to the graph of $y = x^2$.

Solution

a Write $\dfrac{y-6}{3} = \dfrac{1}{(x-1)^2}$ and $y' = \dfrac{1}{(x')^2}$. The points (x, y) satisfying $\dfrac{y-6}{3} = \dfrac{1}{(x-1)^2}$ are mapped to the points (x', y') satisfying $y' = \dfrac{1}{(x')^2}$.

Hence we choose to write
$$y' = \frac{y-6}{3} \quad \text{and} \quad x' = x - 1$$

One transformation is a translation of 6 units in the negative direction of the y-axis and 1 unit in the negative direction of the x-axis followed by a dilation of factor $\frac{1}{3}$ from the x-axis.

b Write $y - 6 = (5x-1)^2$ and $y' = (x')^2$. The points (x, y) satisfying $y - 6 = (5x-1)^2$ are mapped to the points (x', y') satisfying $y' = (x')^2$.

Hence we choose to write
$$y' = y - 6 \quad \text{and} \quad x' = 5x - 1$$

One transformation is a dilation of factor 5 from the y-axis followed by a translation of 6 units in the negative direction of the y-axis and 1 unit in the negative direction of the x-axis.

We note that the transformations we found are far from being the only possible answers. In fact there are infinitely many choices.

Section summary

The notation developed in this chapter can be used to help find the transformation that takes the graph of a function to its image.

For example, if the graph of $y = f(x)$ is mapped to the graph of $y' = 2f(x' - 3)$, we can see that the transformation
$$x' = x + 3 \quad \text{and} \quad y' = 2y$$

is a suitable choice. This is a translation of 3 units to the right followed by a dilation of factor 2 from the x-axis.

There are infinitely many transformations that take the graph of $y = f(x)$ to the graph of $y' = 2f(x' - 3)$. The one we chose is conventional.

Exercise 7D

Example 4

1 For each of the following, find a sequence of transformations that takes:

  a the graph of $y = x^2$ to the graph of

    i $y = 2(x - 1)^2 + 3$ **ii** $y = -(x + 1)^2 + 2$ **iii** $y = (2x + 1)^2 - 2$

  b the graph of $y = \dfrac{1}{x}$ to the graph of

    i $y = \dfrac{2}{x + 3}$ **ii** $y = \dfrac{1}{x + 3} + 2$ **iii** $y = \dfrac{1}{x - 3} - 2$

  c the graph of $y = \sqrt{x}$ to the graph of

    i $y = \sqrt{x + 3} + 2$ **ii** $y = 2\sqrt{3x}$ **iii** $y = -\sqrt{x} + 2$

Example 5

2 **a** Find a sequence of transformations that takes the graph of $y = \dfrac{5}{(x - 3)^2} - 7$ to the graph of $y = \dfrac{1}{x^2}$.

  b Find a sequence of transformations that takes the graph of $y = (3x + 2)^2 + 5$ to the graph of $y = x^2$.

  c Find a sequence of transformations that takes the graph of $y = -3(3x + 1)^2 + 7$ to the graph of $y = x^2$.

  d Find a sequence of transformations that takes the graph of $y = 2\sqrt{4 - x}$ to the graph of $y = \sqrt{x}$.

  e Find a sequence of transformations that takes the graph of $y = 2\sqrt{4 - x} + 3$ to the graph of $y = -\sqrt{x} + 6$.

7E Matrices

This section and the next provide a brief introduction to matrices. Later in this chapter we will see that the transformations we consider in this course can be determined through matrix arithmetic. Additional information and exercises are available in the Interactive Textbook.

▶ **Matrix notation**

A **matrix** is a rectangular array of numbers. The numbers in the array are called the **entries** of the matrix. The following are examples of matrices:

$$\begin{bmatrix} -3 & 4 \\ 5 & 6 \end{bmatrix} \quad \begin{bmatrix} 6 \\ 7 \end{bmatrix} \quad \begin{bmatrix} \sqrt{2} & \pi & 3 \\ 0 & 0 & 1 \\ \sqrt{2} & 0 & \pi \end{bmatrix} \quad \begin{bmatrix} 5 \end{bmatrix}$$

Matrices vary in size. The size, or **dimension**, of the matrix is described by specifying the number of **rows** (horizontal lines) and **columns** (vertical lines) that occur in the matrix.

The dimensions of the above matrices are, in order:

    2×2, 2×1, 3×3, 1×1

The first number represents the number of rows, and the second the number of columns.

In this book we are only interested in 2 × 2 matrices and 2 × 1 matrices.

If **A** is a matrix, then a_{ij} will be used to denote the entry that occurs in row i and column j of **A**. Thus a 2 × 2 matrix may be written as

$$\mathbf{A} = \begin{bmatrix} a_{11} & a_{12} \\ a_{21} & a_{22} \end{bmatrix}$$

A general 2 × 1 matrix may be written as

$$\mathbf{B} = \begin{bmatrix} b_{11} \\ b_{21} \end{bmatrix}$$

A matrix is, then, a way of recording a set of numbers, arranged in a particular way. As in Cartesian coordinates, the order of the numbers is significant. Although the matrices

$$\begin{bmatrix} 1 & 2 \\ 3 & 4 \end{bmatrix} \quad \text{and} \quad \begin{bmatrix} 3 & 4 \\ 1 & 2 \end{bmatrix}$$

have the same numbers and the same number of entries, they are different matrices (just as (2, 1) and (1, 2) are the coordinates of different points).

Two matrices **A** and **B** are **equal**, and we can write **A** = **B**, when:

- they have the same number of rows and the same number of columns, and
- they have the same number or entry at corresponding positions.

▶ Addition, subtraction and multiplication by a scalar

Addition is defined for two matrices *only* when they have the same number of rows and the same number of columns. In this case the sum of the two matrices is found by adding corresponding entries.

For example,

$$\begin{bmatrix} 1 & 0 \\ 0 & 2 \end{bmatrix} + \begin{bmatrix} 0 & -3 \\ 4 & 1 \end{bmatrix} = \begin{bmatrix} 1 & -3 \\ 4 & 3 \end{bmatrix}$$

and

$$\begin{bmatrix} a_{11} \\ a_{21} \end{bmatrix} + \begin{bmatrix} b_{11} \\ b_{21} \end{bmatrix} = \begin{bmatrix} a_{11} + b_{11} \\ a_{21} + b_{21} \end{bmatrix}$$

Subtraction is defined in a similar way. When two matrices have the same number of rows and the same number of columns, their difference is found by subtracting corresponding entries.

Example 6

Find:

a $\begin{bmatrix} 1 & 0 \\ 2 & 0 \end{bmatrix} + \begin{bmatrix} 2 & -1 \\ -4 & 1 \end{bmatrix}$

b $\begin{bmatrix} 2 \\ -1 \end{bmatrix} - \begin{bmatrix} 2 \\ -1 \end{bmatrix}$

Solution

a $\begin{bmatrix} 1 & 0 \\ 2 & 0 \end{bmatrix} + \begin{bmatrix} 2 & -1 \\ -4 & 1 \end{bmatrix} = \begin{bmatrix} 3 & -1 \\ -2 & 1 \end{bmatrix}$

b $\begin{bmatrix} 2 \\ -1 \end{bmatrix} - \begin{bmatrix} 2 \\ -1 \end{bmatrix} = \begin{bmatrix} 0 \\ 0 \end{bmatrix}$

It is useful to define **multiplication of a matrix by a real number**. If **A** is an $m \times n$ matrix and k is a real number (also called a **scalar**), then $k\mathbf{A}$ is an $m \times n$ matrix whose entries are k times the corresponding entries of **A**. Thus

$$3 \begin{bmatrix} 2 & -2 \\ 0 & 1 \end{bmatrix} = \begin{bmatrix} 6 & -6 \\ 0 & 3 \end{bmatrix}$$

These definitions have the helpful consequence that, if a matrix is added to itself, the result is twice the matrix, i.e. $\mathbf{A} + \mathbf{A} = 2\mathbf{A}$. Similarly, the sum of n matrices each equal to **A** is $n\mathbf{A}$ (where n is a natural number).

The $m \times n$ matrix with all entries equal to zero is called the **zero matrix**.

Example 7

If $\mathbf{A} = \begin{bmatrix} 3 & 2 \\ -1 & 1 \end{bmatrix}$ and $\mathbf{B} = \begin{bmatrix} 0 & -4 \\ -2 & 8 \end{bmatrix}$, find the matrix **X** such that $2\mathbf{A} + \mathbf{X} = \mathbf{B}$.

Solution

If $2\mathbf{A} + \mathbf{X} = \mathbf{B}$, then $\mathbf{X} = \mathbf{B} - 2\mathbf{A}$. Therefore

$$\mathbf{X} = \begin{bmatrix} 0 & -4 \\ -2 & 8 \end{bmatrix} - 2\begin{bmatrix} 3 & 2 \\ -1 & 1 \end{bmatrix}$$

$$= \begin{bmatrix} 0 - 2 \times 3 & -4 - 2 \times 2 \\ -2 - 2 \times (-1) & 8 - 2 \times 1 \end{bmatrix}$$

$$= \begin{bmatrix} -6 & -8 \\ 0 & 6 \end{bmatrix}$$

Using the TI-Nspire

The matrix template

- The simplest way to enter a 2×2 matrix is using the 2×2 matrix template as shown. (Access the templates using either (🖩) or (ctrl)(menu) > **Math Templates**.)
- Notice that there is also a template for entering $m \times n$ matrices.

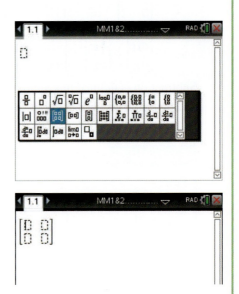

- Define the matrix $\mathbf{A} = \begin{bmatrix} 3 & 6 \\ 6 & 7 \end{bmatrix}$ as shown.
  The assignment symbol := is accessed using (ctrl) (=). Use the touchpad arrows to move between the entries of the matrix.
- Define the matrix $\mathbf{B} = \begin{bmatrix} 3 & 6 \\ 5 & 6.5 \end{bmatrix}$ similarly.

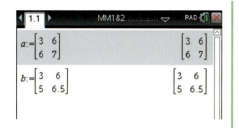

Note: All variables will be changed to lower case.
  Alternatively, you can store ((ctrl) (var)) the matrices if preferred.

Entering matrices directly

- To enter matrix **A** without using the template, enter the matrix row by row as [[3, 6][6, 7]].

Addition, subtraction and multiplication by a scalar

- Once **A** and **B** are defined as above, the matrices $\mathbf{A} + \mathbf{B}$, $\mathbf{A} - \mathbf{B}$ and $k\mathbf{A}$ can easily be determined.

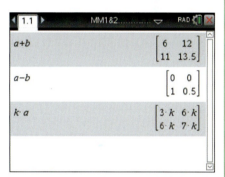

Using the Casio ClassPad

- Matrices are accessed through the (Math2) keyboard.
- Select [▦] and tap on each of the entry boxes to enter the matrix values.

Notes:

- To expand the 2×2 matrix to a 3×3 matrix, tap on the [▦] button twice.
- To increase the number of rows, tap on the [▤] button. To increase the number of columns, tap on the [▥] button.

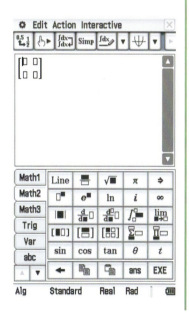

- Matrices can be stored as a variable for later use in operations by selecting the store button (⇒) located in Math1 followed by the variable name (usually a capital letter).
- Once **A** and **B** are defined as shown, the matrices **A** + **B**, **A** − **B** and k**A** can be found.
(Use the Var keyboard to enter the variable names.)

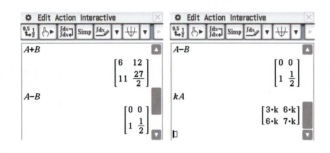
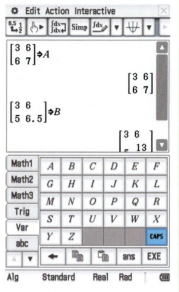

► Multiplication of matrices

Multiplication of a matrix by a real number has been discussed in the previous subsection. The definition for multiplication of matrices is less natural. The procedure for multiplying two 2×2 matrices is shown first.

Let $\mathbf{A} = \begin{bmatrix} 1 & 3 \\ 4 & 2 \end{bmatrix}$ and $\mathbf{B} = \begin{bmatrix} 5 & 1 \\ 6 & 3 \end{bmatrix}$.

Then $\mathbf{AB} = \begin{bmatrix} 1 & 3 \\ 4 & 2 \end{bmatrix} \begin{bmatrix} 5 & 1 \\ 6 & 3 \end{bmatrix}$

$= \begin{bmatrix} 1 \times 5 + 3 \times 6 & 1 \times 1 + 3 \times 3 \\ 4 \times 5 + 2 \times 6 & 4 \times 1 + 2 \times 3 \end{bmatrix}$

$= \begin{bmatrix} 23 & 10 \\ 32 & 10 \end{bmatrix}$

and $\mathbf{BA} = \begin{bmatrix} 5 & 1 \\ 6 & 3 \end{bmatrix} \begin{bmatrix} 1 & 3 \\ 4 & 2 \end{bmatrix}$

$= \begin{bmatrix} 5 \times 1 + 1 \times 4 & 5 \times 3 + 1 \times 2 \\ 6 \times 1 + 3 \times 4 & 6 \times 3 + 3 \times 2 \end{bmatrix}$

$= \begin{bmatrix} 9 & 17 \\ 18 & 24 \end{bmatrix}$

Note that **AB** ≠ **BA**.

7E Matrices

If **A** is an $m \times n$ matrix and **B** is an $n \times r$ matrix, then the product **AB** is the $m \times r$ matrix whose entries are determined as follows:

> To find the entry in row i and column j of **AB**, single out row i in matrix **A** and column j in matrix **B**. Multiply the corresponding entries from the row and column and then add up the resulting products.

Note: The product **AB** is defined only if the number of columns of **A** is the same as the number of rows of **B**.

Example 8

For $\mathbf{A} = \begin{bmatrix} 2 & 4 \\ 3 & 6 \end{bmatrix}$ and $\mathbf{B} = \begin{bmatrix} 5 \\ 3 \end{bmatrix}$, find **AB**.

Solution

A is a 2×2 matrix and **B** is a 2×1 matrix. Therefore **AB** is defined and will be a 2×1 matrix.

$$\mathbf{AB} = \begin{bmatrix} 2 & 4 \\ 3 & 6 \end{bmatrix}\begin{bmatrix} 5 \\ 3 \end{bmatrix} = \begin{bmatrix} 2 \times 5 + 4 \times 3 \\ 3 \times 5 + 6 \times 3 \end{bmatrix} = \begin{bmatrix} 22 \\ 33 \end{bmatrix}$$

Using the TI-Nspire

Multiplication of

$$\mathbf{A} = \begin{bmatrix} 3 & 6 \\ 6 & 7 \end{bmatrix} \quad \text{and} \quad \mathbf{B} = \begin{bmatrix} 3 & 6 \\ 5 & 6.5 \end{bmatrix}$$

The products **AB** and **BA** are shown.

Using the Casio ClassPad

Multiplication of

$$\mathbf{A} = \begin{bmatrix} 3 & 6 \\ 6 & 7 \end{bmatrix} \quad \text{and} \quad \mathbf{B} = \begin{bmatrix} 3 & 6 \\ 5 & 6.5 \end{bmatrix}$$

The products **AB** and **BA** are shown.

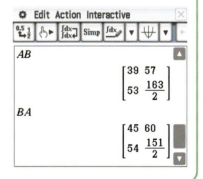

Section summary

- A **matrix** is a rectangular array of numbers.
- Two matrices **A** and **B** are equal when:
  - they have the same number of rows and the same number of columns, and
  - they have the same number or entry at corresponding positions.
- The size or **dimension** of a matrix is described by specifying the number of rows (m) and the number of columns (n). The dimension is written $m \times n$.
- Addition is defined for two matrices only when they have the same dimension. The sum is found by adding corresponding entries.
$$\begin{bmatrix} a & b \\ c & d \end{bmatrix} + \begin{bmatrix} e & f \\ g & h \end{bmatrix} = \begin{bmatrix} a+e & b+f \\ c+g & d+h \end{bmatrix}$$
  Subtraction is defined in a similar way.
- If **A** is an $m \times n$ matrix and k is a real number, then $k\mathbf{A}$ is defined to be an $m \times n$ matrix whose entries are k times the corresponding entries of **A**.
$$k \begin{bmatrix} a & b \\ c & d \end{bmatrix} = \begin{bmatrix} ka & kb \\ kc & kd \end{bmatrix}$$
- If **A** is an $m \times n$ matrix and **B** is an $n \times r$ matrix, then the product **AB** is the $m \times r$ matrix whose entries are determined as follows:

  To find the entry in row i and column j of **AB**, single out row i in matrix **A** and column j in matrix **B**. Multiply the corresponding entries from the row and column and then add up the resulting products.

Exercise 7E

Example 6, 7

1 Let $\mathbf{X} = \begin{bmatrix} 1 \\ -2 \end{bmatrix}$, $\mathbf{Y} = \begin{bmatrix} 3 \\ 0 \end{bmatrix}$, $\mathbf{A} = \begin{bmatrix} 1 & -1 \\ 2 & 3 \end{bmatrix}$ and $\mathbf{B} = \begin{bmatrix} 4 & 0 \\ -1 & 2 \end{bmatrix}$.

Find $\mathbf{X} + \mathbf{Y}$, $2\mathbf{X}$, $4\mathbf{Y} + \mathbf{X}$, $\mathbf{X} - \mathbf{Y}$, $-3\mathbf{A}$ and $-3\mathbf{A} + \mathbf{B}$.

2 Let $\mathbf{A} = \begin{bmatrix} 1 & -1 \\ 0 & 2 \end{bmatrix}$. Find $2\mathbf{A}$, $-3\mathbf{A}$ and $-6\mathbf{A}$.

3 $\mathbf{A} = \begin{bmatrix} 3 & 2 \\ -2 & -2 \end{bmatrix}$ and $\mathbf{B} = \begin{bmatrix} 0 & -3 \\ 4 & 1 \end{bmatrix}$

Calculate:

  a $2\mathbf{A}$ **b** $3\mathbf{B}$ **c** $2\mathbf{A} + 3\mathbf{B}$ **d** $3\mathbf{B} - 2\mathbf{A}$

4 $\mathbf{P} = \begin{bmatrix} 1 & 0 \\ 0 & 3 \end{bmatrix}$, $\mathbf{Q} = \begin{bmatrix} -1 & 1 \\ 2 & 0 \end{bmatrix}$, $\mathbf{R} = \begin{bmatrix} 0 & 4 \\ 1 & 1 \end{bmatrix}$

Calculate:

  a $\mathbf{P} + \mathbf{Q}$ **b** $\mathbf{P} + 3\mathbf{Q}$ **c** $2\mathbf{P} - \mathbf{Q} + \mathbf{R}$

5 If $A = \begin{bmatrix} 3 & 1 \\ -1 & 4 \end{bmatrix}$ and $B = \begin{bmatrix} 0 & -10 \\ -2 & 17 \end{bmatrix}$, find matrices X and Y such that $2A - 3X = B$ and $3A + 2Y = 2B$.

Example 8 **6** If $X = \begin{bmatrix} 2 \\ -1 \end{bmatrix}$, $A = \begin{bmatrix} 1 & -2 \\ -1 & 3 \end{bmatrix}$, $B = \begin{bmatrix} 3 & 0 \\ 0 & 1 \end{bmatrix}$ and $I = \begin{bmatrix} 1 & 0 \\ 0 & 1 \end{bmatrix}$, find the products AX, BX, IX, AI, IB, AB, BA, A^2 and B^2.

7 If $X = \begin{bmatrix} 1 \\ -2 \end{bmatrix}$, $A = \begin{bmatrix} 2 & -1 \\ -1 & 4 \end{bmatrix}$, $B = \begin{bmatrix} -3 & 0 \\ 0 & 2 \end{bmatrix}$ and $C = \begin{bmatrix} 1 & 3 \\ -2 & 1 \end{bmatrix}$, find the products AX, BX, CX, AC, CB, AB, BA, A^2 and B^2.

7F Identities, inverses and determinants for 2×2 matrices

▶ Identities

A matrix with the same number of rows and columns is called a **square matrix**. For square matrices of a given dimension (e.g. 2×2), a multiplicative identity I exists.

For 2×2 matrices, the **identity matrix** is $I = \begin{bmatrix} 1 & 0 \\ 0 & 1 \end{bmatrix}$.

If $A = \begin{bmatrix} 2 & 3 \\ 1 & 4 \end{bmatrix}$, then $AI = IA = A$, and this result holds for any square matrix multiplied by the appropriate multiplicative identity.

▶ Inverses

Given a 2×2 matrix A, is there a matrix B such that $AB = BA = I$?

Let $B = \begin{bmatrix} x & y \\ u & v \end{bmatrix}$ and $A = \begin{bmatrix} 2 & 3 \\ 1 & 4 \end{bmatrix}$.

Then $AB = I$ implies

$$\begin{bmatrix} 2 & 3 \\ 1 & 4 \end{bmatrix} \begin{bmatrix} x & y \\ u & v \end{bmatrix} = \begin{bmatrix} 1 & 0 \\ 0 & 1 \end{bmatrix}$$

i.e. $\begin{bmatrix} 2x + 3u & 2y + 3v \\ x + 4u & y + 4v \end{bmatrix} = \begin{bmatrix} 1 & 0 \\ 0 & 1 \end{bmatrix}$

$\therefore \quad 2x + 3u = 1 \quad$ and $\quad 2y + 3v = 0$
$\quad\quad\quad x + 4u = 0 \quad\quad\quad\quad\quad y + 4v = 1$

These simultaneous equations can be solved to find x, y, u, v and hence B.

$$B = \begin{bmatrix} 0.8 & -0.6 \\ -0.2 & 0.4 \end{bmatrix}$$

The matrix B is said to be the **inverse** of A, as $AB = BA = I$.

In general, for a 2×2 matrix $\mathbf{A} = \begin{bmatrix} a & b \\ c & d \end{bmatrix}$, the inverse of $\mathbf{A}$ is given by

$$\mathbf{A}^{-1} = \frac{1}{ad - bc} \begin{bmatrix} d & -b \\ -c & a \end{bmatrix}$$

provided $ad - bc \neq 0$. The inverse of a 2×2 matrix $\mathbf{A}$ is denoted by $\mathbf{A}^{-1}$. The inverse is unique.

The determinant

The quantity $ad - bc$ that appears in the formula for $\mathbf{A}^{-1}$ has a name: the **determinant** of $\mathbf{A}$. This is denoted $\det(\mathbf{A})$.

So for a 2×2 matrix $\mathbf{A} = \begin{bmatrix} a & b \\ c & d \end{bmatrix}$, we have

$$\det(\mathbf{A}) = ad - bc$$

A 2×2 matrix has an inverse only if $\det(\mathbf{A}) \neq 0$.

A square matrix is said to be **regular** if its inverse exists. A square matrix which does not have an inverse is called a **singular** matrix; for a singular matrix, $\det(\mathbf{A}) = 0$.

Using the TI-Nspire

- The inverse of a matrix is obtained by raising the matrix to the power of -1.
- The determinant command (menu > **Matrix and Vector** > **Determinant**) is used as shown.

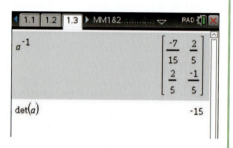

(Here a is the matrix $\mathbf{A} = \begin{bmatrix} 3 & 6 \\ 6 & 7 \end{bmatrix}$ defined on page 283.)

Using the Casio ClassPad

- The inverse of matrix A is obtained by entering $A\wedge-1$ in the entry line.
- The determinant is obtained by typing $\det(A)$.

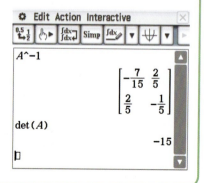

Example 9

For the matrix $\mathbf{A} = \begin{bmatrix} 5 & 2 \\ 3 & 1 \end{bmatrix}$, find:

a $\det(\mathbf{A})$ **b** $\mathbf{A}^{-1}$

Solution

a $\det(\mathbf{A}) = 5 \times 1 - 2 \times 3 = -1$

b $\mathbf{A}^{-1} = \dfrac{1}{-1}\begin{bmatrix} 1 & -2 \\ -3 & 5 \end{bmatrix} = \begin{bmatrix} -1 & 2 \\ 3 & -5 \end{bmatrix}$

Example 10

For the matrix $\mathbf{A} = \begin{bmatrix} 3 & 2 \\ 1 & 6 \end{bmatrix}$, find:

a $\det(\mathbf{A})$ **b** $\mathbf{A}^{-1}$ **c** $\mathbf{X}$, if $\mathbf{AX} = \begin{bmatrix} 5 \\ 7 \end{bmatrix}$

Solution

a $\det(\mathbf{A}) = 3 \times 6 - 2 = 16$

b $\mathbf{A}^{-1} = \dfrac{1}{16}\begin{bmatrix} 6 & -2 \\ -1 & 3 \end{bmatrix}$

c $\mathbf{AX} = \begin{bmatrix} 5 \\ 7 \end{bmatrix}$

Multiply both sides (from the left) by $\mathbf{A}^{-1}$.

$$\mathbf{A}^{-1}\mathbf{AX} = \mathbf{A}^{-1}\begin{bmatrix} 5 \\ 7 \end{bmatrix}$$

$$\therefore \quad \mathbf{IX} = \mathbf{X} = \dfrac{1}{16}\begin{bmatrix} 6 & -2 \\ -1 & 3 \end{bmatrix}\begin{bmatrix} 5 \\ 7 \end{bmatrix}$$

$$= \dfrac{1}{16}\begin{bmatrix} 16 \\ 16 \end{bmatrix}$$

$$= \begin{bmatrix} 1 \\ 1 \end{bmatrix}$$

Section summary

- If $\mathbf{A}$ and $\mathbf{B}$ are 2×2 matrices with $\mathbf{AB} = \mathbf{BA} = \mathbf{I}$, then $\mathbf{A}$ is said to be the inverse of $\mathbf{B}$, and $\mathbf{B}$ is said to be the inverse of $\mathbf{A}$.
- For a 2×2 matrix $\mathbf{A} = \begin{bmatrix} a & b \\ c & d \end{bmatrix}$, the inverse of $\mathbf{A}$ is

$$\mathbf{A}^{-1} = \dfrac{1}{ad - bc}\begin{bmatrix} d & -b \\ -c & a \end{bmatrix}$$

and the **determinant** of $\mathbf{A}$ is $\det(\mathbf{A}) = ad - bc$.

- A square matrix is said to be **regular** if its inverse exists, and said to be **singular** if it does not have an inverse.

Exercise 7F

Example 9

1 For the matrices $\mathbf{A} = \begin{bmatrix} 2 & 1 \\ 3 & 2 \end{bmatrix}$ and $\mathbf{B} = \begin{bmatrix} -2 & -2 \\ 3 & 2 \end{bmatrix}$, find:

   a $\det(\mathbf{A})$ **b** $\mathbf{A}^{-1}$ **c** $\det(\mathbf{B})$ **d** $\mathbf{B}^{-1}$

2 Find the inverse of each of the following regular matrices:

   a $\begin{bmatrix} 3 & -1 \\ 4 & -1 \end{bmatrix}$ **b** $\begin{bmatrix} 3 & 1 \\ -2 & 4 \end{bmatrix}$ **c** $\begin{bmatrix} 1 & 0 \\ 0 & k \end{bmatrix}$, where k is any non-zero real number

3 Let $\mathbf{A}$ and $\mathbf{B}$ be the regular matrices $\mathbf{A} = \begin{bmatrix} 2 & 1 \\ 0 & -1 \end{bmatrix}$ and $\mathbf{B} = \begin{bmatrix} 1 & 0 \\ 3 & 1 \end{bmatrix}$.

   a Find $\mathbf{A}^{-1}$ and $\mathbf{B}^{-1}$.
   b Find $\mathbf{AB}$ and hence find, if possible, $(\mathbf{AB})^{-1}$.
   c From $\mathbf{A}^{-1}$ and $\mathbf{B}^{-1}$, find the products $\mathbf{A}^{-1}\mathbf{B}^{-1}$ and $\mathbf{B}^{-1}\mathbf{A}^{-1}$. What do you notice?

Example 10

4 Let $\mathbf{A} = \begin{bmatrix} 4 & 3 \\ 2 & 1 \end{bmatrix}$.

   a Find $\mathbf{A}^{-1}$. **b** If $\mathbf{AX} = \begin{bmatrix} 3 & 4 \\ 1 & 6 \end{bmatrix}$, find $\mathbf{X}$. **c** If $\mathbf{YA} = \begin{bmatrix} 3 & 4 \\ 1 & 6 \end{bmatrix}$, find $\mathbf{Y}$.

5 Let $\mathbf{A} = \begin{bmatrix} 3 & 2 \\ 1 & 6 \end{bmatrix}$, $\mathbf{B} = \begin{bmatrix} 4 & -1 \\ 2 & 2 \end{bmatrix}$ and $\mathbf{C} = \begin{bmatrix} 3 & 4 \\ 2 & 6 \end{bmatrix}$.

   a Find $\mathbf{X}$ such that $\mathbf{AX} + \mathbf{B} = \mathbf{C}$. **b** Find $\mathbf{Y}$ such that $\mathbf{YA} + \mathbf{B} = \mathbf{C}$.

7G Using matrices with transformations

The following table gives a summary of some basic transformations of the plane.

Mapping	Rule	
Reflection in the x-axis	$x' = x$	$= x + 0y$
	$y' = -y$	$= 0x + -y$
Reflection in the y-axis	$x' = -x$	$= -x + 0y$
	$y' = y$	$= 0x + y$
Dilation of factor k from the y-axis	$x' = kx$	$= kx + 0y$
	$y' = y$	$= 0x + y$
Dilation of factor k from the x-axis	$x' = x$	$= x + 0y$
	$y' = ky$	$= 0x + ky$
Reflection in the line $y = x$	$x' = y$	$= 0x + y$
	$y' = x$	$= x + 0y$
Translation defined by a column matrix $\begin{bmatrix} a \\ b \end{bmatrix}$	$x' = x + a$	
	$y' = y + b$	

We have discussed most of the transformations from this table already in this chapter. Reflection in the line $y = x$ occurred in our consideration of inverse functions in Chapter 5.

The first five mappings given in the table are special cases of a general kind of mapping defined by

$$x' = ax + by$$
$$y' = cx + dy$$

where a, b, c, d are real numbers.

This mapping can be defined equivalently using a matrix equation:

$$\begin{bmatrix} x' \\ y' \end{bmatrix} = \begin{bmatrix} a & b \\ c & d \end{bmatrix} \begin{bmatrix} x \\ y \end{bmatrix}$$

A transformation of the form

$$(x, y) \rightarrow (ax + by, cx + dy)$$

is called a **linear transformation**.

These first five mappings can each be defined by a 2×2 matrix. This is shown in the following table.

Mapping	Rule	Matrix
Reflection in the x-axis	$x' = 1x + 0y$ $y' = 0x - 1y$	$\begin{bmatrix} 1 & 0 \\ 0 & -1 \end{bmatrix}$
Reflection in the y-axis	$x' = -1x + 0y$ $y' = 0x + 1y$	$\begin{bmatrix} -1 & 0 \\ 0 & 1 \end{bmatrix}$
Dilation of factor k from the y-axis	$x' = kx + 0y$ $y' = 0x + 1y$	$\begin{bmatrix} k & 0 \\ 0 & 1 \end{bmatrix}$
Dilation of factor k from the x-axis	$x' = 1x + 0y$ $y' = 0x + ky$	$\begin{bmatrix} 1 & 0 \\ 0 & k \end{bmatrix}$
Reflection in the line $y = x$	$x' = 0x + 1y$ $y' = 1x + 0y$	$\begin{bmatrix} 0 & 1 \\ 1 & 0 \end{bmatrix}$

Example 11

Find the image of the point $(2, 3)$ under:

a a reflection in the x-axis **b** a dilation of factor k from the y-axis.

Solution

a $\begin{bmatrix} 1 & 0 \\ 0 & -1 \end{bmatrix} \begin{bmatrix} 2 \\ 3 \end{bmatrix} = \begin{bmatrix} 2 \\ -3 \end{bmatrix}$

Therefore $(2, 3) \rightarrow (2, -3)$.

b $\begin{bmatrix} k & 0 \\ 0 & 1 \end{bmatrix} \begin{bmatrix} 2 \\ 3 \end{bmatrix} = \begin{bmatrix} 2k \\ 3 \end{bmatrix}$

Therefore $(2, 3) \rightarrow (2k, 3)$.

> **Example 12**
>
> Consider a linear transformation such that $(1, 0) \to (3, -1)$ and $(0, 1) \to (-2, 4)$. Find the image of $(-3, 5)$.
>
> **Solution**
>
> $$\begin{bmatrix} a & b \\ c & d \end{bmatrix} \begin{bmatrix} 1 \\ 0 \end{bmatrix} = \begin{bmatrix} 3 \\ -1 \end{bmatrix} \quad \text{and} \quad \begin{bmatrix} a & b \\ c & d \end{bmatrix} \begin{bmatrix} 0 \\ 1 \end{bmatrix} = \begin{bmatrix} -2 \\ 4 \end{bmatrix}$$
>
> $\therefore \quad a = 3, c = -1 \quad$ and $\quad b = -2, d = 4$
>
> The transformation can be defined by the 2×2 matrix $\begin{bmatrix} 3 & -2 \\ -1 & 4 \end{bmatrix}$.
>
> Let $(-3, 5) \to (x', y')$.
>
> Then $\begin{bmatrix} x' \\ y' \end{bmatrix} = \begin{bmatrix} 3 & -2 \\ -1 & 4 \end{bmatrix} \begin{bmatrix} -3 \\ 5 \end{bmatrix}$
>
> $\qquad = \begin{bmatrix} 3 \times (-3) + (-2) \times 5 \\ (-1) \times (-3) + 4 \times 5 \end{bmatrix}$
>
> $\qquad = \begin{bmatrix} -19 \\ 23 \end{bmatrix}$
>
> The image of $(-3, 5)$ is $(-19, 23)$.

Note that a non-linear transformation cannot be represented by a matrix in the way indicated above. For example, the translation

$x' = x + a$

$y' = y + b$

cannot be represented by a square matrix. However, we can write

$$\begin{bmatrix} x' \\ y' \end{bmatrix} = \begin{bmatrix} x \\ y \end{bmatrix} + \begin{bmatrix} a \\ b \end{bmatrix}$$

using matrix addition.

▶ Composition of mappings

Consider two linear transformations defined by matrices

$$\mathbf{A} = \begin{bmatrix} a_{11} & a_{12} \\ a_{21} & a_{22} \end{bmatrix} \quad \text{and} \quad \mathbf{B} = \begin{bmatrix} b_{11} & b_{12} \\ b_{21} & b_{22} \end{bmatrix}$$

We can compose the transformation of **A** with the transformation of **B**.

The **composition** consists of the transformation of **A** being applied first and then the transformation of **B**. The matrix of the resulting composition is the product **BA**:

$$\mathbf{BA} = \begin{bmatrix} b_{11}a_{11} + b_{12}a_{21} & b_{11}a_{12} + b_{12}a_{22} \\ b_{21}a_{11} + b_{22}a_{21} & b_{21}a_{12} + b_{22}a_{22} \end{bmatrix}$$

Example 13

Find the image of the point $(2, -3)$ under a reflection in the x-axis followed by a dilation of factor k from the y-axis.

Solution

Matrix multiplication gives the matrix of the composition of the transformations.

Let $\mathbf{A}$ be the matrix for reflection in the x-axis, and let $\mathbf{B}$ be the matrix for dilation of factor k from the y-axis.

The required transformation is defined by the product

$$\mathbf{BA} = \begin{bmatrix} k & 0 \\ 0 & 1 \end{bmatrix} \begin{bmatrix} 1 & 0 \\ 0 & -1 \end{bmatrix} = \begin{bmatrix} k & 0 \\ 0 & -1 \end{bmatrix}$$

Since

$$\mathbf{BA} \begin{bmatrix} 2 \\ -3 \end{bmatrix} = \begin{bmatrix} k & 0 \\ 0 & -1 \end{bmatrix} \begin{bmatrix} 2 \\ -3 \end{bmatrix} = \begin{bmatrix} 2k \\ 3 \end{bmatrix}$$

the image of $(2, -3)$ is $(2k, 3)$.

Example 14

Express the composition of the transformations dilation of factor k from the y-axis followed by a translation defined by the matrix $\mathbf{C} = \begin{bmatrix} a \\ b \end{bmatrix}$, mapping a point (x, y) to a point (x', y'), as a matrix equation. Hence find x and y in terms of x' and y' respectively.

Solution

Let $\mathbf{A}$ be the matrix of the dilation transformation, let $\mathbf{X} = \begin{bmatrix} x \\ y \end{bmatrix}$ and let $\mathbf{X}' = \begin{bmatrix} x' \\ y' \end{bmatrix}$.

The equation is $\mathbf{AX} + \mathbf{C} = \mathbf{X}'$.

Thus $\mathbf{AX} = \mathbf{X}' - \mathbf{C}$ and hence $\mathbf{X} = \mathbf{A}^{-1}(\mathbf{X}' - \mathbf{C})$.

Now $\mathbf{A} = \begin{bmatrix} k & 0 \\ 0 & 1 \end{bmatrix}$, giving $\det(\mathbf{A}) = k$ and $\mathbf{A}^{-1} = \frac{1}{k} \begin{bmatrix} 1 & 0 \\ 0 & k \end{bmatrix} = \begin{bmatrix} \frac{1}{k} & 0 \\ 0 & 1 \end{bmatrix}$.

Therefore

$$\mathbf{X} = \begin{bmatrix} \frac{1}{k} & 0 \\ 0 & 1 \end{bmatrix} \left(\begin{bmatrix} x' \\ y' \end{bmatrix} - \begin{bmatrix} a \\ b \end{bmatrix} \right)$$

$$= \begin{bmatrix} \frac{1}{k} & 0 \\ 0 & 1 \end{bmatrix} \begin{bmatrix} x' - a \\ y' - b \end{bmatrix}$$

$$= \begin{bmatrix} \frac{1}{k}(x' - a) \\ y' - b \end{bmatrix}$$

Hence $x = \dfrac{1}{k}(x' - a)$ and $y = y' - b$.

Section summary

Transformation matrices

Mapping	Rule	Matrix
Reflection in the x-axis	$x' = x$ $y' = -y$	$\begin{bmatrix} 1 & 0 \\ 0 & -1 \end{bmatrix}$
Reflection in the y-axis	$x' = -x$ $y' = y$	$\begin{bmatrix} -1 & 0 \\ 0 & 1 \end{bmatrix}$
Dilation of factor k from the y-axis	$x' = kx$ $y' = y$	$\begin{bmatrix} k & 0 \\ 0 & 1 \end{bmatrix}$
Dilation of factor k from the x-axis	$x' = x$ $y' = ky$	$\begin{bmatrix} 1 & 0 \\ 0 & k \end{bmatrix}$
Reflection in the line $y = x$	$x' = y$ $y' = x$	$\begin{bmatrix} 0 & 1 \\ 1 & 0 \end{bmatrix}$

Composition of transformations We can consider the composition of two linear transformations defined by matrices

$$\mathbf{A} = \begin{bmatrix} a_{11} & a_{12} \\ a_{21} & a_{22} \end{bmatrix} \quad \text{and} \quad \mathbf{B} = \begin{bmatrix} b_{11} & b_{12} \\ b_{21} & b_{22} \end{bmatrix}$$

The composition consists of the transformation of **A** being applied first and then the transformation of **B**. The matrix of the resulting composition is the product **BA**:

$$\mathbf{BA} = \begin{bmatrix} b_{11}a_{11} + b_{12}a_{21} & b_{11}a_{12} + b_{12}a_{22} \\ b_{21}a_{11} + b_{22}a_{21} & b_{21}a_{12} + b_{22}a_{22} \end{bmatrix}$$

Exercise 7G

1 Find:

a $\begin{bmatrix} 2 & -3 \\ 5 & 4 \end{bmatrix} \begin{bmatrix} -1 \\ 2 \end{bmatrix}$

b $\begin{bmatrix} -3 & -1 \\ -1 & 3 \end{bmatrix} \begin{bmatrix} a \\ b \end{bmatrix}$

2 If a linear transformation is defined by the matrix $\mathbf{A} = \begin{bmatrix} 2 & -1 \\ -4 & 3 \end{bmatrix}$, find the image of $(1, 0)$, $(0, 1)$ and $(3, 2)$ under this transformation.

3 Find the images of $(1, 0)$ and $(-1, 2)$ under the linear transformation whose matrix is:

a $\begin{bmatrix} 2 & -1 \\ 1 & 1 \end{bmatrix}$

b $\begin{bmatrix} -2 & 0 \\ 0 & 1 \end{bmatrix}$

c $\begin{bmatrix} 2 & 3 \\ 3 & -1 \end{bmatrix}$

7G Using matrices with transformations

Example 11   **4**   Using matrix methods, find the image of the point (6, 7) under each of the following transformations:

    a   dilation of factor 3 from the x-axis
    b   dilation of factor 2 from the y-axis
    c   reflection in the x-axis
    d   reflection in the y-axis
    e   reflection in the line $y = x$

Example 12   **5**   **a**   Find the matrix of the linear transformation that maps $(1, -2) \to (-4, 5)$ and $(3, 4) \to (18, 5)$.

    b   The images of two points are given for a linear transformation. Investigate whether this is sufficient information to determine the matrix of the transformation.

    c   Find the matrix of the linear transformation such that $(1, 0) \to (1, 1)$ and $(0, 1) \to (2, 2)$.

Example 13   **6**   Find the matrix that determines the composition of the transformations (in the given order):

- reflection in the x-axis
- dilation of factor 2 from the x-axis.

7   Write down the matrix of each of the following transformations:

    a   reflection in the line $x = 0$
    b   reflection in the line $y = x$
    c   reflection in the line $y = -x$
    d   dilation of factor 2 from the x-axis
    e   dilation of factor $\frac{1}{2}$ from the x-axis
    f   dilation of factor 3 from the y-axis

8   A transformation T is equivalent to a dilation of factor 2 from the x-axis followed by a reflection in the line $y = -x$.

    a   What matrix defines T?
    b   Find $T(3, 2)$.
    c   If $T(a, b) = (6, 2)$, find the values of a and b.

Example 14   **9**   Express as a matrix equation the composition of the transformations dilation of factor 2 from the y-axis followed by a translation defined by the matrix $\mathbf{C} = \begin{bmatrix} 3 \\ 4 \end{bmatrix}$, mapping a point (x, y) to a point (x', y'). Hence find x and y in terms of x' and y' respectively.

   10   A linear transformation T maps the point $(1, 3)$ to the point $(-2, -3)$ to the point $(2, 4)$ to the point $(-3, -11)$. Find the matrix of the transformation.

7H Transformations of graphs of functions with matrices

Skillsheet Matrix notation for transformations was introduced in Section 7G. In this section the notation is applied to transforming graphs.

Example 15

A transformation is defined by the matrix $\begin{bmatrix} 1 & 0 \\ 0 & 2 \end{bmatrix}$. Find the equation of the image of the graph of the quadratic equation $y = x^2 + 2x + 3$ under this transformation.

Solution

As before, the transformation maps $(x, y) \to (x', y')$.

Using matrix notation,

$$\begin{bmatrix} 1 & 0 \\ 0 & 2 \end{bmatrix} \begin{bmatrix} x \\ y \end{bmatrix} = \begin{bmatrix} x' \\ y' \end{bmatrix}$$

This can be written as the matrix equation $\mathbf{TX} = \mathbf{X'}$. We now solve this equation for $\mathbf{X}$.

Multiply both sides of the equation (from the left) by $\mathbf{T}^{-1}$.

Then $\mathbf{T}^{-1}\mathbf{TX} = \mathbf{T}^{-1}\mathbf{X'}$ and so $\mathbf{X} = \mathbf{T}^{-1}\mathbf{X'}$.

Therefore

$$\begin{bmatrix} x \\ y \end{bmatrix} = \begin{bmatrix} 1 & 0 \\ 0 & \frac{1}{2} \end{bmatrix} \begin{bmatrix} x' \\ y' \end{bmatrix} = \begin{bmatrix} x' \\ \frac{1}{2}y' \end{bmatrix}$$

So $x = x'$ and $y = \dfrac{y'}{2}$.

The curve with equation $y = x^2 + 2x + 3$ is mapped to the curve with equation $\dfrac{y'}{2} = (x')^2 + 2x' + 3$.

This makes quite hard work of an easy problem, but it demonstrates a procedure that can be used for any transformation defined by a 2×2 non-singular matrix.

Example 16

A transformation is described by the equation

$$\mathbf{T(X + B) = X'}, \quad \text{where} \quad \mathbf{T} = \begin{bmatrix} 0 & -3 \\ 2 & 0 \end{bmatrix} \quad \text{and} \quad \mathbf{B} = \begin{bmatrix} 1 \\ 2 \end{bmatrix}$$

Find the image of the straight line with equation $y = 2x + 5$ under this transformation.

Solution

First solve the matrix equation for $\mathbf{X}$:

$$\mathbf{T}^{-1}\mathbf{T(X + B) = T^{-1}X'}$$
$$\mathbf{X + B = T^{-1}X'}$$
$$\mathbf{X = T^{-1}X' - B}$$

Therefore

$$\begin{bmatrix} x \\ y \end{bmatrix} = \begin{bmatrix} 0 & \frac{1}{2} \\ -\frac{1}{3} & 0 \end{bmatrix}\begin{bmatrix} x' \\ y' \end{bmatrix} - \begin{bmatrix} 1 \\ 2 \end{bmatrix} = \begin{bmatrix} \frac{y'}{2} - 1 \\ -\frac{x'}{3} - 2 \end{bmatrix}$$

So $x = \frac{y'}{2} - 1$ and $y = -\frac{x'}{3} - 2$.

The straight line with equation $y = 2x + 5$ is transformed to the straight line with equation

$$-\frac{x'}{3} - 2 = 2\left(\frac{y'}{2} - 1\right) + 5$$

Rearranging gives $y' = -\frac{x'}{3} - 5$.

Exercise 7H

Example 15

1. A transformation is defined by the matrix $\begin{bmatrix} 3 & 0 \\ 0 & -2 \end{bmatrix}$. Find the equation of the image of the graph of the quadratic equation $y = x^2 + x + 2$ under this transformation.

2. A transformation is defined by the matrix $\begin{bmatrix} 4 & 0 \\ 0 & -2 \end{bmatrix}$. Find the equation of the image of the graph of the cubic equation $y = x^3 + 2x$ under this transformation.

3. A transformation is defined by the matrix $\begin{bmatrix} 0 & 2 \\ -3 & 0 \end{bmatrix}$. Find the equation of the image of the straight line with equation $y = 2x + 3$ under this transformation.

4. A transformation is defined by the matrix $\begin{bmatrix} 0 & 4 \\ -2 & 0 \end{bmatrix}$. Find the equation of the image of the straight line with equation $y = -2x + 4$ under this transformation.

Example 16

5. A transformation is described by the equation $\mathbf{T}(\mathbf{X} + \mathbf{B}) = \mathbf{X}'$, where $\mathbf{T} = \begin{bmatrix} 0 & -2 \\ 1 & 0 \end{bmatrix}$ and $\mathbf{B} = \begin{bmatrix} -1 \\ 2 \end{bmatrix}$. Find the image of the straight line with equation $y = -2x + 6$ under the transformation.

6. A transformation is described by the equation $\mathbf{TX} + \mathbf{B} = \mathbf{X}'$, where $\mathbf{T} = \begin{bmatrix} 0 & -2 \\ 1 & 0 \end{bmatrix}$ and $\mathbf{B} = \begin{bmatrix} -1 \\ 2 \end{bmatrix}$. Find the image of the straight line with equation $y = -2x + 6$ under the transformation.

7. A transformation is described by the equation $\mathbf{TX} + \mathbf{B} = \mathbf{X}'$, where $\mathbf{T} = \begin{bmatrix} 2 & 0 \\ 0 & 3 \end{bmatrix}$ and $\mathbf{B} = \begin{bmatrix} -2 \\ 2 \end{bmatrix}$. Find the image of the curve with equation $y = -2x^3 + 6x$ under the transformation.

Chapter summary

- **Transformations of the graphs of functions** In the following table, the rule for each transformation is given and the rule for the image of the graph of $y = f(x)$.

Mapping	Rule	The graph of $y = f(x)$ maps to
Reflection in the x-axis	$x' = x,\ y' = -y$	$y = -f(x)$
Reflection in the y-axis	$x' = -x,\ y' = y$	$y = f(-x)$
Dilation of factor a from the y-axis	$x' = ax,\ y' = y$	$y = f\left(\dfrac{x}{a}\right)$
Dilation of factor b from the x-axis	$x' = x,\ y' = by$	$y = bf(x)$
Reflection in the line $y = x$	$x' = y,\ y' = x$	$x = f(y)$
Translation defined by $\begin{bmatrix} h \\ k \end{bmatrix}$	$x' = x + h$ $y' = y + k$	$y - k = f(x - h)$

- **Matrices** See sections on matrices for summaries.

Technology-free questions

1. Using matrix methods, find the image of the point $(-1, 3)$ under each of the following transformations and give the corresponding transformation matrix:
   a. dilation of factor 4 from the x-axis
   b. dilation of factor 3 from the y-axis
   c. reflection in the x-axis
   d. reflection in the y-axis
   e. reflection in the line $y = x$

2. Sketch the graph of each of the following, labelling asymptotes and axis intercepts:
   a. $y = \dfrac{1}{x} + 3$
   b. $y = \dfrac{1}{x^2} - 3$
   c. $y = \dfrac{1}{(x+2)^2}$
   d. $y = \sqrt{x - 2}$
   e. $y = \dfrac{1}{x - 1}$
   f. $y = \dfrac{1}{x} - 4$
   g. $y = \dfrac{1}{x + 2}$
   h. $y = \dfrac{1}{x - 3}$
   i. $f(x) = \dfrac{1}{(x - 3)^2}$
   j. $f(x) = \dfrac{1}{(x + 4)^2}$
   k. $f(x) = \dfrac{1}{x - 1} + 1$
   l. $f(x) = \dfrac{1}{x - 2} + 2$

3. Sketch the graph of each of the following, stating the equations of asymptotes, the axis intercepts and the range of each function:
   a. $y = \dfrac{1}{x^2} + 1$
   b. $y = \dfrac{3}{x^2}$
   c. $y = \dfrac{1}{(x - 1)^2}$
   d. $y = \dfrac{1}{x^2} - 4$

4 Express as a matrix equation the composition of the transformations dilation of factor 2 from the x-axis followed by a translation defined by the matrix $\mathbf{C} = \begin{bmatrix} 2 \\ 3 \end{bmatrix}$, mapping a point (x, y) to a point (x', y'). Hence find x and y in terms of x' and y' respectively.

5 For each of the following, find a sequence of transformations that takes:
  a the graph of $y = x^2$ to the graph of
    i $y = 3(x + 1)^2 + 2$ **ii** $y = -2(x + 2)^2 + 3$ **iii** $y = (3x + 1)^2 - 1$
  b the graph of $y = \dfrac{1}{x}$ to the graph of
    i $y = \dfrac{4}{x + 2}$ **ii** $y = \dfrac{1}{x + 6} - 12$ **iii** $y = \dfrac{4}{x - 3} - 5$
  c the graph of $y = \sqrt{x}$ to the graph of
    i $y = \sqrt{x - 4} + 2$ **ii** $y = 2\sqrt{2x}$ **iii** $y = -2\sqrt{x} + 3$

6 Express as a matrix equation the composition of the transformations reflection in the x-axis followed by a dilation of factor 3 from the y-axis and then by a translation defined by the matrix $\mathbf{C} = \begin{bmatrix} -2 \\ 3 \end{bmatrix}$, mapping a point (x, y) to a point (x', y'). Hence find x and y in terms of x' and y' respectively.

Multiple-choice questions

1 The point $P(1, 7)$ is translated 3 units in the positive direction of the y-axis and then reflected in the x-axis. The coordinates of the final image of P are
  A $(-1, 7)$ **B** $(-1, -7)$ **C** $(1, -10)$ **D** $(0, 7)$ **E** $(1, 0)$

2 The point $P(4, -3)$ lies on the graph of a function f. The graph of f is translated 4 units in the positive direction of the y-axis and then reflected in the y-axis. The coordinates of the final image of P are
  A $(4, 3)$ **B** $(-4, -1)$ **C** $(-4, -7)$ **D** $(-4, 1)$ **E** $(4, -7)$

3 A transformation of the plane is defined by $(x, y) \to (3x - 1, y + 2)$. If $(a, b) \to (8, 8)$, then
  A $a = 3, b = 6$ **B** $a = -3, b = -6$ **C** $a = 7, b = 6$
  D $a = 6, b = 3$ **E** $a = 23, b = 10$

4 A transformation of the plane is defined by $(x, y) \to (3x - 1, 2y + 2)$. If $(a, b) \to (a, b)$, then
  A $a = \tfrac{1}{2}, b = -2$ **B** $a = \tfrac{3}{2}, b = -6$ **C** $a = -1, b = 2$
  D $a = 5, b = -2$ **E** $a = -\tfrac{1}{2}, b = 2$

5 The square shown is subject to successive transformations. The first transformation has matrix $\begin{bmatrix} -1 & 0 \\ 0 & 1 \end{bmatrix}$ and the second transformation has matrix $\begin{bmatrix} 0 & -1 \\ -2 & 1 \end{bmatrix}$.

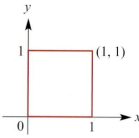

Which one of the following graphs shows the image of the square after these two transformations?

A 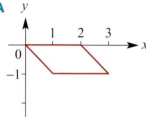 B 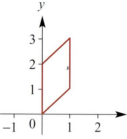 C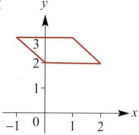

D 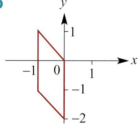 E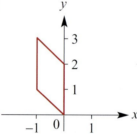

6 The matrix which determines the transformation dilation from the x-axis of factor 2 followed by a dilation from the y-axis of factor 3 is

A $\begin{bmatrix} 2 & 3 \\ 1 & 1 \end{bmatrix}$ B $\begin{bmatrix} 2 & 0 \\ 0 & 3 \end{bmatrix}$ C $\begin{bmatrix} 0 & 3 \\ 2 & 0 \end{bmatrix}$ D $\begin{bmatrix} 3 & 0 \\ 0 & 2 \end{bmatrix}$ E $\begin{bmatrix} 2 & 0 \\ 3 & 0 \end{bmatrix}$

7 The matrix which determines the transformation dilation from the x-axis of factor 2 followed by reflection in the line $y = x$ is

A $\begin{bmatrix} 2 & 0 \\ 0 & 1 \end{bmatrix}$ B $\begin{bmatrix} 0 & 2 \\ 1 & 0 \end{bmatrix}$ C $\begin{bmatrix} 1 & 0 \\ 0 & 2 \end{bmatrix}$ D $\begin{bmatrix} 2 & 1 \\ 0 & 1 \end{bmatrix}$ E $\begin{bmatrix} 1 & 0 \\ 2 & 0 \end{bmatrix}$

8 The matrix which determines the transformation dilation from the x-axis of factor 2 followed by reflection in the x-axis is

A $\begin{bmatrix} 2 & 0 \\ 0 & -1 \end{bmatrix}$ B $\begin{bmatrix} 0 & -2 \\ 1 & 0 \end{bmatrix}$ C $\begin{bmatrix} 1 & 0 \\ 0 & -2 \end{bmatrix}$ D $\begin{bmatrix} -2 & 1 \\ 0 & 1 \end{bmatrix}$ E $\begin{bmatrix} -1 & 0 \\ 2 & 0 \end{bmatrix}$

Extended-response questions

1 Let $f(x) = x^2$.

  a Find the value of k such that the line $y = x$ is tangent to the graph of $y = f(x) + k$.
  b Find the value of h such that the line $y = x$ is tangent to the graph of $y = f(x - h)$.

2 **a** The graph of $f(x) = x^2$ is translated to the graph of $y = f(x + h)$. Find the possible values of h if $f(1 + h) = 8$.
  b The graph of $f(x) = x^2$ is transformed to the graph of $y = f(ax)$. Find the possible values of a if the graph of $y = f(ax)$ passes through the point with coordinates $(1, 8)$.
  c The quadratic with equation $y = ax^2 + bx$ has vertex with coordinates $(1, 8)$. Find the values of a and b.

3 A quadratic function g has rule $g(x) = x^2 + 4x - 6$.

  a Find the value of k for which the equation $g(x) + k = 0$ has one solution.
  b Find the values of h for which the equation $g(x - h) = 0$ has:
   i two positive solutions
   ii two negative solutions
   iii one positive and one negative solution.

4 A cubic function f has rule $f(x) = (x - 3)(x + 4)(x - 5)$.

  a Solve the equation $f(x - 2) = 0$.
  b Solve the equation $f(x + 2) = 0$.
  c It is known that the equation $f(x) + k = 0$ has a solution $x = 0$. Find the value of k and solve the equation $f(x) + k = 0$.
  d The equation $f(x - h) = 0$ has a solution $x = 0$. Find the possible values of h.
  e Find the values of h such that $f(x - h) = 0$ has only one positive solution.

8 Revision of Chapters 2–7

8A Technology-free questions

1. The points $A(-2, 1)$, $B(3, -4)$ and $C(5, 7)$ are the vertices of triangle ABC.
   a. Let M and N be the midpoints of line segments AB and AC respectively. Find the coordinates of M and N.
   b. Show that MN is parallel to BC.

2. Let $P(x) = 8x^3 + 4x - 3$.
   a. Find the remainder when $P(x)$ is divided by $2x + 1$.
   b. Find the remainder when $P(x)$ is divided by $2 - x$.
   c. Find the remainder when $P(x + 1)$ is divided by $x + 2$.

3. If $g(x) = 3x^2 - 4$, then find:
   a. $g(2a)$ b. $g(a - 1)$ c. $g(a + 1) - g(a - 1)$

4. Let $f(x) = 4 - 5x$ and $g(x) = 7 + 2x$.
   a. Is it true that $f(2) + f(3) = f(2 + 3)$?
   b. Solve the equation $f(x) = g(x)$ for x.
   c. Solve the inequality $f(x) \geq g(x)$.
   d. Find the value of k for which $f(2k) = g(3k)$.

5. Solve the simultaneous equations:
$$x + y = 5$$
$$(x + 1)^2 + (y + 1)^2 = 25$$

6. Show that the points $A(0, -5)$, $B(-1, 2)$, $C(4, 7)$ and $D(5, 0)$ form a rhombus $ABCD$.

7 Write each of the following in turning point form:
   a $y = x^2 + 4x - 9$
   b $y = x^2 - 3x - 11$
   c $y = 2x^2 - 3x + 11$

8 Find the coordinates of the points of intersection of the graphs for each of the following pairs of functions:
   a $y = 4x + 1$ and $y = x^2 + 3x - 9$
   b $y = 2x + 2$ and $y = x^2 - 2x + 6$
   c $y = -3x + 2$ and $y = x^2 + 5x + 18$

9 Solve each of the following inequalities:
   a $x^2 + 3x - 5 > 0$
   b $2x^2 - 5x - 5 \geq 0$
   c $(x-3)^2(x+4) \geq 0$
   d $(x-3)(x+4)(2x-1) \leq 0$
   e $(x-2)^3 - 8 \leq 0$

10 State the maximal (implied) domain of each of the following functions:
   a $f(x) = \dfrac{3}{2x-5} - 7$
   b $g(x) = \sqrt{5-x} - 4$
   c $f(x) = x^2 - 4x - 7$
   d $f(x) = \dfrac{2}{(x-2)^2} - 5$
   e $h(x) = 2x^2 - 4x + 2$
   f $h(x) = 4 - \dfrac{5}{3x-2}$

11 Given that $(x+4)$ is a factor of $3x^3 + x^2 + px + 24$, find the value of p and hence factorise the expression completely.

12 If $5x^3 - 3x^2 + ax + 7 = (x+2)Q_1(x) + R$ and $4x^3 + ax^2 + 7x - 4 = (x+2)Q_2(x) + 2R$, find the values of a and R.

13 Find the inverse function of each of the following functions:
   a $f: [1, 2] \to \mathbb{R}, f(x) = x^2$
   b $h: [-1, 2] \to \mathbb{R}, h(x) = 2 - x$
   c $g: \mathbb{R}^- \to \mathbb{R}, g(x) = x^2 - 4$
   d $f: (-\infty, 2] \to \mathbb{R}, f(x) = \sqrt{2-x} + 3$
   e $f: \mathbb{R} \to \mathbb{R}, f(x) = (x-2)^3 + 8$

14 At Big Bob's Burger Bar, a Big Bob burger costs $\$b$ and a regular fries costs $\$f$. Three Big Bob burgers and two regular fries cost $\$18.20$.
   a Write an equation to show this.
   b If one Big Bob burger costs $\$4.20$, what is the cost of one regular fries?

15 $4x + ky = 7$ and $y = 3 - 4x$ are the equations of two lines. Find k if:
   a the lines are parallel
   b the lines are perpendicular.

16 Line ℓ_1 has an x-axis intercept at $(5, 0)$ and a y-axis intercept at $(0, -2)$. Line ℓ_2 is perpendicular to ℓ_1 and passes through the point $(1, 6)$.
   a Find the gradient of line ℓ_1.
   b Find the equation of line ℓ_2 expressing your answer in the form $ax + by + c = 0$, where a, b and c are integers and $a > 0$.

17 A family of parabolas have rules of the form $y = ax^2 + 2x + a$, for $a \neq 0$.

  a Express $ax^2 + 2x + a$ in the form $a(x + b)^2 + c$ for real numbers b and c.

  b Give the coordinates of the turning point of the graph of $y = ax^2 + 2x + a$ in terms of a.

  c For which values of a is $ax^2 + 2x + a$ a perfect square?

  d For which values of a does the graph of $y = ax^2 + 2x + a$ have two x-axis intercepts?

18 a Sketch the graph of $y = 1 + \dfrac{1}{2 + x}$, where $x \neq -2$.

  b The graph crosses the y-axis at A and the x-axis at B. Give the coordinates of A and B.

  c Find the equation of line AB.

  d Find the coordinates of the midpoint M of AB.

  e Find the equation of the straight line passing through M perpendicular to AB.

8B Multiple-choice questions

1 The turning point of a quadratic with rule $y = x^2 - ax$ has coordinates

  A $(0, a)$ **B** $\left(\dfrac{a}{2}, \dfrac{-a^2}{4}\right)$ **C** $(a, 0)$ **D** $\left(a, \dfrac{-a^2}{2}\right)$ **E** $\left(\dfrac{-a}{2}, \dfrac{-a^2}{4}\right)$

2 The quadratic equation $x^2 - 2ax + b = 0$, where a and b are positive constants, has one solution when

  A $b = a$ and $a \neq 1$ **B** $b = \sqrt{a}$ and $b = -\sqrt{a}$ **C** $b = 1$ and $a \neq 1$
  D $a = \sqrt{b}$ **E** $b = a = 2$

3 The simultaneous equations $(m - 2)x + 3y = 6$ and $2x + (m + 2)y = m$ have a unique solution for

  A $m \in \mathbb{R} \setminus \{0\}$ **B** $m \in \mathbb{R} \setminus \{-1, 1\}$ **C** $m \in \mathbb{R} \setminus \{-\sqrt{10}, \sqrt{10}\}$
  D $m \in \mathbb{R} \setminus [-1, 1]$ **E** $m \in \mathbb{R}$

4 The graph of $3x - 2y = -6$ is

  A 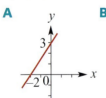   **B**   **C** 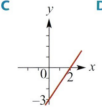   **D** 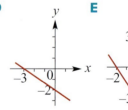   **E**

5 Which of the following points lies on both the line with equation $y = 3x - 1$ and the line with equation $4x + 2y = 8$?

  A $(0, 0)$ **B** $(0, 4)$ **C** $(2, 0)$ **D** $(1, 2)$ **E** $(2, 1)$

6 The factors of $x^3 - 8$ are
  A $(x+2)(x^2 - 2x + 4)$ **B** $(x-2)^3$ **C** $(x^2 - 4)(x+2)$
  D $(x-2)(x^2 + 2x + 4)$ **E** $(x^2 + 4)(x-2)$

7 The linear factors of $2x^2 - 5x - 12$ are
  A $(2x+1)$ and $(x-12)$ **B** $(2x-1)$ and $(x+12)$ **C** $(2x+3)$ and $(x-4)$
  D $2(2x-3)$ and $(x+2)$ **E** $2(x - \frac{1}{2})$ and $(x+6)$

8 The remainder when $4x^3 - 5x + 5$ is divided by $2x + 3$ is
  A 4   **B** 11   **C** -1 **D** 1   **E** 2

9 The equation $x^2 + y^2 + 6x - 2y + 6 = 0$ corresponds to a circle of radius
  A 4   **B** $\sqrt{6}$ **C** 2   **D** 6   **E** 10

10 The gradient of the line with equation $2x + 4y - 6 = 0$ is
  A $-\frac{1}{2}$ **B** 2   **C** 4   **D** -2 **E** 1

11 The equation of the line perpendicular to the line with equation $2x + 4y = 3$ and containing the point $(1, 2)$ is
  A $y = -\frac{1}{2}x + \frac{5}{2}$ **B** $2y = x + 2$ **C** $2y = x$ **D** $y = 2x - 4$ **E** $y = 2x$

12 If $x - 3$ is a factor of $x^3 + ax^2 - x - 6$, then a is equal to
  A 2   **B** -2 **C** 1   **D** -1 **E** -3

13 The linear factors of $x^3 + 8x^2 + 9x - 18$ are
  A $x - 1$, $x + 3$, $x + 6$ **B** $x - 1$, $x - 3$, $x - 6$ **C** $x + 1$, $x - 3$, $x + 6$
  D $x + 1$, $x + 3$, $x - 1$ **E** $x + 1$, $x - 3$, $x - 6$

14 The parabola shown has equation
  A $y = 2(x-2)(x+2)$
  B $y = -2(x-2)^2$
  C $3y = 4(x+2)(x-2)$
  D $3y = 2(x+2)(x-2)$
  E $4y = -3(x+2)(x-2)$

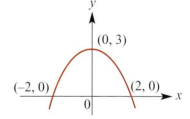

15 The line with equation $y = mx + c$ is perpendicular to the line with equation $y = 4 - 3x$. The value of m is
  A 3   **B** $\frac{1}{3}$ **C** -3 **D** $-\frac{1}{3}$ **E** -1

16 If $f(x) = x^2 - 1$, then $f(x-1)$ is equal to
  A 0   **B** 1   **C** $x - 1$ **D** $x^2 - 2x$ **E** $x^2 - 2x - 2$

17 The graph of $y = x^2 + kx + k + 8$ touches the x-axis. The value of k is
  A -4 **B** 8   **C** 12   **D** -4 or 8   **E** -8 or 12

18 Let $P(x) = 3x^3 - 4x - k$. If $P(x)$ is divisible by $x - k$, the remainder when $P(x)$ is divided by $x + k$ is

A $2k$ **B** k **C** 0 **D** $-k$ **E** $-2k$

19 The turning point of the graph of the quadratic function whose rule is $y = a(x - b)^2 + c$ is the point with coordinates

A $\left(\dfrac{b}{a}, c\right)$ **B** (b, c) **C** (c, b) **D** $(-b, c)$ **E** $\left(\dfrac{b}{a}, \dfrac{c}{a}\right)$

20 If the graphs of $y = 3 + 4x - x^2$ and $y = k$ have only one common point, then k is

A -1 **B** 1 **C** 4 **D** 7 **E** 2

21 The coordinates of the midpoint of the line segment with endpoints $(12, 7)$ and $(-1, 5)$ are

A $(7\tfrac{1}{2}, 6)$ **B** $(9, 12)$ **C** $(15, 2)$ **D** $(7\tfrac{1}{2}, 1)$ **E** $(6\tfrac{1}{2}, 6)$

22 M is the midpoint of XY. The coordinates of M and Y are $(7, -3)$ and $(5, 4)$ respectively. The coordinates of X are

A $(6, \tfrac{1}{2})$ **B** $(4, -14)$ **C** $(1, 0)$ **D** $(9, -10)$ **E** $(6, -5)$

23 The range of the function represented by the set of ordered pairs
$\{(x, y) : y = x^2 + 1, \ x \in [-2, 1]\}$ is

A $[-3, 1]$ **B** $[1, 5]$ **C** $(1, \infty)$ **D** $[12, 5]$ **E** $\mathbb{R}$

24 The equation $x^3 + 2x - 8 = 0$ has only one solution. This solution lies between

A -2 and -1 **B** -1 and 0 **C** 0 and 1 **D** 1 and 2 **E** 2 and 8

25 If $f : \mathbb{R} \to \mathbb{R}$ with $f(x) = x(x - 2)$, then $f(-3)$ is equal to

A -8 **B** 2 **C** 8 **D** 15 **E** -15

26 The circle $x^2 + y^2 - 11x - 10y + 24 = 0$ cuts the y-axis at M and N. The distance between M and N is

A 2 **B** 5 **C** 10 **D** 11 **E** 24

27 The length of the line segment joining the points with coordinates $(-4, -3)$ and $(-5, -10)$ is

A $2\sqrt{5}$ **B** $5\sqrt{2}$ **C** $5\sqrt{10}$ **D** $25\sqrt{2}$ **E** $15\sqrt{2}$

28 The straight line intersects the parabola at points A and B. The length of line segment AB is

A $\sqrt{48}$ **B** $\sqrt{60}$ **C** $\sqrt{180}$
D $\sqrt{320}$ **E** $\sqrt{360}$

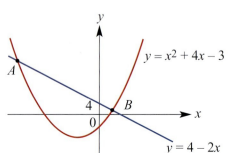

29 Which one of the following ordered pairs **is not** a member of the relation $\{(x, y) : y \leq 2x + 3\}$?

A $(1, 4)$ **B** $(-1, 1)$ **C** $(\frac{1}{2}, 3\frac{1}{2})$ **D** $(-\frac{1}{2}, 2\frac{1}{2})$ **E** $(2, 5)$

30 If the graph of $y = k + 2x - x^2$ touches the x-axis, the value of k is

A -2 **B** -1 **C** 0 **D** 1 **E** 2

31 If the line with equation $kx + y - 4 = 0$ is perpendicular to the line with equation $x - 2y + 3 = 0$, then k equals

A -2 **B** $\frac{1}{2}$ **C** 2 **D** $-\frac{1}{2}$ **E** $\frac{3}{4}$

32 The simultaneous equations $y = x^2 + k$ and $y = x$ have only one solution. The value of k is

A $\frac{1}{4}$ **B** $-\frac{1}{4}$ **C** 4 **D** -4 **E** 1

33 A circle has its centre at $(-4, 2)$ and touches the y-axis. Its equation is

A $x^2 + y^2 = 20$
B $x^2 + y^2 - 8x - 4y = 0$
C $x^2 + y^2 + 8x - 4y + 4 = 0$
D $x^2 + y^2 + 8x - 4y + 16 = 0$
E $x^2 + y^2 - 8x + 4y + 4 = 0$

34 If two lines $2x - y + 3 = 0$ and $ax + 3y - 1 = 0$ are parallel, then the value of a is

A -6 **B** -2 **C** 2 **D** 3 **E** 6

35 The maximal domain of the function with rule $f(x) = \sqrt{4 - x^2}$ is

A $[0, 2]$ **B** $[-2, 2]$ **C** $(2, \infty)$ **D** $(-\infty, 2)$ **E** $(-2, 2)$

36 The range of the function $f : \mathbb{R} \to \mathbb{R}$, $f(x) = 2x^2 + 3x + 4$ is

A $(-\infty, 4]$ **B** $\left[\frac{4}{3}, \infty\right)$ **C** $\left[\frac{23}{8}, \infty\right)$ **D** $[1, \infty)$ **E** $[4, \infty)$

37 When $x^3 - kx^2 - 10kx + 25$ is divided by $x - 2$, the remainder is 9. The value of k is

A 25 **B** $-\frac{1}{2}$ **C** $\frac{7}{4}$ **D** 1 **E** $-\frac{13}{8}$

38 If $f(x) = x^2 - 7x + k$ and $f(k) = -9$, then $f(-1)$ equals

A -9 **B** -3 **C** 3 **D** 5 **E** 11

39 $2xy - x^2 - y^2$ is equal to

A $(x - y)^2$ **B** $(-x - y)^2$ **C** $(-x + y)^2$ **D** $-(x + y)^2$ **E** $-(x - y)^2$

40 $\{x : x^2 - x - 12 \leq 0\}$ is equal to

A $[3, 4]$ **B** $(-\infty, 3) \cup [4, \infty)$ **C** $[-3, 4]$
D $(-\infty, -4] \cup [-3, \infty)$ **E** $[-4, 3]$

41 If $f(x) = \frac{1}{2}x(x - 1)$, then $f(x) - f(x + 1)$ is equal to

A 1 **B** -2 **C** $-x$ **D** $-2x$ **E** $-\frac{x}{2}$

42 The set $\{x : 2x^2 - 2 \leq 0\}$ is equal to

A $(-\infty, 1]$ **B** $[-1, \infty)$ **C** $[-1, 1]$
D $[1, \infty) \cup (-\infty, -1]$ **E** $(-\infty, 1) \cup [1, \infty)$

43 The range of the function $f(x) = -2[(x - \frac{1}{2})^2 - 3]$ is

A $(-\infty, 6]$ **B** $(-\infty, 3]$ **C** $(-3, \infty)$ **D** $[6, \infty]$ **E** $[-6, \infty]$

8C Extended-response questions

1 The general equation of the circle can be written as $x^2 + y^2 + bx + cy + d = 0$. A circle passes through the points with coordinates $(-4, 5)$, $(-2, 7)$ and $(4, -3)$.
  a Write three simultaneous equations in b, c and d.
  b Determine the equation of the circle.

2 A circle passes through the origin. It has equation $x^2 + y^2 + bx + cy = 0$. The circle also passes through the point $(4, 4)$.
  a Find c in terms of b.
  b Find the x-axis intercepts in terms of b.
  c Find the y-axis intercepts in terms of b.
  d For what value of b does the circle touch the y-axis?

3 A family of functions have rules of the form $f(x) = \sqrt{a - x}$, where a is a positive real number.
  a State the maximal domain of f.
  b Find the coordinates of the point of intersection of the graph of $y = f(x)$ with the graph of $y = x$.
  c For what value of a does the line with equation $y = x$ intersect the graph of $y = f(x)$ at the point with coordinates $(1, 1)$?
  d For what value of a does the line with equation $y = x$ intersect the graph of $y = f(x)$ at the point with coordinates $(2, 2)$?
  e For what value of a does the line with equation $y = x$ intersect the graph of $y = f(x)$ at the point with coordinates (c, c), where c is a positive real number?

4 A particular plastic plate manufactured at a factory sells at $11.50. The cost of production consists of an initial cost of $3500 and then $10.50 a plate. Let x be the number of plates produced.
  a Let $\$C$ be the cost of production of x plates. Write an expression for C in terms of x.
  b Let $\$I$ be the income from selling x plates. Write an expression for I in terms of x.
  c On the one set of axes sketch the graphs of I against x and C against x.
  d How many plates must be sold for the income to equal the cost of production?
  e Let $P = I - C$. Sketch the graph of P against x. What does P represent?
  f How many plates must be sold for a profit of $2000 to be made?

5 A swimming pool initially contains 45 000 litres of water. At 12 p.m., an inlet valve is opened letting 40 litres of water per minute into the pool. Assume no water evaporates.
  a Find an expression for the volume, V litres, in the pool m minutes after 12 p.m.
  b When will the pool reach its maximum capacity of 55 000 litres?
  c Sketch the graph of V against m (use the appropriate domain).

6 A tank of capacity 1000 litres is initially empty. Water flows into the tank at 20 litres per minute for 10 minutes, and then the rate is decreased to 15 litres per minute. The water continues to flow in at this rate until the tank is filled.
  a How much water is in the tank after 10 minutes?

The volume of water in the tank can be described by the rule

$$V = \begin{cases} at & 0 \leq t \leq 10 \\ bt + c & 10 < t \leq d \end{cases}$$

  b Find the values of a, b, c and d.
  c Sketch the graph of V against t.

7 From a piece of wire 42 cm long, a length $10x$ cm is cut off and bent into a rectangle whose length is one and a half times its width. The remainder is bent to form a square.
  a State the area of the rectangle in terms of x.
  b State the area of the square in terms of x.
  c State the possible values for x.
  d Find an expression for the total area, A cm^2, of the square and the rectangle.
  e Sketch the graph of A against x.
  f What is the maximum possible total area?
  g If the combined area of the rectangle and the square is 63 cm^2, find their dimensions.

8 A stone is projected from a balcony as shown.
The path is described by the equation

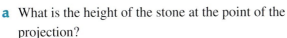

$$y = -\frac{1}{10}(x + 10)(x - 20), \quad x \geq 0$$

where y metres is the height above the ground when the stone has travelled x metres horizontally.

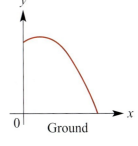

  a What is the height of the stone at the point of the projection?
  b What is the horizontal distance travelled before the stone hits the ground?
  c What is the maximum height reached by the stone?

9 A rectangular block is 2 cm wider than it is high and twice as long as it is wide. Let x cm be the height of the block.
  a Find an expression for the total surface area, A cm^2, in terms of x.
  b Find A if:
    i $x = 1$ **ii** $x = 2$
  c Find the value of x if $A = 190$.
  d Sketch the graph of A against x for suitable values of x.
  e Find an expression for the volume, V cm^3, of the block in terms of x.
  f If the volume of the block is 150 cm^3, find the value of x.
  g If the volume of the block is 1000 cm^3, find the value of x.

10 A region is enclosed as shown.
  a Find expressions for:
    i A (m^2), the area of the region in terms of x and y
    ii P (m), the perimeter of the region in terms of x and y.
  b **i** If the perimeter is 100 m, find A in terms of x.
    ii What is the maximum area possible?
    iii State the possible values for x.
    iv Sketch the graph of A against x for these values.

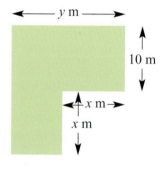

11 The diagram shows a window with six equal square panes divided by equally thick timber framing.
  a Write down the total area of the whole window in terms of x and y.
  b Show that the total area of the dividing wood is $7xy + 2y^2$.
  c The total area of glass is 1.5 m^2 and the total area of the dividing wood is 1 m^2.
    i Find x.   **ii** Find y.

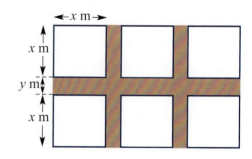

12 A fountain is 5 metres high. Water is coming vertically out of the fountain. The function which describes the height of a drop of water above the spout t seconds after leaving the spout of the fountain is given by $h(t) = -4.9t^2 + 10t + 5$.
  a How high is the drop of water after 3 seconds?
  b When will the drop be back at the height of the spout?
  c Sketch the graph of the height of the drop above the fountain against time.
  d If there is a little wind, the drop will not travel along a vertical line but its time in the air will not be affected and h will still describe its height above the ground. How long will it take for a drop of water to hit the ground?

13 An open rectangular cardboard box is 7 cm high and its length is 5 cm greater than its breadth, which is x cm.
  a Find the length of the box in terms of x.
  b Find the volume (V cm^3) of the box in terms of x.
  c Find the surface area (S cm^2) in terms of x.
  d Sketch the graphs of S against x and V against x for a suitable domain on the one set of axes.
  e For what value of x is $V = S$?
  f If the total surface area is 500 cm^2, find x.

14 Two points A and C have coordinates $(1, 3)$ and $(7, 7)$.
  a Find the equation of the perpendicular bisector of AC.
  b B is a point on the y-axis which is equidistant from A and C, and $ABCD$ is a rhombus. Find:
   i the coordinates of B **ii** the coordinates of D
  c Find the area of the rhombus $ABCD$.
  d Calculate the perpendicular distance of A from BC.

15 a A train travels 300 km at a constant speed of V km/h. If the train had travelled 5 km/h faster, the journey would have taken two hours less. Find the speed of the train travelling at the slower speed.
  b A tank can be filled by two taps A and B in $33\frac{1}{3}$ minutes (33 minutes 20 seconds) when they are running together. Tap A running by itself fills the tank in 15 minutes less than tap B. Find the time taken for each tap running by itself to fill the tank.
  c A hall can be paved with 200 square tiles of a certain size. If each tile were 1 cm longer and wider it would take 128 tiles. Find the length of each tile.

16 A piece of wire 400 cm long is used to make the 12 edges of a cuboid with dimensions as shown.
  a Find h in terms of x.
  b Find the volume, V cm^3, in terms of x.
  c State the possible values for x.
  d Plot the graph of V against x on a CAS calculator for the domain determined in part c.

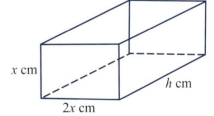

  e State the values of x (correct to 3 decimal places) which will result in a volume of:
   i 30 000 cm^3 **ii** 20 000 cm^3.
  f State the maximum volume (correct to 3 decimal places) and the corresponding value of x.

  g The cuboid is covered in paper.
   i Find the surface area, S cm^2, of the cuboid in terms of x.
   ii Find the maximum value of S and the value of x for which this occurs.
  h Find the values of x for which $S = V$.

17 A section of a path along the edge of a river can be modelled by a cubic function for $x \in [0, 250]$. Measurements are in metres. The following are the coordinates of points on the path: $(0, 0)$, $(100, 33)$, $(50, 57)$ and $(150, -15)$.

a Find the equation of the graph of the cubic function which passes through these points.

b The bank of the river is 5 metres to the north of the centre of the path. Find the equation of the cubic function which models the river bank.

c Find the largest deviation of the path from the x-axis.

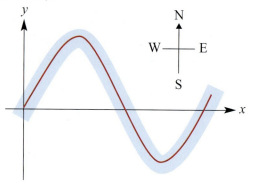

18 ABC is an isosceles triangle. The coordinates of A and B are $(5, 6)$ and $(0, -4)$ respectively. Given that the gradient of BC is $\frac{3}{4}$ and D is the midpoint of BC, find:

a the equation of BC

b the equation of AD

c the coordinates of D

d the length of the perpendicular AD

e the area of triangle ABC.

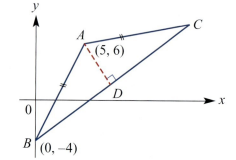

19 A parcel in the form of a rectangular block is held together by three pieces of tape as shown.

The parcel has square ends with side length x cm. The length of the parcel is y cm.

The total length of tape is 500 cm.

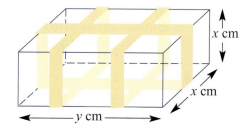

a **i** Find y in terms of x.

ii Find V, the volume of the parcel in cm³, in terms of x.

b Draw the graph of V against x for suitable values of x.

c State the domain of this function.

d Find the values of x for which $V = 25\,000$.

e Find the maximum volume of the parcel and the corresponding values of x and y.

Chapter 9: Probability

Objectives

▶ To understand the basic concepts and notation of **set theory**.
▶ To understand the basic concepts and rules of **probability**.
▶ To introduce **mutually exclusive events**.
▶ To apply the **addition rule** to solve problems.
▶ To use **Venn diagrams**, **tree diagrams** and **probability tables** to calculate probabilities.
▶ To introduce **conditional probability** and **independence**.
▶ To use the **multiplication rule** and the **law of total probability** to calculate probabilities.

Uncertainty is involved in much of the reasoning we undertake every day of our lives. We are often required to make decisions based on the chance of a particular occurrence. Some events can be predicted from our present store of knowledge, such as the time of the next high tide. Others, such as whether a head or tail will show when a coin is tossed, are not predictable.

However, whether through our prior observations or through a theoretical understanding of the circumstances, we are often able to assign a numerical value, or **probability**, to each possible outcome of an experiment. This probability, which will take a value between 0 and 1, gives us an indication as to how likely we are to observe the outcome. A probability of 0 means that the outcome is impossible and a probability of 1 means that it is certain. Generally, the probability will be somewhere in between, with a higher value meaning that the outcome is more likely.

9A Sample spaces and probability

In this section we look at two essential components of probability: a sample space, which is the set of all possible outcomes of an experiment, and a set of probabilities, one for each outcome.

▶ Sample spaces

Suppose we toss a coin to see whether a head (H) or a tail (T) appears uppermost. The toss of the coin can be termed a single **trial** of a **random experiment**. The word 'random' is used here because, while the outcome observed must be either a head or a tail, on a particular toss we don't know which will be observed. However, we do know that the outcome observed will be one of a known set of possible outcomes, and the set of all possible outcomes is called the **sample space** for the experiment.

Set notation can be used in listing all the elements in the sample space. For example, the sample space for the tossing of a coin would be written as

$$\{H, T\}$$

where H indicates head and T indicates tail. Throughout this chapter, the Greek letter ε (epsilon) will be used to denote the sample space.

For example, the following table lists the sample spaces for each of the random experiments described.

Random experiment	Sample space
The number observed when a die is rolled	$\varepsilon = \{1, 2, 3, 4, 5, 6\}$
The number of brown eggs in a carton of 12 eggs	$\varepsilon = \{0, 1, 2, 3, 4, 5, 6, 7, 8, 9, 10, 11, 12\}$
The result when two coins are tossed	$\varepsilon = \{HH, HT, TH, TT\}$
The number of calls to your phone in the next two hours	$\varepsilon = \{0, 1, 2, 3, 4, \ldots\}$
The time, in hours, it takes to complete your homework	$\varepsilon = \{t : t \geq 0\}$

▶ Events

An **event** is a subset of the sample space. It may consist of a single outcome, or it may consist of several outcomes. For example, when rolling a die, the event of interest may be 'getting a six', which consists of just one outcome and is described by the set $\{6\}$. However, the event 'getting an odd number' can be achieved by rolling 1, 3 or 5 and is described by the set $\{1, 3, 5\}$.

It is convenient to use set notation to list the elements of the event. In general we use capital letters, $A, B, C, \ldots$, to denote events.

The following table lists the experiments described earlier and gives the sample space and an example of an event for each one.

Sample space	An event
The number observed when a die is rolled $\varepsilon = \{1, 2, 3, 4, 5, 6\}$	'An even number' = $\{2, 4, 6\}$
The number of brown eggs in a carton of 12 eggs $\varepsilon = \{0, 1, 2, 3, 4, 5, 6, 7, 8, 9, 10, 11, 12\}$	'More than half brown' = $\{7, 8, 9, 10, 11, 12\}$
The result when two coins are tossed $\varepsilon = \{HH, HT, TH, TT\}$	'Two heads' = $\{HH\}$
The number of calls to your phone in the next two hours $\varepsilon = \{0, 1, 2, 3, 4, \dots\}$	'Fewer than two phone calls' = $\{0, 1\}$
The time, in hours, it takes to complete your homework $\varepsilon = \{t : t \geq 0\}$	'More than two hours' = $\{t : t > 2\}$

Note: Both a sample space and an event can be discrete or continuous, finite or infinite.

Example 1

A bag contains seven marbles numbered from 1 to 7 and a marble is withdrawn.
a Give the sample space for this experiment.
b List the outcomes (elements) of the event 'a marble with an odd number is withdrawn'.

Solution

a $\{1, 2, 3, 4, 5, 6, 7\}$

b $\{1, 3, 5, 7\}$

Explanation

Any number from 1 to 7 could be observed.

This set contains the odd numbers in the sample space.

▶ Determining probabilities for equally likely outcomes

There are many situations for which we can develop a simple model that can be used to assign a probability to an event. The most obvious of these is when it is reasonable to assume that all of the outcomes are equally likely, such as when a die is rolled.

We require that the probabilities of all the outcomes in the sample space sum to 1, and that the probability of each outcome is a non-negative number. This means that the probability of each outcome must lie in the interval [0, 1]. Since six outcomes are possible when rolling a die, we can assign the probability of each outcome to be $\frac{1}{6}$. That is,

$$\Pr(1) = \Pr(2) = \Pr(3) = \Pr(4) = \Pr(5) = \Pr(6) = \frac{1}{6}$$

When the sample space is finite, the **probability of an event** is equal to the sum of the probabilities of the outcomes in that event.

For example, let A be the event that an even number is rolled on the die. Then $A = \{2, 4, 6\}$ and $\Pr(A) = \Pr(2) + \Pr(4) + \Pr(6) = \frac{1}{2}$. Since the outcomes are equally likely, we can calculate this more easily as

$$\Pr(A) = \frac{\text{number of outcomes in } A}{\text{total number of outcomes}} = \frac{3}{6} = \frac{1}{2}$$

> **Equally likely outcomes**
>
> In general, if the sample space ε for an experiment contains n outcomes, all of which are equally likely to occur, we assign a probability of $\frac{1}{n}$ to each of these outcomes.
>
> Then the probability of any event A which contains m of these outcomes is the ratio of the number of elements in A to the number of elements in ε. That is,
>
> $$\Pr(A) = \frac{n(A)}{n(\varepsilon)} = \frac{m}{n}$$
>
> where the notation $n(S)$ is used to represent the number of elements in set S.

Of course, there are many situations where the outcomes are not equally likely. For example, it has been established worldwide that the probability of a male birth is in fact 0.51, not 0.5. However, in many situations the assumption of equally likely is justified, and allows us to assign probabilities reasonably.

Example 2

Suppose a number is drawn at random from the numbers 7, 8, 9, 10, 11, 12, 13, 14. What is the probability of choosing a prime number?

Solution	Explanation
Let A be the event the chosen number is prime. Then $\Pr(A) = \frac{3}{8}$	Since the number is drawn at random, we can assume each number is equally likely to be drawn. $A = \{7, 11, 13\}$, $n(A) = 3$, $n(\varepsilon) = 8$

Example 3

Suppose that a card is drawn from a pack of 52 playing cards, and that each card has equal likelihood of being drawn. Find:

a the probability that the card is black
b the probability that the card is a king
c the probability that the card is a black king.

Solution	Explanation
a $\Pr(\text{black card}) = \frac{26}{52} = \frac{1}{2}$	There are 52 cards in a pack and 26 are black.

b Pr(king) = $\frac{4}{52} = \frac{1}{13}$ There are 52 cards in a pack and 4 are kings.

c Pr(black king) = $\frac{2}{52} = \frac{1}{26}$ There are 52 cards in a pack and 2 are black kings.

The following rules of probability hold for finite sample spaces:
- Pr(A) ≥ 0, for any event A.
- The sum of the probabilities of all the outcomes of a random experiment must equal 1.

The second of these two rules can be used to determine probabilities as follows.

Example 4

A random experiment may result in 1, 2, 3 or 4. If Pr(1) = $\frac{1}{13}$, Pr(2) = $\frac{2}{13}$ and Pr(3) = $\frac{3}{13}$, find the probability of obtaining a 4.

Solution

Pr(4) = $1 - \left(\frac{1}{13} + \frac{2}{13} + \frac{3}{13}\right)$

$= 1 - \frac{6}{13} = \frac{7}{13}$

Explanation

The sum of the probabilities is 1.

Example 5

Find the probability that each of the possible outcomes is observed for the following spinners:

a

b

Solution

a Pr(1) = Pr(2) = Pr(3) = Pr(4) = Pr(5) = $\frac{1}{5}$

b Pr(1) = Pr(2) = Pr(3) = $\frac{1}{8}$ = 0.125

Pr(4) = $\frac{2}{8} = \frac{1}{4}$ = 0.25

Pr(5) = $\frac{3}{8}$ = 0.375

Note that in both these cases
Pr(1) + Pr(2) + Pr(3) + Pr(4) + Pr(5) = 1

Explanation

On spinner a, there are five equally likely outcomes.

Since there are 8 equal segments, we assume each has a probability of $\frac{1}{8}$.

The results 1, 2 and 3 appear once.
The result 4 appears twice.
The result 5 appears three times.

Complementary events

When two events have no elements in common and together they make up the entire sample space, they are said to be **complementary events**. The complement of event A is the event A', which consists of all the outcomes in ε that are not in A. Since the sum of the probabilities is 1, we can write

$$\Pr(A') = 1 - \Pr(A)$$

Example 6

A card is drawn at random from a pack of 52 cards. What is the probability that the card is:

a not a heart
b not an ace?

Solution

a Let H be the event a heart is drawn.

Then $\Pr(H') = 1 - \Pr(H)$
$$= 1 - \frac{13}{52}$$
$$= 1 - \frac{1}{4}$$
$$= \frac{3}{4}$$

b Let A be the event an ace is drawn.

Then $\Pr(A') = 1 - \Pr(A)$
$$= 1 - \frac{4}{52}$$
$$= 1 - \frac{1}{13}$$
$$= \frac{12}{13}$$

Combining our knowledge of the rules of probability enables us to solve more complex problems.

Example 7

A random experiment may result in outcomes A, B, C, D or E, where A, B, C, D are equally likely and E is twice as likely as A. Find:

a $\Pr(E)$
b $\Pr(B')$

Solution

a Let $\Pr(A) = \Pr(B) = \Pr(C) = \Pr(D) = x$.
Then $\Pr(E) = 2x$.

$$x + x + x + x + 2x = 1$$
$$6x = 1$$
$$x = \frac{1}{6}$$

Thus $\Pr(E) = 2x = \frac{1}{3}$

b $\Pr(B') = 1 - \Pr(B) = 1 - \frac{1}{6} = \frac{5}{6}$

Explanation

Summarise the information in the question in terms of one unknown.

The sum of the probabilities is 1.

Since B' is the complement of B, the probabilities will add to 1.

Section summary

- The **sample space**, ε, for a random experiment is the set of all possible outcomes.
- An **event** is a subset of the sample space. The probability of an event A occurring is denoted by $\Pr(A)$.
- Rules of probability for finite sample spaces:
  - $\Pr(A) \geq 0$, for each event A.
  - The sum of the probabilities of all the outcomes of a random experiment must be equal to 1.
- **Equally likely outcomes** If the sample space ε for an experiment contains n outcomes, all of which are equally likely to occur, we assign a probability of $\dfrac{1}{n}$ to each outcome. Then the probability of an event A is given by
$$\Pr(A) = \frac{\text{number of outcomes in } A}{\text{total number of outcomes}} = \frac{n(A)}{n(\varepsilon)}$$
- If two events have no elements in common and together they make up the entire sample space, they are said to be **complementary events**. The complement of any event A is denoted A' and we can write
$$\Pr(A') = 1 - \Pr(A)$$

Exercise 9A

Example 1

1 List the sample space for the toss of a coin.

2 List the sample space for the outcomes when a die is rolled.

3 Answer the following for a normal deck of playing cards:
   a How many cards are there?
   b How many suits are there?
   c What are the suits called?
   d Which suits are red and which suits are black?
   e How many cards are there in each suit?
   f Which cards are known as the 'picture cards'?
   g How many aces are there in the deck?
   h How many 'picture cards' are there in the deck?

4 List the sample spaces for the following experiments:
   a the number of picture cards in a hand of five cards
   b the number of female children in a family with six children
   c the number of female students on a committee of three students chosen from a class of 10 male and 10 female students

5 List the sample spaces for the following experiments:
  a the number of cars which pass through a particular intersection in a day
  b the number of people on board a bus licensed to carry 40 passengers
  c the number of times a die is rolled before a six is observed

6 List the outcomes associated with the following events:
  a 'an even number' when a die is rolled
  b 'more than two female students' when three students are chosen for a committee from a class of 10 male and 10 female students
  c 'more than four aces' when five cards are dealt from a standard pack of 52 cards

Example 2

7 A number is drawn at random from the set $\{1, 2, 3, \ldots, 20\}$. What is the probability that the number is:
  a divisible by 2
  b divisible by 3
  c divisible by both 2 and 3?

8 A bag has 15 marbles numbered $1, 2, 3, \ldots, 15$. If one marble is drawn at random from the bag, what is the probability that the number on the marble is:
  a less than 5
  b greater than or equal to 6
  c a number from 5 to 8 inclusive?

Example 3

9 A card is drawn at random from a well-shuffled pack of 52 cards. Find the probability that the card is:
  a a club
  b red
  c a picture card (ace, king, queen, jack)
  d a red picture card.

10 A card is drawn at random from a well-shuffled pack of 52 cards. Find the probability that the card is:
  a less than 10
  b less than or equal to 10
  c an even number
  d an ace.

11 Suppose that in a certain city the same number of people were born on each of the 365 days of the year, and that nobody was born on 29 February. Find the probability that the birthday of a person selected at random:
  a is 29 November
  b is in November
  c falls between 15 January and 15 February, not including either day
  d is in the first three months of the year.

12 One letter is drawn at random from the letters in the word AUSTRALIA. Find the probability that the letter is:

a a T b an A c a vowel d a consonant.

13 A random experiment results in 1, 2, 3, 4, 5 or 6. If $\Pr(1) = \frac{1}{12}$, $\Pr(2) = \frac{1}{6}$, $\Pr(3) = \frac{1}{8}$, $\Pr(5) = \frac{1}{6}$ and $\Pr(6) = \frac{1}{8}$, find the probability of obtaining a 4.

14 A random experiment results in 1, 2, 3 or 4. If $\Pr(1) = 0.2$, $\Pr(3) = 0.1$ and $\Pr(4) = 0.3$, find $\Pr(2)$.

15 Consider the following spinners. In each case, what is the chance of the pointer stopping in region 1?

a b c

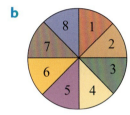
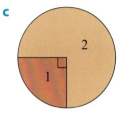

16 Assume that the probability of a baby being born on a certain day is the same for each day of the week. Find the probability that a randomly chosen person was born:

a on a Wednesday b not on the weekend.

17 A card is drawn at random from a well-shuffled pack of 52 cards. Find the probability that the card is:

a not a club
b not red
c not a picture card
d not a red picture card.

18 A random experiment results in 1, 2, 3 or 4. If 1, 2 and 3 are equally likely to occur, and 4 is twice as likely to occur as 3, find the probability of each of the possible outcomes.

19 For a particular biased six-sided die it is known that the numbers 2, 3, 4 and 5 are equally likely to occur, that the number 6 occurs twice as often as the number 2, and that the number 1 occurs half as often as the number 2.

a Find the probability of each of the possible outcomes.
b Find the probability that the number observed is not a 6.

9B Estimating probabilities

Skillsheet — When we are dealing with a random experiment which does not have equally likely outcomes, other methods of estimating probability are required.

▶ Subjective probabilities

Sometimes, the probability is assigned a value just on the basis of experience. For example, a sports journalist may suggest that Australia has a 60% chance of winning the next Ashes series relying on his or her own judgement. Another journalist might well assign this probability an entirely different value. Such probabilities are called subjective probabilities, and whether or not they are accurate estimates of the true probability would be open to dispute.

▶ Probabilities from data

A better way to estimate an unknown probability is by experimentation: by performing the random experiment leading to the event of interest many times and recording the results. This information can then be used to estimate the chances of it happening again in the future. The proportion of trials that resulted in this event is called the **relative frequency** of the event. (For most purposes we can consider proportion and relative frequency as interchangeable.) That is,

$$\text{Relative frequency of event } A = \frac{\text{number of times event } A \text{ occurs}}{\text{number of trials}}$$

Suppose, for example, that we are interested in determining the probability that a drawing pin will land 'point up' when it is tossed. Since a drawing pin is not symmetrical, the assumption of equally likely outcomes cannot be used to determine probabilities.

Our strategy to estimate this probability is to toss the drawing pin many times and count the number of times it lands point up. We can then calculate the relative frequency:

$$\text{Relative frequency of 'point up'} = \frac{\text{number of times drawing pin landed 'point up'}}{\text{number of trials}}$$

This proportion, or relative frequency, is an estimate of the probability of a drawing pin landing with the point up.

The graph opposite shows the results of one experiment where a drawing pin is tossed 150 times, with the probability of the drawing pin landing point up estimated every 10 throws.

From the graph it may be seen that, as the number of trials (repetitions of the experiment) increases, the estimated probability converges to a value and then stays fairly stable.

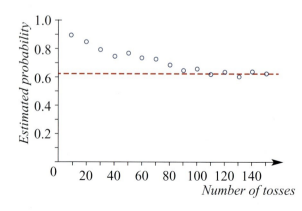

In general, if the same experiment is repeated many, many times, the relative frequency of any particular event will stabilise to a constant value. This limiting value of the relative frequency is then considered to be the probability of the event.

> When the number of trials is sufficiently large, the observed relative frequency of an event A becomes close to the probability Pr(A). That is,
>
> $$\Pr(A) \approx \frac{\text{number of times event } A \text{ occurs}}{\text{number of trials}} \quad \text{for a large number of trials}$$

If the experiment was repeated, it would generally be found that the results were slightly different. One might conclude that relative frequency is not a very good way of estimating probability. In many situations, however, experiments are the only way to get at an unknown probability. One of the most valuable lessons to be learnt is that such estimates are not exact, and will in fact vary from sample to sample.

Understanding the variation between estimates is extremely important in the study of statistics, and will be the topic of your later studies in mathematics. At this stage it is valuable to realise that the variation does exist, and that the best estimates of the probabilities will result from using as many trials as possible.

Example 8

In order to investigate the probability that a drawing pin lands point up, Katia decides to toss it 50 times and to count the number of favourable outcomes, which turns out to be 33. Mikki repeats the experiment, but she tosses the same drawing pin 100 times and counts 62 favourable outcomes.

a What is Katia's estimate of the probability of the drawing pin landing point up?
b What is Mikki's estimate?
c Which of these is the preferred estimate of the probability from these experiments?
d Based on the information available, what would be the preferred estimate of the probability?

Solution

a From Katia's information: $\Pr(\text{point up}) \approx \dfrac{33}{50} = 0.66$

b From Mikki's information: $\Pr(\text{point up}) \approx \dfrac{62}{100} = 0.62$

c Since Mikki has estimated the probability from a larger number of trials, her estimate would be preferred to Katia's.

d Based on the information available, the preferred estimate of the probability would be found by combining the data from both experiments, and so maximising the number of trials. In total, 95 favourable outcomes were observed in 150 tosses, and this gives a 'best' estimate of the probability of $\dfrac{95}{150} = 0.63$.

Thus, probability can be considered as the proportion of times that an event will occur in the long run. This interpretation also defines the minimum and maximum values of probability as 0 (the event never occurs) and 1 (the event always occurs), and confirms that the sum of the probabilities for all possible outcomes will equal 1.

▶ Simulation

The word simulate means to pretend or to imitate. In statistics, simulation is a way to model a random experiment, such that simulated outcomes closely match real-world outcomes. Simulation does not involve repeating the actual experiment. Instead, more complex probabilities can be estimated via multiple trials of an experiment which approximates the actual experiment, but can be carried out quickly and easily. A more detailed discussion of simulation is found in Section 9H.

▶ Probabilities from area

In the previous section we used the model of equally likely outcomes to determine probabilities. We counted both the outcomes in the event and the outcomes in the sample space, and used the ratio to determine the probability of the event.

This idea can be extended to calculate probabilities when areas are involved, by assuming that the probabilities of all points in the region (which can be considered to be the sample space) are equally likely.

Example 9

Suppose that a square dartboard consists of a red square drawn inside a larger white square of side length 12 cm, as shown.

If a dart thrown at the board has equal chance of landing anywhere on the board, what is the probability it lands in the red area? (Ignore the possibility that it might land on the line or miss the board altogether!)

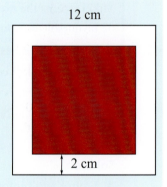

Solution

$$\text{Pr(landing in the red area)} = \frac{\text{area of red square}}{\text{area of dartboard}}$$

$$= \frac{64}{144}$$

$$= \frac{4}{9}$$

Explanation

There are really only two outcomes for this experiment: landing in the red area or landing in the white area.

Assume that the probability of landing in an area is proportional to the size of the area.

Section summary

- When a probability is unknown, it can be estimated by the relative frequency obtained through repeated trials of the random experiment under consideration. In this case,

$$\Pr(A) \approx \frac{\text{number of times event } A \text{ occurs}}{\text{number of trials}} \quad \text{for a large number of trials}$$

- Whichever method of estimating probability is used, the rules of probability hold:
  - $\Pr(A) \geq 0$, for each event A
  - $\Pr(\varepsilon) = 1$
  - The sum of the probabilities of all the outcomes of a random experiment equals 1.

Exercise 9B

1 Estimate the probability of the event specified occurring, using the data given:
  a Pr(head) if a coin is tossed 100 times and 34 heads observed
  b Pr(ten) if a spinner is spun 200 times and lands on the 'ten' 20 times
  c Pr(two heads) if two coins are tossed 150 times and two heads are observed on 40 occasions
  d Pr(three sixes) if three dice are rolled 200 times and three sixes observed only once

2 A student decides to toss two coins and notes the results.
  a Do you think relative frequencies obtained from 20 trials would make for a good estimate of the probabilities?
  b Perform the experiment 20 times and estimate Pr(two heads), Pr(one head) and Pr(no heads).
  c Combine your results with those of your friends, so that you have results from at least 100 trials. Use these results to again estimate the probabilities.
  d Do you think the data from 100 trials give better estimates of the probabilities?
  e How many trials would you need to find the probabilities exactly?

3 Two misshapen six-sided dice were used for the following experiment. The first die was thrown 500 times and 78 sixes were observed. The second die was thrown 700 times and 102 sixes were observed. If you wished to throw a six, which die would you choose to throw, and why?

4 A bowl contains 340 red and 60 black balls.
  a State the proportion of red balls in the bowl.
  b A random sample of 60 balls is taken from the bowl and is found to have 48 red balls. Find the proportion of red balls in the sample.
  c Another random sample of 60 balls is taken from the bowl and is found to have 54 red balls. Find the proportion of red balls in the sample.
  d What is the expected number of red balls in a sample of 60?

5   In a survey of 2000 people, 890 indicated that they regularly use social media to keep in touch with friends. What is an estimate for the probability that the next person surveyed also uses social media?

6   A square of side length 1 metre contains a blue one-quarter of a circular disc centred at the bottom-left vertex of the square, as shown.

   a What proportion of the square is blue?
   b If a dart thrown at the square is equally likely to hit any part of the square, and it hits the square every time, find the probability of it hitting the blue region.

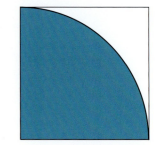

7   A dart is thrown at random onto a board that has the shape of a circle as shown. Calculate the probability that the dart will hit the shaded region.

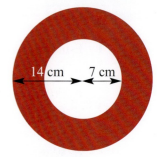

8   A spinner is as shown in the diagram.
Find the probability that when spun the pointer will land on:

   a the red section
   b the yellow section
   c any section except the yellow section.

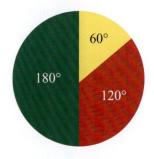

9   In a sideshow at a fete a dart is thrown at a square with side length 1 metre. The circle shown has a radius of 0.4 metres. The dart is equally likely to hit any point on the square. Find the probability that the dart will hit:

   a the shaded part of the square
   b the unshaded part of the square.

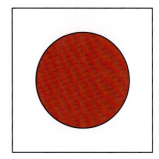

10 A dart is thrown at random onto the board shown. The board is a square of side length x, the larger circle is of radius $\dfrac{x}{2}$ and the smaller circle is of radius $\dfrac{x}{4}$.

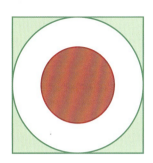

a Find, in terms of x:
  i the area of the square
  ii the area of the larger circle
  iii the area of the smaller circle.

b Hence find the probability that the dart will land:
  i inside the smaller circle
  ii in the white region
  iii in the outer shaded region.

9C Multi-stage experiments

Often we are interested in probabilities which arise from more complex **multi-stage experiments**. That is, they are concerned with experiments which could be considered to take place in more than one stage.

For example, when considering the outcomes from tossing two coins (or tossing one coin twice) we should consider the possible outcomes in two stages:

- the outcome from coin 1
- followed by the outcome from coin 2.

In such cases, it is helpful to list the elements of the sample space systematically by means of a **tree diagram** as shown.

Each path along the branches of the tree gives an outcome, which we determine by reading along the branches, making sure we maintain the order of the outcome at each stage carefully.

Collecting together all the outcomes, we see that the sample space is

$\varepsilon = \{HH, HT, TH, TT\}$

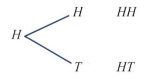
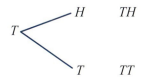

When the outcomes of the multi-stage experiment are equally likely, we can still determine the probability of an event occurring by dividing the number of outcomes in the event by the number of outcomes in the sample space.

Example 10

Find the probability that when a fair coin is tossed twice:

a one head is observed
b at least one head is observed
c both heads or both tails are observed.

Solution	Explanation
a $\Pr(\text{one head}) = \dfrac{2}{4} = \dfrac{1}{2}$	List the outcomes of the event: 'one head' = $\{HT, TH\}$. There are 2 outcomes in the event and 4 in the sample space (see tree diagram).
b $\Pr(\text{at least one head}) = \dfrac{3}{4}$	List the outcomes of the event: 'at least one head' = $\{HH, HT, TH\}$. There are 3 outcomes in the event and 4 in the sample space.
c $\Pr(\text{both heads or both tails}) = \dfrac{2}{4} = \dfrac{1}{2}$	List the outcomes of the event: 'both heads or both tails' = $\{HH, TT\}$. There are 2 outcomes in the event and 4 in the sample space.

When listing the outcomes for a two-stage experiment, it can also be convenient to display the sample space in a table. For example, when rolling two dice (or a single die twice) there is the possibility of $\{1, 2, 3, 4, 5, 6\}$ on die 1 (or the first roll), and $\{1, 2, 3, 4, 5, 6\}$ on die 2 (or the second roll). So the sample space for this experiment can be written as:

		\multicolumn{6}{c}{Die 2}				
		1	2	3	4	5	6
Die 1	1	(1, 1)	(1, 2)	(1, 3)	(1, 4)	(1, 5)	(1, 6)
	2	(2, 1)	(2, 2)	(2, 3)	(2, 4)	(2, 5)	(2, 6)
	3	(3, 1)	(3, 2)	(3, 3)	(3, 4)	(3, 5)	(3, 6)
	4	(4, 1)	(4, 2)	(4, 3)	(4, 4)	(4, 5)	(4, 6)
	5	(5, 1)	(5, 2)	(5, 3)	(5, 4)	(5, 5)	(5, 6)
	6	(6, 1)	(6, 2)	(6, 3)	(6, 4)	(6, 5)	(6, 6)

Example 11

Find the probability that when two fair dice are rolled:

a the same number shows on both dice (a double)

b the sum of the two numbers shown is greater than 10.

Solution	Explanation
a $\Pr(\text{double}) = \dfrac{6}{36} = \dfrac{1}{6}$	'double' = {(1, 1), (2, 2), (3, 3), (4, 4), (5, 5), (6, 6)}. There are 6 outcomes in the event and 36 in the sample space.
b $\Pr(\text{sum} > 10) = \dfrac{3}{36} = \dfrac{1}{12}$	'sum is greater than 10' = {(5, 6), (6, 5), (6, 6)}. There are 3 outcomes in the event and 36 in the sample space.

When the experiment involves more than two stages, it is best to use a **tree diagram** to determine all of the possible outcomes. Suppose, for example, that three coins are tossed and the outcomes noted. The three-stage tree diagram for listing the sample space for this experiment is as follows:

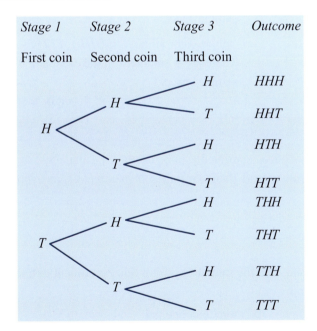

Thus the required sample space is

$$\varepsilon = \{HHH, HHT, HTH, HTT, THH, THT, TTH, TTT\}$$

Example 12

Find the probability that when a coin is tossed three times:
a one head is observed
b at least one head is observed
c the second toss results in a head
d all heads or all tails are observed.

Solution

a Pr(one head) = $\dfrac{3}{8}$

b Pr(at least one head) = $\dfrac{7}{8}$

c Pr(second toss is a head)
$= \dfrac{4}{8} = \dfrac{1}{2}$

d Pr(all heads or all tails)
$= \dfrac{2}{8} = \dfrac{1}{4}$

Explanation

'one head' = $\{HTT, THT, TTH\}$.
There are 3 outcomes in the event and 8 in the sample space.

'at least one head' =
$\{HHH, HHT, HTH, THH, HTT, THT, TTH\}$.
There are 7 outcomes in the event and 8 in the sample space.

'second toss is a head' = $\{HHH, HHT, THH, THT\}$.
There are 4 outcomes in the event and 8 in the sample space.

'all heads or all tails' = $\{HHH, TTT\}$.
There are 2 outcomes in the event and 8 in the sample space.

Section summary

The sample space for a two-stage experiment can be displayed using a tree diagram or a table. If an experiment involves more than two stages, then a tree diagram should be used.

Exercise 9C

Example 10   **1**   Two fair coins are tossed. Use the sample space for this experiment to find the probability of observing:
    a no heads   **b** more than one tail.

2 A fair coin is tossed twice. Find the probability that:
    a the first toss is a head   **b** the second toss is a head   **c** both tosses are heads.

Example 11   **3**   Two regular dice are rolled. Use the sample space for this experiment to find the probability that the sum of the numbers showing is:
    a even   **b** 3   **c** less than 6.

4 Two regular dice are rolled. Use the sample space for this experiment to find the probability that the sum of the numbers showing is:
   a equal to 10
   b odd
   c less than or equal to 7.

5 A fair coin is tossed three times. Use the sample space for this experiment to find the probability that:
   a exactly one tail is observed
   b exactly two tails are observed
   c exactly three tails are observed
   d no tails are observed.

6 A fair coin is tossed three times. Use the sample space for this experiment to find the probability that:
   a the third toss is a head
   b the second and third tosses are heads
   c at least one head and one tail are observed.

7 An experiment consists of rolling a die and tossing a coin. Use a tree diagram to list the sample space for the experiment. Find the probability of obtaining a head and an even number.

8 Two coins are tossed and a die is rolled.
   a Draw a tree diagram to show all the possible outcomes.
   b Find the probability of observing:
      i two heads and a 6
      ii one head, one tail and an even number
      iii two tails and an odd number
      iv an odd number on the die.

9 Madison has a choice of two entrees (soup or salad), three main courses (fish, chicken or steak) and three desserts (ice-cream, lemon tart or cheese).
   a Draw a tree diagram to show all her possible dinner combinations.
   b If Madison chooses all three courses, and is equally likely to choose any of the options at each course, find the probability that:
      i she chooses soup, fish and lemon tart
      ii she chooses fish
      iii she chooses salad and chicken
      iv she doesn't have the lemon tart.
   c Suppose Madison has the choice to omit the entree and/or the dessert course altogether. Find the probability that:
      i she chooses soup, fish and lemon tart
      ii she chooses all three courses
      iii she chooses only two courses
      iv she has only the main course.

10 A bag contains five balls, numbered 1 to 5. A ball is chosen at random, the number noted and the ball replaced. A second ball is then chosen at random and its number noted.

    a Draw up a table of ordered pairs to show the sample space for the experiment.

    b Find the probability that:

        i the sum of the two numbers is 5

        ii the two numbers are different

        iii the second number is two more than the first.

9D Combining events

Before proceeding with the discussion of probability, a review of sets and set notation is necessary.

The **empty set**, denoted by ∅, is the set consisting of no elements. This is different from {0}, which is a set containing one element, 0.

Sets, and the relationships between sets, can be illustrated clearly by using **Venn diagrams**. The universal set ε is usually shown as a rectangle, and a subset of ε as a circle.

If A and B are any two sets, then the **union** of A and B, denoted $A \cup B$, is the set of all elements in A or B (or both). This is shown on a Venn diagram by shading both sets A and B.

For example, if A is the set of students in a school who play hockey, and B the set of students who play tennis, then the union of A and B is the set of students who play either hockey or tennis or both.

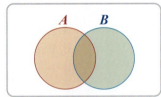

Union

The **intersection** of A and B, denoted $A \cap B$, is the set of elements that are in both A and B. This is shown on a Venn diagram by shading only the area contained in both A and B.

For example, the intersection of the two sets previously described is the set of students who play both hockey and tennis.

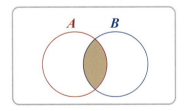

Intersection

As previously, note that the **complement** of A, denoted A', is the set of all elements of ε that are not in A. This is shown on a Venn diagram by shading only the area outside A.

The complement of the set of students who play hockey in a school is the set of students who do not play hockey.

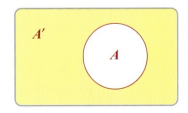

Complement

Two sets A and B are said to be **disjoint** or **mutually exclusive** if they have no elements in common, that is, if $A \cap B = \emptyset$. The Venn diagram opposite shows two sets that are mutually exclusive.

If A is the set of girls who play hockey in a school and B is the set of boys who play hockey, then A and B are mutually exclusive, as no student can belong to both sets.

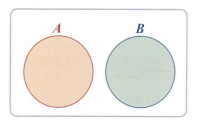

Disjoint sets

Finally, the number of elements in a set A is usually denoted $n(A)$. For example, if $A = \{2, 4, 6\}$, then $n(A) = 3$.

Venn diagrams can be used to help us solve practical problems involving sets.

Example 13

Fifty students were asked what they did on the weekends. A total of 35 said they went to football matches, the movies or both. Of the 22 who went to football matches, 12 said they also went to the movies. Show this information on a Venn diagram.

a How many students went to the movies but not to football matches?
b How many went neither to football matches nor to the movies?

Solution

Let F denote the set of students who attend football matches and M denote the set of students who attend movies.

Hence, from the information given, $n(F \cup M) = 35$, $n(F) = 22$ and $n(F \cap M) = 12$.

a Students who go to the movies but not to football matches are found in the region $F' \cap M$, and from the diagram $n(F' \cap M) = 13$.

b Those who attend neither are found in the region $F' \cap M'$, and from the diagram $n(F' \cap M') = 15$.

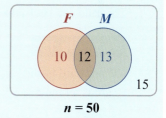

$n = 50$

Example 14

Consider Example 13. What is the probability that a student chosen at random from this group of 50:

a went to the movies but not to football matches
b went neither to football matches nor to the movies?

Solution

a $\Pr(F' \cap M) = \dfrac{n(F' \cap M)}{n(\varepsilon)} = \dfrac{13}{50}$

b $\Pr(F' \cap M') = \dfrac{n(F' \cap M')}{n(\varepsilon)} = \dfrac{15}{50} = \dfrac{3}{10}$

Explanation

To determine the probability of these events, divide by the size of the sample space in each case.

The addition rule

Venn diagrams can be used to illustrate a very important rule that will enable us to calculate probabilities for more complex events. If A and B are two events in a sample space ε and $A \cap B \neq \varnothing$, then the relationship between them can be represented by a Venn diagram, as shown.

From the Venn diagram we can see that

$$n(A \cup B) = n(A) + n(B) - n(A \cap B)$$

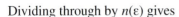

(As the intersection has been counted twice, in both $n(A)$ and $n(B)$, we must subtract it.)

Dividing through by $n(\varepsilon)$ gives

$$\frac{n(A \cup B)}{n(\varepsilon)} = \frac{n(A)}{n(\varepsilon)} + \frac{n(B)}{n(\varepsilon)} - \frac{n(A \cap B)}{n(\varepsilon)}$$

Now, if each of the outcomes in ε is equally likely to occur, then each term in this expression is equal to the probability of that event occurring. This can be rewritten as:

$$\Pr(A \cup B) = \Pr(A) + \Pr(B) - \Pr(A \cap B)$$

> So the probability of A or B or both occurring can be calculated using
>
> $$\Pr(A \cup B) = \Pr(A) + \Pr(B) - \Pr(A \cap B)$$
>
> This is called the **addition rule** for combining probabilities. This rule also applies in situations where the outcomes are not equally likely; it is always true.

This rule can be used to help solve more complex problems in probability.

Example 15

If one card is chosen at random from a well-shuffled deck, what is the probability that the card is a king or a spade?

Solution

Let event K be 'a king'. Then K = {king of spades, king of hearts, king of diamonds, king of clubs} and $n(K) = 4$.

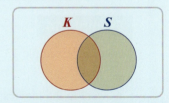

Let event S be 'a spade'. Then S = {ace of spades, king of spades, queen of spades, ... } and $n(S) = 13$.

The event 'a king or a spade' corresponds to the union of sets K and S. We have

$$\Pr(K) = \frac{4}{52}, \quad \Pr(S) = \frac{13}{52}, \quad \Pr(K \cap S) = \frac{1}{52}$$

and so, using the addition rule, we find

$$\Pr(K \cup S) = \frac{4}{52} + \frac{13}{52} - \frac{1}{52} = \frac{16}{52} = 0.3077 \quad \text{(correct to 4 decimal places)}$$

9D Combining events

Section summary

- Venn diagrams are often useful for solving problems involving sets.
- For any two events A and B, the **addition rule** can be applied:

  $\Pr(A \cup B) = \Pr(A) + \Pr(B) - \Pr(A \cap B)$

- If the two events A and B are mutually exclusive, then $\Pr(A \cap B) = 0$ and therefore $\Pr(A \cup B) = \Pr(A) + \Pr(B)$.

Exercise 9D

1 $\varepsilon = \{1, 2, 3, 4, 5, 6, 7, 8, 9, 10\}$, $A = \{1, 2, 3, 4\}$, $B = \{2, 4, 6\}$.

Show these sets on a Venn diagram and use your diagram to find:

- **a** $A \cup B$
- **b** $A \cap B$
- **c** A'
- **d** $A \cap B'$
- **e** $(A \cap B)'$
- **f** $(A \cup B)'$

2 $\varepsilon = \{1, 2, 3, 4, 5, 6, 7, 8, 9, 10, 11, 12\}$, $A = \{\text{multiples of four}\}$, $B = \{\text{even numbers}\}$.

Show these sets on a Venn diagram and use your diagram to find:

- **a** A'
- **b** B'
- **c** $A \cup B$
- **d** $(A \cup B)'$
- **e** $A' \cap B'$

3 $\varepsilon = \{\text{different letters of the word MATHEMATICS}\}$
$A = \{\text{different letters of the word ATTIC}\}$
$B = \{\text{different letters of the word TASTE}\}$

Show ε, A and B on a Venn diagram, entering all the elements. Hence list the sets:

- **a** A'
- **b** B'
- **c** $A \cup B$
- **d** $(A \cup B)'$
- **e** $A' \cup B'$
- **f** $A' \cap B'$

Example 13 **4** In a survey of 100 university students, a market research company found that 70 students owned smartphones, 45 owned cars and 35 owned smartphones and cars. Use a Venn diagram to help you answer the following questions:

- **a** How many students owned neither a car nor a smartphone?
- **b** How many students owned either a car or a smartphone, but not both?

Example 14 **5** Let $\varepsilon = \{1, 2, 3, 4, 5, 6\}$, where the outcomes are equally likely. If $A = \{2, 4, 6\}$ and $B = \{3\}$, find:

- **a** $\Pr(A \cup B)$
- **b** $\Pr(A \cap B)$
- **c** $\Pr(A')$
- **d** $\Pr(B')$

Example 15 **6** Let $\varepsilon = \{1, 2, 3, 4, 5, 6, 7, 8, 9, 10, 11, 12\}$, where the outcomes are equally likely. If A is the event 'an even number' and B is the event 'a multiple of three', find:

- **a** $\Pr(A)$
- **b** $\Pr(B)$
- **c** $\Pr(A \cap B)$ and hence $\Pr(A \cup B)$.

7 In Sam's class at school many of the students are on the swimming team. There are 18 students in the class. Seven of the students swim freestyle and four swim backstroke. Two students swim both freestyle and backstroke. Draw a Venn diagram and use it to find the probability that a student randomly chosen from Sam's class:
  a swims freestyle
  b swims backstroke
  c swims freestyle and backstroke
  d is on the swimming team.

8 Suppose that A is the set of factors of 12, and B is the set of prime numbers less than 10. If a number is chosen at random from the integers from 1 to 20, draw a Venn diagram and use it to find:
  a $\Pr(A)$ b $\Pr(B)$ c $\Pr(A \cap B)$ d $\Pr(A \cup B)$

9 Suppose $\Pr(A) = 0.5$, $\Pr(B) = 0.4$ and $\Pr(A \cap B) = 0.2$. Find $\Pr(A \cup B)$.

10 Suppose $\Pr(A) = 0.35$, $\Pr(B) = 0.24$ and $\Pr(A \cap B) = 0.12$. Find $\Pr(A \cup B)$.

11 Suppose $\Pr(A) = 0.28$, $\Pr(B) = 0.45$ and $A \subseteq B$. Find:
  a $\Pr(A \cap B)$ b $\Pr(A \cup B)$

12 Suppose $\Pr(A) = 0.58$, $\Pr(B) = 0.45$ and $B \subseteq A$. Find:
  a $\Pr(A \cap B)$ b $\Pr(A \cup B)$

13 Suppose $\Pr(A) = 0.3$, $\Pr(B) = 0.4$ and $A \cap B = \emptyset$. Find:
  a $\Pr(A \cap B)$ b $\Pr(A \cup B)$

14 Suppose $\Pr(A) = 0.08$, $\Pr(B) = 0.15$, and A and B are disjoint. Find:
  a $\Pr(A \cap B)$ b $\Pr(A \cup B)$

15 Suppose $\Pr(A) = 0.3$, $\Pr(B) = 0.4$ and $\Pr(A \cup B) = 0.5$. Find $\Pr(A \cap B)$.

16 Suppose $\Pr(A) = 0.24$, $\Pr(B) = 0.44$ and $\Pr(A \cup B) = 0.63$. Find $\Pr(A \cap B)$.

17 Suppose $\Pr(A) = 0.3$, $\Pr(B) = 0.4$ and $\Pr(A \cap B') = 0.2$. Find $\Pr(A \cup B')$.

18 Suppose that in a certain school the probability that a student plays soccer is 0.18, the probability that a student plays tennis is 0.25, and the probability that a student plays both soccer and tennis is 0.11. Find the probability that a student plays either or both of these sports.

19 Suppose that in a certain school the probability that a student studies Chinese is 0.22, the probability that a student studies French is 0.35, and the probability that a student studies both languages is 0.14.
  a Find the probability that a student in that school studies at least one of these languages.
  b Find the probability that a student in that school studies exactly one of these languages.

9E Probability tables

Skillsheet A **probability table** is an alternative to a Venn diagram when illustrating a probability problem diagrammatically. Consider the Venn diagram which illustrates two intersecting sets A and B.

From the Venn diagram it can be seen that the sample space is divided by the sets into four disjoint regions: $A \cap B$, $A \cap B'$, $A' \cap B$ and $A' \cap B'$. These regions may be represented in a table as follows. Such a table is sometimes referred to as a **Karnaugh map**.

	B	B'
A	$A \cap B$	$A \cap B'$
A'	$A' \cap B$	$A' \cap B'$

In a probability table, the entries give the probabilities of each of these events occurring.

		Column 1	Column 2
		B	B'
Row 1	A	$\Pr(A \cap B)$	$\Pr(A \cap B')$
Row 2	A'	$\Pr(A' \cap B)$	$\Pr(A' \cap B')$

Further, from the Venn diagram we can see that set A is the union of the part of set A that intersects with set B and the part of set A that does not intersect with set B. That is,

$$A = (A \cap B) \cup (A \cap B')$$

The sets $A \cap B$ and $A \cap B'$ are mutually exclusive, so

$$\Pr(A \cap B) + \Pr(A \cap B') = \Pr(A) \qquad \text{(row 1)}$$

and thus summing the probabilities in row 1 gives $\Pr(A)$. Similarly:

$$\Pr(A' \cap B) + \Pr(A' \cap B') = \Pr(A') \qquad \text{(row 2)}$$
$$\Pr(A \cap B) + \Pr(A' \cap B) = \Pr(B) \qquad \text{(column 1)}$$
$$\Pr(A \cap B') + \Pr(A' \cap B') = \Pr(B') \qquad \text{(column 2)}$$

Finally, since $\Pr(A) + \Pr(A') = 1$ and $\Pr(B) + \Pr(B') = 1$, the totals for both column 3 and row 3 are equal to 1. Thus, the completed table becomes:

		Column 1	Column 2	Column 3
		B	B'	
Row 1	A	$\Pr(A \cap B)$	$\Pr(A \cap B')$	$\Pr(A)$
Row 2	A'	$\Pr(A' \cap B)$	$\Pr(A' \cap B')$	$\Pr(A')$
Row 3		$\Pr(B)$	$\Pr(B')$	1

Chapter 9: Probability

These tables can be useful when solving problems involving probability, as shown in the next two examples.

Example 16

If A and B are events such that $\Pr(A) = 0.7$, $\Pr(A \cap B) = 0.4$ and $\Pr(A' \cap B) = 0.2$, find:

a $\Pr(A \cap B')$ **b** $\Pr(B)$ **c** $\Pr(A' \cap B')$ **d** $\Pr(A \cup B)$

Solution

		Column 1	Column 2	Column 3
		B	B'	
Row 1	A	$\Pr(A \cap B) = 0.4$	$\Pr(A \cap B')$	$\Pr(A) = 0.7$
Row 2	A'	$\Pr(A' \cap B) = 0.2$	$\Pr(A' \cap B')$	$\Pr(A')$
Row 3		$\Pr(B)$	$\Pr(B')$	1

The given information has been entered in the table in red.

a From row 1: $\Pr(A \cap B') = \Pr(A) - \Pr(A \cap B) = 0.7 - 0.4 = 0.3$

b From column 1: $\Pr(B) = \Pr(A \cap B) + \Pr(A' \cap B) = 0.4 + 0.2 = 0.6$

c From column 3: $\Pr(A') = 1 - \Pr(A) = 1 - 0.7 = 0.3$
From row 2: $\Pr(A' \cap B') = 0.3 - 0.2 = 0.1$

d Using the addition rule: $\Pr(A \cup B) = \Pr(A) + \Pr(B) - \Pr(A \cap B)$
$$= 0.7 + 0.6 - 0.4$$
$$= 0.9$$

The completed table is shown below.

		Column 1	Column 2	Column 3
		B	B'	
Row 1	A	$\Pr(A \cap B) = 0.4$	$\Pr(A \cap B') = 0.3$	$\Pr(A) = 0.7$
Row 2	A'	$\Pr(A' \cap B) = 0.2$	$\Pr(A' \cap B') = 0.1$	$\Pr(A') = 0.3$
Row 3		$\Pr(B) = 0.6$	$\Pr(B') = 0.4$	1

Example 17

Records indicate that, in Australia, 65% of secondary students participate in sport, and 71% of secondary students are Australian by birth. They also show that 53% of students are Australian by birth and participate in sport. Use this information to find:

a the probability that a student selected at random is not Australian by birth

b the probability that a student selected at random is not Australian by birth and does not participate in sport.

Solution

The information in the question may be entered into a table as shown. We use A to represent 'Australian by birth' and S to represent 'participates in sport'.

	S		S'	
A	0.53			0.71
A'				
	0.65			1

All the empty cells in the table may now be filled in by subtraction.

In column 1: $\Pr(A' \cap S) = 0.65 - 0.53 = 0.12$

In column 3: $\Pr(A') = 1 - 0.71 = 0.29$

In row 1: $\Pr(A \cap S') = 0.71 - 0.53 = 0.18$

In row 3: $\Pr(S') = 1 - 0.65 = 0.35$

In row 2: $\Pr(A' \cap S') = 0.29 - 0.12 = 0.17$

	S	S'	
A	0.53	0.18	0.71
A'	0.12	0.17	0.29
	0.65	0.35	1

a The probability that a student selected at random is not Australian by birth is given by $\Pr(A') = 0.29$.

b The probability that a student selected at random is not Australian by birth and does not participate in sport is given by $\Pr(A' \cap S') = 0.17$.

Exercise 9E

1 (Example 16) If A and B are events such that $\Pr(A) = 0.6$, $\Pr(A \cap B) = 0.4$ and $\Pr(A' \cap B) = 0.1$, find:
   a $\Pr(A \cap B')$ **b** $\Pr(B)$ **c** $\Pr(A' \cap B')$ **d** $\Pr(A \cup B)$

2 If A and B are events such that $\Pr(A') = 0.25$, $\Pr(A' \cap B) = 0.12$ and $\Pr(B) = 0.52$, find:
   a $\Pr(A)$ **b** $\Pr(A \cap B)$ **c** $\Pr(A \cup B)$ **d** $\Pr(B')$

3 If C and D are events such that $\Pr(C \cup D) = 0.85$, $\Pr(C) = 0.45$ and $\Pr(D') = 0.37$, find:
   a $\Pr(D)$ **b** $\Pr(C \cap D)$ **c** $\Pr(C \cap D')$ **d** $\Pr(C' \cup D')$

4 If E and F are events such that $\Pr(E \cup F) = 0.7$, $\Pr(E \cap F) = 0.15$ and $\Pr(E') = 0.55$, find:
   a $\Pr(E)$ **b** $\Pr(F)$ **c** $\Pr(E' \cap F)$ **d** $\Pr(E' \cup F)$

5 If A and B are events such that $\Pr(A) = 0.8$, $\Pr(B) = 0.7$ and $\Pr(A' \cap B') = 0.1$, find:
   a $\Pr(A \cup B)$ **b** $\Pr(A \cap B)$ **c** $\Pr(A' \cap B)$ **d** $\Pr(A \cup B')$

6 (Example 17) In a recent survey of senior citizens, it was found that 85% favoured giving greater powers of arrest to police, 60% favoured longer sentences for convicted persons, and 50% favoured both propositions.
   a What percentage favoured at least one of the two propositions?
   b What percentage favoured neither proposition?

7 Suppose a card is selected at random from an ordinary deck of 52 playing cards.
Let A = event a picture card is selected (i.e. jack, queen, king or ace)
C = event a heart is selected
   a List the outcomes corresponding to events A and C.
   b Determine the following probabilities and express your results in words:
   i $\Pr(A)$ **ii** $\Pr(C)$ **iii** $\Pr(A \cap C)$ **iv** $\Pr(A \cup C)$ **v** $\Pr(A \cup C')$

8 The following information applies to a particular class:
- The probability that a student's name begins with M and the student studies French is $\frac{1}{6}$.
- The probability that a student's name begins with M is $\frac{3}{10}$.
- The probability that a student does not study French is $\frac{7}{15}$.

Find the probability that a student chosen at random from this class:
   a studies French
   b has a name which does not begin with M
   c has a name which does begin with M, but does not study French
   d has a name which does not begin with M and does not study French.

9 A frame is chosen at random from a shop where picture frames are sold. It is known that in this shop:
- the probability that the frame is made of wood is 0.72
- the probability that the frame is freestanding is 0.65
- the probability that the frame is not made of wood and is not freestanding is 0.2.

Find the probability that the randomly chosen frame:
   a is made of wood or is freestanding   **b** is made of wood and is freestanding
   c is not made of wood   **d** is not made of wood but is freestanding.

10 A book is chosen at random from a bookshop. It is known that in this bookshop:
- the probability that the book is a hardback but not a novel is 0.05
- the probability that the book is not hardback but is a novel is 0.12
- the probability that the book is not a novel is 0.19.

Find the probability that the randomly chosen book is:
   a a novel   **b** a hardback novel
   c a hardback   **d** a novel or a hardback.

11 At a school camp consisting of 60 students, sailing was offered as an activity one morning, and bushwalking in the afternoon. Every student attended at least one activity. If 32 students went sailing and 40 students went bushwalking, find the probability that a student chosen at random:
   a undertook neither of these activities   **b** has sailed or bushwalked
   c has sailed and bushwalked   **d** has sailed but not bushwalked.

12 At a barbecue attended by 50 people, hamburgers and sausages were available. It was found that 35 hamburgers and 38 sausages were eaten, and six people were noted to have eaten neither a hamburger nor a sausage. If no person ate more than one hamburger or one sausage, find the probability that a person chosen at random ate:

- **a** a hamburger or a sausage
- **b** a hamburger and a sausage
- **c** only one serve of food
- **d** only a hamburger.

9F Conditional probability

> Skillsheet

We are often interested in calculating the probability of one event in the light of whether another event has or has not already occurred. For example, consider tossing a coin twice. What is the probability that the second toss shows a head, if we know that the first toss shows a head? Is the probability the same as if the first toss was a tail?

Suppose that we define event A as 'the second toss is a head', and event B as 'the first toss is a head'. Then the probability that the second toss shows a head, given that the first toss shows a head, is written $\Pr(A \mid B)$ and is an example of conditional probability.

> The probability of an event A occurring when it is known that some event B has occurred is called **conditional probability** and is written $\Pr(A \mid B)$. This is usually read as 'the probability of A given B', and can be thought of as a means of adjusting probability in the light of new information.

Example 18

Suppose we roll a fair die and define event A as 'rolling a six' and event B as 'rolling an even number'. What is the probability of rolling a six given the information that an even number was rolled?

Solution

The events A and B can be shown on a Venn diagram.

We know that event B has already occurred so we know that the outcome was 2, 4 or 6. Thus

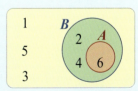

$\Pr(\text{six is rolled given an even number is rolled})$

$= \dfrac{\text{number of favourable outcomes}}{\text{total number of outcomes}}$

$= \dfrac{n(A)}{n(B)}$

$= \dfrac{1}{3}$

Example 19

In Stephen's class 12 students study Chinese, 20 study French, and 8 study both Chinese and French.

a Given that a student in his class studies Chinese (C), what is the probability that they also study French (F)?

b Given that a student in his class studies French, what is the probability that they also study Chinese?

Solution

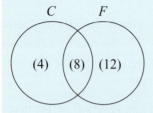

a $\Pr(F \mid C) = \dfrac{8}{12} = \dfrac{2}{3}$

b $\Pr(C \mid F) = \dfrac{8}{20} = \dfrac{2}{5}$

Explanation

Display the information in the question in a Venn diagram. The numbers in brackets indicate the number of elements in each region.

If we know that the student studies Chinese, the sample space is restricted to those 12 students. From the Venn diagram we can see that 8 of these students also study French.

If we know that the student studies French, the sample space is restricted to those 20 students. From the Venn diagram we can see that 8 of these students also study Chinese.

This example clearly demonstrates that, in general, $\Pr(A \mid B) \neq \Pr(B \mid A)$. So care needs to be taken when determining conditional probabilities.

Conditional probabilities can also be calculated from a table, as shown in Example 20.

Example 20

500 people were questioned and classified according to age and whether or not they regularly use social media. The results are shown in the table.

Do you regularly use social media?

	Age < 25	Age ≥ 25	Total
Yes	200	100	300
No	40	160	200
Total	240	260	500

One person is selected at random from these 500. Given that the selected person is less than 25 years of age, what is the probability that they regularly use social media?

Solution

$\Pr(\text{Yes} \mid \text{Age} < 25) = \dfrac{200}{240} = \dfrac{5}{6}$

Explanation

If we know the person is less than 25 years old, then the sample space is restricted to those 240 people. Of these, 200 regularly use social media.

Note that, in Example 20,

$$\Pr(\text{Yes} \cap \text{Age} < 25) = \frac{200}{500} \quad \text{and} \quad \Pr(\text{Age} < 25) = \frac{240}{500}$$

Hence we have

$$\frac{\Pr(\text{Yes} \cap \text{Age} < 25)}{\Pr(\text{Age} < 25)} = \frac{\frac{200}{500}}{\frac{240}{500}} = \frac{200}{240} = \frac{5}{6}$$

which is equal to the conditional probability $\Pr(\text{Yes} \mid \text{Age} < 25)$.

This illustrates a general principle which is always true.

The conditional probability of an event A, given that event B has already occurred, is given by

$$\Pr(A \mid B) = \frac{\Pr(A \cap B)}{\Pr(B)} \quad \text{if } \Pr(B) \neq 0$$

This formula may be rearranged to give the **multiplication rule of probability**:

$$\Pr(A \cap B) = \Pr(A \mid B) \times \Pr(B)$$

Example 21

Given that for two events A and B, $\Pr(A) = 0.7$, $\Pr(B) = 0.3$ and $\Pr(B \mid A) = 0.4$, find:

a $\Pr(A \cap B)$　　　　　　　　**b** $\Pr(A \mid B)$

Solution

a $\Pr(A \cap B) = \Pr(B \mid A) \times \Pr(A)$
$= 0.4 \times 0.7 = 0.28$

b $\Pr(A \mid B) = \dfrac{\Pr(A \cap B)}{\Pr(B)} = \dfrac{0.28}{0.3} = \dfrac{14}{15}$

Example 22

In a particular school 55% of the students are male and 45% are female. Of the male students 13% say mathematics is their favourite subject, while of the female students 18% prefer mathematics. Find the probability that:

a a student chosen at random prefers mathematics and is female

b a student chosen at random prefers mathematics and is male.

Solution

Let us use M to represent male, F for female, and P for prefers mathematics. Then

$$\Pr(M) = 0.55, \quad \Pr(F) = 0.45, \quad \Pr(P \mid M) = 0.13, \quad \Pr(P \mid F) = 0.18$$

We can use the multiplication rule to find the required probabilities:

a The event 'prefers mathematics and is female' is represented by $P \cap F$, with

$$\Pr(P \cap F) = \Pr(P \mid F) \times \Pr(F) = 0.18 \times 0.45 = 0.081$$

b The event 'prefers mathematics and is male' is represented by $P \cap M$, with

$$\Pr(P \cap M) = \Pr(P \mid M) \times \Pr(M) = 0.13 \times 0.55 = 0.0715$$

The law of total probability

As has already been seen, the tree diagram is an efficient way of listing a multi-stage sample space. If the probabilities associated with each stage are also added to the tree diagram, it becomes a very useful way of calculating the probability for each outcome. The probabilities at each stage are conditional probabilities that the particular path will be followed and the multiplication rule says that the probability of reaching the end of a given branch is the product of the probabilities associated with each segment of that branch.

Example 23

Using the information from Example 22, construct a tree diagram and use it to determine:

a the probability that a student selected is female and does not prefer mathematics
b the overall percentage of students who prefer mathematics.

Solution

The situation described can be represented by a tree diagram as follows:

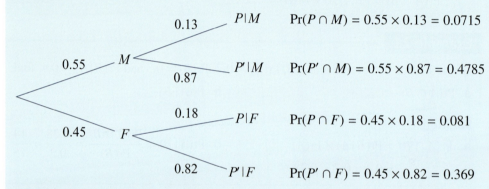

a To find the probability that a student is female and does not prefer mathematics we multiply along the appropriate branches thus:

$$\Pr(F \cap P') = \Pr(F) \times \Pr(P' | F) = 0.45 \times 0.82 = 0.369$$

b Now, to find the overall percentage of students who prefer mathematics we recall that:

$$P = (P \cap F) \cup (P \cap M)$$

Since $P \cap F$ and $P \cap M$ are mutually exclusive,

$$\Pr(P) = \Pr(P \cap F) + \Pr(P \cap M) = 0.081 + 0.0715 = 0.1525$$

Thus 15.25% of all students prefer mathematics.

The solution to part b of Example 23 is an application of a rule known as the law of total probability. This can be expressed in general terms as follows:

> The **law of total probability** states that, in the case of two events A and B,
> $$\Pr(A) = \Pr(A | B) \Pr(B) + \Pr(A | B') \Pr(B')$$

A further example of the use of the law of total probability is given in the following example.

Example 24

In a certain town, the probability that it rains on any Monday is 0.21. If it rains on Monday, then the probability that it rains on Tuesday is 0.83. If it does not rain on Monday, then the probability of rain on Tuesday is 0.3. For a given week, find the probability that it rains:

a on both Monday and Tuesday   **b** on Tuesday.

Solution

Let M represent the event 'rain on Monday' and T represent the event 'rain on Tuesday'.

The situation described in the question can be represented by a tree diagram. You can check that the probabilities are correct by seeing if they add to 1.

$$\begin{array}{ll} 0.83 \; T|M & \Pr(T \cap M) = 0.21 \times 0.83 = 0.1743 \\ 0.21 \; M & \\ 0.17 \; T'|M & \Pr(T' \cap M) = 0.21 \times 0.17 = 0.0357 \\ & \\ 0.3 \; T|M' & \Pr(T \cap M') = 0.79 \times 0.3 = 0.237 \\ 0.79 \; M' & \\ 0.7 \; T'|M' & \Pr(T' \cap M') = 0.79 \times 0.7 = 0.553 \end{array}$$

a The probability that it rains on both Monday and Tuesday is given by

$$\Pr(T \cap M) = 0.21 \times 0.83 = 0.1743$$

b The probability that it rains on Tuesday is given by

$$\Pr(T) = \Pr(T \cap M) + \Pr(T \cap M') = 0.1743 + 0.237 = 0.4113$$

Section summary

- The probability of an event A occurring when it is known that some event B has already occurred is called conditional probability and is written $\Pr(A \mid B)$.
- In general, the **conditional probability** of an event A, given that event B has already occurred, is given by

$$\Pr(A \mid B) = \frac{\Pr(A \cap B)}{\Pr(B)} \quad \text{if } \Pr(B) \neq 0$$

  This formula may be rearranged to give the **multiplication rule of probability**:

$$\Pr(A \cap B) = \Pr(A \mid B) \times \Pr(B)$$

- The **law of total probability** states that, in the case of two events A and B,

$$\Pr(A) = \Pr(A \mid B) \Pr(B) + \Pr(A \mid B') \Pr(B')$$

Exercise 9F

1 Suppose that a fair die is rolled, and event A is defined as 'rolling a six' and event B as 'rolling a number greater than 2'. Find $\Pr(A \mid B)$.

2 Suppose that a fair die is rolled, and event A is defined as 'rolling a three' and event B as 'rolling an odd number'. Draw a Venn diagram and use it to find $\Pr(A \mid B)$.

3 Suppose that a card is drawn from a pack of 52 cards, and event A is defined as 'selecting an ace' and event B as 'selecting a club'. Draw a Venn diagram and use it to find the probability that the card drawn is an ace, given that it is a club.

4 In Sam's class 12 students play violin, 12 play piano and 7 play both. Draw a Venn diagram and use it to find the probability that a randomly chosen student plays the violin given that they play the piano.

5 Two dice are rolled and the outcomes observed. Given that the dice both show the same number, what is the probability that it's a 'double six'?

6 In Annabelle's class 17 students own an iPhone, 7 own an iPad, and 4 own both.
   a What is the probability that a student owns an iPad, given that they own an iPhone?
   b What is the probability that a student owns an iPhone, given that they own an iPad?

7 100 people were questioned and classified according to sex and whether or not they think private individuals should be allowed to carry guns. The results are shown in the table.

Do you think private individuals should be allowed to carry guns?

	Male	Female	Total
Yes	35	30	65
No	25	10	35
Total	60	40	100

One person is selected at random from these 100. Given that the selected person is male, what is the probability that they think private individuals should be allowed to carry guns?

8 A group of 500 students were asked whether they would rather spend their recreational time playing sport or listening to music. The results, as well as the sex of the student, are given in the table.

	Male	Female	Total
Sport	225	150	375
Music	75	50	125
Total	300	200	500

One student is selected at random from these 500. Find:
   a the probability that the student prefers sport
   b the probability that the student prefers sport, given that they are male.

9 The following data was derived from accident records on a highway noted for its above-average accident rate.

Type of accident	Probable cause				Total
	Speed	Alcohol	Reckless driving	Other	
Fatal	42	61	22	12	137
Non-fatal	88	185	98	60	431
Total	130	246	120	72	568

Use the table to estimate:
a the probability that speed is the cause of the accident
b the probability that the accident is fatal
c the probability that the accident is fatal, given that speed is the cause
d the probability that the accident is fatal, given that alcohol is the cause.

Example 21 **10** Given that for two events A and B, $\Pr(A) = 0.6$, $\Pr(B) = 0.3$ and $\Pr(B|A) = 0.1$, find:
a $\Pr(A \cap B)$ **b** $\Pr(A|B)$

11 For events A and B:
a if $\Pr(A) = 0.7$ and $\Pr(A \cap B) = 0.4$, find $\Pr(B|A)$
b if $\Pr(A|B) = 0.6$ and $\Pr(B) = 0.5$, find $\Pr(A \cap B)$
c if $\Pr(A|B) = 0.44$ and $\Pr(A \cap B) = 0.3$, find $\Pr(B)$.

12 In a random experiment $\Pr(A) = 0.5$, $\Pr(B) = 0.4$ and $\Pr(A \cup B) = 0.7$. Find:
a $\Pr(A \cap B)$ **b** $\Pr(A|B)$ **c** $\Pr(B|A)$

13 In a random experiment $\Pr(A) = 0.6$, $\Pr(B) = 0.54$ and $\Pr(A \cap B') = 0.4$. Find:
a $\Pr(A \cap B)$ **b** $\Pr(A|B)$ **c** $\Pr(B|A)$

14 In a random experiment $\Pr(A) = 0.4$, $\Pr(A|B) = 0.6$ and $\Pr(B) = 0.5$. Find:
a $\Pr(A \cap B)$ **b** $\Pr(B|A)$

Example 22 **15** The current football fixture has the local team playing at home for 60% of its matches. When it plays at home, the team wins 80% of the time. When it plays away, the team wins only 40% of the time. What percentage of its games does the team play away and win?

16 The probability that a car will need an oil change is 0.15, the probability that it needs a new oil filter is 0.08, and the probability that both the oil and the filter need changing is 0.03. Given that the oil has to be changed, what is the probability that a new oil filter is also needed?

17 A card is selected from a pack of 52 playing cards. The card is replaced and a second card chosen. Find the probability that:
  a both cards are hearts
  b both cards are aces
  c the first card is red and the second is black
  d both cards are picture cards.

18 A card is selected from a pack of 52 playing cards and **not** replaced. Then a second card is chosen. Find the probability that:
  a both cards are hearts
  b both cards are aces
  c the first card is red and the second is black
  d both cards are picture cards.

19 A person is chosen at random from the employees of a large company. Let W be the event that the person chosen is a woman, and let A be the event that the person chosen is 25 years or older. Suppose the probability of selecting a woman is $\Pr(W) = 0.652$ and the probability of a woman being 25 years or older is $\Pr(A \mid W) = 0.354$. Find the probability that a randomly chosen employee is a woman aged 25 years or older.

20 In a class of 28 students there are 15 girls. Of the students in the class, six girls and eight boys play basketball. A student is chosen at random from the class. If G represents the event that a girl student is chosen and B represents the event that the student chosen plays basketball, find:
  a $\Pr(G)$ **b** $\Pr(B)$ **c** $\Pr(B')$ **d** $\Pr(B \mid G)$
  e $\Pr(G \mid B)$ **f** $\Pr(B \mid G')$ **g** $\Pr(B' \cap G')$ **h** $\Pr(B \cap G)$

21 In a recent survey it was found that 85% of the population eats red meat. Of those who eat red meat, 60% preferred lamb. A person is chosen at random from the population. If R represents the event that the person eats red meat and L represents the event that the person prefers lamb, find:
  a $\Pr(R)$ **b** $\Pr(L \mid R)$ **c** $\Pr(L \cap R)$ **d** $\Pr(L)$

22 In a senior college, 25% of the Year 11 students and 40% of the Year 12 students would prefer not to wear school uniform. This particular college has 320 Year 11 students and 280 Year 12 students. Find the probability that a randomly chosen student is in Year 11 and is in favour of wearing school uniform. What is the overall percentage of students who are in favour of wearing school uniform?

23 At a certain school it was found that 35% of the 500 boys and 40% of the 400 girls enjoyed bushwalking. One student from the school is chosen at random. Let G represent the event that the student is a girl, and B represent the event that the student enjoys bushwalking.

  a Find, correct to two decimal places:
   i $\Pr(G)$ **ii** $\Pr(B|G)$ **iii** $\Pr(B|G')$
   iv $\Pr(B \cap G)$ **v** $\Pr(B \cap G')$
  b Find $\Pr(B)$.
  c Hence find:
   i $\Pr(G|B)$ **ii** $\Pr(G|B')$

24 In a factory two machines produce a particular circuit board. The older machine produces 480 boards each day, of which an average of 12% are defective. The newer machine produces 620 boards each day, of which an average of 5% are defective. A board is chosen at random and checked. Let N represent the event that the board comes from the newer machine, and D represent the event that the board is defective.

  a Find, correct to two decimal places:
   i $\Pr(N)$ **ii** $\Pr(D|N)$
   iii $\Pr(D|N')$ **iv** $\Pr(D \cap N)$
   v $\Pr(D \cap N')$
  b Find $\Pr(D)$.
  c Hence find $\Pr(N|D)$, correct to two decimal places.

25 Jane has three bags of lollies. In bag 1 there are three mints and three toffees, in bag 2 there are three mints and two toffees, and in bag 3 there are two mints and one toffee. Jane selects a bag at random, and then selects a lolly at random. Find:
  a the probability she chooses a mint from bag 1
  b the probability she chooses a mint
  c the probability that Jane chose bag 1, given that she selects a mint.

26 Assuming a finite sample space, describe the relationship between events A and B if:
  a $\Pr(A|B) = 1$ **b** $\Pr(A|B) = 0$ **c** $\Pr(A|B) = \dfrac{\Pr(A)}{\Pr(B)}$

9G Independent events

Let us again consider the question of the probability that the second toss shows a head, given that the first toss shows a head, when tossing a coin twice. If we define A as the event 'the second toss is a head' and B as the event 'the first toss is a head', then what is $\Pr(A \mid B)$?

Using the definition of conditional probability:

$$\Pr(A \mid B) = \frac{\Pr(A \cap B)}{\Pr(B)}$$

$$= \frac{\Pr(\text{both tosses show heads})}{\Pr(\text{first toss shows a head})}$$

$$= \frac{\frac{1}{4}}{\frac{1}{2}} = \frac{1}{2}$$

That is, the probability of the second toss showing a head does not seem to be affected by the outcome of the first toss. This is an example of independent events.

> Two events A and B are **independent** if the occurrence of one event has no effect on the probability of the occurrence of the other, that is, if
>
> $$\Pr(A \mid B) = \Pr(A)$$

If $\Pr(B) \neq 0$, then the multiplication rule of probability gives

$$\Pr(A \mid B) = \frac{\Pr(A \cap B)}{\Pr(B)}$$

Thus, when events A and B are independent, we can equate the two expressions for $\Pr(A \mid B)$ to obtain

$$\Pr(A) = \frac{\Pr(A \cap B)}{\Pr(B)}$$

and therefore

$$\Pr(A \cap B) = \Pr(A) \times \Pr(B)$$

In fact, we can also use this final equation as a test for independence:

> Events A and B are independent if and only if
>
> $$\Pr(A \cap B) = \Pr(A) \times \Pr(B)$$

Notes:
- For events A and B with $\Pr(A) \neq 0$ and $\Pr(B) \neq 0$, the following three conditions are all equivalent conditions for the independence of A and B:
  - $\Pr(A \mid B) = \Pr(A)$
  - $\Pr(B \mid A) = \Pr(B)$
  - $\Pr(A \cap B) = \Pr(A) \times \Pr(B)$
- In the special case that $\Pr(A) = 0$ or $\Pr(B) = 0$, the condition $\Pr(A \cap B) = \Pr(A) \times \Pr(B)$ holds since both sides are zero, and so we say that A and B are independent.
- Sometimes this definition of independence is referred to as **pairwise independence**.

Example 25

500 people were questioned and classified according to age and whether or not they regularly use social media. The results are shown in the table.

Is the regular use of social media independent of the respondent's age?

Do you regularly use social media?

	Age < 25	Age ≥ 25	Total
Yes	200	100	300
No	40	160	200
Total	240	260	500

Solution

From the table:

$$\Pr(\text{Age} < 25 \cap \text{Yes}) = \frac{200}{500} = 0.4$$

$$\Pr(\text{Age} < 25) \times \Pr(\text{Yes}) = \frac{240}{500} \times \frac{300}{500} = 0.48 \times 0.6 = 0.288$$

Hence

$$\Pr(\text{Age} < 25 \cap \text{Yes}) \neq \Pr(\text{Age} < 25) \times \Pr(\text{Yes})$$

and therefore these events are not independent.

Example 26

An experiment consists of drawing a number at random from $\{1, 2, 3, 4, 5, 6, 7, 8\}$. Let $A = \{1, 2, 3, 4\}$, $B = \{1, 3, 5, 7\}$ and $C = \{4, 6, 8\}$.

a Are A and B independent?
b Are A and C independent?
c Are B and C independent?

Solution

$\Pr(A) = \frac{1}{2}$, $\Pr(B) = \frac{1}{2}$, $\Pr(C) = \frac{3}{8}$

a $\Pr(A \cap B) = \frac{1}{4}$

$\Pr(A) \times \Pr(B) = \frac{1}{2} \times \frac{1}{2} = \frac{1}{4}$

∴ $\Pr(A) \times \Pr(B) = \Pr(A \cap B)$

Thus A and B are independent

b $\Pr(A \cap C) = \frac{1}{8}$

$\Pr(A) \times \Pr(C) = \frac{1}{2} \times \frac{3}{8} = \frac{3}{16}$

∴ $\Pr(A) \times \Pr(C) \neq \Pr(A \cap C)$

Thus A and C are not independent

c $\Pr(B \cap C) = 0$

$\Pr(B) \times \Pr(C) = \frac{1}{2} \times \frac{3}{8} = \frac{3}{16}$

∴ $\Pr(B) \times \Pr(C) \neq \Pr(B \cap C)$

Thus B and C are not independent

Explanation

since $A \cap B = \{1, 3\}$

since these two probabilities are equal.

since $A \cap C = \{4\}$

since these two probabilities are not equal.

since $B \cap C = \emptyset$

since these two probabilities are not equal.

The concept of mathematical independence is sometimes confused with that of physical independence. If two events are physically independent, then they are also mathematically independent, but the converse is not necessarily true. The following example illustrates this.

Example 27

Suppose we roll a die twice and define the following events:

A = the first roll shows a 4

B = the second roll shows a 4

C = the sum of the numbers showing is at least 10

a Are A and B independent events?
b What about A and C?

Solution

a Since A and B are physically independent, they must also be mathematically independent, but we can also check this directly.
We have
$$\Pr(A) \times \Pr(B) = \frac{1}{6} \times \frac{1}{6} = \frac{1}{36}$$

If we write the sample space as ordered pairs, in which the first entry is the result of the first throw and the second is the result of the second throw, then
$$\varepsilon = \{(1, 1), (1, 2), (1, 3), \ldots, (6, 5), (6, 6)\}$$
and $n(\varepsilon) = 36$

The event $A \cap B$ corresponds to the outcome $(4, 4)$, and so $n(A \cap B) = 1$.
Thus
$$\Pr(A \cap B) = \frac{1}{36} = \Pr(A) \times \Pr(B)$$

and so A and B are independent.

b We have $C = \{(4, 6), (5, 5), (5, 6), (6, 4), (6, 5), (6, 6)\}$ and so $n(C) = 6$.
Thus
$$\Pr(A) \times \Pr(C) = \frac{1}{6} \times \frac{6}{36} = \frac{1}{36}$$

The event $A \cap C$ corresponds to the outcome $(4, 6)$, and so $n(A \cap C) = 1$.
Thus
$$\Pr(A \cap C) = \frac{1}{36} = \Pr(A) \times \Pr(C)$$

This means that A and C are also independent events.

Knowing that events are independent means that we can determine the probability of their intersection by multiplying together their individual probabilities. This is illustrated in the following example.

Example 28

Suppose that the probability that a family in a certain town owns a television set (T) is 0.75, and the probability that a family owns a station wagon (S) is 0.25. If these events are independent, find the following probabilities:

a A family chosen at random owns both a television set and a station wagon.
b A family chosen at random owns at least one of these items.

Solution

a The event 'owns both a television set and a station wagon' is represented by $T \cap S$, with

$$\Pr(T \cap S) = \Pr(T) \times \Pr(S) \qquad \text{(as } T \text{ and } S \text{ are independent)}$$
$$= 0.75 \times 0.25 = 0.1875$$

b The event 'owns at least one of these items' is represented by $T \cup S$, with

$$\Pr(T \cup S) = \Pr(T) + \Pr(S) - \Pr(T \cap S) \qquad \text{(from the addition rule)}$$
$$= 0.75 + 0.25 - 0.75 \times 0.25 \qquad \text{(as } T \text{ and } S \text{ are independent)}$$
$$= 0.8125$$

Confusion often arises between independent and mutually exclusive events. That two events A and B are mutually exclusive means that $A \cap B = \emptyset$ and hence that $\Pr(A \cap B) = 0$. Thus, if two events are independent, they cannot also be mutually exclusive, unless the probability of at least one of the events is zero.

Section summary

- The probability of an event A occurring when it is known that some event B has already occurred is called **conditional probability** and is written $\Pr(A \mid B)$, where

$$\Pr(A \mid B) = \frac{\Pr(A \cap B)}{\Pr(B)} \qquad \text{if } \Pr(B) \neq 0$$

- Two events A and B are **independent** if the occurrence of one event has no effect on the probability of the occurrence of the other, that is, if

$$\Pr(A \mid B) = \Pr(A)$$

- Events A and B are independent if and only if

$$\Pr(A \cap B) = \Pr(A) \times \Pr(B)$$

Exercise 9G

1 100 people were questioned and classified according to sex and whether or not they think private individuals should be allowed to carry guns. The results are shown in the table.

Do you think private individuals should be allowed to carry guns?

	Male	Female	Total
Yes	35	30	65
No	25	10	35
Total	60	40	100

Is support for private individuals carrying guns independent of sex?

2 A group of 500 students were asked whether they would rather spend their recreational time playing sport or listening to music. The results, as well as the sex of the student, are given in the following table.

	Male	Female	Total
Sport	225	150	375
Music	75	50	125
Total	300	200	500

Is preference for playing sport or listening to music independent of sex?

3 An analysis of traffic accidents in a certain city classified the accident as serious or minor, as well as whether the driver was speeding or not.

Type of accident	Speeding Yes	Speeding No	Total
Serious	42	61	103
Minor	88	185	273
Total	130	246	376

Is the seriousness of the accident independent of whether the driver was speeding or not?

4 An experiment consists of drawing a number at random from $\{1, 2, 3, \ldots, 12\}$. Let $A = \{1, 2, 3, 4, 5, 6\}$, $B = \{1, 3, 5, 7, 9, 11\}$ and $C = \{4, 6, 8, 9\}$.

  a Are A and B independent?   **b** Are A and C independent?

  c Are B and C independent?

5 A die is thrown and the number uppermost is recorded. Events A and B are defined as 'an even number' and 'a square number' respectively. Show that A and B are independent.

6 Two events A and B are such that $\Pr(A) = 0.3$, $\Pr(B) = 0.1$ and $\Pr(A \cap B) = 0.1$. Are A and B independent?

7 If A and B are independent events with $\Pr(A) = 0.6$ and $\Pr(B) = 0.7$, find:
   a $\Pr(A \mid B)$
   b $\Pr(A \cap B)$
   c $\Pr(A \cup B)$

8 If A and B are independent events with $\Pr(A) = 0.5$ and $\Pr(B) = 0.2$, find $\Pr(A \cup B)$.

Example 28

9 A man and a woman decide to marry. Assume that the probability that each will have a specific blood group is as follows:

Blood group	O	A	B	AB
Probability	0.5	0.35	0.1	0.05

If the blood group of the husband is independent of that of his wife, find the probability that:
   a the husband is group A
   b the husband is group A and his wife is group B
   c both are group A
   d the wife is group AB and her husband is group O.

10 The 165 subjects volunteering for a medical study are classified by sex and blood pressure (high (H), normal (N) and low (L)).

	H	N	L
M	88	22	10
F	11	22	12
Total	99	44	22

If a subject is selected at random, find:
   a $\Pr(N)$
   b $\Pr(F \cap H)$
   c $\Pr(F \cup H)$
   d $\Pr(F \mid L)$
   e $\Pr(L \mid F)$

Are F and L independent? Explain.

11 Events A and B are as shown in the Venn diagram. Show that A and B are independent.

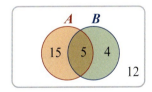

12 The probability that a married woman watches a certain television show is 0.4, and the probability that her husband watches the show is 0.5. The television viewing habits of a husband and wife are clearly not independent. In fact, the probability that a married woman watches the show, given that her husband does, is 0.7. Find the probability that:
   a both the husband and wife watch the show
   b the husband watches the show given that his wife watches it.

13 The 65 middle managers in a company are classified by age and income as follows:

Income	Age		
	30–39 (T)	40–49 (F)	50–69 (S)
Low (L)	13	4	1
Moderate (M)	8	10	3
High (H)	2	16	8
Total	23	30	12

A middle manager is selected at random from the company. Find:

a $\Pr(L)$ **b** $\Pr(S)$ **c** $\Pr(T)$ **d** $\Pr(M)$
e $\Pr(L \cap F)$ **f** $\Pr(T \cap M)$ **g** $\Pr(L|F)$ **h** $\Pr(T|M)$

Is income independent of age? Explain your answer.

14 A consumer research organisation has studied the services provided by the 150 TV repair persons in a certain city and their findings are summarised in the following table.

	Good service (G)	Poor service (G')
Factory trained (F)	48	16
Not factory trained (F')	24	62

a One of the TV repairers is randomly selected. Calculate the following probabilities:

  i $\Pr(G|F)$, the probability that a factory-trained repairer is one who gives good service

  ii $\Pr(G \cap F)$, the probability that the repairer is giving good service and is factory trained

  iii $\Pr(G \cup F)$, the probability that the repairer is giving good service or is factory trained or both

b Are events G and F independent?
c Are the events G and F mutually exclusive?

9H Solving probability problems using simulation

Simulation is a very powerful and widely used procedure which enables us to find approximate answers to difficult probability questions. It is a technique which imitates the operation of the real-world system being investigated. Some problems are not able to be solved directly and simulation allows a solution to be obtained where otherwise none would be possible. In this section some specific probability problems are looked at which may be solved by using simulation, a valuable and legitimate tool for the statistician.

Suppose, for example, we would like to know the probability that a family of five children will include at least four girls. There are ways of determining this probability exactly, which will be discussed in Chapter 11, but we don't know how to do this yet. What we can do, however, is estimate the probability by simulation.

Firstly, we need to make some assumptions so we can decide on a suitable model for the simulation. We will assume:
- There is a probability of 0.5 of each child being female.
- The sex of each child is independent of the sex of the other children. That is, the probability of a female child is always 0.5.

Since the probability of a female child is 0.5, a suitable simulation model would be tossing a fair coin. Let a head represent a female child and a tail a male child. A trial consists of tossing the coin five times to represent one complete family of five children, and the result of the trial is the number of heads obtained in the trial.

To estimate the required probability, several trials need to be conducted. How many trials are needed to estimate the probability? As we have already noted in Section 9B, the more repetitions of an experiment the better the estimate of the probability. Initially about 50 trials could be considered.

An example of the results that might be obtained from 10 trials is:

Trial number	Simulation results	Number of heads
1	T H H T T	2
2	H H H T H	4
3	H H H T H	4
4	H T T T H	2
5	H T H H H	4
6	H T T T H	2
7	T T H H H	3
8	H T H H T	3
9	T T T H H	2
10	H H T T T	2

Continuing in this way, the following results were obtained for 50 trials:

Number of heads	0	1	2	3	4	5
Number of times obtained	1	8	17	13	10	1

The results in the table can be used to estimate the required probability. Since at least four heads were obtained in 11 trials, estimate the probability of at least four female children as $\frac{11}{50}$ or 0.22. Of course, since this probability has been estimated experimentally, repeating the simulations would give a slightly different result, but we would expect to obtain approximately this value most of the time.

Simulation is also widely used to estimate the values of other quantities which are of interest in a probability problem. We may wish to know the average result, the largest result, the number of trials required to achieve a certain result, and so on. An example of this type of problem is given in Example 29.

Example 29

A pizza shop is giving away football cards with each pizza bought. There are six different cards available, and a fan decides to continue buying the pizzas until all six are obtained. How many pizzas will need to be bought, on average, to obtain the complete set of cards?

Solution

As there are more than two outcomes of interest, a coin is not a suitable simulation model, but a fair six-sided die could be used. Each of the six different cards is represented by one of the six sides of the die. Rolling the die and observing the outcome is equivalent to buying a pizza and noting which card was obtained. This simulation model is based on the following assumptions:

- The six cards all occur with equal frequency.
- The card obtained with one pizza is independent of the cards obtained with the other pizzas.

A trial would consist of rolling the die until all of the six numbers 1, 2, 3, 4, 5 and 6 have been observed, and the result of the trial is the number of rolls necessary to do this. The results of one trial are shown:

5 2 5 2 2 2 3 3 1 2 6 3 5 4

In this instance, 14 pizzas were bought before the whole set was obtained. Of course, we would not expect to buy 14 pizzas every time – this is just the result from one trial. To obtain an appropriate estimate, we would need to conduct several trials.

The following is an example of the results that might be obtained from 50 trials. In each case the number listed represents the number of pizzas that were bought to obtain a complete set of football cards:

14	8	12	11	16	8	8	11	15	26	14	20	11	13	35
23	19	14	10	10	20	9	10	14	29	13	7	15	15	22
9	10	14	16	14	17	12	10	24	13	19	27	31	11	9
16	21	22	8	9										

To estimate the number of pizzas that need to be bought, the average of the numbers obtained in these simulations is calculated. Thus we estimate that, in order to collect the complete set of cards, it would be necessary to buy approximately

$$\frac{14 + 8 + 12 + 11 + 16 + \cdots + 16 + 21 + 22 + 8 + 9}{50} \approx 15 \text{ pizzas}$$

In practice there are situations where coins and dice may not be useful. Other methods of simulation need to be adopted to deal with a wide range of situations. Suppose we wished to determine how many pizzas would need to be bought, on average, to obtain a complete set of eight souvenirs. This time we need to generate random numbers from 1 to 8 and a six-sided die would no longer be appropriate, but there are other methods that could be used.

We could construct a spinner with eight equal sections marked from 1 to 8, or we could mark eight balls from 1 to 8 and draw them (with replacement) from a bowl, or one of a number of other methods. Generally, when we wish to simulate we use random number generators on a calculator or computer.

> **Section summary**
>
> - Simulation is a simple and legitimate method for finding solutions to problems when an exact solution is difficult, or impossible, to find.
> - In order to use simulation to solve a problem, a clear statement of the problem and the underlying assumptions must be made.
> - A model must be selected to generate outcomes for a simulation. Possible choices for physical simulation models are coins, dice and spinners. Random number tables, calculators and computers may also be used.
> - Each trial should be defined and repeated several times (at least 50).
> - The results from all the trials should be recorded and summarised appropriately to provide an answer to a problem.

Exercise 9H

1. Use simulation to estimate the probability that a family with three children have all boys.

2. A teacher gives her class a test consisting of five 'true or false' questions. Use simulation to estimate the probability that a student who guesses the answer to every question gets at least three correct.

3. A teacher gives the class a test consisting of 10 multiple-choice questions, each with five alternatives. Use simulation to estimate the probability that a student who guesses the answer to every question gets at least five correct.

4. Use simulation to estimate the number of pizzas we would need to buy if the number of football cards described in Example 29 was extended to 10.

5. Eight players are entered into a tennis tournament.
   In round one, every player plays (four matches).
   In round two, the four winners from round one play (two matches).
   In round three, the two winners from round two play (one match).
   a. Suppose Shaun has a 50% chance of winning each match he plays. Use simulation to determine how many matches he will play, on average, in the tournament.
   b. Suppose he has a 70% chance of winning each match he plays. Use simulation to determine how many matches he will play, on average, in the tournament.

Chapter summary

- Probability is a numerical measure of the chance of a particular event occurring and may be determined experimentally or by symmetry.
- Whatever method is used to determine the probability, the following rules will hold:
  - $0 \leq \Pr(A) \leq 1$ for all events $A \subseteq \varepsilon$
  - $\Pr(\varepsilon) = 1$
  - $\Pr(\varnothing) = 0$
  - $\Pr(A') = 1 - \Pr(A)$, where A' is the complement of A
  - $\Pr(A \cup B) = \Pr(A) + \Pr(B) - \Pr(A \cap B)$, the **addition rule**.
- Probabilities associated with combined events are sometimes able to be calculated more easily from a probability table.
- Two events A and B are **mutually exclusive** if $A \cap B = \varnothing$.
- If events A and B are mutually exclusive, then $\Pr(A \cap B) = 0$ and $\Pr(A \cup B) = \Pr(A) + \Pr(B)$.
- The **conditional probability** of event A occurring, given that event B has already occurred, is
$$\Pr(A \mid B) = \frac{\Pr(A \cap B)}{\Pr(B)} \quad \text{if } \Pr(B) \neq 0$$
giving $\Pr(A \cap B) = \Pr(A \mid B) \times \Pr(B)$ (the **multiplication rule**)
- The probabilities associated with multi-stage experiments can be calculated by constructing an appropriate tree diagram and multiplying along the relevant branches (from the multiplication rule).
- The **law of total probability** states that, in the case of two events A and B,
$$\Pr(A) = \Pr(A \mid B)\Pr(B) + \Pr(A \mid B')\Pr(B')$$
- Two events A and B are **independent** if
$$\Pr(A \mid B) = \Pr(A)$$
so whether or not B has occurred has no effect on the probability of A occurring.
- Events A and B are independent if and only if $\Pr(A \cap B) = \Pr(A) \times \Pr(B)$.

Technology-free questions

1 Two six-sided dice are tossed. Find the probability that:
  a the sum of the values of the uppermost faces is 7
  b the sum is not 7.

2 The probability that a computer chip is operational is 0.993. What is the probability that it is not operational?

3 A whole number between 1 and 300 (inclusive) is chosen at random. Find the probability that the number is:
  a divisible by 3
  b divisible by 4
  c divisible by 3 or by 4.

4 A drawer contains 30 red socks and 20 blue socks.

  a If a sock is chosen at random, its colour noted, the sock replaced and a second sock withdrawn, what is the probability that both socks are red?

  b If replacement doesn't take place, what is the probability that both socks are red?

5 Box A contains five pieces of paper numbered 1, 3, 5, 7, 9.
Box B contains three pieces of paper numbered 1, 4, 9.
One piece of paper is removed at random from each box. Find the probability that the two numbers obtained have a sum that is divisible by 3.

6 A three-digit number is formed by arranging the digits 1, 5 and 6 in a random order.

  a List the sample space.

  b Find the probability of getting a number larger than 400.

  c What is the probability that an even number is obtained?

7 A letter is chosen at random from the word STATISTICIAN.

  a What is the probability that it is a vowel?

  b What is the probability that it is a T?

8 Ivan and Joe are chess players. In any game the probabilities of Ivan beating Joe, Joe beating Ivan or the game resulting in a draw are 0.6, 0.1 or 0.3 respectively. They play a series of three games. Calculate the probability that:

  a they win alternate games, with Ivan winning the first game

  b the three games are drawn   **c** exactly two of the games are drawn

  d Joe does not win a game.

9 A die with two red faces and four blue faces is thrown three times. Each face is equally likely to face upward. Find the probability of obtaining the following:

  a three red faces

  b a blue on the first, a red on the second and a blue on the third

  c exactly one red face   **d** at least two blue faces

10 If Pr(A) = 0.6 and Pr(B) = 0.5, can A and B be mutually exclusive? Why or why not?

11 Events A and B are such that Pr(A) = 0.6, Pr(B) = 0.5 and Pr($A' \cap B$) = 0.4. Construct a probability table and use it to find:

  a Pr($A \cap B'$)   **b** Pr($A' \cap B'$)   **c** Pr($A \cup B$)

12 In Minh's class 18 students study mathematics, 14 study music, and 7 study both mathematics and music.

  a Given that a student in his class studies mathematics, what is the probability that they also study music?

  b Given that a student in his class studies music, what is the probability that they also study mathematics?

Chapter 9: Probability

13 Given $\Pr(B) = \frac{1}{3}$, $\Pr(A|B) = \frac{2}{3}$ and $\Pr(A|B') = \frac{3}{7}$, determine:

  a $\Pr(A \cap B')$ **b** $\Pr(A)$ **c** $\Pr(B'|A)$

14 A group of executives is classified according to body weight and incidence of hypertension. The proportion of the various categories is as shown.

	Overweight	Normal weight	Underweight
Hypertensive	0.10	0.08	0.02
Not hypertensive	0.15	0.45	0.20

  a What is the probability that a person selected at random from this group will have hypertension?

  b A person, selected at random from this group, is found to be overweight. What is the probability that this person is also hypertensive?

15 Given an experiment such that $\Pr(A) = 0.3$, $\Pr(B) = 0.6$ and $\Pr(A \cap B) = 0.2$, find:

  a $\Pr(A \cup B)$ **b** $\Pr(A' \cap B')$ **c** $\Pr(A|B)$ **d** $\Pr(B|A)$

16 For a finite sample space, explain the implication of each of the following in terms of the relationship between events A and B:

  a $\Pr(A|B) = 1$ **b** $\Pr(A|B) = 0$ **c** $\Pr(A|B) = \Pr(A)$

Multiple-choice questions

1 If the probability of Chris scoring 50 or more marks in the exam is 0.7, then the probability he scores less than 50 marks is

  A 0   **B** 0.3   **C** 0.4   **D** 0.7   **E** 0.8

2 A spinner is coloured red, yellow, blue and green. When spun the probability that it lands on red is 0.1, yellow is 0.2 and blue is 0.4. What is the probability that it lands on green?

  A 0.1   **B** 0.2   **C** 0.3   **D** 0.4   **E** 0.5

3 Phillip is making a sign, and has cut the letters of the word THEATRETTE out of wood and placed them in his toolbox. If a letter is selected at random from the toolbox, then the probability that it is a T is

  A $\frac{2}{5}$ **B** $\frac{3}{10}$ **C** $\frac{1}{5}$ **D** $\frac{1}{6}$ **E** $\frac{3}{5}$

4 Of a group of 25 people in a restaurant, three chose a vegetarian meal, five chose fish, ten chose beef and the rest chose chicken for their main course. What is the probability that a randomly chosen diner chose chicken?

  A $\frac{3}{25}$ **B** $\frac{6}{25}$ **C** $\frac{7}{25}$ **D** $\frac{2}{5}$ **E** $\frac{7}{18}$

5 Suppose that a card is chosen at random from a well-shuffled deck of 52 playing cards. What is the probability that the card is a spade or a jack?

   A $\dfrac{1}{4}$ B $\dfrac{1}{13}$ C $\dfrac{17}{52}$ D $\dfrac{4}{13}$ E $\dfrac{9}{26}$

6 A square has side length of 4 metres. Inside the square is a circle of radius 1.5 metres. If a dart thrown at the square is equally likely to land at any point inside the square, then the probability that it will land outside the circle is closest to

   A 0.442   B 0.295   C 0.558   D 0.250   E 0.375

7 An experiment consists of tossing a coin and then rolling a fair six-sided die. What is the probability of observing a head and a 'six'?

   A $\dfrac{1}{2}$ B $\dfrac{1}{4}$ C $\dfrac{1}{35}$ D $\dfrac{1}{12}$ E $\dfrac{7}{12}$

8 If A and B are events such that $\Pr(A) = 0.35$, $\Pr(A \cap B) = 0.18$ and $\Pr(B) = 0.38$, then $\Pr(A \cup B)$ is equal to

   A 0.73   B 0.133   C 0.15   D 0.21   E 0.55

9 If A and B are events such that $\Pr(A) = 0.47$, $\Pr(B) = 0.28$ and $B \subseteq A$, then $\Pr(A \cup B)$ is equal to

   A 0.47   B 0.75   C 0.62   D 0.13   E 0

10 Suppose that 57% of the swimmers in a club are female (F), that 32% of the swimmers in the club swim butterfly (B), and that 11% of the swimmers in the club are female and swim butterfly. Which of the following probability tables correctly summarises this information?

A

	B	B'	
F	0.11	0.21	0.32
F'	0.46	0.22	0.68
	0.57	0.43	1

B

	B	B'	
F	0.11	0.46	0.57
F'	0.21	0.22	0.43
	0.32	0.68	1

C

	B	B'	
F	0.04	0.53	0.57
F'	0.28	0.15	0.43
	0.32	0.68	1

D

	B	B'	
F	0.18	0.39	0.57
F'	0.14	0.29	0.43
	0.32	0.68	1

E

	B	B'	
F	0.11	0.32	0.43
F'	0.21	0.36	0.57
	0.32	0.68	1

11 The following information applies to a particular class:
- The probability that a student studies mathematics is $\frac{2}{3}$.
- The probability that a student studies German is $\frac{3}{10}$.
- The probability that a student studies mathematics and does not study German is $\frac{7}{15}$.

The probability that a randomly chosen student does not study either mathematics or German is

A $\frac{4}{5}$ **B** $\frac{7}{30}$ **C** $\frac{7}{15}$ **D** $\frac{7}{10}$ **E** $\frac{1}{3}$

12 In Imogen's class 15 students play tennis, 14 play basketball and 7 play both. The probability that a randomly chosen student plays basketball, given that they play tennis, is

A $\frac{14}{15}$ **B** $\frac{7}{15}$ **C** $\frac{7}{29}$ **D** $\frac{15}{29}$ **E** $\frac{1}{2}$

13 The following data was derived from accident records on a highway noted for its above-average accident rate.

Type of accident	Probable cause				Total
	Speed	Alcohol	Reckless driving	Other	
Fatal	42	61	22	12	137
Non-fatal	88	185	98	60	431
Total	130	246	120	72	568

The probability that the accident is not fatal, given that reckless driving is the cause, is closest to

A 0.82   **B** 0.17   **C** 0.21   **D** 0.23   **E** 0.29

14 If for two events A and B, $\Pr(A) = \frac{3}{8}$, $\Pr(B) = \frac{4}{7}$ and $\Pr(A \cap B) = \frac{8}{21}$, then $\Pr(A \mid B)$ is equal to

A $\frac{3}{8}$ **B** $\frac{3}{14}$ **C** $\frac{63}{64}$ **D** $\frac{21}{32}$ **E** $\frac{2}{3}$

The following information relates to Questions 15 and 16.

The probability that Miller goes to the gym on Monday is 0.6. If he goes to the gym on Monday, then the probability that he will go again on Tuesday is 0.7. If he doesn't go to the gym on Monday, then the probability that Miller will go on Tuesday is only 0.4.

15 The probability that Miller goes to the gym on both Monday and Tuesday is

A 0.36   **B** 0.24   **C** 0.42   **D** 0.16   **E** 0.28

16 The probability that Miller goes to the gym on Tuesday is

A 0.58   **B** 0.42   **C** 0.16   **D** 0.84   **E** 0.32

17 If A and B are independent events such that $\Pr(A) = 0.35$ and $\Pr(B) = 0.46$, then $\Pr(A \cup B)$ is equal to

A 0.810   **B** 0.649   **C** 0.161

D 0.110   **E** cannot be determined

18 The primary cooling unit in a nuclear power plant has a reliability of 0.95. There is also a back-up cooling unit to substitute for the primary unit when it fails. The reliability of the back-up unit is 0.85. The cooling system of the plant is considered reliable if either one of the systems is working. Assuming that the two systems are independent, the reliability of the cooling system of the power plant is:

A 0.95   **B** 0.85   **C** 0.8075   **D** 0.9925   **E** 1.0

Extended-response questions

1 To have a stage production ready for opening night there are three tasks which must be done and, as the same people are involved in each task, these must be done in sequence. The following probabilities are estimated for the duration of the activities:

Task	6 days	7 days	8 days
Build scenery	0.3	0.3	0.4
Paint scenery	0.6	0.3	0.1
Print programs	0.4	0.4	0.2

a What is the probability that the building and painting of the scenery will together take exactly 15 days?

b What is the probability that all three tasks will together take exactly 22 days?

2 Two bowls each contain eight pieces of fruit. In bowl A there are five oranges and three apples; in bowl B there is one orange and seven apples.

a For each bowl, find the probability that two pieces of fruit chosen at random will both be apples, if the first piece of fruit is not replaced before the second piece of fruit is chosen.

b For each bowl, find the probability that two pieces of fruit chosen at random will both be apples, when the first piece of fruit is replaced before the second is chosen.

c One bowl is chosen at random and from it two pieces of fruit are chosen at random without replacement. If both pieces of fruit are apples, find the probability that bowl A was chosen.

d One bowl is chosen at random and from it two pieces of fruit are chosen at random, the first piece of fruit being replaced before the second is chosen. If both pieces of fruit are apples, find the probability that bowl A was chosen.

3 Rachel is a keen runner. She is supposed to attend running training five days per week. Rachel finds that if she runs one day, the probability that she will run again the next day is $\frac{4}{5}$, and if she does not run one day, the probability that she will not run the next day is $\frac{3}{4}$. Suppose that Rachel runs one day:

a What is the probability that she runs the next day?

b What is the probability that she runs the day after that?

c What is the probability that she runs exactly twice in the next three days?

4 Sixteen players are entered in a tennis tournament.

- In round one, every player plays (eight matches).
- In round two, the eight winners from round one play (four matches).
- In round three, the four winners from round two play (two matches).
- In round four, the two winners from round three play (one match).

Use simulation to estimate how many matches a player will play, on average:

a if the player has a 50% chance of winning each match

b if the player has a 70% chance of winning each match.

5 Consider a finals series of games in which the top four teams play off as follows:

Game 1   Team A vs Team B

Game 2   Team C vs Team D

Game 3   Winner of game 2 plays loser of game 1

Game 4   Winner of game 3 plays winner of game 1

The winner of game 4 is then the winner of the series.

a Assuming all four teams are equally likely to win any game, use simulation to model the series.

b Use the results of the simulation to estimate the probability that each of the four teams wins the series.

Chapter 10
Counting methods

Objectives

▶ To introduce **addition** and **multiplication** principles.
▶ To define and apply the concept of **arrangements** (or permutations).
▶ To define and apply the concept of **selections** (or combinations).
▶ To compute the number of combinations using ^nC_r.
▶ To apply counting methods to **probability**.
▶ To relate combinations to **Pascal's triangle** and the **binomial theorem**.

When determining the probability of an event occurring, we often need to know the number of outcomes contained in the event and in the sample space. To do this in Chapter 9, we listed the sample space using a tree diagram or a table, and counted the number of outcomes.

When dealing with more complicated probability problems, listing the sample space and the event becomes too difficult. There may be hundreds of outcomes for a particular experiment, and even if they were comparatively easy to list we would soon tire of the task. In this chapter we will look at ways of counting the number of outcomes for various experiments and this will enable us to deal with more complicated probability problems.

For example, suppose there are 25 students in a class. The number of different ways of choosing a group of 5 students from the class is 53 130, if it doesn't matter about the order of choice. The number of ways of choosing 5 students in order from the class is 6 375 600. If it takes you 1 minute to choose one ordered group of 5 students, then it would take you over 12 years to obtain every possible ordered group. It is evident that we need to develop some methods to be able to 'count' in these situations.

10A Addition and multiplication principles

Before we start to consider probabilities, we need to formalise some simple rules for determining the number of possible outcomes.

▶ The addition rule

Some people find the decision about what to wear when they get up in the morning to be very difficult, and the more clothes they own, the more complex the decision becomes! Let us consider the number of choices they might have by looking at some examples.

Example 1

Sandi can't decide whether to wear a windcheater or a jacket. She has four windcheaters and two jackets. How many choices does she have?

Solution

As Sandi is going to wear a windcheater *or* a jacket, she has a total of six choices from among these two items.

Example 2

Sandi's next choice is whether to wear jeans or a skirt. She has three pairs of jeans and four skirts. How many choices does she have?

Solution

Once again, as Sandi will wear jeans *or* a skirt, she has a total of seven choices from these two items.

> **Addition rule**
>
> In general, to choose between alternatives simply add up the number of choices available for each alternative.
>
> This rule is generally associated with the use of the word 'or' in the question.

Example 3

At the library Alan is having trouble deciding which book to borrow. He has a choice of three mystery novels, three biographies or two science fiction books. How many choices of book does he have?

Solution

As he is choosing between alternatives (mystery novels *or* biographies *or* science fiction), he has a total of $3 + 3 + 2 = 8$ choices.

▶ The multiplication rule

Sometimes the question arises of determining the number of possibilities when making successive choices, as in multi-stage experiments.

Example 4

When travelling from home to school James first takes a bus or walks to the main road, where he can then catch a train or a tram or another bus to his destination. How many ways does James have for travelling to school?

Solution

A tree diagram may help to answer this question.

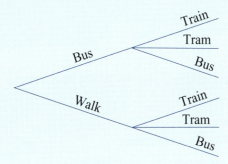

By counting the branches of the tree diagram, it is found that there are six choices.

This answer could also be found by noting that there are two choices for the first part of the journey and three choices for the second, and $2 \times 3 = 6$.

Multiplication rule

When sequential choices are involved, the total number of possibilities is found by multiplying the number of options at each successive stage.

For example, for two stages, if there are m choices for the first stage and n choices for the second stage, then there are $m \times n$ choices altogether.

This rule is generally associated with the word 'and'.

Example 5

Consider Sandi's situation again. She has six choices of windcheaters or jackets, and seven choices of jeans or skirts. How many choices does she have for a complete outfit?

Solution

As Sandi will wear either a windcheater or a jacket *and* jeans or a skirt, we cannot consider these to be alternative choices. We could draw a tree diagram to list the possibilities, but this would be arduous. Using the multiplication rule, however, we can quickly determine the number of choices to be $6 \times 7 = 42$.

Section summary

There are two simple rules which greatly assist in determining the number of possibilities in a sample space.

- **Addition rule** When choosing between alternatives, the total number of possibilities is found by adding the number of options available for each alternative. This rule is generally associated with the use of the word 'or' in the question.
- **Multiplication rule** When sequential choices are involved, the total number of possibilities is found by multiplying the number of options at each successive stage. For example, for two stages, if there are m choices for the first stage and n choices for the second stage, then there are $m \times n$ choices altogether.

Exercise 10A

Example 3

1 Find how many choices of book are possible if one book is to be selected from the following:
   - **a** eight novels, three dictionaries
   - **b** three mysteries, two dramas, seven science fiction
   - **c** twenty-two romances, fourteen mysteries, one autobiography
   - **d** ten novels, three biographies, twelve encyclopedias, four atlases

Example 4, 5

2 Find how many different meals are possible if three courses (one entree, one main course and one dessert) are to be selected from a menu that lists:
   - **a** three entrees, four main courses, five desserts
   - **b** ten entrees, ten main courses, five desserts
   - **c** five entrees, seven main courses, ten desserts
   - **d** eight entrees, eight main courses, eight desserts.

3 The menu in a restaurant lists four choices of entree, eight of main course and four of dessert. Find the number of choices of meal possible:
   - **a** if one of each of the three courses must be chosen
   - **b** if you can choose to omit the entree.

4 John cannot decide how to spend his evening. He can read a book, watch a video or go to the movies. If he can choose between three books, seven videos and ten movies, how many different choices does he have?

5 A student has to select a two-unit study for her course. She has to choose one unit in each semester. In semester one she has to choose one of two mathematics units, three language units and four science units. In semester two she has a choice of two history units, three geography units and two art units. How many choices does she have for the complete study?

6 Dominic is travelling from Melbourne to Brisbane. He could fly directly from Melbourne to Brisbane on one of three airlines, or he could fly from Melbourne to Sydney on one of four airlines and then travel from Sydney to Brisbane with one of five bus lines, or he could go on one of three bus lines directly from Melbourne to Brisbane. In how many ways could Dominic travel from Melbourne to Brisbane?

7 A particular new model of car is available in five choices of colour, three choices of transmission, four types of interior and two types of engine. Air conditioning is optional. How many different types of car are possible?

8 A company uses one letter followed by four digits for product codes. If any of the letters A–Z is allowed in the first position, and any of the digits 0–9 in the next four positions, how many different product codes are possible? (The letters and digits may be used more than once.)

9 In Victoria a licence plate generally consists of three letters followed by three numbers. If any of the letters A–Z is allowed in the first three positions, and any of the digits 0–9 in the second three positions, how many different licence plates are possible? (The letters and digits may be used more than once.)

10 Morse code consists of a succession of dots and dashes. The symbols formed by the code may consist of one, two, three or four dots or dashes. How many different symbols may be represented by this code?

10B Arrangements

Skillsheet The number of **arrangements** of a set of objects is the number of different ways these objects can be arranged in a distinct order. Consider, for example, arrangements of the letters A, B, C. The possibilities are ABC, ACB, BAC, BCA, CAB, CBA. Each of these is considered a different arrangement (even though they all use the same letters), and counting them we can see that there are six arrangements in total.

While it is quite simple to determine the number of arrangements by listing the possibilities when there are only three objects, this is not a good strategy when there are more than three. However, we can work out the number of arrangements by the following logic.

Consider that we have three boxes to be filled:

- We have 3 choices of letter for the first box (A, B or C).
- We only have 2 choices for the second box (because we have already used one letter).
- We only have 1 choice for the third box (because we have already used two letters).

| 3 | 2 | 1 |

Using the multiplication rule, we see that the total number of arrangements (or choices) is

$$3 \times 2 \times 1 = 6$$

Example 6

How many ways are there of arranging four different books on a shelf?

Solution

Consider the bookshelf as having four possible positions in which books can be placed:

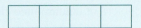

As we have four books:

- There are 4 choices of book to place in position 1.
- There are 3 choices of book to place in position 2.
- There are 2 choices of book to place in position 3.
- There is 1 choice of book to place in position 4.

| 4 | 3 | 2 | 1 |

Using the multiplication rule, we know that the total number of choices will be the product of these individual choices:

Number of arrangements of four books in a row is $4 \times 3 \times 2 \times 1 = 24$.

In general, if n objects are arranged in a row, then there are n choices for the first position, $n - 1$ choices for the second position, $n - 2$ choices for the third position, and so on, until 1 is reached.

Thus, the number of ways of arranging n objects in a row is

$$n \times (n - 1) \times (n - 2) \times (n - 3) \times \cdots \times 2 \times 1$$

Example 7

A photo is to be taken of a group of 12 students. How many ways are there of arranging the group if they all sit in a row?

Solution

As there are 12 students, the number of arrangements is

$$12 \times 11 \times 10 \times 9 \times 8 \times 7 \times 6 \times 5 \times 4 \times 3 \times 2 \times 1 = 479\,001\,600$$

which is rather a large number of choices!

Continuing to write out the expression $n \times (n - 1) \times (n - 2) \times \cdots \times 2 \times 1$ can be rather cumbersome. So for convenience this is written as $n!$, which is read as 'n factorial'.

The notation $n!$ (read as 'n factorial') is an abbreviation for the product of all the integers from n down to 1:

$$n! = n \times (n-1) \times (n-2) \times (n-3) \times \cdots \times 2 \times 1$$

A CAS calculator can be used to evaluate $n!$. See the appropriate appendix in the Interactive Textbook for directions.

Sometimes we wish to arrange objects, but not use all of them every time. Suppose, for example, we wanted to determine how many arrangements there are of the letters A, B, C when taken in groups of two. The possibilities are AB, BA, AC, CA, BC, CB; six in total.

Once again, we can use our 'box' approach to work out the number of arrangements without listing them. This time we have two boxes to be filled:

- We have 3 choices of letter for the first box (A, B or C).
- We have 2 choices for the second box (because we have already used one letter).

Using the multiplication rule again, we see that the total number of arrangements (or choices) is $3 \times 2 = 6$.

Example 8

A painter is to paint the five circles of the Olympic flag. He cannot remember the colours to use for any of the circles, but he knows they should all be different. He has eight colours of paint available. In how many ways can he paint the circles on the flag?

Solution

We represent the painter's choices with five boxes:

- For the first box (paint colour) there are 8 choices.
- For the second box (paint colour) there are 7 choices.
- For the third box (paint colour) there are 6 choices.
- For the fourth box (paint colour) there are 5 choices.
- For the fifth box (paint colour) there are 4 choices.

Thus the total number of arrangements possible is $8 \times 7 \times 6 \times 5 \times 4 = 6720$.

Could the factorial notation be used to express the answer to Example 8? In that example, the number of arrangements of eight objects in groups of five was to determined to be

$$8 \times 7 \times 6 \times 5 \times 4$$

Multiplying this answer by 1, we can write

$$8 \times 7 \times 6 \times 5 \times 4 = (8 \times 7 \times 6 \times 5 \times 4) \times \frac{3 \times 2 \times 1}{3 \times 2 \times 1} = \frac{8!}{3!}$$

Thus, the number of ways of choosing and arranging five objects from eight objects can be written as

$$\frac{8!}{3!} \quad \text{or} \quad \frac{8!}{(8-5)!}$$

> In general, the number of arrangements of n objects in groups of size r is given by
>
> $$\frac{n!}{(n-r)!} = n \times (n-1) \times (n-2) \times \cdots \times (n-r+1)$$

Arrangements are also called **permutations** in mathematics, and so this expression for the number of arrangements of n objects in groups of size r is often denoted by the symbol ^nP_r.

Example 9

Find the number of different four-digit numbers that can be formed from the digits 1, 2, 3, 4, 5, 6, 7, 8, 9, if each digit:

a can only be used once **b** can be used more than once

Solution

a As we are arranging nine objects (n) in groups of four (r):

$$\frac{9!}{(9-4)!} = \frac{9!}{5!} = 9 \times 8 \times 7 \times 6 = 3024$$

b There are nine choices for each of the four positions, so the total number of choices is
$9 \times 9 \times 9 \times 9 = 9^4 = 6561.$

Definition of 0!

For us to be able to use our formula for the number of arrangements in all situations, we need to define a value for 0!. Consider the number of arrangements of n objects in groups of size n. From first principles, we have found that this is equal to $n!$. Using our formula for the number of arrangements of n objects in groups of size n gives us the answer

$$^nP_n = \frac{n!}{(n-n)!} = \frac{n!}{0!}$$

For this to make sense, we need to define

$$0! = 1$$

Arrangements with restrictions

If a more complicated arrangement is required, then it is usually best to deal with the restriction first, as shown in the following example.

Example 10

How many different even four-digit numbers can be formed from the digits 1, 2, 3, 4, 5, 6, 7, 8, if each digit may be used only once?

Solution

We have four boxes to be filled. Dealing with the restriction first, there are 4 choices for the final (fourth) box:

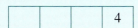

Having now selected the last digit, we have seven digits remaining:

- 7 choices for the first box
- 6 choices for the second box
- 5 choices for the third box.

| 7 | 6 | 5 | 4 |

Multiplying gives $7 \times 6 \times 5 \times 4 = 840$.

Explanation

The restriction is that the number must be even, so it ends in 2, 4, 6 or 8.

The number of choices is reduced by one each time we use a digit.

Section summary

- An **arrangement** is a grouping of objects, such that the order of the objects is important. That is, the arrangements ABC and CBA are different.
- The number of ways of arranging n objects in a row is
$$n! = n \times (n-1) \times (n-2) \times (n-3) \times \cdots \times 2 \times 1$$
- The number of ways of arranging n objects in groups of size r is
$$^nP_r = \frac{n!}{(n-r)!} = n \times (n-1) \times (n-2) \times \cdots \times (n-r+1)$$

Exercise 10B

1 Evaluate:

  a 3!   b 5!   c 7!   d 2!   e 0!   f 1!

2 Evaluate:

  a $\dfrac{5!}{3!}$ b $\dfrac{9!}{7!}$ c $\dfrac{3!}{0!}$ d $\dfrac{8!}{6!}$ e $\dfrac{5!}{0!}$ f $\dfrac{10!}{7!}$

Example 6   **3**   In how many ways can five books be arranged in a row on a shelf?

Example 7   **4**   In how many ways can seven students be seated on a row of seven chairs?

5   In how many ways can four pictures be hung in a row on a wall?

6   In how many ways can six cups be hung on six hooks?

Example 8   **7**   In how many ways can three pictures be hung along a wall if there are ten pictures available?

8   If there are eight swimmers in the final of the 1500 m freestyle event, in how many ways can the first three places be filled?

9   Find the number of ways in which the letters of the word TROUBLE can be arranged:
   a   if they are all used   **b**   if they are used three at a time.

10   Find the number of ways in which the letters of the word PANIC can be arranged:
   a   if they are all used   **b**   if they are used four at a time.

Example 9   **11**   Find the number of four-letter code words that can be made from the letters of the word COMPLEX:
   a   if no letter can be used more than once   **b**   if the letters can be re-used.

12   Find how many code words of three or four letters can be made from the letters of the word NUMBER:
   a   if no letter can be used more than once   **b**   if the letters can be re-used.

Example 10   **13**   If no digit can be used more than once, find how many numbers that can be formed from the digits 3, 4, 5, 6, 7 are:
   a   three-digit numbers   **b**   three-digit numbers and even
   c   greater than 700.

14   If no digit can be used more than once, find how many numbers that can be formed from the digits 3, 4, 5, 6, 7, 8 are:
   a   two- or three-digit numbers   **b**   six-digit numbers and even
   c   greater than 7000.

15   Four boys and two girls sit in a line on stools in front of a counter. Find the number of ways in which they can arrange themselves:
   a   if there are no restrictions   **b**   if the two girls wish to be at the ends.

10C Selections

In the previous section, methods for counting the number of ways in which objects can be chosen and then arranged were discussed. Sometimes the interest is solely in the number of different groups of objects that can be selected. That is, the order is unimportant.

> Skillsheet

Consider again the letters A, B, C when taken in groups of two. We saw that there are six arrangements: AB, BA, AC, CA, BC, CB. However, there are only three distinct selections: $\{A, B\}, \{A, C\}, \{B, C\}$.

Example 11

Four flavours of ice-cream – vanilla, chocolate, strawberry and caramel – are available at the school canteen. How many different double-scoop selections are possible if two different flavours must be used?

Solution

The possibilities are:
- vanilla and chocolate
- vanilla and strawberry
- vanilla and caramel
- chocolate and strawberry
- chocolate and caramel
- strawberry and caramel

giving a total of six different selections.

In this example, the selection 'vanilla and chocolate' is considered to be the same as 'chocolate and vanilla', and so is counted only once. Such choices without regard to order are called **selections** or **combinations**. The notation ^nC_r is used to represent the number of different ways in which groups of size r can be chosen from a total of n objects when order is unimportant.

When the total group size n is not large, the combinations can be listed. But obviously a more efficient method is preferable. Consider again Example 8 concerning the colours on the Olympic flag. Suppose that first the five colours to be used are chosen, and then they are arranged on the flag. This is shown as:

Choose the colours	Arrange them	Possible arrangements
$^8C_5$	$\times\, 5!$	$= \dfrac{8!}{3!}$

So, since $^8C_5 \times 5! = \dfrac{8!}{3!}$, we can find an expression for $^8C_5$ by dividing both sides by $5!$.

$$^8C_5 = \dfrac{8!}{3!\,5!}$$

Note that the two figures on the bottom line (3 and 5) add to 8.

In general, the number of combinations of n objects in groups of size r is

$$^nC_r = \frac{^nP_r}{r!} = \frac{n \times (n-1) \times (n-2) \times \cdots \times (n-r+1)}{r!} = \frac{n!}{r!\,(n-r)!}$$

A commonly used alternative notation for ^nC_r is $\binom{n}{r}$.

A CAS calculator can be used to determine values of ^nC_r. See the appropriate appendix in the Interactive Textbook for directions.

Example 12

Consider the situation from Example 11 again: If four flavours of ice-cream are available, how many double-scoop selections are possible if two different flavours must be used?

Solution
The number of combinations of four flavours in groups of size two is

$$^4C_2 = \frac{4!}{2!2!} = \frac{4 \times 3 \times 2 \times 1}{2 \times 1 \times 2 \times 1} = 6$$

This is the same as the answer we found before by listing the combinations.

Once again, not all combination problems are so straightforward, as shown by the following example.

Example 13

A team of three boys and three girls is to be chosen from a group of eight boys and five girls. How many different teams are possible?

Solution
Three boys can be chosen from eight in $^8C_3$ ways, and three girls from five in $^5C_3$ ways. Since we are choosing boys and girls, the total number of possible teams is

$$^8C_3 \times {^5C_3} = 56 \times 10 = 560$$

▶ Selections of any size

The following result is useful when asked to count all the combinations of any size from a group of n objects.

For n objects,

$$^nC_0 + {^nC_1} + {^nC_2} + \cdots + {^nC_{n-1}} + {^nC_n} = 2^n$$

We can see why it is true using the following argument for three objects.

There are three different books A, B and C, and David can choose whichever ones he likes (including choosing none of them). How many ways can this choice be made?

Let $S = \{A, B, C\}$. The subsets are

$$\emptyset, \quad \{A\}, \quad \{B\}, \quad \{C\}, \quad \{A, B\}, \quad \{A, C\}, \quad \{B, C\}, \quad \{A, B, C\}$$

So there are eight choices.

We can use two different methods to count these choices. First we focus on how many books David chooses:

0 He can choose no books in $^3C_0 = 1$ way. (This corresponds to $\emptyset$.)
1 He can choose one book in $^3C_1 = 3$ ways. (This corresponds to $\{A\}, \{B\}, \{C\}$.)
2 He can choose two books in $^3C_2 = 3$ ways. (This corresponds to $\{A, B\}, \{A, C\}, \{B, C\}$.)
3 He can choose three books in $^3C_3 = 1$ way. (This corresponds to $\{A, B, C\}$.)

By the addition rule, the total number of choices is

$$^3C_0 + {}^3C_1 + {}^3C_2 + {}^3C_3$$

Now, instead, we focus on each book one at a time:

A Book A can be chosen or not (2 ways).
B Book B can be chosen or not (2 ways).
C Book C can be chosen or not (2 ways).

By the multiplication rule, there are a total of $2 \times 2 \times 2 = 2^3$ choices. This gives

$$^3C_0 + {}^3C_1 + {}^3C_2 + {}^3C_3 = 2^3$$

This argument can easily be extended to prove the result for n objects.

Example 14

Nick is making an invitation list for his party, and has seven friends to choose from. If he may choose to invite any number of friends (from one to all seven), how many possible party lists does he have? (Assume he will invite at least one person to his party.)

Solution

Nick may invite one person to the party, and he has $^7C_1 = 7$ ways of doing this. If he invites two people to the party, he has $^7C_2 = 21$ ways of doing this.

Continuing in this way, we can see that Nick's total number of choices is

$$^7C_1 + {}^7C_2 + {}^7C_3 + {}^7C_4 + {}^7C_5 + {}^7C_6 + {}^7C_7$$

Since we know that

$$^7C_0 + {}^7C_1 + {}^7C_2 + {}^7C_3 + {}^7C_4 + {}^7C_5 + {}^7C_6 + {}^7C_7 = 2^7$$

the required answer is

$$\begin{aligned} 2^7 - {}^7C_0 &= 2^7 - 1 \\ &= 128 - 1 \\ &= 127 \end{aligned}$$

> **Section summary**
> - A **selection** (or **combination**) is a grouping of objects, such that the order of the objects is not important. That is, the selections ABC and CBA are the same.
> - Knowing the number of distinct selection of objects, when taking groups of a particular size, may enable us to determine the number of elements in the sample space without having to list them.
> - In general, the number of combinations of n objects in groups of size r is
> $$^nC_r = \frac{^nP_r}{r!} = \frac{n \times (n-1) \times (n-2) \times \cdots \times (n-r+1)}{r!} = \frac{n!}{r!(n-r)!}$$
> - A commonly used alternative notation for ^nC_r is $\binom{n}{r}$.
> - For n objects, $^nC_0 + {}^nC_1 + {}^nC_2 + \cdots + {}^nC_{n-1} + {}^nC_n = 2^n$.

Exercise 10C

1 For each of the following examples, determine the number of selections possible by listing the possibilities:
  a An ice-cream with two different scoops is selected from a choice of vanilla, chocolate and strawberry.
  b Two students from the group of Jaime, Georgia and Wey are chosen to represent the class in debating.
  c Two students from the group of Thomas, William, Jackson and Phillip are chosen for the tennis team.
  d Three scarves are chosen from a blue scarf, a green scarf, a red scarf and a white scarf.

2 Evaluate:
  a $^5C_3$ **b** $^5C_2$ **c** $^7C_4$ **d** $^7C_3$
  Compare your answers for parts a and b, and for parts c and d.

3 Evaluate:
  a $^{20}C_{18}$ **b** $^{100}C_{99}$ **c** $^{100}C_2$ **d** $^{250}C_{248}$

4 Evaluate:
  a $\binom{6}{3}$ **b** $\binom{7}{1}$ **c** $\binom{8}{2}$ **d** $\binom{50}{48}$

5 How many netball teams of seven can be chosen from 13 players?

6 An ice-cream parlour has 25 different flavours of ice-cream available. How many different three-scoop ice-cream sundaes are available if three different flavours are to be used and the order of the scoops does not matter?

7 How many different hands of seven cards can be dealt from a normal pack of 52 cards?

8 In Tattslotto six numbers are selected from 45. How many different possible selections are there? (Do not attempt to consider supplementary numbers.)

Example 13

9 A student has the choice of three mathematics subjects and four science subjects. In how many ways can they choose to study one mathematics and two science subjects?

10 A survey is to be conducted, and eight people are to be chosen from a group of 30.
   a In how many different ways could the eight be chosen?
   b If the group contains 10 men and 20 women, how many groups containing exactly two men are possible?

11 From a standard 52-card deck, how many 7-card hands have 5 spades and 2 hearts?

12 In how many ways can a committee of five be selected from eight women and four men:
   a without restriction   **b** if there must be exactly three women on the committee?

13 Six females and five males are interviewed for five positions. If all are acceptable for any position, in how many ways could the following combinations be selected?
   a three males and two females   **b** four females and one male
   c five females   **d** five people regardless of sex
   e at least four females

14 The selectors of a sporting team need to choose 10 athletes from the 15 track and 12 field athletes who have qualified to compete.
   a How many groups are possible?
   b How many groups would contain track athletes only?
   c How many groups would contain field athletes only?
   d How many groups would contain half track and half field athletes?

15 A student representative committee of five is to be chosen from four male and six female students. How many committees could be selected which contain more female than male students?

Example 14

16 Joanne is offered a selection of five different sweets. She can choose to pass or to select any number of them. In total how many choices does she have?

17 Eight people have auditioned for roles in a play. The director can choose none, or any number of them for the production. In how many ways can selections be made from these eight people, any number at a time?

18 How many colours can be obtained by mixing a set volume of red, blue, green, orange and white paints if any number of paints can be used at a time?

19 How many varieties of fruit salad, using at least two fruits, can be obtained from apples, oranges, pears, passionfruit, kiwifruit and nectarines, taken any number at a time?

20 In how many ways can a group of six people be divided into:
   a two equal groups
   b two unequal groups, if there must be at least one person in each group?

10D Applications to probability

> Skillsheet

As discussed in Chapter 9, for a sample space with equally likely outcomes, the probability of an event occurring may be determined by dividing the number of outcomes in the event by the total number of possible outcomes. Establishing the number of outcomes in the event and the total number of outcomes is often achieved by using permutations and combinations.

Example 15

Four-letter 'words' are to be made by arranging letters of the word SPECIAL. What is the probability that the 'word' will start with a vowel?

Solution

There are 7 letters to be arranged in groups of 4. So the total number of possible arrangements is $7 \times 6 \times 5 \times 4 = 840$.

Now consider words which start with a vowel. Since there are three vowels, we have 3 choices for the first letter. Having done this, we have six letters remaining which are to be placed in the three remaining positions, and this can be done in $6 \times 5 \times 4 = 120$ ways.

Thus the number of arrangements which start with a vowel is

$$3 \times 6 \times 5 \times 4 = 360$$

Hence, the probability of the word starting with a vowel is

$$\frac{\text{number of outcomes in the event}}{\text{total number of outcomes}} = \frac{360}{840} = \frac{3}{7}$$

Example 16

Three students are to be chosen to represent the class in a debate. If the class consists of six boys and four girls, what is the probability that the team will contain:

a exactly one girl **b** at least two girls?

Solution

Since there is a total of 10 students, the number of possible teams is $^{10}C_3 = 120$.

a One girl can be chosen for the team in $^4C_1 = 4$ different ways. Having placed one girl, the other two places must be filled by boys, and this can be done in $^6C_2 = 15$ different ways. Thus the total number of teams containing one girl and two boys is $4 \times 15 = 60$, and the probability that the team contains exactly one girl is $\frac{60}{120} = 0.5$.

b If the team is to contain at least two girls, then it may contain two *or* three girls. The number of teams containing:

- exactly two girls is $^6C_1 \times {}^4C_2 = 36$
- exactly three girls is $^6C_0 \times {}^4C_3 = 4$

Thus the total number of teams containing at least two girls is 40, and the probability of this is $\frac{40}{120} = \frac{1}{3}$.

10D Applications to probability

Section summary

Using our knowledge of arrangements and selections, we can calculate probabilities for sample spaces with equally like outcomes:

- First determine the total number of possible outcomes.
- Then determine the number of outcomes in the event of interest.
- The required probability is equal to

$$\frac{\text{number of outcomes in the event}}{\text{total number of oucomes}}$$

Exercise 10D

1 A four-digit number (with no repetitions) is to be formed from the set of digits $\{1, 2, 3, 4, 5, 6\}$. Find the probability that the number:

  a is even **b** is odd.

Example 15

2 Three-letter 'words' are to be made by arranging the letters of the word COMPUTER. What is the probability that the 'word' will start with a vowel?

3 Three letters are chosen at random from the word HEART and arranged in a row. Find the probability that:

  a the letter H is first **b** the letter H is chosen **c** both vowels are chosen.

4 Three men and three women are to be randomly seated in a row. Find the probability that both the end places will be filled by women.

Example 16

5 A netball team of seven players is to be chosen from six men and seven women. Find the probability that the selected team contains more men than women.

6 Bill is making a sandwich. He may choose any combination of the following: lettuce, tomato, carrot, cheese, cucumber, beetroot, onion, ham. Find the probability that:

  a the sandwich contains ham
  b the sandwich contains three ingredients
  c the sandwich contains at least three ingredients.

7 A bag contains five white, six red and seven blue balls. If three balls are selected at random, without replacement, find the probability they are:

  a all red **b** all different colours.

8 Susie chooses four pieces of bubble gum from a jar containing five red, two blue and three green pieces of bubble gum. Calculate the probability that Susie selects:

  a no green bubble gum
  b at least one green bubble gum
  c at least one green bubble gum and at least one red bubble gum
  d at least one red bubble gum, given that there is at least one green bubble gum.

9 A four-digit number (with no repetitions) is to be formed from the set of digits $\{0, 1, 2, 3, 4, 5, 6, 7\}$. Find the probability that the number:
   a is even
   b is odd
   c is less than 4000
   d is less than 4000, given that it is greater that 3000.

10 A hand of five cards is dealt from a normal pack of 52 cards. Find the probability that the hand will contain:
   a no aces
   b at least one ace
   c the ace of spades
   d the ace of spades, given that there is at least one ace.

11 A committee of three is to be chosen from a group of four men and five women. Find the probability that the committee contains:
   a all women
   b at least one woman
   c exactly two men, given that at least one man is chosen.

10E Pascal's triangle and the binomial theorem*

There is a connection between the selection problems we have encountered and the expansion of expressions of the form $(a + b)^n$. In this section we explore this connection.

▶ Pascal's triangle

Consider the possibilities when choosing from a small group of objects. In the first instance, consider when the group has only one object, A. We can choose either no objects or one object from this group, each in only one way:

$$^1C_0 = 1 \qquad ^1C_1 = 1$$

Next, consider when the group has two objects, A and B. We can choose either no objects, one object or two objects from this group:

$$^2C_0 = 1 \qquad ^2C_1 = 2 \qquad ^2C_2 = 1$$

Choosing from three objects we have:

$$^3C_0 = 1 \qquad ^3C_1 = 3 \qquad ^3C_2 = 3 \qquad ^3C_3 = 1$$

We can continue in this way to create the following pattern of numbers. We also add a top line for a group of 0 objects.

$n = 0$:			$^0C_0$						1			
$n = 1$:		$^1C_0$		$^1C_1$				1		1		
$n = 2$:		$^2C_0$	$^2C_1$		$^2C_2$		1		2		1	
$n = 3$:	$^3C_0$	$^3C_1$		$^3C_2$		$^3C_3$	1		3		3	1
$n = 4$:	$^4C_0$	$^4C_1$	$^4C_2$	$^4C_3$		$^4C_4$	1	4		6		4	1
$n = 5$:	$^5C_0$	$^5C_1$	$^5C_2$	$^5C_3$	$^5C_4$	$^5C_5$	1	5	10		10	5	1

* This section could be omitted but it is useful for further study.

This triangle of numbers is usually called **Pascal's triangle** after the French mathematician Blaise Pascal who made ingenious use of it in his studies of probability.

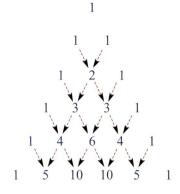

The pattern can be continued indefinitely by noting:
- The first and last numbers in every row are always 1.
- The number in any position in a row is the sum of the two numbers in the row above which are to the left and right of it, as shown.

This is proved by the following result.

> **Pascal's identity**
>
> $^nC_r = {}^{n-1}C_{r-1} + {}^{n-1}C_r$ for $0 < r < n$

Proof Using the formula for ^nC_r, we find

$$^{n-1}C_{r-1} + {}^{n-1}C_r = \frac{(n-1)!}{(n-r)!(r-1)!} + \frac{(n-1)!}{(n-1-r)!\,r!}$$

$$= \frac{(n-1)!}{(n-r-1)!(r-1)!}\left(\frac{1}{n-r} + \frac{1}{r}\right)$$

$$= \frac{(n-1)!}{(n-r-1)!(r-1)!}\left(\frac{n}{(n-r)r}\right)$$

$$= \frac{n!}{(n-r)!\,r!}$$

$$= {}^nC_r$$

▶ The binomial theorem

In Chapter 6, we briefly looked at expansions of $(a + b)^n$ and showed how you could build up the identities. We are now able to apply the techniques of this chapter to obtain the general result that

$$(a+b)^n = a^n + \binom{n}{1}a^{n-1}b + \binom{n}{2}a^{n-2}b^2 + \cdots + \binom{n}{r}a^{n-r}b^r + \cdots + \binom{n}{n-1}ab^{n-1} + b^n$$

This may look very complicated, but by substituting in $n = 3$ and $n = 4$ we obtain the results we know:

$$(a+b)^3 = a^3 + \binom{3}{1}a^{3-1}b + \binom{3}{2}a^{3-2}b^2 + \binom{3}{3}a^{3-3}b^3$$

$$= a^3 + \binom{3}{1}a^2b + \binom{3}{2}ab^2 + \binom{3}{3}b^3$$

$$= a^3 + 3a^2b + 3ab^2 + b^3$$

$$(a+b)^4 = a^4 + 4a^3b + 6a^2b^2 + 4ab^3 + b^4$$

Before proceeding further, we note that the coefficients can be found from Pascal's triangle. We present the triangle in this form so the coefficient of the b^i term can easily be read off.

n	b^0	b^1	b^2	b^3	b^4	b^5
0	1					
1	1	1				
2	1	2	1			
3	1	3	3	1		
4	1	4	6	4	1	
5	1	5	10	10	5	1

From this we could read off the coefficients of $(a + b)^5$, for example:

$$(a + b)^5 = a^5 + 5a^4b + 10a^3b^2 + 10a^2b^3 + 5ab^4 + b^5$$

Using combinations, we can now see why this identity holds without having to multiply out the left-hand side.

If we expand $(a + b)^5$, we know that the terms will be of the form

$$c_0 a^5 \quad c_1 a^4 b \quad c_2 a^3 b^2 \quad c_3 a^2 b^3 \quad c_4 a b^4 \quad c_5 b^5$$

where the c_i are the coefficients. Writing

$$(a + b)^5 = (a + b)(a + b)(a + b)(a + b)(a + b)$$

we can use our knowledge of combinations to find these coefficients.

For finding the coefficient c_1 of a^4b, the relevant terms when multiplying out are

$$aaaab \quad aaaba \quad aabaa \quad abaaa \quad baaaa$$

Each of these terms comes from choosing either a or b from each of the five brackets. There are $\binom{5}{1}$ ways of choosing exactly one b from the five brackets. Therefore the coefficient of a^4b is $c_1 = \binom{5}{1} = 5$.

Similarly, there are $\binom{5}{2}$ ways of choosing exactly two bs from the five brackets. Therefore the coefficient of a^3b^2 is $c_2 = \binom{5}{2} = 10$.

Continuing in this way, we can see that the remaining coefficients are $c_3 = \binom{5}{3} = 10$, $c_4 = \binom{5}{4} = 5$ and $c_5 = \binom{5}{5} = 1$.

This argument in the special case of $(a + b)^5$ can be extended to $(a + b)^n$ to give the following general result.

Binomial theorem

For each positive integer n,

$$(a + b)^n = a^n + \binom{n}{1} a^{n-1} b + \binom{n}{2} a^{n-2} b^2 + \cdots + \binom{n}{r} a^{n-r} b^r + \cdots + \binom{n}{n-1} a b^{n-1} + b^n$$

Example 17

Use the binomial theorem to expand $(2 - 3x)^4$.

Solution

We know $(a + b)^4 = a^4 + 4a^3b + 6a^2b^2 + 4ab^3 + b^4$.

Let $a = 2$ and $b = -3x$. Then
$$\begin{aligned}(2 + (-3x))^4 &= 2^4 + 4 \times 2^3(-3x) + 6 \times 2^2(-3x)^2 + 4 \times 2(-3x)^3 + (-3x)^4 \\ &= 16 + 4 \times 8 \times (-3)x + 6 \times 4 \times (-3)^2 x^2 + 4 \times 2 \times (-3)^3 x^3 + (-3)^4 x^4 \\ &= 16 - 96x + 216x^2 - 216x^3 + 81x^4\end{aligned}$$

Section summary

- **Pascal's triangle**

n	b^0	b^1	b^2	b^3	b^4	b^5
0	1					
1	1	1				
2	1	2	1			
3	1	3	3	1		
4	1	4	6	4	1	
5	1	5	10	10	5	1

- **Binomial theorem**

  For each positive integer n,
  $$(a+b)^n = a^n + \binom{n}{1}a^{n-1}b + \binom{n}{2}a^{n-2}b^2 + \cdots + \binom{n}{r}a^{n-r}b^r + \cdots + \binom{n}{n-1}ab^{n-1} + b^n$$

Exercise 10E

1 Expand each of the following using the binomial theorem:
  - **a** $(x + 2)^4$
  - **b** $(2x + 1)^4$
  - **c** $(2x - 3)^4$
  - **d** $(3x - 1)^3$
  - **e** $(1 - 2x)^4$
  - **f** $(1 - 2x)^5$
  - **g** $(1 - 3x)^5$
  - **h** $(3 - 2x)^4$

Chapter summary

- $n! = n \times (n-1) \times (n-2) \times \cdots \times 2 \times 1$ and $0! = 1$, where the notation $n!$ is read as 'n factorial'.
- An **arrangement** (or **permutation**) is a grouping of objects, such that the order of the objects is important. That is, the arrangements ABC and CBA are different.
- The number of ways of arranging n objects in a row is
$$n! = n \times (n-1) \times (n-2) \times (n-3) \times \cdots \times 2 \times 1$$
- The number of ways of arranging n objects in groups of size r is
$$^nP_r = \frac{n!}{(n-r)!} = n \times (n-1) \times (n-2) \times \cdots \times (n-r+1)$$
- A **selection** (or **combination**) is a grouping of objects, such that the order of the objects is not important. That is, the selections ABC and CBA are the same.
- The number of combinations of n objects in groups of size r is
$$^nC_r = \frac{^nP_r}{r!} = \frac{n \times (n-1) \times (n-2) \times \cdots \times (n-r+1)}{r!} = \frac{n!}{r!(n-r)!}$$
- A commonly used alternative notation for ^nC_r is $\binom{n}{r}$.
- For n objects, $^nC_0 + {}^nC_1 + {}^nC_2 + \cdots + {}^nC_{n-1} + {}^nC_n = 2^n$.
- When the combination problem involves restrictions, deal with these first.
- Combinations may be used when determining probabilities. In the appropriate cases, the probability is given by dividing the number of outcomes in an event by the total number of outcomes.
- Binomial theorem:
$$(a+b)^n = a^n + \binom{n}{1}a^{n-1}b + \binom{n}{2}a^{n-2}b^2 + \cdots + \binom{n}{r}a^{n-r}b^r + \cdots + \binom{n}{n-1}ab^{n-1} + b^n$$

Technology-free questions

1 Evaluate:
   a $^{1000}C_{998}$
   b $^{1\,000\,000}C_{999\,999}$
   c $^{1\,000\,000}C_1$

2 How many integers from 100 to 999, inclusive, have three different digits?

3 How many different three-digit house numbers can be constructed from six brass numerals 1, 2, 3, 4, 5, 6?

4 A supermarket sells n different brands of dishwashing liquid. Each brand offers four different sized bottles (small, medium, large and economy), and each is available as either lemon-scented or pine-scented. How many different types of dishwashing liquid bottles are available at this supermarket?

5 Of the integers from 1000 to 9999, how many have at least one digit a 5 or 7?

6 A bushwalking club has 80 members: 50 men and 30 women. A committee consisting of two men and one woman is to be selected. How many different committees are possible?

7 There are five vowels and 21 consonants in the English alphabet. How many different four-letter 'words' can be formed that contain two different vowels and two different consonants?

8 A pizza restaurant offers the following toppings: onions, green peppers, mushrooms, anchovies and pepperoni.
   a How many different kinds of pizza with three different toppings can be ordered?
   b How many different kinds with any number of toppings (between none and all five) can be ordered?

9 Seven people are to be seated in a row. Calculate the number of ways in which this can be done so that two particular persons, A and B, always have exactly one of the others between them.

10 Three letters are chosen at random from the word OLYMPICS and arranged in a row. What is the probability that:
   a the letter O is first   b the letter Y is chosen   c both vowels are chosen?

Multiple-choice questions

1 For his holiday reading Geoff has selected eight detective novels, three biographies and four science fiction books, but he only has room in his case for three books. If he selects one book from each group, how many combinations of books are possible?
   A 15   B 28   C 56   D 20   E 96

2 Georgia is choosing her five subjects for Year 12. She has already chosen three subjects. For the remaining two she will choose one of the three mathematics subjects, and either one of five languages or one of three science subjects. How many different subject combinations are possible?
   A 11   B 15   C 9   D 24   E 45

3 In how many ways can 10 people be arranged in a queue at the bank?
   A $10!$ B $\dfrac{10!}{2!}$ C $\dfrac{10!}{2!8!}$ D $\dfrac{10!}{8!}$ E $^{10}C_1$

4 How many different licence plates can be made using two letters followed by four digits, if neither the letters nor the digits can be repeated?
   A 8   B 720   C 5690   D 3 276 000   E 6 760 000

5 $^{21}C_3$ is equal to
   A $21!$ B $\dfrac{21!}{3!}$ C $\dfrac{21!}{18!3!}$ D $\dfrac{21!}{18!}$ E $\dfrac{18!3!}{21!}$

390 Chapter 10: Counting methods

6 In how many ways can a hand of six cards be dealt from a pack of 52 cards?

A 6!   **B** $^{52}C_6$ **C** $^{46}C_6$ **D** $\dfrac{52!}{6!}$ **E** 52!

7 In how many ways can three DVDs be chosen from a group of 12 DVDs?

A 12   **B** 36   **C** 220   **D** 1320   **E** 79 833 600

8 A class consists of 10 girls and 14 boys. In how many ways could a committee of two girls and two boys be chosen?

A $^{10}C_2 \times {}^{14}C_2$ **B** $^{24}C_4$ **C** $10! \times 14!$

D $10 \times 9 \times 14 \times 13$ **E** $\dfrac{10!14!}{4!}$

9 Three-letter 'words' are to be made by arranging the letters of the word METHODS. What is the probability that the word begins with a vowel?

A $\dfrac{1}{105}$ **B** $\dfrac{1}{21}$ **C** $\dfrac{1}{2}$ **D** $\dfrac{5}{26}$ **E** $\dfrac{2}{7}$

10 What is the probability that a team of four chosen at random from a group of eight friends, four males and four females, would consist of three women and one man?

A $\dfrac{1}{2}$ **B** $\dfrac{3}{4}$ **C** $\dfrac{3}{8}$ **D** $\dfrac{3}{64}$ **E** $\dfrac{8}{35}$

Extended-response questions

1 Permutations are formed using all of the digits 1, 2, 3, 4, ..., 9 without repetition. Determine the number of possible permutations in each of the following cases:

    a Even and odd digits alternate.

    b The digits 1 and 2 are together but not necessarily in that order.

2 There are 10 chairs in a row.

    a In how many ways can three people be seated?

    b In how many of these will the two end chairs be occupied?

    c In how many of these will the two end chairs be empty?

3 All possible three-digit numbers are formed from the odd digits {1, 3, 5, 7, 9}.

    a How many such numbers are possible if each digit is used only once?

    b How many of the numbers from part a are larger than 350?

4 In how many ways can a committee of four be chosen from five married couples if:

    a all individuals are eligible for selection

    b the committee must consist of two women and two men

    c a husband and wife cannot both be selected?

5 Geoff has five flat batteries and ten charged batteries. Unfortunately his little brother mixes them up, and he can't tell them apart. He selects four batteries at random for his calculator.
   a How many different combinations of the 15 batteries could Geoff select?
   b In how many of these are all four batteries charged?
   c In how many of these is at least one battery flat?

6 There are seven mints and 11 jubes in the lolly jar. Steve puts his hand in the jar and selects four lollies at random.
   a How many different combinations of the lollies are there?
   b In how many of these are there no mints?
   c In how many of these are there two mints and two jubes?

7 In Tattslotto, a player picks a selection of six numbers from the numbers 1 to 45. To determine the winners, eight numbers are chosen at random – the first six are designated as the winning numbers, and the other two as the supplementary numbers. Prizes are determined as follows.

   Division 1:   6 winning numbers
   Division 2:   5 winning numbers and 1 supplementary
   Division 3:   5 winning numbers
   Division 4:   4 winning numbers
   Division 5:   3 winning numbers and 1 supplementary

   Find the number of combinations which satisfy each of the divisions, and hence the probabilities of winning each of the five divisions.

8 In Keno, a player selects between three and ten numbers from 1 to 80. Each selection is called a 'spot'. If you select five numbers, you are playing a 'Spot 5' game.
   To determine the winners, 20 numbers are drawn randomly from the 80 numbers. If all your selected numbers are among the 20, you win. The amount you win depends on the 'spot' you are playing.
   Find the probability of winning:

   a a 'Spot 6' game
   b a 'Spot 5' game.

Chapter 11

Discrete probability distributions

Objectives

▶ To introduce the basic ideas of **discrete random variables**.
▶ To introduce the concept of a **probability distribution** for a discrete random variable.
▶ To investigate and compare the processes of:
   ▷ sampling without replacement (**hypergeometric probability distribution**)
   ▷ sampling with replacement (**binomial probability distribution**).

In Chapter 10 we introduced some strategies for helping us to determine the number of outcomes in an event. This allows us to determine probabilities without listing all of the possible outcomes. In this chapter we extend our ability to calculate probabilities for complex events even further. We do this by introducing useful rules for calculating probabilities in some very commonly encountered situations.

We will again concentrate on finite sample spaces. Therefore we start with a sample space ε and the outcomes are the elements of this sample space. We can assign a probability to each of these outcomes from the interval [0, 1], and the sum of the probabilities of these outcomes is 1. An event is a subset of the sample space, and the probability of an event is equal to the sum of the probabilities of the outcomes in that event.

We will see that a distribution for a random experiment is a description of the probabilities of the outcomes. This is sometimes done by a table and sometimes by a rule.

11A Discrete random variables

An important next step in our study of probability is to assign numerical values to each outcome in the sample space.

▶ Random variables

Consider the sample space obtained when a coin is tossed three times:

$$\varepsilon = \{HHH, HHT, HTH, THH, HTT, THT, TTH, TTT\}$$

Suppose we are particularly interested in the number of heads associated with each outcome. We let X represent the number of heads observed when a coin is tossed three times. Then each outcome in the sample space can be associated with a value of X, as shown in the table.

Outcome	Number of heads
HHH	$X = 3$
HHT	$X = 2$
HTH	$X = 2$
THH	$X = 2$
HTT	$X = 1$
THT	$X = 1$
TTH	$X = 1$
TTT	$X = 0$

From the table we can see that the possible values of X are 0, 1, 2 and 3. Since the actual value that X will take is the result of a random experiment, X is called a random variable.

> A **random variable** is a function that assigns a number to each outcome in the sample space ε.

A random variable can be discrete or continuous:

- A **discrete random variable** is one which may take on only a countable number of distinct values, such as 0, 1, 2, 3, 4. Discrete random variables are usually (but not necessarily) generated by counting. The number of children in a family, the number of brown eggs in a carton of a dozen eggs, and the number times we roll a die before we observe a 'six' are all examples of discrete random variables.
- A **continuous random variable** is one that can take any value in an interval of the real number line, and is usually (but not always) generated by measuring. Height, weight, and the time taken to complete a puzzle are all examples of continuous random variables.

In this chapter we are interested in understanding more about discrete random variables.

Discrete probability distributions

Because the values of a random variable are associated with outcomes in the sample space, we can determine the probability of each value of the random variable occurring.

Let's look again at the results obtained when a coin is tossed three times. Assuming that the coin is fair, we can add probabilities to the previous table.

Outcome	Number of heads	Probability
HHH	$X = 3$	$\frac{1}{8}$
HHT	$X = 2$	$\frac{1}{8}$
HTH	$X = 2$	$\frac{1}{8}$
THH	$X = 2$	$\frac{1}{8}$
HTT	$X = 1$	$\frac{1}{8}$
THT	$X = 1$	$\frac{1}{8}$
TTH	$X = 1$	$\frac{1}{8}$
TTT	$X = 0$	$\frac{1}{8}$

$\Pr(X = 3) = \frac{1}{8}$

$\Pr(X = 2) = \frac{3}{8}$

$\Pr(X = 1) = \frac{3}{8}$

$\Pr(X = 0) = \frac{1}{8}$

The list of all possible values of the random variable X, together with the probability associated with each value, is known as the probability distribution of X. More usually, we would summarise the probability distribution associated with the number of heads observed when a fair coin is tossed three times in a table as follows.

x	0	1	2	3
$\Pr(X = x)$	$\frac{1}{8}$	$\frac{3}{8}$	$\frac{3}{8}$	$\frac{1}{8}$

Note that, since every possible value of the random variable is included, the probabilities must add to 1.

> The **probability distribution** of a discrete random variable X is a function
>
> $p(x) = \Pr(X = x)$
>
> that assigns a probability to each value of X. It can be represented by a rule, a table or a graph, and must give a probability $p(x)$ for every value x that X can take. This function is sometimes referred to as the **mass function**.
>
> For any discrete probability distribution, the following must be true:
> - Each value of $p(x)$ must belong to the interval $[0, 1]$. That is,
>
> $0 \leq p(x) \leq 1$
>
>   for every value x that X can take.
> - The sum of the values of $p(x)$ must be 1.

Example 1

Consider the probability distribution:

x	1	2	3	4	5	6
$\Pr(X = x)$	0.2	0.3	0.1	0.2	0.15	0.05

Use the table to find:
a $\Pr(X = 3)$ **b** $\Pr(X < 3)$ **c** $\Pr(X \geq 4)$
d $\Pr(3 \leq X \leq 5)$ **e** $\Pr(X \neq 5)$

Solution

a $\Pr(X = 3) = 0.1$

b $\Pr(X < 3) = 0.2 + 0.3$
$= 0.5$

c $\Pr(X \geq 4) = 0.2 + 0.15 + 0.05$
$= 0.4$

d $\Pr(3 \leq X \leq 5) = 0.1 + 0.2 + 0.15$
$= 0.45$

e $\Pr(X \neq 5) = 1 - \Pr(X = 5)$
$= 1 - 0.15$
$= 0.85$

Explanation

If X is less than 3, then from the table we see that X can take the value 1 or 2.

If X is greater than or equal to 4, then X can take the value 4, 5 or 6.

Here X can take the value 3, 4 or 5.

The sum of all the probabilities must be 1.

Example 2

Consider the function:

x	1	2	3	4	5
$\Pr(X = x)$	$2c$	$3c$	$4c$	$5c$	$6c$

For what value of c is this a probability distribution?

Solution

$2c + 3c + 4c + 5c + 6c = 1$
$20c = 1$
$c = \dfrac{1}{20}$

Explanation

For a probability distribution, we require that the probabilities add to 1.

Example 3

The table shows a probability distribution for a random variable X.

x	1	2	3	4	5	6
$\Pr(X = x)$	0.2	0.2	0.07	0.17	0.13	0.23

Give the following probabilities:

a $\Pr(X > 4)$ **b** $\Pr(2 < X < 5)$ **c** $\Pr(X \geq 5 \mid X \geq 3)$

Solution

a $\Pr(X > 4) = \Pr(X = 5) + \Pr(X = 6)$
$= 0.13 + 0.23 = 0.36$

b $\Pr(2 < X < 5) = \Pr(X = 3) + \Pr(X = 4)$
$= 0.07 + 0.17 = 0.24$

c $\Pr(X \geq 5 \mid X \geq 3) = \dfrac{\Pr(X \geq 5 \text{ and } X \geq 3)}{\Pr(X \geq 3)}$

$= \dfrac{\Pr(X \geq 5)}{\Pr(X \geq 3)}$ (since $X \geq 5$ implies $X \geq 3$)

$= \dfrac{\Pr(X = 5) + \Pr(X = 6)}{\Pr(X = 3) + \Pr(X = 4) + \Pr(X = 5) + \Pr(X = 6)}$

$= \dfrac{0.13 + 0.23}{0.07 + 0.17 + 0.13 + 0.23}$

$= \dfrac{0.36}{0.6} = \dfrac{3}{5}$

Example 4

The following distribution table gives the probabilities for the number of people on a carnival ride at a particular time of day.

Number of people (t)	0	1	2	3	4	5
$\Pr(T = t)$	0.05	0.2	0.3	0.2	0.1	0.15

Find:

a $\Pr(T > 4)$ **b** $\Pr(1 < T < 5)$ **c** $\Pr(T < 3 \mid T < 4)$

Solution

a $\Pr(T > 4) = \Pr(T = 5) = 0.15$

b $\Pr(1 < T < 5) = \Pr(T = 2) + \Pr(T = 3) + \Pr(T = 4) = 0.6$

c $\Pr(T < 3 \mid T < 4) = \dfrac{\Pr(T < 3 \text{ and } T < 4)}{\Pr(T < 4)}$

$= \dfrac{\Pr(T < 3)}{\Pr(T < 4)} = \dfrac{0.55}{0.75} = \dfrac{11}{15}$

11A Discrete random variables

Section summary

A **discrete probability distribution** is a table, graph or function which lists all the values that a random variable can take, together with the probability that the random variable takes each value.

Exercise 11A

1 A random variable X can take the values $x = 1, 2, 3, 4$. Indicate whether or not each of the following is a probability distribution for such a variable, and if not, give reasons:

  a $p(1) = 0.05$ $p(2) = 0.35$ $p(3) = 0.55$ $p(4) = 0.15$

  b $p(1) = 0.125$ $p(2) = 0.5$ $p(3) = 0.25$ $p(4) = 0.0625$

  c $p(1) = 13\%$ $p(2) = 69\%$ $p(3) = 1\%$ $p(4) = 17\%$

  d $p(1) = 51$ $p(2) = 12$ $p(3) = 34$ $p(4) = 3$

  e $p(1) = 0.66$ $p(2) = 0.32$ $p(3) = -0.19$ $p(4) = 0.2$

2 For each of the following, write a probability statement in terms of the discrete random variable X showing the probability that:

  a X is equal to 2
  b X is greater than 2
  c X is at least 2
  d X is less than 2
  e X is 2 or more
  f X is more than 2
  g X is no more than 2
  h X is greater than or equal to 2
  i X is less than or equal to 2
  j X is no less than 2
  k X is greater than 2 and less than 5

3 A random variable X can take the values 0, 1, 2, 3, 4, 5. List the set of values that X can take for each of the following probability statements:

  a $\Pr(X = 2)$
  b $\Pr(X > 2)$
  c $\Pr(X \geq 2)$
  d $\Pr(X < 2)$
  e $\Pr(X \leq 2)$
  f $\Pr(2 \leq X \leq 5)$
  g $\Pr(2 < X \leq 5)$
  h $\Pr(2 \leq X < 5)$
  i $\Pr(2 < X < 5)$

Example 1   **4** Consider the probability distribution:

x	0	1	2	3	4	5
$\Pr(X = x)$	0.3	0.2	0.2	0.1	0.05	0.15

Use the table to find:

  a $\Pr(X = 2)$
  b $\Pr(X < 2)$
  c $\Pr(X \geq 3)$
  d $\Pr(2 \leq X \leq 4)$
  e $\Pr(X \neq 3)$

Example 2 **5** Consider the following function:

x	1	2	3	4	5
$\Pr(X = x)$	k	$2k$	$3k$	$4k$	$5k$

a For what value of k is this a probability distribution?
b Find $\Pr(2 \leq X \leq 4)$.

6 The number of 'no-shows' on a scheduled airline flight has the following probability distribution:

r	0	1	2	3	4	5	6	7
$p(r)$	0.09	0.22	0.26	0.21	0.13	0.06	0.02	0.01

Find the probability that:
a more than four people do not show up for the flight
b at least two people do not show up for the flight.

7 Suppose Y is a random variable with the distribution given in the table.

y	0.2	0.3	0.4	0.5	0.6	0.7	0.8	0.9
$\Pr(Y = y)$	0.08	0.13	0.09	0.19	0.20	0.03	0.10	0.18

Find:
a $\Pr(Y \leq 0.5)$
b $\Pr(Y > 0.5)$
c $\Pr(0.3 \leq Y \leq 0.8)$

Example 3 **8** The table shows a probability distribution for a random variable X.

x	1	2	3	4	5	6
$\Pr(X = x)$	0.1	0.13	0.17	0.27	0.20	0.13

Give the following probabilities:
a $\Pr(X > 3)$
b $\Pr(3 < X < 6)$
c $\Pr(X \geq 4 \mid X \geq 2)$

9 Suppose that a fair coin is tossed three times.
a List the eight equally likely outcomes.
b If X represents the number of heads shown, determine $\Pr(X = 2)$.
c Find the probability distribution of the random variable X.
d Find $\Pr(X \leq 2)$.
e Find $\Pr(X \leq 1 \mid X \leq 2)$.

10 When a pair of dice is rolled, there are 36 equally likely outcomes. Let Y denote the sum of the dice.
a What are the possible values of the random variable Y?
b Find $\Pr(Y = 7)$.
c Determine the probability distribution of the random variable Y.

11 When a pair of dice is rolled, there are 36 equally likely outcomes. Let X denote the larger of the values showing on the dice. If both dice come up the same, then X denotes the common value.
   a What are the possible values of the random variable X?
   b Find $\Pr(X = 4)$.
   c Determine the probability distribution of the random variable X.

12 Suppose that a fair coin is tossed three times. You lose $3.00 if three heads appear and lose $2.00 if two heads appear. You win $1.00 if one head appears and win $3.00 if no heads appear. Let Y be the amount you win or lose.
   a Find the probability distribution of the random variable Y.
   b Find $\Pr(Y \leq 1)$.

11B Sampling without replacement

In this section we will investigate the type of probability distribution that arises through **sampling without replacement**, that is, when an object is selected from a finite group of objects and not replaced before a subsequent selection is made. The effect of this is that the probability of observing a particular outcome changes after each selection.

Consider, for example, a jar containing three mints and four toffees. Suppose Bob selects two lollies (without looking) and that the random variable X is the number of mints he selects, which can take the value 0, 1 or 2.

There are seven lollies in total. The probability that Bob chooses a mint with his first selection is $\frac{3}{7}$, and the probability that he chooses a toffee is $\frac{4}{7}$.

When Bob makes his second selection, there are only six lollies left, and the probability that he selects a mint or a toffee will depend on what he selected the first time. This problem can readily be illustrated with a tree diagram as shown.

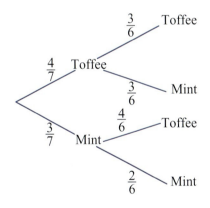

Since this can be considered as a sequence of two trials in which the second is dependent on the first, we can determine the probabilities associated with each outcome using the multiplication rule. Therefore

$$\Pr(X = 0) = \frac{4}{7} \times \frac{3}{6} = \frac{2}{7}$$

$$\Pr(X = 1) = \left(\frac{4}{7} \times \frac{3}{6}\right) + \left(\frac{3}{7} \times \frac{4}{6}\right) = \frac{2}{7} + \frac{2}{7} = \frac{4}{7}$$

and $$\Pr(X = 2) = \frac{3}{7} \times \frac{2}{6} = \frac{1}{7}$$

Thus the probability distribution for the number of mints X is:

x	0	1	2
$\Pr(X = x)$	$\frac{2}{7}$	$\frac{4}{7}$	$\frac{1}{7}$

Note that the probabilities in the table add up to 1. If they did not add to 1, we would know we had made a mistake!

When the sample space is large, listing all possible outcomes using a tree diagram is no longer practical. However, we can also work out the probability for each value of the random variable X by using our knowledge of selections from Chapter 10.

Consider the situation $X = 0$, in which the sample of two lollies contains no mints. Then it must contain two toffees. Thus Bob has selected no mints from the three available, and two toffees from the four available, which gives the number of favourable outcomes as

$$\binom{3}{0}\binom{4}{2}$$

The total number of possible choices Bob has when choosing two lollies from seven is $\binom{7}{2}$. Thus the probability of Bob selecting no mints is

$$\Pr(X = 0) = \frac{\binom{3}{0}\binom{4}{2}}{\binom{7}{2}} = \frac{6}{21} = \frac{2}{7}$$

Similarly, we can determine:

$$\Pr(X = 1) = \frac{\binom{3}{1}\binom{4}{1}}{\binom{7}{2}} = \frac{12}{21} = \frac{4}{7} \quad \text{and} \quad \Pr(X = 2) = \frac{\binom{3}{2}\binom{4}{0}}{\binom{7}{2}} = \frac{3}{21} = \frac{1}{7}$$

The type of distribution illustrated by this example (arising from sampling without replacement) is commonly called the **hypergeometric distribution**.

Example 5

Marine biologists are studying a group of dolphins which live in a small bay. They know there are 12 dolphins in the group, four of which have been caught, tagged and released to mix back into the population. If the researchers return the following week and catch another group of three dolphins, what is the probability that two of these will already be tagged?

Solution

Let X equal the number of tagged dolphins in the second sample. Then

$$\Pr(X = 2) = \frac{\binom{4}{2}\binom{8}{1}}{\binom{12}{3}}$$

$$= \frac{12}{55}$$

Explanation

We wish to know the probability of selecting two of the four tagged dolphins, and one of the eight non-tagged dolphins, when a sample of size 3 is selected from a population of size 12.

Section summary

Sampling without replacement means that successive objects are selected from a finite group of objects without being replaced, with the result that the probability of success changes after each selection. When the sample size is small, we can determine the probability distribution using a tree diagram. However, a more general strategy is to use our knowledge of selections.

Exercise 11B

Example 5

1. A company employs 30 salespersons, 12 of whom are men and 18 are women. Five salespersons are to be selected at random to attend an important conference. What is the probability of selecting two men and three women?

2. An electrical component is packaged in boxes of 20. A technician randomly selects three from each box for testing. If there are no faulty components, the whole box is passed. If there are any faulty components, the box is sent back for further inspection. If a box is known to contain four faulty components, what is the probability it will pass?

3. A pond contains seven gold and eight black fish. If three fish are caught at random in a net, find the probability that at least one of them is black.

4. A researcher has caught, tagged and released 10 birds of a particular species into the forest. If there are known to be 25 of this species of bird in the area, what is the probability that another sample of five birds will contain three tagged ones?

5. A tennis instructor has 10 new and 10 used tennis balls. If he selects six balls at random to use in a class, what is the probability that there will be at least two new balls?

6. A jury of six persons was selected from a group of 18 potential jurors, of whom eight were female and 10 male. The jury was supposedly selected at random, but it contained only one female. Do you have any reason to doubt the randomness of the selection? Explain your reasons.

11C Sampling with replacement: the binomial distribution

In this section we will investigate the type of probability distribution that arises through **sampling with replacement**, that is, when an object is selected from a finite group of objects and replaced before a subsequent selection is made, or is selected from an infinite population, or in fact any situation when the probability of observing a particular outcome remains the same through the course of the experiment. This applies to many of our common scenarios, such as the tossing of a coin or the rolling of a die.

Suppose a fair six-sided die is rolled three times and a random variable X is defined as the number of 3s observed. Let T represent a 3, let N represent not a 3. Consider all of the possible outcomes and the probability for each outcome.

Outcome	Number of 3s	Probability
TTT	$X = 3$	$\frac{1}{6} \times \frac{1}{6} \times \frac{1}{6}$ $\Pr(X = 3) = (\frac{1}{6})^3$
TTN	$X = 2$	$\frac{1}{6} \times \frac{1}{6} \times \frac{5}{6}$
TNT	$X = 2$	$\frac{1}{6} \times \frac{5}{6} \times \frac{1}{6}$ $\Pr(X = 2) = 3 \times (\frac{1}{6})^2 \times \frac{5}{6}$
NTT	$X = 2$	$\frac{5}{6} \times \frac{1}{6} \times \frac{1}{6}$
TNN	$X = 1$	$\frac{1}{6} \times \frac{5}{6} \times \frac{5}{6}$
NTN	$X = 1$	$\frac{5}{6} \times \frac{1}{6} \times \frac{5}{6}$ $\Pr(X = 1) = 3 \times \frac{1}{6} \times (\frac{5}{6})^2$
NNT	$X = 1$	$\frac{5}{6} \times \frac{5}{6} \times \frac{1}{6}$
NNN	$X = 0$	$\frac{5}{6} \times \frac{5}{6} \times \frac{5}{6}$ $\Pr(X = 0) = (\frac{5}{6})^3$

Thus the entire probability distribution can be defined by the following table.

x	0	1	2	3
$\Pr(X = x)$	$\frac{125}{216}$	$\frac{75}{216}$	$\frac{15}{216}$	$\frac{1}{216}$

Once again, it is not necessary to list all of the outcomes in order to determine the probability distribution. We can use our knowledge of selections from Chapter 10.

Consider the probability that $X = 1$, that is, when exactly one 3 is observed. We can see from the table that there are three ways this can occur. Since the 3 could occur on the first, second or third roll of the die, we can consider this as selecting one object from a group of three, which can be done in $\binom{3}{1}$ ways.

Consider the probability that $X = 2$, that is, when exactly two 3s are observed. Again from the table there are three ways this can occur. Since the two 3s could occur on any two of the three rolls of the die, we can consider this as selecting two objects from a group of three, which can be done in $\binom{3}{2}$ ways.

This leads us to a general formula for this probability distribution:

$$\Pr(X = x) = \binom{3}{x}\left(\frac{1}{6}\right)^x\left(\frac{5}{6}\right)^{3-x} \qquad x = 0, 1, 2, 3$$

This is an example of the binomial probability distribution, which arises from a binomial experiment.

> A **binomial experiment** is one that possesses the following properties:
> - The experiment consists of a number, n, of identical trials.
> - Each trial results in one of two outcomes, which are usually designated as either a **success**, S, or a **failure**, F.
> - The probability of success on a single trial, p, is constant for all trials (and thus the probability of failure on a single trial is $1 - p$).
> - The trials are independent (so that the outcome of any trial is not affected by the outcome of any previous trial).
>
> The random variable of interest, X, is the number of successes in n trials of a binomial experiment. Thus, X has a **binomial distribution** and the rule is
>
> $$\Pr(X = x) = \binom{n}{x} p^x (1-p)^{n-x} \qquad x = 0, 1, \ldots, n$$
>
> where $\binom{n}{x} = \dfrac{n!}{x!\,(n-x)!}$

Example 6

Rainfall records for the city of Melbourne indicate that, on average, the probability of rain falling on any one day in November is 0.4. Assuming that the occurrence of rain on any day is independent of whether or not rain falls on any other day, find the probability that rain will fall on any three days of a chosen week.

Solution

Define X as the number of days on which it rains in a given week.

Then X is a binomial random variable with $n = 7$ and $p = 0.4$. Thus

$$\Pr(X = x) = \binom{7}{x}(0.4)^x(0.6)^{7-x} \qquad x = 0, 1, \ldots, 7$$

and so

$$\Pr(X = 3) = \binom{7}{3}(0.4)^3(0.6)^{7-3}$$

$$= \frac{7!}{3!\,4!} \times 0.064 \times 0.1296$$

$$= 0.290304$$

Explanation

There are only two possible outcomes on each day (rain or no rain), and the probability of rain on any day is constant (0.4), regardless of previous outcomes. So this is a binomial experiment. In this example, the occurrence of rain is considered as a success.

Using the TI-Nspire

The calculator can be used to evaluate probabilities for many distributions, including the binomial distribution.

The distributions can be found in a **Calculator** application through either (menu) > **Probability** > **Distributions** or (menu) > **Statistics** > **Distributions**. They can also be found in a **Lists & Spreadsheet** application through (menu) > **Statistics** > **Distributions**.

- **D:Binomial Pdf** is used to determine probabilities for the binomial distribution of the form $\Pr(X = x)$. Here Pdf refers to probability distribution function.
- **E:Binomial Cdf** is used to determine probabilities for the binomial distribution of the form $\Pr(a \leq X \leq b)$. Here Cdf refers to cumulative distribution function.

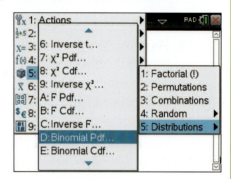

Examples of how and when to use each of these functions are given in Example 7.

Using the Casio ClassPad

The calculator can be used to evaluate probabilities for discrete and continuous distributions.

For the binomial distribution:

- In the main screen $\sqrt{\alpha}$, go to **Interactive** > **Distribution** > **Discrete**.
- Select **binomialPDf** to find the probability for one value of X, that is, to find $\Pr(X = x)$.
- Select **binomialCDf** for cumulative probabilities, that is, to find $\Pr(a \leq X \leq b)$.

An illustration of the use of these functions is given in Example 7.

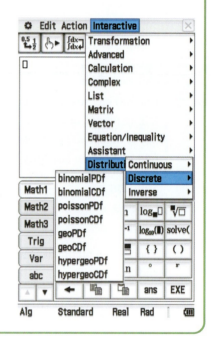

Example 7

For the situation described in Example 6, use a CAS calculator to find the probability that:

a rain will fall on any three days of a chosen week
b rain will fall on no more than three days of a chosen week
c rain will fall on at least three days of a chosen week.

Using the TI-Nspire

a As shown in Example 6, we want to find $\Pr(X = 3)$ where $n = 7$ and $p = 0.4$. Use **Binomial Pdf** and complete as shown to find that $\Pr(X = 3) = 0.290304$.

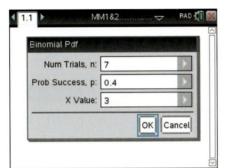 

b Here $\Pr(X \leq 3)$ is required. Use **Binomial Cdf** and complete as shown to find that $\Pr(X \leq 3) = 0.710208$.

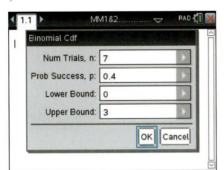 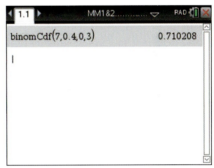

c Here $\Pr(X \geq 3)$ is required. Use **Binomial Cdf** and complete as shown to find that $\Pr(X \geq 3) = 0.580096$.

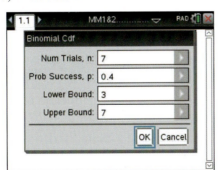 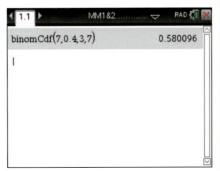

Using the Casio ClassPad

a ■ As shown in Example 6, we want to find $\Pr(X = 3)$, where $n = 7$ and $p = 0.4$.
■ In Main √α, go to **Interactive > Distribution > Discrete** and select **binomialPDf**.
■ Enter the parameters as shown and tap OK.
■ The calculator returns the answer $\Pr(X = 3) = 0.290304$.

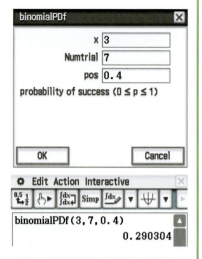

b ■ Here $\Pr(X \leq 3)$ is required.
■ In Main √α, go to **Interactive > Distribution > Discrete**. This time select **binomialCDf**.
■ Enter the parameters as shown and tap OK.
■ The calculator returns the answer $\Pr(X \leq 3) = 0.710208$.

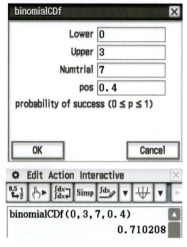

c ■ Here $\Pr(X \geq 3)$ is required.
■ In Main √α, go to **Interactive > Distribution > Discrete** and select **binomialCDf**.
■ Enter the parameters as shown and tap OK.
■ The calculator returns the answer $\Pr(X \geq 3) = 0.580096$.

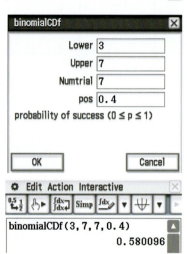

Example 8

Use a CAS calculator to plot the following probability distribution function:

$$\Pr(X = x) = \binom{n}{x} p^x (1-p)^{n-x} \quad x = 0, 1, \ldots, n$$

for $n = 8$ and $p = 0.2$.

Using the TI-Nspire

- Place the numbers 0 to 8 in a list.
- Place the distribution in a list by completing the entry for **Binomial Pdf** without giving a specific value for x.
- In a **Graphs** application, create a scatter plot (menu > **Graph Entry/Edit** > **Scatter Plot**) as shown.
- Use menu > **Trace** > **Graph Trace** to show the data values on the plot.
- Alternatively, the lists can be created in a **Lists & Spreadsheet** application and the scatter plot in a **Data & Statistics** application.

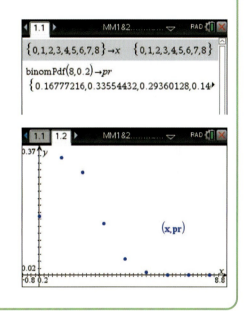

Using the Casio ClassPad

- In $\sqrt{\alpha}$ Main, go to **Interactive** > **Distribution** > **Discrete** and select **binomialPDf**.
- Enter the parameters as shown below and tap OK.
- The calculator will respond with a 'wrong argument type' error as shown below. Ignore this and tap OK.

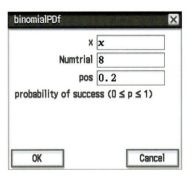
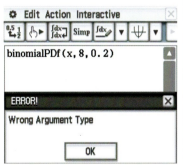

To transfer the binomial distribution into the **Graph & Table** application:

- Highlight the line with the binomialPDf and go to **Edit > Copy**. Open 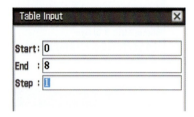 and, with the cursor on y1, go to **Edit > Paste**.
- Tick the box next to y1.

To view the probability distribution table and graph:

- In [icon], set the table input from 0 to 8.

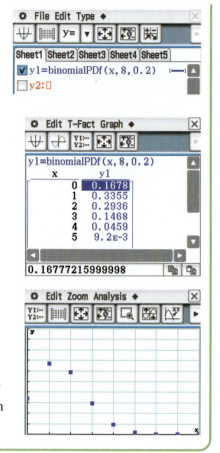

- Tap on the table icon.
- Select the discrete graph icon.
- Tap [icon] to automatically adjust the window.
- In the graph window, use **Analysis > Trace** to view coordinates of the points. Use the cursor arrows on the hard keyboard to navigate around the points.

Example 9

The probability of winning a prize in a game of chance is 0.25. What is the least number of games that must be played to ensure that the probability of winning at least twice is more than 0.9?

Solution

As the probability of winning each game is the same each time the game is played, this is an example of a binomial distribution, with the probability of success $p = 0.25$.

We are being asked to find the smallest value of n such that $\Pr(X \geq 2) > 0.9$, or equivalently, such that

$$\Pr(X < 2) < 0.1$$

We have

$$\Pr(X < 2) = \Pr(X = 0) + \Pr(X = 1)$$
$$= \binom{n}{0}(0.25)^0(0.75)^n + \binom{n}{1}(0.25)^1(0.75)^{n-1}$$
$$= (0.75)^n + 0.25n(0.75)^{n-1}$$

since $\binom{n}{0} = 1$ and $\binom{n}{1} = n$.

So we want to find the smallest value of n such that

$$(0.75)^n + 0.25n(0.75)^{n-1} < 0.1$$

This equation cannot be solved algebraically; however, it can be solved numerically using a CAS calculator as shown. Thus, the game must be played 15 times to ensure that the probability of winning at least twice is more than 0.9.

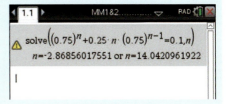

Example 10

The probability of an archer obtaining a maximum score from a shot is 0.4. Find the probability that out of five shots the archer obtains the maximum score:

a three times

b three times, given that she obtains the maximum score at least once.

Solution

Let X be the number of maximum scores from five shots. Then X has a binomial distribution with $n = 5$ and $p = 0.4$.

a $\Pr(X = 3) = \binom{5}{3}(0.4)^3(0.6)^2$

$= 10 \times 0.064 \times 0.36$

$= 0.2304 \quad \left(= \dfrac{144}{625}\right)$

b $\Pr(X = 3 \mid X > 0) = \dfrac{\Pr(X = 3)}{\Pr(X > 0)}$

$= \dfrac{0.2304}{1 - \Pr(X = 0)}$

$= \dfrac{0.2304}{1 - 0.6^5}$

$= 0.2498$

correct to four decimal places.

Section summary

Sampling with replacement means that the probability of success remains constant after each selection. When the sample size is small, we can determine the probability distribution using a table or a tree diagram. However, a more general strategy is to apply the rule for the binomial distribution:

If the random variable X is the number of successes in n trials of a binomial experiment with probability of success p, then X has a **binomial distribution** and probabilities can be determined using the formula

$$\Pr(X = x) = \binom{n}{x} p^x (1-p)^{n-x} \qquad x = 0, 1, \ldots, n$$

where $\binom{n}{x} = \dfrac{n!}{x!\,(n-x)!}$

Exercise 11C

Example 6

1 For the binomial distribution $\Pr(X = x) = \binom{6}{x}(0.3)^x(0.7)^{6-x}$, $x = 0, 1, \ldots, 6$, find:

   a $\Pr(X = 3)$ **b** $\Pr(X = 4)$

Example 7

2 For the binomial distribution $\Pr(X = x) = \binom{10}{x}(0.1)^x(0.9)^{10-x}$, $x = 0, 1, \ldots, 10$, find:

   a $\Pr(X = 2)$ **b** $\Pr(X \leq 2)$

3 A fair die is rolled 60 times. Use your CAS calculator to find the probability of observing:

   a exactly ten 6s   **b** fewer than ten 6s   **c** at least ten 6s.

4 Rainfall records for the city of Melbourne indicate that, on average, the probability of rain falling on any one day in November is 0.35. Assuming that the occurrence of rain on any day is independent of whether or not rain falls on any other day, find the probability that:

   a rain will fall on the first three days of a given week, but not on the other four
   b rain will fall on exactly three days of a given week
   c rain will fall on at least three days of a given week.

5 A die is rolled seven times and the number of 2s that occur in the seven rolls is noted. Find the probability that:

   a the first roll is a 2 and the rest are not
   b exactly one of the seven rolls results in a 2.

6 If the probability of a female child being born is 0.5, use your CAS calculator to find the probability that, if 100 babies are born on a certain day, more than 60 of them will be female.

7 A breakfast cereal manufacturer places a coupon in every tenth packet of cereal entitling the buyer to a free packet of cereal. Over a period of two months a family purchases five packets of cereal.

   a Find the probability distribution of the number of coupons in the five packets.
   b What is the most probable number of coupons in the five packets?

8 If the probability of a female child being born is 0.48, find the probability that a family with exactly three children has at least one child of each sex.

9 An insurance company examines its records and notes that 30% of accident claims are made by drivers aged under 21. If there are 100 accident claims in the next 12 months, use your CAS calculator to determine the probability that 40 or more of them are made by drivers aged under 21.

10 A restaurant is able to seat 80 customers inside, and many more at outside tables. Generally, 80% of their customers prefer to sit inside. If 100 customers arrive one day, use your CAS calculator to determine the probability that the restaurant will seat inside all those who make this request.

11 A supermarket has four checkouts. A customer in a hurry decides to leave without making a purchase if all the checkouts are busy. At that time of day the probability of each checkout being free is 0.25. Assuming that whether or not a checkout is busy is independent of any other checkout, calculate the probability that the customer will make a purchase.

12 An aircraft has four engines. The probability that any one of them will fail on a flight is 0.003. Assuming the four engines operate independently, find the probability that on a particular flight:

  a no engine failure occurs
  b not more than one engine failure occurs
  c all four engines fail.

13 A market researcher wishes to determine if the public has a preference for one of two brands of cheese, brand *A* or brand *B*. In order to do this, 15 people are asked to choose which cheese they prefer. If there is actually no difference in preference:

  a What is the probability that 10 or more people would state a preference for brand *A*?
  b What is the probability that 10 or more people would state a preference for brand *A* or brand *B*?

14 It has been discovered that 4% of the batteries produced at a certain factory are defective. A sample of 10 is drawn randomly from each hour's production and the number of defective batteries is noted. In what percentage of these hourly samples would there be a least two defective batteries? Explain what doubts you might have if a particular sample contained six defective batteries.

15 An examination consists of 10 multiple-choice questions. Each question has four possible answers. At least five correct answers are required to pass the examination.

  a Suppose a student guesses the answer to each question. What is the probability the student will make:
    i at least three correct guesses
    ii at least four correct guesses
    iii at least five correct guesses?
  b How many correct answers do you think are necessary to decide that the student is not guessing each answer? Explain your reasons.

16 An examination consists of 20 multiple-choice questions. Each question has four possible answers. At least 10 correct answers are required to pass the examination. Suppose the student guesses the answer to each question. Use your CAS calculator to determine the probability that the student passes.

Example 8 17 Plot the probability distribution function $\Pr(X = x) = \binom{n}{x} p^x (1-p)^{n-x}$, $x = 0, 1, \ldots, n$, for $n = 10$ and $p = 0.3$.

18 Plot the probability distribution function $\Pr(X = x) = \binom{n}{x} p^x (1-p)^{n-x}$, $x = 0, 1, \ldots, n$, for $n = 15$ and $p = 0.6$.

Example 9 19 What is the least number of times a fair coin should be tossed in order to ensure that:
  a the probability of observing at least one head is more than 0.95
  b the probability of observing more than one head is more than 0.95?

20 What is the least number of times a fair die should be rolled in order to ensure that:
  a the probability of observing at least one 6 is more than 0.9
  b the probability of observing more than one 6 is more than 0.9?

21 Geoff has determined that his probability of hitting an ace when serving at tennis is 0.1. What is the least number of balls he must serve to ensure that:
  a the probability of hitting at least one ace is more than 0.8
  b probability of hitting more than one ace is more than 0.8?

22 The probability of winning in a game of chance is known to be 0.05. What is the least number of times Phillip should play the game in order to ensure that:
  a the probability that he wins at least once is more than 0.90
  b the probability that he wins at least once is more than 0.95?

Example 10 23 The probability of a shooter obtaining a maximum score from a shot is 0.7. Find the probability that out of five shots the shooter obtains the maximum score:
  a three times
  b three times, given that he obtains the maximum score at least once.

24 Each week a security firm transports a large sum of money between two places. The day on which the journey is made is varied at random and, in any week, each of the five days from Monday to Friday is equally likely to be chosen. (In the following, give answers correct to four decimal places.) Calculate the probability that in a period of 10 weeks Friday will be chosen:
  a exactly two times
  b at least two times
  c exactly three times, given it is chosen at least two times.

Chapter summary

- A **discrete** random variable X is one which can take only a countable number of values. Often these values are whole numbers, but not necessarily.
- The **probability distribution** of X is a function $p(x) = \Pr(X = x)$ that assigns a probability to each value of X. It can be represented by a rule, a table or a graph, and must give a probability $p(x)$ for every value x that X can take.
- For *any* discrete probability distribution, the following must be true:
  - Each value of $p(x)$ belongs to the interval $[0, 1]$. That is, $0 \leq p(x) \leq 1$ for all x.
  - The sum of the values of $p(x)$ must be 1.
- The **binomial distribution** arises when counting the number of successes in a sample chosen from an infinite population, or from a finite population with replacement. In either case, the probability, p, of a success on a single trial remains constant for all trials.
  If the experiment consists of a number, n, of identical trials, and the random variable X is the number of successes in n trials, then
  $$\Pr(X = x) = \binom{n}{x} p^x (1-p)^{n-x} \qquad x = 0, 1, \ldots, n$$
  where $\binom{n}{x} = \dfrac{n!}{x!\,(n-x)!}$

Technology-free questions

1 For the probability distribution

x	0	1	2	3	4
$\Pr(X = x)$	0.12	0.25	0.43	0.12	0.08

calculate:

a $\Pr(X \leq 3)$ **b** $\Pr(X \geq 2)$ **c** $\Pr(1 \leq X \leq 3)$

2 A box contains 100 cards. Twenty-five cards are numbered 1, 28 are numbered 2, 30 are numbered 3 and 17 are numbered 4. One card will be drawn from the box and its number X observed. Give the probability distribution of X.

3 From six marbles numbered as shown, two marbles will be drawn without replacement.

① ① ① ① ② ②

Let X denote the sum of the numbers on the selected marbles. List the possible values of X and determine the probability distribution.

4 Two of the integers {1, 2, 3, 6, 7, 9} are chosen at random. (An integer can be chosen twice.) Let X denote the sum of the two integers.
  a List all choices and the corresponding values of X.
  b List the distinct values of X.
  c Obtain the probability distribution of X.

5 For a binomial distribution with $n = 4$ and $p = 0.25$, find the probability of:
  a three or more successes
  b at most three successes
  c two or more failures.

6 Twenty-five per cent of trees in a forest have severe leaf damage from air pollution. If three trees are selected at random, find the probability that:
  a two of the selected trees have severe leaf damage
  b at least one has severe leaf damage.

7 In a large batch of eggs, one in three is found to be bad. What is the probability that of four eggs there will be:
  a no bad egg
  b exactly one bad egg
  c more than one bad egg?

8 In a particular village the probability of rain falling on any given day is $\frac{1}{4}$. Write down an expression for the probability that in a particular week rain will fall on:
  a exactly three days
  b less than three days.

9 Previous experience indicates that, of the students entering a particular diploma course, $p\%$ will successfully complete it. One year, 15 students commence the course. Calculate, in terms of p, the probability that:
  a all 15 students successfully complete the course
  b only one student fails
  c no more than two students fail.

10 The probability of winning a particular game is $\frac{3}{5}$. (Assume all games are independent.)
  a Find the probability of winning at least one game when the game is played three times.
  b Given that, when the game is played m times, the probability of winning exactly two games is three times the probability of winning exactly one game, find the value of m.

Chapter 11 review

Multiple-choice questions

1 Consider the following table, which represents the probability distribution of a random variable X.

x	0	1	2	3	4
$\Pr(X = x)$	k	$2k$	$3k$	$2k$	k

For the table to represent a probability distribution, the value of k is

A $\dfrac{1}{10}$ **B** $\dfrac{1}{9}$ **C** $\dfrac{1}{5}$ **D** $\dfrac{1}{7}$ **E** $\dfrac{1}{8}$

2 Suppose that the random variable X has the probability distribution given in the table:

x	1	2	3	4	5	6
$\Pr(X = x)$	0.05	0.23	0.18	0.33	0.14	0.10

Then $\Pr(X \geq 5)$ is equal to

A 0.24 **B** 0.10 **C** 0.90 **D** 0.76 **E** 0.14

3 Suppose that there are two apples and three oranges in a bag. A piece of fruit is drawn from the bag. If the fruit is an apple, it is not replaced and a second piece of fruit is drawn and the process is repeated until an orange is chosen. If X is the number of pieces of fruit drawn *before* an orange is chosen, then the possible values for X are

A $\{0\}$ **B** $\{0, 1\}$ **C** $\{0, 1, 2\}$ **D** $\{0, 1, 2, 3\}$ **E** $\{1, 2, 3\}$

4 Which one of the following random variables has a binomial distribution?

A the number of tails observed when a fair coin is tossed 10 times
B the number of times a player rolls a die before a 6 is observed
C the number of text messages a students sends in a day
D the number of people at the AFL Grand Final
E the number of accidents which occur per day at a busy intersection

5 Suppose that X is the number of male children born into a family of six children. If the distribution of X is binomial, with probability of success of 0.48, the probability that a family with six children will have exactly three male children is

A 0.48×3 **B** $(0.48)^3$ **C** $(0.48)^6$
D $^6C_3(0.48)^3$ **E** $^6C_3(0.48)^3(0.52)^3$

6 The probability that a student will be left-handed is known to be 0.23. If nine students are selected at random for the softball team, then the probability that at least one of these students is left-handed is given by

A $(0.23)^9$ **B** $^9C_1(0.23)^1(0.77)^8$ **C** $1 - {^9C_0}(0.23)^0(0.77)^9$
D $1 - {^9C_0}(0.23)^0(0.77)^9 - {^9C_1}(0.23)^1(0.77)^8$
E $(0.23)^9 + {^9C_1}(0.23)^1(0.77)^8$

7 Which one of the following graphs best represents the shape of a binomial probability distribution for the random variable X with 10 independent trials and probability of success 0.2?

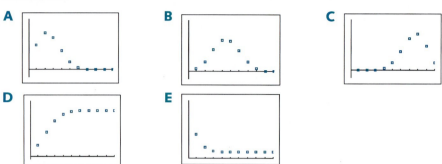

8 If the probability that a mathematics student in a certain state is male is 0.56, and if 60 students are chosen at random from that state, then the probability that at least 30 of those chosen are male is closest to

A 0.066 **B** 0.210 **C** 0.790 **D** 0.857 **E** 0.143

The following information relates to Questions 9 and 10.

Tom is choosing lucky numbers from a box. The probability of winning a prize with any one of the lucky numbers is 0.1, and whether or not a prize is won on a single draw is independent of any other draw.

9 Suppose Tom draws 10 lucky numbers. The probability he wins three or four times is

A 0.0574 **B** 0.0686 **C** 0.0112 **D** 0.0702 **E** 0.9984

10 Suppose Tom plays a sequence of n games. If the probability of winning at least one prize is more than 0.90, then the smallest value n can take is closest to

A 1 **B** 2 **C** 15 **D** 21 **E** 22

Extended-response questions

1 For a particular random experiment, $\Pr(A\,|\,B) = 0.6$, $\Pr(A\,|\,B') = 0.1$ and $\Pr(B) = 0.4$. The random variable X takes the value 4 if both A and B occur, 3 if only A occurs, 2 if only B occurs, and 1 if neither A nor B occur.

a Specify the probability distribution of X.
b Find $\Pr(X \geq 2)$.

2 The number of times a paper boy hits the front step of a particular house in a street in a randomly selected week is given by the random variable X, which can take values 0, 1, 2, 3, 4, 5, 6, 7. The probability distribution for X is given in the table.

x	0	1	2	3	4	5	6	7
$\Pr(X = x)$	0	k	0.1	0.2	0.2	0.3	0.1	0

  a i Find the value of k.
     ii Find the probability that he hits the front step more than three times.
     iii Find the probability that he hits the front step more than four times, given that he hits the front step more than three times.
  b It is found that there are 10 houses on the round for which the paper boy's accuracy is given exactly by the distribution above. Therefore the probability of hitting the front step of any one of these 10 houses three or four times a week is 0.4.
     i Find the probability (correct to four decimal places) that out of 10 houses he hits the front step of exactly *four particular* houses three or four times a week.
     ii Find the probability (correct to four decimal places) that out of 10 houses he hits the front step of any four houses three or four times a week.

3 A bag contains three blue cards and two white cards that are identical in all respects except colour. Two cards are drawn at random and without replacement from the bag.
  a Find the probability that the two cards are different colours.
  If the cards are different colours, then two fair coins are tossed and the number of heads recorded. If the cards are the same colour, then the two fair coins are each tossed twice and the number of heads recorded.
  Let X be the number of heads recorded.
  b Find:
     i $\Pr(X = 0)$ ii $\Pr(X = 2)$
  The events A and B are defined as follows: event A occurs if the two cards drawn are the same colour, and event B occurs if $X = 2$.
  c Find:
     i $\Pr(A \cup B)$ ii $\Pr(B \mid A)$

4 An examination consists of 20 multiple-choice questions. Each question has five possible answers. At least 10 correct answers are required to pass the examination. Suppose the student guesses the answer to each question.
  a Use your CAS calculator to determine the probability that the student passes.
  b Given that the student has passed, what is the probability that they scored at least 80% on the test?

5 Jolanta is playing a game of chance. She is told that the probability of winning at least once in every five games is 0.99968. Assuming that the probability of winning each game is constant, what is her probability of winning in any one game?

6 Suppose that a telephone salesperson has a probability of 0.05 of making a sale on any phone call.

  a What is the probability that they will make at least one sale in the next 10 calls?

  b How many calls should the salesperson make in order to ensure that the probability of making at least one sale is more than 90%?

7 Suppose that, in flight, aeroplane engines fail with probability q, independently of each other, and a plane will complete the flight successfully if at least half of its engines do not fail.

  a Find, in terms of q, the probability that a two-engine plane completes the flight successfully.

  b Find, in terms of q, the probability that a four-engine plane completes the flight successfully.

  c For what values of q is a two-engine plane to be preferred to a four-engine one?

8 In general 45% of people have type O blood. Assuming that donors arrive independently and randomly at the blood bank, use simulation to answer the following questions.

  a If 10 donors came in one day, what is the probability of at least four having type O blood?

  b On a certain day, the blood bank needs four donors with type O blood. How many donors, on average, should they have to see in order to obtain exactly four with type O blood?

12

Revision of Chapters 9–11

12A Technology-free questions

1   A six-sided die is rolled twice. Calculate the probability that:
    a the sum of the numbers showing is 5
    b the sum of the numbers showing is not 5.

2   A number is formed by arranging the digits 3, 4 and 8 in random order.
    a List the sample space.
    b Calculate the probability that a number less than 500 is obtained.
    c What is the probability that the number obtained is even?

3   A card is drawn at random from a pack of 52 cards. What is the probability that the card is:
    a not red
    b not an ace?

4   Consider the following spinners. In each case, what is the chance of the pointer stopping in region A?

    a
    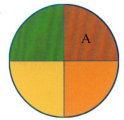

    b
    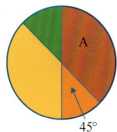
    45°

5 For a particular biased six-sided die, it is known that the numbers 1, 2, 3 and 5 are equally likely to occur, that the number 4 occurs four times as often as the number 2, and that the number 6 occurs half as often as the number 2.
   a Find the probability of each of the possible outcomes.
   b Find the probability that the number observed is not a 4.

6 The dartboard shown consists of two concentric circular regions. The radius of the inner circle is 10 cm, and the radius of the outer circle is 20 cm. If Mike throws a dart, it is equally likely to hit any part of the dartboard, and it hits the dartboard every time. Find the probability of the dart hitting the blue region.

7 Suppose that in a certain school the probability that a student plays basketball is 0.3, the probability that a student plays hockey is 0.4, and probability that a student plays both basketball and hockey is 0.1.
   a Find the probability that a student plays either or both of these sports.
   b Find the probability that a student plays hockey, given that they play basketball.

8 At a school holiday program for 60 students, painting was offered as an additional activity one morning, and music as an additional activity in the afternoon. Every student went to at least one additional activity, with 45 students attending painting and 30 students attending music. Construct a probability table, and use it to find the probability that a student chosen at random:
   a went to music
   b went to painting
   c went to painting but not music
   d went to music but not painting.

9 In a certain town, the probability that it will be sunny on any Saturday is 0.6. If it is sunny on Saturday, then the probability that it is sunny on Sunday is 0.8. If it is not sunny on Saturday, then the probability that it is sunny on Sunday is 0.2. Find the probability that:
   a it is sunny all weekend
   b it is sunny on Sunday.

10 For two events A and B such that $\Pr(A) = 0.5$, $\Pr(B) = 0.2$ and $\Pr(B|A) = 0.1$, find:
   a $\Pr(A \cap B)$
   b $\Pr(A|B)$

11 If A and B are independent events with $\Pr(A) = 0.4$ and $\Pr(B) = 0.5$, find:
   a $\Pr(A|B)$
   b $\Pr(A \cap B)$
   c $\Pr(A \cup B)$

12 If there are ten runners in the final of the 5000 metres, in how many ways can the first three places be filled?

13 How many different hands of seven cards can be dealt from a normal pack of 52 cards? (Give your answer using factorial notation.)

14 A committee of three is to be chosen to represent a class at the School Council. If everyone in the class is equally likely to be chosen, and the class consists of five boys and seven girls, what is the probability that the committee will contain:

  a one girl **b** two girls?

15 For the probability distribution

x	0	1	2	3	4
$\Pr(X = x)$	0.1	0.2	0.4	0.1	0.2

calculate:

  a $\Pr(X \leq 2)$ **b** $\Pr(X \geq 2)$ **c** $\Pr(1 \leq X \leq 3)$

16 For a binomial distribution with $n = 4$ and $p = 0.2$, find the probability of:

  a exactly four successes **b** three or more successes.

17 In a particular city the probability of rain falling on any given day is $\frac{1}{5}$. Write down expression which would enable you to calculate the probability that in a particular week rain will fall on:

  a exactly three days **b** less than three days **c** four or more days.

18 Records show that $x\%$ of people will pass their driver's license on the first attempt. If ten students attempt their driver's license, write down in terms of x the probability that:

  a all 10 students pass **b** only one fails **c** no more than two fail.

12B Multiple-choice questions

Questions marked with a † are based on Chapter 11.

1 Mary and Ann try to guess the month in which the other was born. The probability that both guess correctly is

  A $\frac{1}{2}$ **B** $\frac{1}{6}$ **C** $\frac{1}{4}$ **D** $\frac{1}{24}$ **E** $\frac{1}{144}$

2 Bag A contains 2 white and 3 black balls. Bag B contains 3 white and 2 black balls. If one ball is drawn from each bag, the probability that they are of different colours is

  A $\frac{6}{25}$ **B** $\frac{10}{25}$ **C** $\frac{13}{25}$ **D** $\frac{21}{25}$ **E** $\frac{24}{25}$

3 Two dice are thrown. The probability of getting a sum that is greater than or equal to 12 is

  A 0 **B** $\frac{1}{6}$ **C** $\frac{1}{12}$ **D** $\frac{1}{18}$ **E** $\frac{1}{36}$

4 A group consists of four boys and three girls. If two of them are chosen at random (without replacement), the probability that a boy and a girl are chosen is

A $\dfrac{2}{7}$ **B** $\dfrac{4}{7}$ **C** $\dfrac{12}{49}$ **D** $\dfrac{24}{49}$ **E** $\dfrac{27}{49}$

5 If X and Y are mutually exclusive events such that $\Pr(X) = \Pr(Y')$, then $\Pr(X \cup Y)$ is

A $\Pr(X) \times \Pr(Y)$ **B** $\Pr(X)$ **C** $\Pr(Y)$
D 0 **E** 1

†6 The probability that England wins the toss exactly 250 times in the next 500 Tests is

A 1 **B** $\left(\dfrac{1}{2}\right)^{250}$ **C** $\left(\dfrac{1}{2}\right)^{500}$ **D** $\dbinom{500}{250}\left(\dfrac{1}{2}\right)^{250}$ **E** $\dbinom{500}{250}\left(\dfrac{1}{2}\right)^{500}$

7 If six fair dice are rolled, the probability of getting at least one 4 is

A $\dfrac{4}{6}$ **B** $\left(\dfrac{5}{6}\right)^{6}$ **C** $1 - \left(\dfrac{5}{6}\right)^{6}$ **D** $\dfrac{1}{6}$ **E** $\dfrac{1}{3}$

8 If a card is randomly drawn from a well-shuffled card deck (52 cards), the probability of getting a heart or a jack is

A $\dfrac{1}{52}$ **B** $\dfrac{5}{13}$ **C** $\dfrac{4}{13}$ **D** $\dfrac{7}{52}$ **E** $\dfrac{1}{26}$

9 A bag contains k red marbles and 1 white marble. Two marbles are drawn without replacement. The probability that both are red is

A $\dfrac{k}{(k+1)^2}$ **B** $\dfrac{k-1}{k+1}$ **C** $\dfrac{k}{k+1}$ **D** $\dfrac{2k}{k+1}$ **E** $\dfrac{2}{k+1}$

10 Two cards are drawn at random from a pack. Consider the probabilities when:
- The first card is replaced and the pack shuffled before the second is drawn.
- There is no such replacement.

The ratio of the probabilities that both are aces is

A $8:3$ **B** $5:3$ **C** $4:3$ **D** $17:13$ **E** $52:51$

11 The probability of Bill hitting the bullseye with a single shot is $\tfrac{1}{2}$. The probability that Charles does the same is $\tfrac{1}{4}$. Bill has 2 shots and Charles has 4. The ratio of the probability of each player hitting the bullseye at least once is

A $64:27$ **B** $2:1$ **C** $32:27$ **D** $192:175$ **E** $64:85$

12 The number of arrangements which can be made using all the letters of the word RAPIDS, if the vowels are together, is

A 30 **B** 60 **C** 120 **D** 240 **E** 720

13 The number of ways in which n books can be chosen from $m + n$ different books is

A $\dfrac{(m+n)!}{n!}$ **B** $(m+n)! - m!$ **C** $(m+n)! - n!$

D $\dfrac{(m+n)!}{m!}$ **E** $\dfrac{(m+n)!}{m!n!}$

14 The number of different teams of seven which can be selected from a squad of 12 players is

   A 792   **B** 84   **C** 5040   **D** 120   **E** 396

15 The number of four-letter code words which can be made using the letters P, Q, R, S if repetitions are allowed is

   A 16   **B** 24   **C** 64   **D** 128   **E** 256

16 Six cards labelled 1, 2, 3, 4, 5 and 6 are put into a box. Three cards are then drawn from the box (without replacement). The probability that the three cards are all labelled with odd numbers is

   A $\frac{1}{2}$ **B** $\frac{1}{4}$ **C** $\frac{1}{8}$ **D** $\frac{1}{12}$ **E** $\frac{1}{20}$

17 A football ground has six entry gates (I, J, K, L, M and N) and ten exit gates (Q, R, S, T, U, V, W, X, Y and Z). The number of ways two people can enter by the same entry gate and leave by different exit gates is

   A $6 \times 10 + 1 \times 9$ **B** $6 \times 10 \times 9$ **C** $6 \times 10 + 6 \times 9$
   D $6 + 10 + 9$ **E** $6 \times 10 \times 2$

18 If $\Pr(A \cap B) = \frac{1}{5}$ and $\Pr(B) = \frac{1}{2}$ and $\Pr(B|A) = \frac{1}{3}$, then

   A $\Pr(A|B) = \frac{3}{5}$ and $\Pr(A) = \frac{1}{5}$ **B** $\Pr(A|B) = \frac{1}{3}$ and $\Pr(A) = \frac{2}{5}$

   C $\Pr(A|B) = \frac{2}{5}$ and $\Pr(A) = \frac{3}{5}$ **D** $\Pr(A|B) = \frac{2}{3}$ and $\Pr(A) = \frac{3}{5}$

   E $\Pr(A|B) = \frac{2}{5}$ and $\Pr(A) = \frac{2}{5}$

19 A pair of unbiased dice is thrown. The probability of the sum of the numbers uppermost being 10 is

   A $\frac{1}{36}$ **B** $\frac{2}{36}$ **C** $\frac{3}{36}$ **D** $\frac{10}{36}$ **E** $\frac{18}{36}$

20 If the letters of the word HEADS are arranged in random order, then the probability that the letters are in alphabetical order is

   A $\frac{1}{120}$ **B** $\frac{1}{60}$ **C** $\frac{1}{24}$ **D** $\frac{1}{5}$ **E** $\frac{1}{4}$

21 A box contains twelve red balls and four green balls. A ball is selected at random from the box and not replaced and then a second ball is drawn. The probability that the two balls are both green is equal to

   A $\frac{1}{4}$ **B** $\frac{1}{16}$ **C** $\frac{3}{64}$ **D** $\frac{1}{8}$ **E** $\frac{1}{20}$

†22 A hockey player attempts to score a goal in a practice session. The probability of each shot scoring is $\frac{1}{8}$, independently of the outcome of any other shot. The probability that the player hits four goals out of six shots is

A $\left(\frac{1}{8}\right)^4 \left(\frac{7}{8}\right)^2$
B $15\left(\frac{7}{8}\right)^4 \left(\frac{1}{8}\right)^2$
C $20\left(\frac{7}{8}\right)^4 \left(\frac{1}{8}\right)^2$
D $\left(\frac{7}{8}\right)^4 \left(\frac{1}{8}\right)^2$
E $15\left(\frac{1}{8}\right)^4 \left(\frac{7}{8}\right)^2$

†23 In an experiment the constant probability that a trial will be successful is p. Three trials are to be made. The probability that not more than one will be successful is

A $(1-p)^3$
B $3p(1-p)^2$
C $(1-p)^2(1+2p)$
D $p^2(3-2p)$
E p^3

†24 It is found that an archer hits a target with a probability of 0.8. The probability that he hits the target at least once from 10 shots is

A $1 - {}^{10}C_1(0.8)^1(0.2)^9$
B ${}^{10}C_1(0.8)^9(0.2)^1$
C ${}^{10}C_1(0.8)^1(0.2)^9$
D $1 - (0.2)^{10}$
E $1 - (0.8)^{10}$

25 The probability that Trevor hits the bullseye on a dartboard is 0.15. The least number of darts that Trevor should throw to ensure that the probability he throws at least one bullseye is more than 0.9 is

A 2 **B** 6 **C** 14 **D** 15 **E** 29

12C Extended-response questions

1 The heights (measured to the nearest centimetre) of 56 plants grown under experimental conditions are given in the following table.

Note: The table gives the number of plants for which the measured height lies in a given interval.

Interval	(0, 10]	(10, 20]	(20, 30]	(30, 40]	(40, 50]	(50, 60]	(60, 70]
Number of plants	1	2	4	6	13	22	8

a If one plant is selected at random, find the probability that its height is:
   i greater than 50 cm
   ii either greater than 50 cm or less than or equal to 30 cm
   iii greater than 40 cm, given that it is greater than 30 cm.

b The probability that a randomly selected plant produces a flower is $\frac{6}{7}$ and the probability that it will suffer from a disease is $\frac{1}{4}$. Assume independence.
   i Find the probability that a single plant selected at random produces a flower but does not suffer from disease.
   ii Find the probability that a single plant selected at random produces a flower, does not suffer from disease and has a height greater than 50 cm.

2 Three people, *A*, *B* and *C*, are each given a bag containing six numbered balls as shown in the diagram below, and each of them draws a ball from the bag that they were given.

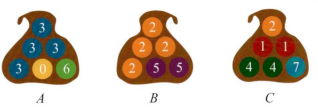

  a Calculate the probability that *B* draws a higher number than *C*.
  b Calculate the probability that *A* draws a higher number than both *B* and *C*.

3 Eight cards bearing the letters P, A, R, A, L, L, E, L are placed in a box. Three cards are drawn out at random without replacement. Calculate the probability that:
  a the second card bears the letter L
  b the three cards bear the letters A, L, E in that order
  c the three cards bear the letters A, L, E in any order
  d the first two cards bear different letters.

4 Bella Scotsimal, a fortune teller, claims to be able to predict the sex of unborn children. In fact, on each occasion she is consulted the probability that she makes a correct prediction is 0.6, independent of any other prediction.
One afternoon Bella is consulted by ten women. Find, correct to two significant figures, the probability that:
  a her first eight predictions are correct and her last two are wrong
  b she makes exactly eight correct predictions
  c she makes at least eight correct predictions
  d she makes exactly eight correct predictions, given that she makes at least eight.

5 Of the employees in a large factory, $\frac{1}{8}$ travel to work by bus, $\frac{3}{8}$ by train, and the remainder by car. Those travelling by bus have a probability of $\frac{1}{3}$ of being late, those by train will be late with probability $\frac{1}{5}$, and those by car will be late with probability $\frac{3}{4}$.
  a Draw and complete a tree diagram and calculate the probability that an employee chosen at random will be late.
  b If an employee is late, calculate the probability that he travelled by car.

6 In order to choose a team for a quiz, a class is split into three groups. Group A contains two boys and three girls, group B contains one boy and three girls, and group C contains two boys and one girl. An unbiased die is thrown. If a 1, 2 or 3 appears, a random choice will be made from group A. If a 4 or 5 appears, a random choice will be made from group C. If a 6 appears, a random choice will be made from group B.
  a Calculate the probability that a boy will be chosen when the choice is made.
  b Given that a girl is chosen when the choice is made, calculate the probability that she will be chosen from:
    i group A   **ii** group B.

7 Suppose that in a game of chance bag A contains balls numbered 1 and 2, bag B contains balls numbered 3, 4 and 5, and bag C contains balls numbered 3 and 5.

a David chooses one bag at random and then draws one ball randomly from the bag.

  i Find the probability that the ball drawn is a 4.
  ii Find the probability that the ball drawn is a 3.

b After David has drawn a ball in the way described in part a, he puts it back into the original bag. Next, Sally chooses one bag at random and then draws one ball randomly from the bag.
Find the probability that:

  i the balls drawn by David and Sally are both numbered 4
  ii the balls drawn by David and Sally are both numbered 3 and from the same bag.

8 Of the 100 students at a particular level in a school, 40 take history, 45 take geography and 10 take both subjects.

a A Venn diagram interpreting this situation is as shown:

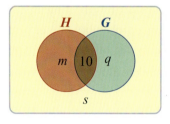

m is the number of students who take history only.

q is the number of students who take geography only.

s is the number of students who take neither subject.

  i Find the values of m, q and s.
  ii Find the number of students who take either history or geography but not both.

b If a student is chosen at random, find the probability that he or she takes history but not geography.

c If a student is chosen randomly from the students who do not take history, find the probability that he or she takes geography.

9 Players *A*, *B* and *C* each have a disc and a spinning arrow which when spun comes to rest with its head pointing towards one sector. The probability of the arrowhead stopping at any sector and the score recorded by the player is shown in the diagram. For example, player *A* scores 1, 4 or 8 with probabilities 0.2, 0.4 or 0.4 respectively.

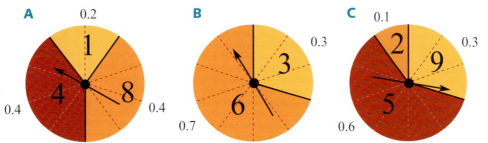

If *A*, *B* and *C* all spin their arrows simultaneously, find the probability (assuming independence) that:

  a the total of the scores is 23
  b *B* scores more than *C*
  c *C* scores more than *A*.

10 The journey from town *A* to town *D* passes through towns *B* and *C*. There are three roads from *A* to *B*, four from *B* to *C* and five from *C* to *D*.

  a Find the number of different routes that can be taken from *A* to *D*.

There are road works on one of the roads between *A* and *B*, on two roads between *B* and *C* and on three roads between *C* and *D*.

  b Find the number of different routes that can be taken from *A* to *D* without encountering any road works.
  c Calculate the probability that a traveller from *A* to *D*, picking a route at random, encounters road works at each stage of their journey.

11 *A*, *B* and *C* fire one shot each at a target. The probability that *A* will hit the target is $\frac{1}{5}$, the probability that *B* will hit the target is $\frac{1}{4}$, and the probability that *C* will hit the target is $\frac{1}{3}$. If they fire together, calculate the probability that:

  a all three shots hit the target
  b only *C*'s shot hits the target
  c at least one shot hits the target
  d given that only one shot hits the target, it is the shot by *C*.

12 In a game at a fair, darts are thrown at a board. The outer square is of side length 100 cm and each of the nine inner squares is of side length 20 cm.

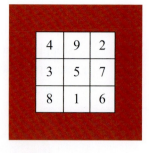

  a Calculate, in cm², the area of:

  i the larger outer square

  ii one of the inner squares

  iii the shaded region.

The number shown in each region is the score obtained by a dart hitting that region. A dart hitting the shaded region scores 0. Assume that all darts hit the board and that each point on the board is equally likely to be hit.

  b Find the probability that with one dart the score will be:

  i 7   **ii** at least 7   **iii** 0

  c Each turn consists of throwing three darts. Calculate the probability of scoring:

  i a total of 18 with the first two darts   **ii** a total of 24 with the three darts.

13 Eighteen numbers are arranged in three groups of six as follows:

Group A: 0, 6, 6, 6, 6, 10

Group B: 1, 1, 1, 7, 7, 11

Group C: 3, 3, 3, 3, 8, 8

One number is drawn at random from each group. Given that a, b and c denote the numbers drawn from groups A, B and C respectively, calculate the probability that:

  a $c < b$ **b** a is greater than both b and c **c** $c > a + b$

14 Philip has noted that when he is fishing the probability that he will catch a trout on any day is 0.2, independent of whether or not he catches a trout on any other day. He stops fishing for the day if he catches a trout.

  a Suppose that Philip goes fishing five days in a row. What is the probability that he will catch:

  i no trout   **ii** exactly two trout   **iii** at least one trout?

  b What is the least number of days on which he should fish to ensure that:

  i the probability of catching at least one trout is more than 0.9

  ii the probability of catching more than one trout is more than 0.9?

15 Suppose that the probability of a team scoring a goal from a corner in a hockey game is 0.3.

  a Suppose that the team has 10 corners. What is the probability, correct to four decimal places, that the team will score:

  i one goal   **ii** at least two goals   **iii** no more than two goals?

  b What is the least number of corners which would be required to ensure that:

  i the probability of scoring at least one goal is more than 0.95

  ii the probability of scoring more than one goal is more than 0.95?

Chapter 13
Exponential functions and logarithms

Objectives

▶ To understand the rules for manipulating **exponential expressions**.
▶ To define **exponential functions** and to sketch their graphs.
▶ To solve **exponential equations**.
▶ To evaluate **logarithmic expressions**.
▶ To solve equations using **logarithmic methods**.
▶ To sketch graphs of functions of the form $y = \log_a x$ and simple transformations of this.
▶ To understand and use a range of **exponential models**.
▶ To apply **logarithmic scales**.

The function $f(x) = ka^x$, where k is a non-zero constant and the base a is a positive real number other than 1, is called an **exponential function**.

Consider the following example of an exponential function. Assume that a particular biological organism reproduces by dividing every minute. The following table shows the population, P, after n one-minute intervals (assuming that all organisms are still alive).

n	0	1	2	3	4	5	6	n
P	1	2	4	8	16	32	64	2^n

Thus P defines a function which has the rule $P = 2^n$, an exponential function.

In this chapter, the work on functions in this course is continued. Many of the concepts introduced in Chapter 5 – such as domain, range, transformations and inverse functions – are used in the context of exponential and logarithmic functions.

There are many applications of exponential and logarithmic functions, and some of these are investigated in the final two sections of this chapter.

13A The index laws

> **Skillsheet**

The expression a^n is called a **power**, where a is a non-zero number called the **base** and n is a number called the **exponent** or **index**. In this section we concentrate on indices that are integers.

We note that, if n is positive, then $0^n = 0$. But if n is negative or zero, then 0^n is undefined.

Index law 1: Multiplying powers

> **Index law 1**
>
> To **multiply** two powers with the same base, **add** the indices.
>
> $$a^m \times a^n = a^{m+n}$$

If m and n are positive integers,

then $\quad a^m = \underbrace{a \times a \times \cdots \times a}_{m \text{ terms}}$

and $\quad a^n = \underbrace{a \times a \times \cdots \times a}_{n \text{ terms}}$

$\therefore \quad a^m \times a^n = \underbrace{(a \times a \times \cdots \times a)}_{m \text{ terms}} \times \underbrace{(a \times a \times \cdots \times a)}_{n \text{ terms}}$

$\qquad\qquad\quad = \underbrace{a \times a \times \cdots \times a}_{(m+n) \text{ terms}}$

$\qquad\qquad\quad = a^{m+n}$

> **Example 1**
>
> Simplify each of the following:
>
> **a** $2^3 \times 2^{12}$ **b** $x^2 y^3 \times x^4 y$ **c** $2^x \times 2^{x+2}$ **d** $3a^2 b^3 \times 4a^3 b^3$
>
> **Solution**
>
> **a** $2^3 \times 2^{12} = 2^{3+12}$
> $\qquad\qquad = 2^{15}$
>
> **b** $x^2 y^3 \times x^4 y = x^2 \times x^4 \times y^3 \times y$
> $\qquad\qquad\quad = x^6 y^4$
>
> **c** $2^x \times 2^{x+2} = 2^{x+x+2}$
> $\qquad\qquad\quad = 2^{2x+2}$
>
> **d** $3a^2 b^3 \times 4a^3 b^3$
> $\quad = 3 \times 4 \times a^2 \times a^3 \times b^3 \times b^3$
> $\quad = 12 a^5 b^6$
>
> **Explanation**
>
> When multiplying powers with the same base, add the indices.
>
> In part b, the indices of the base-x powers are added, and the indices of the base-y powers are added. Note that $y = y^1$.
>
> In part c, we use $x + x + 2 = 2x + 2$.
>
> In part d, the indices of the base-a powers are added, the indices of the base-b powers are added, and the factors that are numerals are multiplied together.

Using the TI-Nspire

Parts b, c and d can be simplified as shown: the TI-Nspire will simplify automatically.

Note: When using ⌃ to enter indices, you need to use either ▶ or ▼ to return to the baseline.

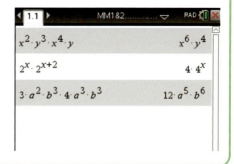

Using the Casio ClassPad

- To enter expressions involving powers, use the power button found in the Math1 keyboard.
- Tap EXE to obtain the simplified expression.

Note: Tap the stylus under the index to return the cursor to the baseline.
The pronumerals a and b must be selected from the Var keyboard.

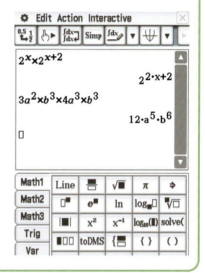

Index law 2: Dividing powers

Index law 2

To **divide** two powers with the same base, **subtract** the indices.

$$a^m \div a^n = a^{m-n}$$

If m and n are positive integers with $m > n$, then

$$a^m \div a^n = \frac{\overbrace{a \times a \times \cdots \times a}^{m \text{ terms}}}{\underbrace{a \times a \times \cdots \times a}_{n \text{ terms}}}$$

$$= \underbrace{a \times a \times \cdots \times a}_{(m-n) \text{ terms}} \quad \text{(by cancelling)}$$

$$= a^{m-n}$$

Example 2

Simplify each of the following:

a $\dfrac{x^4 y^3}{x^2 y^2}$ b $\dfrac{b^{4x} \times b^{x+1}}{b^{2x}}$ c $\dfrac{16a^5 b \times 4a^4 b^3}{8ab}$

Solution

a $\dfrac{x^4 y^3}{x^2 y^2} = x^{4-2} y^{3-2}$

$= x^2 y$

b $\dfrac{b^{4x} \times b^{x+1}}{b^{2x}} = b^{4x+x+1-2x}$

$= b^{3x+1}$

c $\dfrac{16a^5 b \times 4a^4 b^3}{8ab} = \dfrac{16 \times 4}{8} \times a^{5+4-1} \times b^{1+3-1}$

$= 8a^8 b^3$

Explanation

When dividing powers with the same base, subtract the indices.

In part a, the indices of the base-x powers are subtracted, and the indices of the base-y powers are subtracted.

In parts b and c, both index law 1 and index law 2 are used. In part c, the factors that are numerals are grouped together and simplified.

The zero index and negative integer indices

Define $a^0 = 1$ for $a \neq 0$, and define $a^{-n} = \dfrac{1}{a^n}$ for $a \neq 0$.

Index laws 1 and 2 also hold for negative indices m, n.

For example:

$2^4 \times 2^{-2} = \dfrac{2^4}{2^2} = \dfrac{2 \times 2 \times 2 \times 2}{2 \times 2} = 2^2$ (i.e. $2^{4+(-2)}$)

$2^{-4} \div 2^2 = \dfrac{1}{2^4} \times \dfrac{1}{2^2} = \dfrac{1}{2^4 \times 2^2} = 2^{-6}$ (i.e. 2^{-4-2})

$2^3 \div 2^3 = 2^3 \times \dfrac{1}{2^3} = 1 = 2^0$ (i.e. 2^{3-3})

The reciprocal of a fraction such as $\dfrac{2}{3}$ is $\dfrac{3}{2}$. For fractions, the index -1 means 'the reciprocal of'. For example:

$\left(\dfrac{2}{3}\right)^{-1} = \dfrac{3}{2}$

When raising a fraction to other negative indices, take the reciprocal first. For example:

$\left(\dfrac{5}{6}\right)^{-2} = \left(\dfrac{6}{5}\right)^2 = \dfrac{36}{25}$

Example 3

Evaluate each of the following:

a 8^{-2} b $\left(\dfrac{1}{2}\right)^{-4}$ c $\left(\dfrac{3}{4}\right)^{-3}$

Solution

a $8^{-2} = \left(\dfrac{1}{8}\right)^2 = \dfrac{1}{64}$ 　　**b** $\left(\dfrac{1}{2}\right)^{-4} = 2^4 = 16$ 　　**c** $\left(\dfrac{3}{4}\right)^{-3} = \left(\dfrac{4}{3}\right)^3 = \dfrac{64}{27}$

Index law 3: Raising the power

Consider the following:

$(2^3)^2 = 2^3 \times 2^3 = 2^{3+3} = 2^6 = 2^{3 \times 2}$

$(4^3)^4 = 4^3 \times 4^3 \times 4^3 \times 4^3 = 4^{3+3+3+3} = 4^{12} = 4^{3 \times 4}$

$(a^2)^5 = a^2 \times a^2 \times a^2 \times a^2 \times a^2 = a^{2+2+2+2+2} = a^{10} = a^{2 \times 5}$

In general, $(a^m)^n = a^{m \times n}$.

> **Index law 3**
>
> To raise a power to another power, **multiply** the indices.
>
> $(a^m)^n = a^{m \times n}$
>
> This rule holds for all integers m and n.

Example 4

Simplify each of the following:

a $(a^5)^3$ 　　**b** $\left(\left(\dfrac{1}{2}\right)^{-3}\right)^2$ 　　**c** $(b^3)^2 \times (b^2)^{-1}$

Solution	Explanation
a $(a^5)^3 = a^{15}$	Index law 3 is used.
b $\left(\left(\dfrac{1}{2}\right)^{-3}\right)^2 = \left(\dfrac{1}{2}\right)^{-6} = 2^6 = 64$	For part b, the following calculation is probably preferable: $\left(\left(\dfrac{1}{2}\right)^{-3}\right)^2 = (2^3)^2 = 8^2 = 64$
c $(b^3)^2 \times (b^2)^{-1} = b^6 \times b^{-2} = b^4$	In part c, index law 1 is also used.

Index laws 4 and 5: Products and quotients

> **Index law 4**
>
> $(ab)^n = a^n b^n$

If n is a positive integer, then

$(ab)^n = \underbrace{(ab) \times (ab) \times \cdots \times (ab)}_{n \text{ terms}}$

$ = \underbrace{(a \times a \times \cdots \times a)}_{n \text{ terms}} \times \underbrace{(b \times b \times \cdots \times b)}_{n \text{ terms}}$

$ = a^n b^n$

> **Index law 5**
>
> $$\left(\frac{a}{b}\right)^n = \frac{a^n}{b^n}$$

If n is a positive integer, then

$$\left(\frac{a}{b}\right)^n = \frac{a}{b} \times \frac{a}{b} \times \cdots \times \frac{a}{b}$$
$$= \frac{a^n}{b^n}$$

Example 5

Simplify each of the following:

a $(2a^2b^3)^3 \times (3ab^4)^{-2}$ **b** $\left(\dfrac{2a^3b^2}{abc^2}\right)^3 \div (ab^{-1}c)^3$

Solution

a $(2a^2b^3)^3 \times (3ab^4)^{-2} = 8a^6b^9 \times 3^{-2}a^{-2}b^{-8}$
$= \dfrac{8a^4b}{9}$

b $\left(\dfrac{2a^3b^2}{abc^2}\right)^3 \div (ab^{-1}c)^3 = \dfrac{8a^9b^6}{a^3b^3c^6} \times \dfrac{1}{a^3b^{-3}c^3}$
$= \dfrac{8a^3b^6}{c^9}$

Explanation

In part a, index law 4 is used, and then laws 3 and 1 and the fact that $3^{-2} = \dfrac{1}{9}$.

In part b, index law 5 is used. Dividing by a fraction always means multiply by the reciprocal of that fraction.

Working with a negative base

The power $(-a)^n$ can be written as $(-1 \times a)^n = (-1)^n(a)^n$. We note that:

- If n is even, then $(-1)^n = 1$.
- If n is odd, then $(-1)^n = -1$.

Hence, if a is a positive number, then the number $(-a)^n$ is positive when n is even and negative when n is odd.

Example 6

Simplify each of the following:

a $(-3)^4$ **b** $(-5a)^3$ **c** $(-2a)^3 \times 3a^2$

Solution

a $(-3)^4 = 81$ **b** $(-5a)^3 = -125a^3$ **c** $(-2a)^3 \times 3a^2 = -8a^3 \times 3a^2$
$= -24a^5$

Using prime decomposition

Bases that are composite numbers are often best factored into primes before further calculations are undertaken.

Example 7

Simplify the following, expressing the answers in positive-index form:

a $12^n \times 18^{-2n}$

b $\dfrac{3^{-3} \times 6^4 \times 12^{-3}}{9^{-4} \times 2^{-2}}$

c $\dfrac{3^{2n} \times 6^n}{8^n \times 3^n}$

Solution

a
$$\begin{aligned} 12^n \times 18^{-2n} &= (3 \times 2^2)^n \times (3^2 \times 2)^{-2n} \\ &= 3^n \times 2^{2n} \times 3^{-4n} \times 2^{-2n} \\ &= 3^{-3n} \times 2^0 \\ &= \dfrac{1}{3^{3n}} \end{aligned}$$

b
$$\begin{aligned} \dfrac{3^{-3} \times 6^4 \times 12^{-3}}{9^{-4} \times 2^{-2}} &= \dfrac{3^{-3} \times 2^4 \times 3^4 \times 2^{-6} \times 3^{-3}}{3^{-4} \times 3^{-4} \times 2^{-2}} \\ &= \dfrac{3^{-2} \times 2^{-2}}{3^{-8} \times 2^{-2}} \\ &= 3^6 \end{aligned}$$

c
$$\begin{aligned} \dfrac{3^{2n} \times 6^n}{8^n \times 3^n} &= \dfrac{(3^n \times 3^n) \times (3^n \times 2^n)}{2^{3n} \times 3^n} \\ &= \dfrac{3^n \times 3^n}{2^{2n}} \\ &= \left(\dfrac{3}{2}\right)^{2n} \end{aligned}$$

Explanation

The prime decomposition of 12 is
$$12 = 2^2 \times 3$$

The prime decomposition of 18 is
$$18 = 2 \times 3^2$$

Each number in this question can be expressed using powers of 2 and 3.

Index law 4 is used in each of the parts. For example:
$$\begin{aligned} 12^{-3} &= (2^2 \times 3)^{-3} \\ &= (2^2)^{-3} \times 3^{-3} \\ &= 2^{-6} \times 3^{-3} \end{aligned}$$

Section summary

- The expression a^n is called a **power**, where a is a non-zero number called the **base** and n is a number called the **exponent** or **index**.
- **Index laws** The following results hold for all non-zero numbers a and b and all integers m and n:

    1 $a^m \times a^n = a^{m+n}$ **2** $a^m \div a^n = a^{m-n}$ **3** $(a^m)^n = a^{mn}$

    4 $(ab)^n = a^n b^n$ **5** $\left(\dfrac{a}{b}\right)^n = \dfrac{a^n}{b^n}$

- For every non-zero number a and positive integer n:
    - $a^0 = 1$
    - $a^{-n} = \dfrac{1}{a^n}$ and $\dfrac{1}{a^{-n}} = a^n$
- $0^n = 0$, if n is a positive integer, and 0^0 is undefined.

Exercise 13A

1 For each of the following, use the stated rule to give an equivalent expression in simplest form:

- **a** $x^2 \times x^3$
- **b** $2 \times x^3 \times x^4 \times 4$ — Index law 1
- **c** $\dfrac{x^5}{x^3}$
- **d** $\dfrac{4x^6}{2x^3}$ — Index law 2
- **e** $(a^3)^2$
- **f** $(2^3)^2$ — Index law 3
- **g** $(xy)^2$
- **h** $(x^2y^3)^2$ — Index law 4 (also use law 3 for h)
- **i** $\left(\dfrac{x}{y}\right)^3$
- **j** $\left(\dfrac{x^3}{y^2}\right)^2$ — Index law 5 (also use law 3 for j)

Example 1

2 Simplify each of the following:

- **a** $3^5 \times 3^{12}$
- **b** $x^3y^2 \times x^4y^3$
- **c** $3^{x+1} \times 3^{3x+2}$
- **d** $5a^3b^2 \times 6a^2b^4$

Example 2

3 Simplify each of the following:

- **a** $\dfrac{x^5y^2}{x^3y}$
- **b** $\dfrac{b^{5x} \times b^{2x+1}}{b^{3x}}$
- **c** $\dfrac{8a^2b \times 3a^5b^2}{6a^2b^2}$

Example 3

4 Evaluate each of the following:

- **a** 7^{-2}
- **b** $\left(\dfrac{1}{4}\right)^{-3}$
- **c** $\left(\dfrac{5}{2}\right)^{-3}$

Example 4

5 Simplify each of the following:

- **a** $(b^5)^2$
- **b** $\left(\left(\dfrac{1}{3}\right)^{-2}\right)^3$
- **c** $(b^5)^2 \times (b^2)^{-3}$

Example 5

6 Simplify each of the following:

- **a** $(3a^4b^3)^3 \times (4a^2b^4)^{-2}$
- **b** $\left(\dfrac{5a^3b^3}{ab^2c^2}\right)^3 \div (a^2b^{-1}c)^3$

Example 6

7 Simplify each of the following:

- **a** $(-2)^6$
- **b** $(-3a)^3$
- **c** $(-2a)^5 \times 3a^{-2}$

Example 7

8 Simplify the following:

- **a** $36^n \times 12^{-2n}$
- **b** $\dfrac{2^{-3} \times 8^4 \times 32^{-3}}{4^{-4} \times 2^{-2}}$
- **c** $\dfrac{5^{2n} \times 10^n}{8^n \times 5^n}$

9 Simplify the following:

- **a** $x^3 \times x^4 \times x^2$
- **b** $2^4 \times 4^3 \times 8^2$
- **c** $3^4 \times 9^2 \times 27^3$
- **d** $(q^2p)^3 \times (qp^3)^2$
- **e** $a^2b^{-3} \times (a^3b^2)^3$
- **f** $(2x^3)^2 \times (4x^4)^3$
- **g** $m^3p^2 \times (m^2n^3)^4 \times (p^{-2})^2$
- **h** $2^3a^3b^2 \times (2a^{-1}b^2)^{-2}$

10 Simplify the following:

a $\dfrac{x^3 y^5}{xy^2}$
b $\dfrac{16a^5 b \times 4a^4 b^3}{8ab}$
c $\dfrac{(-2xy)^2 \times 2(x^2 y)^3}{8(xy)^3}$
d $\dfrac{(-3x^2 y^3)^2}{(2xy)^3} \times \dfrac{4x^4 y^3}{(xy)^3}$

11 Simplify each of the following, expressing your answer in positive-index form:

a $m^3 n^2 p^{-2} \times (mn^2 p)^{-3}$
b $\dfrac{x^3 yz^{-2} \times 2(x^3 y^{-2} z)^2}{xyz^{-1}}$
c $\dfrac{a^2 b \times (ab^{-2})^{-3}}{(a^{-2} b^{-1})^{-2}}$

d $\dfrac{a^2 b^3 c^{-4}}{a^{-1} b^2 c^{-3}}$
e $\dfrac{a^{2n-1} \times b^3 \times c^{1-n}}{a^{n-3} \times b^{2-n} \times c^{2-2n}}$

12 Simplify each of the following:

a $3^{4n} \times 9^{2n} \times 27^{3n}$
b $\dfrac{2^n \times 8^{n+1}}{32^n}$
c $\dfrac{3^{n-1} \times 9^{2n-3}}{6^2 \times 3^{n+2}}$

d $\dfrac{2^{2n} \times 9^{2n-1}}{6^{n-1}}$
e $\dfrac{25^{2n} \times 5^{n-1}}{5^{2n+1}}$
f $\dfrac{6^{x-3} \times 4^x}{3^{x+1}}$

g $\dfrac{6^{2n} \times 9^3}{27^n \times 8^n \times 16^n}$
h $\dfrac{3^{n-2} \times 9^{n+1}}{27^{n-1}}$
i $\dfrac{8 \times 2^5 \times 3^7}{9 \times 2^7 \times 81}$

13 Simplify and evaluate:

a $\dfrac{(8^3)^4}{(2^{12})^2}$
b $\dfrac{125^3}{25^2}$
c $\dfrac{81^4 \div 27^3}{9^2}$

13B Rational indices

Skillsheet
Let a be a positive real number and let $n \in \mathbb{N}$. Then $a^{\frac{1}{n}}$ is defined to be the nth root of a. That is, $a^{\frac{1}{n}}$ is the positive number whose nth power is a. We can also write this as $a^{\frac{1}{n}} = \sqrt[n]{a}$. For example: $9^{\frac{1}{2}} = 3$, since $3^2 = 9$.

We define $0^{\frac{1}{n}} = 0$, for each natural number n, since $0^n = 0$.

If n is odd, then we can also define $a^{\frac{1}{n}}$ when a is negative. If a is negative and n is odd, define $a^{\frac{1}{n}}$ to be the number whose nth power is a. For example: $(-8)^{\frac{1}{3}} = -2$, as $(-2)^3 = -8$.

In all three cases we can write:

$$a^{\frac{1}{n}} = \sqrt[n]{a} \quad \text{with} \quad \left(a^{\frac{1}{n}}\right)^n = a$$

Using this notation for square roots:

$$\sqrt{a} = \sqrt[2]{a} = a^{\frac{1}{2}}$$

Further, the expression a^x can be defined for rational indices, i.e. when $x = \dfrac{m}{n}$, where m and n are integers, by defining

$$a^{\frac{m}{n}} = \left(a^{\frac{1}{n}}\right)^m$$

To employ this definition we will always first write the fractional power in simplest form.

Example 8

Evaluate:

a $(-64)^{\frac{1}{3}}$ **b** $9^{-\frac{1}{2}}$ **c** $16^{\frac{5}{2}}$ **d** $64^{-\frac{2}{3}}$

Solution

a $(-64)^{\frac{1}{3}} = -4$

b $9^{-\frac{1}{2}} = \dfrac{1}{9^{\frac{1}{2}}} = \dfrac{1}{\sqrt{9}} = \dfrac{1}{3}$

c $16^{\frac{5}{2}} = \left(16^{\frac{1}{2}}\right)^5 = \left(\sqrt[2]{16}\right)^5 = 4^5 = 1024$

d $64^{-\frac{2}{3}} = \dfrac{1}{64^{\frac{2}{3}}} = \dfrac{1}{\left(64^{\frac{1}{3}}\right)^2} = \dfrac{1}{\left(\sqrt[3]{64}\right)^2} = \dfrac{1}{4^2} = \dfrac{1}{16}$

Note: In the previous section, we stated the index laws for m and n integers:

1 $a^m \times a^n = a^{m+n}$ **2** $a^m \div a^n = a^{m-n}$ **3** $(a^m)^n = a^{m \times n}$

These laws are applicable for all rational indices:

1 $a^{\frac{m}{q}} \times a^{\frac{n}{p}} = a^{\frac{m}{q}+\frac{n}{p}}$ **2** $a^{\frac{m}{q}} \div a^{\frac{n}{p}} = a^{\frac{m}{q}-\frac{n}{p}}$ **3** $\left(a^{\frac{m}{q}}\right)^{\frac{n}{p}} = a^{\frac{m}{q} \times \frac{n}{p}}$

Example 9

Simplify:

a $\dfrac{3^{\frac{1}{4}} \times \sqrt{6} \times \sqrt[4]{2}}{16^{\frac{3}{4}}}$ **b** $(x^{-2}y)^{\frac{1}{2}} \times \left(\dfrac{x}{y^{-3}}\right)^4$

Solution

a $\dfrac{3^{\frac{1}{4}} \times \sqrt{6} \times \sqrt[4]{2}}{16^{\frac{3}{4}}} = \dfrac{3^{\frac{1}{4}} \times 3^{\frac{1}{2}} \times 2^{\frac{1}{2}} \times 2^{\frac{1}{4}}}{\left(16^{\frac{1}{4}}\right)^3}$

$= \dfrac{3^{\frac{1}{4}} \times 3^{\frac{1}{2}} \times 2^{\frac{1}{2}} \times 2^{\frac{1}{4}}}{2^3}$

$= \dfrac{3^{\frac{3}{4}} \times 2^{\frac{3}{4}}}{2^3}$

$= \dfrac{3^{\frac{3}{4}}}{2^{\frac{12}{4}-\frac{3}{4}}} = \dfrac{3^{\frac{3}{4}}}{2^{\frac{9}{4}}}$

b $(x^{-2}y)^{\frac{1}{2}} \times \left(\dfrac{x}{y^{-3}}\right)^4 = x^{-1}y^{\frac{1}{2}} \times \dfrac{x^4}{y^{-12}}$

$= x^3 \times y^{\frac{25}{2}}$

Explanation

$\sqrt{6} = \sqrt{3} \times \sqrt{2} = 3^{\frac{1}{2}} \times 2^{\frac{1}{2}}$ and $\sqrt[4]{2} = 2^{\frac{1}{4}}$

$2^3 = 2^{\frac{12}{4}}$

$\dfrac{x^4}{y^{-12}} = x^4 \times y^{12}$

Section summary

- Let a be a positive real number and let $n \in \mathbb{N}$. Then $a^{\frac{1}{n}}$ is defined to be the nth root of a. That is, $a^{\frac{1}{n}}$ is the positive number whose nth power is a.
- Define $0^{\frac{1}{n}} = 0$, for each $n \in \mathbb{N}$.
- If n is odd, then we can define $a^{\frac{1}{n}}$ when a is negative. If a is negative and n is odd, define $a^{\frac{1}{n}}$ to be the number whose nth power is a.
- In all three cases we can write:
$$a^{\frac{1}{n}} = \sqrt[n]{a} \quad \text{with} \quad \left(a^{\frac{1}{n}}\right)^n = a$$
- The index laws can be extended to rational indices:

  1 $a^{\frac{m}{q}} \times a^{\frac{n}{p}} = a^{\frac{m}{q}+\frac{n}{p}}$ **2** $a^{\frac{m}{q}} \div a^{\frac{n}{p}} = a^{\frac{m}{q}-\frac{n}{p}}$ **3** $\left(a^{\frac{m}{q}}\right)^{\frac{n}{p}} = a^{\frac{m}{q} \times \frac{n}{p}}$

Exercise 13B

Example 8   **1** Evaluate each of the following:

a $125^{\frac{2}{3}}$ b $243^{\frac{3}{5}}$ c $81^{-\frac{1}{2}}$ d $64^{\frac{2}{3}}$

e $\left(\dfrac{1}{8}\right)^{\frac{1}{3}}$ f $32^{-\frac{2}{5}}$ g $125^{-\frac{2}{3}}$ h $32^{\frac{4}{5}}$

i $1000^{-\frac{4}{3}}$ j $10\,000^{\frac{3}{4}}$ k $81^{\frac{3}{4}}$ l $\left(\dfrac{27}{125}\right)^{\frac{1}{3}}$

m $(-8)^{\frac{1}{3}}$ n $125^{-\frac{4}{3}}$ o $(-32)^{\frac{4}{5}}$ p $\left(\dfrac{1}{49}\right)^{-\frac{3}{2}}$

Example 9   **2** Simplify:

a $\sqrt[3]{a^2 b} \div \sqrt{ab^3}$ b $(a^{-2}b)^3 \times \left(\dfrac{1}{b^{-3}}\right)^{\frac{1}{2}}$

c $\dfrac{45^{\frac{1}{3}}}{9^{\frac{3}{4}} \times 15^{\frac{3}{2}}}$ d $2^{\frac{3}{2}} \times 4^{-\frac{1}{4}} \times 16^{-\frac{3}{4}}$

e $\left(\dfrac{x^3 y^{-2}}{3^{-3} y^{-3}}\right)^{-2} \div \left(\dfrac{3^{-3} x^{-2} y}{x^4 y^{-2}}\right)^2$ f $\left(\sqrt[5]{a^2}\right)^{\frac{3}{2}} \times \left(\sqrt[3]{a^5}\right)^{\frac{1}{5}}$

3 Simplify each of the following:

a $(2x-1)\sqrt{2x-1}$ b $(x-1)^2 \sqrt{x-1}$

c $(x^2+1)\sqrt{x^2+1}$ d $(x-1)^3 \sqrt{x-1}$

e $\dfrac{1}{\sqrt{x-1}} + \sqrt{x-1}$ f $(5x^2+1)\sqrt[3]{5x^2+1}$

13C Graphs of exponential functions

Two types of graphs of exponential functions will be examined.

▶ Graph of $y = a^x$ when $a > 1$

Example 10

Plot the graph of $y = 2^x$ and examine the table of values for $-3 \leq x \leq 3$. A calculator can be used.

Solution

x	-3	-2	-1	0	1	2	3
$y = 2^x$	$\frac{1}{8}$	$\frac{1}{4}$	$\frac{1}{2}$	1	2	4	8

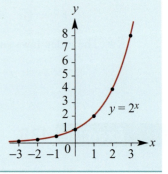

We can make the following observations about graphs of the form $y = a^x$ where $a > 1$:

- As the magnitude of the negative x-values becomes larger and larger, the y-values get closer and closer to zero, but never reach zero. That is, the graph of $y = a^x$ approaches the x-axis from above. The x-axis is said to be an **asymptote**.

  We can write: As $x \to -\infty$, $y \to 0^+$.

  This is read: As x approaches negative infinity, y approaches 0 from the positive side.

- As the x-values increase, the y-values increase.
- The y-axis intercept is at $(0, 1)$.
- The range of the function is $\mathbb{R}^+$.

Example 11

Plot the graph of $y = 10^x$ and examine the table of values for $-1 \leq x \leq 1$. A calculator can be used to obtain approximate values.

Solution

x	-1	-0.5	0	0.5	1
$y = 10^x$	0.1	≈ 0.316	1	≈ 3.16	10

- The x-axis is an asymptote.
- The y-axis intercept is at $(0, 1)$.
- As the x-values increase, the y-values increase.
- For a given value of x, this rate of increase for $y = 10^x$ is greater than that for $y = 2^x$.

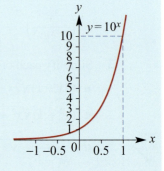

Note that, for any numbers a and b greater than 1, there is a positive number k with $a^k = b$. This can be seen from the graphs of $y = 2^x$ and $y = 10^x$. Using a calculator to solve $2^k = 10$ gives $k = 3.3219\ldots$. Hence $10^x = (2^{3.3219\ldots})^x$ and therefore the graph of $y = 10^x$ can be obtained from the graph of $y = 2^x$ by a dilation of factor $\dfrac{1}{k} = \dfrac{1}{3.3219\ldots}$ from the y-axis.

All graphs of the form $y = a^x$, where $a > 1$, are related to each other by dilations from the y-axis. (This will be discussed again later in the chapter.)

▶ Graph of $y = a^x$ when $0 < a < 1$

Example 12

Plot the graph of $y = (\tfrac{1}{2})^x$ and examine the table of values for $-3 \le x \le 3$. A calculator can be used.

Solution

Note that $y = (\tfrac{1}{2})^x = 2^{-x}$.

x	-3	-2	-1	0	1	2	3
$y = (\tfrac{1}{2})^x$	8	4	2	1	$\tfrac{1}{2}$	$\tfrac{1}{4}$	$\tfrac{1}{8}$

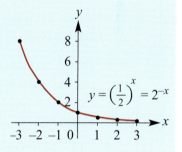

We can make the following observations about graphs of the form $y = a^x$ where $0 < a < 1$:

- The x-axis is an asymptote. As the x-values increase, the graph approaches the x-axis from above. This is written: As $x \to \infty$, $y \to 0^+$.
- The y-axis intercept is at $(0, 1)$.
- The range of the function is $\mathbb{R}^+$.

▶ Graphs of $y = a^x$ in general

In general:

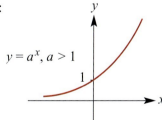
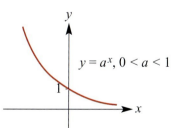

In both cases $a > 1$ and $0 < a < 1$, we can write $y = a^x$ as $y = b^{-x}$, where $b = \dfrac{1}{a}$. The graph of $y = b^{-x}$ is obtained from the graph of $y = b^x$ by a reflection in the y-axis.

Thus, for example, the graph of $y = (\tfrac{1}{2})^x$ is obtained from the graph of $y = 2^x$ by a reflection in the y-axis, and vice versa. Using function notation: Let $f(x) = 2^x$ and $g(x) = (\tfrac{1}{2})^x$. Then

$$g(x) = (\tfrac{1}{2})^x = (2^{-1})^x = 2^{-x} = f(-x)$$

442 Chapter 13: Exponential functions and logarithms

> **Example 13**
>
> Plot the graph of $y = 2^x$ on a CAS calculator and hence find (correct to three decimal places):
>
> **a** the value of y when $x = 2.1$ **b** the value of x when $y = 9$.

Using the TI-Nspire

Plot the graph of $y = 2^x$.

a
- To go to the point with x-coordinate 2.1, use menu > **Trace** > **Graph Trace** and type 2.1 enter.
- Press enter to paste the coordinates to the point.
- Press esc to exit the **Graph Trace** tool.

When $x = 2.1$, $y = 4.287$ (correct to three decimal places).

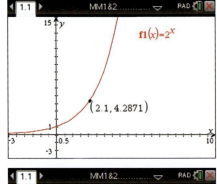

b
- To find the value of x for which $y = 9$, plot the graph of $y = 9$ on the same screen and use menu > **Geometry** > **Points & Lines** > **Intersection Point(s)**.
- Press esc to exit the **Intersection Point(s)** tool.

When $y = 9$, $x = 3.170$ (correct to three decimal places).

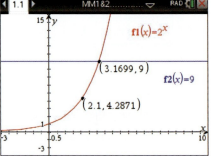

Note: Alternatively, find the intersection point using menu > **Analyze Graph** > **Intersection**.

Using the Casio ClassPad

In [Graph & Table], enter 2^x in y1. Tick the box and select the graph icon.

a Tap in the graph window, select **Analysis** > **G-Solve** > **x-Cal/y-Cal** > **y-Cal** and enter $x = 2.1$.

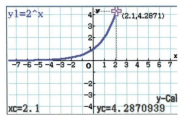

When $x = 2.1$, $y = 4.287$ (correct to three decimal places).

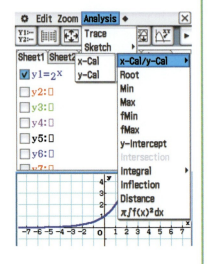

b Select **Analysis** > **G-Solve** > **x-Cal/y-Cal** > **x-Cal** and enter $y = 9$.

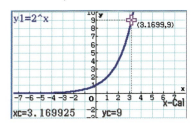

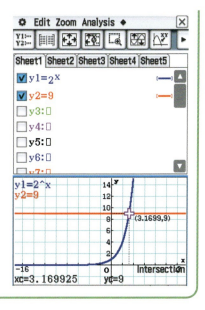

When $y = 9$, $x = 3.170$ (correct to three decimal places).

Note: An alternative method for part b is to enter $y2 = 9$ and use **Analysis** > **G-Solve** > **Intersection**, as shown on the right.

▶ Transformations of exponential graphs

The techniques for transformations that were introduced in earlier chapters are now applied to the graphs of exponential functions.

Example 14

Sketch the graphs of each of the following pairs of functions. For the second function in each pair, state the equation of the asymptote, the y-axis intercept and the range. (The x-axis intercepts need not be given.)

a $f: \mathbb{R} \to \mathbb{R}$, $f(x) = 2^x$ and $g: \mathbb{R} \to \mathbb{R}$, $g(x) = 2^x + 3$
b $f: \mathbb{R} \to \mathbb{R}$, $f(x) = 3^x$ and $g: \mathbb{R} \to \mathbb{R}$, $g(x) = 2 \times 3^x + 1$
c $f: \mathbb{R} \to \mathbb{R}$, $f(x) = 3^x$ and $g: \mathbb{R} \to \mathbb{R}$, $g(x) = -3^x + 2$

Solution

a

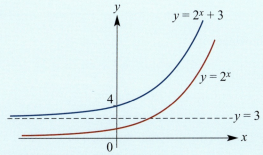

Graph of $g(x) = 2^x + 3$:
- The asymptote has equation $y = 3$.
- The y-axis intercept is $g(0) = 2^0 + 3 = 4$.
- The range of the function g is $(3, \infty)$.

Explanation

The graph of $y = 2^x + 3$ is obtained by transforming the graph of $y = 2^x$ by a translation of 3 units in the positive direction of the y-axis.

The asymptote of $y = 2^x$ is the line with equation $y = 0$, which is transformed to the line with equation $y = 3$.

b

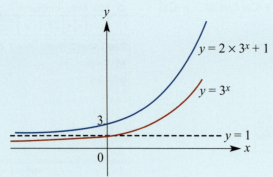

The graph of $y = 2 \times 3^x + 1$ is obtained by transforming the graph of $y = 3^x$ by a dilation of factor 2 from the x-axis, followed by a translation of 1 unit in the positive direction of the y-axis.

The asymptote of $y = 3^x$ is the line $y = 0$, which is transformed to the line $y = 1$.

Graph of $g(x) = 2 \times 3^x + 1$:
- The asymptote has equation $y = 1$.
- The y-axis intercept is $g(0) = 2 \times 3^0 + 1 = 3$.
- The range of the function g is $(1, \infty)$.

c

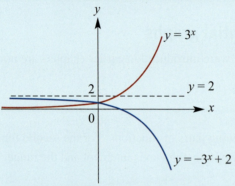

The graph of $y = -3^x + 2$ is obtained by transforming the graph of $y = 3^x$ by a reflection in the x-axis, followed by a translation of 2 units in the positive direction of the y-axis.

The asymptote of $y = 3^x$ is the line $y = 0$, which is transformed to the line $y = 2$.

Graph of $g(x) = -3^x + 2$:
- The asymptote has equation $y = 2$.
- The y-axis intercept is $g(0) = -3^0 + 2 = 1$.
- The range of the function g is $(-\infty, 2)$.

Example 15

Sketch the graph of each of the following:

a $y = 2 \times 3^x$ **b** $y = 3^{2x}$ **c** $y = -3^{2x} + 4$

Solution

a

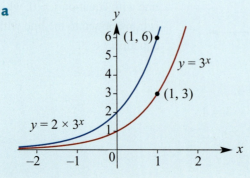

Explanation

The graph of $y = 2 \times 3^x$ is obtained from the graph of $y = 3^x$ by a dilation of factor 2 from the x-axis.

Both graphs have a horizontal asymptote with equation $y = 0$.

b

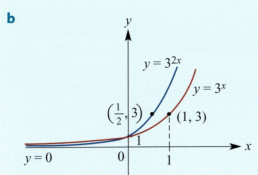

The graph of $y = 3^{2x}$ is obtained from the graph of $y = 3^x$ by a dilation of factor $\frac{1}{2}$ from the y-axis. (See the note below.)

Both graphs have a horizontal asymptote with equation $y = 0$.

c

The graph of $y = -3^{2x} + 4$ is obtained from the graph of $y = 3^x$ by a dilation of factor $\frac{1}{2}$ from the y-axis, followed by a reflection in the x-axis and then a translation of 4 units in the positive direction of the y-axis.

The graph of $y = -3^{2x} + 4$ has a horizontal asymptote with equation $y = 4$.

Note: In the notation introduced in Chapter 7, write the transformation for part b as $(x, y) \to (\frac{1}{2}x, y)$. Then describe the transformation as $x' = \frac{1}{2}x$ and $y' = y$, and hence $x = 2x'$ and $y = y'$. The graph of $y = 3^x$ is mapped to the graph of $y' = 3^{2x'}$.

Section summary

- Graphs of exponential functions:

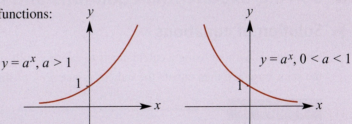

- In both cases $a > 1$ and $0 < a < 1$, the graph of $y = a^x$ has the following properties:
  - The x-axis is an asymptote.
  - The y-values are always positive.
  - The y-axis intercept is 1.
  - There is no x-axis intercept.
- All graphs of the form $y = a^x$, where $a > 1$, are related to each other by dilations from the y-axis. Similarly, all graphs of the form $y = a^x$, where $0 < a < 1$, are related to each other by dilations from the y-axis.
- Let $a > 1$. If $f(x) = a^x$ and $g(x) = (\frac{1}{a})^x$, then $g(x) = f(-x)$ and so the graph of $y = g(x)$ is the reflection in the y-axis of the graph of $y = f(x)$.

Exercise 13C

1. Using a calculator, plot the graphs of the following and comment on the similarities and differences between them:
   a $y = 1.8^x$
   b $y = 2.4^x$
   c $y = 0.9^x$
   d $y = 0.5^x$

2. Using a calculator, plot the graphs of the following and comment on the similarities and differences between them:
   a $y = 2 \times 3^x$
   b $y = 5 \times 3^x$
   c $y = -2 \times 3^x$
   d $y = -5 \times 3^x$

3. Plot the graph of $y = 2^x$ on a CAS calculator and hence find the solution of the equation $2^x = 14$.

4. Plot the graph of $y = 10^x$ on a CAS calculator and hence find the solution of the equation $10^x = 6$.

5. Sketch the graphs of the following functions. Give equations of asymptotes and y-axis intercepts, and state the range of each function. (The x-axis intercepts need not be given.)
   a $f: \mathbb{R} \to \mathbb{R},\ f(x) = 3 \times 2^x + 2$
   b $f: \mathbb{R} \to \mathbb{R},\ f(x) = 3 \times 2^x - 3$
   c $f: \mathbb{R} \to \mathbb{R},\ f(x) = -3^x - 2$
   d $f: \mathbb{R} \to \mathbb{R},\ f(x) = -2 \times 3^x + 2$
   e $f: \mathbb{R} \to \mathbb{R},\ f(x) = (\frac{1}{2})^x + 2$
   f $f: \mathbb{R} \to \mathbb{R},\ f(x) = -2 \times 3^x - 2$

6. Sketch the graph of each of the following:
   a $y = 2 \times 5^x$
   b $y = 3^{3x}$
   c $y = 5^{\frac{x}{2}}$
   d $y = -3^{2x} + 2$

13D Solving exponential equations and inequalities

Solution of equations

One method without using a calculator is to express both sides of the equation as powers with the same base and then equate the indices (since $a^x = a^y$ implies $x = y$, for any $a \in \mathbb{R}^+ \setminus \{1\}$).

Example 16

Find the value of x for which:
a $4^x = 256$
b $3^{x-1} = 81$
c $5^{2x-4} = 25^{-x+2}$

Solution

a
$$4^x = 256$$
$$4^x = 4^4$$
$$\therefore x = 4$$

b
$$3^{x-1} = 81$$
$$3^{x-1} = 3^4$$
$$\therefore x - 1 = 4$$
$$x = 5$$

c
$$5^{2x-4} = 25^{-x+2}$$
$$= (5^2)^{-x+2}$$
$$= 5^{-2x+4}$$
$$\therefore 2x - 4 = -2x + 4$$
$$4x = 8$$
$$x = 2$$

13D Solving exponential equations and inequalities

Sometimes solving an exponential equation involves solving a polynomial equation first. In the following example, the solution of a quadratic equation is necessary.

Example 17

Solve:

a $9^x = 12 \times 3^x - 27$

b $3^{2x} = 27 - 6 \times 3^x$

Solution

a We have $(3^x)^2 = 12 \times 3^x - 27$.
Let $a = 3^x$. The equation becomes

$$a^2 = 12a - 27$$
$$a^2 - 12a + 27 = 0$$
$$(a-3)(a-9) = 0$$

Therefore

$a - 3 = 0$ or $a - 9 = 0$
$a = 3$ or $a = 9$

Hence $3^x = 3^1$ or $3^x = 3^2$
and so $x = 1$ or $x = 2$

b We have $(3^x)^2 = 27 - 6 \times 3^x$.
Let $a = 3^x$. The equation becomes

$$a^2 = 27 - 6a$$
$$a^2 + 6a - 27 = 0$$
$$(a+9)(a-3) = 0$$

Therefore

$a = -9$ or $a = 3$

Hence $3^x = -9$ or $3^x = 3^1$

There is only one solution, $x = 1$, since $3^x > 0$ for all values of x.

Using the TI-Nspire

Use menu > **Algebra** > **Solve** to solve the equation.

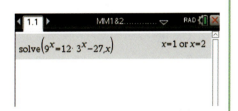

Using the Casio ClassPad

- Go to the $\sqrt{\alpha}$ (Main) screen and turn on the keyboard.
- Enter the equation $9^x = 12 \times 3^x - 27$.
- Highlight the equation using the stylus and select **Interactive** > **Equation/Inequality** > **solve**.
- Tap on OK to obtain the solution. (Note that the default variable is x.)

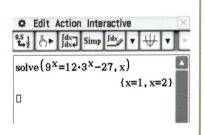

The calculator can be used to obtain approximate answers as shown in the following example. For the equation $5^x = 10$ we can find an exact solution, but logarithms are involved in the final answer. Logarithms are discussed in the following section.

Example 18

Solve $5^x = 10$ correct to two decimal places.

Using the TI-Nspire

Press ctrl enter to obtain the answer as a decimal number.

The solution is $x = 1.43$ (correct to two decimal places).

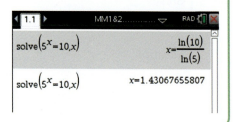

Using the Casio ClassPad

To answer the question as required, you may need to highlight the answer and tap [icon] to convert from the exact solution to a decimal approximation.

The solution is $x = 1.43$ (correct to two decimal places).

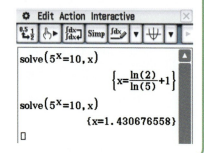

▶ Solution of inequalities

The following two properties are useful when solving inequalities:

- $a^x > a^y \Leftrightarrow x > y$, when $a \in (1, \infty)$
- $a^x > a^y \Leftrightarrow x < y$, when $a \in (0, 1)$.

Example 19

Solve for x in each of the following:

a $16^x > 2$

b $2^{-3x+1} < \dfrac{1}{16}$

Solution

a
$$2^{4x} > 2^1$$
$$\Leftrightarrow 4x > 1$$
$$\Leftrightarrow x > \dfrac{1}{4}$$

b
$$2^{-3x+1} < 2^{-4}$$
$$\Leftrightarrow -3x + 1 < -4$$
$$\Leftrightarrow -3x < -5$$
$$\Leftrightarrow x > \dfrac{5}{3}$$

Note: The CAS calculator can be used to help 'visualise' the inequality. For Example 19a, plot the graphs of $y = 16^x$ and $y = 2$ and then find the point of intersection.

Section summary

- One method for solving an exponential equation, without using a calculator, is first to express both sides of the equation as powers with the same base and then to equate the indices (since $a^x = a^y$ implies $x = y$, for any base $a \in \mathbb{R}^+ \setminus \{1\}$).
  For example: $2^{x+1} = 8 \Leftrightarrow 2^{x+1} = 2^3 \Leftrightarrow x+1 = 3 \Leftrightarrow x = 2$
- To solve an exponential inequality, first proceed as for an equation and then use the appropriate property:
  - $a^x > a^y \Leftrightarrow x > y$, when $a \in (1, \infty)$
  - $a^x > a^y \Leftrightarrow x < y$, when $a \in (0, 1)$.

  For example: $2^{x+1} > 8 \Leftrightarrow 2^{x+1} > 2^3 \Leftrightarrow x+1 > 3 \Leftrightarrow x > 2$

Exercise 13D

Example 16

1 Solve for x in each of the following:
  - **a** $3^x = 27$
  - **b** $4^x = 64$
  - **c** $49^x = 7$
  - **d** $16^x = 8$
  - **e** $125^x = 5$
  - **f** $5^x = 625$
  - **g** $16^x = 256$
  - **h** $4^{-x} = \dfrac{1}{64}$
  - **i** $5^{-x} = \dfrac{1}{125}$

2 Solve for n in each of the following:
  - **a** $5^n \times 25^{2n-1} = 125$
  - **b** $3^{2n-4} = 1$
  - **c** $3^{2n-1} = \dfrac{1}{81}$
  - **d** $\dfrac{3^{n-2}}{9^{1-n}} = 1$
  - **e** $3^{3n} \times 9^{-2n+1} = 27$
  - **f** $2^{-3n} \times 4^{2n-2} = 16$
  - **g** $2^{n-6} = 8^{2-n}$
  - **h** $9^{3n+3} = 27^{n-2}$
  - **i** $4^{n+1} = 8^{n-2}$
  - **j** $32^{2n+1} = 8^{4n-1}$
  - **k** $25^{n+1} = 5 \times 390\,625$
  - **l** $125^{4-n} = 5^{6-2n}$
  - **m** $4^{2-n} = \dfrac{1}{2048}$

3 Solve the following exponential equations:
  - **a** $2^{x-1} \times 4^{2x+1} = 32$
  - **b** $3^{2x-1} \times 9^x = 243$
  - **c** $(27 \times 3^x)^2 = 27^x \times 3^{\frac{1}{2}}$

Example 17

4 Solve for x:
  - **a** $4(2^{2x}) = 8(2^x) - 4$
  - **b** $8(2^{2x}) - 10(2^x) + 2 = 0$
  - **c** $3 \times 2^{2x} - 18(2^x) + 24 = 0$
  - **d** $9^x - 4(3^x) + 3 = 0$

Example 18

5 Use a calculator to solve each of the following, correct to two decimal places:
  - **a** $2^x = 5$
  - **b** $4^x = 6$
  - **c** $10^x = 18$
  - **d** $10^x = 56$

Example 19

6 Solve for x in each of the following:
  - **a** $7^x > 49$
  - **b** $8^x > 2$
  - **c** $25^x \le 5$
  - **d** $3^{x+1} < 81$
  - **e** $9^{2x+1} < 243$
  - **f** $4^{2x+1} > 64$
  - **g** $3^{2x-2} \le 81$

13E Logarithms

Skillsheet Consider the statement

$$2^3 = 8$$

This may be written in an alternative form:

$$\log_2 8 = 3$$

which is read as 'the logarithm of 8 to the base 2 is equal to 3'.

> For $a \in \mathbb{R}^+ \setminus \{1\}$, the **logarithm function** with base a is defined as follows:
>
> $a^x = y$ is equivalent to $\log_a y = x$

Note: Since a^x is positive, the expression $\log_a y$ is only defined when y is positive.

The logarithm function with base a is the inverse of the exponential function with base a. We will discuss this in Section 13G.

Further examples:

- $3^2 = 9$ is equivalent to $\log_3 9 = 2$
- $10^4 = 10\,000$ is equivalent to $\log_{10} 10\,000 = 4$
- $a^0 = 1$ is equivalent to $\log_a 1 = 0$

Example 20

Without the aid of a calculator, evaluate the following:

a $\log_2 32$ **b** $\log_3 81$

Solution

a Let $\log_2 32 = x$
Then $\quad 2^x = 32$
$\quad\quad\quad 2^x = 2^5$
Therefore $x = 5$, giving $\log_2 32 = 5$.

b Let $\log_3 81 = x$
Then $\quad 3^x = 81$
$\quad\quad\quad 3^x = 3^4$
Therefore $x = 4$, giving $\log_3 81 = 4$.

Note: To find $\log_2 32$, we ask 'What power of 2 gives 32?'
To find $\log_3 81$, we ask 'What power of 3 gives 81?'

▶ Laws of logarithms

The index laws are used to establish rules for computations with logarithms.

> **Law 1: Logarithm of a product**
>
> The logarithm of a product is the sum of their logarithms:
>
> $\log_a(mn) = \log_a m + \log_a n$

Proof Let $\log_a m = x$ and $\log_a n = y$, where m and n are positive real numbers. Then $a^x = m$ and $a^y = n$, and therefore

$$mn = a^x \times a^y = a^{x+y} \qquad \text{(using index law 1)}$$

Hence $\log_a(mn) = x + y = \log_a m + \log_a n$.

For example:

$$\log_{10} 200 + \log_{10} 5 = \log_{10}(200 \times 5)$$
$$= \log_{10} 1000$$
$$= 3$$

Law 2: Logarithm of a quotient

The logarithm of a quotient is the difference of their logarithms:

$$\log_a\left(\frac{m}{n}\right) = \log_a m - \log_a n$$

Proof Let $\log_a m = x$ and $\log_a n = y$, where m and n are positive real numbers. Then as before $a^x = m$ and $a^y = n$, and therefore

$$\frac{m}{n} = \frac{a^x}{a^y} = a^{x-y} \qquad \text{(using index law 2)}$$

Hence $\log_a\left(\frac{m}{n}\right) = x - y = \log_a m - \log_a n$.

For example:

$$\log_2 32 - \log_2 8 = \log_2\left(\frac{32}{8}\right)$$
$$= \log_2 4$$
$$= 2$$

Law 3: Logarithm of a power

$$\log_a(m^p) = p \log_a m$$

Proof Let $\log_a m = x$. Then $a^x = m$, and therefore

$$m^p = (a^x)^p = a^{xp} \qquad \text{(using index law 3)}$$

Hence $\log_a(m^p) = xp = p \log_a m$.

For example: $\log_2 32 = \log_2(2^5) = 5$.

Law 4: Logarithm of $\frac{1}{m}$

$$\log_a(m^{-1}) = -\log_a m$$

Proof Use logarithm law 3 with $p = -1$.

For example: $\log_a(\frac{1}{2}) = \log_a(2^{-1}) = -\log_a 2$.

Law 5

$\log_a 1 = 0$ and $\log_a a = 1$

Proof Since $a^0 = 1$, we have $\log_a 1 = 0$. Since $a^1 = a$, we have $\log_a a = 1$.

Example 21

Without using a calculator, simplify the following:

$$2\log_{10} 3 + \log_{10} 16 - 2\log_{10}\left(\frac{6}{5}\right)$$

Solution

$$\begin{aligned}
2\log_{10} 3 + \log_{10} 16 - 2\log_{10}\left(\frac{6}{5}\right) &= \log_{10}(3^2) + \log_{10} 16 - \log_{10}\left(\frac{6}{5}\right)^2 \\
&= \log_{10} 9 + \log_{10} 16 - \log_{10}\left(\frac{36}{25}\right) \\
&= \log_{10}\left(9 \times 16 \times \frac{25}{36}\right) \\
&= \log_{10} 100 \\
&= 2
\end{aligned}$$

Example 22

Solve each of the following equations for x:

a $\log_5 x = 3$
b $\log_5(2x+1) = 2$
c $\log_2(2x+1) - \log_2(x-1) = 4$
d $\log_3(x-1) + \log_3(x+1) = 1$

Solution

a $\log_5 x = 3 \Leftrightarrow x = 5^3 = 125$

b $\log_5(2x+1) = 2 \Leftrightarrow 2x+1 = 5^2$
$\therefore 2x + 1 = 25$
$2x = 24$
$x = 12$

c $\log_2(2x+1) - \log_2(x-1) = 4$
$\log_2\left(\frac{2x+1}{x-1}\right) = 4$
$\therefore \frac{2x+1}{x-1} = 2^4$
$2x + 1 = 16(x-1)$
$17 = 14x$
$x = \frac{17}{14}$

d $\log_3(x-1) + \log_3(x+1) = 1$
$\log_3[(x-1)(x+1)] = 1$
$\log_3(x^2 - 1) = 1$
$x^2 - 1 = 3$
$x = \pm 2$
But the original expression is not defined for $x = -2$, and therefore $x = 2$.

Section summary

- For $a \in \mathbb{R}^+ \setminus \{1\}$, the logarithm function base a is defined as follows:

  $a^x = y$ is equivalent to $\log_a y = x$

- The expression $\log_a y$ is defined for all positive real numbers y.
- To evaluate $\log_a y$ ask the question: 'What power of a gives y?'
- Laws of logarithms

  1. $\log_a(mn) = \log_a m + \log_a n$
  2. $\log_a\left(\dfrac{m}{n}\right) = \log_a m - \log_a n$
  3. $\log_a(m^p) = p \log_a m$
  4. $\log_a(m^{-1}) = -\log_a m$
  5. $\log_a 1 = 0$ and $\log_a a = 1$

Exercise 13E

Example 20

1 Without using a calculator, evaluate the following:
  a $\log_2 128$
  b $\log_3 81$
  c $\log_5 125$
  d $\log_{10} 0.1$

2 Use the stated rule for each of the following to give an equivalent expression in simplest form:

  a $\log_2 10 + \log_2 a$
  b $\log_{10} 5 + \log_{10} 2$ — Law 1
  c $\log_2 9 - \log_2 4$
  d $\log_2 10 - \log_2 5$ — Law 2
  e $\log_2(a^3)$
  f $\log_2(8^3)$ — Law 3
  g $\log_5\left(\dfrac{1}{6}\right)$
  h $\log_5\left(\dfrac{1}{25}\right)$ — Law 4

3 Without using a calculator, evaluate each of the following:
  a $\log_3 27$
  b $\log_5 625$
  c $\log_2\left(\dfrac{1}{128}\right)$
  d $\log_4\left(\dfrac{1}{64}\right)$
  e $\log_x(x^4)$
  f $\log_2 0.125$
  g $\log_{10} 10\,000$
  h $\log_{10} 0.000\,001$
  i $-3 \log_5 125$
  j $-4 \log_{16} 2$
  k $2 \log_3 9$
  l $-4 \log_{16} 4$

Example 21

4 Without using a calculator, simplify each of the following:
  a $\tfrac{1}{2} \log_{10} 16 + 2 \log_{10} 5$
  b $\log_2 16 + \log_2 8$
  c $\log_2 128 + \log_3 45 - \log_3 5$
  d $\log_4 32 - \log_9 27$
  e $\log_b(b^3) - \log_b \sqrt{b}$
  f $2 \log_x a + \log_x(a^3)$
  g $x \log_2 8 + \log_2(8^{1-x})$
  h $\tfrac{3}{2} \log_a a - \log_a \sqrt{a}$

454 Chapter 13: Exponential functions and logarithms

Example 22

5 Solve for x:
   a $\log_3 9 = x$
   b $\log_3 x = 3$
   c $\log_5 x = -3$
   d $\log_{10} x = \log_{10} 4 + \log_{10} 2$
   e $\log_{10} 2 + \log_{10} 5 + \log_{10} x - \log_{10} 3 = 2$
   f $\log_{10} x = \frac{1}{2}\log_{10} 36 - 2\log_{10} 3$
   g $\log_x 64 = 2$
   h $\log_5(2x - 3) = 3$
   i $\log_3(x + 2) - \log_3 2 = 1$
   j $\log_x 0.01 = -2$

6 Solve each of the following for x:
   a $\log_x\left(\dfrac{1}{25}\right) = -2$
   b $\log_4(2x - 1) = 3$
   c $\log_4(x + 2) - \log_4 6 = 1$
   d $\log_4(3x + 4) + \log_4 16 = 5$
   e $\log_3(x^2 - 3x - 1) = 0$
   f $\log_3(x^2 - 3x + 1) = 0$

7 If $\log_{10} x = a$ and $\log_{10} y = c$, express $\log_{10}\left(\dfrac{100x^3 y^{-\frac{1}{2}}}{y^2}\right)$ in terms of a and c.

8 Prove that $\log_{10}\left(\dfrac{ab^2}{c}\right) + \log_{10}\left(\dfrac{c^2}{ab}\right) - \log_{10}(bc) = 0$.

9 If $\log_a\left(\dfrac{11}{3}\right) + \log_a\left(\dfrac{490}{297}\right) - 2\log_a\left(\dfrac{7}{9}\right) = \log_a k$, find k.

10 Solve each of the following equations for x:
   a $\log_{10}(x^2 - 2x + 8) = 2\log_{10} x$
   b $\log_{10}(5x) - \log_{10}(3 - 2x) = 1$
   c $3\log_{10}(x - 1) = \log_{10} 8$
   d $\log_{10}(20x) - \log_{10}(x - 8) = 2$
   e $2\log_{10} 5 + \log_{10}(x + 1) = 1 + \log_{10}(2x + 7)$
   f $1 + 2\log_{10}(x + 1) = \log_{10}(2x + 1) + \log_{10}(5x + 8)$

13F Using logarithms to solve exponential equations and inequalities
Skillsheet

If $a \in \mathbb{R}^+ \setminus \{1\}$, then the statements $a^x = b$ and $\log_a b = x$ are equivalent. This defining property of logarithms may be used in the solution of exponential equations.

Example 23

Solve for x if $2^x = 11$.

Solution

We immediately see that $x = \log_2 11$.

This can be evaluated with a calculator:

$x = \log_2 11 \approx 3.45943$

Note: We will show an alternative method for solving Example 23 because it illustrates the relationship between logarithms of different bases. Take $\log_{10}$ of both sides of the equation $2^x = 11$. Then

$$\log_{10}(2^x) = \log_{10} 11$$
$$x \log_{10} 2 = \log_{10} 11$$
$$x = \frac{\log_{10} 11}{\log_{10} 2}$$

We have shown that

$$\log_2 11 = \frac{\log_{10} 11}{\log_{10} 2}$$

In general, if a, b and c are positive numbers with $a \neq 1$ and $b \neq 1$, then

$$\log_b c = \frac{\log_a c}{\log_a b}$$

Example 24

Solve $3^{2x-1} = 28$.

Solution

$$2x - 1 = \log_3 28$$
$$2x = 1 + \log_3 28$$
$$x = \frac{1 + \log_3 28}{2}$$
$$\approx 2.017 \quad \text{(to three decimal places)}$$

Example 25

Solve the inequality $0.7^x \geq 0.3$.

Solution

Taking $\log_{10}$ of both sides:

$$\log_{10}(0.7^x) \geq \log_{10} 0.3$$
$$x \log_{10} 0.7 \geq \log_{10} 0.3$$
$$x \leq \frac{\log_{10} 0.3}{\log_{10} 0.7} \quad \text{(direction of inequality reversed since } \log_{10} 0.7 < 0\text{)}$$
$$x \leq 3.376 \quad \text{(to three decimal places)}$$

Alternatively, we can solve the inequality $0.7^x \geq 0.3$ directly as follows:

Note that $0 < 0.7 < 1$ and thus, as x decreases, $y = 0.7^x$ increases. Therefore the inequality holds for $x \leq \log_{0.7} 0.3$.

Exponential graphs revisited

In Section 13C we graphed exponential functions, but often we could not find the x-axis intercept. Now that we have defined logarithms this can be done.

Example 26

Sketch the graph of $f(x) = 2 \times 10^x - 4$, giving the equation of the asymptote and the axis intercepts.

Solution

- As $x \to -\infty$, $y \to -4^+$. The equation of the horizontal asymptote is $y = -4$.
- The graph crosses the y-axis when $x = 0$, and so the y-axis intercept is given by $f(0) = 2 \times 10^0 - 4 = 2 - 4 = -2$.
- The graph crosses the x-axis when $f(x) = 0$:

$$2 \times 10^x - 4 = 0$$
$$2 \times 10^x = 4$$
$$10^x = 2$$
$$x = \log_{10} 2 \approx 0.3010$$

(correct to four decimal places)

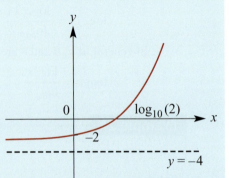

Section summary

- If $a \in \mathbb{R}^+ \setminus \{1\}$ and $x \in \mathbb{R}$, then the statements $a^x = b$ and $\log_a b = x$ are equivalent. This defining property of logarithms may be used in the solution of exponential equations and inequalities.

    For example:
    - $2^x = 5 \Leftrightarrow x = \log_2 5$
    - $(0.3)^x = 5 \Leftrightarrow x = \log_{0.3} 5$
    - $2^x \geq 5 \Leftrightarrow x \geq \log_2 5$
    - $(0.3)^x \geq 5 \Leftrightarrow x \leq \log_{0.3} 5$

- The x-axis intercepts of exponential graphs can now be found.

Exercise 13F

Example 23 **1** Solve each of the following equations correct to two decimal places:
  a $2^x = 7$
  b $2^x = 0.4$
  c $3^x = 14$
  d $4^x = 3$
  e $2^{-x} = 6$
  f $0.3^x = 2$

Example 24 **2** Solve each of the following equations correct to two decimal places:
  a $5^{2x-1} = 90$
  b $3^{x-1} = 10$
  c $0.2^{x+1} = 0.6$

Example 25 3 Solve for x. Give values correct to two decimal places if necessary.
  a $2^x > 8$
  b $3^x < 5$
  c $0.3^x > 4$
  d $3^{x-1} \leq 7$
  e $0.4^x \leq 0.3$

Example 26 4 For each of the following, sketch the graph of $y = f(x)$, giving the equation of the asymptote and the axis intercepts:
  a $f(x) = 2^x - 4$
  b $f(x) = 2 \times 3^x - 6$
  c $f(x) = 3 \times 10^x - 5$
  d $f(x) = -2 \times 10^x + 4$
  e $f(x) = -3 \times 2^x + 6$
  f $f(x) = 5 \times 2^x - 6$

13G Graphs of logarithm functions

▶ Graph of $y = \log_a x$ when $a > 1$

We look at the graphs of $y = \log_2 x$ and $y = \log_{10} x$. We note that $\log_{10} x = \log_{10} 2 \times \log_2 x$, and hence the graph of $y = \log_{10} x$ is the image of the graph of $y = \log_2 x$ under a dilation from the x-axis of factor $\log_{10} 2 \approx 0.3010$.

$y = \log_2 x$

A table of values for $y = \log_2 x$ is given below, and the graphs of $y = 2^x$ and $y = \log_2 x$ are drawn on the one set of axes.

x	$\frac{1}{4}$	$\frac{1}{2}$	1	2	4	8
$y = \log_2 x$	-2	-1	0	1	2	3

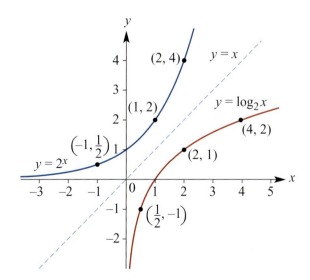

Notes:
- The point $(1, 2)$ is on the graph of $y = 2^x$ and the point $(2, 1)$ is on the graph of $y = \log_2 x$.
- The point $(2, 4)$ is on the graph of $y = 2^x$ and the point $(4, 2)$ is on the graph of $y = \log_2 x$.
- The graph of $y = \log_2 x$ is the reflection of the graph of $y = 2^x$ in the line $y = x$.

$y = \log_{10} x$

A table of values for $y = \log_{10} x$ is given below (the values are correct to two decimal places). Use your calculator to check these values.

x	0.1	1	2	3	4	5
$y = \log_{10} x$	-1	0	≈ 0.30	≈ 0.48	≈ 0.60	≈ 0.70

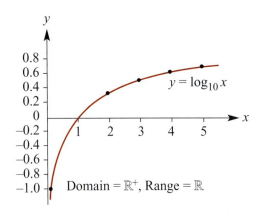

Domain = $\mathbb{R}^+$, Range = $\mathbb{R}$

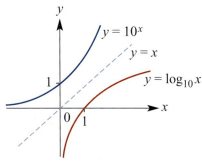

The graph of $y = \log_{10} x$ is the reflection in the line $y = x$ of the graph of $y = 10^x$.

In general

Properties of $y = a^x$, $a > 1$
- domain = $\mathbb{R}$
- range = $\mathbb{R}^+$
- $a^0 = 1$
- as $x \to -\infty$, $y \to 0^+$
- $y = 0$ is an asymptote

Properties of $y = \log_a x$, $a > 1$
- domain = $\mathbb{R}^+$
- range = $\mathbb{R}$
- $\log_a 1 = 0$
- as $x \to 0^+$, $y \to -\infty$
- $x = 0$ is an asymptote

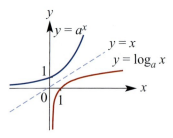

▶ Graph of $y = \log_a x$ when $0 < a < 1$

Consider $y = \log_{\frac{1}{2}} x$. We observe the following:

$$\log_{\frac{1}{2}} x = y \Leftrightarrow \left(\tfrac{1}{2}\right)^y = x$$
$$\Leftrightarrow 2^{-y} = x$$
$$\Leftrightarrow \log_2 x = -y$$
$$\Leftrightarrow y = -\log_2 x$$

So we have $\log_{\frac{1}{2}} x = -\log_2 x$.

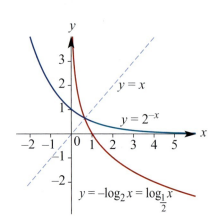

▶ Inverses

The inverse of a one-to-one function was introduced in Section 5G.

- The inverse of $f: \mathbb{R} \to \mathbb{R}$, $f(x) = 2^x$ is the function $f^{-1}: \mathbb{R}^+ \to \mathbb{R}$, $f^{-1}(x) = \log_2 x$.
- The inverse of $f: \mathbb{R} \to \mathbb{R}$, $f(x) = 10^x$ is the function $f^{-1}: \mathbb{R}^+ \to \mathbb{R}$, $f^{-1}(x) = \log_{10} x$.

Let $a \in \mathbb{R}^+ \setminus \{1\}$. The function with rule $y = \log_a x$, for $x > 0$, is the inverse of the function with rule $y = a^x$, for $x \in \mathbb{R}$.

- $\log_a(a^x) = x$ for all x
- $a^{\log_a x} = x$ for all positive values of x

Example 27

Find the inverse of:

a $f(x) = 10^{2x}$ **b** $g(x) = \log_{10}(2x)$

Solution

a Let $y = 10^{2x}$.
Interchanging x and y gives:
$$x = 10^{2y}$$
$$2y = \log_{10} x$$
$$y = \tfrac{1}{2} \log_{10} x$$
Thus $f^{-1}(x) = \tfrac{1}{2} \log_{10} x$.

b Let $y = \log_{10}(2x)$.
Interchanging x and y gives:
$$x = \log_{10}(2y)$$
$$10^x = 2y$$
$$y = \tfrac{1}{2} \times 10^x$$
Thus $g^{-1}(x) = \tfrac{1}{2} \times 10^x$.

Example 28

Find the rule for the inverse function of each of the following and state the domain of f^{-1}:

a $f(x) = \log_2(x - 2)$ **b** $f(x) = 5 \times 2^x + 3$

Solution

a Let $y = \log_2(x - 2)$.
Interchanging x and y gives:
$$x = \log_2(y - 2)$$
$$2^x = y - 2$$
$$y = 2^x + 2$$
$$\therefore f^{-1}(x) = 2^x + 2$$
The domain of f^{-1} is $\mathbb{R}$.

b Let $y = 5 \times 2^x + 3$.
Interchanging x and y gives:
$$x = 5 \times 2^y + 3$$
$$\frac{x - 3}{5} = 2^y$$
$$y = \log_2\left(\frac{x - 3}{5}\right)$$
$$\therefore f^{-1}(x) = \log_2\left(\frac{x - 3}{5}\right)$$
The domain of f^{-1} is $(3, \infty)$.

We observed in Section 13C that all graphs of the form $y = a^x$, where $a > 1$, are related to each other by dilations from the y-axis. This can be established by using the fact that $a^{\log_a x} = x$ for all $x > 0$.

For example, if $y = 2^x$, then
$$y = 2^x = (10^{\log_{10} 2})^x = 10^{(\log_{10} 2)x}$$

Therefore the graph of $y = 2^x$ is the image of the graph of $y = 10^x$ under a dilation of factor $\dfrac{1}{\log_{10} 2}$ from the y-axis.

Transformations of logarithm graphs

Transformations can be applied to the graphs of logarithm functions. This is shown in the following example.

Example 29

Sketch the graph of each of the following. Give the maximal domain, the equation of the asymptote and the axis intercepts.

a $f(x) = \log_2(x - 3)$
b $f(x) = \log_2(x + 2)$
c $f(x) = \log_2(3x)$

Solution

a $f(x) = \log_2(x - 3)$

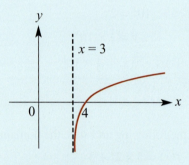

- The maximal domain is $(3, \infty)$.
- Equation of asymptote is $x = 3$.
- x-axis intercept: $\log_2(x - 3) = 0$ implies $x - 3 = 2^0$, i.e. $x = 4$.

b $f(x) = \log_2(x + 2)$

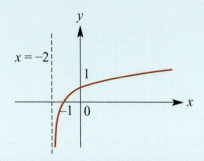

- The maximal domain is $(-2, \infty)$.
- Equation of asymptote is $x = -2$.
- y-axis intercept: $f(0) = \log_2(2) = 1$.
- x-axis intercept: $\log_2(x + 2) = 0$ implies $x + 2 = 2^0$, i.e. $x = -1$.

Explanation

The graph of $y = \log_2 x$ is translated 3 units in the positive direction of the x-axis.

Maximal domain: For $f(x) = \log_2(x - 3)$ to be defined, we need $x - 3 > 0$, i.e. $x > 3$.

Asymptote: As $x \to 3^+$, $y \to -\infty$.

The graph of $y = \log_2 x$ is translated 2 units in the negative direction of the x-axis.

Maximal domain: For $f(x) = \log_2(x + 2)$ to be defined, we need $x + 2 > 0$, i.e. $x > -2$.

Asymptote: As $x \to -2^+$, $y \to -\infty$.

c $f(x) = \log_2(3x)$

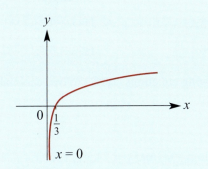

- The maximal domain is $(0, \infty)$.
- Equation of asymptote is $x = 0$.
- x-axis intercept: $\log_2(3x) = 0$ implies $3x = 2^0$, i.e. $x = \frac{1}{3}$.

The graph of $y = \log_2 x$ is dilated by a factor of $\frac{1}{3}$ from the y-axis.

Maximal domain: For $f(x) = \log_2(3x)$ to be defined, we need $3x > 0$, i.e. $x > 0$.

Asymptote: As $x \to 0^+$, $y \to -\infty$.

Section summary

Let $a \in \mathbb{R}^+ \setminus \{1\}$. The functions $f : \mathbb{R} \to \mathbb{R}$, $f(x) = a^x$ and $g : \mathbb{R}^+ \to \mathbb{R}$, $g(x) = \log_a x$ are inverse functions. That is, $g = f^{-1}$.

- $\log_a(a^x) = x$ for all x
- $a^{\log_a x} = x$ for all positive values of x

Exercise 13G

1 Sketch the graph of each of the following and state the domain and range for each:
   a $y = \log_{10}(2x)$
   b $y = 2 \log_{10} x$
   c $y = \log_{10}(\frac{1}{2}x)$
   d $y = 2 \log_{10}(3x)$
   e $y = -\log_{10} x$
   f $y = \log_{10}(-x)$

Example 27

2 Determine the inverse of each of the following:
   a $y = 10^{0.5x}$
   b $y = 3 \log_{10} x$
   c $y = 10^{3x}$
   d $y = 2 \log_{10}(3x)$

Example 28

3 Find the rule for the inverse function of each of the following:
   a $f(x) = 3^x + 2$
   b $f(x) = \log_2(x - 3)$
   c $f(x) = 4 \times 3^x + 2$
   d $f(x) = 5^x - 2$
   e $f(x) = \log_2(3x)$
   f $f(x) = \log_2\left(\frac{x}{3}\right)$
   g $f(x) = \log_2(x + 3)$
   h $f(x) = 5 \times 3^x - 2$

462 Chapter 13: Exponential functions and logarithms

Example 29

4 Sketch the graph of each of the following. Give the maximal domain, the equation of the asymptote and the axis intercepts.
  a $f(x) = \log_2(x - 4)$
  b $f(x) = \log_2(x + 3)$
  c $f(x) = \log_2(2x)$
  d $f(x) = \log_2(x + 2)$
  e $f(x) = \log_2\left(\dfrac{x}{3}\right)$
  f $f(x) = \log_2(-2x)$

5 Use a calculator to solve each of the following equations correct to two decimal places:
  a $2^{-x} = x$
  b $\log_{10}(x) + x = 0$

6 Use a calculator to plot the graphs of $y = \log_{10}(x^2)$ and $y = 2\log_{10} x$ for $x \in [-10, 10]$, $x \neq 0$.

7 On the same set of axes plot the graphs of $y = \log_{10}(\sqrt{x})$ and $y = \tfrac{1}{2}\log_{10} x$ for $x \in (0, 10]$.

8 Use a calculator to plot the graphs of $y = \log_{10}(2x) + \log_{10}(3x)$ and $y = \log_{10}(6x^2)$.

13H Exponential models and applications

Skillsheet In this section we begin by looking at several situations that can be modelled by exponential functions, and then discuss some examples where data is fitted by an exponential function.

▶ Exponential growth and decay

In the following, we consider a variable A that is subject to exponential change.

Let A be the quantity at time t. Then $A = A_0 b^t$, where A_0 is the initial quantity and b is a positive constant.

If $b > 1$, the model represents **growth**:
- growth of cells
- population growth
- continuously compounded interest

If $b < 1$, the model represents **decay**:
- radioactive decay
- cooling of materials

Cell growth

Suppose a particular type of bacteria cell divides into two new cells every T_D minutes. Let N_0 be the initial number of cells of this type. Then after t minutes the number of cells, N, is given by the formula

$$N = N_0 2^{\frac{t}{T_D}}$$

where T_D is called the **generation time**. Here we are only dealing with the type of reproduction where the cell divides in two. For most known bacteria that can be cultured, generation times range from about 15 minutes to 1 hour.

Example 30

What is the generation time of a bacterial population that increases from 5000 cells to 100 000 cells in four hours of growth?

Solution

In this example, $N_0 = 5000$ and $N = 100\,000$ when $t = 240$.

Hence $100\,000 = 5000 \times 2^{\frac{240}{T_D}}$

$$20 = 2^{\frac{240}{T_D}}$$

Thus $T_D = \dfrac{240}{\log_2 20} \approx 55.53$ (correct to two decimal places).

The generation time is approximately 55.53 minutes.

Radioactive decay

Radioactive materials decay so that the amount of radioactive material, A, present at time t (in years) is given by the formula

$$A = A_0 2^{-kt}$$

where A_0 is the initial amount and k is a positive constant that depends on the type of material. A radioactive substance is often described in terms of its **half-life**, which is the time required for half the material to decay.

Example 31

After 1000 years, a sample of radium-226 has decayed to 64.7% of its original mass. Find the half-life of radium-226.

Solution

We use the formula $A = A_0 2^{-kt}$. When $t = 1000$, $A = 0.647 A_0$. Thus

$$0.647 A_0 = A_0 2^{-1000k}$$
$$0.647 = 2^{-1000k}$$
$$-1000k = \log_2 0.647$$
$$k = \dfrac{-\log_2 0.647}{1000} \approx 0.000628$$

To find the half-life, we consider when $A = \tfrac{1}{2} A_0$:

$$A_0 2^{-kt} = \tfrac{1}{2} A_0$$
$$2^{-kt} = \tfrac{1}{2}$$
$$-kt = \log_2(\tfrac{1}{2})$$
$$-kt = -1$$
$$t = \dfrac{1}{k} \approx 1591.95$$

The half-life of radium-226 is approximately 1592 years.

Population growth

It is sometimes possible to model population growth through exponential models.

Example 32

There are approximately ten times as many red kangaroos as grey kangaroos in a certain area. If the population of grey kangaroos increases at a rate of 11% per annum while that of the red kangaroos decreases at 5% per annum, find how many years must elapse before the proportions are reversed, assuming the same rates continue to apply.

Solution

Let G_0 be the population of grey kangaroos at the start.

Then the number of grey kangaroos after n years is $G = G_0(1.11)^n$, and the number of red kangaroos after n years is $R = 10G_0(0.95)^n$.

When the proportions are reversed:

$$G = 10R$$
$$G_0(1.11)^n = 10 \times 10G_0(0.95)^n$$
$$(1.11)^n = 100(0.95)^n$$

Taking $\log_{10}$ of both sides:

$$\log_{10}((1.11)^n) = \log_{10}(100(0.95)^n)$$
$$n \log_{10} 1.11 = \log_{10} 100 + n \log_{10} 0.95$$
$$n \log_{10} 1.11 = 2 + n \log_{10} 0.95$$
$$n = \frac{2}{\log_{10} 1.11 - \log_{10} 0.95} \approx 29.6$$

i.e. the proportions of the kangaroo populations will be reversed after 30 years.

▶ Determining exponential rules

We have looked at determining rules for functions in Chapters 2 to 6. We look at one very useful case for exponential functions.

Example 33

The points $(1, 6)$ and $(5, 96)$ are known to lie on the curve $y = a \times b^x$, where $a > 0$ and $b > 0$. Find the values of a and b.

Solution

We can write

$$a \times b^1 = 6 \quad (1)$$
$$a \times b^5 = 96 \quad (2)$$

Dividing equation (2) by equation (1) gives $b^4 = 16$. Thus $b = 16^{\frac{1}{4}} = 2$, and substituting into equation (1) gives $a = 3$.

Using the TI-Nspire

- Define $f(x) = a \times b^x$.
- Solve for $a > 0$ and $b > 0$ using the simultaneous equations template with $f(1) = 6$ and $f(5) = 96$ as shown.

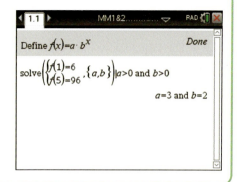

Using the Casio ClassPad

- Define $f(x) = a \times b^x$.
- Solve the simultaneous equations $f(1) = 6$ and $f(5) = 96$ for $a > 0$ and $b > 0$ as shown.

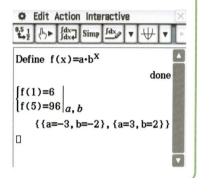

In many practical situations, the relationship between variables is exponential.

Example 34

Take a rectangular piece of paper approximately 30 cm × 6 cm. Fold the paper in half, successively, until you have folded it five times. Tabulate the times folded, f, and the number of creases in the paper, C.

Solution

Times folded, f	0	1	2	3	4	5
Creases, C	0	1	3	7	15	31

The rule connecting C and f is

$$C = 2^f - 1, \quad f \in \mathbb{N} \cup \{0\}$$

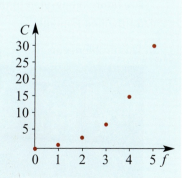

▶ Fitting data

Example 35

The table below shows the increase in weight of Somu, an orang-utan born at the Eastern Plains Zoo. Draw a graph to show Somu's weight increase for the first six months.

Data values

Months, m	0	1	2	3	4	5	6
Weight (kg), w	1.65	1.7	2.2	3.0	3.7	4.2	4.8

Solution

Plotting these data values:

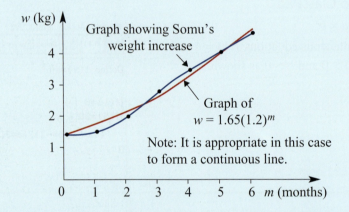

Graph showing Somu's weight increase

Graph of $w = 1.65(1.2)^m$

Note: It is appropriate in this case to form a continuous line.

On the same set of axes is the graph of the exponential function $w = 1.65(1.2)^m$, $0 \leq m \leq 6$. A table of values for this function is shown below.

Values from model

m	0	1	2	3	4	5	6
w	1.65	1.98	2.38	2.85	3.42	4.1	4.93

It can be seen from the graphs in Example 35 that the exponential model $w = 1.65(1.2)^m$ approximates the actual weight gain and would be a useful model to predict weight gains for any future orang-utan births at the zoo. This model describes a growth rate of 20% per month for the first 6 months.

This problem can also be attempted with a CAS calculator.

Using the TI-Nspire

- Enter the data either in a **Calculator** application as lists or in a **Lists & Spreadsheet** application as shown.

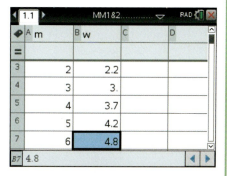

- Insert a **Calculator** page and use menu > **Statistics** > **Stat Calculations** > **Exponential Regression**. Complete as shown:
  - Use tab to move between fields.
  - Use the selection tool to open a field. Then use the arrows ▲ and ▼ to choose the correct entry, and select this entry using the selection tool.

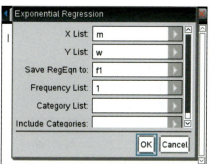

- This now gives the values of a and b, and the equation has been entered in $f_1(x)$.

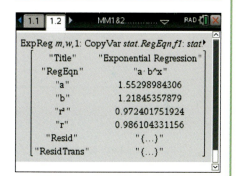

- The curve can be shown in a **Graphs** application together with the scatter plot (menu > **Graph Type** > **Scatter Plot**) using an appropriate window (menu > **Window/Zoom**).

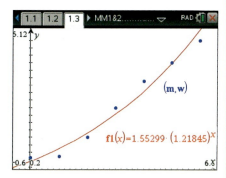

Note: Alternatively, the scatter plot and regression curve can be obtained using the **Data & Statistics** application.

Using the Casio ClassPad

- In **Statistics**, enter the data in lists 1 and 2 as shown below on the left.
- Select the graph icon and ensure that you set the graph type to Scatter and the lists to list 1 and list 2.

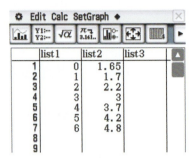
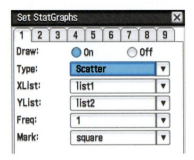

- Now select **Calc > Regression > abExponential Reg**. Confirm the settings by selecting OK.

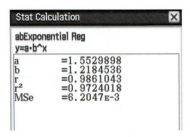
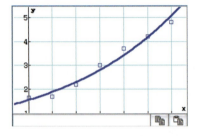

Section summary

There are many situations in which a varying quantity can be modelled by an exponential function. Let A be the quantity at time t. Then $A = A_0 b^t$, where A_0 is the initial quantity and b is a positive constant.

If $b > 1$, the model represents **growth**:
- growth of cells
- population growth
- continuously compounded interest

If $b < 1$, the model represents **decay**:
- radioactive decay
- cooling of materials

Exercise 13H

1 A population of 1000 E. coli bacteria doubles every 15 minutes.
   a Determine the formula for the number of bacteria at time t minutes.
   b How long will it take for the population to reach 10 000? (Give your answer to the nearest minute.)

Example 31   **2** The half-life of plutonium-239 is 24 000 years. If 10 grams are present now, how long will it take until only 10% of the original sample remains? (Give your answer to the nearest year.)

3 Carbon-14 is a radioactive substance with a half-life of 5730 years. It is used to determine the age of ancient objects. A Babylonian cloth fragment now has 40% of the carbon-14 that it contained originally. How old is the fragment of cloth?

4 The pressure, P, in the Earth's atmosphere decreases exponentially as you rise above the surface. The pressure in millibars at a height of h kilometres is given approximately by the function $P(h) = 1000 \times 10^{-0.05428h}$.
  a Find the pressure at a height of 5 km. (Give your answer to the nearest millibar.)
  b Find the height at which the pressure is 400 millibars. (Give your answer to the nearest metre.)

5 A biological culture contains 500 000 bacteria at 12 p.m. on Sunday. The culture increases by 10% every hour. At what time will the culture exceed 4 million bacteria?

6 When a liquid is placed into a refrigerator, its temperature $T°C$ at time t minutes is given by the formula $T = T_0 10^{-kt}$. The temperature is initially 100°C and drops to 40°C in 5 minutes. Find the temperature of the liquid after 15 minutes.

7 Iodine-131 is a radioactive isotope used in the treatment of the thyroid gland. It decays so that, after t days, 1 unit of the isotope is reduced to 0.9174^t units. How many days does it take for the amount to fall to less than 0.2 units?

Example 32   **8** The populations (in millions), p and q, of two neighbouring American states, P and Q, over a period of 50 years from 1950 are modelled by functions $p = 1.2 \times 2^{0.08t}$ and $q = 1.7 \times 2^{0.04t}$, where t is the number of years since 1950.
  a Plot the graphs of both functions using a calculator.
  b Find when the population of state P is:
    i equal to the population of state Q
    ii twice the population of state Q.

Example 33   **9** Each of the following pairs of points is known to lie on a curve $y = a \times b^x$, where $a > 0$ and $b > 0$. Find the values of a and b in each case.
  a (1, 15) and (4, 1875)   **b** (2, 1) and $\left(5, \dfrac{1}{8}\right)$ **c** $\left(1, \dfrac{15}{2}\right)$ and $\left(\dfrac{1}{2}, \dfrac{5\sqrt{6}}{2}\right)$

10 Five kilograms of sugar is gradually dissolved in a vat of water. After t hours, the amount S kg of undissolved sugar remaining is given by $S = 5 \times 10^{-kt}$.
  a Calculate k given that $S = 3.2$ when $t = 2$.
  b At what time will there be 1 kg of sugar remaining?

11 The number of bacteria, N, in a culture increases exponentially with time according to the rule $N = a \times b^t$, where time t is measured in hours. When observation started, there were 1000 bacteria, and five hours later there were 10 000 bacteria.

  a Find the values of a and b.
  b Find, to the nearest minute, when there were 5000 bacteria.
  c Find, to the nearest minute, when the number of bacteria first exceeds 1 000 000.
  d How many bacteria would there be 12 hours after the first observation?

12 Find a and k such that the graph of $y = a10^{kx}$ passes through the points $(2, 6)$ and $(5, 20)$.

13 Find an exponential model of the form $y = ab^x$ to fit the following data:

x	0	2	4	5	10
y	1.5	0.5	0.17	0.09	0.006

14 Find an exponential model of the form $p = ab^t$ to fit the following data:

t	0	2	4	6	8
p	2.5	4.56	8.3	15.12	27.56

15 A sheet of paper 0.2 mm thick is cut in half, and one piece is stacked on top of the other.

  a If this process is repeated, complete the following table:

Cuts, n	Sheets	Total thickness, T (mm)
0	1	0.2
1	2	0.4
2	4	0.8
3	8	
$\vdots$	$\vdots$	$\vdots$
10		

  b Write down a formula which shows the relationship between T and n.
  c Draw a graph of T against n for $n \leq 10$.
  d What would be the total thickness, T, after 30 cuts?

16 In the initial period of its life a particular species of tree grows in the manner described by the rule $d = d_0 10^{mt}$, where d is the diameter (in cm) of the tree t years after the beginning of this period. The diameter is 52 cm after 1 year, and 80 cm after 3 years. Calculate the values of the constants d_0 and m.

13I Logarithmic scales*

A **logarithmic scale** is a scale of measurement that uses the logarithm of a quantity. Familiar examples of logarithmic scales include the Richter scale (earthquakes), decibels (noise) and pH (acidity). In this section, we will show why such scales are useful and study these three examples.

▶ Charts with logarithmic scales

In the chart below we show an example for which the vertical axis has equally spaced increments that are labelled $1 = 5^0$, $5 = 5^1$, $25 = 5^2$, $125 = 5^3$, ... instead of $0, 1, 2, 3, \ldots$.

The major horizontal grid lines, which are equally spaced, are the integer powers of 5.

The straight line is the result of graphing $y = 3 \times 5^{2x}$ but with the vertical axis having a logarithmic scale (base 5).

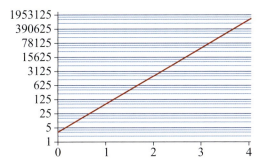 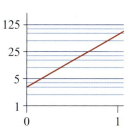

The bottom-left corner of the chart is shown 'blown up' on the right.

- The horizontal grid lines between 1 and 5 represent 2, 3 and 4. Their positions are determined by $\log_5 2$, $\log_5 3$ and $\log_5 4$.
- The horizontal grid lines between 5 and 25 represent 10, 15 and 20. Their positions are determined by $\log_5 10$, $\log_5 15$ and $\log_5 20$.
- The horizontal grid lines between 25 and 125 represent 50, 75 and 100. Their positions are determined by $\log_5 50$, $\log_5 75$ and $\log_5 100$.

Notice that there is the same gap between the grid lines for 1 and 2, for 5 and 10, and for 25 and 50. This is because

$$\log_5 2 - \log_5 1 = \log_5 2 \qquad \log_5 10 - \log_5 5 = \log_5 2 \qquad \log_5 50 - \log_5 25 = \log_5 2$$

This is not what we are used to from working with linear scales.

- For a **linear scale**, the change between two values is determined by the difference between the values. That is, a change from 1 to 2 is the same as a change from 6 to 7. We use linear scales to measure temperature (degrees Celsius) and length (metres) and in standard Cartesian graphs.
- For a **logarithmic scale**, the change between two values is determined by the ratio of the values. That is, a change from 1 to 2 (ratio of 1:2) would be perceived as the same amount of increase as a change from 6 to 12 (also a ratio of 1:2).

---

* This section is not required for Mathematical Methods Units 1 & 2.

The logarithm rule

$$\log_a\left(\frac{x}{y}\right) = \log_a x - \log_a y$$

provides the connections between these types of scale.

Presentation of data on a logarithmic scale can be helpful when the data covers a large range of values. The use of the logarithms of the values rather than the actual values reduces a wide range to a more manageable size.

▶ Graphing with logarithmic scales

We will see how to sketch the graph of an exponential function using a logarithmic scale for the vertical axis and a linear scale for the horizontal axis.

Let $y = b \times a^{mx}$, where a, b and m are positive real numbers. Then taking logarithms base a of both sides gives

$$\log_a y = \log_a b + mx$$

So the graph of $\log_a y$ against x is a straight line with gradient m and with ($\log_a y$)-axis intercept at $(0, \log_a b)$.

In the case of the exponential function $y = 3 \times 5^{2x}$, the equation for the straight line becomes $\log_5 y = \log_5 3 + 2x$. On the chart, we have labelled the vertical axis with powers of 5 rather than the logarithm.

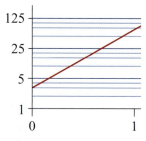

This straight line has gradient 2. The line through points $(0.5, 15)$ and $(1, 75)$ on this chart has actual gradient

$$\frac{\log_5 75 - \log_5 15}{1 - 0.5} = 2\log_5\left(\frac{75}{15}\right) = 2\log_5 5 = 2$$

Of course any two points on the line will give this result.

Example 36

Let $y = 4 \times 3^{2x}$, for $x \geq 0$.

a If $\log_3 y = mx + c$, give the values of m and c.
b Sketch the graph of $\log_3 y$ against x.
c Sketch the graph of $\log_3 y$ against x labelling your vertical axis with powers of 3.

Solution

a Take logarithms base 3 of both sides of the equation:

$$\log_3 y = \log_3(4 \times 3^{2x})$$
$$\log_3 y = \log_3 4 + \log_3(3^{2x})$$
$$\log_3 y = 2x + \log_3 4$$

Therefore $m = 2$ and $c = \log_3 4$.

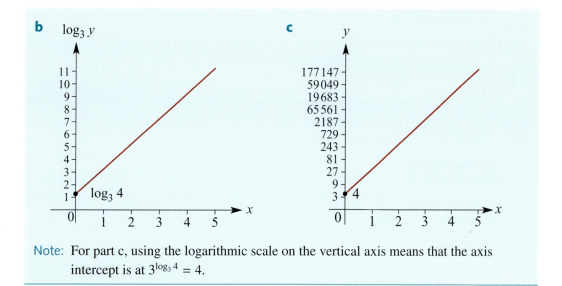

Note: For part c, using the logarithmic scale on the vertical axis means that the axis intercept is at $3^{\log_3 4} = 4$.

▶ **Applications**

We now look at three uses of logarithmic scales.

Decibels

A **decibel** is defined as one-tenth of a bel, which is named after Alexander Graham Bell, the inventor of the telephone.

The decibel is a logarithmic scale for measuring 'loudness of noise'. The intensity of a sound in decibels can be defined by

$$dB = 10 \log_{10}(P \times 10^{16})$$

where P is the power of the sound in watt/cm^2.

Example 37

A power mower generates a noise of 96 dB and a conversation in a restaurant generates noise of 60 dB. Find the power in watt/cm^2 for each of these.

Solution

■ Power mower
We have $96 = 10 \log_{10}(P \times 10^{16})$.
Hence
$$\log_{10}(P \times 10^{16}) = 9.6$$
$$P \times 10^{16} = 10^{9.6}$$
$$P = 10^{-6.4}$$

The power is $10^{-6.4}$ watt/cm^2.

■ Conversation
We have $60 = 10 \log_{10}(P \times 10^{16})$.
Hence
$$\log_{10}(P \times 10^{16}) = 6$$
$$P \times 10^{16} = 10^{6}$$
$$P = 10^{-10}$$

The power is 10^{-10} watt/cm^2.

Note: The maximum intensity which the ear can tolerate is about 10^{-4} watt/cm^2, which corresponds to a loudness level of about 120 dB.

Chapter 13: Exponential functions and logarithms

The Richter scale

Earthquake intensity is often reported on the **Richter scale**. The formula is

$$R = \log_{10}\left(\frac{a}{T}\right) + B$$

where a is the amplitude of the ground motion, T is the period of the seismic wave, and B is a term that allows for the weakening of the seismic wave with increasing distance from the epicentre of the earthquake.

Example 38

Assume that, for a particular earthquake, we have $a = 10$, $T = 1$ and $B = 6.8$. Find the earthquake's magnitude on the Richter scale.

Solution

$$R = \log_{10}\left(\frac{10}{1}\right) + 6.8 = 7.8$$

Example 39

Early in the twentieth century an earthquake in San Francisco registered 8.3 on the Richter scale. In the same year, another earthquake was recorded in South America that was four times stronger. We will take this to mean that the value of $\frac{a}{T}$ for South America is four times that for San Francisco. What was the magnitude of the earthquake in South America? Assume both were measured at the same distance from the epicentre, and so the constant B is the same for both.

Solution

For San Francisco:

$$8.3 = \log_{10}\left(\frac{a_1}{T_1}\right) + B \quad\quad (1)$$

Hence, for South America:

$$\begin{aligned}
R &= \log_{10}\left(\frac{a_2}{T_2}\right) + B \\
&= \log_{10}\left(\frac{4a_1}{T_1}\right) + B \\
&= \log_{10} 4 + \log_{10}\left(\frac{a_1}{T_1}\right) + B \\
&= \log_{10} 4 + 8.3 \quad\quad \text{using equation (1)} \\
&\approx 8.9
\end{aligned}$$

The magnitude was 8.9.

Note: Although the earthquake in South America was four times stronger, the magnitude on the Richter scale only increased by $\log_{10} 4 \approx 0.6$.

The pH scale

The pH scale for measuring the acidity of a solution is logarithmic. The pH of a solution is determined by the concentration of hydronium ions, $[H_3O^+]$, in the solution. (Concentration is measured in moles per litre.) The definition is

$$pH = \log_{10}\left(\frac{1}{[H_3O^+]}\right) = -\log_{10}([H_3O^+])$$

Vinegar has pH 3, and bananas have pH in the interval [4.5, 4.7]. The scale goes from 0.1 for hydrochloric acid up to 14 for sodium hydroxide.

Example 40

The pH of blood normally lies in the interval [7.37, 7.44]. Find the range for the concentration of hydronium ions.

Solution

For pH 7.37, we have

$$-\log_{10}([H_3O^+]) = 7.37$$
$$\log_{10}([H_3O^+]) = -7.37$$
$$[H_3O^+] = 10^{-7.37} \text{ moles per litre}$$

Now, for pH 7.44, we have

$$\log_{10}([H_3O^+]) = -7.44$$
$$[H_3O^+] = 10^{-7.44} \text{ moles per litre}$$

So the concentration of hydronium ions lies in the interval $[10^{-7.44}, 10^{-7.37}]$.

We can write this interval as $[3.63 \times 10^{-8}, 4.27 \times 10^{-8}]$ to three significant figures.

Section summary

- **Linear scale** The change between two values is determined by the difference between the values. That is, a change from 1 to 2 is the same as a change from 6 to 7. We use linear scales for temperature and length.
- **Logarithmic scale** The change between two values is determined by the ratio of the values. That is, a change from 1 to 2 (ratio of 1:2) is the same as a change from 6 to 12 (also a ratio of 1:2). We use logarithmic scales for noise and acidity.
- Consider the exponential function $y = b \times a^{mx}$, where a, b and m are positive real numbers. Taking logarithms base a of both sides gives

    $\log_a y = \log_a b + mx$

    So the graph of $\log_a y$ against x is a straight line with gradient m and with $(\log_a y)$-axis intercept at $(0, \log_a b)$.

Exercise 13I

Example 36

1. Let $y = 3 \times 4^{2x}$, for $x \geq 0$.
   a. If $\log_4 y = mx + c$, give the values of m and c.
   b. Sketch the graph of $\log_4 y$ against x.
   c. Sketch the graph of $\log_4 y$ against x labelling your vertical axis with powers of 4.

2. Let $y = 2 \times 5^{3x}$, for $x \geq 0$.
   a. If $\log_5 y = mx + c$, give the values of m and c.
   b. Sketch the graph of $\log_5 y$ against x.
   c. Sketch the graph of $\log_5 y$ against x labelling your vertical axis with powers of 5.

Example 37

3. A busy street generates noise of 70 dB and a quiet car generates noise of 50 dB. Find the power in watt/cm² for each of these.

4. Use the formula $dB = 10 \log_{10}(P \times 10^{16})$ to answer the following:
   a. If P is increased by a factor of 2, what is the effect on dB?
   b. If P is increased by a factor of 10, what is the effect on dB?
   c. If dB is increased by a factor of 3, what is the effect on P?
   d. For what value of P is $dB = 0$?
   e. For what value of P is $dB = 100$?

5. If $dB_1 - dB_2 = \lambda$, find P_1 in terms of P_2.

Example 38

6. Find the magnitude on the Richter scale of an earthquake with $a = 10$, $T = 2$ and $B = 5$.

Example 39

7. An earthquake in Turkey registered 7.3 on the Richter scale. In the same year, an earthquake in Greece had a quarter of this strength. We will take this to mean that the value of $\dfrac{a}{T}$ for Greece is one-quarter that for Turkey. What was the magnitude of the earthquake in Greece? Assume both were measured at the same distance from the epicentre, and so the constant B is the same for both.

Example 40

8. The pH of a soft drink normally lies in the interval [2.0, 4.0]. Find the range for the concentration of hydronium ions.

Chapter 13 review

Chapter summary

- **Index laws**
  - To **multiply** two powers with the same base, **add** the indices: $a^m \times a^n = a^{m+n}$
  - To **divide** two powers with the same base, **subtract** the indices: $a^m \div a^n = a^{m-n}$
  - To raise a power to another power, **multiply** the indices: $(a^m)^n = a^{m \times n}$

- Rational indices:
$$a^{\frac{1}{n}} = \sqrt[n]{a} \quad \text{and} \quad a^{\frac{m}{n}} = \left(a^{\frac{1}{n}}\right)^m$$

- Graphs of exponential functions:

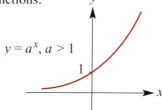
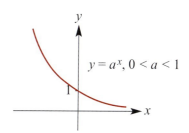

- For $a \in \mathbb{R}^+ \setminus \{1\}$:
$$\text{if } a^x = a^y, \text{ then } x = y$$

- For $a \in \mathbb{R}^+ \setminus \{1\}$:
$$a^x = y \quad \text{is equivalent to} \quad \log_a y = x$$

- Laws of logarithms
  1. $\log_a(mn) = \log_a m + \log_a n$
  2. $\log_a\left(\dfrac{m}{n}\right) = \log_a m - \log_a n$
  3. $\log_a(m^p) = p \log_a m$
  4. $\log_a(m^{-1}) = -\log_a m$
  5. $\log_a 1 = 0$ and $\log_a a = 1$

Technology-free questions

1 Simplify each of the following, expressing your answer with positive index:

- **a** $\dfrac{a^6}{a^2}$
- **b** $\dfrac{b^8}{b^{10}}$
- **c** $\dfrac{m^3 n^4}{m^5 n^6}$
- **d** $\dfrac{a^3 b^2}{(ab^2)^4}$
- **e** $\dfrac{6a^8}{4a^2}$
- **f** $\dfrac{10a^7}{6a^9}$
- **g** $\dfrac{8(a^3)^2}{(2a)^3}$
- **h** $\dfrac{m^{-1} n^2}{(mn^{-2})^3}$
- **i** $(p^{-1} q^{-2})^2$
- **j** $\dfrac{(2a^{-4})^3}{5a^{-1}}$
- **k** $\dfrac{6a^{-1}}{3a^{-2}}$
- **l** $\dfrac{a^4 + a^8}{a^2}$

2 Use logarithms to solve each of the following equations:

- **a** $2^x = 7$
- **b** $2^{2x} = 7$
- **c** $10^x = 2$
- **d** $10^x = 3.6$
- **e** $10^x = 110$
- **f** $10^x = 1010$
- **g** $2^{5x} = 100$
- **h** $2^x = 0.1$

478 Chapter 13: Exponential functions and logarithms

3 Evaluate each of the following:
   a $\log_2 64$
   b $\log_{10}(10^7)$
   c $\log_a(a^2)$
   d $\log_4 1$
   e $\log_3 27$
   f $\log_2\left(\dfrac{1}{4}\right)$
   g $\log_{10} 0.001$
   h $\log_2 16$

4 Express each of the following as a single logarithm:
   a $\log_{10} 2 + \log_{10} 3$
   b $\log_{10} 4 + 2\log_{10} 3 - \log_{10} 6$
   c $2\log_{10} a - \log_{10} b$
   d $2\log_{10} a - 3 - \log_{10} 25$
   e $\log_{10} x + \log_{10} y - \log_{10} x$
   f $2\log_{10} a + 3\log_{10} b - \log_{10} c$

5 Solve each of the following for x:
   a $3^x(3^x - 27) = 0$
   b $(2^x - 8)(2^x - 1) = 0$
   c $2^{2x} - 2^{x+1} = 0$
   d $2^{2x} - 12 \times 2^x + 32 = 0$

6 Sketch the graph of:
   a $y = 2 \times 2^x$
   b $y = -3 \times 2^x$
   c $y = 5 \times 2^{-x}$
   d $y = 2^{-x} + 1$
   e $y = 2^x - 1$
   f $y = 2^x + 2$

7 Solve the equation $\log_{10} x + \log_{10}(2x) - \log_{10}(x+1) = 0$.

8 Given $3^x = 4^y = 12^z$, show that $z = \dfrac{xy}{x+y}$.

9 Evaluate $2\log_2 12 + 3\log_2 5 - \log_2 15 - \log_2 150$.

10 a Given that $\log_p 7 + \log_p k = 0$, find k.
   b Given that $4\log_q 3 + 2\log_q 2 - \log_q 144 = 2$, find q.

11 Solve:
   a $2 \times 4^{a+1} = 16^{2a}$ for a
   b $\log_2(y^2) = 4 + \log_2(y+5)$ for y

Multiple-choice questions

1 $8x^3 \div 4x^{-3} =$
   A 2
   B $2x^0$
   C $2x^6$
   D $2x^{-1}$
   E $\dfrac{2}{x^9}$

2 The expression $\dfrac{a^2 b}{(2ab^2)^3} \div \dfrac{ab}{16a^0}$ simplifies to
   A $\dfrac{2}{a^2 b^6}$
   B $\dfrac{2a^2}{b^6}$
   C $2a^2 b^6$
   D $\dfrac{2}{ab^6}$
   E $\dfrac{1}{128ab^5}$

3 The function $f: \mathbb{R} \to \mathbb{R}$, $f(x) = 3 \times 2^x - 1$ has range
   A $\mathbb{R}$
   B $\mathbb{R} \setminus \{-1\}$
   C $(-1, \infty)$
   D $(1, \infty)$
   E $[1, \infty)$

4 The function $f: \mathbb{R}^+ \to \mathbb{R}$, where $f(x) = \log_2(3x)$, has an inverse function f^{-1}. The rule for f^{-1} is given by

- **A** $f^{-1}(x) = 2^x$
- **B** $f^{-1}(x) = 3^x$
- **C** $f^{-1}(x) = \dfrac{2^x}{3}$
- **D** $f^{-1}(x) = 2^{\frac{x}{3}}$
- **E** $f^{-1}(x) = \log_2\left(\dfrac{x}{3}\right)$

5 If $\log_{10}(x-2) - 3\log_{10}(2x) = 1 - \log_{10} y$, then y is equal to

- **A** $\dfrac{80x^3}{x-2}$
- **B** $1 + \dfrac{8x^3}{x-2}$
- **C** $\dfrac{60x}{x-2}$
- **D** $1 + \dfrac{6x}{x-2}$
- **E** $1 - \dfrac{x-2}{8x^3}$

6 The solution of the equation $5 \times 2^{5x} = 10$ is x equals

- **A** $\dfrac{1}{2}$
- **B** $\dfrac{1}{5}$
- **C** $\dfrac{1}{5}\log_2 10$
- **D** $\dfrac{1}{2}\log_2 5$
- **E** $\dfrac{1}{5} \times 2^5$

7 The equation of the asymptote of $y = 3\log_2(5x) + 2$ is

- **A** $x = 0$
- **B** $x = 2$
- **C** $x = 3$
- **D** $x = 5$
- **E** $y = 2$

8 Which of the following graphs could be the graph of the function $f(x) = 2^{ax} + b$, where a and b are positive?

A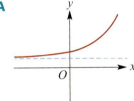

B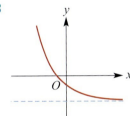

C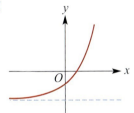

D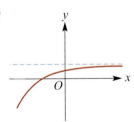

E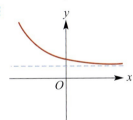

9 Which one of the following functions has a graph with a vertical asymptote with equation $x = b$?

- **A** $y = \log_2(x - b)$
- **B** $y = \dfrac{1}{x+b}$
- **C** $y = \dfrac{1}{x+b} - b$
- **D** $y = 2^x + b$
- **E** $y = 2^{x-b}$

10 The expression $\dfrac{2mh}{(3mh^2)^3} \div \dfrac{mh}{81m^2}$ is equal to

- **A** $\dfrac{6}{mh^6}$
- **B** $\dfrac{6m^2}{h^6}$
- **C** $6m^2h^6$
- **D** $\dfrac{6}{m^2h^6}$
- **E** $\dfrac{1}{128mh^5}$

Extended-response questions

1 This problem is based on the so-called 'Tower of Hanoi' puzzle. Given a number of different sized discs, the problem is to move a pile of discs to a second location (if starting at A, then either to B or C) according to the following rules:

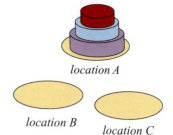
location A

location B   location C

- Only one disc can be moved at a time.
- A total of only three locations (A, B and C) can be used to 'rest' the discs.
- A larger sized disc cannot be placed on top of a smaller disc.
- The task must be completed in the smallest possible number of moves.

a First complete the puzzle using two coins. Repeat with three coins and then with four coins, and thus complete the following table:

Number of discs, n	1	2	3	4
Minimum number of moves, M	1			

b Work out the formula which shows the relationship between M and n. Use your formula to extend the table of values for $n = 5, 6, 7$.

c Plot the graph of M against n.

d Investigate, for both $n = 3$ and $n = 4$, to find whether there is a pattern for the number of times each particular disc is moved.

2 To control an advanced electronic machine, a total of 2187 different switch positions are required. There are two kinds of switches available:

Switch 1   These can be set in 9 different positions.
Switch 2   These can be set in 3 different positions.

If n of switch type 1 and $n + 1$ of switch type 2 are used, calculate the value of n that gives the required total number of switch positions.

3 Research is being carried out to investigate the durability of paints of different thicknesses. The automatic machine shown in the diagram is proposed for producing a coat of paint of a particular thickness.

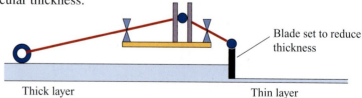

Thick layer   Thin layer

The paint is spread over a plate and a blade sweeps over the plate reducing the thickness of the paint. The process involves the blade moving at three different speeds.

a Operating at the initial setting, the blade reduces the paint thickness to one-eighth of the original thickness. This happens n times. What fraction of the paint thickness remains? Express this as a power of $\frac{1}{2}$.

b The blade is then reset so that it removes three-quarters of the remaining paint. This happens $(n-1)$ times. At the end of this second stage, express the remaining thickness as a power of $\frac{1}{2}$.

c The third phase of the process involves the blade being reset to remove half of the remaining paint. This happens $(n-3)$ times. At what value of n would the machine have to be set to reduce a film of paint 8192 units thick to 1 unit thick?

4 A hermit has little opportunity to replenish supplies of tea and so, to eke out supplies for as long as possible, he dries out the tea leaves after use and then stores the dried tea in an airtight box. He estimates that after each re-use of the leaves the amount of tannin in the used tea will be half the previous amount. He also estimates that the amount of caffeine in the used tea will be one-quarter of the previous amount.
The information on the label of the tea packet states that the tea contains 729 mg of caffeine and 128 mg of tannin.

a Write down expressions for the amount of caffeine when the tea leaves are re-used for the first, second, third and nth times.

b Do the same for the amount of tannin remaining.

c Find the number of times he can re-use the tea leaves if a 'tea' containing more than three times as much tannin as caffeine is undrinkable.

5 A new type of red synthetic carpet was produced in two batches. The first batch had a brightness of 15 units and the second batch 20 units. After a period of time it was discovered that the first batch was losing its brightness at the rate of 5% per year while the second was losing brightness at the rate of 6% per year.

a Write down expressions for the brightness of each batch after n years.

b A person bought some carpet from the first batch when it was a year old and some new carpet from the second batch. How long would it be before the brightness of the two carpets was the same?

6 The value of shares in Company X increased linearly over a two-year period according to the model $x = 0.8 + 0.17t$, where t is the number of months from the beginning of January 2014 and x is the value of the shares at time t.
The value of shares in Company Y increased over the same period of time according to the model $y = 100^{0.03t}$, where y is the value of these shares at time t months.
The value of shares in Company Z increased over the same period according to the model $z = 1.7 \log_{10}(5(t+1))$, where z is the value of the shares at time t months.
Use a calculator to sketch the graphs of the three functions on the one screen.

a Find the values of the shares in each of the three companies at the end of June 2014.

b Find the values of the shares in the three companies at the end of September 2015.

c During which months were shares in Company X more valuable than shares in Company Y?

d For how long and during which months were the shares in Company X the most valuable?

7 In the year 2000, in an African game park it was estimated that there were approximately 700 wildebeest and that their population was increasing at 3% per year. At the same time, in the park there were approximately 1850 zebras and their population was decreasing at the rate of 4% per year. Use a calculator to plot the graphs of both functions.

  a After how many years was the number of wildebeest greater than the number of zebras?

  b It is also estimated that there were 1000 antelope and their numbers were increasing by 50 per year. After how many years was the number of antelope greater than the number of zebras?

8 Students conducting a science experiment on cooling rates measure the temperature of a beaker of liquid over a period of time. The following measurements were taken.

Time (minutes)	3	6	9	12	15	18	21
Temperature (°C)	71.5	59	49	45.5	34	28	23.5

  a Find an exponential model to fit the data collected.
  b Use this model to estimate:

     i the initial temperature of the liquid
     ii the temperature of the liquid after 25 minutes.

  It is suspected that one of the temperature readings was incorrect.

  c Re-calculate the model to fit the data, omitting the incorrect reading.
  d Use the new model to estimate:

     i the initial temperature of the liquid
     ii the temperature of the liquid at $t = 12$.

  e If the room temperature is 15°C, find the approximate time at which the cooling of the liquid ceased.

9 The graph of $y = ab^x$ passes through the points $(1, 1)$ and $(2, 5)$.

  a Find the values of a and b.
  b Let $b^x = 10^z$.

     i Take logarithms of both sides (base 10) to find an expression for z in terms of x.
     ii Find the values of k and a such that the graph of $y = a10^{kx}$ passes through the points $(1, 1)$ and $(2, 5)$.

10 a Find an exponential model of the form $y = a \cdot b^x$ to fit the following data:

x	0	2	4	5	10
y	2	5	13	20	200

  b Express the model you have found in part **a** in the form $y = a10^{kx}$.
  c Hence find an expression for x in terms of y.

Chapter 14

Circular functions

Objectives

- ▶ To use **radians** and **degrees** for the measurement of angle.
- ▶ To convert radians to degrees, and vice versa.
- ▶ To define the circular functions **sine**, **cosine** and **tangent**.
- ▶ To explore the **symmetry properties** of circular functions.
- ▶ To find standard **exact values** of circular functions.
- ▶ To understand and sketch the **graphs of circular functions**.

Following on from our study of polynomial, exponential and logarithmic functions, we meet a further three important functions in this chapter. Again we use the notation developed in Chapter 5 for describing functions and their properties.

You have studied trigonometry in earlier years, mainly for angles between 0° and 90°. In this chapter we see how the trigonometry you have studied may be extended to form three new functions: sine, cosine and tangent. We will see that the first two of these functions have the real numbers as their domain, and the third the real numbers without the odd multiples of $\frac{\pi}{2}$.

An important property of these three functions is that they are periodic. That is, they each repeat their values in regular intervals or periods. In general, a function f is **periodic** if there is a positive constant a such that $f(x + a) = f(x)$. The sine and cosine functions each have period 2π, while the tangent function has period π.

The sine and cosine functions are used to model wave motion, and are therefore central to the application of mathematics to any problem in which periodic motion is involved – from the motion of the tides and ocean waves to sound waves and modern telecommunications.

14A Measuring angles in degrees and radians

The diagram shows a **unit circle**, i.e. a circle of radius 1 unit.

The circumference of the unit circle $= 2\pi \times 1$
$\qquad\qquad\qquad\qquad\qquad\qquad = 2\pi$ units

Thus, the distance in an anticlockwise direction around the circle from

$\qquad A$ to $B = \dfrac{\pi}{2}$ units

$\qquad A$ to $C = \pi$ units

$\qquad A$ to $D = \dfrac{3\pi}{2}$ units

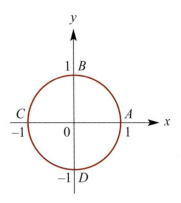

▶ Definition of a radian

In moving around the circle a distance of 1 unit from A to P, the angle POA is defined. The measure of this angle is 1 radian.

> One **radian** (written 1^c) is the angle subtended at the centre of the unit circle by an arc of length 1 unit.

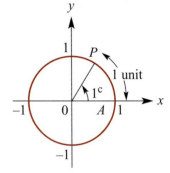

Note: Angles formed by moving **anticlockwise** around the unit circle are defined as **positive**; those formed by moving **clockwise** are defined as **negative**.

▶ Degrees and radians

The angle, in radians, swept out in one revolution of a circle is $2\pi^c$.

$\qquad 2\pi^c = 360°$

$\therefore \qquad \pi^c = 180°$

$\therefore \qquad \boxed{1^c = \dfrac{180°}{\pi} \quad \text{or} \quad 1° = \dfrac{\pi^c}{180}}$

Example 1

Convert $30°$ to radians.

Solution

$\qquad 1° = \dfrac{\pi^c}{180}$

$\therefore \quad 30° = \dfrac{30 \times \pi}{180} = \dfrac{\pi^c}{6}$

Explanation

Multiply by $\dfrac{\pi}{180}$ and simplify by cancelling.

Example 2

Convert $\dfrac{\pi^c}{4}$ to degrees.

Solution	Explanation
$1^c = \dfrac{180°}{\pi}$ $\therefore \dfrac{\pi^c}{4} = \dfrac{\pi \times 180}{4 \times \pi} = 45°$	Multiply by $\dfrac{180}{\pi}$ and simplify by cancelling.

Note: Often the symbol for radians, ^{c}, is omitted.
For example, the angle 45° is written as $\dfrac{\pi}{4}$ rather than $\dfrac{\pi^c}{4}$.

Using the TI-Nspire

To convert 32 degrees to radians, type $32° \blacktriangleright \textbf{Rad}$ as shown.

- The degree symbol ° is found in the symbols palette (ctrl 📖) or the catalog (📖 4).
- The ▶ **Rad** command can be found in the catalog (📖 1 R).

To convert 2 radians to degrees, type $2^r \blacktriangleright \textbf{DD}$ as shown.

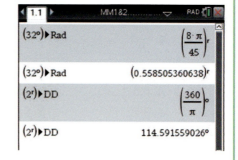

- The radian symbol ^{r} is found in the symbols palette (ctrl 📖) or the catalog (📖 4).
- The ▶ **DD** command can be found in the catalog (📖 1 D).

Note: If the calculator is in radian mode, you can convert 32° to radians by simply typing 32° then enter. If the calculator is in degree mode, type 2^r then enter.

Using the Casio ClassPad

To convert 32 degrees to radians:

- Ensure your calculator is in radian mode (with **Rad** in the status bar at the bottom of the main screen).
- Enter 32° and tap EXE. The degree symbol ° is found in the Math1 keyboard.
- The answer can be displayed exactly, as shown, or highlight the answer and tap 🔢 to convert to decimal.

To convert 2 radians to degrees:

- Ensure your calculator is in degree mode (**Deg**).
- Enter 2^r and tap EXE. The radian symbol ^{r} is found in the Math1 keyboard.

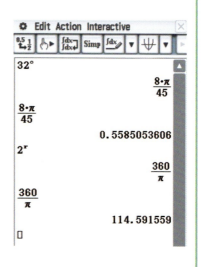

486 Chapter 14: Circular functions   14A

> **Section summary**
> - One **radian** (written 1^c) is the angle subtended at the centre of the unit circle by an arc of length 1 unit.
> - To convert:
>   - degrees to radians, multiply by $\dfrac{\pi}{180}$
>   - radians to degrees, multiply by $\dfrac{180}{\pi}$.

Exercise 14A

Example 1 **1** Express the following angles in radian measure in terms of π:
    a $60°$ **b** $144°$ **c** $240°$ **d** $330°$ **e** $420°$ **f** $480°$

Example 2 **2** Express, in degrees, the angles with the following radian measures:
    a $\dfrac{2\pi}{3}$ **b** $\dfrac{5\pi}{6}$ **c** $\dfrac{7\pi}{6}$ **d** 0.9π
    e $\dfrac{5\pi}{9}$ **f** $\dfrac{9\pi}{5}$ **g** $\dfrac{11\pi}{9}$ **h** 1.8π

3 Use a calculator to convert the following angles from radians to degrees:
    a 0.6 **b** 1.89 **c** 2.9 **d** 4.31
    e 3.72 **f** 5.18 **g** 4.73 **h** 6.00

4 Use a calculator to express the following in radian measure:
    a $38°$ **b** $73°$ **c** $107°$ **d** $161°$
    e $84.1°$ **f** $228°$ **g** $136.4°$ **h** $329°$

5 Express, in degrees, the angles with the following radian measures:
    a $-\dfrac{\pi}{3}$ **b** -4π **c** -3π **d** $-\pi$
    e $\dfrac{5\pi}{3}$ **f** $\dfrac{-11\pi}{6}$ **g** $\dfrac{23\pi}{6}$ **h** $\dfrac{-23\pi}{6}$

6 Express each of the following in radian measure in terms of π:
    a $-360°$ **b** $-540°$ **c** $-240°$ **d** $-720°$ **e** $-330°$ **f** $-210°$

7 **a** On a set of axes, draw a unit circle centred at the origin and indicate the position on the unit circle corresponding to each of the following:
    i $\dfrac{\pi}{4}$ **ii** $\dfrac{3\pi}{4}$ **iii** $\dfrac{5\pi}{4}$ **iv** $\dfrac{7\pi}{4}$

  b On a set of axes, draw a unit circle centred at the origin and indicate the position on the unit circle corresponding to each of the following:
    i $\dfrac{\pi}{3}$ **ii** $-\dfrac{\pi}{3}$ **iii** $\dfrac{2\pi}{3}$ **iv** $\dfrac{4\pi}{3}$

  c On a set of axes, draw a unit circle centred at the origin and indicate the position on the unit circle corresponding to each of the following:
    i $\dfrac{\pi}{6}$ **ii** $-\dfrac{7\pi}{6}$ **iii** $\dfrac{13\pi}{6}$ **iv** $\dfrac{17\pi}{6}$

14B Defining circular functions: sine and cosine

Consider the unit circle.

The position of point P on the circle can be described by relating the angle θ to the Cartesian coordinates x and y.

The point P on the circle corresponding to an angle θ is written $P(\theta)$.

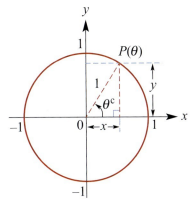

The x-coordinate of $P(\theta)$ is determined by the angle θ. Similarly, the y-coordinate of $P(\theta)$ is determined by the angle θ. So we can define two functions, called sine and cosine, as follows:

> The x-coordinate of $P(\theta)$ is given by $x = \text{cosine } \theta$, for $\theta \in \mathbb{R}$.
>
> The y-coordinate of $P(\theta)$ is given by $y = \text{sine } \theta$, for $\theta \in \mathbb{R}$.

These functions are usually written in an abbreviated form as follows:

$$x = \cos \theta$$
$$y = \sin \theta$$

Hence the coordinates of $P(\theta)$ are $(\cos \theta, \sin \theta)$.

Note: Adding 2π to the angle results in a return to the same point on the unit circle. Thus $\cos(2\pi + \theta) = \cos \theta$ and $\sin(2\pi + \theta) = \sin \theta$.

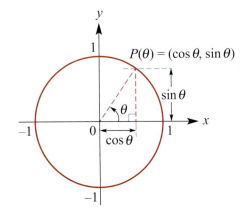

Example 3

Evaluate $\sin \pi$ and $\cos \pi$.

Solution

After moving through an angle of π, the position is $P(\pi) = (-1, 0)$.

$\therefore \cos \pi = -1$ and $\sin \pi = 0$

Example 4

Evaluate $\sin\left(-\dfrac{3\pi}{2}\right)$ and $\cos\left(-\dfrac{\pi}{2}\right)$.

Solution	Explanation
$\sin\left(-\dfrac{3\pi}{2}\right) = 1$	The point $P\left(-\dfrac{3\pi}{2}\right)$ has coordinates $(0, 1)$.
$\cos\left(-\dfrac{\pi}{2}\right) = 0$	The point $P\left(-\dfrac{\pi}{2}\right)$ has coordinates $(0, -1)$.

Example 5

Evaluate $\sin\left(\dfrac{5\pi}{2}\right)$ and $\sin\left(\dfrac{7\pi}{2}\right)$.

Solution

$$\sin\left(\dfrac{5\pi}{2}\right) = \sin\left(2\tfrac{1}{2}\pi\right) = \sin\left(2\pi + \dfrac{\pi}{2}\right) = \sin\left(\dfrac{\pi}{2}\right) = 1$$

$$\sin\left(\dfrac{7\pi}{2}\right) = \sin\left(3\tfrac{1}{2}\pi\right) = \sin\left(2\pi + \dfrac{3\pi}{2}\right) = \sin\left(\dfrac{3\pi}{2}\right) = -1$$

Example 6

Evaluate $\sin\left(\dfrac{9\pi}{2}\right)$ and $\cos(27\pi)$.

Solution

$$\sin\left(\dfrac{9\pi}{2}\right) = \sin\left(4\pi + \dfrac{\pi}{2}\right) = \sin\left(\dfrac{\pi}{2}\right) = 1 \qquad \cos(27\pi) = \cos(26\pi + \pi) = \cos\pi = -1$$

Section summary

- $P(\theta) = (\cos\theta, \sin\theta)$
- $\cos(2\pi + \theta) = \cos\theta$ and $\sin(2\pi + \theta) = \sin\theta$
- If an angle is an odd multiple of $\dfrac{\pi}{2}$, then its sine is either 1 or -1, and its cosine is zero.
- If an angle is an even multiple of $\dfrac{\pi}{2}$, then its sine is zero, and its cosine is either 1 or -1.

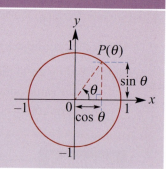

Exercise 14B

Example 4, 5

1 For each of the following angles, t, determine the values of $\sin t$ and $\cos t$:

a $t = 0$
b $t = \dfrac{3\pi}{2}$
c $t = -\dfrac{3\pi}{2}$
d $t = \dfrac{5\pi}{2}$

Example 5, 6

e $t = -3\pi$
f $t = \dfrac{9\pi}{2}$
g $t = \dfrac{7\pi}{2}$
h $t = 4\pi$

2 Evaluate using your calculator. (Check that your calculator is in radian mode.)

a $\sin 1.9$
b $\sin 2.3$
c $\sin 4.1$
d $\cos 0.3$
e $\cos 2.1$
f $\cos(-1.6)$
g $\sin(-2.1)$
h $\sin(-3.8)$

Example 6

3 For each of the following angles, θ, determine the values of $\sin\theta$ and $\cos\theta$:

a $\theta = 27\pi$
b $\theta = -\dfrac{5\pi}{2}$
c $\theta = \dfrac{27\pi}{2}$
d $\theta = -\dfrac{9\pi}{2}$
e $\theta = \dfrac{11\pi}{2}$
f $\theta = 57\pi$
g $\theta = 211\pi$
h $\theta = -53\pi$

14C Another circular function: tangent

Again consider the unit circle.

If we draw a tangent to the unit circle at A, then the y-coordinate of C, the point of intersection of the extension of OP and the tangent, is called **tangent** θ (abbreviated to $\tan \theta$).

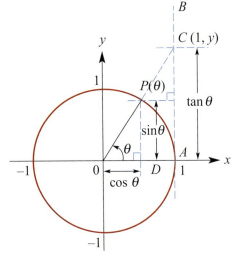

By considering the similar triangles OPD and OCA:

$$\frac{\tan \theta}{1} = \frac{\sin \theta}{\cos \theta}$$

$$\therefore \quad \tan \theta = \frac{\sin \theta}{\cos \theta}$$

Note that $\tan \theta$ is undefined when $\cos \theta = 0$.

Hence $\tan \theta$ is undefined when $\theta = \pm\frac{\pi}{2}, \pm\frac{3\pi}{2}, \pm\frac{5\pi}{2}, \ldots$

The domain of $\tan$ is $\mathbb{R} \setminus \{\theta : \cos \theta = 0\}$.

Example 7

Evaluate using a calculator. (Give answers to two decimal places.)

a $\tan 1.3$ **b** $\tan 1.9$ **c** $\tan(-2.8)$ **d** $\tan 59°$ **e** $\tan 138°$

Solution

a $\tan 1.3 = 3.60$
b $\tan 1.9 = -2.93$
c $\tan(-2.8) = 0.36$
d $\tan 59° = 1.66$
e $\tan 138° = -0.90$

Explanation

Don't forget that your calculator must be in radian mode.
$\cos 1.9$ is negative.
Both $\cos(-2.8)$ and $\sin(-2.8)$ are negative, so $\tan$ is positive.
Calculate in degree mode.

Exercise 14C

1 Evaluate:

a $\tan \pi$ **b** $\tan(-\pi)$ **c** $\tan\left(\frac{7\pi}{2}\right)$ **d** $\tan(-2\pi)$ **e** $\tan\left(\frac{5\pi}{2}\right)$ **f** $\tan\left(-\frac{\pi}{2}\right)$

2 Use a calculator to find correct to two decimal places:

a $\tan 1.6$ **b** $\tan(-1.2)$ **c** $\tan 136°$ **d** $\tan(-54°)$
e $\tan 3.9$ **f** $\tan(-2.5)$ **g** $\tan 239°$

3 For each of the following values of θ, find $\tan \theta$:

a $\theta = 180°$ **b** $\theta = 360°$ **c** $\theta = 0$
d $\theta = -180°$ **e** $\theta = -540°$ **f** $\theta = 720°$

14D Reviewing trigonometric ratios

For right-angled triangles:

$$\sin \theta = \frac{O}{H}$$

$$\cos \theta = \frac{A}{H}$$

$$\tan \theta = \frac{O}{A}$$

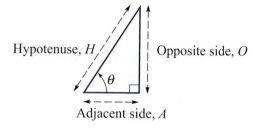

Applying these trigonometric ratios to the right-angled triangle, OAB, in the unit circle:

$$\sin \theta = \frac{O}{H} = \frac{y}{1} = y$$

$$\cos \theta = \frac{A}{H} = \frac{x}{1} = x$$

$$\tan \theta = \frac{O}{A} = \frac{y}{x} = \frac{\sin \theta}{\cos \theta}$$

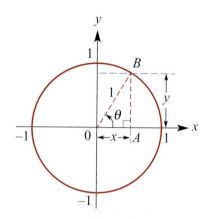

For $0 < \theta < \frac{\pi}{2}$, the functions sin, cos and tan defined by the trigonometric ratios agree with the circular functions introduced in this chapter.

Exercise 14D

1 Find the value of the pronumeral for each of the following:

a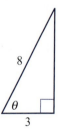

b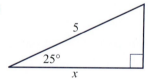

c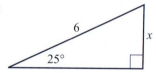

d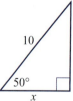

e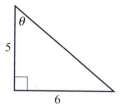

f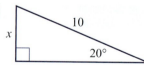

g

h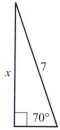

i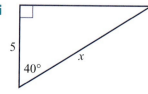

14E Symmetry properties of circular functions

The coordinate axes divide the unit circle into four quadrants. The quadrants can be numbered, anticlockwise from the positive direction of the x-axis, as shown.

Using symmetry, we can determine relationships between the circular functions for angles in different quadrants.

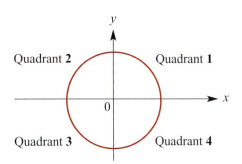

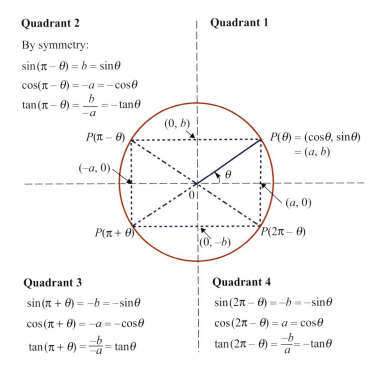

Quadrant 2

By symmetry:
$\sin(\pi - \theta) = b = \sin\theta$
$\cos(\pi - \theta) = -a = -\cos\theta$
$\tan(\pi - \theta) = \dfrac{b}{-a} = -\tan\theta$

Quadrant 3

$\sin(\pi + \theta) = -b = -\sin\theta$
$\cos(\pi + \theta) = -a = -\cos\theta$
$\tan(\pi + \theta) = \dfrac{-b}{-a} = \tan\theta$

Quadrant 4

$\sin(2\pi - \theta) = -b = -\sin\theta$
$\cos(2\pi - \theta) = a = \cos\theta$
$\tan(2\pi - \theta) = \dfrac{-b}{a} = -\tan\theta$

Note: These relationships are true for all values of θ.

▶ Signs of circular functions

Using these symmetry properties, the signs of sin, cos and tan for the four quadrants can be summarised as follows:

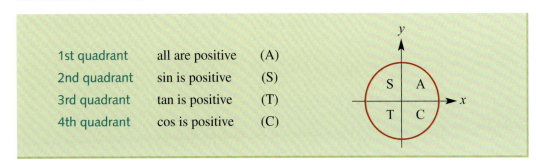

1st quadrant   all are positive   (A)
2nd quadrant   sin is positive   (S)
3rd quadrant   tan is positive   (T)
4th quadrant   cos is positive   (C)

Negative of angles

By symmetry:

$$\cos(-\theta) = \cos\theta$$

$$\sin(-\theta) = -\sin\theta$$

$$\tan(-\theta) = \frac{-\sin\theta}{\cos\theta} = -\tan\theta$$

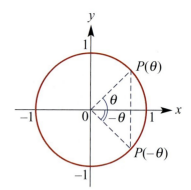

Example 8

If $\sin x = 0.6$, find the value of:

a $\sin(\pi - x)$ **b** $\sin(\pi + x)$ **c** $\sin(2\pi - x)$ **d** $\sin(-x)$

Solution

a $\sin(\pi - x)$
  $= \sin x$
  $= 0.6$

b $\sin(\pi + x)$
  $= -\sin x$
  $= -0.6$

c $\sin(2\pi - x)$
  $= -\sin x$
  $= -0.6$

d $\sin(-x)$
  $= -\sin x$
  $= -0.6$

Example 9

If $\cos x° = 0.8$, find the value of:

a $\cos(180 - x)°$ **b** $\cos(180 + x)°$ **c** $\cos(360 - x)°$ **d** $\cos(-x)°$

Solution

a $\cos(180 - x)°$
  $= -\cos x°$
  $= -0.8$

b $\cos(180 + x)°$
  $= -\cos x°$
  $= -0.8$

c $\cos(360 - x)°$
  $= \cos x°$
  $= 0.8$

d $\cos(-x)°$
  $= \cos x°$
  $= 0.8$

Exercise 14E

Example 8   **1** If $\sin\theta = 0.42$, $\cos x = 0.7$ and $\tan\alpha = 0.38$, write down the values of:

a $\sin(\pi + \theta)$ **b** $\cos(\pi - x)$ **c** $\sin(2\pi - \theta)$ **d** $\tan(\pi - \alpha)$
e $\sin(\pi - \theta)$ **f** $\tan(2\pi - \alpha)$ **g** $\cos(\pi + x)$ **h** $\cos(2\pi - x)$

2 a If $\cos x = -\cos\left(\dfrac{\pi}{6}\right)$ and $\dfrac{\pi}{2} < x < \pi$, find the value of x.

b If $\cos x = -\cos\left(\dfrac{\pi}{6}\right)$ and $\pi < x < \dfrac{3\pi}{2}$, find the value of x.

c If $\cos x = \cos\left(\dfrac{\pi}{6}\right)$ and $\dfrac{3\pi}{2} < x < 2\pi$, find the value of x.

3 For the diagram shown, write down the values of:
  a $a = \cos(\pi - \theta)$
  b $b = \sin(\pi - \theta)$
  c $c = \cos(-\theta)$
  d $d = \sin(-\theta)$
  e $\tan(\pi - \theta)$
  f $\tan(-\theta)$

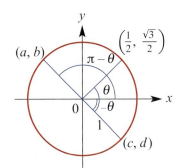

4 For the diagram shown, write down the values of:
  a $d = \sin(\pi + \theta)$
  b $c = \cos(\pi + \theta)$
  c $\tan(\pi + \theta)$
  d $\sin(2\pi - \theta)$
  e $\cos(2\pi - \theta)$

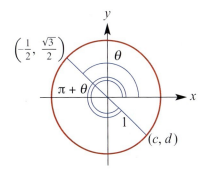

5 a For the diagram shown, use your calculator to find a and b correct to four decimal places.
  b Hence find the values of c and d.
  c **i** Use your calculator to find $\cos 140°$ and $\sin 140°$.
       ii Write $\cos 140°$ in terms of $\cos 40°$.

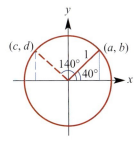

Example 9

6 If $\sin x° = 0.7$, $\cos \theta° = 0.6$ and $\tan \alpha° = 0.4$, write down the values of:
  a $\sin(180 + x)°$
  b $\cos(180 + \theta)°$
  c $\tan(360 - \alpha)°$
  d $\cos(180 - \theta)°$
  e $\sin(360 - x)°$
  f $\sin(-x)°$
  g $\tan(360 + \alpha)°$
  h $\cos(-\theta)°$

7 a If $\sin x° = \sin 60°$ and $90° < x° < 180°$, find the value of x.
  b If $\sin x° = -\sin 60°$ and $180° < x° < 270°$, find the value of x.
  c If $\sin x° = -\sin 60°$ and $-90° < x° < 0°$, find the value of x.
  d If $\cos x° = -\cos 60°$ and $90° < x° < 180°$, find the value of x.
  e If $\cos x° = -\cos 60°$ and $180° < x° < 270°$, find the value of x.
  f If $\cos x° = \cos 60°$ and $270° < x° < 360°$, find the value of x.

14F Exact values of circular functions

A calculator can be used to find the values of the circular functions for different values of θ. For many values of θ, the calculator gives an approximation. We now consider some values of θ such that sin, cos and tan can be calculated exactly.

▶ Exact values for 0 (0°) and $\frac{\pi}{2}$ (90°)

From the unit circle:

$\sin 0° = 0$ $\sin 90° = 1$

$\cos 0° = 1$ $\cos 90° = 0$

$\tan 0° = 0$ $\tan 90°$ is undefined

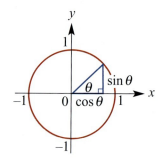

▶ Exact values for $\frac{\pi}{6}$ (30°) and $\frac{\pi}{3}$ (60°)

Consider an equilateral triangle ABC of side length 2 units.
In $\triangle ACD$, by Pythagoras' theorem, $CD = \sqrt{AC^2 - AD^2} = \sqrt{3}$.

$\sin 30° = \dfrac{AD}{AC} = \dfrac{1}{2}$ $\sin 60° = \dfrac{CD}{AC} = \dfrac{\sqrt{3}}{2}$

$\cos 30° = \dfrac{CD}{AC} = \dfrac{\sqrt{3}}{2}$ $\cos 60° = \dfrac{AD}{AC} = \dfrac{1}{2}$

$\tan 30° = \dfrac{AD}{CD} = \dfrac{1}{\sqrt{3}}$ $\tan 60° = \dfrac{CD}{AD} = \dfrac{\sqrt{3}}{1} = \sqrt{3}$

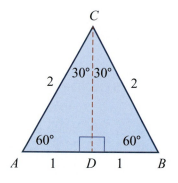

▶ Exact values for $\frac{\pi}{4}$ (45°)

For the triangle ABC shown on the right, we have $AC = \sqrt{1^2 + 1^2} = \sqrt{2}$.

$\sin 45° = \dfrac{BC}{AC} = \dfrac{1}{\sqrt{2}}$

$\cos 45° = \dfrac{AB}{AC} = \dfrac{1}{\sqrt{2}}$

$\tan 45° = \dfrac{BC}{AB} = 1$

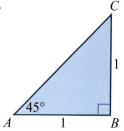

Example 10

Evaluate:

a $\cos 150°$ **b** $\sin 690°$

Solution

a $\cos 150° = \cos(180 - 30)°$

$ = -\cos 30° = -\dfrac{\sqrt{3}}{2}$

b $\sin 690° = \sin(2 \times 360 - 30)°$

$ = \sin(-30°) = -\dfrac{1}{2}$

Example 11

Evaluate:

a $\cos\left(\dfrac{5\pi}{4}\right)$

b $\sin\left(\dfrac{11\pi}{6}\right)$

Solution

a $\cos\left(\dfrac{5\pi}{4}\right) = \cos\left(\pi + \dfrac{\pi}{4}\right)$
$= -\cos\left(\dfrac{\pi}{4}\right)$ (by symmetry)
$= -\dfrac{1}{\sqrt{2}}$

b $\sin\left(\dfrac{11\pi}{6}\right) = \sin\left(2\pi - \dfrac{\pi}{6}\right)$
$= -\sin\left(\dfrac{\pi}{6}\right)$ (by symmetry)
$= -\dfrac{1}{2}$

Section summary

As an aid to memory, the exact values for circular functions can be tabulated.

θ	$\sin\theta$	$\cos\theta$	$\tan\theta$
0	0	1	0
$\dfrac{\pi}{6}$ (30°)	$\dfrac{1}{2}$	$\dfrac{\sqrt{3}}{2}$	$\dfrac{1}{\sqrt{3}}$
$\dfrac{\pi}{4}$ (45°)	$\dfrac{1}{\sqrt{2}}$	$\dfrac{1}{\sqrt{2}}$	1
$\dfrac{\pi}{3}$ (60°)	$\dfrac{\sqrt{3}}{2}$	$\dfrac{1}{2}$	$\sqrt{3}$
$\dfrac{\pi}{2}$ (90°)	1	0	undefined

Exercise 14F

Example 10

1 Without using a calculator, evaluate the sin, cos and tan of each of the following:

a 120° **b** 135° **c** 210° **d** 240° **e** 315°
f 390° **g** 420° **h** −135° **i** −300° **j** −60°

Example 11

2 Write down the exact values of:

a $\sin\left(\dfrac{2\pi}{3}\right)$ **b** $\cos\left(\dfrac{3\pi}{4}\right)$ **c** $\tan\left(\dfrac{5\pi}{6}\right)$

d $\sin\left(\dfrac{7\pi}{6}\right)$ **e** $\cos\left(\dfrac{5\pi}{4}\right)$ **f** $\tan\left(\dfrac{4\pi}{3}\right)$

g $\sin\left(\dfrac{5\pi}{3}\right)$ **h** $\cos\left(\dfrac{7\pi}{4}\right)$ **i** $\tan\left(\dfrac{11\pi}{6}\right)$

3 Write down the exact values of:

a $\sin\left(-\dfrac{2\pi}{3}\right)$ b $\cos\left(\dfrac{11\pi}{4}\right)$ c $\tan\left(\dfrac{13\pi}{6}\right)$ d $\tan\left(\dfrac{15\pi}{6}\right)$

e $\cos\left(\dfrac{14\pi}{4}\right)$ f $\cos\left(-\dfrac{3\pi}{4}\right)$ g $\sin\left(\dfrac{11\pi}{4}\right)$ h $\cos\left(-\dfrac{21\pi}{3}\right)$

14G Graphs of sine and cosine

Graph of the sine function

A table of exact values for $y = \sin x$ is given below.

x	$-\pi$	$-\dfrac{3\pi}{4}$	$-\dfrac{\pi}{2}$	$-\dfrac{\pi}{4}$	0	$\dfrac{\pi}{4}$	$\dfrac{\pi}{2}$	$\dfrac{3\pi}{4}$	π	$\dfrac{5\pi}{4}$	$\dfrac{3\pi}{2}$	$\dfrac{7\pi}{4}$	2π	$\dfrac{9\pi}{4}$	$\dfrac{5\pi}{2}$	$\dfrac{11\pi}{4}$	3π
y	0	$\dfrac{-1}{\sqrt{2}}$	-1	$\dfrac{-1}{\sqrt{2}}$	0	$\dfrac{1}{\sqrt{2}}$	1	$\dfrac{1}{\sqrt{2}}$	0	$\dfrac{-1}{\sqrt{2}}$	-1	$\dfrac{-1}{\sqrt{2}}$	0	$\dfrac{1}{\sqrt{2}}$	1	$\dfrac{1}{\sqrt{2}}$	0

A calculator can be used to plot the graph of $y = \sin x$ (for $-\pi \le x \le 3\pi$). Note that radian mode must be selected.

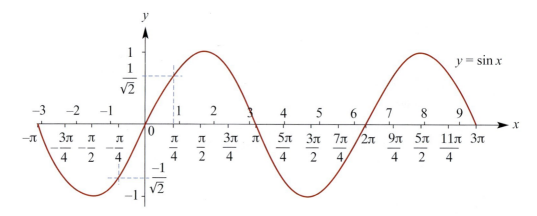

Observations from the graph of $y = \sin x$

- The graph repeats itself after an interval of 2π units.
  A function which repeats itself regularly is called a **periodic** function, and the interval between the repetitions is called the **period** of the function (also called the wavelength). Thus $\sin x$ has a period of 2π units.

- The maximum and minimum values of $\sin x$ are 1 and -1 respectively.
  The distance between the mean position and the maximum position is called the **amplitude**. The graph of $y = \sin x$ has an amplitude of 1.

▶ Graph of the cosine function

A table of exact values for $y = \cos x$ is given below.

x	$-\pi$	$-\dfrac{3\pi}{4}$	$-\dfrac{\pi}{2}$	$-\dfrac{\pi}{4}$	0	$\dfrac{\pi}{4}$	$\dfrac{\pi}{2}$	$\dfrac{3\pi}{4}$	π	$\dfrac{5\pi}{4}$	$\dfrac{3\pi}{2}$	$\dfrac{7\pi}{4}$	2π	$\dfrac{9\pi}{4}$	$\dfrac{5\pi}{2}$	$\dfrac{11\pi}{4}$	3π
y	-1	$\dfrac{-1}{\sqrt{2}}$	0	$\dfrac{1}{\sqrt{2}}$	1	$\dfrac{1}{\sqrt{2}}$	0	$\dfrac{-1}{\sqrt{2}}$	-1	$\dfrac{-1}{\sqrt{2}}$	0	$\dfrac{1}{\sqrt{2}}$	1	$\dfrac{1}{\sqrt{2}}$	0	$\dfrac{-1}{\sqrt{2}}$	-1

Using the TI-Nspire

- A graph of $y = \cos x$ for $-\pi \leq x \leq 3\pi$ can be plotted in a **Graphs** application by entering $f_1(x) = \cos(x) \,|\, -\pi \leq x \leq 3\pi$.
- Change the window to suit (menu > **Window/Zoom > Window Settings**).

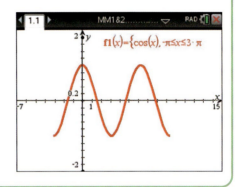

Using the Casio ClassPad

To plot the graph of $y = \cos x$ for $-\pi \leq x \leq 3\pi$:

- In **Graph & Table**, enter the equation in $y1$ as shown, then tick to select and tap to produce the graph.
- Select the icon to adjust the window settings as shown below.

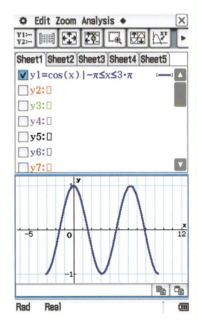

Observations from the graph of $y = \cos x$

- The period is 2π and the amplitude is 1.
- The graph of $y = \cos x$ is the graph of $y = \sin x$ translated $\dfrac{\pi}{2}$ units in the negative direction of the x-axis.

498 Chapter 14: Circular functions

▶ Sketch graphs of $y = a\sin(nt)$ and $y = a\cos(nt)$

The graphs of functions of the forms $y = a\sin(nt)$ and $y = a\cos(nt)$ are transformations of the graphs of $y = \sin t$ and $y = \cos t$ respectively. We first consider the case where a and n are positive numbers.

Transformations: dilations

Graph of $y = 3\sin(2t)$ The image of the graph of $y = \sin t$ under a dilation of factor 3 from the t-axis and a dilation of factor $\frac{1}{2}$ from the y-axis is $y = 3\sin(2t)$.

Note: Let $f(t) = \sin t$. Then the graph of $y = f(t)$ is transformed to the graph of $y = 3f(2t)$.
The point with coordinates (t, y) is mapped to the point with coordinates $\left(\dfrac{t}{2}, 3y\right)$.

t	0	$\dfrac{\pi}{4}$	$\dfrac{\pi}{2}$	$\dfrac{3\pi}{4}$	π
$y = 3\sin(2t)$	0	3	0	-3	0

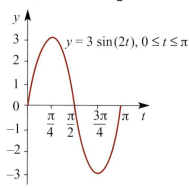

We make the following observations about the graph of $y = 3\sin(2t)$:

- amplitude is 3
- period is π

Graph of $y = 2\cos(3t)$ The image of the graph of $y = \cos t$ under a dilation of factor 2 from the t-axis and a dilation of factor $\frac{1}{3}$ from the y-axis is $y = 2\cos(3t)$.

t	0	$\dfrac{\pi}{6}$	$\dfrac{\pi}{3}$	$\dfrac{\pi}{2}$	$\dfrac{2\pi}{3}$
$y = 2\cos(3t)$	2	0	-2	0	2

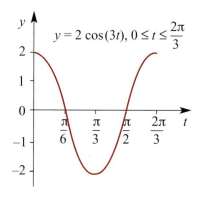

We make the following observations about the graph of $y = 2\cos(3t)$:

- amplitude is 2
- period is $\dfrac{2\pi}{3}$

Amplitude and period Comparing these results with those for $y = \sin t$ and $y = \cos t$, the following general rules can be stated for a and n positive:

Function	Amplitude	Period
$y = a\sin(nt)$	a	$\dfrac{2\pi}{n}$
$y = a\cos(nt)$	a	$\dfrac{2\pi}{n}$

Example 12

For each of the following functions with domain $\mathbb{R}$, state the amplitude and period:

a $f(t) = 2\sin(3t)$ **b** $f(t) = -\dfrac{1}{2}\sin\left(\dfrac{t}{2}\right)$ **c** $f(t) = 4\cos(3\pi t)$

Solution

a Amplitude is 2

Period is $\dfrac{2\pi}{3}$

b Amplitude is $\dfrac{1}{2}$

Period is $2\pi \div \dfrac{1}{2} = 4\pi$

c Amplitude is 4

Period is $\dfrac{2\pi}{3\pi} = \dfrac{2}{3}$

Graphs of $y = a\sin(nt)$ and $y = a\cos(nt)$

In general, for a and n positive numbers, the graph of $y = a\sin(nt)$ (or $y = a\cos(nt)$) is obtained from the graph of $y = \sin t$ (or $y = \cos t$) by a dilation of factor a from the t-axis and a dilation of factor $\dfrac{1}{n}$ from the y-axis.

The point with coordinates (t, y) is mapped to the point with coordinates $\left(\dfrac{t}{n}, ay\right)$.

The following are important properties of both of the functions $f(t) = a\sin(nt)$ and $g(t) = a\cos(nt)$:

- The period is $\dfrac{2\pi}{n}$.
- The amplitude is a.
- The maximal domain is $\mathbb{R}$.
- The range is $[-a, a]$.

Example 13

For each of the following, give a sequence of transformations which takes the graph of $y = \sin x$ to the graph of $y = g(x)$, and state the amplitude and period of $g(x)$:

a $g(x) = 3\sin(2x)$

b $g(x) = 4\sin\left(\dfrac{x}{2}\right)$

Solution

a The graph of $y = 3\sin(2x)$ is obtained from the graph of $y = \sin x$ by a dilation of factor 3 from the x-axis and a dilation of factor $\dfrac{1}{2}$ from the y-axis.

The function $g(x) = 3\sin(2x)$ has amplitude 3 and period $\dfrac{2\pi}{2} = \pi$.

b The graph of $y = 4\sin\left(\dfrac{x}{2}\right)$ is obtained from the graph of $y = \sin x$ by a dilation of factor 4 from the x-axis and a dilation of factor 2 from the y-axis.

The function $g(x) = 4\sin\left(\dfrac{x}{2}\right)$ has amplitude 4 and period $2\pi \div \dfrac{1}{2} = 4\pi$.

500 Chapter 14: Circular functions

Example 14

Sketch the graph of each of the following functions:

a $y = 2\cos(2\theta)$

b $y = \dfrac{1}{2}\sin\left(\dfrac{x}{2}\right)$

In each case, show one complete cycle.

Solution

a $y = 2\cos(2\theta)$

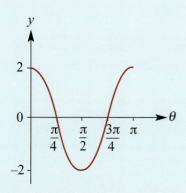

Explanation

The amplitude is 2.

The period is $\dfrac{2\pi}{2} = \pi$.

The graph of $y = 2\cos(2\theta)$ is obtained from the graph of $y = \cos\theta$ by a dilation of factor 2 from the θ-axis and a dilation of factor $\dfrac{1}{2}$ from the y-axis.

b $y = \dfrac{1}{2}\sin\left(\dfrac{x}{2}\right)$

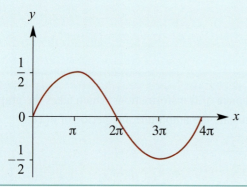

The amplitude is $\dfrac{1}{2}$.

The period is $2\pi \div \dfrac{1}{2} = 4\pi$.

The graph of $y = \dfrac{1}{2}\sin(\dfrac{x}{2})$ is obtained from the graph of $y = \sin x$ by a dilation of factor $\dfrac{1}{2}$ from the x-axis and a dilation of factor 2 from the y-axis.

Example 15

Sketch the graph of $f : [0, 2] \to \mathbb{R}$, $f(t) = 3\sin(\pi t)$.

Solution

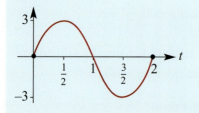

Explanation

The amplitude is 3.

The period is $2\pi \div \pi = 2$.

The graph of $f(t) = 3\sin(\pi t)$ is obtained from the graph of $y = \sin t$ by a dilation of factor 3 from the t-axis and a dilation of factor $\dfrac{1}{\pi}$ from the y-axis.

Transformations: reflection in the horizontal axis

Example 16

Sketch the following graphs for $x \in [0, 4\pi]$:

a $f(x) = -2\sin\left(\dfrac{x}{2}\right)$ **b** $y = -\cos(2x)$

Solution

a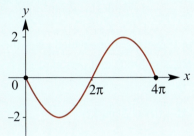

Explanation

The graph of $f(x) = -2\sin(\frac{x}{2})$ is obtained from the graph of $y = 2\sin(\frac{x}{2})$ by a reflection in the x-axis.

The amplitude is 2 and the period is 4π.

b

The graph of $y = -\cos(2x)$ is obtained from the graph of $y = \cos(2x)$ by a reflection in the x-axis.

The amplitude is 1 and the period is π.

Transformations: reflection in the vertical axis

Remember that $\sin(-x) = -\sin x$ and $\cos(-x) = \cos x$.

Hence, when reflected in the y-axis:

- The graph of $y = \cos x$ transforms onto itself. (The point (α, β) is mapped to the point $(-\alpha, \beta)$. This second point is on the curve $y = \cos x$ by the observation above.)
- The graph of $y = \sin x$ transforms onto the graph of $y = -\sin x$. (The point (α, β) is mapped to the point $(-\alpha, \beta)$. This second point is on the curve $y = -\sin x$ by the observation above.)

Section summary

For positive numbers a and n, the graphs of $y = a\sin(nt)$, $y = -a\sin(nt)$, $y = a\cos(nt)$ and $y = -a\cos(nt)$ all have the following properties:

- The period is $\dfrac{2\pi}{n}$.
- The amplitude is a.
- The maximal domain is $\mathbb{R}$.
- The range is $[-a, a]$.

Exercise 14G

1 Write down **i** the period and **ii** the amplitude of each of the following:
  a $2\sin\theta$
  b $3\sin(2\theta)$
  c $\frac{1}{2}\cos(3\theta)$
  d $3\sin\left(\frac{1}{2}\theta\right)$
  e $4\cos(3\theta)$
  f $-\frac{1}{2}\sin(4\theta)$
  g $-2\cos\left(\frac{1}{2}\theta\right)$
  h $2\cos(\pi t)$
  i $-3\sin\left(\frac{\pi t}{2}\right)$

2 For each of the following, give a sequence of transformations which takes the graph of $y = \sin x$ to the graph of $y = g(x)$, and state the amplitude and period of $g(x)$:
  a $g(x) = 3\sin x$
  b $g(x) = \sin(5x)$
  c $g(x) = \sin\left(\frac{x}{3}\right)$
  d $g(x) = 2\sin(5x)$

3 Sketch the graph of each of the following, showing one complete cycle. State the amplitude and period.
  a $y = 3\sin(2x)$
  b $y = 2\cos(3\theta)$
  c $y = 4\sin\left(\frac{\theta}{2}\right)$
  d $y = \frac{1}{2}\cos(3x)$
  e $y = 4\sin(3x)$
  f $y = 5\cos(2x)$
  g $y = -3\cos\left(\frac{\theta}{2}\right)$
  h $y = 2\cos(4\theta)$
  i $y = -2\sin\left(\frac{\theta}{3}\right)$

4 Sketch the graph of:
  a $f: [0, 2] \to \mathbb{R}, \ f(t) = 2\cos(\pi t)$
  b $f: [0, 2] \to \mathbb{R}, \ f(t) = 3\sin(2\pi t)$

5 Sketch the graph of:
  a $f(x) = \sin(2x)$ for $x \in [-2\pi, 2\pi]$
  b $f(x) = 2\sin\left(\frac{x}{3}\right)$ for $x \in [-6\pi, 6\pi]$
  c $f(x) = 2\cos(3x)$ for $x \in [0, 2\pi]$
  d $f(x) = -2\sin(3x)$ for $x \in [0, 2\pi]$

6 Sketch the graph of $f: [0, 2\pi] \to \mathbb{R}, \ f(x) = \frac{5}{2}\cos\left(\frac{2x}{3}\right)$.
  Hint: For the endpoints, find $f(0)$ and $f(2\pi)$.

7 For each of the following, give a sequence of transformations which takes the graph of $y = \sin x$ to the graph of $y = g(x)$, and state the amplitude and period of $g(x)$:
  a $g(x) = -\sin(5x)$
  b $g(x) = \sin(-x)$
  c $g(x) = 2\sin\left(\frac{x}{3}\right)$
  d $g(x) = -4\sin\left(\frac{x}{2}\right)$
  e $g(x) = 2\sin\left(\frac{-x}{3}\right)$

8 a On the one set of axes, sketch the graphs of $f: [0, 2\pi] \to \mathbb{R}, \ f(x) = \sin x$ and $g: [0, 2\pi] \to \mathbb{R}, \ g(x) = \cos x$.
  b By inspection from these graphs, state the values of x for which $\sin x = \cos x$.

14H Solution of trigonometric equations

Skillsheet In this section we introduce methods for solving equations of the form $a \sin(nt) = b$ and $a \cos(nt) = b$.

▶ Solving equations of the form $\sin t = b$ and $\cos t = b$

First we look at the techniques for solving equations of the form $\sin t = b$ and $\cos t = b$. These same techniques will be applied to solve more complicated trigonometric equations later in this section.

Example 17

Find all solutions to the equation $\sin \theta = \dfrac{1}{2}$ for $\theta \in [0, 4\pi]$.

Solution

The solution for $\theta \in \left[0, \dfrac{\pi}{2}\right]$ is $\theta = \dfrac{\pi}{6}$.

The second solution is $\theta = \pi - \dfrac{\pi}{6} = \dfrac{5\pi}{6}$.

The third solution is $\theta = 2\pi + \dfrac{\pi}{6} = \dfrac{13\pi}{6}$.

The fourth solution is $\theta = 2\pi + \dfrac{5\pi}{6} = \dfrac{17\pi}{6}$.

These four solutions are shown on the graph below.

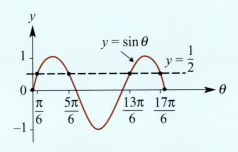

Explanation

By sketching a graph, we can see that there are four solutions in the interval $[0, 4\pi]$.

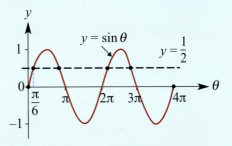

The first solution can be obtained from a knowledge of exact values or by using $\sin^{-1}$ on your calculator.

The second solution is obtained using symmetry. The sine function is positive in the 2nd quadrant and $\sin(\pi - \theta) = \sin \theta$.

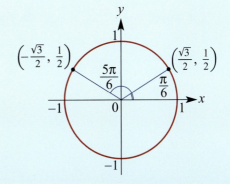

Further solutions are found by adding 2π, since $\sin \theta = \sin(2\pi + \theta)$.

Example 18

Find two values of x:

a $\sin x = -0.3$ with $0 \leq x \leq 2\pi$

b $\cos x° = -0.7$ with $0° \leq x° \leq 360°$

Solution

a First solve the equation $\sin \alpha = 0.3$ for $\alpha \in \left[0, \dfrac{\pi}{2}\right]$. Use your calculator to find the solution $\alpha = 0.30469\ldots$

Now the value of $\sin x$ is negative for $P(x)$ in the 3rd and 4th quadrants. From the symmetry relationships (or from the graph of $y = \sin x$):

3rd quadrant: $\quad x = \pi + 0.30469\ldots$
$\qquad\qquad\qquad = 3.446 \quad$ (to 3 d.p.)

4th quadrant: $\quad x = 2\pi - 0.30469\ldots$
$\qquad\qquad\qquad = 5.978 \quad$ (to 3 d.p.)

$\therefore$ If $\sin x = -0.3$, then $x = 3.446$ or $x = 5.978$.

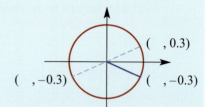

b First solve the equation $\cos \alpha° = 0.7$ for $\alpha° \in [0°, 90°]$. Use your calculator to find the solution $\alpha° = 45.57°$.

Now the value of $\cos x°$ is negative for $P(x°)$ in the 2nd and 3rd quadrants.

2nd quadrant: $\quad x° = 180° - 45.57°$
$\qquad\qquad\qquad = 134.43°$

3rd quadrant: $\quad x° = 180° + 45.57°$
$\qquad\qquad\qquad = 225.57°$

$\therefore$ If $\cos x° = -0.7$, then $x° = 134.43°$ or $x° = 225.57°$.

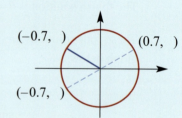

Example 19

Find all the values of $\theta°$ between $0°$ and $360°$ for which:

a $\cos \theta° = \dfrac{\sqrt{3}}{2}$ **b** $\sin \theta° = -\dfrac{1}{2}$ **c** $\cos \theta° - \dfrac{1}{\sqrt{2}} = 0$

Solution	Explanation
a $\cos \theta° = \dfrac{\sqrt{3}}{2}$ $\theta° = 30°$ or $\theta° = 360° - 30°$ $\theta° = 30°$ or $\theta° = 330°$	$\cos \theta°$ is positive, and so $P(\theta°)$ lies in the 1st or 4th quadrant. $\cos(360° - \theta°) = \cos \theta°$

b $\sin \theta° = -\dfrac{1}{2}$

$\theta° = 180° + 30°$ or $\theta° = 360° - 30°$

$\theta° = 210°$ or $\theta° = 330°$

$\sin \theta°$ is negative, and so $P(\theta°)$ lies in the 3rd or 4th quadrant.

$\sin(180° + \theta°) = -\sin \theta°$

$\sin(360° - \theta°) = -\sin \theta°$

c $\cos \theta° - \dfrac{1}{\sqrt{2}} = 0$

$\therefore \cos \theta° = \dfrac{1}{\sqrt{2}}$

$\theta° = 45°$ or $\theta° = 360° - 45°$

$\theta° = 45°$ or $\theta° = 315°$

$\cos \theta°$ is positive, and so $P(\theta°)$ lies in the 1st or 4th quadrant.

Using the TI-Nspire

For Example 19a, make sure the calculator is in degree mode and complete as shown.

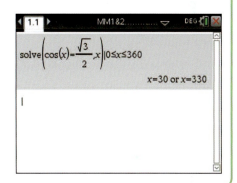

Using the Casio ClassPad

- Ensure your calculator is in degree mode (with **Deg** in the status bar at the bottom of the main screen).
- Use the **Math1** and **Math3** keyboards to enter the equation

$$\cos(x) = \dfrac{\sqrt{3}}{2} \mid 0 \leq x \leq 360$$

- Highlight the equation and domain. Then select **Interactive > Equation/Inequality > solve** and ensure the variable is set to x.

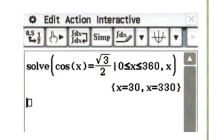

▶ Solving equations of the form $a\sin(nt) = b$ and $a\cos(nt) = b$

The techniques introduced above can be applied in a more general situation. This is achieved by a simple substitution, as shown in the following example.

Example 20

Solve the equation $\sin(2\theta) = -\dfrac{\sqrt{3}}{2}$ for $\theta \in [-\pi, \pi]$.

Solution

It is clear from the graph that there are four solutions.

To solve the equation, let $x = 2\theta$.

Note: If $\theta \in [-\pi, \pi]$, then we have
$$x = 2\theta \in [-2\pi, 2\pi].$$

Now consider the equation
$$\sin x = -\dfrac{\sqrt{3}}{2} \quad \text{for } x \in [-2\pi, 2\pi]$$

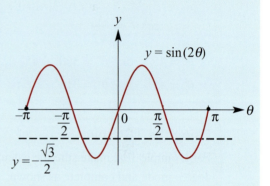

The 1st quadrant solution to the equation $\sin \alpha = \dfrac{\sqrt{3}}{2}$ is $\alpha = \dfrac{\pi}{3}$.

Using symmetry, the solutions to $\sin x = -\dfrac{\sqrt{3}}{2}$ for $x \in [0, 2\pi]$ are

$$x = \pi + \dfrac{\pi}{3} \text{ and } x = 2\pi - \dfrac{\pi}{3}$$

i.e. $x = \dfrac{4\pi}{3}$ and $x = \dfrac{5\pi}{3}$

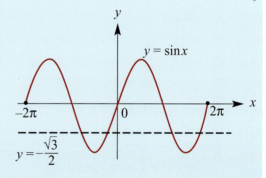

The other two solutions (obtained by subtracting 2π) are $x = \dfrac{4\pi}{3} - 2\pi$ and $x = \dfrac{5\pi}{3} - 2\pi$.

∴ The required solutions for x are $-\dfrac{2\pi}{3}, -\dfrac{\pi}{3}, \dfrac{4\pi}{3}$ and $\dfrac{5\pi}{3}$.

∴ The required solutions for θ are $-\dfrac{\pi}{3}, -\dfrac{\pi}{6}, \dfrac{2\pi}{3}$ and $\dfrac{5\pi}{6}$.

Using the TI-Nspire

Ensure that the calculator is in radian mode and complete as shown.

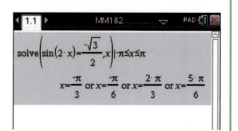

Using the Casio ClassPad

- Ensure your calculator is in radian mode (with **Rad** in the status bar at bottom of the main screen).
- Enter the equation
$$\sin(2x) = \frac{-\sqrt{3}}{2} \mid -\pi \leq x \leq \pi$$
- Highlight the equation and domain. Then select **Interactive** > **Equation/Inequality** > **solve** and ensure the variable is set to x.

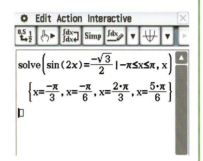

Section summary

- For solving equations of the form $\sin t = b$ and $\cos t = b$:
  - First find the solutions in the interval $[0, 2\pi]$. This can be done using your knowledge of exact values and symmetry properties, or with the aid of a calculator.
  - Further solutions can be found by adding and subtracting multiples of 2π.
- For solving equations of the form $a \sin(nt) = b$ and $a \cos(nt) = b$:
  - First substitute $x = nt$. Work out the interval in which solutions for x are required. Then proceed as in the case above to solve for x.
  - Once the solutions for x are found, the solutions for t can be found.

  For example: To solve $\sin(3t) = \frac{1}{2}$ for $t \in [0, 2\pi]$, first let $x = 3t$. The equation becomes $\sin x = \frac{1}{2}$ and the required solutions for x are in the interval $[0, 6\pi]$.

Exercise 14H

Example 17 **1** Find all the values of x between 0 and 4π for which:

   a $\cos x = \dfrac{1}{2}$ **b** $\sin x = \dfrac{1}{\sqrt{2}}$ **c** $\sin x = \dfrac{\sqrt{3}}{2}$

Example 18 **2** Find, correct to two decimal places, all the values of x between 0 and 2π for which:

   a $\sin x = 0.8$ **b** $\cos x = -0.4$ **c** $\sin x = -0.35$
   d $\sin x = 0.4$ **e** $\cos x = -0.7$ **f** $\cos x = -0.2$

Example 19 **3** Without using a calculator, find all the values of $\theta°$ between $0°$ and $360°$ for each of the following:

   a $\cos \theta° = -\dfrac{\sqrt{3}}{2}$ **b** $\sin \theta° = \dfrac{1}{2}$ **c** $\cos \theta° = -\dfrac{1}{2}$
   d $2\cos(\theta°) + 1 = 0$ **e** $2 \sin \theta° = \sqrt{3}$ **f** $\sqrt{2} \sin(\theta°) - 1 = 0$

4 Without using a calculator, find all the values of x between 0 and 2π for each of the following:

   a $2 \cos x = \sqrt{3}$ **b** $\sqrt{2} \sin(x) + 1 = 0$ **c** $\sqrt{2} \cos(x) - 1 = 0$

5 Find all the values of x between $-\pi$ and π for which:

  a $\cos x = -\dfrac{1}{\sqrt{2}}$
  b $\sin x = \dfrac{\sqrt{3}}{2}$
  c $\cos x = -\dfrac{1}{2}$

6 **a** Sketch the graph of $f : [-2\pi, 2\pi] \to \mathbb{R}$, $f(x) = \cos x$.
  b On the graph, mark the points with y-coordinate $\dfrac{1}{2}$ and give the associated x-values.
  c On the graph, mark the points with y-coordinate $-\dfrac{1}{2}$ and give the associated x-values.

Example 20 **7** Solve the following equations for $\theta \in [0, 2\pi]$:

  a $\sin(2\theta) = -\dfrac{1}{2}$
  b $\cos(2\theta) = \dfrac{\sqrt{3}}{2}$
  c $\sin(2\theta) = \dfrac{1}{2}$

  d $\sin(3\theta) = -\dfrac{1}{\sqrt{2}}$
  e $\cos(2\theta) = -\dfrac{\sqrt{3}}{2}$
  f $\sin(2\theta) = -\dfrac{1}{\sqrt{2}}$

8 Solve the following equations for $\theta \in [0, 2\pi]$:

  a $\sin(2\theta) = -0.8$
  b $\sin(2\theta) = -0.6$
  c $\cos(2\theta) = 0.4$
  d $\cos(3\theta) = 0.6$

14I Sketch graphs of $y = a \sin n(t \pm \varepsilon)$ and $y = a \cos n(t \pm \varepsilon)$

In this section, we consider translations of graphs of functions of the form $f(t) = a \sin(nt)$ and $g(t) = a \cos(nt)$ in the direction of the t-axis.

When a translation of $\dfrac{\pi}{4}$ units in the positive direction of the t-axis is applied to the graph of $y = f(t)$, the resulting image has equation

$$y = f\left(t - \dfrac{\pi}{4}\right)$$

For example, the graph of $f(t) = 3\sin(2t)$ is mapped to the graph of $y = 3 \sin 2\left(t - \dfrac{\pi}{4}\right)$.

Example 21

On separate axes, draw the graphs of the following functions. Use a calculator to help establish the shape. Set the window appropriately by noting the range and period.

a $y = 3 \sin 2\left(t - \dfrac{\pi}{4}\right)$, $\dfrac{\pi}{4} \leq t \leq \dfrac{5\pi}{4}$
b $y = 2 \cos 3\left(t + \dfrac{\pi}{3}\right)$, $-\dfrac{\pi}{3} \leq t \leq \dfrac{\pi}{3}$

Solution

a The range is $[-3, 3]$ and the period is π.

b The range is $[-2, 2]$ and the period is $\dfrac{2\pi}{3}$.

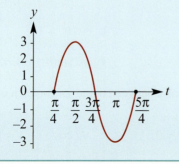

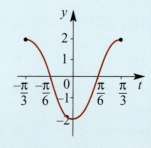

Observations from the example

a The graph of $y = 3 \sin 2\left(t - \dfrac{\pi}{4}\right)$ is the same shape as $y = 3 \sin(2t)$, but is translated $\dfrac{\pi}{4}$ units in the positive direction of the t-axis.

b The graph of $y = 2 \cos 3\left(t + \dfrac{\pi}{3}\right)$ is the same shape as $y = 2 \cos(3t)$, but is translated $\dfrac{\pi}{3}$ units in the negative direction of the t-axis.

The effect of $\pm \varepsilon$ is to translate the graph parallel to the t-axis. (Here $\pm \varepsilon$ is called the phase.)

Note: To determine the sequence of transformations, the techniques of Chapter 7 can also be used. The graph of $y = \sin t$ is transformed to the graph of $y = 3 \sin 2\left(t - \dfrac{\pi}{4}\right)$.

Write the second equation as $\dfrac{y'}{3} = \sin 2\left(t' - \dfrac{\pi}{4}\right)$.

From this it can be seen that $y = \dfrac{y'}{3}$ and $t = 2\left(t' - \dfrac{\pi}{4}\right)$. Thus $y' = 3y$ and $t' = \dfrac{t}{2} + \dfrac{\pi}{4}$.

Hence the sequence of transformations is:

- dilation of factor 3 from the t-axis
- dilation of factor $\dfrac{1}{2}$ from the y-axis
- translation of $\dfrac{\pi}{4}$ units in the positive direction of the t-axis.

Alternatively, we can find this sequence by observing that graph of $y = f(t)$ is transformed to the graph of $y = 3f\left(2\left(t - \dfrac{\pi}{4}\right)\right)$, where $f(t) = \sin t$.

Section summary

The graphs of $y = a \sin n(t \pm \varepsilon)$ and $y = a \cos n(t \pm \varepsilon)$ are translations of the graphs of $y = a \sin(nt)$ and $y = a \cos(nt)$ respectively.

The graphs are translated $\mp \varepsilon$ units parallel to the t-axis, where $\pm \varepsilon$ is called the phase.

Exercise 14I

Example 21

1 Sketch the graph of each of the following, showing one complete cycle. State the period and amplitude, and the greatest and least values of y.

a $y = 3 \sin\left(\theta - \dfrac{\pi}{2}\right)$ **b** $y = \sin 2(\theta + \pi)$ **c** $y = 2 \sin 3\left(\theta + \dfrac{\pi}{4}\right)$

d $y = \sqrt{3} \sin 2\left(\theta - \dfrac{\pi}{2}\right)$ **e** $y = 3 \sin(2x)$ **f** $y = 2 \cos 3\left(\theta + \dfrac{\pi}{4}\right)$

g $y = \sqrt{2} \sin 2\left(\theta - \dfrac{\pi}{3}\right)$ **h** $y = -3 \sin(2x)$ **i** $y = -3 \cos 2\left(\theta + \dfrac{\pi}{2}\right)$

2 For the function $f: [0, 2\pi] \to \mathbb{R}$, $f(x) = \cos\left(x - \dfrac{\pi}{3}\right)$:

a find $f(0)$, $f(2\pi)$ **b** sketch the graph of f.

3 For the function $f: [0, 2\pi] \to \mathbb{R}$, $f(x) = \sin 2\left(x - \dfrac{\pi}{3}\right)$:

a find $f(0)$, $f(2\pi)$ **b** sketch the graph of f.

4 For the function $f: [-\pi, \pi] \to \mathbb{R}$, $f(x) = \sin 3\left(x + \dfrac{\pi}{4}\right)$:

   a find $f(-\pi)$, $f(\pi)$ b sketch the graph of f.

5 Find the equation of the image of $y = \sin x$ for each of the following transformations:

   a dilation of factor 2 from the y-axis followed by dilation of factor 3 from the x-axis
   b dilation of factor $\frac{1}{2}$ from the y-axis followed by dilation of factor 3 from the x-axis
   c dilation of factor 3 from the y-axis followed by dilation of factor 2 from the x-axis
   d dilation of factor $\frac{1}{2}$ from the y-axis followed by translation of $\dfrac{\pi}{3}$ units in the positive direction of the x-axis
   e dilation of factor 2 from the y-axis followed by translation of $\dfrac{\pi}{3}$ units in the negative direction of the x-axis

14J Sketch graphs of $y = a \sin n(t \pm \varepsilon) \pm b$ and $y = a \cos n(t \pm \varepsilon) \pm b$

> Skillsheet   We now consider translations parallel to the y-axis.

Example 22

Sketch each of the following graphs. Use a calculator to help establish the shape.

a $y = 3 \sin 2\left(t - \dfrac{\pi}{4}\right) + 2$, $\dfrac{\pi}{4} \le t \le \dfrac{5\pi}{4}$ b $y = 2 \cos 3\left(t + \dfrac{\pi}{3}\right) - 1$, $-\dfrac{\pi}{3} \le t \le \dfrac{\pi}{3}$

Solution

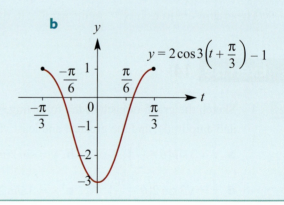

Observations from the example

a The graph of $y = 3 \sin 2\left(t - \dfrac{\pi}{4}\right) + 2$ is the same shape as the graph of $y = 3 \sin 2\left(t - \dfrac{\pi}{4}\right)$, but is translated 2 units in the positive direction of the y-axis.

b The graph of $y = 2 \cos 3\left(t + \dfrac{\pi}{3}\right) - 1$ is the same shape as the graph of $y = 2 \cos 3\left(t + \dfrac{\pi}{3}\right)$, but is translated 1 unit in the negative direction of the y-axis.

In general, the effect of $\pm b$ is to translate the graph $\pm b$ units parallel to the y-axis.

▶ Finding axis intercepts

Example 23

Sketch the graph of each of the following for $x \in [0, 2\pi]$. Clearly indicate axis intercepts.

a $y = \sqrt{2}\sin(x) + 1$ **b** $y = 2\cos(2x) - 1$ **c** $y = 2\sin 2\left(x - \dfrac{\pi}{3}\right) - \sqrt{3}$

Solution

a To determine the x-axis intercepts, the equation $\sqrt{2}\sin(x) + 1 = 0$ must be solved.

$\sqrt{2}\sin(x) + 1 = 0$

$\therefore \quad \sin x = -\dfrac{1}{\sqrt{2}}$

$\therefore \, x = \pi + \dfrac{\pi}{4}$ or $2\pi - \dfrac{\pi}{4}$

$\therefore \, x = \dfrac{5\pi}{4}$ or $\dfrac{7\pi}{4}$

The x-axis intercepts are $\dfrac{5\pi}{4}$ and $\dfrac{7\pi}{4}$.

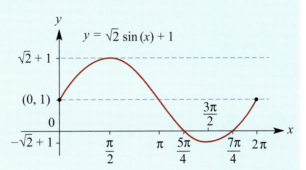

b $2\cos(2x) - 1 = 0$

$\therefore \quad \cos(2x) = \dfrac{1}{2}$

$\therefore \, 2x = \dfrac{\pi}{3}, \dfrac{5\pi}{3}, \dfrac{7\pi}{3}$ or $\dfrac{11\pi}{3}$

$\therefore \, x = \dfrac{\pi}{6}, \dfrac{5\pi}{6}, \dfrac{7\pi}{6}$ or $\dfrac{11\pi}{6}$

The x-axis intercepts are $\dfrac{\pi}{6}, \dfrac{5\pi}{6}, \dfrac{7\pi}{6}$ and $\dfrac{11\pi}{6}$.

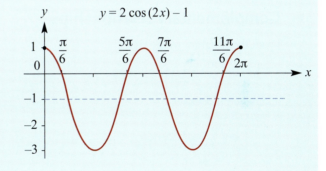

c $\sin 2\left(x - \dfrac{\pi}{3}\right) = \dfrac{\sqrt{3}}{2}$

$\therefore \, 2\left(x - \dfrac{\pi}{3}\right) = \dfrac{\pi}{3}, \dfrac{2\pi}{3}, \dfrac{7\pi}{3}$ or $\dfrac{8\pi}{3}$

$\therefore \, x - \dfrac{\pi}{3} = \dfrac{\pi}{6}, \dfrac{\pi}{3}, \dfrac{7\pi}{6}$ or $\dfrac{4\pi}{3}$

$\therefore \quad x = \dfrac{\pi}{2}, \dfrac{2\pi}{3}, \dfrac{3\pi}{2}$ or $\dfrac{5\pi}{3}$

The x-axis intercepts are $\dfrac{\pi}{2}, \dfrac{2\pi}{3}, \dfrac{3\pi}{2}$ and $\dfrac{5\pi}{3}$.

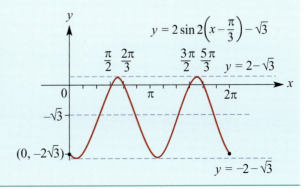

Exercise 14J

Example 23 1 Sketch the graph of each of the following for $x \in [0, 2\pi]$. List the x-axis intercepts of each graph for this interval.
  a $y = 2\sin(x) + 1$
  b $y = 2\sin(2x) - \sqrt{3}$
  c $y = \sqrt{2}\cos(x) + 1$
  d $y = 2\sin(2x) - 2$
  e $y = \sqrt{2}\sin\left(x - \dfrac{\pi}{4}\right) + 1$

2 Sketch the graph of each of the following for $x \in [-\pi, 2\pi]$:
  a $y = 2\sin(3x) - 2$
  b $y = 2\cos 3\left(x - \dfrac{\pi}{4}\right)$
  c $y = 2\sin(2x) - 3$
  d $y = 2\cos(2x) + 1$
  e $y = 2\cos 2\left(x - \dfrac{\pi}{3}\right) - 1$
  f $y = 2\sin 2\left(x + \dfrac{\pi}{6}\right) + 1$

3 Sketch the graph of each of the following for $x \in [-\pi, \pi]$:
  a $y = 2\sin 2\left(x + \dfrac{\pi}{3}\right) + 1$
  b $y = -2\sin 2\left(x + \dfrac{\pi}{6}\right) + 1$
  c $y = 2\cos 2\left(x + \dfrac{\pi}{4}\right) + \sqrt{3}$

14K Further symmetry properties and the Pythagorean identity

▶ Complementary relationships

From the diagram to the right,
$$\sin\left(\dfrac{\pi}{2} - \theta\right) = a$$
and, since $a = \cos\theta$,
$$\sin\left(\dfrac{\pi}{2} - \theta\right) = \cos\theta$$

From the same diagram,
$$\cos\left(\dfrac{\pi}{2} - \theta\right) = b$$
and, since $b = \sin\theta$,
$$\cos\left(\dfrac{\pi}{2} - \theta\right) = \sin\theta$$

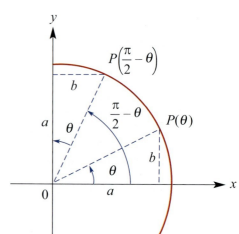

From the diagram to the right:
$$\sin\left(\dfrac{\pi}{2} + \theta\right) = a = \cos\theta$$
$$\cos\left(\dfrac{\pi}{2} + \theta\right) = -b = -\sin\theta$$

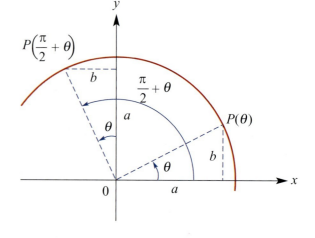

Example 24

If $\sin\theta = 0.3$ and $\cos\alpha = 0.8$, find the values of:

a $\sin\left(\dfrac{\pi}{2} - \alpha\right)$ **b** $\cos\left(\dfrac{\pi}{2} + \theta\right)$ **c** $\sin(-\theta)$

Solution

a $\sin\left(\dfrac{\pi}{2} - \alpha\right) = \cos\alpha$
$= 0.8$

b $\cos\left(\dfrac{\pi}{2} + \theta\right) = -\sin\theta$
$= -0.3$

c $\sin(-\theta) = -\sin\theta$
$= -0.3$

▶ The Pythagorean identity

Consider a point, $P(\theta)$, on the unit circle.

By Pythagoras' theorem,

$$OP^2 = OM^2 + MP^2$$
$$\therefore \quad 1 = (\cos\theta)^2 + (\sin\theta)^2$$

Now $(\cos\theta)^2$ and $(\sin\theta)^2$ may be written as $\cos^2\theta$ and $\sin^2\theta$.

$$\therefore \quad 1 = \cos^2\theta + \sin^2\theta$$

As this is true for all values of θ, it is called an identity. In particular, this is called the **Pythagorean identity**:

$$\cos^2\theta + \sin^2\theta = 1$$

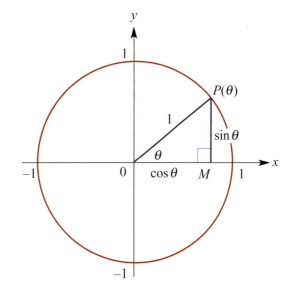

Example 25

Given that $\sin x = \dfrac{3}{5}$ and $\dfrac{\pi}{2} < x < \pi$, find:

a $\cos x$ **b** $\tan x$

Solution

a Substitute $\sin x = \dfrac{3}{5}$ into the Pythagorean identity:

$$\cos^2 x + \sin^2 x = 1$$
$$\cos^2 x + \dfrac{9}{25} = 1$$
$$\cos^2 x = 1 - \dfrac{9}{25}$$
$$= \dfrac{16}{25}$$

Therefore $\cos x = \pm\dfrac{4}{5}$. But x is in the 2nd quadrant, and so $\cos x = -\dfrac{4}{5}$.

b Using part a, we have

$$\tan x = \dfrac{\sin x}{\cos x}$$
$$= \dfrac{3}{5} \div \left(-\dfrac{4}{5}\right)$$
$$= \dfrac{3}{5} \times \left(-\dfrac{5}{4}\right)$$
$$= -\dfrac{3}{4}$$

> **Section summary**
>
> ■ **Complementary relationships**
>
> $$\sin\left(\frac{\pi}{2} - \theta\right) = \cos\theta \qquad \cos\left(\frac{\pi}{2} - \theta\right) = \sin\theta$$
>
> $$\sin\left(\frac{\pi}{2} + \theta\right) = \cos\theta \qquad \cos\left(\frac{\pi}{2} + \theta\right) = -\sin\theta$$
>
> ■ **Pythagorean identity**
>
> $$\cos^2\theta + \sin^2\theta = 1$$

Exercise 14K

Example 24

1 If $\sin x = 0.3$, $\cos \alpha = 0.6$ and $\tan \theta = 0.7$, find the values of:

  a $\cos(-\alpha)$ **b** $\sin\left(\frac{\pi}{2} + \alpha\right)$ **c** $\tan(-\theta)$ **d** $\cos\left(\frac{\pi}{2} - x\right)$

  e $\sin(-x)$ **f** $\tan\left(\frac{\pi}{2} - \theta\right)$ **g** $\cos\left(\frac{\pi}{2} + x\right)$ **h** $\sin\left(\frac{\pi}{2} - \alpha\right)$

  i $\sin\left(\frac{3\pi}{2} + \alpha\right)$ **j** $\cos\left(\frac{3\pi}{2} - x\right)$

2 **a** Given that $0 < \theta < \frac{\pi}{2}$ and $\cos\theta = \sin\left(\frac{\pi}{6}\right)$, find the value of θ.

  b Given that $0 < \theta < \frac{\pi}{2}$ and $\sin\theta = \cos\left(\frac{\pi}{6}\right)$, find the value of θ.

  c Given that $0 < \theta < \frac{\pi}{2}$ and $\cos\theta = \sin\left(\frac{\pi}{12}\right)$, find the value of θ.

  d Given that $0 < \theta < \frac{\pi}{2}$ and $\sin\theta = \cos\left(\frac{3\pi}{7}\right)$, find the value of θ.

Example 25

3 Given that $\cos x = \frac{3}{5}$ and $\frac{3\pi}{2} < x < 2\pi$, find $\sin x$ and $\tan x$.

4 Given that $\sin x = \frac{5}{13}$ and $\frac{\pi}{2} < x < \pi$, find $\cos x$ and $\tan x$.

5 Given that $\cos x = \frac{1}{5}$ and $\frac{3\pi}{2} < x < 2\pi$, find $\sin x$ and $\tan x$.

14L The tangent function

A table of values for $y = \tan x$ is given below. Use a calculator to check these values and plot the graph of $y = \tan x$.

x	$-\pi$	$-\frac{3\pi}{4}$	$-\frac{\pi}{2}$	$-\frac{\pi}{4}$	0	$\frac{\pi}{4}$	$\frac{\pi}{2}$	$\frac{3\pi}{4}$	π	$\frac{5\pi}{4}$	$\frac{3\pi}{2}$	$\frac{7\pi}{4}$	2π	$\frac{9\pi}{4}$	$\frac{5\pi}{2}$	$\frac{11\pi}{4}$	3π
y	0	1	ud	-1	0	1	ud	-1	0	1	ud	-1	0	1	ud	-1	0

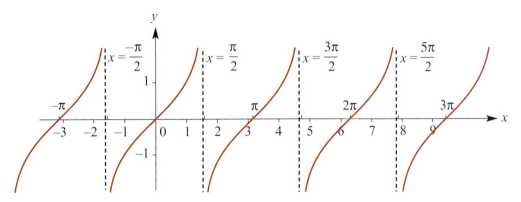

Note: The lines $x = -\frac{\pi}{2}$, $x = \frac{\pi}{2}$, $x = \frac{3\pi}{2}$ and $x = \frac{5\pi}{2}$ are asymptotes.

The x-axis intercepts occur when $\sin x = 0$, which is for $x = 0, \pi, 2\pi$, etc. In general, $x = k\pi$, where k is an integer.

Observations from the graph of $y = \tan x$

- The graph repeats itself every π units, i.e. the period of tan is π.
- The range of tan is $\mathbb{R}$.
- The equations of the asymptotes are of the form $x = \frac{(2k+1)\pi}{2}$, where k is an integer.
- The x-axis intercepts occur for $x = k\pi$, where k is an integer.

▶ Transformations of $y = \tan x$

Consider a dilation of factor $\frac{1}{2}$ from the y-axis and a dilation of factor 3 from the x-axis:

$$(x, y) \rightarrow (\tfrac{1}{2}x, 3y)$$

If the image of (x, y) under the transformation is (x', y'), then $x' = \frac{1}{2}x$ and $y' = 3y$. Hence $x = 2x'$ and $y = \frac{y'}{3}$.

Thus the graph of $y = \tan x$ is transformed to the graph of $\frac{y'}{3} = \tan(2x')$. That is, it is transformed to the graph of $y = 3\tan(2x)$. The period of the graph will be $\frac{\pi}{2}$.

Graph of $y = a\tan(nt)$

In general, for a and n positive numbers, the graph of $y = a\tan(nt)$ is obtained from the graph of $y = \tan t$ by a dilation of factor a from the t-axis and a dilation of factor $\frac{1}{n}$ from the y-axis.

The following are important properties of the function $f(t) = a\tan(nt)$:

- The period is $\frac{\pi}{n}$.
- The range is $\mathbb{R}$.
- The asymptotes have equations $t = \frac{(2k+1)\pi}{2n}$, where k is an integer.
- The t-axis intercepts are $t = \frac{k\pi}{n}$, where k is an integer.

Example 26

Sketch the graph of each of the following for $x \in [-\pi, \pi]$:

a $y = 3\tan(2x)$ **b** $y = -2\tan(3x)$

Solution

a Period $= \frac{\pi}{n} = \frac{\pi}{2}$

Asymptotes: $x = \frac{(2k+1)\pi}{4}$, $k \in \mathbb{Z}$

Axis intercepts: $x = \frac{k\pi}{2}$, $k \in \mathbb{Z}$

b Period $= \frac{\pi}{n} = \frac{\pi}{3}$

Asymptotes: $x = \frac{(2k+1)\pi}{6}$, $k \in \mathbb{Z}$

Axis intercepts: $x = \frac{k\pi}{3}$, $k \in \mathbb{Z}$

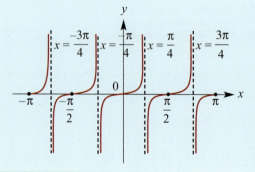
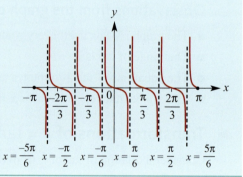

▶ **Solution of equations**

The techniques for solving equations of the form $a\tan(nt) = b$ are similar to those for solving equations of the form $a\sin(nt) = b$ and $a\cos(nt) = b$ discussed in Section 14H. An important difference is that the period of tan is π. The method for obtaining further solutions is to add and subtract multiples of π.

Example 27

Solve each of the following equations for $x \in [-\pi, \pi]$:

a $\tan x = -1$ **b** $\tan(2x) = \sqrt{3}$ **c** $2\tan(3x) = 0$

14L The tangent function

Solution	Explanation
a $\tan x = -1$ $$\therefore \quad x = \frac{3\pi}{4} \text{ or } \frac{-\pi}{4}$$	Since $\tan x$ is negative, the point $P(x)$ lies in the 2nd or 4th quadrant. Solutions are required for $x \in [-\pi, \pi]$. Use $\tan(\pi - x) = -\tan x$ and $\tan(-x) = -\tan x$.
b $\tan(2x) = \sqrt{3}$ Let $a = 2x$. The equation becomes $\tan a = \sqrt{3}$ $$\therefore \quad a = \frac{\pi}{3} \text{ or } \frac{4\pi}{3} \text{ or } \frac{-2\pi}{3} \text{ or } \frac{-5\pi}{3}$$ $$\therefore \quad x = \frac{\pi}{6} \text{ or } \frac{4\pi}{6} \text{ or } \frac{-2\pi}{6} \text{ or } \frac{-5\pi}{6}$$ $$= \frac{\pi}{6} \text{ or } \frac{2\pi}{3} \text{ or } \frac{-\pi}{3} \text{ or } \frac{-5\pi}{6}$$	Consider solutions for $a \in [-2\pi, 2\pi]$. Since $\tan a$ is positive, the point $P(a)$ lies in the 1st or 3rd quadrant. Use $\tan(\pi + x) = \tan x$. Subtract π from each of the first two solutions to obtain the second two.
c $2\tan(3x) = 0$ $3x = -3\pi, -2\pi, -\pi, 0, \pi, 2\pi \text{ or } 3\pi$ $$\therefore \quad x = -\pi, \frac{-2\pi}{3}, \frac{-\pi}{3}, 0, \frac{\pi}{3}, \frac{2\pi}{3} \text{ or } \pi$$	The solutions for $3x$ are to be in the interval $[-3\pi, 3\pi]$.

Example 28

Sketch the graph of $y = \tan(2x) + 1$ for $x \in [-\pi, \pi]$.

Solution

The graph of $y = \tan(2x) + 1$ is obtained from the graph of $y = \tan(2x)$ by a translation of 1 unit in the positive direction of the y-axis.

For the y-axis intercept, let $x = 0$. Then $y = \tan 0 + 1 = 1$.

For the x-axis intercepts, consider $\tan(2x) + 1 = 0$.

This implies $\tan(2x) = -1$.

Hence $2x = \dfrac{3\pi}{4}, \dfrac{-\pi}{4}, \dfrac{7\pi}{4}$ or $\dfrac{-5\pi}{4}$

and so $x = \dfrac{3\pi}{8}, \dfrac{-\pi}{8}, \dfrac{7\pi}{8}$ or $\dfrac{-5\pi}{8}$

The asymptotes are the same as those for $y = \tan(2x)$, that is, $x = \dfrac{(2k+1)\pi}{4}, k \in \mathbb{Z}$

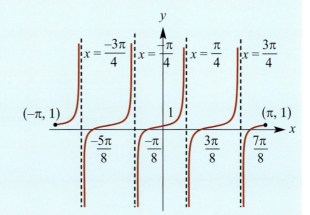

Exercise 14L

1. For each of the following, state the period:

   a $y = \tan(4x)$ **b** $y = \tan\left(\dfrac{2x}{3}\right)$ **c** $y = -3\tan(2x)$

Example 26

2. Sketch the graph of each of the following for $x \in [-\pi, \pi]$:

   a $y = \tan(2x)$ **b** $y = 2\tan(3x)$ **c** $y = -\tan x$

Example 27

3. Solve each of the following equations for $x \in [-\pi, \pi]$:

   a $2\tan(2x) = 2$ **b** $3\tan(3x) = \sqrt{3}$

   c $2\tan(2x) = 2\sqrt{3}$ **d** $3\tan(3x) = -\sqrt{3}$

Example 28

4. Sketch the graph of each of the following for $x \in [-\pi, \pi]$:

   a $y = 3\tan(x) + \sqrt{3}$ **b** $y = \tan(x) + 2$ **c** $y = 3\tan(x) - 3$

14M Numerical methods with a CAS calculator

> **Example 29**
>
> Solve the equation $\dfrac{x}{2} = \sin x$, giving your answer correct to two decimal places.

Using the TI-Nspire

- Use (menu) > **Algebra** > **Solve** to solve as shown.
- Press (ctrl)(enter), if necessary, to obtain the answer as a decimal approximation.

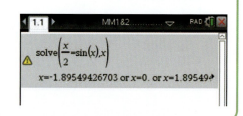

Using the Casio ClassPad

The equation $\dfrac{x}{2} = \sin(x)$ can be solved numerically by drawing a graph for each side of the equation and finding the intersection points.

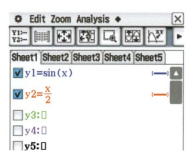
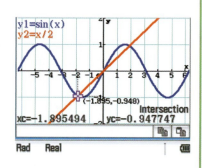

- To see all the intersection points, set the window to $-2\pi \leq x \leq 2\pi$ and $-2 \leq y \leq 2$.
- Select **Analysis > G-Solve > Intersection** to obtain the first point. To find the other points, navigate across using the cursor arrows on the hard keyboard.

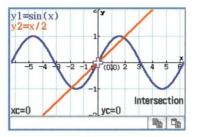 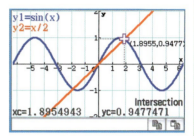

Alternatively, the solutions can be found in the main screen.

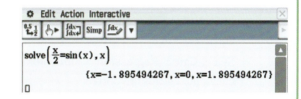

▶ Fitting data

Example 30

Fit a sine curve to the points $(1, 2.08)$, $(2, 2.3)$, $(3, 0.49)$, $(4, -1.77)$ and $(6, -0.96)$.

Using the TI-Nspire

- Enter the data either in a **Calculator** application as lists or in a **Lists & Spreadsheet** application as shown.

- In a **Calculator** application, choose menu > **Statistics > Stat Calculations > Sinusoidal Regression**.
- This now gives the values of a, b, c and d, and the equation has been entered in $f_1(x)$.

Note: This regression analysis can also be done in the **Lists & Spreadsheet** application.

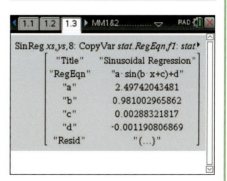

- The curve can be shown in a **Graphs** application together with the scatter plot (menu > **Graph Type** > **Scatter Plot**) using an appropriate window (menu > **Window/Zoom**).

Note: The scatter plot and regression curve can also be obtained using the **Data & Statistics** application.

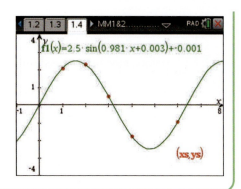

Using the Casio ClassPad

- In **Statistics**, enter the data in lists 1 and 2 as shown.
- Select **Calc** > **Regression** > **Sinusoidal Reg** and check the entries are correct.

Note: Set **Copy Formula** to y1, as this will store the formula for the graph for later use.

- Take note of the formula. Then tap OK again to produce the graph.

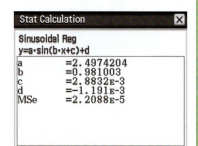

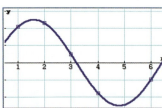

Exercise 14M

Example 29   **1**   Solve each of the following equations for x, correct to two decimal places:

     a $\cos x = x$ **b** $\sin x = 1 - x$ **c** $\cos x = x^2$ **d** $\sin x = x^2$

Example 30   **2**   For each of the following sets of data, find a suitable trigonometric rule (model):

a

θ	0	$\dfrac{\pi}{4}$	$\dfrac{\pi}{2}$	$\dfrac{3\pi}{4}$	π
y	1	2.4	−1	2.4	1

b

θ	0	0.2	0.4	0.6	0.8
y	0	1.77	2.85	2.85	1.77

c

θ	0	0.2	0.4	0.6	0.8
y	5	2.18	0.34	0.13	1.62

14N General solution of trigonometric equations

Solution of equations involving circular functions has been discussed in Section 14H for functions over a restricted domain. In this section, we consider the general solutions of such equations over the maximal domain for each function.

If an equation involving a circular function has one or more solutions in one 'cycle', then it will have corresponding solutions in each cycle of its domain, i.e. there will be an infinite number of solutions.

For example, if $\cos x = \frac{1}{4}$, then the solution in the interval $[0, \pi]$ is given by:

$$x = \cos^{-1}(\tfrac{1}{4})$$

By the symmetry properties of the cosine function, other solutions are given by:

$$-\cos^{-1}(\tfrac{1}{4}),\ \pm 2\pi + \cos^{-1}(\tfrac{1}{4}),\ \pm 2\pi - \cos^{-1}(\tfrac{1}{4}),\ \pm 4\pi + \cos^{-1}(\tfrac{1}{4}),\ \pm 4\pi - \cos^{-1}(\tfrac{1}{4}),\ \ldots$$

In general, we have the following:

- For $a \in [-1, 1]$, the general solution of the equation $\cos x = a$ is

  $$x = 2n\pi \pm \cos^{-1}(a), \quad \text{where } n \in \mathbb{Z}$$

- For $a \in \mathbb{R}$, the general solution of the equation $\tan x = a$ is

  $$x = n\pi + \tan^{-1}(a), \quad \text{where } n \in \mathbb{Z}$$

- For $a \in [-1, 1]$, the general solution of the equation $\sin x = a$ is

  $$x = 2n\pi + \sin^{-1}(a) \quad \text{or} \quad x = (2n+1)\pi - \sin^{-1}(a), \quad \text{where } n \in \mathbb{Z}$$

Note: An alternative and more concise way to express the general solution of $\sin x = a$ is $x = n\pi + (-1)^n \sin^{-1}(a)$, where $n \in \mathbb{Z}$.

Example 31

Find the general solution of each of the following equations:

a $\cos x = 0.5$ **b** $\sqrt{3} \tan(3x) = 1$ **c** $2 \sin x = \sqrt{2}$

Solution

a $\cos x = 0.5$

$x = 2n\pi \pm \cos^{-1}(0.5)$

$= 2n\pi \pm \dfrac{\pi}{3}$

$= \dfrac{(6n \pm 1)\pi}{3}, \quad n \in \mathbb{Z}$

b $\tan(3x) = \dfrac{1}{\sqrt{3}}$

$3x = n\pi + \tan^{-1}\left(\dfrac{1}{\sqrt{3}}\right)$

$= n\pi + \dfrac{\pi}{6}$

$= \dfrac{(6n+1)\pi}{6}$

$x = \dfrac{(6n+1)\pi}{18}, \quad n \in \mathbb{Z}$

c $\sin x = \dfrac{\sqrt{2}}{2} = \dfrac{1}{\sqrt{2}}$

$x = 2n\pi + \sin^{-1}\left(\dfrac{1}{\sqrt{2}}\right)$ or $x = (2n+1)\pi - \sin^{-1}\left(\dfrac{1}{\sqrt{2}}\right)$

$ = 2n\pi + \dfrac{\pi}{4}$ $= (2n+1)\pi - \dfrac{\pi}{4}$

$ = \dfrac{(8n+1)\pi}{4}, \quad n \in \mathbb{Z}$ $= \dfrac{(8n+3)\pi}{4}, \quad n \in \mathbb{Z}$

Using the TI-Nspire

Check that the calculator is in radian mode.

a Use menu > **Algebra** > **Solve** and complete as shown. Note the use of $\tfrac{1}{2}$ rather than 0.5 to ensure that the answer is exact.

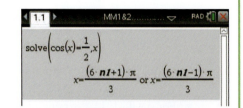

b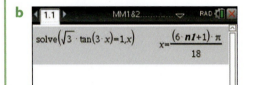

c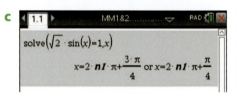

Using the Casio ClassPad

Check that the calculator is in radian mode.

a ■ In Main $\sqrt{\alpha}$, enter and highlight the equation $\cos(x) = 0.5$.
  ■ Select **Interactive** > **Equation/Inequality** > **solve**. Then tap EXE.
  ■ To view the entire solution, rotate the screen by selecting Rotate.

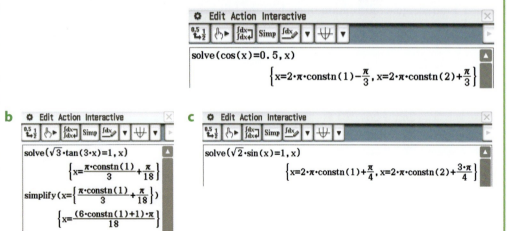

Note: The constn(1) and constn(2) are replaced with n in the written answer.

14N General solution of trigonometric equations

Example 32

Find the first three positive solutions of each of the following equations:

a $\cos x = 0.5$ **b** $\sqrt{3} \tan(3x) = 1$ **c** $2 \sin x = \sqrt{2}$

Solution

a The general solution (from Example 31a) is given by $x = \dfrac{(6n \pm 1)\pi}{3}, n \in \mathbb{Z}$.

When $n = 0$, $x = \pm\dfrac{\pi}{3}$, and when $n = 1$, $x = \dfrac{5\pi}{3}$ or $x = \dfrac{7\pi}{3}$.

Thus the first three positive solutions of $\cos x = 0.5$ are $x = \dfrac{\pi}{3}, \dfrac{5\pi}{3}, \dfrac{7\pi}{3}$.

b The general solution (from Example 31b) is given by $x = \dfrac{(6n + 1)\pi}{18}, n \in \mathbb{Z}$.

When $n = 0$, $x = \dfrac{\pi}{18}$, and when $n = 1$, $x = \dfrac{7\pi}{18}$, and when $n = 2$, $x = \dfrac{13\pi}{18}$.

Thus the first three positive solutions of $\sqrt{3} \tan(3x) = 1$ are $x = \dfrac{\pi}{18}, \dfrac{7\pi}{18}, \dfrac{13\pi}{18}$.

c The general solution (from Example 31c) is $x = \dfrac{(8n + 1)\pi}{4}$ or $x = \dfrac{(8n + 3)\pi}{4}, n \in \mathbb{Z}$.

When $n = 0$, $x = \dfrac{\pi}{4}$ or $x = \dfrac{3\pi}{4}$, and when $n = 1$, $x = \dfrac{9\pi}{4}$ or $x = \dfrac{11\pi}{4}$.

Thus the first three positive solutions of $2 \sin x = \sqrt{2}$ are $x = \dfrac{\pi}{4}, \dfrac{3\pi}{4}, \dfrac{9\pi}{4}$.

Section summary

- For $a \in [-1, 1]$, the general solution of the equation $\cos x = a$ is
$$x = 2n\pi \pm \cos^{-1}(a), \quad \text{where } n \in \mathbb{Z}$$

- For $a \in \mathbb{R}$, the general solution of the equation $\tan x = a$ is
$$x = n\pi + \tan^{-1}(a), \quad \text{where } n \in \mathbb{Z}$$

- For $a \in [-1, 1]$, the general solution of the equation $\sin x = a$ is
$$x = 2n\pi + \sin^{-1}(a) \quad \text{or} \quad x = (2n + 1)\pi - \sin^{-1}(a), \quad \text{where } n \in \mathbb{Z}$$

Exercise 14N

Example 31 **1** Find the general solution of each of the following equations:

a $\sin x = 0.5$ **b** $2\cos(3x) = \sqrt{3}$ **c** $\sqrt{3} \tan x = -3$

Example 32 **2** Find the first two positive solutions of each of the following equations:

a $\sin x = 0.5$ **b** $2\cos(3x) = \sqrt{3}$ **c** $\sqrt{3} \tan x = -3$

524 Chapter 14: Circular functions

3 Find the general solution of $2\cos\left(2x + \dfrac{\pi}{4}\right) = \sqrt{2}$, and hence find all the solutions for x in the interval $(-2\pi, 2\pi)$.

4 Find the general solution of $\sqrt{3}\tan\left(\dfrac{\pi}{6} - 3x\right) - 1 = 0$, and hence find all the solutions for x in the interval $[-\pi, 0]$.

5 Find the general solution of $2\sin(4\pi x) + \sqrt{3} = 0$, and hence find all the solutions for x in the interval $[-1, 1]$.

14O Applications of circular functions

> Skillsheet
>
>
>
> **Example 33**
>
> It is suggested that the height, $h(t)$ metres, of the tide above mean sea level on 1 January at Warnung is given approximately by the rule $h(t) = 4\sin\left(\dfrac{\pi}{6}t\right)$, where t is the number of hours after midnight.
>
> **a** Draw the graph of $y = h(t)$ for $0 \leq t \leq 24$.
> **b** When was high tide?
> **c** What was the height of the high tide?
> **d** What was the height of the tide at 8 a.m.?
> **e** A boat can only cross the harbour bar when the tide is at least 1 metre above mean sea level. When could the boat cross the harbour bar on 1 January?
>
> **Solution**
>
> **a**
>
>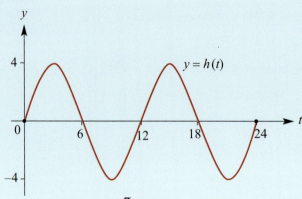
>
> Note: Period $= 2\pi \div \dfrac{\pi}{6} = 12$
>
> **b** High tide occurs when $h(t) = 4$:
>
> $4\sin\left(\dfrac{\pi}{6}t\right) = 4$
>
> $\sin\left(\dfrac{\pi}{6}t\right) = 1$
>
> $\dfrac{\pi}{6}t = \dfrac{\pi}{2}, \dfrac{5\pi}{2}$
>
> $\therefore \; t = 3, 15$
>
> i.e. high tide occurs at 03:00 and 15:00 (3 p.m.).
>
> **c** The high tide has height 4 metres above the mean height.
>
> **d** $h(8) = 4\sin\left(\dfrac{8\pi}{6}\right) = 4\sin\left(\dfrac{4\pi}{3}\right) = 4 \times \dfrac{-\sqrt{3}}{2} = -2\sqrt{3}$
>
> The water is $2\sqrt{3}$ metres below the mean height at 8 a.m.

e We first consider $4\sin\left(\dfrac{\pi}{6}t\right) = 1$.

Thus $\sin\left(\dfrac{\pi}{6}t\right) = \dfrac{1}{4}$

$\therefore \quad \dfrac{\pi}{6}t = 0.2526,\ 2.889,\ 6.5358,\ 9.172$

$\therefore \quad t = 0.4824,\ 5.5176,\ 12.4824,\ 17.5173$

i.e. the water is at height 1 metre at 00:29, 05:31, 12:29, 17:31.
Thus the boat can pass across the harbour bar between 00:29 and 05:31, and between 12:29 and 17:31.

Exercise 14O

1 It is suggested that the height, $h(t)$ metres, of the tide above mean sea level during a particular day at Seabreak is given approximately by the rule

$$h(t) = 5\sin\left(\dfrac{\pi}{6}t\right)$$

where t is the number of hours after midnight.

  a Draw the graph of $y = h(t)$ for $0 \leq t \leq 24$.
  b When was high tide?
  c What was the height of the high tide?
  d What was the height of the tide at 2 a.m.?
  e What was the height of the tide at 2 p.m.?
  f A boat can only cross the harbour bar when the tide is at least 2.5 metres above mean sea level. When could the boat cross the harbour bar on this day?

2 A particle moves on a straight line, OX, and its distance x metres from O at time t seconds is given by $x = 3 + 2\sin(3t)$.

  a Find its greatest distance from O.
  b Find its least distance from O.
  c Find the times at which it is 5 metres from O for $0 \leq t \leq 5$.
  d Find the times at which it is 3 metres from O for $0 \leq t \leq 3$.
  e Describe the motion of the particle.

3 A particle moves on a straight line, OX, and its distance x metres from O at time t seconds is given by $x = 5 + 2\sin(2\pi t)$.

  a Find its greatest distance from O.
  b Find its least distance from O.
  c Find the times at which it is 7 metres from O for $0 \leq t \leq 5$.
  d Find the times at which it is 6 metres from O for $0 \leq t \leq 3$.
  e Describe the motion of the particle.

4 A particle moves in a vertical circle of radius 10 m. The height, $h(t)$ m, of the particle above the ground at time t seconds is given by the function

$$h(t) = 10\sin\left(\frac{\pi t}{3}\right) + 10 \quad \text{where } t \geq 0$$

  a Find the height of the particle above the ground for:
  i $t = 0$ **ii** $t = 1$ **iii** $t = 2$ **iv** $t = 4$ **v** $t = 5$
  b Find the period of the motion of the particle.
  c Find the greatest height of the particle above the ground.
  d Find the first four times that the particle is at a height 15 m above the ground.
  e Find the first four times that the particle is at a height 5 m above the ground.

5 The temperature, $T°C$, in a town over a day is modelled by the function with rule

$$T = 17 - 8\cos\left(\frac{\pi t}{12}\right)$$

where t is the time in hours after midnight, $0 \leq t \leq 24$.
  a What is the temperature at midnight?
  b What are the maximum and minimum temperatures reached?
  c At what times of the day, to the nearest minute, are temperatures warmer than 20°C?
  d Sketch the graph for the temperatures over a day.

6 The depth, $D(t)$ metres, of water at the entrance to a harbour at t hours after midnight on a particular day is given by $D(t) = 10 + 3\sin\left(\frac{\pi t}{6}\right)$, $0 \leq t \leq 24$.
  a Sketch the graph of $D(t)$ for $0 \leq t \leq 24$.
  b Find the values of t for which $D(t) \geq 8.5$.
  c Boats which need a depth of w metres are permitted to enter the harbour only if the depth of the water at the entrance is at least w metres for a continuous period of 1 hour. Find, correct to one decimal place, the largest value of w which satisfies this condition.

7 The depth of water at the entrance to a harbour t hours after high tide is D metres, where $D = p + q\cos(rt)°$ for suitable constants p, q, r. At high tide the depth is 7 m; at low tide, 6 hours later, the depth is 3 m.
  a Show that $r = 30$ and find the values of p and q.
  b Sketch the graph of D against t for $0 \leq t \leq 12$.
  c Find how soon after low tide a ship that requires a depth of at least 4 m of water will be able to enter the harbour.

8 For each of the following, construct a formula involving a circular function which could be used to model the situation described:

  a Water depths in a canal vary between a minimum of 3 metres and a maximum of 6 metres over a 24-hour period.
  b At a certain town just south of the Arctic circle, the number of hours of daylight varies between 2 and 22 hours during a 365-day year.

Chapter 14 review 527

Chapter summary

- **Definition of a radian**

  One radian (written 1^c) is the angle formed at the centre of the unit circle by an arc of length 1 unit.

  $$1^c = \frac{180°}{\pi} \qquad 1° = \frac{\pi^c}{180}$$

  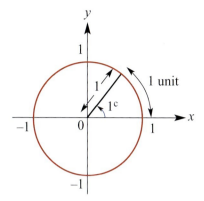

- **Sine and cosine**

  x-coordinate of $P(\theta)$ on unit circle:

  $$x = \text{cosine } \theta, \quad \theta \in \mathbb{R}$$

  y-coordinate of $P(\theta)$ on unit circle:

  $$y = \text{sine } \theta, \quad \theta \in \mathbb{R}$$

  Abbreviated to

  $$x = \cos\theta$$
  $$y = \sin\theta$$

  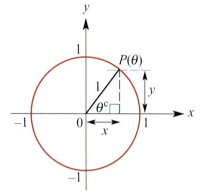

- **Tangent**

  If the tangent to the unit circle at A is drawn, then the y-coordinate of B is called tangent θ (abbreviated to $\tan\theta$). By using similar triangles:

  $$\tan\theta = \frac{\sin\theta}{\cos\theta}$$

  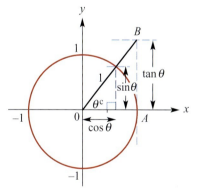

- **Circular functions and trigonometric ratios**

  $$\sin\theta = \frac{O}{H} = \frac{y}{1} = y$$

  $$\cos\theta = \frac{A}{H} = \frac{x}{1} = x$$

  $$\tan\theta = \frac{O}{A} = \frac{y}{x} = \frac{\sin\theta}{\cos\theta}$$

  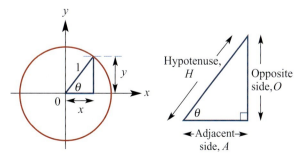

Symmetry properties of circular functions

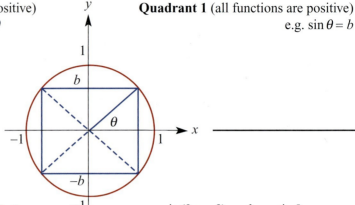

Quadrant 2 (sin is positive)
$\sin(\pi - \theta) = b = \sin\theta$

Quadrant 1 (all functions are positive)
e.g. $\sin\theta = b$

$\sin(\pi + \theta) = -b = -\sin\theta$
Quadrant 3 (tan is positive)

$\sin(2\pi - \theta) = -b = -\sin\theta$
Quadrant 4 (cos is positive)

Further symmetry properties

Negative angles:

$$\cos(-\theta) = \cos\theta$$
$$\sin(-\theta) = -\sin\theta$$
$$\tan(-\theta) = \frac{-\sin\theta}{\cos\theta} = -\tan\theta$$

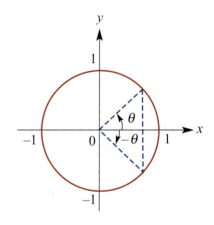

Complementary angles:

$$\sin\left(\frac{\pi}{2} - \theta\right) = \cos\theta, \quad \sin\left(\frac{\pi}{2} + \theta\right) = \cos\theta$$
$$\cos\left(\frac{\pi}{2} - \theta\right) = \sin\theta, \quad \cos\left(\frac{\pi}{2} + \theta\right) = -\sin\theta$$

Pythagorean identity

$$\cos^2\theta + \sin^2\theta = 1$$

Exact values of circular functions

θ	$\sin\theta$	$\cos\theta$	$\tan\theta$
0	0	1	0
$\dfrac{\pi}{6}$	$\dfrac{1}{2}$	$\dfrac{\sqrt{3}}{2}$	$\dfrac{1}{\sqrt{3}}$
$\dfrac{\pi}{4}$	$\dfrac{1}{\sqrt{2}}$	$\dfrac{1}{\sqrt{2}}$	1
$\dfrac{\pi}{3}$	$\dfrac{\sqrt{3}}{2}$	$\dfrac{1}{2}$	$\sqrt{3}$
$\dfrac{\pi}{2}$	1	0	undefined

- Graphs of circular functions

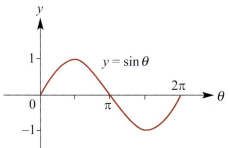

Amplitude = 1
Period = 2π

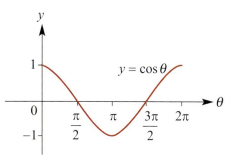

Amplitude = 1
Period = 2π

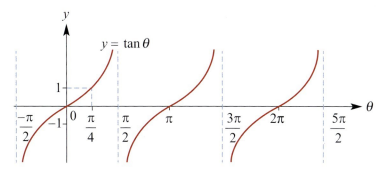

Amplitude is undefined
Period = π

- Graphs of circular functions of the type
  $y = a \sin n(t \pm \varepsilon) \pm b$ and $y = a \cos n(t \pm \varepsilon) \pm b$

  e.g. $y = 2 \cos 3\left(t + \dfrac{\pi}{3}\right) - 1$

  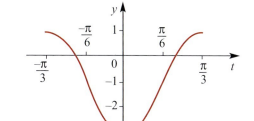

  - Amplitude, $a = 2$
  - Period $= \dfrac{2\pi}{n} = \dfrac{2\pi}{3}$
  - The graph is the same shape as $y = 2\cos(3t)$ but is translated $\dfrac{\pi}{3}$ units in the negative direction of the t-axis and 1 unit in the negative direction of the y-axis.

- Solutions of trigonometric equations of the type $\sin x° = a$ and $\cos x° = a$

  e.g. Solve $\cos x° = -0.7$ for $x \in [0, 360]$.
  First look at the 1st quadrant: If $\cos \alpha° = 0.7$, then $\alpha = 45.6$.
  Since $\cos x°$ is negative for $P(x°)$ in the 2nd and 3rd quadrants, the solutions are
  $$x = 180 - 45.6 = 134.4 \quad \text{and} \quad x = 180 + 45.6 = 225.6$$

Technology-free questions

1 Convert each of the following to radian measure in terms of π:

    a 330°   **b** 810°   **c** 1080°   **d** 1035°   **e** 135°

    f 405°   **g** 390°   **h** 420°   **i** 80°

Review

2 Convert each of the following to degree measure:

a $\dfrac{5\pi^c}{6}$ b $\dfrac{7\pi^c}{4}$ c $\dfrac{11\pi^c}{4}$ d $\dfrac{3\pi^c}{12}$ e $\dfrac{15\pi^c}{2}$

f $-\dfrac{3\pi^c}{4}$ g $-\dfrac{\pi^c}{4}$ h $-\dfrac{11\pi^c}{4}$ i $-\dfrac{23\pi^c}{4}$

3 Give exact values of each of the following:

a $\sin\left(\dfrac{11\pi}{4}\right)$ b $\cos\left(-\dfrac{7\pi}{4}\right)$ c $\sin\left(\dfrac{11\pi}{6}\right)$ d $\cos\left(-\dfrac{7\pi}{6}\right)$

e $\cos\left(\dfrac{13\pi}{6}\right)$ f $\sin\left(\dfrac{23\pi}{6}\right)$ g $\cos\left(-\dfrac{23}{3}\pi\right)$ h $\sin\left(-\dfrac{17}{4}\pi\right)$

4 State the amplitude and period of each of the following:

a $2\sin\left(\dfrac{\theta}{2}\right)$ b $-3\sin(4\theta)$ c $\dfrac{1}{2}\sin(3\theta)$

d $-3\cos(2x)$ e $-4\sin\left(\dfrac{x}{3}\right)$ f $\dfrac{2}{3}\sin\left(\dfrac{2x}{3}\right)$

5 Sketch the graph of each of the following (showing one cycle):

a $y = 2\sin(2x)$ b $y = -3\cos\left(\dfrac{x}{3}\right)$ c $y = -2\sin(3x)$

d $y = 2\sin\left(\dfrac{x}{3}\right)$ e $y = \sin\left(x - \dfrac{\pi}{4}\right)$ f $y = \sin\left(x + \dfrac{2\pi}{3}\right)$

g $y = 2\cos\left(x - \dfrac{5\pi}{6}\right)$ h $y = -3\cos\left(x + \dfrac{\pi}{6}\right)$

6 Solve each of the following equations for θ:

a $\sin\theta = -\dfrac{\sqrt{3}}{2}$, $\theta \in [-\pi, \pi]$ b $\sin(2\theta) = -\dfrac{\sqrt{3}}{2}$, $\theta \in [-\pi, \pi]$

c $\sin\left(\theta - \dfrac{\pi}{3}\right) = -\dfrac{1}{2}$, $\theta \in [0, 2\pi]$ d $\sin\left(\theta + \dfrac{\pi}{3}\right) = -1$, $\theta \in [0, 2\pi]$

e $\sin\left(\dfrac{\pi}{3} - \theta\right) = -\dfrac{1}{2}$, $\theta \in [0, 2\pi]$

Multiple-choice questions

1 In a right-angled triangle, the two shorter side lengths are 3 cm and 4 cm. To the nearest degree, the value of the smallest angle is

   A 1°   **B** 23°   **C** 37°   **D** 53°   **E** 92°

2 The minimum value of $3 - 10\cos(2x)$ is

   A -13 **B** -17 **C** -23 **D** -7 **E** -10

3 The range of the function $f: [0, 2\pi] \to \mathbb{R}$, $f(x) = 4\sin\left(2x - \dfrac{\pi}{2}\right)$ is

   A $\mathbb{R}$ **B** $[0, 4]$ **C** $[-4, 0]$ **D** $[0, 8]$ **E** $[-4, 4]$

4 The period of the graph of $y = 3\sin\left(\dfrac{1}{2}x - \pi\right) + 4$ is

   A π **B** 3   **C** 4π **D** $\pi + 4$ **E** 2π

5 The graph of $y = \sin x$ is dilated by factor $\dfrac{1}{2}$ from the y-axis and translated $\dfrac{\pi}{4}$ units in the positive direction of the x-axis. The equation of the image is

A $y = \sin\left(\dfrac{1}{2}x + \dfrac{\pi}{4}\right)$ **B** $y = \sin\left(\dfrac{1}{2}x - \dfrac{\pi}{4}\right)$ **C** $y = 2\sin\left(x - \dfrac{\pi}{4}\right)$

D $y = \sin\left(2x - \dfrac{\pi}{4}\right)$ **E** $y = \sin\left(2\left(x - \dfrac{\pi}{4}\right)\right)$

6 The period of the function $f : \mathbb{R} \to \mathbb{R}$, where $f(x) = a\sin(bx) + c$ and a, b and c are positive constants, is

A a **B** b **C** $\dfrac{2\pi}{a}$ **D** $\dfrac{2\pi}{b}$ **E** $\dfrac{b}{2\pi}$

7 One cycle of the graph of $y = \tan(ax)$ has vertical asymptotes at $x = -\dfrac{\pi}{6}$ and $x = \dfrac{\pi}{6}$. A possible value of a is

A 6 **B** π **C** $\dfrac{\pi}{6}$ **D** $\dfrac{1}{3}$ **E** 3

8 The equation $3\sin(x) + 1 = b$, where b is a positive real number, has one solution in the interval $[0, 2\pi]$. The value of b is

A 1 **B** 1.5 **C** 2 **D** 3 **E** 4

9 The number of solutions of the equation $b = a\sin x$, where $x \in [-2\pi, 2\pi]$ and a and b are positive real numbers with $a > b$, is

A 2 **B** 3 **C** 4 **D** 5 **E** 6

10 The depth of water, in metres, in a harbour at a certain point at time t hours is given by $D(t) = 8 + 2\sin\left(\dfrac{\pi t}{6}\right)$, $0 \leq t \leq 24$. The depth of the water is first 9 m at

A $t = 0$ **B** $t = 1$ **C** $t = 2$ **D** $t = 3$ **E** $t = 4$

Extended-response questions

1 The number of hours of daylight at a point on the Antarctic Circle is given approximately by $d = 12 + 12\cos\left(\dfrac{1}{6}\pi\left(t + \dfrac{1}{3}\right)\right)$, where t is the number of months which have elapsed since 1 January.

  a **i** Find d on 21 June ($t \approx 5.7$).   **ii** Find d on 21 March ($t \approx 2.7$).

  b When will there be 5 hours of daylight?

2 The temperature, $A°C$, inside a house at t hours after 4 a.m. is given by the rule $A = 21 - 3\cos\left(\dfrac{\pi t}{12}\right)$, for $0 \leq t \leq 24$. The temperature, $B°C$, outside the house at the same time is given by $B = 22 - 5\cos\left(\dfrac{\pi t}{12}\right)$, for $0 \leq t \leq 24$.

  a Find the temperature inside the house at 8 a.m.

  b Write down an expression for $D = A - B$, the difference between the inside and outside temperatures.

  c Sketch the graph of D for $0 \leq t \leq 24$.

  d Determine when the inside temperature is less than the outside temperature.

532 Chapter 14: Circular functions

3 At a certain time of the year the depth of water, d metres, in the harbour at Bunk Island is given by the rule $d = 3 + 1.8\cos\left(\dfrac{\pi}{6}t\right)$, where t is the time in hours after 3 a.m.

  a Sketch the graph of the function $d = 3 + 1.8\cos\left(\dfrac{\pi}{6}t\right)$ over a 24-hour period from 3 a.m. to 3 a.m.

  b At what time(s) does high tide occur for $t \in [0, 24]$?

  c At what time(s) does low tide occur for $t \in [0, 24]$?

  A passenger ferry operates between Main Beach and Bunk Island. It takes 50 minutes to go from Main Beach to Bunk Island. The ferry only runs between the hours of 8 a.m. and 8 p.m., and is only able to enter the harbour at Bunk Island if the depth of water is at least 2 metres.

  d What is the earliest time the ferry should leave Main Beach so that it arrives at Bunk Island and can immediately enter the harbour?

  e The time to go from Bunk Island to Main Beach is also 50 minutes. The minimum time the ferry takes at Bunk Island harbour is 5 minutes. The minimum time at Main Beach is also 5 minutes.

   i What is the latest time the ferry can leave Main Beach to complete a round trip in 105 minutes?

   ii How many complete round trips can the ferry make in a day?

4 The depth of water, D metres, at the end of Brighton pier t hours after low tide is given by the rule $D = p - 2\cos(rt)$, where p and r are suitable constants.
At low tide ($t = 0$) the depth is 2 metres; at high tide, which occurs 8 hours later, the depth is 6 metres.

  a Show that $r = \dfrac{\pi}{8}$ and $p = 4$.

  b Sketch the graph of $D = 4 - 2\cos\left(\dfrac{\pi}{8}t\right)$ for $0 \leq t \leq 16$.

  c If the first low tide occurs at 4 a.m., when will the next low tide occur?

  d At what times will the depth be equal to 4 metres?

  The poles that support the Brighton pier stand 7.5 metres above the sea bed.

  e How much of a particular pole is exposed at:

   i high tide   **ii** 2 p.m.?

  Over the years mussels have attached themselves to the pole. A particular mussel is attached 4 metres from the top of the pole so that some of the time it is exposed and some of the time it is covered by water.

  f For how long will the mussel be covered by water during the time from one low tide to the next?

15 Revision of Chapters 13–14

15A Technology-free questions

1. Simplify the following, expressing the answers in positive-index form:

   a $(-2a^2)^3 \times 3a^4$

   b $\dfrac{5a^4 \times 2ab^2}{20a^2b^4}$

   c $\dfrac{(xy^{-2})^{-1}}{y} \times \dfrac{3x^{-1}y^2}{4(xy)^3}$

   d $\left(\dfrac{4a^2}{ab}\right)^3 \div (2ab^{-1})^3$

   e $\sqrt{x^{-1}y^2} \times \left(\dfrac{y}{x}\right)^{-\frac{1}{3}}$

   f $\sqrt{2x-1} \times (2x-1)^{-1}$

2. Simplify and evaluate:

   a $\left(\dfrac{3}{5}\right)^{-2}$

   b $\left(\dfrac{4^2}{2^6}\right)^{-2}$

   c $\dfrac{27^2 \times 9^3}{81^2}$

   d $(-27)^{-\frac{1}{3}}$

3. Simplify:

   a $\dfrac{9^{2n} \times 8^n \times 16^n}{6^n}$

   b $3\log_2(16)$

   c $2\log_{10} 3 + \log_{10} 4$

   d $\log_3\left(\dfrac{1}{27}\right)$

4. Sketch graphs of the following functions. Give equations of asymptotes and y-axis intercepts, and state the range of each.

   a $f: \mathbb{R} \to \mathbb{R},\ f(x) = 2^x - 3$

   b $f: \mathbb{R} \to \mathbb{R},\ f(x) = -3 \times 2^x + 1$

5. Solve these equations for x:

   a $4^x = 8^{x-1}$

   b $4^x = 5 \times 2^x - 4$

   c $5^{x-1} > 125$

   d $\log_2(x+1) = 3$

   e $\log_4(2x) - \log_4(x+1) = 0$

6. Solve using logarithms:

   a $2^x = 5$

   b $5^{3x+1} = 10$

   c $0.6^x < 0.2$

7 Find the rule for the inverse function of $f(x) = 3^x + 2$. Sketch the graph of both the function and its inverse on the same set of axes, showing asymptotes and intercepts.

8 Convert to radians:
  a $60°$
  b $270°$
  c $140°$

9 Evaluate:
  a $\sin\left(-\dfrac{\pi}{2}\right)$
  b $\cos\left(\dfrac{3\pi}{2}\right)$
  c $\tan(3\pi)$
  d $\tan\left(-\dfrac{\pi}{2}\right)$

10 Find the value of the pronumeral:

  a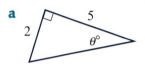
  b
  c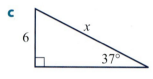

11 Find:
  a $\sin(2\pi - \theta)$ if $\sin\theta = 0.3$
  b $\cos(-\theta)$ if $\cos\theta = -0.5$
  c $\tan(\pi + \theta)$ if $\tan\theta = 1.6$
  d $\sin(\pi + \theta)$ if $\sin\theta = 0.6$
  e $\sin\left(\dfrac{\pi}{2} - \theta\right)$ if $\cos\theta = 0.1$
  f $\cos\theta$ if $\sin\theta = \dfrac{3}{5}$ and $0 < \theta < \dfrac{\pi}{2}$

12 Write down the exact values of:
  a $\sin\left(\dfrac{2\pi}{3}\right)$
  b $\cos\left(\dfrac{5\pi}{6}\right)$
  c $\tan\left(\dfrac{-\pi}{4}\right)$
  d $\sin\left(\dfrac{-7\pi}{6}\right)$
  e $\cos\left(\dfrac{-7\pi}{4}\right)$
  f $\tan\left(\dfrac{5\pi}{3}\right)$

13 Consider the function $f(x) = 2\cos\left(\dfrac{x}{2}\right)$.
  a State the period and amplitude.
  b Sketch a graph for one complete cycle.
  c Give the sequence of transformations which takes the graph of $y = \cos x$ to the graph of $y = f(x)$.

14 Sketch $f(x) = -3\sin(2\pi x)$ for $x \in [0, 2]$.

15 Solve these equations for $\theta \in [-2\pi, 2\pi]$:
  a $\cos\theta = -\dfrac{\sqrt{3}}{2}$
  b $\sqrt{2}\sin\theta = 1$
  c $\sin(2\theta) = -\dfrac{1}{2}$
  d $\tan\theta = -\sqrt{3}$

16 Sketch $y = 2\sin 2\left(x - \dfrac{\pi}{4}\right) + 1$ for $x \in [0, 2\pi]$ and determine the x-axis intercepts.

17 Sketch the graph of $y = \dfrac{1}{2}\tan(2x)$ for $x \in [-\pi, \pi]$.

18 Find the general solution of each of the following equations:
  a $\sin x = \dfrac{1}{2}$
  b $2\cos x = \sqrt{3}$
  c $\tan(2x) = -1$

15B Multiple-choice questions

1 If $\log_a 8 = 3$, then a is equal to
   A 1   **B** 2   **C** 3   **D** 4   **E** 0

2 $5^{n-1} \times 5^{n+1}$ is equal to
   A $5n^2$ **B** 5^{2n} **C** 10^{2n} **D** 25^{2n} **E** 25^{n^2-1}

3 If $2^x = \dfrac{1}{64}$, then x is equal to
   A 6   **B** −6   **C** 5   **D** −5   **E** $\dfrac{1}{6}$

4 $125^a \times 5^b$ is equal to
   A 625^{a+b} **B** 625^{ab} **C** 125^{a+3b} **D** 5^{a+3b} **E** 5^{3a+b}

5 The solution of the equation $4^x = 10 - 4^{x+1}$ is
   A $x = 4$ **B** $x = 2$ **C** $x = \dfrac{1}{4}$ **D** $x = \dfrac{1}{2}$ **E** $x = 1$

6 $\dfrac{7^{n+2} - 35(7^{n-1})}{44(7^{n+2})}$ is equal to
   A $\dfrac{1}{49}$ **B** $\dfrac{1}{44}$ **C** $\dfrac{1}{28}$ **D** $\dfrac{1}{7}$ **E** 7

7 If $f(x) = 2 + 3^x$, then $f(2x) - f(x)$ is equal to
   A 3^x **B** 3^{2x} **C** $2 + 3^x$ **D** $3^x(3^x - 1)$ **E** $3^x(3^x + 1)$

8 If $7^{2x} \times 49^{2x-1} = 1$, then x is equal to
   A −1   **B** $-\dfrac{1}{3}$ **C** $\dfrac{1}{3}$ **D** 1   **E** 3

9 The graphs of $y = 2^x$ and $y = (\tfrac{1}{2})^x$ have
   A the same x-axis intercept
   B the same y-axis intercept
   C no point in common
   D two points in common
   E three points in common

10 If $f(x) = (2x)^0 + x^{-\frac{2}{3}}$, then $f(8)$ is equal to
   A $\dfrac{5}{4}$ **B** $\dfrac{65}{4}$ **C** 5   **D** 20   **E** none of these

11 $\log(a^2) + \log(b^2) - 2\log(ab)$ is equal to
   A 0   **B** 1   **C** a **D** b **E** $a^2 b^2$

12 An angle is measured as $2x$ radians. The measure of the angle in degrees is
   A $\left(\dfrac{\pi x}{90}\right)^\circ$ **B** $\left(\dfrac{90x}{\pi}\right)^\circ$ **C** $\left(\dfrac{\pi}{180x}\right)^\circ$ **D** $\left(\dfrac{360x}{\pi}\right)^\circ$ **E** $\left(\dfrac{\pi x}{360}\right)^\circ$

13 The figure shows the graph of $y = \sin(2x) + 1$.
The coordinates of Q are

A $\left(\dfrac{\pi}{4}, 2\right)$ **B** $\left(\dfrac{\pi}{12}, 2\right)$ **C** $(\pi, 1)$

D $\left(\dfrac{\pi}{4}, 1\right)$ **E** $\left(\dfrac{\pi}{2}, 1\right)$

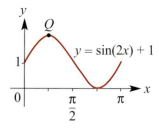

14 The smallest value of $1 - 3\cos\theta$ is

A -5 **B** -4 **C** -3 **D** -2 **E** -1

15 A roller coaster is constructed in such a way that any car is y metres above the ground when it is x metres from the starting point, where $y = 16 + 15\sin\left(\dfrac{\pi}{60}x\right)$.
The height of the car, in metres, when $x = 10$ is

A 31   **B** 1   **C** 16   **D** 23.5   **E** $16 - 5\sqrt{2}$

16 $\sin(\pi + \theta) + \cos(\pi + \theta)$ is equal to

A $\sin\theta + \cos\theta$ **B** $-\sin\theta + \cos\theta$ **C** $\sin\theta - \cos\theta$

D $-\sin\theta - \cos\theta$ **E** $-\sin\theta\cos\theta$

17 For $x \in [0, \pi]$, which of the following equations has exactly two solutions?

A $\sin x = 0$ **B** $\cos x = 0$ **C** $\sin x = 1$

D $\sin x = -1$ **E** $\cos x = 1$

18 Which of the following is the graph of $y = \sin\left(\dfrac{x}{2}\right)$ for one cycle?

A 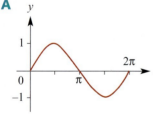 **B** 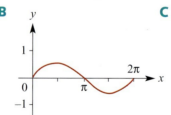 **C**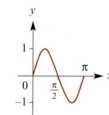

D 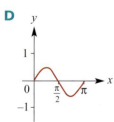 **E**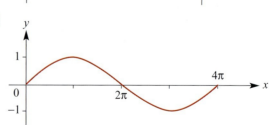

19 The minimum value of $2 - 3\sin\theta$ is

A 2   **B** 1   **C** 0   **D** -1 **E** 3

20 The graph shown is of
  A $y = \cos(x - 30)°$
  B $y = \frac{1}{2}\cos(x + 30)°$
  C $y = \frac{1}{2}\cos(x - 30)°$
  D $y = \cos(x + 30)°$
  E $y = \frac{1}{2}\cos x$

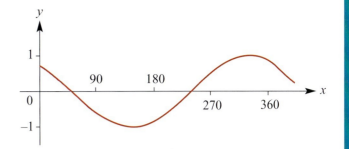

21 The function $f: \mathbb{R} \to \mathbb{R}$, $f(x) = -2\cos(3x)$ has
  A amplitude 2 and period π
  B amplitude -2 and period $\frac{2\pi}{3}$
  C amplitude 2 and period 6π
  D amplitude 3 and period π
  E amplitude 2 and period $\frac{2\pi}{3}$

22 If $C^d = 3$, then $C^{4d} - 5$ equals
  A 76   **B** 7   **C** 22   **D** 86   **E** 35

23 The value of $\log_2 56 - \log_2 7 + \log_2 2$ is
  A $\log_2 51$ **B** 1   **C** 2   **D** 3   **E** 4

24 If $\log_b a = c$ and $\log_x b = c$, then $\log_a x$ equals
  A a **B** c^{-2} **C** b^2 **D** b **E** abc^2

25 If $\cos\theta - \sin\theta = \frac{1}{4}$, then $\sin\theta\cos\theta$ equals
  A $\frac{1}{16}$ **B** $\frac{15}{16}$ **C** $\frac{1}{32}$ **D** $\frac{15}{32}$ **E** $\frac{1}{2}$

26 The coordinates of a point of intersection of the graphs $y = \frac{1}{2}\sin(2x)$ and $y = \frac{1}{2}$ are
  A $\left(\frac{1}{2}, \frac{\pi}{3}\right)$ **B** $\left(\frac{\pi}{4}, \frac{1}{2}\right)$ **C** $\left(\frac{\pi}{2}, \frac{1}{2}\right)$ **D** $\left(\frac{1}{2}, \frac{\pi}{6}\right)$ **E** $\left(2\pi, \frac{1}{2}\right)$

15C Extended-response questions

1 The height of the tide, h metres, at a harbour at any time during a 24-hour period is given by the rule $h(t) = 10 + 4\sin(15t)°$, where t is measured in hours.
  a Sketch the graph of h against t for $0 \leq t \leq 24$.
  b Find the times at which $h = 13$ during the 24-hour period.
  c A boat can leave the harbour when the height of the tide is at 11 metres or more. State the times during the 24 hours when the boat can leave the harbour.

2 Medical researchers studying the growth of a strain of bacteria observe that the number of bacteria present after t hours is given by the formula $N(t) = 40 \times 2^{1.5t}$.
   a State the number of bacteria present at the start of the experiment.
   b State the number of bacteria present after:
      i 2 hours   ii 4 hours   iii 12 hours
   c Sketch the graph of N against t.
   d How many minutes does it take for the number of bacteria to double?

3 For a ride on a Ferris wheel, the height above the ground, h metres, of a person at time t seconds is given by

$$h(t) = 11 + 9\cos\left(\frac{\pi}{30}(t - 10)\right)$$

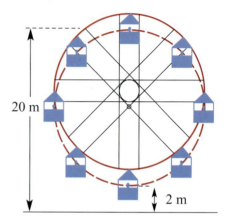

   a How long does it take for the Ferris wheel to make one complete revolution?
   b Sketch the graph of h against t for one revolution.
   c State the range of the function.
   d At what time(s) is the person at a height of 2 metres above the ground?
   e At what time(s) is the person at a height of 15.5 metres above the ground?

4 The voltage, V, in a circuit after t seconds is given by $V = 120\cos(60\pi t)$.
   a Sketch the graph of V against t for one cycle.
   b Find the first time the voltage is 60.
   c Find all times at which the voltage is maximised.

5 The figure shows a waterwheel rotating at 4 revolutions per minute. The distance, d in metres, of a point P from the surface of the water as a function of time, t in seconds, can be modelled by a rule of the form

$$d = a + b\sin c(t - h)$$

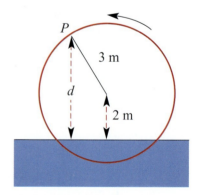

   a Find:
      i the period   ii the amplitude   iii c
   b If $d = 0$ when $t = 0$, find h.
   c Sketch the graph of d against t for $0 \leq t \leq 30$.

6 A forest fire has burned out 30 hectares by 11 a.m. It then spreads according to the formula

$$h(t) = 30(1.65)^t$$

where $h(t)$ is the area burned (in hectares) at time t (in hours after 11 a.m.).

a Find h when:

  i $t = 0$ **ii** $t = 1$ **iii** $t = 2$

b Find k such that $h(t + 1) = k\,h(t)$.

c How long does it take for 900 hectares to be burned?

d Sketch the graph of h against t.

7 A bowl of water is initially at boiling point (i.e. 100°C). The temperature, θ°C, of the water t minutes after beginning to cool is $\theta = 80(2^{-t}) + 20$.

a Copy and complete this table:

t	0	1	2	3	4	5
θ						

b Draw a graph of θ against t.

c At what time is the temperature 60°C?

d Find θ when $t = 3.5$.

8 A, B and C are three countries. Each of them now has a population of 70 million.

- Country A's population grows uniformly by 30 million in every period of 10 years.
- Country B's population grows uniformly by 50 million in every period of 10 years.
- Country C's population is multiplied by 1.3 every 10 years.

a Give an equation for the population of each country at time t.

b On the same set of axes, carefully draw the graphs of the three equations.

c From your graph find out when the population of C overtakes:

  i the population of A **ii** the population of B.

9 An estimate for the population of the Earth, P in billions, is

$$P = 4 \times 2^{\frac{(t-1975)}{32}}$$

where t is the year.

a Evaluate P for:

  i $t = 1975$ **ii** $t = 1995$ **iii** $t = 2005$

b When will the population of the Earth be twice that in 1997?

10 Two tanks simultaneously start to leak. Tank A contains $V_1(t)$ litres of water and tank B contains $V_2(t)$ litres of water, where

$$V_1(t) = 1000 \times 3^{\frac{-t}{10}} \quad t \geq 0$$
$$V_2(t) = 1000 - 40t \quad 0 \leq t \leq 25$$

and t is the time after the tanks start to leak.

a Find $V_1(0)$ and $V_2(0)$.
b Sketch the graphs of $y = V_1(t)$ and $y = V_2(t)$ for $0 \leq t \leq 25$.
c How much water is in tank A when tank B is empty?
d Find the times at which the two tanks have equal amounts of water in them.

11 A river gate is used to control the height of water in a river.

- On one side of the gate, the height of the water is subject to tides. The height of the water (in metres) on this side is given by

$$h_1(t) = 18 + 10 \sin\left(\frac{\pi}{6}t\right)$$

where t is the time in hours past midnight.

- On the other side of the gate, the height of the water (in metres) is rising according to the rule

$$h_2(t) = 8 + 6t$$

where t is the time in hours past midnight.

a Sketch the graphs of $y = h_1(t)$ and $y = h_2(t)$, for $0 \leq t \leq 6$, on the one set of axes.
b Find the time at which $h_1(t) = h_2(t)$.
c When the water levels on both sides of the gate are the same, the gate is opened and the height of the water on both sides is given by $y = h_1(t)$.
  i The gate is closed again when $h_1(t)$ reaches its minimum value. At what time does this happen?
  ii Water flows in on the non-tidal side so that the height increases by 6 metres every hour. What will be the height of the river t hours after the gates have been closed?

Chapter 16

Rates of change

Objectives

▶ To recognise **relationships** between variables.
▶ To calculate average **rates of change**.
▶ To estimate **gradients of tangents** to curves.
▶ To estimate instantaneous rates of change.
▶ To apply the estimation and calculation of rates of change to solving problems.

Throughout Chapters 2–7 and Chapters 13–14, we have been looking at situations where there is a relationship between two variables. We have developed and applied the idea that one variable, say y, is a function of another variable, say x.

Furthermore, we have represented such relationships graphically, and investigated key features such as axis intercepts, turning points and asymptotes.

This graphical representation can also be used to see how the relationship is changing.

In applications, how the relationship is changing is of critical importance in establishing how accurately a given rule models the relationship between the variables in question. For example, if x increases, does y also increase, or does it decrease, or remain unaltered? And, if it does change, does it do so consistently, quickly, slowly, indefinitely, etc.?

This chapter serves as an introduction to the ideas of calculus, which we begin to study more formally in the next chapter. In this chapter, we talk about rates of change informally, based on our intuition. Our study of calculus will enable us to talk about these ideas more precisely.

16A Recognising relationships

In previous chapters, we have studied polynomial, exponential, logarithmic and circular functions, and have seen that many real-life situations may be modelled by these functions.

In this first section, we look at several real-life situations involving two variables, and investigate the form of the relationships between the variables through graphs. The algebraic relationship is not established.

Example 1

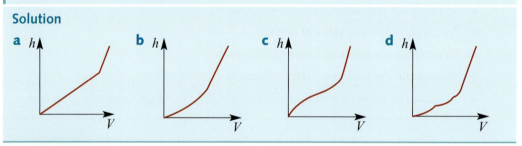

Water is being poured steadily into each of these vessels.

Draw a graph that shows the relationship between the height of the water (h) and the volume (V) that has been poured in.

Solution

(graphs a, b, c, d showing h vs V)

Example 2

A particle travels in a straight line.

The graph shows the distance, D metres, of the particle from a fixed point O over a period of 20 minutes.

Describe the motion of the particle.

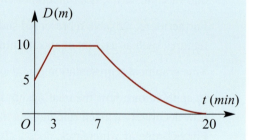

Solution

The particle is initially 5 m from O. It travels away from O for 3 minutes at a constant speed of $\dfrac{5}{3}$ m/min. It then remains stationary at a distance of 10 m from O for 4 minutes, before returning to O at a speed which is gradually decreasing so that it comes to rest at O at time $t = 20$ minutes.

By examining the graph representing a function, it can be
determined whether the rate of change is positive, negative
or neither.

Consider the graph of a function $y = f(x)$.

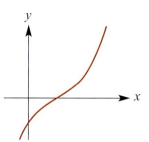

If the graph shows that y is increasing as x increases, then we
can say that the **rate of change** of y with respect to x is **positive**.
(The graph 'slopes upwards'.)

If the graph shows that y is decreasing as x increases, then we
can say that the **rate of change** of y with respect to x is **negative**.
(The graph 'slopes downwards'.)

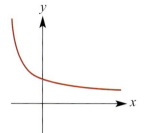

If y remains the same value as x changes, the corresponding graph
is a horizontal line, and we say that the rate of change of y with
respect to x is **zero**.

All of this is consistent with the gradient (rate of change) of a
linear function, which was discussed in Chapter 2.

Example 3

For the graph shown on the right for $x \in [-5, 2]$,
use interval notation to describe the set of values
of x for which:

a the rate of change of y with respect to x is
negative

b the rate of change of y with respect to x is
positive.

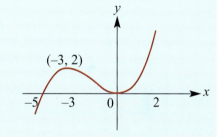

Solution

a The rate of change of y with respect to x is negative for $x \in (-3, 0)$.

b The rate of change of y with respect to x is positive for $x \in [-5, -3) \cup (0, 2]$.

Section summary

Consider the graph of a function with rule $y = f(x)$.

- If the graph shows that y is increasing as x increases over some interval, then the
  rate of change of y with respect to x is **positive** for that interval.
- If the graph shows that y is decreasing as x increases over some interval, then the
  rate of change of y with respect to x is **negative** for that interval.
- If y remains the same value as x changes, the corresponding graph is a horizontal line
  and the rate of change of y with respect to x is **zero**.

Exercise 16A

1 Water is being poured steadily into these vessels:

a   b   c   d

For each of the vessels, draw a graph of the height, h, of water in the vessel and the volume, V, that has been poured in. Label the horizontal axis V and the vertical axis h.

2 A particle travels in a straight line. The graph shows the distance, D metres, of the particle from a fixed point O on the line over a period of 14 minutes.
Describe the motion of the particle.

For Questions 3–6 there may be more than one correct answer. Your written explanations are an important part of the exercise.

3 The manager of a theatre wishes to know what effect changing the price of admission will have on the profit she makes.

  a Which one of the following graphs would show the effect of change?

  b Explain your choice, including comments on scales and axes and what the point of intersection of the axes represents.

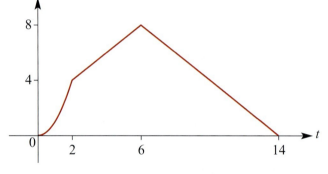

4 Sketch a graph to show how the height of a person might vary with age.

5 A motorist starts a journey at the point marked *A* on a country road, drives 2 km along the route shown, and stops at the point marked *B*. He is able to drive at 100 km/h, but must slow down at corners.

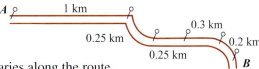

  a Explain briefly how the car's speed varies along the route.
  b Sketch a graph showing how the car's speed varies along the route. (Label the vertical axis *car's speed* and the horizontal axis *distance from A*.)

6 An athlete is a competitor in a 10 000 m race. Below are some graphs which could show the relationship between the speed of the runner and the distance covered.

  a Explain the meaning of each graph in words.
  b Which graph is the most realistic for a winning athlete?

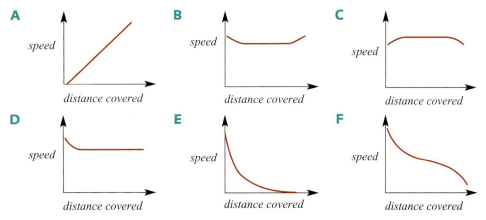

If you do not think any of these graphs are realistic, draw your own and explain it fully.

7 A sprinter covers 100 metres at a constant speed of 10 m/s. Sketch:

  a the distance–time graph   **b** the speed–time graph

8 For the vessel shown, sketch a reasonable curve for the height, *h*, of the water in the vessel as a function of the volume, *V*, of water in the vessel.

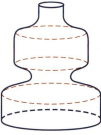

9 The graph relating the distance a car travels to the time taken is a straight line as shown. The graph shows that the car is

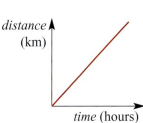

  A speeding up   **B** slowing down
  C travelling uphill   **D** travelling at a constant speed
  E stationary

10 Which one of these graphs best represents the rate of increase in the cost of living slowing down?

A cost of living
B cost of living
C cost of living
D cost of living

11 For the graph shown on the right for $x \in [-7, 3]$, use interval notation to describe the set of values of x for which:

a the rate of change of y with respect to x is negative

b the rate of change of y with respect to x is positive.

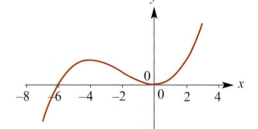

12 For the graph shown on the right for $x \in [-5, 2]$, use interval notation to describe the set of values of x for which:

a the rate of change of y with respect to x is positive

b the rate of change of y with respect to x is negative.

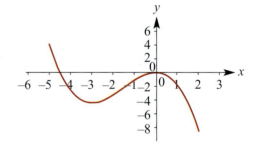

16B Constant rate of change

Any function that is linear will have a **constant rate of change**. That rate of change is simply the gradient of the graph and, given appropriate information, the rate can be calculated from the graph of the function or simply read from the rule of the function if it is stated.

Example 4

A car travels from Copahunga to Charlegum, which is a distance of 150 km, in 2 hours (120 minutes). Assuming the car travels at a constant speed, draw a distance–time graph and calculate the speed.

Solution

We denote the distance function by D. The graph of $y = D(t)$ is shown.

The rule of the function may be written:

$$D(t) = \frac{150}{120}t = \frac{5}{4}t$$

Note that

$$\frac{XY}{YO} = \frac{BA}{AO} = \frac{5}{4}$$

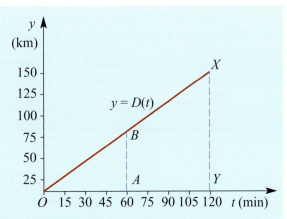

The gradient of the graph gives the speed in kilometres per minute. Therefore, the speed of the car is $\frac{5}{4}$ kilometres per minute.

This speed may be expressed in kilometres per hour (km/h):

$$\text{Speed} = \frac{5}{4} \times 60 = 75 \text{ km/h}$$

Example 5

Three cars are driven over a 2-kilometre straight track. They are all to go from point A to point B. Each car travels with constant speed. It is not a race as:

- the speed of car Y is twice that of car X
- the speed of car Z is half that of car X.

Illustrate this situation with a distance–time graph. Assume that car X travels at 1 km/min.

Solution

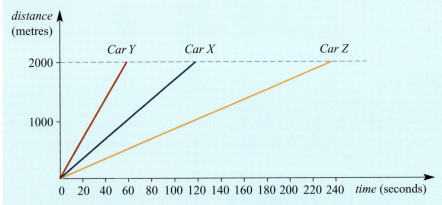

Note: The gradient of the graph for car X is $\dfrac{2000}{120} = 16\tfrac{2}{3}$

The gradient of the graph for car Y is $\dfrac{2000}{60} = 33\tfrac{1}{3}$

The gradient of the graph for car Z is $\dfrac{2000}{240} = 8\tfrac{1}{3}$

An object whose motion can be described by a linear distance–time graph is travelling at a constant speed equal to the gradient of the linear graph.

There are many other examples, as well as motion at a constant speed, in which a real-life situation is usefully modelled by a straight-line graph in such a way that the gradient of the graph is meaningful.

In all these situations the gradient of the straight-line graph represents a **rate**.

For example:

- **Petrol consumption of a car** A straight-line graph has been used as a model, and its gradient represents the rate of consumption of petrol, which is measured in litres per kilometre. Such a model makes fairly large assumptions. What are they?

- **Exchange rates for currencies** The gradient of the graph gives the exchange rate of dollars to yen.

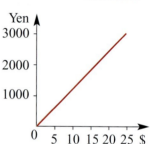

Section summary

A linear function $f(x) = mx + c$ has a constant rate of change, m.

Examples include an object travelling with constant speed and currency exchange rates.

Exercise 16B

Example 4 **1** A car travels from Bombay to Pune, a distance of 200 km, at a constant speed. The journey takes 150 minutes. Draw a distance–time graph and calculate the speed.

Example 5 **2** Two cars are driven in a straight line for 5 kilometres. They both go from point A to point B and start at the same time. (They are actually driving parallel to each other.) Each car travels with constant speed. The speed of car Y is twice that of car X, and the speed of car X is 40 km/h. Illustrate this with a distance–time graph.

3 The exchange rate for the Australian dollar in terms of the American dollar was A$1 = US$0.75.
Draw a straight-line graph that illustrates this relationship. The axes should be as shown.

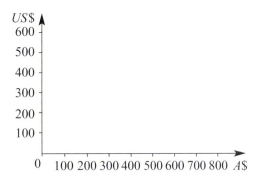

4 Find the speed for each of the following (assume constant speed):
  a distance travelled 120 km, time taken 2 hours
  b distance travelled 60 m, time taken 20 seconds
  c distance travelled 8000 m, time taken 20 minutes
  d distance travelled 200 km, time taken 5 hours 40 minutes
  e distance travelled 6542 m, time taken 5 minutes 20 seconds

5 Find the rate of flow from the following taps in litres per minute:
  a a tap which fills a 40-litre drum in 5 minutes
  b a tap which fills a 600-litre tank in 12 minutes
  c a tap which takes 17 minutes to fill a 200-litre tank
  d a tap which takes 17 minutes 20 seconds to fill a 180-litre tank

6 Water comes out of a tap at the rate of 15 litres per minute.
  a Copy and complete this table showing the amount which has come out at time t:

Time in minutes, t	0	0.5	1	1.5	2	3	4	5
Amount in litres, A	0							

  b Draw a graph from the table.

7 A worker is paid $200 for 13 hours work. What is their rate of pay per hour?

8 An aircraft travelling at a constant speed took 24 seconds to travel 5000 metres. What was the speed of the plane in metres per second?

9 A spherical balloon is blown up so that its volume is increasing by 8 cm³ every second. Sketch a graph to show how the volume of the balloon changes with time.

10 Two cars start together and travel with constant speed over a 1-kilometre straight track. Car 1 has speed 60 km/h, and car 2 travels at three-quarters of this speed. Illustrate this situation with distance–time graphs for both cars on the one set of axes.

16C Average rate of change

Skillsheet Many moving objects do not travel with constant speed. For example, the speedometer of a car being driven in city traffic rarely stays still for long.

Similarly, not all functions are linear, and so not all functions have a constant rate of change. For a function that is non-linear, the rate of change of the function varies, and may in fact be different for every different point on the graph of the function.

▶ Average speed

We will use a distance–time graph to illustrate the idea of average speed.

The graph below shows the motion of two cars both travelling in a straight line away from a fixed point O, where d is the distance travelled (in metres) at time t (in seconds).

The straight-line graph through D shows a constant speed of 60 km/h. By comparison, the graph through points A, B and C shows a motorist travelling at varying speeds. The motorist accelerates to reach 60 km/h at A before slowing for the lights at B, where there is a 10-second standstill. There is then another short burst of speed before another standstill at C.

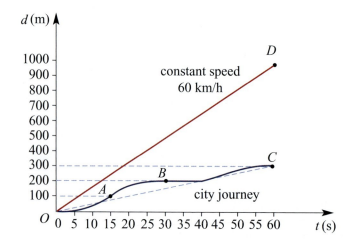

Although we do not know the actual speed of the car travelling in the city at any particular time (other than when it is stationary), we can work out the average speed of the car over the full 60 seconds.

The average speed is given by

$$\frac{\text{distance travelled}}{\text{time taken}} = \frac{300}{60}$$

which gives an average speed of 5 metres per second. The average speed is the gradient of the line OC.

The average speed may also be calculated for any given time interval. For example, for the time interval from $t = 15$ to $t = 30$, the average speed is given by the gradient of the line joining points A and B. This is $\dfrac{100}{15} = 6\tfrac{2}{3}$ metres per second.

In general:

$$\text{average speed} = \frac{\text{total distance travelled}}{\text{total time taken}}$$

So the average speed of an object for $a \leq t \leq b$ is given by the gradient of the line passing through points P and Q.

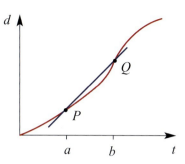

Example 6

The graph of distance travelled (metres) against time (seconds) for the motion of an object is shown.

Find the average speed of the object in m/s over the interval from $t = 2$ to $t = 12$.

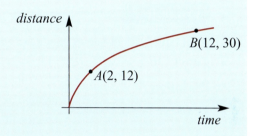

Solution

$$\begin{aligned}\text{Average speed} &= \frac{\text{total distance travelled}}{\text{total time taken}} \\ &= \frac{30 - 12}{12 - 2} \\ &= \frac{18}{10} \\ &= 1.8 \text{ m/s}\end{aligned}$$

▶ Average rate of change for a function

The line which passes through two points on a curve is called a **secant**.

The line segment joining two points on a curve is called a **chord**.

Average rate of change

For any function $y = f(x)$, the **average rate of change** of y with respect to x over the interval $[a, b]$ is the gradient of the line through $A(a, f(a))$ and $B(b, f(b))$ (secant AB).

That is,

$$\text{average rate of change} = \frac{f(b) - f(a)}{b - a}$$

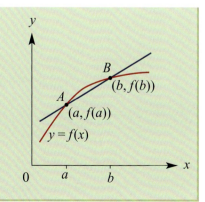

For example, for the function with the graph shown, the average rate of change of y with respect to x over the interval [1, 2] is given by the gradient of the secant PQ:

$$\text{gradient} = \frac{4-1}{2-1} = 3$$

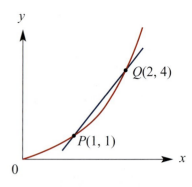

Example 7

Find the average rate of change of the function with rule $f(x) = x^2 - 2x + 5$ as x changes from 1 to 5.

Solution

$$\text{Average rate of change} = \frac{\text{change in } y}{\text{change in } x}$$

$f(1) = (1)^2 - 2(1) + 5 = 4$

$f(5) = (5)^2 - 2(5) + 5 = 20$

$$\text{Average rate of change} = \frac{20 - 4}{5 - 1}$$

$$= 4$$

Example 8

Find the average rate of change of the function depicted in the graph for the interval $[-2, 5]$.

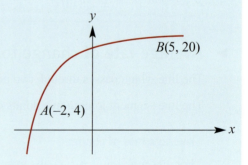

Solution

Average rate of change for the interval $[-2, 5]$

$$= \frac{20 - 4}{5 - (-2)}$$

$$= \frac{16}{7}$$

Example 9

The air temperature, $T\,°C$, at a weather station on a particular evening is modelled by the equation $T = \dfrac{600}{t^2 + 2t + 30}$, where t is the time in hours after 6 p.m.

a Find the temperature at 6 p.m.
b Find the temperature at midnight.
c Find the average rate of change of the air temperature from 6 p.m. until midnight.

Solution

a At 6 p.m., $t = 0$. Hence
$$T = \dfrac{600}{(0)^2 + 2(0) + 30} = 20°C$$

b At midnight, $t = 6$. Hence
$$T = \dfrac{600}{(6)^2 + 2(6) + 30} = \dfrac{100}{13} = 7.69°C \quad \text{(correct to two decimal places)}$$

c Average rate of change of temperature $= \dfrac{\tfrac{100}{13} - 20}{6 - 0} = -\dfrac{80}{39} = -2.05°C$ per hour

Section summary

- The line which passes through two points on a curve is called a **secant**.
- The line segment joining two points on a curve is called a **chord**.
- For a function $y = f(x)$, the **average rate of change** of y with respect to x over the interval $[a, b]$ is the gradient of the secant line through $(a, f(a))$ and $(b, f(b))$. That is,

$$\text{average rate of change} = \dfrac{f(b) - f(a)}{b - a}$$

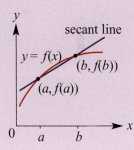

Exercise 16C

Example 6

1 The graph of distance travelled (metres) against time (seconds) for the motion of an object is shown. Find the average speed of the object in m/s over the interval from $t = 3$ to $t = 8$.

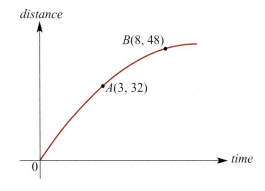

Example 7 2 For each function, find the average rate of change over the stated interval:
  a $f(x) = 2x + 5$, $x \in [0, 3]$
  b $f(x) = 3x^2 + 4x - 2$, $x \in [-1, 2]$
  c $f(x) = \dfrac{2}{(x-3)} + 4$, $x \in [4, 7]$
  d $f(x) = \sqrt{5-x}$, $x \in [0, 4]$

Example 8 3 Find the average rate of change of y with respect to x from point A to point B for each of the following graphs:

  a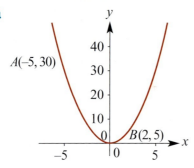
  b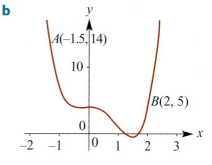
  c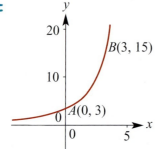
  d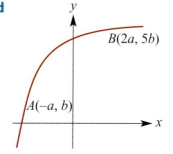

4 The distance (in metres) from a point O of an object t seconds after it starts to move in a straight line is given by the function $S(t) = t^3 + t^2 - 2t + 2$, $t \geq 0$. Find the average rate of change with respect to time of the distance of the object from O:
  a in the first 2 seconds
  b in the next 2 seconds.

5 A person invests $2000 dollars, which increases in value by 7% per year for three years.
  a Calculate the value of the investment after three years.
  b Calculate the average rate of change in the value of the investment over that time.

Example 9 6 The depth, d cm, of water in a bath tub t minutes after the tap is turned on is modelled by the function $d(t) = \dfrac{-300}{(t+6)} + 50$, $t \geq 0$. Find the average rate of change of the depth of the water with respect to time over the first 10 minutes after the tap is turned on.

7 Using the information in the graph on the right, the average speed from $t = 0$ to $t = 3$ is
  A 2 m/s
  B 1 m/s
  C $\dfrac{2}{3}$ m/s
  D $1\tfrac{1}{2}$ m/s

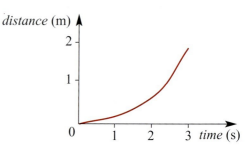

16D Instantaneous rate of change

In the previous section, we investigated the average rate of change of a function over a stated interval. We saw that, in general (except for linear functions), the average rate of change of a function over different intervals in the domain of the function is not constant.

In this section, we investigate the idea of instantaneous rate of change.

▶ Tangent line at a point

We talk about the idea of the tangent to a curve at a point informally here. It is a line which has 'the same slope' as the graph at this point. Of course, we don't know exactly what this means, but if we think of a very, very, ..., very small section of the curve around the point, we can consider it to be a line segment which can be extended out to a straight line. This straight line is what we call the 'tangent line' to the curve at the point.

We can illustrate this idea with a specific example. Part of the graph of $y = x^2$ is shown below. We will find the tangent line at the point $P(1, 1)$.

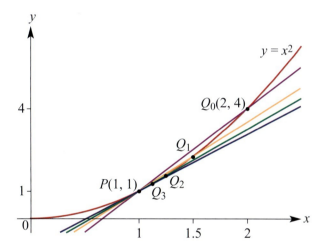

We start with the secant PQ_0 passing through $P(1, 1)$ and $Q_0(2, 4)$.

The gradient of PQ_0 is $\dfrac{4-1}{2-1} = 3$, and so the equation of the secant PQ_0 is $y = 3x - 2$.

The points $Q_1, Q_2, Q_3, \ldots, Q_n, \ldots$ on the curve $y = x^2$ are chosen so that they get closer and closer to P in the following way:

- The x-coordinate of Q_1 is $\dfrac{1}{2}(1 + 2) = \dfrac{3}{2}$.
- The x-coordinate of Q_2 is $\dfrac{1}{2}\left(1 + \dfrac{3}{2}\right) = \dfrac{5}{4}$.
- The x-coordinate of Q_3 is $\dfrac{1}{2}\left(1 + \dfrac{5}{4}\right) = \dfrac{9}{8}$.

We now look at the sequence of secants $PQ_0, PQ_1, PQ_2, PQ_3, \ldots, PQ_n, \ldots$. The following table shows the gradient and the equation for each secant.

Secants of the curve $y = x^2$ through the point $P(1, 1)$

Step	Endpoint	Secant	Gradient	Equation of secant
0	$Q_0(2, 4)$	PQ_0	3	$y = 3x - 2$
1	$Q_1(\frac{3}{2}, \frac{9}{4})$	PQ_1	$\frac{5}{2}$	$y = \frac{5}{2}x - \frac{3}{2}$
2	$Q_2(\frac{5}{4}, \frac{25}{16})$	PQ_2	$\frac{9}{4}$	$y = \frac{9}{4}x - \frac{5}{4}$
3	$Q_3(\frac{9}{8}, \frac{81}{64})$	PQ_3	$\frac{17}{8}$	$y = \frac{17}{8}x - \frac{9}{8}$
n	$Q_n(1 + 2^{-n}, (1 + 2^{-n})^2)$	PQ_n	$2 + 2^{-n}$	$y = (2 + 2^{-n})x - (1 + 2^{-n})$

The sequence of gradients is $3, \frac{5}{2}, \frac{9}{4}, \frac{17}{8}, \ldots, 2 + \frac{1}{2^n}, \ldots$

We can see that the gradients get closer and closer to 2. This is particularly evident from the general gradient, $2 + \frac{1}{2^n}$, since as $n \to \infty$, $\frac{1}{2^n} \to 0$.

We can also see that the secants get closer and closer to the line with equation $y = 2x - 1$. This line is the **tangent line** at the point P, and the gradient of the tangent line is the **instantaneous rate of change** of y with respect to x at the point P. We define these two concepts in Chapters 17 and 18.

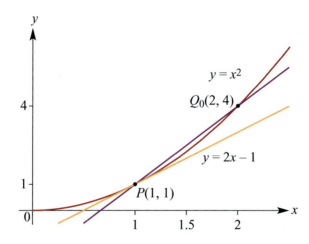

In the examples and exercises in this chapter, we only require approximations to the instantaneous rate of change.

Example 10

Estimate the instantaneous rate of change of y with respect to x at the point $P(2, 9)$ on the curve $y = x^3 + 1$ by considering the secant PQ, where $Q = (2.01, (2.01)^3 + 1)$.

Solution

Gradient of $PQ = \dfrac{(2.01)^3 + 1 - 9}{2.01 - 2} = 12.0601$

Note: An even better approximation can be made by choosing the points $P(2, 9)$ and $Q(2.001, (2.001)^3 + 1)$. Using the approach taken for $y = x^2$ in the discussion above, we would find that the instantaneous rate of change for this example is 12.

Example 11

The graph represents the area covered by a spreading plant. Area is measured in square centimetres and time in weeks.

a Find the gradient of the secant PQ.

b The point Q' has coordinates $(3, 330)$. Find the average rate of change of area with respect to time for the interval $[2, 3]$, and hence estimate the instantaneous rate of change of the area of the plant at $t = 2$.

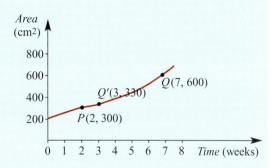

Solution

a Gradient of $PQ = \dfrac{600 - 300}{7 - 2}$

$= \dfrac{300}{5}$

$= 60$

The average rate of change of area from $t = 2$ to $t = 7$ is 60 cm² per week.

b Gradient of $PQ' = \dfrac{330 - 300}{1} = 30$

∴ Gradient at P is approximately 30.

The instantaneous rate of change of the area of the plant with respect to time when $t = 2$ is approximately 30 cm² per week.

Example 12

Consider the curve $y = 2^x$.

a Using the secant through the points where $x = 3$ and $x = 3.1$, estimate the instantaneous rate of change of y with respect to x at the point where $x = 3$.

b Repeat for the points where $x = 3$ and $x = 3.001$.

Solution

a When $x = 3$, $y = 8$ and when $x = 3.1$, $y = 8.5742$ (correct to four decimal places).
The gradient of the line through $(3, 8)$ and $(3.1, 8.5742)$ is 5.7419.
Thus an estimate for the instantaneous rate of change of $y = 2^x$ at $x = 3$ is 5.742.

b When $x = 3.001$, $y = 8.005547$.
The gradient of the line through $(3, 8)$ and $(3.001, 8.005547)$ is 5.547.

Note: The true instantaneous rate of change of y with respect to x at $x = 3$ is 5.5452 (correct to four decimal places).

▶ Using the graph window of your calculator

The graph of $y = 0.5x^3 - 2x + 1$ is shown. We will investigate the gradient at the point $(0, 1)$.

First find the gradient of the secant RS, where
$R = (-0.75, 2.2891)$ and $S = (0.25, 0.5078)$:

gradient of $RS = -1.7813$

(The coordinates of R and S are given to four decimal places.)

Now consider another secant $R_1 S$, where
$R_1 = (-0.25, 1.4922)$ and $S = (0.25, 0.5078)$:

gradient of $R_1 S = -1.9688$

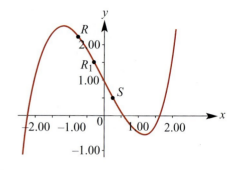

Using a calculator, zoom in on the graph near $x = 0$. As you zoom further in, this section of the curve appears increasingly linear. By assuming that this section of the curve is in fact linear and finding its gradient, we can approximate the gradient of the curve at $x = 0$.

This diagram shows a 'zoomed in' section of the graph around the point $(0, 1)$.

Consider the secant AB where $A = (-0.1, 1.1995)$ and $B = (0.1, 0.8005)$. The gradient of this line is approximately -2.

Therefore we make the approximation that the gradient of the curve $y = 0.5x^3 - 2x + 1$ at the point $(0, 1)$ is -2.

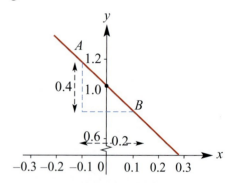

Section summary

For a function $y = f(x)$, the **instantaneous rate of change** of y with respect to x at the point $(a, f(a))$ is the gradient of the tangent line to the graph of $y = f(x)$ at the point $(a, f(a))$.

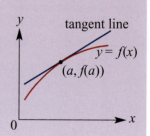

Exercise 16D

Example 10

1 By considering the secant through the points where $x = 1.2$ and $x = 1.3$, estimate the instantaneous rate of change of y with respect to x at the point on the curve $y = x^3 + x^2$ where $x = 1.3$.

2 Cardiac output is an important factor in athletic endurance. The graph shows a stress-test graph of cardiac output (measured in litres/min of blood) versus workload (measured in kg m/min).

a Estimate the average rate of change of cardiac output with respect to workload as the workload increases from 0 to 1200 kg m/min.

b Estimate the instantaneous rate of change of cardiac output with respect to workload at the point where the workload is 450 kg m/min.

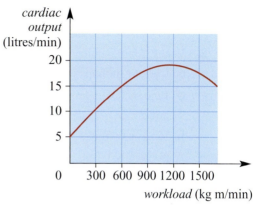

3 Let $y = 10^x$.

a Find the average rate at which y changes with respect to x over each of the following intervals:

  i $[0, 1]$ ii $[0, 0.5]$ iii $[0, 0.1]$

b Estimate the instantaneous rate of change of y with respect to x when $x = 0$.

4 Temperature ($T\,°C$) varies with time (t hours) over a 24-hour period, as illustrated in the graph.

a Estimate the maximum temperature and the time at which this occurs.

b The temperature rise between 10:00 and 14:00 is approximately linear. Estimate the rate at which the temperature is increasing in this period.

c Estimate the instantaneous rate of change of temperature at $t = 20$.

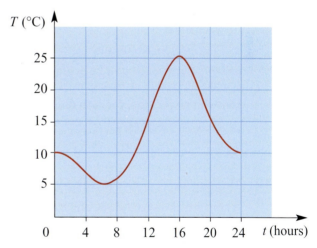

5 By considering the secant through the points at which $x = 1.2$ and $x = 1.4$, estimate the instantaneous rate of change of y with respect to x of the curve $y = \dfrac{1}{x}$ at $x = 1.2$.

6 Draw the graph of $y = \sqrt{16 - x^2}$, $-4 \leq x \leq 4$. Use an appropriate technique to find an estimate of the instantaneous rate of change of y with respect to x at the points:

  a $x = 0$ b $x = 2$ c $x = 3$

7 It is known that the straight line $y = 4x - 4$ touches the curve $y = x^2$ at the point $(2, 4)$. Sketch the graphs of both of these functions on the one set of axes.
Find the instantaneous rate of change of y with respect to x at the point at $(2, 4)$ on the curve $y = x^2$.

8 Water is being collected in a water tank. The volume, V cubic metres, of water in the tank after t minutes is given by $V = 3t^2 + 4t + 2$.
  a Find the average rate of change of volume with respect to time between times $t = 1$ and $t = 3$.
  b Find an estimate for the instantaneous rate of change of volume with respect to time at $t = 1$.

9 A population of bacteria is growing. The population, P million, after time t minutes is given by $P = 3 \times 2^t$.
  a Find the average rate of change of population between times $t = 2$ and $t = 4$.
  b Find an estimate for the instantaneous rate of change of population with respect to time at $t = 2$.

10 Water is flowing out of a water tank. The volume, V cubic metres, of water in the tank after t minutes is given by $V = 5 \times 10^5 - 10^2 \times 2^t$, $0 \leq t \leq 12$.
  a Find the average rate of change of volume with respect to time between times $t = 0$ and $t = 5$.
  b Find an estimate for the instantaneous rate of change of volume with respect to time when $t = 6$.
  c Find an estimate for the rate of change of volume when $t = 12$.

11 Use the technique of Examples 10 and 12 to estimate the instantaneous rate of change of y with respect to x for each of the following at the stated point:
  a $y = x^3 + 2x^2$, $(1, 3)$
  b $y = 2x^3 + 3x$, $(1, 5)$
  c $y = -x^3 + 3x^2 + 2x$, $(2, 8)$
  d $y = 2x^3 - 3x^2 - x + 2$, $(3, 26)$

12 The volume, V, of a cube with edge length x is given by $V = x^3$.
  a Find the average rate at which the volume of the cube changes with respect to x, as x increases from $x = 2$ to $x = 4$.
  b Find an estimate for the instantaneous rate at which V changes with respect to x when $x = 2$.

13 Let $y = 2x^2 - 1$.
  a Find the average rate at which y changes with respect to x over the interval $[1, 4]$.
  b Find an estimate for the instantaneous rate at which y changes with respect to x when $x = 1$.

14 Let $y = \sin x$.

   a Find the average rate at which y changes with respect to x over each of the following intervals:

     i $\left[0, \dfrac{\pi}{2}\right]$ **ii** $\left[0, \dfrac{\pi}{4}\right]$ **iii** $[0, 0.5]$ **iv** $[0, 0.1]$

   b Estimate the instantaneous rate of change of y with respect to x when $x = 0$.

16E Position and average velocity

One of the key applications of rates of change is in the study of the motion of a particle.

In this section, we consider motion in a straight line. The study of motion in a straight line is continued in Chapter 18.

▶ Position

The **position** of a particle is a specification of its location relative to a reference point.

Consider motion on a straight line with reference point O.

We say that position to the right of O is positive and to the left of O is negative.

A particle is moving along the straight line. Let x metres denote its position relative to O at time t (where time is measured in seconds).

- At time $t = 0$, $x = 0$.
- At time $t = 5$, $x = 6.25$.
- At time $t = 8$, $x = -8.96$.

At $t = 0$, the particle starts from rest and moves to the right. At $t = 5$, the particle stops and moves back in the opposite direction. Its position–time graph is shown below.

Note that from $t = 0$ until $t = 7.1$, the position is positive, i.e. the particle is to the right of O.

For $t > 7.1$, the position is negative, i.e. the particle is to the left of O.

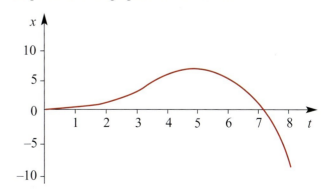

Average velocity

The average velocity of a particle is the average rate of change in position with respect to time:

$$\text{average velocity} = \frac{\text{change in position}}{\text{time elapsed}}$$

For the moving particle we have been considering:

- At time $t = 0$, $x = 0$.
- At time $t = 5$, $x = 6.25$.
- At time $t = 8$, $x = -8.96$.

Therefore the particle's average velocity over the time interval $0 \leq t \leq 5$ is given by

$$\text{average velocity} = \frac{6.25}{5}$$
$$= 1.25 \text{ metres per second (m/s)}$$

and over the time interval $5 \leq t \leq 8$,

$$\text{average velocity} = \frac{-8.96 - 6.25}{3}$$
$$= -5.07 \text{ metres per second (m/s)}$$

Example 13

Let $s(t) = 6t - t^2$ be the position function of a particle moving in a straight line, where t is in seconds and s is in metres.

a Find the average velocity for the time interval $[0, 1]$.
b Find the average velocity for the time interval $[6, 8]$.

Solution

a $s(0) = 0$ and $s(1) = 6 - 1^2 = 5$.
Hence, change in position $= 5$ and

$$\text{average velocity} = \text{average rate of change} = \frac{5}{1} = 5$$

The average velocity for $[0, 1]$ is 5 m/s.

b $s(6) = 0$ and $s(8) = 6 \times 8 - 8^2 = -16$.
Hence, change in position $= -16$ and

$$\text{average velocity} = \text{average rate of change} = \frac{-16}{8-6} = -8$$

The average velocity for $[6, 8]$ is -8 m/s.

▶ Velocity–time graphs

In the next two examples we look at the velocity–time graph obtained from a position–time graph. Each of the position–time graphs is the graph of a piecewise-defined function where each of the components is linear.

Example 14

The graph shown is the position–time graph for the bicycle trip of a boy who lives on a long straight road. The road runs north–south, and north is chosen to be the positive direction.

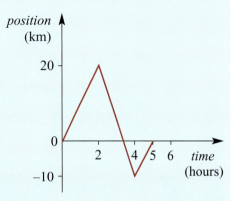

a Describe his trip.
b Draw the corresponding velocity–time graph.

Solution

a ■ The boy heads north for 2 hours.
  His velocity for this period is $\dfrac{20 - 0}{2} = 10$ km/h.

  ■ He then turns and rides south for 2 hours.
  His velocity for this period is $\dfrac{-10 - 20}{2} = -15$ km/h.

  ■ He turns and rides north until he reaches home.
  His velocity for this period is $\dfrac{0 - (-10)}{1} = 10$ km/h.

b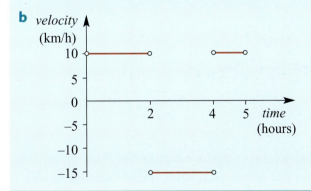

Example 15

A particle is moving in a straight line. It was initially at rest at a point O. It moves to the right of O with a constant velocity and reaches a point A, 15 metres from O, after 5 seconds. It then returns to O. The return trip takes 10 seconds. It stops at O.

On the one set of axes draw the position–time graph and the velocity–time graph for the motion.

Solution

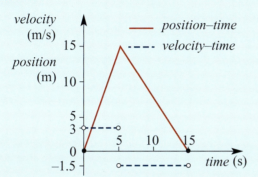

Explanation

The gradient of the position–time graph for $0 < t < 5$ is 3.

The gradient for $5 < t < 15$ is -1.5.

The gradient of the position–time graph determines the velocity–time graph.

▶ Instantaneous velocity

Instantaneous velocity is the instantaneous rate of change in position with respect to time. It can be thought of as the gradient of the tangent to the position–time graph at a particular point. If we know an object's instantaneous velocity at every moment in time, we can sketch a velocity–time graph for an object moving with non-constant velocity.

In the graph shown below, the position–time graph is the same as the one from the start of this section.

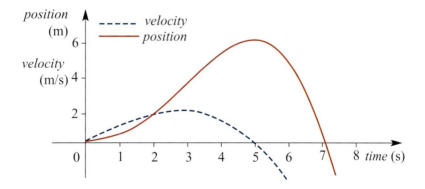

This graph illustrates the relationship between position and velocity. The vertical axis is in both metres per second for velocity and metres for position. In the following, we use velocity to mean instantaneous velocity.

We make the following observations from the graph:

- For $0 < t < 5$, the velocity is positive: the particle is travelling from left to right.
- For $t > 5$, the velocity is negative: the particle is travelling from right to left.
- For $t = 5$, the velocity is zero: the particle is instantaneously at rest.

Example 16

The position of a particle moving in a straight line is given by the function $S(t) = t^3 - 6t^2$, $t \geq 0$. The graph of S against t is shown. The corresponding velocity–time graph is also shown. The function describing the velocity is $V(t) = 3t^2 - 12t$.

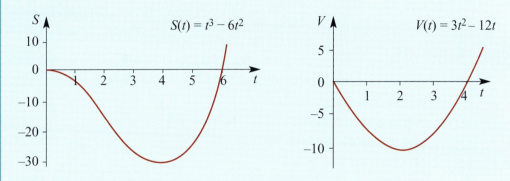

a Find the average velocity of the particle for the intervals:
  i $[3.5, 4.5]$ **ii** $[3.9, 4.1]$ **iii** $[3.99, 4.01]$
b From part a, what is the instantaneous velocity when $t = 4$?
c **i** For what values of t is the velocity positive?
  ii For what values of t is the velocity negative?

Solution

a **i** Average velocity $= \dfrac{S(4.5) - S(3.5)}{1} = \dfrac{-30.375 + 30.625}{1} = 0.25$

  ii Average velocity $= \dfrac{S(4.1) - S(3.9)}{0.2} = \dfrac{-31.939 + 31.941}{0.2} = 0.01$

  iii Average velocity $= \dfrac{S(4.01) - S(3.99)}{0.02} = \dfrac{-31.999399 + 31.999401}{0.02} = 0.0001$

b The results of part a suggest that the instantaneous velocity is zero when $t = 4$, and this is consistent with both graphs.

c **i** From the position–time graph it can be seen that the velocity is positive for $t > 4$.
  ii From the position–time graph it can be seen that the velocity is negative for $0 < t < 4$.

Section summary

- The **position** of a particle moving along a straight line is a specification of its location.
- The average velocity of a particle is the average rate of change in position with respect to time:

  $$\textbf{average velocity} = \dfrac{\text{change in position}}{\text{time elapsed}}$$

- Instantaneous velocity is the instantaneous rate of change in position with respect to time. It can be thought of as the gradient of the tangent to the position–time graph at a particular point.

Exercise 16E

1 Let $s(t) = 6t - 2t^3$ be the position function of a particle moving in a straight line, where t is in seconds and s is in metres.

   a Find the average velocity for the time interval $[0, 1]$.

   b Find the average velocity for the time interval $[0.8, 1]$.

2 The following is the position–time graph for a train travelling on a straight track. Position is measured from the door of the ticket office at Jimbara station.

   a What was the train's velocity over each of the following time intervals:

   i $[0, 2]$

   ii $[2, 5]$

   iii $[5, 8]$

   b Describe the train journey.

   c Draw a velocity–time graph for the train's motion for the interval $[0, 8]$.

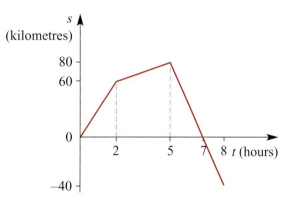

3 The motion of a particle moving in a straight line is described by the following information:

   - For the time period $(0, 2)$, velocity $= -3$.
   - For the time period $(2, 5)$, velocity $= 3$.
   - For the time period $(5, 7)$, velocity $= 4$.

   a Draw the velocity–time graph for the interval $[0, 7]$.

   b Draw the position–time graph for the interval $[0, 7]$.

4 A particle moves along a horizontal straight line. It starts from rest at a point O. The graph is the position–time graph for this motion.

   a At what time is the instantaneous velocity zero?

   b For which values of t is the instantaneous velocity positive?

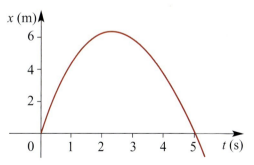

   c How far from O does the particle go to the right?

   d How long does it take to return to O?

   e Estimate the instantaneous velocity of the particle at $t = 1$.

Example 13 1 Let $s(t) = 6t - 2t^2$ be the position function of a particle moving in a straight line, where t is in seconds and s is in metres.

   a Find the average velocity for the time interval $[0, 1]$.

Example 14 2 The following is the position–time graph for a train travelling on a straight track. Position is measured from the door of the ticket office at Jimbara station.

   a What was the train's velocity over each of the following time intervals:

     i $[0, 2]$
     ii $[2, 5]$

   b Describe the train journey.

   c Draw a velocity–time graph.

  3 The motion of a particle moving in a straight line is described by the following information:

  - For the time period $(0, 2)$, velocity $= 3$.
  - For the time period $(2, 5)$, velocity $= 1$.
  - For the time period $(5, 7)$, velocity $= 4$.

   a Draw the velocity–time graph for the interval $[0, 7]$.

Example 15 4 A particle moves along a horizontal straight line. It starts from rest at a point O. The graph is the position–time graph for this motion.

   a At what time is the instantaneous velocity zero?

   b For which values of t is the instantaneous velocity positive?

   c How far from O does the particle go to the right?

   d How long does it take to return to O?

   e Estimate the instantaneous velocity of the particle at $t = 1$.

5 The table shows the distance, d metres, of a ball from its starting position at time t seconds after being thrown into the air.

t	0	1	2	3	4	5	6
d	0	25	40	45	40	25	0

Using the scales 2 cm = 1 second and 1 cm = 5 metres, draw the graph of d against t. From your graph find:

a when the ball returns to the starting point
b the average velocity of the ball from $t = 1$ to $t = 2$
c the average velocity of the ball from $t = 1$ to $t = 1.5$
d an estimate of the velocity of the ball when $t = 1$
e an estimate of the velocity of the ball when $t = 4$
f an estimate of the velocity of the ball when $t = 5$.

6 A stone is thrown vertically upwards from the edge of a platform which is 10 m above the ground. The position–time graph for the motion of the stone is shown. The motion of the stone is in a straight line and the reference point for position is taken as a point at ground level, directly below where the stone was thrown.

a From the graph estimate the instantaneous velocity with which the stone is thrown.
b What is the maximum height reached by the stone?
c At what time does the stone reach its maximum height?
d At what time does the stone hit the ground?
e From the graph estimate the instantaneous speed at which the stone hits the ground.

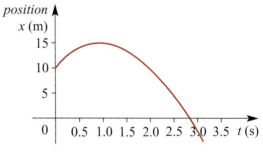

7 A particle is moving in a horizontal straight line. Position is measured from a point O. The particle starts at a point 20 m to the left of O. The position–time graph for the motion of the particle is as shown.

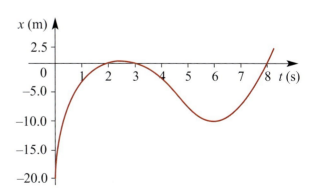

a At which times is the particle at O?
b For which values of t is the particle moving to the right?
c For which values of t is the particle stationary?

Chapter 16: Rates of change

Chapter summary

- Where a real-life situation is modelled by a straight-line graph, the gradient represents the rate of change of one quantity with respect to another.

- Average speed = $\dfrac{\text{total distance travelled}}{\text{total time taken}}$

- For a function $y = f(x)$, the **average rate of change** of y with respect to x over the interval $[a, b]$ is the gradient of the secant line through $(a, f(a))$ and $(b, f(b))$.

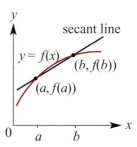

- For a function $y = f(x)$, the **instantaneous rate of change** of y with respect to x at the point $(a, f(a))$ is the gradient of the tangent line to the graph of $y = f(x)$ at the point $(a, f(a))$.

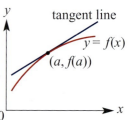

- The **position** of a particle moving along a straight line specifies its location relative to a reference point O.

- The **average velocity** of the particle is the average rate of change in position with respect to time over a given time interval.

- The **instantaneous velocity** is the instantaneous rate of change in position with respect to time at a given moment.

Technology-free questions

1 A liquid is poured at a constant rate into each of the containers shown below. For each container, draw a graph to show how the depth of the water varies with time.

  a

  b

  c

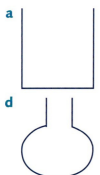

  d

  e

  f

2 a A car travels from New Delhi to Agra, a distance of 200 km, in 3 hours. Assuming the car travels at a constant speed, draw a distance–time graph and calculate this constant speed. For the distance–time graph, use minutes as the unit of time.

b A girl walks at a constant speed of 1.5 m/s for 20 seconds. Draw a distance–time graph to illustrate this.

c A car travels along a road for $6\frac{1}{2}$ hours. The trip can be described in three sections:

Section A Car travels at a constant speed of 40 km/h for 1 hour.
Section B Car travels at a constant speed of 80 km/h for $3\frac{1}{2}$ hours.
Section C Car travels at a constant speed of 90 km/h for 2 hours.

Draw a distance–time graph which illustrates this motion.

3 The surface area, s cm^2, of a cube is given by the formula $s = 6x^2$, where x cm is the length of each edge of the cube. Find the average rate at which the surface area changes with respect to x, as x increases from $x = 2$ to $x = 4$.

4 Let $y = x^3$. Find the average rate at which y changes with respect to x over each of the following intervals:

a [0, 1]   **b** [1, 3]

5 Let $s(t) = 4t - 6t^3$ be the position function of a particle moving in a straight line, where t is in seconds and s is in metres.

a Find the average velocity for the time interval [0, 1].
b Find the average velocity for the time interval [0.9, 1].
c Estimate the instantaneous velocity for $t = 1$.

Multiple-choice questions

1 A bushwalker walks 12 km in 2 hours, stops for 45 minutes and then walks a further 8 km in another 1.25 hours. The average walking speed of the bushwalker over the entire walk is

A 10 km/h   **B** 9 km/h   **C** 5 km/h   **D** 4 km/h   **E** 7.2 km/h

2 Postal workers sort 12 000 letters during the normal day shift of 8 hours and, with a reduced workforce during the 2 hours overtime shift, they sort a further 2500 letters. The average rate of letter sorting per hour is

A 1375 letters per hour   **B** 1450 letters per hour
C 1300 letters per hour   **D** 1400 letters per hour
E 1500 letters per hour

Questions 3 to 5 refer to the following information:

The graph shows the movement of a vehicle over a period of time. It represents the distance (*s*) from a fixed point at a given time (*t*).

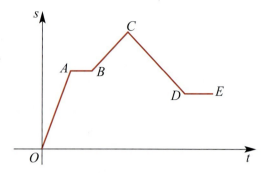

3 The line segment *OA* represents a stage of the movement during which the vehicle is
  A speeding up
  B slowing down
  C travelling north
  D travelling at a constant speed
  E stationary

4 The line segment *AB* represents a stage of the movement during which the vehicle is
  A speeding up
  B slowing down
  C travelling east
  D travelling at a constant speed greater than zero
  E stationary

5 The section(s) of the graph which represent(s) the vehicle when it is stationary is/are
  A at *O*
  B at *A* and *C*
  C between *C* and *D*
  D between *A* and *B* and between *D* and *E*
  E at no time

6 The average rate of change of the function $y = 3 \times 2^x$ over the interval [0, 2] is
  A 9   **B** 4.5   **C** 12   **D** 6   **E** 5

7 The population of trout in a trout pond is growing. If the population, *P*, after *t* weeks is given by $P = 10 \times 1.1^t$, the average rate of growth of the population during the 5th week is closest to
  A 16 trout per week
  B 15 trout per week
  C 1.5 trout per week
  D 4 trout per week
  E 15.35 trout per week

8 Given $f(x) = 2x^3 + 3x$, the average rate of change of $f(x)$ with respect to *x* for the interval [−2, 2] is
  A 0   **B** −22   **C** −11   **D** 22   **E** 11

Extended-response questions

1 The resistance of a copper wire is measured at various temperatures with the following results:

Temperature (°C)	10	20	30	40	50	60
Resistance (ohms)	23.4	23.9	24.4	24.9	25.5	26.0

  a Plot the data to see whether the resistance rises approximately linearly with temperature.

  b If it does, find the rate of increase in ohms per degree.

2 A rock is allowed to fall from the top of a high cliff. It falls y metres in t seconds, where $y = 4.9t^2$.

  a Find the average speed of the rock between:

   i $t = 0$ and $t = 2$ **ii** $t = 2$ and $t = 4$

  b **i** How far has the rock fallen between $t = 4 - h$ and $t = 4$?

   ii What is the average speed between $t = 4 - h$ and $t = 4$?

   iii Find the average speed when $h = 0.2, 0.1, 0.05, 0.01, 0.001$.

3 A vending machine in a bus terminus contains cans of soft drink. On a typical day:

  ■ the machine starts one-quarter full
  ■ no drinks are sold between 1 a.m. and 6 a.m.
  ■ the machine is filled at 2 p.m.

  Sketch a graph to show how the number of cans in the machine may vary from 6 a.m. until midnight.

4 a $P(a, a^2)$ and $Q(b, b^2)$ are two points on the curve with equation $y = x^2$.
  Find the gradient of the line joining the points. (Answer in terms of a and b.)

  b Use this result to find the gradient of the line for points with $a = 1$ and $b = 2$.

  c Use this result to find the gradient of the line if $a = 2$ and $b = 2.01$.

5 The figure shows part of the curve with equation $y = \dfrac{4}{x}$ and P is the point at which $x = 2$.

  a A_1 and A_2 are points on the curve whose x-coordinates are 1.5 and 2.5 respectively. Use your calculator to find their y-coordinates and hence find the gradient of $A_1 A_2$.

  b Repeat for B_1 and B_2 whose x-coordinates are 1.9 and 2.1 respectively.

  c Repeat for C_1 and C_2 whose x-coordinates are 1.99 and 2.01 respectively.

  d Repeat for D_1 and D_2 whose x-coordinates are 1.999 and 2.001 respectively.

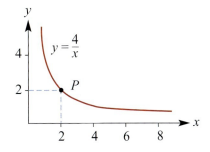

6 These graphs compare the weights of two people over the first 18 years of their lives.

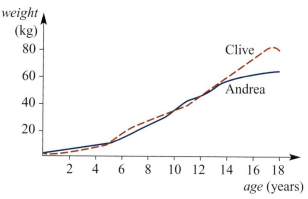

  a What was the average rate of change of weight with respect to time for Andrea between the ages of 0 and 18?

  b What was the average rate of change of weight with respect to time for Clive between the ages of 0 and 18?

  c During which periods did Andrea weigh more than Clive?

  d During which periods of time was Clive growing more rapidly than Andrea?

7 The graph below shows exponential growth in the size of the population of Acubaland. In exponential growth, the rate of increase of the population at any time is proportional to the size of the population at that time.

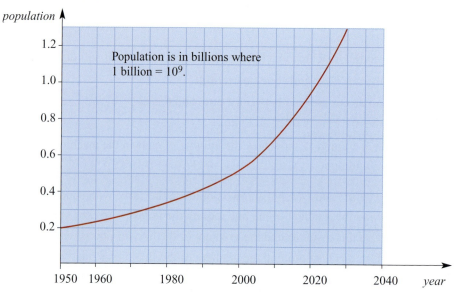

  a From the graph find the population of Acubaland in:

  i 1960   **ii** 2000

  b Calculate the average annual rate of population increase (in billions per year) over the years from 1960 to 2000.

  c From the graph estimate the rate of population increase in:

  i 1960   **ii** 2000

  d How many years do you expect that it will take to double the 2020 population? Explain your reasoning.

8 a Draw the graph of $y = 10^x$ and find the gradient of the secant through the points:
  i $x = 2.5$ and $x = 2.8$
  ii $x = 2.6$ and $x = 2.8$
  iii $x = 2.7$ and $x = 2.8$
  iv $x = 2.75$ and $x = 2.8$
b Comment on your result and investigate further.

9 a Use the result that $a^3 - b^3 = (a - b)(a^2 + ab + b^2)$ to find an expression for the gradient of the line joining points $P(a, a^3)$ and $Q(b, b^3)$ on the curve with equation $y = x^3$.
b Find the gradient of the line for $a = 1, b = 2$.
c Find the gradient of the line for $a = 2, b = 2.01$.
d For your expression for the gradient in terms of a and b (from part a), let $a = b$ and write your new expression in simplest terms. Interpret this result.

10 The rough sketch graph below shows what happens when three swimmers compete in a 100-metre race. (The vertical axis shows distance travelled by a swimmer.)

a Who wins the race?
b Who is in front at the 50 m mark?
c What is the approximate distance separating first and third place when the winner finishes?
d What is the approximate time difference between first and third place?

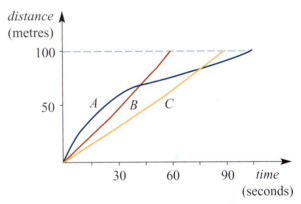

e What is the average speed of each swimmer?
f Describe the race as if you were a commentator.

11 In the following, $f(x)$ is the rule for a well-behaved function f.
Assume that, for $y = f(x)$, the average rate of change of y with respect to x is m, over the interval $[a, b]$. Find the average rate of change of y with respect to x over the same interval $[a, b]$ for:
  a $y = f(x) + c$
  b $y = cf(x)$
  c $y = -f(x)$

Chapter 17

Differentiation and antidifferentiation of polynomials

Objectives

▶ To understand the concept of **limit**.
▶ To understand the definition of the **derivative** of a function.
▶ To understand and use the notation for the **derivative** of a polynomial function.
▶ To find the **gradient of a tangent** to a polynomial function by calculating its derivative.
▶ To apply the rules for differentiating polynomials to solving problems.
▶ To be able to differentiate expressions of the form x^n where n is a negative integer.
▶ To understand and use the notation for the **antiderivative** of a polynomial function.

It is believed that calculus was discovered independently in the late seventeenth century by two great mathematicians: Isaac Newton and Gottfried Leibniz. Like most scientific breakthroughs, the discovery of calculus did not arise out of a vacuum. In fact, many mathematicians and philosophers going back to ancient times made discoveries relating to calculus.

In the previous chapter, we investigated the rate of change of one quantity with respect to another quantity. In this chapter, a technique will be developed for calculating the rate of change for polynomial functions.

To illustrate the idea, we start with an introductory example:

On planet X, an object falls a distance of y metres in t seconds, where $y = 0.8t^2$.
Can we find a general expression for the speed of such an object after t seconds?

(Note that, on Earth, the commonly used model is $y = 4.9t^2$.)

In the previous chapter, we found that we could approximate the gradient of a curve at a given point P by finding the gradient of a secant PQ, where Q is a point on the curve as close as possible to P.

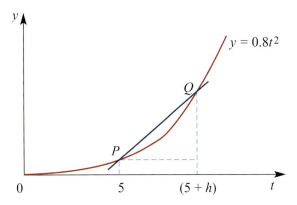

The gradient of PQ approximates the speed of the object at P. The closer we make the point Q to the point P, the better the approximation.

Let P be the point on the curve where $t = 5$. Let Q be the point on the curve corresponding to h seconds after $t = 5$. That is, Q is the point on the curve where $t = 5 + h$.

$$\begin{align}\text{Gradient of } PQ &= \frac{0.8(5+h)^2 - 0.8 \times 5^2}{(5+h) - 5} \\ &= \frac{0.8((5+h)^2 - 5^2)}{h} \\ &= 0.8(10 + h)\end{align}$$

The table gives the gradient of PQ for different values of h. Use your calculator to check these.

If we take values of h with smaller and smaller magnitude, then the gradient of PQ gets closer and closer to 8. So, at the point where $t = 5$, the gradient of the curve is 8.

Thus the speed of the object at the moment $t = 5$ is 8 m/s.

The speed of the object at the moment $t = 5$ is the limiting value of the gradients of PQ, as Q approaches P.

h	Gradient of PQ
0.7	8.56
0.6	8.48
0.5	8.40
0.4	8.32
0.3	8.24
0.2	8.16
0.1	8.08

We want to find a general formula for the speed of the object at any time t.

Let P be the point with coordinates $(t, 0.8t^2)$ on the curve and let Q be the point with coordinates $(t + h, 0.8(t + h)^2)$.

$$\begin{align}\text{Gradient of } PQ &= \frac{0.8(t+h)^2 - 0.8t^2}{(t+h) - t} \\ &= 0.8(2t + h)\end{align}$$

Now consider the limit as h approaches 0, that is, the value of $0.8(2t + h)$ as h becomes arbitrarily small. This limit is $1.6t$.

So the gradient of the tangent to the curve at the point corresponding to time t is $1.6t$. Hence the speed at time t is $1.6t$ m/s.

This technique can be used to investigate the gradient of the tangent at a given point for similar functions.

17A The derivative

We first recall that a **chord** of a curve is a line segment joining points P and Q on the curve. A **secant** is a line through points P and Q on the curve.

In the previous chapter we considered what happened when we looked at a sequence of secants $PQ_1, PQ_2, \ldots, PQ_n, \ldots$, where the points Q_i get closer and closer to P. The idea of instantaneous rate of change at P was introduced.

In this section we focus our attention on the gradient of the tangent at P.

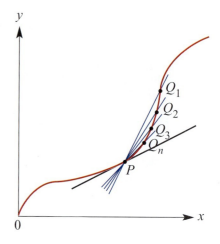

▶ The tangent to a curve at a point

Consider the function $f: \mathbb{R} \to \mathbb{R}$, $f(x) = x^2$.

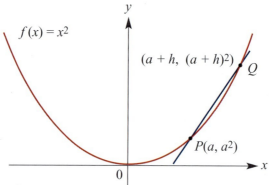

The gradient of the secant PQ shown on the graph is

$$\begin{aligned}
\text{gradient of } PQ &= \frac{(a+h)^2 - a^2}{a+h-a} \\
&= \frac{a^2 + 2ah + h^2 - a^2}{h} \\
&= 2a + h
\end{aligned}$$

The limit of $2a + h$ as h approaches 0 is $2a$, and so the gradient of the tangent at P is said to be $2a$.

The straight line that passes through the point P and has gradient $2a$ is called the **tangent** to the curve at P.

It can be seen that there is nothing special about a here. The same calculation works for any real number x. The gradient of the tangent to the graph of $y = x^2$ at any point x is $2x$.

We say that the **derivative of x^2 with respect to x is $2x$**, or more briefly, we can say that the **derivative of x^2 is $2x$**.

Example 1

By first considering the gradient of the secant PQ, find the gradient of the tangent line to $y = x^2 - 2x$ at the point P with coordinates $(3, 3)$.

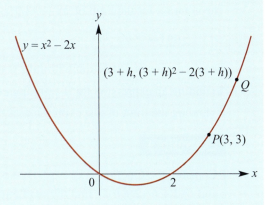

Solution

$$\text{Gradient of } PQ = \frac{(3+h)^2 - 2(3+h) - 3}{3+h-3}$$

$$= \frac{9 + 6h + h^2 - 6 - 2h - 3}{h}$$

$$= \frac{4h + h^2}{h}$$

$$= 4 + h$$

Now consider the gradient of PQ as h approaches 0. The gradient of the tangent line at the point $P(3, 3)$ is 4.

Example 2

Find the gradient of the secant PQ and hence find the derivative of $x^2 + x$.

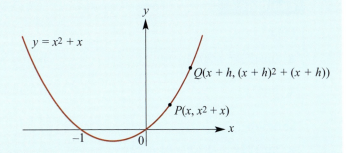

Solution

$$\text{Gradient of } PQ = \frac{(x+h)^2 + (x+h) - (x^2 + x)}{x+h-x}$$

$$= \frac{x^2 + 2xh + h^2 + x + h - x^2 - x}{h}$$

$$= \frac{2xh + h^2 + h}{h}$$

$$= 2x + h + 1$$

From this it is seen that the derivative of $x^2 + x$ is $2x + 1$.

Limit notation

The notation for the limit of $2x + h + 1$ as h approaches 0 is

$$\lim_{h \to 0} (2x + h + 1)$$

The derivative of a function with rule $f(x)$ may be found by:

1 finding an expression for the gradient of the line through $P(x, f(x))$ and $Q(x + h, f(x + h))$
2 finding the limit of this expression as h approaches 0.

Example 3

Consider the function $f(x) = x^3$. By first finding the gradient of the secant through $P(2, 8)$ and $Q(2 + h, (2 + h)^3)$, find the gradient of the tangent to the curve at the point $(2, 8)$.

Solution

$$\begin{aligned}
\text{Gradient of } PQ &= \frac{(2 + h)^3 - 8}{2 + h - 2} \\
&= \frac{8 + 12h + 6h^2 + h^3 - 8}{h} \\
&= \frac{12h + 6h^2 + h^3}{h} \\
&= 12 + 6h + h^2
\end{aligned}$$

The gradient of the tangent line at $(2, 8)$ is $\lim_{h \to 0} (12 + 6h + h^2) = 12$.

The following example provides practice in determining limits.

Example 4

Find:

a $\lim_{h \to 0} (22x^2 + 20xh + h)$

b $\lim_{h \to 0} \dfrac{3x^2 h + 2h^2}{h}$

c $\lim_{h \to 0} 3x$

d $\lim_{h \to 0} 4$

Solution

a $\lim_{h \to 0} (22x^2 + 20xh + h) = 22x^2$

b $\lim_{h \to 0} \dfrac{3x^2 h + 2h^2}{h} = \lim_{h \to 0} (3x^2 + 2h)$
$= 3x^2$

c $\lim_{h \to 0} 3x = 3x$

d $\lim_{h \to 0} 4 = 4$

Using the TI-Nspire

To calculate a limit, use menu > **Calculus** > **Limit** and complete as shown.

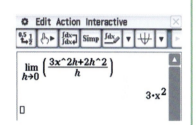

Note: The limit template can also be accessed from the 2D-template palette.
When you insert the limit template, you will notice a superscript field (small box) on the template – generally this will be left empty.

Using the Casio ClassPad

- In $\sqrt{\alpha}$ Main, enter and highlight the expression

  $$\frac{3x^2h + 2h^2}{h}$$

  Note: Use h from the Var keyboard.
- Select lim from the Math2 keyboard and tap EXE.
- Enter h and 0 in the spaces provided as shown.

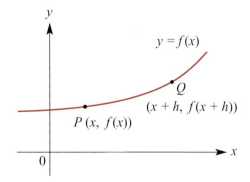

Definition of the derivative

In general, consider the graph $y = f(x)$ of a function $f : \mathbb{R} \to \mathbb{R}$.

Gradient of secant $PQ = \dfrac{f(x+h) - f(x)}{x+h-x}$

$= \dfrac{f(x+h) - f(x)}{h}$

The gradient of the tangent to the graph of $y = f(x)$ at the point $P(x, f(x))$ is the limit of this expression as h approaches 0.

Derivative of a function

The **derivative** of the function f is denoted f' and is defined by

$$f'(x) = \lim_{h \to 0} \frac{f(x+h) - f(x)}{h}$$

The **tangent line** to the graph of the function f at the point $(a, f(a))$ is defined to be the line through $(a, f(a))$ with gradient $f'(a)$.

Warning: This definition of the derivative assumes that the limit exists. For polynomial functions, such limits always exist. But it is not true that for every function you can find the derivative at every point of its domain. This is discussed further in Sections 17F and 17G.

Differentiation by first principles

Determining the derivative of a function by evaluating the limit is called **differentiation by first principles**.

Example 5

For $f(x) = x^2 + 2x$, find $f'(x)$ by first principles.

Solution

$$\begin{aligned}
f'(x) &= \lim_{h \to 0} \frac{f(x+h) - f(x)}{h} \\
&= \lim_{h \to 0} \frac{(x+h)^2 + 2(x+h) - (x^2 + 2x)}{h} \\
&= \lim_{h \to 0} \frac{x^2 + 2xh + h^2 + 2x + 2h - x^2 - 2x}{h} \\
&= \lim_{h \to 0} \frac{2xh + h^2 + 2h}{h} \\
&= \lim_{h \to 0} (2x + h + 2) \\
&= 2x + 2
\end{aligned}$$

$\therefore \quad f'(x) = 2x + 2$

Example 6

For $f(x) = 2 - x^3$, find $f'(x)$ by first principles.

Solution

$$\begin{aligned}
f'(x) &= \lim_{h \to 0} \frac{f(x+h) - f(x)}{h} \\
&= \lim_{h \to 0} \frac{2 - (x+h)^3 - (2 - x^3)}{h} \\
&= \lim_{h \to 0} \frac{2 - (x^3 + 3x^2h + 3xh^2 + h^3) - (2 - x^3)}{h} \\
&= \lim_{h \to 0} \frac{-3x^2h - 3xh^2 - h^3}{h} \\
&= \lim_{h \to 0} (-3x^2 - 3xh - h^2) \\
&= -3x^2
\end{aligned}$$

Using the TI-Nspire

- Define $f(x) = 2 - x^3$.
- Use menu > **Calculus** > **Limit** or the 2D-template palette, and complete as shown.

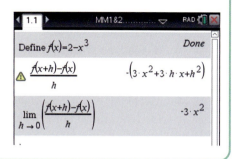

Using the Casio ClassPad

- In Main, enter and highlight the expression $2 - x^3$. Select **Interactive** > **Define** and tap OK.
- Now enter and highlight the expression
$$\frac{f(x+h) - f(x)}{h}$$
  Note: Select f from the abc keyboard and x, h from the Var keyboard.
- Select lim from the Math2 keyboard and tap EXE.
- Enter h and 0 in the spaces provided as shown.

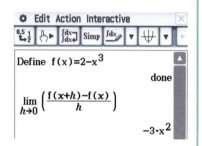

Section summary

- The **derivative** of the function f is denoted f' and is defined by
$$f'(x) = \lim_{h \to 0} \frac{f(x+h) - f(x)}{h}$$
- The **tangent line** to the graph of the function f at the point $(a, f(a))$ is defined to be the line through $(a, f(a))$ with gradient $f'(a)$.

Exercise 17A

Example 1

1 Let $f(x) = -x^2 + 4x$. The graph of $y = f(x)$ is shown opposite.

  a Find the gradient of PQ.

  b Find the gradient of the curve at the point P by considering what happens as h approaches 0.

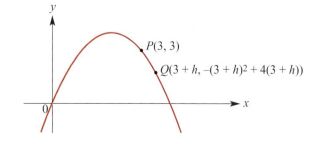

2 Let $f(x) = x^2 - 3x$. Then the points $P(4, 4)$ and $Q(4 + h, (4 + h)^2 - 3(4 + h))$ are on the curve $y = f(x)$.
   a Find the gradient of the secant PQ.
   b Find the gradient of the tangent line to the curve at the point P by considering what happens as h approaches 0.

Example 2

3 The points $P(x, x^2 - 2x)$ and $Q(x + h, (x + h)^2 - 2(x + h))$ are on the curve $y = x^2 - 2x$. Find the gradient of PQ and hence find the derivative of $x^2 - 2x$.

Example 3

4 By first considering the gradient of the secant through $P(2, 16)$ and $Q(2 + h, (2 + h)^4)$ for the curve $y = x^4$, find the gradient of the tangent to the curve at the point $(2, 16)$.
   Hint: $(x + h)^4 = x^4 + 4x^3h + 6x^2h^2 + 4xh^3 + h^4$

5 A space vehicle moves so that the distance travelled over its first minute of motion is given by $y = 4t^4$, where y is the distance travelled in metres and t the time in seconds. By finding the gradient of the secant through the points where $t = 5$ and $t = 5 + h$, calculate the speed of the space vehicle when $t = 5$.

6 A population of insects grows so that the size of the population, P, at time t (days) is given by $P = 1000 + t^2 + t$. By finding the gradient of the secant through the points where $t = 3$ and $t = 3 + h$, calculate the rate of growth of the insect population at time $t = 3$.

Example 4

7 Find:
   a $\lim\limits_{h \to 0} \dfrac{2x^2h^3 + xh^2 + h}{h}$
   b $\lim\limits_{h \to 0} \dfrac{3x^2h - 2xh^2 + h}{h}$
   c $\lim\limits_{h \to 0} (20 - 10h)$
   d $\lim\limits_{h \to 0} \dfrac{30hx^2 + 2h^2 + h}{h}$
   e $\lim\limits_{h \to 0} 5$
   f $\lim\limits_{h \to 0} \dfrac{30hx^3 + 2h^2 + 4h}{h}$

8 Find:
   a $\lim\limits_{h \to 0} \dfrac{(x + h)^2 + 2(x + h) - (x^2 + 2x)}{h}$ i.e. the derivative of $y = x^2 + 2x$
   b $\lim\limits_{h \to 0} \dfrac{(5 + h)^2 + 3(5 + h) - 40}{h}$ i.e. the gradient of $y = x^2 + 3x$ at $x = 5$
   c $\lim\limits_{h \to 0} \dfrac{(x + h)^3 + 2(x + h)^2 - (x^3 + 2x^2)}{h}$ i.e. the derivative of $y = x^3 + 2x^2$

9 For the curve with equation $y = 3x^2 - x$:
   a Find the gradient of the secant PQ, where P is the point $(1, 2)$ and Q is the point $(1 + h, 3(1 + h)^2 - (1 + h))$.
   b Find the gradient of PQ when $h = 0.1$.
   c Find the gradient of the tangent to the curve at P.

10 For the curve with equation $y = \dfrac{2}{x}$:
   a Find the gradient of the chord AB, where $A = (2, 1)$ and $B = \left(2 + h, \dfrac{2}{2 + h}\right)$.
   b Find the gradient of AB when $h = 0.1$.
   c Find the gradient of the tangent to the curve at A.

11 For the curve with equation $y = x^2 + 2x - 3$:

a Find the gradient of the secant PQ, where P is the point $(2, 5)$ and Q is the point $(2 + h, (2 + h)^2 + 2(2 + h) - 3)$.

b Find the gradient of PQ when $h = 0.1$.

c Find the gradient of the tangent to the curve at P.

Example 5, 6 **12** For each of the following, find $f'(x)$ by finding $\lim_{h \to 0} \dfrac{f(x + h) - f(x)}{h}$:

a $f(x) = 3x^2$
b $f(x) = 4x$
c $f(x) = 3$
d $f(x) = 3x^2 + 4x + 3$
e $f(x) = 2x^3 - 4$
f $f(x) = 4x^2 - 5x$
g $f(x) = 3 - 2x + x^2$

13 By first considering the gradient of the secant through $P(x, f(x))$ and $Q(x + h, f(x + h))$ for the curve $f(x) = x^4$, find the derivative of x^4.

Hint: $f(x + h) = x^4 + 4x^3h + 6x^2h^2 + 4xh^3 + h^4$

17B Rules for differentiation

The derivative of x^n where n is a positive integer

From your work in the first section of this chapter, you may have noticed that differentiating from first principles gives the following:

- For $f(x) = x$, $f'(x) = 1$.
- For $f(x) = x^2$, $f'(x) = 2x$.
- For $f(x) = x^3$, $f'(x) = 3x^2$.

This suggests the following general result:

> For $f(x) = x^n$, $f'(x) = nx^{n-1}$, where $n = 1, 2, 3, \ldots$

We can prove this result using the binomial theorem, which was introduced in Section 10E. The proof is not required to be known.

Proof Let $f(x) = x^n$, where $n \in \mathbb{N}$ with $n \geq 2$.

Then
$$f(x + h) - f(x) = (x + h)^n - x^n$$
$$= x^n + {}^nC_1 x^{n-1}h + {}^nC_2 x^{n-2}h^2 + \cdots + {}^nC_{n-1} xh^{n-1} + h^n - x^n$$
$$= {}^nC_1 x^{n-1}h + {}^nC_2 x^{n-2}h^2 + \cdots + {}^nC_{n-1} xh^{n-1} + h^n$$
$$= nx^{n-1}h + {}^nC_2 x^{n-2}h^2 + \cdots + {}^nC_{n-1} xh^{n-1} + h^n$$

and so
$$\dfrac{f(x + h) - f(x)}{h} = \dfrac{1}{h}\left(nx^{n-1}h + {}^nC_2 x^{n-2}h^2 + \cdots + {}^nC_{n-1} xh^{n-1} + h^n\right)$$
$$= nx^{n-1} + {}^nC_2 x^{n-2}h + \cdots + {}^nC_{n-1} xh^{n-2} + h^{n-1}$$

$\therefore \quad \lim_{h \to 0} \dfrac{f(x + h) - f(x)}{h} = \lim_{h \to 0}\left(nx^{n-1} + {}^nC_2 x^{n-2}h + \cdots + {}^nC_{n-1} xh^{n-2} + h^{n-1}\right)$
$$= nx^{n-1}$$

The derivative of a polynomial function

The following results are very useful when finding the derivative of a polynomial function. We will prove two of these results in the final section of this chapter.

- **Constant function:** If $f(x) = c$, then $f'(x) = 0$.
- **Linear function:** If $f(x) = mx + c$, then $f'(x) = m$.
- **Multiple:** If $f(x) = k\,g(x)$, where k is a constant, then $f'(x) = k\,g'(x)$.
  That is, the derivative of a number multiple is the multiple of the derivative.
  For example: if $f(x) = 5x^2$, then $f'(x) = 5(2x) = 10x$.
- **Sum:** If $f(x) = g(x) + h(x)$, then $f'(x) = g'(x) + h'(x)$.
  That is, the derivative of the sum is the sum of the derivatives.
  For example: if $f(x) = x^2 + 2x$, then $f'(x) = 2x + 2$.
- **Difference:** If $f(x) = g(x) - h(x)$, then $f'(x) = g'(x) - h'(x)$.
  That is, the derivative of the difference is the difference of the derivatives.
  For example: if $f(x) = x^2 - 2x$, then $f'(x) = 2x - 2$.

You will meet rules for the derivative of products and quotients in Mathematical Methods Units 3 & 4.

The process of finding the derivative function is called **differentiation**.

Example 7

Find the derivative of $x^5 - 2x^3 + 2$, i.e. differentiate $x^5 - 2x^3 + 2$ with respect to x.

Solution

Let $f(x) = x^5 - 2x^3 + 2$
Then $f'(x) = 5x^4 - 2(3x^2) + 0$
$= 5x^4 - 6x^2$

Explanation

We use the following results:
- the derivative of x^n is nx^{n-1}
- the derivative of a number is 0
- the multiple, sum and difference rules.

Example 8

Find the derivative of $f(x) = 3x^3 - 6x^2 + 1$ and thus find $f'(1)$.

Solution

Let $f(x) = 3x^3 - 6x^2 + 1$
Then $f'(x) = 3(3x^2) - 6(2x) + 0$
$= 9x^2 - 12x$
$\therefore\ f'(1) = 9 - 12$
$= -3$

Using the TI-Nspire

For Example 7:

- Use (menu) > **Calculus** > **Derivative** and complete as shown.

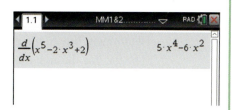

Note: The derivative template can also be accessed from the 2D-template palette. Alternatively, using (shift)(−) will paste the derivative template to the screen.

For Example 8:

- Define $f(x) = 3x^3 - 6x^2 + 1$.
- Use (menu) > **Calculus** > **Derivative** to differentiate as shown.
- To find the value of the derivative at $x = 1$, use (menu) > **Calculus** > **Derivative at a Point**.

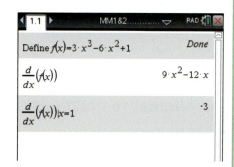

Using the Casio ClassPad

For Example 7:

- In Main, enter and highlight the expression $x^5 - 2x^3 + 2$.
- Go to **Interactive** > **Calculation** > **diff** and tap OK.

For Example 8:

- In Main, enter and highlight the expression $3x^3 - 6x^2 + 1$.
- Go to **Interactive** > **Calculation** > **diff** and tap OK; this will give the derivative only.
- To find the value of the derivative at $x = 1$, tap the stylus at the end of the entry line. Select | from the (Math3) keyboard and type $x = 1$. Then tap (EXE).
- Alternatively, define the derivative as $g(x)$ and find $g(1)$.

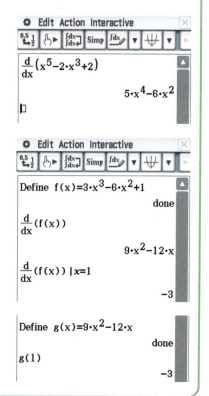

Finding the gradient of a tangent line

We discussed the tangent line at a point on a graph in Section 17A. We recall the following:

The **tangent line** to the graph of the function f at the point $(a, f(a))$ is defined to be the line through $(a, f(a))$ with gradient $f'(a)$.

Example 9

For the curve determined by the rule $f(x) = 3x^3 - 6x^2 + 1$, find the gradient of the tangent line to the curve at the point $(1, -2)$.

Solution

Now $f'(x) = 9x^2 - 12x$ and so $f'(1) = 9 - 12 = -3$.

The gradient of the tangent line at the point $(1, -2)$ is -3.

▶ Alternative notations

It was mentioned in the introduction to this chapter that the German mathematician Gottfried Leibniz was one of the two people to whom the discovery of calculus is attributed. A form of the notation he introduced is still in use today.

Leibniz notation

An alternative notation for the derivative is the following:

If $y = x^3$, then the derivative can be denoted by $\dfrac{dy}{dx}$, and so we write $\dfrac{dy}{dx} = 3x^2$.

In general, if y is a function of x, then the derivative of y with respect to x is denoted by $\dfrac{dy}{dx}$.

Similarly, if z is a function of t, then the derivative of z with respect to t is denoted $\dfrac{dz}{dt}$.

Warning: In this notation, the symbol d is not a factor and cannot be cancelled.

This notation came about because, in the eighteenth century, the standard diagram for finding the limiting gradient was labelled as shown:

- δx means a small difference in x
- δy means a small difference in y

where δ (delta) is the lowercase Greek letter d.

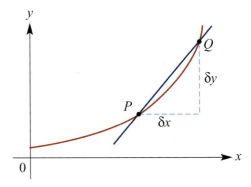

Example 10

a If $y = t^2$, find $\dfrac{dy}{dt}$.

b If $x = t^3 + t$, find $\dfrac{dx}{dt}$.

c If $z = \dfrac{1}{3}x^3 + x^2$, find $\dfrac{dz}{dx}$.

Solution

a $y = t^2$

$\dfrac{dy}{dt} = 2t$

b $x = t^3 + t$

$\dfrac{dx}{dt} = 3t^2 + 1$

c $z = \dfrac{1}{3}x^3 + x^2$

$\dfrac{dz}{dx} = x^2 + 2x$

Example 11

a For $y = (x + 3)^2$, find $\dfrac{dy}{dx}$.

b For $z = (2t - 1)^2(t + 2)$, find $\dfrac{dz}{dt}$.

c For $y = \dfrac{x^2 + 3x}{x}$, find $\dfrac{dy}{dx}$.

d Differentiate $y = 2x^3 - 1$ with respect to x.

Solution

a It is first necessary to write $y = (x + 3)^2$ in expanded form:

$y = x^2 + 6x + 9$

$\therefore \dfrac{dy}{dx} = 2x + 6$

b Expanding:

$z = (4t^2 - 4t + 1)(t + 2)$

$= 4t^3 - 4t^2 + t + 8t^2 - 8t + 2$

$= 4t^3 + 4t^2 - 7t + 2$

$\therefore \dfrac{dz}{dt} = 12t^2 + 8t - 7$

c First simplify:

$y = x + 3$ (for $x \neq 0$)

$\therefore \dfrac{dy}{dx} = 1$ (for $x \neq 0$)

d $y = 2x^3 - 1$

$\therefore \dfrac{dy}{dx} = 6x^2$

Operator notation

'Find the derivative of $2x^2 - 4x$ with respect to x' can also be written as 'find $\dfrac{d}{dx}(2x^2 - 4x)$'.

In general: $\dfrac{d}{dx}(f(x)) = f'(x)$.

Example 12

Find:

a $\dfrac{d}{dx}(5x - 4x^3)$

b $\dfrac{d}{dz}(5z^2 - 4z)$

c $\dfrac{d}{dz}(6z^3 - 4z^2)$

Solution

a $\dfrac{d}{dx}(5x - 4x^3)$

$= 5 - 12x^2$

b $\dfrac{d}{dz}(5z^2 - 4z)$

$= 10z - 4$

c $\dfrac{d}{dz}(6z^3 - 4z^2)$

$= 18z^2 - 8z$

Example 13

For each of the following curves, find the coordinates of the points on the curve at which the gradient of the tangent line at that point has the given value:

a $y = x^3$, gradient = 8
b $y = x^2 - 4x + 2$, gradient = 0
c $y = 4 - x^3$, gradient = −6

Solution

a $y = x^3$ implies $\dfrac{dy}{dx} = 3x^2$

$\therefore \quad 3x^2 = 8$

$\therefore \quad x = \pm\sqrt{\dfrac{8}{3}} = \dfrac{\pm 2\sqrt{6}}{3}$

The points are $\left(\dfrac{2\sqrt{6}}{3}, \dfrac{16\sqrt{6}}{9}\right)$ and $\left(\dfrac{-2\sqrt{6}}{3}, \dfrac{-16\sqrt{6}}{9}\right)$.

b $y = x^2 - 4x + 2$ implies $\dfrac{dy}{dx} = 2x - 4$

$\therefore \quad 2x - 4 = 0$

$\therefore \quad x = 2$

The only point is $(2, -2)$.

c $y = 4 - x^3$ implies $\dfrac{dy}{dx} = -3x^2$

$\therefore \quad -3x^2 = -6$

$\therefore \quad x^2 = 2$

$\therefore \quad x = \pm\sqrt{2}$

The points are $\left(2^{\frac{1}{2}}, 4 - 2^{\frac{3}{2}}\right)$ and $\left(-2^{\frac{1}{2}}, 4 + 2^{\frac{3}{2}}\right)$.

Using the TI-Nspire

- Define $f(x) = 4 - x^3$.
- Solve the equation $\dfrac{d}{dx}(f(x)) = -6$.
- Substitute in $f(x)$ to find the y-coordinates.

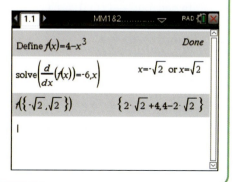

Using the Casio ClassPad

- In $\sqrt{\alpha}$ (Main), enter and highlight the expression $4 - x^3$.
- Go to **Interactive > Define** and tap OK.
- In the next entry line, type and highlight $f(x)$.
- Go to **Interactive > Calculation > diff** and tap OK.
- Type $= -6$ after $\dfrac{d}{dx}(f(x))$. Highlight the equation and use **Interactive > Equation/Inequality > solve**.
- Enter $f(-\sqrt{2})$ and $f(\sqrt{2})$ to find the required y-values.

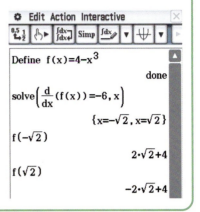

Section summary

- For $f(x) = x^n$, $f'(x) = nx^{n-1}$, where $n = 1, 2, 3, \ldots$
- **Constant function:** If $f(x) = c$, then $f'(x) = 0$.
- **Linear function:** If $f(x) = mx + c$, then $f'(x) = m$.
- **Multiple:** If $f(x) = k\,g(x)$, where k is a constant, then $f'(x) = k\,g'(x)$.
  That is, the derivative of a number multiple is the multiple of the derivative.
- **Sum:** If $f(x) = g(x) + h(x)$, then $f'(x) = g'(x) + h'(x)$.
  That is, the derivative of the sum is the sum of the derivatives.
- **Difference:** If $f(x) = g(x) - h(x)$, then $f'(x) = g'(x) - h'(x)$.
  That is, the derivative of the difference is the difference of the derivatives.

For example, if $f(x) = 5x^3 - 10x^2 + 7$, then $f'(x) = 5(3x^2) - 10(2x) + 0 = 15x^2 - 20x$.

Exercise 17B

Example 7

1 Find the derivative of each of the following with respect to x:

   a $x^2 + 4x$ **b** $2x + 1$ **c** $x^3 - x$

   d $\dfrac{1}{2}x^2 - 3x + 4$ **e** $5x^3 + 3x^2$ **f** $-x^3 + 2x^2$

2 For each of the following, find $f'(x)$:

   a $f(x) = x^{12}$ **b** $f(x) = 3x^7$ **c** $f(x) = 5x$

   d $f(x) = 5x + 3$ **e** $f(x) = 3$ **f** $f(x) = 5x^2 - 3x$

   g $f(x) = 10x^5 + 3x^4$ **h** $f(x) = 2x^4 - \dfrac{1}{3}x^3 - \dfrac{1}{4}x^2 + 2$

Example 8

3 For each of the following, find $f'(1)$:

   a $f(x) = x^6$ **b** $f(x) = 4x^5$ **c** $f(x) = 5x$

   d $f(x) = 5x^2 + 3$ **e** $f(x) = 3$ **f** $f(x) = 5x^2 - 3x$

   g $f(x) = 10x^4 - 3x^3$ **h** $f(x) = 2x^4 - \dfrac{1}{3}x^3$ **i** $f(x) = -10x^3 - 2x^2 + 2$

4 For each of the following, find $f'(-2)$:
   a $f(x) = 5x^3$ **b** $f(x) = 4x^2$ **c** $f(x) = 5x^3 - 3x$ **d** $f(x) = -5x^4 - 2x^2$

5 Find the gradient of the tangent line to the graph of f at the given point:
   a $f(x) = x^2 + 3x$, $(2, 10)$
   b $f(x) = 3x^2 - 4x$, $(1, -1)$
   c $f(x) = -2x^2 - 4x$, $(3, -30)$
   d $f(x) = x^3 - x$, $(2, 6)$

6 For each of the following, find $\dfrac{dy}{dx}$:
   a $y = -x$ **b** $y = 10$ **c** $y = 4x^3 - 3x + 2$
   d $y = \dfrac{1}{3}(x^3 - 3x + 6)$ **e** $y = (x + 1)(x + 2)$ **f** $y = 2x(3x^2 - 4)$
   g $y = \dfrac{10x^5 + 3x^4}{2x^2}$, $x \neq 0$

7 **a** For $y = (x + 4)^2$, find $\dfrac{dy}{dx}$.
   b For $z = (4t - 1)^2(t + 1)$, find $\dfrac{dz}{dt}$.
   c For $y = \dfrac{x^3 + 3x}{x}$, find $\dfrac{dy}{dx}$.

8 **a** For the curve with equation $y = x^3 + 1$, find the gradient of the tangent line at points:
   i $(1, 2)$ **ii** $(a, a^3 + 1)$
   b Find the derivative of $x^3 + 1$ with respect to x.

9 **a** Given that $y = x^3 - 3x^2 + 3x$, find $\dfrac{dy}{dx}$. Hence show that $\dfrac{dy}{dx} \geq 0$ for all x, and interpret this in terms of the graph of $y = x^3 - 3x^2 + 3x$.
   b Given that $y = \dfrac{x^2 + 2x}{x}$, for $x \neq 0$, find $\dfrac{dy}{dx}$.
   c Differentiate $y = (3x + 1)^2$ with respect to x.

10 For each of the following curves, find the y-coordinate of the point on the curve with the given x-coordinate, and find the gradient of the tangent line at that point:
   a $y = x^2 - 2x + 1$, $x = 2$
   b $y = x^2 + x + 1$, $x = 0$
   c $y = x^2 - 2x$, $x = -1$
   d $y = (x + 2)(x - 4)$, $x = 3$
   e $y = 3x^2 - 2x^3$, $x = -2$
   f $y = (4x - 5)^2$, $x = \tfrac{1}{2}$

11 **a** For each of the following, first find $f'(x)$ and $f'(1)$. Then, for $y = f(x)$, find the set $\{(x, y) : f'(x) = 1\}$. That is, find the coordinates of the points where the gradient of the tangent line is 1.
   i $f(x) = 2x^2 - x$
   ii $f(x) = 1 + \dfrac{1}{2}x + \dfrac{1}{3}x^2$
   iii $f(x) = x^3 + x$
   iv $f(x) = x^4 - 31x$
   b What is the interpretation of $\{(x, y) : f'(x) = 1\}$ in terms of the graphs?

Example 12 12 Find:

  a $\dfrac{d}{dt}(3t^2 - 4t)$ **b** $\dfrac{d}{dx}(4 - x^2 + x^3)$ **c** $\dfrac{d}{dz}(5 - 2z^2 - z^4)$

  d $\dfrac{d}{dy}(3y^2 - y^3)$ **e** $\dfrac{d}{dx}(2x^3 - 4x^2)$ **f** $\dfrac{d}{dt}(9.8t^2 - 2t)$

Example 13 13 For each of the following curves, find the coordinates of the points on the curve at which the gradient of the tangent line has the given value:

  a $y = x^2$, gradient $= 8$ **b** $y = x^3$, gradient $= 12$
  c $y = x(2 - x)$, gradient $= 2$ **d** $y = x^2 - 3x + 1$, gradient $= 0$
  e $y = x^3 - 6x^2 + 4$, gradient $= -12$ **f** $y = x^2 - x^3$, gradient $= -1$

17C Differentiating x^n where n is a negative integer

Skillsheet In the previous sections we have seen how to differentiate polynomial functions. In this section we add to the family of functions that we can differentiate. In particular, we will consider functions which involve linear combinations of powers of x, where the indices may be negative integers.

e.g. $f: \mathbb{R} \setminus \{0\} \to \mathbb{R},\ f(x) = x^{-1}$

$f: \mathbb{R} \setminus \{0\} \to \mathbb{R},\ f(x) = 2x + x^{-1}$

$f: \mathbb{R} \setminus \{0\} \to \mathbb{R},\ f(x) = x + 3 + x^{-2}$

Note: We have reintroduced function notation to emphasise the need to consider domains.

Example 14

Let $f: \mathbb{R} \setminus \{0\} \to \mathbb{R},\ f(x) = \dfrac{1}{x}$. Find $f'(x)$ by first principles.

Solution

The gradient of secant PQ is given by

$\dfrac{f(x+h) - f(x)}{x+h-x} = \left(\dfrac{1}{x+h} - \dfrac{1}{x}\right) \times \dfrac{1}{h}$

$= \dfrac{x - (x+h)}{(x+h)x} \times \dfrac{1}{h}$

$= \dfrac{-h}{(x+h)x} \times \dfrac{1}{h}$

$= \dfrac{-1}{(x+h)x}$

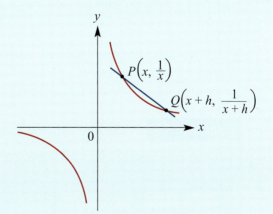

So the gradient of the curve at P is

$\lim\limits_{h \to 0} \dfrac{-1}{(x+h)x} = \dfrac{-1}{x^2} = -x^{-2}$

Hence $f'(x) = -x^{-2}$.

Example 15

Let $f: \mathbb{R} \setminus \{0\} \to \mathbb{R}$, $f(x) = x^{-3}$. Find $f'(x)$ by first principles.

Solution

The gradient of secant PQ is given by

$$\frac{(x+h)^{-3} - x^{-3}}{h}$$

$$= \frac{x^3 - (x+h)^3}{(x+h)^3 x^3} \times \frac{1}{h}$$

$$= \frac{x^3 - (x^3 + 3x^2h + 3xh^2 + h^3)}{(x+h)^3 x^3} \times \frac{1}{h}$$

$$= \frac{-3x^2h - 3xh^2 - h^3}{(x+h)^3 x^3} \times \frac{1}{h}$$

$$= \frac{-3x^2 - 3xh - h^2}{(x+h)^3 x^3}$$

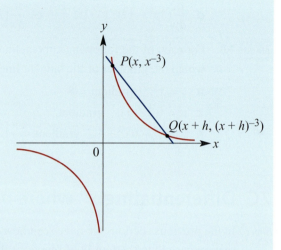

So the gradient of the curve at P is given by

$$\lim_{h \to 0} \frac{-3x^2 - 3xh - h^2}{(x+h)^3 x^3} = \frac{-3x^2}{x^6} = -3x^{-4}$$

Hence $f'(x) = -3x^{-4}$.

We are now in a position to state the generalisation of the result we found in Section 17B.

> For $f(x) = x^n$, $f'(x) = nx^{n-1}$, where n is a non-zero integer.
>
> For $f(x) = c$, $f'(x) = 0$, where c is a constant.

When n is positive, we take the domain of f to be $\mathbb{R}$, and when n is negative, we take the domain of f to be $\mathbb{R} \setminus \{0\}$.

Notes:
- This result can be proved by again using the binomial theorem – the previous example gives the idea of the proof.
- We will consider rational indices in Chapter 20.

Example 16

Find the derivative of $x^4 - 2x^{-3} + x^{-1} + 2$, $x \neq 0$.

Solution

If $\quad f(x) = x^4 - 2x^{-3} + x^{-1} + 2 \qquad$ (for $x \neq 0$)

then $f'(x) = 4x^3 - 2(-3x^{-4}) + (-x^{-2}) + 0$

$\qquad\quad = 4x^3 + 6x^{-4} - x^{-2} \qquad$ (for $x \neq 0$)

Example 17

Find the derivative f' of $f: \mathbb{R} \setminus \{0\} \to \mathbb{R}$, $f(x) = 3x^2 - 6x^{-2} + 1$.

Solution

$$f': \mathbb{R} \setminus \{0\} \to \mathbb{R}, \quad f'(x) = 3(2x) - 6(-2x^{-3}) + 0$$
$$= 6x + 12x^{-3}$$

Example 18

Find the gradient of the tangent to the curve determined by the function $f: \mathbb{R} \setminus \{0\} \to \mathbb{R}$, $f(x) = x^2 + \dfrac{1}{x}$ at the point $(1, 2)$.

Solution

$$f': \mathbb{R} \setminus \{0\} \to \mathbb{R}, \quad f'(x) = 2x + (-x^{-2})$$
$$= 2x - x^{-2}$$

Therefore $f'(1) = 2 - 1 = 1$. The gradient of the curve is 1 at the point $(1, 2)$.

Example 19

Show that the derivative of the function $f: \mathbb{R} \setminus \{0\} \to \mathbb{R}$, $f(x) = x^{-3}$ is always negative.

Solution

$$f': \mathbb{R} \setminus \{0\} \to \mathbb{R}, \quad f'(x) = -3x^{-4}$$
$$= \frac{-3}{x^4}$$

Since x^4 is positive for all $x \neq 0$, we have $f'(x) < 0$ for all $x \neq 0$.

Section summary

For $f(x) = x^n$, $f'(x) = nx^{n-1}$, where n is a non-zero integer.

For $f(x) = c$, $f'(x) = 0$, where c is a constant.

Exercise 17C

Example 14   **1**   **a**   Let $f: \mathbb{R} \setminus \{3\} \to \mathbb{R}$, $f(x) = \dfrac{1}{x - 3}$. Find $f'(x)$ by first principles.

    b   Let $f: \mathbb{R} \setminus \{-2\} \to \mathbb{R}$, $f(x) = \dfrac{1}{x + 2}$. Find $f'(x)$ by first principles.

Example 15   **2**   **a**   Let $f: \mathbb{R} \setminus \{0\} \to \mathbb{R}$, $f(x) = x^{-2}$. Find $f'(x)$ by first principles.

    b   Let $f: \mathbb{R} \setminus \{0\} \to \mathbb{R}$, $f(x) = x^{-4}$. Find $f'(x)$ by first principles.

        Hint: Remember that $(x + h)^4 = x^4 + 4x^3h + 6x^2h^2 + 4xh^3 + h^4$.

594 Chapter 17: Differentiation and antidifferentiation of polynomials

Example 16   **3**   Differentiate each of the following with respect to x:

     a $3x^{-2} + 5x^{-1} + 6$ **b** $\dfrac{3}{x^2} + 5x^2$ **c** $\dfrac{5}{x^3} + \dfrac{4}{x^2} + 1$

     d $3x^2 + \dfrac{5}{3}x^{-4} + 2$ **e** $6x^{-2} + 3x$ **f** $\dfrac{3x^2 + 2}{x}$

4   Find the derivative of each of the following:

     a $\dfrac{3z^2 + 2z + 4}{z^2}, \ z \neq 0$ **b** $\dfrac{3 + z}{z^3}, \ z \neq 0$ **c** $\dfrac{2z^2 + 3z}{4z}, \ z \neq 0$

     d $9z^2 + 4z + 6z^{-3}, \ z \neq 0$ **e** $9 - z^{-2}, \ z \neq 0$ **f** $\dfrac{5z - 3z^2}{5z}, \ z \neq 0$

Example 17   **5**   **a**   Find the derivative f' of $f: \mathbb{R} \setminus \{0\} \to \mathbb{R}, \ f(x) = 3x^4 - 6x^{-3} + x^{-1}$.

         b   Find the derivative f' of $f: \mathbb{R} \setminus \{0\} \to \mathbb{R}, \ f(x) = 5x^4 + 4x^{-2} + x^{-1}$.

     6   Carefully sketch the graph of $f(x) = \dfrac{1}{x^2}, \ x \neq 0$.

         a   Let P be the point $(1, f(1))$ and Q the point $(1 + h, f(1 + h))$. Find the gradient of the secant PQ.

         b   Hence find the gradient of the tangent line to the curve $y = \dfrac{1}{x^2}$ at $x = 1$.

Example 18   **7**   For each of the following curves, find the gradient of the tangent line to the curve at the given point:

     a $y = x^{-2} + x^3, \ x \neq 0, \text{ at } (2, 8\tfrac{1}{4})$ **b** $y = \dfrac{x - 2}{x}, \ x \neq 0, \text{ at } (4, \tfrac{1}{2})$

     c $y = x^{-2} - \dfrac{1}{x}, \ x \neq 0, \text{ at } (1, 0)$ **d** $y = x(x^{-1} + x^2 - x^{-3}), \ x \neq 0, \text{ at } (1, 1)$

8   For the curve with equation $f(x) = x^{-2}$, find the x-coordinate of the point on the curve at which the gradient of the tangent line is:

     a   16   **b** -16

Example 19   **9**   Show that the derivative of the function $f: \mathbb{R} \setminus \{0\} \to \mathbb{R}, \ f(x) = x^{-1}$ is always negative.

17D Graphs of the derivative function

Skillsheet ▶ **Increasing and decreasing functions**

We say a function f is **strictly increasing** on an interval if $x_2 > x_1$ implies $f(x_2) > f(x_1)$.

For example:

- The graph opposite shows a strictly increasing function.
- A straight line with positive gradient is strictly increasing.
- The function $f: (0, \infty) \to \mathbb{R}, \ f(x) = x^2$ is strictly increasing.

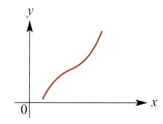

We say a function f is **strictly decreasing** on an interval if $x_2 > x_1$ implies $f(x_2) < f(x_1)$.

For example:

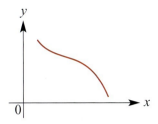

- The graph opposite shows a strictly decreasing function.
- A straight line with negative gradient is strictly decreasing.
- The function $f : (-\infty, 0) \to \mathbb{R}$, $f(x) = x^2$ is strictly decreasing.

Note: The word *strictly* refers to the use of the strict inequality signs $<, >$ rather than $\leq, \geq$.

If $f'(x) > 0$, for all x in the interval, then the function is strictly increasing.
(Think of the tangents at each point – they each have positive gradient.)

If $f'(x) < 0$, for all x in the interval, then the function is strictly decreasing.
(Think of the tangents at each point – they each have negative gradient.)

Warning: The function $f : \mathbb{R} \to \mathbb{R}$, $f(x) = x^3$ is strictly increasing, but $f'(0) = 0$. This means that *strictly increasing does not imply $f'(x) > 0$*.

We can see that $f(x) = x^3$ is strictly increasing from its graph. Alternatively, consider

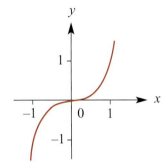

$$a^3 - b^3 = (a - b)(a^2 + ab + b^2)$$
$$= (a - b)\left(a^2 + ab + \left(\tfrac{1}{2}b\right)^2 + b^2 - \left(\tfrac{1}{2}b\right)^2\right)$$
$$= (a - b)\left(\left(a + \tfrac{1}{2}b\right)^2 + \tfrac{3}{4}b^2\right)$$

Hence $a > b$ implies $a^3 > b^3$.

▶ Sign of the derivative

Consider the graph of $y = g(x)$ shown opposite.

At a point $(a, g(a))$ on the graph, the gradient is $g'(a)$.

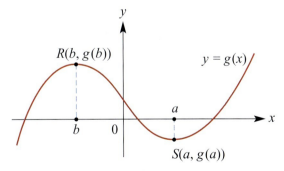

By noting whether the curve is sloping upwards or downwards at a particular point, we can tell the sign of the derivative at that point:

- For $x < b$, $g'(x) > 0$. This implies that g is strictly increasing on the interval $(-\infty, b)$.
- For $x = b$, $g'(b) = 0$.
- For $b < x < a$, $g'(x) < 0$. This implies that g is strictly decreasing on the interval (b, a).
- For $x = a$, $g'(a) = 0$.
- For $x > a$, $g'(x) > 0$. This implies that g is strictly increasing on the interval (a, ∞).

Example 20

For the graph of $f: \mathbb{R} \to \mathbb{R}$, find:

a $\{x : f'(x) > 0\}$
b $\{x : f'(x) < 0\}$
c $\{x : f'(x) = 0\}$

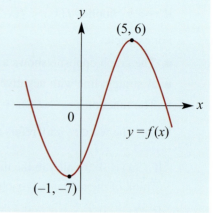

Solution

a $\{x : f'(x) > 0\} = \{x : -1 < x < 5\} = (-1, 5)$
b $\{x : f'(x) < 0\} = \{x : x < -1\} \cup \{x : x > 5\} = (-\infty, -1) \cup (5, \infty)$
c $\{x : f'(x) = 0\} = \{-1, 5\}$

Example 21

Sketch the graph of $y = f'(x)$ for each of the following. (It is impossible to determine all features.)

a 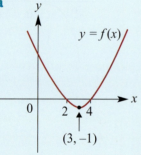   **b** 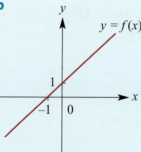   **c**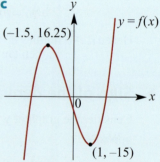

Solution

a $f'(x) > 0$ for $x > 3$
$f'(x) < 0$ for $x < 3$
$f'(x) = 0$ for $x = 3$

b $f'(x) = 1$ for all x

c $f'(x) > 0$ for $x > 1$
$f'(x) < 0$ for $-1.5 < x < 1$
$f'(x) > 0$ for $x < -1.5$
$f'(-1.5) = 0$ and $f'(1) = 0$

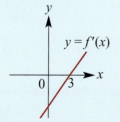   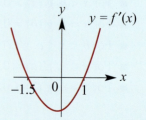

If the rule for the function is given, then a CAS calculator can be used to plot the graph of its derivative function.

Using the TI-Nspire
Plot the graphs of

$$f_1(x) = x^3 - 2x^2 + x - 1$$

$$f_2(x) = \frac{d}{dx}(f_1(x))$$

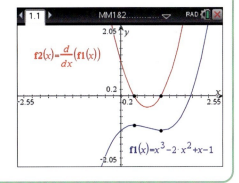

▶ An angle associated with the gradient of a curve at a point

The gradient of a curve at a point is the gradient of the tangent at that point. A straight line, the tangent, is associated with each point on the curve.

If α is the angle a straight line makes with the positive direction of the x-axis, then the gradient, m, of the straight line is equal to $\tan \alpha$. That is, $m = \tan \alpha$.

For example:
- If $\alpha = 45°$, then $\tan \alpha = 1$ and the gradient is 1.
- If $\alpha = 20°$, then the gradient of the straight line is $\tan 20°$.
- If $\alpha = 135°$, then $\tan \alpha = -1$ and the gradient is -1.

Example 22

Find the coordinates of the points on the curve with equation $y = x^2 - 7x + 8$ at which the tangent line:

a makes an angle of $45°$ with the positive direction of the x-axis
b is parallel to the line $y = -2x + 6$.

Solution

a $\dfrac{dy}{dx} = 2x - 7$

$2x - 7 = 1$ (as $\tan 45° = 1$)

$2x = 8$

$\therefore \quad x = 4$

$y = 4^2 - 7 \times 4 + 8 = -4$

The coordinates are $(4, -4)$.

b The line $y = -2x + 6$ has gradient -2.

$2x - 7 = -2$

$2x = 5$

$\therefore \quad x = \dfrac{5}{2}$

The coordinates are $\left(\dfrac{5}{2}, -\dfrac{13}{4}\right)$.

Example 23

The planned path for a flying saucer leaving a planet is defined by the equation

$$y = \frac{1}{4}x^4 + \frac{2}{3}x^3 \quad \text{for } x > 0$$

The units are kilometres. (The x-axis is horizontal and the y-axis vertical.)

a Find the direction of motion when the x-value is:
  i 2   **ii** 3

b Find a point on the flying saucer's path where the path is inclined at 45° to the positive x-axis (i.e. where the gradient of the path is 1).

c Are there any other points on the path which satisfy the situation described in part b?

Solution

a $\dfrac{dy}{dx} = x^3 + 2x^2$

i When $x = 2$, $\dfrac{dy}{dx} = 8 + 8 = 16$

$\tan^{-1} 16 = 86.42°$ (to the x-axis)

ii When $x = 3$, $\dfrac{dy}{dx} = 27 + 18 = 45$

$\tan^{-1} 45 = 88.73°$ (to the x-axis)

b, c When the flying saucer is flying at 45° to the positive direction of the x-axis, the gradient of the curve of its path is given by $\tan 45°$. Thus to find the point at which this happens we consider the equation

$$\frac{dy}{dx} = \tan 45°$$

$$x^3 + 2x^2 = 1$$

$$x^3 + 2x^2 - 1 = 0$$

$$(x + 1)(x^2 + x - 1) = 0$$

$$\therefore \quad x = -1 \text{ or } x = \frac{-1 \pm \sqrt{5}}{2}$$

The only acceptable solution is $x = \dfrac{-1 + \sqrt{5}}{2} \approx 0.62$, as the other two possibilities give negative values for x and we are only considering positive values for x.

Section summary

- A function f is **strictly increasing** on an interval if $x_2 > x_1$ implies $f(x_2) > f(x_1)$.
- A function f is **strictly decreasing** on an interval if $x_2 > x_1$ implies $f(x_2) < f(x_1)$.
- If $f'(x) > 0$ for all x in the interval, then the function is strictly increasing.
- If $f'(x) < 0$ for all x in the interval, then the function is strictly decreasing.

Exercise 17D

1 For which of the following curves is $\dfrac{dy}{dx}$ positive for all values of x?

a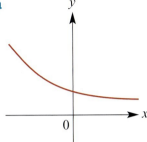

b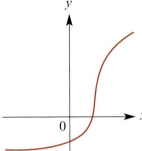

c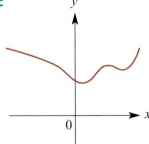

d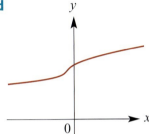

e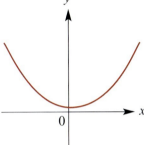

2 For which of the following curves is $\dfrac{dy}{dx}$ negative for all values of x?

a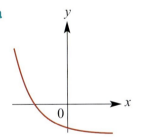

b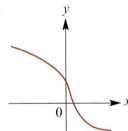

c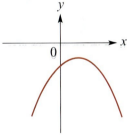

d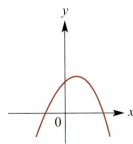

e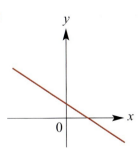

f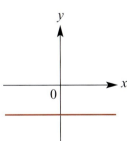

3 For the function $f(x) = 2(x-1)^2$, find the values of x for which:

   a $f(x) = 0$ **b** $f'(x) = 0$ **c** $f'(x) > 0$ **d** $f'(x) < 0$ **e** $f'(x) = -2$

Example 20 4 For the graph of $y = h(x)$ shown here, find:
  a $\{x : h'(x) > 0\}$
  b $\{x : h'(x) < 0\}$
  c $\{x : h'(x) = 0\}$

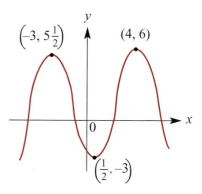

5 Which of the graphs labelled **A–F** correspond to each of the graphs labelled **a–f**?

a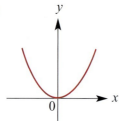

b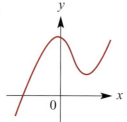

c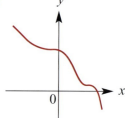

d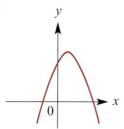

e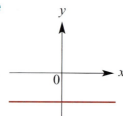

f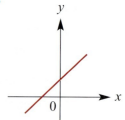

A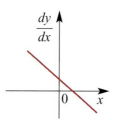

B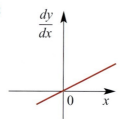

C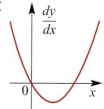

D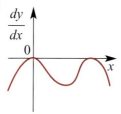

E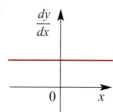

F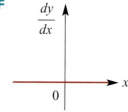

Example 21 **6** Sketch the graph of $y = f'(x)$ for each of the following:

a 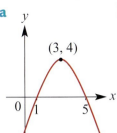 **b** 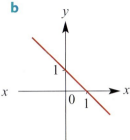 **c** 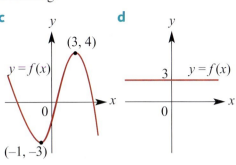 **d**

7 For the graph of $y = f(x)$ shown on the right, find:
  a $\{x : f'(x) > 0\}$
  b $\{x : f'(x) < 0\}$
  c $\{x : f'(x) = 0\}$

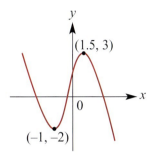

Example 22 **8** Find the coordinates of the points on the curve $y = x^2 - 5x + 6$ at which the tangent:
  a makes an angle of $45°$ with the positive direction of the x-axis
  b is parallel to the line $y = 3x + 4$.

9 Find the coordinates of the points on the parabola $y = x^2 - x - 6$ at which:
  a the gradient of the tangent is zero
  b the tangent is parallel to the line $x + y = 6$.

10 Use a calculator to plot the graph of $y = f'(x)$ where:
  a $f(x) = \sin x$ **b** $f(x) = \cos x$ **c** $f(x) = 2^x$

Example 23 **11** The path of a particle is defined by the equation $y = \frac{1}{3}x^3 + \frac{2}{3}x^2$, for $x > 0$. The units are metres. (The x-axis is horizontal and the y-axis vertical.)
  a Find the direction of motion when the x-value is:
    i 1   **ii** 0.5
  b Find a point on the particle's path where the path is inclined at $45°$ to the positive direction of the x-axis.
  c Are there any other points on the path which satisfy the situation described in part **b**?

12 A car moves away from a set of traffic lights so that the distance, $S(t)$ metres, covered after t seconds is modelled by $S(t) = 0.2 \times t^3$.
  a Find its speed after t seconds.   **b** What will its speed be when $t = 1, 3, 5$?

13 The curve with equation $y = ax^2 + bx$ has a gradient of 3 at the point $(2, -2)$.
  a Find the values of a and b.
  b Find the coordinates of the point where the gradient is 0.

14 A rocket is launched from Cape York Peninsula so that after t seconds its height, $h(t)$ metres, is given by $h(t) = 20t^2$, $0 \leq t \leq 150$. After $2\frac{1}{2}$ minutes this model is no longer appropriate.

a Find the height and the speed of the rocket when $t = 150$.

b After how long will its speed be 1000 m/s?

17E Antidifferentiation of polynomial functions

The derivative of x^2 with respect to x is $2x$. Conversely, given that an unknown expression has derivative $2x$, it is clear that the unknown expression could be x^2. The process of finding a function from its derivative is called **antidifferentiation**.

Now consider the functions $f(x) = x^2 + 1$ and $g(x) = x^2 - 7$.

We have $f'(x) = 2x$ and $g'(x) = 2x$. So the two different functions have the same derivative function.

Both $x^2 + 1$ and $x^2 - 7$ are said to be **antiderivatives** of $2x$.

If two functions have the same derivative function, then they differ by a constant. So the graphs of the two functions can be obtained from each other by translation parallel to the y-axis.

The diagram shows several antiderivatives of $2x$.

Each of the graphs is a translation of $y = x^2$ parallel to the y-axis.

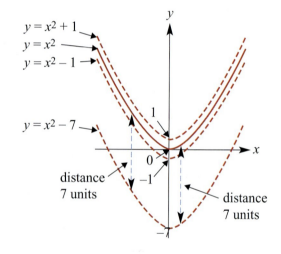

Notation

The general antiderivative of $2x$ is $x^2 + c$, where c is an arbitrary real number. We use the notation of Leibniz to state this with symbols:

$$\int 2x \, dx = x^2 + c$$

This is read as 'the **general antiderivative** of $2x$ with respect to x is equal to $x^2 + c$' or as 'the **indefinite integral** of $2x$ with respect to x is $x^2 + c$'.

To be more precise, the indefinite integral is the set of all antiderivatives and to emphasise this we could write:

$$\int 2x \, dx = \{ f(x) : f'(x) = 2x \} = \{ x^2 + c : c \in \mathbb{R} \}$$

This set notation is not commonly used, but it should be clearly understood that there is not a unique antiderivative for a given function. We will not use this set notation, but it is advisable to keep it in mind when considering further results.

In general:

> If $F'(x) = f(x)$, then $\int f(x)\, dx = F(x) + c$, where c is an arbitrary real number.

Rules for antidifferentiation

We know that:

$$f(x) = x^3 \quad \text{implies} \quad f'(x) = 3x^2$$
$$f(x) = x^8 \quad \text{implies} \quad f'(x) = 8x^7$$
$$f(x) = x \quad \text{implies} \quad f'(x) = 1$$
$$f(x) = x^n \quad \text{implies} \quad f'(x) = nx^{n-1}$$

Reversing this process we have:

$$\int 3x^2\, dx = x^3 + c \quad \text{where } c \text{ is an arbitrary constant}$$
$$\int 8x^7\, dx = x^8 + c \quad \text{where } c \text{ is an arbitrary constant}$$
$$\int 1\, dx = x + c \quad \text{where } c \text{ is an arbitrary constant}$$
$$\int nx^{n-1}\, dx = x^n + c \quad \text{where } c \text{ is an arbitrary constant}$$

We also have:

$$\int x^2\, dx = \frac{1}{3}x^3 + c$$
$$\int x^7\, dx = \frac{1}{8}x^8 + c$$
$$\int 1\, dx = x + c$$
$$\int x^{n-1}\, dx = \frac{1}{n}x^n + c$$

From this we see that:

> $$\int x^n\, dx = \frac{x^{n+1}}{n+1} + c, \quad n \in \mathbb{N} \cup \{0\}$$

Note: This result can be extended to include x^n where n is a negative integer other than -1. The extension is covered in Chapter 20. You will see the antiderivative of x^{-1} in Mathematical Methods Units 3 & 4.

We also record the following results, which follow immediately from the corresponding results for differentiation:

Sum $\quad \int f(x) + g(x)\, dx = \int f(x)\, dx + \int g(x)\, dx$

Difference $\quad \int f(x) - g(x)\, dx = \int f(x)\, dx - \int g(x)\, dx$

Multiple $\quad \int kf(x)\, dx = k\int f(x)\, dx$, where k is a real number

Example 24

Find the general antiderivative (indefinite integral) of each of the following:

a $3x^5$ **b** $3x^2 + 4x^3 + 3$

Solution

a $\int 3x^5 \, dx = 3 \int x^5 \, dx$

$= 3 \times \dfrac{x^6}{6} + c$

$= \dfrac{x^6}{2} + c$

b $\int 3x^2 + 4x^3 + 3 \, dx$

$= 3 \int x^2 \, dx + 4 \int x^3 \, dx + 3 \int 1 \, dx$

$= \dfrac{3x^3}{3} + \dfrac{4x^4}{4} + \dfrac{3x}{1} + c$

$= x^3 + x^4 + 3x + c$

Given extra information, we can find a unique antiderivative.

Example 25

It is known that $f'(x) = x^3 + 4x^2$ and $f(0) = 0$. Find $f(x)$.

Solution

$\int x^3 + 4x^2 \, dx = \dfrac{x^4}{4} + \dfrac{4x^3}{3} + c$

Thus $f(x) = \dfrac{x^4}{4} + \dfrac{4x^3}{3} + c$ for some real number c.

Since $f(0) = 0$, we have $c = 0$.

$\therefore \quad f(x) = \dfrac{x^4}{4} + \dfrac{4x^3}{3}$

Using the Casio ClassPad

- To find the general antiderivative of $x^3 + 4x^2$, enter and highlight the expression in Main $\sqrt{\alpha}$.
- Select **Interactive > Calculation > ∫**.
- Ensure that 'Indefinite integral' is selected, as shown below.

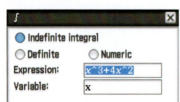

- Remember to add a constant c to the answer.
- To find the specific antiderivative, define the family of functions $f(x)$.
- Solve $f(0) = 0$ for c.

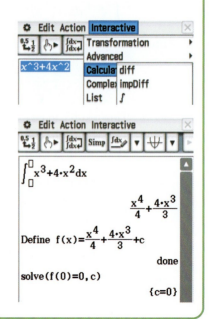

Example 26

If the gradient of the tangent at a point (x, y) on a curve is given by $5x$ and the curve passes through $(0, 6)$, find the equation of the curve.

Solution

Let the curve have equation $y = f(x)$. Then $f'(x) = 5x$.

$$\int 5x\, dx = \frac{5x^2}{2} + c$$

$$\therefore f(x) = \frac{5x^2}{2} + c$$

This describes the family of curves for which $f'(x) = 5x$. Here we are given the additional information that the curve passes through $(0, 6)$, i.e. $f(0) = 6$.

Hence $c = 6$ and so $f(x) = \frac{5x^2}{2} + 6$.

Example 27

Find y in terms of x if:

a $\dfrac{dy}{dx} = x^2 + 2x$, and $y = 1$ when $x = 1$

b $\dfrac{dy}{dx} = 3 - x$, and $y = 2$ when $x = 4$

Solution

a $\int x^2 + 2x\, dx = \dfrac{x^3}{3} + x^2 + c$

$\therefore y = \dfrac{x^3}{3} + x^2 + c$

As $y = 1$ when $x = 1$,

$1 = \dfrac{1}{3} + 1 + c$

$c = -\dfrac{1}{3}$

Hence $y = \dfrac{x^3}{3} + x^2 - \dfrac{1}{3}$

b $\int 3 - x\, dx = 3x - \dfrac{x^2}{2} + c$

$\therefore y = 3x - \dfrac{x^2}{2} + c$

As $y = 2$ when $x = 4$,

$2 = 3 \times 4 - \dfrac{4^2}{2} + c$

$c = -2$

Hence $y = 3x - \dfrac{x^2}{2} - 2$

Using the TI-Nspire

For Example 27a:

- To find the general antiderivative, define the function $f(x)$ using menu > **Calculus** > **Integral** as shown.
- Check that c has not been assigned a value.
- For the specific antiderivative, find the value of c by solving $f(1) = 1$.

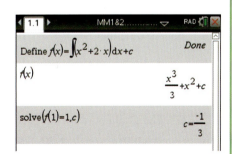

Section summary

- Antiderivative of x^n, for $n \in \mathbb{N} \cup \{0\}$:
$$\int x^n \, dx = \frac{x^{n+1}}{n+1} + c$$

- Rules of antidifferentiation:
  - $\int f(x) + g(x) \, dx = \int f(x) \, dx + \int g(x) \, dx$
  - $\int f(x) - g(x) \, dx = \int f(x) \, dx - \int g(x) \, dx$
  - $\int k f(x) \, dx = k \int f(x) \, dx$, where k is a real number

Exercise 17E

Example 24 **1** Find:

a $\int \frac{1}{2} x^3 \, dx$ b $\int 3x^2 - 2 \, dx$ c $\int 5x^3 - 2x \, dx$

d $\int \frac{4}{5} x^3 - 2x^2 \, dx$ e $\int (x-1)^2 \, dx$ f $\int x(x + \frac{1}{x}) \, dx, \ x \neq 0$

g $\int 2z^2(z-1) \, dz$ h $\int (2t-3)^2 \, dt$ i $\int (t-1)^3 \, dt$

Example 25 **2** It is known that $f'(x) = 4x^3 + 6x^2 + 2$ and $f(0) = 0$. Find $f(x)$.

Example 26 **3** If the gradient at a point (x, y) on a curve is given by $6x^2$ and the curve passes through $(0, 12)$, find the equation of the curve.

Example 27 **4** Find y in terms of x in each of the following:

a $\dfrac{dy}{dx} = 2x - 1$, and $y = 0$ when $x = 1$

b $\dfrac{dy}{dx} = 3 - x$, and $y = 1$ when $x = 0$

c $\dfrac{dy}{dx} = x^2 + 2x$, and $y = 2$ when $x = 0$

d $\dfrac{dy}{dx} = 3 - x^2$, and $y = 2$ when $x = 3$

e $\dfrac{dy}{dx} = 2x^4 + x$, and $y = 0$ when $x = 0$

5 Assume that $\dfrac{dV}{dt} = t^2 - t$ for $t > 1$, and that $V = 9$ when $t = 3$.

a Find V in terms of t.

b Calculate the value of V when $t = 10$.

6 The gradient of the tangent at any point $(x, f(x))$ on the curve with equation $y = f(x)$ is given by $3x^2 - 1$. Find $f(x)$ if the curve passes through the point $(1, 2)$, i.e. $f(1) = 2$.

7 a Which one of the following graphs represents $\frac{dw}{dt} = 2000 - 20t, t > 0$?

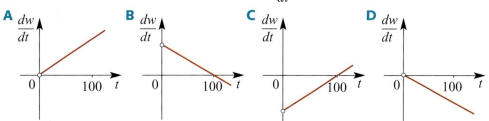

b Find w in terms of t if when $t = 0$, $w = 100\,000$.

8 The graph shows $\frac{dy}{dx}$ against x for a certain curve with equation $y = f(x)$.

Find $f(x)$, given that the point $(0, 4)$ lies on the curve.

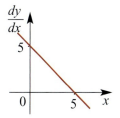

9 Find the equation of the curve $y = f(x)$ which passes through the point $(2, -6)$ and for which $f'(x) = x^2(x - 3)$.

10 The curve $y = f(x)$ for which $f'(x) = 4x + k$, where k is a constant, has a turning point at $(-2, -1)$.

a Find the value of k.

b Find the coordinates of the point at which the curve meets the y-axis.

11 Given that $\frac{dy}{dx} = ax^2 + 1$ and that when $x = 1$, $\frac{dy}{dx} = 3$ and $y = 3$, find the value of y when $x = 2$.

12 The curve for which $\frac{dy}{dx} = 2x + k$, where k is a constant, is such that the tangent at $(3, 6)$ passes through the origin. Find the gradient of this tangent and hence determine:

a the value of k

b the equation of the curve.

13 The curve $y = f(x)$ for which $f'(x) = 16x + k$, where k is a constant, has a turning point at $(2, 1)$.

a Find the value of k.

b Find the value of $f(x)$ when $x = 7$.

14 Suppose that a point moves along some unknown curve $y = f(x)$ in such a way that, at each point (x, y) on the curve, the tangent line has slope x^2. Find an equation for the curve, given that it passes through $(2, 1)$.

17F Limits and continuity

▶ Limits

It is not the intention of this course to provide a formal introduction to limits. We require only an intuitive understanding of limits and some fairly obvious rules for how to handle them.

> The notation $\lim_{x \to a} f(x) = p$ says that the limit of $f(x)$, as x approaches a, is p. We can also say: 'As x approaches a, $f(x)$ approaches p.'
>
> This means that we can make the value of $f(x)$ as close as we like to p, provided we choose x-values close enough to a.

We have met a similar idea earlier in the course. For example, we have seen that $\lim_{x \to \infty} f(x) = 4$ for the function with rule $f(x) = \dfrac{1}{x} + 4$. The graph of $y = f(x)$ can get as close as we like to the line $y = 4$, just by taking larger and larger values of x.

As we will see, for many functions (in particular, for polynomial functions), the limit at a particular point is simply the value of the function at that point.

Example 28

Find $\lim_{x \to 2} 3x^2$.

Solution	Explanation
$\lim_{x \to 2} 3x^2 = 3(2)^2 = 12$	As x gets closer and closer to 2, the value of $3x^2$ gets closer and closer to 12.

If the function is not defined at the value for which the limit is to be found, a different procedure is used.

Example 29

For $f(x) = \dfrac{2x^2 - 5x + 2}{x - 2}$, $x \neq 2$, find $\lim_{x \to 2} f(x)$.

Solution

Observe that

$$f(x) = \dfrac{2x^2 - 5x + 2}{x - 2}$$

$$= \dfrac{(2x - 1)(x - 2)}{x - 2}$$

$$= 2x - 1 \quad \text{(for } x \neq 2\text{)}$$

Hence $\lim_{x \to 2} f(x) = 3$.

The graph of $f : \mathbb{R} \setminus \{2\} \to \mathbb{R}$, $f(x) = 2x - 1$ is shown.

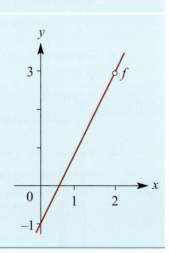

We can investigate Example 29 further by looking at the values of the function as we take x-values closer and closer to 2.

Observe that $f(x)$ is defined for $x \in \mathbb{R} \setminus \{2\}$. Examine the behaviour of $f(x)$ for values of x close to 2.

From the table, it is apparent that, as x takes values closer and closer to 2 (regardless of whether x approaches 2 from the left or from the right), the values of $f(x)$ become closer and closer to 3. That is, $\lim_{x \to 2} f(x) = 3$.

$x < 2$	$x > 2$
$f(1.7) = 2.4$	$f(2.3) = 3.6$
$f(1.8) = 2.6$	$f(2.2) = 3.4$
$f(1.9) = 2.8$	$f(2.1) = 3.2$
$f(1.99) = 2.98$	$f(2.01) = 3.02$
$f(1.999) = 2.998$	$f(2.001) = 3.002$

Note that the limit exists, but the function is not defined at $x = 2$.

▶ Algebra of limits

The following important results are useful for the evaluation of limits.

> Suppose that $f(x)$ and $g(x)$ are functions and that a is a real number. Assume that both $\lim_{x \to a} f(x)$ and $\lim_{x \to a} g(x)$ exist.
>
> ■ **Sum:** $\lim_{x \to a} (f(x) + g(x)) = \lim_{x \to a} f(x) + \lim_{x \to a} g(x)$
> That is, the limit of the sum is the sum of the limits.
>
> ■ **Multiple:** $\lim_{x \to a} kf(x) = k \lim_{x \to a} f(x)$, where k is a given real number.
>
> ■ **Product:** $\lim_{x \to a} (f(x) g(x)) = \lim_{x \to a} f(x) \lim_{x \to a} g(x)$
> That is, the limit of the product is the product of the limits.
>
> ■ **Quotient:** $\lim_{x \to a} \dfrac{f(x)}{g(x)} = \dfrac{\lim_{x \to a} f(x)}{\lim_{x \to a} g(x)}$, provided $\lim_{x \to a} g(x) \neq 0$.
> That is, the limit of the quotient is the quotient of the limits.

Example 30

Find:

a $\lim_{h \to 0} (3h + 4)$
b $\lim_{x \to 2} 4x(x + 2)$
c $\lim_{x \to 3} \dfrac{5x + 2}{x - 2}$

Solution

a $\lim_{h \to 0} (3h + 4) = \lim_{h \to 0} (3h) + \lim_{h \to 0} (4)$
$= 0 + 4$
$= 4$

b $\lim_{x \to 2} 4x(x + 2) = \lim_{x \to 2} (4x) \lim_{x \to 2} (x + 2)$
$= 8 \times 4$
$= 32$

c $\lim_{x \to 3} \dfrac{5x + 2}{x - 2} = \lim_{x \to 3} (5x + 2) \div \lim_{x \to 3} (x - 2)$
$= 17 \div 1$
$= 17$

Example 31

Find:

a $\lim\limits_{x \to 3} \dfrac{x^2 - 3x}{x - 3}$
b $\lim\limits_{x \to 2} \dfrac{x^2 - x - 2}{x - 2}$
c $\lim\limits_{x \to 3} \dfrac{x^2 - 7x + 10}{x^2 - 25}$

Solution

a $\lim\limits_{x \to 3} \dfrac{x^2 - 3x}{x - 3} = \lim\limits_{x \to 3} \dfrac{x(x - 3)}{x - 3} = \lim\limits_{x \to 3} x = 3$

b $\lim\limits_{x \to 2} \dfrac{x^2 - x - 2}{x - 2} = \lim\limits_{x \to 2} \dfrac{(x - 2)(x + 1)}{x - 2} = \lim\limits_{x \to 2} (x + 1) = 3$

c $\lim\limits_{x \to 3} \dfrac{x^2 - 7x + 10}{x^2 - 25} = \lim\limits_{x \to 3} \dfrac{(x - 2)(x - 5)}{(x + 5)(x - 5)} = \dfrac{\lim\limits_{x \to 3} (x - 2)}{\lim\limits_{x \to 3} (x + 5)} = \dfrac{1}{8}$

▶ Left and right limits

An idea which is useful in the following discussion is the existence of limits from the left and from the right. This is particularly useful when talking about piecewise-defined functions.

If the value of $f(x)$ approaches the number p as x approaches a from the right-hand side, then it is written as $\lim\limits_{x \to a^+} f(x) = p$.

If the value of $f(x)$ approaches the number p as x approaches a from the left-hand side, then it is written as $\lim\limits_{x \to a^-} f(x) = p$.

The limit as x approaches a exists only if both the limit from the left and the limit from the right exist and are equal. Then $\lim\limits_{x \to a} f(x) = p$.

Piecewise-defined function

The following is an example of a piecewise-defined function where the limit does not exist for a particular value.

Let $f(x) = \begin{cases} x^3 & \text{if } 0 \leq x < 1 \\ 5 & \text{if } x = 1 \\ 6 & \text{if } 1 < x \leq 2 \end{cases}$

It is clear from the graph of f that $\lim\limits_{x \to 1} f(x)$ does not exist. However, if x is allowed to approach 1 from the left, then $f(x)$ approaches 1. On the other hand, if x is allowed to approach 1 from the right, then $f(x)$ approaches 6. Also note that $f(1) = 5$.

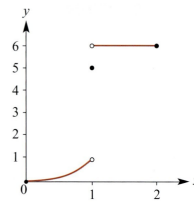

Rectangular hyperbola

As mentioned at the start of this section, the notation of limits is used to describe the asymptotic behaviour of graphs.

First consider $f: \mathbb{R} \setminus \{0\} \to \mathbb{R}$, $f(x) = \dfrac{1}{x^2}$. Observe that, as x approaches 0 both from the left and from the right, $f(x)$ increases without bound. The limit notation for this is $\lim_{x \to 0} f(x) = \infty$.

Now consider $g: \mathbb{R} \setminus \{0\} \to \mathbb{R}$, $g(x) = \dfrac{1}{x}$. The behaviour of $g(x)$ as x approaches 0 from the left is different from the behaviour as x approaches 0 from the right.

With limit notation this is written as:

$$\lim_{x \to 0^-} g(x) = -\infty \quad \text{and} \quad \lim_{x \to 0^+} g(x) = \infty$$

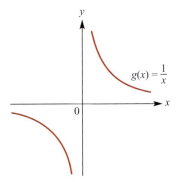

Now examine this function as the magnitude of x becomes very large. It can be seen that, as x increases without bound through positive values, the corresponding values of $g(x)$ approach zero. Likewise, as x decreases without bound through negative values, the corresponding values of $g(x)$ also approach zero.

Symbolically this is written as:

$$\lim_{x \to \infty} g(x) = 0^+ \quad \text{and} \quad \lim_{x \to -\infty} g(x) = 0^-$$

Many functions approach a limiting value or limit as x approaches $\pm\infty$.

▶ Continuity at a point

We only require an intuitive understanding of continuity.

> A function with rule $f(x)$ is said to be continuous at $x = a$ if the graph of $y = f(x)$ can be drawn through the point with coordinates $(a, f(a))$ without a break. Otherwise, there is said to be a discontinuity at $x = a$.

We can give a more formal definition of continuity using limits. A function f is continuous at the point $x = a$ provided $f(a)$, $\lim_{x \to a^+} f(x)$ and $\lim_{x \to a^-} f(x)$ all exist and are equal.

We can state this equivalently as follows:

> A function f is **continuous** at the point $x = a$ if the following conditions are met:
> - $f(x)$ is defined at $x = a$
> - $\lim_{x \to a} f(x) = f(a)$

The function is **discontinuous** at a point if it is not continuous at that point.

A function is said to be **continuous everywhere** if it is continuous for all real numbers. All the polynomial functions are continuous everywhere. In contrast, the function

$$f(x) = \begin{cases} x^3 & \text{if } x < 1 \\ 5 & \text{if } x = 1 \\ 6 & \text{if } x > 1 \end{cases}$$

is defined for all real numbers but is not continuous at $x = 1$.

Example 32

State the values for x for which the functions shown below have a discontinuity:

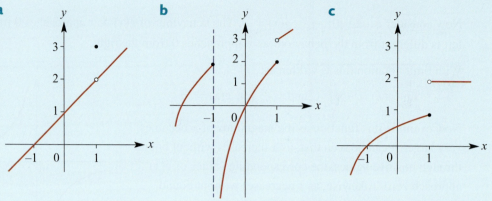

a   **b**   **c**

Solution

a There is a discontinuity at $x = 1$, since $f(1) = 3$ but $\lim_{x \to 1^+} f(x) = \lim_{x \to 1^-} f(x) = 2$.

b There is a discontinuity at $x = 1$, since $f(1) = 2$ and $\lim_{x \to 1^-} f(x) = 2$ but $\lim_{x \to 1^+} f(x) = 3$.
There is also a discontinuity at $x = -1$, since $f(-1) = 2$ and $\lim_{x \to -1^-} f(x) = 2$ but $\lim_{x \to -1^+} f(x) = -\infty$.

c There is a discontinuity at $x = 1$, since $f(1) = 1$ and $\lim_{x \to 1^-} f(x) = 1$ but $\lim_{x \to 1^+} f(x) = 2$.

Example 33

For each function, state the values of x for which there is a discontinuity, and use the definition of continuity in terms of $f(a)$, $\lim_{x \to a^+} f(x)$ and $\lim_{x \to a^-} f(x)$ to explain why:

a $f(x) = \begin{cases} 2x & \text{if } x \geq 0 \\ -2x + 1 & \text{if } x < 0 \end{cases}$

b $f(x) = \begin{cases} x^2 & \text{if } x \geq 0 \\ -2x + 1 & \text{if } x < 0 \end{cases}$

c $f(x) = \begin{cases} x & \text{if } x \leq -1 \\ x^2 & \text{if } -1 < x < 0 \\ -2x + 1 & \text{if } x \geq 0 \end{cases}$

d $f(x) = \begin{cases} x^2 + 1 & \text{if } x \geq 0 \\ -2x + 1 & \text{if } x < 0 \end{cases}$

e $f(x) = \begin{cases} x & \text{if } x \geq 0 \\ -2x & \text{if } x < 0 \end{cases}$

Solution

a $f(0) = 0$ but $\lim_{x \to 0^-} f(x) = 1$, therefore there is a discontinuity at $x = 0$.

b $f(0) = 0$ but $\lim_{x \to 0^-} f(x) = 1$, therefore there is a discontinuity at $x = 0$.

c $f(-1) = -1$ but $\lim_{x \to -1^+} f(x) = 1$, therefore there is a discontinuity at $x = -1$.
$f(0) = 1$ but $\lim_{x \to 0^-} f(x) = 0$, therefore there is a discontinuity at $x = 0$.

d No discontinuity.   **e** No discontinuity.

Section summary

- A function f is **continuous** at the point $x = a$ if the following conditions are met:
  - $f(x)$ is defined at $x = a$
  - $\lim_{x \to a} f(x) = f(a)$
- The function is **discontinuous** at a point if it is not continuous at that point.
- A function is said to be **continuous everywhere** if it is continuous for all real numbers. All the polynomial functions are continuous everywhere.
- **Algebra of limits** Suppose that $f(x)$ and $g(x)$ are functions and that a is a real number. Assume that both $\lim_{x \to a} f(x)$ and $\lim_{x \to a} g(x)$ exist.
  - $\lim_{x \to a} (f(x) + g(x)) = \lim_{x \to a} f(x) + \lim_{x \to a} g(x)$
    That is, the limit of the sum is the sum of the limits.
  - $\lim_{x \to a} k f(x) = k \lim_{x \to a} f(x)$, where k is a given real number.
  - $\lim_{x \to a} (f(x) g(x)) = \lim_{x \to a} f(x) \lim_{x \to a} g(x)$
    That is, the limit of the product is the product of the limits.
  - $\lim_{x \to a} \dfrac{f(x)}{g(x)} = \dfrac{\lim_{x \to a} f(x)}{\lim_{x \to a} g(x)}$, provided $\lim_{x \to a} g(x) \neq 0$.
    That is, the limit of the quotient is the quotient of the limits.

Exercise 17F

1 Find the following limits:

a $\lim_{x \to 3} 15$

b $\lim_{x \to 6} (x - 5)$

c $\lim_{x \to \frac{1}{2}} (3x - 5)$

d $\lim_{t \to -3} \dfrac{t - 2}{t + 5}$

e $\lim_{t \to -1} \dfrac{t^2 + 2t + 1}{t + 1}$

f $\lim_{x \to 0} \dfrac{(x + 2)^2 - 4}{x}$

g $\lim_{t \to 1} \dfrac{t^2 - 1}{t - 1}$

h $\lim_{x \to 9} \sqrt{x + 3}$

i $\lim_{x \to 0} \dfrac{x^2 - 2x}{x}$

j $\lim_{x \to 2} \dfrac{x^3 - 8}{x - 2}$

k $\lim_{x \to 2} \dfrac{3x^2 - x - 10}{x^2 + 5x - 14}$

l $\lim_{x \to 1} \dfrac{x^2 - 3x + 2}{x^2 - 6x + 5}$

2 For each of the following graphs, give the values of x at which a discontinuity occurs. Give reasons.

a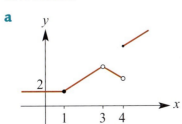

b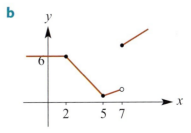

Example 33 3 For the following functions, state each value of x at which there is a discontinuity. Use the definition of continuity in terms of $f(a)$, $\lim_{x \to a^+} f(x)$ and $\lim_{x \to a^-} f(x)$ to explain why each stated value of x corresponds to a discontinuity.

a $f(x) = \begin{cases} 3x & \text{if } x \geq 0 \\ -2x + 2 & \text{if } x < 0 \end{cases}$

b $f(x) = \begin{cases} x^2 + 2 & \text{if } x \geq 1 \\ -2x + 1 & \text{if } x < 1 \end{cases}$

c $f(x) = \begin{cases} -x & \text{if } x \leq -1 \\ x^2 & \text{if } -1 < x < 0 \\ -3x + 1 & \text{if } x \geq 0 \end{cases}$

4 The rule of a particular function is given below. For what values of x is the graph of this function discontinuous?

$$y = \begin{cases} 2 & \text{if } x < 1 \\ (x - 4)^2 - 9 & \text{if } 1 \leq x < 7 \\ x - 7 & \text{if } x \geq 7 \end{cases}$$

17G When is a function differentiable?

A function f is said to be **differentiable** at $x = a$ if $\lim_{h \to 0} \dfrac{f(a + h) - f(a)}{h}$ exists.

The polynomial functions considered in this chapter are differentiable for all real numbers. However, this is not true for all functions.

Let $f: \mathbb{R} \to \mathbb{R}$, $f(x) = \begin{cases} x & \text{if } x \geq 0 \\ -x & \text{if } x < 0 \end{cases}$

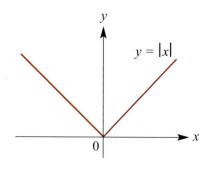

This function is called the modulus function (or the absolute-value function) and is denoted by $f(x) = |x|$.

The function f is not differentiable at $x = 0$, because

$$\dfrac{f(0 + h) - f(0)}{h} = \dfrac{f(h)}{h} = \begin{cases} 1 & \text{if } h > 0 \\ -1 & \text{if } h < 0 \end{cases}$$

and so $\lim_{h \to 0} \dfrac{f(0 + h) - f(0)}{h}$ does not exist.

Note: To the left of 0 the gradient is -1, and to the right of 0 the gradient is 1.

Example 34

Let $f: \mathbb{R} \to \mathbb{R}$, $f(x) = \begin{cases} x & \text{if } x \geq 0 \\ -x & \text{if } x < 0 \end{cases}$

(That is, $f(x) = |x|$.) Sketch the graph of the derivative for a suitable domain.

Solution

$$f'(x) = \begin{cases} 1 & \text{if } x > 0 \\ -1 & \text{if } x < 0 \end{cases}$$

$f'(x)$ is not defined at $x = 0$

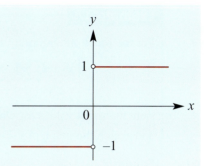

Example 35

Draw a sketch graph of f' where the graph of f is as illustrated. Indicate where f' is not defined.

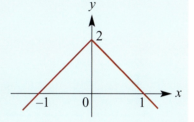

Solution

The derivative does not exist at $x = 0$,
i.e. the function is not differentiable at $x = 0$.

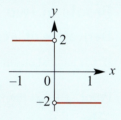

It was shown in the previous section that some piecewise-defined functions are continuous everywhere. Similarly, there are piecewise-defined functions which are differentiable everywhere. The smoothness of the 'joins' determines whether this is the case.

Example 36

For the function with following rule, find $f'(x)$ and sketch the graph of $y = f'(x)$:

$$f(x) = \begin{cases} x^2 + 2x + 1 & \text{if } x \geq 0 \\ 2x + 1 & \text{if } x < 0 \end{cases}$$

Solution

$$f'(x) = \begin{cases} 2x + 2 & \text{if } x \geq 0 \\ 2 & \text{if } x < 0 \end{cases}$$

In particular, $f'(0)$ is defined and is equal to 2. The two sections of the graph of $y = f(x)$ join smoothly at the point $(0, 1)$.

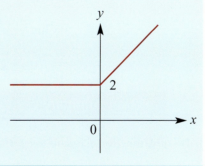

Example 37

For the function with rule

$$f(x) = \begin{cases} x^2 + 2x + 1 & \text{if } x \geq 0 \\ x + 1 & \text{if } x < 0 \end{cases}$$

state the set of values for which the derivative is defined, find $f'(x)$ for this set of values and sketch the graph of $y = f'(x)$.

Solution

$$f'(x) = \begin{cases} 2x + 2 & \text{if } x > 0 \\ 1 & \text{if } x < 0 \end{cases}$$

$f'(0)$ is not defined as the limits from the left and right are not equal.

The function f is differentiable for $\mathbb{R} \setminus \{0\}$.

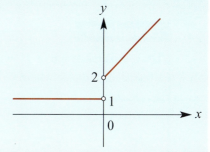

▶ Proofs of two results for derivatives

Derivative of a constant function

If f is a constant function, $f(x) = c$, then $f'(a) = 0$ for all real numbers a.

Proof $\quad f'(a) = \lim\limits_{h \to 0} \dfrac{f(a + h) - f(a)}{h} = \lim\limits_{h \to 0} \dfrac{c - c}{h} = 0$

Derivative of a sum

If f and g are differentiable at a, then $f + g$ is also differentiable at a, and

$$(f + g)'(a) = f'(a) + g'(a)$$

Proof $\quad (f + g)'(a) = \lim\limits_{h \to 0} \dfrac{(f + g)(a + h) - (f + g)(a)}{h}$

$\qquad\qquad\qquad = \lim\limits_{h \to 0} \dfrac{f(a + h) + g(a + h) - f(a) - g(a)}{h}$

$\qquad\qquad\qquad = \lim\limits_{h \to 0} \dfrac{f(a + h) - f(a) + g(a + h) - g(a)}{h}$

$\qquad\qquad\qquad = \lim\limits_{h \to 0} \dfrac{f(a + h) - f(a)}{h} + \lim\limits_{h \to 0} \dfrac{g(a + h) - g(a)}{h}$

$\qquad\qquad\qquad = f'(a) + g'(a)$

Section summary

A function f is said to be **differentiable** at $x = a$ if $\lim\limits_{h \to 0} \dfrac{f(a + h) - f(a)}{h}$ exists.

Exercise 17G

Example 34, 35

1 In each of the figures below, the graph of a function f is given. Sketch the graph of f'. Obviously your sketch of f' cannot be exact; but $f'(x)$ should be zero at values of x for which the gradient of f is zero, and $f'(x)$ should be negative where the original graph slopes downwards, and so on.

a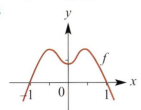

b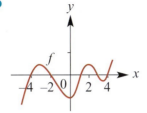

c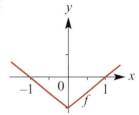

d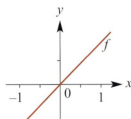

e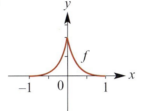

f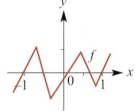

Example 36

2 For the function with following rule, find $f'(x)$ and sketch the graph of $y = f'(x)$:

$$f(x) = \begin{cases} -x^2 + 3x + 1 & \text{if } x \geq 0 \\ 3x + 1 & \text{if } x < 0 \end{cases}$$

Example 37

3 For the function with the following rule, state the set of values for which the derivative is defined, find $f'(x)$ for this set of values and sketch the graph of $y = f'(x)$:

$$f(x) = \begin{cases} x^2 + 2x + 1 & \text{if } x \geq 1 \\ -2x + 3 & \text{if } x < 1 \end{cases}$$

4 For the function with the following rule, state the set of values for which the derivative is defined, find $f'(x)$ for this set of values and sketch the graph of $y = f'(x)$:

$$f(x) = \begin{cases} -x^2 - 3x + 1 & \text{if } x \geq -1 \\ -2x + 3 & \text{if } x < -1 \end{cases}$$

Chapter summary

The derivative

- The notation for the limit as h approaches 0 is $\lim_{h \to 0}$.
- For the graph of $y = f(x)$:
  - The gradient of the secant PQ is given by
  $$\frac{f(x+h) - f(x)}{h}$$
  - The gradient of the tangent to the graph at the point P is given by
  $$\lim_{h \to 0} \frac{f(x+h) - f(x)}{h}$$

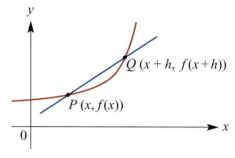

- The **derivative** of the function f is denoted f' and is defined by
$$f'(x) = \lim_{h \to 0} \frac{f(x+h) - f(x)}{h}$$

- At a point $(a, g(a))$ on the curve $y = g(x)$, the gradient is $g'(a)$.

  For the graph shown:
  - $g'(x) > 0$ for $x < b$ and for $x > a$
  - $g'(x) < 0$ for $b < x < a$
  - $g'(x) = 0$ for $x = b$ and for $x = a$.

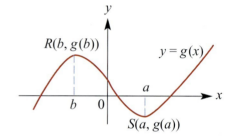

Rules for differentiation

- For $f(x) = c$, $f'(x) = 0$. That is, the derivative of a constant function is zero.
  For example:
  - $f(x) = 1$, $f'(x) = 0$
  - $f(x) = 27.3$, $f'(x) = 0$

- For $f(x) = x^n$, $f'(x) = nx^{n-1}$, where n is a non-zero integer.
  For example:
  - $f(x) = x^2$, $f'(x) = 2x$
  - $f(x) = x^4$, $f'(x) = 4x^3$
  - $f(x) = x^{-1}$, $f'(x) = -x^{-2}$
  - $f(x) = x^{-3}$, $f'(x) = -3x^{-4}$

- For $f(x) = k\,g(x)$, where k is a constant, $f'(x) = k\,g'(x)$.
  That is, the derivative of a number multiple is the multiple of the derivative.
  For example:
  - $f(x) = 3x^2$, $f'(x) = 3(2x) = 6x$

- For $f(x) = g(x) + h(x)$, $f'(x) = g'(x) + h'(x)$.
  That is, the derivative of a sum is the sum of the derivatives.
  For example:
  - $f(x) = x^2 + x^3$, $f'(x) = 2x + 3x^2$
  - $g(x) = 3x^2 + 4x^3$, $g'(x) = 3(2x) + 4(3x^2) = 6x + 12x^2$

Antiderivatives

- If $F'(x) = f(x)$, then $\int f(x)\,dx = F(x) + c$, where c is an arbitrary real number.
- $\int x^n\,dx = \dfrac{x^{n+1}}{n+1} + c$, where $n \in \mathbb{N} \cup \{0\}$
- $\int f(x) + g(x)\,dx = \int f(x)\,dx + \int g(x)\,dx$
- $\int kf(x)\,dx = k\int f(x)\,dx$, where k is a real number.

Algebra of limits

- $\lim\limits_{x \to a}(f(x) + g(x)) = \lim\limits_{x \to a} f(x) + \lim\limits_{x \to a} g(x)$
  That is, the limit of the sum is the sum of the limits.
- $\lim\limits_{x \to a} kf(x) = k \lim\limits_{x \to a} f(x)$, where k is a real number.
- $\lim\limits_{x \to a}(f(x)g(x)) = \lim\limits_{x \to a} f(x) \lim\limits_{x \to a} g(x)$
  That is, the limit of the product is the product of the limits.
- $\lim\limits_{x \to a} \dfrac{f(x)}{g(x)} = \dfrac{\lim\limits_{x \to a} f(x)}{\lim\limits_{x \to a} g(x)}$, provided $\lim\limits_{x \to a} g(x) \neq 0$.
  That is, the limit of the quotient is the quotient of the limits.

Continuity

- A function f is **continuous** at the point $x = a$ if:
  - $f(x)$ is defined at $x = a$
  - $\lim\limits_{x \to a} f(x) = f(a)$
- The function is **discontinuous** at a point if it is not continuous at that point.

Technology-free questions

1 Find the derivative of each of the following by first principles:
  a $y = 3x + 1$
  b $y = 4 - x^2$
  c $y = x^2 + 5x$
  d $y = x^3 + x$
  e $y = x^2 + 2x + 1$
  f $y = 3x^2 - x$

2 Find $\dfrac{dy}{dx}$ when:
  a $y = 3x^2 - 2x + 6$
  b $y = 5$
  c $y = 2x(2 - x)$
  d $y = 4(2x - 1)(5x + 2)$
  e $y = (x + 1)(3x - 2)$
  f $y = (x + 1)(2 - 3x)$

3 Find $\dfrac{dy}{dx}$ when:
  a $y = -x$
  b $y = 10$
  c $y = \dfrac{(x + 3)(2x + 1)}{4}$
  d $y = \dfrac{2x^3 - x^2}{3x}$
  e $y = \dfrac{x^4 + 3x^2}{2x^2}$

4 For each of the following functions, find the y-coordinate and the gradient of the tangent at the point on the curve for the given value of x:
  a $y = x^2 - 2x + 1$, $x = 2$
  b $y = x^2 - 2x$, $x = -1$
  c $y = (x + 2)(x - 4)$, $x = 3$
  d $y = 3x^2 - 2x^3$, $x = -2$

5 Find the coordinates of the points on the curves given by the following equations at which the gradient of the tangent at that point has the given value:

a $y = x^2 - 3x + 1$, $\dfrac{dy}{dx} = 0$
b $y = x^3 - 6x^2 + 4$, $\dfrac{dy}{dx} = -12$
c $y = x^2 - x^3$, $\dfrac{dy}{dx} = -1$
d $y = x^3 - 2x + 7$, $\dfrac{dy}{dx} = 1$
e $y = x^4 - 2x^3 + 1$, $\dfrac{dy}{dx} = 0$
f $y = x(x - 3)^2$, $\dfrac{dy}{dx} = 0$

6 For the function with rule $f(x) = 3(2x - 1)^2$, find the values of x for which:

a $f(x) = 0$
b $f'(x) = 0$
c $f'(x) > 0$
d $f'(x) < 0$
e $f(x) > 0$
f $f'(x) = 3$

7 Find the derivative of each of the following with respect to x:

a x^{-4}
b $2x^{-3}$
c $-\dfrac{1}{3x^2}$
d $-\dfrac{1}{x^4}$
e $\dfrac{3}{x^5}$
f $\dfrac{x^2 + x^3}{x^4}$
g $\dfrac{3x^2 + 2x}{x^2}$
h $5x^2 - \dfrac{2}{x}$

8 The curve with equation $y = ax^2 + bx$ has a tangent with gradient 3 at the point $(1, 1)$. Find:

a the values of a and b
b the coordinates of the points where the gradient is 0.

9 Find:

a $\int \dfrac{1}{2} \, dx$
b $\int \dfrac{1}{2}x^2 \, dx$
c $\int (x^2 + 3x) \, dx$
d $\int (2x + 3)^2 \, dx$
e $\int at \, dt$
f $\int \dfrac{1}{3}t^3 \, dt$
g $\int (t + 1)(t - 2) \, dt$
h $\int (2 - t)(t + 1) \, dt$

10 The curve with equation $y = f(x)$ passes through the point $(3, -1)$ and $f'(x) = 2x + 5$. Find $f(x)$.

11 The curve with equation $y = f(x)$ passes through the origin and $f'(x) = 3x^2 - 8x + 3$.
a Find $f(x)$.
b Find the intercepts of the curve with the x-axis.

12 The graph of $y = f(x)$ is shown. Sketch the graph of $y = f'(x)$. (Not all details can be determined, but the axis intercepts and the shape of graph can be determined.)

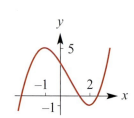

13 For the graph of $y = h(x)$, find:

a $\{x : h'(x) > 0\}$
b $\{x : h'(x) < 0\}$
c $\{x : h'(x) = 0\}$

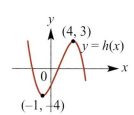

Chapter 17 review 621

Multiple-choice questions

1 The gradient of the curve $y = x^3 + 4x$ at the point where $x = 2$ is
   A 12 **B** 4 **C** 10 **D** 16 **E** 8

2 The gradient of the chord of the curve $y = 2x^2$ between the points where $x = 1$ and $x = 1 + h$ is given by
   A $2(x + h)^2 - 2x^2$ **B** $4 + 2h$ **C** 4 **D** $4x$ **E** $4 + h$

3 If $y = 2x^4 - 5x^3 + 2$, then $\dfrac{dy}{dx}$ equals
   A $8x^3 - 5x^2 + 2$ **B** $4x^4 - 15x^2 + 2$ **C** $4x^4 - 10x^2$
   D $8x^3 - 15x + 2$ **E** $8x^3 - 15x^2$

4 If $f(x) = x^2(x + 1)$, then $f'(-1)$ equals
   A -1 **B** 1 **C** 2 **D** -2 **E** 5

5 If $f(x) = (x - 3)^2$, then $f'(x)$ equals
   A $x - 3$ **B** $x - 6$ **C** $2x - 6$ **D** $2x + 9$ **E** $2x$

6 If $y = \dfrac{2x^4 + 9x^2}{3x}$, then $\dfrac{dy}{dx}$ equals
   A $\dfrac{2x^4}{3} + 6x$ **B** $2x + 3$ **C** $2x^2 + 3$ **D** $\dfrac{8x^3 + 18x}{3}$ **E** $8x^3 + 18x$

7 Given that $y = x^2 - 6x + 9$, the values of x for which $\dfrac{dy}{dx} \geq 0$ are
   A $x \geq 3$ **B** $x > 3$ **C** $x \geq -3$ **D** $x \leq -3$ **E** $x < 3$

8 If $y = 2x^4 - 36x^2$, the points at which the tangent to the curve is parallel to the x-axis are
   A 1, 0 and 3 **B** 0 and 3 **C** -3 and 3 **D** 0 and -3 **E** -3, 0 and 3

9 The coordinates of the point on the graph of $y = x^2 + 6x - 5$ at which the tangent is parallel to the line $y = 4x$ are
   A $(-1, -10)$ **B** $(-1, -2)$ **C** $(1, 2)$ **D** $(-1, 4)$ **E** $(-1, 10)$

10 If $y = -2x^3 + 3x^2 - x + 1$, then $\dfrac{dy}{dx}$ equals
   A $6x^2 + 6x - 1$ **B** $-6x^2 + 6x$ **C** $-6x^2 + 3x - 1$
   D $-6x^2 + 6x - 1$ **E** $6x^2 - 6x - 1$

Extended-response questions

1 The diagram to the right shows part of the graph of $\dfrac{dy}{dx}$ against x.

Sketch a possible shape for the graph of y against x over the same interval if:
- $y = -1$ when $x = -1$
- $y = 0$ when $x = 0$
- $y = 1$ when $x = 2$.

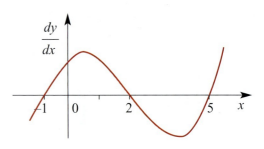

2 The graph shown is that of a polynomial function of the form $P(x) = ax^3 + bx^2 + cx + d$. Find the values of a, b, c and d.

Note: $Q(1, -2)$ is not a turning point.

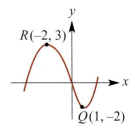

3 A body moves in a path described by the equation $y = \dfrac{1}{5}x^5 + \dfrac{1}{2}x^4$, for $x \geq 0$.

Units are in kilometres, and x and y are the horizontal and vertical axes respectively.

a What will be the direction of motion (give your answer as the angle between the direction of motion and the x-axis) when the x-value is:

i 1 km **ii** 3 km?

b Find a value of x for which the gradient of the path is 32.

4 A trail over a mountain pass can be modelled by the curve $y = 2 + 0.12x - 0.01x^3$, where x and y are the horizontal and vertical distances respectively, measured in kilometres, and $0 \leq x \leq 3$.

a Find the gradients at the beginning and the end of the trail.

b Calculate the point where the gradient is zero, and calculate also the height of the pass.

5 A tadpole begins to swim vertically upwards in a pond and after t seconds it is $25 - 0.1t^3$ cm below the surface.

a How long does the tadpole take to reach the surface, and what is its speed then?

b What is the average speed over this time?

6 **a** Show that the gradients of the curve $y = x(x - 2)$ at the points $(0, 0)$ and $(2, 0)$ only differ in sign. What is the geometrical interpretation for this?

b If the gradients of the curve $y = x(x - 2)(x - 5)$ at the points $(0, 0)$, $(2, 0)$ and $(5, 0)$ are ℓ, m and n respectively, show that $\dfrac{1}{\ell} + \dfrac{1}{m} + \dfrac{1}{n} = 0$.

Chapter 18
Applications of differentiation and antidifferentiation of polynomials

Objectives

▶ To be able to find the equation of the **tangent** and the **normal** at a given point on a polynomial curve.
▶ To use the derivative of a polynomial in **rate of change** problems.
▶ To be able to find the **stationary points** on the curves of certain polynomial functions and to state the nature of such points.
▶ To use differential calculus for **sketching the graphs** of polynomial functions.
▶ To apply differential calculus to the solution of **maximum and minimum** problems.
▶ To use derivatives and antiderivatives in problems involving **motion in a straight line**.

In this chapter we continue our study of calculus. There are two main aspects of this chapter. One is to apply our knowledge of the derivative to sketching graphs and solving maximum and minimum problems. The other is to see that the derivative can be used to define instantaneous rate of change.

The new techniques for sketching graphs of polynomial functions are a useful addition to the skills that were introduced in Chapter 6. At that stage, rather frustratingly, we were only able to determine the coordinates of turning points of cubic and quartic functions using technology. The new techniques are also used for determining maximum or minimum values for problems set in a 'real world' context.

The use of the derivative to determine instantaneous rates of change is a very important application of calculus. One of the first areas of applied mathematics to be studied in the seventeenth century was motion in a straight line. The problems of kinematics were the motivation for Newton's work on calculus.

Chapter 18: Applications of differentiation and antidifferentiation of polynomials

18A Tangents and normals

Skillsheet

The derivative of a function is a new function which gives the measure of the gradient of the tangent at each point on the curve. If the gradient is known, it is possible to find the equation of the tangent for a given point on the curve.

Suppose (x_1, y_1) is a point on the curve $y = f(x)$. Then, if f is differentiable at $x = x_1$, the equation of the tangent at (x_1, y_1) is given by $y - y_1 = f'(x_1)(x - x_1)$.

Example 1

Find the equation of the tangent to the curve $y = x^3 + \frac{1}{2}x^2$ at the point $x = 1$.

Solution

When $x = 1$, $y = \frac{3}{2}$, and so $(1, \frac{3}{2})$ is a point on the tangent.

Since $\dfrac{dy}{dx} = 3x^2 + x$, the gradient of the tangent to the curve at $x = 1$ is 4.

Hence the equation of the tangent is

$$y - \tfrac{3}{2} = 4(x - 1)$$

which becomes $y = 4x - \tfrac{5}{2}$.

Using the TI-Nspire

Use menu > **Calculus** > **Tangent Line** to calculate the tangent to the curve at $x = 1$.

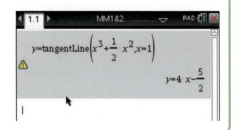

Using the Casio ClassPad

The tangent to the graph of $y = x^3 + \frac{1}{2}x^2$ at the point $x = 1$ can be found in two ways.

Method 1

- In Main $\sqrt{\alpha}$, enter and highlight the expression $x^3 + \frac{1}{2}x^2$.
- Select **Interactive** > **Calculation** > **line** > **tanLine**.
- The pop-up window shown will appear. Enter the value 1 for the point and tap OK.

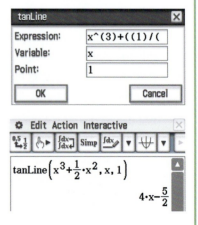

Method 2

- In , enter the expression $x^3 + \frac{1}{2}x^2$ in y1.
- Tick the box for y1 and select the graph icon.
- Select **Analysis > Sketch > Tangent**.
- When the graph appears, press the x-value of interest, in this case $x = 1$, and the window shown below will appear. Tap OK.

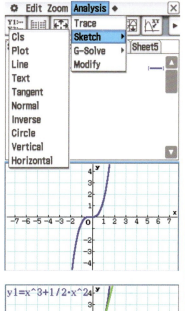

- The tangent at $x = 1$ is drawn on the graph.
- To view the equation of the tangent, tap EXE.
- The tangent equation is shown at the bottom of the screen.

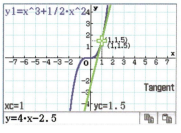

The **normal** to a curve at a point on the curve is the line which passes through the point and is perpendicular to the tangent at that point.

Recall from Chapter 2 that two lines with gradients m_1 and m_2 are perpendicular if and only if $m_1 m_2 = -1$.

Thus, if a tangent has gradient m, the normal has gradient $-\dfrac{1}{m}$.

Example 2

Find the equation of the normal to the curve with equation $y = x^3 - 2x^2$ at the point $(1, -1)$.

Solution

The point $(1, -1)$ lies on the normal.

Since $\dfrac{dy}{dx} = 3x^2 - 4x$, the gradient of the tangent at $x = 1$ is -1.

Thus the gradient of the normal at $x = 1$ is $\dfrac{-1}{-1} = 1$.

Hence the equation of the normal is

$$y - (-1) = 1(x - 1)$$

i.e. the equation of the normal is $y = x - 2$.

Using the TI-Nspire

Use menu > Calculus > Normal Line to calculate the normal to the curve at the point $(1, -1)$, i.e. when $x = 1$.

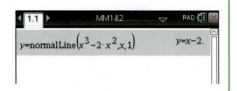

Using the Casio ClassPad

The normal to the graph of $y = x^3 - 2x^2$ at the point $(1, -1)$ can be found in two ways.

Method 1

- In Main, enter and highlight $x^3 - 2x^2$.
- Select **Interactive > Calculation > line > normal**.
- In the pop-up window that appears, enter the value 1 for the point and tap OK.

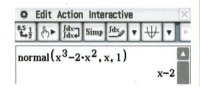

Method 2

- In Graph&Table, enter the expression $x^3 - 2x^2$ in y1.
- Tick the box for y1 and select the graph icon.
- Select **Analysis > Sketch > Normal**.
- When the graph appears, press the x-value of interest, in this case $x = 1$. Tap OK.
- The normal at $x = 1$ is drawn on the graph.
- To view the equation of the normal, tap EXE.

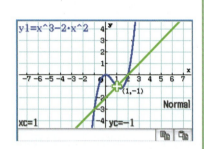

Section summary

- **Equation of a tangent** Suppose (x_1, y_1) is a point on the curve $y = f(x)$. Then, if f is differentiable at $x = x_1$, the equation of the tangent to the curve at (x_1, y_1) is given by $y - y_1 = f'(x_1)(x - x_1)$.
- **Gradient of normal** If a tangent has gradient m, the normal has gradient $-\dfrac{1}{m}$.

Exercise 18A

Example 1, 2

1 Find the equation of the tangent and the normal at the given point for:

a $f(x) = x^2$, $(2, 4)$
b $f(x) = (2x - 1)^2$, $(2, 9)$
c $f(x) = 3x - x^2$, $(2, 2)$
d $f(x) = 9x - x^3$, $(1, 8)$

2 Find the equation of the tangent to the curve with equation $y = 3x^3 - 4x^2 + 2x - 10$ at the point of intersection with the y-axis.

3 Find the equation of the tangent to $y = x^2$ at the point $(1, 1)$ and the equation of the tangent to $y = \frac{1}{6}x^3$ at the point $\left(2, \frac{4}{3}\right)$.
Show that these tangents are parallel and find the perpendicular distance between them.

4 Find the equations of the tangents to the curve $y = x^3 - 6x^2 + 12x + 2$ which are parallel to the line $y = 3x$.

5 The curve with the equation $y = (x - 2)(x - 3)(x - 4)$ cuts the x-axis at the points $P = (2, 0)$, $Q = (3, 0)$ and $R = (4, 0)$.
   a Prove that the tangents at P and R are parallel.
   b At what point does the normal to the curve at Q cut the y-axis?

6 For the curve with equation $y = x^2 + 3$, show that $y = 2ax - a^2 + 3$ is the equation of the tangent at the point $(a, a^2 + 3)$.
Hence find the coordinates of the two points on the curve, the tangents of which pass through the point $(2, 6)$.

7 a Find the equation of the tangent at the point $(2, 4)$ to the curve $y = x^3 - 2x$.
   b Find the coordinates of the point where the tangent meets the curve again.

8 a Find the equation of the tangent to the curve $y = x^3 - 9x^2 + 20x - 8$ at the point $(1, 4)$.
   b At what points on the curve is the tangent parallel to the line $4x + y - 3 = 0$?

18B Rates of change

The derivative of a function was defined geometrically in the previous chapter. But, as seen in Chapter 16, the process of differentiation may be used to tackle many kinds of problems involving rates of change.

> For the function with rule $f(x)$:
> - The **average rate of change** for $x \in [a, b]$ is given by $\dfrac{f(b) - f(a)}{b - a}$.
> - The **instantaneous rate of change** of f with respect to x when $x = a$ is defined to be $f'(a)$.

Average rate of change has been discussed in Chapter 16.

The instantaneous rate of change of y with respect to x is given by $\dfrac{dy}{dx}$, that is, by the derivative of y with respect to x.

- If $\dfrac{dy}{dx} > 0$, the change is an increase in the value of y corresponding to an increase in x.
- If $\dfrac{dy}{dx} < 0$, the change is a decrease in the value of y corresponding to an increase in x.

Example 3

For the function with rule $f(x) = x^2 + 2x$, find:

a the average rate of change for $x \in [2, 3]$
b the average rate of change for the interval $[2, 2 + h]$
c the instantaneous rate of change of f with respect to x when $x = 2$.

Solution

a Average rate of change $= \dfrac{f(3) - f(2)}{3 - 2} = 15 - 8 = 7$

b Average rate of change $= \dfrac{f(2 + h) - f(2)}{2 + h - 2}$

$= \dfrac{(2 + h)^2 + 2(2 + h) - 8}{h}$

$= \dfrac{4 + 4h + h^2 + 4 + 2h - 8}{h}$

$= \dfrac{6h + h^2}{h}$

$= 6 + h$

c The derivative is $f'(x) = 2x + 2$. When $x = 2$, the instantaneous rate of change is $f'(2) = 6$. This can also be seen from the result of part b.

Using the TI-Nspire

- For parts a and b, use the catalog to access the **Average Rate of Change** command (catalog 1 A) and enter as:

  avgRC(*expression, x = initial value, step size*)

- For part c, use menu > **Calculus** > **Derivative at a Point** and complete as shown.

Example 4

A balloon develops a microscopic leak and gradually decreases in volume.
Its volume, V (cm^3), at time t (seconds) is $V = 600 - 10t - \dfrac{1}{100}t^2$, $t > 0$.

a Find the rate of change of volume after:

    i 10 seconds
    ii 20 seconds.

b For how long could the model be valid?

Solution

a $V = 600 - 10t - \dfrac{1}{100}t^2$

$\dfrac{dV}{dt} = -10 - \dfrac{t}{50}$

i When $t = 10$, $\dfrac{dV}{dt} = -10 - \dfrac{1}{5}$

$= -10\dfrac{1}{5}$

i.e. the volume is decreasing at a rate of $10\dfrac{1}{5}$ cm^3 per second.

ii When $t = 20$, $\dfrac{dV}{dt} = -10 - \dfrac{2}{5}$

$= -10\dfrac{2}{5}$

i.e. the volume is decreasing at a rate of $10\dfrac{2}{5}$ cm^3 per second.

b The model will not be meaningful when $V < 0$.

Consider $V = 0$:

$$600 - 10t - \dfrac{1}{100}t^2 = 0$$

$\therefore \quad t = \dfrac{10 \pm \sqrt{100 + 4 \times 0.01 \times 600}}{-0.02}$

$\therefore \quad t = -1056.78 \quad \text{or} \quad t = 56.78 \quad \text{(to two decimal places)}$

Hence the model may be suitable for $0 < t < 56.78$.

Using the TI-Nspire

Define $v(t) = 600 - 10t - (1/100)t^2$.

a Use menu > **Calculus** > **Derivative** and enter the required t-values using the | symbol ((ctrl)(=)) to evaluate the derivative of $v(t)$ at $t = 10$ and $t = 20$.

Press (ctrl)(enter) to obtain the answer as a decimal number.

Note: If you used menu > **Calculus** > **Derivative at a Point** instead, then each t-value would need to be evaluated separately.

b To find the domain, use:

$\text{solve}(v(t) > 0, t) \mid t > 0$

Press (ctrl)(enter) to obtain the answer as a decimal number.

Using the Casio ClassPad

- In $\sqrt{\alpha}$ Main, enter and highlight $600 - 10t - \dfrac{1}{100}t^2$.
- Select **Interactive > Define**: enter the function name V using the `abc` keyboard, set the variable to t using the `Var` keyboard, and then tap OK.
- In the next entry line, enter and highlight $V(t)$.
- Go to **Interactive > Calculation > diff**. Set the variable to t and tap OK.
- To substitute values of t, insert | from the `Math3` keyboard and type $t = 10$ or $t = 20$ after the derivative, as shown.

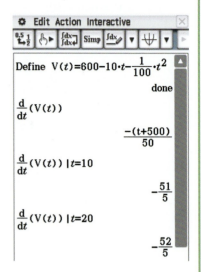

- To find the domain, enter and highlight $V(t) > 0$.
- Go to **Interactive > Equation/Inequality > solve**. Set the variable to t and tap OK.

$$\text{solve}(V(t)>0, t)$$
$$\{-100\cdot\sqrt{31}-500 < t < 100\cdot\sqrt{31}-500\}$$

$$\text{solve}(V(t)>0, t)$$
$$\{-1056.776436 < t < 56.77643628\}$$

- Disregard negative values, since $t > 0$. So the answer is $0 < t < 56.78$.
- The domain can also be obtained graphically by finding where $V = 0$.

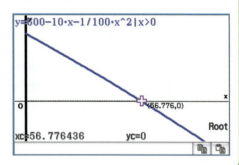

Section summary

For the function with rule $f(x)$:

- The average rate of change for $x \in [a, b]$ is given by $\dfrac{f(b) - f(a)}{b - a}$.
- The instantaneous rate of change of f with respect to x when $x = a$ is $f'(a)$.

Exercise 18B

Example 3

1 Let $y = 35 + 12x^2$.

   a Find the change in y as x changes from 1 to 2. What is the average rate of change of y with respect to x in this interval?

   b Find the change in y as x changes from $2 - h$ to 2. What is the average rate of change of y with respect to x in this interval?

   c Find the rate of change of y with respect to x when $x = 2$.

Example 4

2 According to a business magazine, the expected assets, M, of a proposed new company will be given by $M = 200\,000 + 600t^2 - \dfrac{200}{3}t^3$, where t is the number of months after the business is set up.

   a Find the rate of growth of assets at time t months.

   b Find the rate of growth of assets at time $t = 3$ months.

   c When will the rate of growth of assets be zero?

3 As a result of a survey, the marketing director of a company found that the revenue, R, from pricing 100 produced items at P each is given by the rule $R = 30P - 2P^2$.

   a Find $\dfrac{dR}{dP}$ and explain what it means.

   b Calculate $\dfrac{dR}{dP}$ when $P = 5$ and $P = 10$.

   c For what selling prices is revenue rising?

4 The population, P, of a new housing estate t years after 30 January 2012 is given by the rule $P = 100(5 + t - 0.25t^2)$. Find the rate of change of the population after:

   a 1 year
   b 2 years
   c 3 years.

5 Water is being poured into a flask. The volume, V mL, of water in the flask at time t seconds is given by $V(t) = \dfrac{5}{8}\left(10t^2 - \dfrac{t^3}{3}\right)$, $0 \le t \le 20$.

   a Find the volume of water in the flask at time:

   i $t = 0$ **ii** $t = 20$.

   b Find the rate of flow of water into the flask at time t.

   c Sketch the graph of $V'(t)$ against t for $0 \le t \le 20$.

6 The area, A km^2, of an oil slick is growing according to the rule $A = \dfrac{t}{2} + \dfrac{t^2}{10}$, where t is the time in hours since the leak started.

   a Find the area covered at the end of 1 hour.

   b Find the rate of increase of the area after 1 hour.

18C Stationary points

Skillsheet In the previous chapter, we have seen that the gradient of the tangent at a point $(a, f(a))$ on the curve with rule $y = f(x)$ is given by $f'(a)$.

> A point $(a, f(a))$ on a curve $y = f(x)$ is said to be a **stationary point** if $f'(a) = 0$.
>
> Equivalently, for $y = f(x)$, if $\dfrac{dy}{dx} = 0$ when $x = a$, then $(a, f(a))$ is a stationary point.

In the graph shown, there are stationary points at A, B and C. At such points the tangents are parallel to the x-axis (illustrated as dashed lines).

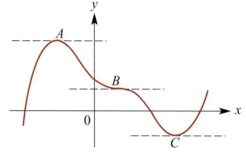

The reason for the name *stationary points* becomes clear later in this chapter when we look at the application to the motion of a particle.

Example 5

Find the stationary points of the following functions:
a $y = 9 + 12x - 2x^2$ **b** $p = 2t^3 - 5t^2 - 4t + 13$ for $t > 0$ **c** $y = 4 + 3x - x^3$

Solution

a $y = 9 + 12x - 2x^2$

$\dfrac{dy}{dx} = 12 - 4x$

The stationary points occur when $\dfrac{dy}{dx} = 0$, i.e. when $12 - 4x = 0$, i.e. at $x = 3$.

When $x = 3$, $y = 9 + 12 \times 3 - 2 \times 3^2 = 27$. Thus the stationary point is at $(3, 27)$.

b $p = 2t^3 - 5t^2 - 4t + 13$ $(t > 0)$

$\dfrac{dp}{dt} = 6t^2 - 10t - 4$ $(t > 0)$

Thus, $\dfrac{dp}{dt} = 0$ implies $2(3t^2 - 5t - 2) = 0$

$(3t + 1)(t - 2) = 0$

$\therefore t = -\dfrac{1}{3}$ or $t = 2$

But $t > 0$, therefore the only acceptable solution is $t = 2$.
When $t = 2$, $p = 16 - 20 - 8 + 13 = 1$.
So the corresponding stationary point is $(2, 1)$.

c $y = 4 + 3x - x^3$

$\dfrac{dy}{dx} = 3 - 3x^2$

Thus, $\dfrac{dy}{dx} = 0$ implies $3(1 - x^2) = 0$

$\therefore \quad x = \pm 1$

The stationary points occur at $(1, 6)$ and $(-1, 2)$.

Example 6

The curve with equation $y = x^3 + ax^2 + bx + c$ passes through $(0, 5)$ and has a stationary point at $(2, 7)$. Find a, b and c.

Solution

When $x = 0$, $y = 5$. Thus $c = 5$.

We have $\dfrac{dy}{dx} = 3x^2 + 2ax + b$ and at $x = 2$, $\dfrac{dy}{dx} = 0$.

Therefore

$0 = 12 + 4a + b \quad (1)$

The point $(2, 7)$ is on the curve and so

$7 = 2^3 + 2^2 a + 2b + 5$

$2 = 8 + 4a + 2b$

$4a + 2b + 6 = 0 \quad (2)$

Subtract (2) from (1):

$-b + 6 = 0$

$\therefore \quad b = 6$

Substitute in (1):

$0 = 12 + 4a + 6$

$-18 = 4a$

$\therefore \quad -\dfrac{9}{2} = a$

Hence $a = -\dfrac{9}{2}$, $b = 6$ and $c = 5$.

Section summary

- A point $(a, f(a))$ on a curve $y = f(x)$ is said to be a **stationary point** if $f'(a) = 0$.
- Equivalently, for $y = f(x)$, if $\dfrac{dy}{dx} = 0$ when $x = a$, then $(a, f(a))$ is a stationary point.

Exercise 18C

1 Find the coordinates of the stationary points of each of the following functions:
  a $f(x) = x^2 - 6x + 3$
  b $y = x^3 - 4x^2 - 3x + 20$ for $x > 0$
  c $z = x^4 - 32x + 50$
  d $q = 8t + 5t^2 - t^3$ for $t > 0$
  e $y = 2x^2(x - 3)$
  f $y = 3x^4 - 16x^3 + 24x^2 - 10$

2 The curve with equation $y = ax^2 + bx + c$ passes through $(0, -1)$ and has a stationary point at $(2, -9)$. Find a, b and c.

3 The curve with equation $y = ax^2 + bx + c$ has a stationary point at $(1, 2)$. When $x = 0$, the slope of the curve is $45°$. Find a, b and c.

4 The curve with equation $y = ax^2 + bx$ has a gradient of 3 at the point $(2, -2)$.
  a Find the values of a and b.
  b Find the coordinates of the turning point.

5 The curve with equation $y = x^2 + ax + 3$ has a stationary point when $x = 4$. Find a.

6 The curve with equation $y = x^2 - ax + 4$ has a stationary point when $x = 3$. Find a.

7 Find the coordinates of the stationary points of each of the following:
  a $y = x^2 - 5x - 6$
  b $y = (3x - 2)(8x + 3)$
  c $y = 2x^3 - 9x^2 + 27$
  d $y = x^3 - 3x^2 - 24x + 20$
  e $y = (x + 1)^2(x + 4)$
  f $y = (x + 1)^2 + (x + 2)^2$

8 The curve with equation $y = ax^2 + bx + 12$ has a stationary point at $(1, 13)$. Find a and b.

9 The curve with equation $y = ax^3 + bx^2 + cx + d$ has a gradient of -3 at $(0, 7\frac{1}{2})$ and a turning point at $(3, 6)$. Find a, b, c and d.

18D Types of stationary points

The graph of $y = f(x)$ below has three stationary points $A(a, f(a))$, $B(b, f(b))$, $C(c, f(c))$.

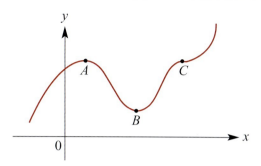

A Point A is called a **local maximum** point.
Notice that $f'(x) > 0$ immediately to the left of A, and that $f'(x) < 0$ immediately to the right of A. This means that f is strictly increasing immediately to the left of A, and strictly decreasing immediately to the right of A.

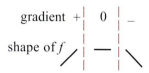

B Point B is called a **local minimum** point.
Notice that $f'(x) < 0$ immediately to the left of B, and that $f'(x) > 0$ immediately to the right of B. This means that f is strictly decreasing immediately to the left of B, and strictly increasing immediately to the right of B.

C The point C is called a **stationary point of inflection**.
Notice that $f'(x) > 0$ immediately to the left and right of C.

Clearly it is also possible to have stationary points of inflection with $f'(x) < 0$ immediately to the left and right.

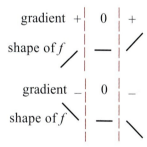

Stationary points of types A and B are referred to as **turning points**.

Before proceeding with some more complicated functions, it is worth referring back to some of the functions we met earlier in this book.

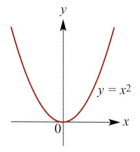
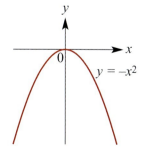
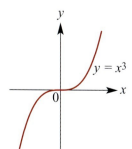

$f : \mathbb{R} \to \mathbb{R}, f(x) = x^2$
Local minimum at $(0, 0)$.

$f : \mathbb{R} \to \mathbb{R}, f(x) = -x^2$
Local maximum at $(0, 0)$.

$f : \mathbb{R} \to \mathbb{R}, f(x) = x^3$
Stationary point of inflection at $(0, 0)$.

Example 7

For the function $f: \mathbb{R} \to \mathbb{R}$, $f(x) = 3x^3 - 4x + 1$:

a Find the stationary points and state their nature.
b Sketch the graph.

Solution

a The derivative is $f'(x) = 9x^2 - 4$.

The stationary points occur where $f'(x) = 0$:

$$9x^2 - 4 = 0$$
$$\therefore \quad x = \pm \frac{2}{3}$$

There are stationary points at $(-\frac{2}{3}, f(-\frac{2}{3}))$ and $(\frac{2}{3}, f(\frac{2}{3}))$, that is, at $(-\frac{2}{3}, 2\frac{7}{9})$ and $(\frac{2}{3}, -\frac{7}{9})$. So $f'(x)$ is of constant sign for each of

$$\{x : x < -\tfrac{2}{3}\}, \quad \{x : -\tfrac{2}{3} < x < \tfrac{2}{3}\} \quad \text{and} \quad \{x : x > \tfrac{2}{3}\}$$

To calculate the sign of $f'(x)$ for each of these sets, simply choose a representative number in the set.

Thus $f'(-1) = 9 - 4 = 5 > 0$
$f'(0) = 0 - 4 = -4 < 0$
$f'(1) = 9 - 4 = 5 > 0$

We can now put together the table shown on the right.

x		$-\frac{2}{3}$		$\frac{2}{3}$	
$f'(x)$	+	0	−	0	+
shape of f	╱	—	╲	—	╱

There is a local maximum at $(-\frac{2}{3}, 2\frac{7}{9})$ and a local minimum at $(\frac{2}{3}, -\frac{7}{9})$.

b To sketch the graph of this function we need to find the axis intercepts and investigate the behaviour of the graph for $x > \frac{2}{3}$ and $x < -\frac{2}{3}$.

The y-axis intercept is $f(0) = 1$.

To find the x-axis intercepts, consider $f(x) = 0$, which implies $3x^3 - 4x + 1 = 0$. Using the factor theorem, we find that $x - 1$ is a factor of $3x^3 - 4x + 1$. By division:

$$3x^3 - 4x + 1 = (x - 1)(3x^2 + 3x - 1)$$

Now $(x - 1)(3x^2 + 3x - 1) = 0$ implies that $x = 1$ or $3x^2 + 3x - 1 = 0$.
We have

$$3x^2 + 3x - 1 = 3\left[\left(x + \frac{1}{2}\right)^2 - \frac{1}{4} - \frac{1}{3}\right]$$

$$= 3\left[\left(x + \frac{1}{2}\right)^2 - \frac{21}{36}\right]$$

$$= 3\left(x + \frac{1}{2} - \frac{\sqrt{21}}{6}\right)\left(x + \frac{1}{2} + \frac{\sqrt{21}}{6}\right)$$

Thus the x-axis intercepts are at

$$x = -\frac{1}{2} + \frac{\sqrt{21}}{6}, \quad x = -\frac{1}{2} - \frac{\sqrt{21}}{6}, \quad x = 1$$

For $x > \frac{2}{3}$, $f(x)$ becomes larger.

For $x < \frac{2}{3}$, $f(x)$ becomes smaller.

Using the TI-Nspire

- Define the function $f(x) = 3x^3 - 4x + 1$.
- Use menu > **Algebra** > **Solve** and menu > **Calculus** > **Derivative** to solve the equation $\frac{d}{dx}(f(x)) = 0$ and determine the coordinates of the stationary points.

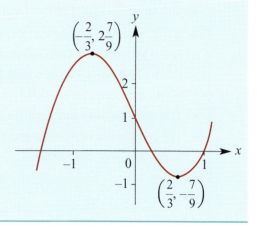

- Find the x-axis intercepts by solving the equation $f(x) = 0$.

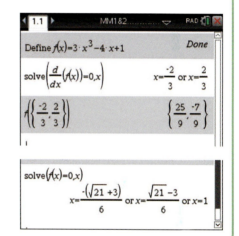

Using the Casio ClassPad

To determine the exact coordinates of the stationary points:

- In Main, define the function $f(x) = 3x^3 - 4x + 1$.
- Solve the equation $\frac{d}{dx}(f(x)) = 0$ for x.
- Evaluate the function f at each x-value to find the corresponding y-value.

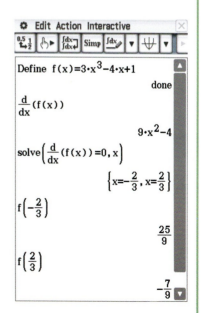

To determine the nature of these stationary points:

- In Main √α, enter and highlight $f(x)$.
- Select **Interactive > Calculation > fMin**.
- Enter a known interval in which the stationary points are located, e.g. start at -1 and end at 1.
- This gives the coordinates of the local minimum.
- The coordinates of the local maximum can be found similarly using **fMax**.

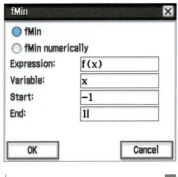

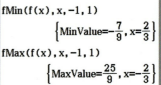

To find the x-axis intercepts:

- Solve the equation $f(x) = 0$.

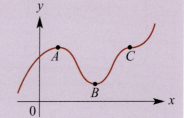

Section summary

A point $(a, f(a))$ on a curve $y = f(x)$ is said to be a **stationary point** if $f'(a) = 0$.

Types of stationary points

A Point A is a **local maximum**:
- $f'(x) > 0$ immediately to the left of A
- $f'(x) < 0$ immediately to the right of A.

B Point B is a **local minimum**:
- $f'(x) < 0$ immediately to the left of B
- $f'(x) > 0$ immediately to the right of B.

C Point C is a **stationary point of inflection**.

Stationary points of types A and B are called **turning points**.

Exercise 18D

Example 7

1 For each of the following, find all stationary points and state their nature. Sketch the graph of each function.

  a $y = 9x^2 - x^3$
  b $y = x^3 - 3x^2 - 9x$
  c $y = x^4 - 4x^3$

2 Find the stationary points (and state their type) for each of the following functions:

  a $y = x^2(x - 4)$
  b $y = x^2(3 - x)$
  c $y = x^4$
  d $y = x^5(x - 4)$
  e $y = x^3 - 5x^2 + 3x + 2$
  f $y = x(x - 8)(x - 3)$

3 Sketch the graph of each of the following functions:
  a $y = 2 + 3x - x^3$
  b $y = 2x^2(x - 3)$
  c $y = x^3 - 3x^2 - 9x + 11$

4 The graph corresponding to each of the following equations has a stationary point at $(-2, 10)$. For each graph, find the nature of the stationary point at $(-2, 10)$.
  a $y = 2x^3 + 3x^2 - 12x - 10$
  b $y = 3x^4 + 16x^3 + 24x^2 - 6$

5 For the function $y = x^3 - 6x^2 + 9x + 10$:
  a Find the values of x for which $\dfrac{dy}{dx} > 0$, i.e. find $\left\{x : \dfrac{dy}{dx} > 0\right\}$.
  b Find the stationary points on the curve corresponding to $y = x^3 - 6x^2 + 9x + 10$.
  c Sketch the curve carefully between $x = 0$ and $x = 4$.

6 For the function $f : \mathbb{R} \to \mathbb{R}$, $f(x) = 1 + 12x - x^3$, determine the values of x for which $f'(x) > 0$.

7 Let $f : \mathbb{R} \to \mathbb{R}$, where $f(x) = 3 + 6x - 2x^3$.
  a Find the values of x such that $f'(x) > 0$.
  b Find the values of x such that $f'(x) < 0$.

8 Let $f(x) = x(x + 3)(x - 5)$.
  a Find the values of x for which $f'(x) = 0$.
  b Sketch the graph of $y = f(x)$ for $-5 \leq x \leq 6$, giving the coordinates of the intersections with the axes and the coordinates of the turning points.

9 Sketch the graph of $y = x^3 - 6x^2 + 9x - 4$. State the coordinates of the axis intercepts and the turning points.

10 Find the coordinates of the points on the curve $y = x^3 - 3x^2 - 45x + 2$ where the tangent is parallel to the x-axis.

11 Let $f(x) = x^3 - 3x^2$.
  a Find:
    i $\{x : f'(x) < 0\}$
    ii $\{x : f'(x) > 0\}$
    iii $\{x : f'(x) = 0\}$
  b Sketch the graph of $y = f(x)$.

12 Sketch the graph of $y = x^3 - 9x^2 + 27x - 19$ and state the coordinates of the stationary points.

13 Sketch the graph of $y = x^4 - 8x^2 + 7$. All axis intercepts and all turning points should be identified and their coordinates given.

18E Applications to maximum and minimum problems

Skillsheet Many practical problems involve finding a maximum or minimum value of a function. We have solved some of these in Chapters 3 and 6. In the case of quadratic functions, we wrote the quadratic in turning point form and hence determined the maximum or minimum value. In the case of cubic functions, we used a CAS calculator to find the maximum or minimum values.

In this section we use calculus to solve problems which involve finding a local maximum or local minimum.

Example 8

A loop of string of length 100 cm is to be formed into a rectangle. Find the maximum area of this rectangle.

Solution

Let the length of the rectangle be x cm and the width y cm.

Then $2x + 2y = 100$. Thus $x + y = 50$ and hence

$$y = 50 - x \quad (1)$$

It is clear that, for this problem, we must have $0 \leq x \leq 50$.

The area, A cm^2, is given by the formula $A = xy$.

Substituting from (1) gives

$$A = x(50 - x)$$
$$= 50x - x^2$$

Differentiating with respect to x:

$$\frac{dA}{dx} = 50 - 2x$$

Thus $\dfrac{dA}{dx} = 0$ implies $x = 25$.

Since the coefficient of x^2 is negative, this stationary point is a local maximum. (Alternatively, we could check the sign of $A'(x)$ immediately to the left and the right of $x = 25$.)

The maximum area is formed when the rectangle is a square with side length 25 cm, and so the maximum area is 625 cm^2.

Note: It is clear that we could have completed this question without calculus by using our knowledge of quadratic functions.

18E Applications to maximum and minimum problems 641

Example 9

Given that $x + 2y = 4$, calculate the minimum value of $x^2 + xy - y^2$.

Solution

Rearranging $x + 2y = 4$, we have $x = 4 - 2y$.

Let $P = x^2 + xy - y^2$. Substituting for x gives
$$P = (4 - 2y)^2 + (4 - 2y)y - y^2$$
$$= 16 - 16y + 4y^2 + 4y - 2y^2 - y^2$$
$$= 16 - 12y + y^2$$
$$\therefore \frac{dP}{dy} = -12 + 2y$$

Stationary values occur when $\frac{dP}{dy} = 0$:

$-12 + 2y = 0$

$y = 6$

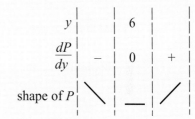

From the diagram, there is a minimum when $y = 6$.

When $y = 6$, $x = -8$. Thus the minimum value of $x^2 + xy - y^2$ is -20.

Example 10

From a square piece of metal of side length 2 m, four squares are removed as shown in the diagram. The metal is then folded along the dashed lines to form an open box with height x m.

a Show that the volume of the box, V m^3, is given by
$V = 4x^3 - 8x^2 + 4x$.

b Find the value of x that gives the box its maximum volume and show that the volume is a maximum for this value.

c Sketch the graph of V against x for a suitable domain.

d Find the value(s) of x for which $V = 0.5$ m^3.

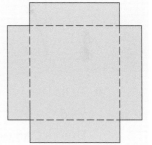

Solution

a The box has length and width $2 - 2x$ metres, and has height x metres. Thus
$$V = (2 - 2x)^2 x$$
$$= (4 - 8x + 4x^2)x$$
$$= 4x^3 - 8x^2 + 4x$$

b Let $V = 4x^3 - 8x^2 + 4x$. The maximum volume will occur when $\dfrac{dV}{dx} = 0$.

We have $\dfrac{dV}{dx} = 12x^2 - 16x + 4$, and so $\dfrac{dV}{dx} = 0$ implies that

$$12x^2 - 16x + 4 = 0$$
$$3x^2 - 4x + 1 = 0$$
$$(3x - 1)(x - 1) = 0$$
$$\therefore \ x = \dfrac{1}{3} \text{ or } x = 1$$

But, when $x = 1$, the length of the box is $2 - 2x = 0$. Therefore the only value to be considered is $x = \dfrac{1}{3}$. We show the entire chart for completeness.

A maximum occurs when $x = \dfrac{1}{3}$.

$\therefore$ Maximum volume $= \left(2 - 2 \times \dfrac{1}{3}\right)^2 \times \dfrac{1}{3}$

$= \dfrac{16}{27}$ m^3

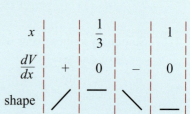

c

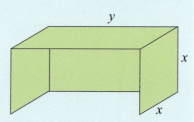

d To find the value(s) of x for which $V = 0.5$ m^3, we need to solve the equation $V = 0.5$, i.e. $4x^3 - 8x^2 + 4x = 0.5$.

Using a CAS calculator gives $x = \dfrac{1}{2}$ or $x = \dfrac{3 \pm \sqrt{5}}{4}$.

But the domain of V is $[0, 1]$. Hence $x = \dfrac{1}{2}$ or $x = \dfrac{3 - \sqrt{5}}{4}$.

Example 11

A canvas shelter is made up with a back, two square sides and a top. The area of canvas available is 24 m^2. Let V m^3 be the volume enclosed by the shelter.

a Find the dimensions of the shelter that will create the largest possible enclosed volume.

b Sketch the graph of V against x for a suitable domain.

c Find the values of x and y for which $V = 10$ m^3.

Solution

a The volume $V = x^2y$. One of the variables must be eliminated.
We know that the area is 24 m².

$$\therefore \quad 2x^2 + 2xy = 24$$

Rearranging gives $y = \dfrac{24 - 2x^2}{2x}$, i.e. $y = \dfrac{12}{x} - x$.

Substituting in the formula for volume gives

$$V = 12x - x^3$$

Differentiation now gives

$$\frac{dV}{dx} = 12 - 3x^2$$

Stationary points occur when $\dfrac{dV}{dx} = 0$, which implies $12 - 3x^2 = 0$.

So stationary points occur when $x^2 = 4$, i.e. when $x = \pm 2$. But negative values have no meaning in this problem, so the only solution is $x = 2$.

Hence the maximum is at $x = 2$. The dimensions are 2 m, 2 m, 4 m.

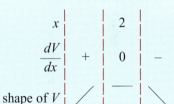

shape of V

b Note that $x > 0$ and $y \geq 0$.
This implies $x > 0$ and $12 - x^2 \geq 0$, i.e. $0 < x \leq 2\sqrt{3}$.

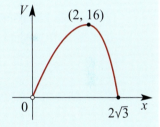

c Using a CAS calculator, solve the equation $12x - x^3 = 10$ numerically.
The solutions are $x = 2.9304\ldots$ and $x = 0.8925\ldots$
Possible dimensions to the nearest centimetre are 2.93 m, 2.93 m, 1.16 m and 0.89 m, 0.89 m, 12.55 m.

▶ Maximum or minimum at an endpoint

Calculus can be used to find a local maximum or local minimum, but these are often not the actual maximum or minimum values of the function.

For a function defined on an interval:

- the actual maximum value of the function is called the **absolute maximum**
- the actual minimum value of the function is called the **absolute minimum**.

The corresponding points on the graph of the function are not necessarily stationary points.

Example 12

Let $f: [-2, 4] \to \mathbb{R}$, $f(x) = x^2 + 2$. Find the absolute maximum value and the absolute minimum value of the function.

Solution

The maximum value is 18 and occurs when $x = 4$.

The minimum value is 2 and occurs when $x = 0$.

The minimum value occurs at a stationary point of the graph, but the endpoint $(4, 18)$ is not a stationary point.

The absolute maximum value is 18 and the absolute minimum value is 2.

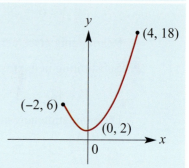

Example 13

Let $f: [-2, 1] \to \mathbb{R}$, $f(x) = x^3 + 2$. Find the maximum and minimum values of the function.

Solution

The maximum value is 3 and occurs when $x = 1$.

The minimum value is -6 and occurs when $x = -2$.

The absolute maximum and the absolute minimum do not occur at stationary points.

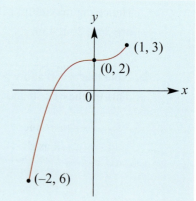

Example 14

In Example 10, the maximum volume of a box was found. The maximum value corresponded to a local maximum of the graph of $V = 4x^3 - 8x^2 + 4x$. This was also the absolute maximum value.

If the height of the box must be at most 0.3 m (i.e. $x \leq 0.3$), what will be the maximum volume of the box?

Solution

The local maximum of $V(x)$ for $x \in [0, 1]$ was at $x = \dfrac{1}{3}$. But $\dfrac{1}{3}$ is greater than 0.3.

For the new problem, we have $V'(x) > 0$ for all $x \in [0, 0.3]$, and so $V(x)$ is strictly increasing on the interval $[0, 0.3]$.

Therefore the maximum volume occurs when $x = 0.3$ and is 0.588 m^3.

18E Applications to maximum and minimum problems

Section summary

Here are some steps for solving maximum and minimum problems:

- Where possible, draw a diagram to illustrate the problem. Label the diagram and designate your variables and constants. Note the values that the variables can take.
- Write an expression for the quantity that is going to be maximised or minimised. Form an equation for this quantity in terms of a single independent variable. This may require some algebraic manipulation.
- If $y = f(x)$ is the quantity to be maximised or minimised, find the values of x for which $f'(x) = 0$.
- Test each point for which $f'(x) = 0$ to determine whether it is a local maximum, a local minimum or neither.
- If the function $y = f(x)$ is defined on an interval, such as $[a, b]$ or $[0, \infty)$, check the values of the function at the endpoints.

Exercise 18E

Example 8   **1**   A loop of string of length 200 cm is to be formed into a rectangle. Find the maximum area of this rectangle.

2   Find the maximum value of the product of two numbers x and $10 - x$.

Example 9   **3**   Given that $x + y = 2$, calculate the minimum value of $x^2 + y^2$.

Example 10   **4**   From a square piece of metal of side length 6 m, four squares are removed as shown in the diagram. The metal is folded along the dashed lines to form an open box with height x m.

    a   Show that the volume of the box, V m^3, is given by
$$V = 4x^3 - 24x^2 + 36x.$$
    b   Find the value of x that gives the box its maximum volume and find the maximum volume.

5   A bank of earth has cross-section as shown in the diagram. The curve defining the bank has equation
$$y = \frac{x^2}{400}(20 - x) \quad \text{for } x \in [0, 20]$$

    a   Find the height of the bank where:
      i $x = 5$ **ii** $x = 10$ **iii** $x = 15$

    b   Find the value of x for which the height is a maximum and state the maximum height of the bank.

    c   Find the values of x for which:
      i $\dfrac{dy}{dx} = \dfrac{1}{8}$ **ii** $\dfrac{dy}{dx} = -\dfrac{1}{8}$

6 A cuboid has a total surface area of 150 cm² and a square base of side length x cm.
  a Show that the height, h cm, of the cuboid is given by $h = \dfrac{75 - x^2}{2x}$.
  b Express the volume of the cuboid in terms of x.
  c Hence determine its maximum volume as x varies.
  d If the maximum side length of the square base of the cuboid is 4 cm, what is the maximum volume possible?

7 The volume of a cylinder is given by the formula $V = \pi r^2 h$. Find the maximum value of V if $r + h = 12$.

8 A rectangular sheet of metal measures 50 cm by 40 cm. Congruent squares of side length x cm are cut from each of the corners and not used further. The sheet is then folded up to make a tray of depth x cm. Find the value of x for which the volume of the tray is a maximum.

9 Let $f: [-2, 2] \to \mathbb{R}$, $f(x) = 2 - 8x^2$. Find the absolute maximum value and the absolute minimum value of the function.

10 Let $f: [-2, 1] \to \mathbb{R}$, $f(x) = x^3 + 2x + 3$. Find the absolute maximum value and the absolute minimum value of the function for its domain.

11 Let $f: [0, 4] \to \mathbb{R}$, $f(x) = 2x^3 - 6x^2$. Find the absolute maximum and the absolute minimum values of the function.

12 Let $f: [-2, 5] \to \mathbb{R}$, $f(x) = 2x^4 - 8x^2$. Find the absolute maximum and the absolute minimum values of the function.

13 A rectangular block is such that the sides of its base are of length x cm and $3x$ cm. The sum of the lengths of all its edges is 20 cm.
  a Show that the volume, V cm³, is given by $V = 15x^2 - 12x^3$.
  b Find the derivative $\dfrac{dV}{dx}$.
  c Find the local maximum for the graph of V against x for $x \in [0, 1.25]$.
  d If $x \in [0, 0.8]$, find the absolute maximum value of V and the value of x for which this occurs.
  e If $x \in [0, 1]$, find the absolute maximum value of V and the value of x for which this occurs.

14 For the variables x, y and z, it is known that $x + y = 20$ and $z = xy$.
  a If $x \in [2, 5]$, find the possible values of y.
  b Find the maximum and minimum values of z.

15 For the variables x, y and z, it is known that $z = x^2 y$ and $2x + y = 50$. Find the maximum value of z if:
  a $x \in [0, 25]$
  b $x \in [0, 10]$
  c $x \in [5, 20]$.

16 A piece of string 10 metres long is cut into two pieces to form two squares.

  a If one piece of string has length x metres, show that the combined area of the two squares is given by $A = \frac{1}{8}(x^2 - 10x + 50)$.

  b Find $\dfrac{dA}{dx}$.

  c Find the value of x that makes A a minimum.

  d What is the minimum total area of the two squares?

18F Applications of differentiation to kinematics

▶ Position

The **position** of a particle moving in a straight line is determined by its distance from a fixed point O on the line, called the **origin**, and whether it is to the right or left of O. By convention, the direction to the right of the origin is considered to be positive.

Consider a particle which starts at O and begins to move. The position of the particle at any instant can be specified by a real number x. For example, if the unit is metres and if $x = -3$, the position is 3 m to the left of O; while if $x = 3$, the position is 3 m to the right of O.

Sometimes there is a rule that enables the position at any instant to be calculated. In this case, we can view x as being a function of t. Hence $x(t)$ is the position at time t.

For example, imagine that a stone is dropped from the top of a vertical cliff 45 metres high. Assume that the stone is a particle travelling in a straight line. Let $x(t)$ metres be the downwards position of the particle from O, the top of the cliff, t seconds after the particle is dropped. If air resistance is neglected, then an approximate model for the position is

$$x(t) = 5t^2 \quad \text{for } 0 \leq t \leq 3$$

Example 15

A particle moves in a straight line so that its position, x cm, relative to O at time t seconds is given by $x = t^2 - 7t + 6$, $t \geq 0$.

a Find its initial position.

b Find its position at $t = 4$.

Solution

a At $t = 0$, $x = +6$, i.e. the particle is 6 cm to the right of O.

b At $t = 4$, $x = (4)^2 - 7(4) + 6 = -6$, i.e. the particle is 6 cm to the left of O.

Distance and displacement

The **displacement** of a particle is defined as the change in position of the particle.

It is important to distinguish between the scalar quantity **distance** and the vector quantity displacement (which has a direction).

For example, consider a particle that starts at O and moves first 5 units to the right to point P, and then 7 units to the left to point Q.

The difference between its final position and its initial position is -2. So the displacement of the particle is -2 units. However, the distance it has travelled is 12 units.

Velocity

In this section we consider instantaneous rates of change which arise when studying the motion of a particle travelling in a straight line. In particular, we define the velocity and acceleration of a particle.

Average velocity

The average rate of change of position with respect to time is **average velocity**.

> A particle's average velocity for a time interval $[t_1, t_2]$ is given by
> $$\text{average velocity} = \frac{\text{change in position}}{\text{change in time}} = \frac{x_2 - x_1}{t_2 - t_1}$$
> where x_1 is the position at time t_1 and x_2 is the position at time t_2.

Instantaneous velocity

The instantaneous rate of change of position with respect to time is **instantaneous velocity**. We will refer to the instantaneous velocity as simply the **velocity**.

If a particle's position, x, at time t is given as a function of t, then the velocity of the particle at time t is determined by differentiating the rule for position with respect to time.

> If x is the position of a particle at time t, then
> $$\text{velocity } v = \frac{dx}{dt}$$

Velocity may be positive, negative or zero. If the velocity is positive, the particle is moving to the right, and if it is negative, the particle is moving to the left. A velocity of zero means the particle is instantaneously at rest.

18F Applications of differentiation to kinematics

Speed and average speed

- **Speed** is the magnitude of the velocity.
- **Average speed** for a time interval $[t_1, t_2]$ is given by $\dfrac{\text{distance travelled}}{t_2 - t_1}$

Units of measurement

Common units for velocity (and speed) are:

$$1 \text{ metre per second} = 1 \text{ m/s} = 1 \text{ m s}^{-1}$$
$$1 \text{ centimetre per second} = 1 \text{ cm/s} = 1 \text{ cm s}^{-1}$$
$$1 \text{ kilometre per hour} = 1 \text{ km/h} = 1 \text{ km h}^{-1}$$

The first and third units are connected in the following way:

$$1 \text{ km/h} = 1000 \text{ m/h}$$
$$= \frac{1000}{60 \times 60} \text{ m/s}$$
$$= \frac{5}{18} \text{ m/s}$$
$$\therefore \quad 1 \text{ m/s} = \frac{18}{5} \text{ km/h}$$

Example 16

A particle moves in a straight line so that its position, x cm, relative to O at time t seconds is given by $x = t^2 - 7t + 6$, $t \geq 0$.

a Find its initial velocity.
b When does its velocity equal zero, and what is its position at this time?
c What is its average velocity for the first 4 seconds?
d Determine its average speed for the first 4 seconds.

Solution

a $x = t^2 - 7t + 6$

$$v = \frac{dx}{dt} = 2t - 7$$

At $t = 0$, $v = -7$. The particle is initially moving to the left at 7 cm/s.

b $\dfrac{dx}{dt} = 0$ implies $2t - 7 = 0$, i.e. $t = 3.5$

When $t = 3.5$, $x = (3.5)^2 - 7(3.5) + 6$
$$= -6.25$$

So, at $t = 3.5$ seconds, the particle is at rest 6.25 cm to the left of O.

c Average velocity = $\dfrac{\text{change in position}}{\text{change in time}}$

Position is given by $x = t^2 - 7t + 6$. So at $t = 4$, $x = -6$, and at $t = 0$, $x = 6$.

∴ Average velocity = $\dfrac{-6 - 6}{4} = -3$ cm/s

d Average speed = $\dfrac{\text{distance travelled}}{\text{change in time}}$

The particle stopped at $t = 3.5$ and began to move in the opposite direction. So we must consider the distance travelled in the first 3.5 seconds (from $x = 6$ to $x = -6.25$) and then the distance travelled in the final 0.5 seconds (from $x = -6.25$ to $x = -6$).

Total distance travelled = $12.25 + 0.25 = 12.5$

∴ Average speed = $\dfrac{12.5}{4} = 3.125$ cm/s

Note: Remember that speed is the magnitude of the velocity. However, we can see from this example that average speed is *not* the magnitude of the average velocity.

▶ ## Acceleration

The acceleration of a particle is the rate of change of its velocity with respect to time.

- **Average acceleration** for the time interval $[t_1, t_2]$ is given by $\dfrac{v_2 - v_1}{t_2 - t_1}$, where v_2 is the velocity at time t_2 and v_1 is the velocity at time t_1.
- **Instantaneous acceleration** $a = \dfrac{dv}{dt} = \dfrac{d}{dt}\left(\dfrac{dx}{dt}\right) = \dfrac{d^2x}{dt^2}$

The second derivative $\dfrac{d^2x}{dt^2}$ is just the derivative of the derivative. It will be discussed further in Chapter 20.

Acceleration may be positive, negative or zero. Zero acceleration means the particle is moving at a constant velocity.

The direction of motion and the acceleration need not coincide. For example, a particle may have a positive velocity, indicating it is moving to the right, but a negative acceleration, indicating it is slowing down.

Also, although a particle may be instantaneously at rest, its acceleration at that instant need not be zero. If acceleration has the same sign as velocity, then the particle is 'speeding up'. If the sign is opposite, the particle is 'slowing down'.

The most commonly used units for acceleration are cm/s^2 and m/s^2.

Example 17

A particle moves in a straight line so that its position, x cm, relative to O at time t seconds is given by $x = t^3 - 6t^2 + 5$, $t \geq 0$.

a Find its initial position, velocity and acceleration, and hence describe its motion.
b Find the times when it is instantaneously at rest and determine its position and acceleration at those times.

Solution

a $x = t^3 - 6t^2 + 5$

$$v = \frac{dx}{dt} = 3t^2 - 12t$$

$$a = \frac{dv}{dt} = 6t - 12$$

So when $t = 0$, we have $x = 5$, $v = 0$ and $a = -12$.
Initially, the particle is instantaneously at rest 5 cm to the right of O, with an acceleration of -12 cm/s^2.

b $v = 0$ implies $3t^2 - 12t = 0$

$$3t(t - 4) = 0$$

$$\therefore \quad t = 0 \text{ or } t = 4$$

The particle is initially at rest and stops again after 4 seconds.
At $t = 0$, $x = 5$ and $a = -12$.
At $t = 4$, $x = (4)^3 - 6(4)^2 + 5 = -27$ and $a = 6(4) - 12 = 12$.
After 4 seconds, the particle's position is 27 cm to the left of O, and its acceleration is 12 cm/s^2.

Example 18

A car starts from rest and moves a distance s metres in t seconds, where $s = \frac{1}{6}t^3 + \frac{1}{4}t^2$.
What is the initial acceleration and the acceleration when $t = 2$?

Solution

We are given

$$s = \frac{1}{6}t^3 + \frac{1}{4}t^2$$

The car's velocity is given by

$$v = \frac{ds}{dt} = \frac{1}{2}t^2 + \frac{1}{2}t$$

The car's acceleration is given by

$$a = \frac{dv}{dt} = t + \frac{1}{2}$$

When $t = 0$, $a = \frac{1}{2}$, and when $t = 2$, $a = 2\frac{1}{2}$.

Hence the required accelerations are $\frac{1}{2}$ m/s^2 and $2\frac{1}{2}$ m/s^2.

Example 19

A particle moves along a straight line so that its position, x m, relative to O at time t seconds is given by the formula $x = t^3 - 6t^2 + 9t$.

a Find at what times and in what positions the particle will have zero velocity.
b Find its acceleration at those instants.
c Find its velocity when its acceleration is zero.

Solution

a Velocity $v = \dfrac{dx}{dt} = 3t^2 - 12t + 9$

When $v = 0$,
$$3(t^2 - 4t + 3) = 0$$
$$(t-1)(t-3) = 0$$
$$\therefore \quad t = 1 \text{ or } t = 3$$

i.e. the velocity is zero when $t = 1$ and $t = 3$, where $x = 4$ and $x = 0$.

b Acceleration $a = \dfrac{dv}{dt} = 6t - 12$

When $t = 1$, $a = -6$ m/s². When $t = 3$, $a = 6$ m/s².

c Acceleration is zero when $6t - 12 = 0$, i.e. when $t = 2$.
When $t = 2$, the velocity is $v = 3 \times 4 - 24 + 9 = -3$ m/s.

Section summary

- The **position** of a particle moving in a straight line is determined by its distance from a fixed point O on the line, called the **origin**, and whether it is to the right or left of O. By convention, the direction to the right of the origin is positive.
- **Average velocity** for a time interval $[t_1, t_2]$ is given by
$$\text{average velocity} = \frac{\text{change in position}}{\text{change in time}} = \frac{x_2 - x_1}{t_2 - t_1}$$
where x_2 is the position at time t_2 and x_1 is the position at time t_1.
- The instantaneous rate of change of position with respect to time is called the **instantaneous velocity**, or simply the **velocity**.
  If x is the position of the particle at time t, then its velocity is $v = \dfrac{dx}{dt}$
- **Speed** is the magnitude of the velocity.
- **Average speed** for a time interval $[t_1, t_2]$ is $\dfrac{\text{distance travelled}}{t_2 - t_1}$
- **Average acceleration** for a time interval $[t_1, t_2]$ is given by $\dfrac{v_2 - v_1}{t_2 - t_1}$, where v_2 is the velocity at time t_2 and v_1 is the velocity at time t_1.
- **Instantaneous acceleration** $a = \dfrac{dv}{dt} = \dfrac{d}{dt}\left(\dfrac{dx}{dt}\right) = \dfrac{d^2x}{dt^2}$

Exercise 18F

Example 15

1 A particle moves in a straight line so that its position, x cm, relative to O at time t seconds is given by $x = t^2 - 12t + 11$, $t \geq 0$.
   a Find its initial position.
   b Find its position at $t = 3$.

Example 16

2 A particle moves in a straight line so that its position, x cm, relative to O at time t seconds is given by $x = t^2 - 12t + 11$, $t \geq 0$.
   a Find its initial velocity.
   b When does its velocity equal zero, and what is its position at this time?
   c What is its average velocity for the first 3 seconds?
   d Determine its average speed for the first 3 seconds.

3 The position of a body moving in a straight line, x cm from the origin, at time t seconds ($t \geq 0$) is given by $x = \frac{1}{3}t^3 - 12t + 6$.
   a Find the rate of change of position with respect to time at $t = 3$.
   b Find the time at which the velocity is zero.

Example 17

4 A particle moves in a straight line so that its position, x cm, relative to O at time t seconds is given by $x = 4t^3 - 6t^2 + 5$, $t \geq 0$.
   a Find its initial position, velocity and acceleration, and hence describe its motion.
   b Find the times when it is instantaneously at rest and determine its position and acceleration at those times.

Example 18

5 A car starts from rest and moves a distance s metres in t seconds, where $s = t^4 + t^2$.
   a What is the acceleration when $t = 0$?
   b What is the acceleration when $t = 2$?

6 Let $s = 10 + 15t - 4.9t^2$ be the height (in metres) of an object at time t (in seconds).
   a Find the velocity at time t.
   b Find the acceleration at time t.

Example 19

7 The position, x metres, at time t seconds ($t \geq 0$) of a particle moving in a straight line is given by $x = t^2 - 7t + 10$.
   a When does its velocity equal zero?
   b Find its acceleration at this time.
   c Find the distance travelled in the first 5 seconds.
   d When does its velocity equal -2 m/s, and what is its position at this time?

8 A particle moves along a straight line so that after t seconds its position, s m, relative to a fixed point O on the line is given by $s = t^3 - 3t^2 + 2t$.
   a When is the particle at O?
   b What is its velocity and acceleration at these times?
   c What is the average velocity during the first second?

9 A particle moves in a straight line so that its position, x cm, relative to O at time t seconds ($t \geq 0$) is given by $x = t^2 - 7t + 12$.
  a Find its initial position.
  b What is its position at $t = 5$?
  c Find its initial velocity.
  d When does its velocity equal zero, and what is its position at this time?
  e What is its average velocity in the first 5 seconds?
  f What is its average speed in the first 5 seconds?

10 A particle moves in a straight line so that after t seconds its position, s metres, is given by $s = t^4 + 3t^2$.
  a Find the acceleration when $t = 1$, $t = 2$, $t = 3$.
  b Find the average acceleration between $t = 1$ and $t = 3$.

11 A particle moving in a straight line has position x cm relative to the point O at time t seconds ($t \geq 0$), where $x = t^3 - 11t^2 + 24t - 3$.
  a Find its initial position and velocity.
  b Find its velocity at any time t.
  c At what times is the particle stationary?
  d What is the position of the particle when it is stationary?
  e For how long is the particle's velocity negative?
  f Find its acceleration at any time t.
  g When is the particle's acceleration zero? What is its velocity and its position at that time?

12 A particle moves in a straight line so that its position, x cm, relative to O at time t seconds ($t \geq 0$) is given by $x = 2t^3 - 5t^2 + 4t - 5$.
  a When is its velocity zero, and what is its acceleration at that time?
  b When is its acceleration zero, and what is its velocity at that time?

13 A particle is moving in a straight line in such a way that its position, x cm, relative to the point O at time t seconds ($t \geq 0$) satisfies $x = t^3 - 13t^2 + 46t - 48$. When does the particle pass through O, and what is its velocity and acceleration at those times?

14 Two particles are moving along a straight path so that their positions, x_1 cm and x_2 cm, relative to a fixed point P at any time t seconds are given by $x_1 = t + 2$ and $x_2 = t^2 - 2t - 2$.
  a Find the time when the particles are at the same position.
  b Find the time when the particles are moving with the same velocity.

18G Applications of antidifferentiation to kinematics

In the previous section we considered examples in which we were given a rule for the position of a particle in terms of time, and from it we derived rules for the velocity and the acceleration by differentiation.

We may be given a rule for the acceleration at time t and, by using antidifferentiation with respect to t and some additional information, we can deduce rules for both velocity and position.

Example 20

A body starts from O and moves in a straight line. After t seconds ($t \geq 0$) its velocity, v m/s, is given by $v = 2t - 4$.

a Find its position x in terms of t.
b Find its position after 3 seconds.
c What is the distance travelled in the first 3 seconds?
d Find its average velocity in the first 3 seconds.
e Find its average speed in the first 3 seconds.

Solution

a Antidifferentiate v to find the expression for position, x m, at time t seconds:

$$x = t^2 - 4t + c$$

When $t = 0$, $x = 0$, and so $c = 0$.

$$\therefore \quad x = t^2 - 4t$$

b When $t = 3$, $x = -3$. The body is 3 m to the left of O.

c First find when the body is at rest: $v = 0$ implies $2t - 4 = 0$, i.e. $t = 2$.

When $t = 2$, $x = -4$. Therefore the body goes from $x = 0$ to $x = -4$ in the first 2 seconds, and then back to $x = -3$ in the next second.

Thus it has travelled 5 m in the first 3 seconds.

d Average velocity $= \dfrac{-3 - 0}{3}$

$= -1$ m/s

e From part c, the distance travelled is 5 m.

$\therefore$ Average speed $= \dfrac{5}{3}$ m/s

Example 21

A particle starts from rest 3 metres from a fixed point and moves in a straight line with an acceleration of $a = 6t + 8$. Find its position and velocity at any time t seconds.

Solution

We are given the acceleration:

$$a = \frac{dv}{dt} = 6t + 8$$

Find the velocity by antidifferentiating:

$$v = 3t^2 + 8t + c$$

At $t = 0$, $v = 0$, and so $c = 0$.

$$\therefore \quad v = 3t^2 + 8t$$

Find the position by antidifferentiating again:

$$x = t^3 + 4t^2 + d$$

At $t = 0$, $x = 3$, and so $d = 3$.

$$\therefore \quad x = t^3 + 4t^2 + 3$$

Example 22

A stone is projected vertically upwards from the top of a 20 m high building with an initial velocity of 15 m/s.

a Find the time taken for the stone to reach its maximum height.
b Find the maximum height reached by the stone.
c What is the time taken for the stone to reach the ground?
d What is the velocity of the stone as it hits the ground?

In this case we only consider the stone's motion in a vertical direction, so we can treat it as motion in a straight line. Also we will assume that the acceleration due to gravity is approximately -10 m/s^2. (Note that downwards is considered the negative direction.)

Solution

We have

$$a = -10$$
$$v = -10t + c$$

At $t = 0$, $v = 15$, so $c = 15$.

$$\therefore \quad v = -10t + 15$$
$$x = -5t^2 + 15t + d$$

At $t = 0$, $x = 20$, so $d = 20$.

$$\therefore \quad x = -5t^2 + 15t + 20$$

a The stone will reach its maximum height when $v = 0$, i.e. when $-10t + 15 = 0$, which implies $t = 1.5$.

The stone reaches its maximum height when $t = 1.5$ seconds.

b At $t = 1.5$, $x = -5(1.5)^2 + 15(1.5) + 20$
$= 31.25$

The maximum height reached by the stone is 31.25 metres.

c The stone reaches the ground when $x = 0$:
$$-5t^2 + 15t + 20 = 0$$
$$-5(t^2 - 3t - 4) = 0$$
$$-5(t - 4)(t + 1) = 0$$

Thus $t = 4$. (The solution of $t = -1$ is rejected, since $t \geq 0$.)

The stone takes 4 seconds to reach the ground.

d At $t = 4$, $v = -10(4) + 15$
$= -25$

Thus its velocity on impact is -25 m/s.

Section summary

Antidifferentiation may be used to go from acceleration to velocity, and from velocity to position.

Exercise 18G

Example 20

1 A body starts from O and moves in a straight line. After t seconds ($t \geq 0$) its velocity, v cm/s, is given by $v = 4t - 6$.
  a Find its position x in terms of t.
  b Find its position after 3 seconds.
  c Find the distance travelled in the first 3 seconds.
  d What is its average velocity in the first 3 seconds?
  e What is its average speed in the first 3 seconds?

2 The velocity of a particle, v m/s, at time t seconds ($t \geq 0$) is given by $v = 3t^2 - 8t + 5$. It is initially 4 m to the right of a point O.
  a Find its position and acceleration at any time t.
  b Find its position when the velocity is zero.
  c What is its acceleration when the velocity is zero?

Example 21   **3**   A body moves in a straight line so that its acceleration, a m/s², after time t seconds ($t \geq 0$) is given by $a = 2t - 3$. If the initial position of the body is 2 m to the right of a point O and its velocity is 3 m/s, find the particle's position and velocity after 10 seconds.

Example 22   **4**   An object is projected vertically upwards with a velocity of 25 m/s. (Its acceleration due to gravity is -10 m/s².)

    a Find the object's velocity at any time t.
    b Find its height above the point of projection at any time t.
    c Find the time it takes to reach its maximum height.
    d What is the maximum height reached?
    e Find the time taken to return to the point of projection.

5   The lift in a tall building passes the 50th floor with a velocity of -8 m/s and an acceleration of $\frac{1}{9}(t-5)$ m/s². If each floor spans a height of 6 metres, find at which floor the lift will stop.

18H Families of functions and transformations

Skillsheet   In the earlier chapters of this book we looked at families of functions. We can now use calculus to explore such families further. It is assumed that a CAS calculator will be used throughout this section.

Example 23

Consider the family of functions with rules of the form $f(x) = (x-a)^2(x-b)$, where a and b are positive constants with $b > a$.

a Find the derivative of $f(x)$ with respect to x.
b Find the coordinates of the stationary points of the graph of $y = f(x)$.
c Show that the stationary point at $(a, 0)$ is always a local maximum.
d Find the values of a and b if the stationary points occur where $x = 3$ and $x = 4$.

Solution

a Use a CAS calculator to find that $f'(x) = (x - a)(3x - a - 2b)$.

b The coordinates of the stationary points are $(a, 0)$ and $\left(\dfrac{a+2b}{3}, \dfrac{4(a-b)^3}{27} \right)$.

c If $x < a$, then $f'(x) > 0$, and if $a < x < \dfrac{a+2b}{3}$, then $f'(x) < 0$.
Therefore the stationary point at $(a, 0)$ is a local maximum.

d Since $a < b$, we must have $a = 3$ and $\dfrac{a+2b}{3} = 4$. Therefore $b = \dfrac{9}{2}$.

Example 24

The graph of the function $y = x^3 - 3x^2$ is translated by a units in the positive direction of the x-axis and b units in the positive direction of the y-axis (where a and b are positive constants).

a Find the coordinates of the turning points of the graph of $y = x^3 - 3x^2$.
b Find the coordinates of the turning points of its image.

Solution

a The turning points have coordinates $(0, 0)$ and $(2, -4)$.
b The turning points of the image are (a, b) and $(2 + a, -4 + b)$.

Exercise 18H

Example 23   **1**   Consider the family of functions with rules of the form $f(x) = (x - 2)^2(x - b)$, where b is a positive constant with $b > 2$.

    a Find the derivative of $f(x)$ with respect to x.
    b Find the coordinates of the stationary points of the graph of $y = f(x)$.
    c Show that the stationary point at $(2, 0)$ is always a local maximum.
    d Find the value of b if the stationary points occur where $x = 2$ and $x = 4$.

Example 24   **2**   The graph of the function $y = x^4 - 12x^3$ is translated by a units in the positive direction of the x-axis and b units in the positive direction of the y-axis (where a and b are positive constants).

    a Find the coordinates of the turning points of the graph of $y = x^4 - 12x^3$.
    b Find the coordinates of the turning points of its image.

3   Consider the function $f: \mathbb{R} \to \mathbb{R}$ defined by $f(x) = x - ax^2$, where a is a real number with $a > 0$.

    a Determine the intervals for which $f'(x)$ is:
        i positive   **ii** negative.
    b Find the equation of the tangent to the graph of f at the point $\left(\dfrac{1}{a}, 0\right)$.
    c Find the equation of the normal to the graph of f at the point $\left(\dfrac{1}{a}, 0\right)$.
    d What is the range of f?

4   Consider the cubic function with rule $f(x) = (x - a)^2(x - 1)$, where $a > 1$.

    a Find the coordinates of the turning points of the graph of $y = f(x)$.
    b State the nature of each of the turning points.
    c Find the equation of the tangent at which:
        i $x = 1$ **ii** $x = a$ **iii** $x = \dfrac{a+1}{2}$

5 A line with equation $y = mx + c$ is a tangent to the curve $y = (x - 2)^2$ at a point P where $x = a$ such that $0 < a < 2$.

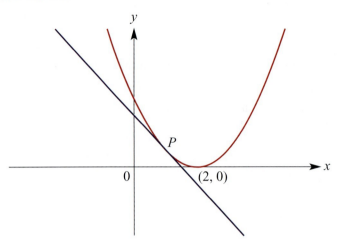

  a i Find the gradient of the curve where $x = a$, for $0 < a < 2$.
  ii Hence express m in terms of a.
  b State the coordinates of the point P, expressing your answer in terms of a.
  c Find the equation of the tangent where $x = a$.
  d Find the x-axis intercept of the tangent.

6 a The graph of $f(x) = x^3$ is translated to the graph of $y = f(x + h)$. Find the value of h if $f(1 + h) = 27$.
  b The graph of $f(x) = x^3$ is transformed to the graph of $y = f(ax)$. Find the value of a if the graph of $y = f(ax)$ passes through the point $(1, 27)$.
  c The cubic with equation $y = ax^3 - bx^2$ has a turning point with coordinates $(1, 8)$. Find the values of a and b.

7 The graph of the function $y = x^4 + 4x^2$ is translated by a units in the positive direction of the x-axis and b units in the positive direction of the y-axis (where a and b are positive constants).
  a Find the coordinates of the turning points of the graph of $y = x^4 + 4x^2$.
  b Find the coordinates of the turning points of its image.

8 Consider the quartic function with rule $f(x) = (x - 1)^2(x - b)^2$, where $b > 1$.
  a Find the derivative of f.
  b Find the coordinates of the turning points of f.
  c Find the value of b such that the graph of $y = f(x)$ has a turning point at $(2, 1)$.

18I Newton's method for finding solutions to equations

Spreadsheet Newton's method is used for finding approximate solutions to equations. The method involves finding the tangent at successive points.

Solving the equation $x^2 - 2 = 0$ for $x > 0$

Let $f(x) = x^2 - 2$. Then $f'(x) = 2x$.

We will use Newton's method to look for an approximation to the solution of the equation $f(x) = 0$, where $x > 0$. Part of the graph of $y = f(x)$ is shown below.

First step Start with $x = 4$. The equation of the tangent to the curve $y = f(x)$ at the point $(4, f(4))$ is $y - f(4) = f'(4)(x - 4)$.

The x-axis intercept of this tangent occurs when $y = 0$:

$$-f(4) = f'(4)(x - 4)$$

$$-\frac{f(4)}{f'(4)} = x - 4$$

$$x = 4 - \frac{f(4)}{f'(4)}$$

$$x = 4 - \frac{14}{8}$$

$$\therefore \quad x = \frac{9}{4}$$

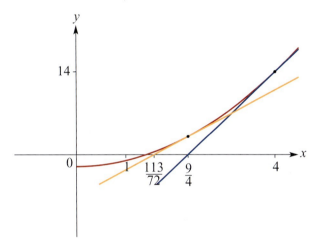

This is our first approximate solution (not counting $x = 4$) to the equation $f(x) = 0$.

Second step Now find the x-axis intercept of the tangent to the curve when $x = \dfrac{9}{4}$.

$$-f\left(\frac{9}{4}\right) = f'\left(\frac{9}{4}\right)\left(x - \frac{9}{4}\right)$$

$$-\frac{f\left(\frac{9}{4}\right)}{f'\left(\frac{9}{4}\right)} = x - \frac{9}{4}$$

$$x = \frac{9}{4} - \frac{f\left(\frac{9}{4}\right)}{f'\left(\frac{9}{4}\right)}$$

$$\therefore \quad x = \frac{113}{72} \approx 1.56944$$

Next step To go from one approximation to the next, we use the iterative formula:

$$x_{n+1} = x_n - \frac{f(x_n)}{f'(x_n)} \qquad \text{where } n = 0, 1, 2, \ldots$$

In the special case for $f(x) = x^2 - 2$, this formula becomes

$$x_{n+1} = x_n - \frac{x_n^2 - 2}{2x_n} \qquad \text{where } n = 0, 1, 2, \ldots$$

In searching for the solution of $x^2 - 2 = 0$, we obtain the sequence of approximations $x_0 = 4$, $x_1 = 1.25$, $x_2 \approx 1.56944$, $x_3 \approx 1.42189$, ...

The process is continued in a spreadsheet as shown. You can see the speed of convergence to a very good approximation.

n	x_n	$f(x_n)$	$f'(x_n)$
0	4.00000000	14.00000000	8.00000000
1	2.25000000	3.06250000	4.50000000
2	1.56944444	0.46315586	3.13888889
3	1.42189036	0.02177221	2.84378073
4	1.41423429	0.00005862	2.82846857
5	1.41421356	0.00000000	2.82842713
6	1.41421356	0.00000000	2.82842712

You can produce this sequence on your calculator by defining the function

$$g(a) = a - \frac{a^2 - 2}{2a}$$

and repeatedly applying this function starting with $x = 4$. Or you can use nests such as $g(g(g(g(4))))$, which gives four iterations at once.

The general procedure

Of course, this process can be used for other functions.

Suppose that the equation $f(x) = 0$ has a solution at $x = \alpha$. Choose x_0 close to α.

Start with the point $P_0(x_0, f(x_0))$ on the curve $y = f(x)$.

Let x_1 be the x-axis intercept of the tangent to the curve at P_0. In general, x_1 will be a better approximation to the solution α.

Next consider the point $P_1(x_1, f(x_1))$.

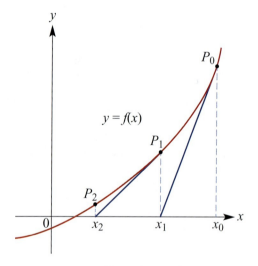

The process is repeated to give a sequence of values $x_1, x_2, x_3, \ldots$ with each one closer to α.

We can go from x_n to x_{n+1} by using the iterative formula:

$$x_{n+1} = x_n - \frac{f(x_n)}{f'(x_n)} \quad \text{where } n = 0, 1, 2, \ldots$$

The process does not always work, as we will see later.

Example 25

Solve the equation $-x^3 + 5x^2 - 3x + 4 = 0$ for $x \in [0, \infty)$.

Solution

Let $f(x) = -x^3 + 5x^2 - 3x + 4$.

The derivative is $f'(x) = -3x^2 + 10x - 3$, and so the iterative formula is

$$x_{n+1} = x_n - \frac{-x_n^3 + 5x_n^2 - 3x_n + 4}{-3x_n^2 + 10x_n - 3}$$

By starting at $x_0 = 3.8$, we obtain the spreadsheet shown.

n	x_n	$f(x_n)$	$f'(x_n)$
0	3.80000000	9.92800000	−8.32000000
1	4.99326923	−10.81199119	−27.86552053
2	4.60526316	−1.44403339	−20.57271468
3	4.53507148	−0.04308844	−19.34990517
4	4.53284468	−0.00004266	−19.31159580
5	4.53284247	0.00000000	−19.31155781
6	4.53284247	0.00000000	−19.31155781

Alternatively, define the function

$$g(a) = a - \frac{-a^3 + 5a^2 - 3a + 4}{-3a^2 + 10a - 3}$$

and apply repeatedly starting with $a = 3.8$.

The solution is $x \approx 4.53284247$.

The graph on the right shows the first two tangent lines when starting at $x_0 = 3.8$. Note that the second tangent line is through a point on the curve below the x-axis.

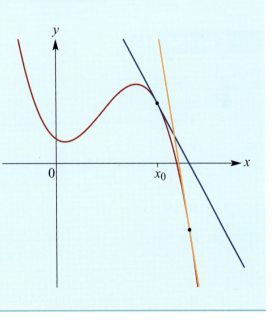

Note: In Example 25, if you start at a point on the other side of the local maximum you can still have 'convergence' to the solution. For example, starting at $x_0 = 2.7$, it takes over 100 iterations to arrive at $x \approx 4.53284247$. Starting at $x_0 = -5$, it takes only 12 iterations.

Newton's method does not always work

The function $f(x) = x^3 - 5x$ can be used to illustrate the problems that can occur when using Newton's method.

1 Oscillating sequence

If you start with $x_0 = 1$, the tangent is $y = -2 - 2x$. This gives $x_1 = -1$.
The tangent at $x = -1$ is $y = 2 - 2x$.
So you get the sequence $1, -1, 1, -1, \ldots$

2 Terminating sequence

There are stationary points at $x = \pm\frac{\sqrt{15}}{3}$.
The tangents at these points are parallel to the x-axis, and you do not get a solution.

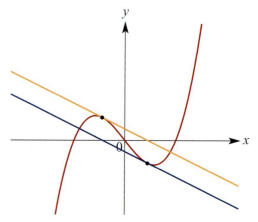

Newton's method can be used successfully with the function $f(x) = x^3 - 5x$:

- For any starting point in the interval $(-1, 1)$, you will get convergence to $x = 0$.
- For any starting point in $(1, \infty)$ except for $\frac{\sqrt{15}}{3}$, you will get convergence to $x = \sqrt{5}$.
- For any starting point in $(-\infty, -1)$ except for $-\frac{\sqrt{15}}{3}$, you will get convergence to $x = -\sqrt{5}$.

Exercise 18I

1 Find approximate solutions for each of the following in the given interval. The desired accuracy is stated.

    a $x^3 - x - 1 = 0$ $[1, 2]$ 2 decimal places
    b $x^4 + x - 3 = 0$ $[1, 3]$ 3 decimal places
    c $x^3 - 5x + 4.2 = 0$ $[1, 2]$ 3 decimal places
    d $x^3 - 2x^2 + 2x - 5 = 0$ $[2, 3]$ 3 decimal places
    e $2x^4 - 3x^2 + 2x - 6 = 0$ $[-2, -1]$ 2 decimal places

2 For $f(x) = x^3 - 3$, show that Newton's method gives the iterative formula

$$x_{n+1} = \frac{2x_n^3 + 3}{3x_n^2}$$

Hence find an approximation for $3^{\frac{1}{3}}$ with your calculator. Start with $x_0 = 2$ and use the function $g(a) = \frac{2a^3 + 3}{3a^2}$ repeatedly.

3 For $f(x) = x^3 - 2x - 1$, show that Newton's method gives the iterative formula

$$x_{n+1} = \frac{2x_n^3 + 1}{3x_n^2 - 2}$$

Hence find an approximation to a solution near $x = 2$ for $x^3 - 2x - 1 = 0$ with your calculator. Start with $x_0 = 2$ and use the function $g(a) = \frac{2a^3 + 1}{3a^2 - 2}$ repeatedly.

Chapter summary

- **Tangents and normals**

  Let (x_1, y_1) be a point on the curve $y = f(x)$. If f is differentiable at $x = x_1$, then
  - the equation of the **tangent** to the curve at (x_1, y_1) is given by $y - y_1 = f'(x_1)(x - x_1)$
  - the equation of the **normal** to the curve at (x_1, y_1) is given by $y - y_1 = \dfrac{-1}{f'(x_1)}(x - x_1)$.

- **Stationary points**

  A point with coordinates $(a, f(a))$ on a curve $y = f(x)$ is a **stationary point** if $f'(a) = 0$.

  The graph shown has three stationary points: A, B and C.

  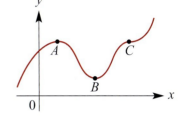

  A Point A is a **local maximum** point. Notice that immediately to the left of A the gradient is positive, and immediately to the right the gradient is negative.

  B Point B is a **local minimum** point. Notice that immediately to the left of B the gradient is negative, and immediately to the right the gradient is positive.

  C Point C is a **stationary point of inflection**.

  Stationary points of types A and B are referred to as **turning points**.

- **Maximum and minimum values**

  For a continuous function f defined on an interval $[a, b]$:
  - if M is a value of the function such that $f(x) \leq M$ for all $x \in [a, b]$, then M is the **absolute maximum** value of the function
  - if N is a value of the function such that $f(x) \geq N$ for all $x \in [a, b]$, then N is the **absolute minimum** value of the function.

- **Motion in a straight line**

  For an object moving in a straight line with position x at time t:

  $$\text{velocity } v = \frac{dx}{dt} \qquad \text{acceleration } a = \frac{dv}{dt}$$

Technology-free questions

1 The graph of $y = 4x - x^2$ is shown.

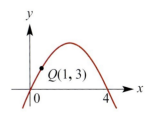

  a Find $\dfrac{dy}{dx}$.

  b Find the gradient of the tangent to the curve at $Q(1, 3)$.

  c Find the equation of the tangent at Q.

2 The graph of $y = x^3 - 4x^2$ is shown.
  a Find $\dfrac{dy}{dx}$.
  b Find the gradient of the tangent to the curve at the point $(2, -8)$.
  c Find the equation of the tangent at the point $(2, -8)$.
  d Find the coordinates of the point Q where the tangent crosses the curve again.

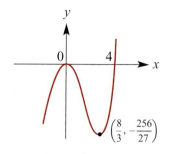

3 Let $y = x^3 - 12x + 2$.
  a Find $\dfrac{dy}{dx}$ and the value(s) of x for which $\dfrac{dy}{dx} = 0$.
  b State the nature of each of these stationary points.
  c Find the corresponding y-value for each of these.

4 Write down the values of x for which each of the following derivative functions are zero. For each of the corresponding stationary points, determine whether it is a local maximum, local minimum or stationary point of inflection.
  a $\dfrac{dy}{dx} = 3x^2$
  b $\dfrac{dy}{dx} = -3x^3$
  c $f'(x) = (x-2)(x-3)$
  d $f'(x) = (x-2)(x+2)$
  e $f'(x) = (2-x)(x+2)$
  f $f'(x) = -(x-1)(x-3)$
  g $\dfrac{dy}{dx} = -x^2 + x + 12$
  h $\dfrac{dy}{dx} = 15 - 2x - x^2$

5 For each of the following, find all stationary points and state the nature of each:
  a $y = 4x - 3x^3$
  b $y = 2x^3 - 3x^2 - 12x - 7$
  c $y = x(2x-3)(x-4)$

6 Sketch the graph of each of the following. Give the coordinates of the stationary points and the axis intercepts.
  a $y = 3x^2 - x^3$
  b $y = x^3 - 6x^2$
  c $y = (x+1)^2(2-x)$
  d $y = 4x^3 - 3x$
  e $y = x^3 - 12x^2$

7 Match each position–time graph shown with its velocity–time graph:

a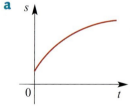
b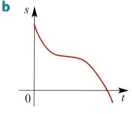
c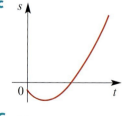

A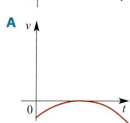
B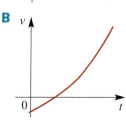
C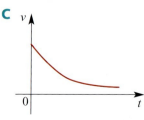

8 A boy stands on the edge of a cliff of height 60 m. He throws a stone vertically upwards so that its distance, h m, above the cliff top is given by $h = 20t - 5t^2$.
   a Calculate the maximum height reached by the stone above the cliff top.
   b Calculate the time which elapses before the stone hits the beach (vertically below).
   c Calculate the speed with which the stone hits the beach.

9 Find the least possible value of $x^2 + y^2$ given that $x + y = 12$.

10 A particle moves in a straight line. It starts from rest at an origin O and its acceleration, a m/s^2, at time t seconds is given by $a = 4 - t$. Calculate:
   a the velocity of the particle when $t = 3$
   b the displacement from O when it next comes to rest
   c the displacement from O when $t = 12$
   d the average speed during the first 12 seconds.

Multiple-choice questions

1 The equation of the tangent to the curve $y = x^3 + 2x$ at the point $(1, 3)$ is
   A $y = x$
   B $y = 5x$
   C $y = 5x + 2$
   D $y = 5x - 2$
   E $y = x - 2$

2 The equation of the normal to the curve $y = x^3 + 2x$ at the point $(1, 3)$ is
   A $y = -5x$
   B $y = -5x + 2$
   C $y = \frac{1}{5}x + \frac{12}{5}$
   D $y = -\frac{1}{5}x + \frac{12}{5}$
   E $y = -\frac{1}{5}x + \frac{16}{5}$

3 The equation of the tangent to the curve $y = 2x - 3x^3$ at the origin is
   A $y = 2$
   B $y = -2x$
   C $y = x$
   D $y = -x$
   E $y = 2x$

4 The average rate of change of the function $f(x) = 4x - x^2$ between $x = 0$ and $x = 1$ is
   A 3
   B −3
   C 4
   D −4
   E 0

5 A particle moves in a straight line so that its position, S m, relative to O at a time t seconds ($t \geq 0$) is given by $S = 4t^3 + 3t - 7$. The initial velocity of the particle is
   A 0 m/s
   B −7 m/s
   C 3 m/s
   D −4 m/s
   E 15 m/s

6 The function $y = x^3 - 12x$ has stationary points at $x =$
   A 0 and 12
   B −4 and 4
   C −2 and 4
   D −2 and 2
   E 2 only

7 The curve $y = 2x^3 - 6x$ has a gradient of 6 at $x =$
   A 2
   B $\sqrt{2}$
   C −2 and 2
   D $-\sqrt{2}$ and $\sqrt{2}$
   E 0 and $\sqrt{2}$

8 The rate of change of the function $f(x) = 2x^3 - 5x^2 + x$ at $x = 2$ is
   A 5
   B −2
   C 2
   D −5
   E 6

9 The average rate of change of the function $y = \frac{1}{2}x^4 + 2x^2 - 5$ between $x = -2$ and $x = 2$ is

    A 0   **B** 5.5   **C** 11   **D** 22   **E** 2.75

10 The minimum value of the function $y = x^2 - 8x + 1$ is

    A 1   **B** 4   **C** −15   **D** 0   **E** −11

A particle moves along a horizontal line. The graph of the particle's position relative to the origin over time is shown.

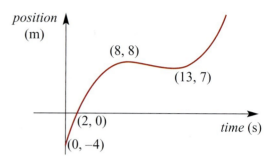

11 The particle has a velocity of zero at

    A 8 s and 13 s   **B** 2 s   **C** 0 s   **D** 8 s and 7 s   **E** −4 s

12 The time interval(s) during which the particle has a negative velocity are

    A $8 < t < 13$ **B** $0 < t < 2$ and $8 < t < 13$ **C** $0 < t < 2$

    D $7 < t < 8$ **E** $(0, \infty)$

Extended-response questions

Rate of change problems

1 The height, in metres, of a stone thrown vertically upwards from the surface of a planet is $2 + 10t - 4t^2$ after t seconds.

    a Calculate the velocity of the stone after 3 seconds.

    b Find the acceleration due to gravity.

2 A dam is being emptied. The quantity of water, V litres, remaining in the dam at any time t minutes after it starts to empty is given by $V(t) = 1000(30 - t)^3$, for $t \geq 0$.

    a Sketch the graph of V against t.

    b Find the time at which there are:

        i 2 000 000 litres of water in the dam   **ii** 20 000 000 litres of water in the dam.

    c At what rate is the dam being emptied at any time t?

    d How long does it take to empty the dam?

    e At what time is the water flowing out at 8000 litres per minute?

    f Sketch the graphs of $y = V(t)$ and $y = V'(t)$ on the one set of axes.

3 In a certain area of Victoria the quantity of blackberries, W tonnes, ready for picking x days after 1 September is given by

$$W = \frac{x}{4000}\left(48\,000 - 2600x + 60x^2 - \frac{x^3}{2}\right) \quad \text{for } 0 \leq x \leq 60$$

a Sketch the graph of W against x for $0 \leq x \leq 60$.
b After how many days will there be 50 tonnes of blackberries ready for picking?
c Find the rate of increase of W, in tonnes per day, when $x = 20$, 40 and 60.
d Find the value of W when $x = 30$.

4 A newly installed central heating system has a thermometer which shows the water temperature as it leaves the boiler ($y°$C). It also has a thermostat which switches off the system when $y = 65$.

The relationship between y and t, the time in minutes, is given by $y = 15 + \frac{1}{80}t^2(30 - t)$.

a Find the temperature at $t = 0$.
b Find the rate of increase of y with respect to t, when $t = 0, 5, 10, 15$ and 20.
c Sketch the graph of y against t for $0 \leq t \leq 20$.

5 The sweetness, S, of a pineapple t days after it begins to ripen is found to be given by $S = 4000 + (t - 16)^3$ units.

a At what rate is S increasing when $t = 0$? **b** Find $\dfrac{dS}{dt}$ when $t = 4, 8, 12$ and 16.
c The pineapple is said to be unsatisfactory when our model indicates that the rate of increase of sweetness is zero. When does this happen?
d Sketch the graph of S against t up to the moment when the pineapple is unsatisfactory.

6 A slow train which stops at every station passes a certain signal box at 12 p.m. The motion of the train between the two stations on either side of the signal box is such that it is s km past the signal box at t minutes past 12 p.m., where $s = \dfrac{1}{3}t + \dfrac{1}{9}t^2 - \dfrac{1}{27}t^3$.

(Note that, before the train reaches the signal box, both s and t will be negative.)

a Use a calculator to help sketch the graphs of s against t and $\dfrac{ds}{dt}$ against t on the one set of axes. Sketch for $t \in [-2, 5]$.
b Find the time of departure from the first station and the time of arrival at the second.
c Find the distance of each station from the signal box.
d Find the average velocity between the stations.
e Find the velocity with which the train passes the signal box.

7 Water is draining from a tank. The volume, V L, of water at time t (hours) is given by $V(t) = 1000 + (2 - t)^3$, for $t \geq 0$ and $V(t) \geq 0$.

a What are the possible values of t?
b Find the rate of draining when:
  i $t = 5$ **ii** $t = 10$

8 A mountain path can be approximately described by the following rule, where y is the elevation, in metres above sea level, and x is the horizontal distance travelled in kilometres:

$$y = \frac{1}{5}(4x^3 - 8x^2 + 192x + 144) \quad \text{for } 0 \leq x \leq 7$$

  a How high above sea level is the start of the track, i.e. $x = 0$?
  b When $x = 6$, what is the value of y?
  c Use a calculator to draw a graph of the path. Sketch this graph.
  d Does this model for the path make sense for $x > 7$?
  e Find the gradient of the graph for the following distances (be careful of units):
      i $x = 0$ ii $x = 3$ iii $x = 7$

Maximum and minimum problems

9 a On the one set of axes sketch the graphs of $y = x^3$ and $y = 2 + x - x^2$.
   b Note that $2 + x - x^2 \geq x^3$ for $x \leq 0$. Find the value of x, with $x \leq 0$, for which the vertical distance between the two curves is a minimum and find the minimum distance.
      Hint: Consider the function with rule $y = 2 + x - x^2 - x^3$ for $x \leq 0$.

10 The number of mosquitos, $M(x)$ in millions, in a certain area depends on the average daily rainfall, x mm, during September and is approximated by

$$M(x) = \frac{1}{30}(50 - 32x + 14x^2 - x^3) \quad \text{for } 0 \leq x \leq 10$$

Find the rainfall that will produce the maximum and the minimum number of mosquitos. (First plot the graph of $y = M(x)$ using a calculator.)

11 Given that $x + y = 5$ and $P = xy$, find:
    a y in terms of x
    b P in terms of x
    c the maximum value of P and the corresponding values of x and y.

12 Given that $2x + y = 10$ and $A = x^2y$, where $0 \leq x \leq 5$, find:
    a y in terms of x
    b A in terms of x
    c the maximum value of A and the corresponding values of x and y.

13 Given that $xy = 10$ and $T = 3x^2y - x^3$, find the maximum value of T for $0 < x < \sqrt{30}$.

14 The sum of two numbers x and y is 8.
    a Write down an expression for y in terms of x.
    b Write down an expression for s, the sum of the squares of these two numbers, in terms of x.
    c Find the least value of the sum of their squares.

15 Find two positive numbers whose sum is 4, such that the sum of the cube of the first and the square of the second is as small as possible.

16 A rectangular patch of ground is to be enclosed with 100 metres of fencing wire. Find the dimensions of the rectangle so that the area enclosed will be a maximum.

17 The sum of two numbers is 24. If one number is x, find the value of x such that the product of the two numbers is a maximum.

18 A factory which produces n items per hour is found to have overhead costs of $\$\left(400 - 16n + \dfrac{1}{4}n^2\right)$ per hour. How many items should be produced every hour to keep the overhead costs to a minimum?

19 For $x + y = 100$, prove that the product $P = xy$ is a maximum when $x = y$, and find the maximum value of P.

20 A farmer has 4 km of fencing wire and wishes to fence in a rectangular piece of land through which a straight river flows. The river is to form one side of the enclosure. How can this be done to enclose as much land as possible?

21 Two positive quantities p and q vary in such a way that $p^3 q = 9$. Another quantity z is defined by $z = 16p + 3q$. Find values of p and q that make z a minimum.

22 A beam has a rectangular cross-section of depth x cm and width y cm. The perimeter of the cross-section of the beam is 120 cm. The strength, S, of the beam is given by $S = 5x^2 y$.
  a Find y in terms of x.
  b Express S in terms of x.
  c What are the possible values for x?
  d Sketch the graph of S against x.
  e Find the values of x and y which give the strongest beam.
  f If the cross-sectional depth of the beam must be less than or equal to 19 cm, find the maximum strength of the beam.

23 The number of salmon swimming upstream in a river to spawn is approximated by $s(x) = -x^3 + 3x^2 + 360x + 5000$, with x representing the temperature of the water in degrees (°C). (This model is valid only if $6 \leq x \leq 20$.) Find the water temperature that results in the maximum number of salmon swimming upstream.

24 A piece of wire 360 cm long is used to make the twelve edges of a rectangular box for which the length is twice the breadth.
  a Denoting the breadth of the box by x cm, show that the volume of the box, V cm^3, is given by $V = 180x^2 - 6x^3$.
  b Find the domain, S, of the function $V: S \to \mathbb{R}$, $V(x) = 180x^2 - 6x^3$ which describes the situation.

  c Sketch the graph of the function with rule $y = V(x)$.
  d Find the dimensions of the box that has the greatest volume.
  e Find the values of x (correct to two decimal places) for which $V = 20\,000$.

25 A piece of wire of length 90 cm is bent into the shape shown in the diagram.

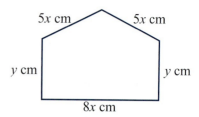

 a Show that the area, A cm², enclosed by the wire is given by $A = 360x - 60x^2$.
 b Find the values of x and y for which A is a maximum.

26 A piece of wire 100 cm in length is to be cut into two pieces, one piece of which is to be shaped into a circle and the other into a square.

 a How should the wire be cut if the sum of the enclosed areas is to be a minimum? (Give your answer to the nearest centimetre.)
 b How should the wire be used to obtain a maximum area?

27 A roll of tape 36 metres long is to be used to mark out the edges and internal lines of a rectangular court of length $4x$ metres and width y metres, as shown in the diagram. Find the length and width of the court for which the area is a maximum.

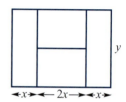

28 A rectangular chicken run is to be built on flat ground. A 16-metre length of chicken wire will be used to form three of the sides; the fourth side, of length x metres, will be part of a straight wooden fence.

 a Let y be the width of the rectangle. Find an expression for A, the area of the chicken run, in terms of x and y.
 b Find an expression for A in terms of x.
 c Find the possible values of x.
 d Sketch the graph of A against x for these values of x.
 e What is the largest area of ground the chicken run can cover?

29 The diagram illustrates a window that consists of an equilateral triangle and a rectangle. The amount of light that comes through the window is directly proportional to the area of the window.
If the perimeter of such a window must be 8000 mm, find the values of h and a (correct to the nearest mm) which allow the maximum amount of light to pass.

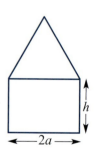

30 The diagram shows a cross-section of an open drainage channel. The flat bottom of the channel is *y* metres across and the sides are quarter circles of radius *x* metres. The total length of the bottom plus the two curved sides is 10 metres.

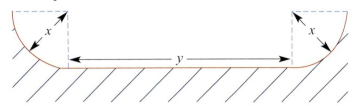

a Express *y* in terms of *x*.
b State the possible values that *x* can take.
c Find an expression for *A*, the area of the cross-section, in terms of *x*.
d Sketch the graph of *A* against *x*, for possible values of *x*.
e Find the value of *x* which maximises *A*.
f Comment on the cross-sectional shape of the drain.

31 A cylinder closed at both ends has a total surface area of 1000 cm². The radius of the cylinder is *x* cm and the height *h* cm. Let *V* cm³ be the volume of the cylinder.

a Find *h* in terms of *x*.
b Find *V* in terms of *x*.
c Find $\dfrac{dV}{dx}$.
d Find $\left\{ x : \dfrac{dV}{dx} = 0 \right\}$.
e Sketch the graph of *V* against *x* for a suitable domain.
f Find the maximum volume of the cylinder.
g Find the value(s) of *x* and *h* for which *V* = 1000, correct to two decimal places.

32 A cylindrical aluminium can able to contain half a litre of drink is to be manufactured. The volume of the can must therefore be 500 cm³.

a Find the radius and height of the can which will use the least aluminium and therefore be the cheapest to manufacture.
b If the radius of the can must be no greater than 5 cm, find the radius and height of the can that will use the least aluminium.

19

Revision of Chapters 16–18

19A Technology-free questions

1. Water is being poured steadily into the vessel shown on the right. Sketch a graph showing the relationship between the height of water and the volume that has been poured in.

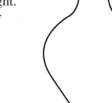

2. A particle moves in a straight line so that its position, x cm, relative to O at time t seconds is given by $x(t) = 2t^3 - t$, $t \geq 0$.
   a. Find the average velocity in the first second.
   b. Find the average velocity in the next three seconds.

3. A curve has rule $y = 9 - x^2$.
   a. Find the average rate of change over the interval:
      i. $[1, 3]$ ii. $[1, 2]$
   b. Find an expression for the average rate of change over the interval $[1, 1 + h]$.
   c. Use your result from part b to find the instantaneous rate of change at $x = 1$.

4. By first considering the gradient of the secant through the points $P(x, f(x))$ and $Q(x + h, f(x + h))$ on the curve $f(x) = \frac{1}{2}x^2 - x$, find the derivative of $\frac{1}{2}x^2 - x$.

5. Find the derivative of each of the following:
   a. $2x^3 - x + 1$
   b. $(x - 1)(x + 2)$
   c. $\frac{x^2 + 5x}{x}$

6. Find the gradient of the tangent to each of the following curves at the given point:
   a. $y = 3x^4 + x$, $(1, 4)$
   b. $y = 2x(1 - x)$, $(-2, -12)$

7. For the function $f(x) = x - 2x^2$, find the values of x for which:
   a. $f(x) = 0$
   b. $f'(x) = 0$
   c. $f'(x) > 0$
   d. $f'(x) < 0$
   e. $f'(x) = -10$

8 Find:

   a $\dfrac{d}{dx}(2x^{-3} - x^{-1})$

   b $\dfrac{d}{dz}\left(\dfrac{3-z}{z^3}\right)$

9 Find the equations of the tangent and the normal to the curve $y = x^2 - 5x$ at $x = 1$.

10 A particle moves in a straight line so that its position, x cm, relative to O at time t seconds is given by $x = \dfrac{1}{6}t^3 - \dfrac{1}{2}t^2 + 1$.

   a At what times does the particle have zero velocity?
   b Find its acceleration at those instants.
   c Find the velocity when the acceleration is zero.

11 For $y = 2(x^3 - 4x)$, find all stationary points and state their nature.

19B Multiple-choice questions

1 The bowl shown in the diagram is being filled with water from a tap flowing at a constant rate. The graph which shows how the depth, d, of water changes with time, t, is

A B C D E

(graphs of d vs t)

2 The point P has coordinates $(3, 30)$.
   The gradient of the graph at P is closest to

   A -10 B -0.1 C 0 D 1 E 10

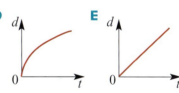

3 For the distance–time graph shown, the average speed from $t = 0$ to $t = 3$ is

   A 0.1 m/s   B 1 m/s   C $\dfrac{1}{3}$ m/s
   D -3 m/s   E 3 m/s

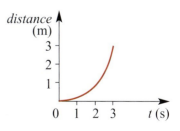

4 Given $f(x) = 3x^2 + 1$, the average rate of change of $f(x)$ with respect to x for the interval $[0, 2]$ is

   A 6 B 6.5 C 12 D 13 E 14

5 On a particular day, the temperature at 7 a.m. was 10°C, and the temperature at noon was 23.5°C. The average rate of increase of temperature, °C per hour, with respect to time is

A 13.5 **B** 2.7 **C** 4.7 **D** 4 **E** 5

6 If $y = 5x^2 + 1$, then $\dfrac{dy}{dx}$ is equal to

A $10x$ **B** $10x + 1$ **C** $\dfrac{5x^3}{3} + x$ **D** $10x^2 + x$ **E** $\dfrac{5x^3}{3} + x + c$

7 If $f(x) = x^2$, then the value of $f(5 + h) - f(5)$ is

A $2x$ **B** 25 **C** h^2 **D** $10h + h^2$ **E** $(5 + h)^2$

8 The graph shown has zero gradient for

A $x = -2$ and $x = 0$ and $x = 2.5$
B $x = -1$ and $x = 1.5$
C $x \in [-1, 1.5]$
D $x = 3$ and $x = -2$
E $x = 0$ only

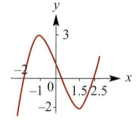

9 Water is flowing into a tank. The volume, V m³, of water in the tank after t minutes is given by $V = 3t^2 + 4t + 2$. The instantaneous rate of change of the volume (m³/min) of water at time $t = 2$ is

A $6t + 4$ **B** 22 **C** 16 **D** 10 **E** $t^3 + 2t^2$

10 Given that $\dfrac{f(3 + h) - f(3)}{h} = 2h^2 + 2h$, the value of $f'(3)$ is

A 0 **B** 14 **C** 2 **D** 5 **E** 6

11 For the graph shown, the gradient is positive for

A $x \in (-\infty, 2)$
B $x \in (-2, 2)$
C $x \in (-\infty, -2) \cup (1, \infty)$
D $x \in (-\infty, -2) \cup (2, \infty)$
E $x \in (-\infty, -2)$

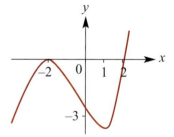

12 The graph of the function $f(x) = x^3 - x^2 - 5$ has stationary points at x equals

A $\dfrac{2}{3}$ only **B** 0 and $\dfrac{2}{3}$ **C** 0 and $-\dfrac{2}{3}$ **D** $-\dfrac{1}{3}$ and 1 **E** $\dfrac{1}{3}$ and -1

13 For the graph shown, $f'(2)$ is equal to

A $-\dfrac{3}{5}$ **B** $\dfrac{5}{3}$ **C** -1.5 **D** 5 **E** -1

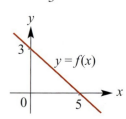

14 The gradient of the curve with equation $y = 2x^3 - 3x^2$ at the point $(1, -1)$ is

  A -3 **B** -1 **C** 0 **D** 1 **E** 12

15 If $y = 7 + 2x - x^2$, then the maximum value of y is

  A $-4\frac{1}{2}$ **B** $4\frac{1}{2}$ **C** 8 **D** $8\frac{1}{2}$ **E** 9

16 A ball was thrown vertically upwards and the height, s metres, it reached after t seconds was given by $s = 28t - 16t^2$. The greatest height reached by the ball was

  A $12\frac{1}{4}$ m   **B** $14\frac{1}{8}$ m   **C** $16\frac{3}{4}$ m   **D** $10\frac{1}{2}$ m   **E** $25\frac{3}{8}$ m

17 The graph of f is shown on the right. The graph of f' is best represented by

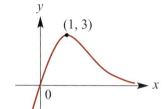

A 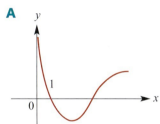   **B** 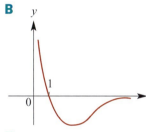   **C**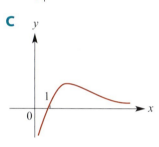

D 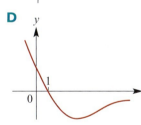   **E**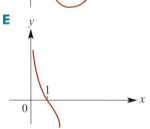

18 The graph of the gradient function for $f(x) = 2x^3 - 6x$ is shown. This means that $f(x)$ has a local maximum at

  A $(1, -4)$ **B** $(0, 0)$ **C** $(0, -6)$
  D $(-3, 0)$ **E** $(-1, 4)$

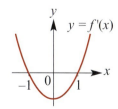

19 If $y = \dfrac{x^2}{2}(x^2 + 2x - 4)$, then $\dfrac{dy}{dx}$ equals

  A $4x^3 + 6x^2 - 8x$ **B** $2x^2 + 2x$ **C** $2x^3 + 3x^2 - 4x$
  D $2x^3 + 4x^2 - 8x$ **E** $x^3 + 2x^2 - 4x$

20 The derivative of $5 + 3x^2$ is

  A $5x + x^3$ **B** $6x$ **C** $5x + 6x$ **D** $6x^3$ **E** $5 + x^3$

21 The graph of $y = f(x)$ shown has stationary points at $(1, 6)$ and $(-1, -5)$.

$f'(x) < 0$ for

A $\left(-3, -\frac{1}{2}\right) \cup (3, \infty)$ **B** $(-1, 1)$

C $\left(-3, -\frac{1}{2}\right)$ **D** $(-\infty, -5) \cup (1, \infty)$

E $(-\infty, -1) \cup (1, \infty)$

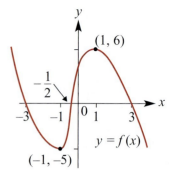

22 The gradient of the chord AB joining points $A(1, 3)$ and $B(1 + h, (1 + h)^2 + 2)$ is

A $1 + h$ **B** $h^2 - 2h$ **C** $h^2 + 2h$
D $2 + h$ **E** 2

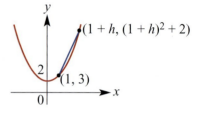

23 The gradient at the point $(1, -1)$ on the curve with equation $y = x^2(2x - 3)$ is

A 0 **B** $\dfrac{2}{3}$ **C** $\dfrac{4}{3}$ **D** $\dfrac{\pi}{2}$ **E** 4

24 The gradient of the chord AB is

A $b + a$ **B** $2a$ **C** $b - a$

D $a - b$ **E** $\lim\limits_{h \to 0} \dfrac{(x + h)^2 + 1 - (x^2 + 1)}{h}$

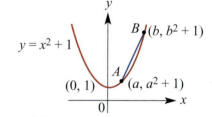

25 The derivative function of $f(x) = 3x^3 + 6x^2 - x + 1$ has rule

A $f'(x) = \dfrac{3x^4}{4} + 2x^3 - \dfrac{x^2}{2} + x$ **B** $f'(x) = 1 + 12x + 9x^2$ **C** $f'(x) = 9x^2 + 12x - 1$
D $f'(x) = 6x^2 + 12x - 1$ **E** $f'(x) = 3x^2 + 2x - 1$

26 Suppose $A = 4xy$ and $y + 3x = 10$. Which one of the following equations can be used to directly calculate the value of x so that the value of A is a maximum?

A $10x - x^2 = 0$ **B** $10 - 3x^2 = 0$ **C** $10 - 3x = 0$
D $5 - 3x = 0$ **E** $5 - x = 0$

27 The gradient of the graph of $y = x^2 + 3$ at the point with coordinates $(3, 12)$ is

A 24 **B** 6 **C** 3 **D** 4 **E** 12

28 The function $y = x^3 + 5x^2 - 8x$ has

A a local minimum when $x = -4$ and a local maximum when $x = \frac{2}{3}$
B a local maximum when $x = -4$ and a local minimum when $x = \frac{2}{3}$
C a local maximum when $x = 4$ and a local minimum when $x = -\frac{2}{3}$
D a local minimum when $x = 4$ and a local maximum when $x = -\frac{2}{3}$
E a stationary point of inflection when $x = -4$ and a local maximum when $x = \frac{2}{3}$

29 The gradient of the curve $y = f(x)$ at the point where $x = 1$ is

A $\lim\limits_{h \to 0} \dfrac{(1+h) - 1}{h}$ **B** $\lim\limits_{h \to 0} \dfrac{f(1+h) - f(1)}{h}$ **C** $\dfrac{f(1+h) - f(1)}{h}$

D $\dfrac{f(1)}{h}$ **E** $\dfrac{1}{h} \lim\limits_{h \to 0} \big(f(1+h) - f(1)\big)$

30 The minimum value of the function $y = x^2 + 4x - 3$ is

A -2 **B** 2 **C** -7 **D** -15 **E** -3

31 The gradient of the normal to the curve $y = x^2$ at the point where $x = 2$ is equal to

A 2 **B** 4 **C** $-\dfrac{1}{2}$ **D** $-\dfrac{1}{4}$ **E** $\dfrac{1}{2}$

32 If $y = \dfrac{2x + 5}{x}$, then $\dfrac{dy}{dx}$ equals

A $2 - \dfrac{5}{x^2}$ **B** 2 **C** $\dfrac{2}{x}$ **D** $2 + \dfrac{5}{x^2}$ **E** $\dfrac{-5}{x^2}$

33 The function $y = x^2 - 3x - 4$ is decreasing when

A $x \in \left(-\infty, \dfrac{3}{2}\right)$ **B** $x \in \left(-\dfrac{3}{2}, \infty\right)$ **C** $x \in (-1, 4)$

D $x \in (-\infty, 1) \cup (4, \infty)$ **E** $x \in \left(\dfrac{3}{2}, \infty\right)$

34 $\lim\limits_{x \to 0} \dfrac{x^2 - x}{x}$ is

A -1 **B** 0 **C** 1 **D** ∞ **E** undefined

35 The graph shown in the diagram is

A discontinuous at $x = 2$ only
B discontinuous at $x = 0$ only
C discontinuous at $x = 0$ and $x = 2$
D continuous for all real values of x
E continuous for all $x < 0$ but discontinuous elsewhere

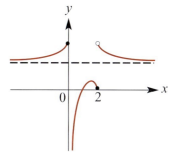

36 The function with the graph as shown in the diagram is

A continuous for all real values of x
B discontinuous for all real values of x
C discontinuous at $x = -1$ and $x = 1$
D discontinuous for all $x \neq -1$ but continuous elsewhere
E discontinuous for all $x \neq 1$ but continuous elsewhere

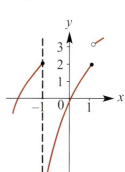

37 The derivative of $y = \dfrac{1}{x^5}$ is equal to

A $\dfrac{1}{5x^4}$ **B** $-\dfrac{4}{x^4}$ **C** $\dfrac{5}{x^4}$ **D** $-\dfrac{5}{x^6}$ **E** $-\dfrac{5}{x^4}$

38 If $f(x) = 4x^3 - 3x + 7 - \dfrac{2}{x}$, then $f'(1)$ equals

A -2 **B** 18 **C** 7 **D** 11 **E** 14

39 If $f'(x) = 6x^2 + 3$ and $f(1) = 7$, then $f(x)$ equals

A $2x^3 + 3x$ **B** $12x$ **C** 84
D $2x^3 + 3x + 2$ **E** $2x^3 + 3x + 7$

19C Extended-response questions

1 An object follows a path (in a vertical plane) described by the equation $y = x - 0.01x^2$, where x is the horizontal distance travelled and y is the height above ground level of the object when it has travelled a horizontal distance x. The object travels from $(0, 0)$, a point at ground level.

  a What is the horizontal distance travelled by the object before it returns to ground level?
  b Find $\dfrac{dy}{dx}$.
  c Find the value of x for which $\dfrac{dy}{dx} = 0$ and the corresponding y-value.
  d Sketch the graph of y against x.
  e State the coordinates of the point on the path for which the gradient is:
   i $\dfrac{1}{2}$ **ii** $-\dfrac{1}{2}$

2 A designer of roller coasters decides to use a polynomial model for a new construction, and tries the polynomial $y = -0.0001(x^3 - 100x^2)$, where $x \in [0, 100]$. The graph is as shown.

  a What are the coordinates of the highest point reached?
  b Find the gradient of the curve at:
   i $x = 20$
   ii $x = 80$
   iii $x = 100$
  c Describe the ride the roller coaster would provide.
  d What alteration would you suggest?

3 A rectangular block is such that the sides of its base are of length x cm and $3x$ cm. The sum of the length of all its edges is 20 cm.
   a Find an expression in terms of x for the height of the block.
   b Show that the volume, V cm^3, is given by $V = 15x^2 - 12x^3$.
   c What values of x should be considered? (That is, find the domain of the function V.)
   d Find $\dfrac{dV}{dx}$.
   e Find $\left\{ x : \dfrac{dV}{dx} = 0 \right\}$ and hence find the maximum volume possible.
   f Sketch the graph of V against x for the values of x determined in part c.

4 A stone is projected vertically upwards with a speed of 30 m/s. Its height, h m, above the ground after t seconds ($t < 6$) is given by $h = 30t - 5t^2$.
   a Find $\dfrac{dh}{dt}$.
   b Find the maximum height reached.
   c Sketch the graph of h against t.

5 A box is made from the net shown.
   a Write down an expression for the surface area of the net in terms of x.
   b Write down an expression for the volume, V cm^3, of the made-up box in terms of x.
   c Sketch the graph of V against x.
   d Find the dimensions and the volume of a box with maximum volume.

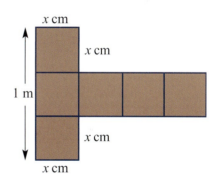

6 A right circular cone lies inside a sphere of radius 1 m as shown. The centre of the sphere, 0, lies x m from the base of the cone. The volume of a cone is given by the formula $V = \dfrac{1}{3}\pi r^2 h$.
   a Find:
       i r in terms of x
       ii h in terms of x
   b Show that $V = \dfrac{\pi}{3}(1 + x - x^2 - x^3)$.
   c State a suitable domain for the function with rule $V = \dfrac{\pi}{3}(1 + x - x^2 - x^3)$.
   d i   Find $\dfrac{dV}{dx}$.
      ii Find $\left\{ x : \dfrac{dV}{dx} = 0 \right\}$.
      iii State the maximum possible volume of the cone.
   e Sketch the graph of V against x.

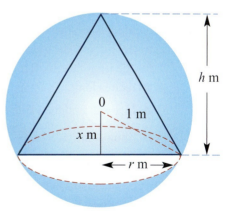

7 The number of insects in a colony at time t days after 1 January 2015 is approximated by the function with rule $P(t) = 1000 \times 2^{\frac{t}{20}}$, where $t = 0$ corresponds to 1 January 2015. This rule for the population is valid for the entire year.

  a Find the approximate number of insects in the colony on 1 January.
  b Find the approximate number of insects on 10 January (i.e. when $t = 9$).
  c For what values of t is $P(t)$ equal to:
   i 4000 **ii** 6000? (Give answer correct to two decimal places.)
  d Find $P(20)$ and $P(15)$ and hence calculate the average rate of change of P with respect to time for the interval of time $[15, 20]$, giving your answer correct to two decimal places.
  e **i** Find the average rate of change of P with respect to t for the interval $[15, 15 + h]$, in terms of h.
   ii Explain how the instantaneous rate of change of P with respect to t, for $t = 15$, could be found by numerical methods.

8 A rectangular block, the length of whose base is twice its width, has total surface area of 300 m². The width of the base is x m and the height of the block is h m.

  a Find h in terms of x, with h the subject of the formula.
  b Find V, the volume of the block, in terms of x.
  c Find $\dfrac{dV}{dx}$.
  d State the positive values of x for which $V > 0$.
  e Find the maximum value of V and the value of x for which this occurs.
  f For the values of x established in part d, sketch the graph of V against x.

9 The metal frame of the front face of a building is as shown. Each length represents a steel girder. The total length of girder used for the front face is 70 metres. The building is 40 metres long.

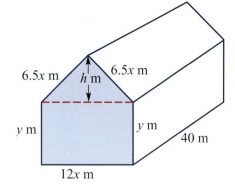

  a If $x = 2$, find the value of y.
  b Show that $y = \dfrac{70 - 25x}{2}$.
  c **i** Find the height h (marked on the diagram) in terms of x.
   ii Show that the area of the front face of the building (shaded in the diagram) in terms of x and y is $A = 15x^2 + 12xy$.
  d Find the volume, V m³, of the building in terms of x.
  e **i** For what value of x is the volume of the building a maximum? What is the corresponding value of y?
   ii State the corresponding maximum volume of the building.

10 The equation of the curve is of the form $y = kx^2(a - x)$.

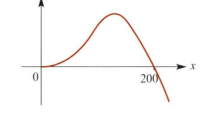

  a Find the values of a and k given that when $x = 170$, $y = 8.67$, and when $x = 200$, $y = 0$.

  b **i** Find the value of x for which there is a local maximum.

  ii State the value of y which corresponds to this value of x.

  c When $x = 105$, find:

  i the y-value   **ii** the gradient of the curve at this point.

  d **i** Find the equation of the tangent at the point where $x = 105$.

  ii State the y-axis intercept of the tangent.

  e Find the average rate of change of y with respect to x for the interval $[0, 105]$.

  f Carefully sketch the graph of $y = kx^2(a - x)$, for $x \in [0, 200]$, and on the same set of axes sketch the graph of the tangent at $x = 105$.

11 The population density (number of residents per unit area) of many cities depends on the distance from the city centre. For a particular city, the population density P (in thousands of people per square kilometre) at a distance of r kilometres from the centre is given approximately by $P = 10 + 40r - 20r^2$.

  a What is the population density in the centre of the city?

  b What are the possible values for r?

  c Sketch a graph of P against r.

  d **i** Find $\dfrac{dP}{dr}$.

  ii Evaluate $\dfrac{dP}{dr}$ when $r = 0.5$, 1 and 2.

  iii Sketch a graph of $\dfrac{dP}{dr}$ against r.

  e Where is the population density greatest?

12 The diagram shows a rectangle with sides a m and x m. The area of the shaded region is y m². In the following, a is a constant.

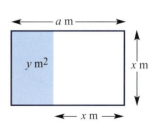

  a Find an expression for y in terms of x.

  b Find the set of possible values for x in terms of a.

  c Find the maximum value of y and the corresponding value of x (in terms of a).

  d Explain briefly why this value of y is a maximum.

  e **i** Sketch the graph of y against x when $a = 9$.

  ii State the set of possible values for y.

13 Water is being poured into a flask. The volume, V mL, of water in the flask at time t seconds is given by $V(t) = 0.6\left(20t^2 - \dfrac{2t^3}{3}\right)$, $0 \leq t \leq 20$.

  a Find the volume of water in the flask when:

   i $t = 0$ **ii** $t = 20$

  b Find the rate of flow of water into the flask, i.e. find $\dfrac{dV}{dt}$.

  c Sketch the graph of V against t for $t \in [0, 20]$.

  d Sketch the graph of $\dfrac{dV}{dt}$ against t for $t \in [0, 20]$.

14 The function $y = ax^3 + bx^2$, where a and b are constants, has a stationary point at $(1, -1)$.

  a Using the fact that $(1, -1)$ lies on the curve, form an equation involving a and b.

  b Using the fact that $(1, -1)$ is also a stationary point, form a second equation and solve the two equations simultaneously to find a and b.

  c Sketch the graph of y against x.

15 A trough is to be made by bending a long sheet of metal 80 cm wide to give a trapezoid cross-section with sides of equal length x cm inclined at $60°$ to the horizontal as shown.

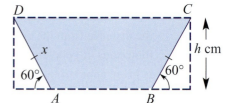

  a Find:

   i length AB in terms of x

   ii h in terms of x

  b Find the cross-sectional area (shaded) in terms of x.

  c Find the value of x for which the cross-sectional area is a maximum.

16 The diagrams opposite show an open cardboard box of dimensions x cm, x cm, y cm and the lid for the box of dimensions x cm, x cm, 2 cm. The total amount of cardboard used for the box and the lid is 1400 cm^2. Let V cm^3 be the volume of the box.

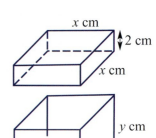

  a Find y in terms of x.

  b Find V in terms of x.

  c Find $\dfrac{dV}{dx}$.

  d Find $\left\{x : \dfrac{dV}{dx} = 0\right\}$.

  e Sketch the graph of V against x.

  f Find the maximum volume of the box.

  g Find the values of x and y such that $V = 1000$.

Chapter 20

Further differentiation and antidifferentiation

Objectives

▶ To understand and use the **chain rule**.
▶ To differentiate **rational powers**.
▶ To antidifferentiate **rational powers**.
▶ To find **second derivatives** of functions.
▶ To use differentiation techniques to **sketch graphs** of functions.
▶ To apply differentiation techniques to **solving problems**.

In this chapter we introduce two important ideas. The first is the chain rule.

What is a **composition** of functions?

If $f(x) = x^5$ and $g(x) = x^2 + 3x$, then the function with rule $f(g(x)) = (x^2 + 3x)^5$ is called the composition of f with g. The other composition from these two functions has rule $g(f(x)) = x^{10} + 3x^5$. We write the new functions as $f \circ g$ and $g \circ f$ respectively.

The chain rule gives a simple method for differentiating expressions such as $(x^2 + 3x)^5$.

We then go on to extend our rule for differentiating powers of x to fractional powers. This is done by using first principles to establish a few results to start with, but then through the chain rule.

For any non-zero rational number $r = \dfrac{p}{q}$, if $f(x) = x^r$, then $f'(x) = rx^{r-1}$.

These two results extend the collection of functions for which we can find the derivative. For example, we will be able to find the derivative of $\sqrt{x}$ and, using the chain rule, the derivative of expressions such as $\sqrt{2x^2 + 3}$.

20A The chain rule

An expression such as $(x^3 + 1)^2$ may be differentiated by expanding and then differentiating each term. This method is a great deal more tiresome for an expression such as $(x^3 + 1)^{30}$.

Instead, we can transform $y = (x^3 + 1)^2$ into two simpler functions defined by

$$u = x^3 + 1 \quad \text{and} \quad y = u^2$$

which are 'chained' together:

$$x \xrightarrow{h} u \xrightarrow{g} y$$

where $h(x) = x^3 + 1 = u$ and $g(u) = u^2 = y$.

We may exploit this connection to differentiate. We use Leibniz notation to explore this idea.

Consider $y = (x^3 + 1)^2$ at the point where $x = 2$.

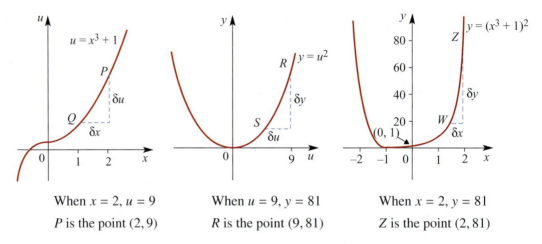

When $x = 2$, $u = 9$ | When $u = 9$, $y = 81$ | When $x = 2$, $y = 81$
P is the point $(2, 9)$ | R is the point $(9, 81)$ | Z is the point $(2, 81)$

A section of a spreadsheet (shown below) illustrates the connection between the gradients of the secants PQ, RS and ZW.

x	u	y	δx	δu	δy	$\dfrac{\delta u}{\delta x}$	$\dfrac{\delta y}{\delta u}$	$\dfrac{\delta u}{\delta x} \times \dfrac{\delta y}{\delta u}$	$\dfrac{\delta y}{\delta x}$
1.60000	5.09600	25.96922	0.40000	3.90400	55.03078	9.76000	14.09600	137.57696	137.57696
1.80000	6.83200	46.67622	0.20000	2.16800	34.32378	10.84000	15.83200	171.61888	171.61888
1.90000	7.85900	61.76388	0.10000	1.14100	19.23612	11.41000	16.85900	192.36119	192.36119
1.99000	8.88060	78.86504	0.01000	0.11940	2.13496	11.94010	17.88060	213.49614	213.49614
1.99900	8.98801	80.78425	0.00100	0.01199	0.21575	11.99400	17.98801	215.74816	215.74816
1.99990	8.99880	80.97840	0.00010	0.00120	0.02160	11.99940	17.99880	215.97480	215.97480
1.99999	8.99988	80.99784	0.00001	0.00012	0.00216	11.99994	17.99988	215.99748	215.99748

It can be seen that, as δx gets smaller, so does δu, and that $\dfrac{\delta y}{\delta x} = \dfrac{\delta y}{\delta u} \times \dfrac{\delta u}{\delta x}$.

By considering δx becoming smaller, and hence δu becoming smaller, we arrive at the following result. We will prove this result at the end of the section.

> **The chain rule for differentiation**
>
> $$\frac{dy}{dx} = \frac{dy}{du} \cdot \frac{du}{dx}$$

From the spreadsheet it can be seen that the gradient of $u = x^3 + 1$ at $x = 2$ is 12, and the gradient of $y = u^2$ at $u = 9$ is 18. The gradient of $y = (x^3 + 1)^2$ at $x = 2$ is 216. The chain rule can be used to confirm this:

$$\frac{du}{dx} = 3x^2 \quad \text{and, at } x = 2, \quad \frac{du}{dx} = 12$$

$$\frac{dy}{du} = 2u \quad \text{and, at } u = 9, \quad \frac{dy}{du} = 18$$

$$\frac{dy}{dx} = \frac{dy}{du} \cdot \frac{du}{dx} = 18 \times 12 = 216$$

Example 1

Find the derivative of $y = (3x + 4)^{20}$.

Solution

Let $u = 3x + 4$ then $y = u^{20}$

So $\dfrac{du}{dx} = 3$ and $\dfrac{dy}{du} = 20u^{19}$

$\therefore \quad \dfrac{dy}{dx} = \dfrac{dy}{du} \cdot \dfrac{du}{dx}$

$\qquad = 20u^{19} \cdot 3$

$\qquad = 60(3x + 4)^{19}$

Example 2

Find the gradient of the curve with equation $y = \dfrac{16}{3x^2 + 1}$ at the point $(1, 4)$.

Solution

Let $u = 3x^2 + 1$ then $y = 16u^{-1}$

So $\dfrac{du}{dx} = 6x$ and $\dfrac{dy}{du} = -16u^{-2}$

$\therefore \quad \dfrac{dy}{dx} = \dfrac{dy}{du} \cdot \dfrac{du}{dx}$

$\qquad = -16u^{-2} \cdot 6x$

$\qquad = \dfrac{-96x}{(3x^2 + 1)^2}$

$\therefore$ At $x = 1$, the gradient is $\dfrac{-96}{16} = -6$.

Example 3

Differentiate $y = (4x^3 - 5x)^{-2}$.

Solution

Let $u = 4x^3 - 5x$ then $y = u^{-2}$

So $\dfrac{du}{dx} = 12x^2 - 5$ and $\dfrac{dy}{du} = -2u^{-3}$

$\therefore \quad \dfrac{dy}{dx} = \dfrac{dy}{du} \cdot \dfrac{du}{dx}$

$\qquad = (-2u^{-3}) \cdot (12x^2 - 5)$

$\qquad = \dfrac{-2(12x^2 - 5)}{(4x^3 - 5x)^3}$

Example 4

Use the chain rule to prove that, if $y = x^n$ where n is a negative integer, then $\dfrac{dy}{dx} = nx^{n-1}$.

(Assume the result in the case that n is a positive integer and the case that $n = -1$.)

Solution

Let $y = x^n$, where n is a negative integer.

Then $y = \dfrac{1}{x^{-n}}$, where $-n$ is a positive integer.

Now let $u = x^{-n}$. Then $y = \dfrac{1}{u} = u^{-1}$.

So we have $\dfrac{du}{dx} = -nx^{-n-1}$, since $-n$ is a positive integer, and $\dfrac{dy}{du} = -u^{-2}$.

Hence

$\dfrac{dy}{dx} = \dfrac{dy}{du} \cdot \dfrac{du}{dx}$

$\qquad = -u^{-2} \cdot (-nx^{-n-1})$

$\qquad = nx^{-n-1}(x^{-n})^{-2}$

$\qquad = nx^{-n-1}(x^{2n})$

$\qquad = nx^{n-1}$

Using function notation, the chain rule is stated as

$(f \circ g)'(x) = f'(g(x))\, g'(x)$

where $(f \circ g)(x) = f(g(x))$.

Example 5

Given that $f(x) = (x^2 + 1)^3$, find $f'(x)$.

Solution

We can write $f = k \circ g$ where $k(x) = x^3$ and $g(x) = x^2 + 1$
giving $k'(x) = 3x^2$ and $g'(x) = 2x$

By the chain rule:
$$f'(x) = k'(g(x)) g'(x)$$
$$= 3(g(x))^2 \times 2x$$
$$= 6x(x^2 + 1)^2$$

Proof of the chain rule

Let f and g be differentiable functions. To find the derivative of their composition $f \circ g$, we must evaluate the limit

$$(f \circ g)'(x) = \lim_{h \to 0} \frac{f(g(x+h)) - f(g(x))}{h}$$

Multiply and divide the expression inside the limit by an extra term:

$$\frac{f(g(x+h)) - f(g(x))}{h} = \frac{f(g(x+h)) - f(g(x))}{g(x+h) - g(x)} \times \frac{g(x+h) - g(x)}{h}$$

Now we can rewrite the limit as

$$(f \circ g)'(x) = \lim_{h \to 0} \frac{f(g(x+h)) - f(g(x))}{g(x+h) - g(x)} \times \lim_{h \to 0} \frac{g(x+h) - g(x)}{h}$$

The second limit is just $g'(x)$. Notice that the expression inside the first limit is the gradient of the secant of the graph of f through the two points $(g(x), f(g(x)))$ and $(g(x+h), f(g(x+h)))$. As $h \to 0$, this approaches the gradient of f at $g(x)$. So the first limit is $f'(g(x))$.

Hence we have shown that

$$(f \circ g)'(x) = f'(g(x)) g'(x)$$

This proof is not without fault: for example, if there are values of h near zero for which $g(x+h) - g(x) = 0$, then we have division by zero in the first limit. However, a completely rigorous proof is beyond the scope of this course.

Section summary

- The chain rule (using Leibniz notation)
$$\frac{dy}{dx} = \frac{dy}{du} \cdot \frac{du}{dx}$$

- The chain rule (using function notation)
$$(f \circ g)'(x) = f'(g(x)) g'(x), \quad \text{where } (f \circ g)(x) = f(g(x))$$

Exercise 20A

1 Differentiate each of the following with respect to x:
  a $(x-1)^{30}$
  b $(x^5 - x^{10})^{20}$
  c $(x - x^3 - x^5)^4$
  d $(x^2 + 2x + 1)^4$
  e $(x^2 + 2x)^{-2}$, $x \neq -2, 0$
  f $\left(x^2 - \dfrac{2}{x}\right)^{-3}$, $x \neq 0$

2
  a Find the derivative of $f: \mathbb{R} \to \mathbb{R}$, $f(x) = (2x^3 + 1)^4$.
  b Find the gradient of $f: \mathbb{R} \to \mathbb{R}$, $f(x) = (2x^3 + 1)^4$ at the point $(1, 81)$.

3
  a Find the gradient of the curve with equation $y = \dfrac{1}{x+3}$ at the point $(1, \tfrac{1}{4})$.
  b Find the gradient of the curve with equation $y = \dfrac{1}{(x+3)^3}$ at the point $(1, \tfrac{1}{64})$.

4 The diagram is a sketch graph of the function $f(x) = \dfrac{1}{2x+3}$.
  a Find the gradient of the curve at the point $(0, \tfrac{1}{3})$.
  b Find the coordinates of the points on the curve at which the gradient is $-\dfrac{2}{9}$.

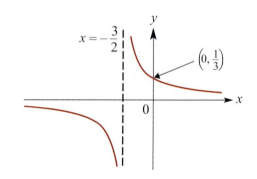

5 The diagram shows graphs of the functions $y = \dfrac{1}{x}$ and $y = -\dfrac{1}{x}$.

  a Find the gradient of $y = \dfrac{1}{x}$ at the point $(2, \tfrac{1}{2})$.
  b Without further calculation, state the gradient of $y = -\dfrac{1}{x}$ at $(2, -\tfrac{1}{2})$.

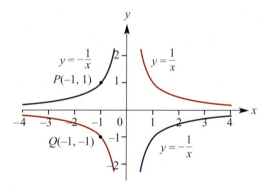

  c Find the equation of the tangent at the point $(1, 1)$ of $y = \dfrac{1}{x}$.
  d Find the equation of the tangent at the point $(1, -1)$ of $y = -\dfrac{1}{x}$.
  e Find the equations of the tangents at points P and Q, and find their point of intersection.
  f Draw sketch graphs of $y = \dfrac{1}{x}$ and $y = -\dfrac{1}{x}$ on the same set of axes and draw in the four tangents.

20B Differentiating rational powers

Before using the chain rule to differentiate rational powers, we will show how to differentiate $x^{\frac{1}{2}}$ and $x^{\frac{1}{3}}$ by first principles.

Example 6

Differentiate each of the following by first principles:

a $f(x) = x^{\frac{1}{2}}$, $x > 0$ **b** $g(x) = x^{\frac{1}{3}}$, $x \neq 0$

Solution

a
$$\frac{f(x+h) - f(x)}{h} = \frac{\sqrt{x+h} - \sqrt{x}}{h}$$
$$= \frac{\sqrt{x+h} - \sqrt{x}}{h} \times \frac{\sqrt{x+h} + \sqrt{x}}{\sqrt{x+h} + \sqrt{x}}$$
$$= \frac{x+h-x}{h(\sqrt{x+h} + \sqrt{x})}$$
$$= \frac{1}{\sqrt{x+h} + \sqrt{x}}$$

$$\therefore \quad f'(x) = \lim_{h \to 0} \frac{f(x+h) - f(x)}{h} = \lim_{h \to 0} \frac{1}{\sqrt{x+h} + \sqrt{x}} = \frac{1}{2\sqrt{x}}$$

b We use the identity
$$a^3 - b^3 = (a - b)(a^2 + ab + b^2)$$

By observing that $\left(a^{\frac{1}{3}}\right)^3 = a$ and $\left(b^{\frac{1}{3}}\right)^3 = b$, we obtain
$$a - b = \left(a^{\frac{1}{3}} - b^{\frac{1}{3}}\right)\left(a^{\frac{2}{3}} + a^{\frac{1}{3}}b^{\frac{1}{3}} + b^{\frac{2}{3}}\right)$$

and therefore
$$a^{\frac{1}{3}} - b^{\frac{1}{3}} = \frac{a - b}{a^{\frac{2}{3}} + a^{\frac{1}{3}}b^{\frac{1}{3}} + b^{\frac{2}{3}}}$$

We now have
$$\frac{g(x+h) - g(x)}{h} = \frac{(x+h)^{\frac{1}{3}} - x^{\frac{1}{3}}}{h}$$
$$= \frac{x + h - x}{h\left((x+h)^{\frac{2}{3}} + (x+h)^{\frac{1}{3}}x^{\frac{1}{3}} + x^{\frac{2}{3}}\right)}$$
$$= \frac{1}{(x+h)^{\frac{2}{3}} + (x+h)^{\frac{1}{3}}x^{\frac{1}{3}} + x^{\frac{2}{3}}}$$

Hence
$$g'(x) = \lim_{h \to 0} \frac{g(x+h) - g(x)}{h} = \lim_{h \to 0} \frac{1}{(x+h)^{\frac{2}{3}} + (x+h)^{\frac{1}{3}}x^{\frac{1}{3}} + x^{\frac{2}{3}}} = \frac{1}{3x^{\frac{2}{3}}}$$

Note: We can prove that $a^n - b^n = (a-b)(a^{n-1} + a^{n-2}b + a^{n-3}b^2 + \cdots + ab^{n-2} + b^{n-1})$ for $n \geq 2$. We could use this result to find the derivative of $x^{\frac{1}{n}}$ by first principles, but instead we will use the chain rule.

▶ Using the chain rule

Using the chain rule in the form $\dfrac{dy}{du} = \dfrac{dy}{dx} \cdot \dfrac{dx}{du}$ with $y = u$, we have

$$1 = \frac{dy}{dx} \cdot \frac{dx}{dy}$$

Thus $\quad \dfrac{dy}{dx} = \dfrac{1}{\dfrac{dx}{dy}} \quad$ for $\dfrac{dx}{dy} \neq 0$

Now let $y = x^{\frac{1}{n}}$, where $n \in \mathbb{Z} \setminus \{0\}$ and $x > 0$.

We have $y^n = x$ and so $\dfrac{dx}{dy} = ny^{n-1}$. Therefore

$$\frac{dy}{dx} = \frac{1}{\dfrac{dx}{dy}} = \frac{1}{ny^{n-1}} = \frac{1}{n\left(x^{\frac{1}{n}}\right)^{n-1}} = \frac{1}{n}x^{\frac{1}{n}-1}$$

For $y = x^{\frac{1}{n}}$, $\dfrac{dy}{dx} = \dfrac{1}{n}x^{\frac{1}{n}-1}$, where $n \in \mathbb{Z} \setminus \{0\}$ and $x > 0$.

This result may now be extended to rational powers.

Let $y = x^{\frac{p}{q}}$, where $p, q \in \mathbb{Z} \setminus \{0\}$.

Write $y = \left(x^{\frac{1}{q}}\right)^p$. Let $u = x^{\frac{1}{q}}$. Then $y = u^p$. The chain rule yields

$$\frac{dy}{dx} = \frac{dy}{du} \cdot \frac{du}{dx}$$

$$= pu^{p-1} \cdot \frac{1}{q}x^{\frac{1}{q}-1}$$

$$= p\left(x^{\frac{1}{q}}\right)^{p-1} \cdot \frac{1}{q}x^{\frac{1}{q}-1}$$

$$= \frac{p}{q}x^{\frac{p}{q}-\frac{1}{q}}x^{\frac{1}{q}-1}$$

$$= \frac{p}{q}x^{\frac{p}{q}-1}$$

Thus the result for integer powers has been extended to rational powers. In fact, the analogous result holds for any non-zero real power:

For $f(x) = x^a$, $f'(x) = ax^{a-1}$, where $a \in \mathbb{R} \setminus \{0\}$ and $x > 0$.

This result is stated for $x > 0$, as $(-3)^{\frac{1}{2}}$ is not defined, although $(-2)^{\frac{1}{3}}$ is defined.

The graphs of $y = x^{\frac{1}{2}}$, $y = x^{\frac{1}{3}}$ and $y = x^{\frac{1}{4}}$ are shown.

The domain of each has been taken to be $\mathbb{R}^+$.

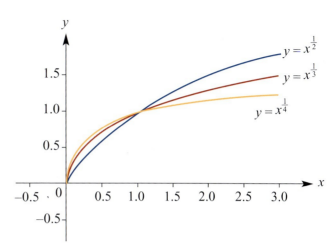

The figure to the right is the graph of the function $f : \mathbb{R} \to \mathbb{R}$, $f(x) = x^{\frac{1}{3}}$.

Note that the values shown here are $-0.08 \leq x \leq 0.08$.

From this it can be seen that the tangent to $y = x^{\frac{1}{3}}$ at the origin is on the y-axis.

Use a calculator to investigate graphs of this type further.

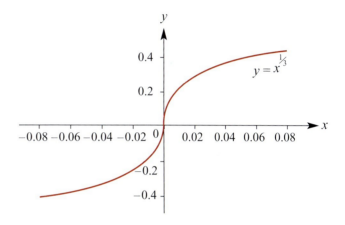

Example 7

Find the derivative of each of the following with respect to x:

a $4x^{\frac{2}{3}}$ **b** $x^{\frac{1}{5}} - 2x^{-3}$

Solution

a Let $y = 4x^{\frac{2}{3}}$

Then $\dfrac{dy}{dx} = 4 \times \dfrac{2}{3} \times x^{\frac{2}{3}-1}$

$= \dfrac{8}{3} x^{\frac{-1}{3}}$

b Let $y = x^{\frac{1}{5}} - 2x^{-3}$

Then $\dfrac{dy}{dx} = \dfrac{1}{5} x^{\frac{1}{5}-1} - 2 \times (-3x^{-3-1})$

$= \dfrac{1}{5} x^{\frac{-4}{5}} + 6x^{-4}$

Section summary

For any non-zero rational number $r = \dfrac{p}{q}$, if $f(x) = x^r$, then $f'(x) = rx^{r-1}$.

Exercise 20B

1 Find the derivative of each of the following with respect to x:
   a $x^{\frac{1}{3}}$
   b $x^{\frac{3}{2}}$, $x > 0$
   c $x^{\frac{5}{2}} - x^{\frac{3}{2}}$, $x > 0$
   d $2x^{\frac{1}{2}} - 3x^{\frac{5}{3}}$, $x > 0$
   e $x^{-\frac{5}{6}}$, $x > 0$
   f $x^{-\frac{1}{2}} - 4$, $x > 0$

2 Find the derivative of each of the following with respect to x:
   a $\sqrt{1 + x^2}$
   b $\sqrt[3]{x + x^2}$
   c $(1 + x^2)^{-\frac{1}{2}}$
   d $(1 + x)^{\frac{1}{3}}$

3 a Find the gradient of $y = x^{\frac{1}{3}}$ at each of the following points:
   i $\left(\frac{1}{8}, \frac{1}{2}\right)$
   ii $\left(-\frac{1}{8}, -\frac{1}{2}\right)$
   iii $(1, 1)$
   iv $(-1, -1)$

   b Comment on your results.

4 Consider the graphs of $y = x^{\frac{1}{2}}$ and $y = x^{\frac{1}{3}}$ for $x > 0$.
   a Find $\left\{x : x^{\frac{1}{2}} < x^{\frac{1}{3}}\right\}$.
   b Find the values for x for which the gradient of $y = x^{\frac{1}{2}}$ is greater than the gradient of $y = x^{\frac{1}{3}}$.

5 Differentiate each of the following with respect to x:
   a $(2 - 5\sqrt{x})^2$
   b $(3\sqrt{x} + 2)^2$
   c $\dfrac{2 + \sqrt{x}}{x^2}$
   d $\dfrac{x^2 + 2}{\sqrt{x}}$
   e $3\sqrt{x}(x^2 + 2)$

20C Antidifferentiating rational powers

In the previous section, we showed that:

If $f(x) = x^r$, where $r \in \mathbb{Q} \setminus \{0\}$, then $f'(x) = rx^{r-1}$.

For example, we know that:

$f(x) = x^{-2}$ implies $f'(x) = -2x^{-3}$

$f(x) = x^{\frac{1}{2}}$ implies $f'(x) = \dfrac{1}{2}x^{-\frac{1}{2}}$

$f(x) = x^{\frac{3}{2}}$ implies $f'(x) = \dfrac{3}{2}x^{\frac{1}{2}}$

Reversing this process we have:

$\displaystyle\int -2x^{-3}\, dx = x^{-2} + c$ where c is an arbitrary constant

$\displaystyle\int \frac{1}{2}x^{-\frac{1}{2}}\, dx = x^{\frac{1}{2}} + c$ where c is an arbitrary constant

$\displaystyle\int \frac{3}{2}x^{\frac{1}{2}}\, dx = x^{\frac{3}{2}} + c$ where c is an arbitrary constant

We also have:

$$\int x^{-3}\, dx = -\frac{1}{2}x^{-2} + c$$

$$\int x^{-\frac{1}{2}}\, dx = 2x^{\frac{1}{2}} + c$$

$$\int x^{\frac{1}{2}}\, dx = \frac{2}{3}x^{\frac{3}{2}} + c$$

From this we see that:

$$\int x^r\, dx = \frac{x^{r+1}}{r+1} + c, \quad r \in \mathbb{Q} \setminus \{-1\}$$

Note: This result can only be applied for suitable values of x for a given value of r.
For example, if $r = \frac{1}{2}$, then $x \in \mathbb{R}^+$ is a suitable restriction. If $r = -2$, we can take $x \in \mathbb{R} \setminus \{0\}$, and if $r = 3$, we can take $x \in \mathbb{R}$.

Example 8

Find y in terms of x if:

a $\dfrac{dy}{dx} = \dfrac{1}{x^2}$, and $y = 1$ when $x = 1$

b $\dfrac{dy}{dx} = 3\sqrt{x}$, and $y = 2$ when $x = 4$

c $\dfrac{dy}{dx} = x^{\frac{3}{4}} + x^{-\frac{3}{4}}$, and $y = 0$ when $x = 0$

Solution

a $\int \dfrac{1}{x^2}\, dx = \int x^{-2}\, dx$

$\qquad = \dfrac{x^{-1}}{-1} + c$

$\therefore\ y = -\dfrac{1}{x} + c$

As $y = 1$ when $x = 1$, we have $c = 2$.

Thus $y = -\dfrac{1}{x} + 2$

b $\int 3\sqrt{x}\, dx = 3\int x^{\frac{1}{2}}\, dx$

$\qquad = 3 \times \dfrac{x^{\frac{3}{2}}}{\frac{3}{2}} + c$

$\therefore\ y = 2x^{\frac{3}{2}} + c$

As $y = 2$ when $x = 4$, we have

$2 = 2(4)^{\frac{3}{2}} + c$

$2 = 2 \times 8 + c$

$\therefore\ c = -14$

Thus $y = 2x^{\frac{3}{2}} - 14$

c $y = \dfrac{4}{7}x^{\frac{7}{4}} + 4x^{\frac{1}{4}} + c$

As $y = 0$ when $x = 0$, we have $c = 0$,

and so $y = \dfrac{4}{7}x^{\frac{7}{4}} + 4x^{\frac{1}{4}}$

Section summary

For any rational number $r \neq -1$:
$$\int x^r \, dx = \frac{x^{r+1}}{r+1} + c$$

Exercise 20C

1 Find:

   a $\int 3x^{-2} \, dx$

   b $\int 2x^{-4} + 6x \, dx$

   c $\int \sqrt{x}(2 + x) \, dx$

   d $\int 3x^{\frac{1}{3}} - 5x^{\frac{5}{4}} \, dx$

   e $\int \frac{3z^4 + 2z}{z^3} \, dz$

   f $\int 3x^{\frac{3}{4}} - 7x^{\frac{1}{2}} \, dx$

2 Find y in terms of x for each of the following:

   a $\frac{dy}{dx} = x^{\frac{1}{2}} + x$, and $y = 6$ when $x = 4$

   b $\frac{dy}{dx} = \frac{1}{x^3}$, and $y = 1$ when $x = 1$

   c $\frac{dy}{dx} = 3x + \frac{1}{x^2}$, and $y = 5$ when $x = 1$

3 A curve with equation $y = f(x)$ passes through the point $(2, 0)$ and $f'(x) = 3x^2 - \frac{1}{x^2}$. Find $f(x)$.

4 Find s in terms of t, if $\frac{ds}{dt} = 3t - \frac{8}{t^2}$ and $s = 1\frac{1}{2}$ when $t = 1$.

5 Given that $\frac{dy}{dx} = \frac{a}{x^2} + 1$ and that, when $x = 1$, $\frac{dy}{dx} = 3$ and $y = 3$, find the value of y when $x = 2$.

6 The curve for which $\frac{dy}{dx} = ax$, where a is a constant, is such that the tangent at $(1, 2)$ passes through the origin. Find the gradient of this tangent and hence determine:

   a the value of a

   b the equation of the curve.

7 Find the equation of the curve which passes through the point $(-1, 2)$ and has the property that, for each point (x, y) on the curve, the gradient equals the square of the distance between the point and the y-axis.

20D The second derivative

For the function $f: \mathbb{R} \to \mathbb{R}$, $f(x) = 2x^2 + 4x + 1$, the derivative has rule $f'(x) = 4x + 4$.

That is, the derivative of $2x^2 + 4x + 1$ is $4x + 4$.

The second derivative of $2x^2 + 4x + 1$ is the derivative of $4x + 4$, which is 4.

The function notation for the second derivative is $f''(x) = 4$.

Using Leibniz notation: If $y = 2x^2 + 4x + 1$, then the first derivative is $\dfrac{dy}{dx} = 4x + 4$ and the second derivative is $\dfrac{d^2y}{dx^2} = 4$.

Example 9

For each of the following, find $f''(x)$:

a $f(x) = 3x^3 + 2x^{-1} + 1$, $x \neq 0$

b $f(x) = x^{\frac{1}{2}} + 3x^{-4} + 1$, $x > 0$

c $f(x) = x^4 + x^{-\frac{3}{2}} + 1$, $x > 0$

Solution

a $f'(x) = 9x^2 - 2x^{-2}$ $(x \neq 0)$
$f''(x) = 18x + 4x^{-3}$ $(x \neq 0)$

b $f'(x) = \dfrac{1}{2}x^{-\frac{1}{2}} - 12x^{-5}$ $(x > 0)$
$f''(x) = -\dfrac{1}{4}x^{-\frac{3}{2}} + 60x^{-6}$ $(x > 0)$

c $f'(x) = 4x^3 - \dfrac{3}{2}x^{-\frac{5}{2}}$ $(x > 0)$
$f''(x) = 12x^2 + \dfrac{15}{4}x^{-\frac{7}{2}}$ $(x > 0)$

▶ Position, velocity and acceleration

We recall the following from Chapter 18. For an object moving in a straight line, if $x(t)$ denotes the position of the object at time t, then:

- $\dfrac{dx}{dt}$ gives the velocity at time t
- $\dfrac{d^2x}{dt^2}$ gives the acceleration at time t.

Exercise 20D

Example 9

1 Find $f''(x)$ for each of the following:

a $f(x) = x^3 + 2x + 1$

b $f(x) = 3x + 2$

c $f(x) = (3x + 1)^4$

d $f(x) = x^{\frac{1}{2}} + 3x^3$, $x > 0$

e $f(x) = (x^6 + 1)^3$

f $f(x) = 5x^2 + 6x^{-1} + 3x^{\frac{3}{2}}$

2 For each of the following, find $\dfrac{d^2y}{dx^2}$:

a $y = 3x^3 + 4x + 1$
b $y = 6$
c $y = 6x^2 + 3x + 1$
d $y = (6x + 1)^4$
e $y = (5x + 2)^4$
f $y = x^3 + 2x^2 + 3x^{-1}$

3 The height of a stone is $20t - 4.9t^2$ metres at a time t seconds after it is thrown. What is the acceleration?

4 After t seconds, the x-coordinate of a particle moving along the x-axis is given by $x(t) = 4t - 3t^3$, where the units on the x-axis are in metres.

a Find:
  i the x-coordinate after 2 seconds of motion
  ii the velocity of the particle at the start
  iii the velocity of the particle after half a second
  iv the velocity of the particle after 2 seconds

b When is the acceleration zero?
c What is the average velocity during the first 2 seconds?

20E Sketch graphs

In Chapter 18 we used calculus to help us sketch the graphs of polynomial functions. In this section we show how the same techniques may be applied to non-polynomial functions.

We will sketch the graph of the function

$$f: \mathbb{R} \setminus \{0\} \to \mathbb{R}, \quad f(x) = \dfrac{1}{x^2} + x$$

Consider the behaviour of the function for very large x

This section of a spreadsheet shows the behaviour of $f(x)$ as the value of x becomes very large positive. This has been done using increasing powers of 2.

We see that as $x \to \infty$, $f(x) \to x$.

This shows us that the line $y = x$ is an **oblique asymptote** for the graph.

It is clear also that as $x \to -\infty$, $f(x) \to x$.

a

x	$f(x)$
1	2.0000000000
2	2.2500000000
4	4.0625000000
8	8.0156250000
16	16.0039062500
32	32.0009765625
64	64.0002441406
128	128.0000610352
256	256.0000152588
512	512.0000038147
1024	1024.0000009537
2048	2048.0000002384

Consider vertical asymptotes

The function is not defined at $x = 0$. The behaviour of the function as x approaches 0 is demonstrated below. The values of x considered are 2^0, 2^{-1}, 2^{-2}, 2^{-3}, etc.

b

x	$f(x)$
1.00000000	2.00000000
0.50000000	4.50000000
0.25000000	16.25000000
0.12500000	64.12500000
0.06250000	256.06250000
0.03125000	1024.03125000
0.01562500	4096.01562500
0.00781250	16384.00781250
0.00390625	65536.00390625

c

x	$f(x)$
−1.00000000	0.00000000
−0.50000000	3.50000000
−0.25000000	15.75000000
−0.12500000	63.87500000
−0.06250000	255.93750000
−0.03125000	1023.96875000
−0.01562500	4095.98437500
−0.00781250	16383.99218750
−0.00390625	65535.99609375

Spreadsheet **b** shows the behaviour as x approaches 0 from the right: $f(x)$ becomes increasingly large. We write $\lim_{x \to 0^+} f(x) = \infty$.

Spreadsheet **c** shows the behaviour as x approaches 0 from the left: again $f(x)$ becomes increasingly large. We write $\lim_{x \to 0^-} f(x) = \infty$.

Find the axis intercepts

The graph does not have a y-axis intercept, as the function is not defined at $x = 0$. The graph crosses the x-axis when $\frac{1}{x^2} + x = 0$, i.e. when $x^3 = -1$, which implies $x = -1$.

Consider the stationary points

For $f(x) = \frac{1}{x^2} + x$, we have $f'(x) = \frac{-2}{x^3} + 1$, and so $f'(x) = 0$ implies $x = 2^{\frac{1}{3}}$. Thus there is a point on the curve at $x = 2^{\frac{1}{3}}$ at which the gradient is zero.

As the graph is not continuous at $x = 0$, we use a gradient chart for $x > 0$ only.

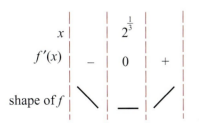

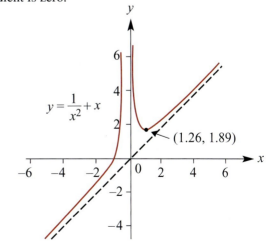

Thus there is a local minimum at the point (1.26, 1.89), with coordinates correct to two decimal places.

Spreadsheet **a** shows how rapidly the graph of $y = f(x)$ moves towards the line $y = x$. At $x = 4$, $f(x) = 4.0625$ and at $x = 8$, $f(x) = 8.015625$.

Example 10

Sketch the graph of $f: \mathbb{R} \setminus \{-1\} \to \mathbb{R}$, $f(x) = \dfrac{x^2 + 3}{x + 1}$.

Solution

By division, $f(x) = x - 1 + \dfrac{4}{x + 1}$.

Behaviour for very large x

As $x \to \infty$, $f(x) \to x - 1$ from above.

As $x \to -\infty$, $f(x) \to x - 1$ from below.

There is an oblique asymptote with equation $y = x - 1$.

Vertical asymptote

$\lim\limits_{x \to -1^+} f(x) = \infty$ and $\lim\limits_{x \to -1^-} f(x) = -\infty$

There is a vertical asymptote with equation $x = -1$.

Axis intercepts

When $x = 0$, $f(x) = 3$. There is no x-axis intercept, as $x^2 + 3 \neq 0$ for all $x \in \mathbb{R}$.

Stationary points

For $f(x) = x - 1 + \dfrac{4}{x + 1}$

$$f'(x) = 1 - \dfrac{4}{(x + 1)^2}$$

Find where $f'(x) = 0$:

$$1 - \dfrac{4}{(x + 1)^2} = 0$$

$$(x + 1)^2 = 4$$

$$x + 1 = \pm 2$$

Therefore $x = 1$ or $x = -3$.

We consider two gradient charts.

First for $x > -1$: Next for $x < -1$:

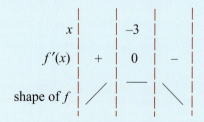

∴ Local minimum at $(1, 2)$ ∴ Local maximum at $(-3, -6)$

Sketch graph

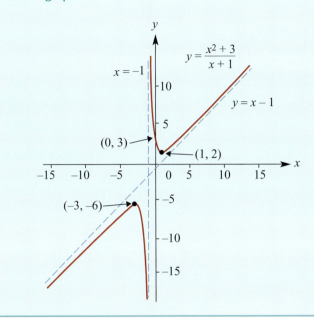

Section summary

Steps for sketching graphs
- Find the x-axis and y-axis intercepts and the stationary points.
- Find where the graph is strictly increasing and where it is strictly decreasing.
- Determine the nature of each stationary point (local maximum, local minimum or stationary point of inflection).
- Identify vertical asymptotes.
- Understand the behaviour as x becomes very large positive and very large negative.

Exercise 20E

Example 10

1 The equation of a curve is $y = 4x + \dfrac{1}{x}$.
  a Find the coordinates of the turning points.
  b Find the equation of the tangent to the curve at the point where $x = 2$.

2 Find the x-coordinates of the points on the curve $y = \dfrac{x^2 - 1}{x}$ at which the gradient of the curve is 5.

3 Find the gradient of the curve $y = \dfrac{2x - 4}{x^2}$ at the point where the curve crosses the x-axis.

4 For the curve $y = x - 5 + \dfrac{4}{x}$, find:

  a the coordinates of the points of intersection with the axes
  b the equations of all asymptotes
  c the coordinates of all turning points.

  Use this information to sketch the curve.

5 If x is positive, find the least value of $x + \dfrac{4}{x^2}$.

6 For positive values of x, sketch the graph of $y = x + \dfrac{4}{x}$ and find the least value of y.

7 Sketch the graph of each of the following, indicating the coordinates of axis intercepts and turning points, and the equations of asymptotes:

  a $y = x + \dfrac{1}{x},\ x \neq 0$
  b $y = \dfrac{1}{x^2} - x,\ x \neq 0$

  c $y = x + 1 + \dfrac{1}{x+3},\ x \neq -3$
  d $y = x^3 + \dfrac{243}{x},\ x \neq 0$

  e $y = x - 5 + \dfrac{1}{x},\ x \neq 0$
  f $y = \dfrac{x^2 - 4}{x+2},\ x \neq -2$

Chapter summary

- **Chain rule**
  - The chain rule is often used to differentiate a complicated function by transforming it into two simpler functions, which are 'chained' together.
    For example: $y = \sqrt{3x^2 + 1}$ can be transformed into $y = \sqrt{u}$ and $u = 3x^2 + 1$.
  - Using Leibniz notation, the chain rule is stated as $\dfrac{dy}{dx} = \dfrac{dy}{du} \cdot \dfrac{du}{dx}$.
  - Using function notation, the chain rule is stated as $(f \circ g)'(x) = f'(g(x))\, g'(x)$, where $(f \circ g)(x) = f(g(x))$.

- **Derivatives and antiderivatives of powers**
  - If $f(x) = x^r$, then $f'(x) = rx^{r-1}$, for any non-zero rational number r.
  - $\int x^r\, dx = \dfrac{x^{r+1}}{r+1} + c$, for any rational number $r \neq -1$.

- **Second derivative**
  - The second derivative of y with respect to x is written as $\dfrac{d^2y}{dx^2}$.
  - Using function notation, the second derivative of f is written as f''.

- **Sketch graphs** When sketching the graph of a function, consider:
  - the behaviour of the function as x becomes large positive and large negative
  - vertical asymptotes
  - axis intercepts
  - stationary points (i.e. where the gradient is zero).

Technology-free questions

1 Find the derivative of each of the following with respect to x:

  a $x^{\frac{1}{2}}$ **b** $\sqrt[3]{x}$ **c** $-\dfrac{2}{x^{\frac{1}{3}}}$ **d** $x^{\frac{4}{3}}$ **e** $x^{-\frac{1}{3}}$ **f** $x^{-\frac{1}{3}} + 2x^{\frac{3}{5}}$

2 Differentiate each of the following with respect to x:

  a $(2x + 3)^2$ **b** $2(3x + 4)^4$ **c** $(3 - 2x)^{-\frac{1}{2}}$ **d** $\dfrac{1}{3 + 2x}$

  e $\dfrac{1}{(2x - 1)^{\frac{2}{3}}}$ **f** $\dfrac{3}{\sqrt{2 + x^2}}$ **g** $\left(2x^2 - \dfrac{3}{x^2}\right)^{\frac{1}{3}}$

3 Find:

  a $\int 2x^{-3}\, dx$ **b** $\int \sqrt{x}\,(x - 2)\, dx$ **c** $\int \dfrac{3x^2 + 2x}{x}\, dx$

  d $\int \dfrac{3x + 1}{x^3}\, dx$ **e** $\int 5x - 2\sqrt{x}\, dx$ **f** $\int 5x^{\frac{3}{4}} - 2x^{\frac{1}{3}}\, dx$

  g $\int 2 - \sqrt{x}\, dx$ **h** $\int \dfrac{3x^2 + 2x}{x^4}\, dx$

Review

4 Find s in terms of t, if $\dfrac{ds}{dt} = t + 3 - \dfrac{1}{t^2}$ and $s = 6$ when $t = 1$.

5 Find the gradient of the tangent to each of the following curves at the given point:

   a $y = \sqrt{x}$, $(9, 3)$ **b** $y = \dfrac{1}{2x+1}$, $(0, 1)$ **c** $y = \dfrac{2}{x^2}$, $(4, \tfrac{1}{8})$

   d $y = 3 + \dfrac{2}{x}$, $(1, 5)$ **e** $y = \sqrt{x+1}$, $(8, 3)$ **f** $y = (x^2 - 7x - 8)^3$, $(8, 0)$

6 Find the coordinates of the point(s) on the curve with equation $y = \dfrac{1}{x}$ for which the gradient is -4.

7 Find the coordinates of the point(s) on the curve with equation $y = \sqrt{x}$ for which the gradient is 2.

Multiple-choice questions

1 If $f(x) = \dfrac{4x^4 - 12x^2}{3x}$, then $f'(x)$ equals

  A $\dfrac{16x^3 - 24x}{3}$ **B** $4x^2 - 4$ **C** $\dfrac{16x^3 - 24x}{3x}$

  D $4x^2 - 8x$ **E** $\dfrac{8x^3 - 16x}{3x}$

2 If $f(x) = 2x^{\frac{p}{q}}$, where p and q are integers, then $f'(x)$ equals

  A $2x^{\frac{(p-q)}{q}}$ **B** $2px^{\frac{p}{q}-1}$ **C** 2 **D** $\dfrac{2p}{q} x^{\frac{(p-q)}{q}}$ **E** $\dfrac{2p}{q} x$

3 If $f: \mathbb{R} \setminus \{2\} \to \mathbb{R}$ with $f(x) = 4 + \dfrac{4}{2-x}$, then $f'(x) > 0$ for

  A $\mathbb{R} \setminus \{2\}$ **B** $\mathbb{R}$ **C** $x < 2$ **D** $x > 2$ **E** $x > 4$

4 A particle moves in a straight line so that its position, x cm, relative to a fixed point O at time t seconds ($t \geq 0$) is given by $x = -t^3 + 7t^2 - 14t + 6$. The particle's acceleration at $t = 3$ is

  A -4 cm/s^2 **B** 3 cm/s^2 **C** 4 cm/s^2 **D** 8 cm/s^2 **E** 0 cm/s^2

5 Let $y = f(g(x))$, where $g(x) = x^3$. Then $\dfrac{dy}{dx}$ equals

  A $3x^2 f'(x^3)$ **B** $3x^2 f(x^3)$ **C** $2x f(x) f'(x^3)$

  D $2f(x) f'(x^3)$ **E** $3x^2$

6 The graph defined by the rule $f(x) = x + \dfrac{1}{x}$ has a local minimum at $(a, f(a))$. The value of a is

  A -1 **B** 2 **C** $-\dfrac{5}{2}$ **D** $\dfrac{5}{2}$ **E** 1

7 Which of the following is *not true* for the curve of $y = f(x)$, where $f(x) = x^{\frac{1}{5}}$?
  A The gradient is defined for all real numbers.
  B The curve passes through the origin.
  C The curve passes through the points with coordinates $(1, 1)$ and $(-1, -1)$.
  D For $x > 0$, the gradient is positive.
  E For $x > 0$, the gradient is decreasing.

8 Which of the following is *not true* for $y = f(x)$, where $f(x) = x^{\frac{3}{4}}$?
  A The maximal domain of the function is $\mathbb{R}^+ \cup \{0\}$.
  B $f(x) > x$ for all $x > 1$.
  C The curve of $y = f(x)$ passes through the point with coordinates $(1, 1)$.
  D For $x > 0$, the gradient of the curve is positive.
  E For $x > 0$, the gradient of the curve is decreasing.

9 The derivative of $(5x^2 + 2x)^n$ is
  A $n(10x + 2)(5x^2 + 2x)^{n-1}$ B $(5x^2 + 2x)^{n-1}$ C $(10x + 2)^n$
  D $n(5x^2 + 2x)^{n-1}$ E $10x^{2n-1} + 2x^{n-1}$

10 The graph of the function with rule $y = \dfrac{k}{2(x^2 + 1)}$ has gradient 1 when $x = 1$. The value of k is
  A 1 B -1 C 4 D -4 E $-\dfrac{1}{4}$

Extended-response questions

1 A solid circular cylinder has radius r cm and height h cm. It has a fixed volume of 400 cm^3.
  a Find h in terms of r.
  b Show that the total surface area, A cm^2, of the cylinder is given by $A = 2\pi r^2 + \dfrac{800}{r}$.
  c Find $\dfrac{dA}{dr}$.
  d Solve the equation $\dfrac{dA}{dr} = 0$ for r.
  e Find, correct to three significant figures, the minimum surface area of the cylinder.
  f Sketch the graph of A against r.

2 A rectangle has sides of length x cm and y cm, and the area of the rectangle is 16 cm^2.
  a Find y in terms of x.
  b Show that the perimeter, P cm, is given by $P = 2x + \dfrac{32}{x}$.
  c Find the value of x for which the value of P is a minimum and find this value of P.
  d Sketch the graph of P against x for $x > 0$.

3 The area of rectangle $OABC$ is 120 cm², the length of CZ is 5 cm and the length of AX is 7 cm. Let the length of OC be x cm.

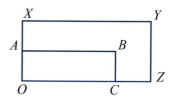

  a Find the length of OA in terms of x.
  b Find the length of OX in terms of x.
  c Find the length of OZ in terms of x.
  d Find the area, y cm², of rectangle $OXYZ$ in terms of x.
  e Find the value of x for which the area, y cm², is a minimum.

4 The curve with equation $y = \sqrt{x+2}$ meets the x-axis at A and the y-axis at B.
  a Find the coordinates of A and B.
  b By using the chain rule, find $\dfrac{dy}{dx}$.
  c **i** Find the gradient of the curve where $x = -1$.
   ii Find the equation of the tangent at the point where $x = -1$.
   iii If this tangent meets the x-axis at C and the y-axis at D, find the distance CD.
  d Find the values of x for which $\dfrac{dy}{dx} < 1$.

5 An open rectangular box of height h cm has a horizontal rectangular base with side lengths x cm and $2x$ cm. The volume of the box is 36 cm³.
  a Express h in terms of x.
  b Show that the total surface area, A cm², of the box is given by $A = 2x^2 + \dfrac{108}{x}$.
  c Calculate the values of x and h which make the total surface area a minimum.
  d Sketch the graph of A against x for $x > 0$.

6 The prism shown in the diagram has a triangular cross-section. The 'ends' of the prism shown are congruent right-angled triangles with the right angles at C and Z.
The lengths of some edges are $AX = CZ = BY = y$ cm, $AC = XZ = 3x$ cm and $CB = ZY = 4x$ cm.
The volume of the prism is 1500 cm³.

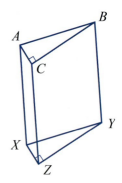

  a Express y in terms of x.
  b Show that the total surface area, S cm², is given by
   $S = 12x^2 + \dfrac{3000}{x}$.
  c Find $\dfrac{dS}{dx}$.
  d Find the minimum value of S.

Integration

Objectives

▶ To use **numerical methods** to estimate the area under the graph of a function.
▶ To be able to calculate **definite integrals**.
▶ To use the definite integral to find the **exact area** under the graph of a function.

We have used the derivative to find the gradients of tangents to curves, and in turn this has been used in graph sketching. The derivative has also been used to define instantaneous rate of change and to solve problems involving motion in a straight line.

We have also worked with antiderivatives. These provided a method for going from a rate of change of a variable back to the variable itself: for example, from velocity to position.

It comes as a surprise that these same ideas can be used to determine areas. In this chapter we define an area function A for a given function f on an interval $[a, b]$, and show that the derivative of the area function is the original function f. Hence, you can go from the function f to its area function by antidifferentiating. This result is so important that it carries the title **fundamental theorem of calculus**.

The result was developed over many centuries, and some of the methods discussed in this chapter date back to Archimedes. The final result was brought together by both Leibniz and Newton in the seventeenth century. The wonder of it is that the two seemingly distinct ideas – calculation of areas and calculation of gradients – were shown to be so closely related.

21A Estimating the area under a graph

Consider a function $f: \mathbb{R} \to \mathbb{R}$ and its graph $y = f(x)$. We want to find the area under the graph. For now we'll assume that the graph $y = f(x)$ is always *above the x-axis*, and we will estimate the area between the graph $y = f(x)$ and the x-axis. We set left and right endpoints and estimate the area between those endpoints.

Below is the graph of $f(x) = 9 - 0.1x^2$. We consider three methods for determining the area under this graph between $x = 2$ and $x = 5$.

▶ The left-endpoint estimate

We first find an approximation for the area under the graph between $x = 2$ and $x = 5$ by dividing the region into rectangles as illustrated. The width of each rectangle is 0.5.

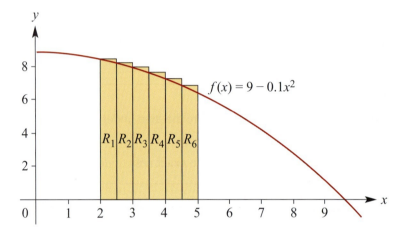

Areas of rectangles:

- Area of $R_1 = 0.5 \times f(2.0) = 0.5 \times 8.60 = 4.30$ square units
- Area of $R_2 = 0.5 \times f(2.5) = 0.5 \times 8.38 = 4.19$ square units
- Area of $R_3 = 0.5 \times f(3.0) = 0.5 \times 8.10 = 4.05$ square units
- Area of $R_4 = 0.5 \times f(3.5) = 0.5 \times 7.78 = 3.89$ square units
- Area of $R_5 = 0.5 \times f(4.0) = 0.5 \times 7.40 = 3.70$ square units
- Area of $R_6 = 0.5 \times f(4.5) = 0.5 \times 6.98 = 3.49$ square units

The sum of the areas of the rectangles is 23.62 square units.

This is called the **left-endpoint estimate** for the area under the graph.

The left-endpoint estimate will be larger than the actual area for a graph that is decreasing over the interval, and smaller than the actual area for a graph that is increasing.

▶ The right-endpoint estimate

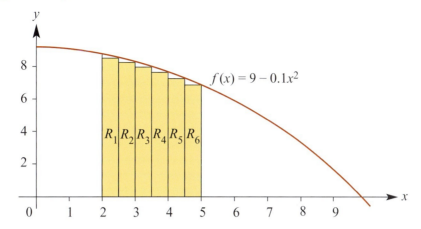

Areas of rectangles:

- Area of $R_1 = 0.5 \times f(2.5) = 0.5 \times 8.38 = 4.19$ square units
- Area of $R_2 = 0.5 \times f(3.0) = 0.5 \times 8.10 = 4.05$ square units
- Area of $R_3 = 0.5 \times f(3.5) = 0.5 \times 7.78 = 3.89$ square units
- Area of $R_4 = 0.5 \times f(4.0) = 0.5 \times 7.40 = 3.70$ square units
- Area of $R_5 = 0.5 \times f(4.5) = 0.5 \times 6.98 = 3.49$ square units
- Area of $R_6 = 0.5 \times f(5.0) = 0.5 \times 6.50 = 3.25$ square units

The sum of the areas of the rectangles is 22.67 square units.

This is called the **right-endpoint estimate** for the area under the graph.

> For f decreasing over $[a, b]$: left-endpoint estimate ≥ true area ≥ right-endpoint estimate
>
> For f increasing over $[a, b]$: left-endpoint estimate ≤ true area ≤ right-endpoint estimate

It is clear that, if narrower strips are chosen, we obtain an estimate that is closer to the true value. This is time-consuming to do by hand, but a computer program or spreadsheet makes the process quite manageable. In the following spreadsheet, the right-endpoint estimate is calculated using rectangles of width 0.1 units.

x	$f(x)$	$0.1 \times f(x)$	x	$f(x)$	$0.1 \times f(x)$	x	$f(x)$	$0.1 \times f(x)$
2.1	8.559	0.8559	3.1	8.039	0.8039	4.1	7.319	0.7319
2.2	8.516	0.8516	3.2	7.976	0.7976	4.2	7.236	0.7236
2.3	8.471	0.8471	3.3	7.911	0.7911	4.3	7.151	0.7151
2.4	8.424	0.8424	3.4	7.844	0.7844	4.4	7.064	0.7064
2.5	8.375	0.8375	3.5	7.775	0.7775	4.5	6.975	0.6975
2.6	8.324	0.8324	3.6	7.704	0.7704	4.6	6.884	0.6884
2.7	8.271	0.8271	3.7	7.631	0.7631	4.7	6.791	0.6791
2.8	8.216	0.8216	3.8	7.556	0.7556	4.8	6.696	0.6696
2.9	8.159	0.8159	3.9	7.479	0.7479	4.9	6.599	0.6599
3	8.1	0.81	4	7.4	0.74	5	6.5	0.65

The sum of the areas of the rectangles is 22.9945 square units.

The trapezoidal estimate

For this estimate we work with trapeziums instead of rectangles.

The area of a trapezium is $\frac{1}{2}(a + b)h$, where a and b are the lengths of the two parallel sides and h is their distance apart.

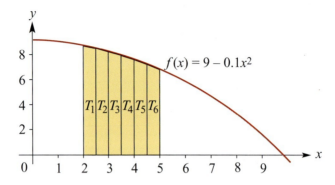

Areas of trapeziums:

- Area of $T_1 = \frac{1}{2}[f(2.0) + f(2.5)] \times 0.5 = 4.24375$ square units
- Area of $T_2 = \frac{1}{2}[f(2.5) + f(3.0)] \times 0.5 = 4.11875$ square units
- Area of $T_3 = \frac{1}{2}[f(3.0) + f(3.5)] \times 0.5 = 3.96875$ square units
- Area of $T_4 = \frac{1}{2}[f(3.5) + f(4.0)] \times 0.5 = 3.79375$ square units
- Area of $T_5 = \frac{1}{2}[f(4.0) + f(4.5)] \times 0.5 = 3.59375$ square units
- Area of $T_6 = \frac{1}{2}[f(4.5) + f(5.0)] \times 0.5 = 3.36875$ square units

The sum of the areas is 23.0875 square units.

This is called the **trapezoidal estimate** for the area under the graph.

We can see that the trapezoidal estimate for this example can also be calculated as

$$\frac{1}{2}\Big[f(2) + 2f(2.5) + 2f(3) + 2f(3.5) + 2f(4) + 2f(4.5) + f(5)\Big] \times 0.5$$

Example 1

Find the sum of the areas of the shaded rectangles to approximate the area under the curve

$$y = (x - 2)(x + 2)(x - 1)^2 + 10$$

between $x = 0$ and $x = 3$.

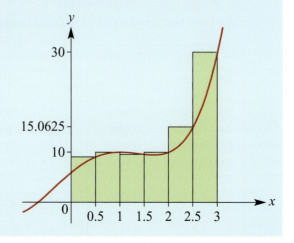

Solution

We use the right-endpoint method with rectangles of width 0.5:

$$\text{Area} = f(0.5) \times 0.5 + f(1) \times 0.5 + f(1.5) \times 0.5 + f(2) \times 0.5 + f(2.5) \times 0.5 + f(3) \times 0.5$$
$$= \big(f(0.5) + f(1) + f(1.5) + f(2) + f(2.5) + f(3)\big) \times 0.5$$
$$= 83.6875 \times 0.5$$
$$= 41.84375$$

Notes:
- The left-endpoint estimate with the same intervals is 29.84375.
- The actual area under the curve is 35.1.

Section summary

Divide the interval $[a, b]$ on the x-axis into n equal subintervals $[a, x_1]$, $[x_1, x_2]$, $[x_2, x_3]$, ..., $[x_{n-1}, x_n]$ as illustrated.

Estimates for the area under the graph of $y = f(x)$ between $x = a$ and $x = b$:

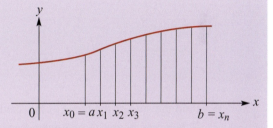

- **Left-endpoint estimate**

$$L_n = \frac{b-a}{n}\big[f(x_0) + f(x_1) + \cdots + f(x_{n-1})\big]$$

- **Right-endpoint estimate**

$$R_n = \frac{b-a}{n}\big[f(x_1) + f(x_2) + \cdots + f(x_n)\big]$$

- **Trapezoidal estimate**

$$T_n = \frac{b-a}{2n}\big[f(x_0) + 2f(x_1) + 2f(x_2) + \cdots + 2f(x_{n-1}) + f(x_n)\big]$$

These methods are not limited to situations in which the graph is either increasing or decreasing for the whole interval. They may be used to determine the area under the curve for any continuous function on an interval $[a, b]$.

Exercise 21A

Example 1

1 Find the sum of the areas of the shaded rectangles to approximate the area under the curve $y = x^2 + 2$ between $x = 1$ and $x = 5$.

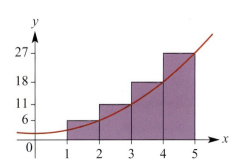

2 Find the sum of the areas of the shaded rectangles to approximate the area under the curve $y = 2x^2 + 2x$ between $x = 1$ and $x = 5$.

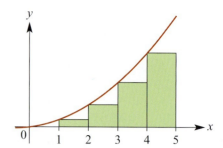

3 Find the sum of the areas of the shaded rectangles to approximate the area under the curve $y = (x - 1)(x + 2)(x - 3)^2 + 20$ between $x = 0$ and $x = 3$.

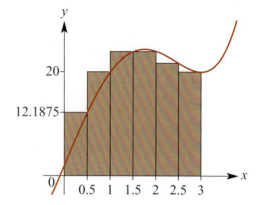

4 Find the sum of the areas of the shaded trapeziums to approximate the area under the curve $y = 2x^2 + 3x$ between $x = 0$ and $x = 4$.

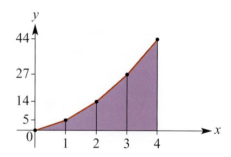

5 To approximate the area of the shaded region, use the subintervals shown to calculate:
  a the left-endpoint estimate
  b the right-endpoint estimate
  c the trapezoidal estimate.

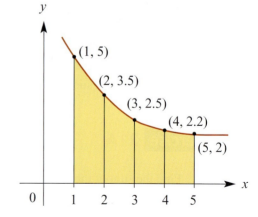

6 Calculate an approximation to the area under the graph of $y = x(3 - x)$ between $x = 0$ and $x = 3$ using strips of width:
  a 0.5
  b 0.2

7 A table of values is given for the rule $y = f(x)$.

x	0	1	2	3	4	5	6	7	8	9	10
y	3	3.5	3.7	3.8	3.9	3.9	4.0	4.0	3.7	3.3	2.9

Find the area enclosed by the graph of $y = f(x)$, the lines $x = 0$ and $x = 10$, and the x-axis by using:

   a the left-endpoint estimate   **b** the trapezoidal estimate.

8 The graph is that of $y = \dfrac{1}{1 + x^2}$. It is known that the area of the shaded region is $\dfrac{\pi}{4}$.

Apply the trapezoidal estimate with strips of width 0.25, and hence find an approximate value for π.

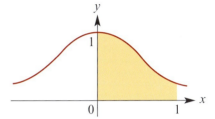

9 Use the trapezoidal estimate to find approximate values for the area under the graph of:

   a $y = 2^x$ between $x = 0$ and $x = 2$, using intervals of width 0.5

   b $y = \dfrac{1}{\sqrt{1 - x^2}}$ between $x = 0$ and $x = 0.9$, using intervals of width 0.1.

10 An engineer takes soundings at intervals of 3 metres across a river 30 metres wide to obtain the data in the following table. Use the trapezoidal estimate to give an approximate value for the area of the cross-section of the river's channel.

Distance from bank in metres	0	3	6	9	12	15	18	21	24	27	30
Depth of sounding in metres	1	2	3	4	5	5	6	4	4	2	2

21B Finding the exact area: the definite integral

▶ Definition of the integral

Assume that we want to find the area under the graph of a continuous function f. Using one of the three methods from the previous section, we can make better and better estimates of the area by taking narrower and narrower strips. In the limit (i.e. as $n \to \infty$), these estimates will converge to an answer for the exact area under the graph. Furthermore, it does not matter which of the three methods we choose, we will obtain the same answer in each case.

> The limit we obtain for the exact area under the graph of $y = f(x)$ between $x = a$ and $x = b$ is denoted by
>
> $$\int_a^b f(x)\, dx$$
>
> This is called the **definite integral** of $f(x)$ with respect to x from $x = a$ to $x = b$.

The symbol $\int$ is called the **integral sign**, the numbers a and b are called the **terminals** or **endpoints** of the integral, and the function f is called the **integrand**.

The exact area

In the previous section we looked at ways of approximating the area under the graph of $f(x) = 9 - 0.1x^2$ between $x = 2$ and $x = 5$. We now can denote the exact area by

$$\int_2^5 f(x)\,dx$$

We will show this area can be found by an antiderivative of f.

The derivative of the area function

Let $f : [a, b] \to \mathbb{R}$ be a continuous function such that $f(x) \geq 0$ for all $x \in [a, b]$.

We define the function $A(x)$ geometrically by saying that it is the measure of the area under the curve between a and x. We thus have $A(a) = 0$. We will see that $A'(x) = f(x)$, and thus that $A(x)$ is an antiderivative of $f(x)$.

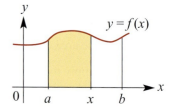

First consider the quotient $\dfrac{A(x+h) - A(x)}{h}$ for $h > 0$.

By our definition of $A(x)$, it follows that $A(x + h) - A(x)$ is the area between x and $x + h$.

Let c be the point in the interval $[x, x + h]$ such that $f(c) \geq f(z)$ for all $z \in [x, x + h]$, and let d be the point in the same interval such that $f(d) \leq f(z)$ for all $z \in [x, x + h]$.

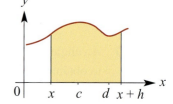

Thus $f(d) \leq f(z) \leq f(c)$ for all $z \in [x, x + h]$.

Therefore $hf(d) \leq A(x + h) - A(x) \leq hf(c)$.

That is, the shaded region has an area less than the area of the rectangle with base h and height $f(c)$ and an area greater than the area of the rectangle with base h and height $f(d)$.

Dividing by h gives

$$f(d) \leq \frac{A(x+h) - A(x)}{h} \leq f(c)$$

As $h \to 0$, both $f(c)$ and $f(d)$ approach $f(x)$.

Thus we have shown that $A'(x) = f(x)$, and therefore $A(x)$ is an antiderivative of $f(x)$.

The example again

Now we return to the example $f(x) = 9 - 0.1x^2$ from Section 21A.

Let $A(x)$ be the function giving the area under this curve between 2 and x. Then $A(x)$ is an antiderivative of $f(x)$ such that $A(2) = 0$. The function defined by

$$A(x) = 9x - \frac{x^3}{30} - \frac{266}{15} = \frac{1}{30}\left(-x^3 + 270x - 532\right)$$

is an antiderivative of $f(x)$ such that $A(2) = 0$. (Check this for yourself.) So the area between $x = 2$ and $x = 5$ is given by $A(5) = 23.1$ square units.

We can write $\int_2^5 9 - 0.1x^2 \, dx = 23.1$.

▶ The fundamental theorem of calculus

A general method to find the area under a graph $y = f(x)$ between $x = a$ and $x = b$ is given by the following important theorem.

> **Fundamental theorem of calculus**
>
> Let $f(x)$ be a continuous function on an interval $[a, b]$. Then
>
> $$\int_a^b f(x)\, dx = \big[F(x)\big]_a^b = F(b) - F(a)$$
>
> where $F(x)$ is any antiderivative of $f(x)$.

Proof Let $A(x)$ be the area function we defined above. Since both $A(x)$ and $F(x)$ are antiderivatives of $f(x)$, they must differ by a constant. That is,

$$A(x) = F(x) + k$$

where k is a constant. First let $x = a$. We then have

$$0 = A(a) = F(a) + k$$

and so $k = -F(a)$.

Thus $A(x) = F(x) - F(a)$, and letting $x = b$ yields

$$A(b) = F(b) - F(a)$$

Therefore the area under the curve $y = f(x)$ between a and b is equal to $F(b) - F(a)$, where $F(x)$ is an antiderivative of $f(x)$.

The notation $[F(x)]_a^b$ in the statement of this theorem helps with setting out integral calculations. It is just another way of writing $F(b) - F(a)$. The use of this notation is illustrated in the following example.

Example 2

Evaluate each of the following definite integrals:

a $\int_2^3 x^2\, dx$ **b** $\int_3^2 x^2\, dx$ **c** $\int_0^1 x^{\frac{1}{2}} + x^{\frac{3}{2}}\, dx$

Solution

a $\int_2^3 x^2\, dx$

$= \left[\dfrac{x^3}{3}\right]_2^3$

$= \dfrac{27}{3} - \dfrac{8}{3}$

$= 9 - 2\tfrac{2}{3}$

$= 6\tfrac{1}{3}$

b $\int_3^2 x^2\, dx$

$= \left[\dfrac{x^3}{3}\right]_3^2$

$= \dfrac{8}{3} - \dfrac{27}{3}$

$= -6\tfrac{1}{3}$

c $\int_0^1 x^{\frac{1}{2}} + x^{\frac{3}{2}}\, dx$

$= \left[\dfrac{2}{3}x^{\frac{3}{2}} + \dfrac{2}{5}x^{\frac{5}{2}}\right]_0^1$

$= \dfrac{2}{3} + \dfrac{2}{5}$

$= \dfrac{16}{15}$

Example 3

Find the area of the shaded region.

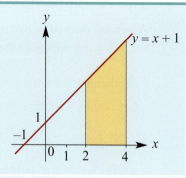

Solution

Area = $\int_2^4 x + 1 \, dx$

An antiderivative of $x + 1$ is $\dfrac{x^2}{2} + x$.

We write $\int_2^4 x + 1 \, dx = \left[\dfrac{x^2}{2} + x\right]_2^4$

$= \left(\dfrac{4^2}{2} + 4\right) - \left(\dfrac{2^2}{2} + 2\right)$

$= 12 - 4$

$= 8$

The shaded region has area 8 square units. (Note that you do not have to write 'square units'. This is understood from the context.)

This area can also be found without using calculus, since the region is a trapezium with area $\frac{1}{2}(3 + 5) \times 2 = 8$.

Example 4

Part of the graph of $y = 4 - x^2$ is shown to the right. Find the area of the shaded region.

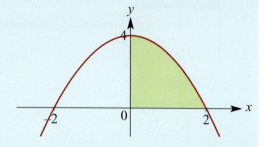

Solution

By the fundamental theorem of calculus, the shaded area is given by

$\int_0^2 4 - x^2 \, dx = \left[4x - \dfrac{x^3}{3}\right]_0^2$

$= 8 - \dfrac{8}{3}$

$= \dfrac{16}{3}$

Exercise 21B

1 Evaluate each of the following:

a $\int_1^2 x^2 \, dx$

b $\int_{-1}^3 x^3 \, dx$

c $\int_0^1 x^3 - x \, dx$

d $\int_{-1}^2 (x+1)^2 \, dx$

e $\int_1^2 x^3 \, dx$

f $\int_1^4 x + 2x^2 \, dx$

g $\int_0^2 x^3 + 2x^2 + x + 2 \, dx$

h $\int_1^4 2x + 5 \, dx$

2 Part of the graph of $y = x + 1$ is shown to the right. Find the area of the shaded region.

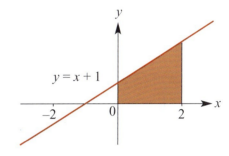

3 Part of the graph of $y = x^2$ is shown to the right. Find the area of the shaded region.

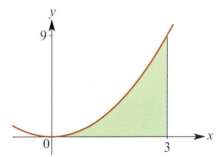

4 Part of the graph of $y = 1 - x^2$ is shown to the right. Find the area of the shaded region.

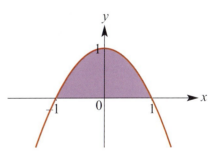

5 Part of the graph of $y = 4x - x^3$ is shown to the right. Find the area of the shaded region.

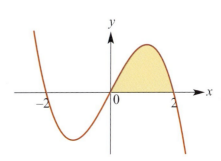

718 Chapter 21: Integration

21C Signed area

We now look at regions below the x-axis as well as those above the x-axis.

Consider the graph of $y = x + 1$ shown to the right.

$A_1 = \frac{1}{2} \times 3 \times 3 = 4\frac{1}{2}$ (area of a triangle)

$A_2 = \frac{1}{2} \times 1 \times 1 = \frac{1}{2}$

The total area is $A_1 + A_2 = 5$.

The **signed area** is $A_1 - A_2 = 4$.

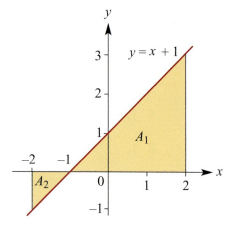

- Regions above the x-axis have *positive* signed area.
- Regions below the x-axis have *negative* signed area.

The total area of the shaded region is $A_1 + A_2 + A_3 + A_4$.

The signed area of the shaded region is $A_1 - A_2 + A_3 - A_4$.

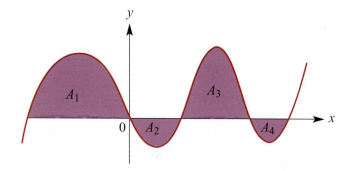

The left-endpoint, right-endpoint and trapezoidal estimates from Section 21A clearly give negative values when the graph lies below the x-axis, and so our definition of the integral is satisfactory in this situation.

The definite integral $\int_a^b f(x)\, dx$ gives the **signed area** enclosed by the graph of $y = f(x)$ between $x = a$ and $x = b$.

Example 5

Find the area of the shaded region.

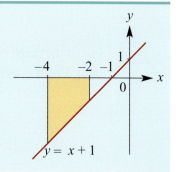

Solution

Area $= -\int_{-4}^{-2} x+1 \; dx$

$= -\left[\dfrac{x^2}{2} + x\right]_{-4}^{-2}$

$= -(0 - 4)$

$= 4$

The area of the shaded region is 4 square units.

Explanation

The integral gives the signed area. Since the region is below the x-axis, its signed area is negative, and so its area is the negative of the integral from -4 to -2.

Example 6

a Find the total area of the shaded regions.

b Find the signed area of the shaded regions.

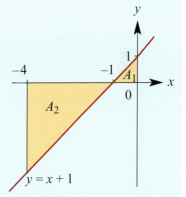

Solution

Area A_1 is above the x-axis and area A_2 is below the x-axis.

Therefore

$A_1 = \int_{-1}^{0} x+1 \; dx$

$= \left[\dfrac{x^2}{2} + x\right]_{-1}^{0}$

$= 0 - \left(\dfrac{1}{2} - 1\right)$

$= \dfrac{1}{2}$

$A_2 = -\int_{-4}^{-1} x+1 \; dx$

$= -\left[\dfrac{x^2}{2} + x\right]_{-4}^{-1}$

$= -\left(\left(\dfrac{1}{2} - 1\right) - \left(\dfrac{16}{2} - 4\right)\right)$

$= -\left(-\dfrac{1}{2} - 4\right)$

$= 4\dfrac{1}{2}$

a Total area $= A_1 + A_2 = \dfrac{1}{2} + 4\dfrac{1}{2} = 5$

b Signed area $= A_1 - A_2 = \dfrac{1}{2} - 4\dfrac{1}{2} = -4$

Note: You can also find the signed area directly by evaluating $\int_{-4}^{0} x+1 \; dx$.

Finding areas

- If $f(x) \geq 0$ for all $x \in [a, b]$, then the area of the region contained between the curve, the x-axis and the lines $x = a$ and $x = b$ is given by $\int_a^b f(x)\,dx$.
- If $f(x) \leq 0$ for all $x \in [c, d]$, then the area of the region contained between the curve, the x-axis and the lines $x = c$ and $x = d$ is given by $-\int_c^d f(x)\,dx$.
- If $c \in (a, b)$ with $f(c) = 0$ and $f(x) \geq 0$ for $x \in (c, b]$ and $f(x) \leq 0$ for $x \in [a, c)$, then the area of the shaded region is given by $\int_c^b f(x)\,dx + -\int_a^c f(x)\,dx$.

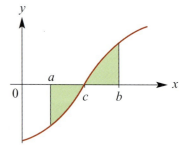

Note: The important aspect is the sign of $f(x)$ in the given interval.

Example 7

Find the area of the shaded region.

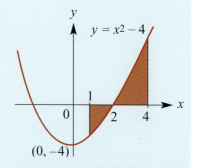

Solution

$$\text{Area} = \int_2^4 (x^2 - 4)\,dx + -\int_1^2 (x^2 - 4)\,dx$$

$$= \left[\frac{x^3}{3} - 4x\right]_2^4 - \left[\frac{x^3}{3} - 4x\right]_1^2$$

$$= \left(\frac{64}{3} - 16\right) - \left(\frac{8}{3} - 8\right) - \left(\left(\frac{8}{3} - 8\right) - \left(\frac{1}{3} - 4\right)\right)$$

$$= \frac{56}{3} - 8 - \left(\frac{7}{3} - 4\right) = \frac{37}{3}$$

The area is $\dfrac{37}{3}$ square units.

Using the TI-Nspire

Use menu > **Calculus** > **Integral** and complete the definite integral as shown.

Note: The definite integral template can also be accessed using the 2D-template palette or shift + .

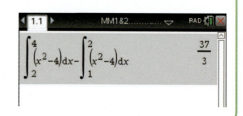

Using the Casio ClassPad

- In Main √☐, enter and highlight the expression $x^2 - 4$.
- Select **Interactive** > **Calculation** > ∫.
- Select the definite integral button and enter the endpoints 2 and 4. Tap OK.

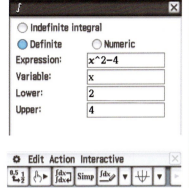

- Go back to the first entry line and add $-(x^2 - 4)$. Highlight $x^2 - 4$ and repeat the process above with the endpoints 1 and 2.
- Tap OK again to find the answer to the complete question.

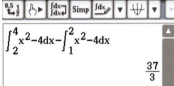

Example 8

Find the area enclosed by the graph of $y = x(2 - x)(x - 3)$ and the x-axis.

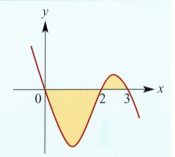

Solution

$y = x(-x^2 + 5x - 6)$
$= -x^3 + 5x^2 - 6x$

Area $= \int_2^3 (-x^3 + 5x^2 - 6x)\,dx + -\int_0^2 (-x^3 + 5x^2 - 6x)\,dx$

$= \left[\dfrac{-x^4}{4} + \dfrac{5x^3}{3} - \dfrac{6x^2}{2}\right]_2^3 - \left[\dfrac{-x^4}{4} + \dfrac{5x^3}{3} - \dfrac{6x^2}{2}\right]_0^2$

$= \left(\dfrac{-81}{4} + 45 - 27\right) - \left(-4 + \dfrac{40}{3} - 12\right) - \left(-4 + \dfrac{40}{3} - 12\right)$

$= \dfrac{-81}{4} + 18 + 32 - \dfrac{80}{3}$

$= 50 - \dfrac{243 + 320}{12} = \dfrac{37}{12}$

The area is $\dfrac{37}{12}$ square units.

Note: There is no need to find the coordinates of stationary points.

▶ Properties of the definite integral

We present these properties without proof. The proofs are straightforward.

- $\int_a^b f(x)\, dx = \int_a^c f(x)\, dx + \int_c^b f(x)\, dx$
- $\int_a^a f(x)\, dx = 0$
- $\int_a^b k f(x)\, dx = k \int_a^b f(x)\, dx$
- $\int_a^b f(x) \pm g(x)\, dx = \int_a^b f(x)\, dx \pm \int_a^b g(x)\, dx$
- $\int_a^b f(x)\, dx = -\int_b^a f(x)\, dx$

Example 9

Given that $\int_1^3 f(x)\, dx = 6$, evaluate:

a $\int_1^3 2f(x)\, dx$ **b** $\int_1^3 f(x) + 3\, dx$ **c** $\int_3^1 f(x)\, dx$

Solution

a $\int_1^3 2f(x)\, dx$
$= 2\int_1^3 f(x)\, dx$
$= 2 \times 6$
$= 12$

b $\int_1^3 f(x) + 3\, dx$
$= \int_1^3 f(x)\, dx + \int_1^3 3\, dx$
$= 6 + \left[3x\right]_1^3$
$= 6 + (9 - 3)$
$= 12$

c $\int_3^1 f(x)\, dx$
$= -\int_1^3 f(x)\, dx$
$= -6$

Exercise 21C

Example 5

1 On a graph of $y = x^2 - 4x$, shade the region corresponding to $\int_0^4 x^2 - 4x\, dx$ and calculate its value.

Example 6, 7

2 On a graph of $y = x^2 - 9$, shade the region corresponding to $\int_{-3}^3 x^2 - 9\, dx$ and calculate its value.

3 On a graph of the line $y = 2t + 3$, shade the trapezium between the line and the t-axis bounded by $t = 1$ and $t = 5$. Use geometry to find the area of this trapezium and verify your result by integration.

Example 8

4 The figure shows part of the graph of the curve with equation $y = x(x-1)(3-x)$. Calculate the area of the shaded region.

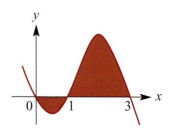

21C

5 Given that $\int_1^5 h(x)\, dx = 4$, evaluate:
  a $\int_1^5 2h(x)\, dx$
  b $\int_1^5 h(x) + 3\, dx$
  c $\int_5^1 h(x)\, dx$

6 Given that $\int_2^5 f(x)\, dx = 12$, evaluate:
  a $\int_5^2 f(x)\, dx$
  b $\int_2^5 3f(x)\, dx$
  c $\int_2^4 (f(x) + 4)\, dx + \int_4^5 f(x)\, dx$

7 Calculate the values of $\int_1^3 f(x)\, dx$, $\int_3^4 f(x)\, dx$ and $\int_1^4 f(x)\, dx$ for:
  a $f(x) = 6x$
  b $f(x) = 6 - 2x$
  What is the relationship between your three answers in each case?

8 Sketch the graph of $y = 5x - x^2 - 4$ and find the area enclosed by the x-axis and the portion of the curve above the x-axis.

9 Sketch the graph of $y = x(10 - x)$ and hence find the area enclosed between the x-axis and the portion of the curve above the x-axis.

10 Sketch the graph of $y = x(x - 2)(x + 1)$ and find the area of the region contained between the graph and the x-axis. (Do not attempt to find the coordinates of the turning points.)

11 Evaluate each of the following:
  a $\int_1^2 \dfrac{(2 - x)(2 + x)}{x^2}\, dx$
  b $\int_1^4 2x - 3\sqrt{x}\, dx$
  c $\int_1^3 \dfrac{4x^2 + 9}{x^2}\, dx$
  d $\int_1^4 6x - 3\sqrt{x}\, dx$
  e $\int_1^4 \dfrac{x^2 - 1}{x^2}\, dx$
  f $\int_1^4 \dfrac{2x - 3\sqrt{x}}{x}\, dx$

12 Find the area bounded by the x-axis and the graph of each of the following functions:
  a $f(x) = x^2 - 2x$
  b $f(x) = (4 - x)(3 - x)$
  c $f(x) = (x + 2)(7 - x)$
  d $f(x) = x^2 - 5x + 6$
  e $f(x) = 3 - x^2$
  f $f(x) = x^3 - 6x^2$

Chapter summary

- **Numerical methods for approximating the area under a graph:**
  The interval $[a, b]$ on the x-axis is divided into n equal subintervals $[a, x_1]$, $[x_1, x_2]$, $[x_2, x_3]$, ..., $[x_{n-1}, x_n]$.

  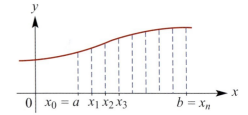

  - Left-endpoint estimate
    $$L_n = \frac{b-a}{n}\left[f(x_0) + f(x_1) + \cdots + f(x_{n-1})\right]$$
  - Right-endpoint estimate
    $$R_n = \frac{b-a}{n}\left[f(x_1) + f(x_2) + \cdots + f(x_n)\right]$$
  - Trapezoidal estimate
    $$T_n = \frac{b-a}{2n}\left[f(x_0) + 2f(x_1) + 2f(x_2) + \cdots + 2f(x_{n-1}) + f(x_n)\right]$$

- **Definite integral** The signed area enclosed by the graph of $y = f(x)$ between $x = a$ and $x = b$ is denoted by $\int_a^b f(x)\, dx$.

- **Fundamental theorem of calculus**
  Let $f(x)$ be a continuous function on an interval $[a, b]$. Then
  $$\int_a^b f(x)\, dx = \left[F(x)\right]_a^b = F(b) - F(a)$$
  where $F(x)$ is any antiderivative of $f(x)$.

- **Finding areas:**
  - If $f(x) \geq 0$ for all $x \in [a, b]$, then the area of the region contained between the curve, the x-axis and the lines $x = a$ and $x = b$ is given by $\int_a^b f(x)\, dx$.
  - If $f(x) \leq 0$ for all $x \in [c, d]$, then the area of the region contained between the curve, the x-axis and the lines $x = c$ and $x = d$ is given by $-\int_c^d f(x)\, dx$.
  - If $c \in [a, b]$ with $f(c) = 0$ and $f(x) \geq 0$ for $x \in (c, b]$ and $f(x) \leq 0$ for $x \in [a, c)$, then the area of the shaded region is given by $\int_c^b f(x)\, dx + -\int_a^c f(x)\, dx$.

  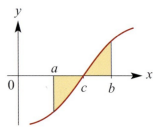

- **Properties of the definite integral:**
  - $\int_a^b f(x)\, dx = \int_a^c f(x)\, dx + \int_c^b f(x)\, dx$
  - $\int_a^a f(x)\, dx = 0$
  - $\int_a^b k f(x)\, dx = k \int_a^b f(x)\, dx$
  - $\int_a^b f(x) \pm g(x)\, dx = \int_a^b f(x)\, dx \pm \int_a^b g(x)\, dx$
  - $\int_a^b f(x)\, dx = -\int_b^a f(x)\, dx$

Technology-free questions

1 Evaluate each of the following definite integrals:

a $\int_1^2 2x\, dx$ **b** $\int_2^5 2\, dx$ **c** $\int_3^5 (3x^2 + 2x)\, dx$

d $\int_1^5 (x^2 + 2x)\, dx$ **e** $\int_{-3}^{-2} 5\, dx$

2 Evaluate each of the following definite integrals:

a $\int_1^4 \sqrt{x}\, dx$ **b** $\int_1^4 x^3 - 2x\, dx$ **c** $\int_1^2 \dfrac{1}{x^2}\, dx$

d $\int_1^4 \dfrac{2}{x^3}\, dx$ **e** $\int_0^1 \sqrt{x}\,(x+1)\, dx$

3 On a graph of $y = x^3$, shade the region corresponding to $\int_1^2 x^3\, dx$ and calculate its value.

4 The figure shows the graph of the function $y = (1 - x)(2 + x)$.
Find the area of the shaded region.

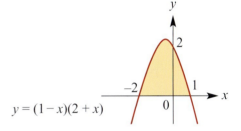

5 The figure shows the curve with equation $y = x(x - 3)(x + 2)$.
Calculate the area of the shaded region.

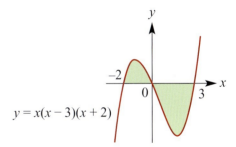

6 **a** Find the coordinates of points B and C.
    b Find the area of rectangle $ABCD$.
    c Find the area of the shaded region.

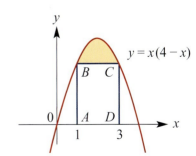

Multiple-choice questions

1 An antiderivative of $x^3 + 3x$ is

    A $x(x^2 + 3)$ **B** $3(x^2 + 1)$ **C** $\dfrac{x^4}{4} + \dfrac{3x^2}{2} + c$

    D $x^3 + 3 + c$ **E** $3x^3 + x^2 + c$

2 $\int \sqrt{x} + x \, dx$ equals

    A $\dfrac{\sqrt{x^2} + x^2}{2} + c$ **B** $x^{\frac{3}{2}} + x^2 + c$ **C** $\dfrac{1}{2}x + 1$

    D $\dfrac{2}{3}x^{\frac{3}{2}} + \dfrac{1}{2}x^2 + c$ **E** 2

3 $3 \int x^{-4} \, dx$ equals

    A $\dfrac{-1}{x^3} + c$ **B** $-x^3 + c$ **C** $-12x^{-3} + c$ **D** $-12x^{-5} + c$ **E** $\dfrac{-3x^{-4}}{5} + c$

4 An expression for y, if $\dfrac{dy}{dx} = 2x + 5$ and if $y = 1$ when $x = 0$, is

    A $y = x^2 + 5x$ **B** $y = 2$ **C** $y = x^2 + 5x - 1$

    D $y = x^2 + 5x + 1$ **E** $y = x^2 + 5x - 5$

5 If $f'(x) = 5x^4 - 9x^2$ and $f(1) = 2$, then $f(x)$ is equal to

    A $x^5 - 3x^2 + 2$ **B** $x^5 - 3x^3 + 4$ **C** $x^5 - 9x^2 + 5$

    D $x^5 - 3x^3$ **E** $x^5 - 3x^2 + 2$

6 An expression for y, if $\dfrac{dy}{dx} = \dfrac{4}{x^3}$ and if $y = 0$ when $x = 1$, is

    A $y = \dfrac{-2}{x^2}$ **B** $y = \dfrac{-2}{x^2} + 2$ **C** $y = \dfrac{-2}{3x^2} - \dfrac{2}{3}$

    D $y = \dfrac{-4}{x^2} - 2$ **E** $y = 2x$

7 If $F'(x) = f(x)$, then $\int_3^5 f(x) \, dx$ is

    A $f(5) - f(3)$ **B** $f(5) + c$ **C** $f(5) - f(3) + c$

    D $F(5) - F(3)$ **E** $F(5) + F(3)$

8 $\int_0^2 (3x^2 - 2x) \, dx =$

    A 12   **B** 4   **C** 8   **D** 32   **E** 2

9 An equivalent expression for $\int_0^2 3f(x) + 2 \, dx$ is

    A $3 \int_0^2 f(x) \, dx + 2x$ **B** $3 \int_0^2 f(x) \, dx + 2x$ **C** $3 \int_0^2 f(x) \, dx + 4$

    D $2f'(x) + 3$ **E** $\int_0^2 f(x) + 6$

10 The graph with the equation $y = k(x - 3)^2$ is shown. If the area of the shaded region is 36 square units, the value of k is

A 4   **B** −4   **C** 9   **D** $\dfrac{4}{7}$ **E** 32

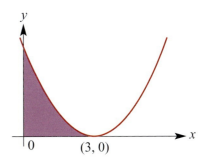

Extended-response questions

1 The slope of a children's slide is given by
$$\frac{dy}{dx} = \frac{9}{32}(x^2 - 4x) \quad \text{for } x \in [0, 4]$$
where the origin is taken to be at ground level beneath the highest point of the slide, which is 3 m above the ground. All units are in metres.

  a Find the equation of the curve which describes the slide.
  b Sketch the curve of the slide, labelling stationary points.
  c Does the slope of the slide ever exceed 45°?

2 A swimming pool has a cross-sectional area as shown.

  a Find the area of the rectangle $OABC$.
  b Find the equation of the curve given that it is of the form $y = k(x - 4)^2$.
  c Find the total area of the region enclosed between the curve and the x-axis for $x \in [0, 9]$.
  d Find the area of the cross-section of the pool (i.e. the shaded region).

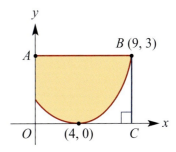

3 a Water flows into a container at the constant rate (R) of 2 litres per second. A graph of the rate of flow is as shown.

  i How much water has flowed into the container after 1 minute?
  ii Illustrate this quantity as an area under the graph of $R = 2$.

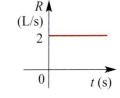

  b Water flows into a container at a rate R L/s, where $R = \dfrac{t}{2}$ and t is the time measured in seconds.
  The graph is as shown.

  i How much water has flowed into the container after 1 minute?
  ii Illustrate this quantity as an area under the graph of $R = \dfrac{t}{2}$.
  iii How much water has flowed into the container after a minutes?

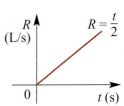

c Water flows into a container at a rate R L/s, where $R = \dfrac{t^2}{10}$ and t is the time measured in seconds.

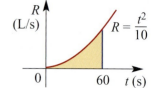

  i Find the area of the shaded region.
  ii What does the area represent?
  iii After how many seconds will 10 000 litres have flowed into the container?

4 a i A car travels on a straight road at 60 km/h for 2 hours. Sketch the speed–time graph illustrating this.
  ii Shade the region which indicates the total distance travelled by the car after 2 hours.
 b i Sketch the speed–time graph of a car travelling for 5 minutes, if the car starts from rest and accelerates at a rate of 0.3 km/min^2.
  ii How far has the car travelled at the end of 5 minutes?
 c A particle starts from a point O and travels at a velocity V m/s given by $V = 20t - 3t^2$, where t seconds is the time the particle has been travelling.
  i Find the acceleration of the particle at time t.
  ii Sketch the graph of V against t for $0 \leq t \leq \dfrac{20}{3}$.
  iii How far has the particle travelled after 6 seconds? Illustrate this quantity by shading a suitable region under the graph.

5 A large mound of earth has a constant cross-sectional area. The cross-section is described by the rule

$$y = \dfrac{x^2}{1000}(50 - x)$$

where y denotes the height of the mound in metres at a distance of x metres from the edge at 0.

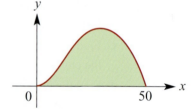

 a Find the height of the mound when:
  i $x = 10$ **ii** $x = 40$
 b Find the gradient of the boundary curve $y = \dfrac{x^2}{1000}(50 - x)$ when:
  i $x = 10$ **ii** $x = 40$
 c i Find the value of x for which the height of the mound is a maximum.
  ii Find the maximum height of the mound.
 d Find the cross-sectional area of the mound.
 e It is decided to take the 'top' off the mound as shown.
  i Point A has coordinates $(20, 12)$. Find the coordinates of point B.
  ii Find values p, q and R such that the area of the cross-section of the top is determined by
  $$\int_q^p \dfrac{x^2}{1000}(50 - x)\,dx - R.$$

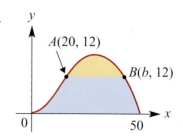

6 a The curve with equation $y = f(x)$ passes through the point with coordinates $(1, 6)$ and $f'(x) = 6x + 3$.

  i Find the gradient of the curve at the point with coordinates $(1, 6)$.
  ii Find the equation of the tangent to the curve $y = f(x)$ at this point.
  iii Find the equation of the curve.

b The curve with equation $y = f(x)$ is such that the tangent to the curve at the point with coordinates $(2, 10)$ passes through the origin and $f'(x) = 6x + k$.

  i Find the gradient of this tangent in terms of k.
  ii Find the value of k.
  iii Find the equation of the curve.

7 An irrigation channel 2 metres deep is constructed. Its cross-section, trapezium $ABCD$, is shown in the diagram.
The length AD is 5 metres and the length BC is 1 metre.

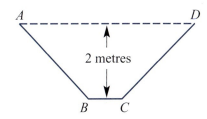

a Calculate the area enclosed by this cross-section.

b The cross-section is placed symmetrically on coordinate axes as shown.

  i Find the equation of the line CD.
  ii Calculate the area of the cross-section of the water (shaded) when the water is y metres deep. Give your answer in terms of x.

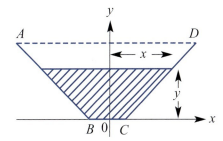

c In an attempt to improve water flow, a metal chute is added. Its cross-section has the shape of a parabola $PQORS$ and it just touches the original channel at Q, O and R.

  i Given that the x-coordinate of R is 1, find the equation of the parabola and find the coordinates of P and S.
  ii Calculate the area of the cross-section $PQORS$.

    Hint: You could find the area of rectangle $PTVS$ and subtract the area 'under' the parabola.

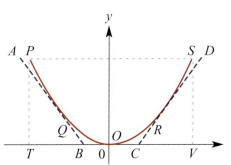

8 A small hill has a cross-section as shown. The coordinates of four points are given. Measurements are in metres.

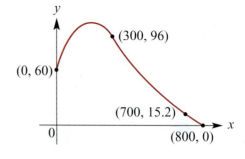

a Find the equation of the cubic.

b Find the maximum height of the hill correct to the nearest metre.

c **i** Using a CAS calculator, plot the graph of the gradient function.

　ii State the coordinates of the point on the curve where the magnitude of the gradient is a maximum.

d Use a CAS calculator to find the cross-sectional area correct to the nearest square metre.

9 **a** Use a CAS calculator to plot the graph of $g(x) = \int_0^x f(t)\, dt$, where $f(t) = 2^t$, for $x \in [0, 5]$.

b Solve the equation $\int_0^x f(t)\, dt = 10$.

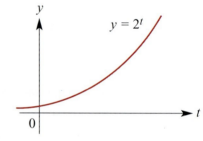

22

Revision of Chapters 20–21

22A Technology-free questions

1. This graph shows the area under the curve $y = \dfrac{1}{x+1}$ between $x = 0$ and $x = 4$.
   Using the intervals shown, calculate:

   a the left-endpoint estimate
   b the right-endpoint estimate
   c the trapezoidal estimate.

2. Find the derivative of each of the following with respect to x:

   a $3x^{\frac{3}{2}}$ b $\sqrt[5]{x}$ c $-\dfrac{2}{x^{\frac{5}{3}}}$ d $6x^{\frac{5}{3}}$ e $x^{-\frac{1}{5}}$ f $x^{-\frac{2}{3}} - 2x^{\frac{3}{2}}$

3. Differentiate each of the following with respect to x:

   a $(3x+5)^2$ b $-(2x+7)^4$ c $(5-2x)^{-\frac{1}{3}}$ d $\dfrac{4}{5+3x}$

   e $\dfrac{1}{(x-1)^{\frac{2}{3}}}$ f $\dfrac{3}{\sqrt{2+3x^2}}$ g $\left(2x^3 - \dfrac{5}{x}\right)^{\frac{1}{3}}$

4. Find x in terms of t, if $\dfrac{dx}{dt} = t + 4 - \dfrac{3}{t^2}$ and $x = 6$ when $t = 1$.

5. Find the gradient of the tangent to each of the following curves at the given point:

   a $y = \sqrt[3]{x}$, $(27, 3)$ b $y = \dfrac{1}{3x+1}$, $(0, 1)$ c $y = \dfrac{2}{x^3}$, $(2, \tfrac{1}{4})$

6. Find the coordinates of the point(s) on the curve with equation $y = \dfrac{1}{x^2}$ for which the gradient is 4.

7 Find the coordinates of the point(s) on the curve with equation $y = \sqrt[3]{x}$ for which the gradient is 2.

8 Find:
 a $\int 3x^2 + 1 \, dx$
 b $\int (t+1)(2-3t) \, dt$
 c $\int \sqrt{x} \, dx$
 d $\int 2x^{\frac{3}{2}} + x^{\frac{1}{3}} \, dx$

9 Evaluate:
 a $\int_1^3 x^{-2} \, dx$
 b $\int_{-3}^{-2} \left(\dfrac{x^2 - 1}{x^2}\right) dx$

10 Find the area between these curves and the x-axis:
 a $y = (x-1)(2-x)$
 b $y = x(x-1)(x-2)$

22B Multiple-choice questions

1 If $f(x) = \sqrt{9x^2 + 4}$, then $f'(x)$ is equal to
 A $18x(9x^2 + 4)^{\frac{1}{2}}$
 B $3x + 2$
 C $\sqrt{18x}$
 D $-9x(9x^2 + 4)^{-\frac{1}{2}}$
 E $9x(9x^2 + 4)^{-\frac{1}{2}}$

2 If $f(x) = (3x^2 - 7)^4$, then $f'(x)$ is equal to
 A $6x(3x^2 - 7)^3$
 B $(6x - 7)^4$
 C $24x(3x^2 - 7)^3$
 D $24x(6x - 7)^3$
 E $(6x)^4$

3 The derivative of $\dfrac{2}{3+x}$ is
 A $\dfrac{2}{(3+x)^2}$
 B $\dfrac{2}{3}$
 C $\dfrac{1}{2}$
 D $\dfrac{2}{3-x}$
 E $\dfrac{-2}{(x+3)^2}$

4 The derivative of $\dfrac{x-1}{\sqrt{x}}$ is
 A $2\sqrt{x}$
 B $\dfrac{x+1}{x\sqrt{x}}$
 C $\dfrac{3x-1}{2\sqrt{x}}$
 D $\dfrac{x+1}{2x\sqrt{x}}$
 E $\dfrac{3x-1}{2x\sqrt{x}}$

5 $\int 3x^2 + 6 \, dx =$
 A $x^3 + 6x + c$
 B $6x$
 C $6x + c$
 D $\dfrac{x^3}{3} + \dfrac{6}{x} + c$
 E $x^3 + 6x + c$

6 $\int_1^3 x - 2 \, dx =$
 A 0
 B 1
 C $-\dfrac{1}{2}$
 D $\dfrac{1}{2}$
 E 2

7 If $g(x)$ is such that $g'(x) = f(x)$, then $\int_1^3 f(x) \, dx$ is equal to
 A $f(3) - f(1)$
 B $f(3) + c$
 C $g(3) - g(1) + c$
 D $f(3) - f(1) + c$
 E $g(3) - g(1)$

8 The total area of the shaded regions is determined by

A $\int_{-2}^{1}(x^2 + 2x)\,dx$

B $\int_{0}^{1}(x^2 + 2x)\,dx + \int_{-2}^{0}(x^2 + 2x)\,dx$

C $\int_{0}^{1}(x^2 + 2x)\,dx + \int_{0}^{-2}(x^2 + 2x)\,dx$

D $\int_{0}^{-2}(x^2 + 2x)\,dx$

E $\int_{1}^{0}(x^2 + 2x)\,dx + \int_{0}^{-2}(x^2 + 2x)\,dx$

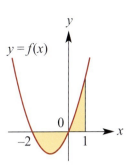

9 $\int_{1}^{4} 5f(x) + 2\,dx$ can be written as

A $4\int_{1}^{4} f(x)\,dx + 2f(x)$ B $\int_{1}^{4} f(x) + 10\,dx$ C $3f'(x) - 2x + c$

D $\int_{1}^{4} 5f(x)\,dx - 5\int_{1}^{4} 2\,dx$ E $5\int_{1}^{4} f(x)\,dx + 6$

10 The graph with the equation $y = k(1 - x^2)$ is shown. If the area of the shaded region is 40 square units, then k is

A $-\dfrac{80}{3}$ B $\dfrac{80}{3}$ C 60 D 10 E $\dfrac{2}{3}$

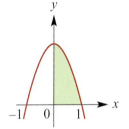

11 The curve with equation $y = 5x - x^2$ is shown. The area of the shaded region is

A 5.4 square units B 4.5 square units C 16.5 square units
D 6.0 square units E 12 square units

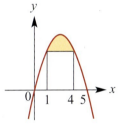

12 $\int 4x^2(2x + 1)\,dx$ is equal to

A $\dfrac{x^3}{3}\left(\dfrac{x^2}{2} + x\right) + c$ B $4(x^4 + x^3) + c$ C $2x^4 + \dfrac{4x^3}{3} + c$

D $\dfrac{x^4}{4} + \dfrac{x^3}{3} + c$ E $\dfrac{x^2(x + 1)^2}{2}$

13 The total area of the shaded region is

A $\int_{0}^{7} f(x)\,dx$

B $\int_{7}^{0} f(x)\,dx$

C $\int_{0}^{3} f(x)\,dx - \int_{3}^{7} f(x)\,dx$

D $\int_{0}^{3} f(x)\,dx - \int_{7}^{3} f(x)\,dx$

E $\int_{0}^{3} f(x)\,dx + \int_{3}^{7} f(x)\,dx$

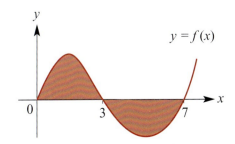

23
Revision of Chapters 1–22

23A Technology-free questions

1. Solve the linear equation $2x + 3(4 - x) = 8$ for x.

2. Solve the equation $\dfrac{at + b}{ct + d} = 2$ for t.

3. Solve the inequality $\dfrac{4x}{3} - 4 \leq 2x - 3$.

4. Given that $-4 \leq x \leq 6$ and $2 \leq y \leq 8$, calculate:
   a. the smallest possible value of $x - y$
   b. the largest possible value of $\dfrac{x}{y}$
   c. the largest possible value of $x^2 + y^2$.

5. A man bought 20 books. Some of the books cost $72 each and the other books cost $24 each. If the man spent a total of $720 on these books, how many of the $24 books did he buy?

6. Solve the inequality $\dfrac{1 - 5x}{3} \geq -12$.

7. If $a = \dfrac{y^2 - xz}{10}$, find a when $x = -5$, $y = 7$ and $z = 6$.

8. a. Find the coordinates of the midpoint of the line segment joining $(8, 14)$ and (a, b) in terms of a and b.
   b. If $(5, 10)$ is the midpoint, find the values of a and b.

9 The line passing through the points $A(-2, 6)$ and $B(10, 15)$ meets the axes at P and Q.
   a Find the equation of AB.
   b Find the length of PQ.

10 If $A = (-7, 6)$ and $B = (11, -5)$, find:
   a the coordinates of the midpoint of AB
   b the distance between A and B
   c the equation of AB
   d the equation of the perpendicular bisector of AB.

11 Sketch the graph of $y = -x^2 + 4x + 2$, clearly labelling the x-axis and y-axis intercepts and the turning point.

12 A parabola has turning point $(2, -6)$ and passes through the point $(6, 12)$. Find its equation.

13 Find the value of a in the polynomial $ax^3 + 4x^2 + 3$ if the remainder is 3 when the polynomial is divided by $x - 2$.

14 A piece of wire 6000 cm long is used to make the edges of a cuboid. The length is $5x$ cm, the width is $4x$ cm and the height is w cm.
   a Find w in terms of x.
   b Find the volume, V cm^3, of the cuboid in terms of x.
   c State the possible values of x.
   d Find the volume if $x = 100$.

15 A box contains 8 red cups and 10 blue cups.
   a If a cup is chosen at random, the colour observed, the cup replaced and a second cup withdrawn, what is the probability that both cups drawn are red?
   b If the first cup is not replaced, what is the probability that both cups drawn are red?

16 Box A contains three pieces of paper numbered 1, 3, 5.
Box B contains three pieces of paper numbered 2, 4, 6.
One piece of paper is removed at random from each box.
Find the probability that the two numbers obtained have a sum that is divisible by 3.

17 A letter is chosen at random from the word GOOGLE.
   a What is the probability that the letter is a vowel?
   b What is the probability that the letter is an O?

18 David has either a sandwich or fruit salad for lunch. If he has a sandwich for lunch one day, the probability he has a sandwich for lunch the next day is 0.4. If he has fruit salad for lunch one day, the probability he has fruit salad for lunch the next day is 0.3. Suppose he has a sandwich for lunch on a Monday. What is the probability that he has fruit salad for lunch on the following Wednesday?

19 Solve the equation $\cos(3x) = \dfrac{1}{2}$ for $x \in \left[-\dfrac{\pi}{2}, \dfrac{\pi}{2}\right]$.

20 The graph of $y = ax^3 + bx + c$ has axis intercepts at $(0, 6)$ and $(-2, 0)$ and has a stationary point where $x = 1$.
  a Find the value of c.
  b Write down two simultaneous equations in a and b from the given information.
  c Hence find the values of a and b.

21 A tangent to the graph of $y = x^4$ has equation $y = -32x + a$. Find the value(s) of a.

22 For the function $f : [-\pi, \pi] \to \mathbb{R}$, $f(x) = 4\cos(2x)$:
  a Write down the amplitude and period of the function.
  b Sketch the graph of the function f on a set of axes. Label the axis intercepts and the endpoints with their coordinates.

23 Four identical balls are numbered 1, 3, 5 and 7 and put into a box. A ball is randomly drawn from the box, and not returned to the box. A second ball is then randomly drawn from the box.
  a What is the probability that the second ball drawn is numbered 1?
  b What is the probability that the sum of the numbers on the two balls is 8?
  c Given that the sum of the numbers on the two balls is 8, what is the probability that the second ball drawn is numbered 1?

24 The line $y = x + 1$ cuts the circle $x^2 + y^2 + 2x - 4y + 1 = 0$ at the points A and B.
  a Find the midpoint of line segment AB.
  b Sketch the graphs of $y = x + 1$ and $x^2 + y^2 + 2x - 4y + 1 = 0$ on the same axes.

25 Solve the following equations:
  a $4^x - 5 \times 2^x - 24 = 0$
  b $2^{5-3x} - 4^{x^2} = 0$

26 The curve for which $\dfrac{dy}{dx} = -4x + k$, where k is a constant, has a stationary point at $(1, 5)$. Find the value of k and the equation of the curve.

27 The curve $y = ax^3 - 2x^2 - x + 7$ has a gradient of 4 when $x = -1$. Find the value of a.

28 Find the image of the curve $y = x^2$ under the transformation of the plane defined by the matrix $\begin{bmatrix} 3 & 0 \\ 0 & -2 \end{bmatrix}$.

29 The polynomial $3x^2 + x + 10$ leaves the same remainder when divided by $x + b$ and by $x - 2b$, where $b \neq 0$. Calculate the value of b.

30 Show that the curves $y = x^3$ and $y = x^3 + x^2 + 6x + 9$ intersect at one point and find the gradient of each of these curves at that point.

31 a Find the coordinates of the stationary points on the graph of $y = x^3 - 75x - 10$ and sketch the graph.
 b Find the values of p for which the equation $x^3 - 75x - 10 = p$ has more than one real solution.

32 Find the maximal domains of the functions with the following rules:
 a $f(x) = \dfrac{1}{x - 3}$
 b $f(x) = \dfrac{1}{(x - 2)^2}$
 c $f(x) = \sqrt{2 - x}$
 d $f(x) = \sqrt{x - 4}$
 e $f(x) = \dfrac{1}{\sqrt{5 - x}}$

23B Multiple-choice questions

1 The function $f(x) = 5\sin\left(\dfrac{x}{4}\right)$ has period
 A $\dfrac{\pi}{4}$ B 8π C 5 D 4π E $\dfrac{\pi}{2}$

2 For the function $f(x) = x^2 + 2x$, the average rate of change for $f(x)$ with respect to x for the interval $[0, 3]$ is
 A 5 B 8 C 10 D 15 E 7.5

3 The range of the function $f : [1, 4) \to \mathbb{R}$, $f(x) = (x - 2)^2 + 3$ is
 A $[2, \infty)$ B $\mathbb{R}^+$ C $[3, \infty)$ D $[3, 7)$ E $\mathbb{R}$

4 A function g with domain $\mathbb{R}$ has the following properties: $g'(x) = 3x^2 - 4x$ and the graph of $y = g(x)$ passes through the point $(1, 0)$. The rule for $g(x)$ is
 A $6x - 4$
 B $x^3 - 2x^2$
 C $3x^3 - 5x^2 + 2$
 D $x^3 - 2x^2 + 1$
 E $x^3 - x^2 - 1$

5 The simultaneous equations $(m - 2)x + y = 0$ and $2x + (m - 3)y = 0$ have infinitely many solutions for
 A $m \in \mathbb{R}$
 B $m \in \mathbb{R} \setminus \{1\}$
 C $m \in \mathbb{R} \setminus \{4\}$
 D $m = 4$ or $m = 1$
 E $m \in \mathbb{R} \setminus \{0\}$

6 The function f has rule $f(x) = 2\log_{10}(3x)$. If $f(5x) = \log_{10}(y)$, then y is equal to

A $30x$ **B** $12x$ **C** $225x^2$ **D** $50x^2$ **E** $1000x^2$

7 A bag contains 2 white balls and 4 black balls. Three balls are drawn from the bag without replacement. The probability they are all black is

A $\dfrac{1}{6}$ **B** $\dfrac{27}{125}$ **C** $\dfrac{1}{5}$ **D** $\dfrac{8}{216}$ **E** $\dfrac{1}{2}$

8 The gradient of $f: \mathbb{R} \to \mathbb{R}$, $f(x) = \frac{1}{3}x^3 - 2x^2 + 1$ is negative for

A $0 < x < 4$ **B** $x > 0$ or $x < 4$ **C** $x > \sqrt{3}$

D $x < -\sqrt{2}$ or $x > \sqrt{2}$ **E** $x > 0$ or $x < \dfrac{1}{3}$

9 The maximal domain D of the function $f: D \to \mathbb{R}$ with rule $f(x) = \sqrt{2x+1}$ is

A $\mathbb{R} \setminus \{-\frac{1}{2}\}$ **B** $[-\frac{1}{2}, \infty)$ **C** $\mathbb{R}$ **D** $(0, \infty)$ **E** $(-\infty, -\frac{1}{2})$

10 In algebraic notation, 11 is four times 9 more than x can be written as

A $11 = 4(x+9)$ **B** $4x + 9 = 11$ **C** $11 = 9(x+4)$

D $\dfrac{4}{x+9} = 11$ **E** $11 - \dfrac{9}{4} = x$

11 A car covers a distance of 120 km at a speed of a km/h, and a train covers the same distance at $(a-4)$ km/h. If the time taken by the train is one hour more than the time taken by the car, then a is equal to

A 20   **B** 24   **C** 10   **D** 15   **E** 25

12 The equation of the parabola that passes through the point $(-3, 12)$ and has its vertex at $(-2, 8)$ is

A $y = 4(x+2)^2 + 8$ **B** $y = (x+2)^2 + 4$ **C** $y = 4(x-2)^2 + 4$

D $y = (x-2)^2 - 4$ **E** $y = -4(x-2)^2 + 4$

13 The range of the function $f: [-3, 5) \to \mathbb{R}$, $f(x) = 5 - 2x$ is

A $(-5, 11]$ **B** $[-5, 11)$ **C** $(-5, \infty)$ **D** $(-5, 11)$ **E** $\mathbb{R}$

14 For $f: [-3, 2) \to \mathbb{R}$, $f(x) = 2x^2 + 7$, the range is

A $\mathbb{R}$ **B** $[7, \infty)$ **C** $[0, 25)$ **D** $[15, 25]$ **E** $[7, 25]$

15 Which of the following functions is not a one-to-one function?

A $y = 11x^2 - 11x$, $x > 11$ **B** $y = \sqrt{11 - x^2}$

C $y = 11x^2$, $x > 0$ **D** $y = 11\sqrt{x}$

E $y = 11x$

16 The function with rule $f(x) = mx + 2$, where $m > 0$, has an inverse function with rule $f^{-1}(x) = ax + b$, for some $a, b \in \mathbb{R}$. Which one of the following statements is true?

A $a > 0, b > 0$ **B** $a < 0, b < 0$ **C** $a > 0, b < 0$

D $a < 0, b > 0$ **E** $a = \dfrac{1}{m}, b = -2$

17 If $x + 1$ is a factor of $x^2 + ax + b$, then $-a + b + 7$ equals

A -7 **B** 6 **C** 1 **D** 7 **E** 9

18 A possible equation of the graph shown is

A $y = -2(x + 1)^3 + 2$
B $y = -(x + 1)^3 + 2$
C $y = -(x - 1)^3 + 2$
D $y = -(x - 1)^3 - 1$
E $y = -2(x + 1)^3 - 2$

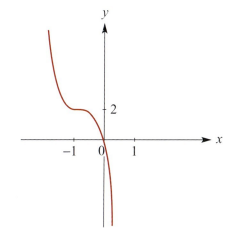

19 A linear transformation T is defined by $\begin{bmatrix} x' \\ y' \end{bmatrix} = \begin{bmatrix} 5 & 0 \\ 0 & 3 \end{bmatrix} \begin{bmatrix} x \\ y \end{bmatrix} + \begin{bmatrix} 7 \\ 1 \end{bmatrix}$.

The equation of the image of the curve $y = x^2$ under T is

A $5y = 3(x - 7)^2 + 1$ **B** $3y = (x - 1)^2 + 7$ **C** $25y = 3(x - 7)^2 + 25$

D $2y = (x - 7)^2 + 7$ **E** $y = 2\left(\dfrac{x}{5} - 5\right)^2 + 2$

20 The transformation which maps the curve with equation $y = 5^x$ to the curve with equation $y = 5^{(2x+4)} - 3$ could have the rule $\begin{bmatrix} x' \\ y' \end{bmatrix} =$

A $\begin{bmatrix} 0.5 & 0 \\ 0 & 1 \end{bmatrix} \begin{bmatrix} x \\ y \end{bmatrix} - \begin{bmatrix} 2 \\ 3 \end{bmatrix}$ **B** $\begin{bmatrix} 0.5 & 0 \\ 0 & 1 \end{bmatrix} \begin{bmatrix} x \\ y \end{bmatrix} + \begin{bmatrix} 2 \\ 3 \end{bmatrix}$ **C** $\begin{bmatrix} 1 & 0 \\ 0 & 2 \end{bmatrix} \begin{bmatrix} x \\ y \end{bmatrix} + \begin{bmatrix} -4 \\ 3 \end{bmatrix}$

D $\begin{bmatrix} 1 & 0 \\ 0 & 2 \end{bmatrix} \begin{bmatrix} x \\ y \end{bmatrix} + \begin{bmatrix} -2 \\ 3 \end{bmatrix}$ **E** $\begin{bmatrix} 2 & 0 \\ 0 & 1 \end{bmatrix} \begin{bmatrix} x \\ y \end{bmatrix} - \begin{bmatrix} 4 \\ 3 \end{bmatrix}$

21 Let $f: \mathbb{R} \to \mathbb{R}$ be defined by $f(x) = x$. Which one of the following is *not* true?

A $f(xy) = f(x)f(y)$ **B** $f(x) - f(-x) = 0$
C $f(7x) = 7f(x)$ **D** $f(x - y) = f(x) - f(y)$
E $f(x + y) + f(x - y) = 2f(x)$

22 The tangent at the point $(1, 5)$ on the curve $y = f(x)$ has equation $y = 6 + x$. The tangent at the point $(3, 6)$ on the curve $y = f(x - 2) + 1$ has equation

A $y = 2x - 4$
B $y = x + 5$
C $y = -2x + 14$
D $y = 2x + 4$
E $y = 2x + 2$

23 The graph of the derivative function f' of the cubic function with rule $y = f(x)$ crosses the x-axis at $(1, 0)$ and $(-3, 0)$. The maximum value of the derivative function is 12. The value of x for which the graph of $y = f(x)$ has a local maximum is

A -3
B 0
C -1
D 1
E 12

24 The random variable X has the following probability distribution:

x	0	2	4
$\Pr(X = x)$	a	$2a$	0.1

The value of a is

A 0
B 0.1
C 0.2
D 0.3
E 0.4

25 Assume that $f'(x) = 5g'(x) + 4$ and $f(1) = 5$ and $g(x) = x^2 f(x)$. Then $f(x) =$

A $5g(x) + 4x - 24$
B $5g'(x) + 4$
C $5g(x) + 4x - 4$
D $5g(x) + 20$
E $5g(x) + 20$

26 The set of solutions to the equation $25^x - 7 \times 5^x + 12 = 0$ is

A $\{3, 4\}$
B $\{-3, -4\}$
C $\{\log_5 4, \log_5 3\}$
D $\{1, \log_5 2\}$
E $\{-\log_5 4, \log_5 3\}$

27 A particle moves in a straight line so that its position, s m, relative to O at a time t seconds ($t > 0$) is given by $s = 4t^3 - 5t - 10$. The acceleration at $t = 1$ is

A 12 m/s²
B 24 m/s²
C -11 m/s²
D -10 m/s²
E 0 m/s²

28 The average rate of change of the function $y = 2x^4 + x^3 - 1$ between $x = -1$ and $x = 1$ is

A 1
B 0
C 4
D 3
E -6

29 A function $f: \mathbb{R} \to \mathbb{R}$ is such that:

- $f'(x) = 0$ where $x = 3$
- $f'(x) = 0$ where $x = 5$
- $f'(x) > 0$ where $3 < x < 5$
- $f'(x) < 0$ where $x > 5$
- $f'(x) < 0$ where $x < 3$.

Which one of the following is true?

A The graph of f has a stationary point of inflection where $x = 3$.
B The graph of f has a local maximum point where $x = 3$.
C The graph of f has a stationary point of inflection where $x = 5$.
D The graph of f has a local minimum point where $x = 5$.
E The graph of f has a local minimum point where $x = 3$.

30 The number of pets, X, that a family has is a random variable with the following probability distribution:

x	0	1	2	3
$\Pr(X = x)$	0.3	0.2	0.4	0.1

If two families are selected at random, the probability that they have the same number of pets (each family having 0 pets is a favourable outcome for this event) is

A 0.10   **B** 0.20   **C** 0.30   **D** 0.40   **E** 0.50

23C Extended-response questions

1 The diagram shows the graph of the function $f : [0, 4] \to \mathbb{R}$, $f(x) = 16 - x^2$.

The line segment AB is drawn from the point $A(0, 16)$ to the point $B(b, f(b))$, where $0 < b < 4$.

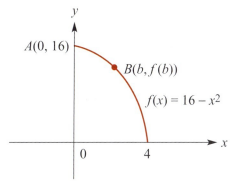

  a **i** What is the gradient of AB?

      ii At what value of x between 0 and b does the tangent to the graph of f have the same gradient as AB?

  b **i** What is the area, $S(b)$, of the trapezium bounded by line segment AB, the x-axis, the line $x = 0$ and the line $x = b$?

      ii For what value of b does this area equal 28?

2 Consider the function $f : \mathbb{R}^+ \to \mathbb{R}$ given by $f(x) = (\sqrt{x} - 2)^2(\sqrt{x} + 1)^2$. The graph of $y = f(x)$ is shown.

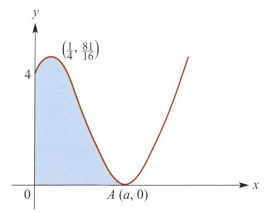

  a Point $A(a, 0)$ is the x-axis intercept of $y = f(x)$. Find the value of a.

  b There is a stationary point at $x = \dfrac{1}{4}$. State the interval for which the graph of f has negative gradient.

  c The area of the shaded region of the graph is $\dfrac{136}{15}$.

Let O be the origin, C a point on the positive y-axis and B the point such that $OABC$ is a rectangle. Find the length OC such that the area of the rectangle $OABC$ is the same as the area of the shaded region.

3 A body starts from O and moves in a straight line. After t seconds its velocity, v cm/s, is given by $v = 4t - 6$. Find:
   a its position x at time t seconds
   b its position after 3 seconds
   c its average velocity in the first 3 seconds
   d the distance travelled in the first 3 seconds
   e its average speed in the first 3 seconds.

4 For the function $f: \mathbb{R} \to \mathbb{R}$, $f(x) = -x^3 + ax^2$, where a is a positive real number:
   a Determine the intervals on which f has:
      i negative gradient
      ii positive gradient.
   b Find the equation of the tangent to the graph of f at the point $(a, 0)$.
   c Find the equation of the normal to the graph of f at the point $(a, 0)$.
   d Find the area of the region contained between the graph and the x-axis from $x = 0$ to $x = a$.

5 A piece of wire of length 52 cm is bent to form a trapezium in which the lengths of the two parallel sides are $2y$ cm and $(16x + 2y)$ cm. The other two sides both have length $10x$ cm.
   a Find y in terms of x.
   b Find the area, A cm^2, in terms of x.
   c Find the values of x and y for which A is a maximum.

6 Kerrie has 5200 m of fencing to make two square enclosures using an existing wall as one side of the enclosure. The squares have side lengths x m and y m with $x \leq y$, as shown.
   a Show that the total area, A m^2, of the two enclosures is given by
   $$A = x^2 + \frac{(5200 - 2x)^2}{9}$$
   b Find the minimum area and the values of x and y for which this occurs.
   c Sketch the graph of A against x.

7 A die has six faces numbered 0, 2, 4, 6, 8 and 10. A second die has faces numbered 1, 3, 5, 7, 9 and 11. Both dice are tossed and the results recorded.
   a List the sample space of the experiment as a set of ordered pairs.
   b Find the probability that the sum of the values from the two dice is:
      i 1   **ii** 13   **iii** 9
   c Find the probability of obtaining a sum of 15 given that the sum is greater than 7.

8 a Find **AB**, given that

$$A = \begin{bmatrix} 2 & -1 & 1 \\ 4 & 2 & 2 \\ 1 & 3 & 1 \end{bmatrix} \text{ and } B = \begin{bmatrix} 2 & 1 & 1 \\ 1 & -1 & -2 \\ -5 & 2 & 1 \end{bmatrix}$$

b Write the following equations as a matrix equation **BX = C**:

$$2x + y + z = 7$$
$$x - y - 2z = -7$$
$$-5x + 2y + z = 2$$

c Multiply both sides of the matrix equation by **A**.

d Hence solve the equations in part b.

9 Consider the family of functions with rules of the form $f(x) = \sqrt{x - 2a}$, where a is a positive number.

a Find the maximal domain of such a function.

b Solve the equation $f(x) = x$ for x.

c For what value of a does the equation $f(x) = x$ have one solution?

d Sketch the graphs of $f(x) = \sqrt{x - \dfrac{1}{4}}$ and $y = x$ on the one set of axes and label the point at which they touch with its coordinates.

10 Each night Frederick goes to the library or the study hall. If he goes to the library one night, the probability he goes to the library the next night is 0.7, and if he goes to the study hall one night, the probability he goes to the study hall the next night is 0.4. Suppose he goes to the library one Wednesday night.

a What is the probability that he goes to the library on each of the next three nights?

b What is the probability that he goes to the library on exactly two of the next three nights?

11 Platypus Sports sells hockey sticks directly to hockey clubs on a yearly basis. If a hockey club buys its sticks from Platypus one year, there is a 75% chance it will buy sticks from Platypus the next year. If a hockey club does not buy its sticks from Platypus one year, there is a 20% chance it will buy its sticks from Platypus the next year.

Suppose the Cross-Sticks club buys its hockey sticks from Platypus this year ($n = 0$).

a What is the probability, correct to four decimal places, that Cross-Sticks buys its sticks from Platypus for the next three years?

b What is the probability, correct to four decimal places, that it buys its sticks from Platypus for exactly two of the next three years?

c What is the probability, correct to four decimal places, that it buys its sticks from Platypus in the third year ($n = 2$)?

12 Consider the function $f : [a, b] \to \mathbb{R}$, $f(x) = -mx + 3$ where $0 \leq a < b$ and $m > 0$.
It defines the line segment with endpoints $A(a, -ma + 3)$ and $B(b, -mb + 3)$.

  a Find the range of f.
  b Find the equation of the inverse function of f.
  c Find the coordinates of the midpoint of AB.
  d Find the equation of the line that passes through the midpoint of AB and is perpendicular to the line through A and B.
  e Find the equation of the image of the line through A and B under a translation of 3 units in the negative direction of the x-axis and 5 units in the positive direction of the y-axis. Give the coordinates of the endpoints of the line segment under this transformation.
  f Find the equation of the image of the line through A and B under a reflection in the y-axis. Give the coordinates of the endpoints of the line segment under this transformation.
  g If $a = 0$, find the values of b and m if the midpoint of AB has coordinates $(6, -4)$.

13 Consider the family of quadratics with rules of the form $f(x) = (p - 1)x^2 + 4x + (p - 4)$, where p is an arbitrary constant.

  a Sketch the graph of f when:
    i $p = 0$ **ii** $p = 2$
  b Find the coordinates of the turning point of the graph of $y = f(x)$ in terms of p.
  c For which values of p does the turning point of the graph of $y = f(x)$ lie on the x-axis?
  d For which values of p are there two distinct solutions to the equation $f(x) = 0$?
  e Let $f(x) = 2x^2 + 4x - 1$. (This is when $p = 3$.) Now let $y = g(x)$ be the image of the graph of $y = f(x)$ under a reflection in the y-axis. Find the equation for $y = g(x)$ and sketch the graphs of both $y = f(x)$ and $y = g(x)$ on the same set of axes.

14 A road near the shoreline is sometimes covered by water, and then the road is closed until it is uncovered again. The height, h metres, of the tide above mean sea level is modelled by the equation $h(t) = 2.3 \cos(kt)$, where t hours is the time measured from 1 p.m. on a particular day. It is assumed that high tides occur every 12 hours.

  a Find the value of k.
  b If on this day the road was closed for 1 hour 30 minutes after 1 p.m., find the height of the road above mean sea level. Give your answer in centimetres.
  c A raised footpath along the road is only under water for 1 hour after 1 p.m. Find the height of the footpath above mean sea level. Give your answer in centimetres.

Further polynomials and systems of linear equations

A1 Synthetic substitution and division

Synthetic division gives a quick way to divide polynomials. We start this section by motivating the method and comparing it with long division.

You can proceed directly to Example 1 if you just want to see the method.

▶ Synthetic substitution

As an example, consider the cubic polynomial

$$P(x) = 2x^3 + x^2 - 5x - 3$$

We can reorganise the expression as shown here:

$$\begin{aligned} P(x) &= 2x^3 + x^2 - 5x - 3 \\ &= (2x^2 + x - 5)x - 3 \\ &= ((2x + 1)x - 5)x - 3 \end{aligned}$$

Now we evaluate this step-by-step at $x = 3$:

$$P(3) = ((2 \times 3 + 1) \times 3 - 5) \times 3 - 3 = 45$$

Step 1	Multiply 2 by 3 and add 1:	$2 \times 3 + 1 = 7$
Step 2	Multiply the result of Step 1 by 3 and add -5:	$7 \times 3 + (-5) = 16$
Step 3	Multiply the result of Step 2 by 3 and add -3:	$16 \times 3 + (-3) = 45$

At each step, the result is multiplied by 3 and then the next coefficient is added.

The steps for substituting $x = 3$ into
$$P(x) = 2x^3 + x^2 - 5x - 3$$
can be set out in a table:

$$\begin{array}{c|cccc} & 2 & 1 & -5 & -3 \\ 3 & & 6 & 21 & 48 \\ \hline & 2 \nearrow & 7 \nearrow & 16 \nearrow & 45 \end{array}$$

- The number 3 to the left of the vertical line is the number being substituted.
- The **first row** of the table contains the coefficients of $P(x)$.
- Each entry in the **second row** is obtained by multiplying the number diagonally below and to the left by 3. For example: $2 \times 3 = 6$ and $7 \times 3 = 21$.
- The **third row** is the sum of the first two rows. For example: $1 + 6 = 7$ and $-5 + 21 = 16$.
- You work from left to right following these rules.

To see what is really going on here, we can add the corresponding powers of x to the table:

$$\begin{array}{c|cccc} & 2x^3 & 1x^2 & -5x & -3 \\ 3 & & 6x^2 & 21x & 48 \\ \hline & 2x^3 & 7x^2 & 16x & 45 \end{array}$$

The following is now evident:
$$\begin{aligned} P(x) &= 2x^3 + x^2 - 5x - 3 \\ &= (2x^3 + 7x^2 + 16x + 45) - (6x^2 + 21x + 48) \\ &= x(2x^2 + 7x + 16) - 3(2x^2 + 7x + 16) + 45 \\ &= (x - 3)(2x^2 + 7x + 16) + 45 \end{aligned}$$

Therefore we can write
$$(2x^3 + x^2 - 5x - 3) \div (x - 3) = 2x^2 + 7x + 16 + \frac{45}{x - 3}$$

This will work with every cubic, and thus gives a method for dividing. This method is called **synthetic division**. Before we proceed, let us compare it with the long-division algorithm:

$$\begin{array}{r} 2x^2 + 7x + 16 \\ x - 3 \overline{\smash{)}2x^3 + x^2 - 5x - 3} \\ \underline{2x^3 - 6x^2} \\ 7x^2 - 5x - 3 \\ \underline{7x^2 - 21x} \\ 16x - 3 \\ \underline{16x - 48} \\ 45 \end{array}$$

You can see the 'parallel structure' of the two methods.

A1 Synthetic substitution and division

▶ **Synthetic division**

Example 1

Divide $x^3 + 2x^2 - 1$ by $x - 3$ using synthetic division.

Solution

Step 1

$$\begin{array}{c|cccc} & 1 & 2 & 0 & -1 \\ 3 & & & & \\ \hline & 1 & & & \end{array}$$

Explanation

Enter the coefficients in the first row:

the coefficient of x^3 is 1, the coefficient of x^2 is 2, the coefficient of x is 0, the constant is -1.

Then the '3' from $x - 3$ is placed to the left, and the leading coefficient 1 is placed below the line.

Step 2

$$\begin{array}{c|cccc} & 1 & 2 & 0 & -1 \\ 3 & & 3 & & \\ \hline & 1 & & & \end{array}$$

Multiply the 1 in the row below the line by 3, and enter the result in the second row.

Step 3

$$\begin{array}{c|cccc} & 1 & 2 & 0 & -1 \\ 3 & & 3 & & \\ \hline & 1 & 5 & & \end{array}$$

Enter 5 below the line, as it is the sum of the numbers 2 and 3 above.

Step 4

$$\begin{array}{c|cccc} & 1 & 2 & 0 & -1 \\ 3 & & 3 & 15 & \\ \hline & 1 & 5 & 15 & \end{array}$$

Multiply the 5 below the line by 3, place the result below the 0, and then add the two values as shown.

Step 5

$$\begin{array}{c|cccc} & 1 & 2 & 0 & -1 \\ 3 & & 3 & 15 & 45 \\ \hline & 1 & 5 & 15 & 44 \end{array}$$

Multiply the 15 below the line by 3, place the result below the -1, and then add the two values as shown.

Therefore

$(x^3 + 2x^2 - 1) \div (x - 3)$

$= x^2 + 5x + 15 + \dfrac{44}{x - 3}$

Now read off the answer from the bottom row of the table as shown.

Example 2

Divide $2x^3 + 2x^2 - 1$ by $x + 3$ using synthetic division.

Solution

Using synthetic division:

$$\begin{array}{c|cccc} & 2 & 2 & 0 & -1 \\ -3 & & -6 & 12 & -36 \\ \hline & 2 & -4 & 12 & -37 \end{array}$$

The result of the division is

$(2x^3 + 2x^2 - 1) \div (x + 3)$

$= 2x^2 - 4x + 12 - \dfrac{37}{x + 3}$

Example 3

Divide $4x^3 + 4x^2 + 7x - 1$ by $x - \frac{1}{2}$ using synthetic division.

Solution

Using synthetic division:

$$\begin{array}{c|cccc} & 4 & 4 & 7 & -1 \\ \frac{1}{2} & & 2 & 3 & 5 \\ \hline & 4 & 6 & 10 & 4 \end{array}$$

The result of the division is

$$(4x^3 + 4x^2 + 7x - 1) \div (x - \tfrac{1}{2}) = 4x^2 + 6x + 10 + \frac{4}{x - \frac{1}{2}}$$

Note that

$$(4x^3 + 4x^2 + 7x - 1) \div (2x - 1) = 2x^2 + 3x + 5 + \frac{4}{2x - 1}$$

Exercise A1

1 Use synthetic division to carry out the following divisions, where the first polynomial is divided by the second. Give the quotient and the remainder.

a $3x^3 + 4x - 6$, $x - 2$
b $3x^3 + 4x^2 - 6x + 24$, $x + 3$
c $x^3 - 5x^2 + 72$, $x - 3$
d $4x^3 - 4x^2 + 7x - 72$, $x - \frac{1}{2}$
e $4x^3 - 4x^2 + 7x - 72$, $2x - 1$

A2 The rational-root theorem

Rational-root theorem

Let $P(x) = a_n x^n + a_{n-1} x^{n-1} + \cdots + a_1 x + a_0$ be a polynomial of degree n with all the coefficients a_i integers. Let p and q be integers such that the highest common factor of p and q is 1 (i.e. p and q are relatively prime).

If $px + q$ is a factor of $P(x)$, then p divides a_n and q divides a_0.

Where can this theorem be used?

It may happen that a cubic equation has no integer solutions, but does have rational solutions. For example, consider the cubic equation

$$P(x) = 2x^3 - x^2 - x - 3 = 0$$

It is easily verified that $P(1) \neq 0$, $P(-1) \neq 0$, $P(3) \neq 0$ and $P(-3) \neq 0$. Hence this equation has no solution which is an integer.

If the equation has a rational solution $\frac{-q}{p}$, where p and q are relatively prime, then the rational-root theorem tells us that p must divide 2 and q must divide -3. So the only value of p that needs to be considered is 2, and $q = \pm 3$ or $q = \pm 1$.

We can test these using the factor theorem. That is, we check $P(\pm\frac{1}{2})$ and $P(\pm\frac{3}{2})$. We find

$$P\left(\frac{3}{2}\right) = 2\left(\frac{3}{2}\right)^3 - \left(\frac{3}{2}\right)^2 - \left(\frac{3}{2}\right) - 3$$

$$= 2 \times \frac{27}{8} - \frac{9}{4} - \frac{3}{2} - 3$$

$$= 0$$

Thus $2x - 3$ is a factor of $P(x)$.

We can use synthetic division to divide through:

$$\begin{array}{c|cccc} & 2 & -1 & -1 & -3 \\ \frac{3}{2} & & 3 & 3 & 3 \\ \hline & 2 & 2 & 2 & 0 \end{array}$$

Therefore

$$P(x) = (x - \tfrac{3}{2})(2x^2 + 2x + 2)$$
$$= (2x - 3)(x^2 + x + 1)$$

Since the discriminant of $x^2 + x + 1$ is negative, we cannot factorise $P(x)$ any further.

▶ ## The proof

We prove the rational-root theorem for a cubic polynomial, but the proof given can easily be extended to a polynomial of any degree.

Let $P(x) = ax^3 + bx^2 + cx + d$, where a, b, c, d are integers. Assume that $px + q$ is a factor of $P(x)$ such that p and q are relatively prime.

Then we know that $P\left(-\frac{q}{p}\right) = 0$ by the factor theorem. That is,

$$a\left(-\frac{q}{p}\right)^3 + b\left(-\frac{q}{p}\right)^2 + c\left(-\frac{q}{p}\right) + d = 0$$

Therefore

$$aq^3 = p(bq^2 - cpq + dp^2) \qquad (1)$$

Now $bq^2 - cpq + dp^2$ is an integer, and so p divides aq^3. Since p and q are relatively prime, it follows that p is relatively prime to q^3. Hence p divides a.

We can also write equation (1) as

$$dp^3 = q(aq^2 - bpq + cp^2)$$

So a similar argument can be used to show that q divides d.

Exercise A2

1. Use the rational-root theorem to help solve each of the following equations for x:
   a. $2x^3 - 5x^2 - 7x + 15 = 0$
   b. $3x^3 + 2x^2 - 4x + 1 = 0$
   c. $6x^3 + x^2 - 16x + 5 = 0$
   d. $2x^3 + x^2 - 7x + 3 = 0$
   e. $30x^3 - 13x^2 - 5x + 2 = 0$
   f. $18x^3 - 3x^2 - 7x + 2 = 0$

A3 Systems of equations

Consider the general system of three linear equations in three unknowns:

$$a_1 x + b_1 y + c_1 z = d_1$$
$$a_2 x + b_2 y + c_2 z = d_2$$
$$a_3 x + b_3 y + c_3 z = d_3$$

In this section we look at how to solve such systems of simultaneous equations. In some cases, this can be done easily by elimination, as shown in Examples 4 and 5. In these cases, you could be expected to find the solution by hand. We will see that in some cases using a calculator is the best choice.

Example 4

Solve the following system of three equations in three unknowns:

$$2x + y + z = -1 \quad (1)$$
$$3y + 4z = -7 \quad (2)$$
$$6x + z = 8 \quad (3)$$

Solution

Subtract (1) from (3):

$$4x - y = 9 \quad (4)$$

Subtract (2) from $4 \times (3)$:

$$24x - 3y = 39$$
$$8x - y = 13 \quad (5)$$

Subtract (4) from (5) to obtain $4x = 4$. Hence $x = 1$.

Substitute in (4) to find $y = -5$, and substitute in (3) to find $z = 2$.

Explanation

The aim is first to eliminate z and obtain two simultaneous equations in x and y only.

Having obtained equations (4) and (5), we solve for x and y. Then substitute to find z.

It should be noted that, just as for two equations in two unknowns, there is a geometric interpretation for three equations in three unknowns. There is only a unique solution if the three equations represent three planes intersecting at a point.

Example 5

Solve the following simultaneous linear equations for x, y and z:

$$x - y + z = 6, \quad 2x + z = 4, \quad 3x + 2y - z = 6$$

Solution

$$x - y + z = 6 \quad (1)$$
$$2x + z = 4 \quad (2)$$
$$3x + 2y - z = 6 \quad (3)$$

Eliminate z to find two simultaneous equations in x and y:

$$x + y = -2 \quad (4) \quad \text{subtracted (1) from (2)}$$
$$5x + 2y = 10 \quad (5) \quad \text{added (2) to (3)}$$

Solve to find $x = \dfrac{14}{3}$, $y = -\dfrac{20}{3}$, $z = -\dfrac{16}{3}$.

A CAS calculator can be used to solve a system of three equations in the same way as for solving two simultaneous equations.

Using the TI-Nspire

Use the simultaneous equations template (menu > **Algebra** > **Solve System of Equations** > **Solve System of Equations**) as shown.

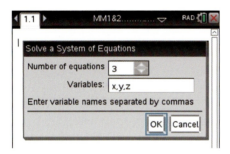 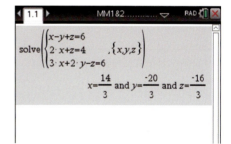

Note: The result could also be obtained using:
solve($x - y + z = 6$ and $2x + z = 4$ and $3x + 2y - z = 6$, $\{x, y, z\}$)

Using the Casio ClassPad

- From the Math1 keyboard, tap twice to create a template for three simultaneous equations.
- Enter the equations using the Var keyboard.

As a linear equation in two variables defines a line, a linear equation in three variables defines a plane.

The coordinate axes in three dimensions are drawn as shown.

The point $P(2, 2, 4)$ is marked.

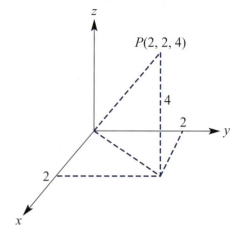

An equation of the form $ax + by + cz = d$ defines a plane.

As an example, we will look at the plane $x + y + z = 4$. We get some idea of how the graph sits by considering

- $x = 0$, $y = 0$, $z = 4$
- $x = 0$, $y = 4$, $z = 0$
- $x = 4$, $y = 0$, $z = 0$

and plotting these three points.

This results in being able to sketch the plane as shown opposite.

We can use a CAS calculator to plot a plane.

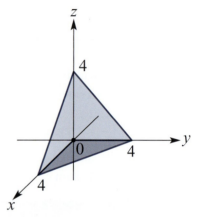

Using the TI-Nspire

To plot the plane $x - y + z = 6$:

- Rearrange the equation of the plane to $z = 6 - x + y$.
- Insert a Graphs page, select 3D view (menu > **View** > **3D Graphing**) and enter the formula as shown for $z1$.

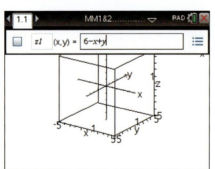 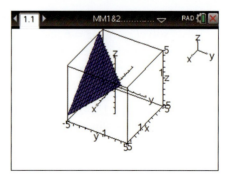

- Use R and the touchpad arrows to rotate the plot.
- Use A to auto-rotate the plot.
- Use X, Y or Z to orientate the plot to an axis.

The solution of simultaneous linear equations in three variables can correspond to:

- a point
- a line
- a plane

There also may be no solution. The situations are as shown in the following diagrams. Examples 4 and 5 provide examples of three planes intersecting at a point (Diagram 1).

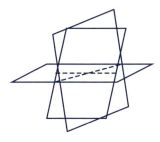
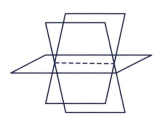
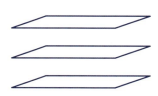

Diagram 1: Intersection at a point

Diagram 2: Intersection in a line

Diagram 3: No intersection

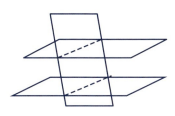
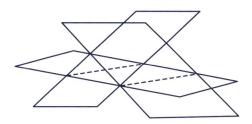

Diagram 4: No common intersection

Diagram 5: No common intersection

Example 6

The simultaneous equations $x + 2y + 3z = 13$, $-x - 3y + 2z = 2$ and $-x - 4y + 7z = 17$ have infinitely many solutions. Describe these solutions through the use of a parameter.

Solution

The point $(-9, 5, 4)$ satisfies all three equations, but it is certainly not the only solution.

We can use a CAS calculator to find all the solutions in terms of a fourth variable λ.

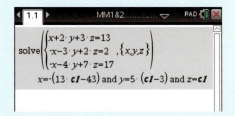
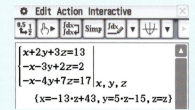

Let $z = \lambda$. Then $x = 43 - 13\lambda$ and $y = 5\lambda - 15$.

For example, if $\lambda = 4$, then $x = -9$, $y = 5$ and $z = 4$.

Note that, as z increases by 1, x decreases by 13 and y increases by 5. All of the points that satisfy the equations lie on a straight line. This is the situation shown in Diagram 2.

Exercise A3

1 Solve each of the following sets of simultaneous equations:

   a $2x + 3y - z = 12$
       $2y + z = 7$
       $2y - z = 5$

   b $x + 2y + 3z = 13$
       $-x - y + 2z = 2$
       $-x + 3y + 4z = 26$

   c $x + y = 5$
       $y + z = 7$
       $z + x = 12$

2 Solve the following system of equations:

$$x - y - z = 0, \quad 5x + 20z = 50, \quad 10y - 20z = 30$$

3 The parabola with equation $y = ax^2 + bx + c$ passes through the points with coordinates $(1, 2), (-1, 6)$ and $(2, 3)$. Find the values of a, b and c.

4 The cubic with equation $y = x^3 + bx^2 + cx + d$ passes through the points with coordinates $(-2, -3), (-1, 3)$ and $(1, 9)$. Find the values of b, c and d.

5 Solve the following simultaneous linear equations for x, y and z:

$$2x + 3y + z = 5, \quad x + 2y = 1, \quad x + y - 2z = 1$$

6 The cubic with equation $y = x^3 + bx^2 + cx + d$ passes through the points with coordinates $(-2, -13), (-1, 0)$ and $(1, 2)$. Find the values of b, c and d.

7 Consider the following simultaneous equations:

$$x + 2y + 3z = 13 \quad (1)$$
$$-x - 3y + 2z = 2 \quad (2)$$
$$-x - 4y + 7z = 17 \quad (3)$$

   a Add equation (2) to equation (1), and subtract equation (2) from equation (3).
   b Comment on the two equations obtained in part a.
   c Let $z = \lambda$ and find y in terms of λ.
   d Substitute for z and y, in terms of λ, in equation (1) to find x in terms of λ.

8 Consider the simultaneous equations $x + 2y - 3z = 4$ and $x + y + z = 6$.

   a Subtract the second equation from the first to find y in terms of z.
   b Let $z = \lambda$. Solve the equations to give the solution in terms of λ.

Glossary

A

Acceleration [p. 650] The acceleration of a particle is defined as the rate of change of its velocity with respect to time.

Acceleration, average [p. 650] The average acceleration of a particle for the time interval $[t_1, t_2]$ is given by $\dfrac{v_2 - v_1}{t_2 - t_1}$, where v_2 is the velocity at time t_2 and v_1 is the velocity at time t_1.

Acceleration, instantaneous [p. 650] $a = \dfrac{dv}{dt}$

Addition rule for choices [p. 368] To determine the total number of choices from disjoint alternatives, simply add up the number of choices available for each alternative.

Addition rule for probability [p. 334] The probability of A or B or both occurring is given by $\Pr(A \cup B) = \Pr(A) + \Pr(B) - \Pr(A \cap B)$

Amplitude of circular functions [p. 496] The distance between the mean position and the maximum position is called the amplitude. The graph of $y = \sin x$ has an amplitude of 1.

Antiderivative [p. 602] To find the general antiderivative of $f(x)$: If $F'(x) = f(x)$, then $\int f(x)\, dx = F(x) + c$
where c is an arbitrary real number.

Arrangements [p. 371] counted when order is important. The number of ways of selecting and arranging r objects from a total of n objects is $\dfrac{n!}{(n-r)!} = n \times (n-1) \times (n-2) \times \cdots \times (n-r+1)$

Asymptote [pp. 146, 698] A straight line is an asymptote of the graph of a function $y = f(x)$ if the graph of $y = f(x)$ gets arbitrarily close to the straight line. An asymptote can be horizontal, vertical or oblique.

B

Binomial distribution [p. 403] The probability of observing x successes in n binomial trials, each with probability of success p, is given by
$$\Pr(X = x) = \binom{n}{x} p^x (1-p)^{n-x}, \quad x = 0, 1, \ldots, n$$
where $\binom{n}{x} = \dfrac{n!}{x!\,(n-x)!}$

Binomial experiment [p. 403]
- The experiment consists of a number, n, of identical trials.
- Each trial results in one of two outcomes, which are usually designated either a success, S, or a failure, F.
- The probability of success on a single trial, p, is constant for all trials.
- The trials are independent (so that the outcome of any trial is not affected by the outcome of any previous trial).

Bisection method [p. 257] A numerical method for solving equations. If values a and b are found such that $f(a)$ and $f(b)$ have opposite signs, then the equation $f(x) = 0$ has a solution in the interval $[a, b]$. The method is to bisect the interval and replace it with one half or the other.

C

Chain rule [p. 685] The chain rule can be used to differentiate a complicated function $y = f(x)$ by transforming it into two simpler functions, which are 'chained' together:
$$x \xrightarrow{h} u \xrightarrow{g} y$$
Using Leibniz notation, the chain rule is stated as
$$\frac{dy}{dx} = \frac{dy}{du} \cdot \frac{du}{dx}$$

Circle, general equation [p. 154] The general equation for a circle is
$$(x - h)^2 + (y - k)^2 = r^2$$
where the centre of the circle is the point (h, k) and the radius is r.

Coefficient [p. 210] the number that multiplies a power of x in a polynomial. E.g. for $2x^5 - 7x^2 + 4$, the coefficient of x^2 is -7.

Combinations [p. 377] *see* selections

Complement, A' [pp. 318, 332] the set of outcomes that are in the sample space, ε, but not in A. The probability of the event A' is
$$\Pr(A') = 1 - \Pr(A)$$

Conditional probability [p. 341] the probability of an event A occurring when it is known that some event B has occurred, given by
$$\Pr(A \mid B) = \frac{\Pr(A \cap B)}{\Pr(B)}$$

Constant function [p. 182] a function $f: \mathbb{R} \to \mathbb{R}$, $f(x) = a$

Continuous function [p. 611] A function f is continuous at the point $x = a$ if the following three conditions are met:
- $f(x)$ is defined at $x = a$
- $\lim_{x \to a} f(x)$ exists
- $\lim_{x \to a} f(x) = f(a)$

We say that a function is continuous everywhere if it is continuous for all real numbers.

Coordinates [p. 33] an ordered pair of numbers that identifies a point in the Cartesian plane; the first number identifies the position with respect to the x-axis, and the second number identifies the position with respect to the y-axis

Cosine and sine functions [p. 487]
- cosine θ is defined as the x-coordinate of the point P on the unit circle where OP forms an angle of θ radians with the positive direction of the x-axis
- sine θ is defined as the y-coordinate of the point P on the unit circle where OP forms an angle of θ radians with the positive direction of the x-axis

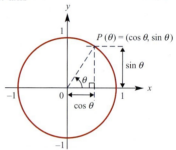

Cubic function [p. 209] A polynomial of degree 3 is called a cubic, and is a function f with rule $f(x) = ax^3 + bx^2 + cx + d$, where $a \neq 0$.

D

Definite integral [pp. 713, 718] $\int_a^b f(x)\, dx$ denotes the signed area enclosed by the graph of $y = f(x)$ between $x = a$ and $x = b$.
See also fundamental theorem of calculus

Degree of a polynomial [p. 210] given by the highest power of x with a non-zero coefficient. For example, the polynomial $2x^5 - 7x^2 + 4$ has degree 5.

Dependent trials or events [p. 399] The probability of one event is influenced by the outcome of another event. *See* sampling without replacement

Derivative function [p. 579] also called the gradient function. The derivative f' of a function f is given by
$$f'(x) = \lim_{h \to 0} \frac{f(x + h) - f(x)}{h}$$

Determinant of a 2×2 matrix [p. 288]
If $\mathbf{A} = \begin{bmatrix} a & b \\ c & d \end{bmatrix}$, then $\det(\mathbf{A}) = ad - bc$.

Difference of two cubes [p. 226]
$$x^3 - y^3 = (x - y)(x^2 + xy + y^2)$$

Difference of two squares [pp. 84, 88]
$$x^2 - y^2 = (x - y)(x + y)$$

Differentiable [p. 614] A function f is said to be differentiable at the point $x = a$ if $\lim\limits_{h \to 0} \dfrac{f(a+h) - f(a)}{h}$ exists.

Differentiation rules [pp. 583, 692]
- $f(x) = x^n$, $f'(x) = nx^{n-1}$, for $n = 1, 2, 3, \ldots$
- $f(x) = x^a$, $f'(x) = ax^{a-1}$, for $a \in \mathbb{R} \setminus \{0\}$, $x > 0$
- Constant: $f(x) = c$, $f'(x) = 0$
- Sum: $f(x) = g(x) + h(x)$, $f'(x) = g'(x) + h'(x)$
- Multiple: $f(x) = k\, g(x)$, $f'(x) = k\, g'(x)$

Dilation from the x-axis [p. 272] A dilation of factor b from the x-axis is described by the rule $(x, y) \to (x, by)$. The curve with equation $y = f(x)$ is mapped to the curve with equation $y = bf(x)$.

Dilation from the y-axis [p. 272] A dilation of factor a from the y-axis is described by the rule $(x, y) \to (ax, y)$. The curve with equation $y = f(x)$ is mapped to the curve with equation $y = f\left(\dfrac{x}{a}\right)$.

Dimension of a matrix [p. 280] The size, or dimension, of a matrix is described by specifying the number of rows (horizontal lines) and columns (vertical lines). A matrix with m rows and n columns is said to be an $m \times n$ matrix.

Discontinuity [p. 611] A function is said to be discontinuous at a point if it is not continuous at that point.

Discrete random variable [p. 393] a random variable X which can take only a countable number of values, usually whole numbers

Discriminant, Δ, of a quadratic [p. 116] the expression $b^2 - 4ac$, which is part of the quadratic formula. For the quadratic equation $ax^2 + bx + c = 0$:
- If $b^2 - 4ac > 0$, there are two solutions.
- If $b^2 - 4ac = 0$, there is one solution.
- If $b^2 - 4ac < 0$, there are no real solutions.

Disjoint sets [pp. 170, 333] If sets A and B have no elements in common, we say A and B are disjoint and write $A \cap B = \emptyset$.

Distance between two points [p. 35] The distance between the given points $A(x_1, y_1)$ and $B(x_2, y_2)$ is $AB = \sqrt{(x_2 - x_1)^2 + (y_2 - y_1)^2}$

Division of polynomials [p. 215] When we divide the polynomial $P(x)$ by the polynomial $D(x)$ we obtain two polynomials, $Q(x)$ the quotient and $R(x)$ the remainder, such that
$P(x) = D(x)Q(x) + R(x)$
and either $R(x) = 0$ or $R(x)$ has degree less than $D(x)$. The polynomial $P(x)$ is the dividend.

Domain [p. 174] the set of all the first coordinates of the ordered pairs in a relation

E

Element [p. 170] a member of a set.
- If x is an element of a set A, we write $x \in A$.
- If x is *not* an element of a set A, we write $x \notin A$.

Empty set, $\emptyset$ [pp. 170, 332] the set that has no elements

Even function [p. 249] A function f is even if $f(-x) = f(x)$. This means that the graph is symmetric about the y-axis.

Event [p. 314] a subset of the sample space. It may consist of a single outcome, or it may consist of several outcomes.

Exponential function [p. 429] a function $f(x) = ka^x$, where k is a non-zero constant and the base a is a positive real number other than 1

F

Factor [pp. 215, 216] a number or expression that divides another number or expression without remainder

Factor theorem [p. 222] If $\beta x + \alpha$ is a factor of $P(x)$, then $P\left(-\dfrac{\alpha}{\beta}\right) = 0$. Conversely, if $P\left(-\dfrac{\alpha}{\beta}\right) = 0$, then $\beta x + \alpha$ is a factor of $P(x)$.

Factorise [p. 87] express as a product of factors

Formula [p. 23] an equation containing symbols that states a relationship between two or more quantities; e.g. $A = \ell w$ (area = length × width). The value of A, the subject of the formula, can be found by substituting given values of ℓ and w.

Function [p. 180] a relation such that for each x-value there is only one corresponding y-value. This means that, if (a, b) and (a, c) are ordered pairs of a function, then $b = c$.

Function, one-to-one [p. 188] different x-values map to different y-values. For example, the function $y = x + 1$ is one-to-one. But $y = x^2$ is not one-to-one, as both 2 and -2 map to 4.

Function, vertical-line test [p. 180] used to identify whether a relation is a function or not. If a vertical line can be drawn anywhere on the graph and it only ever intersects the graph a maximum of once, then the relation is a *function*.

Fundamental theorem of calculus [p. 715] If f is a continuous function on an interval $[a, b]$, then
$\int_a^b f(x)\, dx = F(b) - F(a)$
where F is any antiderivative of f and $\int_a^b f(x)\, dx$ is the definite integral from a to b.

G

Gradient function *see* derivative function

Gradient of a line [p. 37] The gradient is
$$m = \frac{\text{rise}}{\text{run}} = \frac{y_2 - y_1}{x_2 - x_1}$$
where (x_1, y_1) and (x_2, y_2) are the coordinates of two points on the line.

Gradient of a vertical line [p. 38] The gradient of a vertical line (parallel to the y-axis) is undefined.

H

Horizontal-line test [p. 188] If a horizontal line can be drawn anywhere on the graph of a function and it only ever intersects the graph a maximum of once, then the function is *one-to-one*.

Hybrid function *see* piecewise-defined function

I

Implied domain *see* maximal domain

Indefinite integral *see* antiderivative

Independence [p. 350] Two events A and B are independent if $\Pr(A \cap B) = \Pr(A) \times \Pr(B)$ or $\Pr(A \mid B) = \Pr(A)$ or $\Pr(B \mid A) = \Pr(B)$

Independent trials *see* sampling with replacement

Index laws [p. 430]
- To multiply two powers with the same base, add the indices: $a^m \times a^n = a^{m+n}$
- To divide two powers with the same base, subtract the indices: $a^m \div a^n = a^{m-n}$
- To raise a power to another power, multiply the indices: $(a^m)^n = a^{m \times n}$
- Rational indices: $a^{\frac{m}{n}} = (\sqrt[n]{a})^m$
- For base $a \in \mathbb{R}^+ \setminus \{1\}$, if $a^x = a^y$, then $x = y$.

Inequality [p. 20] a mathematical statement that contains an inequality symbol rather than an equals sign; e.g. $2x + 1 < 4$

Integers [p. 171] the elements of
$\mathbb{Z} = \{\ldots, -2, -1, 0, 1, 2, \ldots\}$

Integration, general results [pp. 603, 695]
- $\int x^r \, dx = \dfrac{x^{r+1}}{r+1} + c, \quad r \in \mathbb{Q} \setminus \{-1\}$
- $\int f(x) + g(x) \, dx = \int f(x) \, dx + \int g(x) \, dx$
- $\int k f(x) \, dx = k \int f(x) \, dx$

Integration (definite), general results [p. 722]
- $\int_a^b f(x) \, dx = \int_a^c f(x) \, dx + \int_c^b f(x) \, dx$
- $\int_a^a f(x) \, dx = 0$
- $\int_a^b k f(x) \, dx = k \int_a^b f(x) \, dx$
- $\int_a^b f(x) \pm g(x) \, dx = \int_a^b f(x) \, dx \pm \int_a^b g(x) \, dx$
- $\int_a^b f(x) \, dx = -\int_b^a f(x) \, dx$

Intersection of sets [pp. 170, 332] The intersection of two sets A and B, written $A \cap B$, is the set of all elements common to A and B.

Interval [p. 172] a subset of the real numbers of the form $[a, b]$, $[a, b)$, (a, ∞), etc.

Inverse function [p. 196] For a one-to-one function f, the inverse function f^{-1} is defined by $f^{-1}(x) = y$ if $f(y) = x$, for $x \in \text{ran } f$, $y \in \text{dom } f$.

Irrational number [p. 171] a real number that is not rational; e.g. π and $\sqrt{2}$

K

Karnaugh map [p. 337] a probability table

L

Law of total probability [p. 344] In the case of two events, A and B:
$\Pr(A) = \Pr(A \mid B) \Pr(B) + \Pr(A \mid B') \Pr(B')$

Leading term [p. 210] The leading term, $a_n x^n$, of a polynomial is the term of highest index among those terms with a non-zero coefficient. E.g. the leading term of $2x^5 - 7x^2 + 4$ is $2x^5$.

Limits, properties of [p. 609]
- Sum: $\lim\limits_{x \to a}(f(x) + g(x)) = \lim\limits_{x \to a} f(x) + \lim\limits_{x \to a} g(x)$
- Multiple: $\lim\limits_{x \to a}(k f(x)) = k \lim\limits_{x \to a} f(x)$
- Product: $\lim\limits_{x \to a}(f(x) g(x)) = \lim\limits_{x \to a} f(x) \lim\limits_{x \to a} g(x)$
- Quotient: $\lim\limits_{x \to a} \dfrac{f(x)}{g(x)} = \dfrac{\lim\limits_{x \to a} f(x)}{\lim\limits_{x \to a} g(x)}$, if $\lim\limits_{x \to a} g(x) \neq 0$

Linear equation [p. 2] a polynomial equation of degree 1; e.g. $2x + 1 = 0$

Linear function [p. 182] a function $f : \mathbb{R} \to \mathbb{R}$, $f(x) = mx + c$; e.g. $f(x) = 3x + 1$

Literal equation [p. 5] an equation for the variable x in which the coefficients of x, including the constants, are pronumerals; e.g. $ax + b = c$

Logarithm [p. 450] If $a \in \mathbb{R}^+ \setminus \{1\}$ and $x \in \mathbb{R}$, then the statements $a^x = y$ and $\log_a y = x$ are equivalent.

Logarithm laws [p. 450]
- $\log_a(mn) = \log_a m + \log_a n$
- $\log_a\left(\dfrac{m}{n}\right) = \log_a m - \log_a n$
- $\log_a\left(\dfrac{1}{n}\right) = -\log_a n$
- $\log_a(m^p) = p \log_a m$

M

Matrices, addition [p. 281] Addition is defined for two matrices of the same dimension (same number of rows and same number of columns). The sum is found by adding corresponding entries. For example:
$$\begin{bmatrix} 1 & 0 \\ 0 & 2 \end{bmatrix} + \begin{bmatrix} 0 & -3 \\ 4 & 1 \end{bmatrix} = \begin{bmatrix} 1 & -3 \\ 4 & 3 \end{bmatrix}$$

Matrices, equal [p. 281] Two matrices **A** and **B** are equal, and we can write **A** = **B**, when:
- they have the same number of rows and the same number of columns, and
- they have the same number or entry at corresponding positions.

Matrices, multiplication [p. 284] The product of two matrices **A** and **B** is only defined if the number of columns of **A** is the same as the number of rows of **B**. If **A** is an $m \times n$ matrix and **B** is an $n \times r$ matrix, then the product **AB** is the $m \times r$ matrix whose entries are determined as follows:

To find the entry in row i and column j of **AB**, single out row i in matrix **A** and column j in matrix **B**. Multiply the corresponding entries from the row and column and then add up the resulting products.

Matrix, identity [p. 287]
For square matrices of a given dimension (e.g. 2×2), a multiplicative identity **I** exists.
For 2×2 matrices, the identity is $\mathbf{I} = \begin{bmatrix} 1 & 0 \\ 0 & 1 \end{bmatrix}$
and **AI** = **IA** = **A** for each 2×2 matrix **A**.

Matrix, inverse [p. 287] If **A** is a square matrix and there exists a matrix **B** such that **AB** = **BA** = **I**, then **B** is called the inverse of **A**. The inverse of a square matrix **A** is denoted by $\mathbf{A}^{-1}$. The inverse is unique. It does not exist for every square matrix.

Matrix, multiplication by a scalar [p. 282] If **A** is an $m \times n$ matrix and k is a real number, then $k\mathbf{A}$ is an $m \times n$ matrix whose entries are k times the corresponding entries of **A**. For example:
$$3\begin{bmatrix} 2 & -2 \\ 0 & 1 \end{bmatrix} = \begin{bmatrix} 6 & -6 \\ 0 & 3 \end{bmatrix}$$

Matrix, regular [p. 288] A square matrix is said to be regular if its inverse exists.

Matrix, singular [p. 288] A square matrix is said to be singular if it does not have an inverse.

Matrix, square [p. 287] A matrix with the same number of rows and columns is called a square matrix; e.g. 2×2 matrices.

Matrix, zero [p. 282] The $m \times n$ matrix with all entries equal to zero is called the zero matrix.

Maximal domain [pp. 178, 189] When the rule for a relation is given and no domain is specified, then the domain taken is the largest for which the rule has meaning.

Maximum and minimum value [p. 643] For a continuous function f defined on an interval $[a, b]$:
- if M is a value of the function such that $f(x) \leq M$ for all $x \in [a, b]$, then M is the *absolute maximum* value of the function
- if N is a value of the function such that $f(x) \geq N$ for all $x \in [a, b]$, then N is the *absolute minimum* value of the function.

Midpoint of a line segment [p. 34] If $P(x, y)$ is the midpoint of the line segment joining $A(x_1, y_1)$ and $B(x_2, y_2)$, then
$$x = \dfrac{x_1 + x_2}{2} \quad \text{and} \quad y = \dfrac{y_1 + y_2}{2}$$

Monic polynomial [p. 210] a polynomial whose leading term has coefficient 1; e.g. $x^3 + 4x^2 + 5$

Multiplication rule for choices [p. 369] When sequential choices are involved, the total number of possibilities is found by multiplying the number of options at each successive stage.

Multiplication rule for probability [p. 343] the probability of events A and B both occurring is
$\Pr(A \cap B) = \Pr(A \mid B) \times \Pr(B)$

Multi-stage experiment [p. 327] an experiment that could be considered to take place in more than one stage; e.g. tossing two coins

Mutually exclusive [p. 333] Two sets are said to be mutually exclusive if they have no elements in common.

N

n! [p. 373] The notation $n!$ (read as 'n factorial') is an abbreviation for the product of all the integers from n down to 1:
$n! = n \times (n-1) \times (n-2) \times (n-3) \times \cdots \times 2 \times 1$

Natural numbers [p. 171] the elements of
$\mathbb{N} = \{1, 2, 3, 4, \ldots\}$

^nC_r [p. 378] the number of combinations of n objects in groups of size r:
$$^nC_r = \frac{n!}{r!(n-r)!}$$

Newton's method [p. 661] A method for finding successive approximations to a solution of an equation $f(x) = 0$ using the iterative formula
$$x_{n+1} = x_n - \frac{f(x_n)}{f'(x_n)}$$

Normal, equation of [p. 625] Let (x_1, y_1) be a point on the curve $y = f(x)$. If f is differentiable at $x = x_1$, the equation of the normal at (x_1, y_1) is
$$y - y_1 = \frac{-1}{f'(x_1)}(x - x_1)$$

Null factor theorem [p. 92] If $ab = 0$, then $a = 0$ or $b = 0$.

O

Odd function [p. 249] A function f is odd if $f(-x) = -f(x)$. The graph of an odd function has rotational symmetry with respect to the origin.

Ordered pair [p. 174] An ordered pair, denoted (x, y), is a pair of elements x and y in which x is considered to be the first coordinate and y the second coordinate.

P

Period of a function [p. 496] A function f with domain $\mathbb{R}$ is periodic if there is a positive constant a such that $f(x + a) = f(x)$ for all x. The smallest such a is called the period of f. For example, the period of the sine function is 2π, as $\sin(x + 2\pi) = \sin x$.

Permutations [p. 371] *see* arrangements

Piecewise-defined function [p. 192] a function which has different rules for different subsets of its domain

Polynomial function [p. 210] A polynomial has a rule of the type
$$y = a_n x^n + a_{n-1} x^{n-1} + \cdots + a_1 x + a_0, \quad n \in \mathbb{N} \cup \{0\}$$
where $a_0, a_1, \ldots, a_n$ are numbers called coefficients.

Power function [p. 249] a function of the form $f(x) = x^r$, where r is a non-zero real number

Probability [p. 313] a numerical value assigned to the likelihood of an event occurring. If the event A is impossible, then $\Pr(A) = 0$; if the event A is certain, then $\Pr(A) = 1$; otherwise $0 < \Pr(A) < 1$.

Probability distribution [p. 394] a function, denoted $p(x)$ or $\Pr(X = x)$, which assigns a probability to each value of a discrete random variable X. It can be represented by a rule, a table or a graph, and must give a probability $p(x)$ for every value x that X can take.

Probability table [p. 337] a table used for illustrating a probability problem diagrammatically

Q

$\mathbb{Q}$ [p. 171] the set of all rational numbers

Quadratic formula [p. 112] $x = \dfrac{-b \pm \sqrt{b^2 - 4ac}}{2a}$ is the solution of the quadratic equation $ax^2 + bx + c = 0$

Quadratic function [p. 81] A quadratic has a rule of the form $y = ax^2 + bx + c$, where a, b and c are constants and $a \neq 0$.

Quadratic, turning point form [p. 96] The turning point form of a quadratic function is $y = a(x - h)^2 + k$, where (h, k) is the turning point.

Quartic function [p. 209] A polynomial of degree 4 is called a quartic, and is a function f with rule $f(x) = ax^4 + bx^3 + cx^2 + dx + e$, where $a \neq 0$.

R

$\mathbb{R}^+$ [p. 172] $\{x : x > 0\}$, positive real numbers

$\mathbb{R}^-$ [p. 172] $\{x : x < 0\}$, negative real numbers

$\mathbb{R} \setminus \{0\}$ [p. 172] the set of real numbers excluding 0

$\mathbb{R}^2$ [p. 268] $\{(x, y) : x, y \in \mathbb{R}\}$; i.e. $\mathbb{R}^2$ is the set of all ordered pairs of real numbers

Radian [p. 484] One radian (written 1^c) is the angle subtended at the centre of the unit circle by an arc of length 1 unit.

Random experiment [p. 314] an experiment, such as the rolling of a die, in which the outcome of a single trial is uncertain but observable

Random variable [p. 393] a variable that takes its value from the outcome of a random experiment; e.g. the number of heads observed when a coin is tossed three times

Range [p. 174] the set of all the second coordinates of the ordered pairs in a relation

Rational number [p. 171] a number that can be written as $\dfrac{p}{q}$, for some integers p and q with $q \neq 0$

Rational-root theorem [p. 224]
Let $P(x) = a_nx^n + a_{n-1}x^{n-1} + \cdots + a_1x + a_0$ be a polynomial of degree n with all coefficients a_i integers. Let α and β be integers such that the highest common factor of α and β is 1. If $\beta x + \alpha$ is a factor of $P(x)$, then β divides a_n and α divides a_0.

Rectangular hyperbola [p. 146] The basic rectangular hyperbola has equation $y = \dfrac{1}{x}$.

Reflection in the x-axis [p. 273] A reflection in the x-axis is described by the rule $(x, y) \to (x, -y)$. The curve with equation $y = f(x)$ is mapped to the curve with equation $y = -f(x)$.

Reflection in the y-axis [p. 273] A reflection in the y-axis is described by the rule $(x, y) \to (-x, y)$. The curve with equation $y = f(x)$ is mapped to the curve with equation $y = f(-x)$.

Relation [p. 174] a set of ordered pairs; e.g. $\{(x, y) : y = x^2\}$

Remainder theorem [p. 220] When a polynomial $P(x)$ is divided by $\beta x + \alpha$, the remainder is $P\left(-\dfrac{\alpha}{\beta}\right)$.

Repeated factor of a polynomial [p. 239] a factor that occurs more than once in the factorised form of a polynomial. For example, $x - a$ is a repeated factor of $P(x) = (x - a)^3(x - b)$.

S

Sample space [p. 314] the set of all possible outcomes for a random experiment, sometimes denoted ε

Sampling with replacement [p. 402] selecting individual objects sequentially from a group of objects, and replacing the selected object, so that the probability of obtaining a particular object does not change with each successive selection

Sampling without replacement [p. 399] selecting individual objects sequentially from a group of objects, and not replacing the selected object, so that the probability of obtaining a particular object changes with each successive selection

Secant [p. 551] a straight line that passes through two points $(a, f(a))$ and $(b, f(b))$ on the graph of a function $y = f(x)$

Selections [p. 377] counted when order is not important. The number of ways of selecting r objects from a total of n objects is
$${}^nC_r = \dfrac{n!}{r!\,(n-r)!}$$

Set difference [p. 171] The set difference of two sets A and B is $A \setminus B = \{x : x \in A \text{ and } x \notin B\}$.

Simulation [p. 356] the process of finding an approximate solution to a probability problem by repeated trials using a simulation model

Simulation model [p. 356] a simple model which is analogous to a real-world situation. For example, the outcomes from a toss of a coin (head, tail) could be used as a simulation model for the sex of a child (male, female) under the assumption that in both situations the probabilities are 0.5 for each outcome.

Simultaneous equations [p. 11] equations of two or more lines or curves in the Cartesian plane, the solutions of which are the points of intersection of the lines or curves

Sine function [p. 487] *see* cosine and sine

Speed, average [p. 649]
$$\text{average speed} = \dfrac{\text{total distance travelled}}{\text{total time taken}}$$

Stationary point [pp. 632, 635] A point with coordinates $(a, f(a))$ on a curve $y = f(x)$ is said to be a stationary point if $f'(a) = 0$.

Straight line, equation given two points [p. 46]
$y - y_1 = m(x - x_1)$, where $m = \dfrac{y_2 - y_1}{x_2 - x_1}$

Straight line, gradient–intercept form [p. 43] The gradient–intercept form of the equation of a straight line is $y = mx + c$, where m is the gradient and c is the y-axis intercept.

Straight lines, perpendicular [p. 56] If two straight lines are perpendicular, the product of their gradients is -1. Conversely, if the product of the gradients of two lines is -1, the lines are perpendicular.

Strictly decreasing [p. 595] A function f is strictly decreasing on an interval if $x_2 > x_1$ implies $f(x_2) < f(x_1)$.

Strictly increasing [p. 594] A function f is strictly increasing on an interval if $x_2 > x_1$ implies $f(x_2) > f(x_1)$.

Subset [p. 170] A set B is called a subset of set A if every element of B is also an element of A. We write $B \subseteq A$.

Sum of two cubes [p. 226]
$x^3 + y^3 = (x + y)(x^2 - xy + y^2)$

T

Tangent, equation of [p. 624] Let (x_1, y_1) be a point on the curve $y = f(x)$. Then, if f is differentiable at $x = x_1$, the equation of the tangent at (x_1, y_1) is given by
$$y - y_1 = f'(x_1)(x - x_1)$$

Tangent function [p. 489] The tangent function is given by
$$\tan\theta = \frac{\sin\theta}{\cos\theta}$$

Translation [p. 268] A translation of h units in the positive direction of the x-axis and k units in the positive direction of the y-axis is described by the rule $(x, y) \to (x + h, y + k)$, where h and k are positive numbers. The curve with equation $y = f(x)$ is mapped to the curve with equation $y - k = f(x - h)$.

Tree diagram [pp. 329, 344] a diagram representing the outcomes of a multi-stage experiment

U

Union of sets [pp. 170, 332] The union of two sets A and B, written $A \cup B$, is the set of all elements which are in A or B or both.

V

Velocity, average [pp. 562, 648]
$$\text{average velocity} = \frac{\text{change in position}}{\text{change in time}}$$

Velocity, instantaneous [p. 564] $v = \dfrac{dx}{dt}$

Venn diagram [pp. 170, 332] a diagram showing sets and the relationships between sets

Vertical-line test [p. 180] *see* function

Z

 [p. 171] the set of all integers

Zero polynomial [p. 210] The number 0 is called the zero polynomial.

Answers

Chapter 1

Exercise 1A

1. **a** 3 **b** 9 **c** 1 **d** −8 **e** 5 **f** 2 **g** $\dfrac{5}{3}$ **h** $\dfrac{-7}{2}$ **i** $\dfrac{7}{3}$ **j** $\dfrac{20}{3}$ **k** $\dfrac{-10}{3}$ **l** $\dfrac{14}{5}$

2. **a** $a+b$ **b** $a-b$ **c** $\dfrac{b}{a}$ **d** ab **e** $\dfrac{bc}{a}$

3. **a** $y=5$ **b** $t=5$ **c** $y=-\dfrac{3}{2}$ **d** $x=2$ **e** $t=\dfrac{11}{2}$ **f** $y=\dfrac{8}{3}$ **g** $y=136$ **h** $t=1$ **i** $x=12$ **j** $y=-\dfrac{9}{5}$ **k** $x=-7$ **l** $y=2$

4. **a** $\dfrac{4}{3}$ **b** −5 **c** 2

5. **a** −1 **b** 18 **c** $\dfrac{6}{5}$ **d** 23 **e** 0 **f** 10 **g** 12 **h** 8 **i** $-\dfrac{14}{5}$ **j** $\dfrac{12}{5}$ **k** $\dfrac{7}{2}$

6. **a** $\dfrac{-b}{a}$ **b** $\dfrac{e-d}{c}$ **c** $\dfrac{c}{a}-b$ **d** $\dfrac{b}{c-a}$ **e** $\dfrac{ab}{b+a}$ **f** $a+b$ **g** $\dfrac{b-d}{a-c}$ **h** $\dfrac{bd-c}{a}$

7. **a** −18 **b** −78.2 **c** 16.75 **d** 28 **e** 34 **f** $\dfrac{3}{26}$

8. $x=\dfrac{a^2+b^2+2ab}{ac+bc}=\dfrac{a+b}{c}$

9. $x=\dfrac{ab}{a-b-c}$

Exercise 1B

1. **a** $x+2=6,\ 4$ **b** $3x=10,\ \dfrac{10}{3}$ **c** $3x+6=22,\ \dfrac{16}{3}$ **d** $3x-5=15,\ \dfrac{20}{3}$ **e** $6(x+3)=56,\ \dfrac{19}{3}$ **f** $\dfrac{x+5}{4}=23,\ 87$

2. $A=\$8,\ B=\$24,\ C=\$16$ 3. 14 and 28
4. 8 kg 5. 1.3775 m² 6. 49, 50, 51
7. 17, 19, 21, 23 8. 4200 L 9. 21
10. 3 km 11. 9 and 12 dozen
12. 7.5 km/h 13. 3.6 km 14. 30, 6

Exercise 1C

1. **a** $x=-1,\ y=-1$ **b** $x=5,\ y=21$ **c** $x=-1,\ y=5$ **d** $x=5,\ y=19$ **e** $x=-4,\ y=-13$ **f** $x=-\dfrac{8}{5},\ y=-\dfrac{2}{5}$

2. **a** $x=8,\ y=-2$ **b** $x=-1,\ y=4$ **c** $x=7,\ y=\dfrac{1}{2}$

3. **a** $x=2,\ y=-1$ **b** $x=2.5,\ y=-1$ **c** $m=2,\ n=3$ **d** $x=2,\ y=-1$ **e** $s=2,\ t=5$ **f** $x=10,\ y=13$ **g** $x=\dfrac{4}{3},\ y=\dfrac{7}{2}$ **h** $p=1,\ q=-1$ **i** $x=-1,\ y=\dfrac{5}{2}$

4. **a** No solutions **b** Infinitely many solutions **c** One solution **d** One solution

Exercise 1D

1. 25, 113 2. 22.5, 13.5
3. **a** $70 **b** $12 **c** $3
4. **a** $168 **b** $45 **c** $15

5 17 and 28 **6** 44 and 12
7 5 pizzas, 25 hamburgers
8 Started with 60 and 50; finished with 30 each
9 134 adults, 16 children **10** $\frac{7}{10}$
11 26 **12** 420 adults, 540 children
13 $17 000 **14** 120 shirts, 300 ties
15 360 Outbacks, 300 Bush Walkers
16 2800 in Mydney, 3200 in Selbourne
17 20 kg at $10, 40 kg at $11 and 40 kg at $12

Exercise 1E

1 **a** $x < 1$ **b** $x > 13$ **c** $x \geq 3$ **d** $x \leq 12$
 e $x \leq -6$ **f** $x > 3$ **g** $x < -2$ **h** $x \geq -8$
 i $x \leq \frac{3}{2}$

2 **a** $x < 2$
 b $x < -1$
 c $x < -1$
 d $x \geq 3$
 e $x < 4$
 f $x > 1$
 g $x < 3\frac{1}{2}$
 h $x \geq 3$
 i $x > \frac{1}{6}$

3 **a** $x > \frac{-1}{2}$ **b** $x < 2$ **c** $x > -5$
4 $3x < 20$, $x < \frac{20}{3}$, 6 pages **5** 87

Exercise 1F

1 **a** 18 **b** 9 **c** 3 **d** −18
 e 3 **f** 81 **g** 5 **h** 20
2 **a** $S = a + b + c$ **b** $P = xy$ **c** $C = 5p$
 d $T = dp + cq$ **e** $T = 60a + b$
3 **a** 15 **b** 31.4 **c** 1000 **d** 12
 e 314 **f** 720

4 **a** $V = \dfrac{c}{p}$ **b** $a = \dfrac{F}{m}$ **c** $P = \dfrac{I}{rt}$
 d $r = \dfrac{w - H}{C}$ **e** $t = \dfrac{S - P}{Pr}$ **f** $r = \dfrac{R(V - 2)}{V}$
5 **a** $T = 48$ **b** $b = 8$ **c** $h = 3.82$ **d** $b = 10$
6 **a** $(4a + 3w)$ m **b** $(h + 2b)$ m
 c $3wh$ m^2 **d** $(4ah + 8ab + 6wb)$ m^2
7 **a i** $T = 2\pi(p + q) + 4h$ **ii** $88\pi + 112$
 b $p = \dfrac{A}{\pi h} - q$
8 **a** $D = \dfrac{2}{3}$ **b** $b = 2$ **c** $n = \dfrac{60}{29}$ **d** $r = 4.8$
9 **a** $D = \dfrac{1}{2}bc(1 - k^2)$ **b** $k = \sqrt{1 - \dfrac{2D}{bc}}$
 c $k = \sqrt{\dfrac{2}{3}} = \dfrac{\sqrt{6}}{3}$
10 **a** $P = 4b$ **b** $A = 2bc - c^2$ **c** $b = \dfrac{A + c^2}{2c}$
11 **a** $b = \dfrac{a^2 - a}{2}$ **b** $x = \dfrac{-ay}{b}$
 c $r = \pm\sqrt{3q - p^2x^2}$ **d** $v = \pm\sqrt{u^2\left(1 - \dfrac{x^2}{y^2}\right)}$

Chapter 1 review

Technology-free questions

1 **a** 1 **b** $\dfrac{-3}{2}$ **c** $\dfrac{-2}{3}$ **d** −27
 e 12 **f** $\dfrac{44}{13}$ **g** $\dfrac{1}{8}$ **h** 31
2 **a** $t = a - b$ **b** $\dfrac{cd - b}{a}$ **c** $\dfrac{d}{a} + c$
 d $\dfrac{cb - a}{c - 1}$ **e** $\dfrac{2b}{c - a}$ **f** $\dfrac{1 - cd}{ad}$
3 **a** $x < \dfrac{2}{3}$ **b** $x \leq -148\frac{1}{2}$ **c** $x < \dfrac{22}{29}$ **d** $x \geq \dfrac{-7}{17}$
4 $x = 2(z + 3t)$, -10
5 **a** $d = e^2 + 2f$ **b** $f = \dfrac{d - e^2}{2}$ **c** $f = \dfrac{1}{2}$
6 400π cm^2
7 **a** 196π **b** $\dfrac{975\pi}{2}$
8 **a** $r = \dfrac{A}{\pi s}$ **b** $w = \dfrac{T - P}{Pr}$
 c $r = \dfrac{n - p}{v^2}$ **d** $x = \dfrac{ac - b^2}{b}$
9 **a** $s = 75$ **b** $t = 8$
10 $5\sqrt{2}$ cm
11 12 m and 17 m
12 $m = 2$ and $n = 15$
13 Mr Apollo earns $100 000, Mr Adonis earns $107 200 and Ms Aphrodite earns $96 000
14 **a** $a = \dfrac{28}{11}, b = -\dfrac{9}{11}$ **b** $a = -\dfrac{11}{5}, b = -\dfrac{33}{5}$
15 5 hours travelling on highways

Answers

Multiple-choice questions
1 D 2 D 3 C 4 A 5 C 6 C
7 B 8 B 9 A 10 B 11 E 12 B

Extended-response questions
1 a $C = \dfrac{-10}{9}$ b $F = 86$ c $x = -40$
  d $x = -62.5$ e $x = \dfrac{-160}{13}$ f $k = 5$
2 a $r = \dfrac{2uv}{u+v}$ b $m = \dfrac{v}{u}$
3 a $T = 6w + 6\ell$
  b i $T = 8w$ ii $\ell = \dfrac{25}{6}, w = 12\tfrac{1}{2}$
  c i $y = \dfrac{L-6x}{8}$ ii $y = 22$
  d $x = 10, y = 5$
4 a Distance Tom travelled = ut km
    Distance Julie travelled = vt km
  b i $t = \dfrac{d}{u+v}$ h
    ii Distance from $A = \dfrac{ud}{u+v}$ km
  c $t = 1.25$ h, distance from $A = 37.5$ km
5 a Average speed $= \dfrac{2uv}{u+v}$
  b i $\dfrac{uT}{v}$ ii $\dfrac{vT + uT}{v}$
6 a $\dfrac{3}{a} + \dfrac{3}{b}$ c i $c = \dfrac{2ab}{a+b}$ ii $\dfrac{40}{3}$
7 a $\dfrac{x}{8}, \dfrac{y}{10}$ b $\dfrac{80(x+y)}{10x + 8y}$
  c $x = \dfrac{320}{9}, y = \dfrac{310}{9}$
8 The three lines intersect at the point (4, 3)

Chapter 2

Exercise 2A
1 a (5, 8) b $(\tfrac{1}{2}, \tfrac{1}{2})$ c (1.6, 0.7)
  d (−0.7, 0.85)
2 $M_{AB}(3, 3), M_{BC}(8, 3\tfrac{1}{2}), M_{AC}(6, 1\tfrac{1}{2})$
3 Coordinates of C are (6, 8.8)
4 a (4, 4) b (2, −0.2) c (−2, 5) d (−4, −3)
5 $\left(\dfrac{1+a}{2}, \dfrac{4+b}{2}\right), a = 9, b = -6$
6 a $5\sqrt{2} \approx 7.07$ b $\sqrt{17} \approx 4.12$
  c $\sqrt{34} \approx 5.83$ d 13
7 $\sqrt{97} + \sqrt{85} + \sqrt{104} \approx 29.27$
8 $PM = \sqrt{145} \approx 12.04$ 9 DN

Exercise 2B
1 a 4 b 2 c $\dfrac{1}{4}$ d −4 e 1 f −1
  g $\dfrac{5}{4}$ h −2 i $\dfrac{-5}{4}$ j $\dfrac{4}{3}$ k 0

2 Any line parallel to the one shown
$y = x - 1$

3

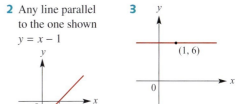

4 a $-\dfrac{1}{4}$ b $-\dfrac{5}{2}$ c −2 d −8 e 0 f −1
  g 7 h 11 i −13 j 11 k 111 l 61
5 a −2 b $\dfrac{2}{5}$
6 a 54 b $\dfrac{5}{6}$
7 a 45° b 45° c 26.57° d 135°
8 a 45° b 26.57° c 161.57° d 49.4°
  e 161.57° f 135°
9 a 1 b −1 c $\sqrt{3}$ d $-\sqrt{3}$

Exercise 2C
1 a $m = 3, c = 6$ b $m = -6, c = 7$
  c $m = 3, c = -6$ d $m = -1, c = -4$
2 a $y = 3x + 5$ b $y = -4x + 6$ c $y = 3x - 4$
3 a $m = 3, c = -6$ b $m = 2, c = -4$
  c $m = \dfrac{1}{2}, c = -2$ d $m = \dfrac{1}{3}, c = -\dfrac{5}{3}$
4 a $m = 2, c = -9$ b $m = -\dfrac{3}{4}, c = \dfrac{5}{2}$
  c $m = -\dfrac{1}{3}, c = -2$ d $m = \dfrac{5}{2}, c = -2$
5 a $y = 3x - 11$ b $y = -2x + 9$
6 a $y = -\dfrac{1}{3}x + \dfrac{11}{3}$ b $y = -\dfrac{7}{5}x + 4$
  c $y = -2x + 4$ d $y = \dfrac{11}{3}x - \dfrac{61}{3}$
7 a 2 b $y = 2x + 6$
8 a $y = 2x + 4$ b $y = -2x + 8$
9 a $y = 2x + 6$ b $y = -2x + 4$
  c $y = -5x + 15$
10 a $y = -\dfrac{2}{3}x + 4$ b $y = -2x - 6$
   c $y = -x + 4$ d $y = -\dfrac{3x}{2} + 3$
11 a $y = \dfrac{2}{3}x + 4$ b $y = \dfrac{2}{3}x - \dfrac{2}{3}$
   c $y = \dfrac{1}{2}x + 1\tfrac{1}{2}$ d $y = -\dfrac{1}{2}x + 2$
   e $y = x + 3.5$ f $y = -0.5x + 0.25$
12 a $y = 4x + 4$ b $y = -\dfrac{2}{3}x$ c $y = -x - 2$
   d $y = \dfrac{1}{2}x - 1$ e $y = 3\tfrac{1}{2}$ f $x = -2$
13 Yes 14 Only c
15 a $x = 4$ b $y = 11$ c $x = 11$ d $y = -1$

Answers

Exercise 2D

1 a (0, 4), (4, 0) **b** (0, −4), (4, 0)
  c (0, −6), (−6, 0) **d** (0, 8), (−8, 0)

2 a   **b**

  c   **d**

  e 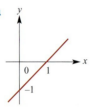 **f**

3 a 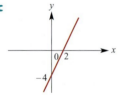 **b**

  c

4 a 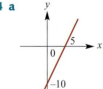 **b**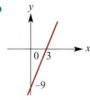

  c   **d**

5 a 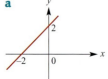 **b**

6 a   **b**

  c   **d**

  c   **d**

7 a   **b**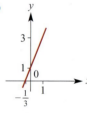

  c   **d**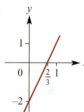

  e   **f**

  g   **h**

8 a  **b**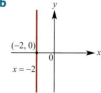

c 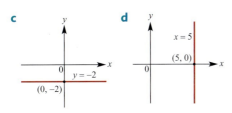 **d**

9 a 45° **b** 135° **c** 45° **d** 135°
e 63.43° (to 2 d.p.) **f** 116.57° (to 2 d.p.)
10 a 71.57° **b** 135° **c** 45° **d** 161.57°
11 $a = -4, b = \frac{4}{3}, d = -1, e = \frac{14}{3}$

Exercise 2E

1 a $y = 2x - 10$ **b** $y = -\frac{1}{2}x$
  c $y = -2x + 6$ **d** $y = \frac{1}{2}x - 4$
  e $y = \frac{2}{3}x - \frac{14}{3}$ **f** $y = -\frac{3}{2}x + 4$
  g $y = -\frac{1}{3}x - \frac{2}{3}$ **h** $y = 3x - 14$
2 Parallel lines: a, b, c; non-parallel lines: d
3 a $y = 4$ **b** $x = 2$ **c** $y = 4$ **d** $x = 3$
4 $y = 2x + 2$
5 Midpoint of AB is $(-1, 6)$; $y = 2x + 8$
6 $m_{BC} = -\frac{3}{5}, m_{AB} = \frac{5}{3}$
  $\therefore m_{BC} \times m_{AB} = -\frac{3}{5} \times \frac{5}{3} = -1$
  $\therefore \triangle ABC$ is a right-angled triangle
7 $m_{AB} = -2, m_{BC} = \frac{1}{2}$
8 $m_{RS} = -\frac{1}{2}, m_{ST} = 2 \therefore RS \perp ST$
  $m_{UT} = -\frac{1}{2}, m_{ST} = 2 \therefore UT \perp ST$
  (Also need to show $SR = UT$.)
  $\therefore RSTU$ is a rectangle
9 $\ell = -\frac{16}{3}, m = \frac{80}{3}$
10 a $y = -\frac{1}{2}x + \frac{11}{2}$ **b** $B(1, 5)$ **c** $C(2, 7)$

Exercise 2F

1 $m = 5$
2 $c = 5$
3 a $y = -\frac{1}{m}x + 3$ **b** $m = \frac{1}{7}$
4 $m = 2$
5 a $x = \frac{3}{m}$ **b** $m = \frac{9}{5}$ **c** $m \geq 3$
  d $y = -\frac{x}{m} - 3$
6 a $x = -\frac{c}{2}$ **b** $c = -4$ **c** $c \geq -2$
  d $y = -\frac{1}{2}x + c$
7 a $x = 4a$ **b** $m = \frac{12}{a}$ **c i** $a = 6$ **ii** $a = -6$
8 a $x = \frac{c}{2}$ **b** $c = 9$ **c** $c \leq 2$ **d** $y = \frac{1}{2}x + c$
  e i $c = 12$ **ii** $c = 4$ **iii** $c = 8$
9 a $\frac{12}{b}$ **b** $-\frac{3}{b}$ **c i** $b = -3$ **ii** $b = \frac{3}{2}$
  d $y = \frac{b}{3}x - \frac{4b}{3}$

Exercise 2G

1 $w = 20n + 350$ for $n \in \mathbb{N} \cup \{0\}$
2 a $d_1 = 50t$ **b** $d_2 = 80 - 40t$
  c Gradient = 50   Gradient = -40

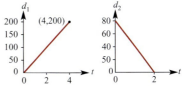

3 a $V = 5t$ **b** $V = 10 + 5t$
4 a $v = 500 - 2.5t$
  b Domain $0 \leq t \leq 200$; Range $0 \leq v \leq 500$
  c

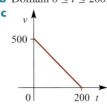

5 $C = 1.5n + 2.6$
6 a $C = 0.24x + 85$ **b** $145
7 $d = 200 - 5t$
8 a

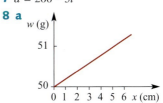

  b $w = 0.2x + 50$ **c** $x = 12.5$ cm
9 a $C = 0.06n - 1$ **b** $59
10 a $C = 5n + 175$ **b** Yes **c** $175

Exercise 2H

1 Both lines have gradient -1, but their y-axis intercepts are 6 and $\frac{13}{2}$
2 $(t, 6 - t)$ where t is a real number
3 a $m = 4$ **b** $m \neq 4$ **c** $m = \frac{9}{5}$
4 $k = 2, m = 5$
5 $k = 24, m = 0$
6 $m = -3$
7 a $m = -5$ **b** $m = 3$

8 a 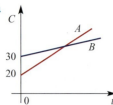   **b** $t = 5$

9 $b = 0.28$ and $a = 0.3$, $\dfrac{25}{7}$ m/s

10 a 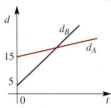   **b** 2 p.m.

11 a $C_1 = 210 + 1.6x$, $C_2 = 330$

b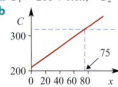

c Fixed-charge method is cheaper for $x > 75$

12 a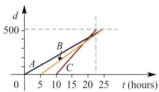

b C wins the race

d C leaves 5 hours after B, and overtakes B $13\tfrac{1}{2}$ hours after B had started, then overtakes A 20 hours after A had started. C wins with a total time of $22\tfrac{1}{2}$ hours ($12\tfrac{1}{2}$ hours for journey + 10 hours handicap), with A and B deadheating for second place, each with a total time of 25 hours.

13 Both craft will pass over the point $(5\tfrac{1}{3}, -4)$

14 a $C_T = 2.8x$, $C_B = 54 + x$

b 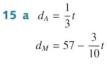   **c** More than 30

15 a $d_A = \dfrac{1}{3}t$ **b**

$d_M = 57 - \dfrac{3}{10}t$

c 10:30 a.m.   **d** Anne 30 km, Maureen 27 km

Chapter 2 review

Technology-free questions

1 a Midpoint $= (3, 2)$; Length $= 4$

b Midpoint $= \left(-\dfrac{1}{2}, -\dfrac{9}{2}\right)$; Length $= \sqrt{74}$

c Midpoint $= \left(5, \dfrac{5}{2}\right)$; Length $= 5$

2 a $\dfrac{9}{4}$ **b** $-\dfrac{10}{11}$ **c** Undefined

d -1 **e** $\dfrac{b}{a}$ **f** $\dfrac{-b}{a}$

3 a $y = 4x$ **b** $y = 4x + 5$

c $y = 4x + 2$ **d** $y = 4x - 5$

4 a $a = -2$ **b** $\dfrac{20}{3}$

5 $4y + 3x = -7$

6 $3y + 2x = -5$

7 a $y = 11$ **b** $y = 6x - 10$ **c** $3y + 2x = -3$

8 $\sqrt{3}y - x = 3\sqrt{3} - 2$

9 $y + x = 1$

10 $y = \dfrac{1}{3}x + \dfrac{20}{3}$

11 $a = 1$, $b = -\dfrac{1}{2}$, $d = 5$, $e = 3$

12 a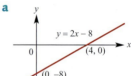

b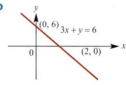

c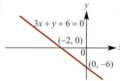

d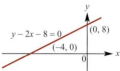

e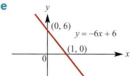

f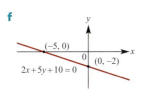

13 a $y = -9$

b $x = 8$
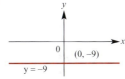

c i $y = 3x$ **ii** $y = -3x$
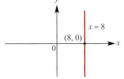

14 a $d = 60t$ **b** $m = 60$
15 $S = 800 + 500n$
16 a $y = 2x + 2$ **b i** $\dfrac{-2}{a}$ **ii** $-2 < a < 0$
  c $\left(\dfrac{1}{a-1}, \dfrac{1}{a-1} + 3\right)$

Multiple-choice questions

1 D **2** E **3** A **4** E **5** C **6** D
7 B **8** E **9** C **10** E **11** C

Extended-response questions

1 a $C = 550 + 190n$ **b** 12 days
  c Fewer than 5 days
2 a Cost of the plug
  b Cost per metre of cable **c** 1.8 **d** $11\tfrac{1}{9}$ m
3 a The maximum profit (when $x = 0$)
  b 43 seats
  c The profit reduces by $24 for each empty seat
4 a i $C = 0.091n$
    ii $C = 1.65 + 0.058n$
    iii $C = 6.13 + 0.0356n$
  b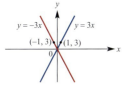
    i For 30 kWh, $C = 2.73$
    ii For 90 kWh, $C = 6.87$
    iii For 300 kWh, $C = 16.81$
  c 389.61 kWh

5 a $y = -\dfrac{7}{3}x + 14\tfrac{2}{3}$ **b** $20\tfrac{1}{3}$ km south
6 a $s = 100 - 7x$
  b 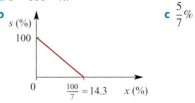 **c** $\dfrac{5}{7}\%$
  d $14\tfrac{2}{7}\%$
  e Probably not a realistic model when $s = 0$
  f $0 \le x \le 14\tfrac{2}{7}$
7 a AB, $y = x + 2$; CD, $y = 2x - 6$
  b Intersection is at $(8, 10)$, on the near bank
8 a $\dfrac{128}{19}$
  b $y = -\dfrac{199}{190}x + \dfrac{128}{19}$
  c No, since gradient of AB is $\dfrac{20}{19} \approx 1.053$,
    whereas the gradient of VC is -1.047
9 a No **b** $1\dfrac{41}{71}$ km to the east of H
10 a $y = x - 38$ **b** $B(56, 18)$
  c $y = -2x + 166$ **d** $(78, 10)$
11 a $y = 3x + 2$ **b** $(0, 2)$
  c $y = 3x - 8$ **d** $(2, -2)$
  e Area = 10 square units
  f Area = 40 square units
12 a $C = 40x + 30\,000$ **b** $45 **c** 5000
  d $R = 80x$
  e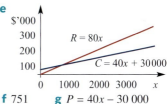
  f 751 **g** $P = 40x - 30\,000$
13 a Cost with method 1 is $226.75; cost with method 2 is $227; so method 1 is cheaper
  b

	0	1000	2000	3000
Method 1	100	181.25	262.50	343.75
Method 2	110	185	260	335

  c Cost the same for approx. 1600 units
  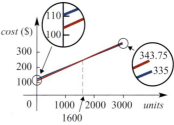
  d $C_1 = 0.08125x + 100$, $C_2 = 0.075x + 110$, $x = 1600$

14 a (17, 12)   **b** $3y = 2x + 2$

15 a PD: $y = \frac{2}{3}x + 120$; DC: $y = \frac{2}{5}x + 136$;
CB: $y = -\frac{5}{2}x + 600$; AB: $y = \frac{2}{5}x + 20$;
AP: $y = -\frac{3}{5}x + 120$

b At B and C, since product of gradients is -1
E.g. $m_{DC} = \frac{2}{5}$, $m_{CB} = -\frac{5}{2}$, $m_{DC} \times m_{CB} = -1$

Chapter 3

Exercise 3A

1 a $2x - 8$ **b** $-2x + 8$ **c** $6x - 12$
d $-12 + 6x$ **e** $x^2 - x$ **f** $2x^2 - 10x$

2 a $6x + 1$ **b** $3x - 6$ **c** $x + 1$ **d** $5x - 3$

3 a $14x - 32$ **b** $2x^2 - 11x$
c $32 - 16x$ **d** $6x - 11$

4 a $2x^2 - 11x$ **b** $3x^2 - 15x$
c $-20x - 6x^2$ **d** $6x - 9x^2 + 6x^3$
e $2x^2 - x$ **f** $6x - 6$

5 a $6x^2 - 2x - 28$ **b** $x^2 - 22x + 120$
c $36x^2 - 4$ **d** $8x^2 - 22x + 15$
e $x^2 - (\sqrt{3} + 2)x + 2\sqrt{3}$
f $2x^2 + \sqrt{5}x - 5$ **g** $3x^2 + \sqrt{7}x - 14$
h $5x^2 + (10\sqrt{2} - 3)x - 6\sqrt{2}$
i $5x^2 - (3\sqrt{5} + 32\sqrt{10})x + 96\sqrt{2}$

6 a $6x^3 - 5x^2 - 14x + 12$ **b** $x^3 - 1$
c $24 - 20x - 8x^2 + 6x^3$ **d** $3x^2 + 4x + 3$
e $-10x^2 + 5x - 2$

7 a $x^2 - 8x + 16$ **b** $4x^2 - 12x + 9$
c $36 - 24x + 4x^2$ **d** $x^2 - x + \frac{1}{4}$
e $x^2 - 2\sqrt{5}x + 5$ **f** $x^2 - 4\sqrt{3}x + 12$

8 a $x^2 - 9$ **b** $4x^2 - 16$ **c** $81x^2 - 121$
d $4x^2 - 9$ **e** $4x^2 - 25$ **f** $x^2 - 5$
g $4x^2 - 27$ **h** $3x^2 - 7$

9 a $x^2 + y^2 - z^2 - 2xy$ **b** $4a^2 - 4ab + b^2 - c^2$
c $9w^2 + 8uz - 16z^2 - u^2$
d $4a^2 - 5b^2 + 4ac + c^2$

10 a i $x^2 + 2x + 1$ **ii** $(x + 1)^2$
b i $(x - 1)^2 + 2(x - 1) + 1$ **ii** x^2

Exercise 3B

1 a $2(x + 2)$ **b** $4(a - 2)$ **c** $3(2 - x)$
d $2(x - 5)$ **e** $6(3x + 2)$ **f** $8(3 - 2x)$

2 a $2x(2x - y)$ **b** $8x(a + 4y)$ **c** $6b(a - 2)$
d $2xy(3 + 7x)$ **e** $x(x + 2)$ **f** $5x(x - 3)$
g $-4x(x + 4)$ **h** $7x(1 + 7x)$ **i** $x(2 - x)$

3 a $6x^2y^2(x + 2)$ **b** $xy(7x - 6y)$
c $2xy^2(4x + 3)$

4 a $(x^2 + 1)(x + 5)$ **b** $(x + 3)(y + 2)$

c $(x - 1)(x + 1)(y - 1)(y + 1)$
d $(a + b)(x + y)$ **e** $(a^2 + 1)(a - 3)$
f $(2a - 5)(b - 6)$ **g** $(2x + 5)(x - 1)$
h $(x + 2)(x - 2)(x + 2)$
i $(x - a)(x + a)(x - b)$

5 a $(x - 6)(x + 6)$ **b** $(x - 9)(x + 9)$
c $(x - a)(x + a)$ **d** $(2x - 9)(2x + 9)$
e $(3x - 4)(3x + 4)$ **f** $(5x - y)(5x + y)$
g $3(x - 4)(x + 4)$ **h** $2(x - 7)(x + 7)$
i $3a(x - 3)(x + 3)$ **j** $(a - \sqrt{7})(a + \sqrt{7})$
k $(\sqrt{2}a - \sqrt{5})(\sqrt{2}a + \sqrt{5})$
l $(x - 2\sqrt{3})(x + 2\sqrt{3})$

6 a $(x - 6)(x + 2)$ **b** $(7 + x)(3 - x)$
c $3(x - 1)(x + 3)$ **d** $-5(2x + 1)$
e $-24x$ **f** $-5(x + 7)(x + 1)$

7 a $(x - 9)(x + 2)$ **b** $(y - 16)(y - 3)$
c $(a - 2)(a - 12)$ **d** $(a + 9)^2$
e $(x - 8)(x + 3)$ **f** $(x - 12)(x + 10)$

8 a $(3x - 1)(x - 2)$ **b** $(2x + 1)(3x + 2)$
c $(5x + 3)(x + 4)$ **d** $(2x + 1)(x + 4)$
e $(3x - 2)(2x - 5)$ **f** $(3x + 1)(2x - 3)$
g $(3x - 2)(4x - 3)$ **h** $(x - 2)(5x + 6)$
i $x(5x - 6)(x - 2)$

9 a $3(y - 6)(y + 2)$ **b** $2(x - 7)(x - 2)$
c $4(x - 3)(x - 6)$ **d** $3(x + 2)(x + 3)$
e $a(x + 3)(x + 4)$ **f** $3x(4 - x)^2$

10 a $x(x + 2)$ **b** $(2x - 3)(x + 2)$
c $2(2x + 5)(x + 2)$

Exercise 3C

1 a 2 or 3   **b** 0 or 2   **c** 4 or 3   **d** 4 or 3
e 3 or -4 **f** 0 or 1   **g** $\frac{5}{2}$ or 6   **h** -4 or 4

2 a $-0.65, 4.65$ **b** $-0.58, 2.58$ **c** $-2.58, 0.58$

3 a $9, -8$ **b** $4, 2$ **c** $11, -3$ **d** $4, -16$
e $2, -7$ **f** $-3, 8$

4 a $-\frac{3}{2}, -1$ **b** $\frac{1}{2}, \frac{3}{2}$ **c** $-\frac{2}{3}, -\frac{3}{2}$ **d** $-\frac{3}{2}, 2$
e $\frac{5}{6}, 3$ **f** $-\frac{3}{2}, 3$ **g** $\frac{1}{2}, \frac{3}{5}$ **h** $-\frac{3}{4}, \frac{2}{3}$
i $\frac{1}{2}$ **j** $-5, 1$ **k** $0, 3$ **l** $-5, -3$
m $\frac{1}{5}, 2$

5 3   **6** 4 or 9   **7** $2, 2\frac{3}{8}$
8 13   **9** 50   **10** 6 cm, 2 cm
11 5   **12** $90, $60   **13** 42

Exercise 3D

1 a i $(0, -4)$
ii $x = 0$
iii $(-2, 0), (2, 0)$

b **i** (0, 2)
   ii $x = 0$
   iii None

c **i** (0, 3)
   ii $x = 0$
   iii $(-\sqrt{3}, 0), (\sqrt{3}, 0)$

d **i** (0, 5)
   ii $x = 0$
   iii $\left(-\sqrt{\tfrac{5}{2}}, 0\right), \left(\sqrt{\tfrac{5}{2}}, 0\right)$

e **i** (0, 4)
   ii $x = 0$
   iii $(-2, 0), (2, 0)$

f **i** (0, −9)
   ii $x = 0$
   iii $(-\sqrt{3}, 0), (\sqrt{3}, 0)$

2 a **i** (2, 0)
   ii $x = 2$
   iii (2, 0)

b **i** (−3, 0)
   ii $x = -3$
   iii (−3, 0)

c **i** (−1, 0)
   ii $x = -1$
   iii (−1, 0)

d **i** (4, 0)
   ii $x = 4$
   iii (4, 0)

3 a **i** (2, 1)
   ii $x = 2$
   iii None

b **i** (2, −1)
   ii $x = 2$
   iii (1, 0), (3, 0)

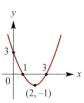

c **i** (1, 2)
   ii $x = 1$
   iii None

d **i** (−1, −1)
   ii $x = -1$
   iii (−2, 0), (0, 0)

e **i** (3, 1)
   ii $x = 3$
   iii (2, 0), (4, 0)

f **i** (−2, −4)
   ii $x = -2$
   iii (−4, 0), (0, 0)

g **i** (−2, −18)
   ii $x = -2$
   iii (−5, 0), (1, 0)

h i (4, 3)
  ii $x = 4$
  iii (3, 0), (5, 0)

i i (−5, −2)
  ii $x = −5$
  iii None

j i (−2, −12)
  ii $x = −2$
  iii (0, 0), (−4, 0)

k i (2, 8)
  ii $x = 2$
  iii $(2 − \sqrt{2}, 0)$, $(2 + \sqrt{2}, 0)$

l i (1, −3)
  ii $x = 1$
  iii (−2, 0), (4, 0)

Exercise 3E

1 a $x^2 − 2x + 1$ **b** $x^2 + 4x + 4$
  c $x^2 − 6x + 9$ **d** $x^2 − 6x + 9$
  e $x^2 + 4x + 4$ **f** $x^2 − 10x + 25$
  g $x^2 − x + \frac{1}{4}$ **h** $x^2 − 3x + \frac{9}{4}$

2 a $(x − 2)^2$ **b** $(x − 6)^2$ **c** $−(x − 2)^2$
  d $2(x − 2)^2$ **e** $−2(x − 3)^2$ **f** $\left(x − \frac{1}{2}\right)^2$
  g $\left(x − \frac{3}{2}\right)^2$ **h** $\left(x + \frac{5}{2}\right)^2$

3 a $1 \pm \sqrt{2}$ **b** $2 \pm \sqrt{6}$ **c** $3 \pm \sqrt{7}$
  d $\dfrac{5 \pm \sqrt{17}}{2}$ **e** $\dfrac{2 \pm \sqrt{2}}{2}$ **f** $-\dfrac{1}{3}, 2$
  g $-1 \pm \sqrt{1 − k}$ **h** $\dfrac{-1 \pm \sqrt{1 − k^2}}{k}$
  i $\dfrac{3k \pm \sqrt{9k^2 − 4}}{2}$

4 a $y = (x − 1)^2 + 2$ **b** $y = (x + 2)^2 − 3$
  t. pt (1, 2)   t. pt (−2, −3)

c $y = \left(x − \dfrac{3}{2}\right)^2 − \dfrac{5}{4}$
  t. pt $\left(\dfrac{3}{2}, -\dfrac{5}{4}\right)$

5 a $y = 2\left(x − \dfrac{1}{2}\right)^2 − \dfrac{11}{2}$
  t. pt $\left(\dfrac{1}{2}, -\dfrac{11}{2}\right)$

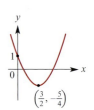

b $y = 4(x + 1)^2 + 4$ **c** $y = 3(x − 1)^2 − 7$
  t. pt (−1, 4)   t. pt (1, −7)

 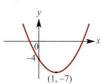

6 a $y = (x − 4)^2 − 4$ **b** $y = \left(x − \dfrac{1}{2}\right)^2 − \dfrac{9}{4}$
  t. pt (4, −4)   t. pt $\left(\dfrac{1}{2}, -\dfrac{9}{4}\right)$

 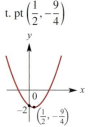

c $y = 2(x + 1)^2 − 4$ **d** $y = −(x − 2)^2 + 5$
  t. pt (−1, −4)   t. pt (2, 5)

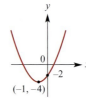 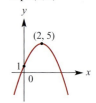

e $y = -2(x+3)^2 + 6$
t. pt $(-3, 6)$

f $y = 3(x-1)^2 + 9$
t. pt $(1, 9)$

Exercise 3F

1 a 7 **b** 7 **c** 1
2 a −2 **b** 8 **c** 4
3 a   **b**

c   **d**

e   **f**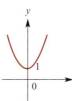

g 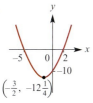 **h**

4 a   **b**

c   **d**

e   **f**

g 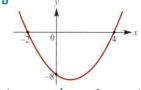 **h**

Exercise 3G

1 a −2, 4 **b**

c $-2 \leq x \leq 4$ **d** $x < -2$ or $x > 4$
2 a $x \leq -2$ or $x \geq 3$ **b** $-4 < x < -3$
c $-4 \leq x \leq \dfrac{1}{2}$ **d** $x < 2$ or $x > 6$
e $2 < x < 3$ **f** $\dfrac{3}{2} \leq x \leq \dfrac{7}{2}$
g $-\dfrac{7}{2} < x < 2$ **h** $-2 \leq x \leq \dfrac{5}{2}$
i $x < -5$ or $x > \dfrac{5}{2}$ **j** $-2 \leq x \leq \dfrac{7}{2}$
k $x < \dfrac{2}{5}$ or $x > \dfrac{7}{2}$ **l** $x \leq \dfrac{5}{2}$ or $x \geq \dfrac{11}{2}$
3 a $x < -5$ or $x > 5$ **b** $-\dfrac{2}{3} \leq y \leq \dfrac{2}{3}$
c $y < -4$ or $y > 4$ **d** $-\dfrac{6}{5} \leq x \leq \dfrac{6}{5}$
e $y \leq -\dfrac{1}{4}$ or $y \geq \dfrac{1}{4}$ **f** $y < -\dfrac{5}{6}$ or $y > \dfrac{5}{6}$
4 a $x \geq 2$ or $x \leq -4$ **b** $-3 < x < 8$
c $-2 \leq x \leq 6$ **d** $x > 3$ or $x < -\dfrac{3}{2}$
e $-\dfrac{3}{2} < x < -\dfrac{2}{3}$ **f** $-3 \leq x \leq -2$
g $x > \dfrac{2}{3}$ or $x < -\dfrac{3}{4}$ **h** $\dfrac{1}{2} \leq x \leq \dfrac{3}{5}$
i $-4 \leq x \leq 5$
j $\dfrac{1}{2}(5 - \sqrt{41}) \leq p \leq \dfrac{1}{2}(5 + \sqrt{41})$
k $y < -1$ or $y > 3$ **l** $x \leq -2$ or $x \geq -1$
5 a $x \leq \dfrac{-3 - \sqrt{29}}{2}$ or $x \geq \dfrac{-3 + \sqrt{29}}{2}$
b $\dfrac{5 - \sqrt{17}}{2} < x < \dfrac{5 + \sqrt{17}}{2}$
c $\dfrac{3 - \sqrt{17}}{4} \leq x \leq \dfrac{3 + \sqrt{17}}{4}$

d $\dfrac{-3-\sqrt{41}}{2} < x < \dfrac{-3+\sqrt{41}}{2}$
e $\dfrac{-7-\sqrt{41}}{4} < x < \dfrac{-7+\sqrt{41}}{4}$
f $x \le \dfrac{4-\sqrt{6}}{2}$ or $x \ge \dfrac{4+\sqrt{6}}{2}$

6 The square of any number is greater than or equal to zero.

7 The negative of the square of any number is less than or equal to zero.

8 $x^2 + 2x + 7 = (x+1)^2 + 6$. For all x, we have $(x+1)^2 \ge 0$ and so $(x+1)^2 + 6 \ge 6$

9 $-x^2 - 2x - 7 = -(x+1)^2 - 6$. For all x, we have $-(x+1)^2 \le 0$ and so $-(x+1)^2 - 6 \le -6$

Exercise 3H

1 a i 40   **ii** $2\sqrt{10}$
  b i 28   **ii** $2\sqrt{7}$
  c i 172 **ii** $2\sqrt{43}$
  d i 96   **ii** $4\sqrt{6}$
  e i 189 **ii** $3\sqrt{21}$

2 a $1+\sqrt{5}$ **b** $\dfrac{3-\sqrt{5}}{2}$ **c** $\dfrac{1+\sqrt{5}}{2}$ **d** $1+2\sqrt{2}$

3 a $-3 \pm \sqrt{13}$ **b** $\dfrac{7 \pm \sqrt{61}}{2}$ **c** $\dfrac{1}{2}, 2$
  d $-1 \pm \dfrac{3}{2}\sqrt{2}$ **e** $-2 \pm \dfrac{3}{2}\sqrt{2}$ **f** $1 \pm \dfrac{\sqrt{30}}{5}$
  g $1 \pm \dfrac{\sqrt{2}}{2}$ **h** $1, \dfrac{-3}{2}$ **i** $\dfrac{-3 \pm \sqrt{6}}{5}$
  j $\dfrac{-13 \pm \sqrt{145}}{12}$ **k** $\dfrac{2 \pm \sqrt{4-2k^2}}{2k}$
  l $\dfrac{2k \pm \sqrt{6k^2-2k}}{2(1-k)}$

4 a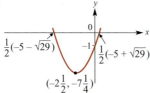

b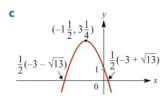

c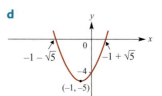

d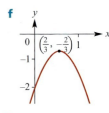

e 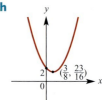   **f**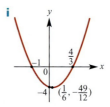

g

h

i

Exercise 3I

1 a 20   **b** −12   **c** 25   **d** 41   **e** 41

2 a Crosses the x-axis   **b** Does not cross
  c Just touches the x-axis
  d Crosses the x-axis   **e** Does not cross
  f Does not cross

3 a Two real solutions   **b** No real solutions
  c Two real solutions   **d** Two real solutions
  e Two real solutions   **f** No real solutions

4 a $\Delta = 0$, one rational solution
  b $\Delta = 1$, two rational solutions
  c $\Delta = 17$, two irrational solutions
  d $\Delta = 0$, one rational solution
  e $\Delta = 57$, two irrational solutions
  f $\Delta = 1$, two rational solutions

5 a i $-\sqrt{5} < m < \sqrt{5}$ **ii** $m = \pm\sqrt{5}$
  iii $m > \sqrt{5}$ or $m < -\sqrt{5}$
  b i $0 < m < \dfrac{4}{3}$ **ii** $m = \dfrac{4}{3}$
  iii $m > \dfrac{4}{3}$ or $m < 0$
  c i $-\dfrac{4}{5} < m < 0$ **ii** $m = 0$ or $m = -\dfrac{4}{5}$
  iii $m < -\dfrac{4}{5}$ or $m > 0$
  d i $-2 < m < 1$ **ii** $m = -2$ or $m = 1$
  iii $m > 1$ or $m < -2$

6 $\Delta = (2m - n)^2$, a perfect square   **7** $p > \dfrac{4}{3}$

8 $p = \dfrac{-1}{2}$

9 a $p = \pm 3$ **b** $p > 1$ **c** $p > \dfrac{2}{3}$ **d** $p > 1$

10 $-2 < p < 8$

11 $\Delta = -4q^2 < 0$ for all values of q

12 a $\Delta = 16m^2 - 96m + 176 = 16(m - 3)^2 + 32$
  b $\Delta \geq 32$; therefore two solutions

13 a $\Delta = 16$
  b $\Delta > 0$; therefore two solutions

14 $\Delta = (m + 4)^2$, a perfect square; therefore rational solutions

15 $\Delta = (m - 2n)^2$, a perfect square; therefore rational solutions

16 The graph will cross the x-axis twice

17 The graph will cross the x-axis twice

Exercise 3J

1 a $(1 - \sqrt{5}, -1 - \sqrt{5}), (1 + \sqrt{5}, -1 + \sqrt{5})$
  b $(-3, 9), (2, 4)$ **c** $(-3, 9), \left(\dfrac{7}{4}, \dfrac{49}{16}\right)$
  d $(1, 3), (2, 5)$

2 a $(2, 0), (-5, 7)$ **b** $(1, -3), (4, 9)$
  c $(1, -3), (-3, 1)$ **d** $(-1, 1), (-3, -3)$
  e $\left(\dfrac{1 + \sqrt{33}}{2}, -3 - \sqrt{33}\right), \left(\dfrac{1 - \sqrt{33}}{2}, -3 + \sqrt{33}\right)$
  f $\left(\dfrac{5 + \sqrt{33}}{2}, 23 + 3\sqrt{33}\right), \left(\dfrac{5 - \sqrt{33}}{2}, 23 - 3\sqrt{33}\right)$

3 a Touch at $(2, 0)$ **b** Touch at $(3, 9)$
  c Touch at $(-2, -4)$ **d** Touch at $(-4, -8)$

4 a $x = 8, y = 16$ and $x = -1, y = 7$
  b $x = -\dfrac{16}{3}, y = 37\dfrac{1}{3}$ and $x = 2, y = 30$
  c $x = \dfrac{4}{5}, y = 10\dfrac{2}{5}$ and $x = -3, y = 18$
  d $x = 10\dfrac{2}{3}, y = 0$ and $x = 1, y = 29$
  e $x = 0, y = -12$ and $x = \dfrac{3}{2}, y = -7\dfrac{1}{2}$
  f $x = 1.14, y = 14.19$ and $x = -1.68, y = 31.09$

5 a -13
  b i

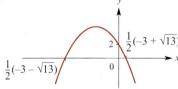

  ii $m = -6 \pm \sqrt{32} = -6 \pm 4\sqrt{2}$

6 a $c = \dfrac{-1}{4}$ **b** $c > \dfrac{-1}{4}$

7 $a = 3$ or $a = -1$

8 $b = 1$

9 $y = (2 + 2\sqrt{3})x - 4 - 2\sqrt{3}$ and
     $y = (2 - 2\sqrt{3})x - 4 + 2\sqrt{3}$

Exercise 3K

1 $a = -4, c = 6$

2 a $\Delta = b^2 - 16a$ **b** $a = \dfrac{b^2}{16}$ **c** $a = \dfrac{1}{4}, b = 2$

3 a $y = 2(x + 2)(x - 6)$ **b** $y = -2(x + 2)^2 + 4$
  c $y = -x^2 + 2x - 3$

4 2 **5** $a = \dfrac{4}{7}, b = \dfrac{-24}{7}$

6 $a = -2, b = 1, c = 6$

7 a $y = -\dfrac{5}{16}x^2 + 5$ **b** $y = x^2$
  c $y = \dfrac{1}{11}x^2 + \dfrac{7}{11}x$ **d** $y = x^2 - 4x + 3$
  e $y = -\dfrac{5}{4}x^2 - \dfrac{5}{2}x + \dfrac{15}{4}$ **f** $y = x^2 - 4x + 6$

8 $y = \dfrac{5}{16}(x + 1)^2 + 3$ **9** $y = -\dfrac{1}{2}(x^2 - 3x - 18)$

10 $y = (x + 1)^2 + 3$ **11** $y = \dfrac{1}{180}x^2 - x + 75$

12 $y = 2x^2 - 4x$ **13** $y = x^2 - 2x - 1$

14 a C   **b** B   **c** D   **d** A

15 a $y = a\left(x + \dfrac{1}{a}\right)^2 + a - \dfrac{1}{a}$ **b** $\left(-\dfrac{1}{a}, a - \dfrac{1}{a}\right)$
  c $a = \pm 1$ **d** $-1 < a < 1$

16 $y = -2x^2 + 8x - 6$

17 a $y = ax(x - 10), a > 0$
  b $y = a(x + 4)(x - 10), a < 0$
  c $y = \dfrac{1}{18}(x - 6)^2 + 6$ **d** $y = a(x - 8)^2, a < 0$

18 a $y = -\dfrac{1}{4}x^2 + x + 2$ **b** $y = x^2 + x - 5$

19 $r = -\dfrac{1}{8}t^2 + 2\dfrac{1}{2}t - 6\dfrac{3}{8}$ **20 a** B   **b** D

21 a $y = -2x^2 - x + 5$ **b** $y = 2x^2 - x - 5$
  c $y = 2x^2 + \dfrac{5}{2}x - \dfrac{11}{2}$

Exercise 3L

1 a $A = 60x - 2x^2$ **b**

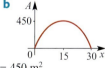

  c Maximum area $= 450$ m²

2 $A = x(10 - x)$; Maximum area $= 25$ m²

3 a [graph of E vs x, peak 100 between 0 and 1]   **b** 0 and 1   **c** 0.5
  d 0.23 and 0.77

4 a $A = 34x - x^2$ **b** [graph peak 289, 0 to 34]
  c 289 cm²

5 a $4x + 10y = 80$
  b i $A = 1.64x^2 - 25.6x + 256$
    ii 31.22 and 48.78

6 a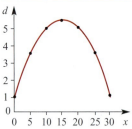
The domain depends on the height of the alpine area. In Victoria, the highest mountain is approx. 2 km high and the minimum alpine height would be approx. 1 km. Thus, for Victoria, domain = [1, 2].
  b Theoretically, no. But of course there is a practical maximum.
  c $1225

7 a 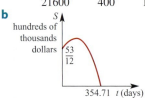 **b** 8874 units

8 a

x	0	5	10	15	20	25	30
d	1	3.5	5	5.5	5	3.5	1

  b i 5.5 m
    ii $15 - 5\sqrt{7}$ m or $15 + 5\sqrt{7}$ m from the bat
    iii 1 m above the ground

9 $a = -\dfrac{16}{15}, b = \dfrac{8}{5}, c = 0$

10 a $a = -\dfrac{7}{21600}, b = \dfrac{41}{400}, c = \dfrac{53}{12}$
  b
  c i $S = \$1\,236\,666$ **ii** $S = \$59\,259$

Chapter 3 review

Technology-free questions

1 a $\left(x + \dfrac{9}{2}\right)^2$ **b** $(x+9)^2$ **c** $\left(x - \dfrac{2}{5}\right)^2$
  d $(x+b)^2$ **e** $(3x-1)^2$ **f** $(5x+2)^2$

2 a $-3x + 6$ **b** $-ax + a^2$
  c $49a^2 - b^2$ **d** $x^2 - x - 12$
  e $2x^2 - 5x - 12$ **f** $x^2 - y^2$

g $a^3 - b^3$ **h** $6x^2 + 8xy + 2y^2$
i $3a^2 - 5a - 2$ **j** $4xy$
k $2u + 2v - uv$ **l** $-3x^2 + 15x - 12$

3 a $4(x-2)$ **b** $x(3x+8)$
  c $3x(8a-1)$ **d** $(2-x)(2+x)$
  e $a(u + 2v + 3w)$
  f $a^2(2b - 3a)(2b + 3a)$
  g $(1 - 6ax)(1 + 6ax)$ **h** $(x+4)(x-3)$
  i $(x+2)(x-1)$ **j** $(2x-1)(x+2)$
  k $(3x+2)(2x+1)$ **l** $(3x+1)(x-3)$
  m $(3x-2)(x+1)$ **n** $(3a-2)(2a+1)$
  o $(3x-2)(2x-1)$

4 a $x = 5$ or $x = -3$ **b** $x = 9$ or $x = 0$
  c $x = 2$ or $x = 3$ **d** $x = -1$ or $x = 25$
  e $x = -3$ or $x = -2$ **f** $x = 6$
  g $x = -\dfrac{1}{2}$ or $x = 3$ **h** $x = -\dfrac{5}{6}$ or $x = \dfrac{3}{2}$
  i $x = -\dfrac{12}{5}$ or $x = 1$

5 a   **b**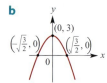

c   **d**

e 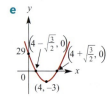 **f**

g   **h**

6 a 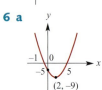 **b**

c 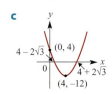 **d**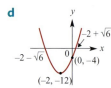

14 225   **15** $y = 5(x-1)^2 + 5$
16 a $(3, 9), (-1, 1)$
   b $\left(\dfrac{4-\sqrt{38}}{2}, 27 - 4\sqrt{38}\right)\left(\dfrac{4+\sqrt{38}}{2}, 27 + 4\sqrt{38}\right)$
   c $\left(\dfrac{-7-\sqrt{73}}{6}, 2\right)\left(\dfrac{-7+\sqrt{73}}{6}, 2\right)$
   d $(\tfrac{1}{2}, \tfrac{1}{2}), (-2, 8)$
17 a $y = 2(x+4)(x-1)$ **b** $y = -2(x+1)^2 + 3$
   c $y = 2x^2 - 2x - 3$
18 2.16 m
19 a $m = \pm\sqrt{8} = \pm 2\sqrt{2}$ **b** $m \leq -\sqrt{5}$ or $m \geq \sqrt{5}$
20 a $x = 0$ and $x = -b$ **b** $\left(-\dfrac{b}{2}, -\dfrac{b^2}{4}\right)$
   c i $(0, 0), (1-b, 1-b)$ **ii** $b = 1$ **iii** $b \neq 1$

Multiple-choice questions

1 A   **2** C   **3** C   **4** E   **5** B
6 C   **7** E   **8** E   **9** D   **10** A
11 B **12** E **13** D

Extended-response questions

1 a $y = -0.0072x(x - 50)$
   b
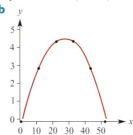
   c 10.57 m and 39.43 m $\left(25 \pm \dfrac{25\sqrt{3}}{3}\text{ m}\right)$
   d 3.2832 m   **e** 3.736 m (correct to 3 d.p.)
2 a Width of rectangle $= \dfrac{12 - 4x}{6}$ cm
   Length of rectangle $= \dfrac{12 - 4x}{3}$ cm
   b $A = \dfrac{17}{9}x^2 - \dfrac{16}{3}x + 8$
   c Length for square $= \dfrac{96}{17} \approx 5.65$ cm and
   length for rectangle $= \dfrac{108}{17} \approx 6.35$ cm
3 a $V = 0.72x^2 - 1.2x$ **b** 22 hours
4 a $V = 10\,800x + 120x^2$
   b $V = 46.6x^2 + 5000x$ **c** $\ell = 55.18$ m
5 a $\ell = 50 - \dfrac{5x}{2}$ **b** $A = 50x - \dfrac{5}{2}x^2$
   c
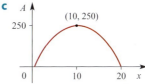
   d Maximum area $= 250$ m² when $x = 10$ m
6 $x = \dfrac{-1 + \sqrt{5}}{2}$

---

e 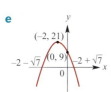   **f**

7 a $x = \dfrac{7}{2}$ **b** $x = -\dfrac{1}{2}$

c $x = \dfrac{5}{2}$ **d** $x = 5$

e $x = -\dfrac{1}{4}$ **f** $x = \dfrac{13}{12}$

g $x = 0$ **h** $x = 0$

8 $p = 1$ or $p = -\dfrac{3}{10}$
9 a $x < 0$ or $x > 1$
   b $-2 - \sqrt{34} \leq x \leq -2 + \sqrt{34}$
   c $-2 \leq x \leq \dfrac{1}{3}$ **d** $\dfrac{3}{2} \leq x \leq 5$
10 a $-3 + \sqrt{6}, -3 - \sqrt{6}$
   b $\dfrac{-9 + \sqrt{33}}{2}, \dfrac{-9 - \sqrt{33}}{2}$
   c $2 - \sqrt{2}, 2 + \sqrt{2}$
   d $\dfrac{-7 - \sqrt{33}}{4}, \dfrac{-7 + \sqrt{33}}{4}$
   e $\dfrac{-7 - \sqrt{17}}{4}, \dfrac{-7 + \sqrt{17}}{4}$
   f $\dfrac{-9 - \sqrt{93}}{6}, \dfrac{-9 + \sqrt{93}}{6}$
11 $y = \dfrac{5}{3}x(x - 5)$ **12** $y = 3(x-5)^2 + 2$
13 $m < -21 - 4\sqrt{29}$ or $m > -21 + 4\sqrt{29}$

7 a $\sqrt{25+x^2}$
  b i $16-x$ **ii** $\sqrt{x^2-32x+265}$
  c 7.5 **d** 10.840 **e** 12.615
8 a i $y = \sqrt{64t^2 + 100(t-0.5)^2}$
    $= \sqrt{164t^2 - 100t + 25}$
  ii

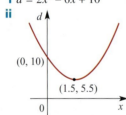

  iii $t = \dfrac{1}{2}$, 1:30 p.m.; $t = \dfrac{9}{82}$, 1:07 p.m.
  iv 0.305; 1:18 p.m.; distance 3.123 km
  b i $0, \dfrac{25}{41}$ **ii** $\dfrac{25 \pm 2\sqrt{269}}{82}$
9 b $2x + 2y = b$
  c $8x^2 - 4bx + b^2 - 16a^2 = 0$
  e i $x = 6 \pm \sqrt{14}, y = 6 \mp \sqrt{14}$
    ii $x = y = \sqrt{2}a$
  f $x = \dfrac{(5 \pm \sqrt{7})a}{4}, y = \dfrac{(5 \mp \sqrt{7})a}{4}$
10 a $b = -2, c = 4, h = 1$
  b i $(x, -6 + 4x - x^2)$ **ii** $(x, x-1)$
    iii $(0, -1), (1, 0), (2, 1), (3, 2), (4, 3)$
    iv $y = x - 1$
  c i $d = 2x^2 - 6x + 10$
    ii

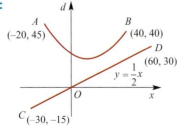

    iii Min value of $d = 5.5$ when $x = 1.5$
11 a $45\sqrt{5}$
  b i $y = \dfrac{1}{600}(7x^2 - 190x + 20\,400)$
    ii $\left(\dfrac{190}{14}, \dfrac{5351}{168}\right)$
  c

  d i The distance (measured parallel to the y-axis) between path and pond
    ii Minimum value $= \dfrac{473}{24}$ when $x = 35$

Chapter 4

Exercise 4A

1 a 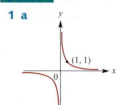 **b**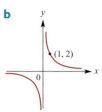

c 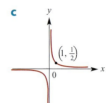 **d**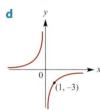

e 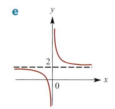 **f**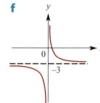

g 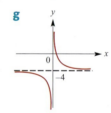 **h**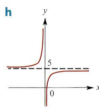

i 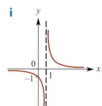 **j**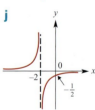

k 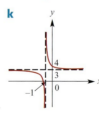 **l**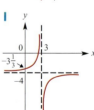

2 a $y = 0, x = 0$ **b** $y = 0, x = 0$
  c $y = 0, x = 0$ **d** $y = 0, x = 0$
  e $y = 2, x = 0$ **f** $y = -3, x = 0$
  g $y = -4, x = 0$ **h** $y = 5, x = 0$
  i $y = 0, x = 1$ **j** $y = 0, x = -2$
  k $y = 3, x = -1$ **l** $y = -4, x = 3$

3 a 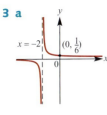 **b**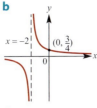

c 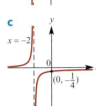 **d**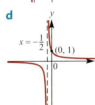

4 a 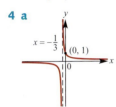 **b**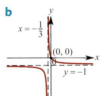

c 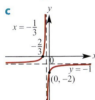 **d**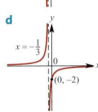

e x-axis intercept $-\frac{1}{2}$
y-axis intercept -6
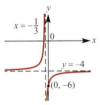

f x-axis intercept $-\frac{1}{9}$
y-axis intercept 1
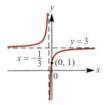

g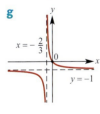

h x-axis intercept $-\frac{1}{3}$
y-axis intercept $-\frac{1}{4}$
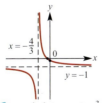

5 x-axis intercept -3
y-axis intercept -3
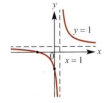

6 x-axis intercept $-\frac{3}{2}$
y-axis intercept 3

7 x-axis intercept $\frac{3}{2}$
y-axis intercept $-\frac{3}{2}$

Exercise 4B

1 a 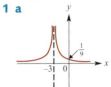 **b**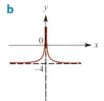

c 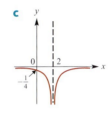 **d**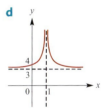

e 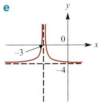 **f**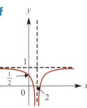

g 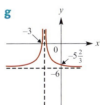 **h**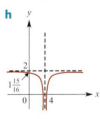

2 a $y = 0, x = -3$ **b** $y = -4, x = 0$
c $y = 0, x = 2$ **d** $y = 3, x = 1$
e $y = -4, x = -3$ **f** $y = 1, x = 2$
g $y = -6, x = -3$ **h** $y = 2, x = 4$

3 a **b**

c

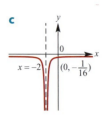

Exercise 4C

1 a $x \geq 0$ and $y \geq 3$ **b** $x \geq 2$ and $y \geq 3$

c $x \geq 2$ and $y \geq -3$ **d** $x \geq -2$ and $y \geq 1$

 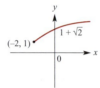

e $x \geq -2$ and $y \leq 3$ **f** $x \geq -2$ and $y \geq -3$

2 a $x \geq 2$ and $y \leq 3$ **b** $x \leq 4$ and $y \geq -2$

c $x \leq -4$ and $y \leq -1$ **d** $x \leq 3$ and $y \geq 0$

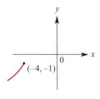

e $x \leq 3$ and $y \leq 0$ **f** $x \leq 3$ and $y \geq -4$

 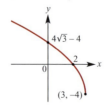

3 a $x \geq 0$ and $y \geq 0$ **b** $x \geq 1$ and $y \geq 0$

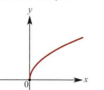 

c $x \geq 0$ and $y \leq 0$ **d** $x \leq 3$ and $y \geq 0$

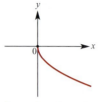 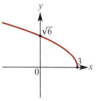

e $x \leq 2$ and $y \leq 0$ **f** $x \leq 3$ and $y \geq -4$

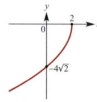 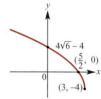

Exercise 4D

1 a $x^2 + y^2 = 9$ **b** $x^2 + y^2 = 16$
c $(x-1)^2 + (y-3)^2 = 25$
d $(x-2)^2 + (y+4)^2 = 9$
e $(x+3)^2 + (y-4)^2 = \dfrac{25}{4}$
f $(x+5)^2 + (y+6)^2 = (4.6)^2$

2 a $C(1, 3), r = 2$ **b** $C(2, -4), r = \sqrt{5}$
c $C(-3, 2), r = 3$ **d** $C(-5, 4), r = \sqrt{8}$

3 a **b**

 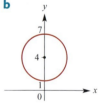

c **d**

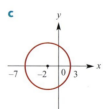 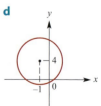

e **f**

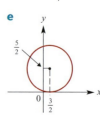 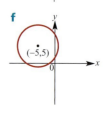

4 a $C(0, 3)$, $r = 5$ **b** $C(4, -6)$, $r = \sqrt{42}$
  c $C(3, -2)$, $r = 2$ **d** $C(-2, 3)$, $r = 5$
  e $C(4, -2)$, $r = \sqrt{19}$ **f** $C(\frac{1}{2}, -2)$, $r = \frac{3}{2}$

5 a 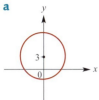 **b**

c

c 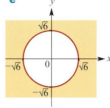 **d**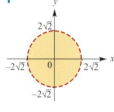

e   **f**

Exercise 4E

1 $a = 5$ **2** $a = -6$, $h = 3$, $k = 4$
3 $a = \dfrac{1}{2}$, $k = \dfrac{15}{2}$ **4** $a = -16$, $h = 2$, $k = -4$
5 $a = 4\sqrt{2}$ **6** $a = \dfrac{2\sqrt{3}}{3}$, $h = -2$
7 $(x - 2)^2 + (y - 1)^2 = 20$
8 $(x + 2)^2 + (y - 3)^2 = 1$
9 $(x + 2)^2 + (y - 3)^2 = 16$
10 $(x - 2)^2 + (y + 3)^2 = 9$
11 $(x - 4)^2 + (y - 4)^2 = 20$
12 $(x - 4)^2 + (y - 5)^2 = 25$ and $(x + 4)^2 + (y - 5)^2 = 25$
13 $(x + 1)^2 + (y + 1)^2 = 10$
14 a $(x - 2)^2 + (y + 2)^2 = 49$
  b $y = 3\sqrt{x - 1} - 2$ **c** $y = \dfrac{1}{x - 2} + 2$
  d $y = -\dfrac{2}{x - 1} - 2$ **e** $y = \sqrt{2 - x} + 1$
  f $y = \dfrac{1}{(x - 2)^2} - 3$

6 a   **b**

c   **d**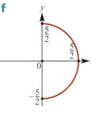

e   **f**

7 a   **b**

8 a   **b**

Chapter 4 review

Technology-free questions

1 a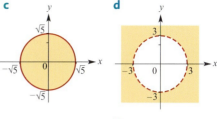

e   **f**

g 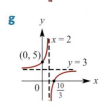   **h**

i   **j**

k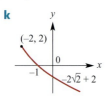

2 a $(x-3)^2 + (y+2)^2 = 25$
  b $\left(x - \frac{3}{2}\right)^2 + \left(y + \frac{5}{2}\right)^2 = \frac{50}{4}$
  c $\left(x - \frac{1}{4}\right)^2 + \left(y + \frac{1}{4}\right)^2 = \frac{17}{8}$
  d $(x+2)^2 + (y-3)^2 = 13$
  e $(x-3)^2 + (y-3)^2 = 18$
  f $(x-2)^2 + (y+3)^2 = 13$

3 $2y + 3x = 0$

4 $2x + 2y = 1$ or $y = x - \frac{5}{2}$

5 a $(x-3)^2 + (y-4)^2 = 25$

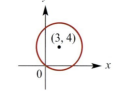

  b $(x+1)^2 + y^2 = 1$

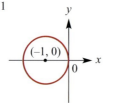

c $(x-4)^2 + (y-4)^2 = 4$

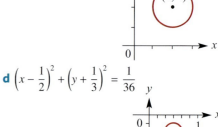

d $\left(x - \frac{1}{2}\right)^2 + \left(y + \frac{1}{3}\right)^2 = \frac{1}{36}$

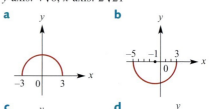

6 $C(-2, 3)$, $r = 6$

7 y-axis: $4\sqrt{6}$; x-axis: $2\sqrt{21}$

8 a   **b**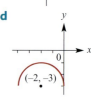

c   **d**

Multiple-choice questions

1 E **2** B **3** E **4** A **5** A
6 D **7** D **8** C **9** E **10** B

Extended-response questions

1 a $(x-10)^2 + y^2 = 25$ **c** $m = \pm\frac{\sqrt{3}}{3}$
  d $P\left(\frac{15}{2}, \frac{\pm 5\sqrt{3}}{2}\right)$ **e** $5\sqrt{3}$

2 a $x^2 + y^2 = 16$
  b ii $m = \pm\frac{\sqrt{3}}{3}$; $y = \frac{\sqrt{3}}{3}x - \frac{8\sqrt{3}}{3}$
  $y = -\frac{\sqrt{3}}{3}x + \frac{8\sqrt{3}}{3}$

3 a $\frac{4}{3}$ **b** $\frac{-3}{4}$ **c** $4y + 3x = 25$ **d** $\frac{125}{12}$

4 a i $\frac{y_1}{x_1}$ **ii** $\frac{-x_1}{y_1}$
  c $\sqrt{2}x + \sqrt{2}y = 8$ or $\sqrt{2}x + \sqrt{2}y = -8$

5 a $y = \dfrac{-\sqrt{3}}{3}x + \dfrac{2\sqrt{3}}{3}a,\ y = \dfrac{\sqrt{3}}{3}x - \dfrac{2\sqrt{3}}{3}a$
  b $x^2 + y^2 = 4a^2$
6 b ii

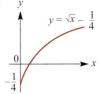

  c i $\dfrac{-1}{4} < k < 0$ **ii** $k = 0$ or $k < \dfrac{-1}{4}$
  iii $k > 0$
7 a $0 < k < \dfrac{1}{4}$ **b** $k = \dfrac{1}{4}$ or $k \le 0$

Chapter 5

Exercise 5A

1 a $\{7, 11\}$ **b** $\{7, 11\}$
  c $\{1, 2, 3, 5, 7, 11, 25, 30\}$
  d $\{1, 2, 3, 5, 7, 11, 15, 25, 30, 32\}$
  e $\{1, 2, 3, 5, 7, 11, 15, 25, 30, 32\}$
  f $\{1, 7, 11, 25, 30\}$
2 a $\{1, 2, 3, 5, 15\}$ **b** $\{25, 30, 32\}$
  c $\{2, 3, 5, 15\}$ **d** $\{25, 30\}$
3 a

  b

  c

  d

  e

  f

4 a $(-2, 1]$ **b** $[-3, 3]$ **c** $[-3, 2)$ **d** $(-1, 2)$
5 a $[-1, 2]$ **b** $(-4, 2]$ **c** $(0, \sqrt{2})$
  d $\left(-\dfrac{\sqrt{3}}{2}, \dfrac{1}{\sqrt{2}}\right]$ **e** $(-1, \infty)$ **f** $(-\infty, -2]$
  g $(-\infty, \infty)$ **h** $[0, \infty)$ **i** $(-\infty, 0]$
6 a $\{7\}$ **b** B, i.e. $\{7, 11, 25, 30, 32\}$
  c $(2, \infty)$ **d** $\{30, 32\}$
7 a

  b

c

  d

8 a $(-\infty, -2) \cup (-2, \infty)$ **b** $(-\infty, 3) \cup (3, \infty)$
  c $(-\infty, 4) \cup (4, \infty)$
9 a

  b

  c

  d

  e

  f

10 a $(-6, -3)$ **b** $\varnothing$ **c** $[-6, 0]$
  d $[-1, 2]$ **e** $\{1\}$ **f** $(-10, -1)$

Exercise 5B

1 a Domain $= \{-3, -1, -6, 1\}$;
  Range $= \{-4, -1, 7, 5\}$

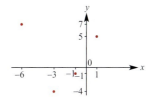

  b Domain $= \{-4, -6\}$; Range $= \{-1, 1, 7, 8\}$

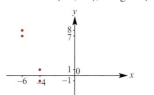

  c Domain $= [-2, 2]$ **d** Domain $= [0, \infty)$
  Range $= [-2, 2]$ Range $= (-\infty, 6]$

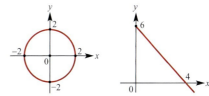

e Domain = $[-1, 2]$
Range = $[-5, -2]$
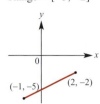

f Domain = $[-4, 1]$
Range = $[-5, 5]$
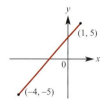

g Range = $[2, 14]$
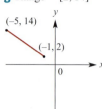

h Range = $(-11, 19)$
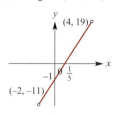

2 a Domain = $[-2, 2]$; Range = $[-1, 2]$
b Domain = $[-2, 2]$; Range = $[-2, 2]$
c Domain = $\mathbb{R}$; Range = $[-1, \infty)$
d Domain = $\mathbb{R}$; Range = $(-\infty, 4]$

3 a $y = (x + 3)^2 + 1$
Range = $[1, \infty)$

b $y = -(x + 2)^2 - 2$
Range = $(-\infty, -2]$

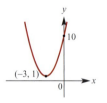

c $y = 2(x - 1)^2 + 4$
Range = $[4, \infty)$

5 a Range = $[3, 4]$

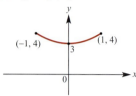

b Range = $[4, 8]$

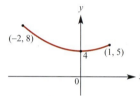

c Range = $[-4, 0]$

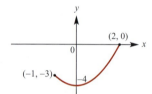

4 a Range = $[3, \infty)$

b Range = $(-\infty, -1]$

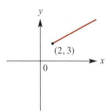
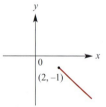

d Range = $[1, 19]$

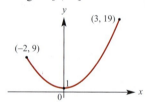

c Range = $[-7, \infty)$

d Range = $(-\infty, 11)$

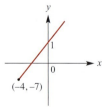
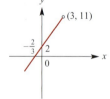

6 a Range = $[1, \infty)$ **b** Range = $[0, \infty)$

e Range = $(-\infty, 4]$ **f** Range = $[-19, 5]$

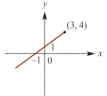
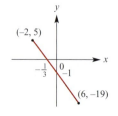

c Range = $[0, 4]$ **d** Range = $[2, \infty)$

e Range = $(-\infty, 4]$ **f** Range = $[-2, 2]$

 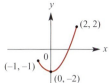

g Range = $\left[\dfrac{39}{8}, \infty\right)$ **h** Range = $\left[\dfrac{15}{4}, \infty\right)$

7 a Domain $-3 \leq x \leq 3$ **b** Domain $-2 \leq x \leq 6$
Range $-3 \leq y \leq 3$ Range $-1 \leq y \leq 7$

c Domain $0 \leq x \leq 1$ **d** Domain $-5 \leq x \leq 5$
Range $1\tfrac{1}{2} \leq y \leq 2\tfrac{1}{2}$ Range $0 \leq y \leq 5$

e Domain $-5 \leq x \leq 5$ **f** Domain $-3 \leq x \leq 7$
Range $-5 \leq y \leq 0$ Range $-5 \leq y \leq 0$

8 a Domain = $\mathbb{R} \setminus \left\{\dfrac{5}{2}\right\}$; Range = $\mathbb{R} \setminus \{3\}$

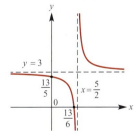

b Domain = $\left[\dfrac{5}{2}, \infty\right)$ **c** Domain = $\left(-\infty, \dfrac{5}{2}\right]$
Range = $\mathbb{R}^+ \cup \{0\}$ Range = $\mathbb{R}^+ \cup \{0\}$

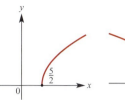 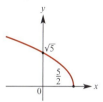

d Domain = $[3, 7]$; Range = $[0, 2]$

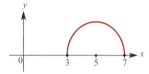

e Domain = $\mathbb{R} \setminus \left\{\dfrac{5}{2}\right\}$ **f** Domain = $(-\infty, 2]$
Range = $(0, \infty)$ Range = $\mathbb{R}^+ \cup \{0\}$

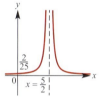 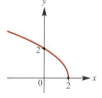

9 a Domain = $[0, \infty)$ **b** Domain = $[1, \infty)$
Range = $\mathbb{R}$ Range = $\mathbb{R}$

 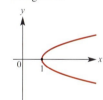

c Domain = $[-1, \infty)$ **d** Domain = $[1, \infty)$
Range = $\mathbb{R}$ Range = $\mathbb{R}$

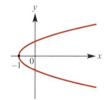

Exercise 5C

1 a Not a function; Domain = $\{0, 1, 2, 3\}$;
Range = $\{1, 2, 3, 4\}$
b A function; Domain = $\{-2, -1, 0, 1, 2\}$;
Range = $\{-5, -2, -1, 2, 4\}$
c Not a function; Domain = $\{-1, 0, 3, 5\}$;
Range = $\{1, 2, 4, 6\}$
d A function; Domain = $\{1, 2, 4, 5, 6\}$;
Range = $\{3\}$

2 a A function
Domain = [0, 4]
Range = [0, 16]

b Not a function
Domain = [0, 2]
Range = [−2, 2]

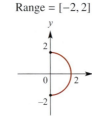

6 a 5, $2t + 1$ **b** $x = \dfrac{5}{2}$ **c** $x = -\dfrac{1}{2}$
d $t = -1$ **e** $x \geq -1$ **f** $x \geq 1$

7 a 1   **b** $\dfrac{1}{6}$ **c** ± 3 **d** $-1, 4$ **e** $-1, 3$ **f** $-2, 3$

8 a $g(-1) = -1$, $g(2) = 8$, $g(-2) = 0$
b $h(-1) = 3$, $h(2) = 18$, $h(-2) = -14$
c **i** $g(-3x) = 9x^2 - 6x$
ii $g(x - 5) = x^2 - 8x + 15$
iii $h(-2x) = -16x^3 - 4x^2 + 6$
iv $g(x + 2) = x^2 + 6x + 8$
v $h(x^2) = 2x^6 - x^4 + 6$

9 a $f(2) = 5$, $f(-4) = 29$ **b** Range = $[-3, \infty)$
10 a $f(2) = 7$ **b** $x = 2$ **c** $x = -1$
11 a 2   **b** ± 1 **c** $x = \pm\sqrt{3}$
12 a $x = -1$ **b** $x > -1$ **c** $x = -\dfrac{6}{7}$
13 a Range = $[0, 4]$ **b** Range = $[-1, 8]$

c A function
Domain = $[0, \infty)$
Range = $(-\infty, 2]$

d A function
Domain = $(0, \infty)$
Range = $(0, \infty)$

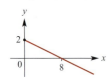

e A function
Domain = $\mathbb{R} \setminus \{0\}$
Range = $\mathbb{R}^+$

f A function
Domain = $\mathbb{R}^+$
Range = $\mathbb{R}^+$

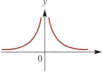

g A function
Domain = $[-1, 4]$
Range = $[0, 16]$

h Not a function
Domain = $[0, \infty)$
Range = $\mathbb{R}$

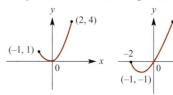

c Range = $\left[\dfrac{1}{3}, \infty\right)$ **d** Range = $[2, \infty)$

e Range = $[2, 18]$ **f** Range = $[0, 25]$

 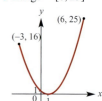

3 a $f: \mathbb{R} \to \mathbb{R}$, $f(x) = 3x + 2$
b $f: \mathbb{R} \to \mathbb{R}$, $f(x) = -\dfrac{3}{2}x + 6$
c $f: [0, \infty) \to \mathbb{R}$, $f(x) = 2x + 3$
d $f: [-1, 2] \to \mathbb{R}$, $f(x) = 5x + 6$
e $f: [-5, 5] \to \mathbb{R}$, $f(x) = -x^2 + 25$
f $f: [0, 1] \to \mathbb{R}$, $f(x) = 5x - 7$

4 a A function; Domain = $\mathbb{R}$; Range = $\{-2\}$
b Not a function; Domain = $\{3\}$; Range = $\mathbb{Z}$
c Function; Domain = $\mathbb{R}$; Range = $\mathbb{R}$
d A function; Domain = $\mathbb{R}$; Range = $[5, \infty)$
e Not a function; Domain = $[-3, 3]$;
Range = $[-3, 3]$

5 a i -3 **ii** 5   **iii** -5 **iv** 9
v $2x - 5$ **vi** $\dfrac{2}{a} - 3$
b i 4   **ii** -4 **iii** $\dfrac{4}{3}$ **iv** 2
c i 4   **ii** 36   **iii** 36   **iv** $(a - 2)^2$
d i 0   **ii** $\dfrac{a}{1+a}$ **iii** $\dfrac{-a}{1-a}$ **iv** $1 - a$

Exercise 5D

1 One-to-one functions: b, d, e, g
2 i Functions: a, c, d, f, g
ii One-to-one functions: c, g
3 a Domain = $\mathbb{R}$; Range = $\mathbb{R}$
b Domain = $\mathbb{R}^+ \cup \{0\}$; Range = $\mathbb{R}^+ \cup \{0\}$
c Domain = $\mathbb{R}$; Range = $[1, \infty)$
d Domain = $[-3, 3]$; Range = $[-3, 0]$
e Domain = $\mathbb{R}^+$; Range = $\mathbb{R}^+$
f Domain = $\mathbb{R}$; Range = $(-\infty, 3]$
g Domain = $[2, \infty)$; Range = $\mathbb{R}^+ \cup \{0\}$
h Domain = $[\tfrac{1}{2}, \infty)$; Range = $[0, \infty)$
i Domain = $(-\infty, \tfrac{3}{2}]$; Range = $[0, \infty)$
j Domain = $\mathbb{R} \setminus \{\tfrac{1}{2}\}$; Range = $\mathbb{R} \setminus \{0\}$

k Domain = $\mathbb{R} \setminus \{\frac{1}{2}\}$; Range = $(-3, \infty)$
l Domain = $\mathbb{R} \setminus \{\frac{1}{2}\}$; Range = $\mathbb{R} \setminus \{2\}$
4 a Domain = $[4, \infty)$; Range = $[0, \infty)$
  b Domain = $(-\infty, 4]$; Range = $[0, \infty)$
  c Domain = $[2, \infty)$; Range = $[3, \infty)$
  d Domain = $\mathbb{R} \setminus \{4\}$; Range = $\mathbb{R} \setminus \{0\}$
  e Domain = $\mathbb{R} \setminus \{4\}$; Range = $\mathbb{R} \setminus \{3\}$
  f Domain = $\mathbb{R} \setminus \{-2\}$; Range = $\mathbb{R} \setminus \{-3\}$
5 a Domain = $\mathbb{R}$; Range = $\mathbb{R}$
  b Domain = $\mathbb{R}$; Range = $[2, \infty)$
  c Domain = $[-4, 4]$; Range = $[-4, 0]$
  d Domain = $\mathbb{R} \setminus \{-2\}$; Range = $\mathbb{R} \setminus \{0\}$
6 $y = \sqrt{2-x}$, Domain $(-\infty, 2]$, Range $[0, \infty)$
   $y = -\sqrt{2-x}$, Domain $(-\infty, 2]$, Range $(-\infty, 0]$
7 a
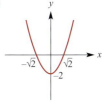
  b $f_1: [0, \infty) \to \mathbb{R}, f_1(x) = x^2 - 2$
     $f_2: (-\infty, 0] \to \mathbb{R}, f_2(x) = x^2 - 2$
8 a $f_1: [1, \infty) \to \mathbb{R}, f_1(x) = x^2 - 2x + 4$
     $f_2: (-\infty, 1] \to \mathbb{R}, f_2(x) = x^2 - 2x + 4$
9 a $f_1: (2, \infty) \to \mathbb{R}, f_1(x) = \dfrac{1}{(x-2)^2}$
     $f_2: (-\infty, 2) \to \mathbb{R}, f_2(x) = \dfrac{1}{(x-2)^2}$
10 a Domain = $[-2, 2]$
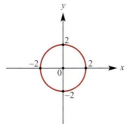
  b $f_1: [0, 2] \to \mathbb{R}, f_1(x) = \sqrt{4-x^2}$
     $f_2: [0, 2] \to \mathbb{R}, f_2(x) = -\sqrt{4-x^2}$
  c $f_1: [-2, 0] \to \mathbb{R}, f_1(x) = \sqrt{4-x^2}$
     $f_2: [-2, 0] \to \mathbb{R}, f_2(x) = -\sqrt{4-x^2}$

Exercise 5E

1 a Range = $[0, \infty)$ **b** Range = $[0, \infty)$
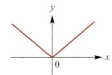 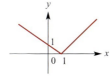

c Range = $(-\infty, 0]$ **d** Range = $[1, \infty)$
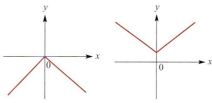

e Range = $[1, \infty)$
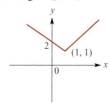

2 Range = $(-\infty, 4]$ **3**
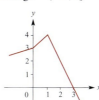

4 Range $[1, \infty)$ **5** Range = $\mathbb{R}$
 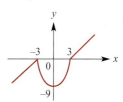

6 a Range = $(-\infty, 0) \cup (2, \infty)$
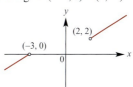

  b Range = $\mathbb{R} \setminus \{0\}$
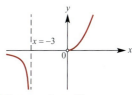

  c Range = $(-\infty, 5]$
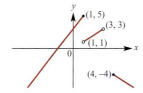

d Range = $\mathbb{R}\setminus[0,1]$

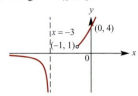

7 Range = $(-\infty, 1]$

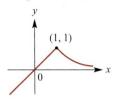

8 $f(x) = \begin{cases} x+3, & -3 \le x \le -1 \\ -x+1, & -1 < x \le 2 \\ -\frac{1}{2}x, & 2 \le x \le 4 \end{cases}$

Exercise 5F

1 b i 25.06 **ii** 25.032 **iii** 25.2 **iv** 26
2 a $a = -3, b = \frac{1}{2}$ **b** 6
3 $f(x) = 7 - 5x$
4 a i $f(0) = -\frac{9}{2}$ **ii** $f(1) = -3$ **b** 3
5 $f(x) = -7(x-2)(x-4)$
6 $f(x) = (x-3)^2 + 7$, Range = $[7, \infty)$
7 $a = \frac{1}{10}, b = -\frac{9}{10}, c = 2$
8 $f(x) = -2(x-1)(x+5)$
$g(x) = -50(x-1)\left(x+\frac{1}{5}\right)$
9 a $k < \frac{-37}{12}$ **b** $k = -\frac{25}{12}$

Exercise 5G

1 a $\{(3,1), (6,-2), (5,4), (1,7)\}$
Domain = $\{3, 6, 5, 1\}$; Range = $\{1, -2, 4, 7\}$
b $\{(3,2), (6,-1), (-5,4), (7,1), (-4,6)\}$
Domain = $\{3, 6, -5, 7, -4\}$
Range = $\{-1, 1, 2, 4, 6\}$
c $\{(3,3), (-4,-2), (-1,-1), (1,-8)\}$
Domain = $\{3, 1, -1, -4\}$
Range = $\{3, -2, -1, -8\}$
d $\{(3,1), (-7,-10), (-6,-7), (8,2), (4,11)\}$
Domain = $\{3, -7, -6, 8, 4\}$
Range = $\{1, -10, -7, 2, 11\}$
2 a $f^{-1}(x) = \frac{6-x}{2}$; Domain = $\mathbb{R}$; Range = $\mathbb{R}$
b $f^{-1}(x) = 3 - x$
Domain = $[-2, 2]$; Range = $[1, 5]$
c $f^{-1}(x) = x - 4$
Domain = $(4, \infty)$; Range = $\mathbb{R}^+$

d $f^{-1}(x) = x - 4$
Domain = $(-\infty, 8]$; Range = $(-\infty, 4]$
e $f^{-1}(x) = 8 - \frac{x}{2}$
Domain = $[2, 18]$; Range = $[-1, 7]$
3 a $f^{-1}(x) = \sqrt{x}$
Domain = $\mathbb{R}^+ \cup \{0\}$; Range = $\mathbb{R}^+ \cup \{0\}$
b $f^{-1}(x) = 2 + \sqrt{x-3}$
Domain = $[3, \infty)$; Range = $[2, \infty)$
c $f^{-1}(x) = 4 - \sqrt{x-6}$
Domain = $[6, \infty)$; Range = $(-\infty, 4]$
d $f^{-1}(x) = 1 - x^2$
Domain = $[0, 1]$; Range = $[0, 1]$
e $f^{-1}(x) = \sqrt{16 - x^2}$
Domain = $[0, 4]$; Range = $[0, 4]$
f $f^{-1}(x) = -4 + \sqrt{x-6}$
Domain = $[22, \infty)$; Range = $[0, \infty)$
4 a

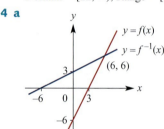

b $(6, 6)$
5 a

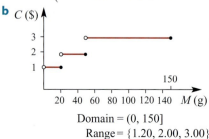

b $(0,0), (1,1)$
6 $a = \frac{-1}{2}, b = \frac{5}{2}$
7 a $f^{-1}(x) = a - x^2$ **b** $a = 1$ or $a = 2$

Exercise 5H

1 $C = 0.15n + 45$ where n is the number of calls
2 a $C(m) = \begin{cases} 1.20 & \text{for } 0 < m \le 20 \\ 2.00 & \text{for } 20 < m \le 50 \\ 3.00 & \text{for } 50 < m \le 150 \end{cases}$
b

Domain = $(0, 150]$
Range = $\{1.20, 2.00, 3.00\}$

3 a i $C_1 = 64 + 0.25x$ **ii** $C_2 = 89$
b
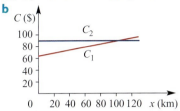
c $x > 100$ km
4 a Length = $(50 - x)$ cm
b $A(x) = x(50 - x)$ **c** $0 \leq x \leq 50$
d Maximum area = 625 cm^2 when $x = 25$
5 a i $A = (8 + x)y - x^2$
  ii $P = 2x + 2y + 16$
b i $A = 192 + 16x - 2x^2$ **ii** $0 < x < 12$
  iii
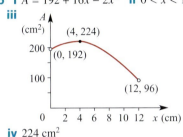
  iv 224 cm^2

Chapter 5 review

Technology-free questions

1 a $[-2, 4)$ **b** $[-2, 4]$ **c** $[1, 8)$ **d** $(-1, 6]$
  e $(-4, -2] \cup (1, 5]$ **f** $(-4, -2] \cup (2, \infty)$
  g $(-\infty, -3] \cup (1, \infty)$
2 a -16 **b** 26 **c** $-\frac{2}{3}$
3 a
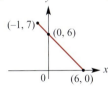
  b Range = $[0, 7]$
4 a Range = $\mathbb{R}$ **b** Range = $[-5, 4]$
  c Range = $[0, 4]$ **d** Range = $(-\infty, 9]$
  e Range = $[2, \infty)$ **f** Range = $\{-6, 2, 4\}$
  g Range = $[0, \infty)$ **h** Range = $\mathbb{R} \setminus \{2\}$
  i Range = $[-5, 1]$ **j** Range = $[-1, 3]$
5 a $a = -15$, $b = \dfrac{33}{2}$ **b** Domain = $\mathbb{R} \setminus \{0\}$
6 a

[Graph showing parabola with vertex $(1,1)$ and x-intercept $(2,0)$]

  b Range = $[0, 1]$
7 $a = 3$, $b = -5$

8 $a = -\frac{1}{2}$, $b = 2$, $c = 0$
9 a $\mathbb{R} \setminus \{2\}$ **b** $[2, \infty)$ **c** $[-5, 5]$ **d** $\mathbb{R} \setminus \{\frac{1}{2}\}$
  e $[-10, 10]$ **f** $(-\infty, 4]$
10 One-to-one functions: b, c, d, e, f, g, j
11 a   **b**
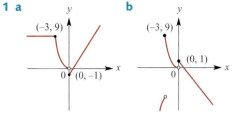

12 a Range = $[0, 4]$

[Graph with point $(3, 4)$]

  b Range = $[1, 10]$
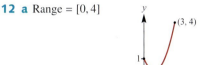

  c Range = $[\frac{1}{81}, 1]$

[Graph with points $(1, 1)$ and $(5, \frac{1}{81})$]

  d Range = $[-6, 3]$
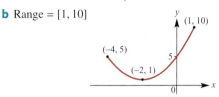

13 a Domain = $[1, \infty)$; Range = $[0, \infty)$
  b Domain = $(-\infty, 1]$; Range = $[0, \infty)$
  c Domain = $[0, \infty)$; Range = $(-\infty, 1]$
14 a Domain = $\mathbb{R} \setminus \{1\}$; Range = $\mathbb{R} \setminus \{0\}$
  b Domain = $\mathbb{R} \setminus \{-1\}$; Range = $\mathbb{R} \setminus \{0\}$
  c Domain = $\mathbb{R} \setminus \{1\}$; Range = $\mathbb{R} \setminus \{3\}$
15 a Domain = $[-1, 1]$; Range = $[0, 1]$
  b Domain = $[-3, 3]$; Range = $[0, 3]$
  c Domain = $[-1, 1]$; Range = $[3, 4]$
16 a $f^{-1}(x) = \dfrac{x+2}{3}$; Domain = $[-5, 13]$
  b $f^{-1}(x) = (x-2)^2 - 2$; Domain = $[2, \infty)$
  c $f^{-1}(x) = \sqrt{\dfrac{x}{3}} - 1$; Domain = $[0, \infty)$
  d $f^{-1}(x) = -\sqrt{x} + 1$; Domain = $(0, \infty)$
17 a $2p + 5$ **b** $2(p + h) + 5$ **c** $2h$ **d** 2
18 -2

19 a $\left(-\infty, -\frac{15}{8}\right]$ **b** $\left[3\frac{7}{8}, \infty\right)$
c $(-\infty, 20]$ **d** $(-\infty, 3]$

20 a
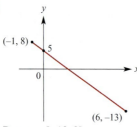
b Range $= [-13, 8]$

21 a
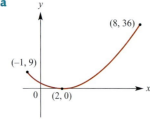
b Range $= [0, 36]$

22 a Domain $-3 \le x \le 3$; Range $-3 \le y \le 3$
b Domain $1 \le x \le 3$; Range $-1 \le y \le 1$
c Domain $0 \le x \le 1$; Range $0 \le y \le 1$
d Domain $-1 \le x \le 9$; Range $-5 \le y \le 5$
e Domain $-4 \le x \le 4$; Range $-2 \le y \le 6$

23 a $\{2, 4, 6, 8\}$ **b** $\{4, 3, 2, 1\}$
c $\{-3, 0, 5, 12\}$ **d** $\{1, \sqrt{2}, \sqrt{3}, 2\}$

Multiple-choice questions
1 B **2** E **3** D **4** B **5** E **6** C
7 E **8** B **9** D **10** C **11** D

Extended-response questions
1 a
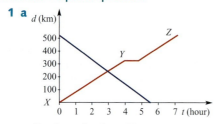

Coach starting from X:
$$d = \begin{cases} 80t & \text{for } 0 \le t \le 4 \\ 320 & \text{for } 4 < t \le 4\frac{3}{4} \\ 80t - 60 & \text{for } 4\frac{3}{4} < t \le 7\frac{1}{4} \end{cases}$$
Range $= [0, 520]$

Coach starting from Z:
$$d = 520 - \frac{1040t}{11} \text{ for } 0 \le t \le 5\frac{1}{2}$$
Range $= [0, 520]$

b The coaches pass $238\frac{1}{3}$ km from X

2 a $P = \frac{1}{2}n$
b
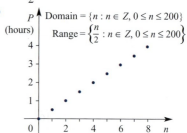
Domain $= \{n : n \in Z, 0 \le n \le 200\}$
Range $= \{\frac{n}{2} : n \in Z, 0 \le n \le 200\}$

3 a i $C(n) = 1000 + 5n, n > 0$
ii
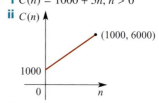

b i $P(n) = 15n - (1000 + 5n)$
$= 10n - 1000$
ii
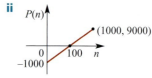

4 $V = 8000(1 - 0.05n) = 8000 - 400n$

5 a $R = (50000 - 2500x)(15 + x)$
$= 2500(x + 15)(20 - x)$
b
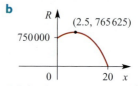
c Price for max revenue $= \$17.50$

6 a $A(x) = \frac{x}{4}(2a - (6 - \sqrt{3})x)$ **b** $0 < x < \frac{a}{3}$

7 a i $d(x) = \sqrt{x^2 + 25} + \sqrt{(16 - x)^2 + 9}$
ii $0 \le x \le 16$

b i
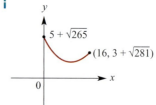
ii 1.54
iii 3.40 or 15.04

c i Minimum is $8\sqrt{5}$, occurs when $x = 10$
ii Range $= [8\sqrt{5}, 5 + \sqrt{265}]$

8 a $A\left(\dfrac{3+\sqrt{33}}{2}, 3+\sqrt{33}\right)$, $B\left(\dfrac{3-\sqrt{33}}{2}, 3-\sqrt{33}\right)$

 b i $d(x) = -x^2 + 3x + 6$
  ii

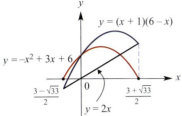

 c i Maximum value of $d(x)$ is 8.25
  ii Range $= [0, 8.25]$
 d $A(2.45, 12.25)$, $B(-2.45, -12.25)$
  $d(x) = -x^2 + 6$
  Maximum value of $d(x)$ is 6; Range $= [0, 6]$

Chapter 6

Exercise 6A

1 a -3 **b** -1 **c** -7 **d** -15
2 a 0 **b** 0
3 a 6 **b** 9 **c** 26 **d** 11
 e $a^3 + 4a^2 - 2a + 6$ **f** $8a^3 + 16a^2 - 4a + 6$
4 a $a = 4$ **b** $a = 4$ **c** $c = 6$
 d $a = -33, b = -15$ **e** $a = -9, b = 23$
5 a $x^3 - 2x^2 - 2x + 2$ **b** $x^3 - x^2 + 2x$
 c $x^3 - 2x^2 + 4x - 2$ **d** $3x^3 - 6x^2 + 3x$
 e $-3x^4 + 8x^3 - 7x^2 + 2x$
 f $-3x^3 - x^2 + 2x$ **g** $x^3 - x^2 - x + 2$
 h $x^5 - x^4 - x^3 + x^2$
6 a $x^3 - 4x^2 + 7x - 6$ **b** $x^3 - 6x^2 + 11x - 12$
 c $2x^3 - 5x^2 - x + 4$
 d $x^3 + (b-2)x^2 + (c-2b)x - 2c$
 e $2x^3 - 7x^2 - 10x - 3$
7 a $x^3 + (b+1)x^2 + (c+b)x + c$
 b $b = -8, c = 12$ **c** $(x+1)(x-6)(x-2)$
8 $b = -3, c = -11$
9 a $a^5 + 5a^4b + 10a^3b^2 + 10a^2b^3 + 5ab^4 + b^5$
 b $a^6 + 6a^5b + 15a^4b^2 + 20a^3b^3 + 15a^2b^4 + 6ab^5 + b^6$
10 a $(x - y)^4 = x^4 - 4x^3y + 6x^2y^2 - 4xy^3 + y^4$
 b $(2x + y)^4 = 16x^4 + 32x^3y + 24x^2y^2 + 8xy^3 + y^4$

Exercise 6B

1 a $x^2 + 2x + \dfrac{3}{x-1}$ **b** $2x^2 - x - 3 + \dfrac{6}{x+1}$
 c $3x^2 - 10x + 22 - \dfrac{43}{x+2}$
 d $2x^2 + 3x + 10 + \dfrac{28}{x-3}$
2 a $x^2 - x + 4 - \dfrac{8}{x+1}$
 b $2x^2 - 8x + 49 - \dfrac{181}{x+4}$
 c $x^2 + x - 3 + \dfrac{11}{x+3}$ **d** $x^2 - x + 4 + \dfrac{8}{x-2}$
3 a $x^2 - 2x + 5$ **b** $2x^2 - 2x - 6$
 c $x^2 - 2x - 6$ **d** $3x^2 - x - 6$
4 a Quotient $x^2 - 3$; Remainder 7
 b Quotient $x^2 + 2x + 15$; Remainder 71
 c Quotient $2x^2 - 3x$; Remainder -7
 d Quotient $5x^2 + 20x + 77$; Remainder 315
5 a $\dfrac{1}{2}x^2 + \dfrac{7}{4}x - \dfrac{3}{8} + \dfrac{103}{8(2x+5)}$
 b $x^2 + 2x - 3 - \dfrac{2}{2x+1}$ **c** $x^2 + 2x - 15$
 d $\dfrac{1}{3}x^2 - \dfrac{8}{9}x - \dfrac{8}{27} + \dfrac{19}{27(3x-1)}$
6 a $x^2 + 3x + 8 + \dfrac{9}{x-1}$
 b $x^2 - \dfrac{x}{2} + \dfrac{9}{4} + \dfrac{21}{4(2x-1)}$
7 a Quotient $2x - 6$; Remainder 0
 b Quotient $x - 6$; Remainder -2
 c Quotient $2x - 6$; Remainder 42
 d Quotient $x^2 - 4x + 2$; Remainder $-x + 7$
 e Quotient $x^2 - 3x + 7$; Remainder $-10x + 9$
 f Quotient $x^2 + x - \dfrac{3}{2}$; Remainder $\dfrac{15}{2}x + 16$

Exercise 6C

1 a -2 **b** -29 **c** 15 **d** 4 **e** 7
 f -12 **g** 0 **h** -5 **i** -8
2 a $a = -3$ **b** $a = 2$ **c** $a = 4$ **d** $a = -10$
3 a $P(1) = 0$ **b** $P(1) = 0$
 c $P(-2) = 0$ **d** $P(\tfrac{3}{2}) = 0$
4 a 6 **b** 28 **c** $-\dfrac{1}{3}$
5 a $(x-1)(x+1)(2x+1)$ **b** $(x+1)^3$
 c $(x-1)(6x^2 - 7x + 6)$
 d $(x-1)(x+5)(x-4)$
 e $(x+1)^2(2x-1)$ **f** $(x+1)(x-1)^2$
 g $(x-2)(4x^2 + 8x + 19)$
 h $(x+2)(2x+1)(2x-3)$
6 1
7 a $(2x-3)(x^2 - 2x + 5)$
 b $(2x+1)(x^2 - 2x + 5)$
 c $(2x+1)(x - 1 - \sqrt{6})(x - 1 + \sqrt{6})$
 d $(2x+3)(x - 1 - \sqrt{2})(x - 1 + \sqrt{2})$
8 a $(x-1)(x^2 + x + 1)$
 b $(x+4)(x^2 - 4x + 16)$
 c $(3x-1)(9x^2 + 3x + 1)$
 d $(4x-5)(16x^2 + 20x + 25)$
 e $(1 - 5x)(1 + 5x + 25x^2)$
 f $(3x+2)(9x^2 - 6x + 4)$
 g $(4m - 3n)(16m^2 + 12mn + 9n^2)$
 h $(3b + 2a)(9b^2 - 6ab + 4a^2)$

9 a $(x+2)(x^2-x+1)$
   b $(3x+2)(x-1)(x-2)$
   c $(x-3)(x+1)(x-2)$
   d $(3x+1)(x+3)(2x-1)$
10 $a=3, b=-3, P(x)=(x-1)(x+3)(x+1)$
11 b i n odd   ii n even
12 a $a=1, b=1$
   b i $P(x)=x^3-2x^2+3$

Exercise 6D

1 a $1, -2, 4$ b $4, 6$ c $\frac{1}{2}, 3, -\frac{2}{3}$ d $0, -3, \frac{5}{2}$

2 a $-2, 0, 4$ b $0, -1 \pm 2\sqrt{3}$ c $-5, 0, 8$
   d $0, -1 \pm \sqrt{17}$

3 a 1 b -1 c $5, \pm\sqrt{10}$ d $\pm 4, a$

4 a $2, 3, -5$ b $-1, -\frac{2}{3}, 3$ c $1, -\sqrt{2}, \sqrt{2}$
   d $-\frac{2}{5}, -4, 2$ e $-\frac{1}{2}, \frac{1}{3}, 1$ f $-2, -\frac{3}{2}, 5$

5 a $-6, 2, 3$ b $-2, -\frac{2}{3}, \frac{1}{2}$ c 3
   d -1 e $-1, 3$ f $3, -2 \pm \sqrt{3}$

6 a $0, \pm 2\sqrt{2}$ b $1 + 2\sqrt[3]{2}$ c -2
   d -5 e $\frac{1}{10}$

7 a $2(x-9)(x-13)(x+11)$
   b $(x+11)(x+3)(2x-1)$
   c $(x+11)(2x-9)(x-11)$
   d $(2x-1)(x+11)(x+15)$

Exercise 6E

1 a
  b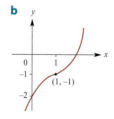
  c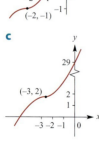
  d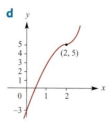
  e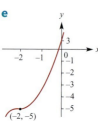

2 a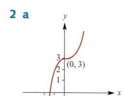
  b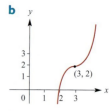
  c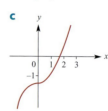
  d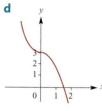
  e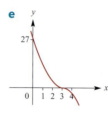
  f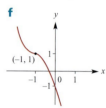
  g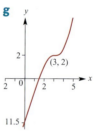

3 a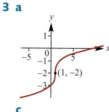
  b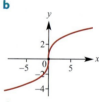
  c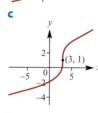
  d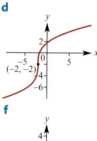
  e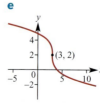
  f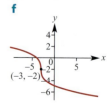

4 a $f^{-1}(x) = \left(\dfrac{x-3}{2}\right)^{\frac{1}{3}}$ **b** $f^{-1}(x) = \dfrac{x^3}{27}$

c $f^{-1}(x) = \left(\dfrac{x-1}{2}\right)^{\frac{1}{3}} - 1$

d $f^{-1}(x) = \dfrac{(x+2)^3}{8} - 3$

e $f^{-1}(x) = 1 - \dfrac{(x-4)^3}{8}$

f $f^{-1}(x) = -\dfrac{(x+1)^3}{8} - 2$

Exercise 6F

1 a 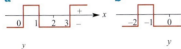   **b**

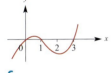 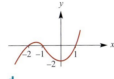

c 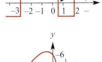   **d**

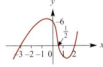 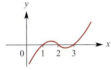

2 a 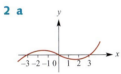   **b**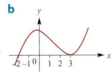

c 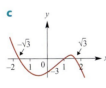   **d**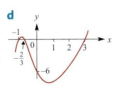

e 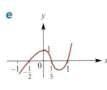   **f**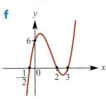

3 a 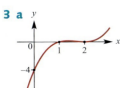   **b**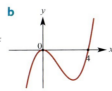

4 a 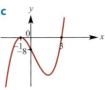   **b**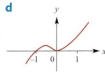

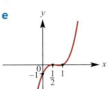 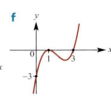

5 a 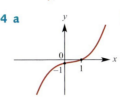   **b**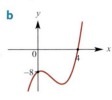

c 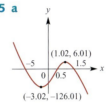   **d**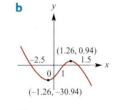

e 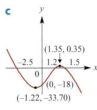   **f**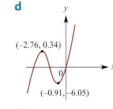

6 $f(x) = (x+1)^2(x-3)$, so graph just touches the x-axis at $x = -1$ and cuts it at $x = 3$

Exercise 6G

1 a $(-\infty, -2] \cup [1, 3]$ **b** $[-2, -1] \cup [4, \infty)$
c $(-\infty, 1)$ **d** $(-2, 0) \cup (3, \infty)$
e $(-\infty, -1]$ **f** $[1, \infty)$
g $(4, \infty)$ **h** $(-\infty, -3]$

2 a $(-2, 0) \cup (2, \infty)$ **b** $(-\infty, 0) \cup (0, 5)$
c $(-\infty, 0] \cup \{2\}$ **d** $(-3, 0) \cup (3, \infty)$
e $[6, \infty)$ **f** $(-\infty, -\sqrt{2}) \cup (\sqrt{2}, 3)$

Exercise 6H

1 a $a = 11$ **b** $a = 2$ **c** $a = \dfrac{4}{3}, b = \dfrac{44}{3}$

2 a $y = -\frac{1}{8}(x+2)^3$ b $y - 2 = -\frac{1}{4}(x-3)^3$
3 $y = 2x(x-2)^2$ **4** $y = -2x(x+4)^2$
5 $y = -2(x-1)(x-3)(x+1)$ **6** a $= 36$
7 a $y = (x-3)^3 + 2$ b $y = \frac{23}{18}x^3 + \frac{67}{18}x^2$
  c $y = 5x^3$
8 a $y = -\frac{1}{3}x^3 + \frac{4}{3}x$ b $y = \frac{1}{4}x(x^2 + 2)$
9 a $y = -4x^3 - 50x^2 + 96x + 270$
  b $y = 4x^3 - 60x^2 + 80x + 26$
  c $y = x^3 - 2x^2 + 6x - 4$
  d $y = 2x^3 - 3x$
  e $y = 2x^3 - 3x^2 - 2x + 1$
  f $y = x^3 - 3x^2 - 2x + 1$
  g $y = -x^3 - 3x^2 - 2x + 1$

Exercise 6I

1 a, b
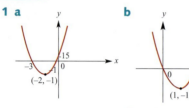

c, d
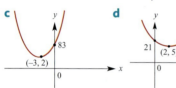

e
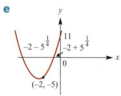

2 a, b, c, d, e, f
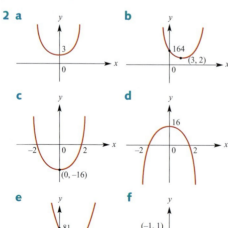

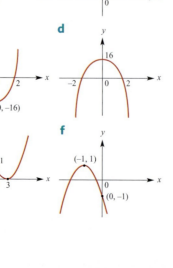

3 a $x = 0$ or $x = 3$
  b $x = 2$ or $x = -1$ or $x = 5$ or $x = -3$
  c $x = 0$ or $x = -2$ d $x = 0$ or $x = 6$
  e $x = 0$ or $x = 3$ or $x = -3$
  f $x = 3$ or $x = -3$
  g $x = 0$ or $x = 4$ or $x = -4$
  h $x = 0$ or $x = 4$ or $x = 3$
  i $x = 0$ or $x = 4$ or $x = 5$
  j $x = 2$ or $x = -2$ or $x = 3$ or $x = -3$
  k $x = 4$ l $x = -4$ or $x = 2$

4 a, b
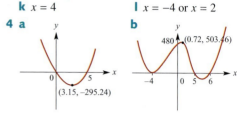

c, d
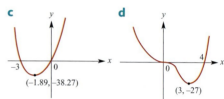

e, f
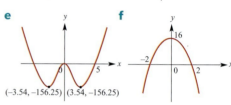

g, h
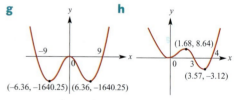

i, j, k, l
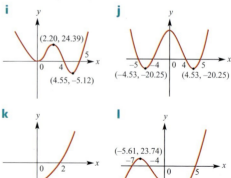

5
a Even   b Odd   c Even   d Odd

6 a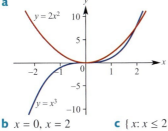
b $x = 0, x = 2$ **c** $\{x: x \le 2\}$

7 a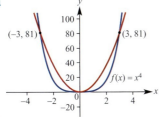
b $x = 0, x = 3, x = -3$
c $\{x : -3 \le x \le 3\}$

8 a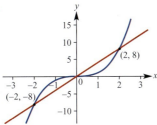
b $x = 0, x = 2, x = -2$
c $\{x : x \le -2\} \cup \{x : 0 \le x \le 2\}$

Exercise 6J

1 a Length of each edge $= 20 - 2x$
b $V(x) = 4x(10 - x)^2$
c $V(5) = 500$; Volume of box $= 500$ cm^3
d $x = 5$ or $x = \dfrac{5}{2}(3 - \sqrt{5})$

2 a $\ell = 12 - 2x$, $w = 10 - 2x$
b $V = 4x(6 - x)(5 - x)$
c

(graph of V (cm³) vs x (cm), peaking near 100 around x=2)

d $V = 80$ **e** $x = 3.56$ or $x = 0.51$
f $V_{\max} = 96.8$ cm^3 when $x = 1.81$

3 a Surface area $= x^2 + 4xh$
b $h = \dfrac{75 - x^2}{4x}$ **c** $V = \dfrac{1}{4}(75x - x^3)$
d i $\dfrac{71}{2}$ **ii** $\dfrac{125}{2}$ **iii** 22
e $x = -2 + 3\sqrt{7}$

4 a $h = 60 - 20x$ **b** $V = 600x^2(3 - x)$
c 0 **d** $x = 1$ or $x = 1 + \sqrt{3}$

5 a $x = \sqrt{64 - h^2}$ **b** $V = \dfrac{\pi h}{3}(64 - h^2)$
c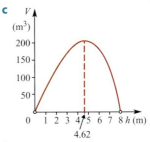

d Domain $= \{h : 0 < h < 8\}$ **e** 64π
f $h = 2.48$ or $h = 6.47$
g $V_{\max} \approx 206.37$ m^3 when $h = 4.62$

6 a $h = 160 - 2x$ **b** $V = x^2(160 - 2x)$
c Domain $= (0, 80)$
d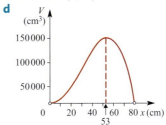

e $x = 20.498$ or $x = 75.63$
f $V_{\max} \approx 151\,703.7$ cm^3 when $x \approx 53$

Exercise 6K

1 a 1.32 **b** 1.164 **c** 1.124 or 1.451
d 2.151 **e** -1.75

Chapter 6 review

Technology-free questions

1 a (graph with $\sqrt[3]{2}+1$, $(0,-3)$, $(1,-2)$)

b

c (graph with $\sqrt[3]{\frac{1}{3}}+1$, $(0,-4)$, $(1,-1)$)

d

e (graph with $(-1,4)$, $(0,1)$, $\sqrt[3]{\frac{1}{3}}$)

f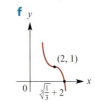

g 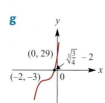 **h**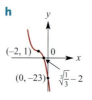

7 a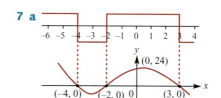

2 a 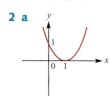 **b**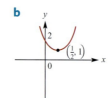

b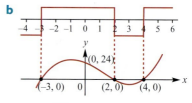

c **d**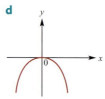

c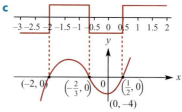

e 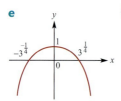 **f**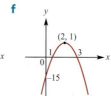

d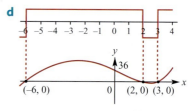

g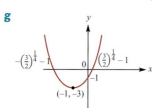

8 a -41 **b** 12 **c** $\dfrac{43}{9}$

9 $y = -\dfrac{2}{5}(x+2)(x-1)(x-5)$

10 $y = \dfrac{2}{81}x(x+4)^2$

11 a $a = 3, b = 8$ **b** $(x+3)(2x-1)(x-1)$

12 a $(\infty, -4] \cup \{3\}$ **b** $(-\infty, -4] \cup [-3, 2]$
 c $(-\infty, -1) \cup (2, 3)$

h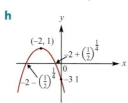

13 a Dilation of factor 2 from the x-axis, then translation of 1 unit in the positive direction of the x-axis and 3 units in the positive direction of the y-axis

b Reflection in the x-axis, then translation of 1 unit in the negative direction of the x-axis and 2 units in the positive direction of the y-axis

c Dilation of factor $\tfrac{1}{2}$ from the y-axis, then translation of $\tfrac{1}{2}$ unit in the negative direction of the x-axis and 2 units in the negative direction of the y-axis

3 a $x = 2, x = -\dfrac{1}{2}, x = -3$

 b $x = 2, x = \dfrac{\sqrt{17}+1}{4}, x = \dfrac{1-\sqrt{17}}{4}$

 c $x = -1, x = 2, x = 6$

4 a $P\left(\dfrac{3}{2}\right) = 0$ and $P(-2) = 0$; $(3x+1)$

 b $x = -2, \dfrac{1}{2}, 3$

 c $x = -1, -\sqrt{11}, +\sqrt{11}$

 d i $P\left(\dfrac{1}{3}\right) = 0$ **ii** $(3x-1)(x+3)(x-2)$

5 a $f(1) = 0$ **b** $(x-1)(x^2 + (1-k)x + k + 1)$

6 $a = 3, b = -24$

Multiple-choice questions

| 1 B | 2 D | 3 A | 4 D | 5 A |
| 6 C | 7 B | 8 B | 9 D | 10 B |

Extended-response questions

1 a $V = \pi r^2(6 - r)$ **b** $0 \leq r \leq 6$
  c $V(3) = 27\pi$ **d** $r = 3$ or $r = \dfrac{3}{2}(1 + \sqrt{5})$
  e Maximum ≈ 100.53 (correct to 2 d.p.)

2 a $v = \dfrac{1}{32\,400}(t - 900)^2$
  b $s = \dfrac{t}{32\,400}(t - 900)^2$
  c

  s (cm), Domain = $\{t : 0 < t < 900\}$
  (300, 3333.3)
  3000
  2000
  1000
  0 200 400 600 800 t (s)
     105   560

  d No, it is not feasible as the maximum range of the taxi is less than 3.5 km (≈ 3.33 km)
  e Maximum speed $\approx \dfrac{2000}{105} = 19$ m/s
   Minimum speed $\approx \dfrac{2000}{560} = 3.6$ m/s

3 a $R = a(x - 5)^3 + 10$ **b** $a = \dfrac{2}{25}$
  c $R = \dfrac{12}{343}(x - 7)^3 + 12$

4 a 4730 cm^3
  b $V = \ell^2(\sqrt{2365} - \ell)$
  c

  V (cm^3)
  20 000
  15 000
  10 000
  5 000
  0 10 20 30 40 50 l (cm)

  d i $\ell = 23.69$ or $\ell = 39.79$
    ii $\ell = 18.1$ or $\ell = 43.3$
  e $V_{\max} \approx 17\,039$ cm^3 when $\ell \approx 32.42$ cm

5 a $a = \dfrac{-43}{15\,000}$, $b = 0.095$, $c = \dfrac{-119}{150}$, $d = 15.8$
  b i $(5.59, 13.83)$ **ii** $(0, 15.8)$

6 a $V = (96 - 4x)(48 - 2x)x = 8x(24 - x)^2$
  b

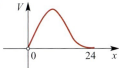

  i $0 < x < 24$
  ii $V_{\max} = 16\,384$ cm^3 when $x = 8.00$
  c 15 680 cm^3 **d** 14 440 cm^3 **e** 9720 cm^3

Chapter 7

Exercise 7A

1 a $(-1, 1)$ **b** $(-5, 8)$ **c** $(-6, 2)$ **d** $(-7, 9)$
  e $(-5, 3)$

2 a $g(x) = \dfrac{1}{x - 2} - 1$ **b** $g(x) = \dfrac{1}{(x - 4)^2} + 3$
  c $g(x) = (x + 2)^2 - 3$ **d** $g(x) = (x - 4)^2 - 2$
  e $g(x) = \sqrt{x - 2} - 1$

3 a 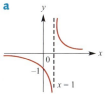   **b**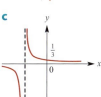

  c 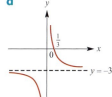   **d**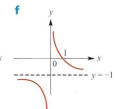

  e 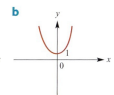   **f**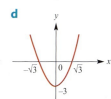

4 a 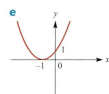   **b**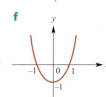

  c

  y
  9
  -3 0 x

  d

  y
  $-\sqrt{3}$ 0 $\sqrt{3}$ x
  -3

  e

  y
  1
  -1 0 x

  f

  y
  -1 0 1 x
  -1

5 a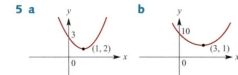
b
c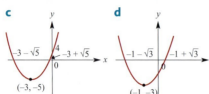
d
e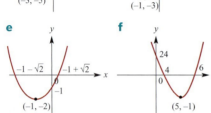
f

Exercise 7B

1 a $(-2, 3)$ **b** $(2, -3)$ **c** $(-2, -12)$ **d** $(-8, -3)$

2 a i $y = 4x^2$ **ii** $y = \dfrac{x^2}{25}$ **iii** $y = \dfrac{2x^2}{3}$
   iv $y = 4x^2$ **v** $y = -x^2$ **vi** $y = x^2$

b i $y = \dfrac{1}{4x^2}$ **ii** $y = \dfrac{25}{x^2}$ **iii** $y = \dfrac{2}{3x^2}$
   iv $y = \dfrac{4}{x^2}$ **v** $y = \dfrac{-1}{x^2}$ **vi** $y = \dfrac{1}{x^2}$

c i $y = \dfrac{1}{2x}$ **ii** $y = \dfrac{5}{x}$ **iii** $y = \dfrac{2}{3x}$
   iv $y = \dfrac{4}{x}$ **v** $y = \dfrac{-1}{x}$ **vi** $y = \dfrac{-1}{x}$

d i $y = \sqrt{2x}$ **ii** $y = \sqrt{\dfrac{x}{5}}$
   iii $y = \dfrac{2\sqrt{x}}{3}$ **iv** $y = 4\sqrt{x}$
   v $y = -\sqrt{x}$ **vi** $y = \sqrt{-x},\ x \le 0$

3 a
b
c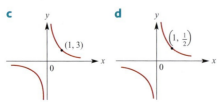
d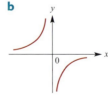

Exercise 7C

1 a $y = 3\sqrt{x - 2}$ **b** $y = -\sqrt{x + 3}$
  c $y = -3\sqrt{x}$ **d** $y = -\sqrt{\dfrac{x}{2}}$
  e $y = 2\sqrt{x - 2} - 3$ **f** $y = \sqrt{\dfrac{x + 2}{2}} - 3$

2 a $y = \dfrac{3}{x - 2}$ **b** $y = \dfrac{-1}{x + 3}$
  c $y = -\dfrac{3}{x}$ **d** $y = -\dfrac{2}{x}$
  e $y = \dfrac{2}{x - 2} - 3$ **f** $y = \dfrac{2}{x + 2} - 3$

3 a $y = 3(x - 2)^{\frac{1}{3}}$ **b** $y = -(x + 3)^{\frac{1}{3}}$
  c $y = -3x^{\frac{1}{3}}$ **d** $y = -\left(\dfrac{x}{2}\right)^{\frac{1}{3}}$
  e $y = 2(x - 2)^{\frac{1}{3}} - 3$ **f** $y = \left(\dfrac{x + 2}{2}\right)^{\frac{1}{3}} - 3$

Exercise 7D

1 a i A dilation of factor 2 from the x-axis, then a translation of 1 unit in the positive direction of the x-axis and 3 units in the positive direction of the y-axis
   ii A reflection in the x-axis, then a translation of 1 unit in the negative direction of the x-axis and 2 units in the positive direction of the y-axis
   iii A dilation of factor $\tfrac{1}{2}$ from the y-axis, then a translation of $\tfrac{1}{2}$ unit in the negative direction of the x-axis and 2 units in the negative direction of the y-axis

b i A dilation of factor 2 from the x-axis, then a translation of 3 units in the negative direction of the x-axis
   ii A translation of 3 units in the negative direction of the x-axis and 2 units in the positive direction of the y-axis
   iii A translation of 3 units in the positive direction of the x-axis and 2 units in the negative direction of the y-axis

c i A translation of 3 units in the negative direction of the x-axis and 2 units in the positive direction of the y-axis
   ii A dilation of factor $\tfrac{1}{3}$ from the y-axis, then a dilation of factor 2 from the x-axis

iii A reflection in the x-axis, then a translation of 2 units in the positive direction of the y-axis

2 a $(x, y) \to \left(x - 3, \dfrac{y + 7}{5}\right)$

b $(x, y) \to (3x + 2, y - 5)$

c $(x, y) \to \left(3x + 1, -\dfrac{y - 7}{3}\right)$

d $(x, y) \to \left(-(x - 4), \dfrac{y}{2}\right)$

e $(x, y) \to \left(-(x - 4), \dfrac{15 - y}{2}\right)$

Exercise 7E

1 $\mathbf{X} + \mathbf{Y} = \begin{bmatrix} 4 \\ -2 \end{bmatrix}$ $2\mathbf{X} = \begin{bmatrix} 2 \\ -4 \end{bmatrix}$ $4\mathbf{Y} + \mathbf{X} = \begin{bmatrix} 13 \\ -2 \end{bmatrix}$

$\mathbf{X} - \mathbf{Y} = \begin{bmatrix} -2 \\ -2 \end{bmatrix}$ $-3\mathbf{A} = \begin{bmatrix} -3 & 3 \\ -6 & -9 \end{bmatrix}$

$-3\mathbf{A} + \mathbf{B} = \begin{bmatrix} 1 & 3 \\ -7 & -7 \end{bmatrix}$

2 $2\mathbf{A} = \begin{bmatrix} 2 & -2 \\ 0 & 4 \end{bmatrix}$ $-3\mathbf{A} = \begin{bmatrix} -3 & 3 \\ 0 & -6 \end{bmatrix}$

$-6\mathbf{A} = \begin{bmatrix} -6 & 6 \\ 0 & -12 \end{bmatrix}$

3 a $\begin{bmatrix} 6 & 4 \\ -4 & -4 \end{bmatrix}$ **b** $\begin{bmatrix} 0 & -9 \\ 12 & 3 \end{bmatrix}$

c $\begin{bmatrix} 6 & -5 \\ 8 & -1 \end{bmatrix}$ **d** $\begin{bmatrix} -6 & -13 \\ 16 & 7 \end{bmatrix}$

4 a $\begin{bmatrix} 0 & 1 \\ 2 & 3 \end{bmatrix}$ **b** $\begin{bmatrix} -2 & 3 \\ 6 & 3 \end{bmatrix}$ **c** $\begin{bmatrix} 3 & 3 \\ -1 & 7 \end{bmatrix}$

5 $\mathbf{X} = \begin{bmatrix} 2 & 4 \\ 0 & -3 \end{bmatrix}$ $\mathbf{Y} = \begin{bmatrix} -\dfrac{9}{2} & -\dfrac{23}{2} \\ -\dfrac{1}{2} & 11 \end{bmatrix}$

6 $\mathbf{AX} = \begin{bmatrix} 4 \\ -5 \end{bmatrix}$ $\mathbf{BX} = \begin{bmatrix} 6 \\ -1 \end{bmatrix}$ $\mathbf{IX} = \begin{bmatrix} 2 \\ -1 \end{bmatrix}$

$\mathbf{AI} = \begin{bmatrix} 1 & -2 \\ -1 & 3 \end{bmatrix}$ $\mathbf{IB} = \begin{bmatrix} 3 & 0 \\ 0 & 1 \end{bmatrix}$

$\mathbf{AB} = \begin{bmatrix} 3 & -2 \\ -3 & 3 \end{bmatrix}$ $\mathbf{BA} = \begin{bmatrix} 3 & -6 \\ -1 & 3 \end{bmatrix}$

$\mathbf{A}^2 = \begin{bmatrix} 3 & -8 \\ -4 & 11 \end{bmatrix}$ $\mathbf{B}^2 = \begin{bmatrix} 9 & 0 \\ 0 & 1 \end{bmatrix}$

7 $\mathbf{AX} = \begin{bmatrix} 4 \\ -9 \end{bmatrix}$ $\mathbf{BX} = \begin{bmatrix} -3 \\ -4 \end{bmatrix}$ $\mathbf{CX} = \begin{bmatrix} -5 \\ -4 \end{bmatrix}$

$\mathbf{AC} = \begin{bmatrix} 4 & 5 \\ -9 & 1 \end{bmatrix}$ $\mathbf{CB} = \begin{bmatrix} -3 & 6 \\ 6 & 2 \end{bmatrix}$

$\mathbf{AB} = \begin{bmatrix} -6 & -2 \\ 3 & 8 \end{bmatrix}$ $\mathbf{BA} = \begin{bmatrix} -6 & 3 \\ -2 & 8 \end{bmatrix}$

$\mathbf{A}^2 = \begin{bmatrix} 5 & -6 \\ -6 & 17 \end{bmatrix}$ $\mathbf{B}^2 = \begin{bmatrix} 9 & 0 \\ 0 & 4 \end{bmatrix}$

Exercise 7F

1 a 1   **b** $\begin{bmatrix} 2 & -1 \\ -3 & 2 \end{bmatrix}$ **c** 2   **d** $\dfrac{1}{2}\begin{bmatrix} 2 & 2 \\ -3 & -2 \end{bmatrix}$

2 a $\begin{bmatrix} -1 & 1 \\ -4 & 3 \end{bmatrix}$ **b** $\begin{bmatrix} \dfrac{2}{7} & -\dfrac{1}{14} \\ \dfrac{1}{7} & \dfrac{3}{14} \end{bmatrix}$ **c** $\begin{bmatrix} 1 & 0 \\ 0 & \dfrac{1}{k} \end{bmatrix}$

3 a $\mathbf{A}^{-1} = \begin{bmatrix} \dfrac{1}{2} & \dfrac{1}{2} \\ 0 & -1 \end{bmatrix}$ $\mathbf{B}^{-1} = \begin{bmatrix} 1 & 0 \\ -3 & 1 \end{bmatrix}$

b $\mathbf{AB} = \begin{bmatrix} 5 & 1 \\ -3 & -1 \end{bmatrix}$ $(\mathbf{AB})^{-1} = \begin{bmatrix} \dfrac{1}{2} & \dfrac{1}{2} \\ -\dfrac{3}{2} & -\dfrac{5}{2} \end{bmatrix}$

c $\mathbf{A}^{-1}\mathbf{B}^{-1} = \begin{bmatrix} -1 & \dfrac{1}{2} \\ 3 & -1 \end{bmatrix}$ $\mathbf{B}^{-1}\mathbf{A}^{-1} = (\mathbf{AB})^{-1}$

4 a $\begin{bmatrix} -1 & 3 \\ \dfrac{3}{2} & \dfrac{3}{2} \\ 1 & -2 \end{bmatrix}$ **b** $\begin{bmatrix} 0 & 7 \\ 1 & -8 \end{bmatrix}$ **c** $\begin{bmatrix} \dfrac{5}{2} & -\dfrac{7}{2} \\ \dfrac{11}{2} & -\dfrac{21}{2} \end{bmatrix}$

5 a $\begin{bmatrix} -\dfrac{3}{8} & \dfrac{11}{8} \\ \dfrac{1}{16} & \dfrac{7}{16} \end{bmatrix}$ **b** $\begin{bmatrix} -\dfrac{11}{16} & \dfrac{17}{16} \\ -\dfrac{1}{4} & \dfrac{3}{4} \end{bmatrix}$

Exercise 7G

1 a $\begin{bmatrix} -8 \\ 3 \end{bmatrix}$ **b** $\begin{bmatrix} -3a - b \\ -a + 3b \end{bmatrix}$

2 $(1, 0) \to (2, -4)$, $(0, 1) \to (-1, 3)$,
$(3, 2) \to (4, -6)$

3 a $(2, 1), (-4, 1)$ **b** $(-2, 0), (2, 2)$
c $(2, 3), (4, -5)$

4 a $(6, 21)$ **b** $(12, 7)$ **c** $(6, -7)$
d $(-6, 7)$ **e** $(7, 6)$

5 a $\begin{bmatrix} 2 & 3 \\ 3 & -1 \end{bmatrix}$ **c** $\begin{bmatrix} 1 & 2 \\ 1 & 2 \end{bmatrix}$

6 $\begin{bmatrix} 1 & 0 \\ 0 & -2 \end{bmatrix}$

7 a $\begin{bmatrix} -1 & 0 \\ 0 & 1 \end{bmatrix}$ **b** $\begin{bmatrix} 0 & 1 \\ 1 & 0 \end{bmatrix}$ **c** $\begin{bmatrix} 0 & -1 \\ -1 & 0 \end{bmatrix}$

d $\begin{bmatrix} 1 & 0 \\ 0 & 2 \end{bmatrix}$ **e** $\begin{bmatrix} 1 & 0 \\ 0 & \dfrac{1}{2} \end{bmatrix}$ **f** $\begin{bmatrix} 3 & 0 \\ 0 & 1 \end{bmatrix}$

8 a $\begin{bmatrix} 0 & -2 \\ -1 & 0 \end{bmatrix}$ **b** $(-4, -3)$ **c** $a = -2, b = -3$

9 $\begin{bmatrix} 2 & 0 \\ 0 & 1 \end{bmatrix} \mathbf{X} + \begin{bmatrix} 3 \\ 4 \end{bmatrix} = \mathbf{X}'$

$\Rightarrow \mathbf{X} = \dfrac{1}{2}\begin{bmatrix} 1 & 0 \\ 0 & 2 \end{bmatrix}\left(\mathbf{X}' - \begin{bmatrix} 3 \\ 4 \end{bmatrix}\right)$

$\Rightarrow x = \tfrac{1}{2}(x' - 3), \; y = y' - 4$

10 $\dfrac{1}{2}\begin{bmatrix} -1 & -1 \\ -21 & 5 \end{bmatrix}$

Exercise 7H

1 $y = \dfrac{-2x^2}{9} - \dfrac{2x}{3} - 4$ **2** $y = \dfrac{-x^3}{32} - x$

3 $y = \dfrac{-3x + 18}{4}$ **4** $y = \dfrac{x}{4} - 4$ **5** $y = \dfrac{x}{4} + 3$

6 $y = \dfrac{x + 21}{4}$ **7** $y = \dfrac{-3x^3}{4} - \dfrac{9x^2}{2} + 14$

Chapter 7 review

Technology-free questions

1 a $\begin{bmatrix} 1 & 0 \\ 0 & 4 \end{bmatrix}$, $(-1, 12)$ **b** $\begin{bmatrix} 3 & 0 \\ 0 & 1 \end{bmatrix}$, $(-3, 3)$

c $\begin{bmatrix} 1 & 0 \\ 0 & -1 \end{bmatrix}$, $(-1, -3)$ **d** $\begin{bmatrix} -1 & 0 \\ 0 & 1 \end{bmatrix}$, $(1, 3)$

e $\begin{bmatrix} 0 & 1 \\ 1 & 0 \end{bmatrix}$, $(3, -1)$

2 a 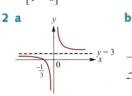 **b**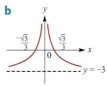

c   **d**

e   **f**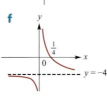

g 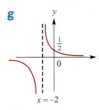 **h**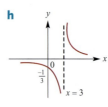

i 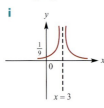 **j**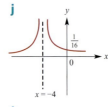

k 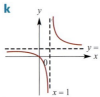 **l**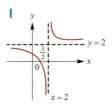

3 a Range = $(1, \infty)$ **b** Range = $(0, \infty)$

c Range = $(0, \infty)$ **d** Range = $(-4, \infty)$

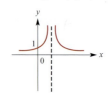 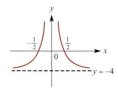

4 $\begin{bmatrix} 1 & 0 \\ 0 & 2 \end{bmatrix} \begin{bmatrix} x \\ y \end{bmatrix} + \begin{bmatrix} 2 \\ 3 \end{bmatrix} = \begin{bmatrix} x' \\ y' \end{bmatrix}$, $x = x' - 2$, $y = \dfrac{y' - 3}{2}$

5 a **i** $(x, y) \to (x - 1, 3y + 2)$
ii $(x, y) \to (x - 2, -2y + 3)$
iii $(x, y) \to \left(\dfrac{x - 1}{3}, y - 1\right)$

b **i** $(x, y) \to (x - 2, 4y)$
ii $(x, y) \to (x - 6, y - 12)$
iii $(x, y) \to (x + 3, 4y - 5)$

c **i** $(x, y) \to (x + 4, y + 2)$
ii $(x, y) \to \left(\dfrac{x}{2}, 2y\right)$
iii $(x, y) \to (x, -2y + 3)$

6 $\begin{bmatrix} 3 & 0 \\ 0 & 1 \end{bmatrix} \begin{bmatrix} x \\ y \end{bmatrix} + \begin{bmatrix} -2 \\ 3 \end{bmatrix} = \begin{bmatrix} x' \\ y' \end{bmatrix}$, $x = \dfrac{x' + 2}{3}$, $y = y' - 3$

Multiple-choice questions

1 C **2** D **3** A **4** A
5 E **6** D **7** B **8** C

Extended-response questions

1 a $k = \dfrac{1}{4}$ **b** $h = \dfrac{-1}{4}$

2 a $h = -1 \pm 2\sqrt{2}$ **b** $a = \pm 2\sqrt{2}$
c $a = -8, b = 16$

3 a $k = 10$
b **i** $h > 2 + \sqrt{10}$ **ii** $h < 2 - \sqrt{10}$
iii $2 - \sqrt{10} < h < 2 + \sqrt{10}$

4 a $x = 5$ or $x = -2$ or $x = 7$
b $x = 1$ or $x = -6$ or $x = 3$
c $k = -60$,
$x = 0$ or $x = 2 + \sqrt{21}$ or $x = 2 - \sqrt{21}$
d $h = -3$ or $h = -5$ or $h = 4$
e $-5 < h < -3$

Chapter 8

Technology-free questions

1 a $M\left(\dfrac{1}{2}, -\dfrac{3}{2}\right), N\left(\dfrac{3}{2}, 4\right)$ **b** $m_{BC} = m_{MN} = \dfrac{11}{2}$

2 a -6 **b** 69 **c** -15

3 a $12a^2 - 4$ **b** $3a^2 - 6a - 1$ **c** $12a$

4 a No **b** $x = -\frac{3}{7}$ **c** $x \leq -\frac{3}{7}$ **d** $k = -\frac{3}{16}$
5 $x = 2$ and $y = 3$, or $x = 3$ and $y = 2$
6 $AB = BC = CD = DA = 5\sqrt{2}$,
$m_{BC} = m_{AD} = 1$ and $m_{AB} = m_{CD} = -7$
7 a $y = (x + 2)^2 - 13$ **b** $y = \left(x - \frac{3}{2}\right)^2 - \frac{53}{4}$
  c $y = 2\left(x - \frac{3}{4}\right)^2 + \frac{79}{8}$
8 a $\left(\frac{1 - \sqrt{41}}{2}, 3 - 2\sqrt{41}\right), \left(\frac{\sqrt{41} + 1}{2}, 2\sqrt{41} + 3\right)$
  b $(2, 6)$ **c** $(-4, 14)$
9 a $x < \frac{-3 - \sqrt{29}}{2}$ or $x > \frac{-3 + \sqrt{29}}{2}$
  b $x \leq \frac{5 - \sqrt{65}}{4}$ or $x \geq \frac{5 + \sqrt{65}}{4}$ **c** $x \geq -4$
  d $\frac{1}{2} \leq x \leq 3$ or $x \leq -4$ **e** $x \leq 4$
10 a $\mathbb{R} \setminus \{\frac{5}{2}\}$ **b** $(-\infty, 5]$ **c** $\mathbb{R}$
  d $\mathbb{R} \setminus \{2\}$ **e** $\mathbb{R}$ **f** $\mathbb{R} \setminus \{\frac{2}{3}\}$
11 $p = -38, (x - 3)(x + 4)(3x - 2)$
12 $a = -5, R = -35$
13 a $f^{-1}: [1, 4] \to \mathbb{R}, f^{-1}(x) = \sqrt{x}$
  b $f^{-1}: [0, 3] \to \mathbb{R}, f^{-1}(x) = 2 - x$
  c $f^{-1}: (-4, \infty) \to \mathbb{R}, f^{-1}(x) = -\sqrt{x + 4}$
  d $f^{-1}: [3, \infty) \to \mathbb{R}, f^{-1}(x) = 2 - (x - 3)^2$
  e $f^{-1}: \mathbb{R} \to \mathbb{R}, f^{-1}(x) = (x - 8)^{\frac{1}{3}} + 2$
14 a $3b + 2f = 18.20$ **b** $\$2.80$
15 a $k = 1$ **b** $k = -16$
16 a $\frac{2}{5}$ **b** $2y + 5x - 17 = 0$
17 a $a\left(x + \frac{1}{a}\right)^2 + \frac{a^2 - 1}{a}$ **b** $\left(-\frac{1}{a}, \frac{a^2 - 1}{a}\right)$
  c $a = \pm 1$ **d** $a \in (-1, 1)$
18 a

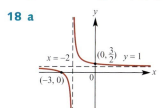

  b $A\left(0, \frac{3}{2}\right), B(-3, 0)$ **c** $y = \frac{1}{2}x + \frac{3}{2}$
  d $\left(-\frac{3}{2}, \frac{3}{4}\right)$ **e** $y = -2x - \frac{9}{4}$

Multiple-choice questions

1 B	2 D	3 C	4 A	5 D
6 D	7 C	8 C	9 C	10 A
11 E	12 B	13 A	14 E	15 B
16 D	17 D	18 E	19 B	20 D
21 E	22 D	23 B	24 D	25 D
26 A	27 B	28 D	29 D	30 B
31 C	32 A	33 C	34 A	35 B
36 C	37 D	38 E	39 E	40 C
41 C	42 C	43 A		

Extended-response questions

1 a $4b - 5c - d = 41, 2b - 7c - d = 53$,
    $-4b + 3c - d = 25$
  b $x^2 + y^2 - 2x - 4y - 29 = 0$
2 a $c = -b - 8$ **b** $x = 0$ or $x = -b$
  c $y = 0$ or $y = b + 8$ **d** $b = -8$
3 a $x \leq a$ **b** $\left(\frac{\sqrt{4a + 1} - 1}{2}, \frac{\sqrt{4a + 1} - 1}{2}\right)$
  c $a = 2$ **d** $a = 6$ **e** $a = c^2 + c$
4 a $C = 3500 + 10.5x$ **b** $I = 11.5x$
  c

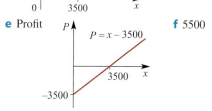

  d 3500
  e Profit

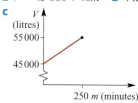

  f 5500
5 a $V = 45\,000 + 40m$ **b** 4 hours 10 minutes
  c

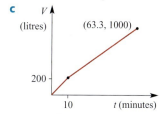

6 a 200 L **b** $V = \begin{cases} 20t & 0 \leq t \leq 10 \\ 15t + 50 & 10 < t \leq \frac{190}{3} \end{cases}$
  c

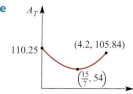

7 a $A_R = 6x^2$
  b $A_S = (10.5 - 2.5x)^2$
  c $0 \leq x \leq 4.2$
  d $A_T = 12.25x^2 - 52.5x + 110.25$
  e

  (graph of A_T with points $(0, 110.25)$, minimum $\left(\frac{15}{7}, 54\right)$, and $(4.2, 105.84)$)

  f 110.25 cm^2 (when area of rectangle = 0)
  g Rectangle 9×6 and square 3×3,
     or rectangle $\frac{27}{7} \times \frac{18}{7}$ and square $\frac{51}{7} \times \frac{51}{7}$

8 a 20 m **b** 20 m **c** 22.5 m
9 a $A = 10x^2 + 28x + 16$
  b i 54 cm^2 **ii** 112 cm^2
  c 3 cm **d**

  e $V = 2x^3 + 8x^2 + 8x$ **f** $x = 3$ **g** $x = 6.66$
10 a i $A = (10 + x)y - x^2$ **ii** $P = 2(y + x + 10)$
  b i $A = 400 + 30x - 2x^2$
    ii $512\frac{1}{2}$ m^2 **iii** $0 \leq x \leq 20$
    iv
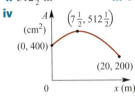
11 a $A = 6x^2 + 7xy + 2y^2$
  c i $x = 0.5$ m **ii** $y = 0.25$ m
12 a 50.9 m **b** $t = 6.12$ seconds
  c
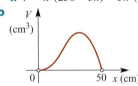
  d 6.285 seconds
13 a $x + 5$ **b** $V = 35x + 7x^2$
  c $S = x^2 + 33x + 70$
  d

  e 3.25 cm **f** 10 cm
14 a $2y + 3x = 22$
  b i $B(0, 11)$ **ii** $D(8, -1)$
  c 52 units^2
  d 6.45 units
15 a 25 km/h **b** Tap A 60 min; Tap B 75 min
  c 4 cm
16 a $h = 100 - 3x$ **b** $V = 2x^2(100 - 3x)$
  c $0 < x < \dfrac{100}{3}$ **d**

  e i $x = 18.142$ or $x = 25.852$
    ii $x = 12.715$ or $x = 29.504$
  f $V_{max} = 32\,921.811$ cm^3 when $x = 22.222$

  g i $S = 600x - 14x^2$
    ii $S_{max} = \dfrac{45000}{7}$ cm^2 when $x = \dfrac{150}{7}$
  h $x = 3.068$ or $x = 32.599$
17 a $y = (7.6 \times 10^{-5})x^3 - 0.0276x^2 + 2.33x$
  b $y = (7.6 \times 10^{-5})x^3 - 0.0276x^2 + 2.33x + 5$
  c 57.31 m
18 a $y = \dfrac{3}{4}x - 4$ **b** $y = -\dfrac{4}{3}x + \dfrac{38}{3}$
  c $D(8, 2)$ **d** 5 units **e** 50 units^2
19 a i $y = 250 - 5x$
    ii $V = x^2(250 - 5x) = 5x^2(50 - x)$
  b

  c $(0, 50)$
  d $x = 11.378$ or $x = 47.813$
  e $V_{max} = 92\,592.59$ cm^3 when $x = 33.33$ and $y = 83.33$

Chapter 9

Exercise 9A

1 $\{H, T\}$
2 $\{1, 2, 3, 4, 5, 6\}$
3 a 52 **b** 4
  c clubs ♣, hearts ♥, spades ♠, diamonds ♦
  d clubs and spades are black;
    diamonds and hearts are red   **e** 13
  f ace, king, queen, jack   **g** 4 **h** 16
4 a $\{0, 1, 2, 3, 4, 5\}$ **b** $\{0, 1, 2, 3, 4, 5, 6\}$
  c $\{0, 1, 2, 3\}$
5 a $\{0, 1, 2, 3, \ldots\}$ **b** $\{0, 1, 2, 3, \ldots, 41\}$
  c $\{1, 2, 3, \ldots\}$
6 a $\{2, 4, 6\}$ **b** $\{FFF\}$ **c** $\varnothing$
7 a $\dfrac{1}{2}$ **b** $\dfrac{3}{10}$ **c** $\dfrac{3}{20}$
8 a $\dfrac{4}{15}$ **b** $\dfrac{2}{3}$ **c** $\dfrac{4}{15}$
9 a $\dfrac{1}{4}$ **b** $\dfrac{1}{2}$ **c** $\dfrac{4}{13}$ **d** $\dfrac{2}{13}$
10 a $\dfrac{9}{13}$ **b** $\dfrac{10}{13}$ **c** $\dfrac{5}{13}$ **d** $\dfrac{1}{13}$
11 a $\dfrac{1}{365}$ **b** $\dfrac{30}{365}$ **c** $\dfrac{30}{365}$ **d** $\dfrac{90}{365}$
12 a $\dfrac{1}{9}$ **b** $\dfrac{1}{3}$ **c** $\dfrac{5}{9}$ **d** $\dfrac{4}{9}$
13 $\dfrac{1}{3}$
14 0.4

15 a $\frac{1}{3}$ b $\frac{1}{8}$ c $\frac{1}{4}$

16 a $\frac{1}{7}$ b $\frac{5}{7}$

17 a $\frac{3}{4}$ b $\frac{1}{2}$ c $\frac{10}{13}$ d $\frac{23}{26}$

18 $\frac{1}{5}, \frac{1}{5}, \frac{1}{5}, \frac{2}{5}$

19 a $\frac{1}{13}, \frac{2}{13}, \frac{2}{13}, \frac{2}{13}, \frac{2}{13}, \frac{4}{13}$ b $\frac{9}{13}$

Exercise 9B

1 a $\frac{17}{50}$ b $\frac{1}{10}$ c $\frac{4}{15}$ d $\frac{1}{200}$

2 a No b Answers will vary
c Answers will vary d Yes
e As the number of trials approaches infinity, the relative frequency approaches the value of the probability

3 Pr(a 6 from first die) $\approx \frac{78}{500} = 0.156$

Pr(a 6 from second die) $\approx \frac{102}{700} \approx 0.146$

Choose first die, as higher probability of a 6

4 a $\frac{17}{20}$ b $\frac{4}{5}$ c $\frac{9}{10}$ d 51

5 0.445

6 a $\frac{\pi}{4}$ b $\frac{\pi}{4} \approx 0.7855$

7 $\frac{3}{4}$

8 a $\frac{1}{3}$ b $\frac{1}{6}$ c $\frac{5}{6}$

9 a $\frac{4\pi}{25}$ b $1 - \frac{4\pi}{25} \approx 0.4973$

10 a i x^2 ii $\frac{1}{4}\pi x^2$ iii $\frac{1}{16}\pi x^2$

b i $\frac{\pi}{16}$ ii $\frac{3\pi}{16}$ iii $1 - \frac{\pi}{4}$

Exercise 9C

1 a $\frac{1}{4}$ b $\frac{1}{4}$

2 a $\frac{1}{2}$ b $\frac{1}{2}$ c $\frac{1}{4}$

3 a $\frac{1}{2}$ b $\frac{1}{18}$ c $\frac{5}{18}$

4 a $\frac{1}{12}$ b $\frac{1}{2}$ c $\frac{7}{12}$

5 a $\frac{3}{8}$ b $\frac{3}{8}$ c $\frac{1}{8}$ d $\frac{1}{8}$

6 a $\frac{1}{2}$ b $\frac{1}{4}$ c $\frac{3}{4}$

7 $\frac{1}{4}$

8 a [tree diagram with H/T branching to dice rolls 1–6]

b i $\frac{1}{24}$ ii $\frac{1}{4}$ iii $\frac{1}{8}$ iv $\frac{1}{2}$

9 a [tree diagram: so/sa → fi/cn/st → ic/lt/ce]

b i $\frac{1}{18}$ ii $\frac{1}{3}$ iii $\frac{1}{6}$ iv $\frac{2}{3}$

c i $\frac{1}{36}$ ii $\frac{1}{2}$ iii $\frac{15}{36}$ iv $\frac{1}{12}$

10 a

		2nd ball				
		1	2	3	4	5
1st ball	1	(1, 1)	(1, 2)	(1, 3)	(1, 4)	(1, 5)
	2	(2, 1)	(2, 2)	(2, 3)	(2, 4)	(2, 5)
	3	(3, 1)	(3, 2)	(3, 3)	(3, 4)	(3, 5)
	4	(4, 1)	(4, 2)	(4, 3)	(4, 4)	(4, 5)
	5	(5, 1)	(5, 2)	(5, 3)	(5, 4)	(5, 5)

b i $\frac{4}{25}$ ii $\frac{4}{5}$ iii $\frac{3}{25}$

Exercise 9D

1 a {1, 2, 3, 4, 6} b {2, 4}
c {5, 6, 7, 8, 9, 10} d {1, 3}
e {1, 3, 5, 6, 7, 8, 9, 10} f {5, 7, 8, 9, 10}

2 a {1, 2, 3, 5, 6, 7, 9, 10, 11}
b {1, 3, 5, 7, 9, 11} c {2, 4, 6, 8, 10, 12}
d {1, 3, 5, 7, 9, 11} e {1, 3, 5, 7, 9, 11}

3 a {E, H, M, S} b {C, H, I, M}
c {A, C, E, I, S, T} d {H, M}
e {C, E, H, I, M, S} f {H, M}

4 a 20 b 45
5 a $\frac{2}{3}$ b 0 c $\frac{1}{2}$ d $\frac{5}{6}$
6 a $\frac{1}{2}$ b $\frac{1}{3}$ c $\frac{1}{6}, \frac{2}{3}$
7 a $\frac{7}{18}$ b $\frac{4}{18} = \frac{2}{9}$ c $\frac{2}{18} = \frac{1}{9}$ d $\frac{1}{2}$
8 a $\frac{3}{5}$ b $\frac{1}{5}$ c $\frac{1}{10}$ d $\frac{2}{5}$
9 $\Pr(A \cup B) = 0.7$
10 $\Pr(A \cup B) = 0.47$
11 a $\Pr(A \cap B) = 0.28$ b $\Pr(A \cup B) = 0.45$
12 a $\Pr(A \cap B) = 0.45$ b $\Pr(A \cup B) = 0.58$
13 a $\Pr(A \cap B) = 0$ b $\Pr(A \cup B) = 0.7$
14 a $\Pr(A \cap B) = 0$ b $\Pr(A \cup B) = 0.23$
15 $\Pr(A \cap B) = 0.2$
16 $\Pr(A \cap B) = 0.05$
17 $\Pr(A \cup B') = 0.7$
18 0.32
19 a 0.43 b 0.29

Exercise 9E

1 a 0.2 b 0.5 c 0.3 d 0.7
2 a 0.75 b 0.4 c 0.87 d 0.48
3 a 0.63 b 0.23 c 0.22 d 0.77
4 a 0.45 b 0.40 c 0.25 d 0.70
5 a 0.9 b 0.6 c 0.1 d 0.9
6 a 95% b 5%
7 a $A = \{J\heartsuit, Q\heartsuit, K\heartsuit, A\heartsuit, J\spadesuit, Q\spadesuit, K\spadesuit, A\spadesuit,$
  $J\diamondsuit, Q\diamondsuit, K\diamondsuit, A\diamondsuit, J\clubsuit, Q\clubsuit, K\clubsuit, A\clubsuit\}$
  $C = \{2\heartsuit, 3\heartsuit, 4\heartsuit, 5\heartsuit, 6\heartsuit, 7\heartsuit, 8\heartsuit,$
  $9\heartsuit, 10\heartsuit, J\heartsuit, Q\heartsuit, K\heartsuit, A\heartsuit\}$
  b i $\Pr(\text{a picture card}) = \frac{4}{13}$
     ii $\Pr(\text{a heart}) = \frac{1}{4}$
     iii $\Pr(\text{a heart picture card}) = \frac{1}{13}$
     iv $\Pr(\text{a picture card or a heart}) = \frac{25}{52}$
     v $\Pr(\text{a picture card or a club, diamond or spade}) = \frac{43}{52}$
8 a $\frac{8}{15}$ b $\frac{7}{10}$ c $\frac{2}{15}$ d $\frac{1}{3}$
9 a 0.8 b 0.57 c 0.28 d 0.08
10 a 0.81 b 0.69 c 0.74 d 0.86
11 a 0 b 1 c $\frac{1}{5}$ d $\frac{1}{3}$
12 a 0.88 b 0.58 c 0.30 d 0.12

Exercise 9F

1 $\frac{1}{4}$ 2 $\frac{1}{3}$ 3 $\frac{1}{13}$ 4 $\frac{7}{19}$ 5 $\frac{1}{6}$
6 a $\frac{4}{17}$ b $\frac{4}{7}$
7 $\frac{7}{12}$
8 a $\frac{375}{500} = \frac{3}{4}$ b $\frac{225}{300} = \frac{3}{4}$
9 a $\frac{65}{284}$ b $\frac{137}{568}$ c $\frac{21}{65}$ d $\frac{61}{246}$
10 a 0.06 b 0.2
11 a $\frac{4}{7}$ b 0.3 c $\frac{15}{22}$
12 a 0.2 b 0.5 c 0.4
13 a 0.2 b $\frac{10}{27}$ c $\frac{1}{3}$
14 a 0.3 b 0.75
15 16%
16 $\frac{1}{5}$
17 a $\frac{1}{16}$ b $\frac{1}{169}$ c $\frac{1}{4}$ d $\frac{16}{169}$
18 a $\frac{1}{17}$ b $\frac{1}{221}$ c $\frac{13}{51}$ d $\frac{20}{221}$
19 $0.230\,808 \approx 0.231$
20 a $\frac{15}{28}$ b $\frac{1}{2}$ c $\frac{1}{2}$ d $\frac{2}{5}$
  e $\frac{3}{7}$ f $\frac{8}{13}$ g $\frac{5}{28}$ h $\frac{3}{14}$
21 a 0.85 b 0.6 c 0.51 d 0.51
22 0.4, 68%
23 a i 0.444 ii 0.4 iii 0.35 iv 0.178 v 0.194
  b 0.372
  c i 0.478 ii 0.425
24 a i 0.564 ii 0.05 iii 0.12 iv 0.0282 v 0.052
  b 0.081
  c 0.35
25 a $\frac{1}{6}$ b $\frac{53}{90}$ c $\frac{15}{53}$
26 a $B \subseteq A$ b $A \cap B = \emptyset$ c $A \subseteq B$

Exercise 9G

1 $\Pr(\text{male and support guns}) = 0.35$;
  $\Pr(\text{male}) \times \Pr(\text{support guns}) = \frac{60}{100} \times \frac{65}{100} = 0.39 \neq 0.35$;
  therefore not independent
2 $\Pr(\text{male and prefer sport}) = 0.45$;
  $\Pr(\text{male}) \times \Pr(\text{prefer sport}) = 0.45$;
  therefore independent
3 $\Pr(\text{speeding and serious}) = \frac{42}{376} \approx 0.112$;
  $\Pr(\text{speeding}) \times \Pr(\text{serious}) = \frac{130}{376} \times \frac{103}{376} \approx 0.095 \neq 0.112$;
  therefore not independent
4 a Yes b Yes c No
5 $\Pr(A) \times \Pr(B) = \frac{3}{6} \times \frac{2}{6} = \frac{1}{6} = \Pr(A \cap B)$
6 No
7 a 0.6 b 0.42 c 0.88
8 0.6
9 a 0.35 b 0.035 c 0.1225 d 0.025

Answers

10 a $\frac{4}{15}$ **b** $\frac{1}{15}$ **c** $\frac{133}{165}$ **d** $\frac{6}{11}$ **e** $\frac{4}{15}$
No, as $\Pr(L|F) \neq \Pr(L)$
11 $\Pr(A) \times \Pr(B) = \frac{20}{36} \times \frac{9}{36} = \frac{5}{36} = \Pr(A \cap B)$
12 a 0.35 **b** 0.875
13 a $\frac{18}{65}$ **b** $\frac{12}{65}$ **c** $\frac{23}{65}$ **d** $\frac{21}{65}$ **e** $\frac{4}{65}$
f $\frac{8}{65}$ **g** $\frac{2}{15}$ **h** $\frac{8}{21}$; No
14 a i 0.75 **ii** 0.32 **iii** 0.59 **b** No **c** No

Exercise 9H

1 Approx. 0.125 **2** Approx. 0.172
3 Approx. 0.0009 **4** Approx. 29.29
5 a Approx. 1.75 **b** Approx. 2.19

Chapter 9 review

Technology-free questions

1 a $\frac{1}{6}$ **b** $\frac{5}{6}$
2 0.007
3 a $\frac{1}{3}$ **b** $\frac{1}{4}$ **c** $\frac{1}{2}$
4 a 0.36 **b** $\frac{87}{245}$
5 $\frac{4}{15}$
6 a {156, 165, 516, 561, 615, 651} **b** $\frac{2}{3}$ **c** $\frac{1}{3}$
7 a $\frac{5}{12}$ **b** $\frac{1}{4}$
8 a 0.036 **b** 0.027 **c** 0.189 **d** 0.729
9 a $\frac{1}{27}$ **b** $\frac{4}{27}$ **c** $\frac{4}{9}$ **d** $\frac{20}{27}$
10 No
11 a 0.5 **b** 0 **c** 1
12 a $\frac{7}{18}$ **b** $\frac{1}{2}$
13 a $\frac{2}{7}$ **b** $\frac{32}{63}$ **c** $\frac{9}{16}$
14 a 0.2 **b** 0.4
15 a 0.7 **b** 0.3 **c** $\frac{1}{3}$ **d** $\frac{2}{3}$
16 a $B \subseteq A$ **b** $A \cap B = \emptyset$
c A and B are independent

Multiple-choice questions

1 B **2** C **3** A **4** C **5** D **6** A
7 D **8** E **9** A **10** B **11** B **12** B
13 A **14** E **15** C **16** A **17** B **18** D

Extended-response questions

1 a 0.15 **b** 0.148
2 a A: $\frac{3}{28}$; B: $\frac{3}{4}$ **b** A: $\frac{9}{64}$; B: $\frac{49}{64}$
c $\frac{1}{8}$ **d** $\frac{9}{58}$
3 a $\frac{4}{5}$ **b** 0.69 **c** 0.208

4 a 1.6 **b** 2.9
5 A and B: $\frac{3}{8}$; C and D: $\frac{1}{8}$

Chapter 10

Exercise 10A

1 a 11 **b** 12 **c** 37 **d** 29
2 a 60 **b** 500 **c** 350 **d** 512
3 a 128 **b** 160
4 20 **5** 63 **6** 26 **7** 240 **8** 260 000
9 17 576 000 **10** 30

Exercise 10B

1 a 6 **b** 120 **c** 5040 **d** 2 **e** 1 **f** 1
2 a 20 **b** 72 **c** 6 **d** 56 **e** 120 **f** 720
3 120 **4** 5040 **5** 24
6 720 **7** 720 **8** 336
9 a 5040 **b** 210
10 a 120 **b** 120
11 a 840 **b** 2401
12 a 480 **b** 1512
13 a 60 **b** 24 **c** 252
14 a 150 **b** 360 **c** 1560
15 a 720 **b** 48

Exercise 10C

1 a 3 **b** 3 **c** 6 **d** 4
2 a 10 **b** 10 **c** 35 **d** 35
3 a 190 **b** 100 **c** 4950 **d** 31 125
4 a 20 **b** 7 **c** 28 **d** 1225
5 1716 **6** 2300
7 133 784 560 **8** 8 145 060 **9** 18
10 a 5 852 925 **b** 1 744 200
11 100 386
12 a 792 **b** 336
13 a 150 **b** 75 **c** 6 **d** 462 **e** 81
14 a 8 436 285 **b** 3003 **c** 66 **d** 2 378 376
15 186 **16** 32 **17** 256 **18** 31 **19** 57
20 a 20 **b** 21

Exercise 10D

1 a 0.5 **b** 0.5
2 0.375
3 a 0.2 **b** 0.6 **c** 0.3
4 0.2 **5** $\frac{329}{858}$
6 a $\frac{2^7}{2^8 - 1} \approx 0.502$ **b** $\frac{56}{255}$ **c** $\frac{73}{85}$
7 a $\frac{5}{204}$ **b** $\frac{35}{136}$
8 a $\frac{1}{6}$ **b** $\frac{5}{6}$ **c** $\frac{17}{21}$ **d** $\frac{34}{35}$

9 a $\dfrac{25}{49}$ **b** $\dfrac{24}{49}$ **c** $\dfrac{3}{7}$ **d** $\dfrac{1}{6}$
10 a 0.659 **b** 0.341 **c** 0.096 **d** 0.282
11 a $\dfrac{5}{42}$ **b** $\dfrac{20}{21}$ **c** $\dfrac{15}{37}$

Exercise 10E

1 a $x^4 + 8x^3 + 24x^2 + 32x + 16$
 b $16x^4 + 32x^3 + 24x^2 + 8x + 1$
 c $16x^4 - 96x^3 + 216x^2 - 216x + 81$
 d $27x^3 - 27x^2 + 9x - 1$
 e $16x^4 - 32x^3 + 24x^2 - 8x + 1$
 f $-32x^5 + 80x^4 - 80x^3 + 40x^2 - 10x + 1$
 g $-243x^5 + 405x^4 - 270x^3 + 90x^2 - 15x + 1$
 h $16x^4 - 96x^3 + 216x^2 - 216x + 81$

Chapter 10 review

Technology-free questions

1 a 499 500 **b** 1 000 000 **c** 1 000 000
2 648 **3** 120 **4** $8n$
5 5416 **6** 36 750 **7** 50 400
8 a 10 **b** 32
9 1200
10 a $\dfrac{1}{8}$ **b** $\dfrac{3}{8}$ **c** $\dfrac{3}{28}$

Multiple-choice questions

1 E **2** D **3** A **4** D **5** C
6 B **7** C **8** A **9** E **10** E

Extended-response questions

1 a 2880 **b** 80 640
2 a 720 **b** 48 **c** 336
3 a 60 **b** 45
4 a 210 **b** 100 **c** 80
5 a 1365 **b** 210 **c** 1155
6 a 3060 **b** 330 **c** 1155
7 Div. 1: 1.228×10^{-7} Div. 2: 1.473×10^{-6}
  Div. 3: 2.726×10^{-5} Div. 4: 1.365×10^{-3}
  Div. 5: 3.362×10^{-3}
8 a 1.290×10^{-4} **b** 6.449×10^{-4}

Chapter 11

Exercise 11A

1 a No **b** No **c** Yes **d** No **e** No
2 a $\Pr(X = 2)$ **b** $\Pr(X > 2)$ **c** $\Pr(X \geq 2)$
 d $\Pr(X < 2)$ **e** $\Pr(X \geq 2)$ **f** $\Pr(X \geq 2)$
 g $\Pr(X \leq 2)$ **h** $\Pr(X \geq 2)$ **i** $\Pr(X \leq 2)$
 j $\Pr(X \geq 2)$ **k** $\Pr(2 < X < 5)$
3 a $\{2\}$ **b** $\{3, 4, 5\}$ **c** $\{2, 3, 4, 5\}$
 d $\{0, 1\}$ **e** $\{0, 1, 2\}$ **f** $\{2, 3, 4, 5\}$
 g $\{3, 4, 5\}$ **h** $\{2, 3, 4\}$ **i** $\{3, 4\}$
4 a 0.2 **b** 0.5 **c** 0.3 **d** 0.35 **e** 0.9

5 a $\dfrac{1}{15}$ **b** $\dfrac{3}{5}$
6 a 0.09 **b** 0.69
7 a 0.49 **b** 0.51 **c** 0.74
8 a 0.6 **b** 0.47 **c** $\dfrac{2}{3}$
9 a $\{HHH, HTH, HHT, HTT,$ **b** $\dfrac{3}{8}$
  $THH, TTH, THT, TTT\}$

c
x	0	1	2	3
$p(x)$	$\dfrac{1}{8}$	$\dfrac{3}{8}$	$\dfrac{3}{8}$	$\dfrac{1}{8}$

d $\dfrac{7}{8}$ **e** $\dfrac{4}{7}$

10 a $\{2, 3, 4, 5, 6, 7, 8, 9, 10, 11, 12\}$ **b** $\dfrac{1}{6}$

c
y	2	3	4	5	6	7	8	9	10	11	12
$p(y)$	$\dfrac{1}{36}$	$\dfrac{2}{36}$	$\dfrac{3}{36}$	$\dfrac{4}{36}$	$\dfrac{5}{36}$	$\dfrac{6}{36}$	$\dfrac{5}{36}$	$\dfrac{4}{36}$	$\dfrac{3}{36}$	$\dfrac{2}{36}$	$\dfrac{1}{36}$

11 a $\{1, 2, 3, 4, 5, 6\}$ **b** $\dfrac{7}{36}$

c
x	1	2	3	4	5	6
$p(x)$	$\dfrac{1}{36}$	$\dfrac{3}{36}$	$\dfrac{5}{36}$	$\dfrac{7}{36}$	$\dfrac{9}{36}$	$\dfrac{11}{36}$

12 a
y	-3	-2	1	3
$p(y)$	$\dfrac{1}{8}$	$\dfrac{3}{8}$	$\dfrac{3}{8}$	$\dfrac{1}{8}$

b $\dfrac{7}{8}$

Exercise 11B

1 0.378 **2** $\dfrac{28}{57} \approx 0.491$ **3** $\dfrac{12}{13} \approx 0.923$
4 $\dfrac{60}{253} \approx 0.237$ **5** 0.930 **6** 0.109

Exercise 11C

1 a 0.185 **b** 0.060
2 a 0.194 **b** 0.930
3 a 0.137 **b** 0.446 **c** 0.554
4 a 0.008 **b** 0.268 **c** 0.468
5 a 0.056 **b** 0.391
6 0.018
7 a $\Pr(X = x) = \binom{5}{x}(0.1)^x(0.9)^{5-x}$
  for $x = 0, 1, 2, 3, 4, 5$

x	0	1	2	3	4	5
$p(x)$	0.591	0.328	0.073	0.008	0.000	0.000

 b Most probable number is 0

8 0.749 **9** 0.021 **10** 0.5398 **11** $\dfrac{175}{256}$
12 a 0.988 **b** 0.9999 **c** 8.1×10^{-11}
13 a 0.151 **b** 0.302
14 5.8%
15 a i 0.474 **ii** 0.224 **iii** 0.078
 b Answers will vary – about 5 or more

16 0.014

17 [scatter plot] **18** [scatter plot]

19 a 5 **b** 8
20 a 13 **b** 22
21 a 16 **b** 29
22 a 45 **b** 59
23 a 0.3087 **b** $\dfrac{0.3087}{1-(0.3)^5} \approx 0.3095$
24 a 0.3020 **b** 0.6242 **c** 0.3225

Chapter 11 review
Technology-free questions
1 a 0.92 **b** 0.63 **c** 0.8

2
x	1	2	3	4
$p(x)$	0.25	0.28	0.30	0.17

3
x	2	3	4
$p(x)$	$\dfrac{2}{5}$	$\dfrac{8}{15}$	$\dfrac{1}{15}$

4 a

		\multicolumn{5}{c}{2nd choice}

		1	2	3	6	7	9
1st choice	1	2	3	4	7	8	10
	2	3	4	5	8	9	11
	3	4	5	6	9	10	12
	6	7	8	9	12	13	15
	7	8	9	10	13	14	16
	9	10	11	12	15	16	18

b {2, 3, 4, 5, 6, 7, 8, 9, 10, 11, 12, 13, 14, 15, 16, 18}

c
x	2	3	4	5	6	7	8	9
$p(x)$	$\dfrac{1}{36}$	$\dfrac{2}{36}$	$\dfrac{3}{36}$	$\dfrac{2}{36}$	$\dfrac{1}{36}$	$\dfrac{2}{36}$	$\dfrac{4}{36}$	$\dfrac{4}{36}$

x	10	11	12	13	14	15	16	18
$p(x)$	$\dfrac{4}{36}$	$\dfrac{2}{36}$	$\dfrac{3}{36}$	$\dfrac{2}{36}$	$\dfrac{1}{36}$	$\dfrac{2}{36}$	$\dfrac{2}{36}$	$\dfrac{1}{36}$

5 a 0.051 **b** 0.996 **c** $\dfrac{243}{256} \approx 0.949$
6 a $\dfrac{9}{64}$ **b** $\dfrac{37}{64}$
7 a $\dfrac{16}{81}$ **b** $\dfrac{32}{81}$ **c** $\dfrac{11}{27}$
8 a $\binom{7}{3}\left(\dfrac{1}{4}\right)^3 \left(\dfrac{3}{4}\right)^4$
  b $\left(\dfrac{3}{4}\right)^7 + 7\left(\dfrac{1}{4}\right)\left(\dfrac{3}{4}\right)^6 + 21\left(\dfrac{1}{4}\right)^2\left(\dfrac{3}{4}\right)^5$
9 a $\left(\dfrac{p}{100}\right)^{15}$ **b** $15\left(\dfrac{p}{100}\right)^{14}\left(1-\dfrac{p}{100}\right)$
  c $\left(\dfrac{p}{100}\right)^{15} + 15\left(\dfrac{p}{100}\right)^{14}\left(1-\dfrac{p}{100}\right)$
    $+ 105\left(\dfrac{p}{100}\right)^{13}\left(1-\dfrac{p}{100}\right)^2$

10 a $\dfrac{117}{125}$ **b** $m=5$

Multiple-choice questions
1 B **2** A **3** C **4** A **5** E
6 C **7** A **8** D **9** B **10** E

Extended-response questions
1 a
x	1	2	3	4
$p(x)$	0.54	0.16	0.06	0.24

  b 0.46

2 a i 0.1 **ii** 0.6 **iii** $\dfrac{2}{3}$ **b i** 0.0012 **ii** 0.2508
3 a $\dfrac{3}{5}$ **b i** $\dfrac{7}{40}$ **ii** $\dfrac{3}{10}$ **c i** $\dfrac{11}{20}$ **ii** $\dfrac{3}{8}$
4 a 0.003 **b** 5.320×10^{-6}
5 0.8
6 a 0.401 **b** $n \geq 45$
7 a $1-q^2$ **b** $1-4q^3+3q^4$ **c** $\dfrac{1}{3} < q < 1$
8 a 0.734 (exact answer)
  b About 7 (by simulation)

Chapter 12
Technology-free questions
1 a $\dfrac{1}{9}$ **b** $\dfrac{8}{9}$
2 a {348, 384, 438, 483, 834, 843}, $n(\varepsilon) = 6$
  b $\dfrac{2}{3}$ **c** $\dfrac{2}{3}$
3 a $\dfrac{1}{2}$ **b** $\dfrac{12}{13}$
4 a $\dfrac{1}{4}$ **b** $\dfrac{3}{8}$
5 a $\Pr(1) = \Pr(2) = \Pr(3) = \Pr(5) = \dfrac{2}{17}$,
    $\Pr(4) = \dfrac{8}{17}$, $\Pr(6) = \dfrac{1}{17}$
  b $\dfrac{9}{17}$
6 $\dfrac{1}{4}$
7 a 0.6 **b** $\dfrac{1}{3}$
8 a $\dfrac{1}{2}$ **b** $\dfrac{3}{4}$ **c** $\dfrac{1}{2}$ **d** $\dfrac{1}{4}$
9 a 0.48 **b** 0.56
10 a $\Pr(A \cap B) = 0.05$ **b** $\Pr(A \mid B) = 0.25$
11 a 0.4 **b** 0.2 **c** 0.7
12 720
13 $\dfrac{52!}{7!45!}$
14 a $\dfrac{7}{22}$ **b** $\dfrac{21}{44}$
15 a 0.7 **b** 0.7 **c** 0.7
16 a $\Pr(X=4) = 0.0016$ **b** $\Pr(X \geq 3) = 0.0272$

17 a $\Pr(X = 3) = {}^7C_3\, 0.2^3 0.8^4$
  b $\Pr(X < 3) = {}^7C_0\, 0.2^0 0.8^7 + {}^7C_1\, 0.2^1 .8^6 + {}^7C_2\, 0.2^2 0.8^5$
  c $\Pr(X \geq 4) = {}^7C_4\, 0.2^4 0.8^3 + {}^7C_5\, 0.2^5 .8^2 + {}^7C_6\, 0.2^6 0.8^1 + {}^7C_7\, 0.2^7 0.8^0$

18 a $\left(\dfrac{x}{100}\right)^{10}$ **b** $10\left(\dfrac{x}{100}\right)^9\left(1 - \dfrac{x}{100}\right)$
  c $\left(\dfrac{x}{100}\right)^{10} + 10\left(\dfrac{x}{100}\right)^9\left(1 - \dfrac{x}{100}\right) + 45\left(\dfrac{x}{100}\right)^8\left(1 - \dfrac{x}{100}\right)^2$

Multiple-choice questions

1 E	**2** C	**3** E	**4** B	**5** E
6 E	**7** C	**8** C	**9** B	**10** D
11 D	**12** D	**13** E	**14** A	**15** E
16 E	**17** B	**18** C	**19** C	**20** A
21 E	**22** E	**23** C	**24** D	**25** D

Extended-response questions

1 a i $\dfrac{15}{28}$ **ii** $\dfrac{37}{56}$ **iii** $\dfrac{43}{49}$
  b i $\dfrac{9}{14}$ **ii** $\dfrac{135}{392}$

2 a $\dfrac{1}{2}$ **b** $\dfrac{13}{36}$

3 a $\dfrac{3}{8}$ **b** $\dfrac{1}{56}$ **c** $\dfrac{3}{28}$ **d** $\dfrac{6}{7}$

4 a 0.0027 **b** 0.12 **c** 0.17 **d** 0.72

5 a $\dfrac{59}{120}$ **b** $\dfrac{45}{59}$

6 a $\dfrac{167}{360}$
  b i $\dfrac{108}{193}$ **ii** $\dfrac{45}{193}$

7 a i $\dfrac{1}{9}$ **ii** $\dfrac{5}{18}$
  b i $\dfrac{1}{81}$ **ii** $\dfrac{13}{324}$

8 a i $m = 30, q = 35, s = 25$
  ii $m + q = 65$
  b $\dfrac{3}{10}$
  c $\dfrac{7}{12}$

9 a 0.084 **b** 0.52 **c** 0.68

10 a 60 **b** 8 **c** 0.1

11 a $\dfrac{1}{60}$ **b** $\dfrac{1}{5}$ **c** $\dfrac{3}{5}$ **d** $\dfrac{6}{13}$

12 a i $10\,000\ \text{cm}^2$ **ii** $400\ \text{cm}^2$ **iii** $6400\ \text{cm}^2$
  b i 0.04 **ii** 0.12 **iii** 0.64
  c i 0.0016 **ii** $0.000\,64$

13 a $\dfrac{7}{18}$ **b** $\dfrac{13}{36}$ **c** $\dfrac{23}{108}$

14 a i 0.328 **ii** 0.205 **iii** 0.672
  b i 11 **ii** 18

15 a i 0.121 **ii** 0.851 **iii** 0.383
  b i 9 **ii** 14

Chapter 13

Exercise 13A

1 a x^5 **b** $8x^7$ **c** x^2 **d** $2x^3$ **e** a^6
  f 2^6 **g** x^2y^2 **h** x^4y^6 **i** $\dfrac{x^3}{y^3}$ **j** $\dfrac{x^6}{y^4}$

2 a 3^{17} **b** x^7y^5 **c** 3^{4x+3} **d** $30a^5b^6$

3 a x^2y **b** b^{4x+1} **c** $4a^5b$

4 a $\dfrac{1}{49}$ **b** 64 **c** $\dfrac{8}{125}$

5 a b^{10} **b** 729 **c** b^4

6 a $\dfrac{27a^8b}{16}$ **b** $\dfrac{125b^6}{c^9}$

7 a 64 **b** $-27a^3$ **c** $-96a^3$

8 a 2^{-2n} **b** 2^4 **c** $\dfrac{5^{2n}}{2^{2n}}$

9 a x^9 **b** 2^{16} **c** 3^{17} **d** q^8p^9 **e** $a^{11}b^3$
  f 2^8x^{18} **g** $m^{11}n^{12}p^{-2}$ **h** $2a^5b^{-2}$

10 a x^2y^3 **b** $8a^8b^3$ **c** x^5y^2 **d** $\dfrac{9}{2}x^2y^3$

11 a $\dfrac{1}{n^4p^5}$ **b** $\dfrac{2x^8z}{y^4}$ **c** $\dfrac{b^5}{a^5}$ **d** $\dfrac{a^3b}{c}$
  e $a^{n+2}b^{n+1}c^{n-1}$

12 a 3^{17n} **b** 2^{3-n} **c** $\dfrac{3^{4n-11}}{2^2}$
  d $2^{n+1}3^{3n-1}$ **e** 5^{3n-2} **f** $2^{3x-3} \times 3^{-4}$
  g $3^{6-n} \times 2^{-5n}$ **h** $3^3 = 27$ **i** 6

13 a $2^{12} = 4096$ **b** $5^5 = 3125$ **c** $3^3 = 27$

Exercise 13B

1 a 25 **b** 27 **c** $\dfrac{1}{9}$ **d** 16
  e $\dfrac{1}{2}$ **f** $\dfrac{1}{4}$ **g** $\dfrac{1}{25}$ **h** 16
  i $\dfrac{1}{10\,000}$ **j** 1000 **k** 27 **l** $\dfrac{3}{5}$
  m -2 **n** $\dfrac{1}{625}$ **o** 16 **p** 343

2 a $a^{\frac{1}{6}}b^{-\frac{7}{6}}$ **b** $a^{-6}b^{\frac{9}{2}}$ **c** $3^{-\frac{7}{3}} \times 5^{-\frac{7}{6}}$
  d $\dfrac{1}{4}$ **e** x^6y^{-8} **f** $a^{\frac{14}{15}}$

3 a $(2x-1)^{\frac{3}{2}}$ **b** $(x-1)^{\frac{5}{2}}$ **c** $(x^2+1)^{\frac{3}{2}}$
  d $(x-1)^{\frac{7}{2}}$ **e** $x(x-1)^{-\frac{1}{2}}$ **f** $(5x^2+1)^{\frac{4}{3}}$

Exercise 13C

1

$y = 0.5^x$ $y = 2.4^x$
$y = 0.9^x$ $y = 1.8^x$

- All pass through $(0, 1)$
- Horizontal asymptote $y = 0$
- Increasing for base > 1
- Decreasing for base < 1

2

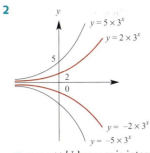

- $y = a \times b^x$ has y-axis intercept at $(0, a)$
- Horizontal asymptote $y = 0$
- Graphs c and d are reflections in the x-axis of graphs a and b

3 $x = 3.807$ **4** $x = 0.778$

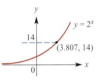 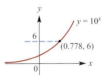

5 a

b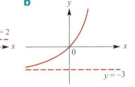

c

d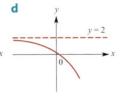

e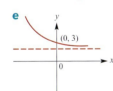

f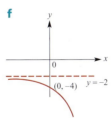

6 a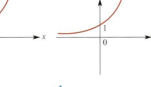

b

c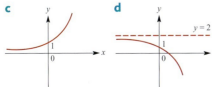

d

Exercise 13D

1 a 3   **b** 3   **c** $\frac{1}{2}$ **d** $\frac{3}{4}$ **e** $\frac{1}{3}$
   f 4   **g** 2   **h** 3   **i** 3

2 a 1   **b** 2   **c** $-\frac{3}{2}$ **d** $\frac{4}{3}$ **e** -1
   f 8   **g** 3   **h** -4 **i** 8   **j** 4
   k $3\frac{1}{2}$ **l** 6   **m** $7\frac{1}{2}$

3 a $\frac{4}{5}$ **b** $\frac{3}{2}$ **c** $5\frac{1}{2}$

4 a 0   **b** 0, -2 **c** 1, 2   **d** 0, 1

5 a 2.32   **b** 1.29   **c** 1.26   **d** 1.75

6 a $x > 2$ **b** $x > \frac{1}{3}$ **c** $x \leq \frac{1}{2}$ **d** $x < 3$
   e $x < \frac{3}{4}$ **f** $x > 1$ **g** $x \leq 3$

Exercise 13E

1 a 7   **b** 4   **c** 3   **d** -1

2 a $\log_2(10a)$ **b** 1   **c** $\log_2\left(\frac{9}{4}\right)$ **d** 1
   e $3\log_2 a$ **f** 9   **g** $-\log_5 6$ **h** -2

3 a 3   **b** 4   **c** -7 **d** -3
   e 4   **f** -3 **g** 4   **h** -6
   i -9 **j** -1 **k** 4   **l** -2

4 a 2   **b** 7   **c** 9   **d** 1
   e $\frac{5}{2}$ **f** $\log_x(a^5)$ **g** 3   **h** 1

5 a 2   **b** 27   **c** $\frac{1}{125}$ **d** 8
   e 30   **f** $\frac{2}{3}$ **g** 8   **h** 64
   i 4   **j** 10

6 a 5   **b** 32.5   **c** 22   **d** 20
   e $\frac{3 + \sqrt{17}}{2}$ **f** 3 or 0

7 $2 + 3a - \frac{5c}{2}$ **9** 10

10 a 4   **b** $\frac{6}{5}$ **c** 3   **d** 10
   e 9   **f** 2

Exercise 13F

1 a 2.81   **b** -1.32 **c** 2.40   **d** 0.79
   e -2.58 **f** -0.58

2 a 1.90   **b** 3.10   **c** -0.68

3 a $x > 3$ **b** $x < 1.46$ **c** $x < -1.15$
   d $x \leq 2.77$ **e** $x \geq 1.31$

4 a   **b**

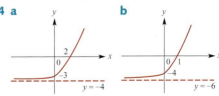

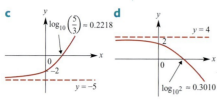

c Domain = $(0, \infty)$ **d** Domain = $(-2, \infty)$

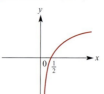

e Domain = $(0, \infty)$ **f** Domain = $(-\infty, 0)$

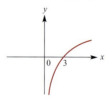
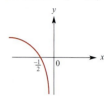

Exercise 13G

1 a 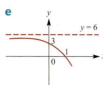   **b**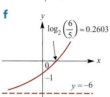

Domain = R^+, Range = R

5 a 0.64   **b** 0.40

6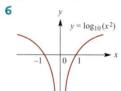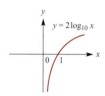

c 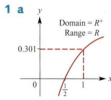   **d**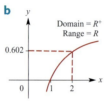

Domain = R^+, Range = R

7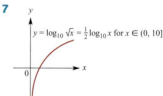

$y = \log_{10}\sqrt{x} = \tfrac{1}{2}\log_{10} x$ for $x \in (0, 10]$

e 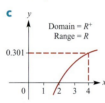   **f**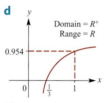

Domain = R^+, Range = R Domain = R^-, Range = R

8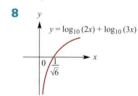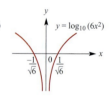

2 a $y = 2\log_{10} x$ **b** $y = 10^{\frac{1}{3}x}$
c $y = \tfrac{1}{3}\log_{10} x$ **d** $y = \tfrac{1}{3} 10^{\frac{1}{2}x}$

Exercise 13H

1 a $N = 1000 \times 2^{\frac{t}{15}}$ **b** 50 minutes

3 a $f^{-1}(x) = \log_3(x - 2)$
b $f^{-1}(x) = 2^x + 3$
c $f^{-1}(x) = \log_3\!\left(\dfrac{x-2}{4}\right)$
d $f^{-1}(x) = \log_5(x + 2)$
e $f^{-1}(x) = \tfrac{1}{3} \times 2^x$ **f** $f^{-1}(x) = 3 \times 2^x$
g $f^{-1}(x) = 2^x - 3$
h $f^{-1}(x) = \log_3\!\left(\dfrac{x+2}{5}\right)$

2 79 726 years
3 7575 years
4 a 535 millibars   **b** 7331 metres
5 22 hours
6 6.4°C
7 $t > 18.668\ldots$

8 a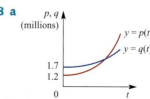

4 a Domain = $(4, \infty)$ **b** Domain = $(-3, \infty)$

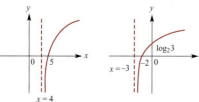

b i $t = 12.56\ldots$ (mid 1962)
  ii $t = 37.56\ldots$ (mid 1987)

9 a $y = 3 \times 5^x$ **b** $y = 4 \times (\tfrac{1}{2})^x$ **c** $y = 5 \times (\tfrac{3}{2})^x$

10 a $k = \log_{10}\left(\frac{5}{4}\right)$ **b** 7.212 hours

11 a $N = 1000 \times 10^{\frac{t}{5}}$ **b** 210 minutes
  c 15 hours **d** 251 189 bacteria

12 $a = 6 \times \left(\frac{10}{3}\right)^{-\frac{2}{3}}$ and $k = \frac{1}{3}\log_{10}\left(\frac{10}{3}\right)$

13 $y = 1.5 \times 0.575^x$ **14** $p = 2.5 \times 1.35^t$

15 a

Cuts, n	Sheets	Thickness, T (mm)
0	1	0.2
1	2	0.4
2	4	0.8
3	8	1.6
4	16	3.2
5	32	6.4
6	64	12.8
7	128	25.6
8	256	51.2
9	512	102.4
10	1024	204.8

b $T = 0.2 \times 2^n$

c

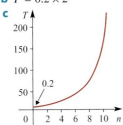

d 214 748.4 m

16 $d_0 = 41.92$, $m = 0.094$

Exercise 13I

1 a $m = 2$ and $c = \log_4 3$
  b $\log_4(y)$
  c

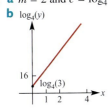
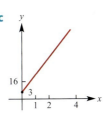

2 a $m = 3$ and $c = \log_5 2$
  b $\log_5(y)$
  c

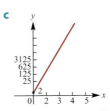

3 Street 10^{-9} watt/cm^2; Quiet car 10^{-11} watt/cm^2

4 a Increases by $10\log_{10} 2 \approx 3$ dB
  b Increases by $10\log_{10} 10 = 10$ dB
  c $P_{\text{new}} = (P_{\text{old}})^3 \times 10^{32}$
  d $P = 10^{-16}$ **e** $P = 10^{-6}$

5 $P_1 = 10^{\frac{\lambda}{10}} \times P_2$ **6** $5 + \log_{10} 5$

7 $7.3 - \log_{10} 4$ **8** $[10^{-4}, 10^{-2}]$

Chapter 13 review

Technology-free questions

1 a a^4 **b** $\frac{1}{b^2}$ **c** $\frac{1}{m^2 n^2}$ **d** $\frac{1}{ab^6}$
  e $\frac{3a^6}{2}$ **f** $\frac{5}{3a^2}$ **g** a^3 **h** $\frac{n^8}{m^4}$
  i $\frac{1}{p^2 q^4}$ **j** $\frac{8}{5a^{11}}$ **k** $2a$ **l** $a^2 + a^6$

2 a $\log_2 7$ **b** $\frac{1}{2}\log_2 7$ **c** $\log_{10} 2$
  d $\log_{10}\left(\frac{18}{5}\right)$ **e** $1 + \log_{10} 11$ **f** $1 + \log_{10} 101$
  g $\frac{1}{5}\log_2 100$ **h** $-\log_2 10$

3 a 6 **b** 7 **c** 2 **d** 0
  e 3 **f** -2 **g** -3 **h** 4

4 a $\log_{10} 6$ **b** $\log_{10} 6$ **c** $\log_{10}\left(\frac{a^2}{b}\right)$
  d $\log_{10}\left(\frac{a^2}{25000}\right)$ **e** $\log_{10} y$ **f** $\log_{10}\left(\frac{a^2 b^3}{c}\right)$

5 a $x = 3$ **b** $x = 3$ or $x = 0$
  c $x = 1$ **d** $x = 2$ or $x = 3$

6 a

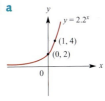

b

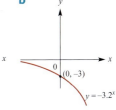

c

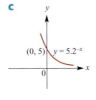

d

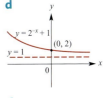

e

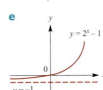

f

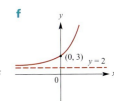

7 $x = 1$ **9** 3

10 a $k = \frac{1}{7}$ **b** $q = \frac{3}{2}$

11 a $a = \frac{1}{2}$ **b** $y = -4$ or $y = 20$

Multiple-choice questions

1 C **2** A **3** C **4** C **5** A
6 B **7** A **8** A **9** A **10** A

Extended-response questions

1 a

n	1	2	3	4
M	1	3	7	15

b $M = 2^n - 1$

n	5	6	7
M	31	63	127

c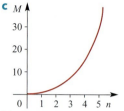

d

Three discs	1	2	3
Times moved	4	2	1

Four discs	1	2	3	4
Times moved	8	4	2	1

2 $n = 2$

3 a $(\tfrac{1}{2})^{3n}$ **b** $(\tfrac{1}{2})^{5n-2}$ **c** $n = 3$

4 a $729(\tfrac{1}{4})^n$ **b** $128(\tfrac{1}{2})^n$ **c** 4 times

5 a Batch 1: $15(0.95)^n$; Batch 2: $20(0.94)^n$
b 32 years

6 a X $1.82   Y $1.51   Z $2.62
b X $4.37   Y $4.27   Z $3.47
c Intersect at $t = 21.784\ldots$ and $t = 2.090\ldots$; therefore Feb 2014 until Sept 2015
d Feb 2015 until Sept 2015; approx. 8 months

7 a 13.81 years   **b** 7.38 years

8 a Temperature $= 87.065 \times 0.94^t$
b i 87.1°C   **ii** 18.56°C
c Temperature $= 85.724 \times 0.94^t$
d i 85.72°C   **ii** 40.82°C
e 28.19 minutes

9 a $a = 0.2$ and $b = 5$
b i $z = x \log_{10} b$ **ii** $a = 0.2$ and $k = \log_{10} 5$

10 a $y = 2 \times 1.585^x$ **b** $y = 2 \times 10^{0.2x}$
c $x = 5 \log_{10}\left(\dfrac{y}{2}\right)$

Chapter 14

Exercise 14A

1 a $\dfrac{\pi}{3}$ **b** $\dfrac{4\pi}{5}$ **c** $\dfrac{4\pi}{3}$ **d** $\dfrac{11\pi}{6}$ **e** $\dfrac{7\pi}{3}$ **f** $\dfrac{8\pi}{3}$

2 a 120°   **b** 150°   **c** 210°   **d** 162°
e 100°   **f** 324°   **g** 220°   **h** 324°

3 a 34.38°   **b** 108.29°   **c** 166.16°   **d** 246.94°
e 213.14°   **f** 296.79°   **g** 271.01°   **h** 343.78°

4 a 0.66   **b** 1.27   **c** 1.87   **d** 2.81
e 1.47   **f** 3.98   **g** 2.38   **h** 5.74

5 a −60°   **b** −720°   **c** −540°   **d** −180°
e 300°   **f** −330°   **g** 690°   **h** −690°

6 a -2π **b** -3π **c** $-\dfrac{4\pi}{3}$ **d** -4π
e $-\dfrac{11\pi}{6}$ **f** $-\dfrac{7\pi}{6}$

7 a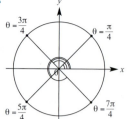

b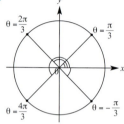

c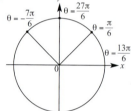

Exercise 14B

1 a 0, 1   **b** −1, 0   **c** 1, 0   **d** 1, 0
e 0, −1   **f** 1, 0   **g** −1, 0   **h** 0, 1

2 a 0.95   **b** 0.75   **c** −0.82   **d** 0.96
e −0.5   **f** −0.03   **g** −0.86   **h** 0.61

3 a 0, −1   **b** −1, 0   **c** −1, 0   **d** −1, 0
e −1, 0   **f** 0, −1   **g** 0, −1   **h** 0, −1

Exercise 14C

1 a 0   **b** 0   **c** Undefined   **d** 0
e Undefined   **f** Undefined

2 a −34.23   **b** −2.57   **c** −0.97   **d** −1.38
e 0.95   **f** 0.75   **g** 1.66

3 a 0   **b** 0   **c** 0   **d** 0   **e** 0   **f** 0

Exercise 14D

1 a 67°59′   **b** 4.5315   **c** 2.5357
d 6.4279   **e** 50°12′   **f** 3.4202
g 2.3315   **h** 6.5778   **i** 6.5270

Exercise 14E

1 a −0.42   **b** −0.7   **c** −0.42   **d** −0.38
e 0.42   **f** −0.38   **g** −0.7   **h** 0.7

2 a $\dfrac{5\pi}{6}$ **b** $\dfrac{7\pi}{6}$ **c** $\dfrac{11\pi}{6}$

3 a $-\dfrac{1}{2}$ **b** $\dfrac{\sqrt{3}}{2}$ **c** $\dfrac{1}{2}$ **d** $\dfrac{-\sqrt{3}}{2}$
  e $-\sqrt{3}$ **f** $-\sqrt{3}$

4 a $-\dfrac{\sqrt{3}}{2}$ **b** $\dfrac{1}{2}$ **c** $-\sqrt{3}$ **d** $-\dfrac{\sqrt{3}}{2}$ **e** $-\dfrac{1}{2}$

5 a $a = 0.7660, b = 0.6428$
  b $c = -0.7660, d = 0.6428$
  c i $\cos 140° = -0.7660, \sin 140° = 0.6428$
    ii $\cos 140° = -\cos 40°$

6 a -0.7 **b** -0.6 **c** -0.4 **d** -0.6
  e -0.7 **f** -0.7 **g** 0.4 **h** 0.6

7 a $120°$ **b** $240°$ **c** $-60°$ **d** $120°$
  e $240°$ **f** $300°$

Exercise 14F

1 a $\sin = \dfrac{\sqrt{3}}{2}, \cos = -\dfrac{1}{2}, \tan = -\sqrt{3}$

  b $\sin = \dfrac{1}{\sqrt{2}}, \cos = -\dfrac{1}{\sqrt{2}}, \tan = -1$

  c $\sin = -\dfrac{1}{2}, \cos = -\dfrac{\sqrt{3}}{2}, \tan = \dfrac{1}{\sqrt{3}}$

  d $\sin = -\dfrac{\sqrt{3}}{2}, \cos = -\dfrac{1}{2}, \tan = \sqrt{3}$

  e $\sin = -\dfrac{1}{\sqrt{2}}, \cos = \dfrac{1}{\sqrt{2}}, \tan = -1$

  f $\sin = \dfrac{1}{2}, \cos = \dfrac{\sqrt{3}}{2}, \tan = \dfrac{1}{\sqrt{3}}$

  g $\sin = \dfrac{\sqrt{3}}{2}, \cos = \dfrac{1}{2}, \tan = \sqrt{3}$

  h $\sin = -\dfrac{1}{\sqrt{2}}, \cos = -\dfrac{1}{\sqrt{2}}, \tan = 1$

  i $\sin = \dfrac{\sqrt{3}}{2}, \cos = \dfrac{1}{2}, \tan = \sqrt{3}$

  j $\sin = -\dfrac{\sqrt{3}}{2}, \cos = \dfrac{1}{2}, \tan = -\sqrt{3}$

2 a $\dfrac{\sqrt{3}}{2}$ **b** $-\dfrac{1}{\sqrt{2}}$ **c** $-\dfrac{1}{\sqrt{3}}$ **d** $-\dfrac{1}{2}$ **e** $-\dfrac{1}{\sqrt{2}}$
  f $\sqrt{3}$ **g** $-\dfrac{\sqrt{3}}{2}$ **h** $\dfrac{1}{\sqrt{2}}$ **i** $-\dfrac{1}{\sqrt{3}}$

3 a $-\dfrac{\sqrt{3}}{2}$ **b** $-\dfrac{1}{\sqrt{2}}$ **c** $\dfrac{1}{\sqrt{3}}$ **d** Undefined
  e 0 **f** $-\dfrac{1}{\sqrt{2}}$ **g** $\dfrac{1}{\sqrt{2}}$ **h** -1

Exercise 14G

1 a i 2π **ii** 2 **b i** π **ii** 3 **c i** $\dfrac{2\pi}{3}$ **ii** $\dfrac{1}{2}$
  d i 4π **ii** 3 **e i** $\dfrac{2\pi}{3}$ **ii** 4 **f i** $\dfrac{\pi}{2}$ **ii** $\dfrac{1}{2}$
  g i 4π **ii** 2 **h i** 2 **ii** 2 **i i** 4 **ii** 3

2 a Dilation of factor 3 from the x-axis;
  Amplitude = 3; Period = 2π
  b Dilation of factor $\tfrac{1}{5}$ from the y-axis;
  Amplitude = 1; Period $\dfrac{2\pi}{5}$
  c Dilation of factor 3 from the y-axis;
  Amplitude = 1; Period = 6π
  d Dilation of factor 2 from the x-axis and
  dilation of factor $\tfrac{1}{5}$ from the y-axis;
  Amplitude = 2; Period = $\dfrac{2\pi}{5}$

3 a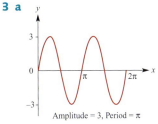
Amplitude = 3, Period = π

b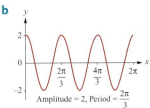
Amplitude = 2, Period = $\dfrac{2\pi}{3}$

c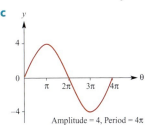
Amplitude = 4, Period = 4π

d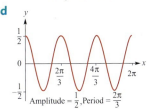
Amplitude = $\dfrac{1}{2}$, Period = $\dfrac{2\pi}{3}$

e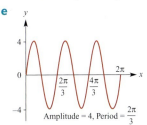
Amplitude = 4, Period = $\dfrac{2\pi}{3}$

f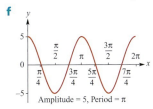
Amplitude = 5, Period = π

g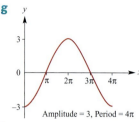
Amplitude = 3, Period = 4π

h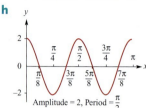
Amplitude = 2, Period = $\dfrac{\pi}{2}$

i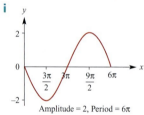
Amplitude = 2, Period = 6π

4 a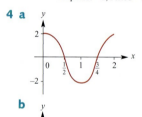

b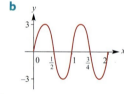

c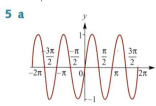

5 a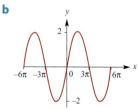

b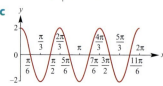

c

d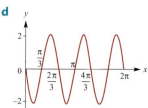

6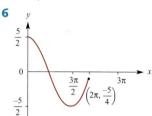

7 a Dilation of factor $\dfrac{1}{5}$ from the y-axis and reflection in the x-axis; Amplitude = 1; Period = $\dfrac{2\pi}{5}$

b Reflection in the y-axis; Amplitude = 1; Period = 2π

c Dilation of factor 3 from the y-axis and dilation of factor 2 from the x-axis; Amplitude = 2; Period = 6π

d Dilation of factor 2 from the y-axis, dilation of factor 4 from the x-axis and reflection in the x-axis; Amplitude = 4; Period = 4π

e Dilation of factor 3 from the y-axis, dilation of factor 2 from the x-axis and reflection in the y-axis; Amplitude = 2; Period = 6π

8 a 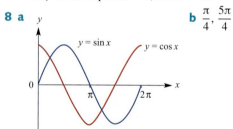   **b** $\dfrac{\pi}{4}, \dfrac{5\pi}{4}$

Exercise 14H

1 a $\dfrac{\pi}{3}, \dfrac{5\pi}{3}, \dfrac{7\pi}{3}, \dfrac{11\pi}{3}$ **b** $\dfrac{\pi}{4}, \dfrac{3\pi}{4}, \dfrac{9\pi}{4}, \dfrac{11\pi}{4}$
c $\dfrac{\pi}{3}, \dfrac{2\pi}{3}, \dfrac{7\pi}{3}, \dfrac{8\pi}{3}$

2 a 0.93, 2.21   **b** 4.30, 1.98   **c** 3.50, 5.93
d 0.41, 2.73   **e** 2.35, 3.94   **f** 1.77, 4.51

3 a 150, 210   **b** 30, 150   **c** 120, 240
d 120, 240   **e** 60, 120   **f** 45, 135

4 a $\dfrac{\pi}{6}, \dfrac{11\pi}{6}$ **b** $\dfrac{5\pi}{4}, \dfrac{7\pi}{4}$ **c** $\dfrac{\pi}{4}, \dfrac{7\pi}{4}$

5 a $\dfrac{3\pi}{4}, -\dfrac{3\pi}{4}$ **b** $\dfrac{\pi}{3}, \dfrac{2\pi}{3}$ **c** $\dfrac{2\pi}{3}, -\dfrac{2\pi}{3}$

6

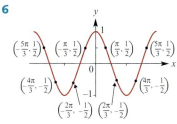

7 a $\dfrac{7\pi}{12}, \dfrac{11\pi}{12}, \dfrac{19\pi}{12}, \dfrac{23\pi}{12}$

  b $\dfrac{\pi}{12}, \dfrac{11\pi}{12}, \dfrac{13\pi}{12}, \dfrac{23\pi}{12}$

  c $\dfrac{\pi}{12}, \dfrac{5\pi}{12}, \dfrac{13\pi}{12}, \dfrac{17\pi}{12}$

  d $\dfrac{5\pi}{12}, \dfrac{7\pi}{12}, \dfrac{13\pi}{12}, \dfrac{15\pi}{12}, \dfrac{21\pi}{12}, \dfrac{23\pi}{12}$

  e $\dfrac{5\pi}{12}, \dfrac{7\pi}{12}, \dfrac{17\pi}{12}, \dfrac{19\pi}{12}$

  f $\dfrac{5\pi}{8}, \dfrac{7\pi}{8}, \dfrac{13\pi}{8}, \dfrac{15\pi}{8}$

8 a 2.034, 2.678, 5.176, 5.820
  b 1.892, 2.820, 5.034, 5.961
  c 0.580, 2.562, 3.721, 5.704
  d 0.309, 1.785, 2.403, 3.880, 4.498, 5.974

Exercise 14I

1 a Period = 2π, Amplitude = 3, $y = \pm 3$

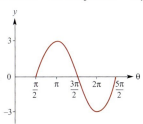

  b Period = π, Amplitude = 1, $y = \pm 1$

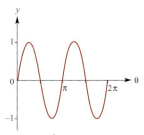

  c Period = $\dfrac{2\pi}{3}$, Amplitude = 2, $y = \pm 2$

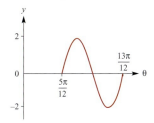

  d Period = π, Amplitude = $\sqrt{3}$, $y = \pm\sqrt{3}$

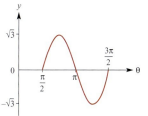

  e Period = π, Amplitude = 3, $y = \pm 3$

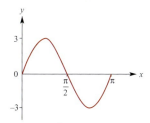

  f Period = $\dfrac{2\pi}{3}$, Amplitude = 2, $y = \pm 2$

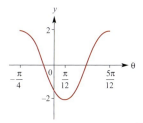

  g Period = π, Amplitude = $\sqrt{2}$, $y = \pm\sqrt{2}$

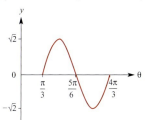

  h Period = π, Amplitude = 3, $y = \pm 3$

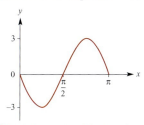

  i Period = π, Amplitude = 3, $y = \pm 3$

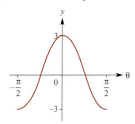

2 a $f(0) = \dfrac{1}{2}$, $f(2\pi) = \dfrac{1}{2}$

b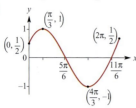

3 a $f(0) = -\dfrac{\sqrt{3}}{2}$, $f(2\pi) = -\dfrac{\sqrt{3}}{2}$

b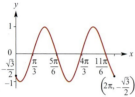

4 a $f(-\pi) = -\dfrac{1}{\sqrt{2}}$, $f(\pi) = -\dfrac{1}{\sqrt{2}}$

b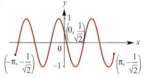

5 a $y = 3\sin\dfrac{x}{2}$ **b** $y = 3\sin(2x)$

c $y = 2\sin\dfrac{x}{3}$ **d** $y = \sin 2\left(x - \dfrac{\pi}{3}\right)$

e $y = \sin\dfrac{1}{2}\left(x + \dfrac{\pi}{3}\right)$

Exercise 14J

1 a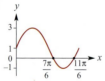

b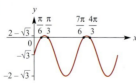

c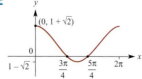

d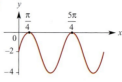

e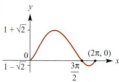

2 a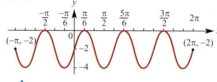

b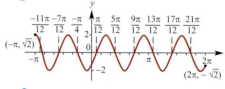

c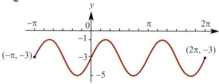

d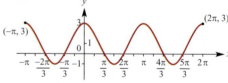

e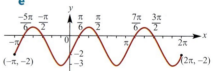

f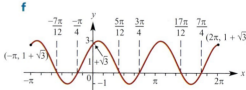

3 a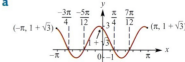

b
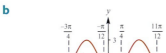

c
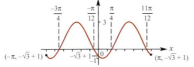

Exercise 14K

1 **a** 0.6   **b** 0.6   **c** −0.7   **d** 0.3
   e −0.3   **f** $\frac{10}{7}$ (1.49)   **g** −0.3
   h 0.6   **i** −0.6   **j** −0.3

2 **a** $\frac{\pi}{3}$ **b** $\frac{\pi}{3}$ **c** $\frac{5\pi}{12}$ **d** $\frac{\pi}{14}$

3 $\sin x = \frac{-4}{5}$, $\tan x = \frac{-4}{3}$

4 $\cos x = \frac{-12}{13}$, $\tan x = \frac{-5}{12}$

5 $\sin x = \frac{-2\sqrt{6}}{5}$, $\tan x = -2\sqrt{6}$

Exercise 14L

1 **a** $\frac{\pi}{4}$ **b** $\frac{3\pi}{2}$ **c** $\frac{\pi}{2}$

2 **a**
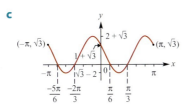

b
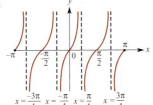

c
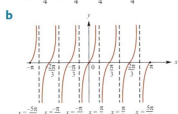

3 **a** $\frac{-7\pi}{8}, \frac{-3\pi}{8}, \frac{\pi}{8}, \frac{5\pi}{8}$

b $\frac{-17\pi}{18}, \frac{-11\pi}{18}, \frac{-5\pi}{18}, \frac{\pi}{18}, \frac{7\pi}{18}, \frac{13\pi}{18}$

c $\frac{-5\pi}{6}, \frac{-\pi}{3}, \frac{\pi}{6}, \frac{2\pi}{3}$

d $\frac{-13\pi}{18}, \frac{-7\pi}{18}, \frac{-\pi}{18}, \frac{5\pi}{18}, \frac{11\pi}{18}, \frac{17\pi}{18}$

4 **a**
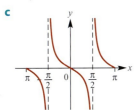

b

c

Exercise 14M

1 **a** 0.74   **b** 0.51   **c** 0.82, −0.82   **d** 0, 0.88

2 $y = a\sin(b\theta + c) + d$
   a $a = 1.993$, $b = 2.998$, $c = 0.003$, $d = 0.993$
   b $a = 3.136$, $b = 3.051$, $c = 0.044$, $d = -0.140$
   c $a = 4.971$, $b = 3.010$, $c = 3.136$, $d = 4.971$

Exercise 14N

1 **a** $x = \frac{(12n+1)\pi}{6}$ or $x = \frac{(12n+5)\pi}{6}$, $n \in \mathbb{Z}$

   b $x = \frac{(12n \pm 1)\pi}{18}$, $n \in \mathbb{Z}$

   c $x = \frac{(3n+2)\pi}{3}$, $n \in \mathbb{Z}$

2 **a** $\frac{\pi}{6}, \frac{5\pi}{6}$ **b** $\frac{\pi}{18}, \frac{11\pi}{18}$ **c** $\frac{2\pi}{3}, \frac{5\pi}{3}$

3 $x = n\pi$ or $x = \frac{(4n-1)\pi}{4}$, $n \in \mathbb{Z}$;
   $x = -\frac{5\pi}{4}, -\pi, -\frac{\pi}{4}, 0, \frac{3\pi}{4}, \pi$ or $\frac{7\pi}{4}$

4 $x = \frac{n\pi}{3}, n \in \mathbb{Z}$; $x = -\pi, -\frac{2\pi}{3}, -\frac{\pi}{3}$ or 0

Exercise 14O

1 a (graph)   **b** $t = 3$ and $t = 15$
  c 5 m above mean sea level
  d $\dfrac{5\sqrt{3}}{2}$ m above mean sea level
  e $\dfrac{5\sqrt{3}}{2}$ m above mean sea level
  f $t \in [1, 5] \cup [13, 17]$

2 a 5 metres   **b** 1 metres
  c $t = 0.524, 2.618$ or 4.712 seconds
  d $t = 0, 1.047$ or 2.094 seconds
  e Particle oscillates between $x = 1$ and $x = 5$

3 a 7 m   **b** 3 m
  c $t = \dfrac{1}{4}, \dfrac{5}{4}, \dfrac{9}{4}, \dfrac{13}{4}$ or $\dfrac{17}{4}$
  d $t = \dfrac{1}{12}, \dfrac{5}{12}, \dfrac{13}{12}, \dfrac{17}{12}, \dfrac{25}{12}$ or $\dfrac{29}{12}$
  e Particle oscillates between $x = 3$ and $x = 7$

4 a i 10   **ii** $10 + 5\sqrt{3}$ **iii** $10 + 5\sqrt{3}$
      iv $10 - 5\sqrt{3}$ **v** $10 - 5\sqrt{3}$
  b 6 seconds   **c** 20 metres
  d $\dfrac{1}{2}, \dfrac{5}{2}, \dfrac{13}{2}, \dfrac{17}{2}$ s   **e** $\dfrac{7}{2}, \dfrac{11}{2}, \dfrac{19}{2}, \dfrac{23}{2}$ s

5 a 9°C   **b** Maximum = 25°C; Minimum = 9°C
  c Between 7:28 and 16:32
  d (graph)

5 $x = \dfrac{6n - 1}{12}$ or $x = \dfrac{3n + 2}{6}$, $n \in \mathbb{Z}$;
  $x = -\dfrac{2}{3}, -\dfrac{7}{12}, -\dfrac{1}{6}, -\dfrac{1}{12}, \dfrac{1}{3}, \dfrac{5}{12}, \dfrac{5}{6}$ or $\dfrac{11}{12}$

6 a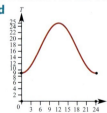
  b $\{t : D(t) \geq 8.5\} = [0, 7] \cup [11, 19] \cup [23, 24]$
  c 12.9 m

7 a $p = 5, q = 2$ **b**
  c A ship can enter 2 hours after low tide

Chapter 14 review

Technology-free questions

1 a $\dfrac{11\pi}{6}$ **b** $\dfrac{9\pi}{2}$ **c** 6π **d** $\dfrac{23\pi}{4}$ **e** $\dfrac{3\pi}{4}$
  f $\dfrac{9\pi}{4}$ **g** $\dfrac{13\pi}{6}$ **h** $\dfrac{7\pi}{3}$ **i** $\dfrac{4\pi}{9}$

2 a 150°   **b** 315°   **c** 495°   **d** 45°
  e 1350°   **f** −135°   **g** −45°   **h** −495°
  i −1035°

3 a $\dfrac{1}{\sqrt{2}}$ **b** $\dfrac{1}{\sqrt{2}}$ **c** $-\dfrac{1}{2}$ **d** $-\dfrac{\sqrt{3}}{2}$
  e $\dfrac{\sqrt{3}}{2}$ **f** $-\dfrac{1}{2}$ **g** $\dfrac{1}{2}$ **h** $-\dfrac{1}{\sqrt{2}}$

4 a $2, 4\pi$ **b** $3, \dfrac{\pi}{2}$ **c** $\dfrac{1}{2}, \dfrac{2\pi}{3}$ **d** $3, \pi$
  e $4, 6\pi$ **f** $\dfrac{2}{3}, 3\pi$

5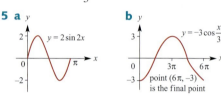
  c 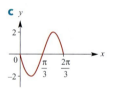   **d**
  e 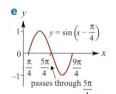   **f**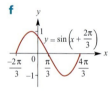
  g 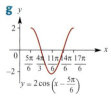   **h**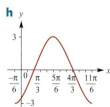

6 a $-\dfrac{2\pi}{3}, -\dfrac{\pi}{3}$ **b** $-\dfrac{\pi}{3}, -\dfrac{\pi}{6}, \dfrac{2\pi}{3}, \dfrac{5\pi}{6}$
  c $\dfrac{\pi}{6}, \dfrac{3\pi}{2}$ **d** $\dfrac{7\pi}{6}$ **e** $\dfrac{\pi}{2}, \dfrac{7\pi}{6}$

Multiple-choice questions

1 C   **2** D   **3** E   **4** C   **5** E
6 D   **7** E   **8** E   **9** C   **10** B

Answers

Extended-response questions

1 a i 1.83×10^{-3} hours **ii** 11.79 hours
  b 26 April ($t = 3.86$), 14 August ($t = 7.48$)
2 a 19.5°C **b** $D = -1 + 2\cos\left(\dfrac{\pi t}{12}\right)$
  c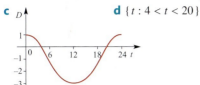
  d $\{t : 4 < t < 20\}$
3 a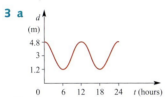
  b 3 a.m., 3 p.m., 3 a.m.
  c 9 a.m., 9 p.m. **d** 10:03 a.m.
  e i 6:12 p.m. **ii** 5 trips
4 b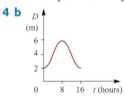
  c $t = 16$ (8 p.m.)
  d $t = 4$ and $t = 12$ (8 a.m. and 4 p.m.)
  e i 1.5 m **ii** 2.086 m
  f 9 hours 17 minutes

Chapter 15

Technology-free questions

1 a $-24a^{10}$ **b** $\dfrac{a^3}{2b^2}$ **c** $\dfrac{3}{4x^5}$ **d** 8
  e $\dfrac{y^{\frac{2}{3}}}{x^{\frac{1}{6}}}$ **f** $\dfrac{1}{(2x-1)^{\frac{1}{2}}}$
2 a $\dfrac{25}{9}$ **b** 16 **c** 81 **d** $-\dfrac{1}{3}$
3 a $2^{6n} \times 3^{3n}$ **b** 12 **c** $\log_{10} 36$ **d** -3
4 a Range $(-3, \infty)$ **b** Range $(-\infty, 1)$
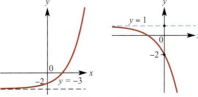
5 a $x = 3$ **b** $x = 0, 2$ **c** $x > 4$ **d** $x = 7$ **e** $x = 1$
6 a $x = \log_2 5$ **b** $x = \dfrac{1}{3}(\log_5(10) - 1)$
  c $x > \dfrac{\log_{10} 0.2}{\log_{10} 0.6}$

7 $f^{-1}(x) = \log_3(x-2)$
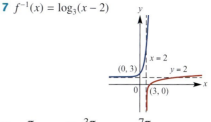
8 a $\dfrac{\pi}{3}$ **b** $\dfrac{3\pi}{2}$ **c** $\dfrac{7\pi}{9}$
9 a -1 **b** 0 **c** 0 **d** Undefined
10 a 21.80° **b** 3.06 **c** 9.97
11 a -0.3 **b** -0.5 **c** 1.6 **d** -0.6 **e** 0.1 **f** $\dfrac{4}{5}$
12 a $\dfrac{\sqrt{3}}{2}$ **b** $-\dfrac{\sqrt{3}}{2}$ **c** -1 **d** $\dfrac{1}{2}$ **e** $\dfrac{1}{\sqrt{2}}$ **f** $-\sqrt{3}$
13 a Period $= 4\pi$; Amplitude $= 2$
  b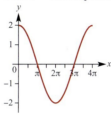
  c Dilation of factor 2 from the x-axis and dilation of factor 2 from the y-axis
14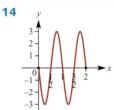
15 a $\dfrac{-7\pi}{6}, \dfrac{-5\pi}{6}, \dfrac{5\pi}{6}, \dfrac{7\pi}{6}$
  b $\dfrac{-7\pi}{4}, \dfrac{-5\pi}{4}, \dfrac{\pi}{4}, \dfrac{3\pi}{4}$
  c $\dfrac{-17\pi}{12}, \dfrac{-13\pi}{12}, \dfrac{-5\pi}{12}, \dfrac{-\pi}{12}, \dfrac{7\pi}{12}, \dfrac{11\pi}{12}, \dfrac{19\pi}{12}, \dfrac{23\pi}{12}$
  d $\dfrac{-4\pi}{3}, \dfrac{-\pi}{3}, \dfrac{2\pi}{3}, \dfrac{5\pi}{3}$
16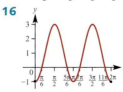
17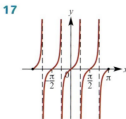

18 a $x = \dfrac{\pi}{6} + 2n\pi$ or $x = \dfrac{5\pi}{6} + 2n\pi$, $n \in \mathbb{Z}$

b $x = \pm\dfrac{\pi}{6} + 2n\pi$, $n \in \mathbb{Z}$

c $x = -\dfrac{\pi}{8} + \dfrac{n\pi}{2}$, $n \in \mathbb{Z}$

Multiple-choice questions

1 B **2** B **3** B **4** E **5** D **6** A
7 D **8** C **9** B **10** A **11** A **12** D
13 A **14** D **15** D **16** D **17** A **18** E
19 D **20** D **21** E **22** A **23** E **24** B
25 D **26** B

Extended-response questions

1 a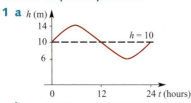

b $t = 3.2393$ and $t = 8.7606$

c $t \in [0.9652, 11.0348]$

2 a 40 bacteria

b i 320   **ii** 2560   **iii** 10 485 760

c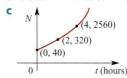

d 40 minutes ($= \tfrac{2}{3}$ hours)

3 a 60 seconds

b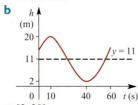

c [2, 20]

d First at height 2 metres after 40 seconds; then every 60 seconds after this first time

e At $t = 0$, $t = 20$ and $t = 60$, for $t \in [0, 60]$

4 a 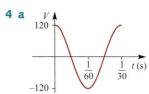   **b** $t = \dfrac{1}{180}$ s

c $t = \dfrac{k}{30}$ s, for $k = 0, 1, 2, \ldots$

5 a i Period = 15 seconds

  ii Amplitude = 3   **iii** $c = \dfrac{2\pi}{15}$

b $h = 1.74202$

c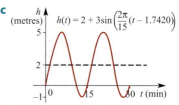

6 a i 30   **ii** 49.5   **iii** 81.675

b $k = 1.65$

c 6.792 hours

d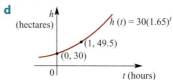

7 a

t	0	1	2	3	4	5
θ	100	60	40	30	25	22.5

b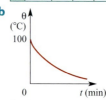

c 1 minute   **d** 27.071

8 a $P_A = 70\,000\,000 + 3\,000\,000t$
$P_B = 70\,000\,000 + 5\,000\,000t$
$P_C = 70\,000\,000 \times 1.3^{\frac{t}{10}}$

b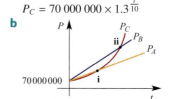

c i 35 years   **ii** 67 years

9 a i 4 billion   **ii** 5.944 billion   **iii** 7.25 billion

b 2032

10 a $V_1(0) = V_2(0) = 1000$

b 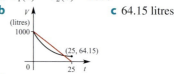   **c** 64.15 litres

d $t = 0$ and $t = 23.00$

11 a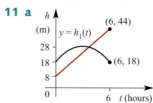

b 3:19 a.m. to nearest minute ($t = 3.31$)

c i 9 a.m.   **ii** $8 + 6t$ metres

Chapter 16

Exercise 16A

1 a, b, c, d

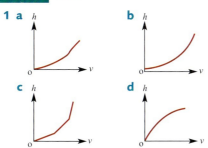

2 For the first 2 minutes, the particle travels a distance of 4 m with its speed increasing. For the next 4 minutes, it travels 4 m at constant speed. Then it turns back and returns to its starting point O, travelling at a constant speed and taking 8 minutes to reach O.

Note: For questions 3–6, there may be more than one correct answer.

3 C is the most likely

4

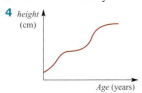

5

6 C and B are the most likely

7 a, b

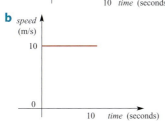

8

9 D

10 C

11 a $(-4, 0)$ b $[-7, -4) \cup (0, 3]$

12 a $(-3, 0)$ b $[-5, -3) \cup (0, 2]$

Exercise 16B

1

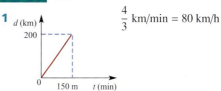

$\frac{4}{3}$ km/min = 80 km/h

2

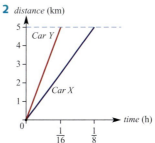

3

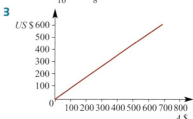

4 a 60 km/h b 3 m/s
  c 400 m/min = 24 km/h = $6\frac{2}{3}$ m/s
  d 35.29 km/h (correct to 2 d.p.)
  e 20.44 m/s (correct to 2 d.p.)

5 a 8 litres/min b 50 litres/min
  c $\frac{200}{17}$ litres/min d $\frac{135}{13}$ litres/min

6 a

t	0	0.5	1	1.5	2	3	4	5
A	0	7.5	15	22.5	30	45	60	75

b

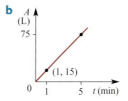

7 $\frac{\$200}{13}$ per hour = $15.38 per hour

8 $208\frac{1}{3}$ m/s

9

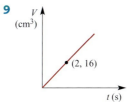

10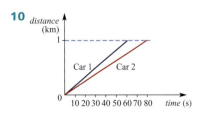

Exercise 16C

1 3.2 m/s

2 a 2   **b** 7   **c** $\dfrac{-1}{2}$ **d** $\dfrac{1-\sqrt{5}}{4}$

3 a $\dfrac{-25}{7}$ **b** $\dfrac{-18}{7}$ **c** 4   **d** $\dfrac{4b}{3a}$

4 a 4 m/s   **b** 32 m/s

5 a $2450.09   **b** $150.03 per year

6 3.125 cm/min

7 C

Exercise 16D

1 7.19

2 a 0.015   **b** $\dfrac{1}{60} \approx 0.0167$

3 a i 9   **ii** 4.3246   **iii** 2.5893
   b 2.30

4 a 25°C at 16:00   **b** $\approx 3°C/h$ **c** $-2.5°C/h$

5 −0.5952

6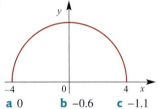
   a 0   **b** −0.6   **c** −1.1

7 4

8 a 16 m³/min   **b** 10 m³/min

9 a 18 million/min   **b** 8.3 million/min

10 a 620 m³/min flowing out
   b 4440 m³/min flowing out
   c 284 000 m³/min flowing out

11 a 7   **b** 9   **c** 2   **d** 35

12 a 28   **b** 12

13 a 10   **b** 4

14 a i $\dfrac{2}{\pi} \approx 0.637$ **ii** $\dfrac{2\sqrt{2}}{\pi} \approx 0.9003$
   iii 0.959   **iv** 0.998
   b 1

Exercise 16E

1 a 4 m/s   **b** 1.12 m/s

2 a i 30 km/h   **ii** $\dfrac{20}{3}$ km/h   **iii** −40 km/h

c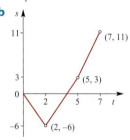

3 a (graph)

b (graph)

4 a $t = 2.5$ **b** $0 \le t < 2.5$ **c** 6 m
   d 5 s   **e** 3 m/s

5 a $t = 6$ **b** 15 m/s   **c** 17.5 m/s
   d 20 m/s   **e** −10 m/s   **f** −20 m/s

6 a 11 m/s   **b** 15 m   **c** 1 s   **d** 2.8 s   **e** 15 m/s

7 a $t = 2$, $t = 3$ and $t = 8$
   b $0 < t < 2.5$ and $t > 6$
   c $t = 2.5$ and $t = 6$

Chapter 16 review

Technology-free questions

1 a depth (graph)   **b** depth (graph)
   c depth (graph)   **d** depth (graph)
   e depth (graph)   **f** depth (graph)

2 a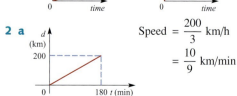

Speed $= \dfrac{200}{3}$ km/h $= \dfrac{10}{9}$ km/min

b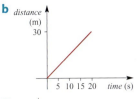

c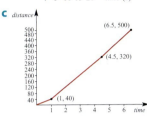

3 36 cm²/cm
4 a 1   **b** 13
5 a −2 m/s   **b** −12.26 m/s   **c** −14 m/s

Multiple-choice questions
1 C   **2** B   **3** D   **4** E
5 D   **6** B   **7** C   **8** E

Extended-response questions
1 a Yes, the relation is linear
   b 0.05 ohm/°C
2 a i 9.8 m/s   **ii** 29.4 m/s
   b i $4.9(8h - h^2)$
     ii $4.9(8 - h)$
     iii 38.22 m/s, 38.71 m/s, 38.995 m/s, 39.151 m/s, 39.1951 m/s

3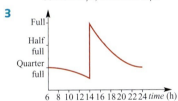

4 a $b + a$ $(a \neq b)$ **b** 3   **c** 4.01
5 a $2\frac{2}{3}, 1\frac{3}{5}$; Gradient $= -1\frac{1}{15}$
   b 2.1053, 1.9048; Gradient $= -1.003$
   c -1.000025 **d** -1.0000003
6 a $\approx 3\frac{1}{3}$ kg/year   **b** ≈ 4.4 kg/year
   c $(0, 5) \cup (10, 12)$ **d** $(5, 7) \cup (11, 17\frac{1}{2})$
7 a i 2.5×10^8 **ii** 5×10^8
   b 0.007 billion/year
   c i 0.004 billion/year   **ii** 0.015 billion/year
   d 25 years after 2020
8 a i 1049.1   **ii** 1164.3   **iii** 1297.7   **iv** 1372.4
   b At 2.8 the gradient is 1452.8
9 a $a^2 + ab + b^2$ **b** 7   **c** 12.06
   d $3b^2$
10 a B   **b** A   **c** 25 m   **d** 45 s
   e 0.98 m/s, 1.724 m/s, 1.136 m/s
11 a m **b** cm **c** $-m$

Chapter 17

Exercise 17A
1 a $-2 - h$ **b** -2
2 a $5 + h$ **b** 5
3 $2x - 2$ **4** 32   **5** 2000 m/s
6 7 per day
7 a 1   **b** $3x^2 + 1$ **c** 20
   d $30x^2 + 1$ **e** 5   **f** $30x^3 + 4$
8 a $2x + 2$ **b** 13   **c** $3x^2 + 4x$
9 a $5 + 3h$ **b** 5.3   **c** 5
10 a $\dfrac{-1}{2+h}$ **b** -0.48 **c** $\dfrac{-1}{2}$
11 a $6 + h$ **b** 6.1   **c** 6
12 a $6x$ **b** 4   **c** 0   **d** $6x + 4$
   e $6x^2$ **f** $8x - 5$ **g** $-2 + 2x$
13 $4x^3$

Exercise 17B
1 a $2x + 4$ **b** 2   **c** $3x^2 - 1$ **d** $x - 3$
   e $15x^2 + 6x$ **f** $-3x^2 + 4x$
2 a $12x^{11}$ **b** $21x^6$ **c** 5   **d** 5
   e 0   **f** $10x - 3$ **g** $50x^4 + 12x^3$
   h $8x^3 - x^2 - \frac{1}{2}x$
3 a 6   **b** 20   **c** 5   **d** 10   **e** 0
   f 7   **g** 31   **h** 7   **i** -34
4 a 60   **b** -16 **c** 57   **d** 168
5 a 7   **b** 2   **c** -16 **d** 11
6 a -1 **b** 0   **c** $12x^2 - 3$
   d $x^2 - 1$ **e** $2x + 3$ **f** $18x^2 - 8$
   g $15x^2 + 3x$
7 a $2(x + 4)$ **b** $48t^2 + 16t - 7$ **c** $2x$
8 a i 3   **ii** $3a^2$ **b** $3x^2$
9 a $\dfrac{dy}{dx} = 3(x-1)^2 \geq 0$ for all x;
     therefore gradient of graph ≥ 0 for all x
   b $\dfrac{dy}{dx} = 1$ for $x \neq 0$
   c $18x + 6$
10 a 1, Gradient $= 2$ **b** 1, Gradient $= 1$
   c 3, Gradient $= -4$ **d** -5, Gradient $= 4$
   e 28, Gradient $= -36$ **f** 9, Gradient $= -24$
11 a i $4x - 1$, 3, $(\frac{1}{2}, 0)$
     ii $\frac{1}{2} + \frac{2}{3}x$, $\frac{7}{6}$, $\left(\frac{3}{4}, \frac{25}{16}\right)$
     iii $3x^2 + 1$, 4, $(0, 0)$
     iv $4x^3 - 31$, -27, $(2, -46)$
   b Coordinates of the point where gradient is 1
12 a $6t - 4$ **b** $-2x + 3x^2$ **c** $-4z - 4z^3$
   d $6y - 3y^2$ **e** $6x^2 - 8x$ **f** $19.6t - 2$
13 a $(4, 16)$ **b** $(2, 8), (-2, -8)$ **c** $(0, 0)$
   d $\left(\frac{3}{2}, -\frac{5}{4}\right)$ **e** $(2, -12)$ **f** $\left(-\frac{1}{3}, \frac{4}{27}\right)$, $(1, 0)$

Exercise 17C

1 a $-\dfrac{1}{(x-3)^2}$ **b** $-\dfrac{1}{(x+2)^2}$

2 a $-\dfrac{2}{x^3}$ **b** $-\dfrac{4}{x^5}$

3 a $-6x^{-3} - 5x^{-2}$ **b** $-6x^{-3} + 10x$
   c $-15x^{-4} - 8x^{-3}$ **d** $6x - \dfrac{20}{3}x^{-5}$
   e $-12x^{-3} + 3$ **f** $3 - 2x^{-2}$

4 a $-2z^{-2} - 8z^{-3}, z \neq 0$ **b** $-9z^{-4} - 2z^{-3}, z \neq 0$
   c $\dfrac{1}{2}, z \neq 0$ **d** $18z + 4 - 18z^{-4}, z \neq 0$
   e $2z^{-3}, z \neq 0$ **f** $-\dfrac{3}{5}, z \neq 0$

5 a $f'(x) = 12x^3 + 18x^{-4} - x^{-2}$
   b $f'(x) = 20x^3 - 8x^{-3} - x^{-2}$

6

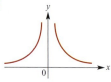

   a Gradient of $PQ = \dfrac{-2-h}{(1+h)^2}$ **b** -2

7 a $11\dfrac{3}{4}$ **b** $\dfrac{1}{8}$ **c** -1 **d** 5

8 a $-\dfrac{1}{2}$ **b** $\dfrac{1}{2}$

9 $f'(x) = -\dfrac{1}{x^2} < 0$ for all $x \neq 0$

Exercise 17D

1 Graphs b and d

2 Graphs a, b and e

3 a $x = 1$ **b** $x = 1$ **c** $x > 1$ **d** $x < 1$ **e** $x = \dfrac{1}{2}$

4 a $(-\infty, -3) \cup (\tfrac{1}{2}, 4)$ **b** $(-3, \tfrac{1}{2}) \cup (4, \infty)$
   c $\{-3, \tfrac{1}{2}, 4\}$

5 a B   **b** C   **c** D   **d** A   **e** F   **f** E

6 a   **b**   **c**   **d**

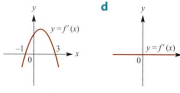

7 a $(-1, 1.5)$ **b** $(-\infty, -1) \cup (1.5, \infty)$ **c** $\{-1, 1.5\}$

8 a $(3, 0)$ **b** $(4, 2)$

9 a $(\tfrac{1}{2}, -6\tfrac{1}{4})$ **b** $(0, -6)$

10 a   **b**

   c

11 a i $66.80°$ **ii** $42.51°$
   b $(0.5352, 0.2420)$
   c No

12 a $(0.6)t^2$ **b** 0.6 m/s, 5.4 m/s, 15 m/s

13 a $a = 2, b = -5$ **b** $\left(\dfrac{5}{4}, -\dfrac{25}{8}\right)$

14 a Height = $450\,000$ m; Speed = 6000 m/s
   b $t = 25$ s

Exercise 17E

1 a $\dfrac{x^4}{8} + c$ **b** $x^3 - 2x + c$ **c** $\dfrac{5x^4}{4} - x^2 + c$
   d $\dfrac{x^4}{5} - \dfrac{2x^3}{3} + c$ **e** $\dfrac{x^3}{3} - x^2 + x + c$
   f $\dfrac{x^3}{3} + x + c$ **g** $\dfrac{z^4}{2} - \dfrac{2z^3}{3} + c$
   h $\dfrac{4t^3}{3} - 6t^2 + 9t + c$ **i** $\dfrac{t^4}{4} - t^3 + \dfrac{3t^2}{2} - t + c$

2 $f(x) = x^4 + 2x^3 + 2x$

3 $y = 2x^3 + 12$

4 a $y = x^2 - x$ **b** $y = 3x - \dfrac{x^2}{2} + 1$
   c $y = \dfrac{x^3}{3} + x^2 + 2$ **d** $y = 3x - \dfrac{x^3}{3} + 2$
   e $y = \dfrac{2x^5}{5} + \dfrac{x^2}{2}$

5 a $V = \dfrac{t^3}{3} - \dfrac{t^2}{2} + \dfrac{9}{2}$ **b** $\dfrac{1727}{6} \approx 287.83$

6 $f(x) = x^3 - x + 2$

7 a B   **b** $w = 2000t - 10t^2 + 100\,000$

8 $f(x) = 5x - \dfrac{x^2}{2} + 4$

9 $f(x) = \dfrac{x^4}{4} - x^3 - 2$

10 a $k = 8$ **b** $(0, 7)$

11 $8\tfrac{2}{3}$

12 a $k = -4$ **b** $y = x^2 - 4x + 9$

13 a $k = -32$ **b** $f(7) = 201$

14 $y = \tfrac{1}{3}(x^3 - 5)$

Exercise 17F

1 a 15 **b** 1 **c** $-3\tfrac{1}{2}$ **d** $-2\tfrac{1}{2}$
   e 0 **f** 4 **g** 2 **h** $2\sqrt{3}$
   i -2 **j** 12 **k** $\dfrac{11}{9}$ **l** $\dfrac{1}{4}$

2 a 3, 4   **b** 7
3 a Discontinuity at 0, as $f(0) = 0$,
$\lim_{x \to 0^+} f(x) = 0$ but $\lim_{x \to 0^-} f(x) = 2$
b Discontinuity at 1, as $f(1) = 3$,
$\lim_{x \to 1^+} f(x) = 3$ but $\lim_{x \to 1^-} f(x) = -1$
c Discontinuity at 0, as $f(0) = 1$,
$\lim_{x \to 0^+} f(x) = 1$ but $\lim_{x \to 0^-} f(x) = 0$
4 $x = 1$

Exercise 17G

1 a 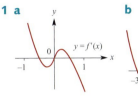   **b**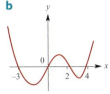

c, **d**, **e**, **f**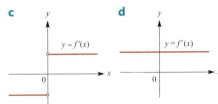

2 $f'(x) = \begin{cases} -2x + 3 & \text{if } x \geq 0 \\ 3 & \text{if } x < 0 \end{cases}$

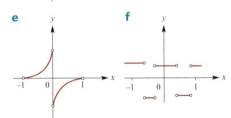

3 $f'(x) = \begin{cases} 2x + 2 & \text{if } x > 1 \\ -2 & \text{if } x < 1 \end{cases}$

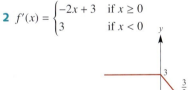

4 $f'(x) = \begin{cases} -2x - 3 & \text{if } x > -1 \\ -2 & \text{if } x < -1 \end{cases}$

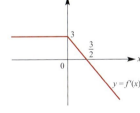

Chapter 17 review

Technology-free questions

1 a 3   **b** $-2x$ **c** $2x + 5$
  d $3x^2 + 1$ **e** $2x + 2$ **f** $6x - 1$
2 a $6x - 2$ **b** 0   **c** $4 - 4x$
  d $4(20x - 1)$ **e** $6x + 1$ **f** $-6x - 1$
3 a -1 **b** 0   **c** $\dfrac{4x + 7}{4}$ **d** $\dfrac{4x - 1}{3}$ **e** x
4 a 1; 2   **b** 3; -4 **c** -5; 4   **d** 28; -36
5 a $\left(\dfrac{3}{2}, -\dfrac{5}{4}\right)$ **b** $(2, -12)$ **c** $\left(-\dfrac{1}{3}, \dfrac{4}{27}\right)$, $(1, 0)$
  d $(-1, 8), (1, 6)$ **e** $(0, 1), \left(\dfrac{3}{2}, -\dfrac{11}{16}\right)$
  f $(3, 0), (1, 4)$
6 a $x = \dfrac{1}{2}$ **b** $x = \dfrac{1}{2}$ **c** $x > \dfrac{1}{2}$ **d** $x < \dfrac{1}{2}$
  e $x \in \mathbb{R} \setminus \left\{\dfrac{1}{2}\right\}$ **f** $x = \dfrac{5}{8}$
7 a $-4x^{-5}$ **b** $-6x^{-4}$ **c** $\dfrac{2}{3x^3}$ **d** $\dfrac{4}{x^5}$
  e $-\dfrac{15}{x^6}$ **f** $-\dfrac{2}{x^3} - \dfrac{1}{x^2} = -\dfrac{2 + x}{x^3}$
  g $-\dfrac{2}{x^2}$ **h** $10x + \dfrac{2}{x^2}$
8 a $a = 2, b = -1$ **b** $\left(\dfrac{1}{4}, -\dfrac{1}{8}\right)$
9 a $\dfrac{x}{2} + c$ **b** $\dfrac{x^3}{6} + c$ **c** $\dfrac{x^3}{3} + \dfrac{3x^2}{2} + c$
  d $\dfrac{4x^3}{3} + 6x^2 + 9x + c$ **e** $\dfrac{at^2}{2} + c$ **f** $\dfrac{t^4}{12} + c$
  g $\dfrac{t^3}{3} - \dfrac{t^2}{2} - 2t + c$ **h** $\dfrac{-t^3}{3} + \dfrac{t^2}{2} + 2t + c$
10 $f(x) = x^2 + 5x - 25$
11 a $f(x) = x^3 - 4x^2 + 3x$ **b** 0, 1, 3
12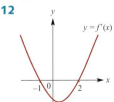

13 a $(-1, 4)$ **b** $(-\infty, -1) \cup (4, \infty)$ **c** $\{-1, 4\}$

Multiple-choice questions

1 D   2 B   3 E   4 B   5 C
6 C   7 A   8 E   9 A   10 D

Extended-response questions

1

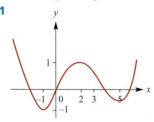

2 $y = \dfrac{7}{36}x^3 + \dfrac{1}{36}x^2 - \dfrac{20}{9}x$

3 a i 71.57°   **ii** 89.58°   **b** 2 km

4 a 0.12, −0.15
  b $x = 2$, $y = 2.16$; Height 2.16 km

5 a $t = \sqrt[3]{250}$, 11.9 cm/s   **b** 3.97 cm/s

6 a At $x = 0$, gradient is −2; at $x = 2$, gradient is 2. Angles of inclination to the positive direction of the x-axis are supplementary.

Chapter 18

Exercise 18A

1 a $y = 4x - 4$, $4y + x = 18$
  b $y = 12x - 15$, $12y + x = 110$
  c $y = -x + 4$, $y = x$
  d $y = 6x + 2$, $6y + x = 49$

2 $y = 2x - 10$

3 $y = 2x - 1$, $y = 2x - \dfrac{8}{3}$;
  Both have gradient 2; Distance apart $= \dfrac{\sqrt{5}}{3}$

4 $y = 3x + 2$, $y = 3x + 6$

5 a Tangents both have gradient 2   **b** $(0, -3)$

6 $(3, 12)$, $(1, 4)$

7 a $y = 10x - 16$ **b** $(-4, -56)$

8 a $y = 5x - 1$ **b** $(2, 4)$, $(4, -8)$

Exercise 18B

1 a 36; $\dfrac{36}{1} = 36$ **b** $48 - 12h$ **c** 48

2 a $1200t - 200t^2$ **b** $1800 per month
  c At $t = 0$ and $t = 6$

3 a $30 - 4P$
  b 10, -10
  c For $P < 7.5$ revenue increases as P increases

4 a 50 people per year   **b** 0 people per year
  c Decreasing by 50 people per year

5 a i 0 mL   **ii** $833\tfrac{1}{3}$ mL
  b $V'(t) = \dfrac{5}{8}(20t - t^2)$
  c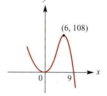

6 a 0.6 km²   **b** 0.7 km²/h

Exercise 18C

1 a $(3, -6)$ **b** $(3, 2)$ **c** $(2, 2)$ **d** $(4, 48)$
  e $(0, 0)$, $(2, -8)$ **f** $(0, -10)$, $(2, 6)$

2 $a = 2$, $b = -8$, $c = -1$

3 $a = -\tfrac{1}{2}$, $b = 1$, $c = 1\tfrac{1}{2}$

4 a $a = 2$, $b = -5$ **b** $\left(\dfrac{5}{4}, -\dfrac{25}{8}\right)$

5 $a = -8$

6 $a = 6$

7 a $(2.5, -12.25)$ **b** $\left(\dfrac{7}{48}, -\dfrac{625}{96}\right)$
  c $(0, 27)$, $(3, 0)$ **d** $(-2, 48)$, $(4, -60)$
  e $(-3, 4)$, $(-1, 0)$ **f** $(-1.5, 0.5)$

8 $a = -1$, $b = 2$

9 $a = -\dfrac{2}{9}$, $b = \dfrac{3}{2}$, $c = -3$, $d = 7\tfrac{1}{2}$

Exercise 18D

1 a min $(0, 0)$ **b** min $(3, -27)$
    max $(6, 108)$ max $(-1, 5)$

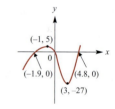

  c inflection $(0, 0)$
    min $(3, -27)$

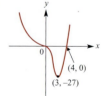

2 a $(0, 0)$ max; $\left(\dfrac{8}{3}, -\dfrac{256}{27}\right)$ min
  b $(0, 0)$ min; $(2, 4)$ max   **c** $(0, 0)$ min
  d $\left(\dfrac{10}{3}, \dfrac{-200\,000}{729}\right)$ min; $(0, 0)$ inflection
  e $(3, -7)$ min; $\left(\dfrac{1}{3}, \dfrac{67}{27}\right)$ max
  f $(6, -36)$ min; $\left(\dfrac{4}{3}, \dfrac{400}{27}\right)$ max

3 a max at $(1, 4)$
 min at $(-1, 0)$
 intercepts $(2, 0), (-1, 0)$

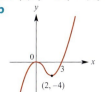

b min at $(2, -8)$
 max at $(0, 0)$
 intercepts $(3, 0), (0, 0)$

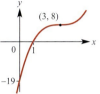

c min at $(3, -16)$
 max at $(-1, 16)$
 intercepts $(0, 11)$,
 $(1 \pm 2\sqrt{3}, 0), (1, 0)$

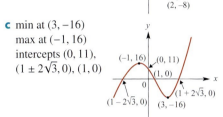

4 a Local maximum
 b Stationary point of inflection

5 a $(-\infty, 1) \cup (3, \infty)$
 b $(1, 14)$ max; $(3, 10)$ min
 c

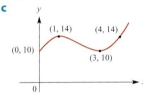

6 $\{x : -2 < x < 2\}$
7 a $x \in (-1, 1)$ **b** $x \in (-\infty, -1) \cup (1, \infty)$
8 a $x = -\dfrac{5}{3}$, $x = 3$
 b max at $\left(-\dfrac{5}{3}, \dfrac{400}{27}\right)$, min at $(3, -36)$
 intercepts $(5, 0), (0, 0), (-3, 0)$

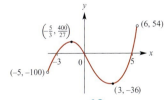

9

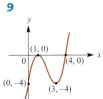

10

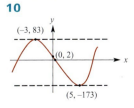

11 a i $(0, 2)$ **ii** $(-\infty, 0) \cup (2, \infty)$ **iii** $\{0, 2\}$
 b

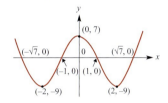

12 Stationary point of inflection at $(3, 8)$

13 min at $(-2, -9)$ and $(2, -9)$; max at $(0, 7)$
 intercepts $(\pm\sqrt{7}, 0), (\pm 1, 0), (0, 7)$

Exercise 18E

1 2500 cm²
2 25
3 2
4 a $V(x) = (6 - 2x)^2 x$
 b $V_{\max} = 16$ m³ when $x = 1$
5 a i 0.9375 m **ii** 2.5 m **iii** 2.8125 m
 b $x = \dfrac{40}{3}, y = \dfrac{80}{27}$
 c i $x = 11.937, x = 1.396$ **ii** $x = 14.484$
6 b $V = \dfrac{75x - x^3}{2}$ **c** 125 cm³ **d** 118 cm³
7 256π
8 $x = \dfrac{5}{3}(9 - \sqrt{21})$
9 Absolute max = 2; Absolute min = -30
10 Absolute max = 6; Absolute min = -9
11 Absolute max = 32; Absolute min = -8
12 Absolute max = 1050; Absolute min = -8
13 b $\dfrac{dV}{dx} = 30x - 36x^2$ **c** $\dfrac{125}{36}$ **d** $\dfrac{432}{125}$
 e $\dfrac{125}{36}$ when $x = \dfrac{5}{6}$
14 a $15 \le y \le 18$ **b** Max 75, min 36
15 a $\dfrac{125\,000}{27}$ **b** 3000 **c** $\dfrac{125\,000}{27}$
16 b $\dfrac{dA}{dx} = \dfrac{1}{8}(2x - 10)$ **c** $x = 5$ **d** $\dfrac{25}{8}$ m²

Exercise 18F

1. **a** $x = 11$ **b** $x = -16$
2. **a** -12 cm/s **b** $t = 6, x = -25$
   c -9 cm/s **d** 9 cm/s
3. **a** -3 cm/s **b** $2\sqrt{3}$ s
4. **a** $x = 5$ cm, $v = 0$ cm/s, $a = -12$ cm/s^2
   b $t = 0, x = 5, a = -12$; $t = 1, x = 3, a = 12$
5. **a** 2 m/s^2 **b** 50 m/s^2
6. **a** $(15 - 9.8t)$ m/s **b** -9.8 m/s^2
7. **a** 3.5 s **b** 2 m/s^2 **c** 14.5 m
   d When $t = 2.5$ s; the particle is 1.25 m to the left of O
8. **a** 0 s, 1 s, 2 s
   b 2 m/s, -1 m/s, 2 m/s; -6 m/s^2, 0 m/s^2, 6 m/s^2
   c 0 m/s
9. **a** 12 cm to the right of O
   b 2 cm to the right of O
   c Moving to the left at 7 cm/s
   d $t = 3.5$ s; particle is 0.25 cm to the left of O
   e -2 cm/s **f** 2.9 cm/s
10. **a** 18 m/s^2, 54 m/s^2, 114 m/s^2, **b** 58 m/s^2
11. **a** 3 cm to the left of O, moving to the right at 24 cm/s
    b $v = 3t^2 - 22t + 24$
    c After $\frac{4}{3}$ s and 6 s
    d $11\frac{22}{27}$ cm to the right of O and 39 cm to the left of O
    e $4\frac{2}{3}$ s
    f $a = 6t - 22$
    g When $t = \frac{11}{3}$ s and the particle is $13\frac{16}{27}$ cm left of O moving to the left at $16\frac{1}{3}$ cm/s
12. **a** When $t = \frac{2}{3}$ s and $a = -2$ cm/s^2, and when $t = 1$ and $a = 2$ cm/s^2
    b When $t = \frac{5}{6}$ and the particle is moving to the left at $\frac{1}{6}$ cm/s
13. When $t = 2$ s, $v = 6$ cm/s, $a = -14$ cm/s^2
    When $t = 3$ s, $v = -5$ cm/s, $a = -8$ cm/s^2
    When $t = 8$ s, $v = 30$ cm/s, $a = 22$ cm/s^2
14. **a** $t = 4$ s and $t = -1$ s **b** $t = \frac{3}{2}$ s

Exercise 18G

1. **a** $x = 2t^2 - 6t$ **b** At the origin O
   c 9 cm **d** 0 cm/s **e** 3 cm/s
2. **a** $x = t^3 - 4t^2 + 5t + 4$, $a = 6t - 8$
   b When $t = 1, x = 6$; when $t = \frac{5}{3}, x = 5\frac{23}{27}$
   c When $t = 1, a = -2$ cm/s^2; when $t = \frac{5}{3}, a = 2$ cm/s^2
3. $x = 215\frac{1}{3}, v = 73$
4. **a** $v = -10t + 25$ **b** $x = -5t^2 + 25t$
   c 2.5 s **d** $31\frac{1}{4}$ m **e** 5 s
5. The 29th floor

Exercise 18H

1. **a** $(x - 2)(3x - 2(b + 1))$
   b $(2, 0), \left(\dfrac{2(b + 1)}{3}, \dfrac{-4(b - 2)^3}{27}\right)$ **d** $b = 5$
2. **a** $(0, 0)$ and $(9, -2187)$
   b (a, b) and $(9 + a, -2187 + b)$
3. **a** **i** $\left(-\infty, \dfrac{1}{2a}\right)$ **ii** $\left(\dfrac{1}{2a}, \infty\right)$
   b $y = -x + \dfrac{1}{a}$ **c** $y = x - \dfrac{1}{a}$ **d** $\left(-\infty, \dfrac{1}{4a}\right]$
4. **a** $(a, 0)$ and $\left(\dfrac{a + 2}{3}, \dfrac{4(a - 1)^3}{27}\right)$
   b Local minimum at $(a, 0)$
   Local maximum at $\left(\dfrac{a + 2}{3}, \dfrac{4(a - 1)^3}{27}\right)$
   c **i** $y = (a - 1)^2(x - 1)$ **ii** $y = 0$
   iii $y = \dfrac{-(a - 1)^2}{4}(x - a)$
5. **a** **i** $2(a - 2)$ **ii** $m = 2(a - 2)$
   b $(a, (a - 2)^2)$
   c $y = 2(a - 2)x - a^2 + 4$ **d** $\dfrac{a + 2}{2}$
6. **a** $h = 2$ **b** $a = 3$ **c** $a = -16, b = -24$
7. **a** $(0, 0)$ **b** (a, b)
8. **a** $2(x - 1)(x - b)(2x - b - 1)$
   b $(1, 0), (b, 0), \left(\dfrac{b + 1}{2}, \dfrac{(b - 1)^4}{16}\right)$ **c** $b = 3$

Exercise 18I

1. **a** 1.32 **b** 1.164 **c** 1.124 or 1.451
   d 2.151 **e** -1.75
2. 1.44225 3. 1.618

Chapter 18 review

Technology-free questions

1. **a** $\dfrac{dy}{dx} = 4 - 2x$ **b** 2 **c** $y = 2x + 1$
2. **a** $3x^2 - 8x$ **b** -4 **c** $y = -4x$ **d** $(0, 0)$
3. **a** $3x^2 - 12; x = \pm 2$
   b Local minimum when $x = 2$
   Local maximum when $x = -2$
   c $x = 2, y = -14$; $x = -2, y = 18$
4. **a** Stationary point of inflection at $x = 0$
   b Maximum at $x = 0$
   c Min at $x = 3$, max at $x = 2$
   d Min at $x = 2$, max at $x = -2$
   e Max at $x = 2$, min at $x = -2$
   f Max at $x = 3$, min at $x = 1$
   g Max at $x = 4$, min at $x = -3$
   h Max at $x = 3$, min at $x = -5$
5. **a** $\left(-\dfrac{2}{3}, -\dfrac{16}{9}\right)$ minimum, $\left(\dfrac{2}{3}, \dfrac{16}{9}\right)$ minimum
   b $(-1, 0)$ maximum, $(2, -27)$ minimum
   c $\left(\dfrac{2}{3}, \dfrac{100}{27}\right)$ maximum, $(3, -9)$ minimum

6 a 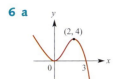 **b**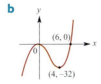

c **d**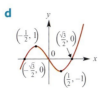

e

7 a C **b** A **c** B
8 a 20 m **b** 6 s **c** 40 m/s
9 72
10 a $\dfrac{15}{2}$ m/s **b** $\dfrac{128}{3}$ m **c** 0 m **d** $\dfrac{64}{9}$ m/s

Multiple-choice questions
1 D **2** E **3** E **4** A **5** C **6** D
7 D **8** A **9** A **10** C **11** A **12** A

Extended-response questions
1 a −14 m/s **b** −8 m/s²

2 a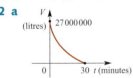

b i 17.4 minutes **ii** 2.9 minutes
c $\dfrac{dV}{dt} = -3000(30 - t)^2$
d 30 minutes
e 28.36 minutes
f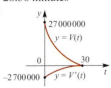

3 a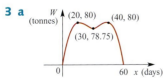

b From 5.71 days until 54.29 days
c When $x = 20$ and when $x = 40$, $\dfrac{dW}{dx} = 0$;
When $x = 60$, $\dfrac{dW}{dx} = -12$ tonnes per day
d When $x = 30$, $W = 78.75$

4 a 15°C
b 0°C/min, $\dfrac{45}{16}$ °C/min, $\dfrac{15}{4}$ °C/min, $\dfrac{45}{16}$ °C/min, 0°C/min

c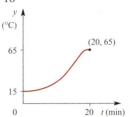

5 a 768 units/day **b** 432, 192, 48, 0
c $t = 16$ **d**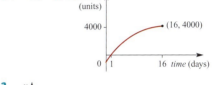

6 a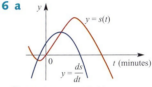

b 11:59 a.m., 12:03 p.m.
c $\dfrac{5}{27}$ km, 1 km
d $\dfrac{8}{27}$ km/min = $17\tfrac{7}{9}$ km/h
e $\dfrac{1}{3}$ km/min = 20 km/h

7 a $0 \le t \le 12$
b i 27 L/h **ii** 192 L/h

8 a 28.8 m
b 374.4
c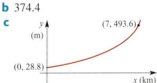

d Path gets too steep after 7 km
e i 0.0384 **ii** 0.0504 **iii** 0.1336

9 a

b For $x \le 0$, the minimum vertical distance occurs when $x = -1$; Min distance = 1 unit

10 8 mm for maximum and $\tfrac{4}{3}$ mm for minimum

11 a $y = 5 - x$ **b** $P = x(5 - x)$
c Max value is 6.25 when $x = 2.5$ and $y = 2.5$

12 a $y = 10 - 2x$ b $A = x^2(10 - 2x)$
   c $A = \dfrac{1000}{27}, x = \dfrac{10}{3}, y = \dfrac{10}{3}$
13 $20\sqrt{10}$
14 a $y = 8 - x$ b $s = x^2 + (8-x)^2$ c 32
15 $\dfrac{4}{3}, \dfrac{8}{3}$
16 Maximum area is 625 m^2 for 25 m $\times$ 25 m
17 $x = 12$ **18** 32
19 Maximum value of P is 2500
20 Maximum area is 2 km^2 for 2 km $\times$ 1 km
21 $p = \dfrac{3}{2}, q = \dfrac{8}{3}$
22 a $y = 60 - x$ b $S = 5x^2(60 - x)$
   c $0 < x < 60$ d

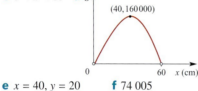

   e $x = 40, y = 20$ f $74\,005$
23 $12°$C
24 b $0 < x < 30$ c

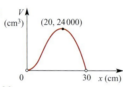

   d 20 cm, 40 cm, 30 cm
   e $x = 14.82$ or $x = 24.4$
25 b Maximum when $x = 3$ and $y = 18$
26 a Use 44 cm for circle and 56 cm for square
   b Use all the wire for the circle
27 Length 7.2 metres, width 4.5 metres
28 a $A = xy$ b $A = \left(8 - \dfrac{x}{2}\right)x$
   c $0 < x < 16$ d

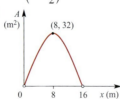

   e 32 m^2
29 $h = 1188, a = 937$
30 a $y = 10 - \pi x$ b $0 \le x \le \dfrac{10}{\pi}$
   c $A = \dfrac{x}{2}(20 - \pi x)$ d

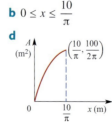

   e Maximum at $x = \dfrac{10}{\pi}$ f A semicircle

31 a $h = \dfrac{500}{\pi x} - x$ b $V = 500x - \pi x^3$
   c $\dfrac{dV}{dx} = 500 - 3\pi x^2$ d $x = 10\sqrt{\dfrac{5}{3\pi}} \approx 7.28$
   e

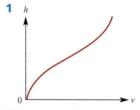

   f 2427.89 cm^3
   g $x = 2.05, h = 75.41$ or $x = 11.46, h = 2.42$
32 a $r = 4.3$ cm, $h = 8.6$ cm
   b $r = 4.3$ cm, $h = 8.6$ cm

Chapter 19

Technology-free questions

1

2 a 1 m/s   b 41 m/s
3 a i -4 ii -3 b $-2 - h$ c -2
4 $x - 1$
5 a $6x^2 - 1$ b $2x + 1$ c 1
6 a 13 b 10
7 a $x = 0$ or $x = \dfrac{1}{2}$ b $x = \dfrac{1}{4}$ c $x < \dfrac{1}{4}$
   d $x > \dfrac{1}{4}$ e $x = \dfrac{11}{4}$
8 a $-6x^{-4} + x^{-2}$ b $\dfrac{2z - 9}{z^4}$
9 Tangent $y = -3x - 1$; Normal $y = \dfrac{1}{3}x - \dfrac{13}{3}$
10 a $t = 0$ and $t = 2$
   b $t = 0, a = -1$ cm/s^2; $t = 2, a = 1$ cm/s^2
   c $-\tfrac{1}{2}$ cm/s
11 Local minimum $\left(\dfrac{2}{\sqrt{3}}, -\dfrac{32}{3\sqrt{3}}\right)$
   Local maximum $\left(-\dfrac{2}{\sqrt{3}}, \dfrac{32}{3\sqrt{3}}\right)$

Multiple-choice questions

1 B   **2** A   **3** B   **4** A   **5** B   **6** A
7 D   **8** B   **9** C   **10** A   **11** C   **12** B
13 A   **14** C   **15** C   **16** A   **17** D   **18** E
19 C   **20** B   **21** E   **22** D   **23** A   **24** A
25 C   **26** D   **27** B   **28** B   **29** B   **30** C
31 D   **32** E   **33** A   **34** A   **35** C   **36** C
37 D   **38** D   **39** D

Extended-response questions

1 a 100   **b** $\dfrac{dy}{dx} = 1 - 0.02x$

   c $x = 50, y = 25$ **d**

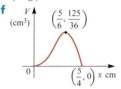

   e i (25, 18.75)   **ii** (75, 18.75)

2 a $\left(66\dfrac{2}{3}, 14\dfrac{22}{27}\right)$

   b i 0.28   **ii** −0.32   **iii** −1

   c A gradual rise to the turning point and a descent which becomes increasingly steep (in fact, alarmingly steep)

   d Smooth out the end of the trip

3 a $h = 5 - 4x$ **c** $0 < x < \dfrac{5}{4}$

   d $\dfrac{dV}{dx} = 30x - 36x^2$

   e $\left\{0, \dfrac{5}{6}\right\}$; Maximum volume = $3\dfrac{17}{36}$ cm^3

   f

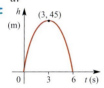

4 a $\dfrac{dh}{dt} = 30 - 10t$ **b** 45 m

   c

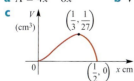

5 a $A = 4x - 6x^2$ **b** $V = x^2 - 2x^3$

   c

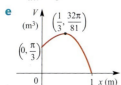

   d $\dfrac{1}{3}$ cm × $\dfrac{1}{3}$ cm × $\dfrac{1}{3}$ cm; Volume = $\dfrac{1}{27}$ cm^3

6 a i $r = \sqrt{1 - x^2}$ **ii** $h = 1 + x$

   c $0 < x < 1$

   d i $\dfrac{dV}{dx} = \dfrac{\pi}{3}(1 - 2x - 3x^2)$ **ii** $\{\tfrac{1}{3}\}$ **iii** $\dfrac{32\pi}{81}$ m^3

   e

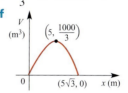

7 a 1000 insects

b 1366 insects

c i $t = 40$ **ii** $t = 51.70$

d 63.64

e i $\dfrac{1000 \times 2^{\tfrac{3}{4}}\left(2^{\tfrac{h}{20}} - 1\right)}{h}$

   ii Consider h decreasing and approaching zero; instantaneous rate of change = 58.286 insects/day

8 a $h = \dfrac{150 - 2x^2}{3x}$ **b** $V = \dfrac{2}{3}(150x - 2x^3)$

   c $\dfrac{dV}{dx} = 2(50 - 2x^2)$ **d** $0 < x < 5\sqrt{3}$

   e $\dfrac{1000}{3}$ m^3 when $x = 5$

   f

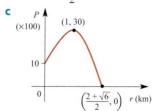

9 a 10

   c i $h = 2.5x$

   d $V = 40(420x - 135x^2)$

   e i $x = \dfrac{14}{9}, y = \dfrac{140}{9}$ **ii** $13\,066\tfrac{2}{3}$ m^3

10 a $a = 200, k = 0.000\,01$

   b i $\dfrac{400}{3}$ **ii** $\dfrac{320}{27}$ **c i** $\dfrac{8379}{800}$ **ii** $\dfrac{357}{4000}$

   d i $y = \dfrac{357}{4000}x + \dfrac{441}{400}$ **ii** $\dfrac{441}{400}$

   e 0.09975

   f

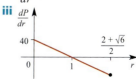

11 a 10 000 people/km^2

   b $0 \leq r \leq \dfrac{2 + \sqrt{6}}{2}$

   c

   d i $\dfrac{dP}{dr} = 40 - 40r$ **ii** 20, 0, −40

   iii

   e At $r = 1$

12 a $y = ax - x^2$ **b** $0 < x < a$ **c** $\dfrac{a^2}{4}, \dfrac{a}{2}$
d Negative coefficient of x^2 for quadratic function
e i 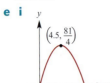 **ii** $\left(0, \dfrac{81}{4}\right]$

13 a i 0 **ii** 1600
b $\dfrac{dV}{dt} = 0.6(40t - 2t^2)$
c 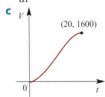 **d**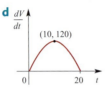

14 a $-1 = a + b$ **b** $0 = 3a + 2b$, $a = 2$, $b = -3$
c

15 a i $80 - 2x$ **ii** $h = \dfrac{\sqrt{3}}{2}x$
c $A = \dfrac{\sqrt{3}}{4}x(160 - 3x)$ **d** $x = \dfrac{80}{3}$

16 a $y = \dfrac{1400 - 2x^2 - 8x}{4x}$
b $V = -\dfrac{x^3}{2} - 2x^2 + 350x$
c $\dfrac{dV}{dx} = -\dfrac{3}{2}x^2 - 4x + 350$
d $x = 14$
e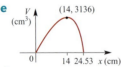
f Maximum volume is 3136 cm³
g $x = 22.83$ and $y = 1.92$, or $x = 2.94$ and $y = 115.45$

Chapter 20

Exercise 20A

1 a $30(x - 1)^{29}$ **b** $100(x^4 - 2x^9)(x^5 - x^{10})^{19}$
c $4(1 - 3x^2 - 5x^4)(x - x^3 - x^5)^3$
d $8(x + 1)^7$ **e** $-4(x + 1)(x^2 + 2x)^{-3}$
f $-6(x + x^{-2})(x^2 - 2x^{-1})^{-4}$

2 a $24x^2(2x^3 + 1)^3$ **b** 648
3 a $-\dfrac{1}{16}$ **b** $-\dfrac{3}{256}$
4 a $-\dfrac{2}{9}$ **b** $\left(-3, -\dfrac{1}{3}\right), \left(0, \dfrac{1}{3}\right)$
5 a $-\dfrac{1}{4}$ **b** $\dfrac{1}{4}$ **c** $y = -x + 2$ **d** $y = x - 2$
e At P, $y = x + 2$; at Q, $y = -x - 2$; $(-2, 0)$
f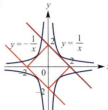

Exercise 20B

1 a $\dfrac{1}{3}x^{-\frac{2}{3}}$ **b** $\dfrac{3}{2}x^{\frac{1}{2}}$, $x > 0$
c $\dfrac{5}{2}x^{\frac{3}{2}} - \dfrac{3}{2}x^{\frac{1}{2}}$, $x > 0$ **d** $x^{-\frac{1}{2}} - 5x^{\frac{2}{3}}$, $x > 0$
e $-\dfrac{5}{6}x^{-\frac{11}{6}}$, $x > 0$ **f** $-\dfrac{1}{2}x^{-\frac{3}{2}}$, $x > 0$

2 a $x(1 + x^2)^{-\frac{1}{2}}$ **b** $\dfrac{1}{3}(1 + 2x)(x + x^2)^{-\frac{2}{3}}$
c $-x(1 + x^2)^{-\frac{3}{2}}$ **d** $\dfrac{1}{3}(1 + x)^{-\frac{2}{3}}$

3 a i $\dfrac{4}{3}$ **ii** $\dfrac{4}{3}$ **iii** $\dfrac{1}{3}$ **iv** $\dfrac{1}{3}$
4 a $\{x : 0 < x < 1\}$ **b** $\{x : x > \left(\dfrac{2}{3}\right)^6\}$
5 a $-5x^{-\frac{1}{2}}(2 - 5\sqrt{x})$ **b** $3x^{-\frac{1}{2}}(3\sqrt{x} + 2)$
c $-4x^{-3} - \dfrac{3}{2}x^{-\frac{5}{2}}$ **d** $\dfrac{3}{2}x^{\frac{1}{2}} - x^{-\frac{3}{2}}$
e $\dfrac{15}{2}x^{\frac{3}{2}} + 3x^{-\frac{1}{2}}$

Exercise 20C

1 a $-\dfrac{3}{x} + c$ **b** $3x^2 - \dfrac{2}{3x^3} + c$
c $\dfrac{4}{3}x^{\frac{3}{2}} + \dfrac{2}{5}x^{\frac{5}{2}} + c$ **d** $\dfrac{9}{4}x^{\frac{4}{3}} - \dfrac{20}{9}x^{\frac{9}{4}} + c$
e $\dfrac{3}{2}z^2 - \dfrac{2}{z} + c$ **f** $\dfrac{12}{7}x^{\frac{7}{4}} - \dfrac{14}{3}x^{\frac{3}{2}} + c$

2 a $y = \dfrac{2}{3}x^{\frac{3}{2}} + \dfrac{1}{2}x^2 - \dfrac{22}{3}$
b $y = \dfrac{3}{2} - \dfrac{1}{2x^2}$ **c** $y = \dfrac{3}{2}x^2 - \dfrac{1}{x} + \dfrac{9}{2}$

3 $f(x) = x^3 + \dfrac{1}{x} - \dfrac{17}{2}$
4 $s = \dfrac{3t^2}{2} + \dfrac{8}{t} - 8$ **5** $y = 5$
6 a 2 **b** $y = x^2 + 1$
7 $y = \dfrac{x^3}{3} + \dfrac{7}{3}$

Answers

Exercise 20D

1 a $6x$ **b** 0 **c** $108(3x+1)^2$
d $-\frac{1}{4}x^{-\frac{3}{2}} + 18x$
e $306x^{16} + 396x^{10} + 90x^4$
f $10 + 12x^{-3} + \frac{9}{4}x^{-\frac{1}{2}}$

2 a $18x$ **b** 0 **c** 12 **d** $432(6x+1)^2$
e $300(5x+2)^2$ **f** $6x + 4 + 6x^{-3}$

3 -9.8 m/s^2

4 a i -16 **ii** 4 m/s **iii** $\frac{7}{4}$ m/s **iv** -32 m/s
b $t = 0$
c -8 m/s

Exercise 20E

1 a $(\frac{1}{2}, 4), (-\frac{1}{2}, -4)$ **b** $y = \frac{15}{4}x + 1$

2 $\pm\frac{1}{2}$

3 $\frac{1}{2}$

4 a $(4, 0), (1, 0)$ **b** $y = x - 5, x = 0$
c $(2, -1)$ min
$(-2, -9)$ max

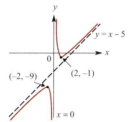

5 3
6 4

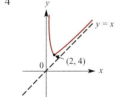

7 a

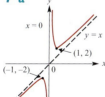

b

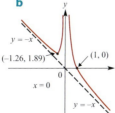

c

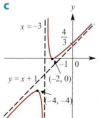

d

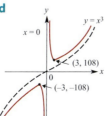

e

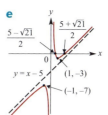

f

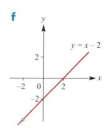

Chapter 20 review

Technology-free questions

1 a $\frac{1}{2x^{\frac{1}{2}}}$ **b** $\frac{1}{3x^{\frac{2}{3}}}$ **c** $\frac{2}{3x^{\frac{4}{3}}}$ **d** $\frac{4}{3}x^{\frac{1}{3}}$
e $-\frac{1}{3x^{\frac{4}{3}}}$ **f** $-\frac{1}{3x^{\frac{4}{3}}} + \frac{6}{5x^{\frac{2}{5}}}$

2 a $8x + 12$ **b** $24(3x+4)^3$
c $\frac{1}{(3-2x)^{\frac{3}{2}}}$ **d** $\frac{-2}{(3+2x)^2}$
e $\frac{-4}{3(2x-1)^{\frac{5}{3}}}$ **f** $\frac{-3x}{(2+x^2)^{\frac{3}{2}}}$
g $\frac{1}{3}\left(4x + \frac{6}{x^3}\right)\left(2x^2 - \frac{3}{x^2}\right)^{-\frac{2}{3}}$

3 a $\frac{-1}{x^2} + c$ **b** $\frac{2x^{\frac{5}{2}}}{5} - \frac{4x^{\frac{3}{2}}}{3} + c$
c $\frac{3x^2}{2} + 2x + c$ **d** $\frac{-6x - 1}{2x^2} + c$
e $\frac{5x^2}{2} - \frac{4x^{\frac{3}{2}}}{3} + c$ **f** $\frac{20x^{\frac{7}{4}}}{7} - \frac{3x^{\frac{4}{3}}}{2} + c$
g $2x - \frac{2x^{\frac{3}{2}}}{3} + c$ **h** $-\frac{(3x+1)}{x^2} + c$

4 $s = \frac{1}{2}t^2 + 3t + \frac{1}{t} + \frac{3}{2}$

5 a $\frac{1}{6}$ **b** -2 **c** $-\frac{1}{16}$ **d** -2 **e** $\frac{1}{6}$ **f** 0

6 $\left(\frac{1}{2}, 2\right)$ and $\left(-\frac{1}{2}, -2\right)$

7 $\left(\frac{1}{16}, \frac{1}{4}\right)$

Multiple-choice questions

1 B **2** D **3** A **4** A **5** A
6 E **7** A **8** B **9** A **10** D

Extended-response questions

1 a $h = \frac{400}{\pi r^2}$
c $\frac{dA}{dr} = 4\pi r - \frac{800}{r^2}$
d $r = \left(\frac{200}{\pi}\right)^{\frac{1}{3}} \approx 3.99$
e $A = 301$ cm^2

f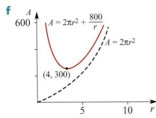

2 a $y = \dfrac{16}{x}$ **c** $x = 4, P = 16$

d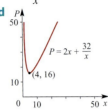

3 a $OA = \dfrac{120}{x}$ **b** $OX = \dfrac{120}{x} + 7$
c $OZ = x + 5$ **d** $y = 7x + \dfrac{600}{x} + 155$
e $x = \dfrac{10\sqrt{42}}{7} \approx 9.26$ cm

4 a $A(-2, 0), B(0, \sqrt{2})$ **b** $\dfrac{1}{2\sqrt{x+2}}$
c i $\dfrac{1}{2}$ **ii** $2y - x = 3$ **iii** $\dfrac{3\sqrt{5}}{2}$
d $x > -\dfrac{7}{4}$

5 a $h = \dfrac{18}{x^2}$ **c** $x = 3, h = 2$

d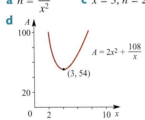

6 a $y = \dfrac{250}{x^2}$ **c** $\dfrac{dS}{dx} = 24x - \dfrac{3000}{x^2}$
d $S_{min} = 900$ cm²

Chapter 21

Exercise 21A

1 62 square units **2** 80 square units
3 60.90623 square units **4** 68 square units
5 a 13.2 **b** 10.2 **c** 11.7
6 a 4.375 **b** 4.536
7 a 36.8 **b** 36.75
8 $\pi \approx 3.13$
9 a 4.371 **b** 1.128
10 109.5 m²

Exercise 21B

1 a $\dfrac{7}{3}$ **b** 20 **c** $-\dfrac{1}{4}$ **d** 9 **e** $\dfrac{15}{4}$
f $\dfrac{297}{6} = 49.5$ **g** $15\tfrac{1}{3}$ **h** 30
2 4 **3** 9 **4** $\dfrac{4}{3}$ **5** 4

Exercise 21C

1 $-\dfrac{32}{3}$

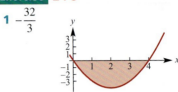

2 -36

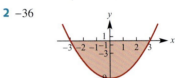

3 36
4 $\dfrac{37}{12}$
5 a 8 **b** 16 **c** -4
6 a -12 **b** 36 **c** 20
7 a 24, 21, 45 **b** 4, -1, 3
8 4.5 square units **9** $166\tfrac{2}{3}$ square units
10 $\dfrac{37}{12}$ square units
11 a 1 **b** 1 **c** 14 **d** 31 **e** $2\tfrac{1}{4}$ **f** 0
12 a $\dfrac{4}{3}$ **b** $\dfrac{1}{6}$ **c** $121\tfrac{1}{2}$ **d** $\dfrac{1}{6}$
e $4\sqrt{3} \approx 6.93$ **f** 108

Chapter 21 review

Technology-free questions

1 a 3 **b** 6 **c** 114 **d** $\dfrac{196}{3}$ **e** 5
2 a $\dfrac{14}{3}$ **b** $48\tfrac{3}{4}$ **c** $\dfrac{1}{2}$ **d** $\dfrac{15}{16}$ **e** $\dfrac{16}{15}$
3 $\dfrac{15}{4}$ square units

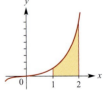

4 $4\tfrac{1}{2}$ square units **5** $21\tfrac{1}{12}$ square units
6 a $B(1, 3), C(3, 3)$ **b** 6 **c** $\dfrac{4}{3}$

Multiple-choice questions

1 C **2** D **3** A **4** D **5** B
6 B **7** D **8** B **9** C **10** A

Extended-response questions

1 a $y = \dfrac{9}{32}\left(\dfrac{x^3}{3} - 2x^2\right) + 3$

  b 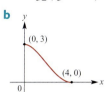   c Yes, for $x \in \left[\dfrac{4}{3}, \dfrac{8}{3}\right]$

2 a 27 square units   b $y = \dfrac{3}{25}(x-4)^2$

  c $\dfrac{189}{25}$ square units   d $\dfrac{486}{25}$ square units

3 a i 120 L   ii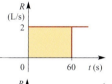

  b i 900 L   ii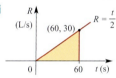

    iii $900a^2$ L

  c i 7200 square units
    ii Volume of water which has flowed in
    iii 66.94 s

4 a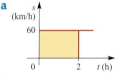

  b i 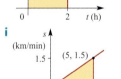   ii 3.75 km

  c i $20 - 6t$ m/s^2
    ii   iii 144 metres

5 a i 4 m   ii 16 m
  b i 0.7   ii −0.8
  c i $\dfrac{100}{3}$ ii $\dfrac{500}{27}$
  d $\dfrac{3125}{6}$ m^2
  e i $(15 + 5\sqrt{33}, 12)$
    ii $R = 60\sqrt{33} - 60$, $q = 20$, $p = 15 + 5\sqrt{33}$

6 a i 9   ii $y = 9x - 3$ iii $y = 3x^2 + 3x$
  b i $12 + k$ ii $k = -7$ iii $y = 3x^2 - 7x + 12$

7 a 6 m^2 b i $y = x - \dfrac{1}{2}$ ii $\left(x^2 - \dfrac{1}{4}\right)$ m^2

  c i $y = \dfrac{1}{2}x^2$, $P(-2, 2)$, $S(2, 2)$ ii $\dfrac{16}{3}$ m^2

8 a $y = 7 \times 10^{-7}x^3 - 0.00116x^2 + 0.405x + 60$
  b 100 m
  c i 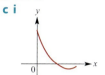   ii $(0, 60)$

  d 51 307 m^2

9 a   b $x = 2.988$

Chapter 22

Technology-free questions

1 a $\dfrac{25}{12}$ b $\dfrac{77}{60}$ c $\dfrac{101}{60}$

2 a $\dfrac{9}{2}x^{\frac{1}{2}}$ b $\dfrac{1}{5}x^{-\frac{4}{5}}$ c $\dfrac{10}{3}x^{-\frac{8}{3}}$ d $10x^{\frac{2}{3}}$

  e $-\dfrac{1}{5}x^{-\frac{6}{5}}$ f $-\dfrac{2}{3}x^{-\frac{5}{3}} - 3x^{\frac{1}{2}}$

3 a $6(3x+5)$ b $-8(2x+7)^3$

  c $\dfrac{2}{3}(5-2x)^{-\frac{4}{3}}$ d $\dfrac{-12}{(5+3x)^2}$

  e $-\dfrac{2}{3}(x-1)^{-\frac{5}{3}}$ f $-9x(2+3x^2)^{-\frac{3}{2}}$

  g $\dfrac{1}{3}\left(2x^3 - \dfrac{5}{x}\right)^{-\frac{2}{3}}\left(6x^2 + \dfrac{5}{x^2}\right)$

4 $x = \dfrac{t^2}{2} + 4t + \dfrac{3}{t} - \dfrac{3}{2}$

5 a $\dfrac{1}{27}$ b -3 c $-\dfrac{3}{8}$

6 $\left(-\left(\dfrac{1}{2}\right)^{\frac{1}{3}}, 4^{\frac{1}{3}}\right)$

7 $\left(\left(\dfrac{1}{6}\right)^{\frac{3}{2}}, \left(\dfrac{1}{6}\right)^{\frac{1}{2}}\right)$ and $\left(-\left(\dfrac{1}{6}\right)^{\frac{3}{2}}, -\left(\dfrac{1}{6}\right)^{\frac{1}{2}}\right)$

8 a $x^3 + x + c$ b $-t^3 - \dfrac{1}{2}t^2 + 2t + c$

  c $\dfrac{2}{3}x^{\frac{3}{2}} + c$ d $\dfrac{4}{5}x^{\frac{5}{2}} + \dfrac{3}{4}x^{\frac{4}{3}} + c$

9 a $\dfrac{2}{3}$ b $\dfrac{5}{6}$

10 a $\dfrac{1}{6}$ square units   b $\dfrac{1}{2}$ square units

Multiple-choice questions

1 E   2 C   3 E   4 D   5 A
6 A   7 E   8 C   9 E   10 C
11 B   12 C   13 C

Chapter 23

Technology-free questions

1. $x = 4$
2. $t = \dfrac{2d - b}{a - 2c}$
3. $x \geq -\dfrac{3}{2}$
4. **a** -12 **b** 3 **c** 100
5. 15
6. $x \leq \dfrac{37}{5}$
7. $a = 7.9$
8. **a** $\left(\dfrac{a+8}{2}, \dfrac{b+14}{2}\right)$ **b** $a = 2, b = 6$
9. **a** $4y - 3x = 30$ **b** $\dfrac{25}{2}$
10. **a** $(2, \tfrac{1}{2})$ **b** $\sqrt{445}$ **c** $11x + 18y = 31$
    d $22y - 36x + 61 = 0$
11.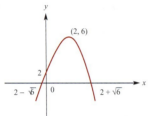
12. $y = \dfrac{9}{8}(x - 2)^2 - 6$
13. $a = -2$
14. **a** $w = 1500 - 9x$ **b** $V = 20x^2(1500 - 9x)$
    c $0 \leq x \leq \dfrac{500}{3}$ **d** $120\,000\,000$ cm^3
15. **a** $\dfrac{16}{81}$ **b** $\dfrac{28}{153}$
16. $\dfrac{1}{3}$
17. **a** $\dfrac{1}{2}$ **b** $\dfrac{1}{3}$
18. 0.42
19. $-\dfrac{\pi}{9}, \dfrac{\pi}{9}$
20. **a** $c = 6$ **b** $0 = -8a - 2b + 6, 0 = 3a + b$
    c $a = 3, b = -9$
21. $a = -48$
22. **a** Amplitude $= 4$; Period $= \pi$
    b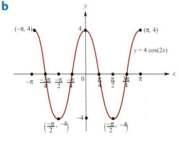
23. **a** $\dfrac{1}{4}$ **b** $\dfrac{1}{3}$ **c** $\dfrac{1}{4}$
24. **a** $(0, 1)$ **b**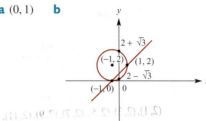
25. **a** $x = 3$ **b** $x = -\dfrac{5}{2}$ or $x = 1$
26. $k = 4$ and $y = -2x^2 + 4x + 3$
27. $a = \dfrac{1}{3}$ 28. $y = \dfrac{-2x^2}{9}$ 29. $b = -\dfrac{1}{3}$
30. Intersect at $(-3, -27)$; both curves have gradient 27 at this point
31. **a** $(5, -260)$ and $(-5, 240)$
    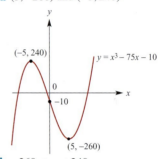
    b $-260 \leq p \leq 240$
32. **a** $\mathbb{R} \setminus \{3\}$ **b** $\mathbb{R} \setminus \{2\}$ **c** $(-\infty, 2]$
    d $[4, \infty)$ **e** $(-\infty, 5)$

Multiple-choice questions

1 B	2 A	3 D	4 D	5 D	6 C
7 C	8 A	9 B	10 A	11 B	12 A
13 A	14 E	15 B	16 C	17 B	18 A
19 C	20 A	21 B	22 B	23 D	24 D
25 A	26 C	27 B	28 A	29 E	30 C

Extended-response questions

1. **a** **i** $-b$ **ii** $x = \dfrac{b}{2}$
   b **i** $S(b) = \dfrac{b}{2}(32 - b^2)$ **ii** $b = 2$
2. **a** $a = 4$ **b** $\left(\dfrac{1}{4}, 4\right)$ **c** $\dfrac{34}{15}$
3. **a** $2t^2 - 6t$ **b** O **c** 0 cm/s **d** 9 cm **e** 3 cm/s
4. **a** **i** $(-\infty, 0) \cup \left(\dfrac{2a}{3}, \infty\right)$ **ii** $\left(0, \dfrac{2a}{3}\right)$
   b $y = -a^2(x - a)$ **c** $y = \dfrac{x}{a^2} - \dfrac{1}{a}$ **d** $\dfrac{a^4}{12}$
5. **a** $y = 13 - 9x$ **b** $A = 156x - 60x^2$
   c $x = \dfrac{13}{10}$ and $y = \dfrac{13}{10}$
6. **b** $2\,080\,000$ m^2 when $x = 800$ and $y = 1200$

c

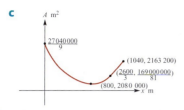

7 a {(0, 1), (0, 3), (0, 5), (0, 7), (0, 9), (0, 11),
(2, 1), (2, 3), (2, 5), (2, 7), (2, 9), (2, 11),
(4, 1), (4, 3), (4, 5), (4, 7), (4, 9), (4, 11),
(6, 1), (6, 3), (6, 5), (6, 7), (6, 9), (6, 11),
(8, 1), (8, 3), (8, 5), (8, 7), (8, 9), (8, 11),
(10, 1), (10, 3), (10, 5), (10, 7), (10, 9), (10, 11)}

b i $\dfrac{1}{36}$ **ii** $\dfrac{5}{36}$ **iii** $\dfrac{5}{36}$ **c** $\dfrac{2}{13}$

8 a $AB = \begin{bmatrix} -2 & 5 & 5 \\ 0 & 6 & 2 \\ 0 & 0 & -4 \end{bmatrix}$ **d** $x = 1, y = 2, z = 3$

9 a $x \geq 2a$

b $x = \dfrac{1 + \sqrt{1 - 8a}}{2}$ or $x = \dfrac{1 - \sqrt{1 - 8a}}{2}$

c $a = \dfrac{1}{8}$ **d**

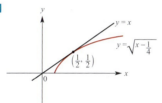

10 a 0.343 **b** 0.399
11 a 0.4219 **b** 0.2156 **c** 0.6125
12 a $[-mb + 3, -ma + 3]$

b $f^{-1}(x) = -\dfrac{1}{m}x + \dfrac{3}{m}$

c $\left(\dfrac{a+b}{2}, \dfrac{-m(a+b)+6}{2}\right)$

d $2ym - 2x = -m^2(a+b) + 6m - (a+b)$
e $y = -mx - 3m + 8$
$A'(a - 3, -ma + 8), B'(b - 3, -mb + 8)$
f $y = mx + 3$
$A'(-a, -ma + 3), B'(-b, -mb + 3)$

g $b = 12, m = \dfrac{7}{6}$

13 a i

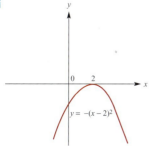

ii

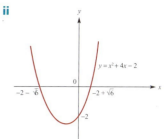

b $\left(\dfrac{2}{1-p}, \dfrac{p^2 - 5p}{p - 1}\right)$ **c** $p = 0$ or $p = 5$

d $0 < p < 5$ and $p \neq 1$
e $y = 2x^2 - 4x - 1$

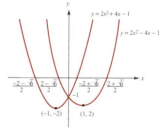

14 a $\dfrac{\pi}{6}$ **b** $115\sqrt{2}$ cm **c** $115\sqrt{3}$ cm

Appendix A

Exercise A1

1 a Quotient $3x^2 + 6x + 16$; Remainder 26
b Quotient $3x^2 - 5x + 9$; Remainder -3
c Quotient $x^2 - 2x - 6$; Remainder 54
d Quotient $4x^2 - 2x + 6$; Remainder -69
e Quotient $2x^2 - x + 3$; Remainder -69

Exercise A2

1 a $\dfrac{3}{2}, \dfrac{1 \pm \sqrt{21}}{2}$ **b** $\dfrac{1}{3}, \dfrac{-1 \pm \sqrt{5}}{2}$

c $\dfrac{1}{3}, \dfrac{-1 \pm \sqrt{41}}{4}$ **d** $\dfrac{1}{2}, \dfrac{-1 \pm \sqrt{13}}{2}$

e $\dfrac{1}{2}, \dfrac{1}{3}, -\dfrac{2}{5}$ **f** $\dfrac{1}{2}, \dfrac{1}{3}, -\dfrac{2}{3}$

Exercise A3

1 a $x = 2, y = 3, z = 1$ **b** $x = -3, y = 5, z = 2$
c $x = 5, y = 0, z = 7$
2 $x = 6, y = 5, z = 1$ **3** $a = 1, b = -2, c = 3$
4 $b = 1, c = 2, d = 5$ **5** $x = 5, y = -2, z = 1$
6 $b = -2, c = 0, d = 3$
7 a $-y + 5z = 15$ and $-y + 5z = 15$
b The solution is a straight line
c $y = 5\lambda - 15$ **d** $x = 43 - 13\lambda$
8 a $y = -2 + 4z$
b $x = 8 - 5\lambda, y = -2 + 4\lambda, z = \lambda$, for $\lambda \in \mathbb{R}$